Dictionary
of the
Middle Ages

AMERICAN COUNCIL OF LEARNED SOCIETIES

The American Council of Learned Societies, organized in 1919 for the purpose of advancing the study of the humanities and of the humanistic aspects of the social sciences, is a nonprofit federation comprising forty-six national scholarly groups. The Council represents the humanities in the United States in the International Union of Academies, provides fellowships and grants-in-aid, supports research-and-planning conferences and symposia, and sponsors special projects and scholarly publications.

MEMBER ORGANIZATIONS
AMERICAN PHILOSOPHICAL SOCIETY, 1743
AMERICAN ACADEMY OF ARTS AND SCIENCES, 1780
AMERICAN ANTIQUARIAN SOCIETY, 1812
AMERICAN ORIENTAL SOCIETY, 1842
AMERICAN NUMISMATIC SOCIETY, 1858
AMERICAN PHILOLOGICAL ASSOCIATION, 1869
ARCHAEOLOGICAL INSTITUTE OF AMERICA, 1879
SOCIETY OF BIBLICAL LITERATURE, 1880
MODERN LANGUAGE ASSOCIATION OF AMERICA, 1883
AMERICAN HISTORICAL ASSOCIATION, 1884
AMERICAN ECONOMIC ASSOCIATION, 1885
AMERICAN FOLKLORE SOCIETY, 1888
AMERICAN DIALECT SOCIETY, 1889
AMERICAN PSYCHOLOGICAL ASSOCIATION, 1892
ASSOCIATION OF AMERICAN LAW SCHOOLS, 1900
AMERICAN PHILOSOPHICAL ASSOCIATION, 1901
AMERICAN ANTHROPOLOGICAL ASSOCIATION, 1902
AMERICAN POLITICAL SCIENCE ASSOCIATION, 1903
BIBLIOGRAPHICAL SOCIETY OF AMERICA, 1904
ASSOCIATION OF AMERICAN GEOGRAPHERS, 1904
HISPANIC SOCIETY OF AMERICA, 1904
AMERICAN SOCIOLOGICAL ASSOCIATION, 1905
AMERICAN SOCIETY OF INTERNATIONAL LAW, 1906
ORGANIZATION OF AMERICAN HISTORIANS, 1907
AMERICAN ACADEMY OF RELIGION, 1909
COLLEGE ART ASSOCIATION OF AMERICA, 1912
HISTORY OF SCIENCE SOCIETY, 1924
LINGUISTIC SOCIETY OF AMERICA, 1924
MEDIAEVAL ACADEMY OF AMERICA, 1925
AMERICAN MUSICOLOGICAL SOCIETY, 1934
SOCIETY OF ARCHITECTURAL HISTORIANS, 1940
ECONOMIC HISTORY ASSOCIATION, 1940
ASSOCIATION FOR ASIAN STUDIES, 1941
AMERICAN SOCIETY FOR AESTHETICS, 1942
AMERICAN ASSOCIATION FOR THE ADVANCEMENT OF SLAVIC STUDIES, 1948
METAPHYSICAL SOCIETY OF AMERICA, 1950
AMERICAN STUDIES ASSOCIATION, 1950
RENAISSANCE SOCIETY OF AMERICA, 1954
SOCIETY FOR ETHNOMUSICOLOGY, 1955
AMERICAN SOCIETY FOR LEGAL HISTORY, 1956
AMERICAN SOCIETY FOR THEATRE RESEARCH, 1956
SOCIETY FOR THE HISTORY OF TECHNOLOGY, 1958
AMERICAN COMPARATIVE LITERATURE ASSOCIATION, 1960
MIDDLE EAST STUDIES ASSOCIATION OF NORTH AMERICA, 1966
AMERICAN SOCIETY FOR EIGHTEENTH-CENTURY STUDIES, 1969
ASSOCIATION FOR JEWISH STUDIES, 1969

The sea resting on twelve oxen. Champlevé enamel on gold: detail from the altarpiece of Klosterneuburg Abbey by Nicholas of Verdun, completed 1181 (now in the Stiftsmuseum, Klosterneuburg). PHOTO BY WLADIMIR NARBUTT-LIEVEN AND INGRID SCHINDLER, VIENNA

Dictionary of the Middle Ages

JOSEPH R. STRAYER, *EDITOR IN CHIEF*

Volume 4

CROATIA—FAMILY SAGAS, ICELANDIC

CHARLES SCRIBNER'S SONS · NEW YORK

Copyright © 1984 American Council of Learned Societies

Library of Congress Cataloging in Publication Data
Main entry under title:

Dictionary of the Middle Ages.

Includes bibliographies and index.
1. Middle Ages—Dictionaries.   I. Strayer,
Joseph Reese, 1904–1987

D114.D5   1982   909.07   82-5904
ISBN 0-684-16760-3 (v. 1)   ISBN 0-684-18169-X (v. 7)
ISBN 0-684-17022-1 (v. 2)   ISBN 0-684-18274-2 (v. 8)
ISBN 0-684-17023-X (v. 3)   ISBN 0-684-18275-0 (v. 9)
ISBN 0-684-17024-8 (v. 4)   ISBN 0-684-18276-9 (v. 10)
ISBN 0-684-18161-4 (v. 5)   ISBN 0-684-18277-7 (v. 11)
ISBN 0-684-18168-1 (v. 6)   ISBN 0-684-18278-5 (v. 12)

3 5 7 9 11 13 15 17 19   B/C   20 18 16 14 12 10 8 6 4 2

PRINTED IN THE UNITED STATES OF AMERICA.

The *Dictionary of the Middle Ages* has been produced with
support from the National Endowment for the Humanities.

The paper in this book meets the guidelines for
permanence and durability of the Committee on
Production Guidelines for Book Longevity of the
Council on Library Resources.

Maps prepared by Sylvia Lehrman.

Editorial Board

Advisory Committee

Editorial Staff

Contributors to Volume 4

MUHAMMAD ABDUL-RAUF
International Islamic University
FAMILY, ISLAMIC

ROBERT W. ACKERMAN
EXCALIBUR

GUSTAVE ALEF
University of Oregon
DMITRII IVANOVICH DONSKOI;
DUMA

THEODORE M. ANDERSSON
Stanford University
DROPLAUGARSONA SAGA

GRACE M. ARMSTRONG
Bryn Mawr College
FABLES

FRANZ H. BÄUML
University of California, Los Angeles
DUKUS HORANT

TERENCE BAILEY
University of Western Ontario
EVOVAE

CARL F. BARNES, JR.
ERWIN, MASTER; EUDES OF MONTREUIL

M. P. BARNES
University College, London
DRAUMKVÆDE

ELIEZER BASHAN
Bar-Ilan University
EXILARCH

WILLIAM W. BASSETT
University of San Francisco
EXCHEQUER, COURT OF

MICHAEL L. BATES
American Numismatic Society
DINAR; DIRHAM

SILVIO A. BEDINI
Smithsonian Institution
DONDI, GIOVANNI DE'

JEANETTE M. A. BEER
Purdue University
DIALECT; EULALIE, LA SÉQUENCE DE STE.

HANS BEKKER-NIELSEN
Odense Universitet
DUNSTANUS SAGA

CAROL MANSON BIER
George Washington University
DĪBĀJ

FOSTER W. BLAISDELL
Indiana University
EREX SAGA

RENATE BLUMENFELD-KOSINSKI
Columbia University
ELEANOR OF AQUITAINE

M.-C. BODDEN
University of British Columbia
ETHELWOLD AND THE BENEDICTINE RULE

DIANE BORNSTEIN
Queens College
FAMILY, WESTERN EUROPEAN

CHARLES BOWEN
University of Massachusetts, Harbor Campus
DINDSHENCHAS

MARY BOYCE
DĒNKARD

CHARLES M. BRAND
Bryn Mawr College
DOUKAS

PAUL A. BRAND
EXCHEQUER OF THE JEWS

CYNTHIA J. BROWN
University of California, Santa Barbara
DÉBAT

JEROME V. BROWN
University of Windsor
DUNS SCOTUS, JOHN

ROBERT BROWNING
University of London
ENCYCLOPEDIAS AND DICTIONARIES, BYZANTINE

LESLIE BRUBAKER
Wheaton College, Norton, Massachusetts
CROCKET; CROSS, FORMS OF; CROSS, PROCESSIONAL; CROSSING; CROWN, MURAL; CROZIER; CRUCIFIXION; CRYPT; CUBICULUM; CUPOLA; CUSP; DALMATIC; DEMETRIOS PRESBYTER; DEPOSITION FROM THE CROSS; DIACONICON; DIAPER PATTERN; DIONYSIOS OF FOURNA; DIONYSIOS THE GREEK; DIPTYCH; DIPTYCH, CONSULAR; DOME; DOME OF HEAVEN; DOME OF THE ROCK; DOMUS ECCLESIAE; DONOR PORTRAIT; DURANDUS; DURROW, BOOK OF; EBO OF RHEIMS; ÉCHOPPE; EGBERT OF TRIER; ELEOUSA; ELEVATION OF THE HOLY CROSS; ÉMAIL BRUN; EMMANUEL, CHRIST; ENAMEL, BASSE-TAILLE; ENAMEL, CHAMPLEVÉ; ENAMEL, CLOISONNÉ; ENAMEL, LIMOGES; ENAMEL, MILLEFIORI; ENAMEL, VERMICULÉ; ENCAUSTIC; ENCOLPIUM; ENTRY INTO JERUSALEM; EPHREM (EPHRAIM); EPIPHANY IN ART; EUTYCHIOS; EVANGELIARY; EVANGELIST SYMBOLS; EX VOTO; EXEDRA; EXONARTHEX; EXULTET ROLL; FALCHION

CONTRIBUTORS TO VOLUME 4

JAMES A. BRUNDAGE
*University of Wisconsin,
Milwaukee*
CRUSADE PROPAGANDA

GLYN S. BURGESS
University of Liverpool
ESPURGATOIRE ST. PATRICE; FABLES,
FRENCH

ROBERT G. CALKINS
Cornell University
DINANDERIE; DROLLERY

JAMES E. CATHEY
*University of Massachusetts,
Amherst*
FÁFNIR

A. C. CAWLEY
University of Leeds
EVERYMAN

ROBERT CHAZAN
Queens College
EXPULSION OF JEWS

FREDRIC L. CHEYETTE
Amherst College
ÉTABLISSEMENTS DE ST. LOUIS

STANLEY CHODOROW
*University of California, San
Diego*
DECRETALS; DECRETISTS; DECRETUM

DOROTHY CLOTELLE CLARKE
University of California, Berkeley
DECIR

CAROL J. CLOVER
University of California, Berkeley
DARRAÐARLJÓÐ; FAMILY SAGAS,
ICELANDIC

LAWRENCE I. CONRAD
American University of Beirut
DĪNAWARĪ, ABŪ ḤANĪFA AḤMAD
IBN DĀWŪD AL-

PATRICIA L. CONROY
University of Washington
FÆREYINGA SAGA

DANIEL COQUILLETTE
Boston University
EQUITY

RAYMOND J. CORMIER
Wilson College
ENÉAS, ROMAN D'

ART COSGROVE
University College, Dublin
DUBLIN

EDWARD J. COWAN
University of Guelph
DURHAM, TREATIES OF

EUGENE L. COX
Wellesley College
DAUPHINÉ

LUCY DER MANUELIAN
EREROYKᶜ

JAMES DICKIE
DERVISH

WACHTANG DJOBADZE
*California State University, Los
Angeles*
DAWID-GAREDJA; DJVARI

MICHAEL W. DOLS
*California State University,
Hayward*
EGYPT, ISLAMIC

JOHN J. DONOHUE
Université Saint Joseph
DAYR

A. A. M. DUNCAN
University of Glasgow
DONALD III (DONALDBANE);
DUNCAN I OF SCOTLAND;
EDINBURGH

LAWRENCE M. EARP
Princeton University
DESCORT

ANDREW S. EHRENKREUTZ
University of Michigan
CRUSADES AND CRUSADER STATES:
NEAR EAST

ROBERT FALCK
University of Toronto
DIAPHONIA; DIASTEMY

ZEᵓEV W. FALK
Hebrew University of Jerusalem
FAMILY AND FAMILY LAW, JEWISH

R. S. FIELD
Yale University
ETCHING

JOHN V. A. FINE, JR.
University of Michigan
CROATIA

EVELYN SCHERABON FIRCHOW
University of Minnesota
EINHARD

RUTH H. FIRESTONE
University of Missouri, Columbia
ECKENLIED

SEYMOUR L. FLAXMAN
City University of New York
DUTCH LITERATURE; ELCKERLIJC

JAROSLAV FOLDA
University of North Carolina
CRUSADER ART AND ARCHITECTURE

CLIVE FOSS
*University of Massachusetts,
Harbor Campus*
EPHESUS

DENTON FOX
University of Toronto
DOUGLAS, GAVIN; DUNBAR,
WILLIAM

ROBERTA FRANK
*University of Toronto, Centre for
Medieval Studies*
DRÓTTKVÆTT; EDDIC METERS;
EGILL SKALLAGRÍMSSON; EILÍFR
GOÐRÚNARSON; EINARR HELGASON
SKÁLAGLAMM; EYVINDR FINNSSON
SKÁLDASPILLIR

JOHN B. FREED
Illinois State University
ELECTIONS, ROYAL

EDWARD FRUEH
Columbia University
DONIZO (DOMNIZO); EMBRICHO OF
MAINZ; ERCHAMBERT OF FREISING;
EUSEBIUS BRUNO

CHIARA FRUGONI
Università degli Studi di Pisa
ECCLESIA AND SYNAGOGA

STEPHEN GARDNER
Columbia University
DURHAM CATHEDRAL; ERNULF

NINA G. GARSOÏAN
Columbia University
DWIN

ADELHEID M. GEALT
Indiana University
DADDI, BERNARDO; DUGENTO
(DUECENTO) ART

x

CONTRIBUTORS TO VOLUME 4

PATRICK GEARY
University of Florida
DUCHY

STEPHEN GERSH
Notre Dame University
DUALISM; ESSENCE AND EXISTENCE

ALAN GEWIRTH
University of Chicago
DEFENSOR PACIS

PETER B. GOLDEN
Rutgers University
DANISHMENDIDS; EMIR

VIVIAN H. H. GREEN
Lincoln College
ELECTIONS, CHURCH

KATHLEEN GREENFIELD
Drexel University
EMBER DAYS

JAMES GRIER
University of Toronto
DISCANTOR; DUPLUM

KAAREN GRIMSTAD
University of Minnesota
EUFEMIAVISOR

MARY GRIZZARD
University of New Mexico
DALMÁU, LUIS; DESTORRENTS,
RAMÓN

BJARNI GUÐNASON
Háskoli Íslands
EIRÍKR ODDSSON

NATHALIE HANLET
Columbia University
DUDO OF ST. QUENTIN;
ERCHENBERT OF MONTE CASSINO

JOSEPH HARRIS
Cornell University
EDDIC POETRY; EIRÍKSMÁL AND
HÁKONARMÁL

RALPH S. HATTOX
Princeton University
DIETARY LAWS, ISLAMIC

HUBERT HEINEN
University of Texas
DIETMAR VON AIST; ELEONORE OF
AUSTRIA; ELISABETH OF NASSAU-
SAARBRÜCKEN

JOHN BELL HENNEMAN
Princeton University Library
ENGUERRAND VII OF COUCY

DAVID HERLIHY
Harvard University
DEMOGRAPHY

MICHAEL HERREN
York University
DICUIL; DUBIIS NOMINIBUS, DE

ROBERT H. HEWSEN
Glassboro State College
DERBENT; ERZINCAN (ERZINJAN)

BENNETT D. HILL
St. Anselm's Abbey
DOMINIC, ST.; ETHELRED OF
RIEVAULX, ST.

JOHN H. HILL
CRUSADES AND CRUSADER STATES:
TO 1192

WILLIAM A. HINNEBUSCH
St. Gertrude Priory
DOMINICANS

GERALD A. J. HODGETT
King's College
ESTATE MANAGEMENT

ROBERT HOLLANDER
Princeton University
DANTE ALIGHIERI

NORMAN HOUSLEY
University of Liverpool
CRUSADES OF THE LATER MIDDLE
AGES

ANDREW HUGHES
University of Toronto
CUSTOS; DIABOLUS IN MUSICA;
DIFFERENTIA

R. STEPHEN HUMPHREYS
University of Chicago
DAMASCUS

W. T. H. JACKSON
Columbia University
EBARCIUS OF ST. AMAND; EPIC,
LATIN; ERMENRICH OF ELLWANGEN

FRANK RAINER JACOBY
ECBASIS CAPTIVI

MICHAEL JEFFREYS
University of Sydney
DIGENIS AKRITAS

JENNY M. JOCHENS
Towson State University
DENMARK

JAMES J. JOHN
Cornell University
DATARY, APOSTOLIC; DIONYSIUS
EXIGUUS

D. W. JOHNSON
Catholic University of America
DOCETISM; EUTYCHES; EUTYCHIOS
THE MELCHITE

GEORGE JONES
University of Maryland
FACHSCHRIFTTUM

JENNIFER E. JONES
Indiana University
DAW, JOHN; DOWN, ROGER;
DROUET OF DAMMARTIN

WILLIAM CHESTER JORDAN
Princeton University
CRUSADES AND CRUSADER STATES:
1212 TO 1272; EUDES RIGAUD

PETER A. JORGENSEN
University of Georgia
DRAUMA-JÓNS SAGA

WALTER EMIL KAEGI, JR.
University of Chicago
DOMESTIC; DRUNGARIOS;
EXARCHATE

RICHARD W. KAEUPER
University of Rochester
DISTRESS; ESCHEAT, ESCHEATOR

MARIANNE E. KALINKE
*University of Illinois at Urbana-
Champaign*
ELIS SAGA OK ROSAMUNDU

STEPHEN J. KAPLOWITT
University of Connecticut
DER VON KÜRENBERG; EZZOLIED

TRUDY S. KAWAMI
CTESIPHON

ALEXANDER P. KAZHDAN
*Dumbarton Oaks Research
Center*
EPARCH, BOOK OF THE

JOHN KELLER
University of Kentucky
EXEMPLUM

CONTRIBUTORS TO VOLUME 4

THOMAS KELLY
Purdue University
DESCHAMPS, EUSTACHE

MARILYN KAY KENNEY
University of Toronto, Centre for Medieval Studies
CUNEDDA WLEDIG; CYNDDELW BRYDYDD MAWR; DYFED

HERBERT L. KESSLER
The Johns Hopkins University
CUMDACH; DRAWINGS AND MODEL BOOKS; DURA EUROPOS; EARLY CHRISTIAN ART

G. L. KEYES
University of Toronto
DOCTORS OF THE CHURCH

MAJID KHADDURI
The Johns Hopkins Foreign Policy Institute
DIPLOMACY, ISLAMIC

FRANCES KIANKA
DEMETRIOS KYDONES

R. P. KINKADE
University of Connecticut
ELUCIDARIUM AND SPANISH LUCIDARIO

DALE KINNEY
Bryn Mawr College
DIOTISALVI (DEOTISALVI)

DAVID N. KLAUSNER
University of Toronto, Centre for Medieval Studies
DAFYDD AP GWILYM; EISTEDDFOD

ALAN E. KNIGHT
Pennsylvania State University
DRAMA, FRENCH

LINDA KOMAROFF
Metropolitan Museum of Art
EYVĀN

F. F. KREISLER
DOMESDAY BOOK

BARIŠA KREKIĆ
University of California, Los Angeles
DALMATIA; DUBROVNIK; DYRRACHIUM

ANGELIKI LAIOU
Harvard University
DUNATOI; FAMILY, BYZANTINE

TRAUGOTT LAWLER
Yale University
ENCYCLOPEDIAS AND DICTIONARIES, WESTERN EUROPEAN

ROBERT E. LERNER
Northwestern University
EIKE VON REPGOWE; EKKEHARD OF AURA

P. OSMUND LEWRY, O.P.
Pontifical Institute of Mediaeval Studies, Toronto
DIALECTIC

F. DONALD LOGAN
Emmanuel College
EXCOMMUNICATION

ANNE LOMBARD-JOURDAN
FAIRS; FAIRS OF CHAMPAGNE

H. R. LOYN
Westfield College
DANEGELD; DANELAW; ENGLAND: ANGLO-SAXON; ETHELRED THE UNREADY

BRYCE LYON
Brown University
ÉCHEVIN; ENGLAND: NORMAN-ANGEVIN; EXCHEQUER

TIMOTHY J. McGEE
University of Toronto
DANCE; DRAMA, LITURGICAL; FAENZA CODEX

HUGH MAGENNIS
The Queen's University of Belfast
EXEGESIS, OLD ENGLISH

GEORGE P. MAJESKA
University of Maryland
DAROKHRANITELNITSA; EPITRAKHIL

KRIKOR H. MAKSOUDIAN
DAVID OF SASUN; DAVID THE INVINCIBLE; ĒJMIACIN; EZNIK OF KOŁB

IVAN G. MARCUS
The Jewish Theological Seminary of America
ELEAZAR BEN JUDAH OF WORMS

T. L. MARKEY
University of Michigan
ERIKSKRÖNIKAN

DENNIS D. MARTIN
Bethany Theological Seminary
DEVOTIO MODERNA

JOHN RUPERT MARTIN
Princeton University
DEESIS

H. SALVADOR MARTÍNEZ
New York University
CUADERNA VÍA

THOMAS F. MATHEWS
New York University
EARLY CHRISTIAN AND BYZANTINE ARCHITECTURE

RALPH WHITNEY MATHISEN
University of South Carolina
DESIDERIUS OF MONTE CASSINO; DONATUS OF FIESOLE; EIGEL; ENDELECHIUS; ENGELMODUS; ENNODIUS, MAGNUS FELIX; ERMOLDUS NIGELLUS; EUGENIUS II OF TOLEDO; EUGENIUS VULGARIUS; EUGIPPIUS; EUPOLEMIUS

BRIAN MERRILEES
University of Toronto
CRUSADE AND DEATH OF RICHARD I; DISCIPLINA CLERICALIS; DONNEI DES AMANTS

JOHN MEYENDORFF
Fordham University
CYRIL AND METHODIOS, STS.; CYRIL OF ALEXANDRIA, ST.; ECUMENICAL PATRIARCH; EUSEBIUS OF CAESAREA

DAVID MILLS
University of Liverpool
DRAMA, WESTERN EUROPEAN

ALASTAIR J. MINNIS
University of Bristol
EXEGESIS, LATIN; EXEGESIS, MIDDLE ENGLISH

ROBERT P. MULTHAUF
Smithsonian Institution
DISTILLED LIQUORS; DYES AND DYEING

DONALD M. NICOL
University of London
EPIROS, DESPOTATE OF

DONNCHADH Ó CORRÁIN
University College, Cork
DÁL CAIS; DÁL RIATA; EÓGANACHT

RICHARD O'GORMAN
University of Iowa
ENVOI

CONTRIBUTORS TO VOLUME 4

THOMAS H. OHLGREN
Purdue University
DUNSTAN, LIFE OF

NICOLAS OIKONOMIDES
Université de Montréal
CUROPALATES; DESPOT; DUX;
ECLOGUE; EPANAGOGE

PÁDRAIG P. Ó NÉILL
*University of North Carolina,
Chapel Hill*
DUODECIM ABUSIVIS SAECULI, DE

HERMANN PÁLSSON
University of Edinburgh
EGILS SAGA EINHENDA OK
ÁSMUNDAR BERSERKJABANA; EGILS
SAGA SKALLAGRÍMSSONAR

OLAF PEDERSON
University of Aarhus
CROSS-STAFF; EQUATORIUM

EDWARD PETERS
University of Pennsylvania
DEPOSITION OF RULERS, THEORIES
OF

E. J. POLAK
*Queensborough Community
College*
DICTAMEN

H. BOONE PORTER
EXTREME UNCTION

VENETIA PORTER
FAIENCE

WADĀD AL-QĀḌĪ
American University of Beirut
DRUZES

DONALD E. QUELLER
*University of Illinois at Urbana-
Champaign*
CRUSADES AND CRUSADER STATES:
FOURTH; DIPLOMACY, WESTERN
EUROPEAN

MARY LYNN RAMPOLLA
*University of Toronto, Centre for
Medieval Studies*
EADMER OF CANTERBURY

THOMAS RENNA
*Saginaw Valley State College,
Michigan*
DISPUTATIO INTER CLERICUM ET
MILITEM; EGIDIUS COLONNA

ROGER E. REYNOLDS
*Pontifical Institute of Mediaeval
Studies, Toronto*
CUSTOMARY; DEAD, OFFICE OF THE;
DEATH AND BURIAL, IN EUROPE;
DIVINE OFFICE

JEAN RICHARD
Université de Dijon
CYPRUS, KINGDOM OF

ELAINE GOLDEN ROBISON
DEUSDEDIT, CARDINAL; DICTATUS
PAPAE; EGBERT OF LIÈGE; EKKEHARD
I OF ST. GALL; EKKEHARD IV OF ST.
GALL; ENGELBERT OF ADMONT

PAUL ROREM
EASTER

LINDA C. ROSE
DARDANELLES; DEMES; DIOCESE,
SECULAR; DIONYSIOS OF TEL-
MAHRÉ; DIYARBAKIR; EDESSA;
EKTHESIS; EPARCH; EPIBOLÉ;
EUPHRATES RIVER

ROY ROSENSTEIN
American College in Paris
DIT; ESTRABOT

JAY ROVNER
Princeton University Library
DIETARY LAWS, JEWISH

TEOFILO F. RUIZ
Brooklyn College
EULOGIUS OF CÓRDOBA

FREDERICK H. RUSSELL
Rutgers University
CRUSADE, CHILDREN'S; CRUSADE,
CONCEPT OF

NAHUM M. SARNA
Brandeis University
EXEGESIS, JEWISH

PAUL SCHACH
University of Nebraska
EYRBYGGJA SAGA

BERNHARD SCHIMMELPFENNIG
Universität Augsburg
DEGRADATION OF CLERICS

MARIANNE SHAPIRO
New York University
ERMENGAUD, MATFRE

MICHAEL M. SHEEHAN
*Pontifical Institute of Mediaeval
Studies, Toronto*
DISPENSATION; FAMILY AND
MARRIAGE, WESTERN EUROPEAN

DANIEL J. SHEERIN
Catholic University of America
DEDICATION OF CHURCHES

SERGEI SHUISKII
Princeton University
ENCYCLOPEDIAS AND DICTIONARIES,
ARABIC AND PERSIAN

LARRY SILVER
Northwestern University
DANSE MACABRE; ECCE HOMO

ECKEHARD SIMON
Harvard University
DRAMA, GERMAN

BARRIE SINGLETON
*University of London, Courtauld
Institute*
ESSEX, JOHN

LOIS K. SMEDICK
University of Windsor
CURSUS

JOSEPH SNOW
University of Georgia
DINIS

ROBERT J. SNOW
University of Texas at Austin
DOMINICAN CHANT

JAMES SNYDER
Bryn Mawr College
DARET, JACQUES; DAVID, GERARD;
EYCK, JAN VAN AND HUBERT VAN

JOSEP M. SOLA-SOLÉ
Catholic University of America
DANÇA GENERAL DE LA MUERTE

PRISCILLA P. SOUCEK
New York University
DAWĀT

ERNST H. SOUDEK
University of Virginia
ECKHART, MEISTER

EDDA SPIELMANN
*California State University,
Northridge*
ERMENRÎKES DÔT

xiii

CONTRIBUTORS TO VOLUME 4

J. STEYAERT
University of Minnesota
DIJON, CHARTREUSE DE CHAMPMOL

JOSEPH R. STRAYER
Princeton University
CRUSADES, POLITICAL; CURFEW;
CURIA, LAY; CURIA, PAPAL;
DAUPHIN; DIOCESE, ECCLESIASTICAL;
DOCTOR; DONATISM; DUNGEON

JAMES H. STUBBLEBINE
Rutgers University
DUCCIO DI BUONINSEGNA

RONALD G. SUNY
University of Michigan
DAVID II (IV) THE BUILDER; DAVID
OF TAO; ERIST^{C}AW

SANDRA CANDEE SUSMAN
DALLE MASEGNE, PIERPAOLO AND
JACOBELLO; DELLA ROBBIA, LUCA,
ANDREA, GIOVANNI

DONALD W. SUTHERLAND
University of Iowa
ENGLISHRY, PRESENTMENT OF

EMILY ZACK TABUTEAU
Michigan State University
CUSTUMALS OF NORMANDY

GEORGE S. TATE
Brigham Young University
EINARR SKÚLASON; EYSTEINN
ÁSGRÍMSSON

GEORGE H. TAVARD
Methodist Theological School
ECCLESIOLOGY

ELAINE C. TENNANT
University of California, Berkeley
DRESDENER HELDENBUCH

R. W. THOMSON
Harvard University
ERISE

KARL D. UITTI
Princeton University
FABLIAU AND COMIC TALE

KRISTINE T. UTTERBACK
*University of Toronto, Centre for
Medieval Studies*
CYPRIAN, ST.

GEORGES VAJDA
DĀWŪD IBN MARWĀN AL-
MUQAMMIȘ

JOHN VAN ENGEN
University of Notre Dame
DECRETALS, FALSE; DONATION OF
CONSTANTINE

ARJO VANDERJAGT
Filosofisch Instituut, Groningen
DURAND OF ST. POURÇAIN

PHILIPPE VERDIER
ENAMEL

CHARLES VERLINDEN
*Commission Internationale
d'Histoire Maritime*
EXPLORATION BY WESTERN
EUROPEANS

BRUCE WEBSTER
University of Kent
DAVID I OF SCOTLAND; DAVID II OF
SCOTLAND

JILL R. WEBSTER
University of Toronto
EIXIMENIS, FRANCESC

ESTELLE WHELAN
New York University
CUERDA SECA

J. E. CAERWYN WILLIAMS
University College of Wales
EINON AP GWALCHMAI; ELIDIR SAIS

JOHN WILLIAMS
University of Pittsburgh
DOMINICUS; EMETERIUS OF TÁBARA;
ENDE

GABRIELE WINKLER
*St. John's University, Collegeville,
Minnesota*
EPIPHANY, FEAST OF

BRUCIA WITTHOFT
Framingham State College
DONATELLO

MARTHA WOLFF
The National Gallery of Art
E. S., MASTER; ENGRAVING

CHARLES T. WOOD
Dartmouth College
EDWARD THE CONFESSOR, ST;
EDWARD I OF ENGLAND; EDWARD II
OF ENGLAND; EDWARD III OF
ENGLAND; EDWARD THE BLACK
PRINCE; ENGLAND: 1216–1485

FRANK E. WOZNIAK
University of New Mexico
DIPLOMACY, BYZANTINE

RONALD JOHN ZAWILLA, O.P.
*Pontifical Institute of Mediaeval
Studies, Toronto*
DOMINICAN RITE; DURAND, GUILLAUME

RONALD EDWARD ZUPKO
Marquette University
DUCAT

Dictionary
of the
Middle Ages

Dictionary of the Middle Ages

CROATIA. In the middle of the sixth century the Balkans (including the western regions, comprising what is now Croatia, Dalmatia, Istria, and Bosnia) were part of the Byzantine Empire. The Slavs, who had been living north of the Danube, began settling in the eastern Balkans around 550. Though in this period they carried out sporadic raids into the western Balkans—some even reaching the Dalmatian coast—occupation of the western regions began later. The Avars appeared in Pannonia in the late 560's and subjugated many Slavs dwelling there. This caused the large-scale flight of Slavs into the Balkans, and by the 580's other Slavs, under Avar command, were invading the Balkans. A major invasion of Dalmatia occurred in 614, leading to the conquest of Salona, the Byzantine provincial capital. In Dalmatia and its environs there followed settlement by both Avars and Slavs. The Slavic component was probably the same as that which settled the more central Balkans and which later was to become the Serbs. Thus the Slavs who occupied what is now Croatia, Dalmatia, Bosnia, Hercegovina, Serbia, and Montenegro were of the same stock.

In the second quarter of the seventh century, during the reign of the Byzantine emperor Heraklios (610–641), if we can believe Constantine Porphyrogenitos (writing *ca.* 950), the Croatians arrived from north of the Carpathians, driving out most of the Avars and establishing their rule over the northwestern Balkans. They seem to have been an Iranian people, though some scholars consider them Slavs. Their numbers were small but they owed their success to tight military organization. They did not yet establish a single state, but set up various smaller units called *župas* or *županijas* (counties).

In a relatively short period of time (certainly by the end of the eighth century) most, if not all, of the Croatians had been assimilated by the Slavs. However, they left their name for the Slavic people whom they had conquered and for the language of these Slavs. In this article the term "Croatian" refers to the Slavic people who thus resulted. Whereas in northern and central Dalmatia the Slavs who came to be under Croatian *župans* (county lords) eventually came to consider themselves Croatians, most Slavs of southern Dalmatia came to consider themselves Serbs. The descendants of the indigenous populations (probably chiefly Illyrians) who did not flee or die in conflict with the invaders were also in time assimilated. Archaeology shows that they had considerable influence on the material culture of the Slavs, and indicates a continuity of various settlements from the pre-Slavic into the Slavic period.

The Dalmatian Croatians continued for a century or so to live independently in their separate counties while the Croatians to the north in Pannonian Croatia (roughly between the Sava and Drava rivers), though under their own leaders, remained somewhat dependent on the Avars. Moreover, in the midst of the Slavic settlement that encompassed most of the Dalmatian coast there remained various walled cities retained by the Byzantines: Zadar, Trogir, Split, Dubrovnik, Budva, Kotor. They formed what is known as the archonate (later theme) of Dalmatia. From these Byzantine cities Christianity and an urban literate culture gradually penetrated into the Slavic interior.

In 788 Charlemagne, having conquered Lombardy, turned farther east, subjugating Istria. This brought him into contact with the declining but still extant Avar khanate in Pannonia. After campaigns of 791 and 795–796 he more or less destroyed Avar power. Thus the Franks became overlords of the territory as far east as the Tisza River. The Pannonian Croatians were ruled by a prince named Vojnomir, who had supported Charlemagne in the campaigns against the Avars. After the Avars' defeat he accepted Frankish overlordship. The Franks placed these

1

Croatians under the margrave of Friuli. Soon, with Frankish blessing, missionaries began entering the territory of the Pannonian Croatians from Aquileia, whose bishop was given jurisdiction over this region by the Franks.

Meanwhile the Franks pressed into Dalmatia. From 803 Frankish overlordship was recognized in most of northern Dalmatia. As a result of this expansion Frankish missionaries under the jurisdiction of the bishop of Aquileia appeared in Dalmatia as well. Nin, a port near Zadar, became the residence of a Croatian prince named Višeslav (*ca.* 800–*ca.* 810), who is spoken of as a Christian. Most of Croatian Dalmatia was under Višeslav. It seems his territory stretched from the Adriatic inland to the Vrbas River and extended roughly from what is now Rijeka down the coast as far south as the Cetina River. Possibly he was pro-Frank and had obtained Frankish aid in extending his authority over Dalmatia. It is reasonable to conclude that the campaigns of the Franks, followed by their recognition of a single Croatian prince in Dalmatia, had done much to unite under one Croatian leader the many Croatian counties or tribes in Dalmatia, which previously had been separate and under various leaders. Thus in the first decade of the ninth century the two Croatian states of the future (Dalmatian Croatia and Pannonian Croatia) existed separately, each under Frankish suzerainty and each under a single native prince.

When Charlemagne died in 814, the Pannonian Croatians were ruled by Prince Ljudevit (*ca.* 810–823), whose chief residence was at Sisak. Concurrently Višeslav's successor, Borna (*ca.* 810–821), who resided at Nin, seems to have ruled most of the Croatians in northern Dalmatia. In 819 Ljudevit revolted against the Franks. The Franks took no action at first, so Ljudevit pressed on to unite to his Pannonian state the Slavs of Istria and Dalmatia. This led to open conflict with Borna, whom he defeated. He also repelled small Frankish expeditions sent against him in 820 and 821. But a major Frankish expedition in 822 put an end to his rebellion and forced him to flee; Frankish overlordship over the Croatians was thereby restored; Borna's nephew was confirmed by the Franks as ruler over Croatian Dalmatia. In 843, when the Frankish empire was divided, Frankish Italy became suzerain of Istria and Dalmatian Croatia, while Frankish Germany possessed Pannonian Croatia.

The most active Slavic fleet in the Adriatic was that of the Neretljani. They took to piracy, striking across the Adriatic at Italy, especially Venice. Still pagan, they occupied the territory between the Cetina and Neretva rivers. They became so troublesome that finally in 839 Venice launched a major campaign against them; the Venetians succeeded in forcing a treaty upon the Neretljani, but it was to be short-lasting, and in the 840's they were again raiding the Italian coast.

The Slavs along the Dalmatian coast, though still under Frankish suzerainty, began developing friendly relations with the Byzantines in the 830's. One gets the impression that despite their overlordship, the Franks had almost no role in Dalmatia in this period, leaving the Dalmatian Croatians to follow their own policies. The prince Trpimir I (845–864), founder of the Trpimirović dynasty, moved the princely residence from Nin to Klis. On his death his son Zdeslav succeeded, only to be immediately overthrown by a Knin nobleman, Domagoj (864–876). Zdeslav fled to Constantinople.

In the 860's Arab raids along the Dalmatian coast led the Byzantines to send a fleet to relieve their Dalmatian towns. Various local Slavic tribes now accepted Byzantine suzerainty. The Neretljani refused until, in 871, the Byzantine fleet forced them to end their resistance. At this time Slavs from Dalmatia participated in Byzantine military operations against the Arabs in the Adriatic. They seem to have served both on their own ships and on regular imperial ships. The Byzantine cities in Dalmatia had long been pillaged by the Slavic tribes who lived around them. Basil I in the early 880's ordered the Byzantine towns to pay the tribute owed to Byzantium to the Slavic tribes. Thus their raiding was reduced by buying them off.

In 875 the Franks, who had played virtually no role in Dalmatia for years, tried to reassert their authority there. Their action precipitated a revolt, led by Prince Domagoj, that succeeded in ending forever Frankish overlordship in Dalmatia. Domagoj tried, but failed, to liberate Istria. Frankish suzerainty continued for a while longer over Pannonian Croatia. Domagoj died within a year of achieving independence; his son was promptly overthrown by Zdeslav of the legitimate dynasty. Zdeslav in his turn was overthrown in 879 by a nobleman, Branimir. In 879, under him, Croatia received papal recognition as a state. Branimir ruled until Mutimir of the legitimate dynasty overthrew him in about 892. At some time between 910 and 914 his heir, Tomislav, the greatest of medieval Croatia's rulers, came to the throne.

The Magyars, meanwhile, in the 890's had migrated into present-day Hungary. They immediately

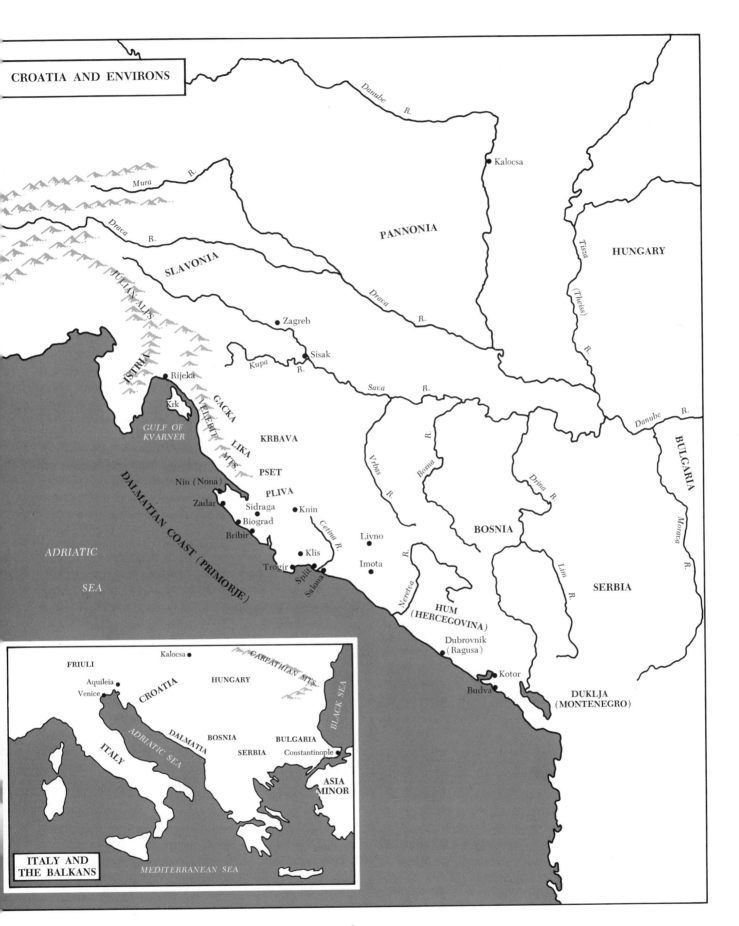

CROATIA AND ENVIRONS

Danube R.

Kalocsa

PANNONIA

HUNGARY

Tisza (Theiss) R.

Mura R.

Drava R.

SLAVONIA

JULIAN ALPS

Zagreb

Drava R.

ISTRIA

Rijeka

Krk

GULF OF KVARNER

Kupa R.

Sisak

VELEBIT

GACKA

Sava R.

LIKA MTS.

KRBAVA

Vrbas R.

Bosna R.

Danube R.

BULGARIA

PSET

DALMATIAN COAST (PRIMORJE)

Nin (Nona)

PLIVA

Zadar

Sidraga

Knin

Biograd

Bribir

Cetina R.

Livno

Klis

BOSNIA

Drina R.

ADRIATIC

SEA

Trogir

Split

Salona

Imota

Neretva R.

Lim R.

Morava R.

SERBIA

HUM (HERCEGOVINA)

Dubrovnik (Ragusa)

Kotor

Budva

DUKLJA (MONTENEGRO)

ITALY AND THE BALKANS

FRIULI

Kalocsa

CARPATHIAN MTS.

Aquileia

CROATIA

HUNGARY

Venice

BLACK SEA

ADRIATIC SEA

ITALY

DALMATIA

BOSNIA

BULGARIA

SERBIA

Constantinople

ASIA MINOR

MEDITERRANEAN SEA

3

began raiding, threatening the other states in the area. They particularly endangered the Pannonian Croatians, still under nominal Frankish suzerainty. These Croatians received aid against the Magyars from Tomislav, who defeated them in several battles and established a lasting border between the Croatians and Magyars along the Drava River. In so doing he took over all Pannonian Croatia and added it to his own state, thereby eliminating all Frankish overlordship over Pannonian Croatia. Thus, Tomislav became master of both Croatias, which were united for the first time. Other than the Drava border, it is not known where exactly his state borders lay. To the south of the Drava he held what we think of as modern Croatia, Slavonia, northern and western Bosnia, and the territory along the Dalmatian coast from what is now Rijeka to at least the mouth of the Cetina River (excluding the scattered Byzantine towns).

Tomislav's state was divided into three main regions. The first, Slavonia, the northernmost territory, extended from the Drava beyond the Sava and Kupa rivers; it seems to have retained considerable local autonomy, simply rendering tribute to the Croatian ruler. Constantine Porphyrogenitos calls it an archonate. It was to keep this autonomous, but subordinate, position until the mid tenth or early eleventh century. Second, there was the *banovina* of Lika, Krbava, and Gacka; it too seems to have retained considerable autonomy. Its ban (ruler) held a high position at court, and after Tomislav's death seems to have become a more or less independent figure. Third, there were Tomislav's original Dalmatian lands, including the northwestern Bosnian territory. The eleven *župas* that Constantine Porphyrogenitos mentions lay within this region. Under their own local nobles, who presumably had less autonomy than the rulers of the other two regions, the eleven *župas* were Livno, Cetina, Imotska, Pliva, Pset, Primorje (the coast), Bribir, Nona, Knin, Sidraga, and Nin. Quite possibly more *župas* existed than those named by Constantine.

Tomislav maintained no permanent capital; rather he traveled from one residence to another, collecting taxes, ensuring that things were in order, and judging legal disputes. His household and retinue traveled with him. Until this time there had been little or no distinction between palace servants and state officials. Under Tomislav some specific offices and some sort of state administration began to develop. He had a chancellery with permanent scribes to draw up charters and decrees.

During the war between Byzantium and Symeon of Bulgaria (*ca.* 923) the Byzantines sent an embassy to Tomislav that concluded an alliance between the two states. In the following year a pro-Byzantine ruler of Serbia, Zaharije, was driven from Serbia by Symeon. He sought refuge with Tomislav. As a result of this alliance and Tomislav's asylum to Zaharije, in 926 Symeon invaded Croatia. Tomislav soundly defeated the invading Bulgarian army. This success demonstrates that Tomislav had created a powerful Croatian military force. Writing twenty-five years later, Constantine Porphyrogenitos claims, probably with considerable exaggeration, that this army consisted of 60,000 horsemen and 100,000 foot soldiers. His navy was said to include 80 galleys and 100 cutters.

As we have seen, politically there were two Dalmatias (one Byzantine, the other Croatian). Yet despite Byzantine political suzerainty over specific towns and islands, it seems that the churches in Byzantine Dalmatia remained under the jurisdiction of the pope. The chief ecclesiastic in Dalmatia was the bishop (probably archbishop) of Split, who may have stood over the other Byzantine Dalmatian towns as well. However, he did not have authority over the Croatian Dalmatian towns. Nevertheless, since some of the missionary activity into the Slavic hinterland originated from Split, some of the early Croatian Christian communities seem to have been under Split's jurisdiction. In Croatian Dalmatia the chief missionary activity had been conducted by the Franks under the direction of the bishop of Aquileia. These efforts dated from the beginning of the ninth century. The Frankish mission seems to have been centered in the princely residence of Nin, where about 850 a bishopric had been established by the pope for Dalmatian Croatia. It is not certain whether this bishop was subordinate to Aquileia or directly under the pope's control.

In 925—if the texts of two letters given in the sixteenth-century *Historia Salonitana maior (HSM)* are authentic—Pope John X sent a legate to convene a church council in Split. The main purpose of the council seems to have been to establish a rational hierarchy for Dalmatia by ending the overlapping jurisdictions between Split and Nin. The council, with Tomislav's support, made the archbishop of Split metropolitan for all Dalmatia (both Byzantine and Croatian) from Istria to Kotor. Nin's Bishop Grgur protested vehemently against the council's decision; as a result a second council was held in 928, also in Split, that abolished the see of Nin. According to

HSM, in 928 the archbishop of Split was placed also over the whole Croatian state, for the bishop of Sisak, the leading bishop in Pannonian Croatia, was subjected to Split. Until recently many scholars have depicted these councils primarily as scenes of a language battle in which Grgur of Nin, supposedly a great defender of Slavic, was crushed by the establishment supporting Latin. However, recent scholarship has shown that the major issue of contention at the councils was the jurisdictional quarrel between the ancient see of Split and the ambitious Croatian bishop of Nin. Language, if it was an issue at all, was a very minor one.

Tomislav seems to have been crowned king by 924 or 925. It is not known when or by whom he was crowned. In fact, the title itself could be called into question. The only evidence for it is a letter— the authenticity of which has been questioned— from Pope John X, allegedly written in 925, calling him "king." It seems that Tomislav died in 928, though Farlati, whose information is often suspect, has him live to 940. Constantine Porphyrogenitos and Farlati each give totally different lists of rulers after Tomislav, just as both give differing lists of his predecessors and different dates for his accession.

Constantine Porphyrogenitos says a civil war broke out in 949 in which an important nobleman, Pribina (ban of Lika, Krbava, and Gacka), overthrew and killed a ruler named Miroslav and put Miroslav's brother Kresimir (949–969) on the throne. Thus, in the period after Tomislav, this ban had great influence in the state and had risen to become a kingmaker. However, since he was a most powerful nobleman, the ruler of three districts, he may have been a special case. Thus one probably should not infer from this that the nobles in general must have increased their power. However, the civil wars after Tomislav's death most likely did hasten the decline of central authority. Various peripheral territories took advantage of unsettled conditions to secede. The Neretljani and possibly Slavonia broke away, and at least part of Croatia's Bosnian holdings were lost to Časlav's revived Serbia. However, Časlav's death (*ca.* 960) led to unsettled conditions among the Serbs that allowed Kresimir of Croatia to regain western (if not all) Bosnia in the 960's.

Very little is known about either part of Croatia in the late tenth century. Stjepan Držislav ruled Croatia from 969 to 997 and was crowned king about 988. Upon his death his lands were divided among his three sons; they were ordered to cooperate with each other and the eldest, Svetoslav, was to

have primacy over the younger two, Kresimir and Gojislav. Svetoslav soon tried to oust his brothers, causing them to revolt. Since Svetoslav had close ties with the Neretljani pirates, the latter's enemies, the Byzantine towns and Venice, turned against him. The Byzantines, involved in a major war with Samuil of Bulgaria, allowed Venice to intervene, and soon gave the doge of Venice the title dux of Dalmatia, making him the imperial representative in Dalmatia. The more active presence of this leading commercial power in Byzantine Dalmatia seemed a threat to the Dalmatians, both those of Croatia and those of the Byzantine theme.

Venice first defeated the Neretljani, who as a consequence entered a period of decline. In 1000 Svetoslav was ousted by his brothers as king of Croatia. It is not known whether Venice had any role in his deposition. In any case, having been deposed and needing support, he turned to Venice, recognizing Venetian overlordship over his lands—a nominal act, since he no longer held them. Svetoslav then disappears from the sources; perhaps he died. However, his son Stjepan was in Venice, where he married the doge's daughter. Stjepan's close ties with Venice increased the danger to his two uncles ruling Croatia, Kresimir (1000–1030) and Gojislav (1000–*ca.* 1020). Their opposition to Venetian activity in Dalmatia caused Venice to direct more attention to the Croatian ports. Soon Venice became overlord of the important Slavic port of Biograd; possibly other Slavic ports fell to Venice as well. As far as we can tell, no Venetian representatives entered any Croatian town; the local citizens merely swore allegiance to Venice and continued to govern themselves.

In 1019, after defeating Samuil, the Byzantine emperor Basil II asserted his own authority in Dalmatia. Immediately Kresimir sent his submission to Basil, who accepted it and bestowed upon Kresimir the patrician rank, leaving him to rule Croatia as a Byzantine vassal. Kresimir's relations with Venice remained tense until 1024. Then a civil war broke out in Venice; Kresimir took advantage of it to regain whatever possessions he had lost to the Venetians. After Basil's death (1025) Byzantium entered a period of decline and took little interest in distant Dalmatia. Kresimir ceased paying homage to the empire and became an independent ruler again. He suffered the loss of some territory to his nephew Stjepan, who had fled the Venetian civil war to Hungary in 1024. The Hungarian king seized part or all of Slavonia— possibly already seceded from Croatia—which he awarded to Stjepan as an appanage. Under Kresimir's son and successor, Stjepan I (1030–1058)—not to be confused with Svetoslav's son Stjepan—the Croatians expanded further to the northwest, annexing Carinthia.

Byzantium reestablished cordial relations with Stjepan I's son Peter Kresimir (1058–1074), known as Kresimir IV. Tied down by two major enemies, the Normans and the Seljuks, the empire was in no position to act in Dalmatia, which was now being threatened by the Normans. Therefore, in 1069 the empire appointed Kresimir IV imperial representative in Dalmatia (that is, over the Dalmatian theme). Kresimir respected the autonomy of the towns that composed it.

In the mid eleventh century the Slavic liturgy became an issue in Croatian Dalmatia. Written in Glagolitic letters, it was widely used, particularly in northern Dalmatia, where its chief centers were on the islands in the Gulf of Kvarner, an inlet formed by the Istrian peninsula. In this regard the isle of Krk was the most important. In the 1060's when the papacy was demanding general church reform, many high clerics in the Byzantine towns of Dalmatia, which had always used the Latin liturgy, wanted to prohibit Slavic and to standardize church practices. Kresimir sympathized with the reformers. A synod was held at Split in 1060 that declared that priests must know Latin and declared it the language of the church. The council condemned Slavic in the service and also priestly beards and marriages. Some churches were closed as a result, and there seems to have been some unrest.

In 1063 the pope demanded application of these decisions and he too called Slavic (as a religious language) heretical. In 1064 a rebellion for the Slavic church broke out on the isle of Krk under a certain Vuk, who set up an autonomous church. A naval expedition directed by Kresimir put an end to this venture. In 1074 a second council was held at Split that reissued the edicts of the 1060 council against Slavic. But though Latin triumphed officially, Slavic survived in many churches, owing either to local toleration or to the impossibility of finding enough clerics knowing Latin. Glagolitic religious manuscripts from Croatia survive from each subsequent century throughout the Middle Ages. But as an established, accepted movement the Slavic church collapsed. Its demise came about because the leading Croatian political and religious figures opposed it.

By 1065 Slavonia, the region between the Sava and the Drava, was administered by the autonomous ban Zvonimir, son-in-law of the late Hungarian king, Bela I. In the course of the next four years Zvonimir came to accept Croatian suzerainty. It seems he submitted to this in an agreement by which his region (Slavonia) was restored to the Croatian state, though in such a way as to retain its autonomy, leaving him as its ruler. It also appears that the region the Croatian king confirmed as Zvonimir's *banovina* was more extensive than his original territory, which suggests he was given further lands by the Croatian king. Zvonimir joined his territory to Croatia in exchange for continued local independence, an important role in general Croatian state affairs, and his own succession to the Croatian throne should Kresimir be childless. Croatian charters were thereafter issued in the names of both the king and the ban.

Kresimir disappears from the sources after 1074. In the fall of 1075 Zvonimir was crowned king of Croatia by a papal legate. He accepted the status of papal vassal and maintained close ties with the papacy. Zvonimir aimed to subdue the nobility—the hereditary provincial nobles, the *župans,* who for generations had been governing in the provinces. They had their own local power bases and exercised great internal independence. It seems that Zvonimir sought to gain firmer control over his state by ousting various local nobles from local administration and replacing them with his own supporters—court nobles and high clerics. Needless to say, his policy was opposed by the provincial nobles.

In 1089 or 1090 Zvonimir died. Legend has him killed in a brawl during a council. He had been married to the sister of the king of Hungary; they had one young son, his heir. The boy—the last of the Trpimirović dynasty—died almost immediately after his succession in 1090, setting off a time of troubles. Zvonimir's widow tried to take over, but she was unpopular with the nobles, who had hated her husband. This was a moment of weakness for the central government, and a fine chance for the nobles to reassert their traditional rights in their own counties. The Hungarian king quickly intervened to protect his sister's interests (a fine excuse for what were surely his own ambitions) and occupied much of Croatia, including part of Dalmatia.

However, the Cumans attacked Hungary, causing a partial withdrawal of the Hungarians. They withdrew from Dalmatia, but kept Pannonian Croatia. Between the Drava and the Gvozd Mountain they created a special Croatian *banovina* ruled by the King's nephew, Almos. This *banovina* existed from 1091 to 1095. The Hungarians also established a bishopric at Zagreb in 1094; its territory coincided with that of Almos' *banovina.* To separate the church in Pannonian Croatia from Split, the Zagreb bishopric was placed under a Hungarian archbishop in Ostrogon. Later Zagreb was to be subjected to another Hungarian archbishopric, Kalocsa.

What was left of Croatia (primarily Dalmatia and any part of the interior not included in the Hungarian *banovina*) was then taken over by a certain Peter (1093–1097), who bore the title "king" and resided in Knin. He soon expelled Almos, and recovered the territory of the *banovina* in 1095. But late that year Koloman (1095–1116) succeeded to the Hungarian throne. In 1096 his armies retook Pannonian Croatia and pushed into Dalmatia. Peter was killed in this warfare on the Gvozd Mountain (renamed Petrova Gora after him). The Hungarians, who had long lacked a port, took Biograd in 1097.

In 1102 Koloman moved against Croatia again, but this time he stopped at the Drava; and there, a fourteenth-century source reports, he met with twelve leading Croatian nobles. As a result of this meeting, Koloman obtained Croatia by agreement (the so-called *Pacta conventa*). He then proceeded to occupy the Dalmatian towns one by one. The process of obtaining submission from them was probably completed between 1105 and 1107. These acquisitions included the Byzantine towns of northern Dalmatia as well as the Croatian towns. There seems to have been no attempt at common action by the Dalmatian towns. Koloman allowed them to keep their former autonomy and issued charters guaranteeing this.

Thus, by 1107 Koloman had annexed Croatia and secured his overlordship over Dalmatia. But, though it is certain that he acquired these territories, the circumstances surrounding his annexation of Croatia remain problematical. He is said to have met with the Croatian nobles and to have obtained their acquiescence in his taking the Croatian crown by promising to respect their ancestral privileges. Having received these promises, the nobles elected him king of Croatia and Dalmatia. However, the source for this agreement is a fourteenth-century document that contains various items that seem anachronistic. Thus it appears that this document is not the original text of the surrender—though that is what it purports to be—but a fourteenth-century version that describes contemporary relations between king and nobility, and then traces that fourteenth-century reality back to an initial agreement. Some of the features of the document probably did go back to 1102,

but other items (including a diet) could have been subsequent developments that were later attributed to 1102 to give them an aura of tradition. But though the text probably includes some questionable historical events and various later features, much of its content does depict the situation that actually was created in 1102.

The document stipulates that the two kingdoms were not to be merged; they were to remain distinct realms with a common king. Thus Croatia was still an independent state; however, the Hungarian dynasty had succeeded the Croatian kings. Each Hungarian king would have to come to Croatia for a separate coronation. The separate coronation in Croatia was retained until 1235. Latin was made the official language of state.

The Croatian nobles (that is, the hereditary provincial leaders and landlords) were thus recognized in their positions by the Hungarian king, and they in turn recognized him as king of Croatia. These nobles were probably relatively content, since they had just escaped from an attack by the Croatian rulers (particularly Zvonimir) on their positions and privileges. Thus they were allowed to remain as basically independent lords on their lands and as local leaders. They were to continue in this position throughout the medieval period, up to the Ottoman conquest of most of Croatia.

By owing loyalty to a Hungarian king they sacrificed little. First, foreign affairs were in the king's hands. Second, the king was the commander in chief of the army, and the nobles owed him military service when summoned (but this had been owed earlier to the Croatian ruler); however, if they crossed the Drava, the Hungarian king was obliged to pay. The king had the mutual obligation to defend Croatia from attack. Third, the Hungarian king appointed a ban of Croatia, but it seems that other than being a military leader for campaigns and the recipient of some income, this ban interfered little in local affairs. In the later twelfth century the ban was frequently a younger son of the Hungarian king. In the thirteenth century this position was often held by the heir to the Hungarian throne. Later the ban was often a Croatian nobleman. Fourth, general Croatian matters were to be discussed at the Croatian Diet (whenever this section of the treaty appeared, be it originally or later). The Hungarian king had to confirm its decisions before they became law, but he did so as king of Croatia.

But besides these few items everything else was left in the hands of the Croatian nobles: internal administration, judicial matters, land policy, and the like. There was no integration of the Croatian state with the Hungarian. Except for the ban and his court, no Hungarians were sent to administer in Croatia. In fact there was very little integration in Croatia at all. Power remained basically on a county level under local nobles, and this was essentially how matters had been until then. Though the king received some taxes and customs duties in Croatia, it seems the nobles owed no tax to the king. They thus rendered him only military service. The king, however, did receive for his personal use the estates of the extinct Croatian royal family.

Occasionally individual nobles tried to break away from Hungary. For example, some of those living near Bosnia later accepted the suzerainty of the king of Bosnia instead of that of the Hungarian king. Some succeeded for a while, and at times the Hungarian kings had to send troops there to reassert their authority. At times there also were civil wars over the Hungarian throne. On these occasions the Croatian nobles often split, and civil wars were then fought throughout Croatia. There also were to be civil wars within or between Croatian families for local power. Thus, despite the long-lasting system established by the Hungarians, there often was anything but tranquillity in Croatia. But throughout these stormy events Croatia continued to be a region ruled by its own nobility and not integrated into the Hungarian state.

Only Pannonian Croatia remained with Hungary until the Ottoman Conquest. Two other regions were also acquired by Koloman: (1) Bosnia was taken in 1102. By 1180 it had for all practical purposes become an independent state. However, through much of its independent period, suzerainty was still claimed by Hungary. (2) Dalmatia was under Koloman's control by 1107. For the rest of the Middle Ages, Dalmatia was to be a battleground for Hungary and Venice.

Throughout the Middle Ages in the Croatian interior there existed a typical feudal society with a warrior class of hereditary nobles standing over, both as administrators and as landlords, a largely peasant population. The surviving documentation does not allow us to be specific as to the nature of peasant obligations to their lords or to the extent, if any, that a free peasantry may also have existed. In the interior there was little urban development; the towns that existed were small, serving as royal residences, fortresses, or local markets. On the coast, towns were larger and busier, being involved in the commerce of the Adriatic. Shipping for commerce and fishing, and in some cases for piracy, was well developed. Trade was profitable, and there was considerable development of crafts.

In the ninth and tenth centuries in Dalmatian Croatia (for instance, the churches of the Holy Cross and of St. Nicholas in Nin, and various other examples in the region of Knin) as well as in Byzantine Dalmatia, a distinctive style of church architecture emerged. Since these churches differed from those of western Europe and Byzantium, many scholars have seen Slavic inspiration in their architecture. By the middle of the eleventh century, presumably as a result of Kresimir IV's close ties with the papacy, Croatian church architecture began to follow the styles of western Europe. It continued to do so for the remainder of the Middle Ages.

Croatian bas-reliefs from Dalmatia attained a high artistic level, reflecting talented carving and original motifs and symbolism (for example, the sculptured work surviving from the Church of the Holy Cross in Nin). Croatian manuscripts, many in Glagolitic, have survived. Their artistic quality improved over the centuries, reaching its height in the fourteenth and fifteenth centuries.

BIBLIOGRAPHY

Francis Dvornik, *Byzantine Missions Among the Slavs* (1970); John V. A. Fine, Jr., *The Early Medieval Balkans: A Critical Survey from the Sixth to the Late Twelfth Century* (1983); Nada Klaić, *Povijest Hrvata u ranom srednjem vijeku* (1971); Ferdinand Šišić, *Pregled povijesti hrvatskoga naroda* (1920).

JOHN V. A. FINE, JR.

[See also **Avars; Bosnia; Dalmatia; Dubrovnik; Hungary; Magyars; Slavs; Tomislav; Venice.**]

CROCKET, a carved ornament, usually leaf-shaped, that projects from the side of a Gothic pinnacle, gable, or spire. Crockets were normally spaced at regular intervals along the angle of inclination, springing from the arris.

LESLIE BRUBAKER

CROSSBOW. See Bow—Crossbow.

CROSS-DOMED CHURCH. See Church, Types of.

CROSS-IN-SQUARE CHURCH. See **Church, Types of.**

CROSS, FORMS OF. The cross appears in both Christian and non-Christian art; in the latter, the cross normally had apotropaic or cosmic significance. The principal Christian uses and forms follow.

Altar cross. On a flat base to rest upon the altar. The earliest known example is pictured in the ninth-century Sacramentary of Marmoutier (Autun, Bibliothèque Municipale, MS 19bis, fol. 1v). By the tenth century, use of altar crosses seems to have been common, though the twelfth-century silver repoussé cross at the Great Lavra on Mt. Athos is among the earliest extant examples. Numerous altar crosses, usually decorated with enamel, are preserved from the Gothic period.

Andrew cross. Shaped like the letter *X*, to replicate the form of cross on which St. Andrew is supposed to have been martyred.

Ankh. Shaped like the letter *T* surmounted by a circle or oval. The ankh was the Egyptian symbol for life; it was adopted for Christian use by the Copts (Egyptian Christians) and in this form is also called a *crux ansata.*

Archiepiscopal cross. Special cross carried by an archbishop.

Calvary cross. A Gothic form showing the Crucifixion on a base shaped to resemble Mt. Golgotha. The Virgin and St. John are depicted either on the base or on the crossarms.

Celtic cross. Essentially a Latin cross, with a circle enclosing the intersection of the upright and the crossbar.

Consecration cross. One of twelve crosses painted on the walls of a church to indicate the places where the building was anointed during its consecration.

Crux fourchette. A cross with flared or forked ends.

Crux gemmata. A cross inlaid with gems or stones, or a painted image of such a cross. This glorification of the cross denotes an image of triumph; the form was apparently inspired by the cult of the cross that arose after St. Helena's discovery of the true cross in Jerusalem in 327.

Crux hasta. A cross with a long descending arm, a cross-staff.

Crux pattée. A Greek cross with flared ends.

Double cross. With two crossbars, the upper one shorter to represent the plaque nailed to Christ's cross bearing the legend "Jesus of Nazareth King of the Jews." Also known as a *crux gemina.*

Gammadion. A hooked cross or swastika; also known as a *crux gammata.*

Greek cross. With arms of equal length. One of the most popular basic shapes for the cross, in common Christian use by the fourth century. With a long handle attached, the Greek cross was often used for episcopal blessing.

Latin cross. With a descending arm longer than the other three. With the Greek cross, the most common basic shape. The Latin cross represents the cross of Christ's crucifixion.

Living cross. A cross either formed of living, unplaned branches or with vines or plants sprouting from its base. The former refers to the legend that Christ's cross was made from the Tree of Life; the latter contrasts the "new" Tree of Life (the cross) with the Old Testament Tree of Life, source of the apple of original sin. In both cases a typological statement is produced, showing Christ's death as a redemption for original sin.

Maltese cross. A Greek cross with arms that taper to a point in the center; the outer ends of the arms may be forked.

Papal cross. A Latin cross with two additional crossbars above the main one; each crossbar is shorter than the one below.

Peter cross. With an ascending arm longer than the other three (an upside-down Latin cross), so called because St. Peter was crucified upside-down.

Stepped cross. A cross resting on a base composed of several steps, apparently in imitation of a monumental cross erected by Constantine in Constantinople.

Suppedaneum cross. A Russian and Byzantine form with an additional short crossbar, either horizontal or slanted, near the base to represent Christ's footrest (suppedaneum).

Tau cross. Shaped like the letter *T*. The Tau cross is apparently the actual form used by the Romans for crucifixions; it is also known as a *crux commissa.*

BIBLIOGRAPHY

Erich Dinkler, *Signum crucis* (1967); Erich Dinkler and Erika Dinkler-von Schubert, "Kreuz," in *Lexikon der christlichen Ikonographie*, II (1969), 562–590; F. J. Dölger, "Beiträge zur Geschichte des Kreuzzeichens," in *Jahrbuch für Antike und Christentum*, 1–10 (1958–1967).

LESLIE BRUBAKER

[See also **Christogram; Cross, Processional; Staurogram.**]

Greek Cross

Latin Cross

Peter Cross

Stepped Cross

Double Cross

Tau Cross

Suppedaneum (a)

Suppedaneum (b)

Papal Cross

Ankh

Crux Fourchette

Crux Pattée

Andrew Cross

Maltese Cross

Gammadion

Living Cross (a)

Living Cross (b)

Crux Gemmata

CROSS, PROCESSIONAL. From at least the sixth century, a special cross was reserved for liturgical processions, often with a detachable handle so that the cross could be removed and set up at the site where Mass was to be said. In the East, the cross was apparently then placed on the altar; in the Latin West this practice was followed only from the thirteenth century, before which time the cross was placed next to the altar.

LESLIE BRUBAKER

CROSSING, that area of a church where nave and transepts intersect, often surmounted by a tower or dome.

LESLIE BRUBAKER

CROSS-STAFF, an instrument for measuring angular distances invented by the Provençal scholar Levi ben Gerson and described in the astronomical book V (called *Sefer tekunah*) of his huge Hebrew encyclopedia *The Wars of the Lord*. Also called the Jacob's Staff (*Genesis* 32:10), it consisted of a transversal rod perpendicular to a long wooden staff along which it could be moved. Seen from one end of the staff, the rod subtends in any position a certain angle that can be read off a graduated scale on the staff. To obtain greater accuracy, the graduation was provided with transversal lines, a device also invented by Levi and later used with great results in Tycho Brahe's instruments.

Levi says that he made his instrument in order to make astronomy more precise, having noticed that a lunar eclipse in 1321 did not occur at the predicted time. He described how the angular distance between two stars could be found with the staff held in the hands of the observer, and also how his invention could be mounted as a meridian instrument for measuring altitudes with the staff fastened in a horizontal position (verified by a plumb line attached to the now vertical rod).

The section on the cross-staff in the *Sefer tekunah* was translated into Latin in 1342 by Peter of Alexandria and dedicated to Pope Clement VI. This treatise became widely known, and the instrument was used by many late medieval and Renaissance astronomers. About 1500 it found a new use in navigation, enabling pilots to determine the geographical latitude of their position from observations of the altitude of the sun or the pole star. Accordingly the many seamen's manuals of fifteenth-century writers like Peter of Medina, Martín Cortés, and others usually described the construction and use of the staff. About 1590 John Davis developed it into the more comfortable backstaff, or Davis' staff, which prevented the observer from looking directly at the sun.

BIBLIOGRAPHY

M. Curtze, "Die Abhandlungen ... über den Jakobsstab," in *Bibliotheca mathematica*, 2nd ser., **12** (1898); Eva G. R. Taylor and M. W. Richey, *The Geometrical Seaman* (1962).

OLAF PEDERSEN

[See also **Astrology/Astronomy; Levi ben Gerson; Navigation: Western European.**]

CROWN, MURAL, a crown that imitates the shape of city walls, used to identify a figure, normally female, as a personification or protector of a city. The convention, known throughout the early Christian and Byzantine world, stems from Hellenistic tradition, especially a statue of the *tyche* of Antioch done in 296 B.C. by Eutychides.

LESLIE BRUBAKER

CROWNS. See **Regalia, Temporal and Religious.**

CROZIER, a bishop's staff, occasionally also carried by abbots and abbesses, in the shape of a shepherd's crook or a cross. The former shape, found in the Latin West since the seventh century, symbolically linked the bishop to Christ as the Good Shepherd.

LESLIE BRUBAKER

CRUCIFIXION, Christ's death on the cross, described in the Gospels and numerous apocrypha. In addition to Christ on the cross, basic components of Crucifixion images include the Virgin and St. John; the two thieves, Dysmus and Gestas; the centurion Longinus; Stephaton, the soldier who offered Christ

Crozier: Annunciation, champlevé enamel on copper. From Limoges, 1250–1300. THE METROPOLITAN MUSEUM OF ART, GIFT OF J. PIERPONT MORGAN, 1917

vinegar; and the sun and moon, in reference to the darkness that followed Christ's death.

Except for a few inscribed gems—probably amulets of a heretical sect—and an early-third-century satirical graffito in Rome depicting the veneration of a crucified ass, the earliest images of the Crucifixion date from the fifth century: the oldest representation of Christ nailed to the cross occurs on an ivory plaque of about 420–430 in the British Museum. Early Christian images show a triumphant, living Christ clad in a simple loincloth (*perizoma*). Byzantine images from the sixth to the ninth century (such as the Rabula Gospels, see illustration to "Colobium" article) present Christ in a long, sleeveless garment (*colobium*); beginning in the seventh century, and especially after the end of iconoclasm in 843, Christ was increasingly shown as dead rather than alive, to emphasize his human suffering. With the new concern for Christ's human nature came the substitution of the loincloth for the *colobium*, as in

the Khludov Psalter of about 860–870. From the ninth century, Byzantine images also show Adam's skull at the base of the cross, a reference to Adam's supposed burial in Mt. Golgotha, and, perhaps, to the name (skull) itself; occasionally a personification of Hades is shown pierced by the cross to show Christ's triumph over death. In the middle and late Byzantine periods, Christ's body sags from the cross and the pathos of the Crucifixion is stressed.

In the Latin West, the loincloth was always the standard garment worn by Christ except in such Byzantine-influenced examples as the eighth-century frescoes at S. Maria Antiqua in Rome and some Hiberno-Saxon and Ottonian pieces. From the ninth century, the Crucifixion gradually became the most important religious image of the Western church and a great variety of forms were introduced; in the tenth century monumental sculptures appear. Among the ninth-century additions to the Crucifixion were the Hand of God, angels, and the symbols of the evangelists, to show Christ's divinity; Oceanus and Gaia (water and earth), who, with the sun and moon, represented the four elements and stressed the cosmic significance of the Crucifixion; personifications of Ecclesia (church) and Synagogue to contrast the new and the old law; Adam's skull and the temptation of Adam and Eve, to demonstrate that Christ's death redeemed Original Sin; and the Lamb of God (*Agnus Dei*) to emphasize Christ's sacrifice. In the eleventh century, figures of Vita (life) and Mors (death) were added to signify the life-giving properties of Christianity and Christ's victory over death. The twelfth century appended the pelican, who sacrifices its life for its young as Christ gave his life for all Christians, and images of the Virtues. The twelfth century also saw the development of the *croce dipinta* (monumental painted crucifixes) in Italy. From the thirteenth century on, Western artists began to avoid symbolism in representations of the Crucifixion and to stress the historical event and its dramatic potential.

BIBLIOGRAPHY

Gertrud Schiller, *Iconography of Christian Art,* II (1972), 88–164; Stanley Ferber, "Crucifixion Iconography in a Group of Carolingian Ivory Plaques," in *Art Bulletin,* **48** (1966); John Martin, "The Dead Christ on the Cross in Byzantine Art," in Kurt Weitzmann, ed., *Late Classical and Medieval Studies in Honor of Albert Mathias Friend, Jr.* (1955), 189–196.

LESLIE BRUBAKER

[See also **Cross, Forms of; Iconography.**]

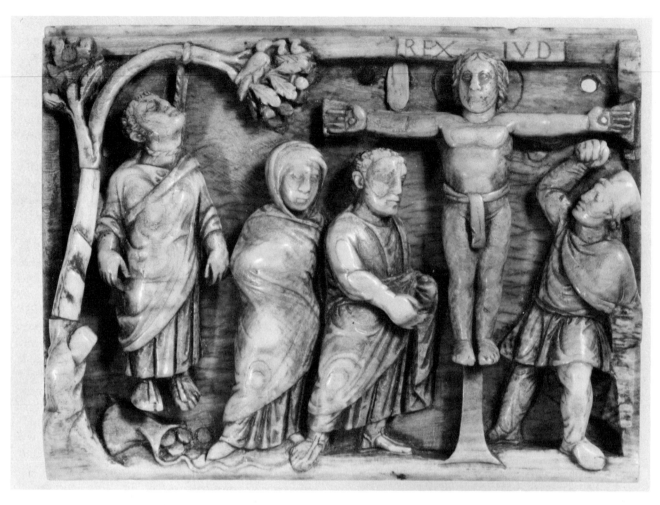

Crucifixion. Ivory panel from a casket. *Ca.* 420–430. THE BRITISH MUSEUM, MS IC 1.10

CRUSADE, CHILDREN'S. The usual view of the Children's Crusade of 1212 depicts the departure of thousands of children from France and Germany to follow a boy prophet who would lead them to Jerusalem and convert the Muslims. Armed only with the conviction that God would part the waters and allow them to cross to the Holy Land without wetting their feet, the children streamed south to the Mediterranean amid great suffering. The anticipated miracle did not occur; and, instead, greedy merchants lured them into ships with promises of free passage to the Holy Land. The children were then shipwrecked or sold into slavery in North Africa.

Scholarship shows this picture to be more legend than fact. There seem to have been in 1212 at least two popular movements, one in Germany and one in France. Their similarities allowed later chroniclers to lump them together as the Children's Crusade.

The German movement began first, in the early spring, led by a boy named Nicholas from around Cologne. Wearing the sign of the cross and carrying banners, the growing throng wended its way amid great tumult up the Rhine and crossed the Alps into Lombardy. Some 7,000 arrived in Genoa in late August. The waters did not part as promised by Nicholas, and the band seems to have broken up. Some left for home, while others may have gone to Rome or Brindisi. Still others may have traveled down the Rhône to Marseilles, where they were probably sold into slavery. Few returned home, and none reached the Holy Land.

In France, a shepherd boy named Stephen from Cloyes, a village near Châteaudun, claimed in June that he bore a letter from Jesus Christ for the king of France. Eventually attracting a reported crowd of 30,000, Stephen proceeded to St. Denis, where he was seen to work many miracles. Acting on advice from the University of Paris, Philip II ordered the crowds to go home, and most of them evidently did. The movement caused less commotion in France than in Germany; none of the contemporary sources mentions any plans of the French throngs to go to Jerusalem.

Later chroniclers embellished the scanty facts of these processions with flights of fantasy and imagination. While firm conclusions are difficult to draw, recent research indicates that most participants were not children—at least not very young children. The throngs were composed of people of both sexes and all ages drawn from the marginal classes of rural society—shepherds, younger sons, laborers, wage earners, drifters—who had little wealth or security to lose by leaving home.

The movement probably spread from Germany to France, where popular religious emotions had been excited by itinerant preachers and the Albigensian Crusade. Most of the participants were probably imbued with the ideal of apostolic poverty, whereby the unarmed poor could accomplish in the Holy Land what the wealthy, well-armed, and powerful had been unable to do in the Third and Fourth official Crusades. Thus they hoped to purge the crusading movement of its materialistic and chivalric motives by resuscitating the power of the pilgrim armed only with divine aid.

The Children's Crusade was never an official crusade, though its genesis and appearance resembled one. Clerical observers saw in its sufferings and failure the work of the devil. Yet the religious hysteria it evoked shows that the poor could be agitated by the ideals of their superiors. Its events are less important than the ideals that motivated it and the legends that later chroniclers based on it. Later movements of the poor, for example that of the Pastoureaux in 1251, as well as the popular imagination, both medieval and modern, were similarly intoxicated by the supposed power of the poor, the pure, and the young.

BIBLIOGRAPHY

Peter Raedts, "The Children's Crusade of 1212," in *Journal of Medieval History,* **3** (1977), summarizes the sources, issues, and literature. George Zabriskie Gray, *The Children's Crusade* (1870, repr. 1972), is fanciful and unreliable.

FREDERICK H. RUSSELL

[See also **Pastoureaux**.]

CRUSADE, CONCEPT OF. The crusade that Urban II called into existence at Clermont in 1095 was a novel event that became a major institution of Western medieval Christendom. Yet earlier experiences constituted an ample body of precedents on which the crusading movement could draw. Suspicion and fear of strangers were common in the ancient world, and often led to wars of conquest and enslavement. The ancient Greeks considered wars against non-Hellenes to be just, and Romans viewed barbarians and foreigners as enemies to be combated in a *bellum justum,* a just war. The Old Testament records many Israelite wars waged with divine aid against nonbelievers. In the New Testament Jesus is pictured as punishing sinners (John 2:15) and as having been sent to bring "not peace but a sword" (Matthew 10:34). However, the Christian doctrine of charity generally led the early church to condemn warfare and military service.

After Constantine's conversion churchmen came to embrace the Roman Empire's wars against barbarian heretics. Augustine resuscitated the Roman concept of just war, defining it as one that avenged injuries. Further, in his notion of true justice, injuries done to God could be avenged. God could authorize wars, and the church had the authority to command imperial persecution of heretics. Pope Gregory I directed warfare against heretics and enemies of the papacy, and encouraged missionary wars against pagans. Charlemagne launched numerous wars of conquest and conversion against pagans on the borders of his empire. He also fought to defend the church and, with active ecclesiastical aid, against papal enemies in Italy. Ninth-century popes promised salvation to those who died fighting infidels.

By the eleventh century the Carolingian and papal ideals of holy war and defense of the church were generally accepted, but churchmen continued to harbor a deep suspicion of the turbulent warrior aristocracy, a suspicion reinforced by the frequent attacks of the petty lay lords on clerics and church properties. In the course of that century, a revaluation of the role of lay military service took place. Seeking to decrease the incidence of violence and to draw on deepening lay piety and desire for expiation of sins and for salvation, churchmen came to advocate a justification for armed force based on its usefulness in defending the faith, the church, and the weak and helpless. Hence weapons were blessed, and church banners, often honoring a patron saint, were carried into battle. The holy war in defense of the church was now the calling of every pious knight.

To complement this ecclesiastical benediction of feudal military service, local bishops initiated the Peace Movement, to protect unarmed Christians (including pilgrims) from violence (Peace of God), and to stop all fighting at certain specified times (Truce of God). Knights who continued in their unholy violence were to be prosecuted violently.

For the peace movement to have any chance of success, it was thus necessary to find another, ecclesiastically sanctioned, outlet for feudal martial vigor. Popes organized campaigns against their enemies, such as the Normans in southern Italy. Gregory VII proposed to lead a force of Christian knights to defend Christians in the Eastern Empire. He also hoped to enlist a *militia Saneti Petri* to do battle against the enemies of the papacy. More broadly, he evisaged the formation of a *militia Christi* to wage the *bellum Christi* against heretics and other enemies of God, the church, and the papacy. At about the same time several popes offered material and spiritual benefits to Christian warriors waging the Reconquest against the Muslims in Spain. Pilgrimages to holy places had become popular means of serving ecclesiastical penances for sin, for example, the Cluniac championing of the pilgrimage to Santiago de Compostela.

The stage was set for the convergence of holy war and pilgrimage effected in 1095, when the former Cluniac monk Urban II preached the First Crusade. His exhortation there and his subsequent actions seemed to envision an armed pilgrimage to the East to support the eastern Christians against the Turks, and to liberate the Holy Land, especially Jerusalem, from the Muslim yoke. To attract followers he promised an indulgence granting remission of sins, or at least remission of penances to those who confessed their sins. Urban's synthesis went beyond its antecedents in calling on pilgrims, heretofore usually unarmed, to fight a war that was not only just but justifying, that endowed the Crusader with special spiritual merit, and that could lead to his salvation. Islam's parallel form of holy war, the jihad, does not appear to have had any direct causal influence on the Christian crusade.

With Urban's preaching the crusading movement was born, and took on added dimensions in the course of subsequent experiences. The First Crusade was to become an unstable amalgam of collective eschatological hope, individual mystical experience, and military venture. Its successes were never to be repeated, yet hope of repeating them was a major impetus for later crusades.

To convert Urban's preaching into an ongoing institution capable of realizing its immediate goal, the conquest of the Holy Land, and also to allow it to become a more versatile instrument of papal policy were tasks to which popes and canon lawyers addressed themselves in the twelfth and thirteenth centuries. The privileges to induce enlistments, the chain of command, and the fiscal status of the enterprises all had to be worked out. The crusade as a Christian form of warfare had to be justified in its goals and methods.

Even before the launching of the First Crusade, Anselm II of Lucca compiled an assemblage of texts (*ca.* 1085) that, among other things, supported the right of the church to invoke violence against heretics, excommunicates, enemies of peace, and infidels. His collection was used extensively in the *Decretum* of Gratian (*ca.* 1140). Gratian defended the right of church officials to punish heretics and infidels, though he refused to allow clerics to become directly involved in killing. Later canonists made the church and the papacy even more directly responsible for the task of punishing infidels and sinners, and though they, too, harbored reservations about direct clerical involvement in actual warfare, these were often disregarded in practice. These canonists did claim that since the Holy Land rightfully belonged to Christians, Muslims held it illicitly and could be conquered and expelled.

With the manifold crusading activity of Innocent III (1198-1216) came further clarification of the status of crusader and crusade in canonistic commentaries on papal crusading bulls. A person became a crusader by making a vow to go on a crusade. This vow created both obligations and rights for the crusader. He was bound to participate in a crusade on pain of ecclesiastical and civil censure for his nonperformance. He was obliged to worship at the Holy Sepulcher in Jerusalem. If he could not or would not fulfill his vow, he could redeem it by a money payment or by performing some other service for the papacy. While the vow put the crusader in debt to the papacy, it also entitled him to the crusade indulgence and other spiritual privileges, as well as to such temporal privileges as papal protection for himself, his family, and his property.

Canon lawyers attempted to clarify the chain of command of a crusade by stressing the necessity of the papal initiative, signified by the preaching of the cross. The pope was also to appoint military commanders and clerical advisers. Thus, as in the just war requirement, a clearly legitimate authority was necessary to declare the crusade, and since only the pope could promulgate the crusade indulgence, only the pope could declare a crusade. Other wars waged on church authority could be holy or just, but the crusade, with its special indulgence, was strictly a papal prerogative.

Paralleling practical developments, canonists lengthened the list of enemies that could be combated in a crusade. Heretics, merely as heretics or because they infringed the peace of orthodox Christians, threatened the Christian faith. Princes who had heretics in their territories must wage a crusade against them on papal command or themselves become the target of a crusade. Even schismatics and enemies of the papacy's political power merited the punishment of a crusade. The papacy could commute a vow to fight in the Holy Land into a duty to participate in a European crusade. The papal monopoly over the crusade indulgence and vow enabled the pope to transform the crusade into an all-purpose instrument for the implementation of papal policy.

Although church officials as leaders constructed the justification and mechanism of the crusades, the potential followers and supporters of the crusades had to be provided with compelling psychological or spiritual incentives. Outwardly symbolized by the wearing of the cross, the vow, with its promise of the remission of sins and even of salvation, was a strong motivation. There was also the widespread assumption that God would aid the crusaders' cause and grant them victory. Success indicated God's activity and benevolence, while failure showed his displeasure at Christian sins. Jerusalem (literally "vision of peace") had a double meaning: geographically it meant worship at the site of Christ's triumph, and spiritually it symbolized the attainment of a better life, one free of earthly care, strife, and sin, which prepared the Christian for paradise. The terrestrial Jerusalem prefigured the celestial. As both temporal quest and spiritual experience, Jerusalem strongly influenced the Christian desire for redemptive purification. To worship at the Holy Sepulcher simultaneously fulfilled the requirements of the vow and stimulated eschatological hopes that the crusader could actually imitate the experiences of Christ.

The need for a more stable and dependable corps of crusaders in the Holy Land led to the formation of military orders whose members were both monks and warriors. Bernard of Clairvaux contrasted the evils of secular fighting with the glory of warfare waged in defense of God and church. In Bernard's view, by joining the Templars, those who had been

criminals in Europe became true Israelites in the Holy Land. The Templars were to safeguard Jerusalem for the sake of all Christians. In Bernard's mystical amalgam the connection between the peace movement and the crusader was made clear, while the distinction between clergy and laity lost its force. Other military orders were soon founded, and carried on their mission of both converting and fighting the infidels not only in the Holy Land but also from the Baltic (where the Teutonic Knights combined the crusade with a missionary war of conquest and conversion) to Spain and well beyond.

For many Europeans desirous of enjoying the benefits of crusader status, service in the Holy Land was impractical, but the thirteenth-century transformation of the crusade into a more general institution gave them a new opportunity to participate closer to home. This is shown most clearly in southern France, where Albigensian heretics attacked orthodox churches and Christians. Since heretics by definition threatened Christian unity, military operations against them were easily justified. In a sense the thirteenth-century crusades were a direct survival of the peace movement and Gregorian reform movement of the eleventh century. Crusade vows taken by those who could not physically participate in a crusade could be redeemed by a money payment which the papacy could use for other purposes. In this climate the papacy could justify and prosecute political crusades against such enemies of its temporal authority as the Hohenstaufens.

Whether in the Holy Land or in Europe, participation in the crusade offered the prospect both of a collective spiritual experience in which one was bound to one's fellows by a feeling of community and fraternal love, and of individual spiritual purification, absolution, and glory.

The medieval crusade as event and institution was a strange hybrid of holy war, just war, pilgrimage, and vow that defies neat categorization. Most basically it was a spiritual quest for Christian unity carried on by God's warriors. Before about 1200 there was not even a specific Latin word to describe what is meant by "crusade." Its broad and diverse purposes—defense of the faith, the church, the papacy, Christian lands—were understood on many levels by different segments of Christian society, all of which recognized that the crusade, as the uniquely papal just war, was the most spiritually meritorious form of military service. At least since Augustine, Christians had recognized that temporal peace was often attainable only through warfare. The crusades offered the further hope that spiritual peace was possible through participation in Christian military service. The historical development of the crusades throughout the Middle Ages is permeated with papal activity. With the decline of papal political power, overseas expansion, and the Protestant Reformation, the assumptions that underlay the medieval crusades were strongly altered, yet the crusade continued to influence men's actions well into the modern period.

BIBLIOGRAPHY

Paul Alphandéry and A. Dupront, *La chrétienté et l'idée de croisade*, 2 vols. (1954–1959); E. O. Blake, "The Formation of the 'Crusade Idea,'" in *Journal of Ecclesiastical History*, **21** (1970); James A. Brundage, *Medieval Canon Law and the Crusader* (1969); Giles Constable, "The Second Crusade as Seen by Contemporaries," in *Traditio*, **9** (1953), 213–279; H. E. J. Cowdrey, "Pope Urban II's Preaching of the First Crusade," in *History*, **55** (1970), and "Cluny and the First Crusade," in *Revue Bénédictine*, **83** (1973); Carl Erdmann, *The Origin of the Idea of Crusade*, trans., with intro. and notes, by Marshall W. Baldwin and Walter Goffart (1977), the fundamental point of departure for all research into the crusade idea; James T. Johnson, *Ideology, Reason, and the Limitation of War* (1975), esp. ch. 2; Thomas P. Murphy, ed., *The Holy War* (1976), esp. H. E. J. Cowdrey, "The Genesis of the Crusades: The Springs of Western Ideas of Holy War," and James A. Brundage, "Holy War and Medieval Lawyers"; *Paix de Dieu et guerre sainte en Languedoc au xiii*ᵉ *siècle* (1969), esp. E. Delaruelle, "Paix de Dieu et croisade dans la chrétienté du xii*ᵉ *siècle*," G. Sicard, "Paix et guerre dans le droit canon du xii*ᵉ *siècle*," and Raymonde Foreville, "Innocent III et la croisade des Albigeois"; Edward M. Peters, ed., *The First Crusade* (1971), a collection of narrative sources, and *Christian Society and the Crusades, 1198–1229* (1971), sources for the crusades to the Holy Land and the Albigensian Crusade; Maureen Purcell, "Changing Views of Crusade in the Thirteenth Century," in *Journal of Religious History*, **7** (1972); Jonathan S. C. Riley-Smith, *What were the Crusades?* (1977), an overview of the entire crusading movement; Ian S. Robinson, "Gregory VII and the Soldiers of Christ," in *History*, **58** (1973); Paul Rousset, ed., "L'idée de croisade," in *X Congresso Internazionale di scienze storiche, Relazione*, III (1955), esp. Rousset's "L'idée de croisade chez les chroniquers d'Occident," and Michel Villey, "L'idée de croisade chez les juristes du moyen âge"; Frederick H. Russell, *The Just War in the Middle Ages* (1975); Joseph R. Strayer, "The Political Crusades of the Thirteenth Century," in Kenneth M. Setton, gen. ed., *A History of the Crusades*, 2nd ed., II (1969); Robert Wolff and Harry W. Hazard, eds., *The Later Crusades* (1969).

FREDERICK H. RUSSELL

[See also Augustine of Hippo, St.; Bernard of Clairvaux, St.; Crusades and Crusader States: To 1187; Gregory I the Great, Pope; Indulgences; Law, Canon; Military Orders; Peace of God, Truce of God; Urban II, Pope.]

CRUSADE AND DEATH OF RICHARD I, a mid-thirteenth-century Anglo-Norman prose chronicle. It relates the journey of Richard I the Lionhearted of England to the Holy Land in 1190–1191 by way of France, Sicily, and Cyprus, the siege and capture of Acre, Richard's own capture and imprisonment in Austria on the journey homeward, his eventual return to England, his final campaigns against Philip II Augustus of France in Normandy and central France, and his death at Châlus in 1199. The work is based on the writings of Roger of Howden (Hoveden), Roger of Wendover, and Matthew Paris.

BIBLIOGRAPHY

Ronald C. Johnston, ed., *The Crusade and Death of Richard I* (1961).

BRIAN MERRILEES

[See also Anglo-Norman Literature.]

CRUSADE PROPAGANDA. Recruitment of volunteers for crusading armies required efforts by the pope and the church hierarchy to popularize the expeditions and to persuade people in large numbers to offer both their personal service and their financial support to these enterprises. Propaganda was accordingly part of the apparatus of the crusades from the beginning and continued to be a feature of papal policy well into the sixteenth century.

Even before the proclamation of the First Crusade in 1095, popes had occasionally faced the problem of recruiting volunteer armies to combat Muslim invaders in Italy. In 853 Pope Leo IV had appealed to the Franks for military assistance in order to defend Rome from Saracen marauders; in 878 Pope John VIII offered inducements to soldiers who would defend the church against its enemies. In both instances the principal favor promised in return for the service of recruits was assurance that those who died while fighting on behalf of the church would merit remission of sins and might expect to receive a heavenly reward for their efforts. Both pontiffs stopped well short of guaranteeing the salvation of those who responded to their appeals, and neither pope proclaimed an indulgence for participants in the wars against the Muslims. It is clear, nonetheless, that in both cases spiritual inducements were used to attract soldiers to fight in behalf of the papal cause.

When Pope Urban II proclaimed the First Crusade at Clermont on 27 November 1095, he also set in motion the machinery to propagandize the expedition. Both in his public address on 27 November and, apparently in greater detail, in a speech to the clergy on the following day, Urban instructed the bishops and other clerics at Clermont to preach the crusade on their return home. He cautioned them to be selective in their recruitment efforts: they were to discourage elderly, feeble, and poverty-stricken persons from participating. They were also to be cautious about enlisting women, priests, and monks, except under special circumstances. Thus crusade propaganda at the beginning was aimed principally at able-bodied males, preferably those with military experience and sufficient means to pay their own expenses during the crusade.

The pope's speech at Clermont provided examples of the propaganda devices that other crusade preachers might employ. Although the surviving accounts of his speech were written later, there is a substantial core of agreement among the chief witnesses about the subjects with which the pope dealt. Urban strongly stressed the need for Western Christians to aid their brethren in the East. He buttressed this appeal with graphic accounts of Turkish victories over the Eastern Christians and the sufferings of those subjected to Turkish rule. The pope also emphasized the desecration and destruction of Christian shrines and holy places by the Turkish conquerors, assuring his audience that God wanted them to avenge this insult.

Moreover, Urban admonished his hearers that while fighting fellow Christians in Europe was sinful, combating the infidel in the East was a righteous cause that God would reward. Participants might expect to profit in this world as well as in the next from the conquest of Turkish-held territory. Finally, the pope assured his listeners that participation in the crusade would count as full penance for their sins.

These themes became staples of crusade propaganda for the next 500 years. We have no reliable accounts of the recruiting sermons preached by other bishops and clerics for the First Crusade, but the chroniclers who narrated the events of the expedition commonly emphasized and amplified the points made in Urban's sermon. The propaganda devices used by popular preachers were perhaps cruder and less cautious than those employed by the pope. Certainly the chronicles make it clear that rank-and-file crusaders believed that they had been promised not merely that participation would satisfy the penance owed for their sins, but that they would unquestionably go to heaven if they died on crusade. There is also evidence that some preachers linked their message to eschatalogical predictions: they foretold the imminent end of the world and final judgment, and convinced at least some of their hearers that participation in the crusade would enable them to meet their maker most propitiously on his own home ground.

Urban II issued no bull for the First Crusade, but solemn written proclamations were regularly employed both to announce later crusades and to outline the privileges that participants would enjoy. These documents, in addition, usually outlined the reasons for the crusade and elaborated the major themes that crusade preachers would employ in their appeals. The bulls often enjoyed wide circulation and were propaganda instruments in their own right. The earliest bull of this type, *Quantum praedecessores,* issued by Pope Eugenius III on 1 December 1145 and reissued the following March, stressed the success of the First Crusade and recounted the reverses that the crusader states had suffered as a result of the loss of Edessa to the Turks in December 1144.

The pope called on the French king, Louis VII, and all the faithful to avenge these insults to the Christian faith and promised numerous benefits to those who responded to the call. Not only would they enjoy the remission of sins promised to soldiers in the First Crusade, but in addition the pope took members of the crusading army under his protection, forbade attempts to harm their wives, families, or possessions during their absence, and guaranteed the help of the church at all levels in making good these assurances. Crusaders were also granted the right to sell or mortgage their lands and estates in order to finance their participation. Moreover, they were exempted from interest on loans made to them, even if they had taken an oath to make such payments. The bull also outlined a code of conduct for crusaders: they were to avoid displays of wealth, hunting, and entertainments that hinted of licentiousness.

Similar crusade bulls were issued by subsequent popes and several general councils, notably the Fourth Lateran Council (1215), the First Council of

Lyons (1245), and the Second Council of Lyons (1274), incorporated crusade proclamations into their constitutions and decrees. Documents of this sort laid down the rules under which crusades operated, enumerated the privileges that crusaders enjoyed, provided both spiritual and temporal inducements for recruits, and promised lesser benefits to those who assisted the crusade with financial contributions and other forms of help. Thus they served both organizational and propaganda purposes.

Chronicles and narratives of crusades also served as propaganda vehicles. Accounts of the successes of previous crusades furnished examples of what participants might expect to achieve, and the authors of such accounts often detailed the opportunities implicit in their histories. Fulcher of Chartres, writing about the Latin settlers in the Levant following the First Crusade, pointed out that:

> Those who were needy have here been enriched by God. Those who had a few pennies, here possess countless bezants. He who had not a village, here possesses a God-given city.... Nor does God wish to burden with poverty those who have vowed to follow (or, rather, pursue) Him with their crosses.... For God wishes to make us all rich and to draw us to Himself as the dearest of friends. (*Historia Hierosolymitana* 3.37)

Not only might crusaders hope to enjoy wealth, comfort, and power in this world as a result of their labors, but the chroniclers also stressed the immense spiritual gains that they could expect. In addition, chronicles served to glorify individual crusader heroes. Some manuscripts of the anonymous *Gesta Francorum et aliorum Hierosolymitanorum* gave special attention to the role played in the First Crusade by Duke Robert of Normandy, and there is reason to believe that copies of the same work were circulated in western Europe by Bohemond of Tarentum to support the legitimacy of his claims to Antioch.

Letters written by crusaders served as additional vehicles for popularizing the expeditions and for justifying the actions of the writers. The letters written by Count Stephen of Blois to his wife Adele during the First Crusade and the collective letter of that crusade's leaders to Pope Urban following the capture of Jerusalem in 1099 are examples of the propagandistic uses of correspondence.

Even more widely circulated types of crusade propaganda were poems and songs. The earliest of these date from the period of the First Crusade or shortly thereafter and were adaptations of traditional pilgrimage songs and hymns. Others, more specifically linked to the crusade, began to appear during the early twelfth century. Although a few of these poems and songs are in Latin, the majority were composed in the vernacular. Many of the most notable poets of the twelfth and thirteenth centuries tried their hands at writing crusade poems, including such well-known figures as Marcabru, Rutebeuf, Conon de Béthune, Walther von der Vogelweide, and Wolfram von Eschenbach.

But unquestionably the most important medium for crusade propaganda was the spoken word, especially the sermon. From the beginning crusade preachers were the principal recruiting officers for the expeditions. The preachers of the First Crusade, apparently, were the bishops and other prelates who attended the Council of Clermont; but in addition a crew of self-appointed popular preachers took up the work. Some of the popular preachers manipulated the crusade message to their personal advantage. The preaching of the Second Crusade was better organized. In 1145 Pope Eugenius II appointed St. Bernard of Clairvaux the principal preacher of the expedition, and Bernard discharged much of this responsibility personally, though he also delegated some of the task to others whom he chose. What we know of the preaching of the Third Crusade suggests that it was even more formally structured. Gerald of Wales's account of his part in the effort makes it clear that there were organized teams of preachers who followed planned itineraries to carry the message of the crusade.

From the beginning of the pontificate of Pope Innocent III in 1198, crusade preaching, which had previously been organized on an ad hoc basis to meet the needs of each major expedition, became a permanent, ongoing enterprise and was increasingly entrusted to members of the mendicant orders, especially the Dominicans and Franciscans. In the mid thirteenth century Humbert of Romans, the fifth master general of the Dominican order, wrote a manual for crusade preachers, *De predicatione sanctae crucis*. In Humbert's treatise the art of crusade preaching is set forth systematically for the guidance of novices. Humbert furnishes his readers with explicit guidelines, complete with tips on topics to emphasize and to avoid, lists of biblical passages to cite, stories to illustrate important points, and answers to criticisms that they might meet.

The fall of Acre on 18 May 1291 brought an end to the Latin states in the Holy Land, but propaganda for the crusades continued. Pope Clement VI (1342–1352), a former crusade preacher, sought to promote new crusades as a weapon in his plans for a renewal of papal Eastern policy. His ambitious schemes failed to materialize, however, as his crusade preachers found their audiences unresponsive. The last full-scale effort to launch a new crusade was undertaken by Pope Pius II; although he succeeded in raising an army, Pius' project died with him at Ancona in 1464.

Crusade propaganda, however, outlived the crusades. Sixteenth-century efforts to mobilize resistance to the Ottoman Turks made use of the strategies and the methods of medieval crusade preaching. The most successful survival of medieval crusade propaganda, however, was directed at a different goal: the Christianization of the Philippines and the New World by the Spanish and Portuguese. True heirs of the crusade tradition, the organizers of the Spanish Empire employed the symbolism of the cross and the methods of the crusades as an integral part of their successful effort to continue the crusades by other means and in a new direction.

BIBLIOGRAPHY

The fundamental bibliography for this, as for other aspects of the crusades, is Hans Eberhard Mayer, *Bibliographie zur Geschichte der Kreuzzüge* (1960). On crusade propaganda and preaching see esp. nos. 4091–4119. See also Mayer's supplement to his main bibliography, "Literaturbericht über die Geschichte der Kreuzzüge: Veröffentlichungen 1958–1967," in *Historische Zeitschrift*, Sonderheft 3 (1969). Some major crusade propaganda motifs are described by Paul Alphandéry, *La chrétienté et l'idée de croisade*, Alphonse Dupront, ed., 2 vols. (1954–1959). See also Paul Rousset, *Les origines et les caractères de la première croisade* (1945), esp. 110–151; as well as Jonathan S. C. Riley-Smith, *What Were the Crusades?* (1977), and "Crusading as an Act of Love," in *History*, 65 (1980).

On crusader privileges, see James A. Brundage, *Medieval Canon Law and the Crusader* (1969), esp. 140–190; and Maureen Purcell, *Papal Crusading Policy* (1975).

Some crusading chronicles that have special significance as propaganda pieces are Fulcher of Chartres, *A History of the Expedition to Jerusalem, 1095–1127*, Frances Rita Ryan, trans., Harold S. Fink, ed. (1969, repr. 1973); *Gesta Francorum et aliorum Hierosolymitanorum*, Rosalind Hill, ed. and trans. (1962); and William of Tyre, *A History of Deeds Done Beyond the Sea*, Emily A. Babcock and A. C. Krey, trans., 2 vols. (1943). Crusaders' letters from the First Crusade are published in *Epistulae et chartae ad historiam primi belli sacri spectantes*, Heinrich Hagenmeyer, ed. (1901). Some of these letters are translated in *Letters of the Crusaders*, rev. ed. by Dana Carleton Munro (1896). Another collection of propagandistic importance is the *Lettres de Jacques de Vitry (1160/70–1240)*, Robert B. C. Huygens, ed. (1960).

On crusader songs and poetry see Joseph Bédier and Pierre Aubry, *Les chansons de croisade* (1909); Richard L. Crocker, "Early Crusade Songs," in *The Holy War*, Thomas P. Murphy, ed. (1976), 78–98.

For Pope Innocent III's crusade policy and its implications for propaganda purposes, see Helmut Roscher, *Papst Innocenz III. und die Kreuzzüge* (1969). Criticism of the crusades and the responses of crusade propagandists are dealt with in Palmer A. Throop, *Criticism of the Crusade: A Study of Public Opinion and Crusade Propaganda* (1940); George B. Flahiff, "*Deus non vult*: A Critic of the Third Crusade," in *Mediaeval Studies*, 9 (1947).

The crusade preachers' manual by Humbert of Romans has been printed only once: *De praedicatione sanctae crucis (ca.* 1945). This edition is exceedingly rare; the only copy in North America is at the Newberry Library, Chicago. The work is partially analyzed by Throop, *op. cit.* See also Albert de la Marche, *La chaire française au moyen âge, spécialement au XIIIᵉ siècle*, 2nd ed. (1886), and "La prédication de la croisade au 13ᵉ siècle," in *Revue des questions historiques*, 48 (1890). Another crusade preacher is treated by Frederick J. Boehlke, Jr., *Pierre de Thomas, Scholar, Diplomat, and Crusader* (1966). On the crusades and Spanish colonization, see James Muldoon, *Pope, Lawyers, and Infidels: The Church and the Non-Christian World, 1250–1550* (1979).

JAMES A. BRUNDAGE

[See also **Bernard of Clairvaux, St.; Crusade, Concept of; Crusades and Crusader States: To 1192; Crusades and Crusader States: Fourth; Fulcher of Chartres; Indulgences; Innocent III, Pope; Preaching, Sermon Literature: Western European; Urban II, Pope.**]

CRUSADER ART AND ARCHITECTURE. The establishment of Frankish colonial states in the eastern Mediterranean area during the period 1099–1291, resulting from crusading expeditions to regain the Holy Land, set the stage for vigorous artistic activity. The Latin Kingdom of Jerusalem contained the holiest sites—in Jerusalem, Bethlehem, and Nazareth—which constituted the focus of crusader aspirations. The most important artistic work was done here and in the county of Tripoli to the north.

Crusader art was patronized mainly by the resident Frankish political leaders, ecclesiastical officials of the Latin church, and, after about 1140, the Hospitalers and Templars. Many patrons, whether newly arrived or born locally, were of French stock, some were Italian, and a few were English or German. The artists who carried out these commissions were of more diverse origins. Besides many from

Deesis. Psalter of Queen Melisende, 1131–1143. THE BRITISH LIBRARY, MS Egerton 1139, fol. 12v

western Europe, others were surely from the Levant, especially Byzantine Greeks and indigenous Christians. From this amalgamation of East and West a distinctive crusader art took form. Faithfully reflecting aspects of Romanesque and Gothic art, it never broke ties to developments in the West. On the other hand, the influence of Byzantine, Armenian, and even Islamic art, local traditions in Syria-Palestine, the practicalities of reusing captured places, and the special requirements of Christian holy sites all gave to crusader art a Levantine dimension not found in Western architecture, sculpture, or painting.

After the capture of Jerusalem on 15 July 1099, the crusaders were challenged to settle and defend newly won territory while expanding their control to defensible positions. The architectural response was impressive. Not since Roman times had there been such building activity in Syria-Palestine. Neither Herod nor Constantine built as much. From 1099 to 1131, while the crusaders were at war to establish themselves, defensive architecture had high priority. Fortifications of newly captured cities were repaired. Castles were important as military out-

posts, administrative centers, and secure residences. Baldwin I built Krak de Montreal in 1115 to protect the kingdom and levy tribute from the nearby caravan route. Erected on the summit of a rocky hill above the village of Shaubak, the irregular plan and stout walls of the castle (later extensively rebuilt by the Mamluks) illustrate the crusader practice of making best use of a naturally commanding site. Also early but very different is the castle at Jubail (Gibelet), on the site of ancient Byblos. The overall plan—corner towers and massive central keep, all roughly rectangular—represents a Western castrum concept translated into impressive reused masonry with stone vaults.

Meanwhile, extensive church building was under way. In Jerusalem the Holy Sepulcher, the holiest church in Christendom and the goal of the crusaders, was to become the foremost product of their architectural endeavors. Sometime after 1112 Patriarch Arnulf apparently initiated a full-scale rebuilding of the Byzantine structures dating from 1048. The crusader concept boldly unified the great rotunda containing the tomb, and the Calvary Chapel, as part of a pointed-arch, rib-vaulted French type of pilgrimage church with a dome over the main nave bay and the high altar in an apse with an ambulatory and radiating chapels. It was a splendid integration of this complex site under one roof. By 1131 the church was far enough along to be the site of the coronation of King Fulk and Queen Melisende. The Church of the Nativity at Bethlehem, captured intact in 1099, had been the place of earlier crownings.

At Nazareth, which the crusaders had found in ruins, the Church of the Annunciation was rebuilt by 1107, modest in size and simple in plan. Of the type, St. Anne's in Jerusalem is the best preserved of contemporary Frankish work, apparently started not long after King Baldwin's repudiated first wife, Arda, entered the convent there in 1113. The nave of four bays with two flanking aisles has ribless groin vaults and slightly pointed arches, and at the east end there are three semicircular apses embedded in the thick, heavy walls. The dome over the easternmost bay is unusual, but along with aspects of the facade, it parallels features of the Church of the Holy Sepulcher.

In contrast with the architecture, little monumental sculpture is known from this early period. As for painting, some nave columns of the Church of the Nativity were decorated early. One image of the Virgin and Child enthroned, in a linear Romanesque style possibly by an Italian artist, is dated 15 May 1130. The Holy Sepulcher seems to have had a scrip-

Ivory cover, the Works of Mercy. Psalter of Queen Melisende, 1131–1143. THE BRITISH LIBRARY, MS Egerton 1139

torium from the 1120's, but only undecorated codices, such as a breviary now in Lucca (MS 5), are known before 1131.

The richest and most diverse artistic output by the crusaders occurred between 1131 and the early 1180's. When Melisende came to the throne, her personal patronage apparently stimulated much activity in and around Jerusalem. At her death in 1161, many of the main crusader monuments in Jerusalem were completed. The most famous work directly associated with her name is the Psalter now in the British Library, done between 1131 and 1143. Three Western-trained artists did the decorations, and one of them, Basilius, signed the deesis in Latin. The obvious Byzantine influence on Basilius is displayed to some degree by the other two painters, one of whom does sumptuous and exotic illuminated initials and the other of whom does images of saints in a more patently Romanesque style. Taken together, the

paintings, the text of the calendar with its notable English features, and the ivory covers with a Byzantine-looking prince engaged in works of mercy (a Western iconographical concept) epitomize the mélange of East and West that characterizes crusader art.

Melisende's name is associated with such important works as St. Anne's Church, which must have been completed during her reign; the tomb of the Virgin, where the queen was eventually buried; and the Convent of St. Lazarus, where her sister Yvette was abbess. Royal patronage clearly set a high and vigorous standard.

The most important project of the 1130's and 1140's was the completion of the Holy Sepulcher. The main facade was conceived with a double portal echoing the Golden Gate. The rich sculptural decoration included Roman-style cornices, an early Christian-style hood molding, voussoirs of Arab-inspired gadroons, late antique-type acanthus capitals, and two Romanesque lintels. The west lintel includes six scenes leading up to the Crucifixion and the Resurrection, the sites of which could be visited

Main (south transept) facade. Church of the Holy Sepulcher, Jerusalem, first half of the 12th century. THE MATSON PHOTO SERVICE

23

inside. Along with many carved capitals, the interior received fine mosaics, of which only the imposing Byzantine-style Christ in the vault of the Latin Calvary Chapel survives. At its dedication on 15 July 1149, the Holy Sepulcher must have been a spectacular statement of the blend of artistic traditions seen on a small scale in Melisende's Psalter.

Elsewhere in Jerusalem major work was under way. The Hospitaler complex (now almost completely destroyed) was decorated with figural sculpture in a robust French Romanesque style of which only fragments survive. On the Ḥaram, the Dome of the Rock was dedicated as the Templum Domini in the 1140's and a large iron grille, surely the masterpiece of crusader metalwork, was put up between the columns. A monastery was erected at the north end of the platform, and on the southern end of the Ḥaram the Templars started building. Only sculp-

Mosaic, Christ of the Ascension. Vault of the Latin Calvary Chapel, Church of the Holy Sepulcher, Jerusalem, first half of the 12th century. DEPARTMENT OF ART, UNIVERSITY OF NORTH CAROLINA

tural fragments later reused by the Arabs survive, but a wet-leaf acanthus style, some of the most beautiful nonfigural crusader work, was apparently introduced at mid century and developed into the 1180's.

Outside Jerusalem architecture flourished. At Tyre the Byzantine cathedral was rebuilt, becoming one of the four largest crusader churches. At Ramla the smaller Church of St. John had its three apses embedded in a more typical rectangular chevet. In concept such churches were mainly Romanesque, but a distinctive Levantine character was introduced by their flat stone roofs and a Near Eastern vocabulary of decorative sculpture.

Some of the best-known castles were built or begun in this period, developing earlier ideas on a new and impressive scale. Kerak (Al-Karak) was started in 1142. Sited on a ridge spur, the massive fortifications, which included rough stone masonry and rectangular towers, produced a defensive position vulnerable, in the end, only to starvation or treachery. Saone (Sahyun) has the most spectacular spur castle site; with its enormous size it is an extraordinary example of a baronial defensive stronghold. Krak des Chevaliers, justifiably the most famous crusader fortress, was ceded in 1142 to the Hospitalers, who after 1170 rebuilt the walls of what is now the inner core on the site of earlier Arab and baronial Frankish work. Belvoir Castle was also ceded to the Hospitalers, who rebuilt it after 1168. Its castrum-within-a-castrum plan is very different from that of Krak, and indicates the importance of the site and preexisting structures for castle design.

Outside Jerusalem, Nazareth and Bethlehem emerged between about 1160 and Saladin's conquest in 1187 as centers of significant artistic activity. Archbishop Lietard apparently enlarged the Church of the Annunciation at Nazareth and planned the most extensive program of figural sculpture yet seen in the crusader states. The figural capitals and several life-size torsos indicate that the artists, working in a French Romanesque style, were innovative and had great talent. In Bethlehem painting came to the fore. Besides continuation of the column paintings, extensive mosaics were done by 1169 in the Church of the Nativity, patronized jointly by the local bishop, King Amalric I, and Emperor Manuel Komnenos. A mosaic artist named Basilius executed the angels of the nave, a certain Ephrem worked in the apse and transepts, and a Nativity scene was done for the grotto itself. The strong Byzantine influence here and nearby in the frescoes of the Hospitaler church at Abū Ghōsh, along with the contemporary products of the Holy Sepulcher scriptorium, reflect the close ties between the Latin Kingdom and the Byzantine Empire through the 1160's to the death of Amaury in 1174.

Saladin's conquest in 1187–1189 sharply reduced but did not halt artistic work by the crusaders. Only a few major castles, such as Krak des Chevaliers, and three main cities—Tripoli, Tyre, and Antioch—held out. The Third Crusade (1189–1192) quickly restored Acre in 1191, but not Jerusalem. For a century Acre functioned as the political and artistic capital of the Latin Kingdom.

As the crusaders struggled to reestablish themselves, there was again a surge of castle building. At Krak des Chevaliers the Hospitalers, working in ashlar masonry, erected a complete circuit of outer defense walls; the inner fortifications were expanded, receiving a massive talus; and both were anchored by a series of round towers. In the main courtyard the new great hall had windows with Gothic tracery and handsome sculpture in the loggia. The nearby chapel received Byzantine-style frescoes. By 1250 Krak was the most formidable Frankish castle anywhere.

St. Thomas, detail. St. Thomas Capital, Church of the Annunciation, Nazareth, third quarter of the 12th century. GARO NALBADIAN AND THE UNIVERSITY OF NORTH CAROLINA PHOTOGRAPH ARCHIVE

Meanwhile, in 1217–1218 the Pilgrim's Castle was built on a virgin site at ᶜAtlīt. The sea being on three sides, the main fortifications consisted of a system of eastern walls with rectangular towers. The Templars held ᶜAtlīt, and with the Hospitalers they controlled the main castles, though they did not develop separate architectural styles.

The exclusive choice of the spur castle in the thirteenth century reflects the embattled Frankish defensive position. As artistic centers the role of these castles was obviously limited. Chapels sometimes were decorated with frescoes, as at Krak and Marqab. But whereas in the twelfth century only Belvoir had significant figural carving, Krak, ᶜAtlīt, and Montfort (the last built about 1229 by the Teutonic Knights) all received notable figural sculpture. The most important church completed during this period, Notre Dame at Tartūs, has naturalistic foliate capitals but, surprisingly, almost no figural work.

Overall artistic output during this time of adversity was predictably limited. Even Jerusalem, regained by treaty in 1229 until overrun by Turks in 1244, produced little. In painting, for example, only the handsome Psalter possibly commissioned about 1235 by Frederick II for his third wife, the English princess Isabella, may have been done there. Despite English and Byzantine aspects reminiscent of Melisende's Psalter, the German approach to the decoration—scenes of Christ's life presented sequentially through the psalms—gives this manuscript a distinctive character that is no less crusader in its blend of East and West.

Artistic output, so sharply diminished between 1191 and 1250, surprisingly increased dramatically during the years 1250–1291, a time of relentless Mamluk incursions. The focus of this activity was Acre, and the pivotal figure Louis IX, who resided in the Latin Kingdom from 1250 to 1254. The defenses of Jaffa, Caesarea, and Sidon were rebuilt or strengthened under his energetic direction, and at Acre the entire northern suburb was fortified. (The exact building phases of St. Jean d'Acre have been little studied even though the bulk of the crusader city survives today within rebuilt walls.) Foremost in the artistic upsurge was painting. The illustrations for an Old French Bible commissioned by Louis IX were done in an accomplished Franco-Byzantine style strongly related to frescoes painted in Constantinople during the Latin Empire. Subsequent painting of codices and icons in Acre retained with variations this blend of Byzantine and Western traditions. A missal now in Perugia seems to be the work of Venetian and French artists jointly, both under Byzantine influence. Icons on wood panels demonstrate the strength of the Italo-Byzantine style. A fine double-faced icon with the Crucifixion and the Anastasis shows distinctive crusader characteristics.

These works reflect the Italian presence in the merchant quarters of Acre. Secular codices became increasingly popular, paralleling developments in the West. An *Histoire universelle,* possibly executed as a gift for King Henry II of Lusignan, has illustrations in a Franco-Byzantine style along with certain Islamic features seen especially in the frontispiece. The climax of French painting in Acre came with an artist who worked for the Hospitalers. Purely Gothic in conception, his images increasingly incorporated visual aspects of his crusader ambience.

It is striking that whereas the greatest output of architecture, sculpture, and monumental painting occurred in the crusader states during the twelfth century, more extant manuscripts and icons by far

are products of the thirteenth. The painting strongly indicates that crusader art blended Eastern and Western traditions. Looked at with this in mind, the architecture and sculpture appear less the product of wholesale colonial transferrals and more the distinctive result of this interaction. Moreover, it is impressive that these characteristics, established early, developed continuously until the demise of the Latin Kingdom.

On 18 May 1291 Acre fell to the invading Mamluks, and within months the mainland crusader states were effectively wiped out. Crusader artistic activity in Syria-Palestine ceased. Much has been lost through destruction during the twelfth and thirteenth centuries and subsequent devastation in the area. Some portable objects no doubt await identification in external collections, and much study of what survives remains to be done. Meanwhile, there was other "crusader" art in Cyprus, Greece, Rhodes, Turkey, and Egypt, not to mention the West. Our strict definition derives from the importance of the Holy Land for the crusades and the culture of medieval Europe.

Our understanding of the art and architecture surveyed above has changed radically since the 1920's. Fifty years ago crusader art was described as a separate French colonial product, very little of which could be dated after 1187. In light of recent studies (1957–1983), we see by contrast what diversity there is in artists, stylistic influences, even patrons. We are discovering gradually the full range of crusader artistic production, which shows unexpected continuity even through the hardest of times in the twelfth and thirteenth centuries. Finally, we have begun to recognize distinctive aspects of crusader style and iconography deriving from the special circumstances of the crusader states, where East and West came together in the unique Levantine context of the medieval Christian holy sites.

Bible, frontispiece to the Book of Judith. Commissioned by Louis IX, *ca.* 1250. BIBLIOTHÈQUE DE L'ARSENAL, PARIS, MS 5211, fol. 252r

BIBLIOGRAPHY

Survey and bibliography. A History of the Crusades, Kenneth M. Setton, gen. ed., IV, *The Art and Architecture of the Crusader States,* Harry W. Hazard, ed. (1977).

Art. Crusader Art in the Twelfth Century, Jaroslav Folda, ed., British Archaeological Reports, International Series, CLII (1982).

Architecture. Meron Benvenisti, *The Crusaders in the Holy Land* (1970); Paul Deschamps, *Les châteaux des croisés en Terre Sainte,* 3 vols. (1934–1973); Camille Enlart, *Les monuments des croisés dans le royaume de Jérusalem: Architecture religieuse et civile,* 2 vols. (1925–1928) and atlas, 2 vols. (1926–1927); William Harvey *et al., The*

Church of the Nativity at Bethlehem, Robert Weir Schultz, ed. (1910); Santino Lange, *Architettura delle crociate in Palestina* (1965); Thomas Edward Lawrence, *Crusader Castles*, 2 vols. (1936); Wolfgang Müller-Wiener, *Castles of the Crusaders*, John Maxwell Brownjohn, trans. (1966); Emmanuel Rey, *Étude sur les monuments de l'architecture militaire des croisés en Syrie et dans l'île de Chypre* (1871); Karl Schmaltz, *Mater ecclesiarum: Die Grabeskirche in Jerusalem* (1918); Prosper Viaud, *Nazareth et ses deux églises de l'Annonciation et de St. Joseph* (1910); Louis Hugues Vincent and Félix Marie Abel, *Bethléem: Le sanctuaire de nativité* (1914); and *Jerusalem: Recherches de topographie, d'archéologie et d'histoire, II, Jérusalem nouvelle*, 2 pts. (1914–1926); Charles Jean Melchior de Vogüé, *Les églises de la Terre Sainte* (1860).

Sculpture. Moshe Barasch, *Crusader Figural Sculpture in the Holy Land* (1971); Helmut Buschhausen, *Die süditalienische Bauplastik im Königreich Jerusalem von König Wilhelm II. bis Kaiser Friedrich II.* (1978); Paul Deschamps, "La sculpture française en Palestine et en Syrie à l'époque des croisades," in *Fondation Eugène Piot, monuments et mémoires, 31* (1930).

Painting. Hugo Buchthal, *Miniature Painting in the Latin Kingdom of Jerusalem* (1957); Jaroslav Folda, *Crusader Manuscript Illumination at Saint-Jean d'Acre, 1275–1291* (1976); Kurt Weitzmann, "Thirteenth-century Crusader Icons on Mount Sinai," in *Art Bulletin,* **45** (1963), and "Icon Painting in the Crusader Kingdom," in *Dumbarton Oaks Papers,* **20** (1966).

Minor arts and inscriptions. Hans Eberhard Meyer, *Das Siegelwesen in den Kreuzfahrerstaaten* (1978); Gustave Schlumberger, *Numismatique de l'Orient latin* (1878).

JAROSLAV FOLDA

[See also **Castles and Fortifications; Castrum; Crusades and Crusader States: To 1192; Dome of the Rock; Jerusalem; Krak des Chevaliers; Military Orders; William of Tyre.**]

CRUSADES AND CRUSADER STATES. The chronological account of the crusades and the crusader states in the Middle East is covered in four separate articles: **Crusades and Crusader States: Near East; Crusades and Crusader States: To 1192; Crusades and Crusader States: Fourth;** and **Crusades and Crusader States: 1212 to 1272.**

CRUSADES AND CRUSADER STATES: NEAR EAST. Although the crusades constitute a very important chapter of medieval European history, they primarily affected the political, social, and economic developments of the Near East. They were impor-

tant in the process of reestablishing the European presence there, after it had been virtually eliminated following the Arab conquest and the victory of Islam. In the course of the eleventh century this process began to gain momentum. Naval squadrons of the Italian mercantile republics raided the coastal towns of North Africa—for instance, the attack against Al-Mahdīyah (Mahdia, Tunisia) in 1087. The Normans of Sicily harassed the North African coast and launched an invasion of Byzantine territories in the Balkans—for instance, the conquest of Dyrrachium (Durrës) in 1081.

Individual pilgrims from various walks of life, as well as mass pilgrimages under the leadership of the west European church hierarchy, either sailed to the Egyptian or the Palestinian coast or traveled overland across the Balkans, Anatolia, and Syria to visit the holy sites in Palestine. They benefited from an increasing number of "tourist" facilities established in Jerusalem with the permission of benevolent Muslim authorities. European sea merchants, especially those from Italy, frequented east Mediterranean ports, successfully gaining commercial privileges from Byzantine and Muslim rulers. Besides yielding spiritual, cultural, and material advantages to European visitors, such contacts served as channels of transmission to Christian Europe of information about the impressive civilization of the Near East, as well as about the declining political and military power of its masters.

In the eleventh century unstable political conditions in Syria were aggravated by the enduring conflict between the Abbasid caliphate of Baghdad and the Fatimid caliphate of Cairo. In the second half of that century the eruption of Seljukid tribes eliminated the Fatimids from Syria but failed to establish a cohesive and stable political regime. Fratricidal struggles between various Seljukid princes—for instance, between Duqāq of Damascus and Riḍwān of Aleppo—and other ambitious military, political, and tribal leaders led to a proliferation of many semiautonomous orthodox and sectarian Muslim and Christian petty states in Syria and northern Mesopotamia. Finally, the crushing victory of the Seljukids over the Byzantines at Manazkert in 1071 dramatically destabilized the political situation in Anatolia. The supremacy of the Byzantine Empire was replaced by a tenuous regime of the Seljukid sultanate of Asia Minor with its capital first at Nicaea (Iznik) and later at Iconium (Konya). The Seljukid sultanate was confronted with the challenge of the Danishmendid emirate of Cappadocia. By the end of

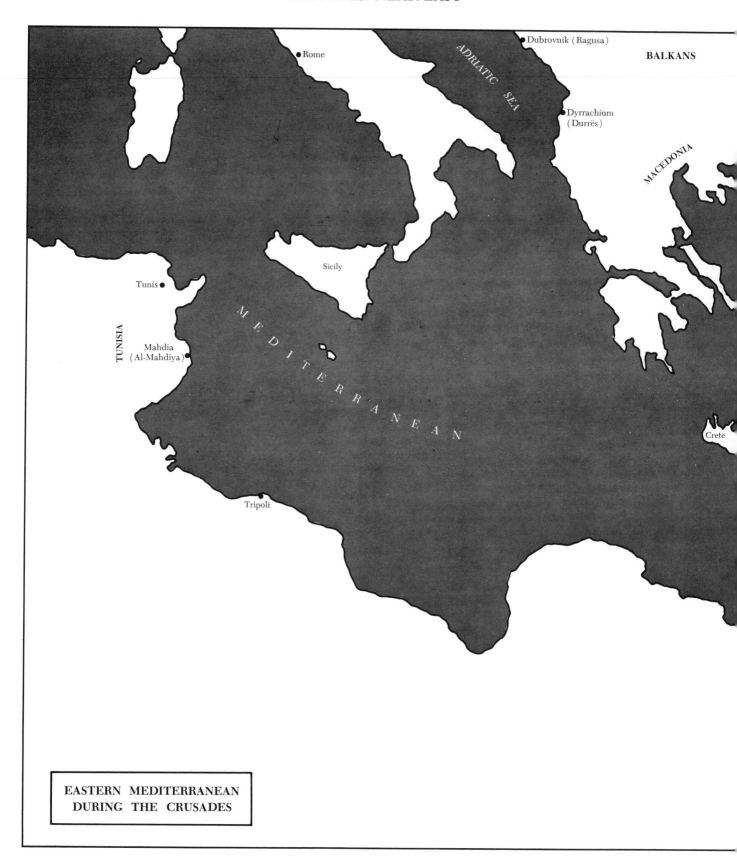

**EASTERN MEDITERRANEAN
DURING THE CRUSADES**

the eleventh century, the eastern Mediterranean Muslim world was too embroiled in internal struggles and rivalries to stand up to a foreign invasion.

This foreign invasion was initially precipitated by the Byzantine Empire. With Constantinople imperiled by the Muslim presence across the Bosporus, Emperor Alexios I Komnenos turned to west European leaders and to the papacy for military assistance. His diplomacy resulted in international consultations involving Byzantine embassies to Italy—for instance, to the Council of Piacenza in March 1095—and Pope Urban II's visits to the courts of the French feudal elite. At a popular level, charismatic preaching by a monk, Peter the Hermit, aroused the masses to act on behalf of Near Eastern Christians reportedly suffering from Seljukid oppression. Finally Urban II delivered an emotional sermon exhorting the faithful to set out on a military expedition to deliver Jerusalem from the Muslim yoke.

In May 1097, after concentrating at Constantinople, a powerful Christian army consisting of west European and Sicilian Norman contingents, was ferried by the Byzantines across the Bosporus to Anatolia. This opened a period of two centuries of direct military intervention of Christian Europe in the Near East, activity that acquired the name of the crusades.

During that period almost incessant fighting went on in various Near Eastern regions belonging to or adjacent to crusader dominions. It was caused either by aggressive initiatives of the crusaders or by Muslim attacks. Eight major campaigns are here discussed, since they acted as catalysts of major developments in the history of the crusades.

The First Crusade, led by Godfrey of Bouillon, Raymond of Toulouse, Bohemond I of Sicily, the papal legate Adémar of Le Puy, and a number of other French, Norman, and Flemish commanders, scored its first success on 19 June 1097, when it forced the Seljukid capital of Nicaea to surrender. On 1 July the crusaders established their military superiority by inflicting a major defeat on the army of the Seljukid sultan, Ķĭlĭj Arslan, at Dorylaeum (Eskişehir). Beginning in October 1097, the main body of the crusader expedition became involved in a difficult and protracted siege of the powerful fortress of Antioch.

On 10 March 1098 a separate contingent, commanded by Baldwin of Boulogne, imposed its power over the Armenian principality of Edessa (Urfa) and founded the first crusader dominion in the Near East, the county of Edessa. On 3 June 1098 the crusaders captured Antioch, and on 28 June they followed this success with an unexpected victory over a powerful relief army made up of a coalition of Muslim leaders. In January 1099, after formally instituting the principality of Antioch under Bohemond of Sicily, the crusaders resumed their march to Jerusalem, which they conquered, after a siege of several weeks, on 15 July.

That the crusaders accomplished their mission against almost insurmountable geophysical and logistic odds, such as the difficult and unfamiliar terrain, thirst, famine, epidemics, and lack of necessary siege machines, was due to their fanatical determination, military superiority, and naval support. The latter proved crucial at the sieges of Antioch and Jerusalem. Also decisive for the outcome of the First Crusade was a hopeless lack of cooperation among the Muslim leaders, who failed to foresee the decisive consequences of a successful European invasion.

In historical perspective, the resulting foundation of a durable state, the Latin Kingdom of Jerusalem, within the Muslim world was more significant than the liberation of the Holy City. Although its first ruler, Godfrey of Bouillon, refused to be crowned as king, his successors, beginning with Baldwin of Boulogne, assumed royal titles and prerogatives. The feudal organizational structure of the kingdom consisted of four fundamental units: the county of Edessa, the principality of Antioch, the county of Tripoli (established in 1109), and the royal territories. At the height of its power the kingdom of the crusaders included parts of northern Mesopotamia, the entire Syro-Palestinian littoral, Palestine, and parts of Transjordan extending south to the Gulf of ᶜAqaba.

In December 1144 a dynamic Muslim war leader, Zangī, captured Edessa. Further reconquests of crusader territories were achieved by Zangī's son, Nūr al-Dīn. Enjoying undivided authority over the military and economic resources of northern Syria and northern Mesopotamia, Nūr al-Dīn began to encroach on territories around Antioch.

The news of the loss of Edessa and the critical position of the principality of Antioch led to the preaching and launching of the Second Crusade (1147–1149). It involved a German army commanded by Emperor Conrad III and a French army led by King Louis VII. However, instead of attacking Nūr al-Dīn, the Second Crusade conducted (July 1148) an abortive siege of Damascus, which at that time was allied with the kingdom of Jerusalem. The outcome of the crusade was utterly negative. It neither recovered Edessa nor curtailed the rising power of Nūr al-Dīn. To make the situation of the Latin Kingdom worse, the crusade pushed Damascus into the arms of Nūr al-Dīn, to whom the great Syrian capital surrendered on 25 April 1154. Such a southward extension of the Muslim front under the unified command of this dedicated leader began to turn the ultimate success of the Muslim holy war, the jihad, into reality.

Under the new circumstances the mastery over Egypt became of crucial strategic importance. In the winter of 1168–1169 an expeditionary army dispatched by Nūr al-Dīn frustrated the crusader attempt to conquer Egypt and established its authority over the moribund Fatimid caliphate. This accomplishment constituted yet another decisive step in the strategy of the Syrian leader to devote military and economic resources of Muslim lands to the overriding goal of the jihad.

A dramatic role in the final implementation of that strategy was played by Saladin, who on 26 March 1169 took command of the Syrian expeditionary force and also became the vizier of the Egyptian caliphate. After ruthlessly suppressing internal revolts and repelling Christian naval offensives (in 1169 a Byzantine attack against Damietta, and in 1174 a Norman assault against Alexandria), Saladin revitalized the political, economic, military, and naval organization of Egypt to suit his political plans and the ambitions of his Kurdish Ayyubid family. In September 1171 he abolished the Fatimid caliphate, the decline of which had to a large extent been precipitated by the activities of the crusaders.

In October 1174, after the death of Nūr al-Dīn (15 May), Saladin took possession of Damascus, and during the following twelve years conducted annual campaigns, mainly against his Muslim rivals. In 1187, having subdued opposition in Syria (Aleppo was taken in 1183), and in northern Mesopotamia (Mosul was taken in 1186), Saladin proceeded to a showdown with the crusaders. On 4 July, having successfully lured King Guy and his crusader army into a fatal tactical move, Saladin wiped out almost all the crusader field forces at Ḥiṭṭīn. This victory was followed by easy reconquests of various crusader lands and towns, including Acre (10 July 1187) and, above all, the holy city of Jerusalem, which surrendered on 2 October of the same year.

The crippling blows inflicted by Saladin on the Latin Kingdom of Jerusalem and surrounding regions, in 1187–1189, aroused western Europe and led to the Third Crusade. It started in the summer of 1189 with an attack against Acre by a crusader force reorganized behind the walls of unconquered Tyre. This operation developed into a two-year siege. But neither the powerful walls of Acre, nor the elite troops committed to their defense, nor the outside assistance rendered by Saladin's huge feudal army and his Egyptian fleet, could withstand the onslaught of this new crusade that involved three crowned heads: Frederick I Barbarossa of the Holy Roman Empire, Philip II Augustus of France, and Richard I the Lionhearted of England.

In addition to land forces the crusade attracted a mass participation of naval squadrons from Italy. But in spite of the recapture of Acre (12 July 1191) and a number of humiliating reverses inflicted by Richard on Saladin, the showdown between the crusaders and the Muslims ended on 2 September 1192 with a negotiated settlement. The crusaders regained possession of the coast between Jaffa and Tyre, but Jerusalem remained in Muslim hands. Its holy shrines were to be accessible to Christian visitors and pilgrims. Shortly after the conclusion of the truce, on 4 March 1193, Saladin, the most celebrated hero of the jihad, died at Damascus.

In 1202 the Fourth Crusade, led by Boniface of Montferrat and Baldwin IX of Flanders, was launched. Its primary target was Ayyubid Egypt, in the belief that its subjugation would prompt an easy recovery of Jerusalem. But instead of pursuing this goal, the crusade conquered and pillaged Constantinople (13 April 1204). Far from attacking the Muslim enemy, the Fourth Crusade accelerated the decline of the Byzantine Empire, founded the Latin Empire of Constantinople (1204–1261), and diverted the attention of prospective crusaders from the Holy Land.

All subsequent crusades between 1204 and 1250 were directed against the Ayyubid sultans of Egypt. Apart from military operations they involved significant diplomatic initiatives. Embroiled in rivalries with other Ayyubid pretenders, the Egyptian sultans showed a willingness to strike diplomatic deals with the crusaders. Christian secular leaders, such as Louis IX, and popes, such as Innocent IV, attempted to promote an alliance with the Mongols, who during that period advanced across Iran in the direction of Iraq, Anatolia, and Syria.

On 5 November 1219, following a difficult siege of seventeen months, John of Brienne (king of Jerusalem 1210–1212; regent of Jerusalem 1212–1225) seized Damietta, a naval base and important economic center. Sultan al-Kāmil (1218–1238) offered to trade Jerusalem for Damietta. The crusaders rejected this offer and advanced on Cairo, only to be defeated on 30 August 1221 near Al-Manṣūra. They were allowed to return to Palestine in exchange for the surrender of Damietta.

On 7 September 1228 the Sicilian-born German emperor Frederick II, excommunicated by Pope Gregory IX for delaying the launching of a crusade, landed with a powerful army in Palestine. Determined to avoid military confrontation, Sultan al-Kāmil offered to negotiate, and on 18 February 1229 the Muslims and Christians concluded a remarkable treaty that surrendered Jerusalem, Bethlehem, Nazareth, part of Sidon, and Toron to the crusaders.

On 7 December 1239 Jerusalem fell to the Ayyubid ruler of Transjordan in spite of the presence in Palestine of a fresh crusader army commanded by Thibaut IV of Champagne. But once again the crusaders benefited from a rivalry between Ayyubid princes who were anxious to secure the neutrality or even the military assistance of Thibaut. Consequently, in 1240 the crusaders recovered not only Jerusalem but also Galilee. On 8 February 1241 these concessions were reaffirmed by a treaty between Sultan al-Ṣāliḥ Ayyūb of Egypt and Richard of Cornwall, the leader of the last crusade to see a Christian Jerusalem.

Successful as those last three crusades were, they did little to avert the rapid decline of the Latin Kingdom of Jerusalem. In the summer of 1244, Khorezmian warriors, displaced by the Mongols, exploited the weakness of the Christian kingdom and captured Jerusalem, which from then until the twentieth century was to remain in Muslim hands.

Nor was the process of decline reversed by the efforts of the idealist crusader, King Louis IX of France. Although on 6 June 1249 his army easily captured Damietta, it embarked on an ill-advised offensive against Cairo. During that expedition the king and his army became trapped at Al-Manṣūra, and on 6 April 1250 they were forced to lay down their arms. The main result of this crusade was the precipitation of a coup d'état in Egypt and the rise of the ruthless militaristic regime of Mamluk sultans (1250–1517). By that time the threat of the crusaders was overshadowed by the unstoppable hordes of the Mongols. Concerned with this archenemy of Islam, the Mamluks saw the necessity of eradicating the feeble vestiges of the crusader kingdom. Beginning with Sultan Baybars (1260–1277) and ending with Sultan al-Ashraf (1290–1294), their fierce warriors conquered, forced into surrender, or caused evacua-

tion of all crusader towns and fortresses on the Near Eastern mainland. With the capitulation of Acre on 18 May 1291, the presence of the crusaders in the Near East came to an end.

That a viable crusader kingdom could operate for nearly 200 years in an entirely alien and hostile environment can be attributed to a number of factors: initial military superiority; the effectiveness of the military orders, such as the Hospitalers and the Templars; naval supremacy achieved by Italian naval squadrons; the seasonal influx of manpower from Europe for defensive or offensive actions against the Muslims; and an ingenious system of strategic castles constructed along the coast and the inland mountain ranges. Also essential for the successes of the crusaders were their psychological or religious commitments to the ideal of the holy war, combined with diplomatic flexibility that allowed them to discern internal dissensions in the Muslim camp and to conclude advantageous agreements with their enemies.

The lack of Muslim unity, as well as the initial misconception and underestimation of the phenomenon of the crusades, was crucial for the rise and longevity of the kingdom of Jerusalem. But once the military and economic resources of Syria and Egypt became integrated under a single command, especially when this integration coincided with a decline of internal cohesion among the crusader leaders, the kingdom of Jerusalem was doomed. In Saladin's time there was enough crusading zeal to avert the catastrophe, but this zeal was largely absent during the exterminatory operations launched by the Mamluks.

Islam emerged triumphant from its confrontation with the crusades. The feelings of military superiority were later reinforced by the victories of the Ottomans over the Byzantines and Christian kingdoms in the Balkans. However, the military outcome of the crusades does not constitute the most significant result of the struggles between Christendom and Islam. Far more important was the fact that the crusades served as a catalyst of rapid cultural and civilizational progress experienced by Christian Europe in the late Middle Ages. This was particularly true of Mediterranean trade developments.

In the eleventh century European sea merchants had merely challenged the Near Eastern hegemony over the Mediterranean sea routes, but during the crusades they succeeded in gaining naval and commercial preponderance at the expense of indigenous Near Eastern competitors. They achieved it mainly by cynically exploiting the conflict between Christianity and Islam to their commercial advantage. They provided the crusaders with naval support to fight the Muslims, but they also supplied strategic war matériel to Egypt, as well as male slaves for the army of the Mamluk sultans, which ultimately exterminated the kingdom of the crusaders.

In the late Middle Ages, as Europe was entering the Renaissance, the Near East was sinking into a period of backwardness. In light of these contrasting civilizational and economic trends, the outcome of the crusades, despite the military victory of the Muslims, was a long-term setback for the Islamic Near East.

BIBLIOGRAPHY

Hans Eberhard Mayer, *The Crusades,* John Gillingham, trans. (1971); Joshua Prawer, *The Latin Kingdom of Jerusalem: European Colonialism in the Middle Ages* (1973); Steven Runciman, *A History of the Crusades,* 3 vols. (1964); Kenneth M. Setton, gen. ed., *A History of the Crusades,* II, *The Later Crusades,* Robert Wolff and Harry Hazard, eds., 2nd ed. (1969).

ANDREW S. EHRENKREUTZ

[See also **Ayyubids; Chivalry, Orders of; Egypt, Islamic; Hittin; Jihad; Mamluks; Saladin.**]

CRUSADES AND CRUSADER STATES: TO 1192. The origin of the crusades is obscure. Historians have attempted to show that they go back to the time of the return of the True Cross to Jerusalem in 627. There is more validity to the view that pilgrimages and holy war were the motives for the crusades. Pilgrims wanted to visit the land of Jesus in peace and safety. The church, meanwhile, had been developing the concept of holy war for at least a century. Therefore a holy war to protect the holy places was the logical result.

The question arises why these pilgrimages to the Holy Land had not led to crusades before the eleventh century. There is no definitive answer. However, conditions in the eleventh century created a favorable environment. Chaos of the earlier years gave way to order and expansion, and signs of urban development appeared. The growth of feudalism led to a martial spirit and a degree of loyalty to authority. William the Conqueror, Emperor Henry IV, and Roger I of Sicily used this new spirit to increase their power.

In the meantime, the church, beset by secularism, turned to reform. The rise of Cluny, with its emphasis on spiritual efforts, gave the papacy power comparable with that of the lay leaders. The church now had two new forces—the reform movement within the church and the need of feudal lords for new lands—to aid in the expansion of Christendom. Pacifist Christianity turned to holy war and sought to expand its frontiers. Spanish knights pushed back Islam in the Reconquest, and the Normans began the conquest of Sicily. The athletes of Christ found life more exciting and profitable as soldiers of Christ.

Conditions in the Near East also favored the expansion of Christendom. Alp Arslan, a son of Chaghri-Beg, unified the Seljuk Turks and began to encroach on the Byzantine Empire. In 1071 he routed a Byzantine army at Manazkert. This defeat left Byzantium militarily weak and opened Asia Minor to the Turks. Jerusalem, however, remained in the hands of the Fatimid caliph of Cairo. The transition was by no means catastrophic. The Seljuks replaced the unpopular Byzantines and life went on as usual. There is little evidence that pilgrims suffered more than in the past. However, the Seljuk penchant for tribal rule led to great division in the Islamic world and made conditions favorable for the crusades.

THE FIRST CRUSADE

Immediate events leading to the First Crusade are well recorded but subject to various interpretations. Legend credited Peter the Hermit with going on a pilgrimage, being subjected to Turkish abuse, and returning to convince the pope of the necessity of a crusade. This story has been discredited. In fact Pope Urban II launched the crusades to free the holy places and perhaps also in the hope of uniting the Greek and Latin churches by freeing Byzantium from the Muslim threats. Urban journeyed to southern France, enlisted the aid of its leaders, and on 27 November 1095 issued at Clermont the call for the crusade. He called for the recovery of the Holy Sepulcher and urged a militant Christendom to fight Islam. The enthusiasm of the crowd rose as the pope spoke of Turkish atrocities. Cries of "Deus vult" rang out. Adhémar, bishop of Le Puy, took the cross, and emissaries of Raymond IV, count of Toulouse and St. Gilles, offered his services. The next few months were spent in preparation.

The First Crusade (1096–1099) is perhaps the best recorded and was the most successful of the crusades. No kings took the cross, but the list of feudal nobility is impressive. Godfrey of Bouillon, duke of

Lower Lorraine, imposed heavy taxes on monasteries to finance his contingent. His brother, Baldwin I, also took the cross. Bohemond I, son of Robert Guiscard, leader of the Norman conquest of south Italy, brought Norman contingents eager to wrest territory from the Byzantines. His nephew Tancred accompanied the Normans. Raymond IV of Toulouse brought the largest number of crusaders and the greatest wealth. Northern France was represented by Robert, duke of Normandy; Robert, count of Flanders; Hugh the Great of Vermandois, brother of the king of France; and Stephen of Blois, son-in-law of the king of England. The church sent no great clerics. The clerics who did take the cross, and the accompanying poor, were mainly a hindrance to secular lords who cared more for new lands than for spiritual rewards.

The preaching of the crusade occupied several months and brought an unexpected response. Plenary indulgence and hope of material gain assured the success of Urban's call. Plans called for departure on 15 August 1096 and the cooperation of Latins and Greeks. The hopes for an orderly crusade soon faded. Peter the Hermit and other itinerant preachers urged the peasants to take the cross. Ill-planned and poorly executed, the Peasants' Crusade became a disaster. Walter the Penniless, supposedly a capable knight, led a band of French peasants across Germany and Hungary. They arrived in the environs of Constantinople in July 1096, then awaited the arrival of Peter the Hermit, who had enlisted large numbers of German peasants. After clashes with the Hungarians and Byzantine mercenaries, Peter's group arrived before Constantinople on 30 July.

The preaching of Peter led other leaders to take the cross. Gottschalk, a priest, led a band of peasants to Hungary, where they were massacred. Volkmar and his rabble persecuted Jews en route to Bohemia. They were dispersed at Nitra (Nyitra). Emich of Leisingen led knights and peasants through Germany and into Hungary. In Germany the mob persecuted the Jews, sacked ghettos, and killed many of the inhabitants. The Hungarians destroyed the band.

The Byzantine emperor, Alexios I Komnenos, advised Peter the Hermit to await the arrival of the better-armed main contingents. On 6 August the impatient pilgrims crossed the Bosporus and marched toward Nicomedia (modern Izmit). One group, consisting of French and Italians under an Italian nobleman named Reginald, split from the main body and captured the castle of Xerigordon, only to be besieged by the forces of Kīlīj Arslan on 29 September.

The heat and lack of water led to surrender and death for many pilgrims. Reginald and a few survivors turned apostate and remained in captivity. The rest of the peasant army, left without Peter, who had returned to Constantinople, marched out of Civetot (Citobus), only to be ambushed by the Turks on 21 October. The few survivors, mostly children, became captives.

The success of the crusade depended on the arrival of the knights, the cooperation of the Greeks and Latins, and the division of the Turks. Hugh the Great of Vermandois, the first of the princes to arrive, received a royal welcome and took an oath that he would help to restore Byzantine lands and would be loyal to Alexios. The new arrivals posed a problem for the emperor. Godfrey of Bouillon arrived before Constantinople on 23 December with his brothers Eustace and Baldwin. Unwilling to take the oath of loyalty, he engaged in minor skirmishes with Byzantine mercenaries. Finally a Byzantine show of force caused Godfrey to take the oath on Easter Sunday 1097, and shortly thereafter he crossed the Bosporus and marched to Pelecanum.

On 9 April 1097 Bohemond arrived and, to the surprise of Alexios, took the oath. His army soon crossed into Asia Minor along with that of Tancred, who refused to take the oath. The army of Raymond IV arrived at roughly the same time. Raymond's forces had marched down the Dalmatian coast, where they encountered hostile Slavs. Expecting a friendly welcome from the Greeks, the Provençals found themselves surrounded by Byzantine mercenaries. Following clashes with the Imperials, Raymond left his army and journeyed to Constantinople.

The meeting of Raymond and Alexios was unfriendly, and the count refused to take an oath. Finally, on 26 April Raymond took an oath similar to those taken among great lords in southern France. He swore that he would respect the life and honor (which is to say the lands) of Alexios, and promised not to cause him injury. Perhaps Raymond understood the need for Greek and Latin friendship better than any other leader. His loyal support of Alexios, however, later caused trouble.

In May the contingents of Robert of Normandy and Stephen of Blois arrived. Robert II of Flanders had reached Constantinople in early April. The Normans soon crossed the Bosporus, and shortly thereafter Raymond followed. The united forces, now ready for booty and glory, had no idea of the hardships that awaited them.

The vanguard under Godfrey marched toward

Nicaea on 26 April and soon thereafter laid siege to the city. Ķîlîj Arslan, governor of Nicaea, left his wife and treasure in the city while he collected a Turkish relief force. His efforts to crush the combined forces of Godfrey and Raymond failed, however, and Nicaea was left at the mercy of the crusaders. On 19 June when the hopes of capturing Nicaea were high, the Westerners saw the imperial standards fly from the ramparts. Manuel Butumites, the Greek commander, had struck a deal with the Turks that restored Nicaea to Alexios and saved the city from looting by the crusaders. Infuriated by what they considered Greek treachery the Latins cursed Alexios.

In a council of war the Latins decided to take the perilous route across Anatolia. Bohemond was to lead, and Raymond took position in the rear guard. Ķîlîj Arslan, waiting in the nearby hills, attacked the forces of Bohemond at Dorylaeum. The Norman leader wisely kept his troops in a tight circle and awaited reinforcements. Godfrey, and then Raymond, attacked the Turks, and finally a diversionary movement by Adhémar routed the enemy. The victory at Dorylaeum left the road open to Antioch.

During the next four months the crusaders suffered from the heat, then torrential rains in October, and ever-present hunger and illness. The success of the march may be attributed to the cooperation of the Greek leader, Tatikios, with the Latins. Towns captured along the route became possessions of Alexios, and Greek and Latin relations were friendly for the moment.

In the meantime Baldwin and Tancred led forces into Cilicia, where Tancred hoped to establish a principality. In the course of this adventure the two quarreled, and Tancred's hopes faded. He rejoined the army while Baldwin marched eastward. On 6 February Baldwin received an enthusiastic welcome in Edessa. The citizens made him joint ruler with Thoros, a local noble, and on 10 March made him sole head of the government after overthrowing Thoros. The county of Edessa became the first Latin state in the Near East.

In late October 1097 the main contingents of the crusaders besieged Antioch on the Orontes River, an ancient city defended by Yāghîsîyān. The siege lasted for months. Shortages of food, inclement weather, quarrels between the Greeks and Latins, and Turkish counterattacks left the crusaders unsure of God's will. During the siege many atrocities were committed in the name of God and Allah. In the darkest moment Bohemond revealed a plan: a traitor, Firuz, would open the gates of Antioch. Under Bohemond's leadership the Latins entered the city on 3 June 1098, massacred the inhabitants, and gave praise to God for his mercy.

The Christians had little time to celebrate. Kerbogha, atabeg of Mosul, arrived before the Iron Bridge on 5 June and two days later laid siege to the city. Alexios, who had promised aid, returned to Constantinople, accompanied by Stephen of Blois and other Christian deserters. In the following days of famine, fear, and illness, a Provençal peasant, Peter Bartholomew, reported that the place where the Holy Lance was hidden had been revealed to him. Despite the skepticism of many, Peter and a small group found a lance that supposedly had pierced Christ's side. The result was dramatic. The crusaders took new hope and on 28 June marched out of Antioch. Kerbogha, rather than attacking divisions as they emerged, waited until all the Christians were assembled outside the walls. The poorly organized Turkish forces proved to be no match for the Western knights, and the ensuing rout of Kerbogha's troops left Antioch in Latin hands. Since Alexios had abandoned the siege, Antioch was left open to rival princes.

The death at Antioch of Adhémar of Le Puy, who had tried to settle the Norman-Provençal quarrel, left the Latins without a conciliatory force. Raymond of Toulouse captured Albara and Maᵓarrat al-Nuᶜmān while the main army delayed the march to Jerusalem. Bohemond strengthened his hold on Antioch and refused to resume the journey. Thus a second Latin state, the principality of Antioch, was formed; and hopes for Latin and Greek cooperation faded.

On 13 January 1099 Raymond of Toulouse marched out of the burning ruins of Maᵓarrat al-Nuᶜmān as a barefoot pilgrim and spurred some of the other leaders to move on. The march to Jerusalem was broken by the siege of Arqa in the spring of 1099. During this time Peter Bartholomew agreed to undergo the ordeal by fire to prove the authenticity of the Holy Lance. His ensuing death left the Normans skeptical, and the Provençals staunch, in their faith in the relic.

On 13 May a reluctant Raymond abandoned the siege of Arqa and resumed the journey. On 7 June a happy Christian army besieged Jerusalem following a year and several months of quarrels and tribulation. The city could expect no aid from either Turks or Egyptians and awaited capture. The end came when Godfrey and his troops entered the city on 15

July. The ensuing slaughter was recorded by Christian clerics who looked on the destruction of the enemy as the will of God. Figures on the massacre are unreliable, and stories of blood flowing to the bridles of horses are drawn from the Book of Revelation. Certainly, the Latins soon learned to live and to let live in an alien land.

The Holy Sepulcher, now in the hands of the Latins, was no longer a goal. Many Westerners returned to Europe, Godfrey and Raymond quarreled, and the stability of Latin states seemed in jeopardy. Finally, Godfrey became defender of the Holy Sepulcher and rallied the Christians to defeat a Fatimid force under al-Afḍal Shānānshāh at the battle of Ascalon on 12 August 1099. Furthermore, Urban had died before the capture of Jerusalem, and his successor, Paschal II, had the problem of sending new recruits to ensure the success of the crusade. Godfrey also died and was succeeded by his brother, Baldwin, who took the title king of Jerusalem.

THE CRUSADE OF 1101

The capture of Jerusalem was a remarkable feat but the climate for a new crusade was not favorable. The monarchs had little interest and Spain was preoccupied with the Reconquest. Paschal turned to other sources to initiate the Crusade of 1101. The popes kept crusading zeal alive for decades to ensure possession of the Holy Sepulcher and to repel Islam. In Lombardy, Anselm, archbishop of Milan, preached the crusade and enlisted clergymen, women, and a few petty lay leaders. Paschal sent some of the latter to preach in France, and through their efforts a council was held at Poitiers on 18 November 1100. Enthusiasm similar to that of Clermont seized the crowd, and Duke William IX of Aquitaine, who had interfered in Languedoc during Raymond's absence, took the oath. One of the first troubadours, William was neither pious nor devoted to the church. Accompanied by a large army and many females, he marched east for new conquests and adventure.

In northern France, Stephen of Blois, at the urging of his wife, took the cross again and swore to carry out the pledge that he had abandoned at Antioch. Hugh of Vermandois, another deserter, also rejoined the cause. In central and eastern France, Count William II of Nevers, Duke Odo of Burgundy, and Count Stephen of Burgundy took the cross. In Germany, Welf IV of Bavaria, Ida of Austria, Arch-

bishop Thiemo of Salzburg, and the bishop of Passau answered the call. Conrad, perhaps a constable of Henry IV, led another force.

The poorly planned crusade was a disaster from the beginning. The Lombards left Milan on 13 September 1100, pillaged the lands of Alexios en route to Constantinople and arrived there in early March 1101. Following clashes with the imperial forces, the Lombards crossed the Bosporus and encamped at Nicomedia, where their ranks were increased by the forces of Conrad, the Burgundians, and Stephen of Blois.

Raymond of Toulouse and a Greek contingent led the motley group, and at the insistence of the Lombards the crusaders decided to attack Pontus. They had learned that Bohemond was held prisoner by Ghāzī Gûmûshtegin (or Dānishmend), the Danishmendid emir of Sivas, and despite opposition from Raymond and Stephen, they turned to rescue him. Encouraged by the capture of Angora (Ankara), they took up a position on the plain below the mountains of Paphlagonia, where they encountered a Turkish force under Ghāzī, Ruḍwān of Aleppo, and Qaraja of Haran.

The ensuing battle went against the Christians. Panic seized the Westerners; the most prominent knights, including Raymond and Stephen, and the high churchmen fled, leaving women and children to the mercy of the Turks. The remnants of the scattered forces returned to Constantinople.

In the meantime the forces of William of Nevers reached Constantinople in June 1101, crossed the Bosporus, and marched to Iconium (Konya) and Heraclea Pontica, where they met defeat. William and a few followers fled to Antioch, where they were received by Tancred.

The united forces of William IX and Welf IV also arrived at Constantinople in June 1101, crossed the Bosporus, and marched to Heraclea Pontica. There the Turks ambushed the Christians, massacred many, and routed the rest. Ida of Austria was taken captive. Hugh of Vermandois, a deserter in the First Crusade, died at Tarsus of an arrow wound.

Survivors of the several disasters reassembled at Antioch and continued the journey to Jerusalem. Tortosa fell to the crusaders, who gave the town to Raymond. King Baldwin received the crusaders and urged them to remain in the Near East. Having fulfilled their vows, many of the Westerners returned home, but some chose to help Baldwin strengthen the kingdom of Jerusalem.

An ill-advised attack on a superior Egyptian force near Ascalon turned into a disaster. Stephen of Blois, who had deserted during the First Crusade, erased his former cowardice by his death. Many noblemen, including Hugh of Lusignan, lost their lives; others were captured and taken to Cairo. The Crusade of 1101 was a futile gesture marked by stupidity. Many died on the long journey, and few crusaders remained to strengthen the Latin states.

The initial enthusiasm for the crusades waned after the recovery of the Holy Sepulcher, and the papacy, with the aid of ambitious knights, struggled to consolidate territorial gains. Fifty years after Urban's call, the West could boast of a tenuous hold on Islamic lands. The county of Edessa, the principality of Antioch, and the kingdom of Jerusalem were established by 1099. Raymond of Toulouse, faithful to his vow to remain in the Near East, devoted the rest of his life to the conquest of Tripoli. At his death in 1105 at Mt. Pilgrim, his task was still unfinished. His cousin, William-Jordan, besieged Tripoli, which fell in 1109. The fourth Latin state, the county of Tripoli, became the possession of Bertrand, son of Raymond IV.

The history of the Latin states reveals the problems of the feudal system. Theoretically, the kingdom of Jerusalem claimed loyalty from the other states, but the claim was a hollow technicality. The deaths of Raymond and Bohemond and internal rivalries marked by deals with the Muslims made the Latins vulnerable. The crusaders were poor colonizers, and at best built castles from which they sallied forth to make raids. The Latin and Greek churches clashed, and Byzantium was a fickle partner.

The crusades were doomed from the beginning because while the objective, the recovery of the Holy Sepulcher, was only a short-term incentive, the holding of the Sepulcher became a monumental, long-term task. Surrounded by the Muslim world, the Latin states depended on outside aid for survival. Enthusiasm for causes soon abates, and within a century Europeans had lost their zest for the crusades. At the same time the Islamic world, earlier racked by divisions and vulnerable to attack, turned to oust the Latins. While the Latins quarreled, Muslims found a strong leader. ⁾Imād al-Dīn Zangī (or Zengī), son of a governor of Aleppo, took Mosul in 1127 and Aleppo perhaps in 1128. His ambitious plans were realized in 1144 when he captured Edessa and, as defender of the faith, began the long task of ousting the Franks from the Near East. The fall of Edessa was a shock to the West and a harbinger of the dismantling of the Latin states decades later.

THE SECOND CRUSADE

The fall of Edessa brought a papal bull authorizing the Second Crusade. Pope Eugenius III initiated it, but St. Bernard of Clairvaux popularized the movement far beyond papal hopes. Unlike the First Crusade, the new venture attracted royalty. The preaching of Bernard of Vézelay on 31 March 1146 brought an enthusiastic response. King Louis VII, his wife, Eleanor of Aquitaine, and many important noblemen and churchmen enrolled. Bernard continued his enthusiastic preaching and finally enlisted Conrad III of Germany, who at best was a reluctant crusader.

Expeditions against the Moors and the Wends kept many Christians from answering Bernard's call. In May 1147 the Germans started their journey, marched across Hungary and Bulgaria, and after minor quarrels with the Imperials and Emperor Manuel, crossed into Asia Minor at the end of September. In the meantime the forces of Louis assembled in June, crossed into Germany, and followed the route taken by Conrad. News of Manuel's treaty with the Seljuks of Iconium caused ill will between the Greeks and Latins, but failed to divert Louis from the crusade. He arrived at Constantinople on 4 October, crossed the Bosporus, and after several weeks negotiated a treaty with Manuel. Conrad decided to attack Iconium without French support. In the ensuing march the Germans suffered heavy losses at Dorylaeum, and only a few survivors reached Nicaea.

The remnants of Conrad's troops soon joined forces with the newly arrived French contingents. Conrad became ill at Ephesus and returned to Constantinople; Louis marched toward Adalia (Antalya). The Turks ambushed the Christians near Cadmus and inflicted heavy losses. On 20 January Louis's troops entered Adalia to a cold reception. The natives furnished few provisions and little goodwill. Louis sailed to Antioch, leaving the remnants of his army to be massacred or sold into slavery. His stay in Antioch proved to be a triumph for Eleanor, who found Antioch society enjoyable.

Recovered from his illness, Conrad sailed to Acre and marched from there to Jerusalem. Louis hastened to Jerusalem to join forces with Conrad and attempt to salvage something from the past defeats.

The crusaders believed that an assault on Damascus would relieve pressure on the Latin states. In July they moved to attack the city. But this decision ignored the real objective of the crusade, the recapture of Edessa. Louis and Conrad, following the advice of the Palestinian nobility, ignored the plight of Edessa and Antioch as well as the internal problems of Tripoli. Welf, who disagreed with the new plan, abandoned the crusade and returned to Europe. The combined forces of the Westerners and the Syrian Franks probably numbered 50,000. The nobles of Jerusalem led the march, Louis followed closely, and Conrad brought up the rear.

The decision to attack Damascus from the west, where orchards sheltered the defenders, proved costly. The Damascenes shot arrows from the trees and took a heavy toll. Finally driven from the orchards, the defenders of the city took up positions along the Barada River, but the troops of Conrad routed them. The Christians had gained the initial advantage, and fear seized the defenders of Damascus.

Mu⊂īn al-Dīn Unur, the vizier of the city, raised the morale of the frightened inhabitants by showing them the Koran of Uthmān. Unwilling to place faith in divine aid, Unur summoned Saif al-Dīn Ghāzī I and Nūr al-Dīn, rival sons of Zangī, to come to his aid. The ambitions of Saif al-Dīn left Unur in a predicament. He suggested to the Palestinian Franks that Saif al-Dīn posed a threat to them if he took control of Damascus, and that if Damascus fell to the crusaders, Saif al-Dīn would certainly take revenge. Unur suggested that the fall of Damascus would benefit the Westerners, not the Christians of the kingdom of Jerusalem. Unur added weight to his argument by sending money to the Palestinian knights to encourage them to withdraw from the siege. The crusaders aided Unur's efforts by abandoning their positions to the west of Damascus and attacking from the east. This foolish move resulted in the abandonment of the siege and a costly retreat.

The grand alliance of the Western crusaders and the Palestinian barons was shattered. Conrad, embittered by the treachery of the Syrian Franks, left Jerusalem and formed an alliance with his former enemy, the Greek emperor Manuel. Louis tarried in the Near East, hoping to aid the crusading cause. Finally, at the insistence of Suger he reluctantly left Palestine on a Sicilian ship, narrowly escaping capture by the Byzantines, who were at war with Roger II of Sicily. This experience turned Louis against

Manuel and resulted in his friendship with the Normans.

The failure of the Second Crusade ended the enthusiastic response of great crowds of knights and peasants. Broken by petty rivalries, the Second Crusade could not equal the gains of the First Crusade. Growing Muslim strength, the Frankish inability to colonize, and strife between Syrian Franks and Western crusaders pointed the way to the end of Pope Urban's dream of a unified Christian world.

THE LATIN STATES

The next four decades brought a modus vivendi in the Near East. Tripoli, Antioch, and Jerusalem became preoccupied with their own affairs and disregarded the need for a unified Christian state in the midst of a hostile Islamic world. The idealism of the First Crusade was replaced by a compromise with the realities of life. Accommodation with Muslim leaders took place, and Byzantine diplomacy replaced military strength. Two factors threatened the existence of the Latin states: the insecure military position of the Syrian Franks and the rise of able Muslim leaders. Nūr al-Dīn, the son of Zangī, and Saladin, the nephew of Asad al-Dīn Shīrkūh, Kurdish emir, rallied Muslim forces and threatened a holy war. Their success depended on conquests in Syria and a friendly Egypt.

The survival of the Latin states after the fall of Edessa may be explained in part by the work of King Baldwin III and his brother Amalric I. Baldwin, faced with disaster after the Second Crusade, attempted to make an alliance with the Greeks and to extend the frontiers of Jerusalem to the south. Highly respected by friend and foe alike, he managed to strengthen the kingdom of Jerusalem and to assure prosperity for the Latin states.

Amalric I, successor of Baldwin, did not possess the political finesse of his brother, but he understood the dangers confronting the kingdom. He learned from the past the danger of Syria and Egypt's combining forces, consequently he devoted a large part of his time to an attempted conquest of Egypt. Nūr al-Dīn, aware of the importance of Syria in the defeat of Amalric's plans, threatened from the north. He succeeded in capturing Bohemond III of Antioch, Raymond III of Tripoli, Joscelin III of Edessa, and many Frankish noblemen. He also besieged and took Harim in 1164. The fall of Harim opened the way for an attack on Antioch, a city that was vital to Latin survival. Amalric turned his attention from

Egypt to Syria, and for a short time checked the advance of Nūr al-Dīn. In the meantime Shīrkūh took advantage of the situation and attempted to conquer Egypt. Amalric responded immediately, and forced a peace treaty on Shīrkūh in 1167.

The success of Nūr al-Dīn and the threat to Antioch caused the Latins to turn to friendship with the Greeks. Fears of a Byzantine seizure of Antioch were allayed by plans for a joint campaign against Egypt. In 1186 the Greeks and Latins ratified a treaty of friendship and cooperation, but as in the past, the effort failed. On 4 November 1168, Amalric moved against Egypt without the aid of the Byzantines, and captured Bilbais. The ensuing slaughter of Muslim and Christian inhabitants solidified Muslim resistance. The resistance of Shīrkūh prevented the capture of Cairo and caused Amalric to abandon his Egyptian campaign. Shīrkūh seized Cairo in 1169 but died only two months later. His nephew Saladin (Ṣalāḥ al-Dīn) brought a new problem to the Syrian Franks, for Jerusalem now faced two powerful leaders: Saladin in Egypt and Nūr al-Dīn in Syria.

SALADIN AND THE FALL OF JERUSALEM

Events of the next two decades centered on Saladin and his efforts to unify the Muslims against the Latin intruders. His life and exploits are clouded by fiction and by later notions of his chivalric behavior. His father, Ayyūb, governed Baalbek, a city rich in ruins of past civilizations. The young Saladin spent his early years at Baalbek, and there is a temptation to believe that the magnificent monuments of the past stirred his ambitions and dreams. At the age of fourteen he joined his uncle, Shīrkūh, and began his long struggle with the Franks. His succession to power in Egypt after the death of Shīrkūh gave scope for his ambitious schemes, which called for a holy war. His first problem arose from the opposition of the Fatimids, the nominal rulers of Egypt. Saladin ruthlessly suppressed them and built an army loyal to himself.

Saladin and Nūr al-Dīn held divergent views on the best way to expel the Franks. Saladin thought that Egypt was of prime importance; Nūr al-Dīn believed that Syria was the key to the overthrow of the Franks. Fate kept the two strong Muslim leaders from clashing. Nūr al-Dīn died 15 May 1174, leaving a young son, al-Malik al-Ṣāliḥ. Under the pretense of protecting the young heir, Saladin clashed with the lieutenants of Nūr al-Dīn. Saladin was also opposed by the emirs of Syria, and faced a divided

Islam. In 1174 he occupied Damascus and soon thereafter took Homs and Hama. The house of Zangī, now threatened by the ambitious schemes of Saladin, hired assassins to kill him. When their efforts failed, they met Saladin in battle at the Horns of Hama (1175). Saladin's military victory brought his formal investiture as head of the governments of Egypt and Syria. Legally ensconced in office, he governed by Islamic law and thereby laid the foundation for a holy war against the crusaders. The ensuing years brought internal problems that left him little time to pursue his dream of expelling the Franks. In fact, he was forced to make peace treaties with his Frankish neighbors while he attempted to unite Islamic forces.

By 1186 Saladin had built a formidable military force and had achieved a degree of unity. He awaited an excuse for breaking peaceful coexistence with the Franks. The following year Reginald of Châtillon, lord of Krak, broke the truce by attacking a caravan bound from Cairo to Damascus and refusing to return the booty, thus giving Saladin an excuse to wage holy war. The vassals of Saladin responded, and by the end of May a formidable Muslim army confronted the Latins.

The two armies met on 4 July 1187 south of the Horns of Ḥiṭṭīn. Saladin hoped to draw the combined forces of the crusaders into a pitched battle at a place where he held the advantage. The Christians made the mistake of engaging in open battle and failing to pick a favorable terrain for the fight. The infantry, plagued by heat and thirst, broke ranks and fell victim to the Muslim forces. The Christian knights fought valiantly but were no match for Saladin's troops. Saladin killed Reginald and had 200 Templars and Hospitalers executed. The remaining knights were well treated, and many were released after paying tribute. The slave markets were crowded with the surviving Christian infantrymen.

Saladin moved swiftly to consolidate his gains. By September the main Christian strongholds except Tyre were in his hands. He besieged Jerusalem in September 1187, and on 2 October occupied it without a frontal assault. The defender of Jerusalem, Balian of Ibelin, struck a deal with Saladin that permitted the Christians to depart unharmed. Sufficient ransom money was raised to free 7,000, but many Christians became slaves. Many of the refugees fled to Antioch after hardships made worse by fellow Christians who refused to share supplies and food. Saladin's generosity caused great problems for the remaining Christian states. Food and shelter for the victims posed a real problem, further weakening their position. Many Syrian and Greek Christians remained in Saladin's realm to pay tribute or turn apostate. Saladin turned to besiege Tyre but failed. His first major reverse left the Latins a foothold for continued crusades.

The success of Saladin did not bring the immediate downfall of the Latin states, but it weakened them for future Islamic attacks. The hopes raised by the emotionalism of the First Crusade were on the wane, and the ensuing crusades continued the futile dream of Latin Christianity's flourishing in an Islamic world. Skepticism, ennui, growing national interests, and the heavy cost in manpower and materials led to the final expulsion of the Latins a century later. Latin rivalries, poor planning, the incompatibility of the various cultures, and the genius of Saladin ended Urban's dream of a united Christendom.

Saladin's victory at Ḥiṭṭīn caused archbishop Joscius of Tyre to issue a call for a new crusade. Henry II of England and Philip II Augustus of France took the Cross on 22 January 1189 and initiated the Third Crusade.

Rivalry of the English and French kings marked the course of the crusade. Henry II died on 6 July 1189 and on 3 September his son Richard took the throne. In the ensuing months Richard and Philip resolved their differences and made preparations for the crusade.

In the meantime, the aging emperor, Frederick Barbarossa, led his forces from Regensburg in May 1189, crossed the straits into Asia Minor, and drowned in the Salef River (modern name: Gök Su). Frederick of Swabia, unable to hold the army together, arrived in Jerusalem with only 300 knights. The first phase of the crusade ended in failure.

Finally, on 4 July 1190 Philip and Richard met at Vézelay and began the long journey to the Holy Land. They traveled to Lyons and then separated. Philip went to Genoa and Richard marched to Marseilles. Later Richard sailed to Genoa and then journeyed to Naples. Following an illness Philip rejoined the crusading forces at Messina.

The crusaders' stay in Sicily gave Richard an opportunity to take Messina and to force Tancred, Count of Lecce, to pay the dowry of Richard's sister Joan. In addition Richard persuaded Philip to release him from his marriage to the French king's half-sister, Alice. On 30 March 1191 Philip sailed from Messina, while Richard awaited the arrival of his mother (Eleanor of Aquitaine) and his fiancée, Berengaria, daughter of Sancho VI of Navarre. On 10 April 1191 Richard sailed from Messina only to have part of his fleet destroyed by a storm. Isaac Komnenos, ruler of Cyprus, and his men robbed the survivors who came ashore there. Richard, on hearing of the disaster, landed on Cyprus, defeated and imprisoned Isaac, and left a garrison to protect his interests there.

In the meantime Philip arrived at Acre on 20 April 1191 and took command of the siege operations. Weeks later, in early June, Richard rejoined the crusading army. The two kings continued to quarrel but eventually forced the garrison at Acre to surrender despite Saladin's efforts to save the city. Shortly thereafter Philip lost his enthusiasm for crusading and for various reasons departed on 31 July 1191, promising to respect Richard's possessions in France (a promise that was not kept).

Richard, apparently happy because of Philip's departure, turned to the task of defeating Saladin. His slaughter of Moslem hostages in Acre heightened Saladin's efforts to prevent the crusaders from marching down the coast. However, Saladin was repulsed at Arsūf, just north of Jaffa, and the conflict reached an impasse. Despite bickering of the barons Richard gained Ascalon and harassed the forces of Saladin. Eventually, Richard realized that he could not take Jerusalem and then moved to make peace with Saladin.

On 2 September 1192 Richard and Saladin signed a truce for three years. The Christians held a narrow strip from Tyre to Jaffa, and free passage for Moslems and Christians in Palestine was assured. In October 1192 Richard sailed from Acre and brought an end to the Third Crusade.

The Third Crusade had not been a complete failure. It strengthened the kingdom of Jerusalem, denied Saladin the full benefits of his victory at Ḥiṭṭīn, and delayed the conquest of the Latin states for decades.

BIBLIOGRAPHY

General works. René Grousset, *Histoire des croisades et du royaume franc de Jérusalem*, 3 vols. (1934–1936); Hans Eberhard Mayer, *Bibliographie zur Geschichte der Kreuzzüge* (1960), and *Geschichte der Kreuzzüge* (1965), the latter available in English as *The Crusades,* John Gillingham, trans. (1973); Steven Runciman, *A History of the Crusades,* I and II (1951–1952), well written and somewhat controversial; Kenneth M. Setton, gen. ed., *A History of* the Crusades, I, The First Hundred Years, Marshall W. Baldwin, ed. (1955), the best work for the serious student.

The First Crusade. Sources include The Alexiad of the Princess Anna Comnena, Elizabeth A. S. Dawes, trans. (1928); Ekkehard von Aura, Hierosolymita, Heinrich Hagenmayer, ed. (1877); Fulcher of Chartres, Historia Hierosolymitana, in Recueil des historiens des croisades—historiens occidentaux, III (1866), also ed. by Heinrich Hagenmayer (1913) and trans. by Frances Rita Ryan as A History of the Expedition to Jerusalem, 1095–1127, Harold S. Fink, ed. (1969); Heinrich Hagenmayer, Die Kreuzzugsbriefe aus den Jahren 1088–1100 (1901); Histoire anonyme de la première croisade, Louis Brehier, ed. and trans. (1924); Raymond of Aguilers, Historia Francorum qui ceperunt Iherusalem, in Recueil des historiens des croisades—historiens occidentaux, III (1866), also ed. and trans. by John H. Hill and Laurita L. Hill, in Memoirs of the American Philosophical Society, 71 (1968); and Le "Liber" de Raymond d'Aguilers, John H. Hill and Laurita L. Hill, eds., in Documents relatifs à l'histoire des croisades publiés par l'Académie des inscriptions et belles-lettres, IX (1969); Recueil des historiens des croisades—historiens occidentaux, III (1866), the standard work for Latin texts; Peter Tudebode, Historia de Hierosolymitana itinere, in Recueil des historiens des croisades—historiens occidentaux, III (1866), also ed. by John H. Hill and Laurita L. Hill, in Documents relatifs à l'histoire, XII (1977), and idem, ed. and trans., in Memoirs of the American Philosophical Society, 101 (1974).

Biographies of leaders of the First Crusade are John C. Andressohn, The Ancestry and Life of Godfrey of Bouillogne (1947); John H. Hill and Laurita L. Hill, Raymond IV, Count of Toulouse (1962); Ralph Bailey Yewdale, Bohemond I, Prince of Antioch (1917).

The Crusade of 1101. The Alexiad of the Princess Anna Comnena; Bartolf of Nangis, Gesta Francorum expugnantium Iherusalem, in Recueil des historiens des croisades—historiens occidentaux, III (1866); J. L. Cate, "A Gay Crusader," in Byzantion, 16 (1942–1943); Fulcher of Chartres, Historia Hierosolymitana; Guibert de Nogent, Gesta Dei per Francos, in Recueil des historiens des croisades—historiens occidentaux, IV (1879); Ordericus Vitalis, Historia ecclesiastica, Augustus Le Prevost, ed., assisted by B. E. C. Guérard and Léopold V. Delisle, IV (1852); William of Malmesbury, Gesta regum Anglorum, William Stubbs, ed. (1889); William of Tyre, Historia rerum in partibus transmarinis gestarum, in Recueils des historiens des croisades—historiens occidentaux, I (1844), ed. and trans. by E. A. Babcock and A. C. Krey as A History of Deeds Done Beyond the Sea, 2 vols. (1943).

The Second Crusade. Albertus Aquensis, Historia Hierosolymitana, in Recueil des historiens des croisades—historiens occidentaux, IV (1879); Samuel J. Eales, ed., The Life and Works of St. Bernard, 3 vols. (1889–1896); De expugnatione Lysbonensi, C. W. David, ed. and trans. (1936); Helmold of Bosau, The Chronicle of the Slavs, F. J. Tschan, trans. (1935); Odo of Deuil, De profectione Ludovici in orientem, V. G. Berry, trans. (1948); Otto of Freising, The Two Cities: A Chronicle of Universal History to the Year 1146, C. C. Mierow, trans. (1928); William of Tyre, Historia . . . gestarum.

Biographies include Curtis Howe Walker, Eleanor of Aquitaine (1950); and A. R. Kelly, Eleanor of Aquitaine and the Four Kings (1950, 2nd ed. 1957).

The Latin states. Claude Cahen, La Syrie du nord à l'époque des croisades et la principauté d'Antioche (1940); John L. La Monte, Feudal Monarchy in the Latin Kingdom of Jerusalem, 1100–1291 (1932); Jean Richard, Le royaume latin de Jérusalem (1953); Reinhold Röhricht, Geschichte des Königreichs Jerusalem, 1100–1291 (1898); W. B. Stevenson, The Crusaders in the East (1907).

Saladin and the fall of Jerusalem. Marshall W. Baldwin, Raymond III of Tripolis and the Fall of Jerusalem, 1140–1187 (1936); H. A. R. Gibb, "The Arabic Sources for the Life of Saladin," in Speculum, 25 (1950); Stanley Edward Lane-Poole, Saladin and the Fall of the Kingdom of Jerusalem, new ed. (1926); Gustave Schlumberger, Renaud de Châtillon (1898).

The Third Crusade. Morton Jerome Hubert, The Crusades of Richard Lion Heart (1941); Lionel Landon, The Itinerary of King Richard I (1935); Kate Norgate, Richard the Lion Heart (1924).

JOHN H. HILL

[See also Aleppo; Alexios I Komnenos; Antioch; Baldwin I of Jerusalem; Bernard of Clairvaux, St.; Bohemond I, Prince of Antioch; Damascus; Edessa; Eleanor of Aquitaine; Jerusalem; Manuel I Komnenos; Peter the Hermit; Richard I, the Lionhearted; Saladin; Seljuks; Tancred (Crusader); Tripoli; Urban II, Pope.]

CRUSADES AND CRUSADER STATES: FOURTH

THE PREACHING AND TAKING OF THE CROSS

Pope Innocent III's proclamation of a Fourth Crusade to Jerusalem in 1198 stemmed essentially from a deeply felt responsibility to rid the Holy Land of the infidel and at the same time aimed to resolve the conflicts between the Christian heads of Europe by uniting them in a religious cause. There was virtually no response, however, to Innocent's repeated demands for men and money, until religious fervor was fanned by a charismatic preacher, Fulk of Neuilly. His eloquence touched the hearts of the common people, though it failed to have an enduring effect.

The enlistment of a real crusading army began at a tournament held at the castle of Écry in Champagne on 28 November 1199 by Count Thibaut, at which an illustrious assemblage of knights, gathered to display their military prowess, spontaneously laid down their weapons and committed themselves to the crusade. Led by Thibaut and his cousin, Count Louis of Blois, the French knights converted a momentary passion into vows of a lasting and enforceable obligation.

Naturally the salvation of Jerusalem was not the sole motivation of these knights. Each crusader was fully aware of his privileged temporal and spiritual status, besides which chivalric ideals, the joy of battle, and the winning of lands and power were factors. Nevertheless, we should not devalue the spiritual motives of these medieval Christians whose religious impulses were stronger than is easily comprehensible to us.

Other nobles in northern France, most notably Count Baldwin of Flanders and Count Hugh of St. Pol, were soon inspired to follow Thibaut's example, and at a meeting in Compiègne in the following year it was decided to seek transportation to the Levant from one of the great maritime cities. Six envoys—among them Geoffroi de Villehardouin, later chronicler of the crusade—were given full powers to contract for transportation in the names of their principals.

Their choice of Venice was based on the practical consideration that it was the only port able to serve the crusaders' purpose, as Pisa and Genoa were engaged in a maritime struggle. It is likely that Pope Innocent III neither encouraged nor discouraged the choice (although there has been considerable controversy over his attitude), and in any case the crusaders did not deem it necessary to ask his opinion. Innocent's vision of papal leadership was anachronistic in an increasingly secular society.

THE ILL-FATED TREATY OF VENICE

The crusaders' envoys were greeted by Doge Enrico Dandolo of Venice in February 1201. The doge was very old and virtually blind, but still a skilled statesman and ardent patriot. Although undoubtedly ambitious for his own glory and for the profit of the republic, he was not the unscrupulous manipulator that historians have depicted.

To the envoys' request the doge replied that Venice would provide transport for 33,500 men and 4,500 horses and provision the army for a year, in addition to supplying fifty war galleys at the republic's own expense, on condition that the Venetians

should receive a half share in any conquests made. The agreed price of 85,000 marks was not extortionate. The contract represented the committing by Venice of virtually all its resources.

Once the treaty had been approved by the Venetian Great Council, Dandolo summoned the popular assembly in St. Mark's, where, in a highly emotional scene, he and the Venetian people pledged themselves as allies to the crusaders. On the following day a treaty was concluded, and although it did not name a specific destination, Dandolo and the envoys secretly agreed on Egypt as the most strategic point of attack. Recent years had seen a change in the ideal of the crusade, which was now less specifically associated with the Holy Land and was seen in broader terms of war against the enemies of Christendom. The less liberal-minded, especially among the lower ranks of the crusaders, however, still retained a romantic fascination with the holy places and would not have readily accepted the Egyptian objective.

Papal confirmation of the treaty has been the subject of much discussion, but it is probable that Innocent willingly confirmed the treaty, at the same time imposing a condition prohibiting any attack on Christian lands. In the final reckoning, however, practical solutions were to become more important to the crusaders than papal prohibitions.

THE ELECTION OF BONIFACE OF MONTFERRAT

Returning home by the Mont Cenis pass, Villehardouin and his companions would have had to pass through the marquessate of Montferrat, and it seems reasonable to speculate that they stopped to visit Marquess Boniface—a relative by marriage of Thibaut—who very probably expressed interest in the crusade.

Thibaut's untimely death on 24 May 1201 forced the crusaders to seek a replacement for him. First the duke of Burgundy and then the count of Bar-le-Duc were offered the command of Thibaut's contingent. When they declined, the French crusaders assembled in June at Soissons, where Villehardouin proposed that Thibaut's troops and the supreme command should be offered to Boniface of Montferrat, who, he was confident, would accept. And so it was agreed.

Boniface of Montferrat was an excellent choice. A man in his early fifties with a long experience of command, he was a chivalrous, fearless, and renowned Christian knight. He was also one of the greatest of the Italian nobles and commanded the allegiance of a large fighting force. It was not for the crusading ideal alone that Boniface assumed the cross. Most crusaders were driven by a complex of religious and secular motives, and ambition ran deep in the souls of the Montferrats, whose interests in the Holy Land and the Byzantine Empire were unsurpassed among the Latin nobility.

The crusaders agreed to meet at Venice in the summer of 1202. Boniface stopped on his return journey to spend Christmas with the German king, Philip of Swabia, at Hagenau. It was here that he met the exiled Prince Alexios, son of the deposed Byzantine emperor Isaac II Angelos and brother of Philip's wife, Irene. Boniface and Alexios shared a common resentment against Byzantium, for two of Boniface's brothers had married into the imperial family with unhappy consequences. The question of moving the crusading army to Jerusalem by the accustomed route through Constantinople, where the young Alexios should be installed as an ally of the crusaders, could scarcely fail to arise. That Alexios was later rejected by the Byzantines does not alter the significance of the crusaders' firm belief that he would be welcomed as the rightful heir.

Historians have often attributed the Latin conquest of Constantinople to a plot laid by Boniface and Philip of Swabia at Hagenau to install Alexios in Constantinople by means of the crusading army. The subject was undoubtedly discussed, though probably not with any firm conclusion; for Philip was powerless and Boniface was well aware that, in spite of his status, he did not have a disciplined army that would respond to such a command. At any rate, neither was capable of maneuvering events at will.

Alexios thus found commiseration but no promise of aid at Philip's court. A journey to Rome also did not gain him support, for Innocent was unimpressed by the prince's claims. The pope later expressed to Boniface his displeasure that the crusaders should consider an attack on Christians.

THE POVERTY OF THE ARMY AT VENICE

Synchronizing the movements of any army is enormously difficult; for a crusading army it was impossible. Departures were tardy, and even though the first crusaders arrived in Venice before the scheduled date, 29 June 1202, they had to await the latecomers. Tents were pitched on the island of St. Nicholas—the Lido—because it was not feasible to host a large alien army in the city proper, especially considering that a force of 33,500 was expected to descend upon a population of about 100,000. Venetians felt that

they—and their wives and daughters—would sleep more soundly if the lagoon divided them from these foreigners.

The Venetians had fulfilled their contract to the letter and assembled a formidable fleet of about 500 vessels, a number that was not needed, because the expected passengers were lacking. Already in June 1202 it was clear that the crusade was in trouble, because crusaders were not arriving soon enough or in sufficient numbers. Some never set out, and others either sailed from another port or were detained by adverse circumstances. It has often been suggested that some of the crusaders avoided Venice out of distaste for the Italian marquess who was now in command of a predominantly French undertaking. This is not a very plausible argument. It implies a decidedly modern "nationalistic" approach and fails to recognize the high rank of the marquess in the international brotherhood of chivalry.

Moreover, an abundance of good reasons for the paucity of crusaders at Venice can be found. It must be remembered that Villehardouin's loyalty to the Venetian ally was not necessarily shared by the mass of crusaders. The cost of transportation, paid by the crusaders themselves, in many cases decisively affected the decision to sail from other ports. In addition, rumors of the intended destination in Egypt influenced those who believed that Palestine was the only legitimate goal to find other ways of reaching the Holy Land directly. Although Villehardouin judges these men harshly, they acted according to their conscience and best judgment, and it is the unrealistic treaty that plays the villain's role. The assembled army was only one-third as great as anticipated.

Sometime during this period the refugee Prince Alexios sent messengers to the crusaders to seek the aid of the army, assuring them that he would be welcomed in Constantinople as a liberator and that he would then aid their enterprise in Palestine.

To the barons, now in extreme financial straits, it was an alluring proposal. Dandolo was demanding payment, and the crusaders were unable to pay the remaining 34,000 marks that they owed. The evil consequences of the unrealistic treaty now stood starkly revealed, for the Venetians could not be expected to renounce payment for this enterprise in which they had invested so much. Indeed, if the crusaders did not pay, Venice faced a financial disaster. On the other hand, as the summer dragged on, the languishing army grumbled against what they regarded as the avariciousness of the Venetians.

THE CONQUEST OF ZARA

Doge Dandolo realized that the crusaders could pay no more. Despite the complaints of the ill-informed, the Venetians were not responsible for this plight; indeed, they stood to suffer with the crusaders in the face of impending crisis.

Searching for a solution that would enable the crusade to get under way, Dandolo raised the question of the Venetian desire to reconquer Zara (Zadar). Control of this Adriatic port was essential to Venice's maritime supremacy. Payment of the crusaders' debt could be deferred in return for their help; thus the interest of Christendom in the holy war and the self-interest of Venice in reconquering Christian Zara coincided. It did not take the crusaders' leaders long to conclude that their options were extremely limited, and they agreed to lend aid.

When rumors of the plan to attack Zara leaked, there was widespread disaffection. For crusaders to become involved in an attack on a Christian city seemed detestable to many, and those who were unwilling to soil their consciences turned back. The more sophisticated, aware that men often find themselves in situations where no ethically commendable choices are open to them, were prepared to make the best of it.

The papal legate, Peter Capuano, accepted the plan, for he wished, at all costs, to prevent the disintegration of the army. There is no evidence that he was repudiated by the pope, even though Innocent, as head of the church, could not condone an offensive against a Catholic city. The pope's letter forbidding the attack did not reach the army until it stood before Zara, too late to have any effect, and it is likely that the prohibition was merely for the record.

The fleet finally set sail in the first week of October 1202. Numbering more than 200 major vessels, it was an imposing armada that swarmed into the harbor of Zara on 10 November and landed unopposed. Some disaffected crusaders assured the Zarans that, as Christians, they would not be harmed, but Dandolo demanded that the agreement to conquer Zara be honored and the city was forced to surrender. The crusading soldiers unleashed upon the defenseless town snatched, plundered, and destroyed, and citizens particularly hateful to the Venetians were exiled or killed.

The conquest of Zara has been represented by many as a moral abomination, but it must be remembered that the Venetians considered they had just grievances against the rebellious and hostile city. If we do not find them guiltless, we should at least comprehend the Venetian point of view.

THE TREATY OF ZARA

A letter from Pope Innocent, written about the end of 1202 or beginning of 1203, vigorously condemned the crusaders for the attack on Zara, though it was not a formal bull of excommunication. His reaction once again reveals the ambiguous situation in which Innocent was placed by his moral duty and his desire to preserve the crusade.

While the fleet wintered in Zara, a riot broke out between embittered crusaders in the ranks and their Venetian allies, in which about 100 men were killed, and in mid December, when Boniface rejoined the army, the camp was still restive. This gave the marquess, encouraged by Philip of Swabia, an opportunity to raise once more the issue of an alliance with the Greek pretender. In return for aid in gaining the Byzantine throne, young Alexios would provide needed financial and military support for the crusade, while the Latins would be performing a work of charity and justice. Neither was aware of the prince's overestimation of his resources and of his influence among the Greeks.

The merits and demerits of the German proposal were argued in the camp. One side spoke of the disgrace of attacking a Christian city, while the other pointed out that the army must accept the proposal in order to survive. A handful of leaders decided to accept the offer, a decision that resulted in the desertion of about 2,000 men. Although Doge Dandolo was certainly aware of Venice's economic interests in the Eastern Empire, it is unfair to accuse him of diverting the crusade.

Innocent III was wisely prepared to be indulgent toward those barons who requested absolution for the attack on Zara, provided they confessed their guilt and desisted from any further attack on Christians. The unrepentant Venetians were punished by a bull of excommunication, although its suppression by Boniface reveals that Innocent still exercised only the most minimal influence over the crusade.

Late in April 1203 the host departed from Zara. Dandolo and Boniface remained behind to wait for young Alexios and together they soon joined the main body at Corfu, where they were initially well received by the Greeks, although some hostile incidents later revealed the depth of bitterness between East and West and the antipathy that any Latin-supported pretender would kindle among the Greeks.

When the Constantinopolitan question was once more raised, more than half the crusaders refused to accept the decision of the leaders. It was only when Boniface and others humbly begged the dissenters not to abandon the army that they agreed to go to Constantinople, on condition that they remain no longer than a month. The army was saved from its gravest crisis so far.

TAKING THE TOWER OF GALATA

The fleet set sail for Constantinople on 24 May 1203. The arrival of Innocent's letter of prohibition too late to stop them has given rise to accusations by Byzantinists of papal misuse of the crusade in order to subjugate the Greek church. The best interpretation of the pope's action is that he simply allowed to happen what he had no power to prevent.

In Constantinople, Alexios III awaited the attack helplessly. He could muster no fleet to oppose the Latins, and the effectiveness of his army was dubious. Alexios probably hoped that the walls that had withstood assaults for eight centuries would prevail once more.

These lofty walls astounded the crusaders when they first caught sight of the magnificent city on the Bosporus. The fleet made port at Scutari, disturbed that no supporters of young Alexios came to welcome him. This surprise and consternation are crucial to my interpretation of the crusade, for the leaders had never planned to conquer the city, much less subject it to Latin rule; they hoped only to restore a rightful ruler who, they expected, would be welcomed by his rightful subjects.

At Dandolo's suggestion the young pretender was taken on the doge's galley and rowed back and forth under the walls of the city, to be shown to his people, while the citizens were urged to recognize their emperor. The ship was greeted with hoots, whistles, insults, and a shower of missiles. In fact, presenting Alexios as a puppet of the Latins only served to unify the Greeks against him, but it reveals how even the sagacious Dandolo expected the prince to be greeted with rejoicing. This abortive attempt to incite revolt precluded the possibility of a bloodless coup and made battle inevitable.

The strategy agreed upon was to attack the shore of the city north of the Golden Horn, defended only by the strong tower of Galata. An army of 10,000 men was assembled in seven battalions, not including the Venetians, who were to be responsible for the fleet, which was vital to success and the survival of all. In the hour of battle all disaffection with the course of the crusade seemed to disappear. All realized that now they must either conquer or die.

Just after sunrise on 5 July 1203 the Venetian ships advanced across the strait in order of battle. The crusaders landed without opposition and their thunderous mounted charge caused the Greeks to flee, abandoning the northern shore except for the tower of Galata. On the following day the crusaders took the tower and broke the chain barring the mouth of the Golden Horn. The Venetian fleet now sailed into the harbor, protected from the elements, while the crusaders occupied the northern shore.

THE FIRST CONQUEST OF CONSTANTINOPLE

Turning their attention to the city on the opposite shore, the crusaders disagreed over their plan of action and finally found a compromise. The Venetians were to assault the harbor walls while the crusaders would attack the fortifications from the landward side.

Crossing the Golden Horn, the crusaders set up camp facing the section of the wall that protected the palace of Blachernae. On 16 July 1203 they began the attack. While crossbowmen opened fire on the walls, the crusaders managed to plant two of their scaling ladders against the battlements close to the sea. In the face of fierce resistance, a handful of men were able to scale the walls, only to be repulsed by the double-headed axes of the Varangian mercenaries.

The Venetian effort was more successful. Led by Dandolo, who stood at the prow of his galley, grasping the staff of the Venetian banner and shouting angrily to his men to put him ashore, the Venetians gained a foothold on the ramparts and soon held about a quarter of the entire harbor wall. Setting fire to the nearest houses, the soldiers started a blaze, which swept as far as the interior of the town, destroying everything in its path.

Never had the people of Constantinople been faced by such peril. The vacillating emperor Alexios III was eventually spurred to action by their condemnations and led onto the plain a force that seemed so overwhelming to the crusaders that they sent a plea for help to the Doge, who withdrew from the walls to aid them. Nevertheless, the Western knights themselves presented a glorious spectacle of colorful shields and silk cloth as, led by Baldwin of Flanders, they rode to meet their enemy.

Reaching the top of a ridge, the crusading army

confronted the Greeks. Both forces were seized with indecision, but it was the emperor who turned back. The crusaders maintained that he was overcome with fear by the size and strength of their army, but Alexios III's sally may well have been merely a successful tactical maneuver to draw the Venetians away from the harbor walls.

Nevertheless, Alexios was widely regarded as a coward in Constantinople. Anxious to save his skin, he fled during the night, leaving the alarmed magnates and ministers to restore to the throne the blind Isaac II Angelos, father of young Alexios. This was a brilliant stroke of statecraft, which would take away the Latin excuse for capturing Constantinople.

The crusaders rejoiced at the news, for their chivalric zeal to aid the oppressed against the powerful had been real; but still the leaders were cautious, realizing the complexity of their situation. They had staked the future of the crusade on young Alexios, not on his father, whom they had never met and who was not their creature. It was not until a delegation, led by Villehardouin, succeeded in obtaining a promise from Isaac II to abide by the Treaty of Zara that the crusaders would let young Alexios enter the city. Isaac knew, better than Alexios, that this promise could not be fulfilled, and his protestations were a dire warning of the problems that would follow.

THE UNEASY ALLIANCE OF LATINS AND GREEKS

Before long the mutually abrasive attitudes of Greeks and Latins within the city prompted Isaac Angelos to persuade the crusaders to move to the northern shore of the Golden Horn; in return the Greeks reluctantly agreed to the coronation of Alexios IV as coemperor. Henceforth, the crusaders tended to ignore Isaac and address themselves to Alexios.

The soldiers spent their time visiting the centers of imperial and ecclesiastical magnificence, marveling at the wonders of the greatest city in Christendom. As pilgrims they were drawn to venerate the illustrious holy relics of Hagia Sophia, no doubt finding comfort in their spiritual benefits.

Although Villehardouin speaks of friendly relations, and some of the money promised to the Latins was paid, the long-developing animosity between the East and the West soon prevailed. The bitterness of the citizens was directed toward their new emperor, Alexios IV, who was degrading the imperial dignity by his vulgar behavior, drinking and gambling with his Latin friends. He tried to meet the Latins' de-

mands for money by plundering the wealthy families and even confiscating ecclesiastical treasures. Besides this, Alexios was already branded as a traitor by the Byzantines for his open submission to the pope, even if he did nothing to give the pontiff real control over the Byzantine church.

Alexios was sure that he would be killed if the crusaders deserted him. He proposed to pay for the retention of the Venetian fleet, whose contract had almost expired, for another year and to provision the crusaders until spring, by which time he believed that he would surely have secured his authority over the whole empire and thus be able to provide the wealth to fulfill his obligations. This seemed a sensible agreement to the crusade's leaders, but it understandably outraged those who had already waited long enough to fulfill their vows. The achievement of a base in Constantinople, however, with an emperor friendly to the West and submissive to Rome, was too important to abandon. It was agreed to extend the treaty with the Venetians for another year.

An expeditionary force of crusaders, led by Alexios and Boniface, pursued the usurper Alexios III, capturing castles and towns in an effort to establish the new emperor's control over the empire. Meanwhile, the fragile foundations of cooperation between Greeks and Latins in Constantinople were undermined by two incidents. A vicious attack on the Latin inhabitants by a Greek mob forced them to flee to the other side of the harbor, and a few days later the Muslim quarter of the city was plundered by a small band of crusaders.

During the second episode a fire was started by crusaders. The blaze spared nothing in its path, consuming hovels and mansions alike. Villehardouin later wrote that the material damage was beyond the power of man to calculate. Certainly it signaled the end of all amicable relations between the crusaders and the Greeks. Few Westerners dared remain to face the retribution of the incensed populace.

HOSTILITIES RESUME

Greek animosity toward the foreigners in the city had now reached a peak, and the crusaders called back the expeditionary force. Alexios' attitude toward his benefactors changed from the day of his return. The haughty manner he now adopted was perhaps the result of a feeling that they had not adequately appreciated his transformation from suppliant to emperor.

It was a fatal conceit to believe that he could succeed unassisted, for Alexios now had to contend with undependable troops and a demoralized populace who blamed the hated foreigners, to whom he owed his throne, for all their hardships. Although the Latins were universally despised, the more moderate Byzantines felt compelled to appease them, while the attitudes of the radicals made it increasingly difficult for Alexios to consort with his Latin benefactors. The young emperor was well aware that he could gain badly needed support by inclining toward the popular anti-Latin party led by Mourtzouphlos. He also came to the tardy realization that he had made extravagant promises that he could never keep.

The termination of even token payments to the crusaders increased the emperor's popularity but gave rise to extreme anxiety within the Latin camp. The crusaders began to realize that they must break with the young emperor, but the Western knights' punctilious regard for honor compelled them to confront Alexios once more before declaring war. During an interview with him, the crusaders' envoys warned that they would commence hostilities unless he honored his agreements. In the angry scene that followed, Alexios ordered them from the land. Undoubtedly the episode had a crucial effect on the standing of Boniface in the crusading army. The marquess' close identification with the young prince and the failure of his policy cost him dearly.

The new year began with a Greek attempt to burn the Venetian fleet, which was saved only by the courage and skill of the Venetian seafarers. Still, the crusaders felt they had not sufficient force to besiege the city, though food was becoming scarcer. Within Constantinople the mob was in an ugly mood, demanding action against the plunderers outside their walls and even electing a new emperor. A young noble, Kanobos, was compelled to accept the crown, but his reign lasted only six days. Nevertheless, Alexios' position was seriously threatened and, seeking protection wherever he could, he turned back to the Latins. This gave the ambitious Mourtzouphlos the opportunity to reveal to the Greek nobles the treachery of Alexios, who was imprisoned.

By blackening Alexios' character, firing the people's hatred of foreigners, and bribing the magnates, Mourtzouphlos convinced the Greeks to elect him emperor. During a meeting between the crusaders and the new emperor, Dandolo demanded full payment of the remaining debt and probably submission to the Roman church, conditions utterly unacceptable to Mourtzouphlos and the Greeks.

The fighting continued to rage intermittently, and hardly a day passed without some skirmish. A foraging party of Latin knights was ambushed on their return by Mourtzouphlos but heroically repelled the far superior numbers of Greek attackers and managed to capture the victory-giving icon of the Virgin.

Fearing a popular insurrection, on the night of 8 February 1204 Mourtzouphlos had young Alexios murdered. Although many of the barons would not mourn Alexios, others deplored the manner of his death, for treachery ranked as one of the most despicable crimes in their feudal society. They now determined not to abandon the siege of Constantinople until they had taken the city, avenged Alexios, and secured the money that was owed them. However, prospects were bleak for the pilgrims. Isolated in a hostile land in the midst of winter, they lacked the basic necessities of life; and before them loomed the fortified walls, the strength of which they had already tested.

THE SECOND CONQUEST OF CONSTANTINOPLE

It would take much courage for this small army to make another attempt to conquer the greatest city they had ever seen. To the Venetians attack was imperative, for the cornerstone of their commercial prosperity was threatened. The crusaders, however, had to be persuaded that such an act possessed religious sanction and were urged to fight only by the bishops' assurance that it would be honorable to die in the attempt to subjugate schismatic Constantinople to Rome.

Before planning their attack the crusaders decided upon the distribution of the spoils. Six Venetians and six crusaders would elect an emperor, and a similarly mixed committee was to allocate fiefs and offices. The emperor would receive one-quarter of the conquest, and the crusaders and the Venetians would share the other three-quarters equally.

On the basis of previous experience, the army agreed to concentrate its forces against the walls fronting the Golden Horn. The important tactical advantage of the Venetian assault bridges, which allowed the attackers to approach on a level with the defenders, was only too clear to Mourtzouphlos. In order to combat this, he built wooden superstructures on his towers and added temporary towers between the permanent ones.

On the morning of Friday, 9 April 1204, the crusaders prepared for battle by confessing their sins and taking Communion. Having crossed the Golden Horn, the assault troops had to splash ashore, burdened with scaling ladders, pickaxes, and other gear while the defenders hurled great stones down from above, smashing their protective covers and forcing the engineers to flee. Handicapped by a wind from the south, the few ships that managed to get close enough to fight were soon driven back. The crusaders' leaders were forced to give the order to retreat while the Greeks jeered at their defeated attackers. The disheartened pilgrims had lost nearly 100 dead.

In spite of the wave of fear that swept the demoralized army, it was decided to resume the attack on the same walls after two days' rest. Sunday was spent at divine services, the most eloquent preachers assuring the men that making war on the Greeks, traitors and schismatics from Rome, was an act of penance in itself. The pilgrims accepted the explanation, although the Pope had specifically forbidden the army to attack Christians.

At sunrise on Monday, 12 April 1204, the fighting began again. The Venetian ships were now lashed together two by two, and the more concentrated forces managed to take several towers. Meanwhile, a party on the shore had made a small hole in the wall. A few crusaders entered the city and outfaced Mourtzouphlos, who retreated to his command post. The gates were opened and the attackers swarmed into the city. Mourtzouphlos' Greek army, though greater in number, fled before the charge of Western knights. The crusaders were free to run riot, massacring and pillaging, while the emperor and his followers took refuge in the Boukeleon.

The crusaders' leaders decided to make camp and renew their fight the next morning. Not daring to seek quarters or disperse, they slept close by their weapons, fearing the worst and fully expecting to face a hard battle the next day. However, during the night a third devastating fire completed the demoralization of the Greeks. Mourtzouphlos had left hurriedly under cover of darkness, and a new leader, (Theodore or Constantine) Laskaris, was unable to rally the frightened people, who had lost the will to resist.

Somewhat anticlimactically, Constantinople had fallen. Although the pilgrims did not know it, their crusade had ended here, where they would found an ill-fated Latin Empire, the defense of which would require all their energies, all their resources, and many of their lives.

EPILOGUE

For three days the hardened and embittered army plundered the imperial city. Although the Venetians were sophisticated enough to seize works of art, the rest pillaged indiscriminately, destroying relics, raping women, and desecrating sacred buildings.

The electoral body chose Baldwin of Flanders as new emperor; Boniface had lost support by his close connection throughout the crusade with the ill-fated Alexios IV. Although Venice received its promised three-eighths of Constantinople, including the significant harbor area, besides—by purchase from Boniface—the strategic island of Crete, the planned partition of the empire among the victorious Latins was largely ignored in the scramble for territories. By the end of 1204 the crusaders had won a large part of the empire, but it was only a weak structure that they established, a complex and decentralized system of fiefs without a strong head. The Latins' disdain for political and diplomatic realities brought disaster upon them. They failed to gain the support of at least some Greeks and rejected foreign alliances, compelling them to face hostility on both fronts.

Within two years the great leaders of the crusade—Dandolo, Baldwin, and Boniface—were dead. The Latin Empire, which had never become a workable reality, declined steadily. When the Greeks reconquered Constantinople in 1261, they found the city in ruins. For years the Latin emperors had lived in abject poverty, selling relics and stripping the lead from roofs to meet their most urgent needs. It would be wrong, however, to assume that the future weakness of the new Byzantine Empire was a result of Latin conquest. A fundamentally sound society would have recovered from the sack of Constantinople and if, when the Greeks recovered their capital, they found that Byzantium's former greatness escaped them, it was because they had merely restored a position that had proved untenable before 1203–1204.

The Latin conquest of Constantinople did not supply a base for the successful conclusion of a crusade to the Holy Land (although it did force the Muslims into a new truce in September 1204 with the king of Jerusalem). The crusaders themselves, however, believed they had wrought a great achievement as instruments of God and became enmeshed in securing and extending their conquests, not only because they were greedy for lands but also because they could not otherwise consider proceeding to the

Holy Land. The irony, of course, is that they were never able to do so.

BIBLIOGRAPHY

The indispensable starting point for studying the Fourth Crusade is Geoffroi de Villehardouin, *La conquête de Constantinople,* Edmond Faral, ed., 2 vols. (1938–1939), of which there are English translations by Margaret R. B. Shaw (1963) and Sir Frank Marzials (1958). Almost equally interesting, though in most respects less reliable, is Robert de Clari, *La conquête de Constantinople,* Philippe Lauer, ed. (1924), of which there is an English translation by Edgar H. McNeal (1966) that should be used with the Lauer edition, which lacks a scholarly apparatus. Those who read Italian can use the translation by Anna Maria Nada Patrone (1972) for its introduction and apparatus, which is extensive, if not always careful. There are many other narrative and documentary sources, for which see Donald E. Queller, *The Fourth Crusade* (1977), 219–222; for a full bibliography to 1977, see pp. 222–241.

An extended discussion of the modern historiography of the Fourth Crusade up to 1969 is Donald E. Queller and Susan J. Stratton, "A Century of Controversy on the Fourth Crusade," in *Studies in Medieval and Renaissance History,* 6 (1969). Charles M. Brand, *Byzantium Confronts the West, 1180–1204* (1968), sets the stage from the standpoint of Constantinople. A brief account is Edgar H. McNeal and Robert Lee Wolff, "The Fourth Crusade," in *A History of the Crusades,* Kenneth M. Setton, ed., II (1962). Among older works is Walter Norden, *Der vierte Kreuzzug im Rahmen der Beziehungen des Abendlandes zu Byzanz* (1898), the first attempt to synthesize the findings of the treason theorists in a modified theory of accidents. The attempt to analyze the influence of the cult of relics on the crusade by Augustin Frolow, *Recherches sur la déviation de la IVe croisade vers Constantinople* (1955), is interesting. Jean Longnon, *Les compagnons de Villehardouin* (1978), is useful.

DONALD E. QUELLER

[See also **Baldwin I of Flanders; Boniface of Montferrat; Constantinople; Crusade Propaganda; Innocent III, Pope; Isaac II Angelos; Venice; Villehardouin, Geoffroi de.**]

CRUSADES AND CRUSADER STATES: 1212 TO 1272

THE FIFTH CRUSADE

Troubled by the diversion of the Fourth Crusade to Constantinople, Pope Innocent III took infinite care in planning the next war against the infidel. By doing so he set the tone for the crusading movement of the thirteenth century. The crusades of the future would depend very much, though by no means exclusively, on papal initiative. The pope announced his desire for a new expedition in April 1213, in the letters that set in motion preparations for the Fourth Lateran Council. Ecclesiastics organized processions and public prayers in order to encourage participation. The pontiff imposed a three-year tax of one-twentieth on ecclesiastical income to finance the war; and he promised the appropriate spiritual benefits to potential warriors in what historians would ultimately call the Fifth Crusade.

Reactions in Christendom differed. King John, newly returned to the papal fold after the interdict, encouraged the preaching of the crusade in England with excellent results. Philip II Augustus of France permitted its preaching in his domains, but allied himself with elements in the French clergy who exploited the opportunity to bargain with the pope for relief of financial burdens. The apparent arrogance and cupidity of the legate, Robert de Courçon (Curzon), whom Innocent had sent to France to organize preparations, further dampened the response. People of various ranks took the cross in France, but the warrior class—the nobility—did so in small numbers. The crusader preacher Oliver of Paderborn, on the other hand, rallied considerable support in the Rhineland and among Frisians and Flemings. And King Andrew II of Hungary and Duke Leopold VI of Austria made earnest preparations in their domains as well.

After Innocent's death (16 July 1216) Honorius III carried on the work. Nevertheless, the earliest of the crusaders to leave Europe in the summer of 1217, found Acre in a state of near famine. The lack of food, combined with the enthusiastic preaching of Jacques de Vitry, stimulated the Christians to make forays into the hinterland. The first military venture was a small expedition that set out in November. The temporary incapacity of the sultan to marshal his forces allowed the little group of fighters to make considerable progress—they came within forty miles of Damascus—but they achieved no permanent advantage by doing so. Similar unproductive expeditions continued through December.

King Andrew and the Hungarian contingents among the early crusaders returned home after this brief season of fighting. In April 1218 new soldiers, mainly Germans, Flemings, and Frisians, reached Acre after a long and often interrupted voyage from the North Atlantic coast. A council of war decided that the most effective strategy to break Muslim power was an attack on the Nile delta city of Damietta, the key to Egypt.

In late May the crusaders took ship from Acre and, on disembarking, succeeded in fortifying a camp in sight of the city walls. John of Brienne, titular king of Jerusalem, took command. A successful assault on the main external defense of the city (the so-called Chain Tower) after three months of frustrating siege warfare did not bring about the surrender of the city itself, which enjoyed the protection of a vast system of walls. Moreover, the arrival of Christian reinforcements in September 1218, led by the papal legate Cardinal Pelagius, brought dissension and conflict at the highest levels. Pelagius insisted on the leadership of the clergy, rather than of laymen, in the expedition. For this and other reasons—not the least the counterattacks of the Muslims—the crusade bogged down during the rainy winter of 1218–1219. For most of the winter the Muslims effectively cut supply by sea to the crusaders, more and more of whom became desperately ill under the difficult conditions.

Revolt in the Muslim army gave the crusaders the chance to improve their position and maintain the siege. Starvation now threatened Damietta. Rather than see it fall, the Muslims, having recovered from the abortive coup, kept offering generous truces, even the return of Jerusalem for the Christians' lifting of the siege. Pelagius answered with repeated refusals. (It is in this period that one dates the mission to the sultan by Francis of Assisi, mistaken by the Muslims for an official emissary.) Pelagius, whom scholars usually berate for his intransigence, deserves better. In these days he never forgot why a crusader army was in Egypt in the first place: Christians could not hope to retain Jerusalem if Egypt remained under Muslim domination.

On 5 November 1219 a truce became irrelevant. The starving city capitulated, its defenders too weak to fight. The crusaders plundered, pillaged, committed atrocities, and sent many of the inhabitants into exile. Damietta became a Christian city and its mosque a cathedral. But hardly had the crusaders achieved victory when the old enemy of jealousy reappeared. Partisans of King John clashed with those of Pelagius over disposition of spoils and over jurisdiction in the city.

The crusade as a war now entered a kind of dormancy. There were plans alive in Europe for a large new contingent under Emperor Frederick II's command. But dissension never ceased in Damietta itself.

King John left in disgust (29 March 1220), only to return on 7 July 1221. The year 1220 and early 1221 saw little action except some modestly successful forays into the hinterland around Damietta. For the Muslims, however, this was a time of careful preparation. They transformed the little outpost of Al-Mansūra, to the south of Damietta, into a fortified gathering center for reinforcements. On the true dimensions of this effort, the crusaders had no dependable information.

In May 1221 a part of the expected German contingents arrived, and Pelagius decided, despite serious objections, to risk the invasion of Egypt. The crusaders left Damietta in early summer, and by 24 July had pushed to Al-Mansūra. Here they realized at last the strength of the reinforced Muslim army. In a brilliant stroke the enemy, aware that a swollen stream was temporarily capable of accommodating vessels of modest displacement, used it to move ships into the Nile and thereby cut off the Christians' supplies and their best route of retreat.

The crusaders before Al-Mansūra were now at the mercy of the Muslims, but neither side quite knew what to do next. The Muslim predicament was strategic: whether to destroy the Christian army and then besiege Christian Damietta—which might be a long, costly, and perhaps ultimately unsuccessful plan of action—or to let a large Christian army go free, on condition that the defenders of Damietta surrender the city. They decided on the latter. For the Christians the choices were equally stark. They could fight and die, hoping against hope that help might arrive before the end. Or they could offer to surrender, the acceptance of which by the Muslims was, of course, dependent on the yielding of Damietta. They chose surrender, unaware that more troops had arrived at Damietta from Europe. They assumed, of course, that the garrison they had left behind would raise no problem.

In fact, the newly arrived crusaders at Damietta—Sicilians and Germans loyal to Frederick II—balked. They had no love for the ecclesiastical leadership of the crusade. Pelagius' ill-conceived decision to attack had shocked them, for Frederick had intended the Germans who arrived in May to await further substantial reinforcements. Finally, they argued that holding Damietta might be worth the price of sacrificing the army in the field. It was this suggestion that pitted Christian against Christian in the city in a minor civil war, the ultimate consequence of which was the acceptance of the Muslim peace offer. At the end of August 1221 the Fifth Crusade came to a close. All of Egypt was in Muslim control by 8 September.

THE CRUSADE OF FREDERICK II

After this debacle the burden of a new crusade fell on Emperor Frederick II, who repeatedly promised to redeem Christian arms in the East; but in the years that followed, he repeatedly failed to fulfill those promises. In doing so he exasperated the papacy. It was nearly seven years before he made the considerable preparations that were required for a major expedition. He departed, under great papal pressure, on 28 June 1228.

This bald summary obscures the fact that Frederick had felt compelled by political uncertainties in Europe to delay his crusade. Also, the papacy was part and parcel of the problem: generations of historians have criticized its almost paranoid hatred of Frederick. But the emperor was far from guiltless. He schemed to get the title of king of Jerusalem, only to mistreat the wife and father-in-law through whom he secured it. If the papacy forced him (or tried to force him) to make concessions that in retrospect seem excessive, we must remember that his contemporaries took the very reasonable line that agreements with the emperor had to have a punitive component or he would not honor them.

In any case, in June 1228 Frederick and his crusader army went to Cyprus. His activities provoked some discontent. Perhaps it was hard for an emperor to be anything but imperious. By the time he reached Acre, a vague apprehension that something was awry became a confirmed threat. Frederick aimed at the subjugation of the crusader states to his authority, not as a prelude to war with the Muslims but as the principal object of his policy. He opened negotiations with the Muslims—or, rather, reopened them, for there had been a flurry of diplomatic activity even before the emperor departed Europe. In the reopening of these talks in the Holy Land in 1228, we know that Frederick took part directly, but the details of the negotiations remained secret. The veil of secrecy and the perceived untrustworthiness of the emperor in talking to, rather than fighting, the enemy further estranged Frederick and the crusader barons.

The negotiations, however, were a success when measured by territory gained. By promising to aid the sultan in his conflicts, perhaps even against certain uncompromising crusaders, and by promising to permit freedom of worship for Muslims, Frederick achieved a ten-year truce and the concession of Je-

rusalem, Bethlehem, Nazareth, and associated territories. Measured by reactions on both sides, the agreement was a less happy one. For many Muslims it was a disgrace to cede so holy a city as Jerusalem and to curry the favor of the infidel leader of the Christians. Frederick's arrogant treatment of the crusader barons, the suspicious secrecy of his negotiations, and his toleration of Islam in the newly conceded territories also left a bitter legacy that he could not overcome. When he left Acre in order to deal with rebellion and invasion at home in Sicily, many crusader barons renounced his rulership but continued to enjoy the peace that his negotiations had brought to them. Thus ended the crusade of Frederick II.

THE CRUSADE OF THIBAUT OF CHAMPAGNE AND RICHARD OF CORNWALL

In the first few years of Frederick's truce there was no obvious urgency for a new crusade. But as time wore on, this complacency gave way. Many books dismiss the expeditions led by Thibaut IV of Champagne, the king of Navarre (1239), and by Richard of Cornwall (1240) that followed the truce. Partly this results from hindsight. Jerusalem fell in 1244 and has never returned to Christian domination. Surely, expeditions with such ephemeral success could not have been serious. Partly, too, some of the bitter feelings that accompanied the expeditions taint evaluations of whatever material success they enjoyed. Yet, men of great substance organized these crusades. Thibaut was not only king of Navarre but also count of Champagne; and Earl Richard was a younger brother of the English king Henry III. Later in the century Richard became a papal ally in the struggle against the Hohenstaufen and received as a reward the (disputed) title of king of the Romans. Neither man, however, had the qualities of leadership necessary for success on this scale (or so overall historical evaluations of their lives suggest). One historian has called their crusades a "burlesque"—that is, a failure with the illusion of victory.

The story of their crusades opens with the efforts of Pope Gregory IX, who, like Innocent III and Honorius III before him, was intent upon arranging a papal expedition. As early as 1234 the pope authorized the preaching of the crusade, with the appropriate promises of indulgences. And he devised various clever ways of raising money besides the traditional taxes on clerical income. Among the people to take the cross was Thibaut. Being a man of such eminence (he had just succeeded to the throne of Navarre), it was natural that he should have a place of honor and leadership in the war. But if this was obvious, little else was. One could hardly predict where a Muslim blow might fall. There is some evidence that Gregory intended to send relief to the fragile Latin Empire of Constantinople in preference to an attack in the Holy Land or Egypt. In the end, however, it became clear that Jerusalem needed reinforcement.

It was not until late summer of 1239 that the expedition began in earnest. The crusaders left behind them a Europe in turmoil from the political squabbles in Italy (the pope had excommunicated Frederick II in March of that year). What they found in Acre was not much more propitious. Jerusalem was Christian, but its fortifications and provisioning were terribly inadequate. To save the situation, the crusaders decided on attack, with the idea that a quick victory would give them time to shore up the defenses of the Holy City. In November they won a small battle that relieved shortages of food, but this success inspired a foolhardy thrust, contrary to the advice of Thibaut, against a large Muslim army.

However, the internal politics of Islam played into the crusaders' hands. In 1240 some Muslim leaders were willing to support the crusaders—indeed, to give them almost whatever they wanted in return for help against their coreligionist foes. The internal enmity suggested by this maneuvering was by no means limited to the Muslims. The great Christian orders—the Hospitalers and Templars—quarreled violently and at times were not averse to seeing each other slaughtered by the common enemy. But in 1240 the most damaging internal struggles, at least temporarily, were on the Muslim side. By playing off the sultan of Egypt against the sultan of Damascus, the crusaders managed to elicit promises that they should retain Jerusalem and other lands that far exceeded even what Frederick II had achieved in 1229. A year after they arrived, the crusade seemed to have been successfully concluded, and Thibaut returned home.

What had really changed? There had been no battles to speak of. The Muslim threat was still very real. The illusory stability of a truce and the continued hostility among Christians effectively undermined the possibility that Jerusalem would be properly fortified and defended. And the next group of crusaders to arrive, those under Richard, earl of Cornwall, disparaged the return of Thibaut's crusaders. Yet, they could hardly upset agreements so recently hammered out. They did little, in fact, except

confirm these agreements and try unsuccessfully to assuage Templar/Hospitaler antagonisms. The more important point is that refortifying Jerusalem never proceeded with the necessary vigor. In retrospect it is not hard to recognize the exposed position of the Christians.

THE CRUSADES OF LOUIS IX

The illusion of stability persisted, but for only a very few years. Increasingly Muslim counterthrusts began to achieve their objectives. In the end the tide turned swiftly—more quickly, perhaps, than could have been imagined. Not only did an alliance of Khorezmian Turks from northern Syria and troops of the sultan of Egypt recapture Jerusalem in August 1244, but in October of the same year a combined army of Christians and dissident Muslims was nearly annihilated near Gaza. The total loss of the Holy Land seemed possible. It was with reports of these events in his mind that King Louis IX of France, lying ill, promised God to redeem the Holy Land if he would prolong Louis' days.

The crusade that resulted from this concatenation of events was better prepared than any in the past. It amassed extraordinarily large military contingents for the time, perhaps 15,000 troops. Its leader, the pious French king, did not need the aid of Pope Innocent IV except for tax purposes: a tenth on ecclesiastical income in Gaul for three years, later extended to five, added substantially to revenues exacted from the royal domain. In other ways Innocent IV was a hindrance. The focus of his attention was riveted on events in the empire and Sicily, for the struggle with Frederick II was coming to a head.

Louis IX planned the crusade for 1247, but as preparations proved more complicated and time-consuming than originally supposed, he delayed his departure until August 1248. He embarked from Aigues-Mortes, a port built especially for his crusade. The rendezvous for these forces and subsequent crusaders was Cyprus. The target of the expedition was, as in the Fifth Crusade, Damietta. A sustained period of continued preparations in Cyprus preceded the invasion of Egypt, which did not begin until late May 1249. On 5 June the attack on the city began—or, rather, the attack on forces defending it outside the walls. Success, in contrast with the Fifth Crusade, was swift. The Muslims were forced to retreat, and the Damietta garrison, alarmed at the probable consequences of the breach of the outer defense, abandoned the city.

The crusading army settled down in Damietta for the summer while awaiting reinforcements. The Muslims, badly shaken, used the time to regroup; Al-Mansūra emerged, as three decades earlier, a major staging point for their army. It was not until November that the crusaders, despite some lingering opposition, began their move southward, seeking this Muslim army. Their advance was slow and not without losses, but until they reached Al-Mansūra it was steady. The new year opened with skirmishes not far from the garrison town.

On the Muslim side a potentially difficult political situation occasioned by the death of the sultan of Egypt, aṣ-Ṣāliḥ Ayyūb, was defused owing to the bold action of his widow. And even more to the Muslim advantage, the Christians had maneuvered themselves into a poor defensive position when their main advance finally stopped. They remained bogged down until February 1250. Yet fortune—an enemy's treachery—salvaged the Christian situation. The turncoat made known to the crusaders a ford across the branch of the Nile on which they were encamped, whereby the army might have access to the Muslim rear.

The advance attack that resulted from this information was a spectacular success against the Muslims stationed on the river, and it might have proved of lasting value had the Christians consolidated their position. Consolidation was all the more important because the main concentration of Muslim troops was in the garrison town itself. It is the grievous sin of hindsight (common to historians) that interprets what the Christians did next as inane. Had élan carried the day, historians would hardly talk of the foolhardy cavalry charge that the king's brother, Robert of Artois, led into the town in the heat of the successful attack across the river. However, his force was annihilated; and the main Christian army continued under heavy pressure and suffered substantial casualties from Muslim counterthrusts.

It became now a war of attrition, a war that, steadily, the Christians began to lose. Retreat in March was ineffective (the Muslims had cut off retreat by river). The king, after desperate fighting, surrendered in April together with most of the army, after which he and they remained captives for a month while engaged in negotiations for their release. A revolt in the Muslim army temporarily disturbed these negotiations, but the agreement that was finally reached promised Damietta to the Muslims as the king's ransom and 800,000 gold bezants for the release of the army. That the crusaders could use the promise of the return of Damietta as a negotiating point was due to fortune, for it was only through the French queen's efforts in the city that the garrison did not desert on hearing of the disaster of Christian arms at Al-Mansūra. In any case, after half the money ransom was paid, the king was released.

The remainder of the crusade (more than three years) requires less space. The king, on his release, sailed for Palestine and spent considerable time, money, and effort in trying to bring harmony to contesting factions in the crusader kingdom. He strove to improve the fortifications of Christian outposts as well. This is not to say that no progress was made in the larger struggle. The other half of the ransom, 400,000 gold bezants, remained unpaid because the Egyptian Muslims enlisted Louis IX's aid against their Syrian rivals. Besides canceling this sum and returning captives, they promised the cession of Jerusalem for his support. However, the war between Egypt and Syria that would have given effect to the promise came to an end too quickly for it to be kept.

It remained the case, therefore, that the king's efforts during his years in Palestine had about them a kind of tinkering or even wait-and-see quality, in sharp contrast with the boldness and enthusiasm with which he had commenced his adventure. He returned home in 1254 utterly disappointed. The first crusade of Louis IX was over.

Louis, however, was not a common sort of man. Failure chastened him, but it also stiffened his resolve. It made him rethink the quality of his rulership, and it gave him the justification to try again. A contingent of French troops remained in Acre after the king's departure, and Louis supported it financially for the next sixteen years. But as long as he was in France, the situation in the East seemed to degenerate. In the 1260's it grew desperate. In 1267 he once more took the cross.

Louis assiduously made preparations for three years. He enlisted foreign support (the English under the future Edward I were important in this regard); and he again convinced the papacy to levy a tenth for three years in support of the expedition. The controversial aspect of the second of Louis' crusades is the target: Tunisia. It is difficult to be certain why Tunisia was chosen, though there were rumors that the bey was willing to convert, and that the supplies of Tunisia were essential to the Muslim army in Egypt.

But generations of historians have hinted at a different explanation: that Charles of Anjou, the king of Sicily, deliberately induced, even misled, his brother, Louis IX, to invade Tunisia because that fitted in well with his own plans or, at least, was less at variance with them than a traditional assault against the Holy Land or Egypt. Tunisia, we now know, was less important in Sicilian foreign and trade policy than earlier scholars believed. Though Charles often showed himself to be ambitious to expand his lordships, Tunisia was certainly not very high in his priorities.

For whatever reason, the target did become Tunisia. The king's troops set sail from Aigues-Mortes for Sardinia on 2 July 1270. After a brief stopover the army set sail for Tunisia, where it landed 18 July. The fighting was indecisive and light. Christians began the siege of Tunis, but slightly more than a month after landing, the king died of illness, as did one of his sons. Charles of Anjou arrived with reinforcements very soon after, but he recognized the ominous signs: illness in the army and the prospect of a long and debilitating siege from a poor position. He had no wish to prolong the war if he could achieve some part of the objective. The Muslims, delighted at the possibility of a truce, agreed to pay a large indemnity and granted extensive commercial rights to Charles's Sicilian subjects in return for the crusaders' withdrawal.

As in earlier expeditions, new crusaders who arrived (in this case under the command of Prince Edward of England) were scornful of truces. The prince joined the withdrawal from Tunisia to Sicily, but after only a brief sojourn he continued on to the Holy Land. He stayed for several months, aiding the remaining crusader outposts, but a truce in 1272 between Acre and the sultan undercut his justification for being in Palestine. In the tradition of Louis IX, he provided the means to support a garrison in Acre after he departed. But with his departure the second crusade of Louis IX came to its true end—and, for that matter, leaving aside much vain talk in the years to come, so did the crusades of the thirteenth century.

BIBLIOGRAPHY

An excellent introduction to the thirteenth-century crusades is Kenneth M. Setton, gen. ed., *A History of the Crusades*, II, *The Later Crusades, 1189–1311*, Robert Wolff and Harry Hazard, eds., 2nd ed. (1969), chs. 11–14, though the chapters on the Fifth Crusade and the Crusade of Frederick II are rabidly antipapal, and the bibliographies are reasonably good but not definitive. Fundamental bibliographies are Hans E. Mayer, *Bibliographie zur Geschichte der Kreuzzüge* (1960); and his "Literaturbericht über die Geschichte der Kreuzzüge," in *Historische Zeitschrift Sonderheft,* 3 (1969).

Two fine studies aimed at a general readership are Hans E. Mayer, *The Crusades,* John Gillingham, trans. (1972); and Jonathan Riley-Smith, *What Were the Crusades?* (1977), both with selected references to the most important literature. An equally readable book concentrating on the world in which the crusaders lived and fought is Joshua Prawer, *The World of the Crusaders* (1972).

On the theology of the crusade and its relationship to papal policy, see Maureen Purcell, *Papal Crusading Policy* (1975). On canon law, James Brundage, *Medieval Canon Law and the Crusader* (1969). Art and architecture in the crusader principalities are treated in Kenneth M. Setton, gen. ed., *A History of the Crusades,* IV, *The Art and Architecture of the Crusader States,* Harry M. Hazard, ed. (1977); also good is Thomas S. Boase, *Kingdoms and Strongholds of the Crusaders* (1971).

WILLIAM CHESTER JORDAN

[See also **Edward I of England; Egypt, Islamic; Frederick II of Sicily; Gregory IX, Pope; Innocent III, Pope; Jacques de Vitry; Louis IX of France; Taxation, Church.**]

CRUSADES OF THE LATER MIDDLE AGES. In 1291 the Mamluk sultan of Egypt conquered the last remaining Christian strongholds in Syria, including the great port of Acre. Nearly two centuries of Latin rule in the Holy Land had come to an end, and the Western powers never managed to recover what they had lost. But the crusading movement survived the blow. For several decades popes and secular rulers actively planned crusades with the aim of reconquering the Holy Land. As the hopelessness of that endeavor became plain, they turned their attention to other parts of the eastern Mediterranean where Christian lives, possessions, and commerce were being attacked by Muslims. And when the Ottoman Turks emerged as a serious threat to Christendom, crusading activity was focused on them. The persistence of the crusading movement in the East was thus assured by the fact that the crusade was not solely a means of securing Christian tenure of the holy places of Palestine, but was also an instrument for the protection of Christians considered to be the victims of infidel aggression, wherever it took place.

A characteristic of projects to reconquer the Holy Land was the dissemination of written treatises in which real or self-appointed experts analyzed the formidable problems involved and put forward solutions. Pope Nicholas IV issued an appeal for such tracts in 1291, and they were particularly abundant during the next forty years, though they continued to be written in the fifteenth century and later. The widespread appeal of the crusade is clear from the nationalities and social status of these theorists; they included a king of Naples, an Armenian prince, a Catalan mystic and missionary, a French publicist, a Venetian man of affairs, and the masters of the military orders. Despite their differing views, these writers tended to come up with similar ideas: that the military orders should be united to improve their efficiency; that there should be a naval blockade of Egypt to weaken the Mamluk sultanate before an assault was launched on Syria; and that a crusade should be divided into stages, a preliminary attack to establish a bridgehead and a "general passage" to complete the conquest.

The Western power most attracted by the idea of launching a crusade of recovery was the French monarchy. Between 1291 and 1336 virtually every French king planned a major expedition to the eastern Mediterranean, but all their projects foundered on basic problems of organization. There were two major obstacles: the irresolvable dispute with England, which exploded into full-scale war in 1337, and the very high cost of the expedition, which would be greater than the French crown's limited and overstrained resources could handle. Even if a French crusade had set sail, it could have achieved little against the enormous power of the Mamluk sultanate, sustained as it was by Christian trade with Alexandria, which the papacy was totally unable to prevent. The only powers capable of enforcing a blockade were the Italian maritime republics, which depended on commerce with Egypt for their livelihood.

In 1362 King Peter de Lusignan of Cyprus revived the idea of a crusade of recovery and succeeded in gathering the men, money, and shipping for the task. He sailed to Alexandria in 1365, captured and sacked the city, but then had to abandon it as a Mamluk army approached. This was the greatest crusading victory of the century and made a tremendous impression, despite the savagery of the sack and the futility of the whole enterprise. But it remains unclear what Peter was trying to achieve. Possibly he adopted the thirteenth-century strategy of making conquests in Egypt and then exchanging them for the Holy Land. Or he may simply have aimed to incapacitate the chief trading rival of his own port of Famagusta, using the lure of Jerusalem as a recruiting device to get Western aid for his expedition. The

second suggestion fits the general trend of this period, in which the recapture of the holy places changed from a genuine military objective to a potent propaganda symbol.

Gradually, therefore, Western exponents of the crusade, whose efforts centered as always on the papal court, advocated more feasible objectives, especially Armenia and Latin Greece. Cilician Armenia was a Christian kingdom under constant pressure from Mamluk, Mongol, and Turkish attack. Its rulers sent a stream of envoys to Western courts pleading for aid. The papacy responded by issuing crusade indulgences, sending money and food supplies, and urging powers in the Levant, such as the Hospitalers, to provide the Armenians with military and naval help. Some aid reached Cilician Armenia, but the internal problems of the kingdom and its exposed position led to its conquest by the Mamluks in 1375. The chances of organizing crusades in defense of Latin Greece were greater because there were Western powers with substantial interests in the area. In the 1320's this patchwork of tiny states and colonies began to suffer piratical raids directed from the Turkish emirates of Anatolia. Venice appealed to the papal court for a crusade against the Turks, and Popes John XXII and Clement VI organized naval leagues with contributions from the major threatened powers. The first such league scored a naval victory over the Turks in 1334, and its more ambitious successor of 1342–1345 captured the port of Smyrna (İzmir), which the Christians held until 1402.

These important successes proved that Christians could still cooperate in a crusade and that they could employ their naval superiority to good effect. But the leagues tended to collapse after their initial victories, partly because of the heavy costs involved and partly because the Venetians preferred diplomacy to military action. From the early 1340's, moreover, the West entered a prolonged period of economic and social crisis which, together with the Anglo-French and other conflicts, proved insuperable obstacles to crusading activity on a large scale. It was largely due to these difficulties that the crusade led by the dauphin Humbert of Vienne in 1345–1347, with the aim of exploiting the capture of Smyrna, proved an almost total failure.

The worst phase of crisis in the West coincided with an alarming series of successes by the Osmanlis, or Ottoman Turks. The Osmanlis profited from the internal problems of the Byzantine Empire to seize Gallipoli in 1354, thereby securing a European bridgehead that they rapidly expanded. The Byzantines appealed for Western aid, but Latins and Greeks still distrusted each other intensely, and it was not until 1366 that appreciable Western aid arrived in the crusade led by Amadeo of Savoy. Amadeo recaptured Gallipoli for the Greeks and rescued John V Palaiologos from semicaptivity in Bulgaria. But resistance to the Ottoman Turks continued to be slight, and in 1371 they smashed the Serbs at the battle of Chernomen. Pope Gregory XI responded by trying to organize a new naval league of threatened Christian powers, without any success.

The Great Schism (1378–1417) was less of an obstacle to the crusade than might be expected, since popes of both obediences sanctioned resistance to the Turks and even allowed their followers to cooperate for this purpose. The great Ottoman victory over the Serbs at Kossovo in 1389 showed that Christendom had to fight to defend itself, and although energies were diverted by a fruitless expedition to Tunisia in 1390—masterminded by the Genoese for their own interests—the biggest crusade of the century, a joint Hungarian-Burgundian attempt to drive the Turks from the Balkans, occurred in 1396. The crusading army engaged the Turks at Nicopolis in Bulgaria on 25 September and was soundly defeated.

As Ottoman pressure on Constantinople increased, the Greek emperors stepped up their attempts to get Western aid. There was a notable French expedition to Constantinople under Marshal Jean Boucicaut in 1399, but large-scale aid depended, as it had since the 1320's, on the end of the schism between Constantinople and Rome. This was achieved at the Council of Florence in 1439, and Pope Eugenius IV set about organizing a crusade. There was a strong foundation for such an enterprise in the heroic defense of Hungary by John Hunyadi, who inflicted three defeats on Sultan Murad between 1438 and 1442. In 1443 Hunyadi and Western crusaders led by Cardinal Julian Cesarini won another victory, which compelled Murad to make a truce. Cesarini persuaded the Poles and Hungarians to break the truce and invade Bulgaria, in the confident expectation of Burgundian and French reinforcements. In November 1444 the crusaders were met in battle by a massive Turkish army at Varna and suffered a heavy defeat in which both the king of Hungary and Cesarini died. Four years later Hunyadi was beaten again, at the second battle of Kossovo, and Hungarian resistance was shattered. The Turks now turned to Constantinople, and the city fell to Sultan Mehmed II in May 1453.

The fall of Constantinople shocked the Christian world and led to the last major crusading initiative in the West. In 1458 Aeneas Sylvius Piccolomini, an active propagandist for the crusade, became pope as Pius II. He worked hard for a crusade against the Turks, devoting to that purpose the proceeds of the alum mines recently opened up in the Papal State and taking the cross himself in St. Peter's in June 1464. But most Western powers showed no interest in the project, and those that did backed out as the departure date drew near. In July 1464 Pius left Rome for Ancona, where his fleet was assembling, but died en route. His death proved the last straw for a crusade sustained from the beginning by the pope alone.

It is easy to find convincing reasons why the crusading movement achieved so little in this period in the eastern Mediterranean: the strength of its main opponents, first the Mamluk sultanate of Egypt and later the rising Ottoman Empire; the economic, social, and religious problems facing the Christian world; the corrosive disunity that characterized attempts to coordinate Christian military activity; the opposition or lukewarm support of the great trading powers; the heavy cost of warfare and the difficulty of waging war at such a distance from the West's main centers of power; and the rival claims on limited resources of other crusading fronts, Granada, Lithuania, and Italy. It is harder to explain why the crusade remained such a persistent feature of Latin Christian life and thought until the mid fifteenth century. For while the great age of crusading had ended in the latter part of the thirteenth century, it is clear from the foregoing account that the expeditions of the later Middle Ages were more than just an epilogue.

One reason certainly was that the twin concepts of Christendom as a religiopolitical unit, and the crusade as that unit's defensive mechanism, continued to exert influence in Western courts. The rise of the Ottoman Turks and their frightening advance from the 1360's onward thus called forth a military response couched in traditional terms: appeals to the papacy for crusade bulls, the recruitment of armies by crusade preaching, and their finance by crusade taxes and the sale of the indulgence. These processes were encouraged by the writings of theorists and propagandists who claimed that a crusading revival was a means of solving Christendom's many internal ills.

There was, however, a more practical explanation. The crusading movement had its own vested interests, notably the military orders, which lost their main raison d'être if crusading ceased to attract support. More important, engaging in a crusade, or promising to do so, brought secular rulers a valuable range of material and moral resources: the service of volunteers, church taxes, lay donations and legacies, papal diplomatic support, and the intercessory prayers of the church. One of the reasons why the Burgundian dukes evinced such a keen interest in the crusade was the prestige that they derived from it. Some court circles in the later Middle Ages were pervaded by the lay spirit, which viewed the crusade almost entirely in terms of profit and propaganda.

The crusade had many faces: ideal; institution; defense mechanism; justification; and source of revenues, political advantage, and prestige. Yet none of these would have ensured its survival for so long had there not endured a residual deposit of enthusiasm for the crusade among the laity. Many fighting men continued to regard the crusade as a desirable activity, so that crusading on several fronts, including the East, was one of the attributes which Chaucer gave to his ideal Knight in the *Canterbury Tales*.

The crusading movement was finally brought to an end by the profound changes taking place in Western society in the fifteenth and sixteenth centuries. The crusade as a military enterprise directed by the papacy became redundant as the national state included among its prerogatives the sole responsibility for warfare. When this occurred, the various features of the crusade either vanished or merged with new forces and ideas. The indulgence and the clerical tenth became sources of state finance, especially in Spain. The defense of Christendom became an aspect of Habsburg imperial ideology. The Hospitalers set up an independent state on Malta. Actual crusaders, volunteer fighters, had no place in the armies of the early modern state and ceased to play an important role even in the continuing struggle with the Ottoman Turks.

BIBLIOGRAPHY

General. Aziz S. Atiya, *The Crusade in the Later Middle Ages* (1938); William E. Lunt, *Financial Relations of the Papacy with England 1327–1534* (1962), 525–620, valuable for details of crusade bulls and indulgences; Donald M. Nicol, *The Last Centuries of Byzantium 1261–1453* (1972); Kenneth M. Setton, gen. ed., *A History of the Crusades*, III, *The Fourteenth and Fifteenth Centuries*, Harry W. Hazard, ed. (1975); Kenneth M. Setton, *The Papacy and the Levant (1204–1571)*, I–II (1976–1978).

Fourteenth century. P. W. Edbury, "The Crusading Policy of King Peter I of Cyprus, 1359–1369," in Peter M. Holt, ed., *The Eastern Mediterranean Lands in the Period*

of the Crusades (1977), 90–105; N. Housley, "Pope Clement V and the Crusades of 1309–1310," in *Journal of Medieval History,* 8 (1982); Anthony T. Luttrell, "The Crusade in the Fourteenth Century," in John R. Hale *et al.,* eds., *Europe in the Late Middle Ages* (1965), 122–154; and numerous other articles by Luttrell on the Hospitalers, Latin Greece, and the papacy, conveniently assembled in his *The Hospitallers in Cyprus, Rhodes, Greece, and the West, 1291–1440* (1978), and *Latin Greece, the Hospitallers, and the Crusades, 1291–1440* (1982). The following older works are still important: Jules Gay, *Le pape Clément VI et les affaires d'Orient (1342–1352)* (1904); Oskar Halecki, *Un empereur de Byzance à Rome* (1930); and Nicolae Jorga, *Philippe de Mézières, 1327–1405, et la croisade au XIVe siècle* (1896).

Fifteenth century. This is a very neglected field. Fundamental research remains to be done on the crusade indulgence, crusade preaching, recruitment and finance, papal policy, Western attitudes toward the crusade, and the Burgundian and Hungarian contributions. But see Joseph Gill, *The Council of Florence* (1959); Steven Runciman, *The Fall of Constantinople, 1453* (1965); R. J. Walsh, "Charles the Bold and the Crusade: Politics and Propaganda," in *Journal of Medieval History,* 3 (1977).

NORMAN HOUSLEY

[See also **Bulgaria; Byzantine Empire: History; John Hunyadi; Lusignans; Mamluks; Military Orders; Navies, Western; Nicopolis; Ottomans; Serbia.**]

CRUSADES, POLITICAL. All crusades were in one sense political: they aimed at conquest, at seizing lands held by enemies of the church and turning them over to orthodox Christian rulers. But there was an obvious difference between a crusade to capture Jerusalem or to crush the Albigensian heretics, and a crusade against a king of Sicily or a king of Aragon. In the first case political means were used for a religious purpose, the redemption of the Holy Land or the destruction of heresy. The political consequences were not part of the original plan. The First Crusade was not preached in order to establish Baldwin I as king of Jerusalem, nor were the Albigensian Crusades designed to add the Midi to the French royal domain. On the other hand, the primary purpose of the political crusades was to bring about political change, to replace a ruler who was disobedient or hostile to the pope with one who would be an ally and a protector.

The political crusades grew out of the insecurity of the papal position in Rome. Theoretically the pope ruled a strip of territory running diagonally across Italy from the Tyrrhenian Sea to the Adriatic. In practice he seldom had full control of these Papal States, and even if he did, he would have been less powerful than most European kings and princes. Theoretically the emperor was supposed to protect the pope, but the emperor was king of Germany and could not spend much time in Italy.

However, the emperor's presence in Italy was not an unmixed blessing. The emperors of the tenth century had controlled the papacy; those of the eleventh century had quarreled with it. Emperors had a nasty habit of setting up antipopes when their wishes were crossed. The towns of northern Italy were natural allies of the popes, since they did not wish to be dominated by the emperor, but they were unreliable allies. Putting their own interests first, they spent much of their energy in fighting each other or in factional struggles within their walls. A defeated town or faction that had been propapal might seek imperial support to regain its old position. There was little political stability in northern Italy.

The south was more stable and thus could be more menacing. Norman adventurers had conquered the southern part of the peninsula and, after a long struggle with the Saracens, the island of Sicily. The Norman kingdom of Sicily was, by 1100, one of the strongest and best-administered states in Europe. It had supported the papacy during the quarrels with the emperor but was quite independent in its policy, and the king of Sicily had received papal privileges that had given him effective control over the Sicilian church. On the other hand, Sicily could be considered a fief of the church; it was the pope who had given the Norman leader the title of king. An independent Sicily was a welcome counterbalance to the threat from the north; a Sicily united to the empire would put Rome in a trap.

That union took place at the beginning of the thirteenth century. Emperor Henry VI, son of Frederick I Barbarossa, married Constance, the heiress of the Norman kingdom of Sicily, in 1186. Barbarossa died when their son, the future Frederick II, was two years old. Pope Innocent III, as was his duty as overlord, established a regency to govern Sicily until Frederick came of age. Unfortunately, Henry VI had brought a number of German troops with him when he came to Sicily, and one of the German leaders, Markward of Anweiler, tried to upset the regency. He also wanted to keep open a corridor along the east coast of Italy, a corridor that would have given him a chance to draw support from the turbulent north of Italy or from Germany.

This seemed to Innocent an intolerable threat. He was convinced that it was absolutely essential to the security and independence of the papacy to keep control of central Italy (thus blocking a union of north and south) and to preserve its superiority over Sicily. These convictions became a permanent part of papal policy and were the cause of most of the political crusades.

The first of these crusades was a trifling affair. Innocent ordered a crusade against Markward of Anweiler in 1199. The crusaders wore the cross and received the same indulgences as those fighting in the Holy Land. However, since the Fourth Crusade was being organized at this time, few men wanted to bother with what seemed to be a sideshow. Some hundreds of crusaders, largely Frenchmen, did attack Markward and kept up a desultory war until he died in 1202. The church had contributed little of its prestige and resources to this operation, but a dangerous precedent had been set.

If the young Frederick II had shown proper gratitude for the protection given him by the papacy, there might have been no more political crusades. Innocent's successor, Honorius III, allowed Frederick to consolidate his position in Sicily and to claim, and receive, the imperial crown. Frederick agreed not to keep both Sicily and Germany, but he never fulfilled this promise, though he did make his son Henry titular king of Germany. He also tried to gain lands in central Italy and to acquire support from north Italian cities and nobles. Gregory IX became sufficiently annoyed to declare war on Frederick in 1228. This was, however, not quite a crusade. Gregory did speak of remission of sins for those who aided him, and he did use money raised for the Albigensian Crusade for his army. He did not promise a full crusade indulgence, and his soldiers wore the papal insignia (the keys of Peter) rather than the cross.

The war ended in an unstable compromise, the Treaty of San Germano (1230). Frederick abandoned some of his enterprises against the Papal States and, in effect, promised to be good. All he did, however, was to shift his aggressive policy to Lombardy, where he won a great victory over the north Italian towns in 1237. Now Frederick could draw soldiers from Germany, pay for them with the wealth of Sicily, and thereby dominate Lombardy. The nightmare of a union of north and south Italy against Rome and the Papal States seemed to have become a reality. Frederick did nothing to allay these fears; in fact, he tried to stir up the Romans against the pope. Therefore Gregory excommunicated Frederick in March 1239 and started a series of wars that did not end until 1285.

Gregory did not immediately proclaim a crusade; his first step was to circulate letters explaining his grievances throughout Europe. He may have preached a crusade late in 1239; certainly a crusade with full crusade privileges and indulgences was proclaimed in 1240. Gregory even allowed Hungarians who had taken the vow to go to the Holy Land to satisfy their obligations by warring on Frederick. Crusade preachers were especially active in Lombardy and Germany. They had little success in Germany and in Lombardy merely managed to stir up a series of local civil wars. Frederick, on the whole, was not seriously disturbed by the crusade either in Germany or in Italy. Gregory realized that he needed more support and called a general council of the church to meet at Rome in March 1241.

A council would certainly have strengthened the papal cause, especially in the transalpine kingdoms. Frederick, however, overreacted to this threat. He sent a Pisan fleet to attack the Genoese ships that were bearing many of the prelates to the council. (Pisa and Genoa were old rivals; since Genoa was helping the pope, Pisa was automatically on Frederick's side.) The Genoese ships were sunk or captured; some bishops drowned; others, and two cardinals, were taken prisoner. Gregory, shocked and disappointed, died in August 1241. The cardinals, also shocked and perplexed, took almost two years to choose a new pope. Frederick had apparently won an overwhelming victory.

Actually Frederick had made a serious mistake. He had changed a local war over Lombardy into an international crisis. Many of the captured prelates were from the transalpine kingdoms and especially from the strongest of these kingdoms, France. He had changed what many had regarded as a personal conflict between himself and Gregory into a war on the church. As a result the new pope, Innocent IV, was unwilling to make any compromise; he insisted that Frederick cease his encroachments on the Papal States and end his attempts to control Lombardy. Innocent soon realized that negotiations were useless; he fled to Genoa and then took refuge in the even safer city of Lyons, not yet a French city but on the borders of France and under the protection of the French king. Innocent issued a call for a general council to meet at Lyons in 1245.

This time Frederick could not interfere. The council accepted the papal decree deposing Frederick as emperor and as king of Sicily. The charges ranged from attacks on papal lands to suspicion of heresy, but the real issue was Frederick's attempt to dominate Italy. The deposition was a declaration of war and was taken as such by both sides.

There were three theaters of war: southern Italy, Lombardy, and Germany. A crusade against Frederick was preached in all these areas; but it had almost no effect in the kingdom of Sicily, where Frederick controlled the clergy, and it was scarcely needed in Lombardy, where rival towns and ambitious nobles would have tried in any case to extend their holdings and acquire independence from the emperor. It had some success in the Papal States, where Frederick's forces were pushed out of Ancona and Spoleto, but this activity did not spill over into the kingdom of Sicily or into Lombardy. Until his death in 1250, Frederick kept complete control of the south and held parts of Lombardy and Tuscany.

Germany was another matter. Frederick had never been greatly concerned with German affairs. He had spent little time there, and there was no central bureaucracy (as there was in Sicily) to make up for his absences. The great princes were practically independent and were glad to have an excuse to demonstrate their power. They elected an antiking, Count William of Holland, who was able to take Aachen (the ancient capital) in 1248 with the help of an army of crusaders. Since the pope allowed Germans to fulfill their crusade vows by fighting in Germany rather than in the Holy Land, it is easy to see why William had no trouble raising troops. What is surprising is that very few crusaders remained in William's service after the capture of Aachen. William never held all of Germany, and by 1251 Conrad IV, Frederick's son and heir, had a strong position in most of the country.

Given the charges against Frederick, and the pope's conviction that he was an incorrigible enemy of the church, it seems curious that Innocent IV put so little emphasis on his crusade. The reason is probably that the war with Frederick overlapped the first years of the crusade of Louis IX of France. It would have been difficult to justify diverting men and money from a crusade led by a saintly king to regain Jerusalem. France had always been the chief source of extraordinary revenues for the papacy, and Frenchmen had always been the largest element in crusading armies. Without French participation and leadership a crusade had little chance of success. Papal legates, such as Gregory of Montelongo in Lombardy and Cardinal Peter Capocci in Germany (and later on the Sicilian frontier), showed some skill in raising armies but no great ability in commanding them. Innocent was probably right in not tying his wars too closely to crusade ideology. He thus avoided blunting a weapon that proved useful to his successors.

Frederick's death in 1250, and the unexpected death of Conrad IV in 1254 (he was only twenty-six) solved two of the problems that had worried the church. There was no generally recognized king in Germany for a generation after Conrad's death, and when the Germans finally agreed on a ruler, they picked a second-rank prince, Rudolf I of Habsburg, who had no ambitions in Italy. Lombardy was still torn by feuds between cities and among the "tyrants" (rulers who had no legitimate claim to authority), but it was almost certain that no one could unite Lombardy and make it a threat to papal independence.

This left Sicily as the enemy, and Sicily was as strong and as dangerous as ever. It had been held for Conrad IV by his illegitimate half brother, Manfred, who had no legal claim to the kingdom after Conrad's death. He surrendered the kingdom to Innocent IV in October 1254 and received the principality of Taranto (the heel of Italy) in return. But no pope could trust a descendant of Frederick, and by November, Manfred and Innocent were at war. Manfred almost annihilated the papal army early in December; Innocent IV died a few days later, and Manfred became ruler, and in 1258 king, of Sicily. The miserable "Sicilian business" still had to be settled by the papacy.

Innocent's successors realized from the beginning that they could not remove the Sicilian threat by their own efforts. They needed an army from the north, and the only possibilities were England and France. But neither country was especially eager to enter the quagmire of Italian politics, and Manfred meanwhile not only had strengthened his position in Sicily but also had begun to gain support in Lombardy. A minor crusade in 1256 defeated Manfred's chief supporter in Lombardy, but this did not damage Manfred's hold on the south. Henry III of England had played with the idea of leading a crusade to secure Sicily for his second son, Edmund, but his attempts to raise money for it led only to the barons' rebellion of 1258. Meanwhile, a small crusading army led by Cardinal Ottaviani was completely routed, and Henry gave up all claims to Sicily.

The next and most obvious candidate was a French prince, and by 1264 Urban IV (a Frenchman) had reached an agreement with the younger brother of Louis IX, Charles of Anjou. Charles promised loyal service to the pope and complete abstention from interference in Lombardy and Germany. The fear of encirclement that had dogged the popes since the beginning of the thirteenth century would thus be ended. In return, Charles was to have full crusade privileges for himself and his men, and a tenth of the revenues of the clergy of France for three years. The pope also put pressure on Italian bankers to lend money to Charles before the tenth was paid.

Urban died in 1264 and his successor, Clement IV (also a Frenchman), carried on his policies. Charles was proclaimed king of Sicily in June 1265, but his army did not reach Rome until January 1266. Charles did not hesitate; he invaded the kingdom in February and encountered Manfred at Benevento. Charles won a complete victory. Manfred was killed in the battle, and the inhabitants of the kingdom accepted Charles as their ruler. The papacy had achieved its great political objective and had done so by means of a well-planned and well-organized crusade.

There were no unmanageable problems for the next few years. Conradin, the sixteen-year-old son of Conrad IV, invaded Italy early in 1268 and rebellions broke out on the island of Sicily and on the mainland. Events came so rapidly that there was scarcely time to organize a crusade, but Clement IV ordered crusade preaching in April. Conradin perhaps advanced too rapidly; he invaded the kingdom in August, and his army was crushed at Tagliacozzo on the twenty-third. Conradin escaped from the field of battle but was captured a few days later and executed at Naples in October. Now the papacy was safe on all fronts.

Or, rather, it appeared to be safe. Charles of Anjou should have been content with possession of a prosperous kingdom. He was, however, an ambitious man. Not only did he try to gain influence in Lombardy (as Frederick and Manfred had done before him); he also wanted to restore the Latin Empire of Constantinople, which had fallen to the Greeks in 1261. Most of his energy and income were devoted to schemes for the reconquest of Constantinople. He pushed his subjects beyond the limits of their endurance while trying to raise money for this enterprise, and his French deputies enforced his orders with great harshness. As a result a bloody rebellion, the Sicilian Vespers, broke out in March 1282. Charles's garrisons were wiped out. After some hesitation the leaders of the rebellion offered the crown of Sicily to King Peter III of Aragon, who had married Manfred's daughter, Constance, and thus could claim to be the rightful successor of Frederick II.

Pope Martin IV, a Frenchman, reacted more violently to this rebellion than he should have done. Charles of Anjou had not been an easy ally. His intrigues in northern Italy had been troublesome, and his plans for reconquering Constantinople had been a disturbing factor in papal diplomacy for some years. In some ways Peter's occupation of Sicily was helpful to the pope, since it soon became evident that Peter did not have the slightest chance of conquering the mainland part of the kingdom. A divided kingdom was much less of a threat to the papacy than the old united kingdom of south Italy, but Martin IV took his stand on higher ground than that of expediency. A papal vassal had been attacked; the sentence of the Council of Lyons depriving Frederick II and his heirs of all their rights had been flouted. Peter of Aragon was excommunicated in 1282 and deprived—in theory—of the kingdom of Aragon in 1283.

But who was going to enforce the papal decrees? The obvious answer was to turn again to France. France was "the principal column of the church," to quote most publicists of the period, and it was a member of the French royal family who had been dispossessed. Negotiations followed very much the same pattern that they had with Charles of Anjou. Charles of Valois, the second son of Philip III of France, would receive Aragon as a papal fief. Philip and his followers would have full crusade privileges. The French clergy would pay a tenth of their revenues for four years to finance the expedition.

Philip accepted these terms on behalf of his minor son in February 1284 and spent the rest of the year raising an army and hiring ships to carry supplies. He was able to begin the invasion of Aragon in May 1285. Peter of Aragon did not make the mistake of attacking the crusading army while it was fresh and full of enthusiasm. He retreated to the strongly fortified town of Gerona, where the French advance was halted. The French spent the summer besieging the town. Illness and incessant raids by Peter's troops diminished their strength. By September, Peter was able to recall his fleet, which had been guarding Sicily, to the western Mediterranean. The ships that Philip had hired were almost annihilated in a naval battle, and this cut off most supplies for the French

army. Philip had to retreat. He withdrew his army safely but died at Perpignan on 5 October 1285.

The new king of France, Philip IV the Fair, showed no eagerness to resume the crusade. He managed to get another grant from the revenues of the French church but, except for a few border raids, the fighting was over. Philip wanted peace, and eventually a settlement was reached in which the Aragonese kept Sicily; the descendants of Charles of Anjou kept Naples and south Italy; and Charles of Valois was consoled for the loss of a crown by receiving the county of Anjou from his Neapolitan kinsmen.

This was the last of the great political crusades. The popes had gained their chief objectives; neither the divided kingdom of Sicily nor the shattered kingdom of Germany was any threat to Rome. After 1292 the Germans finally got around to choosing emperors, but these feeble emperors or emperors-elect (most of them never even came to Rome for coronation) had almost no influence in Italy. The absence of any strong ruler meant that there was no security in Italy. City attacked city; warlords built up principalities that collapsed after a few decades; the Papal States fell into the hands of local tyrants. The situation became so dangerous that the popes took refuge at Avignon, on the Rhone border of France, for much of the fourteenth century; and even when they returned to Rome, they had to fight for almost another century to regain any control over their old possessions.

As bad as the lack of security in Italy was the decrease in respect for the papacy outside Italy. The political crusades had been financed by taxes on the clergy. The kings of France and England kept on collecting these taxes after the crusades had ceased. If it was proper to tax the clergy in order to make Charles of Anjou king of Sicily, why was it improper for an English king to tax his clergy so that he could become king of France, or for the king of France to tax his clergy to defend France, "the principal column of the church"?

With taxation went interference in the choice of bishops and abbots. It was tacitly agreed that kings should be consulted before prelates were selected, and that men who had been useful in royal administration should be rewarded with high office in the church. In return the pope was allowed to reward cardinals and other leading members of the papal curia with bishoprics and other high positions in the lands beyond the Alps. This division of spoils prevented another investiture conflict; it prevented quarrels of the kind that had led to the political crusades of the thirteenth century. It did not, however, prevent the clamor for reform that led to the Protestant Revolt of the sixteenth century.

BIBLIOGRAPHY

Norman Housley, *The Italian Crusades: The Papal-Angevin Alliance and the Crusades Against Christian Lay Powers* (1982), denies that they should be called political crusades; Joseph R. Strayer, "The Crusade Against Aragon," in *Speculum*, 28 (1953), and "Political Crusades," in K. M. Setton, gen. ed., *A History of the Crusades*, II, *The Later Crusades*, Robert Wolff and Harry Hazard, eds., 2nd ed. (1969), both repr. in Strayer's *Medieval Statecraft* (1971). There is a full bibliography at the end of "Political Crusades" in both books.

JOSEPH R. STRAYER

[See also Aragon, Crown of (1137–1479); France; Frederick II of Sicily; Germany; Gregory IX, Pope; Indulgences; Innocent III, Pope; Innocent IV, Pope; Papal States; Philip IV the Fair; Sicilian Vespers; Sicily, Kingdom of.]

CRUX ANSATA; CRUX FOURCHETTE; CRUX GEMMATA; CRUX HASTA; and CRUX PATTÉE. See Cross, Forms of.

CRYPT, from the Latin *crypta* and the Greek *kryptē*, a chamber or vault beneath the main floor of a church, usually containing tombs, especially of saints, or relics. Though frequently subterranean, the floor level of the church was often raised to accommodate a crypt fully or partly above ground (St. Michael's, Hildesheim). Crypts are normally found below the apse or chancel (St. Germain, Auxerre) but may also be located beneath transept wings (Hagios Demetrios, Thessaloniki) and naves (St. Gilles-du-Gard). Known in the early Christian period, especially in North Africa (Orléansville; Djémila), and in Byzantium (St. John Studios, Constantinople), crypts were most common in the early medieval Latin West, particularly in Burgundy (Dijon; Tournus). After the tenth century, ecclesiastical authorities permitted relics held in crypts to be exalted; many were

translated to the main level of the church and the need for crypts diminished. Some Romanesque churches omit a crypt (Hirsau); by the Gothic period relics were customarily housed in the church proper, and crypts were rarely built unless required by the site or a special need for chapels (Bourges, where the town moat did not permit extension of the cathedral). The disappearance of the crypt facilitated a uniform floor level and aided Gothic architects in their attempt to unify church interiors.

BIBLIOGRAPHY

Kenneth J. Conant, *Carolingian and Romanesque Architecture, 800–1200*, rev. ed. (1974); R. Wallrath, "Zur Entwicklungsgeschichte der Krypta," in *Jahrbuch des Kölnischen Geschichtsvereins*, 22 (1940), 273ff.

LESLIE BRUBAKER

CRYPTO JEWS. See New Christians.

CTESIPHON (medieval Tusfun, Taisabun, etc.), originally a Greek settlement (to judge from its name), was the Parthian and later Sasanian winter capital. It is located in southern Mesopotamia on the west bank of the Tigris, in present-day Iraq, opposite the Greek settlement of Seleucia on the Tigris. Now divided and partially destroyed by the river, Ctesiphon is notable for the vast Taq-e Khusro (Ṭāq-i Kisrā), the vaulted brick audience hall attributed to the Sasanian king Xusrō I (531–579). Although Xusrō II Abarwēz (590/591–628) moved the capital 107 kilometers (65 miles) eastward to Dastagird, the city remained an important royal seat. The Arab historians who recorded the capture of the city in 637 described the marble incrustations, figural mosaics, carpets, and a treasury with a golden throne and a great crown. The city contained a significant Christian population during the Sasanian period and was the seat of a Nestorian bishop. Remains claimed to be those of an early church have been excavated.

BIBLIOGRAPHY

Andrea Bruno, "The Preservation and Restoration of Ṭāq-Kiṣrā," in *Mesopotamia*, 1 (1966); Giorgio Gullini, "Problems of an Excavation in Northern Babylonia," *ibid.*; Jens Kröger, "Stucco," in Prudence O. Harper, ed., *The*

Royal Hunter: Art of the Sasanian Empire (1978), 101–104; Gernot Wiesner, *Zur Märtyrerüberlieferung aus der Christenverfolgung Schapur II* (1967).

TRUDY S. KAWAMI

[See also **Sasanian Art.**]

CUADERNA VÍA, a Spanish verse form originating in the twelfth century. The name comes from the *Libro de Alexandre* (thirteenth century), in which the author proudly defines his versification technique as "mester fermoso" based on "fablar curso rimado por la *quaderna via,* / a silabas contadas, qua es grant maestria" (stanza 2, C–D). The double aim of this new form of versification was to compose narrative poetry along the lines of the rhythmic pattern *(cursus rythmicus)* of Latin prose and to do so by counting the exact number of syllables in each line, in opposition to other vernacular poetic forms such as the heroic and lyric verse used by the *juglares* and *trovadores.* From its inception the *cuaderna vía* was, therefore, the quintessence of learned poetry, not only because of its form, but also because the works in which it was employed presented a wider cultural spectrum than other vernacular poetry. In addition, the poetic language and the elaboration of lines and stanzas were much more sophisticated in the *cuaderna vía.* The very idea of the stanza *(estrofa),* as opposed to the irregular laisse *(tirada),* was undoubtedly a learned feature.

The *cuaderna vía* was the preferred verse form of the *clerecía* poets from Gonzalo de Berceo (1169?–1264?) to Pero López de Ayala (1332–1407). It is also known as alexandrine verse, having appeared for the first time in the French *Roman d'Alexandre* (second half of the twelfth century), from which the Spanish *Libro de Alexandre* derives. In its origins, however, alexandrine verse goes back to the popular Latin rhythmic verse of the Middle Ages, exemplified by St. Augustine's *Hymn Against the Donatists,* wherein the tetrameter (trochaic or octonary) is regularly used; St. Peter Damian's *Easter Song (Paschalis rhythmus ad procedendrum);* and the well-known *Visio Filiberti* (twelfth century). The most commonly used stanzas in these Latin compositions were the couplet and the monorhymic quatrain, wherein internal rhymes are often found. Lines were commonly divided into two approximately equal hemistichs as well. A dominant characteristic of these popular Latin compositions, later inherited by

the *clerecía* poets, especially during the thirteenth century, was their syllabic regularity. There are also many examples of irregular lines, as in St. Dionysius Aeropagita's (ninth century) song containing twenty-two lines of unequal hemistichs and internal rhyme.

In the Romance literatures in general, and more particularly in Castilian literature, the alexandrine verse adopted a polyrhythmic meter. Each hemistich generally had the regular accent on the sixth syllable, and the two hemistichs could be of the same or of a different number of syllables, thus resulting in three types of rhythm: trochaic, dactylic, or mixed.

In the *Roman d'Alexandre* the alexandrines make up a series of monorhymes with a variable number of lines, but in the Spanish version the monorhymic lines are systematically grouped in stanzas of four lines *(cuartetos monorrimos,* hence *cuaderna vía).* The classic alexandrine verse, exemplified by the *Libro de Alexandre,* required that the stanza have a consonantic rhyme and an exact number of syllables, typically fourteen-syllable lines, a consonantic rhyme *(a a a a, b b b b,* etc.), and a caesura in the middle. Later examples, such as the *Libro de Apolonio,* the *Poema de Fernán González,* and the fourteenth-century works of Juan Ruiz and López de Ayala, did not achieve such a high degree of regularity.

The *cuaderna vía,* often adopted for prestigious long poems (narrative, didactic, and hagiographic), represented an innovative link between the freer rhythmic prose and the tighter, more difficult *cancioneril* verse. Because its scope was wider than epic verse, it also contributed to the establishment of a learned literature in a Romance language.

BIBLIOGRAPHY

Gonzalo de Berceo, *El libro de Alixandre,* Dana Arthur Nelson, ed. (1979); Tomás Navarro Tomás, *Métrica española: Reseña histórica y descriptiva* (1966), 59–64; Édelestand P. Du Méril, *Poésies populaires latines antérieures au douzième siècle* (1843).

H. SALVADOR MARTÍNEZ

[See also **Alexandre, Libro de; Alexander Romances; Berceo, Gonzalo de; Latin Literature; López de Ayala, Pero; Mester de Clerecía; Spanish Versification and Poetry.**]

CUBICULUM (Latin, "bedchamber"), a small square or rectangular chamber branching from a corridor in a catacomb, containing the tomb of an affluent citizen or the tombs of a family.

LESLIE BRUBAKER

[See also **Catacombs.**]

CUERDA SECA (Spanish, "dry cord"), a term known only since the sixteenth century, refers to a technique for ensuring the separation of colors on polychrome glazed ceramics. The design was drawn on the surface of the unfired object in a greasy manganese-oxide compound. The sections of the design were then filled in with the different colored glazes. When the glazes liquefied during firing, they were prevented from mingling by the greasy outlines; at the same time, the oil base itself was evaporating, so that in the finished piece the compartments of the design were separated only by "dry" lines.

This technique may have been known in antiquity but seems to have been reinvented in Andalusia in the tenth century. It had a long life in Spain and, from the fourteenth century, was popular in Iran as well.

Hispano-Moresque tile. Spain, Seville or Toledo, 16th century. THE METROPOLITAN MUSEUM OF ART, GIFT OF HENRY G. MARQUAND

BIBLIOGRAPHY
Ars Hispaniae, III (1951), 323, and IV (1949), 62–64; Dorothea Duda, *Spanisch-islamische Keramik aus Almería vom 12. bis 15. Jahrhundert* (1970); Alice W. Frothingham, *Catalogue of Hispano-Moresque Pottery in the Collection of the Hispanic Society of America* (1936), 9–11; "Khazaf," in *Encyclopedia of Islam,* new ed., IV (1978).

ESTELLE WHELAN

[See also **Ceramics, European; Ceramics, Islamic.**]

CUMANS. See **Russia, Nomadic Invasions of.**

CUMDACH, a richly ornamented casket used in Ireland to protect books. The earliest known example was made for the Book of Durrow at the behest of Flann Sinna, king of Ireland (879–916).

HERBERT L. KESSLER

CUNEDDA WLEDIG. Cunedda or Cunedag, whose epithet Wledig means ruler, is believed to have founded a ruling dynasty in Gwynedd that extended from about 450 until the establishment of a new dynasty by Merfyn Frych in the early ninth century. According to Welsh genealogical tradition preserved in London, British Library, MS Harley 3859 and the ninth-century *Historia Brittonum,* Cunedda together with eight of his sons and one grandson came from the territory of the Votadini near Din Eidyn (modern Edinburgh) known as Manaw Gododdin. They settled in northwest Wales after having "expelled the Irish with immense slaughter from those regions." The names of his sons and grandson are found in Welsh kingdoms such as Rhufoniog (from Rhufon), Ceredigion (from Ceredig), and Meirionydd (from Meirion). The historicity of Cunedda is still a matter of debate.

BIBLIOGRAPHY
D. P. Kirby, "British Dynastic History in the Pre-Viking Period," in *Bulletin of the Board of Celtic Studies,* 27 (1976–1978); John E. Lloyd, *A History of Wales from the Earliest Times to the Edwardian Conquest* (1948), 100, 102, 117–118; Molly Miller, "Historicity and the Pedigrees of the Northcountrymen," in *Bulletin of the Board of Celtic Studies,* 26 (1974–1976); "Date-guessing and Pedi-

grees," in *Studia celtica,* **10–11** (1975–1976); and "The Foundation-legend of Gwynedd in the Latin Texts," in *Bulletin of the Board of Celtic Studies,* **27** (1976–1978).

MARILYN KAY KENNEY

[See also **Wales: History of.**]

CUPOLA, a dome, especially a small one surmounting a chapel or tower. Cupolas were standard features of middle and late Byzantine buildings and were also common in Islam and Russia.

LESLIE BRUBAKER

CUPOLA CHURCH. See Church, Types of.

CURFEW (French: *couvre-feu,* to extinguish or bank a fire). Since most medieval houses were made of wood, ranging from timber frames filled with rubble and plaster to interwoven branches covered with clay, fire was a great danger. Cooking and heating depended on open fireplaces; an unobserved spark could cause a conflagration. Therefore in many communities a bell was rung at some hour in the evening (often about nine o'clock) to order all fires put out or covered. This curfew bell was also used for police purposes. Anyone found in the streets after curfew was considered a suspicious character; he would have to explain his errand and indicate his residence.

JOSEPH R. STRAYER

[See also **Urbanism, Western European.**]

CURIA, LAY. The best translation of *curia* is "court," if one remembers that both terms have many meanings—social, political, and judicial. Basically, a curia was the group of men who attended a ruler at any one time. There were more or less permanent members, who took care of the ruler's personal needs (chamberlains, butlers, stewards), managed his affairs (treasurers, clerks, military leaders), or provided companionship that the ruler enjoyed. However, when important policy decisions were to be made (war, peace, treaties, marriage alliances, relations with the church) or when important legal

problems had to be settled, many or all of the ruler's important subjects were summoned. Such large meetings were rare—and expensive; ordinary business was conducted by a small group, often comprising no more than ten members.

Whatever the size of a curia, its decision was legally binding. Thus the curia of a powerful ruler, such as a king, duke, or count, might become very active as a court of law. It could become so active that judicial business had to be handed over to a special group of judges, such as the King's Bench in England or the Parlement in France. These bodies, however, were still part of the curia regis, the king's court. Financial affairs might also devolve on a select group—the English Exchequer or the Curia in Compotis in France—but again, these were only committees of the curia.

Any lord who had vassals, rights of justice, and an income above bare subsistence had a curia. It would not be as active or powerful as that of a king or duke, but on a small scale it performed the same functions.

BIBLIOGRAPHY

Raoul van Caenegem, *The Birth of the English Common Law* (1973); Charles H. Haskins, *Norman Institutions* (1918, repr. 1925); Jan Frederick Niermeyer, *Mediae Latinitatis lexicon minus* (1976), s.v. "curia."

JOSEPH R. STRAYER

[See also **Exchequer; Exchequer, Court of; Law, Civil; Law, English Common; Parlement, French.**]

CURIA, PAPAL. Like all important men, the pope needed advisers, administrators, legal and financial specialists, secretaries, and bookkeepers as soon as the church had become a large and increasingly complicated organization. Naturally, as bishop of Rome, he drew first on the clergy of his own city, the deacons who had been charged with welfare activities, the priests who held the city's principal churches, and the bishops of the small dioceses that surrounded Rome. These men gradually became known as cardinals because they were permanently attached to their churches, as a door is to its hinges (*cardines*). They formed the council of the pope and assisted him in all his duties. During the Investiture Conflict they gained the right to elect the pope, free from imperial interference. As their authority grew they ceased to be drawn exclusively from the clergy of the Roman area; any outstanding bishop could become a cardinal, though he was always given the title of a bishopric or a church in the Roman region.

At first the cardinals carried on the business of the papacy with no formal division of powers, but by the beginning of the eleventh century it was obvious that greater specialization was necessary. The pope had always needed a corps of secretaries, but they were headed by the librarian; now, around 1005, a chancellor appeared, as the head of a group of notaries. As papal administrative authority grew, the importance and size of the chancery increased steadily. By the late eleventh century the revenues of the papacy were both greater and more diversified than before, so that a financial department, the camera, had to be created.

These two developments were clearly institutionalized during the pontificate of Urban II (1088–1099); so was the growing importance of the papal chaplains, who served as subordinate administrators and often became cardinals. The only thing lacking by 1100 was a permanent court to hear cases arising under canon law. It was not until the 1260's that a separate court, the Rota Romana, was set up to deal with this business; until then the pope had to appoint special commissions to deal with cases that came to Rome.

There is considerable resemblance between the development of the Roman curia and that of lay rulers such as the kings of England and France. The cardinals by 1100 were like the great feudal lords, advisers and representatives of the ruler in dealing with his subjects. The papal chancery was not unlike lay chanceries; the papal treasury (camera) appeared at about the same time as the English Exchequer. There was a lag in setting up a papal high court (the Rota); on the other hand treatises on canon law were written much earlier than books on the English common law or the laws of French provinces.

Some contemporaries realized that the papal curia was more or less a copy of the lay curia and were bothered by the use of the term. Around 1158, Gerhoh von Reichersberg said that there was no precedent for calling the Holy See a "court" and that the Roman church should be ashamed of letting itself be referred to by this name. The protest had no effect; the term was universally accepted by 1200.

The basic patterns of the papal curia were well established by the thirteenth century; from then on the system became more complicated. The amount of business, the number of officials, and the need for money all increased, and offices were sold. The cardinals became unruly, eventually, in 1378, reaching

the point of schism. Here again, the parallels with lay governments are interesting. The eventual recovery of papal control over the curia was also not unlike the recovery of the French and English monarchies. Beginning with Martin V (1417–1431) old departments, for example the chancery, lost importance, the secretary or secretaries became the chief men in the curia, and the financial organization of the curia was revised. And just as in France and England, reforms that made the curia more efficient (especially in increasing its income) also made it more unpopular and led to resistance to its orders (in France, for example) and eventually to the German Reformation.

BIBLIOGRAPHY

Geoffrey Barraclough, *The Medieval Papacy* (1968); William E. Lunt, *Papal Revenues in the Middle Ages*, 2 vols. (1934); Walter Ullmann, *The Growth of Papal Government in the Middle Ages* (1955).

JOSEPH R. STRAYER

[See also **Cardinals, College of; Chancery; Papacy, Origins and Development of; Urban II, Pope.**]

CUROPALATES, high office of the Byzantine court (commander of the palace guards under Justinian I) that became an honorific title in the ninth century. It was reserved to the imperial family until the tenth century, when it was granted to the Georgian princes. The superior title of *protocuropalates* appears in the eleventh century.

BIBLIOGRAPHY

Rodophe Guillard, "Le curopalate," in *Byzantina,* 2 (1970), repr. in his *Titres et fonctions de l'empire byzantin* (1976); Nicolas Oikonomides, *Les listes de préséance byzantines des IXᵉ et Xᵉ siècles* (1972), 293.

NICOLAS OIKONOMIDES

[See also **Byzantine Bureaucracy.**]

CURSUS. In modern usage the term "cursus" denotes a system of rhythmical clause endings and sentence endings that was employed by some writers of Latin prose from the end of antiquity until the Renaissance. In classical and medieval theoretical texts the term is used more generally, to describe the flow of speech; when used specifically in the Middle Ages, cursus refers to the rhythm of the whole sentence or, occasionally, to that of endings. Cursus defined as rhythmical endings is thought to derive from the use of quantitative or metrical clausulae by classical authors.

The three accentual patterns most commonly recognized as cursus are: ́- - ́- (planus); ́- - ́- - (tardus or ecclesiasticus); and ́- - - - - ́- (velox). A fourth pattern, ́- - - ́- (trispondaicus), is sometimes included in the recognized system of endings. Medieval theorists of the dominant Italian tradition characterized the preferred cadences according to the length of the final word and the placement of accent on both words. The "French school" of theorists, associated especially with Orléans, expressed the preferred cadences, as well as initial and internal rhythms, in terms of "dactyls" and "spondees"—that is, words accented on the antepenultimate and penultimate syllable, respectively. Also recognized by this school are extended cadences composed of a sequence of spondees—used here as a unit of syllabic measurement—following a dactyl and including sometimes a "half spondee." Modern theorists often modify the medieval description to consider, instead of constituent word types, the total number of syllables in relation to the position of accents. Such description has the effect of recognizing endings with variant word divisions as normal forms of cursus.

Whether an author uses cursus may be determined by extensive statistical comparison, either of the supposedly rhythmical text with "unrhythmical" ones, or of the endings within the rhythmical text itself. Using such comparisons, scholars have established the continuity of cadenced prose throughout the Middle Ages. Because there is a lack of theoretical discussion from before the end of the classical period until the latter part of the twelfth century, it had formerly been assumed that the use of cursus was discontinued and then revived through adoption of the system by the papal chancery and through discussion of the theory in twelfth-century Italian artes dictandi. According to the Liber pontificalis, John of Gaèta (later Pope Gelasius II) reintroduced Cursus leoninus, generally interpreted as cursus, in his role as papal chancellor under Urban II (1088–1099). Yet internal comparison has shown that cursus was used in papal documents before this time. Nevertheless, from the pontificate of Urban onward continuous development of the chancery usage, with a marked preference for velox, can be shown.

Detailed discussion of cursus first appears in the Forma dictandi attributed to Albert of Morra (later Pope Gregory VIII) and dated about 1180. In con-

trast with later theoretical texts in the Italian tradition, the Forma dictandi gives instruction concerning the whole sentence and uses the terminology of dactyls and spondees that is later associated exclusively with the French tradition. Scholars are less inclined now than formerly to dismiss the difference between the two traditions as a question of minor detail. It is the chancery tradition, however, concentrating on endings, that was codified by the thirteenth-century artes dictandi and popularized by the proliferation of those artes.

BIBLIOGRAPHY

A thorough account of medieval theory and practice is Tore Janson, Prose Rhythm in Medieval Latin from the 9th to the 13th Century (1975), with extensive bibliography. For the fourteenth to the sixteenth century, see also Gudrun Lindholm, Studien zum mittellateinischen Prosarhythmus (1963). For the transition from classical to medieval prose rhythm, see Mathieu G. Nicolau, L'origine du "cursus" rythmique et les débuts de l'accent d'intensité en latin (1930). Clarification of the relationship between French and Italian traditions is made by Marian Plezia, "L'origine de la théorie du cursus rythmique au XIIᵉ siècle," in Archivum Latinitatis Medii Aevi, 39 (1974).

LOIS K. SMEDICK

[See also **Latin Meter**.]

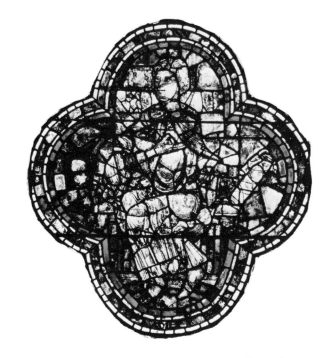

Stained glass quatrefoil cusp of Cosam(?). Clerestory of Canterbury Cathedral, 12th century. DEAN AND CHAPTER OF CANTERBURY

CUSP, a projecting point at which two arcs (foils) meet in Gothic tracery or arches. A circle may be cusped (indented) into a varying number of arcs or foils; a circle with four cusps is called a quatrefoil, and with three cusps a trefoil.

LESLIE BRUBAKER

CUSTOMARY, a book of rules or customs directed to the ordering of ecclesiastical functions and services. Often it is anonymous and designed to supplement established or ancient rules or constitutions. Customaries are called by a variety of names, the most common being *consuetudines* and *ordines.* When they pertain to monastic or religious orders, *consuetudines* are usually modified by place of origin or use, such as the *Consuetudines cluniacenses* or *farfenses. Consuetudines* were often copied and sent to religious houses of the same order, there to be used and recopied. Major (and sometimes minor) churches often had their own customaries or *ordines.* Among the subjects touched in the customaries might be the personnel of the community, their functions and obligations, liturgical regulations, descriptions of the liturgical year, dress regulations, and norms for the spiritual life.

BIBLIOGRAPHY

Kassius Hallinger, *Corpus consuetudinum monachorum,* I (1963), esp. xiii–lxxiv; P. Schmitz, "Coutumiers du moyen âge," in *Dictionnaire de droit canonique,* II, 307–310; Mateo Alamo, "Coutumiers monastiques et religieux," in *Dictionnaire de spiritualité,* II, 2, pp. 2454–2459.

ROGER E. REYNOLDS

CUSTOS, musical term also known as the direct. From the eleventh century a symbol was sometimes placed at the end of the stave to indicate the pitch of the next note. It took various shapes, such as a checkmark, a *W,* or a small note. Occasionally it served instead of a clef on the following stave. A tabulation of variations in the shape could help with localizing and dating manuscripts.

ANDREW HUGHES

[See also **Musical Notation, Western.**]

CUSTUMALS OF NORMANDY. Two medieval custumals survive from Normandy. The earlier one is known as the *Très ancien coutumier* or *Statuta et consuetudines;* the later one, as the *Summa de legibus* or *Grand coutumier.* Both were unofficial in origin and both are anonymous, so that all knowledge of their dates and authorship must be deduced from internal evidence.

The *Très ancien coutumier* is extant in three versions: the Latin original, a translation into French, and fragments of a translation into the Norman dialect. Its two parts were originally separate treatises. The first, the earliest of all northern French custumals, was written between 1199 and 1204. Its author, almost certainly a cleric, was personally acquainted with the practice of the ducal court. The organization of the treatise is not particularly systematic, though chapters on similar subjects are sometimes grouped together. Its principal subjects are private and feudal law, criminal law, and procedure; it also contains a few chapters on ducal rights and one on tenure in alms. The second part was written shortly after 1218. Its author, again almost certainly a cleric, was considerably more influenced by Roman law than the author of the first part. Better organized than the first part, it commences with several official documents and then discusses, in a procedural framework, possessory actions and proprietary actions.

In subject matter the two parts of the *Très ancien coutumier* overlap considerably. The union of the two parts occurred not long after the production of the second: the French translation, made between 1248 and 1270, treats them as one work. The fragments of the Norman translation that survive amount to about a quarter of the custumal but include some material found in no other extant version. In their extant form they date from between 1316 and 1330, but the full Norman version was probably made in the late thirteenth century.

The *Summa de legibus* also exists in three forms: the Latin original and translations into French prose and French verse. The earliest redaction of the Latin text was completed before 1258; it is certainly later than 1226, almost certainly later than 1235, and perhaps later than 1254. The text was subject to some reworking, either by its author (but after 1258) or by a series of redactors working in the later thirteenth and fourteenth centuries. The *Summa de legibus* is the principal monument of medieval Norman law, and the author of the original Latin text has won high praise from modern commentators for the quality of the custumal he produced, which has often been called one of the most important legal treatises of medieval France. He is praised especially for his clarity, his systematic approach, and his creativity. Indeed, on some points he is thought not merely to have recorded but also to have devised the rules that he wrote down and that, on his authority, were subsequently accepted as the custom of Normandy.

The work is comparatively well organized; and the organization, though little of the contents, reflects the author's training in Roman law. Using a procedural approach, it covers most aspects of Norman custom in the thirteenth century, grouped into three principal blocks: judicial organization and competence; rights over things, including regalian and episcopal rights as well as rights enjoyed by all; and procedure both in general and in actions concerning crimes, in actions concerning chattels, and in possessory and proprietary actions concerning real property. This procedural approach means that treatment of substantive topics is sometimes scattered among different chapters; in a few instances treatment of substantive topics is incomplete.

Despite its unofficial origin, by the end of the thirteenth century or shortly thereafter the *Summa de legibus* was taken to be an official codification made at the order of King Philip Augustus after the French conquest of Normandy in 1204. As such, it was the authoritative source for Norman custom in the period before the official redaction of the custom of Normandy, the *Coutume réformée* of 1583, and it remains to this day the foundation of the law of the Channel Islands. Both French translations were made in the late thirteenth century. The importance of the work is attested by the number of surviving copies and by its early publication: manuscripts of the Latin and the French prose versions number more than sixty; and the work was published for the first time before the end of the fifteenth century, perhaps in 1483, along with the extensive commentary, the *Glose* (gloss), which developed around the text in the fifteenth century.

BIBLIOGRAPHY

Sources. The standard edition of both custumals is Ernest-Joseph Tardif, *Coutumiers de Normandie,* I, *Le Très ancien coutumier,* pts. 1 and 2 (1881–1903), and II, *La Summa de legibus Normanniae in curia laicali* (1896): the whole edition is reprinted in 2 vols. (1977). The best available edition of the French version is William Laurence de Gruchy, *L'ancienne coutume de Normandie* (1881).

Studies. Robert Besnier, *La Coutume de Normandie: Histoire externe* (1935); Paul Viollet, "Les coutumiers de Normandie," in *Histoire littéraire de la France,* 33 (1906); Jean Yver, "Le 'Tres ancien coutumier' de Normandie, miroir de la legislation ducale?" in *Tijdschrift voor Rechtsgeschiedenis, Revue d'histoire du droit,* 39 (1971).

EMILY ZACK TABUTEAU

[See also **Law, French: In North.**]

CYNDDELW BRYDYDD MAWR (*fl.* 1155–1200). Although Cynddelw did not possess a bardic pedigree, his origins did not prevent him from obtaining a thorough schooling in the traditions of his native Powys and a mastery of the Welsh bardic craft. Indeed, he is known as *Brydydd Mawr* (the great poet) in manuscripts preserving his poetry.

He began his career as *bardd teulu* (court poet) to Madog ap Maredudd in Powys, and remained at court until Madog's death (1160) and the subsequent fall of Powys. While there Cynddelw won the title of *pencerdd* (chief of song) in a bardic competition with Seisyll Bryffwrch. This brought him not only wealth and the most honored position among poets at Madog's court but also a welcome at the courts of other Welsh princes—a privilege on which he would call frequently throughout his prolific career. Cynddelw composed for many leading figures of his day, including Owain Gwynedd, Owain Cyfeiliog, Gwenwynwyn, and Rhys ap Gruffydd.

Cynddelw's poetry reflects the values and styles of composition common to poets of his age, known as the Gogynfeirdd in Welsh literary history. Consequently, the long, rhythmical passages full of alliterating compound words characteristic of Gogynfeirdd verse often sound leaden and false to modern ears. Yet Cynddelw's images of savage battle, ladies fluttering about court, or the luminous curve of a lady's breast still burst with vitality.

While Cynddelw drew heavily on the lore and poetic techniques known to the Gogynfeirdd, he was also influenced by continental practices, particularly the troubadour poetic conceit of an animal messenger (Welsh: *llatai*) sent to woo one's beloved. His "Rhieingerdd Efa Ferch Madog ap Maredudd" (Love song to Efa, daughter of Madog ap Maredudd) skillfully used both a *llatai* and *dyfalu,* the native method of simile, in a way only the much later fourteenth-century poet Dafydd ap Gwilym could rival.

Cynddelw's poetic talents remained vigorous to the end of his life. So, with the same confidence with which he had always approached Welsh princes, he was able to seek, in "On His Deathbed," entrance to the court of his Creator.

BIBLIOGRAPHY

Sources. John Morris-Jones, ed., *Llawysgrif Hendregadredd* (1971), 81–181; John Gwenogvryn Evans, ed., *The Poetry in the Red Book of Hergest* (1911), 33–36, cols. 1165–1172. Joseph P. Clancy, *The Earliest Welsh Poetry* (1970), translates some poems, 136–151, and provides notes, 209–212.

Studies. D. Myrddin Lloyd, "Barddoniaeth Cynddelw Brydydd Mawr," in *Llenor,* **11** (1932) and **13** (1934), and "The Poets of the Princes," in A. O. H. Jarman, ed., *A Guide to Welsh Literature,* I (1976).

MARILYN KAY KENNEY

[See also **Welsh Literature: Poetry.**]

CYNFEIRDD. See **Welsh Literature: Poetry.**

CYPRIAN, ST., bishop of Carthage from 249 to 258. Before converting to Christianity in 246, he had received an excellent pagan eduation. In 249 he was elected bishop of Carthage, and was forced underground during the Decian persecutions of 250–251. During the Novatian schism Cyprian demanded rebaptism of those baptized by heretics, a stance in conflict with that of Pope Stephen I. After Stephen's death in 257, however, Cyprian returned to the good graces of Rome. He was exiled to Curubis on 30 August 257 during Valerian's persecutions, then returned to Carthage for trial. He refused to wait quietly for his death at the hands of his persecutors, lest he deprive his people of the sight of their bishop being martyred. He finally was executed at Carthage on 14 September 258. His feast day is 16 September.

Cyprian's treatises indicate his strong concern for the unity of the universal church. The standard collection of his letters includes eighty-one examples by him, as well as by some of his correspondents.

BIBLIOGRAPHY

Opera omnia, Wilhelem Hartel, ed., 3 vols. (1868–1871, repr. 1965); *Letters (1–81),* Sister Rose Bernard Donna, trans. (1964); Edward White Benson, *Cyprian: His Life, His Times, His Work* (1897); Josef Ludwig, *Der heilige Märtyerbischof Cyprian von Karthago* (1951).

KRISTINE T. UTTERBACK

[See also **Church Fathers.**]

CYPRUS, KINGDOM OF. The island of Cyprus, which fell under the sovereignty of the Eastern emperor, was from the death of Muḥammad the object of repeated Muslim attacks. The capital, Constantia (now Salamis), was sacked in 647/648, and in the eighth century the Muslims appear to have installed a permanent base there, which was in turn eliminated in 964 by Nikephoros Phokas. The Muslim threat prompted the building of large fortresses such as St. Hilarion and Kantara in the mountains; military colonies of Armenians and Maronites were established at the repeated behests of the emperors.

In the eleventh and especially the twelfth centuries, Cyprus enjoyed a measure of prosperity: it was made a theme; great monasteries were founded (Kykkou, Makheras); the Latin states of the Middle East obtained provisions of wheat there; and the Venetians had a trading center at Limassol, a port of call for their commerce with Alexandria and Syria. But the Byzantine prince Isaac Komnenos, governor of Cyprus, rebelled against Emperor Andronikos I Komnenos about 1184 and declared the island independent.

On his way to the Third Crusade, Richard I the Lionhearted, king of England, landed on Cyprus in 1191 and captured Isaac, on the pretext that Isaac had mistreated pilgrims. After conquering the island, Richard promised to respect the customs of the inhabitants. Soon, however, he found himself forced to sell the island, first to the Templars, whose financial demands touched off a rebellion, and then in 1192 to the former king of Jerusalem, Guy de Lusignan, who made himself the vassal of the English king. Guy attracted settlers to Cyprus. Richard, captured by Leopold of Austria on his way home from the crusade, eventually surrendered his suzerainty over Cyprus. In 1194 Emperor Henry VI gave the crown to Aimery, the brother of Guy.

In 1228 Emperor Frederick II (son of Henry VI) visited the island and dismissed the regent, Jean d'Ibelin, who had been chosen by the barons, and named a successor, as he had a right to do by imperial law. Jean resisted, and after a long war defeated the imperial forces (1233). In 1247, as part of his general attack on Frederick II, Pope Innocent IV abolished imperial suzerainty. King Henry I, Aimery's grandson, was no longer a vassal.

Henry's son, Hugh II, died without heirs. His cousin, Hugh of Antioch, became king in 1267, and in 1268 he inherited the title of king of Jerusalem. When Acre and Tyre, the last remnants of the kingdom of Jerusalem, fell to the Muslims in 1291, Henry II, Hugh's son, made the town of Famagusta the symbol of the lost kingdom. From then on, the crown of Jerusalem was given to the king in the cathedral there.

Henry II, an epileptic, was deposed by his brother Amalric and deported to Armenia in 1306. He was called back after the assassination of Amalric in 1310, and he punished his opponents harshly. Henry's nephew, Hugh IV (1324–1359), and Hugh's son, Peter I, took part in the struggle of Christian powers against Turkish piracy. Peter raided the coast of Asia Minor and occupied Adalia (modern Antalya) and Korykos (northeast of Seleucia, ruled by Cyprus until 1448). He was drawn into a war with the sultan of Egypt and took Alexandria in 1365. He made a triumphal tour of the West, but gained little assistance. On his return in 1369 he was assassinated by his barons, who had been irritated by his financial demands and his abuses of authority. The barons then made the *Book of Jean d'Ibelin*, a treatise of feudal law written about 1265, which was highly favorable to the vassals' rights, the basic law of the kingdom. Genoa, however, took advantage of these disturbances, and sent a fleet that captured Famagusta and the young king, Peter II. Cyprus was pillaged, and Peter had to pawn Famagusta to the Genoese. In 1384 Peter's uncle, James I (1382–1398), ceded the city to the Genoese, who held it until 1464.

King Janus (1398–1432), by protecting Catalan pirates, incurred the enmity of the sultan. He was defeated and captured at Khirokhitia (1426), and had to recognize Egyptian suzerainty and pay tribute. At the death of Janus' son John II in 1458, the throne went to John's daughter Charlotte, wife of Louis of Savoy; but the king's bastard son, James II, obtained investiture from the sultan in 1460 and succeeded in taking Kyrenia, where the followers of Charlotte had taken refuge (1464). James died in 1473; his supporters hoped to marry his widow, Caterina Cornaro, to one of the Aragonese royal family of Naples. Venetian officials, however, brought Caterina under their control and in the end forced her to abdicate and annexed Cyprus (1489).

Cyprus was a feudal monarchy. The Lusignan

kings, Guy and Aimery, had confiscated the greater estates, including those of the church, and had redistributed them as fiefs to "Frankish" knights from the Holy Land or from the West. But they reserved for themselves a rich royal domain, which included towns, castles, many villages (casaux), and taxes on economic activities. They still had to levy general taxes in periods of crisis. The "royal tenth," first taken in 1388, became a permanent tax. The restraints that the barons had tried to impose on the kings in 1306 and 1369 had no permanent effect.

The Lusignan kings had preserved a Byzantine institution, the *sekretikon*, whose head (the *praktoras*) became the "bailiff of the collectorship." This was a company of officials that administered the royal domain and finances. It oversaw expenditures and kept a register of its acts (the register of 1468 has been preserved). The "court"—that is, the royal household—was managed by a bailiff, later by a master of the household. It included several divisions: the butlery, the pantry (food services), the chamber, the royal stables. Each of these had its secretary. The defense of the kingdom was based on the service of the vassals, but the kings hired mercenaries at a very early date, and James II had what were in effect companies of condottieri. The kingdom also had a small navy to assure the safety of commercial shipping, but at times the navy was used for piratical operations.

The kingdom had its great officers: the seneschal, the constable, the marshal, the butler, the "turcoplier" (commander of the cavalry composed of Syrians who fought "in the Turkish way"), the admiral, and the "auditor," who was responsible for petitions to the king. The king also named high officers for the nominal kingdom of Jerusalem and, when Peter I and James I had acquired the title of king of Armenia, for marshals and other officials of that phantom kingdom. From the time of Peter I he also granted titles based on the lost kingdom and principalities of Frankish Syria.

Cases involving fiefs and vassals of the king were heard by the high court, composed of the king's liege men. In the end this court was composed only of the king's councillors. Cyprus never accepted the Western system of notaries (even though the Genoese merchants used Genoese notaries and the Greeks used Greek notaries). Thus private contracts were given legal status by the courts. These courts were held by viscounts, castellans, and the king's bailiff. The island was divided into five bailiwicks (one of these called the Vicomté) at least during the fourteenth century; after that, the judicial functions of the bailiffs were given to the *chevetains*. Commercial contracts were decided before the bailiff of the *comerc*, who was responsible for import duties and market dues (like the Byzantine *kommerkion*).

Most of the knights and other holders of fiefs belonged to families that had been established since the foundation of the kingdom, but foreign lords came to join them. James II gave fiefs confiscated from the early nobility to adventurers or to men descended from Greek or Syrian businessmen. If the wealth of the nobility at times astonished foreign visitors, the bourgeoisie of the merchant cities also accumulated enormous fortunes. Paphos and Limassol were harbors for ships going to Alexandria or to Acre in the thirteenth century. By the beginning of the fourteenth century Famagusta, which had been given privileges and a protective wall by Henry II, became the port that received merchandise coming from Mongol Asia. There one could find Syrian merchants (especially Nestorians) who had built churches of their own rite. The prosperity of Famagusta, however, did not survive Genoese occupation, even though the Genoese tried to maintain the rule that all foreign ships must discharge their cargo in that port. And the port of Les Salines (Larnaca) became the harbor for Venetian ships, which took on salt and sugar there.

Cyprus was not just a place for transshipping Oriental goods, as Francesco Balducci Pegolotti said about 1330; it also provided enough to meet its own needs: wheat, barley, wine, and oil. Moreover, the Latin lords had introduced the cultivation of sugarcane. Cyprus wine was famous in western Europe by the thirteenth century. Cyprus also produced valuable textiles, such as spun gold.

Many of the artisans of Cyprus were Syrians; the peasants, for the most part, were Greek. The latter paid the fees imposed by the Byzantine administrations: head taxes and taxes on property (chevage, *demosion*). These made up the *catepanagium*, collected for the benefit of the lords. Slaves were used on the lords' holdings. But the financial problems of the kings led them to multiply charters of freedom, and by the end of the fifteenth century freemen *(francomates)* were more numerous than serfs *(parèques)*. The latter were bound to the lordship, and their names were listed, in a book called *Prahtico (Praktikon)*.

Peter I gave charters of freedom to the Greek inhabitants of the towns. They then had the same privileges as the French and Syrian burgesses. Burgesses of the Latin faith, as in Jerusalem, were judged in the court of the viscount or the castellan; Syrians (who had arrived at the same time as the Franks), in the court of the *rais* (at least at Nicosia and Famagusta). Franks were judged according to the *Assises des bourgeois* (reedited in the fourteenth century in the *Livre du plédéant et du plaidoyer*). Greeks were under Roman-Byzantine law and had their own judges. But the Greek burgesses seem to have gained access to the jurors' offices during the fifteenth century, and differences in legal procedures, thanks to mixed marriages, became less noticeable in the fifteenth century.

Each community had its own religious organization and each preserved its own usages. Armenians, Maronites, Syrians, Jacobites, and Nestorians had their churches, their bishops, and their monasteries. For the Greeks it would have been desirable to find common ground with the Roman church, the hierarchy of which was established in 1197. The Latin church in Cyprus had an archbishop and three bishops. Since canon law considered Greek bishops as vicars of the Latin bishops for the Greek population, the fourteen existing dioceses should have been reduced to four. The Greek bishops were willing to accept the primacy of the pope, but not to obey Latin bishops. Pope Innocent IV favored the Greeks, but Alexander IV, in the *Bulla Cypria* (1260), ruled in favor of the Latins. This bull established a Greek bishop in each diocese; he was to live in a different city than the Latin bishop. In fact, however, the Latin bishops were satisfied by a formal submission and allowed their Greek colleagues full jurisdiction over all priests and laymen of the Greek rite (although papal legates at times tried to interfere with this arrangement).

By virtue of a concordat negotiated in 1223, the Latin bishops had the tithes of the revenues of the king and the lords. They had to support their cathedral, their canons, and the clergy of the four rural parishes (their vicars being called priors) that followed the Latin rite. There were few Latin monasteries—Stavrovouni, Lapais—at first. Their number grew as religious groups fled from the Latin states of Syria. The Dominicans, Franciscans, and Carmelites established the headquarters of their Holy Land province in Cyprus. But Latin monasteries were becoming less numerous in the fifteenth century.

Greek monasteries remained numerous after the Latin conquest and soon began to prosper. Latin lords venerated the Greek sanctuaries, contributing paintings and making financial donations. The affair of Kantara, where monks who had reopened the old quarrel about the use of unleavened bread (azymes) in the Eucharist were executed in 1231, was a unique case of intolerance. By the fourteenth century there were members of Latin families in Greek monasteries, and it was in such places that one could find the earliest examples of the mingling of rites and cultures that became fully apparent in the next century.

Latin domination had increased the prosperity of the island by freeing it from exploitation by Byzantium. Thus, there was a remarkable burst of artistic activity: building of royal palaces and castles, mansions for the lords, Gothic churches such as the cathedrals of Nicosia and Famagusta and the monastery of Lapais, and production of numerous icons and murals in the Greek churches. French influence inspired such works as the *Gestes des Chiprois,* the *Livre en forme de plaid* of Philippe de Novare and the *Chansonnier* now preserved at Turin. Fine copies were made of Greek manuscripts, and the chroniclers Leontios Makhairas and George Boustron wrote their works in Greek.

BIBLIOGRAPHY

George Hill, *A History of Cyprus,* 4 vols. (1940–1952), is the basic work; see also Louis de Mas-Latrie, *Histoire de l'île de Chypre,* 3 vols. (1852–1861). Leontios Makhairas, *Recital Concerning the Sweet Land of Cyprus,* Richard M. Dawkins, trans., 2 vols. (1932); and Jean Richard, *Documents chypriotes* (1962), and *Le livre des remembrances* (1983), have very useful material in their introductions. Kenneth M. Setton, gen. ed., *A History of the Crusades,* has three good articles on Cyprus: the first by E. C. Furber, II, 2nd ed. (1969), 599–629; the next two by Harry Luke, III (1975), 340–395. An article by Jean Richard on the institutions of the kingdom will appear in vol. V of this series. See also John Hackett, *History of the Orthodox Church in Cyprus* (1901); A. H. S. Megaw and T. R. S. Boase, "The Arts in Cyprus," in *History of the Crusades,* IV, (1977), 165–207; and David Talbot Rice, *The Icons of Cyprus* (1937).

JEAN RICHARD

[See also **Byzantine Empire: History; Crusades and Crusader States; Guy de Lusignan; Lusignans; Richard I the Lionhearted; Trade, European.**]

CYRIL AND METHODIOS, STS., two brothers who served as Byzantine Christian missionaries to the Slavs in the ninth century. Natives of Thessaloniki, where they received a bilingual education, Constantine (*b.* 826 or 827) (Cyril was a monastic name assumed only before his death) and Methodios were first entrusted, around 860, with a diplomatic mission to the Khazars, north of the Caucasus. In 863, following a request by Prince Rastislav of Moravia, Byzantine Emperor Michael III and Patriarch Photios sent them on a religious mission to central Europe, where the expansion of Byzantine Christianity was in competition with the activities of Frankish clergy. Even before the mission Constantine and Methodios were translating scriptural and liturgical texts into the Slavic language, and had composed a totally new Slavonic alphabet, known today as Glagolitic. (The "Cyrillic" alphabet, named after Cyril and used by most Slavic peoples, is of a later composition.) On their arrival in Moravia, they laid the foundation of Slavic Christianity by introducing worship in the vernacular.

After Louis the German conquered Moravia in 864, the activity of the brothers was curtailed by the Frankish clergy. The Franks used Latin in the liturgy and were opposed to the use of the vernacular. Obliged to leave Moravia, the two brothers traveled through Venice, where in 867 they had discussions with Latin clerics and accused them of "the heresy of the three languages"—that is, the belief that Christian worship was possible only in Hebrew, Greek, and Latin. In Venice, however, they also received an invitation from Pope Nicholas I to visit Rome; the pontiff showed particular interest in the relics of St. Clement of Rome, a saintly martyr of the first century, which were purported to have been found by the brothers in the Crimea. The missionaries were met in Rome by Adrian II, Nicholas' successor. They left the relics as a gift to the pope, who then gave his full support to the cause of the Slavonic liturgy. Constantine, having been tonsured a monk under the name of Cyril, died in Rome on 14 February 869. Methodios, meanwhile, was consecrated by Pope Adrian as archbishop of Sirmium, with jurisdiction over several Slavic regions including Moravia, Pannonia, and Slovakia.

By 870, however, the situation in Moravia had changed. In that year, the new prince, Svatopluk, who supported Frankish policies, had Methodios arrested and tried by a council of German bishops in Regensburg. He was imprisoned in Swabia until 873, when the intercession of Pope John VIII won his liberation.

The last twelve years of the great missionary were spent not only in strengthening and expanding the Slavic mission but also in contending with the Franks. The latter continued to oppose the principle of a vernacular liturgy, and they also promoted among the Slavs the Latin version of the Nicene Creed, which had been interpolated with the word *Filioque,* affirming the procession of the Holy Spirit from the Father and the Son. Patriarch Photios and Pope Nicholas I had clashed on the issue in connection with missionary activity in Bulgaria (867). Methodios was facing it in Moravia, even after the reconciliation between Photios and Rome in 879–880. Indeed, the Franks continued to ignore the disapproval of the *Filioque* clause by Pope John VIII, the sponsor and protector of Methodios.

In 881 Methodios returned to Constantinople, where he was warmly received by Emperor Basil I and Patriarch Photios. He got the assurance of Byzantine sympathy and support for his mission. He died in Moravia 6 April 885. His disciples, including particularly Gorazd, Clement, and Naum, were persecuted and imprisoned. The last two eventually emigrated to Ochrid, in the western Bulgarian Empire, where they continued the task of translations and development of the Slavic mission. The use of the Slavic liturgy survived in Moravia until the eleventh century, but eventually disappeared in favor of the linguistic uniformity of Latin Christendom. It continued among eastern and southern Slavs.

The Cyrillo-Methodian mission occurred at a time when the churches of Rome and Constantinople were drifting apart. It is significant, however, that the two brothers, who began their mission precisely when mutual excommunications were launched at each other by Pope Nicholas and Patriarch Photios (863–867), remained in communion with both sides. Furthermore, the fact that in 881 Methodios was fully recognized in Constantinople as archbishop of Sirmium—a position received from the pope—indicates that the reconciliation between Photios and Pope John VIII included Byzantine acceptance of the papal jurisdiction over Illyricum, a long-contested issue.

The heritage left by Sts. Cyril and Methodios to Eastern Christendom is of even greater importance, both symbolic and practical: the liturgy in the vernacular. The arguments used by the brothers in their discussions with proponents of the "three languages" theory remained alive in Eastern Christendom: on Pentecost the apostles were heard preaching in many languages (Acts 2:5), and the apostle Paul considered that "he that speaketh in an unknown tongue edifieth [only] himself" (1 Cor. 14:4). Paraphrasing him, Constantine-Cyril said: "If I pray in an unknown tongue, my spirit prayeth, but my un-

derstanding is unfruitful. . . . Yet in the church I had rather speak five words with my understanding, that with my voice I might teach others also, than 10,000 words in an unknown tongue" (*Vita Constantini,* XVI, 45–58, F. Grivec and F. Tomšič, eds., in *Constantinus et Methodius Thessalonicenses: Fontes* [1960], 135–136). The missionary method of Cyril and Methodios implied the rooting of Christianity in local cultures. In contrast with the cultural and administrative unification of the Latin world, it laid a foundation for national churches, which were free to develop indigenous cultures but had no immediate access to the heritage of classical antiquity.

BIBLIOGRAPHY

Francis Dvornik, *Les légendes de Constantin et de Méthode vues de Byzance* (1933, repr. 1969), which includes a French translation of the *Lives* of Cyril and Methodios; and *Byzantine Missions Among the Slavs: SS. Constantine-Cyril and Methodius* (1970); Franc Grivec, *Konstantin und Method: Lehrer der Slaven* (1960); Dmitri Obolensky, *The Byzantine Commonwealth: Eastern Europe, 500–1453* (1971); Alexis P. Vlasto, *The Entry of the Slavs into Christendom* (1970).

JOHN MEYENDORFF

[See also **Byzantine Church; Glagolitic Rite; Missions and Missionaries, Christian; Moravia; Nicholas I, Pope; Photios.**]

CYRIL OF ALEXANDRIA, ST. (*ca.* 376–444). A prominent theologian and father and doctor of the church, Cyril was elevated to the position of archbishop of Alexandria in 412. A nephew of Theophilus, the preceding archbishop, Cyril had taken part in his uncle's activities, including the deposition of St. John Chrysostom in 403, and soon became one of the most forceful personalities to head the populous, rich, and turbulent Christian community of Egypt. As archbishop of the Alexandrian metropolis, he exercised direct jurisdiction over a country of mixed Greek and Coptic population. Fighting relentlessly against the remnants of paganism, he challenged the imperial prefect Orestes, and is even accused of indirect responsibility for the murder of the philosopher Hypatia by an Alexandrian Christian mob.

After 428, when Nestorius became archbishop of Constantinople, Cyril wrote a series of letters criticizing his doctrine about the person of Christ. The latent animosity between the churches of Alexandria and Constantinople may have played a role in this polemic, but a serious theological difference between the two protagonists is also obvious. Nestorius, following his teacher Theodore of Mopsuestia, saw Christ, the Son of God, as clearly distinct from the "son of Mary." Mary, he said, could not be properly called *Theotokos,* "mother of God," but only the mother of Christ's humanity. Cyril, on the contrary, insisted on personal unity of Christ as the one incarnate Word of God: this unique and divine person was born of Mary and died on the cross "according to the flesh"—that is, having assumed the fullness of humanity.

The union of divinity and humanity in Christ is described by Cyril as a "union according to hypostasis" or "union by nature." Sometimes he uses a formula formerly used by Apollinaris of Laodicea: "one nature incarnate of God the Word." His intention was to affirm the assumption by God himself of human reality (or "nature") in its fullness, but some of his expressions were later used by the Monophysites in their opposition to the doctrine of the "two natures" of Christ, defined at Chalcedon (451).

Cyril's activities against Nestorius led to the condemnation of the latter at the ecumenical Council of Ephesus (431), where Cyril's theology was approved. Archbishop John of Antioch, who was prevented from participating in the decision, opposed Cyril until 433. In that year an exchange of letters, which proves that the turbulent archbishop of Alexandria was also capable of moderation, sanctioned their reconciliation.

His very numerous writings include commentaries on several Old Testament books (Isaiah, the minor prophets). His treatise *Adoration and Worship in Spirit and Truth* explains the Christian typological understanding of the Old Testament. Most important theologically is Cyril's *Commentary on the Gospel of John.* His polemics against Nestorius are found in a series of short tracts and letters. His Third Letter to Nestorius (430) contains his famous Twelve Anathemas, which formulate the main points of his Christology. Cyril also wrote a large *Apology Against Julian,* where he criticizes the views of Emperor Julian the Apostate (361–363), which had apparently remained popular in pagan circles.

BIBLIOGRAPHY

An edition of Cyril's writings is in *Patrologia graeca,* LXVIII–LXXVII (1859). Studies include Alois Grillmeier, *Christ in Christian Tradition* (1965), 329–452; Jaroslav Pelikan, *The Christian Tradition,* I, *The Emergence of the* *Catholic Tradition* (1971); Johannes Quasten, *Patrology,* III (1960); 116–142.

JOHN MEYENDORFF

[See also **Councils (Ecumenical, 325–787); John Chrysostom, St.; Monophysitism; Nestorianism; Theotokos.**]

DADDI, BERNARDO (*ca.* 1290–*ca.* 1348), Florentine painter recorded in volumes of the guild of doctors and apothecaries for the years 1312–1320 and 1320–1353. Daddi was a prolific and popular painter who developed a decorative alternative to Giotto's monumental style. His forms are based on Giotto's inventions but are sweeter and less demanding, demonstrating his attraction to contemporary Sienese painting.

An extensive oeuvre still survives, including Daddi's documented *Madonna and Child* painted in 1347 to replace a miracle-working image destroyed by fire in Or San Michele. His signature appears on the 1348 polyptych *Crucifixion with Saints* now in the Gambier-Parry Collection at Highnam Court.

Daddi's early career is reconstructed by using his

Madonna and Child enthroned with eight angels. Or San Michele, Florence, 1347. SCALA/ART RESOURCE

signed and dated (1328) triptych for the Church of Ognissanti (now in the Uffizi) and the portable triptych of 1333 probably executed for the Ospedale del Bigallo as guides. Other dated works include the 1334 *Madonna and Child with Saints* now in the Galleria dell'Accademia. His generally accepted oeuvre includes the frescoes depicting the martyrdoms of St. Lawrence and St. Stephen in the Pulci-Berardi Chapel of S. Croce and the half-length *Madonna and Child* in the Berenson Collection, I. Tatti. These are generally placed in the 1330's.

Charming, anecdotal, sturdy, and uncomplicated, Daddi's style found its ideal expression in the small, intimate format of the portable altarpiece, of which numerous examples survive.

BIBLIOGRAPHY
Richard Offner, *A Critical and Historical Corpus of Florentine Painting*, sec. 3, vols. III and IV (1930–1934).

ADELHEID M. GEALT

DAFYDD AP GWILYM (*ca.* 1320–*ca.* 1380), the greatest poet of the Welsh Middle Ages, was born, according to early traditions, at Bro Gynin in Cardiganshire. His family was of the *uchelwyr,* the native Welsh nobility, and a sixteenth-century pedigree lists his father as Gwilym Gam ap Gwilym ap Einion. Little else is known of Dafydd's life; internal evidence in his poetry shows a familiarity with the area around Bro Gynin and its parish, Llanbadarn Fawr, as well as with Anglesey and Caernarvonshire. Part of his youth was spent with his uncle, Llywelyn ap Gwilym, constable of Newcastle Emlyn. It is also clear that Dafydd lived for some time in Glamorganshire at the estate of his principal patron, Ifor Hael, to whom he addressed several poems. According to tradition he is buried in the cemetery of the Cistercian abbey of Strata Florida, not far from his birthplace.

The corpus of Dafydd's poetry has not yet been authoritatively established; Thomas Parry's 1952 edition includes just over 150 poems out of almost 250 in the *editio princeps* of 1789. His poetry is often contrasted with the formal bardic work of the previous century. In both form and content Dafydd was often an innovator, adopting ideas from the troubadours and the *clerici vagantes,* but at the same time he adapted and continued many of the traditions of his predecessors. Although much of his poetry is in the new *cywydd* meter, he also wrote in the older

awdl meters; more important, many of his poems in these older forms are examples of elegy and praise in the same vein as the poetry of the previous century. Similarly, although the details of Dafydd's relationship with his patron Ifor ap Llywelyn of Gwern-y-clepa in Glamorgan are not known, the poet clearly saw it in the traditional terms of *pencerdd* (chief of song) to prince. It may well have been Dafydd who gave Ifor his epithet *hael* (the generous).

Nonetheless, although his links with the court poets of the twelfth and thirteenth centuries are clear, Dafydd is of even greater importance as an innovator. Love and nature, not praise and elegy, are his principal subjects. Although neither love poetry nor nature poetry was unknown to the court poets, Dafydd elevated these subjects to a new stature. He describes himself as *dyn Ofydd* (Ovid's man), he writes of love messengers *(llatai)* and thwarted husbands in a manner that is often humorous, and his consideration of nature seems more derived from close observation than from medieval tradition. His love poetry is never spiritual; it is a celebration of physical love.

Although such contemporaries as Madog Benfras and Gruffudd ap Adda wrote both love poetry and nature poetry, neither achieved the power and immediacy of Dafydd's praise of his ladies, Morfydd the fair and Dyddgu the dark. In a series of flyting poems exchanged with Gruffudd Gryg, Gruffudd jokes that Dafydd suffers so much in the bonds of love that he ought to be dead.

Dafydd's poetry in the newer *cywydd* meter shows extraordinary technical mastery of this complex form. Indeed, it is probably because of this complexity of form that he has not been more widely recognized as one of the great medieval vernacular poets. The meter, alternating rhymes on stressed and unstressed syllables, includes complex patterns of consonance, assonance, and internal rhyme (*cynghanedd*) and parenthetical comment (*sangiad*), which make his poetry exceedingly difficult to translate adequately.

Dafydd held strong views on poetry. One poem involves a conversation between the poet and an ascetic friar who advises him to give up worldly pursuits like poetry, for prayer. Dafydd eloquently justifies his poetry and its worldly concerns, pointing out that God himself does not scorn praise in poetry: "For what are hymns and sequences but *englynion* and *awdlau,* and the psalms of the prophet David *cywyddau* to the Holy God."

Dafydd was certainly known to his contemporaries. Two poets, Iolo Goch and Madog Benfras, wrote death songs (marwnadau) to him, in which he is fondly called "the nightingale of Dyfed," "the hawk of the women of the south," and "the pillar of song of the southland."

BIBLIOGRAPHY

Sources. Thomas Parry, ed., *Gwaith Dafydd ap Gwilym* (1952); Rachel Bromwich, *Dafydd ap Gwilym: A Selection of Poems* (1982); Richard M. Loomis, *Dafydd ap Gwilym: The Poems* (1982).

Studies. Rachel Bromwich, *Tradition and Innovation in the Poetry of Dafydd ap Gwilym* (1967), and *Dafydd ap Gwilym* (1974); Theodor M. Chotzen, *Recherches sur la poésie de Dafydd ap Gwilym* (1927); John Rowlands, ed., *Dafydd ap Gwilym: A chanu serch yr Oesoedd Canol* (1975).

DAVID N. KLAUSNER

[See also **Iolo Goch; Welsh Literature: Poetry.**]

DÁL CAIS. According to the theories of the genealogists, the Dál Cais were a branch of the Eóganacht, sprung from one Cormac Cas, brother of Ailill Ólom, the legendary progenitor of the Eóganacht. This dynastic name first appears in the annals in 934, and it and the genealogical legend are a response to a dramatic change in the political fortunes of a minor group formerly known as In Déis (a branch of a people known as Déisi, whose string of petty kingdoms stretched from the sea at Waterford north and west to Limerick). Their slow rise to power began in the eighth century, and from their homeland in Limerick they moved north of the Shannon, filling the power vacuum left by the decline of the great southern Connacht overkingdom of Uí Fiachrach Aidni. They pushed back the local dynasties of Corcu Baiscind and Corcu Modruad (they massacred the latter in 744) and established themselves in eastern Clare. By about the middle of the ninth century there were some fifty landholding families of the Dál Cais in east Clare. With the coming of the Vikings and the development of sea and river traffic, they found themselves in control of the great strategic waterway of the Shannon and its lakes.

In the early tenth century, now ruled by a dynastic family called Uí Thairdelbaig, Dál Cais, largely on account of the decline of the Eóganacht, who had hitherto ruled Munster without a serious competitor and because of the political fragmentation of their neighbors, became a power to be reckoned with in Munster politics. When Cennétig mac Lorcáin, king

of Dál Cais, died in 951, the annalists entitled him "king of Thomond" and "royal heir of Munster." Cennétig's sons, Mathgamain (murdered 976) and Brian (killed 1014), displaced the Eóganacht from the kingship of Munster and turned their father's high-sounding titles into a political reality. Mathgamain was firmly established as king of Munster by 972. He was killed four years later by an Eóganacht alliance and succeeded by his brother Brian, a far more able ruler.

Brian's twelfth-century biographer makes Alfred the Great the model of his hero. His meteoric rise to power fundamentally changed Irish politics. By 978 he had firmly established himself as king of Munster, by 996 he dominated the southern half of Ireland, and by 1005 he could claim with some reason to be king of Ireland. He was killed in the battle of Clontarf in 1014, a battle that was as much part of Irish domestic politics as a struggle against the Vikings. His immediate successor, his son Donnchad, was merely king of Munster, but his successors in turn, Tairdelbach Ua Briain (1064–1086) and Muirchertach Ua Briain (1086–1119), were the most powerful kings in the Ireland of their day. In the early twelfth century Munster was divided between the Dál Cais and the Eóganacht by the increasingly powerful king of Connacht, and by the time of the Norman invasion the Dál Cais had been reduced to kings of north Munster. Throughout the later medieval period the Dál Cais (now known as Uí Briain) maintained themselves as powerful territorial lords in north Munster.

BIBLIOGRAPHY

Francis J. Byrne, *Irish Kings and High-Kings* (1973); John V. Kelleher, "The Rise of Dál Cais," in Etienne Rynne, ed., *North Munster Studies* (1967); Donnchadh Ó Corráin, *Ireland Before the Normans* (1972), and "Dál Cais: Church and Dynasty," in *Eriu,* 24 (1973); John Ryan, "The O'Briens in Munster After Clontarf," in *North Munster Antiquarian Journal,* 2 (1941) and 3 (1942–1943), and "Brian Bóruma, King of Ireland," in Rynne, ed., *op. cit.*

DONNCHADH Ó CORRÁIN

[See also **Eóganacht; Ireland, Early History.**]

DÁL RIATA. The early history of Dál Riata is shrouded in the mists of antiquity and pseudohistory. They originated as petty kings in the extreme northwest of Ireland, but the historical records of their activities in this area are sparse. At an early period they migrated to western Scotland and eventually established a kingdom that was to become the kingdom of Scotland. The date of the migration is uncertain.

There are three dissentient traditions, or rather etiologies, for none is historical. Bede states that their leader was Reuda, "from whom they are still called Dalreudini," but he gives no date for their arrival in Britain. An Irish genealogical legend states that their leader was Cairpre Riata, who arrived in Scotland some ten generations before A.D. 500. Finally, genealogies and other historical materials compiled in Scotland in the seventh century state that the founder was Fergus Mór mac Eirc, and it is generally accepted by Scottish historians that "it was in the person of Fergus Mór that the Dalriadic dynasty removed from Ireland to Scotland," though some (notably Bannerman) have maintained that important segments of the dynasty (Cenél nÓengusa and Cenél Loairn) were already in Scotland before the arrival of Fergus Mór. The best that can be said of these theories is that they reflect the beliefs—as transmitted by traditional historians—of the leading families in Scottish Dál Riata in the seventh century, and have no validity for the migration period and its immediate aftermath.

Genuine historical materials—Adamnan's *Vita Columbae,* the Irish annals (largely based on a chronicle compiled in Iona), and *Senchas Fer nAlban,* a detailed genealogical tract on the ruling dynasties—become available in the seventh century. According to these records, three major dynastic segments had emerged—Cenél Gabráin, Cenél Comgaill, and Cenél Loairn—all claiming a most unlikely descent from a common set of ancestors. Cenél Gabráin dominated the group in the sixth and seventh centuries. Cenél Comgaill, who shared the kingship for a period, lost power by the middle of the seventh century and left the expanding branches of Cenél Gabráin in sole possession.

The dynasts of Cenél Gabráin are depicted as friends and patrons of Iona and of Columba, its founder, a tradition that is best interpreted as a powerful origin legend supporting the legitimacy of Cenél Gabráin and its title to rule Dál Riata. The sources depict Áedán mac Gabráin (*d. ca.* 608) as a dynastic founder, a warrior-king leading an aggressive and plunder-hungry aristocracy engaged in warfare with the Picts, the British, and the Angles. He also had Irish interests, and at the famous convention of Druim Cett (575) he allied himself with the northern Uí Néill to contain Báetán mac Cairill,

king of the Ulaid and the most powerful king in Ireland, who very probably was attempting to extend his suzerainty to Scottish Dál Riata.

For a century or more after the death of Áedán's grandson, Domnall Brecc (*ca.* 642), Dál Riata was racked by intense struggles between Cenél Gabráin and Cenél Loairn, who first appear in the annals in 678 and soon began to share in the overkingship of Dál Riata. The history of the eighth century is one of confused and obscure struggles and interrelationships with the Picts. Óengus mac Fergusa (729–761), king of the Picts, who is curiously given a southern Irish pedigree by the genealogists—perhaps as much a political statement as evidence of Dalriadic-Pictish integration—was the most powerful king in Scotland. He brought all Scotia under his rule and seriously weakened Dál Riata.

Indeed, only one major figure is recorded among the kings of Dál Riata in the eighth century: Áed Find (*d.* 778), who fought a major battle against the Picts in 768 and is credited with a reputation as a lawgiver. After the death of his brother and successor, Fergus (*d.* 781), the succession to the kingship of Dál Riata becomes very obscure and the identity of its kings uncertain. By now Dál Riata and the kingdom of the Picts were closely integrated in their much intermarried royal lineages, and the kings of the first half of the ninth century seem to be a mixed breed ruling over both kingdoms by hereditary right. The stage was now set for the reign of Cináed mac Ailpín (Kenneth mac Alpin, *ca.* 843–858), who united the Picts and the Scots under his rule, and laid the foundations of the kingdom of Scotland.

BIBLIOGRAPHY

Marjorie O. Anderson, *Kings and Kingship in Early Scotland* (1973); John Bannerman, *Studies in the History of Dalriada* (1974); Archibald A. M. Duncan, *Scotland: The Making of the Kingdom* (1975); Kenneth Jackson, "The Duan Albanach," in *Scottish Historical Review,* 36 (1957).

DONNCHADH Ó CORRÁIN

[See also **Áedán mac Gabráin; Scotland, History of.**]

DALLE MASEGNE, PIERPAOLO AND JACOBELLO (*d. ca.* 1403 and *ca.* 1409, respectively), sculptor brothers of Venetian origin, possibly followers of Andriolo de Sanctis in Venice. Their works consist of marble statues of St. John the Bap-

DALLE MASEGNE

Tomb of Giovanni da Legnano, by Pierpaolo and Jacobello Dalle Masegne. Civic Museum, Bologna, *ca.* 1383. ALINARI/ART RESOURCE

tist and St. Anthony of Padua in the sacristy of S. Stefano, Venice, by Jacobello (*ca.* 1380); the monument of Giovanni da Legnano in S. Domenico, Bologna (now in the Museo Civico), by both (*ca.* 1383); the altar of the Coronation of the Virgin in S. Francisco, Bologna, by Pierpaolo (1388–1392); the iconostasis of S. Marco, Venice, by Jacobello (1394–before 1399); sculpture for the facade of the cathedral at Mantua by both (1401); the construction of S. Petronio, Bologna, by Pierpaolo (1398); work on the cathedral at Milan by both (contracted 26 July 1399); work for Gian Galleazzo Visconti in Pavia by Jacobello (1399); the south window of the Doge's Palace, Venice, by Pierpaolo (1400); Virgin and Child with St. Peter and St. Paul above the monument of Antonio Venier (*d.* 1400) in SS. Giovanni e Paolo, Venice; the statue of Antonio Venier, by Jacobello.

The naturalistic Gothic style of the Dalle Masegne brothers spread to Milan, where they were employed in 1399; reached the marches, as seen in the doorway of S. Domenico, Pesaro; and penetrated Tuscany through the works of Jacopo della Quercia at Lucca and Leonardo Riccomanni at Sarzana.

BIBLIOGRAPHY

C. Gnudi, "Jacobello e Pietro Paolo da Venezia," in *Critica d'Arte,* 2 (1937), and "Nuovi appunti sui fratelli dalle Masegne," in *Proporzioni,* 3 (1950); E. Marani, "Nuovi documenti mantovani su Jacomello e Pietropaolo dalle Masegne," in *Accademia Virgiliana . . . di Mantova,*

DALMATIA

Atti e memorie, n.s. 32 (1960), 71–102; P. Toesca, *Storia dell'arte italiana; Il Trecento* (1951), 420–427.

SANDRA CANDEE SUSMAN

DALMATIA, Roman province on the eastern coast of the Adriatic Sea, bordering on Pannonia, Upper Moesia, and Macedonia. In Diocletian's time its southern part was separated and formed the province of Praevalitana, with Scodra (Scutari) as capital, while Salona was the capital of Dalmatia. For a while dominated by Odoacer, then by the Ostrogoths, Dalmatia returned to Byzantine rule about 538. A Byzantine proconsular province was organized from Istria to Kotor, including coastal cities, surrounding territories, and nearby islands, while Slavs and others invaded the hinterland and moved south. Dalmatia prospered throughout this period and later, thanks mainly to naval trade. Ecclesiastically it was under Roman jurisdiction, but because of conflicts between Rome and Constantinople there was alternation of influences over the centuries. Avar-Slavic invasions led to the fall of Salona (612–615) and other Roman coastal cities and to the building of new ones, such as Aspalaton (Split) and Ragusium (Dubrovnik). Surviving cities, together with new ones and islands, were united in a new Byzantine province of Dalmatia while Slavs settled nearby and started organizing their states.

By the first half of the ninth century at the latest, Dalmatia was a Byzantine archonate, and it became a theme in the 870's. It was prosperous, its cities well fortified and with strong commercial fleets. Their ecclesiastical importance is evident from the role they played in Croatian church affairs in the tenth century and later. In the late tenth century Dalmatia was administered by the prior of Zadar, the most powerful local functionary in the theme. The Venetian conquest in 1000 was short-lived but set an important precedent and increased the separation of Dubrovnik, seat of a Byzantine theme, from the rest of Dalmatia, where Byzantine presence was substantially weakened. Byzantine emperors, however, never gave up their claims to sovereignty, either at the time of Venetian domination or when the Croatian kings Peter Kresimir IV (1058–1074) and Dmitar Zvonimir (1075–1089) extended their power in that region, but real Byzantine authority disappeared in the 1060's.

After the union of Croatia with Hungary (1102),

Dalmatia was divided into three zones: the north (Quarnero to Zadar) under Venice; the center (Šibenik to Omiš) under Hungaro-Croatian kings; and the south (Omiš to Bar) nominally under Byzantium but in fact autonomous. The croatization of the cities quickened, while the territory outside the cities belonged predominantly to the Croatians north of the river Neretva, and predominantly to the Serbs south of that river. Byzantine presence in Dalmatia was partly restored between 1067 and 1180, but its collapse resulted in a renewed Hungaro-Venetian struggle for supremacy. Taking advantage of the Fourth Crusade in 1204, Venice put Dalmatia under its domination, where it remained until 1358 when the Hungaro-Croatian king Louis the Great (1342–1382) conquered the area, except for Dubrovnik which became an independent city-republic.

In 1409 the pretender to the Hungaro-Croatian throne, Ladislas of Naples, sold the right to Dalmatia to Venice; by 1420 the Venetians occupied most Dalmatian cities and islands, and remained there until 1797. The Venetian influence is visible in architecture and paintings. The croatization of the cities, together with influences from Italy, created a special cultural symbiosis in Dalmatia that is reflected best in many literary works. Marko Marulić (1450–1524), from Split, was the author of numerous Latin works (among them the *De institutione bene beateque vivendi* and *Davidias*), as well as works in Croatian (*Judita*). Hanibal Lucić (*ca.* 1485–1553), from Hvar, was the author of several works, among them *Robinja*.

For maps of this region, please refer to the articles on Bosnia and Croatia.

BIBLIOGRAPHY

Jadran Ferluga, *L'amministrazione bizantina in Dalmazia*, 2nd ed. (1978); Nada Klaić, *Povijest Hrvata u ranom srednjem vijeku* (1971), and *Povijest Hrvata u razvijenom srednjem vijeku* (1976); J. J. Wilkes, *Dalmatia* (1969.)

BARIŠA KREKIĆ

[See also **Avars; Croatia; Dubrovnik; Slavs; Venice.**]

DALMATIC, a calf-length, sleeved garment, often richly decorated with embroidery, worn by deacons as the principal vestment and by priests, bishops, and archbishops beneath a hip-length mantle (chasuble); it is worn over an ankle-length tunic (alb). The dalmatic was recommended for deacons by Pope Sylvester I (314–335); it seems to have become common for all clergy by the end of the sixth century. By the twelfth century the dalmatic had assumed its modern form as a slightly flared garment, often open beneath the arms. Early examples are known from art (such as the sixth-century mosaic of Ecclesius at S. Vitale, Ravenna); numerous examples are preserved from the twelfth century on.

BIBLIOGRAPHY

Jane Hayward, "Sacred Vestments as They Developed in the Middle Ages," in *Metropolitan Museum Bulletin*, n.s. **29** (1971).

LESLIE BRUBAKER

[See also **Vestments.**]

DALMAÚ, LUIS (active *ca.* 1428–1461), a Catalan painter of the Hispano-Flemish style. He is recorded as having visited Flanders in 1431, and subsequently familiarity with Van Eyck's compositions is revealed in his work. His best-known painting, the *Verge dels Consellers* (documented 1443) for the Casa de la Ciudad, Barcelona, is credited with being the first major example of the Hispano-Flemish style in Spain.

MARY GRIZZARD

DAMASCENE, JOHN. See John of Damascus, St.

DAMASCUS. Located at 36°19′E. × 33°30′N., Damascus (Dimashq) shares to some degree a typical eastern Mediterranean climate: short, cold winters with moderate rainfall, and long, arid summers with no rain for six months or more at a stretch. Although Damascus is only 90 kilometers (about 60 miles) from the coast, it receives but 250 millimeters (under 10 inches) average annual rainfall because of its location just east of the high parallel ridges of the Lebanon and the Anti-Lebanon, which intercept almost all the moisture carried by the westerly winds of the winter months.

In spite of this, Damascus is one of the best-watered spots in the Middle East; its verdant gardens and orchards have traditionally made it recognized as one of the three earthly paradises (along with Samarkand and al-Ubulla). It is situated within a broad oasis (the Ghūṭa) some thirty kilometers (about nineteen miles) east to west and twenty kilometers (twelve miles) north to south. The Ghūṭa is created by a small river, the Baradā, which emerges from a spring in the Anti-Lebanon and flows eastward into a shallow bowl. Since at least the fourth millennium B.C., settlers have been simultaneously draining the basin and extending the cultivable area within it by diverting the waters of the Baradā into a fan-shaped system of canals laid out along low artificial terraces. There are six major canals of this type, five dating back to antiquity and one added in early Muslim times. Two of the canals flow underground through the city, providing water to every part of it by means of an ingenious and extremely intricate system of channels and dividers.

The Ghūṭa was (and is) thickly sprinkled with villages, some of them as ancient as Damascus itself. The eastern portion of the Ghūṭa, at the far end of the irrigation system, was given over to grain production, but the oasis was most renowned for its fruits, especially apricots. Poplar trees grew widely, and their wood was the basis for ordinary construction in Damascus, being used both for roofing material and for wall frameworks, which were filled with mud brick and plastered over with a mixture of clay and reeds.

Damascus owed its importance first of all to the Ghūṭa, but it was fortunately situated in other ways as well. It lay close to, and in a sense connected, two other major agricultural zones: the Bika Valley of central Lebanon to the west, and the fertile, rain-fed Ḥaurān plateau to the south. The role of Damascus as the principal market and administrative center of central Syria was thus all but assured.

In addition, Damascus was the nexus of several important overland routes. Chief of these in Islamic times was the long road from Anatolia to the Hejaz, which made Damascus (along with Cairo and Baghdad) one of the three main termini for the pilgrimage to Mecca. It was also the interior entrepôt for the ports of Acre, Tyre, and Beirut—a particularly significant role during the era of the crusades. Finally, Damascus lay astride the only overland channel of communications between Egypt and Palestine to the south and Syria, Anatolia, and Mesopotamia to the north.

The position of Damascus on the edge of the vast interior steppe of Syria meant that the nomads of this region were an inescapable part of its life.

Throughout the Islamic period they variously ensured or disrupted its trade, protected or threatened its villages, supported or attacked its rulers. They were at all times suppliers and purchasers in its markets, and to some degree they were a source of new settlers and immigrants.

DAMASCUS IN THE FRAMEWORK OF ISLAMIC POLITICAL HISTORY, 634–1516

The political history of Damascus during the Islamic period was turbulent and confusing, but the main determinants of this history can be stated fairly simply. First, the city's strategic location and regional economic importance ensured that it would play a vital role in the rivalries and conflicts of the Nile-to-Tigris area. Second, its population had a strong sense of their identity as Damascenes, took intense pride in their city's distinctive cultural tradition, and could exhibit considerable solidarity vis-à-vis outsiders. Third, the financial resources supplied by the city's immediate dependencies (the Ghūṭa, Bika, and Ḥaurān) could underwrite only a modest administrative-military establishment; left to itself Damascus might dominate Syria, but it was no match for Cairo or even distant Baghdad. The result was that Damascus was constantly being drawn into larger political systems, dominated by Cairo or Baghdad, in which it could not really hold its own. The rulers of Damascus were therefore commonly outsiders appointed from Cairo or (less often) Baghdad. As such, they had to cope with a cohesive and fractious populace that was at times organized into an effective militia.

The political history of Damascus under Islam began very differently. Conquered by the Arab armies in 635, it became the capital of the entire Muslim empire in 661 when its governor Muʿāwiya became uncontested caliph. For the strategic and political imperatives of the Umayyad regime Damascus was admirably situated. First, the dynasty's expansionary thrust was aimed (at least until the failure of Maslama's expedition against Constantinople in 717) as much at Anatolia and the Mediterranean as at Iran. Second, the Umayyads' crucial power base was with the Arab tribal forces stationed in Syria, and the position of Damascus on the edge of the steppe allowed the dynasty's ties with these troops to be constantly nourished. These forces were of course supported not only by the resources of central Syria but also by the tribute of a vast empire.

With the collapse of Umayyad power in 750, the Abbasid dynasty removed the imperial capital to

Baghdad, reducing Damascus to a provincial center for more than 300 years. Abbasid governors (750–878, 905–936), Egyptian Tulunids (878–905) and Ikhshidids (936–970), and the Fatimid counter-caliphate (from 970) subsequently enjoyed contested periods of dominance until 1079, when the city was occupied by the Seljukid prince Tutush (brother of Sultan Malikshāh).

It was during these centuries that the Damascenes gained their reputation as a violent and ungovernable people. The Arab troops of Syria, strongly pro-Umayyad in sentiment, were progressively demobilized under the early Abbasids, and the city was policed by the dynasty's regular forces from Iraq. There were a number of revolts against Abbasid rule during the late eighth and ninth centuries. By the beginning of the tenth century there appeared the first signs of the urban militias (the *ahdāth*) that were to prove such formidable opponents to the city's official governors. By the last decade of Ikhshidid rule (*ca.* 960) they were well-armed bands, both infantry and cavalry, organized under their own chiefs, and they remained a major factor in the internal politics of Damascus until at least the middle of the twelfth century.

The early Seljukid princes and their successors down to 1154 were usually very weak. From 1099, moreover, they were compelled to confront as best they could the aggressive crusader states along the coast. On the other hand, after the death of Sultan Malikshāh in 1092, they were effectively independent of both Baghdad and Cairo. Damascus was now a power center in its own right, and its rulers were able to act autonomously within a regional framework, looking to their peers in Mosul, Aleppo, or the crusader states for allies or rivals.

In 1154 Damascus was occupied without resistance by the prince of Aleppo, Nūr al-Dīn Maḥmūd, who made it his principal residence until his death in 1174. Damascus was not merely the capital of a united Syria in these years, for Nūr al-Dīn was in effect the suzerain of his Zangid relatives in Mosul, and in 1168 his troops occupied Egypt. Nūr al-Dīn's firm hand, his wide popularity among the Sunni Muslim populace, and his relatively ample resources allowed him to control the city's militia groups; thus less and less is heard of them during his and the succeeding reigns, though they certainly never disappeared altogether. The basis of his power was a regular army composed of his personal regiment plus the regiments of his officers; these excluded the indigenous Arabic-speaking population who served only as irregulars, but were instead made up of Turkish *mamlūk*s, Kurds, and Turkmans.

Shortly after Nūr al-Dīn's death Damascus was occupied in 1174 by his erstwhile lieutenant in Egypt, Saladin, and became the main base of operations for his vast conquests in Syria and Mesopotamia. More significantly, when Saladin distributed his domains among his kinsmen in the 1180's to form the Ayyubid confederation, Damascus was one of the major principalities. Cairo was normally the capital, but Damascus was the center of confederation politics because it was the linchpin of resistance by the Syrian prince against domination and control by the ruler of Egypt. The city's importance created some problems for it, to be sure: between 1193 and 1260, it was besieged twelve times, all but twice by Ayyubid armies.

After the Ayyubids were swept away by Mongols in 1260, Damascus was occupied by the armies of the Mamluk sultanate, founded in Egypt a decade earlier. Until the Ottoman conquest in 1516, Damascus would be no more than the capital of one of the sultanate's Syrian provinces. On the other hand, its position was far better than it had been under the Abbasid and Fatimid regimes. On the whole it received more effective protection and control than in the period 750–1079. It was crucial to the defense of Egypt, and was the usual staging ground for the extensive Mamluk campaigns against crusaders, Mongols, and rival Muslims.

As the sultanate's second city, Damascus received a wealth of endowments and benefactions from the Mamluk elite. On the other hand, it was often the base for rebellions against the current sultan by ambitious governors. On two occasions the city was briefly occupied by Mongol armies—the second of these occupations, under Tamerlane (1401), being fearsomely destructive. Finally, there was reemergence of popular factions and youth gangs, notably the *zuᶜar*, appearing at the end of the fifteenth century and clearly symptomatic of a breakdown of the sociopolitical order.

URBAN TOPOGRAPHY AND SETTLEMENT
PATTERNS
The appearance of Damascus at the time of the Arab conquest is a much-disputed topic. It is uncertain whether the wall was rectangular and the street plan classically Roman or whether the medieval ovoid wall and irregular streets had already appeared. However these issues are resolved, the Roman heritage in Islamic Damascus was profound.

Fragments of Roman ornament and masonry are everywhere visible, especially in the northwest quarter of the walled city, while the exterior wall and gate complexes of the Umayyad Mosque still reflect the vast Temple of Jupiter.

It does not seem that the Umayyads greatly altered the Roman city. Muᶜāwiya (661–680) built the caliphal residence, al-Khaḍrāᵓ (the green palace), adjacent to the old temple compound, then shared by a mosque and the Church of St. John the Baptist. Under al-Walīd (705–715) this compound was entirely taken over and converted into a vast and stunningly decorated mosque. Relatively few of the conquerors settled in Damascus, those who did so occupying the northwestern quarter around the mosque-palace complex. Unlike the contemporary camp-cities of Iraq and Egypt or the later caliphal capitals of Baghdad and Cairo, Umayyad Damascus did not balloon into a vast agglomeration—the bulk of the Syrian troops were mustered at al-Jābiya (eighty kilometers [fifty miles] to the south), and there was, in contrast with Iraq, little rural emigration to the capital. Doubtless all this was the result of caliphal policy.

It is difficult to trace the topographical changes that must have occurred in the dark age of Abbasid and Fatimid domination. Two related trends can be noted, however: the emergence of a Muslim majority and the influx of peasant migrants fleeing the insecurity and poverty of the countryside. Both tendencies led to the four-part settlement pattern that characterized it for many centuries: (1) in the northwest quarter, around the Umayyad Mosque and the government buildings, lived the Muslim elite of officials, landowners, and ashrāf (descendants of the Prophet and his close kin), merchants, and ᶜulamāᵓ; (2) in the southwest quarter between Straight Street and Bāb Ṣaghīr lived the Muslim poor, including day laborers and rural migrants; (3) in the northeast quarter between Straight Street and Bāb Tūmā was the Christian quarter, always under pressure on its western boundary; (4) in the southwest corner was the Jewish sector.

Damascus, like most other medieval Islamic cities, should not be identified strictly with the walled area. This was properly only the core of a settlement complex consisting of the immediately adjacent suburbs, nearby villages (several within an hour's walk), and the gardens and pavilions of the city's elite along the Baradā. More generally the society, economy, and religious life of the entire Ghūṭa was dominated by the officials, landowners, merchants, and

ᶜulamāᵓ of the walled city, but at the same time the Ghūṭa provided the economic and demographic resources to sustain the urban core.

The Seljukid period of growth and rebuilding between about 1075 and 1250 led to the emergence of the city as we now know it. The Roman walls had been largely dismantled by the Abbasids for fear of revolts, but in the mid tenth century they were rebuilt (presumably on the ancient foundations) in mud brick. Following the terrible earthquake of 1157, Nūr al-Dīn's reconstruction, which included at least an extension of the north wall, rebuilt gates, and many new towers, was all done in solid stone masonry. Under Tutush (1079–1095) a new citadel—really a fortified royal residence and government compound—was built in the northwest corner; many times worked over during the twelfth century, the citadel was completely reconstructed on the most massive scale (200 meters by 150 meters) early in the reign of the Ayyubid al-ᶜĀdil (1200–1218).

Under the Seljukid princes the city received its first madrasahs. The first was built in 1098. By the time of Nūr al-Dīn's arrival (1154) there were twelve such institutions; at his death (1174) there were twenty-four; under the Ayyubids (1174–1260) sixty-three more were added. These madrasahs and related religious structures were concentrated in two areas: the northwest quarter of the walled city in the vicinity of the revered Umayyad Mosque; and the new suburb of Ṣāliḥīya, about two kilometers (a mile and a quarter) northwest of the walled city on the slopes of Mt. Qāsyūn, which had been founded in the 1160's by Hanbali refugees from crusader Palestine.

Under the early Mamluks, Damascus continued to flourish. To the three old suburbs adjoining the walls (al-ᶜUqayba on the north, Shāghūr and Qaṣr Ḥajjāj to the southwest), which dated back to late Abbasid times, was added the new military marketplace (the sūq al-khayl) west of the citadel. This marketplace provided the focus for a new urban expansion west of the walled city. Among prestige manufactures Damascus was esteemed for its silk and brocade in the twelfth century; in the thirteenth and fourteenth, its enameled glass, inlaid metalwork, and leather achieved fame as well.

The population of Damascus at its medieval apogee can be only roughly estimated. We know from the Ottoman registers that its population about 1525 was approximately 57,000 (for the walled city and the adjacent built-up area). Damascus had been afflicted by recurrent plague epidemics since 1348 and it had been ravaged by Tamerlane in 1401, when much of its artisan class was deported to Samarkand. By the time of the Ottoman conquest, much of the city was apparently deserted. So it can be assumed that at its peak (about 1340) the population was considerably greater, not less than 66,000.

SOCIAL AND POLITICAL INSTITUTIONS

As with all cities of medieval Islam, Damascus had no legally defined corporate status. Whether its ruler was a resident monarch or a provincial governor, the city was simply part of some larger territorial circumscription. The public security of the urban area was looked after by a military officer from the ruler's entourage, who may be called the urban prefect (Arabic: *shiḥna, wālī al-madīna*). The *qadi* and *muḥtasib* were normally drawn from the local notables. These officials had a sort of autonomous political base, but they served at the pleasure of the ruler. A strong ruler could appoint a *qadi* from among the *ᶜulamāᵓ* in his own entourage; thus he might come to dominate the city's judicial and educational system through a man almost entirely dependent on him for his status and livelihood.

Strong rulers were seldom in evidence between the mid tenth and mid twelfth centuries. In this period urban society was dominated by the local notables, who owed their wealth to landholding and commerce, and their social status to religious learning and piety. From these families were drawn not only the religious officials of the state but also a figure called *raᵓīs al-balad* (mayor), officially nominated by the prince or governor, but in fact chosen by consensus of the local notables to represent their own interests. The *raᵓīs* was able to enforce this role in moments of confrontation by calling on the *aḥdāth,* more numerous than and often nearly as well armed as the ruler's own troops. The *aḥdāth* were not always the docile servants of the notables, for they were drawn largely from the poor and disaffected of the city's southwest quarter. They never mounted a systematic revolt against the established social order, but they were always a potential source of violence and turmoil, both a threat and a support for the city's notables.

Far more than their predecessors, Nūr al-Dīn and the Ayyubids succeeded in co-opting the urban notables into their own relatively effective military-administrative apparatus. Thus the visible institutions of urban autonomy disappeared for about two centuries. Under the Mamluks some reemergence of these institutions can be detected, though in a far more fragmented and less effective form. The armed youth gangs of the fourteenth and fifteenth centuries apparently represented not the whole urban populace but particular quarters, and they engaged in factional fighting as much as in protest against the Mamluk rulers. Nor was there a single *raᵓīs al-balad,* but instead many chiefs of quarters, chosen by the Mamluks largely to carry out official policies in their districts. The Mamluk state had vastly greater force at its disposal than did the local populace, and therefore urban solidarity had little opportunity to flourish. The social basis of the quarters is little understood; to some extent they seem to have formed around ethnic groups, occupational groups, or immigrants from the same tribe or village. In spite of the endemic interquarter tensions of Mamluk times, the quarters seem not to have become walled compounds before the Ottoman conquest.

DAMASCUS AS A CENTER OF ISLAMIC LIFE

From an early period Damascus had a tradition of Islamic learning: the historian Ibn Shihāb al-Zuhrī (671–742), though a native of Medina, spent the last two decades of his life there; and the jurist al-Awzāᶜī (*d.* 774), one of the "founding fathers" of *sharīᶜa* jurisprudence, was born there. That Damascus should develop such a tradition is not surprising, considering the presence there of the caliphal court until 750 and the interest in Islamic issues among a number of the Umayyads. But even in the early eighth century Damascus was far outclassed as a center of Islamic thought by Al-Kufa, Basra, Medina, and even Egypt. During the Abbasid and Fatimid periods, Damascus was very much an intellectual backwater.

As Damascus became a Muslim town, it adhered solidly to a Sunni outlook—partly in protest, perhaps, against Abbasid and Fatimid pretensions. By the early eleventh century the city's notables were generally committed to the legal doctrine of al-Shāfiᶜī and the theology of al-Ashᶜarī, and this outlook remained strongly imbedded in Damascene society throughout the Middle Ages. The early Seljukid period brought some competition, however— the first Hanbali scholars (harsh opponents of Ashᶜarī theology), and the emergence of a local Hanafite school as a result of the establishment of a Turkish court and army.

Damascus became a major center of Islamic learning only with the arrival of Nūr al-Dīn. Not only did he establish numerous madrasahs and related institutions, but he also strongly encouraged local scholars such as Ibn ᶜAsāqir (*d.* 1176) and the Hanbalis of

Ṣāliḥīya. More important, he appointed as madrasah professors many outstanding scholars who had been attracted to his court from Mesopotamia and Iran. Under the Ayyubids Damascus became perhaps the leading center of religious learning in the Muslim world, a place where scholars from all four "orthodox" schools produced many of the definitive syntheses in grammar, methodology of ḥadīth studies, and applied jurisprudence. In early Mamluk times Cairo became an increasingly important rival, but Damascus retained an undimmed luster until the mid fourteenth century.

The religious significance of Damascus was not entirely connected with its stature as a center of learning, however. The city and its environs had many sacred sites, some Islamic, others very ancient indeed. These sites were noted in Islamic literature as early as the tenth century; by the twelfth a considerable body of writing was devoted to them. Among the Islamic sites were the tombs of several companions of Muḥammad. A nice irony was the reverence paid both to the tomb of Muᶜāwiya and to shrines devoted to ᶜAlī and his family. The figure of Jesus had considerable importance in local lore, and the head of John the Baptist was supposed to be preserved in a shrine in the Umayyad Mosque. On Mt. Qāsyūn there were shrines variously associated with Adam, Cain and Abel, Abraham, the Seven Sleepers, and al-Khiḍr. By the mid twelfth century Damascus enjoyed a sanctity surpassed in Syria only by Jerusalem and Hebron. For the modern scholar the religious life of Damascus between 1150 and 1350 has a further significance, for in it is represented the whole range of behavior, values, and doctrines to be found in Sunni Islam during the later Middle Ages.

BIBLIOGRAPHY

Sources in translation. Maurice Gaudefroy-Demombynes, *La Syrie à l'époque des Mamelouks d'après les auteurs arabes* (1923); Ibn ᶜAsāqir, *La description de Damas d'Ibn ᶜAsākir,* Nikita Elisséeff, trans. (1959), describes the city in the late twelfth century, with an invaluable map of the medieval city; Ibn al-Qalānisī, *Dhayl Tāᵓrīkh Dimashq:* excerpts trans. by H. A. R. Gibb, *The Damascus Chronicle of the Crusades* (1932), French trans. by Roger Le Tourneau, *Damas de 1075 à 1154* (1952); Guy Le Strange, *Palestine Under the Moslems* (1890, repr. 1970); Henri Sauvaire, "Description de Damas," in *Journal asiatique,* 9th ser. 3–7 (1894–1896).

Studies. Eliyahu Ashtor-Strauss, "L'administration urbaine en Syrie médiévale," in *Rivista degli studi orientali,* 31 (1956); Thierry Bianquis, "Notables ou malandrins d'origine rurale à Damas à l'époque fatimide," in *Bulletin d'études orientales,* 26 (1973); Claude Cahen, "Mouvements populaires et autonomisme urbain dans l'Asie musulmane du moyen âge," in *Arabica,* 5 (1958) and 6 (1959); Nikita Elisséeff, "Dimashḳ," in *Encyclopedia of Islam,* new ed. II (1965), and *Nūr ad-Dīn* (in French), 3 vols. (1967); Joan Gilbert, "Institutionalization of Muslim Scholarship and Professionalization of the ᶜUlamāᵓ in Medieval Damascus," in *Studia islamica,* 52 (1980); Axel Havemann, *Riᵓasa und Qaḍāᵓ* (1975); R. Stephen Humphreys, *From Saladin to the Mongols* (1977); Ira M. Lapidus, *Muslim Cities in the Later Middle Ages* (1967); Jean Sauvaget, "Esquisse d'une histoire de la ville de Damas," in *Revue des études islamiques,* 8 (1934), and *Les monuments historiques de Damas* (1932); Peter von Sievers, "Military, Merchants, and Nomads: The Social Evolution of the Syrian Cities and Countryside During the Classical Period, 780–969/164–358," in *Der Islam,* 56 (1979); Janine Sourdel-Thomine, "Les anciens lieux de pèlerinage damascains d'après les sources arabes," in *Bulletin d'études orientales,* 14 (1952–1954); Karl Wulzinger and Carl Watzinger, *Damaskus, die islamische Stadt* (1924).

R. STEPHEN HUMPHREYS

[See also **Abbasids; Ayyubids; Fatimids; Ikhshidids; Muᶜāwiya; Saladin; Seljuks; Syria; Tulunids; ᶜUlamāᵓ; Umayyads; Yazīd ibn Muᶜāwiya.**]

DAMMARTIN, DROUET DE. See **Drouet of Dammartin.**

DAMMARTIN, GUY DE. See **Guy of Dammartin.**

DANÇA GENERAL DE LA MUERTE, a Spanish dance of death preserved in a manuscript from the second half of the fifteenth century. It consists of seventy-nine stanzas of *arte mayor* with the rhyme scheme *a b a b b c c b.*

After a short moral introduction, Death opens the dance by calling for two maidens, who symbolize fleeting beauty and pride. He then invites each social class to come forward, alternating between clergy (from the pope to the humblest churchman) and laymen (from the emperor to a Muslim doctor of law). In the final stanzas Death summons a rabbi and an *alfaquí* (typical figures of medieval Spanish society), along with "anyone remaining who has not been specifically called." The last ones are asked to dedicate themselves to God.

Invited to participate in the dance, each person looks for excuses. This reluctance gives Death the opportunity to criticize each group. The only one to escape his remarks is a black friar (a Benedictine monk).

The *Dança general de la Muerte* differs from the French *danse macabre* in that there is a reprimand of Death, who in turn launches a scathing and relentless criticism against all strata of society. The democratic aspect of the work is also shown by its indicting equally the powerful and the weak.

Written about 1400, the *Dança general* may be the earliest dance of death known. It also gives the impression that its author could have been a monk from eastern Spain. In 1520 an enlarged edition was printed at Seville by Juan Varela de Salamanca. It has additional lay characters of very popular nature, upsetting the careful balance between the religious and civil figures of the original.

BIBLIOGRAPHY

Joël Saugnieux, *Les danses macabres de France et d'Espagne et leurs prolongements littéraires* (1972); Josep M. Sola-Solé, *La Dança general de la Muerte* (1981); Florence Whyte, *The Dance of Death in Spain and Catalonia* (1931, repr. 1977).

JOSEP M. SOLA-SOLÉ

[See also **Danse Macabre; Spanish Satirical Literature.**]

DANCE. Archival records, iconography, and literary sources indicate that dance was an important part of daily life in Europe throughout the Middle Ages and earlier. Unfortunately, relatively few pieces of known dance music have been preserved from before the fifteenth century, and detailed knowledge of dance steps does not exist from prior to the middle of that century.

Dances and dance songs were not part of secular festivities exclusively; they were also important in religious ceremonies from the very beginning of Christianity. Numerous lyrics have survived in which dancing is mentioned as a part of festive occasions of all kinds; there are many liturgical texts with terms that suggest dancing as a probable accompaniment to the sung text; and throughout the Middle Ages there is documentation of dances as a part of the celebrations of Easter and Christmas. Frequent church warnings against dancing because of its pagan reference suggest that it was often prac-

ticed, and in 1325 the general chapter in Paris forbade clerics, under pain of excommunication, from participation in dances, with the exceptions of Christmastime and the feasts of St. Nicholas and St. Catherine. There is no evidence to suggest that the dance steps performed in a sacred context were different from those in the secular, nor that there was a significant difference between the dances of the lower and upper classes prior to the fifteenth century.

In literature such as Boccaccio's *Decameron* we are told that dancing was performed sometimes to dance songs and at other times to dance tunes played on a variety of instruments. The instruments most often mentioned and depicted for dances are the vielle, rebec, bagpipe, pipe and tabor, portative organ, harp, and lute-type plucked instruments, large and small. Percussion instruments are also mentioned in many texts and depicted in the iconography, and it is probable that some dances were performed to percussion instruments such as nakers (a pair of small pitched drums), tambourine, or tabor (small hand drum), without melody, while the dancers sang. In two well-known frescoes of the fourteenth century, *The Effects of Good Government* in the Palazzo Pubblico of Siena, and *The Way to Salvation* in the Spanish Chapel of S. Maria Novella in Florence, the dancers are accompanied only by a tambourine player whose open mouth indicates that she is singing a dance song while keeping a rhythm for the dancers.

Many late-medieval secular song forms are thought to have been dance songs at one time, perhaps from their origin. The French word *ballade* and its Italian counterpart *ballata* (both from Latin: *ballare*, to dance) are known to have meant "dance song" in the thirteenth and fourteenth centuries in addition to their specific reference in the fourteenth century to set forms of poetry and music (the two forms are not identical). The majority of these early dance songs have multiple verses and a refrain, and one possible performance mode may have been by a solo singer for the verses, followed by the entire group singing the refrain. Any number of dance steps and formations are possible to these songs, but the common refrain suggests the possibility of group dances, with circle or line formations, as in the frescoes mentioned above. The names "rondeau" (from Latin: *rondellus,* "round") and "carol" for two of the earliest known medieval dance songs also indicate round dances, in which the dancers join hands in a circle and perform a series of steps in unison; the

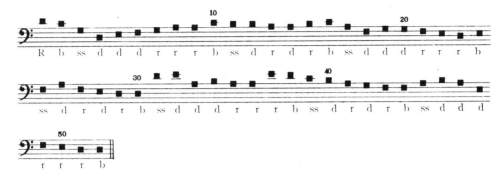

"La haulte Bourgongne." From Frederick Crane, *Materials for the Study of the Fifteenth-century Basse Danse* (1968), 52. REPRODUCED WITH PERMISSION OF THE INSTITUTE OF MEDIEVAL MUSIC, BROOKLYN

song form "virelai" also suggests a dance—*virer* means "to twist." Iconographic evidence shows three kinds of dances: solo, couples, and line or round dances, but there is no clear information about which dances are associated with which ceremonies or songs.

The only clear theoretical statement about dance prior to the fifteenth century is by Johannes de Grocheio in his *De musica* (*ca.* 1300), in which he provides descriptions of dance songs and instrumental dance music under the heading of secular music. He gives the names of dance songs as *rotundellus* (round), *stantipes* (*estampie*), and *ductia*. Johannes states that all of the forms have a refrain, and differ from one another in their length and the amount of line agreement—presumably he refers to poetic feet and rhyme. He does not state how these forms are danced other than that the round and *ductia* are performed in chorus—that is, round or line steps. His description of *stantipes* is that it has a diversity in both melody and rhyme of its "parts" (verse lines?), and a refrain, but there is no mention of dance steps or formation.

No examples of *ductia* have been identified, but a number of round texts with music survive. Grocheio's description is rather vague as to the particulars of the round form, other than that it turns back on itself in the manner of a circle, but it has been suggested that the repertory includes the sixty *rondeaux* in the eleventh fascicle of Florence, Biblioteca Medicea-Laurenziana, MS Pluteo 29. 1. Twenty texts from the thirteenth and early fourteenth centuries have been identified as *estampies*, one with music, none of which agree exactly with either Grocheio's description of the vocal *estampie* or with two other medieval descriptions contained in the early-fourteenth-century poetry treatises, the *Leys d'amours* and the *Doctrina de dictatz*. They all lack

both the rhyme scheme and the refrain called for in the contemporary descriptions. The only *estampie* for which both music and text survive, *Kalenda maya* (*ca.* 1200), conforms more to Grocheio's description of the instrumental *estampie* than to the vocal version, and there is evidence that it may originally have been an instrumental composition. The text, by troubadour Raimbaut de Vaqueiras (*fl.* 1180–1207), is reported to have been composed to the tune of an *estampida* (*estampie*) that he heard performed by two vielle players.

Grocheio describes two untexted instrumental forms as well, also called *ductia* and *stantipes* (*estampie*). He differentiates between them only inasmuch as the *ductia* has an "appropriate percussive beat" and the *estampie* has not, and the *ductia* has three or four double versicles (repeated musical phrases with different endings for the first and second closings), while the *estampie* has six or seven. Siegmund Levarie suggests that the musical differ-

Guglielmo da Pesaro, Jewish dancing master and two of his pupils performing a basse danse. From Guglielmo da Pesaro, *Treatise on Dancing, ca.* 1463. BIBLIOTHÈQUE NATIONALE, FONDS ITAL. 973, fol. 21v

ence between the two dances indicated by Grocheio's enigmatic statement about "percussive beat" refers to the *ductia*'s having the same number of beats in each versicle whereas the *estampie* has an irregular number. Part of this theory is supported by Grocheio's statement that the *estampie* has an uneven rhythm that requires the dancers to be very attentive, and the fact that all of the known *estampies* have versicles of irregular length. Although no music survives with the designation *ductia,* some dance pieces may be tentatively identified as such in the light of Levarie's theory.

Thirty-six extant textless compositions from before 1400 are believed to be instrumental dances. Twenty-six are actually identified in their sources as dances, and the other ten can tentatively be added because of their musical similarities to the others. Sixteen are identified as *estampies;* eight are found in the thirteenth-century French source Paris, Bibliothèque Nationale, MS 844, and eight in the late-fourteenth-century Italian MS London, British Library, Add. 29987. The French *estampies* agree with Grocheio's description in that they all have double versicles with different open *(ouvert)* and close *(clos)* endings. The number of versicles varies from four to seven, compared with Grocheio's description of six or seven, but the actual number may not be very important. They have relatively short versicles of from eight to twenty units of measure, and are all in triple meter. The eight Italian dances, identified in the manuscript as *istanpitte,* are somewhat different. They have four and five double versicles ranging in length from twenty to more than one hundred units of measure, and are all in duple meter (sometimes triply subdivided). These *estampies* are unusual in that they employ complex formal schemes of melodic repetition and melodic and scalar formations that resemble traditional instrumental forms from the eastern Mediterranean countries more clearly than the music of western Europe.

All but three of the other named dances are found in the Italian MS London, British Library, Add. 29987, and are not described in any theoretical sources. Four of them, titled *salterello (sic),* have four and six double versicles varying in length from eight to fifty units of measure, and are in duple meter (sometimes triply subdivided). Another is named *trotto,* but is otherwise musically identical to the *salterelli,* and there are two dance pairs: *Lamento di Tristano* and *La Manfredina,* each followed by a *rotta.* The main dances are in duple meter and have three relatively short double versicles. The *rotte* are

similarly constructed, having melodic material related to the main dance in the fashion found in the dance pairs of later centuries—that is, a stately principal dance followed by a quick after-dance. These two are the earliest known dance pairs, and are possibly related to the sets of dances described as fifteenth-century Italian *balli* and to the sets of dances that flourished all over Europe from the sixteenth century on.

Two additional dances in the French Paris, Bibliothèque Nationale, MS fr. 844, are named *dansse real* and *danse.* They are in triple rhythm, as are the *estampies* in the same manuscript, but they have only three versicles each; the versicles are of equal length, and therefore they may be *ductia.* The remaining named dance is *Bel fiore dança* in the Faenza Codex (Faenza, Biblioteca Comunale, MS 117), which does not resemble any other known dance. It is not separated into versicles and may be incomplete.

Of the unnamed instrumental compositions, one in Paris, Bibliothèque Nationale, MS fr. 844, and three in London, British Library, MS Harley 978, with three, four, and five double versicles of equal length, may also be *ductia.* Three compositions in the Robertsbridge Codex (London, British Library, MS Add. 28550), and two in the Faenza Codex resemble the more complex formal makeup of the Italian *estampies,* and a thirteenth-century English composition in Oxford, Bodleian Library, MS Douce 139, with ten versicles, may have a repeating refrain in the nature of the dance songs described by Grocheio.

All surviving medieval instrumental dance pieces are unique. The extremely small number may be accounted for by the tradition in which dance musicians improvised much of their repertory and learned the remainder by rote. In no surviving iconography is a dance musician depicted playing from music.

There appears to have been a substantial change in the dances of the aristocrats by the fifteenth century. The lower classes continued to dance in their traditional manner, but a new form, the *bassedanse* (Italian: *bassadanza*), replaced whatever may have preceded it as the principal dance of the upper classes.

The *bassedanse* developed some time in the early fifteenth century in two centers, Burgundy and Lombardy, from which it spread quickly throughout the rest of Europe. The name refers to the stately steps, in which the feet were kept relatively low *(basses)* to the floor, as distinguished from the jumping or leaping steps of the more energetic dances. The similarity of the names and the basic steps in both France and Italy suggests that the dance had a single original format, but the descriptions from the mid fifteenth century show that by that time the two traditions were separate.

Detailed information concerning the steps and the music of the *bassedanse* are preserved in several music manuscripts and dance instruction manuals, beginning in the middle of the fifteenth century, from Italy, France, Spain, England, and Germany. The first dated source is the 1463 copy of Guglielmo Ebreo's *De pratica seu arte tripudii vulgare opusculum*, though an earlier dance manual, now lost, is known to have been presented to Ippolita Sforza in 1455.

The *bassedanse* of the northern areas required the dancers to proceed in couples through a series of different kinds of steps: *révérence* (R), a formalized bow; *simple* (ss), a slow step forward with the left foot, joined by the right; *double* (d), three steps forward and a joining of the feet; *branle* (b), turning of the body left, right, left, right, while the heels remain joined together and the feet do not move; and *reprise* (r), one foot moves behind the other, rise to the toes, then return to standing position with feet together. The steps were arranged in series differently for each particular *bassedanse*, thus requiring the dancers to rehearse frequently in order to learn the step variations and the sequences for the many dances. In some courts the nobles apparently attended dance lessons for several hours each day. A typical arrangement of the steps would be as shown in the accompanying illustration taken from Frederick Crane's book (1968).

In Italy the *bassadanza* included the steps and motions of the *bassedanse*, but it was sectional and had steps in addition to the stately steps of the French court dance described above. The original low steps of the northern dance were alternated with sections of *saltarello* and *quadinaria* in which more vigorous steps, including leaps, were used. Whereas the northern dance was performed only by couples who moved always forward, hand in hand in procession, the Italian dance included sections of dancing in file or in groups of three or more, and the steps moved in a variety of directions.

There was an additional Italian dance in the late fifteenth century called *ballo*, originally related to the *bassadanza*. The *ballo* also involved a series of contrasting steps, though it usually began with a quick step, in contrast to the opening slow step of the *bassadanza*. Some of the *balli* had thematic or programmatic organization such as *gelosia* (jealousy) or *malgratiosa* (ungraciousness), and the steps were choreographed in order to depict the theme. The programmatic aspect of the dance was not supplemented by mime, however, but carried out only by the steps, the patterns formed by the dancers, and body movements. The number of *ballo* steps were nine: in addition to the five *bassedanse* steps (in medieval Italian called *reverentia*, *sempio*, *doppio*, *meza volta*, and *represa*), the *ballo* included *continentia*, steps to the side; *volta tonda*, full turn; *movimento* and *salto*, leaping and skipping steps.

The extant repertory of fifteenth-century dance music includes nearly a hundred examples each of the *bassedanse* and the *bassadanza*, and seventy of the *ballo*. There is some correspondence between the French and Italian repertories, but for the most part they are separate. Some of the *bassedanse*, *bassadanza*, and *ballo* music was fully written out in two or three parts, but the largest portion of the repertories existed as a series of sustained notes to which a second, and often a third, part was improvised. The written long notes are directly related to the dance steps and determine the length of the dance. In performance the long notes were played by one instrument, elongated as written, and the other instrument(s) provided florid, improvised embellishment to enhance the written notes. The most frequently pictured instruments of the fifteenth century in performance of *bassedanse* are shawms and trombones, though other instrumental ensembles depicted are trumpet and shawms and flute and drum. The *bassedanse*, *bassadanza*, and *ballo* extended well into the sixteenth century until they were finally replaced by new dance forms of the late Renaissance.

BIBLIOGRAPHY

Pierre Aubry, *Estampies et danses royales* (1907); Jan ten Bokum, *De dansen van het trecento* (1967); Ingrid Brainard, "Bassedanse, Bassadanza, and Ballo in the 15th Century," in Joann W. Kealiinohomaku, ed., *Dance History Research* (1970), 64–79; Howard M. Brown, *Music in the French Secular Theater, 1400–1550* (1963); Manfred F. Bukofzer, "A Polyphonic Basse Dance of the Renaissance," in *Studies in Medieval and Renaissance Music* (1950); Frederick Crane, *Materials for the Study of the Fifteenth-century Basse Danse* (1968); Peter Dronke, *The Medieval Lyric* (1978); Robert Falck, "*Rondellus*, Canon, and Related Types," in *Journal of the American Musicological Society*, 25 (1972); Daniel Heartz, "The Basse Dance: Its Evolution Circa 1450–1550," in *Annales musicologiques*, 6

(1958–1963); Lloyd Hibberd, "*Estampie* and *Stantipes,*" in *Speculum,* **19** (1944); Johannes de Grocheio, *De musica,* ed. and trans. into German by Ernst Rohloff as *Die Quellenhandschriften zum Musiktraktat des Johannes de Grocheio* (1972); trans. by Albert Seay as *Concerning Music* (1973); Otto Kinkeldey, "Dance Tunes of the Fifteenth Century," in David G. Hughes, ed., *Instrumental Music* (1959), 3–30, 89–152; Siegmund Levarie, "Communications," in *Journal of the American Musicological Society,* **27** (1974); Timothy J. McGee, "Eastern Influences in Medieval European Dances," in Robert Falck and Timothy Rice, eds., *Cross-cultural Perspectives in Music* (1982), 79–100, and *Medieval Instrumental Dances* (forthcoming); Raymond Meylan, *L'énigme de la musique des basses danses du quinzième siècle* (1968); Gilbert Reaney, "Concerning the Origins of the Rondeau, Virelai, and Ballades Forms," in *Musica disciplina,* **6** (1952); Yvonne Rokseth, "Danses cléricales du XIIIᵉ siècle," in *Mélanges 1945 des publications de la Faculté des lettres de Strasbourg* (1947); Curt Sachs, *World History of the Dance* (1937).

TIMOTHY J. MCGEE

[See also **Ballade; Ballata; Ballette; Johannes de Grocheio; Musical Instruments, European; Rondeau; Virelai.**]

DANEGELD. The credit for originally suggesting the payment of danegeld is normally given to Sigeric, archbishop of Canterbury, who in 991, after the defeat of the English forces under Byrhtnoth at the Battle of Maldon, is said to have been the first to advise King Ethelred to buy off the marauding Danes. In fact this is a shade unfair, as there was a long history of tribute being paid to the Vikings in Britain and on the Continent. Alfred had bought peace for his people in the 870's, and there are many parallels in Frankish history. What distinguishes Ethelred's reign is the frequency and regularity of the imposts that finally resulted in the institutionalization of the custom. In the record preserved in the Anglo-Saxon Chronicle there are many references from the reign of Ethelred and its immediate aftermath: £10,000 in 991, £16,000 in 994, £24,000 in 1002, £36,000 in 1007, £3,000 (from East Kent) in 1009, £48,000 in 1012, and £72,000 in 1018 from all England after Cnut's succession, with an extra £10,500 from London. These payments are distinguished from the tribute, booty, and treasure that passed into Danish hands.

Some scholars have pointed out that the regularity of the figures (£16,000, £24,000, £36,000, £48,000, £72,000) may suggest approximations on the part of the chronicler, but they are better read as indication that the payments were keyed to the basic administrative and financial structure of the kingdom. The sums were no figment of the chronicler's imagination; massive numbers of silver coins from Ethelred's reign have turned up in Scandinavia. Inscriptions on memorial stones, notably in Sweden, tell of Scandinavians who did very well indeed from English geld. Estates in England were sold so that landowners could meet their obligations under the geld.

Methods of assessment and collection were based on long-established English systems of geld exaction, a land tax that worked, and the term "danegeld" was retained virtually as a synonym for "geld" (tax, tribute) long after the Danish menace had passed. In the eleventh century the history of danegeld is complicated for this reason. In the strict sense it meant a payment made to prevent attack, to buy off the Danes, but the geld system was also used to pay protecting crews to defend the English coast (heregeld), a tax element repealed by Edward the Confessor in 1049 and 1050 when he placed major responsibility for naval defense on the Cinque Ports.

The term "danegeld" nevertheless survived. The *Laws* of Henry I defined it as a tax formerly given to the Danish armies (the thingmen, that is, housecarls) at the rate of twelve pence for each hide per annum, and declared that penalties were incurred if the payment was not made at the appointed time. The assessment pattern was still in use in the 1160's, and the author of the *Dialogue of the Exchequer* (ca. 1179) described danegeld as a tax that had been paid annually up to the time of William I at the rate of two shillings of silver (twenty-four pence) for each hide, but one that was rarely paid in his day (or in the reigns of his successors). In fact danegeld was still recognized as an annual payment in the reign of Henry I, though it seems to have been collected only twice in the reign of his grandson, Henry II (1155 and 1162). The 1162 levy was the last true imposition of danegeld, though the assessments on which it was based were used for the "carucages" (land taxes) of Richard I's reign in 1194 and 1198.

BIBLIOGRAPHY

H. R. Loyn, *The Governance of England* (1984); Peter H. Sawyer, *The Age of the Vikings,* 2nd ed. (1971); Frank M. Stenton, *Anglo-Saxon England,* 3rd ed. (1971).

H. R. LOYN

[See also **Taxation, English; Vikings.**]

DANELAGH. See **Danelaw.**

DANELAW, a term of law in English history and also a geographical term. Legal thinkers in the post-Norman period saw England as divided into three parts: Wessex, Mercia, and the Danelaw. In extent the Danelaw was defined as England north and east of a line along the Thames estuary up the Lea (immediately east of London) to its source, and from there straight to Bedford and then up the Ouse to Watling Street and thence northwest across the country, leaving Warwickshire, Staffordshire, Oxford, Shropshire, and Cheshire within English England. The origins of the division rest firmly with the treaty made in the 880's between the West Saxon king, Alfred the Great, and Guthrum, the newly converted Danish king of East Anglia. The extraordinary persistence of social and legal distinctions along this rather nebulous border is one of the chief indicators of the depth and intensity of Danish settlement in England.

There was, as far as can be judged, little difference between West Saxon and Mercian law, but in the Danelaw such distinctions as a list of higher penalties than elsewhere for infringements of royal rights, a tendency to stereotype penalties for lesser offenses into a standard *lahslit* (an Anglo-Saxon borrowing from Old Norse, "a penalty for breaking the law"), and the imposition of some penalties according to a man's own rank rather than the rank of his lord testify to the strength of Danish custom. The presence of special panels of lawmen (iudices) in boroughs that owed much to Danish settlement, such as York, Lincoln, Stamford, and Chester, also suggests Scandinavian influence.

The Danelaw was far from uniform in its social and racial patterns, but some characteristics tended to identify it as a whole at the time of the Domesday survey in the late eleventh century, and to some extent right through the Middle Ages. There was no difference from English England in basic agrarian techniques, but overall the Danelaw was the home of a freer peasantry and was less heavily manorialized. The reasons for these social phenomena are complex, but it seems evident that the dislocation (though temporary) caused to royal and ecclesiastical tenure by the Scandinavian settlement in the late ninth and early tenth centuries was an important contributory cause. This is particularly true of areas of heavy settlement, such as parts of Yorkshire, the

territory dependent on the Five Boroughs (Lincoln, Nottingham, Derby, Stamford, and Leicester), and parts of East Anglia.

Patterns of assessment (six-carucate units in place of five hides), accountancy methods (the popularity of units of sixteen pence corresponding to the Scandinavian *ora*), the basic language structure, the existence of wapentakes as subdivisions of shires in place of the English hundreds, and personal name customs among the peasantry also served to distinguish the Danelaw from the rest of England well into the Middle Ages.

BIBLIOGRAPHY

H. R. Loyn, *The Vikings in Britain* (1977); Frank M. Stenton, *Anglo-Saxon England*, 3rd ed. (1971).

H. R. LOYN

[See also **Alfred the Great; England: Anglo-Saxon; Vikings.**]

DANISHMENDIDS, a Turkoman dynasty of northern, central, and eastern Anatolia. The main branch of the family (Sivas-Ankara-Kayseri) flourished from about 1071 to about 1174; the Malatya branch may be dated from about 1142 to about 1178. Their origins are obscure. According to some accounts, the founder of the family's fortunes, Aḥmed Dānishmend ibn ᶜAlī ibn Miẓrāb, the son of a Turkoman *beg* from Khwarizm and of the daughter of the Arabian emir of Malatya, married an Armenian princess. These fanciful tales point to the symbiotic nature of the Islamic-Christian culture of the frontier.

The Danishmendids were on the scene by the late 1080's, in possession of Ankara, Kayseri, and Sivas. The First Crusade prevented a growing Seljukid-Danishmendid rivalry from erupting into open war. The Danishmendids figured prominently in the Anatolian theater of the crusade, capturing Bohemond I of Antioch in 1100 and defeating the last crusader forces in Cappadocia. In 1102 Malatya fell to them, but was lost about 1106. The Danishmendid emir Ghāzī Gümüshtegin (1104–1134) successfully campaigned against Seljuks, other Turkish groups, and Christians. In 1124 he regained Malatya. In recognition of his victories over Christians, Caliph al-Mustarshid and Sultan Sanjar granted Gümüshtegin the title *malik* (king) in 1134. His son Muḥammad (1134–1142) ably defended himself against domestic

York

Lincoln

Nottingham

Derby

Leicester

Stamford

Chester

CHESHIRE

STAFFORDSHIRE

SHROPSHIRE

MERCIA

WARWICKSHIRE

WATLING STREET

D A N E L A W

EAST ANGLIA

Bedford

Thames   R.

Ouse

R.

London

WESSEX

THE DANELAW

revolts and the aggressive policies of Byzantine Emperor John II Komnenos. His death, however, signaled the fragmentation of the Danishmendid state. His brothers Yaghïbasan and ᶜAyn al-Dawla, and his son Dhu 'l-Nūn, vied for power. Seljukid and Byzantine interventions led to the creation of three separate branches of the dynasty.

Yaghïbasan's death in 1164 paved the way for the Seljukid acquisition of his lands, and then those of Dhu 'l-Nūn in 1168. Only the intervention of the Zangid Nūr al-Dīn prevented a complete takeover. When the latter died in 1174, the Seljuk Kïlïj Arslan II seized the central Anatolian possessions. Dhu 'l-Nūn was poisoned. After their victory at Myriokephalon (1176), a confrontation produced in part by Kïlïj Arslan's activities in Danishmendid lands, the Seljuks seized Malatya in 1178.

BIBLIOGRAPHY
Dânishmendnâme: as yet unpublished; see Virineia S. Garbuzova, *Skazanie o Melike Danishmende* (1959); Irène Mélikoff (-Sayar), ed., *La Geste de Melik Dāniṣmend* (1960); A. D. Mordtmann, "Die Dynastie der Danischmende," in *Zeitschrift der Deutschen morgenländischen Gesellschaft,* **30** (1876).

PETER B. GOLDEN

[See also **Bohemond I, Prince of Antioch; Crusades and Crusader States: To 1192.**]

DANSE MACABRE. Part of a late-medieval preoccupation with mortality, the dance of death united men of all stations in a step with skeletons. Its origins are postulated in illustrated sermon texts, but the earliest artistic example was the frescoed cemetery of the Church of the Holy Innocents in Paris (1424, destroyed; copied in Marchant woodcuts published in 1485). There are also cycles by Witz in Basel (1440) and Bernt Notke in Lübeck (1463), and woodcuts by Holbein the Younger (1538).

BIBLIOGRAPHY
James M. Clark, *The Dance of Death in the Middle Ages and the Renaissance* (1950); Hellmut Rosenfeld, *Der mittelalterliche Totentanz* (1954); Alberto Tenenti, *Il senso della morte e l'amore della vita nel Rinascimento* (1957).

LARRY SILVER

[See also **Dança General de la Muerte; Death and Burial, in Europe.**]

The Peddler and the Knight. Hans Holbein, *The Dance of Death,* 1538. THE BRITISH LIBRARY

DANTE ALIGHIERI. Universally acknowledged to have been the most important poet of the Middle Ages, Dante was born in Florence, probably near the end of May 1265, and died in Ravenna, 13 or 14 September 1321. These dates are now generally accepted, if still occasionally debated. Almost all the information we have about the man and his works is limited and problematic. While the next generation of major literary figures, including the other two "crowns" of Florence, Petrarch and Boccaccio, left a reasonable number of autograph manuscripts, there exists not a single shred of parchment bearing Dante's own hand. This is but one indication of the difficulty that students of his work confront. There is not even meaningful consensus concerning the dates and order of his various compositions, though recent research has made some progress in this area.

Without having written the *Comedy* (the epithet "Divine" was added to the title only in the Venetian edition of 1555), Dante would still be an extraordinary figure in the history of medieval literature.

Page from manuscript of the *Divine Comedy*, 14th century. FLORENCE, BIBLIOTECA MEDICEA LAURENZIANA, MS TEMPE. 1, c. 2

Nonetheless, the vast poem removes its author from the field of ordinary literary accomplishment and places him, along with Homer, Vergil, Ovid, Chaucer, Shakespeare, Cervantes, Goethe, Dostoevski, and perhaps a very few others, in the pantheon of the very greatest Western writers. The *Comedy* has created extraordinary enthusiasm in its readers since its first fragmentary divulgation during the author's lifetime. And while it was less read during the period 1570–1790, its audience since then probably exceeds that of any other single literary text.

The task of this presentation is not to explore the reasons for such enormous and enduring popularity, but to tell something of Dante's most pressing concerns. The narrative, occupying 100 cantos and told in the first person, recounts Dante's own imagined voyage (he is named at *Purgatorio,* XXX, 55) through Hell, Purgatory, and Paradise during Easter week of the year 1300. The first guide in the poem is the shade of Vergil, who presides over *Inferno* and the first thirty cantos of *Purgatorio*. Dante's choice of a pagan as guide in this passionately Christian poem has been, and continues to be, a wonder to his readers. And while many of Vergil's qualifications (poet of the Roman Empire, recorder of a visit to the underworld in *Aeneid* VI, master of the long narrative poem) help to give grounds for a defense of the surprising choice, they do not fully explain the desire to take so daring a poetic chance. We are forced to conclude that his readings in Vergil's texts had a deeply personal resonance for Dante, one in which the *Aeneid* and the Fourth Eclogue as well became instruments of a major reshaping of his plans and priorities.

The second guide causes no consternation on religious grounds, but might on others. She is Beatrice, the young woman whom Dante had celebrated in some of his earlier poems and in the *Vita nuova*. That he should have chosen her as his instructor as he moves from the Earthly Paradise (*Purgatorio,* XXX) through the nine spheres of the created heavens to the first version of the Empyrean (*Paradiso,* XXX) is indicative of the deeply personal nature of Dante's vision. It is only with the final guide, St. Bernard of Clairvaux (*Paradiso,* XXX–XXXIII), that we confront a being whose presence in a doctrinal poem would come as a surprise to almost no one. Had the progression of guides been, for example, Gregory the Great, Thomas Aquinas, and Bernard, a reader would have considerably less ground for suspension of belief. But Dante is not a poet who makes the task of the reader an easy one.

The *Comedy* culminates a series of reflections on a number of issues that are apparent in almost every stage of Dante's development. The more usual understandings of this development tend to see a unitary whole in the corpus, while some more recent ones—especially those advanced by several American critics—perceive a dialectical movement in Dante's thought in which earlier hypotheses are so greatly modified that they seem to be turned into their opposites. Nonetheless, and whatever one's own view of the matter, there is a remarkable tenacity of obsessive concerns throughout Dante's work. Controversial theoretical positions (in areas that may seem to be only distantly related to the major theological concerns of the works but are in fact vitally connected to them) are the hallmark of his thought. Three of the most noteworthy of these are the assertion of the cognitive worth of poetry (against those theologians who deny to poetry any significant function with respect to knowledge); the claim that the empire derives its independent authority directly from God and thus is not, in temporal things, under the direction of the church; the view that the vernacular is even more worthy of respect as a literary vehicle than the greatest examples of classical eloquence.

Almost nothing that Dante wrote is without the traces of at least one of these polemical positions, and the *Comedy* harmonizes all three in his widest and most daring arc. To select these three concerns from a corpus that is rich in others involves some foreshortening. Yet they do offer a related series of subjects that help to explain the power and uniqueness of Dante's thought, especially as this is translated into the poetry of the *Comedy*. And they are all centrally related to his most profound moral concerns, anchored in the quest for personal salvation, and to the theology that, drawn from St. Thomas' Christianized Aristotle more than any other source, accounts for so much of the structure of his actual and poetic universe.

Since Dante's autobiography, whether overtly or tacitly, serves as a (sometimes hidden) thread that pulls the various works together, this treatment will, benefiting from the previous labors of others, discuss his life in its relationship to the works. There will be no attempt here to offer précis of these works; treatment of them will be limited to characterizations of some of their essential concerns. Not only is the task facing anyone who would describe accurately the life and works of Dante nearly impossible, but it has already been accomplished in the best form it is likely to have in our time. With regard to such matters, Giorgio Petrocchi is, in the opinion of all who work on Dante, *il maestro di color che sanno* (Dante's phrase describing Aristotle at *Inferno*, IV, 131, "the master of those who know"). He has single-handedly produced not only the current best text of the *Comedy* (*La Commedia secondo l'antica vulgata*, 4 vols. [1966–1967]) but also the best available biographical-literary presentation of its author (first in *Itinerari danteschi* [1969]; now in "Biografia: Attività politica e letteraria," in *Enciclopedia Dantesca*, VI [1978]). While others have of course been consulted in the preparation of this article, many of its biographical data represent Petrocchi's judgments. Nonetheless, there are also opinions expressed here that are different in focus or even contrary to his.

1260–1270: THE POLITICAL SITUATION IN TUSCANY

Dante was baptized in S. Giovanni (see *Inferno*, XIX, 16f.; *Paradiso*, XXV, 8f.) 26 March 1266, Holy Saturday. The decade of his birth was marked, as the rest of his life would be, by nearly continual civil strife in Italy, a fact that may help to explain his later fascination with the works of Vergil, Statius, and Lucan, all of whose epics mirror the civil wars of ancient Rome. The principal parties to the dispute throughout the region were the Guelphs (loyal to the pope) and the Ghibellines (loyal to the emperor, or at least to the imperial cause). The year 1260 saw the great battle of Montaperti, near Siena, at which an allied force of Ghibellines, under Farinata degli Uberti (*Inferno*, X), totally defeated the Florentine Guelphs, whose casualties amounted to some 20,000—a staggering loss, perhaps one-fourth the population of the city.

Less than a year after Dante's birth the Guelph party, to which his family belonged, began its successful recuperation. On 26 February 1266 the battle of Benevento brought defeat and death to Manfred (*Purgatorio*, III), former king of Sicily and champion of the empire, at the hands of Charles of Anjou (brother of King Louis IX of France), who had come to Italy as champion of the papacy and to find land of his own to govern. Charles's victory over Manfred gave him the crown of Sicily and Naples; his subsequent defeat of Conradin at Tagliacozzo on 23 August 1268 consolidated his position (though he would lose Sicily in the Sicilian Vespers of 1282) and consolidated Guelph power in the south. (Charles's decision to behead Conradin—*Purgatorio*, XX—

also put an end to nearly 200 years of the house of Hohenstaufen's involvement in Italy.) Florentine Guelphs finally gained a measure of military revenge for Montaperti at the battle of Colle Val d'Elsa, 8 June 1269, where they inflicted a terrible defeat on the Sienese Ghibellines. In Florence they had expelled first part, then all, of the Ghibelline citizens in 1266 and 1267; then the city was given over to the protection of Charles of Anjou. Thus, by 1270 Florence was totally Guelph and would remain so throughout Dante's lifetime.

1270–1280

With the major exception of his early lyrics and the *Vita nuova* (for the early and continuing importance of Beatrice, see below), Dante's youth and young maturity were primarily devoted to action, not contemplation. The life of the mind would account for most of his effort only after his exile, which would take away, most fortunately for posterity, the opportunity for major and continuous political enterprise. Thus Dante, like his Paduan precursor Albertino Mussato, is one of the first Italian exemplars of what would become a modern European tradition, based in classical precedents, of the man of letters whose literary career is closely related to concrete experience of the complexities of human personality and, at times, inhuman event.

Little is known of Dante's education, but it seems likely that he began his study of grammar (that is, the elementary study of Latin) in 1277, the year his family arranged his eventual marriage to Gemma Donati (there exists a copy, dating from 1329, of this arrangement of 9 January 1277). It is a mere if pleasing coincidence that his formal relations with love and letters were thus probably initiated in the same year. The precise dates are not known, but Dante lost his mother (*ca.* 1270) and father (*ca.* 1281 or 1282) before he was eighteen; as the eldest of four or five children, he was not by wealth, family, or education left in the most promising of situations in a Florence that had been savagely torn by civil strife.

1280–1290

As Petrocchi has shown, the 1280's contained many important events in Dante's life for which there is little confirming testimony; the tentative approximations that follow are his: the first lyrics (perhaps under the influence of a second "encounter" with Beatrice) in 1283; marriage to Gemma Donati in 1285; birth of his first child, Giovanni, about 1287; presence in Bologna the same year; presence at mil-

itary engagements in 1286–1287 (the Florentine/ Sienese siege of Poggio S. Cecilia) and 1289 (as a cavalry officer at the battles of Campaldino and Caprona); first meetings that would be major influences on his poetry with Brunetto Latini, Guido Cavalcanti, perhaps Cino da Pistoia, in 1289; death of Beatrice in 1290.

Petrocchi's forceful and welcome point is that too many attempts to develop a chronology for these years are based on preconceived notions of "development" in Dante that pay no heed to the patent fact that he was capable of thinking along several paths at the same time and, in any case, was not constrained to make his mind run in lines narrowly parallel to his absolute experience. Amid the confused and confusing suppositions that characterize any effort to order many possibilities, Petrocchi has offered evidence for what he considers an indisputable stay at Bologna in 1287, a visit that brought Dante into contact with the currents of thought of that city and its university. The year 1290 found Dante married, possibly a father, a man of some (informal) education but more than a little literary inclination and ability, a citizen-soldier who had twice been tried in battle. It is in the following decade that the probable course of his life, had it not been drastically altered by the events of 1300–1302, begins to become manifest.

BEATRICE

The only longer work composed during Dante's years in Florence is the *Vita nuova*. The truly extraordinary achievement wrought in what he referred to as a "little book" (*libello*) is of course overshadowed by the magnificence of the *Comedy*. Had Dante died or been put to death during the early years of exile, were the *Vita nuova* all that had been preserved of his work, at least some literary historians would have realized that in this young Florentine, Italian literature had taken a momentous turn. Here, for the first time in the vernacular, a poet has put a series of his own poems into a meaningful sequence surrounded by glosses of his own devising that are—at least as strikingly—also in the vernacular. There is nothing like this, on formal grounds alone, in previous vernacular literature.

Yet the momentousness of the *libello* resides not only in its form. For here, after nearly two centuries of Italian love poetry, is another kind of revolution. Where previous poets had proclaimed that their ladies were quite extraordinary, even, on occasion (as in the case of Guido Guinizelli), angelic in their capacity to make their lovers aspire toward a higher good, none had gone as far as Dante would dare in his claims for Beatrice. A careful reading of the *Vita nuova*—especially of the forty-two prose chapters that, composed probably in 1292 or 1293, inform the meaning of the thirty-one assembled earlier poems—reveals the full scope of Dante's extravagant claims: his Beatrice is no conventional poet's lady, but the chosen representative of Jesus Christ on earth. The christological iconography with which Dante imbues Beatrice's actions and being is strikingly clear, so much so that later Renaissance editors of the text (rather like some later purveyors of a bowdlerized Shakespeare) were pleased to edit away such indications when they were distressed by them.

Scholars are still divided concerning the historicity of the "love story" recorded in the *Vita nuova,* even though most tend to support the notion that Beatrice was a real woman, Beatrice Portinari, born in 1266, married to Simone de' Bardi in 1287, died in 1290. Perhaps more important than the issue is the patent fact, which has received insufficient attention, that by dealing with the events that he records in a historical narrative, Dante has attempted to move fiction into another realm, one shared by the truest, even sacrosanct, histories, those found in the Bible and in such earlier Italian writings as the lives of St. Francis. For a poet to be aware of possessing such a possibility in his creative choice is to challenge the conventional boundaries of his vision and craft. It is not a long step from the *Vita nuova* to the *Comedy,* although it would take Dante fifteen years to return to the promise with which he concluded the earlier work: " . . . if my life last some years, I hope to say of her what has never been said of another woman." The *Comedy* centrally and richly fulfills this promise; but not before it was, apparently, abandoned.

1290–1300

These two dates, within the fictions of the *Vita nuova* and the *Comedy,* are crucial: the death of Beatrice, the date of the vision of the afterworld. Looking back to the years that followed the completion of the *Vita nuova* from the vantage point of the *Comedy* (for instance, *Inferno,* I, XV; *Purgatorio,* XXX–XXXI), Dante seems to see them principally as a time of error in his life (and perhaps in his work as well). The question of the exact nature of this wandering from the true path has long vexed the commentators, and perhaps always will.

One thing—and perhaps only one—is clear: whatever Dante later berates himself for having done

(or not having done) involved some form of rejection of Beatrice, whether on moral (love for other women), intellectual (following a "wrong" philosophical path), or even stylistic grounds (deserting vernacular poetry for philosophical prose). Still other hypotheses have been advanced; these three are perhaps the most likely ones, and all of them may well be involved in his later self-criticism. Yet if, from the later viewpoint, Dante may have felt that his literary or personal activities at this period were less than praiseworthy, the second half of the 1290's was also the time of his most intense civic service to Florence and must have offered him considerable satisfaction.

Between 1295 and 1301, inscribed as a member of a guild (that of the doctors and apothecaries), Dante profited from an antiaristocratic trend in Florentine politics to the extent that he served his city in various councils and embassies. Here a word is appropriate in order to clarify a secondary division in Tuscan politics, that of Guelphs into Blacks and Whites. This additional factionalism originated in 1300 in Pistoia, where, according to Benvenuto da Imola, it arose from an event so trivial that he must have smiled to report it—a snowball fight. The resulting civil war was more between leagues of allied families than between opposing political philosophies. When the leaders of both factions were imprisoned in Florence, in the hopes of repacifying Pistoia, the dispute spilled over into the streets of Dante's city in a common street brawl.

Florentine Guelphs split into Black and White factions along family lines, not political ones. (Once they were exiled in 1302, however, the Whites tended to take on a new political coloration out of necessity, as they found themselves unwillingly allied with their former enemies, the now equally banished Ghibellines.) Dante's partisanship for the Whites would shortly prove to have been at his own cost. At that time, his literary career, though it had come to seem promising, nonetheless appeared to him less appealing than a political one. In any case the last years of the thirteenth century and the first of the fourteenth were not marked by major literary activity on his part, at least not when they are compared to the years in which exile would make political activity difficult, if not impossible.

Still, there are the lyrics and odes (*canzoni*) that are probably to be assigned to this period, the poems to Lisetta and to the *pargoletta,* as well as the stupefying longer poems to the "stony lady" (the so-called *rime petrose*), works that are as disturbing and powerful today as when they were written (perhaps *ca.* 1297), as well as the lengthy "moral odes." What impresses most in the poems of this period is the experimental nature of Dante's work. We become aware of a writer capable of several, even many, voices, capable of giving himself entirely to each, and yet perhaps not convinced that any is eventually "right" for him. Such a view, which may be advanced only tentatively (the problems in dating these compositions remain severe), would help explain, at least generally, Dante's later desire to censure the works that followed the *Vita nuova.* For if that was the writing that held to the true way (*Purgatorio,* XXX, 130), any other path was a false one. All that can be said is that the dates offered in the *Vita nuova* (death of Beatrice in June 1290) and the *Comedy* (descent into hell undertaken under Vergil's guidance and at Beatrice's instigation 8 April [or, as is perhaps more likely, 25 March] 1300) insist on a ten-year divergence from the true way. It was to be the next five years that witnessed the climactic and crucial events in his personal life, events that had the greatest importance in determining his future as a writer.

1300–1305

With the banishment in 1300 of Corso Donati, the principal figure among the Black Guelphs, Dante's party strengthened its position. (While some believe that Dante made the pilgrimage to Rome during this jubilee year declared by Pope Boniface VIII, even that he was in Rome on Good Friday, 8 April 1300, there is no positive evidence to support this attractive legend. And there is the following negative argument: Would Dante have failed to communicate his pleasure and pride in having been in that city on this significant day? The reference to two-way traffic on the bridge before Castel Sant'Angelo during the jubilee [*Inferno,* XVIII, 28–33] is probably better explained as the result of the descriptions that Dante heard from returned pilgrims or from Romans when he visited the city the following year.)

On 7 May 1300 Dante took part in an embassy on behalf of the ruling White faction to San Gimignano. On 13 June he was elected one of the six priors of Florence, thus coming to the high point of his political career; his success led swiftly and dramatically to his exile. For the next two months (the term of office of the popularly elected priors) were tumultuous, marked in particular by another street brawl, this one between a group of aristocrats and members of the popular faction. The result was the

banishment by the priors of fifteen aristocrats and their families, Black and White alike. Among those banished—and, indeed, soon to die as a direct result of his banishment and exposure to malaria in the pestilential climate of Sarzana—was Dante's former "first friend," Guido Cavalcanti. Some sense of his troubled feelings about his involvement in Guido's death undoubtedly informed his imagined meeting with the dead poet's father in *Inferno, X.*

During these and later events Dante's role seems to have grown in importance. Historians of the period see him as increasingly opposed to the entreaties of Pope Boniface VIII, so much so that he became the center of antagonism to the pope within the White faction. The *Comedy* offers some confirming testimony for this view, for hardly another mortal is treated as scathingly so many times as is Boniface. His first overt presence in the poem occurs in a brilliantly malicious scene (*Inferno, XIX*) in which Pope Nicholas III mistakes the visiting Dante for Boniface, who has arrived to serve his sentence for simony in the eternal prison. (Boniface was elected in 1294 and died in 1303; thus, at the time of the imagined journey, he was the incumbent pope.) Dante's obsessive disapproval of Boniface is evident in several other vituperations throughout the poem, ending only with St. Peter's declamation against Boniface as usurper of the papal prerogatives that he himself had established (*Paradiso,* XXVII, 22) and Beatrice's very last words in the poem (*Paradiso,* XXX, 148), so strikingly cruel a moment of invective that it has turned even some of Dante's commentators against him.

If Dante's campaign against Boniface in his poem has succeeded in making generations of readers see this impressive pope as the enemy of Christendom, his actual efforts were totally unsuccessful. His warnings against Boniface were not heeded by his fellow Whites; the papal forces, represented by Matteo d'Acquasparta and the landless French prince Charles of Valois (despised by Dante as the secular agent of Boniface's nefarious schemes), proved to be devious and clever in their attempt to gain political control of Florence. As alarm grew among the Whites, they planned—too late—to appeal directly to the pope in an attempt to reduce the pressure that Charles and his associates were putting on the city on behalf of the Blacks and of their own ends.

While no finally convincing positive evidence exists, a long tradition supposes that Dante was one of those present in an embassy sent to Boniface in Rome in the autumn of 1301 and, further, that as a particularly virulent opponent of the pope's cause, he was "invited" to remain behind at the papal court while the other ambassadors were allowed to return to Florence. During his absence Charles and the Blacks had their way. On 1 November 1301 Charles entered the city to restore "peace." A few days later, and clearly with the consent of the pope's legate, Corso Donati and a group of exiled Blacks sneaked into the city, robbed, murdered, and pillaged for five days, and drove the surviving Whites into exile.

Whether he was in Rome during these dreadful events, on the way home, or simply out of the city for some other reason, Dante was condemned to exile in January 1302 by the Black priorate, which had been installed in November. Thus Dante saw his native city for the last time late in 1301; the accusation of barratry (misuse of the goods of the state) lodged aginst him (see *Inferno*, XXI–XXII) was almost certainly the result of the desire for political revenge, instant revisionism applied to one who was seen by his enemies as having used his priorate as a means of implementing his personal hostility toward the Blacks. When Dante did not return to pay the fine imposed as penalty and as "reentry fee" (his return would not have been treated with equanimity in any case), his sentence, two years of exile, was revised to a far harsher penalty: to be burned at the stake if ever he returned to Florence (10 March 1302). All his goods were confiscated. He became a man without a home.

Dante and other exiled Whites were almost certainly in contact in 1302, first at Gargonza, then at S. Godenzo, in an effort to organize military operations that would regain the city for them. In the autumn of 1302 the campaign was already losing ground; Dante was at Forlì, which was governed by Scarpetta degli Ordelaffi, a Ghibelline who found little difficulty in siding with White Guelphs out of common cause against the papal forces. Dante was probably still there when, in the spring of 1303, the Blacks defeated the forces of the Whites and Ghibellines at the battle of the Mugello. Petrocchi has established what is now likely to stand as the probable, even definitive, chronology of these complicated years in Dante's life: in May–June 1303, Dante left Forlì and went to Verona, where he stayed until the death of Bartolomeo della Scala, lord of the city, 7 March 1304.

At this point, either because of the hostility of Alboino della Scala, the new ruler of Verona, or (as is more likely in Petrocchi's view) because of hopes aroused by the plans of the new pope, Benedict XI

(1303–1304), to "repacify" Florence by agency of Cardinal Niccolò da Prato, Dante returned to Tuscany, probably to Arezzo. By June 1304 the Blacks had consolidated their triumphs. It was probably at this period that Dante broke with his fellow White exiles, who still desired to do battle, and who did so disastrously on 20 July 1304 at La Lastra. Petrocchi calls attention to the historical coincidence of the date of this battle and the birth of Petrarch, a coincidence that may also have included the presence of Dante in Arezzo, in which case Italy's two greatest poets occupied the same geographical place for the only time in their lives.

1304–1308: DE VULGARI ELOQUENTIA AND CONVIVIO

While little enough is known of Dante's activities in the earlier stages of his life in Florence and in the first years of exile, almost nothing is known with certainty about the next phase, except that it included the composition of two major unfinished works and the beginning of the *Comedy*. It is also at this time (1305) that the pope left Rome for Avignon, the city from which Pope Clement V (1305–1314) was to have, in Dante's eyes, so malevolent an influence on church and empire (see *Inferno*, XIX; *Purgatorio*, XX, XXXII; *Paradiso*, XVII, XXVII, XXX). If Dante left Arezzo in 1304, it is not known where he settled next. Treviso, Lunigiana, Lucca, Padua, and Venice were some of his possible temporary homes during the next few years. Petrocchi tentatively advances the following possible chronology: 1303–1304, Verona, *De vulgari eloquentia*; 1304–1308 (?), Lunigiana, *Convivio*; 1306–1309 (?), Lucca, *Inferno*.

Wherever he wrote them, the first two extended works of the exile, though vastly overshadowed by the *Comedy* and underattended also because they were never finished, are of more than passing interest. *De vulgari eloquentia*, Dante's Latin treatise in defense of the vulgar tongue, was intended, on internal evidence, to contain four books. Two of these exist, the second unfinished. Internal evidence also indicates that he began work no earlier than 1303 and concluded no later than early 1305; the work seems to have been begun after Dante had begun work on the *Convivio*: a passage in that work (I, v, 9) refers to his intention to write a little book concerning vernacular eloquence.

While there is thus good reason to believe that Dante in fact began the *Convivio* first, it is not necessary to think that he completed his work on it before turning to *De vulgari eloquentia*. The contrary would seem to have been the case. This treatise on language, for all its incompleteness and brevity, is of great importance in revealing both Dante's theory of language and his practical views on style, which are those of a working poet-critic. The work begins, as does the *Convivio*, boastfully: Dante, inspired by the Holy Spirit (*Verbo aspirante de celia*) will offer us his hydromel to drink. Nor does his wildly idiosyncratic version of the history of human speech blench at rewriting the Bible (I, iv, 2–4): even though Genesis records that Eve was the first speaker, it is only reasonable to believe that in fact man would have spoken before woman did; therefore, Adam must have been the first speaker and must have uttered the name of God.

For all its seriously playful trampling of convention, the work is of central importance in revealing the strength of Dante's desire to create a theoretical and practical defense of the literary use of the vernacular. This desire was already implicit in the *Vita nuova*, which, simply by virtue of being written in the vulgar tongue, startled a reader who expected to find the prose of the work written in Latin. (In order to remind less suggestible readers of what they expected and did not find, Dante included twenty Latin phrases and sentences in the prose.) And, at one moment in the *Vita nuova* (chapter XXV), Dante explicitly grants the vernacular poet all the rights and privileges previously allowed only to the Latin *poeta*. In that passage and now in *De vulgari eloquentia*, vernacular eloquence is seen as possessing all the virtues of classical eloquence; but now the vernacular is praised as being even more noble than Latin by virtue of its being the first tongue spoken by man (Adam), because it is natural to all humans (grammatical language is learned only at school), and because it is universal (in that all peoples have a vulgar tongue, only some a grammatical one). Latent in these three positions is a view that may remain latent in the *Comedy* yet makes itself felt nonetheless: the theological appropriateness of the vulgar tongue, the language of humility, when it is contrasted with the loftiness of pagan eloquence.

As came to be the case with the *Convivio*, many of Dante's particular judgments were revised, indeed contradicted, in the *Comedy*. Even Adam's first name for God (*El*) became I (*Paradiso*, XXVI, 134), and Dante employed various words proscribed from use in the "illustrious vernacular," which he had attempted to legislate (I, xvi–xix), in the great poem— hardly unintentionally, one must surmise (for in-

stance, from II, vii, 4, *mamma, babbo, greggia, cetra, femina, corpo;* these six words are used a total of seventy-seven times in the *Comedy*, as is the derided Florentine Latinism *introque* of I, xiii, 2, which becomes the last word in *Inferno*, XX, and the *manicare* from the same sentence, resurrected in *Inferno*, XXXIII, 60). The common denominator of Dante's later inclusions of what had been excised would seem to have been the exigencies of the comic, or low, style of the *Comedy* (see *Epistola*, XIII, 28–32), with its theological implications and inherent opposition to the tragic, or high, style recommended in *De vulgari* as alone befitting true vernacular eloquence.

The dates of the composition of the *Convivio* are now agreed upon by most scholars: 1304–1307. Of the fifteen tractates that Dante said explicitly (*Convivio* I, i, 14) would eventually comprise the work, only the first four are extant. Since these comprise, in modern editions, 160 fairly dense pages, the completed work would probably have been 500 pages or more. It is thus clear that when he began it, Dante conceived of the *Convivio* as a magnum opus, an encyclopedic treatment of the literary, philosophical, and moral issues that pressed upon him (and, parenthetically, the longest work yet to be composed in Italian).

Nothing like an adequate characterization of what remains of the *Convivio* can be given briefly. The initial treatise, which serves as proem, is boldly proud in offering us other mortals a banquet (for that is what the title means) of the crumbs of philosophical wisdom that Dante has been able to gather at the feast of the wise. In what follows, his own *canzoni* (odes) will be the meat, his (lengthy) commentaries on them the bread. The primary subject of the first two odes is the greatness of Lady Philosophy, now explained as being the *donna gentile* (noble lady) who consoled him after the death of Beatrice (*Vita nuova*, XXXIV–XXXVIII). While the *Convivio* does not disclaim the earlier work, it does clearly imply (I, i, 16–17) that its Boethian championing of philosophic wisdom is to be preferred to the less mature concerns of the earlier work. The third ode and the accompanying fourth tractate of commentary move away from this subject and toward an exposition of true nobility. The text of the commentary begins to show, for the first time in Dante's career, a lively and present interest in the classical authors, especially Vergil.

Why Dante did not finish *Convivio* is uncertain. It would seem that he abandoned the work (perhaps spurred on by his rereading of Vergil, shortly to become his guide in *Inferno*) in order to begin writing the *Comedy,* and it has frequently been observed that a number of phrases and images in *Inferno,* I pick up similar formulations near the end of *Convivio,* IV. Further, since *Convivio* is at best lukewarm toward Beatrice while the *Comedy* is predicated upon her absolutely central importance, it seems to some scholars that the *Convivio* had to be rejected and abandoned in light of the new and the renewed concerns that prompted Dante to write the great poem.

A number of moments in the *Comedy* look back at passages in the *Convivio* with what seems, at least to some, to be antagonism, especially *Purgatorio,* II, XIX, XXX–XXXI, and the opening verses of *Paradiso,* I, which tend to consider the new poem to be a far better completion of the *Convivio* than would originally have been accomplished. These are matters for conjecture. Nonetheless, the *Convivio* was too large and important a project to have been forsaken without good reason; perhaps the most important fact about the work is that it is unfinished.

VOYAGE TO FRANCE?

The importance and the confused state of the question justify a brief digression. Petrocchi is of the opinion that Dante probably did visit Paris, about 1309–1310. One may object that the few references to the city in the *Comedy* (the only geographic one is to "the Street of Straw," *Paradiso,* X, 137) are so generic as to seem to reflect common knowledge. Further, those early commentators who claim that Dante did visit Paris seem possibly to have been motivated by a desire to explain his expertise in theology as resulting from direct contact with Paris, the queen city of such learning. However, at least as much as Dante knew about the city and Parisian teaching of theology was available to him in Florence, especially at S. Maria Novella in the person of Remigio de' Girolami, who had studied at Paris under St. Thomas.

Further, had Dante actually been in Paris, it seems more than likely that he would have contrived to make it evident to his readers that he had indeed had so important an experience; St. Thomas, in the heaven of the sun (*Paradiso,* X–XIV), might easily have been made to refer, for instance, to Dante's firsthand acquaintance with Dominican teachers there; Bernard of Clairvaux (*Paradiso,* XXX–XXXIII) might have mentioned ecclesiastical edifices seen on such a pilgrimage. In any case, there is

no positive external evidence nor any internal evidence that makes such a journey seem even likely.

The whole question of Dante's relationship to France and French culture remains an important and difficult one. If Dante is in fact the author of the *Fiore,* a sonnet sequence offering a truncated translation of the *Roman de le Rose,* as Contini and most Italian scholars now believe, then he was an author fully conversant, in his formative years (*ca.* 1285), with the greatest work in the French vernacular canon. If that is the case, what had happened to Dante's knowledge of the French poetic tradition of about 1304, when he wrote *De vulgari eloquentia?* Of the many earlier poets referred to there, all are either Provençal or Italian, with the single exception of the French king of Navarre (I, ix, 3); the only other reference to French writing is, rather pointedly, to prose (I, x, 2).

And if Dante had translated the *Roman de la Rose* in his youth, it is unthinkable that he would not have had it in mind as he composed the *Comedy.* Yet few, if any, reminiscences have been demonstrated to exist before the passage in *Paradiso,* II, concerning the spots on the moon (*Roman,* 16,707–16,894). One possible argument, that Dante knew the French poetic tradition but intended to pay it no heed, has some difficulty explaining why, beginning in *Paradiso,* Dante does fairly obviously allude to the *Roman.* It seems altogether possible that he became aware of the French work only late in his life, that it was an important rival and analogue in the *Paradiso,* and that he was not the author of the *Fiore.* The whole question, like so many concerning Dante, is in need of further study.

1308–1313: EMERGENCE, CORONATION, AND DEATH OF HENRY VII

Born in the 1270's, son of Henry, count of Luxembourg, and a French noblewoman named Beatrice (his maternity must have seemed propitious to Dante), Henry probably came to Dante's attention when he was chosen king of Germany in a surprising political compromise among the Capetians, the Habsburgs, and the papacy in 1308. The following year Henry announced that he would go to Italy to receive the imperial crown in Rome. His intention was greeted with delight by Italian Ghibellines and by the imperial-minded Dante. This gesture had not been made since the time of Frederick II, crowned at Rome in 1220; Dante's opinion of Frederick, however, was that, though he was a true emperor, he had failed to live up to his political, moral, and theological responsibilities, (he is found in hell among the heretics, *Inferno*, X, 119). For Dante, Henry's true imperial ancestor was Charlemagne, who dwells in heaven (*Paradiso*, XVIII, 43) and was crowned in Rome on Christmas Day 800, the very model of the Christian emperor.

Henry's Italian voyage, delayed by the intrigues of various enemies, finally began in the autumn of 1310 when he crossed the Alps with some 5,000 troops (not as another Hannibal, but as the new Scipio—see the indirect reference at *Paradiso*, VI, 52–53). He was first crowned at Milan on Epiphany; the symbolically more important Roman coronation met with delay and difficulty, and was finally effectuated in St. John Lateran (rather than St. Peter's) in June 1312. The opposition of Robert of Naples and his fellow Guelphs, now including the pope, proved to be formidable. Clement V, who had been instrumental in Henry's accession, had become, with increasing openness, his enemy. Having come as peacemaker on behalf of all the Italians, Henry now found himself without Guelph support and forced to play out his hand with Ghibelline aid alone. Florence, the center of Guelph strength in the north, became his target; in September 1312 he laid siege to the city.

It is not difficult to imagine Dante's excitement at this time. (His three "political epistles"—*epistole* V–VII, written in 1310–1311—give a perhaps alarming glimpse of his unbridled political passion for the success of Henry and for the defeat of his fellow Florentines.) His imperial dream reached its climax with Henry before the gates of the city; it quickly turned to nightmare. The emperor was forced by his lack of preparation and the Florentines' careful defensive efforts to lift the siege within a month. He wintered at Pisa. The following summer he set out with his troops to assault Naples, the center of Guelph power in the south. His death, probably brought on by malarial fever contracted in Rome the year before, occurred at Buonconvento, near Siena, 24 August 1313.

Henry's years in Italy coincide roughly with the composition of most of the *Inferno* and the *Purgatorio*. While his name is heard only in postmortem praise (*Paradiso*, XVII, 82; XXX, 137), the hopes that Dante lodged in his cause are perhaps present from the opening canto of the *Inferno*, first in the prophecy of the *veltro* (*Inferno*, I, 101). This vexed passage, which has drawn intense speculation and disagreement, should more often be regarded in the light of Jupiter's imperial prophecy in *Aeneid*, I, 257–296. Whomever Dante had in mind—and he probably did have his political hopes pinned on a particular individual, though not yet Henry—the burden of the prophecy is to suggest that Italy, ravaged by forces marshaled under the ensigns of avarice and envy, will be united under a benevolent temporal ruler, who is probably to be understood as the token of the second coming of the true "Emperor," Jesus Christ.

Much of the *Inferno* describes the punishments of those who opposed or violated the sacred imperial principle; this program culminates in the presence of Brutus and Cassius on either side of Judas in Satan's three jaws (*Inferno*, XXXIV). *Purgatorio* is still more open in its championing of the empire. In its last canto Beatrice speaks a prophecy that complements Vergil's *veltro*, the enigmatic "five hundred ten and five" whom many now believe to point to Henry. These remain difficult texts and perhaps will never be resolved to the satisfaction of all. Nevertheless, it is fair to say that the first two *cantiche* of the poem reveal Dante's deeply felt belief in the divine sanction of the imperial cause.

This position is specifically manifest in [*De*] *Monarchia*. As is so often the case with Dante's works, dating of the composition of this treatise on the true relationship between papacy and empire is problematical. Some argue that it was written after *De vulgari eloquentia* and *Convivio* but before Dante began *Inferno*; others that it was done between Henry's coronation and death (1312–1313), and thus either as Dante was completing *Purgatorio* or after he had finished it; still others (on the evidence of I, xii, 6, which explicitly refers to verses found at *Paradiso*, V, 19–22) argue for 1317, after a portion of *Paradiso* had been written, or even later.

Only the first argument may safely be discarded. Boccaccio, who, it must be noted, is rarely to be trusted in matters of historical detail, says that *Monarchia* was composed during Henry's stay in Italy, thus between 1311 and 1313 (*Trattatello in laude di Dante*, 195–197). And while there is no good reason not to belive that the parenthetic remark in the text citing his *Paradiso* is Dante's own, there is also no finally persuasive argument that denies that Dante could have held his text back from the public for some years and added the remark later in his stay in Verona. However, the absence of any reference to Henry probably urges a dating after his death, since it is difficult to believe that Dante would have omitted all reference to his emperor, in the very work that proclaimed the scope of his sovereigny, while he was still living.

The three books of *Monarchia* seem, unlike the

components of *De vulgari eloquentia* and *Convivio,* certainly to be the parts of a completed work. In it Dante's prime purpose is to raise the role of the emperor from the subordinate status reserved to him by one ecclesiastical tradition, in which the empire is metaphorically identified with the moon, the church with the sun. Instead, Dante elevates the imperial jurisdiction to an independent and equally sacrosanct position, even if its territory of operation is the lesser one of this world, while the church is authoritative in questions pertaining to salvation. Yet even this disclaimer gives less than it takes away when one considers the church's eagerness to involve itself in political and other mundane concerns. That such was perceived to be the case is evidenced by the responses of Cardinal Bertrando del Poggetto, who condemned the work as heretical in 1328, and of the Dominican Guido Vernani, who wrote the tract *De reprobatione Monarchiae* at roughly the same time.

1314–1317

Dante's second stay in Verona was almost certainly the longest sojourn at a single court that he had yet enjoyed. The political situation there was as propitious as any he would have then found in Italy. After 1311 Can Grande della Scala was sole ruler. The Scaligeri had welcomed Henry; Can Grande served as one of his imperial vicars. Now, even after the emperor's death, he maintained the title. The new pope, John XXII (1316–1334), would order him to relinquish it in 1317; he refused, and was excommunicated the following year. The Verona to which Dante returned was thus under the governance of a leader with whom Dante was in strong basic agreement, and who stood at the center of what remained of Ghibelline hope and power after Henry's death.

If, as Francesco Mazzoni has argued, the *Letter to Can Grande* (*Epistola* XIII) was composed in 1316, at least two other important facts result. First, Dante must already have been in Verona for a reasonable amount of time, in order to make his extravagant praise of his host seem meaningful; second, he had written the first canto of *Paradiso,* which was accompanied by this dedicatory epistle, at least by then. This extraordinary document, which is now, after years of debate, accepted as authentic by its most knowledgeable students, remains the briefest and most cogent exposition of Dante's poem ever put forward.

This remark is not itself uncontroversial. When one studies the letter with care, either for its general comments about the work's genre, style, technique

of signifying, overall meaning, or for its expert glosses on the opening verses of *Paradiso,* I, it is difficult to believe, as so many, uncomfortable with its striking claims, have done, that anyone else could have written it. (The single most striking of these claims is that the poet has employed the "allegory of the theologians," reserved absolutely to the interpretation of the Bible, and not the conventional "allegory of the poets," as the *Comedy*'s mode of signifying. It is a claim that, considered calmly, makes surprisingly good sense.)

Petrocchi believes that Dante returned to Verona in 1312 and there witnessed from afar the final fifteen months of Henry's Italian campaign. Dante's stay in Verona would thus have lasted until 1318; the final three years of his life were spent at Ravenna, with the time, measured in poetic output, accounted for as follows: 1312–1314, revision of *Inferno* (published second half of 1314) and *Purgatorio* (published autumn 1315); 1315–1318, *Paradiso* I–XVII ("farewell" to Can Grande in the last canto); 1318–1320, Ravenna, *Paradiso* XVIII–XXXIII.

While some have chosen to promulgate the opinion that after Henry's death Dante's imperial hopes either sharply diminished or ceased altogether, it is far more accurate to perceive that he was never without these hopes. If the *Monarchia* is indeed to be dated about 1317, it alone would reveal their tenacity. But even an earlier dating would not remove the prospect of a writer who had not ceased to be vitally concerned with the political future of Italy. The "Letter to the Italian Cardinals" (*Epistola* XI, 1314) reveals the ecclesiastical side of his program, urging vehemently the return of the papacy from Avignon to Rome. And the text of the *Paradiso* itself speaks to his steadfastness: XVII, great deeds of Can Grande foretold (if not spelled out); XXVII, prophecy of the *fortuna,* or "tempest," which will redirect the course of the human "fleet" (this prophecy, while usually overlooked, completes the prophetic program in the poem along with *veltro* and "515"); XXX, the vacant throne of Henry in the empyrean, which, described in terms that reflect the prophecy of the *fortuna,* tacitly asserts that another emperor will come to save Italy.

The victory of the Ghibellines under Uguccione della Faggiuola at Montecatini (August 1315) soon resulted in an amnesty offered by the Florentines to their exiled townsmen on condition that they pay a fine. Dante's response (*Epistola* XII) reveals his stubbornness (derogation of so unworthy an offer) and his pride (he refers to "the fame and glory of

Dante"—hardly an approach calculated to soothe his adversaries) as well as his probable continuing hopes for a solution of the question of his exile by military force. If such was the case, he was shortly to be disappointed. Uguccione failed to besiege Florence, and was himself beset by rebellion among his followers. Montecatini turned out to be the last tangible sign that Dante's personal hopes for a return to his city on his own terms might be rewarded.

Nevertheless, such texts as *Paradiso,* XXV, 1–9, in which he imagines his eventual laureation in Florence, speak to the persistence of this dream. That none of his most strongly felt hopes, whether for Italy or for himself, was to be realized in anything like a near future (Italian unification waited until 1870) should not obscure the vitality of these hopes, which is so readily apparent in his work. Despite the overarching importance of theological matters to so much of that work, it is nonetheless true that political concerns left their continuing mark on the *Comedy,* from *Inferno,* I, to *Paradiso,* XXX.

1317–1321

Some of Dante's desires for his own success must surely have been pleasantly met when he resettled at the court of Guido Novello da Polenta in Ravenna. Not only was he much honored by his hosts and entrusted by Guido with various diplomatic missions, but he was rejoined there by two of his children, Jacopo and Pietro (both of whom were to write commentaries on their father's poem), and was perhaps also reunited with his daughter Antonia, who perhaps later became a nun, taking the name Beatrice, at S. Stefano degli Ulivi. Here, with charm and wit, Dante answered Giovanni del Virgilio's invitation to recast his poem into the more noble tongue, Latin, and thus be rewarded with the laurel in Bologna. His negative and graceful response took the form of two Latin eclogues (*ca.* 1319–1320). (At roughly the same time he also returned briefly to Verona, apparently having first been in Mantua, to deliver his scientific paper, *Questio de situ aque et terre,* on 20 January 1320.)

The major task of the years in Ravenna was, of course, the completion of the *Comedy.* Dante's final obligation was, however, a political one. He took part in an embassy for Guido Novello to Venice, sent in the hope of reducing hostilities between the two cities. Venice probably was the source of the fever that brought on his death in Ravenna on 13 or 14 September 1321. With the *Comedy* at last finished, he must, at the age of fifty-six, have had other plans in mind. What these might have been is an open question. Had he lived longer, it is likely that Dante would finally have been laureated, if not in Florence, then by Guido in Venice.

Some have speculated that he would have turned to autobiography, along the lines of Gibbon, now that the great task was done. That seems at least unlikely, since his own works are so compounded of his life. Given the nature of the commentaries of which the major portions of *Vita nuova* and *Convivio* consist, another theory is that he might have planned similar self-exegesis for the *Comedy,* on the model of what he had already done in the *Letter to Can Grande.* The deliberately enigmatic character of so many passages in the work probably warns us against this hypothesis; he very likely preferred to leave the glossing to others.

Perhaps no poet has ever more clearly invited commentators to pursue his meanings; surely no other poet has had so many takers. From shortly after his death to the present there have been published well over one hundred complete or partial commentaries on the poem, hundreds of books, many thousands of articles. No poem in the history of the Western world has received so much assiduous attention, yet remains so often in dispute with respect to matters large and small. More significantly, no poem remains as fresh and appealing to thousands of new readers every year, a work that commentary can neither exhaust nor kill.

BIBLIOGRAPHY

A full listing of only the works of major importance would cover more than 100 pages. See, for instance, the bibliography in the *Enciclopedia dantesca,* VI (1978), 501–618. The most complete Dante collection is at Cornell University, cataloged only through 1920: Theodore W. Koch, comp., *Catalogue of the Dante Collection Presented by Willard Fiske,* 2 vols. (1898–1900); and Mary Fowler, comp., *Additions, 1898–1920* (1921).

Later publications that serve as supplements to the Cornell catalog include Niccolò D. Evola, *Bibliografia dantesca (1920–1930)* (1932), "Dante" [for 1931–1934], in his *Bibliografia degli studi sulla letteratura italiana* (1938), 292–333, and "Bibliografia dantesca (1935–1939)," in *Aevum,* **15** (1941); Helene Wieruszowski, "Bibliografia dantesca" [1931–1937], in *Giornale dantesco,* **39** (1936 [1938]), and "Bibliografia dantesca" [1938–1939], in *ibid.,* **41** (1938 [1940]); Aldo Vallone, *Gli studi danteschi dal 1940 al 1949* (1950); Enzo Esposito, *Gli studi danteschi dal 1950 al 1964* (1965).

The following works offer information on Dante's fortune in other countries: Paget Toynbee, *Dante in English*

Literature from Chaucer to Cary (1909), repr. as *Britain's Tribute to Dante in Literature and Art: A Chronological Record of 540 Years* (1921); Theodor Ostermann, *Dante in Deutschland* (1929); Vittore Branca and E. Caccia, eds., *Dante nel mondo* (1965).

Current bibliography is available in various periodicals, particularly the following: *L'Alighieri, Rassegna della letteratura italiana,* and *Studi danteschi* (all published in Italy); *Dante Studies* (U.S.A.); *Deutsches Dante-Jahrbuch* (Germany); *MLA International Bibliography* (U.S.A.), and *The Year's Work in Modern Language Studies* (U.K.).

For those without Italian who want information about Dante, his works, and his times, an extraordinarily helpful English text is Paget Toynbee, *A Dictionary of Proper Names and Notable Matters in the Works of Dante,* rev. by Charles S. Singleton (1968). By far the most complete and helpful aid of this kind ever assembled is *Enciclopedia dantesca,* 6 vols. (1970–1978), with bibliographical indications following almost all major entries.

For the *Comedy* the most helpful commentary in English is that included in Charles S. Singleton, ed., *The Divine Comedy,* 6 vols. (1970–1975). For each *cantica* there is a facing prose translation, with the commentary included in a separate volume.

ROBERT HOLLANDER

[See also **Allegory; Florence; Guelphs and Ghibellines; Italian Language; Italian Literature: Allegorical and Didactic; Italian Literature: Religious Poetry; Italy in the Fourteenth and Fifteenth Centuries; Vergil in the Middle Ages; Visions, Literary Form.**]

DARBAND. See Derbent.

DARDANELLES, known also as the Hellespont, the link between the Sea of Marmara and the Aegean Sea, separating Europe from Asia. Its location has made it, throughout history, a strategic point of defense for the city of Constantinople. In 674 the Arab fleet managed to get through and to besiege the city. In the division of the Byzantine Empire after the Fourth Crusade, Baldwin, the Latin emperor, received the Hellespont, but Venice obtained its important ports, including Gallipoli. In the fourteenth century the Ottomans built fortresses there that they used as bases for their attacks against the Byzantines. In addition to its strategic importance, the Hellespont was vital for commercial reasons.

BIBLIOGRAPHY
George Ostrogorsky, *History of the Byzantine State,* Joan Hussey, trans. (1957, rev. ed. 1969).

LINDA C. ROSE

[See also **Bosporus** (with map).]

DARET, JACQUES, a Flemish painter born between 1400 and 1403 at Tournai, where he later took his apprenticeship with Robert Campin and was admitted to the guild of painters in 1432. The only paintings attributed to Daret with certainty are four panels, dated 1435, that decorated the wings of an altarpiece for St. Vaast at Arras (*Visitation,* Berlin; *Nativity,* Thyssen-Bornemisza Collection at Lugano; *Adoration of the Magi,* Berlin; and *Presentation,* Petit Palais, Paris). Stylistically these paintings are closely related to works of Campin and Rogier van der Weyden.

BIBLIOGRAPHY
Max J. Friedländer, *Early Netherlandish Painting,* II (1967), 34–44.

JAMES SNYDER

[See also **Flemish Painting.**]

DAROKHRANITELNITSA (Greek: artophorion), also called a "Zion," the type of tabernacle usually kept on the high altar of an Orthodox church. The medieval *darokhranitelnitsa* is usually in the shape of a domed or multidomed church and contains the consecrated bread intincted with consecrated wine to be used in the Lenten liturgy of the presanctified and for administering communion to the sick. Whenever possible it is made of gold or silver.

GEORGE P. MAJESKA

DARRAÐARLJÓÐ is the name given to an eleven-stanza poem in the *fornyrðislag* meter found in chapter 157 of *Njáls saga.* According to the saga, a certain Dǫrruðr of Caithness, while out walking, sees twelve riders approach a hut and disappear inside. Peering through the window, he sees twelve Valkyries weaving at a loom that, as both the saga and the poem state, has men's heads in place of weights, intestines for the weft and warp, a sword as the weaver's reed and an arrow as the shuttle. As they weave, the women chant the stanzas of the poem, in which their weaving is imaged as a web of war and they themselves as weavers of destiny.

Understood to be a projection on the mythic plane of a particular battle, the chant evokes a field hung with red clouds and drenched in a bloody rain. It prophesies the outcome of that battle ("A great king is fated to die . . . an earl is felled by spears . . . Irish men will endure a grief that will never fade from memory"), and it recounts the Valkyries' activities as choosers of the slain. At the end of the chant, the women tear the cloth from the loom and, each taking a shred, ride off to battle, six to the north and six to the south. The occasion, according to the saga, is the Battle of Clontarf, which took place outside Dublin in 1014 and is commemorated in both Irish and Scandinavian sources.

The poem is certainly older than the saga, and the prose context can be questioned on several points. One is the figure of Dǫrruðr. "Dǫrruðr" is not elsewhere attested as a proper name, and the person so called in the saga appears to be an erroneous adumbration of a word in the poem's thrice-repeated line *vindum vindum vef darraðar* (we weave, we weave a web of spears, "web of spears" being a kenning for battle, or, alternatively, we weave, we weave a battle banner [or Odin's web]). Doubts have also been raised about the saga's association of the poem with the Battle of Clontarf. The poem does not mention a place, only "Irish men," and it has been argued that the reference might just as well be to an earlier battle between Norse and Irish, such as that at Confey (Cenn Fuait) in 917. Yet another question concerns the panegyric quality of certain of the phrases in the poem, which has led to the speculation that it was originally composed in honor of a specific person. If this is so, the saga author seems unaware of it, and has either ignored or not recognized the praise dimension.

Of some interest are the poem's British elements. If the kenning *vefr darraðar* means "web of spears" (battle), it may derive from Anglo-Saxon usage. The exaggerated quality of the imagery is more characteristic of Irish than of Norse poetic practice. Its main idea, women weaving a web of war, appears to be an amalgam of Norse and Irish traditions: Norse in the idea of fate women (Valkyries who select heroes on the battlefield, Norns who spin out the threads of men's destinies), and Irish in the idea of war as a fate weaving.

Formally, however, and in its overall content and diction as well as in its visionary quality, the poem is fully Scandinavian. Some scholars believe that it originated among Scandinavians in the British Isles, perhaps the Orkneys, where heathen traditions were tolerated long after the introduction of Christianity. The age of the poem is unknown; the usual eleventh-century dating rests on the assumption that it refers to the Battle of Clontarf.

BIBLIOGRAPHY

Sources. Einar Ól. Sveinsson, ed., *Brennu-Njáls saga* (1954). The saga is available in a translation by Magnus Magnusson and Hermann Pálsson, *Njal's Saga* (1960).

Studies. Anne Holtsmark, "Vefr Darraðar," in *Maal og minne* (1939), 74–96, repr. in her *Studier i norrøn diktning* (1956), 177–197; Eiríkr Magnússon, "Darraðarljóð," in *Old Lore Miscellany of Shetland, Caithness, and Sutherland*, 3 (1910); Klaus von See, "Das Walkürenlied," in *Beiträge zur Geschichte der deutschen Sprache und Literatur* (Tübingen), 81 (1959), repr. in his *Edda, Saga, Skaldendichtung* (1981).

CAROL J. CLOVER

[See also **Njáls Saga; Norns; Valkyrie.**]

DATARY, APOSTOLIC, the official *(datarius)*—in the fifteenth century normally a bishop—who presided over a bureau or congregation in the papal curia concerned with the dispensing of graces or favors in the external forum, or the bureau itself *(dataria)*. The name comes from the date *(data)* that the datary entered on supplications or petitions, a date that determined when the concession of the petition, if it was granted, would take effect.

No record survives of the formal establishment of the datary. Already in the mid fourteenth century there was an official within the chancery entrusted with at least some of the functions later attached to the datary, but not until the first years of Martin V (1417–1431) is there evidence that this position had been made into a permanent office, the holder of which bore the title of datary. Only in the late sixteenth century did the datary achieve complete independence from the chancery, but even then there had to be cooperation in the dispatch of certain kinds of letters.

The original task of the datary, besides dating, was to present the supplications to the pope or his authorized representative (usually the vice-chancellor) for consideration and signature. Other tasks were added later—including that of keeping the register in which approved supplications were recorded—and an elaborate network of subordinate officials evolved. Requests for benefices and for dispensations of various kinds, such as from the disability of illegitimacy and especially from marriage impediments, constituted the main business of the datary. It also dealt with certain kinds of absolutions, pensions, and indulgences. The development of the datary as a special bureau within the chancery undoubtedly reflected an increase in the amount of business to be conducted, and particularly in the number of papal provisions to church offices.

The datary was in principle a *curia gratiosa,* a court or tribunal bestowing gratuitous papal favors. A custom developed, however, whereby the recipient of the favor made an offering intended for alms or other pious uses. By the end of the fifteenth century this offering had become more of a prescribed fee. To avoid the charge that favors were being bought and sold, the contribution was called a *compositio* (meaning a payment mutually and voluntarily agreed upon) rather than a fee. Because of the crucial role that the date played in putting an approved petition into effect, it was at the dating stage that the composition was collected.

The conservation and allocation of the fees came to be entrusted to the datary. The considerable income thereby generated, which around 1500 seems to have been devoted especially to building the new basilica of St. Peter, enhanced the importance of the datary but also left him in a compromising position, since there was an inherent tension between his financial interests and the gratuitous nature of the papal acts handled by his office. A proposal was made in 1497 to deprive the datary of his role in compositions, but nothing came of it.

BIBLIOGRAPHY

Harry Bresslau, *Handbuch der Urkundenlehre für Deutschland und Italien,* II, pt. 1, 2nd ed. (1915, repr. 1958), 104–115; Léonce Celier, *Les dataries du XVe siècle et les origines de la daterie apostolique* (1910); Emil von Ottenthal, *Regulae cancellariae apostolicae: Die päpstlichen Kanzleiregeln von Johannes XXII. bis Nikolaus V.* (1888, repr. 1968); Nicola Storti, *La storia e il diritto della dataria apostolica dalle origini ai nostri giorni* (1969); Michael Tangl, *Die päpstlichen Kanzleiordnungen von 1200–1500* (1894, repr. 1959).

JAMES J. JOHN

[See also **Chancery; Curia, Papal.**]

DAUPHIN was a title taken by the counts of Albon, sometimes called counts of Vienne, and later by the heirs to the French throne. The counts never ruled the city of Vienne, which was held by its bishop, but they possessed all the district around it, a region later called the Dauphiné. (The count of Clermont-Auvergne was also called dauphin, but he had less power and the name faded away in his district.)

Originally the name seems to have been only a way to distinguish the counts, most of whom were called Guigues, from other men of the same name. One would write *Guigues Dauphin (Guigo Dalphinus)* in the twelfth century, but the title of these Guigues was count. By 1248 *dalphinus* was becoming a title; by the 1280's it had supplanted that of count. The origin of the word is unknown; it certainly did not come from "dolphin" (*delphinus*), a creature unknown in inland France and one not originally depicted in the arms and banner of the dauphin.

The Dauphiné was part of the phantom kingdom of Arles, which in turn was part of the German-Roman Empire. The emperor had some influence there and talked vaguely of reviving the kingdom of Arles, but did nothing. The king of France was pushing down from the north and had acquired Lyons and the county of Burgundy soon after 1308; he also tried to gain influence over the nobles of the kingdom of Arles. The last independent dauphins attempted to profit from this unsettled situation by forming alliances or threatening wars with their neighbors. None of these operations was very successful and all of them were expensive. By 1343 it was obvious that the emperor could do nothing to help the dauphin, that other rulers in the region had no desire to help him, and that he was hopelessly in debt. The dauphin Humbert II had lost his only remaining son and he had no political influence. Thus it was not difficult for the French to persuade him to give up the game and enjoy a peaceful and comfortable old age. In 1343 he sold his hereditary right to the Dauphiné to Philip VI of France for 120,000 florins and an annual pension of 10,000 pounds. The Dauphiné was to keep its privileges and its customs, but was eventually to be ruled by a younger son of the king of France. In 1349 Humbert, still in debt, sold his right to rule the Dauphiné for his lifetime for 200,000 florins and another pension.

Philip soon saw that the provision giving the Dauphiné to a younger son was dangerous; an independent prince of the blood royal might found a dynasty that in the end would threaten the king of France. Therefore in 1344 the treaty was modified. The Dauphiné was to be held by the eldest son of the king, or by the king himself if he had no son. Thus "dauphin" became the title of the heir to the French throne. It is interesting to note that a similar arrangement had already been made in England: when Wales was conquered by Edward I, he made his eldest son prince of Wales, and this has remained the title of the heir to the throne in England ever since.

BIBLIOGRAPHY

Paul Fournier, *Le royaume d'Arles et de Vienne (1138–1378)* (1891); Jules J. Guiffrey, *Histoire de la réunion du Dauphiné à la France* (1868); A. Prudhomme, "De l'origine et du sens des mots dauphin et Dauphiné," in *Bibliothèque de l'École des Chartes,* **28** (1893).

Joseph R. Strayer

[See also **Dauphiné; France; Philip IV the Fair; Philip VI of Valois.**]

DAUPHINÉ. The region that came to be known as the Dauphiné is bounded roughly by the Rhône on the west, Savoy on the north, the Cottian Alps on the east, and Provence on the south. This territory was originally included in the province of Gallia Narbonensis, but by the fifth century Vienne and other Roman settlements had given their names to districts that formed comital and/or ecclesiastical jurisdictions throughout the Middle Ages: Valence (Valentinois), Vapincum (Gap), Brigantio (Briançon), Eburodunum (Embrun), Dea Vocontiorum (Die). The Rhône Valley was ravaged by Vandals, Visigoths, and Alani before falling under the dominion of the Burgundians (443) and the Franks (534).

Following the partition of the Carolingian empire in 843, the territory between the Rhône and the Alps came to form the new kingdom of Provence (also called the First Kingdom of Burgundy or Cisjurane

Burgundy). In 888 the northern regions were detached to form part of the kingdom of Transjurane Burgundy, which in 933 absorbed the remainder to the south and constituted a theoretical unity known variously as the Second Kingdom of Burgundy or the Kingdom of Arles and Vienne.

In 1032 this kingdom passed under the theoretical authority of the Holy Roman emperor, though in fact it continued to be controlled by regional warlords. By 1029/1030 Archbishop Brouchard of Vienne, who also held the title of count, had given comital authority outside the walls of Vienne in fief to two neighboring magnates. The northern part went to his brother-in-law, Count Humbert White Hands (*d.* 1048), founder of the house of Savoy,

while the southern part went to Guigues the Old (*d. ca.* 1060/1070), who established himself at Albon, south of Vienne. Brouchard's enfeoffment was the beginning of the Dauphiné as a political entity.

Count Guigues IV was the first (in 1110) to use the name "dauphin" (*Guigo Dalphinus*), for reasons that remain unknown. His English mother, Matilda, is known to have had a cousin whose name was Dolfin, giving rise to the supposition that she may have wished to recall both her faraway homeland and her English kin by adding that name to her son's. However, "dauphin" was not used as a title until the end of the thirteenth century, and the first appearance of the word *Dalphinatus* to designate a principality occurred in 1293.

The Dauphiné passed by marriage to the house of Burgundy when Beatrice, the only child of Guigues V (*d.* 1162), had a son by Duke Hugh III of Burgundy. The new dauphin was known both as André and as Guigues VI. By 1225 his holdings in the duchy of Burgundy were bought out, and by 1282 Duke Robert II of Burgundy claimed the inheritance for himself. In 1284, however, the succession was secured for Humbert de La Tour du Pin, and the house of La Tour ruled until 1349, when, childless and wifeless, Humbert II sold the Dauphiné to Philip VI of France. By then it had increased considerably in size to include the counties of Embrunais and Gapençais (1202), the Faucigny in Savoy (1268), and the baronies of Tour du Pin (1268), Montauban (1300), and Mévouillon (1317), bringing the Dauphiné to the borders of the Comtat Venaissin.

The "transport" of the Dauphiné to the king of France was a triumph for Valois diplomacy. Humbert II (1333–1355), reared at the Angevin court in Naples, had a taste for regal splendor, and as dauphin he quickly exceeded the capacities of his treasury. As early as 1337 he approached King Robert of Sicily and then Pope Benedict XII, offering to sell his inheritance for a financially secure future, but both found the price too high. Philip VI of France was willing to meet the dauphin's conditions and in 1349 secured the principality for his grandson, the future Charles V (1364–1380), who thus became the first dauphin of the French royal line.

In 1378 Emperor Charles IV conferred upon Prince Charles, the next dauphin, the position of imperial vicar for the kingdom of Arles-Vienne, preparing the way for the eventual transfer of sovereignty over that region to the French monarchy and perhaps explaining why "dauphin" was adopted as the title of the royal heir apparent. Thereafter, the only French dauphin to reside in the Dauphiné and interest himself in its affairs was Louis II (1440–1457), the future King Louis XI, who attempted to revive it as an independent principality by reorganizing its administration and engineering its final annexations: the counties of Valentinois and Diois and the cities of Montélimar and Vienne.

As early as the eleventh century delphinal authority on the local level was exercised by castellans having revocable commissions in *mandamenta* that varied from two or three parishes to more than twenty in the mountains. By the fourteenth century the *mandamenta* had been grouped into seven bailliages. The baillis supervised the castellans, but in the administration of justice they were increasingly supplanted by *juges-mages,* whose jurisdictions were often coterminous with the bailliages.

In the fourteenth century institutions of centralized government appeared that gradually reduced the independence of both the prelates and the great feudal lords. By 1310 there was a military "governor" acting as a permanent lieutenant of the dauphin. By 1318 there was also a *juge-mage des appellations* to hear appeals from lower courts, and by 1306 a Chambre des Comptes that was reorganized by Humbert II in 1340 and installed at Grenoble, as was the Conseil Delphinal in the same year. After the Battle of Poitiers the first Estates General in the Dauphiné was convoked (1357) to sanction a special tax for the war effort. This institution came to play an important part in the government of the region during the next century.

The presence of Christians in the Dauphiné is attested from 177. By the end of the fourth century there were seven dioceses in the archbishoprics of Embrun and Vienne. In the sixth century monasticism appeared, notably at Grenoble (St. Oyand) and Vienne (St. Pierre). Cluniac reformers and Cistercians put down roots, but the most important indigenous contribution was the Grande Chartreuse, founded (1084) by St. Bruno in the mountains just north of Grenoble. Another important new order was the Antonine Hospitalers (Antonines), founded in the late eleventh century at Motte St. Didier (renamed St. Antoine), which became a major pilgrimage center. With new religious orders there also came heretics, such as the Albigensians and Waldensians, often suppressed yet sometimes resurgent. Christian art and architecture flourished in the Dauphiné nonetheless, with notable examples of Romanesque style at Valence, Die, Léoncel, St. Restitut, and St. Paul-Trois-Châteaux, and remarkable Gothic churches and sculpture at Vienne, St. Antoine, Embrun, and Grenoble.

Despite its considerable size the Dauphiné was not a very rich province. Two-thirds of its territory is mountainous and severe in climate, with only the Rhône Valley and the Isère Valley near Grenoble notable for their fertility. The great international trade routes tended to skirt its frontiers, along the Rhône and across the northern Viennois. The Durance valley route from Italy to Avignon only became a major one after the establishment of the papacy there. Thus agriculture was of prime importance, with herding the principal occupation in the mountain regions, though there were hemp mills in the Grésivaudan; and by the twelfth century coal, silver, and iron mines were operating there and in the Briançonais, Oisans, and Embrunais.

Serfdom persisted in the Diois and Baronnies, but elsewhere tended to be replaced by franchises, communal charters, and, in the fourteenth century, life leases called *albergamenta*. The earliest communal charters were those of Moirans (1164) and Montélimar (1198), but by 1355 some 548 such charters had been granted to 183 different places, mostly small rural communities. The only sizable towns were Vienne, Valence, Grenoble, and Romans, although important fairs existed at Briançon and Bourg d'Oisans.

As early as the twelfth century the southern regions of the Dauphiné were centers of troubadour music and literature. Albert de Sisteron came from Gap and the Comtessa di Dia, one of the most important women troubadours, may have come from Die. The literary tradition was continued in the thirteenth century by Ogier de St. Donat, Folquet de Romans, and the innkeeper, jongleur, and poet Guillaume Magret. In 1339 Humbert II obtained from Pope Benedict XII a charter founding a university at Grenoble, the fifth oldest in France.

BIBLIOGRAPHY

Robert-Henri Bautier and Janine Sornay, *Les sources de l'histoire économique et sociale du moyen âge*, I, Provence, Comtat Venaissin, Dauphiné, et états de la maison de Savoie (1968); Raoul Blanchard, *Les Alpes occidentales*, 6 vols. (1938–1945); Bernard Bligny, ed., *Histoire du Dauphiné* (1973); Cyr Ulysse J. Chevalier, *Étude historique sur la constitution de l'église métropolitaine et primatiale de Vienne en Dauphiné (origines–1500)*, 2 vols. (1922–1923); idem, ed., *Régeste dauphinois . . . dès origines chrétiennes à l'année 1349*, 5 vols. (1913–1926); Paul Dreyfus, *Histoire du Dauphiné* (1976); Georges de Manteyer, *Les origines du Dauphiné de Viennois* (1925); Pierre Vaillant, *Les libertés des communautés dauphinoises dès origines au 5 Janvier 1355* (1951).

EUGENE L. COX

[See also **Burgundy, Duchy of; Carthusians; Dauphin; France; Louis XI of France.**]

DAVID I OF SCOTLAND (*ca.* 1080/1085–1153), sixth son of Malcolm III Canmore and St. Margaret of Scotland, daughter of Edward Atheling. He ascended the throne in 1124. He gained experience in England, first as a member of the Scottish royal family in exile (while Scotland was ruled by his half brother Donald III, 1094–1097); then as the brother of Henry I's queen, Matilda; and ultimately as the husband of Matilda, daughter of Earl Waltheof of Northumbria and widow of Simon of St. Liz, earl of Northampton and Huntingdon. In her right David came in turn to hold both earldoms. He was thus a leading member of the Anglo-Norman aristocracy.

As brother of Alexander I, a king who had no legitimate heir, David also acquired a position in Scotland, coming to rule what was almost the heir apparent's appanage of Lothian, Strathclyde, and Cumbria. Here he revealed his interest in religion. His first monastic foundation was made at Selkirk in 1113; many more followed after he succeeded his brother. David was also concerned with the organization of the church, refounding the ancient bishopric of Glasgow before 1118 and creating others once he became king. By the time of his death there were nine dioceses in the country, though it was not yet formally recognized as a separate province because the traditional claims of York to authority over the whole of northern Britain were still accepted by the papacy.

These religious interests impressed contemporaries, but they have perhaps been overemphasized. As a ruler David could be masterful as well as pious. He established his authority in Moray (1130) with a display of violence succinctly recorded in an Irish source as "slaughter of the men of Moray." In 1138, according to the chronicle of Melrose, "King David miserably wasted the whole of Northumbria" when he intervened in the struggle between Stephen and Matilda for the English throne. David was observing the oath he had taken in 1127 to support Matilda, but he was also pursuing the interests of his family in the north of England. His defeat in the Battle of the Standard (1138) was a setback, though his son

Henry received the earldom of Northumberland as part of a settlement with Stephen in 1139.

To extend his authority within Scotland, David granted fiefs to members of many Anglo-Norman and French families, so that, by the end of his reign, much of the land south of the Forth was in the hands of foreign settlers holding by feudal tenures. David also remodeled the government of the country along lines familiar in England and France, with sheriffs based at royal castles, and burghs as centers of trade and bases for foreign merchants and artisans.

At his death David's dynasty was secure enough for the succession to pass to his grandson Malcolm IV, a boy of about eleven.

BIBLIOGRAPHY

Alan O. Anderson, ed., *Early Sources of Scottish History*, II (1922), 169–222; G. W. S. Barrow, *The Anglo-Norman Era in Scottish History* (1980), and *Kingship and Unity: Scotland 1000–1306* (1981), 32–42; idem, ed., *Regesta regum Scottorum*, I (1960), 131–172; A. A. M. Duncan, *Scotland: The Making of the Kingdom* (1975), 133–173 and bibliography; Archibald C. Lawrie, ed., *Early Scottish Charters Prior to A.D. 1153* (1905).

BRUCE WEBSTER

[See also **Malcolm III of Scotland; Scotland, History of.**]

DAVID II OF SCOTLAND (1324–1371), eldest son of Robert I and Elizabeth de Burgh, ascended the throne in 1329. The succession of a child encouraged a revival of English aggression, and by 1334 David was forced to flee to France, where he maintained a small court at Château Gaillard in Normandy. The whole of his reign was to be dominated by the ambitions of Edward III.

By the late 1330's Edward's efforts to conquer Scotland had clearly failed. In 1341 David was able to return and engage in intermittent raids on northern England. On one of these, in 1346, he was defeated at Neville's Cross, near Durham, and taken prisoner. He spent the next eleven years in captivity in England; his release was eventually achieved by the Treaty of Berwick in 1357, at the cost of a ransom of 100,000 marks, to be paid in ten annual installments. This was not a final peace, nor did it give formal recognition of David's title or of Scotland's independence, but it did mark the end of hostilities until the late 1370's. Negotiations continued over the payment of the ransom, which soon fell into arrears, and also about the possible succession of one of Edward's sons to the childless David. This pro-

posal, first raised around 1350, was decisively rejected by the Scottish parliament in 1364.

The war with England raised problems beyond the immediate fighting. For long periods Scotland was under attack and without a king to organize resistance. Many of the nobles stood firm, and they maintained the integrity of the country. But English claims raised problems of allegiance, and some Scots, particularly in the Borders and in the far west, where loyalty to the crown was tenuous, were prepared or forced to make their peace with Edward. The lack of a king disrupted administration and led to lawlessness. It says something for David that he was able to restore the machinery of government after 1357 and to win back the allegiance of those who had wavered.

His absences had also allowed some of the nobles to increase their personal power and lands. David had to rule very circumspectly after 1357, but he was gradually able to build up his own base of support. Late in 1362 or early in 1363 he seized the earl of Mar's castle of Kildrummy, and a few months later he fairly easily suppressed a more general revolt.

Matrimonial difficulties, however, did not enhance his authority. A mistress, Katherine Mortimer, was murdered in 1360. His first wife, Joanna, sister of Edward III, died in England in 1362. His second marriage (1363), to Margaret Drummond, widow of John Logie, was also childless and unhappy. The marriage was dissolved by the Scottish bishops in 1369, but Margaret appealed to Rome, and the case was still disputed when the king died.

David has generally been poorly regarded in contrast to his famous father, yet medieval writers speak well of him, and he maintained his authority and his kingdom in very difficult circumstances.

BIBLIOGRAPHY

David Dalrymple, *Annals of Scotland,* 3rd ed. (1819), II, 165–322; Ranald Nicholson, "David II, the Historians and the Chroniclers," in *Scottish Historical Review,* 45 (1966), and *Scotland: The Later Middle Ages* (1974), 123–183 and bibliography; Bruce Webster, "David II and the Government of Fourteenth-century Scotland," in *Transactions of the Royal Historical Society,* 5th ser., 16 (1966); idem, ed., *Regesta regum Scottorum,* VI (1982).

BRUCE WEBSTER

[See also **Edward III of England; Scotland, History of.**]

DAVID II (IV) THE BUILDER (1073–1125). David, also known as "the Restorer" (*aghmashenebeli*) and, sometimes, as David III, was the Bagratid king of Georgia from 1089, at a time when his small kingdom was emerging from internal disorder and external threats from the Seljuk Turks. Soon after he became coruler with his father, Giorgi II, at age sixteen, David began to organize a military force to drive the Seljuks from his lands. Employing a Qipchaq cavalry of 40,000, the king was able not only to defeat the Turks (most decisively at the Battle of Didgori, 1121) and to retake the capital, Tbilisi (1122), but also to force the Georgian nobility to subordinate itself more completely to the monarchy.

In contrast with the fragmented kingdoms of Armenia that had fallen before the Turks, David's resurgent Georgia emerged to become the strongest and most stable state in Caucasia. David expanded his realm and invited Armenians to settle in his lands. Georgia became for a time a multi-national empire that briefly included the Armenian city of Ani in Širak, Šamaxi in Shirvan, and part of the northern Caucasus. The newfound security aided the development of towns and trade, and the monastery at Gelati, built by the king, became a center of learning. The king's portrait can still be seen among the frescoes in the cathedral at Gelati.

To his heirs David the Builder bequeathed not only a renewed and expanded Georgia but also a vastly increased royal power and prestige. Royal lands (sakhaso) had grown enormously; churches, roads, and bridges had been built; and the army had been expanded. But the Builder's immediate descendants were unable to preserve the gains of their illustrious ancestor, and the period of decline was halted only at the end of the century by Queen T^camar (1184–1212).

BIBLIOGRAPHY

N. A. Berdzenishvili, *Ocherk iz istorii razvitiia feodal'nykh otnoshenii v Gruzii* (1938); René Grousset, *Histoire de l'Armenie dès origines à 1071* (1947); David Marshall Lang, *The Georgians* (1966); Mariam D. Lordkipanidze, *Istoriia Gruzii XI—nachalo XIII veka* (1974); Cyril Toumanoff, "Armenia and Georgia," in *The Cambridge Medieval History*, IV, 1 (1966), 593–637, 983–1009.

RONALD G. SUNY

[See also **Bagratids (Bagratuni), Georgian; Gelati; Georgia: Political History.**]

DAVID OF SASUN (Sasunc^ci Dawit^c in Armenian) is the major hero of the third cycle of the Armenian national folk epic *Sasna Cŕer* (The daredevils of Sasun). Since its first publication in 1874 the entire epic has been popularly identified by the name of this hero, and thus it has been transmitted to the West.

Sasna Cŕer was not recorded until 1873; the ethnographer Garegin Sruanjteanc^c first chanced upon it in the village of Aŕnist, located in the plain of Muš, and published his notes in 1874 in Constantinople. From 1874 to 1951 over sixty different versions and fragments were gathered and published by ethnographers. Manuk Abełean, the first editor of the critical edition of the corpus of the versions, reached the conclusion that what he and his colleagues had salvaged were the vestiges of a dying tradition, but subsequent research and field work in Soviet Armenia sponsored by the Institute of Archaeology and Ethnography of the Armenian Academy of Sciences during 1971–1973, revealed that the tradition had not ended. The researchers gathered eighty-one new versions from peasants who were all above the age of sixty and were originally from western Armenia. Fourteen of these newly discovered versions were published in 1979.

David of Sasun and the other major heroes and villains in the epic—Covinar, the mother of the heroes; her twin sons Sanasar and Pałtasar; Mher; David; Msra Melik^c; P^cok^cr Mher—are all mythical figures. The etymology of the name Covinar suggests a sea or a water deity, and Mher is a variant of Mihr, the Armenized form of the Zoroastrian god Mithra.

The Armenian folk epic reflects an illiterate medieval Armenian peasant society coping with the eternal problems created by foreign oppression. The struggle of the people against the oppressors, the heavy burden of taxes, the lack of water, which is regarded as the source of life, and the difficulty of survival in a hostile environment constitute some of the basic themes in *David of Sasun*. The memory of the great rebellion of 849 by the people of Sasun and Xoyt^c—the mountainous areas to the south and southeast of the plain of Muš—against the caliphate, the emergence of the Mamikonean feudal family in Sasun during the eleventh and twelfth centuries, and the defiant restless and semiautonomous modus vivendi of the people of Sasun until the end of the nineteenth century were all factors in the emergence and development of this epic. According to the information given by two Portuguese travelers of the sixteenth century, the story of "King David" and his heroic deeds was quite well known in the region of Sasun.

The subject matter of the Armenian folk epic is based on the central theme of conflict between the people of Sasun and those of Msr, a non-Christian realm that is one day's journey away. On her way to a forced marriage with the caliph of Baghdad, Covinar, the daughter of an Armenian king, drinks water from a "life-giving spring" and conceives. She gives birth to the twins Sanasar and Paltasar, whom she raises as Christians. The twins are forced to flee the court of the caliph in order to avoid being sacrificed to his idols. They head for Armenia, where they found Sasun. In a dream the older brother, Sanasar, goes down to the underworld, where he meets the Mother of God, the Christianized version of the goddess of the underworld, and returns with superhuman qualities.

The second cycle of the epic is about Sanasar's son Mher, whose life is marked by various heroic exploits and conflict with the *melik*^{C} of Msr, to whom Sasun is obliged to pay taxes. The conflict remains unresolved, since neither Mher nor Msra Melik^C is able to vanquish the other. They come to terms: Msra Melik^C relieves Sasun of the heavy taxes, and in return Mher promises to become the guardian of the *melik*^{C}'s wife and children after he passes away. Soon thereafter the *melik*^{C} dies and Mher goes to Msr, where the wife of the *melik*^{C} lures him and he begets an illegitimate son. Several years later Mher returns home, and shortly before his death he begets David of Sasun from his legitimate wife. His illegitimate son rules in Msr as the new *melik*^{C} and oppresses the people of Sasun.

In the third cycle of the epic there is a struggle between the two half brothers. David finally emerges victorious over his antagonist and liberates Sasun. The fourth cycle concerns P^{C}ok^{C}r Mher, the son of David. He is intolerant of the wickedness in this world. The story ends with his incarceration inside a rock where he shall remain until the present world is destroyed and a better one emerges.

BIBLIOGRAPHY

Critical texts. Sasna Cṙer, Manuk Abelean and Karapet Melik^C-Ohanǰanean, eds., 2 vols. in 3 (1936–1951); *Sasna Cṙer*, Sargis Yarut^{C}iwnean and Aruseak Sahakaen, eds., III (1979); *Sasunc^{C}i Dawit^C, haykakan žołovrdakan ēpos*, 2nd ed. (1961). *English translations. David of Sassoun*, Artin K. Shalian, trans. (1964); *Daredevils of Sassoun, the Armenian National Epic*, Leon Surmelian, trans. (1964).

Krikor H. Maksoudian

[See also **Armenian Literature**.]

DAVID OF TAO (Armenian: Tayk^C) (*d.* 1000) was a Georgian Bagratid prince ruling in the marchlands between Georgia and Armenia proper. He was descended from the Iberian Bagratids and was the son of Adarnase of Tao. According to the chronicles, David was pious, merciful to the poor, compassionate, without resentment, generous, a great friend of monks, a great builder of churches, and magnanimous with everyone. In 975 the viceroy of Iberia ceded that land to David, who in turn made Gurgeni I king. David was actively involved in political and dynastic affairs not only in Georgia and Armenia but in the Byzantine Empire as well. When Basil II was engaged in civil war against the rebels led by Bardas Skleros (976–979), David sent 12,000 cavalry troops to aid the emperor. Basil rewarded David with extensive lands on the frontier of Byzantium extending from Tao toward Lake Van and including Theodosiopolis and Manazkert, though David was only able to retake that city from the Marawanid emirs by 992–994.

David thus became the most powerful ruler in Caucasia. In 978 he replaced Tevdos (Theodosios) III as king of Abkhazeti with Bagrat, heir to the throne of Iberia. David, himself childless, considered Bagrat a son and made him heir to Tao and his other holdings. In the east he collaborated with Gagik I of Armenia in settling the disputed Iberian succession. In 987–989 David supported his friend Bardas Phokas in his rebellion against Basil II, and when David and Bardas were defeated by a joint Russo-Byzantine force, David agreed to cede his lands to the empire at his death. In 990 the emperor named or confirmed David as curopalate of Iberia. But at David's death in 1000, perhaps instigated by the pro-Byzantine party among his nobles, the kings of Georgia hoped to gain David's legacy. Basil II marched eastward to claim his inheritance. Bagrat III of Abkhazeti (978–1014) and his father Gurgeni of Iberia (K^{C}art^{C}li) (994–1008) met with Basil but were unable to prevent the Byzantine annexation of Tao. The real legacy of David of Tao, however, was realized within the decade when, on the death of Gurgeni, his heir Bagrat III became the first ruler of a united Georgian kingdom.

BIBLIOGRAPHY

Z. Avalichvili, "La succession du curopalate David d'Ibérie, dynast de Tao," in *Byzantion*, 8 (1933); John Harper Forsyth, "The Byzantine-Arab Chronicle (938–1034) of Yaḥyā B. Sa^{C}īd al-Anṭaki," 2 vols. (diss., Univ. of Michigan, 1977); René Grousset, *Histoire de l'Arménie dès ori-*

gines à 1071 (1947); Cyril Toumanoff, "Armenia and Georgia," in *The Cambridge Medieval History,* IV, 1 (1966), 593–637, 983–1009.

RONALD G. SUNY

[See also **Bagratids (Bagratuni), Georgian; Bardas Phokas; Bardas Skleros; Basil II "Killer of Bulgars"; Georgia; Political History.**]

DAVID THE INVINCIBLE (Dawit^c Anyałt^c), according to the Armenian tradition dating from as early as the tenth century, was the author of several philosophical and theological works, commentaries, and scholia on the *Grammar* of Dionysius Thrax, and the translator of the works of Aristotle and Porphyry. The same tradition maintains that David was a pupil of Mesrop Maštoc^c, the inventor of the Armenian alphabet, that he was among the Armenian students sent to Constantinople in the 420's, and that he also studied in Athens. David was given the epithet "Invincible" because of his excellence in rhetoric, and after the Council of Chalcedon (451) he returned to Armenia, where he taught philosophy. David's name appears among the saints of the Armenian church.

It is impossible to establish the veracity of the above tradition through the fifth-century sources. Koriwn, the fifth-century biographer and pupil of Maštoc^c, mentions no one named David among his schoolmates. The late-fifth-century historian Łazar P^carpec^ci is also unaware of the existence of such a person.

In the corpus of philosophical texts attributed to David the Invincible there are at least four works that have attracted the interest of modern scholars. Two of these, *Prolegomena tēs philosophias (Sahmank^c Imastasirut^cean)* and *Scholia tēs Porphyriou eisogogēs (Verlucut^ciwn neracut^ceann Porp^ciwri)* are translations from the Greek and were written by a Christian Neoplatonist named David *theophilestatos* and *theophrōn* (philosopher), affiliated with the school of Alexandria. A third work, a commentary on the *Categories* of Aristotle, also bears the name of David as its author. The extant Armenian translation of this, *Meknut^ciwn Storogut^ceanc^cn Aristoteli,* is without the name of the author. According to modern scholars, the author is either Elias or Olympiodorus, both of the school of Alexandria. In the Armenian corpus of

David the Invincible there is a commentary on the *Analytics* of Aristotle, *Meknut^ciwn i Verlucakann Aristoteli,* that is similar in style to the above three works, but its Greek original has not been discovered. The Armenian translations of these four works probably date from the seventh century. According to Yakob Manandean, they were produced in an Armenian Chalcedonian milieu. The identity of the Neoplatonist David, who wrote in the second half of the sixth century, is otherwise unknown.

Modern scholars are divided on the question of the identity and authorship of the works of David the Invincible. Soviet Armenian scholars accept the medieval tradition as historically valid and consider David a late-fifth- or early-sixth-century Armenian philosopher identical with the Neoplatonist David. Earlier researchers and scholars outside the Soviet Union, however, were never certain about the national origin of the Neoplatonist David. Moreover, on the basis of the extant philosophical, theological, and grammatical corpus of David the Invincible's works, they have shown several Armenian Davids who flourished during the sixth and seventh centuries. Among these they have distinguished a scholiast, a poet called Dawt^cak, a theologian named David of Hark^c (probably identical with David of Tarōn), and an early-eighth-century translator David Hypatos. One of these Davids is probably the prototype of the composite figure of David the Invincible.

BIBLIOGRAPHY

P. Nersēs Akinian, *David Harkazi unbesiegter Philosoph, Leben und Werken* (1959); Sen S. Arevshatian, *Formirovanie filosofskoi nauki v drevnei Armenii (V–VI vv.)* (1973); V. Chaloian, *Filosofiia Davida Nepobedimogo* (1946); Missak Khostikian, *David der Philosoph* (1907).

KRIKOR H. MAKSOUDIAN

[See also **Armenian Hellenizing School.**]

DAVID, GERARD (*ca.* 1460–1523), Dutch painter born in Oudewater. Gerard David received his training in the environs of Haarlem and in 1484 settled in Bruges, where he came under the influence of Hans Memling. His earliest paintings (such as the *Crucifixion,* Reinhart Collection, Winterthur, Switzerland) are close in style to Geertgen tot Sint Jans. His major works are the panels of the *Judg-*

Virgo inter Virgines. Gerard David, 1509. MUSÉE DES BEAUX ARTS, ROUEN: LAUROS-GIRAUDON

ment of Cambyses (1498) in Bruges, the *Altarpiece of the Baptism* in Bruges (between 1502 and 1507), and the *Virgo inter virgines* in Rouen (1509). His style exhibits the hearty traits of the Haarlem school in the treatment of figures in space, and the refinements of drapery and head types of Memling. David has been characterized as the last great master of the early Bruges school.

BIBLIOGRAPHY
Max J. Friedländer, *Early Netherlandish Painting,* VI pt. 2 (1971).

JAMES SNYDER

[See also **Flemish Painting; Geertgen tot Sint Jans; Memling, Hans.**]

DAW, JOHN, an early-sixteenth-century English woodcarver from Lawhitton, Cornwall. With John Parwa (Pares or Parrys), a carver of North Lew, Daw is known to have executed the carved screen, the rood-loft, and other woodwork for the parish of Stratton, Cornwall, between 1531 and 1538. In the early sixteenth century Cornwall and Devon were known as great woodcarving areas with a number of prolific local workshops of renown.

BIBLIOGRAPHY
Bishop Hobhouse, *Churchwardens Accounts* (1890), 74; Lawrence Stone, *Sculpture in Britain: The Middle Ages,* 2nd ed. (1972), 224.

JENNIFER E. JONES

[See also **Screen.**]

DAWĀT, Arabic term for a portable inkwell. Often the word was used to describe narrow rectangular boxes provided with compartments not only for inkwells but also for reed pens and other scribal implements. Most surviving examples are made of brass and some have inlaid silver inscriptions or decorations. In Fatimid Egypt a *dawāt* was placed before the ruler in audiences and carried in front of him in processions, thus becoming an emblem of

Dawāt. Brass inlaid with silver and gold, Damascus, late 13th or early 14th century. THE METROPOLITAN MUSEUM OF ART, GIFT OF J. PIERPONT MORGAN, 1917

royal power. The *dawāt* was used by high officials, such as the vizier, as well as by professional scribes. In Iran the same object was sometimes identified by a Persian term, *qalāmdan* (pen box).

PRISCILLA P. SOUCEK

[See also **Writing Materials, Islamic.**]

DAWID-GAREDJA, a monastic complex in Georgia cut out of living rock. The earliest monastery was established in the sixth century by one of the Syrian Fathers, David of Garedja, and rapidly expanded. In David's lifetime two sizable dependencies were added: Dodos Rka and St. John the Baptist. These monasteries grew, attaining their peak between 1000 and 1300, though they remained active until the eighteenth century. The monasteries contain many wall paintings executed in the twelfth and thirteenth centuries, such as those in the main church and refectory in Bertubani and in the Church of the Annunciation and refectory in Udabno. Dawid-Garedja is rich in portrait representations of donors and contemporary rulers. The monasteries were active until the eighteenth century.

BIBLIOGRAPHY

G. Tshubinashvili, *Pescernye monastyri David-Garedji* (1948); G. Abramishvili, *Davit Garedjelis cikli Kartul Kedlis mhatvrobashi* (1972), 167–172, with English summary.

WACHTANG DJOBADZE

[See also **Georgian Art and Architecture; Georgian Church.**]

DĀWŪD IBN MARWĀN AL-MUQAMMIṢ (full name: Dāwūd ibn Marwān al-Raqqī al-Shīrāzī al-Muqammiṣ), a Jewish theologian writing in Syria/Iraq around the last third of the ninth century. Only one of his works, written in Arabic, has survived, the fragmentary ᶜ*Ishrūn Maqālāt* (Twenty exposés). It is a compendium of Judaic theology and apologetics in which he combines the technique of Greek philosophy manuals of late antiquity with the dialectic of Muslim *Kalām*. He uses his knowledge of Monophysite theology, acquired during the Christian period of his career, to refute the dogma of the Trinity, as well as to contend against Manichaean dualism, Islam, and the free thought that negates prophecy. As a Neoplatonist he professes the doctrine of the negative attributes of God. His ethics are basically Hellenistic. He alludes to Jewish messianism in general terms and he states the problem of eternal retribution in the hereafter. Traces of his thought were preserved until the twelfth century and sporadically even later.

BIBLIOGRAPHY

Salo W. Baron, *A Social and Religious History of the Jews*, 2nd ed., VIII (1958), 91–98, 297–298, 327; Julius Guttmann, *Philosophies of Judaism*, David W. Silverman, trans. (1964), 74–75; Isaac Husik, *History of Mediaeval Jewish Philosophy*, 2nd ed. (1930), 17–22; Moritz Steinschneider, *Die arabische Literatur der Juden* (1902), 37, and *Die hebraeischen Uebersetzungen des Mittelalters* (1893), 259–262; George Vadja, in Alexander Altmann, ed., *Jewish Medieval and Renaissance Studies* (1967), "'Le Pari de Pascal' dans un texte judéo-arabe du IXᵉ siècle," in *Mélanges d'histoire des religions offerts à Henri-Charles Puech* (1974), and "La prophétologie de Dāwūd ibn Marwān al Raqqī *al-Muqammiṣ*," in *Journal asiatique*, 265 (1977).

GEORGES VAJDA

[See also **Philosophy-Theology, Jewish, in the Islamic World.**]

DAYR, an Arabic word of Syriac origin designating a Christian monastery in the Middle East. The monastic movement flourished in this area in the sixth and seventh centuries, and continued to maintain numerous active centers of Christian liturgical and intellectual life after the Arab Muslim conquest of Iraq, upper Mesopotamia, Syria, Palestine, and Egypt. The word originally signified a hermitage but came to be applied as well to the complex of church, cells, inn, and exterior shops that characterized the typical *dayr*.

The relative solitude of farming, prayer, and intellectual pursuits gave way to large, festive gatherings on major Christian feasts, when Muslims as well as Christians shared in the celebration. From such accounts there emerged a genre of Muslim literature, the book of monasteries, which assembled bacchic poetry classified according to the monastery in which it was composed. Monastery libraries transmitted much of the Greek classical heritage, in Syriac, to Arab philosophers, and men educated in monastery schools staffed the bureaucracies of Muslim caliphs.

Eastern monasticism declined from the eleventh century on. Nevertheless, monasteries are still active today in northern Iraq, Egypt, and especially Lebanon.

JOHN J. DONOHUE, S.J.

[See also **Minorities; Monastery.**]

DEACON. See **Clergy.**

DEAD, OFFICE OF THE. Although it is sometimes stated that this, the oldest of the supererogatory Offices, was of purely Roman origin and might antedate Gregory I, the first evidence of a structured office like that practiced throughout the Middle Ages dates to about 800 in the *Ordo* of Angilbert of St.

Riquier. Before that time there are references to such services as the recitation of the psalter or parts thereof on the death of a monk, but it is not until Angilbert's *Ordo* that a structured vespers, matins, and lauds of the dead are mentioned. Shortly thereafter it seems that the Office was introduced at Inde by Benedict of Aniane, and it appears again in the series of decrees of the Council of Aachen (816–817) known as the *Institutio canonicorum*. In this early period, it is not certain on what occasions the office was used or whether it was obligatory. But by the tenth century the Office of the Dead was fully established in Benedictine, especially Cluniac, monasteries.

Throughout the Middle Ages there were three hours of this Office: vespers or *Placebo* (from the first word of its antiphon); matins or *Dirige* (whence "dirge") or *Vigiliae mortuorum;* and lauds or *Exultabunt*. These Offices could be interspersed at var-

Office of the Dead. From the book of hours of the Master of Catherine of Cleves, *ca.* 1440. THE PIERPONT MORGAN LIBRARY, MS M. 917, fol. 101

ious times in the regular Office, but the usual arrangement came to be that matins and lauds of the dead were said together at night during the winter after the matins of the day but before lauds; during the summer the matins of the dead was detached and said after the vespers of the dead as the last prayer in the evening. The Office of the Dead was recited on the death of a person as well as daily, either in a solemn or in a simple form. It was usually omitted, however, on Sundays and on principal feasts and their octaves.

The structure of the three hours was very similar, the major differences coming in the variation of versicles and psalms at all the hours and the responses at matins. All three Offices began directly with the antiphon for the first psalm, the introductory versicle being omitted. Vespers and lauds had five psalms, each with antiphon; matins had three nocturns, each with three psalms with antiphons, and three lessons with responses. In vespers and lauds the Magnificat and Benedictus respectively would follow the psalms and antiphons. There would then be additional psalms, versicles, and collects, and the *Requiescant in pace* would conclude Vespers.

BIBLIOGRAPHY

Edmund Bishop, "On the Origin of the Prymer," in his *Liturgica historica* (1918), 211–223; Camillus Callewaert, *Sacris erudiri* (1960), 69–77; Geoffrey Rowell, *The Liturgy of Christian Burial* (1977), 66ff.; John B. L. Tolhurst, ed., *The Monastic Breviary of Hyde Abbey, Winchester,* VI (1942), 107–113.

ROGER E. REYNOLDS

[See also **Death and Burial, in Europe; Divine Office.**]

DEADLY SINS. See Seven Deadly Sins.

DEATH AND BURIAL, IN EUROPE. During the Middle Ages ideas, practices, and depictions of death and burial fluctuated according to evolving concepts in Christian anthropology, ecclesiology, soteriology, and eschatology. As some of the most profound and emotive of mysteries, death and burial impinge on many areas of scholarship, and the field for research in medieval customs and thought is vast, drawing on such sources as religious and secular writings, legal materials (including wills), and visual representa-

tions. Drawing on such material, this article will focus on theories, liturgical practice, and artistic portrayals of death and burial.

THEORIES OF DEATH AND BURIAL

In the early Middle Ages reflection on death and burial was largely dominated by the patristic heritage. As the church had come to be the official religion of the Roman Empire, where both burial and cremation were practiced, her ideas and attitudes toward death and burial had come to supplant those of the pagans, though many of the practices—the preparation of the body, the wake, the funeral procession—continued or were modified by Christians. One of the most distinctive traits of early Christianity was its view of death. Although the emotions of sorrow and grief could not be denied, Christian writers emphasized positive elements within the context of the resurrection of Christ, who had conquered death. For Christians death was not to be feared but was a joyful and victorious experience. Augustine, for example, emphasized the joyful element in the funeral of his mother, Monica (*Confessions* 9.12.29–32), and repeatedly Christians were told to dress in colors of joy and not the black and mournful garb of the pagans.

Reflecting this joyful, victorious attitude, patristic thought viewed death in a variety of ways. As countless funerary inscriptions attest, death was seen as a sleep of those awaiting the resurrection. In the commentaries of the Fathers and in the lives of the saints, such as the Life of St. Melania the Younger, death was the summoning of the soul by Christ and the angels who guided its passage to paradise over a way made dangerous by lurking demons. This journey was seen as a migration to the Lord. Both Christ and the church were compared to ships or the Ark of Noah, on which the faithful made their voyage toward the East. Finally, death was called a *dies natalis,* or day of birth, a day on which peace and light were attained, a day on which the anniversaries of both saints and common Christians were celebrated.

As to the patristic attitude toward the body inherited by the Middle Ages, Augustine's is typical of many a Christian anthropology, and in both the *De civitate dei* (City of God) and *De cura pro mortuis gerenda* (On the care of the dead) he dealt with the issue. On the one hand he stressed that at death the soul was absolutely separated from the body and the world, and that strictly speaking the lack of a funeral or burial could not affect the dead. On the other hand, he said that one should not despise or cast aside the bodies of the dead, especially those of Christians, since they had been temples of the Holy Spirit and were part of the very nature of man. Thus, in the case of the bodies of saints God might even work miracles through contact with the relics of the earthly body.

In the early Middle Ages this heritage of patristic thought continued to be reflected in the liturgical formularies used in the ministrations to the dying and in burial services. To the ninth century there were, according to Damien Sicard, three focuses around which themes in liturgical formularies seemed to cluster: theology (the role of God), anthropology (the dead and the dying person), and ecclesiology (the role of the church). From the fifth to the seventh century God was seen as one who makes man live, one who creates and recreates, purifying sinful man and leading him into the holy city, Jerusalem, and the company of saints. The church, to-

Guardian angel and demon battling over a corpse. From the book of hours of the Master of Catherine of Cleves, *ca.* 1440. THE PIERPONT MORGAN LIBRARY, MS M. 917, p. 206

gether with God and the angels, was the guide, its ministers assisting in and celebrating the passage.

These themes of the formularies from the very early Middle Ages passed into the liturgical books of the Carolingian period, which then became the basis for later medieval development. But to these themes others were added. On the theological level, there was a new emphasis on the grandeur of God, the judge and dispenser of mercy and indulgence. On the anthropological level, there was a growing disdain for the body and stress on the liberation of the person both from his body and from his sins. Further, in the liturgical formularies there appeared an atmosphere of fear with images of Gehenna, darkness, and the judgment to come. And finally, on the ecclesiological level, in the prayers, there was a new emphasis on the community of all the departed (the communion of saints or church triumphant), not simply on the deceased individual.

These new emphases intensified as the Middle Ages wore on. Although synods exhorted pastors to play down the fear of death and emphasize the mercy of God while ministering to the dying, they also stressed the majesty of the final judge and the sinful state of man. Hence, a new emphasis was placed on the necessity of confession and absolution before death. Prayers for the dead were intensified. As for the body itself, Thomas Aquinas wrote of the insensibility of the corpse and distinguished between the body as matter and the soul as form; but more and more there was a growing and almost macabre fascination with the dead body itself, a phenomenon reflected in popular literature and art.

THE RITES OF DEATH AND BURIAL

The rites of death and burial varied as to their sequence and content but generally included the last rites for the dying, preparation of the body, procession to and services in the church, procession to and rites at the cemetery, burial, and postburial rites.

Last rites for the dying. In the earliest Western liturgies the sequence of rites was constantly changing, but basically there was a reading of the Passion according to John, the recitation of psalms and litanies (sometimes immediately after death), and the administration of the last communion, called "viaticum" from the Latin word for traveling provisions.

This simple early practice grew more elaborate as additional ceremonies and prayers were added: processions to the house or room of the dying, unction, and most important, confession and absolution of sin. In Cluniac practice, for example, the dying monk confessed his sins and was anointed. He was then brought before the monastic chapter and publicly confessed his faults and received absolution. Thereafter, he was taken back to his bed, where he received a procession consisting of a priest, servers carrying holy water, cross, and candles, and the remainder of the community. While psalms were sung, the dying monk was anointed and given the viaticum. After the community withdrew, a cross and lighted candles were left at the head of his bed. At the approach of death the body was placed on a hair shirt and was sprinkled with ashes. The community was summoned by a loud knocking at the cloister door and they gathered at the infirmary to say the creed, litanies, responses, and psalms. At the moment of death the soul was commended to God, and the community went to the chapel to say the Office of the Dead. Also there might be the tolling of bells.

In the later Middle Ages, outside the monastic complex, there might be a preliminary visit to the dying man by a priest, who would hear his confession and perhaps inquire if a will had been made. The priest then returned to his church and rang the bells; a procession of the community, very much like those for the feast of Corpus Christi, would form to carry communion to the dying. Among the rites at the bedside the role of unction diminished in the later Middle Ages, while emphasis was placed on confession and penance and on the procession and reception of the Eucharist. Moreover, the recitation of the Passion was to be done only if the dying person was literate.

Preparation of the body. After death a variety of commendatory prayers were read and to these were added psalms, *capitula,* and antiphons, among which was the *Requiem aeternam,* noted as early as the eighth century. Thereafter, in the earliest liturgies the body was washed as psalms and antiphons were sung, some with baptismal and paschal overtones. Then, much as in baptismal rites, the body was clothed in dress appropriate to the station of the deceased. In Cluniac practice, for example, this was a shirt and habit with cowl. Finally the body was placed on a bier either to lie at home to be waked or to be borne in procession to the church.

In the preparation of the body, embalming could take place, especially for those of wealth and status (as witnessed by the graphic stitching on the tomb effigies of King Louis XII and his wife at St. Denis). A more unusual preparation of the body, practiced from the twelfth century on, especially for those of high civil and ecclesiastical rank, was dismember-

ment. Parts and bones might be carried to various places for interment, with subsequent boiling down of the remainder. Among the reasons for this practice were the necessity of transporting the remains over considerable distances, the wish of the departed to have certain parts of the body, such as the head, heart, or viscera, buried at different places, the clamor of individual churches or orders (especially the mendicants) to have a portion of the body, and the desire of the deceased to have multiple prayers said for his soul at a variety of locations. Although dismemberment was condemned by Boniface VIII in 1299 and by a host of canonists and theologians, the practice could not be suppressed, and, in fact, dispensations were given by the church.

Procession and services. When ready for removal to the church, the body was borne in procession to the accompaniment of psalms and antiphons by men of equal rank or dignity. Although in most cases the procession had no special significance, the bearing of the king (or his effigy if he had died sometime before) signified the death of the body natural and at least a preliminary validation of the authority of the new king.

On reaching the church, the bier was arranged according to the status of the deceased (for example, a priest facing the altar), candle and cross to the sides. Thereafter services of different types might be held. In Cluniac practice there was a continuous recitation of psalms until burial, interrupted only by the Office and Mass. The night was divided into three watches, one to each side of the choir and one to the children with their masters.

Characteristic of the funeral or requiem Mass was the censing of the deceased after the censing of the altar, the sequence *Dies irae* used in the later Middle Ages, and the words *dona eis requiem* ("grant them rest") substituted for the more usual *miserere nobis* ("have mercy on us") in the Agnus dei.

Rites at the cemetery. Before the body was borne in procession to the grave, there could be a variety of prayers. In the ancient Gelasian Sacramentary, for example, there are prayers asking that the departed might be given a share in Christ's resurrection and that he be granted peace, light, refreshment, and a place with the patriarchs and saints. After this a procession was formed: accompanied with psalms and antiphons, the body was carried to the grave preceded by lights and incense. According to the thirteenth-century commentator, Guillaume Durand, the bier was to be carried by males of equal rank and three stops were to be made on the way to the grave.

At the grave site prayers, psalms, and antiphons were sung, the grave itself was sprinkled with holy water and censed to cover the stench of the body, and laurel was placed in it signifying the victory of those dying in Christ.

Burial. In most simple burials the body was lowered into the grave in a sheet or coffin. There could, however, be enormous variation. The poor man might simply be placed in the bare earth or covered with a tent of tiles. Large earthen jars or more elaborate sarcophagi might be used for the more wealthy. And for the very rich and important, highly ornate sarcophagi above ground might be used. According to the tradition of the High and later Middle Ages the body was to be placed with the feet toward the east in expectation of the last day, although clearly this was not always possible when burial took place in a church or cloister and architectural restraints came into play. Durand noted that those in sacred orders were to be buried with the *instrumenta* of their rank, such as a small wooden chalice for a priest. Also, Christians were to be dressed in clothes befitting their rank and with boots or shoes on their feet so that they might stand properly clad at the Last Judgment.

Postburial rites. With the increase of votive masses from the ninth century on, Christians were especially encouraged to remember the dead. This was to be accomplished in a diversity of ways. In the Divine Office the Office of the Dead was recited regularly. Masses were to be said for the deceased on the day of his departure and on the thirtieth day thereafter. Into the *Hanc igitur* and *Memento mortuorum* formulas of the Mass books, the names of the departed were entered. The diptychs (so-called after ancient winged panels) were read at Mass with the names of those to be commemorated. And obituaries or lists of the dead arranged according to the months of the year were kept so that prayers for the deceased might be said on the anniversaries of their deaths.

ARTISTIC PORTRAYALS

From patristic antiquity, death and the themes connected with it played a major role in Christian art. In the catacombs themselves, even with their images and symbols of victory over death, there are still depictions of *fossarii*, or gravediggers, and symbols of their office. And although they were decorated with symbols of triumph, early Christian sarcophagi still remained somber vessels of death.

In the Middle Ages death and its associated themes were constantly depicted. In manuscript illumination, for example, beyond the scenes of the crucifixion, burial, and resurrection of Christ, there might be portrayed death in battle, death by execution, and the related eschatological themes of the resurrection of the dead, hell and heaven, and the Last Judgment. But perhaps the most striking manuscript depictions of death and burial occur in the books of hours, where extensive series showing the various stages of death and burial accompany the appropriate texts.

Related to this miniature painting in manuscripts was fresco and panel painting, which used many of the same themes. A particularly somber genre in later medieval wall painting was the dance of death, with its macabre skeletons dancing with or dragging away members of various grades of society.

Sculpture, too, was filled with images of death. Besides the less ornate sarcophagi there could be extremely elaborate sepulchers for the wealthy. Sometimes a sculpted effigy of the deceased dressed appropriately to his rank and bearing the symbols of his office would be borne by or surrounded by sculpted hooded mourners. In the fifteenth century tombs with double depictions of important deceased persons became common, the upper effigy an ideal or realistic depiction and the lower a gruesome rotting cadaver or skeleton. Besides the sculptured tombs there were highly ornate memorial crosses and crosses to mark locations where the cortege had stopped, and chantry chapels where Masses for the dead could be said. Themes associated with death were frequently depicted in sculpture: the Last Judgment was often found on the tympana of churches, along with representations of hell and heaven.

In medieval literature some of the greatest works centered on death and its related themes. Dante's *Divine Comedy* is, of course, among the most important of these; others, such as the thirteenth-century *Le Dit des trois mors et des trois vifs,* were the inspiration for paintings of the dance of death or for masques played by men dressed as skeletons.

Finally, some of the most moving achievements in the realm of poetry and music were written for the rituals of death and burial: the antiphon *Dirige* for the Office of the Dead, the response *Libera me,* and finally the sequence *Dies irae,* formerly attributed to the Franciscan Thomas of Celano.

BIBLIOGRAPHY

Thomas S. R. Boase, *Death in the Middle Ages: Mortality, Judgment, and Remembrance* (1972); H. Braef and

W. Verbreke, eds., *Death in the Middle Ages* (1983); Elizabeth A. R. Brown, "Death and the Human Body in the Later Middle Ages: The Legislation of Boniface VIII on the Division of the Corpse," in *Viator*, 12 (1981); Richard Huntington and Peter Metcalf, *Celebrations of Death: The Anthropology of Mortuary Ritual* (1979), 159–172; Theodor Klauser, *Die Cathedra im Totenkult der Heidnischen und christlichen Antike* (1971); Leonard P. Kurtz, *The Dance of Death and the Macabre Spirit in European Literature* (1975), and *La Maladie et la mort du chrétien dans la liturgie*, in *Bibliotheca "Ephemerides liturgicae" Subsid.*, I (1975); Aimé G. Martimort, *L'église en prière: Introduction à la liturgie*, 3rd ed. (1965), 618–630; *La mort au moyen âge, Colloque de l'Association des historiens médiévistes français réunis à Strasbourg en juin 1975* (1977); Jaroslav Pelikan, *The Shape of Death: Life, Death, and Immortality in the Early Fathers* (1961); Richard W. Pfaff, *Medieval Latin Liturgy: A Select Bibliography* (1982), 42–44; Roger E. Reynolds, "Sarcophagi of the Roman Empire," in Oscar W. Muscarella, ed., *Ladders to Heaven: Art Treasures from Lands of the Bible* (1981), 296–304; Geoffrey Rowell, *The Liturgy of Christian Burial* (1977), 19–30, 57–73; Alfred C. Rush, *Death and Burial in Christian Antiquity* (1941); Damien Sicard, *La liturgie de la mort dans l'église latine des origines à la réforme carolingienne* (1978); Karl Stüber, *Commendatio animae: Sterben im Mittelalter* (1976). See also the *International Bibliography of Liturgy*, class 57.

ROGER E. REYNOLDS

[See also **Black Death; Catacombs; Danse Macabre; Inheritance, Western European; Unction of the Sick.**]

DÉBAT, a medieval French lyric form that likely derived from the more satirical twelfth-century Provençal *tenson* (discussion). It features a series of verses or stanzas pronounced alternately by two human or abstract disputants. The subject often involves amorous predicaments, although a wide variety of topics are discussed in the *débat*. Examples range from an exchange between Colin Muset and Jacques d'Amiens about faithlessness in love to Villon's celebrated "Débat du cuer et du corps." Other related forms include the *pastourelle*, the *jeu parti*, and the *conflictus*.

BIBLIOGRAPHY

Alfred Jeanroy, *Les origines de la poésie lyrique en France au moyen âge* (1965), 45–60, 462–478.

CYNTHIA J. BROWN

[See also **Courtly Love; French Literature; Owl and the Nightingale, The; Provençal Literature.**]

DECIR, a poem to be read or recited, not sung, normally composed in *coplas de arte mayor* or *coplas de arte menor* or one of their variations. A short *finida* (ending) is optional. The term *decir* indicates mode of transmission and is not to be confused with *copla* (stanza), the metric form in which the *decir* is composed.

Thematically and stylistically versatile, despite limited metric form, the *decires*, contributing to the *mester de clerecía* tradition, flourished in early- and mid-fifteenth-century Spanish court poetry. They accommodated all genres and modes of nonsong learned poetry. Well known are the allegorical *decires* by Imperial, Páez de Ribera, and Santillana.

BIBLIOGRAPHY

José María Azáceta, ed., *Cancionero*, 3 vols. (1966), containing numerous *decires* and bibliographical notes; Raymond Foulché-Delbosc, *Cancionero castellano del siglo XV*, 2 vols. (1912–1915); Pierre Le Gentil, *La poésie lyrique espagnole et portugaise à la fin du moyen âge* (1949–1953), I, 8–10, 334–336; II, 180–186.

DOROTHY CLOTELLE CLARKE

[See also **Copla; Mester de Clerecía; Spanish Lyric Poetry.**]

DECRETALS are papal letters, but exactly what type of letters is hard to define. This problem of definition has been of concern to historians of canon law and the papacy for generations; it was also a problem for Gratian, the founder of modern canonical jurisprudence. In his *Decretum*, published about 1140, Gratian discussed the question "whether [decretals] have the force of law when they are not included in the corpus of canons?" This question reveals that for Gratian all papal letters were decretals. The real problem was that of defining the binding force of decretals. Was a papal letter binding in law because of its source or because an expert had chosen it for his law collection? Gratian answered that decretals were legally binding because they were papal letters, but he recognized that law collections, and not the papal registers or archives, were where people looked when a legal problem arose. His theory countered the effect of practice.

Studies of the decretal collections of the twelfth century show that no definition of the decretal according to content or form, or as a response to a judicial appeal or to queries forwarded by a lower judge, will suffice to explain why canonists treated some letters as authorities and ignored others. Episcopal and monastic archives contain many judicial responses—mandates, commissions, grants of authority, and the like—that have lain hidden from the eager eyes of lawyers, judges, and litigants other than those to whom they were originally sent.

Decretal collections contain many pieces that had no doctrinal or institutional significance. Some of these merely confirmed a sentence by a judge delegate or commanded that one be executed. Others dealt with liturgical matters, such as when the feast of the Holy Trinity ought to be celebrated, or with matters of purely local interest, such as when feasts begin and end in northern Norway, where the setting and rising sun offer no help. If the decretal must be defined by the characteristics common to all of them, then the choice of commonalities is narrowed to two, its author or its placement in a specialized collection. At the very beginning of the modern canon law system, Gratian recognized and made this choice.

Despite Gratian's definition of the decretal, it did not function as a precedent in the canon law system. To say that any papal letter was a decretal did not mean that the pope could not decide a case against the doctrine of previous decisions. The canon law system was not built with decisions, but was realized in them and in the other forms of legal texts, conciliar decrees, and snippets from patristic writings. Thus, collection of new decretals was important as a supplemental revelation of the canon law, revealed in its basic structure in Gratian's *Decretum*.

Early in the history of the new canonical jurisprudence, users of the *Decretum* created appendixes of decretal texts. By the pontificate of Alexander III (1159–1181), these supplements had grown too large to serve as appendixes. For example, the collection called the *Berolinensis prima* consists of 126 texts, and although it follows a copy of the *Decretum* in its MS, it can hardly be considered an appendix to it. Another collection, *Dertusensis prima*, is about the same size and, in its extant copy, has no connection with a copy of the *Decretum*.

About fifty-five collections of decretals survive, not counting multiple copies and the many fragments. The earliest date from the 1170's, and the filial relationships among them, forming them into several groups, show that lawyers passed them around. The early ones were not topically organized and usually contain full copies of the letters they transmit. These unsystematic ("primitive") collections were never simply copied as they circulated,

but were used as the basis of new collections that were enlarged at each stage by material from local archives and from other collections available to the compiler. As a result there is only one copy of each known primitive collection. These unique productions continued to be made well into the 1180's, when they were becoming obsolete because of the creation of better, systematic works.

The systematization of the decretal law began toward the end of the pontificate of Alexander III, when a progressive teacher and legal scholar at Bologna, probably Bernard of Pavia, made the collection called *Parisiensis secunda*. This work predates the Third Lateran Council (March 1179); the latest datable letter in it was issued after 11 May 1177. Bernard used the collection in his *Summa de electione* (published before the council). The main features of the new collection were the organization in titles and the use of cross-references to indicate texts that treated more than one topic. The letters themselves were copied in full under the first title to which each was relevant. This system had a great advantage over the unsystematic collections, some of which contained rudimentary rubrics and titles, but it could obviously be improved. The active development of systematic collections after 1179 realized the potential of the new way of presenting the decretal law.

The decrees of the Third Lateran Council formed a new element in the tradition of post-Gratian law. Churches throughout Europe received copies of the decrees, and these became part of their legal reference libraries. The new, systematic decretal collections developed in conjunction with this expansion of legal sources; and the spirit of reform embodied in the decrees was transferred to the new works. The *Bambergensis* and its derivatives, the Tanner Collection and the *Appendix Laterani concilii*, are decretal collections that follow the decrees of the council and treat the decretals in a systematic way. In these works the decretals that treat more than one subject are divided into parts that are distributed among the appropriate titles. Here the legal scholarship of the period reached a significant stage, at which an attempt was made to present the new law as it was realized in the decretals. This presentation was accomplished by organization and editing of the decretals. The editing made the organization effective and the presentation efficient.

The scholar credited with having created the first systematic collection, Bernard of Pavia, was also the one to establish the basic structure of the decretal law. Between 1188 and 1192 he created the *Breviar-*

ium extravagantium, which later came to be known as the *Compilatio prima.* This collection was the textbook for the first course on the decretals at Bologna, and although there is evidence that the teachers in the northern law schools had already established such courses, Bernard's text became the standard teaching and reference work on the decretal law. The growth of the decretal law did not, of course, stop with the publication of Bernard's book, which went through several editions before the Englishman Gilbert compiled a supplement to it in 1202. Several further textbooks followed soon after this, since Pope Innocent III (1198–1216) produced a stupendous number of important decretals.

These textbooks from Bologna dominated the field, but a welter of small collections as well as the older works continued to circulate. These undermined the systematic presentation of the decretal law and led Pope Gregory IX (1227–1241) to commission a leading lawyer, Raymond of Peñafort, to compile a definitive collection of the decretals. Based on the Bolognese textbooks, the "five compilations," the Decretals of Gregory IX were issued in 1234 as a papal lawbook. All earlier collections not only became obsolete after this, but also were no longer binding in the courts. Later popes, up to John XXII, added to this body of decretal law, but none did so by revising or replacing it. The Decretals of Gregory IX, representing the decretal law up to 1234, became a part of the *Corpus iuris canonici.*

BIBLIOGRAPHY

Gerard Fransen, *Les décrétales et les collections de décrétales* (1972); W. Holtzmann, *Studies in the Collections of Twelfth-Century Decretals,* C. R. Cheney and M. G. Cheney, eds., in Monumenta juris canonici, ser. B, III (1979); Stephan Kuttner, *Repertorium der Kanonistik (1140–1234)* (1937), 272–385; K. W. Norr, "Päpstliche Dekretalen und römisch-kanonischer Zivilprozess," in Walter Wilhelm, ed., *Studien zur europäischen Rechtsgeschichte* (1972), 53–65.

STANLEY CHODOROW

[See also **Gratian; Law, Canon; Papacy, Origins and Development of; Raymond of Peñafort, St.**]

DECRETALS, FALSE. The False Decretals form the most influential portion of numerous spurious documents from the mid ninth century known collectively as the Pseudo-Isidorian forgeries. "Isidorus Mercator," later often confused with Isidore of Se-

Page from the so-called False Decretals, the Harmony of the Spheres. Pen drawing, Rheims, *ca.* 1180. BIBLIOTHÈQUE MUNICIPALE, RHEIMS, MS 672, fol. 1r

ville, claimed to have gathered into a single volume all major conciliar decisions down to the Second Council of Seville (619—in fact the Thirteenth Council of Toledo [683]) and all papal decretals down to Pope Gregory II (*d.* 731), thus making his the largest historical-chronological collection of early medieval canon law. He modeled his beginning and ending on the then widely used and quasi-official *Dionysio-Hadriana* collection, and parts II and III of his three-part work on the Gallican version of the *Hispana* collection. Indeed, a falsified version of the canons in the Gallican *Hispana,* now extant in a single manuscript that originated at Corbie (Biblioteca Apostolica Vaticana, MS Vat. lat. 1341, tenth century) but of which there were once at least three additional copies in the ecclesiastical province of Rheims, may well have represented the first stage in the forgers' work. The final version of the falsified canons (*Hispana* part I became Pseudo-Isidore part II) is prefaced by the *De primitiua ecclesia et synodo Nicena* and the *Constitutum Constantini* (or Donation of Constantine), forged about a century earlier; through their inclusion those two documents acquired enormous influence in later medieval history. Unfortunately, Hinschius published these canons (pp. 258–444) in their authentic (as available in nineteenth-century editions) rather than their falsified version, a major editorial blunder that still often misleads scholars. Also associated with the Pseudo-Isidorean forgeries are seventy-one or seventy-two sentences (according to which tradition is accepted) on judicial procedure known as the *Capitula Angilramni* and three books of forged capitularies ascribed to Benedictus Levita.

The False Decretals as such make up virtually all of the first part and a fair portion of the third in Pseudo-Isidore's collection. To the authentic decretals of popes Damasus (366–384) through Gregory I (590–604), compiled in part II of the *Hispana*, Pseudo-Isidore added numerous spurious letters in what became his own part III. His boldest step, however, was to forge for his own wholly unprecedented part I some sixty decretal letters ascribed to the earliest popes. He began with an earlier forgery, the *Canons of the Apostles;* then he adapted for his purposes the *Pseudo-Clementines,* spurious fourth-century letters (with layers going back to the late second or early third centuries) claiming to describe in homiletic fashion the transmission of power from Christ through St. Peter to Clement (the fourth pope) and the ideal form for each ecclesiastical office; and finally he followed the *Liber pontificalis* from Anacletus (who actually reigned before Clement) to Melchiades (or Miltiades, *d.* 314), preparing for each pope wholly forged letters that depict the law and structure of the church as fully formed and papally authorized from its very earliest days.

The exact form in which these forged letters first appeared remains uncertain; indeed, scholars continue to discover fragments of similar theme and style that somehow never became a part of the larger collection. Fully ninety to one hundred manuscripts of Pseudo-Isidore's collection still survive, making it the most frequently copied historical-chronological collection; and, notably, more than a dozen of those manuscripts date to the late ninth or early tenth century—that is, to the first two generations after the forgery was done. Most scholars agree that the desired final form of the work was the one that Hinschius labeled the *A-1* version (the three-part collection of forged early decretals, falsified canons, and partially forged later decretals described above). Unfortunately Hinschius dismissed the manuscript of this version now considered among the oldest and best (Biblioteca Apostolica Vaticana, MS Vat. lat.

Ottobon. 93, from *ca.* 860), selected as his base a faulty north Italian manuscript, and published a decidedly "mixed" edition.

Hinschius' *A/B* class can also be traced back to the ninth century through a highly regarded manuscript from Corbie (now in the Biblioteca Apostolica Vaticana, MS Vat. lat. 630); to judge from its conciliar sections, this may represent a preparatory stage rather than the final version of the forgery. The *A-2* class contains only false decretals from Clement to Damasus, numbered consecutively and supplied with rubrics (as in Hinschius' edition)—the heart, in effect, of the False Decretals. There are nine ninth-century manuscripts of this version, mostly from northern Italy, still extant. By the 870's or 880's (judging from the two oldest manuscripts) someone gathered seventy-five excerpts from this version into what became known as the Pseudo-Remedius of Chur collection. Eventually Hinschius' *B* and *C* classes also derived from *A-2,* with the latter providing the basis for the first printed edition by J. Merlin in 1524. In sum, no previous canonistic collection, and certainly no other medieval forgery, was transmitted so rapidly, in such numbers, and with such diversity as Pseudo-Isidore's collection.

It is all the more surprising, then, that scholars still cannot determine exactly where the forgeries originated and what immediate impact, if any, they had on the church. The Pseudo-Isidorian forgers probably belonged to a mid-ninth-century reform party determined to bolster the rights and privileges of bishops in the Frankish empire against clerical and lay rivals. Hence they paid little or no attention to aspects of canon law not pertinent to the bishop's office, and they consistently celebrated bishops as "high priests," "thrones of God," and "eyes of the Lord." The deposition, forced recantation, and exspoliation of Ebo of Rheims (*d.* 851) seem to lie behind certain particular points stressed in Pseudo-Isidore. It was also in the ecclesiastical province of Rheims that the False Decretals were first cited, and there too that several of the earliest manuscripts originated, with a noteworthy concentration of connections, first pointed out by Fuhrmann, to the abbey of Corbie. It is among the followers of Ebo and the adversaries of Archbishop Hincmar of Rheims, therefore, that the forgers were most likely to be found, and historians have dated their work roughly to the years 847–852.

To protect bishops against attack, Pseudo-Isidore "recalled" the law and structure of the church's early golden years. Charges brought by "infamous witnesses" and those based on forced written confessions were to be thrown out of court. Only laymen and lower clerics of utterly spotless character could bring charges against lower clergymen and bishops, respectively. Deposed and exspoliated bishops could not be put on trial until their offices and properties had been restored (the *exceptio spolii*). If all these obstacles were overcome, the trial could then take place only if both accuser and accused agreed to appear together; and a conviction could not be obtained unless there were seventy-two irreproachable witnesses against the bishop! Even then conviction and deposition became binding only upon papal confirmation. As chief among the rivals to episcopal authority, chorepiscopi were banished from the hierarchy and reduced to simple priestly status.

Metropolitans constituted the most serious threats to bishops from above. Pseudo-Isidore invented the office of primate as a higher check on their authority; primates held sees in the first cities of old Roman provinces—thus Trier (where Ebo's followers had fled) was superior to Rheims in Belgica. Moreover, provincial synods presided over by metropolitans could investigate bishops only within their own ecclesiastical provinces, and then only when all bishops of the province were present. Pseudo-Isidore also enhanced the authority of Rome: bishops could appeal to Rome at any point in their trials; the approval of Rome was needed to convene valid provincial synods; and confirmation by Rome was necessary finally to depose bishops. In short, through these and numerous other procedural details, Pseudo-Isidore sought to invoke the authority of the earliest popes to render the trial and deposition of bishops a virtual impossibility.

Pseudo-Isidore drew on a large variety of sources to concoct his False Decretals: Scripture, authentic (but later) decretals and canons, the church fathers, and Irish penitentials. Liturgical and sacramental matters peculiar to episcopal authority also received considerable attention, and the homiletic, even hagiographic, style of the letters aimed to show the earliest popes and contemporary bishops at their best. The Reformed theologian David Blondel (1628) first proved by thorough source analysis that the decretals prior to Damasus I had no historical authenticity whatsoever.

Scholars have long debated the impact of the False Decretals. Protestant and secular historians once ascribed the making of the Roman papal monarchy largely to these forgeries, while Catholics insisted that the Roman church owed nothing of its claims and powers to this "pious fraud." In fact the quantitative impact of the False Decretals cannot be lightly dismissed; they made up, for instance, about one-tenth of Gratian's *Decretum*, the standard textbook of medieval canon law. But their qualitative influence requires more nuanced judgment, as Fuhrmann has shown. Quite possibly almost every Frankish see was initally provided with a copy. Hincmar of Rheims, the likely object of the forgers' activity, was the first to use—and also the first to question—several of the False Decretals. The crushing defeat of his suffragan nephew, Hincmar of Laon, in 871, however, effectively obstructed the use of Pseudo-Isidore's collection as a platform for the promotion of episcopal reform and privilege. Henceforth reception of the False Decretals depended largely on their inclusion individually in systematic collections, culminating in Gratian's *Decretum* (*ca.* 1140).

In the collections of the later ninth, tenth, and eleventh centuries, the False Decretals had their greatest impact on procedural law, complicating immeasurably the formal process of accusation, trial, and conviction. The False Decretals in fact created wholly new law only in detailed matters of procedure and in the invented office of primate. In the late eleventh century, however, the Gregorian reformers, in their zeal for the liberty of the church, rediscovered the privileges and honors Pseudo-Isidore had heaped upon the Roman church, in particular the right to appeal to Rome at any time, the need for Roman confirmation of provincial synods (later to influence the question of conciliarism), and the required approval of Rome for episcopal depositions. The claims of the reformers sprang from religious conviction, but the False Decretals seemed to support their views with the authority of the earliest popes.

There was still another, more imponderable way in which the False Decretals were to influence the Western church throughout the later Middle Ages. These decretals created the impression that papal rulings had governed the life of the church from the beginning and that the hierarchical church had sprung directly from the precepts of St. Peter and his earliest successors.

BIBLIOGRAPHY

Edition. Paulus Hinschius, ed., *Decretales Pseudo-Isidoriana et Capitula Angilramni* (1863, repr. 1963).

Studies. The best overview, with literature down to 1905, is E. Seckel, "Pseudoisidor," in Johann Herzog, ed.,

Realenzyklopädie für protestantische Theologie und Kirche, XVI (1905), 265–307. On the question of influence and for more recent scholarship, see Horst Fuhrmann, *Einfluss und Verbreitung der pseudoisidorischen Fälschungen*, 3 vols. (1972–1974), esp. 43–51. Other important publications include J. Richter, "Stufen pseudoisidorischer Fälschung: Untersuchungen zum Konzilsteil der pseudoisidorischen Dekretalen," in *Zeitschrift für Rechtsgeschicht*, Kan. Abt., 95 (1978); K.-G. Schon, "Eine Redaktion der pseudoisidorischen Dekretalen aus der Zeit der Fälschung," in *Deutsches Archiv für Erforschung des Mittelalters*, 34 (1978); Schafer Williams, *Codices Pseudo-Isidoriani: A Paleographico-historical Study* (1971).

JOHN VAN ENGEN

[See also **Benedictus Levita; Ebo of Rheims; Forgery; Hincmar of Rheims; Law, Canon; Papacy, Origins and Development of.**]

DECRETISTS were legal scholars who wrote commentaries on the *Decretum Gratiani*, the basic textbook of canon law. The *Decretum*, completed about 1140, became the basis for a new canonical jurisprudence. Its system of organization and the method of treating the mass of conciliar decrees, papal letters, and snippets of patristic literature that constituted the law of the church made it an ideal textbook. Teachers at Bologna and elsewhere seized on the book as a text from which to lecture in the basic course on canon law.

In its original form the *Decretum* was a series of treatises gathered under the title *Concordia discordantium canonum*. The masters who used it revised the book, first by dividing it into small sections and second by adding material to it. This revision was the first activity of the decretists, and it took place so early in the transmission of the *Decretum* that no manuscript preserves the original version. But the principal work of the decretists was to provide explanatory material and summaries of the text.

The canons collected in the *Decretum* presented many problems, since they had accumulated over a period of ten centuries, and therefore represented many types of documents and many stages in the development of medieval Latin. The earliest comments on the work were glosses, interlinear and marginal, that explained the meaning of words and cited parallel or contrary texts found elsewhere in the book. As the glosses grew more important and expansive, they became established in the margins, and copyists produced *Decretum* texts with ample margins for the comments. The first explanatory glosses were succeeded by *notabilia*, which summarized the texts; *solutiones contrariorum*, which resolved contradictions; and statements of the legal rules contained in the texts. These basic types of glosses developed into independent genres representing the instructional techniques used in the law schools.

The main types of literature derived from the glosses were collections of *notabilia, casus, brocarda, distinctiones*, and *quaestiones*. *Notabilia* often began with "Nota" or "Notandum quod" and set forth the salient points of individual *capitula* in the *Decretum*. From this basic type derived the *brocarda*, which set out the legal rules based on the *capitula*, and the *casus*, which functioned as summaries and rubrics. From the *solutiones contrariorum* came two forms of gloss that were transmitted separately: the large body of *distinctiones* that reconciled contradictions and provided solutions to problems of law, and the *quaestio*, also a major genre, which treated legal problems generated by the individual *capitula* and by the rules of law they contained.

The body of glosses by the decretists grew as a natural product of their teaching activities. In the 1160's scholars began to compile glosses into large exegetical works called apparatuses, which brought together the glosses of many masters and represented the complete course on the *Decretum*. The authorship of the various segments of the apparatus was indicated by *sigla* (initials), many of which have not yet been deciphered; many parts of the extant apparatuses therefore remain effectively anonymous. The steady growth of the apparatus led, as it had in biblical exegesis, to the formation of a *glossa ordinaria*. This standard work, the companion of every medieval student of the *Decretum*, was compiled by Johannes Teutonicus (after 1215). Bartholomeus Brixiensis gave it its final form soon after 1245.

The rise of the gloss was paralleled by the development of the summa (summary) of the *Decretum*. These works stood separate from Gratian's book and provided an overall résumé of its contents. The earliest summa was that of Paucapalea, written in Bologna before 1148. The summa called the *Stroma magistri Rolandi* also predates 1148, though it relies on Paucapalea. From the late 1150's a series of influential summae—by Rufinus (1157–1159), Stephen of Tournai (*ca.* 1160), Simon of Bisignano (before 1179), and several anonymous authors—led to the greatest example of the genre in the work of Huguccio, completed after 1188. This work contributed to all the large apparatuses up to the *glossa ordinaria* and influenced Pope Innocent III (1198–1216).

BIBLIOGRAPHY

Stephan Kuttner, *Repertorium der Kanonistik (1140–1234)* (1937), and "Les débuts de l'école canoniste française," in *Studia et documenta historiae et iuris,* **13** (1938); Stephan Kuttner and Eleanor Rathbone, "Anglo-Norman Canonists of the Twelfth Century," in *Traditio,* 7 (1949–1951); C. Lefebvre, "Formation du droit classique," in Gabriel Le Bras, ed., *Histoire du droit et des institutions de l'église en occident,* VII, *L'âge classique, 1140–1378* (1965), 266–291.

STANLEY CHODOROW

[See also **Gloss; Gratian; Law, Canon; Law Schools.**]

DECRETUM. In Roman law the term *decretum* originally signified a judicial decision of the emperor sitting as a magistrate. The term also came to be used for imperial decisions on appeals or on petitions *(supplicationes)* of individuals. A *decretum* could be interlocutory, issued to intervene in a case in process. It could also, apparently, be issued in a declaratory manner to correct an injustice, in which event the emperor acted as if a particular case of the wrong were before him.

In canon law *decretum* was applied to papal pronouncements. In the ninth-century collections of forged documents known as the False Decretals, transmitted under the name of "Isidorus Mercator" (the Pseudo-Isidorean collections), are the "decreta Anastasii pape," which include a response to a consultation with German and Burgundian bishops and a hortatory letter to a layman. The term is also used to describe the supposed products of other early popes. Among the "decreta Gelasii pape" is one entitled "Decretum generale," which has the appearance of a series of conciliar decrees set out under a greeting of Pope Gelasius to episcopal recipients. By the Carolingian period, then, the word *decretum* had lost its peculiarly judicial use, becoming a title for virtually any legally binding pronouncement of the pope. In this usage its most common form became the adjectival *decretalis,* employed to modify *epistola* in order to signify that the contents of the letter were law.

The use of *decretum* for a variety of canon law texts achieved its final stage when it became the title of large, miscellaneous collections of legal documents. Such collections contained conciliar decrees, papal letters, and snippets of patristic writings, and they provided a source for those engaged in ecclesiastical legal business. The first of these collections to be called *Liber decretorum* or *Decretum* was that of Burchard of Worms. Burchard became bishop of Worms in 1000 and undertook a reform of his diocese. The *Decretorum libri XX,* which he completed between 1008 and 1012, was a complement of the reform, designed as a guide on ecclesiastical discipline for his successors and episcopal colleagues. It became the principal collection of canon law in the eleventh century, and its texts passed into the next collection to bear the title *Decretum,* that attributed to Ivo of Chartres.

The *Decretum* attributed to Ivo was completed between 1093 and 1095; the latest datable document in it is a letter of Urban II from 1093, and it was finished before the Council of Clermont (1095). Its author had much more material at his disposal than had Burchard; the material from the latter's *Decretum,* nearly all of which was used, constitutes only about two-fifths of the new work. The other main sources for the new *Decretum* were a collection related to the *Collectio Britannica* (a product of the eleventh-century reform movement) and the first two parts of the *Tripartita* (which Paul Fournier called Collection A), also attributed to Ivo. This *Decretum* contains 3,760 texts (compared with 1,784 in Burchard's work) distributed in seventeen parts, and was the largest collection of canon law texts in its time. Its organization derives from the plan of Burchard, but its author reversed the sequence of the two main elements. Burchard treated the rules of ecclesiastical organization and discipline first, then faith and the sacraments; the *Decretum* attributed to Ivo reverses this order. The new *Decretum* is known in only a few manuscripts, which leads scholars to conclude that it was little known or used in the Middle Ages. Its size and the relative disorder of texts within each part may explain this neglect.

The definitive stage in the use of *decretum* as a title was attained when the term became attached to the work of the Bolognese master Gratian. About 1140 he completed a series of treatises on canon law under the general title *Concordia discordantium canonum;* his successors in the school of Bologna imposed both a new order and a new title on the collection. In the hands of the law teachers, the treatises were welded into a comprehensive textbook of canon law called, to indicate its function as a book of sources for teaching and legal business, the *Decreta* or *Decretum*. This work became the first part of the medieval *Corpus iuris canonici,* which was replaced as the primary body of canon law only in 1917.

In the extant manuscripts of Gratian's *Decretum,* of which there are several hundred from the twelfth century alone, the work is divided into three parts: the *Distinctiones,* comprising 101 sections (each called a *distinctio);* the *Causae,* comprising 36 cases subdivided into questions treating the various aspects of each case; and the *De consecratione,* consisting of 5 *distinctiones.* In each part the compiler states a doctrine, issue, or case, then proceeds by using the Scholastic method to arrange the canonistic texts on both sides of each question and to provide a commentary designed to resolve the contradictions, both real and apparent, in the tradition of the laws. Thus, the work alternates between dicta of Gratian and capitula, each of which is provided with a rubric and is identified by author or source.

The organization of the work as it stands does not hide an underlying division. In the first two parts, the *Distinctiones* and *Causae,* subdivisions are discernible. The first twenty distinctions deal with the kinds and sources of law, and form a work on laws *(tractatus de legibus).* The next eighty-one treat the character, promotion, and relationships of the members of the ecclesiastical hierarchy. This long section is referred to by Gratian himself as the work on those who are ordained *(tractatus ordinandorum,* C. 11, *q.* 3, *c.* 15). The *Causae* also reveal an earlier organization as a series of treatises. *Causae* 2–7 constitute a series on the judiciary *(ordo iudiciarius); Causae* 12–14 form a treatise on ecclesiastical and clerical property; *Causae* 16–20 treat monks; and *Causae* 27–36 can be distinguished as a work on marriage *(tractatus de matrimonio).*

In the thirty-third *causa* there is a long treatise on penitence that makes up the third section (question) of the discussion of the *causa.* Many of the texts used in this tract, which is subdivided into seven *distinctiones,* are treated differently than in other parts of the *Decretum,* and this characteristic, along with the theological nature of much of the material, raises questions about the authenticity of the *De penitentia.* Thus, Gratian's successors transformed his work not only by introducing new divisions but also by adding material.

Scholars who have studied the text of the *Decretum* have concluded that the extant work does not represent the original, even though no manuscript preserves Gratian's first version. (There is no evidence about the role that the master himself might have taken in the revision of his work.) The questions raised by the *De penitentia* are also raised by the third part of the work, the *De consecratione.* This section treats a theological subject, the sacraments; and in it too the texts are handled differently than in other parts of the *Decretum.* In addition, the earliest abbreviations of and commentaries on the work contain no trace of the *De consecratione.* Only a small number of the texts in the *De penitentia* are treated in these early works. Finally, careful study has shown that the Roman law texts now in the *Decretum* were not put there by the master. They too were additions by the lawyers who turned Gratian's series of treatises into a textbook suitable for the teaching and research activities of the generation after him. It has even been suggested that the sharp distinction between dicta and capitula, which appears in the textbook version and facilitates both teaching and research, was not made by Gratian.

The addition of the *De penitentia* and the *De consecratione* was the most extensive, but not the only, addition made by later lawyers. During the first quarter century of its use, they inserted individual capitula throughout the work. The most recent study of these texts, called *paleae* (chaff) by the commentators on the *Decretum,* counted 148 of them. Most of these pieces were from the sources used by Gratian himself, and their interpolation shows that his successors judged certain texts overlooked or intentionally excluded by him to be important in the teaching or development of doctrine. A few of the new canons were from papal letters written after the completion of the *Decretum,* but two processes soon ended the practice of inserting material of this sort in the work.

First, the process of centralization, begun by the eleventh-century reformers, reached a significant stage by the middle of the twelfth century. One effect of this centralization was a rise in the number of appeals for justice made to the Roman curia and the concomitant rise in the number of papal judgments of interest to lawyers. St. Bernard of Clairvaux complained of the clamor of litigants in the curia in his *De consideratione,* a book of instruction to the Cisterician pope Eugenius III (1145–1153), but the problem he perceived in the time of Eugenius was a mere shadow of what happened in the pontificate of Alexander III (1159–1181). The canon lawyers used more than 700 letters of Alexander in their collections, and these were a fraction of the number issued. Under the growing pressure of new law in the decretal letters, the canonists ceased trying to insert material into the *Decretum* and began constructing appendixes of new papal documents. The latter soon outgrew the role of supplement and by the 1170's became separate works.

Second, the new law was based on the old, but as it became clear that a new body of law was forming, the distinction between the old, basic law of the *Decretum* and the new revisions and expansions of the decretal tradition became increasingly pronounced. This process of distinction between the old and the new was formalized in the establishment, about 1190 (perhaps earlier in the law schools of northern Europe), of a new law course devoted to the decretals, which made it unnecessary to cover the new doctrines in the standard course on the *Decretum.* But the process had taken effect by about 1170, after which little new material was added to Gratian's work and the new collections of decretals came into existence. By that time the *Decretum* had become the basic and comprehensive repository of the law of the church, the first segment of the *Corpus iuris canonici.*

BIBLIOGRAPHY

Texts. Burchard of Worms, *Decretorum libri XX,* in Patrologia latina, CXL (1853), 537–1058; Gratian, *Decretum (Concordia discordantium canonum),* E. Friedberg, ed., in *Corpus iuris canonici,* I (1879); Ivo of Chartres, *Decretum,* in Patrologia latina, CLXI (1855), 47–1036.

Studies. Stanley Chodorow, *Christian Political Theory and Church Politics in the Mid-twelfth Century* (1972); Paul Fournier and Gabriel Le Bras, *Histoire des collections canoniques en occident,* 2 vols. (1931–1932); Stephan Kuttner, *Repertorium der Kanonistik (1140–1234)* (1937), and "The Father of the Science of Canon Law," in *The Jurist,* 1 (1941); J. Rambaud, "Le legs de l'ancien droit: Gratien," in Gabriel Le Bras, ed., *L'âge classique (1140–1378): Sources et théorie du droit* (1965), 5–129.

STANLEY CHODOROW

[See also **Burchard of Worms; Gratian; Ivo of Chartres, St.; Law, Canon; Law, Schools of.**]

DEDICATION OF CHURCHES. Later legends of the apostolic dedication of churches and claims of a primitive Christian precedent for such dedication or consecration notwithstanding, no evidence exists for the practice by the early church. Pagan practices and rites of dedication would have been rejected out of hand, and Jewish rites for the consecration of sacred places and objects were ignored, exercising an influence only later, in Byzantine and Gallican rites.

For all that, the lavish celebration of the dedication of churches appears in the fourth century immediately following the Peace of the Church (Eusebius, *Historia ecclesiastica,* 10.3–4), and the pattern was set early for the festive and spectacular character of the dedication of major churches. Also, from the latter part of that century on, there appeared the common association with the dedication of churches of the solemn translation of relics of the saints, which was eventually to become an essential feature of the rite. Roman reluctance to disturb the graves of the saints, though not as absolute as sometimes portrayed, prevented the translation and division of relics commonly practiced elsewhere, and led to the initial substitution of secondary relics for the actual corporeal remains of the saints when translation of relics came to be a part of the Roman dedication rite. Dedication of churches in honor of the saint(s) whose relics were there enshrined became the universal practice, and these dedications provide valuable evidence for the development and extent of the cults of particular saints.

The earliest evidence for the Roman rite of dedication is found in a letter of Pope Vigilius to Profuturus of Braga, dated 538. This document, though difficult to interpret, seems to suggest two rites for the dedication of churches: dedication without the deposition of relics, in which case the celebration of Mass alone sufficed to accomplish the dedication; and the deposition of relics, followed by the celebration of Mass. Vigilius seems to exclude from the rite lustration of the church with holy water, a feature perhaps familiar to Profuturus but alien to Roman practice. Gregory the Great required the lustration of pagan temples being converted to Christian churches (hence the term *aqua Gregoriana* for the peculiar type of lustral water used in the developed dedication rite), and lustration eventually came to be a part of the Roman dedication rite.

A detailed description of the later (second half of the eighth century) Roman rite is found in Michel Andrieu's ordo XLII (" ... ordo quomodo in sancta Romana ecclesia reliquiae conduntur"), which provides complicated instructions for enclosing relics in the altar, and includes anointing the altar with chrism and lustration of the church; it concludes with a dedication Mass, to be repeated through an octave. Apart from the dedication Mass, always the sine qua non of the dedication rite, the dominant element in ordo XLII is the elaborate burial or reinterment of the relics.

The Gallican rite of dedication is found in its simpler form in the Sacramentary of Angoulême (eighth century), and in its more elaborate form in Andrieu's ordo XLI ("Ordo quomodo ecclesia debeat dedicari," second half of the eighth century). The Gallican rite displays clear Byzantine influence, as well as direct borrowings from the Old Testament ritual, especially from Exodus 29:12–13 and 18, and Leviticus 8:11. Commentators, medieval and modern alike, agree on the close analogy of the Gallican dedication rite to the rites of baptism. The Gallican ritual emphasizes the consecration of the church building and altar, with the deposition of relics playing a role clearly subordinate to the elaborate patterns of lustrations and anointings of altar and church.

The two more influential ordos, the Roman ordo XLII and the Gallican ordo XLI, circulated independently as well as paired in early medieval pontificals. They underwent a fusion in the compilation of the very influential Romano-Germanic Pontifical at Mainz (950–962); this fused rite, with added elaborations, was adopted by Guillaume Durand for his compilation of the pontifical (1293–1295) and found its way thence into the printed Roman pontificals.

The dedication of churches was not universally required until the Council of Trent, but it was mandated much earlier by many provincial councils and became the practice everywhere. The privilege of dedication was reserved to bishops, local ordinaries, or their delegates; hence its inclusion in the pontifical.

Notices and descriptions of church dedications, whether dedicatory inscriptions, formal archival records, or literary accounts, provide valuable data for ecclesiastical history and prosopography, for the history of art and architecture, and, given the festive character of the dedications as communal or even national celebrations, for social and political history.

The permanent memorials of the fact of dedication remaining from the dedication rite—the twelve consecration crosses painted, inscribed, or attached to the interior (and in England the exterior) walls of the church—have been relatively little studied, save for those of English churches, and so their archaeological significance and their role in decorative schemes have yet to be assessed.

Depictions of the events of the dedication ritual are available, but no systematic effort to collect and study the many medieval illustrations of the rite has been undertaken.

BIBLIOGRAPHY

Michel Andrieu, *Les Ordines Romani du haut moyen âge,* 5 vols. (1931–1961), esp. IV, 315–336, 359–394; S. Benz, "Zur Geschichte der römischen Kirchweihe nach den Texten des 6. bis 7. Jahrhunderts," in Hilarius Emonds, ed., *Enkainia: Gesammelte Arbeiten zum 800 jährigen Weihegedächtnis der Abteikirche Maria Laach am 24. August 1956* (1956), 62–109; Lee Bowen, "The Tropology of Mediaeval Dedication Rites," in *Speculum,* 16 (1941); "Kirchweihe," in Engelbert Kirschbaum, *et al.,* eds., *Lexikon der christlichen Ikonographie,* II (1970), 538–539; Séverien Salaville, *Cérémonial de la consécration d'une église selon le rite byzantin* (1937); Daniel J. Sheerin, "The Church Dedication 'Ordo' Used at Fulda, 1 Nov., 819," in *Revue bénédictine,* 92 (1982); Geoffrey G. Willis, "The Consecration of Churches down to the Ninth Century," in his *Further Essays in Early Roman Liturgy* (1968), 133–173.

DANIEL J. SHEERIN

[See also **Gallican Rite; Liturgy, Byzantine; Translation of Saints.**]

DEESIS. The Byzantine image of the Deesis (Greek, "supplication" or "entreaty") alludes to the Last Judgment. Christ appears between the Virgin Mary and John the Baptist, who intercede with him for the salvation of mankind. According to Charles Rufus Morey, Mary is present "as guarantee of Christ's humanity and the Baptist as type of the old dispensation completed and justified in the new." The subject was given monumental form in the mural decoration of Byzantine churches, a particularly fine example being the fragmentary mosaic in the south gallery of Hagia Sophia in Istanbul (illustrated in this *Dictionary,* vol. 2, p. 448). On a smaller scale are the numerous representations of the Deesis in Byzantine illuminated manuscripts, in enamels, and in ivory carvings of the type of the Harbaville Triptych in the Louvre. The composition was also adopted in Western medieval art, and there is a late reflection of it in the *Ghent Altarpiece* of 1432 by the brothers van Eyck.

BIBLIOGRAPHY

John Beckwith, *Early Christian and Byzantine Art* (1970); Otto Demus, *Byzantine Mosaic Decoration* (1948); Charles Rufus Morey, *Medieval Art* (1942).

JOHN RUPERT MARTIN

[See also **Byzantine Art; Ghent Altarpiece.**]

DEFENSOR PACIS, a major treatise of political philosophy by Marsilius of Padua, was completed in 1324. Marsilius probably studied medicine at the University of Padua and in 1313 was rector of the University of Paris. When his authorship of the *Defensor pacis* became known in 1326, he was forced to flee to the court of Louis of Bavaria at Nuremberg. Pope John XXII thereupon branded him a heretic. Marsilius subsequently assisted Louis in various imperial ventures in Italy.

The primary purpose of the *Defensor pacis* was to refute the papalist claims to "plenitude of power" as these claims had been advanced by Pope Innocent IV, Egidius Colonna (Giles of Rome), and others in the thirteenth and fourteenth centuries. The papalist position had held that secular rulers must be subject to the papacy even in "temporal" affairs, so that they must be established, judged, and, if necessary, deposed by the pope. Marsilius, in contrast, undertook to demonstrate that the papacy and the priesthood in general must be subject not only in temporal, but even in "spiritual," affairs to the whole people and to the secular ruler acting by the people's authority. The powers of the priesthood were to be reduced to the administration of the sacraments and the teaching of divine law, and even in these functions the priests were to be regulated by the people and their elected government.

As important as these revolutionary conclusions are the premises from which Marsilius derived them. These premises are found in his general political theory, which is noteworthy for its fusing of three themes. The first is the Aristotelian teleological view of the state (*civitas sive regnum*) as subserving the good life. The various parts of the state, including government, are defined by the contribution they make to the rational "fulfillment" of men's natural desire for a "sufficient life." The second theme emphasizes the inevitability of conflicts among men and the consequent need for the formal instrumentalities of coercive law and government in order to regulate these conflicts. Without such regulation, Marsilius repeatedly insists, human society must be destroyed. The third theme is the republican position that the people are the only legitimate source of all political authority. It is the people, the whole body of citizens or its "weightier part," that must make the laws either by itself or through elected representatives, and it is also the people that must elect, "correct," and, if necessary, depose the government.

The full consequence of these three themes emerges in the applications Marsilius makes of his general political theory to the problems of ecclesiastical politics. In keeping with his first theme, he views the Christian priesthood as one of the parts of the state dedicated to achieving the "sufficient life" for all believers. Unlike the other parts of the state, however, the priesthood subserves the "sufficient life" to be attained primarily in the future world rather than the present one. Taken in conjunction with the teleological doctrine of his first theme, accepting that the priesthood subserves the highest end of man would have required Marsilius to accept the papalist doctrine that the secular government, subserving the lesser end of this-worldly happiness, must be politically subordinate to the priesthood.

At this point, however, Marsilius' second and third themes have their effect. Since the essence of political authority is the coerciveness required for the minimal end of preserving society, it follows that the higher end subserved by the priesthood does not entitle it to superior political authority. What determines the order of political authority is not the greater excellence of one end over another but, rather, the specifically political need for unified coercive authority in order to prevent unresolved conflicts from destroying society.

Hence, the secular government, as bearer of this coercive authority, must be politically superior to the priesthood. If the priests refuse to obey the government and its laws, then they must be compelled to do so, because such disobedience threatens that unity of coercive authority without which society cannot survive. Indeed, it is because of this disobedience and because of its claim to a rival, superior "plenitude of power" that Marsilius convicts the papacy of being the gravest enemy of civil peace. In addition to this political argument against diverse centers of coercive power in any society, Marsilius stresses, from within the religious tradition itself, that religious belief, in order to be meritorious, must be purely voluntary. Hence, in order to fulfill its mission, divine law and the priesthood that teaches and administers it cannot be coercive in this world.

Marsilius' third theme, republicanism, also plays an important role in the political subordination of the priesthood and papacy. The only rules and persons that are entitled to the status of being coercive laws and government officials are those ultimately chosen by the people; hence, there can be no crediting the claims of divine law and the priesthood to a separate derivation of coercive political authority from God. Although Marsilius subsequently holds that secular rulers govern by divine right, he views this only as a divine confirmation of the people's ultimate electoral authority.

This republicanism operates not only in the relation of the priesthood to the secular state but also in its relation to religious affairs. Because the whole people is superior in virtue to any of its parts and because freedom requires popular consent or election, the priesthood must be elected by the people of each community rather than be appointed by an oligarchically chosen pope, and the pope himself must be elected by the whole of Christendom. Similarly, the whole people must elect general councils to provide authoritative interpretations of the meaning of divine law.

In these ways Marsilius' general political theory leads to a republican structure for the church as against its traditional monarchic structure. In effect, this also means that the secular government, acting by the people's authority, secures hegemony over the priesthood and papacy in all spheres.

The *Defensor pacis* was influential among the conciliarists of the fifteenth century and during the Reformation.

BIBLIOGRAPHY

Sources. The *Defensor pacis* is available in two critical editions: by C. W. Previté-Orton (1928), and by Richard Scholz, 2 vols., in *Monumenta Germaniae historica, Fontes iuris Germanici antiqui,* VII (1932–1933), and in an English translation by Alan Gewirth, *Defensor pacis* (1956).

Studies. Alan Gewirth, *Marsilius of Padua and Medieval Political Philosophy* (1951); Georges de Lagarde, *Le Defensor pacis,* new ed. (1970); Jeannine Quillet, "Marsilio da Padova: Atti del Convegno internazionale su Marsilio da Padova, 1980," in *Medioevo,* 5–6 (1979–1980), and *La philosophie politique e Marsile de Padoue* (1970).

ALAN GEWIRTH

[See also **Marsilius of Padua; Papacy; Political Theory, Western European.**]

DEGRADATION OF CLERICS. Degradation remains, to the present day, the severest penalty for a cleric because only by this act does he lose all ecclesiastical privileges. This penalty, as well as others, was first set in canon law in the late twelfth century. Previously, degradation was synonymous with deposition and merely signified the clergyman's removal from office. Furthermore, until that time a secular judge could degrade a cleric.

In 1176–1177 Alexander III universally forbade the *traditio curie* following a degradation. His prohibition was instigated by the murder of Thomas Becket in 1170 and was connected to the formation of a class consciousness among clergymen. As a result, his successors from Celestine III on and the canonists had to reclassify ecclesiastical penal law. This development was concluded with Boniface VIII's *Liber sextus* in 1298. From that time, four penalties were distinguished: suspension, privation, deposition, and degradation. Through suspension, a cleric was temporarily or permanently removed from office. Through privation, he lost his church income. Deposition constituted an intensification of both penalties and could be removed only by restitution. Deposition, more often than not, included imprisonment, usually in a cloister. All three penalties could be meted out for spiritual or criminal transgressions. For the worst criminal offenses— such as murder, theft, abduction, and rape, which all carried a death sentence for laymen—deposition was the only punishment for ecclesiastics. Consequently, clerics—even if they only wore a tonsure or had taken the lower orders and led a secular life—received milder punishments than laymen. This state of affairs, already existing in the thirteenth century, led to full-scale conflicts with civilian courts in the fifteenth century. It is important that none of the three penalties brought with it a loss of clerical class privileges.

Such a loss was possible only through degradation, which, to the vexation of secular courts, was administered only in cases of spiritual transgressions. Such offenses were only the relapse of an already deposed cleric *(incorrigibilitas),* insubordination to one's own bishop, falsification of papal documents, and, above all, heresy. In connection with heresy, assassination (perfidious murder for religious reasons as practiced by the Assassins), homosexuality, and witchcraft were punishable by degradation. Secular judges attempted to make murder and high treason punishable by degradation from around 1230 in Spain and from the time of Philip the Fair in France. These undertakings slowly achieved success in the fifteenth century. For this reason, the struggle to administer degradation, and with it the struggle to establish the civilian courts' jurisdiction over the clergy, are important indexes for the implementation of secular sovereignty over all inhabitants in a particular area.

From Boniface VIII, two acts were distinguished in degradation: *degradatio verbalis* and *degradatio realis* or *actualis*. During the *degradatio verbalis*, which included the court proceedings, the degradation sentence was pronounced. Theoretically, in addition to the degradator himself, twelve bishops had to take part in the proceedings in the case of a bishop; in the case of a priest, six bishops; in the case of a deacon or subdeacon, three or two bishops, respectively. Dispensations were granted from the time of Gregory IX in order to combat heretics better. Degradation in the case of a pope was not permissible, though it was attempted by canonists after 1378 as a result of the Great Schism.

The second act, *degradatio realis*, effected the actual degradation and was performed liturgically by a bishop, probably in a church. Since the code was not completed until Boniface VIII, the ordines of degradation were drawn up chiefly from the early fourteenth century, initially in southern France, which was one of the strongholds of heresy. It can be gleaned from sources that the delinquent party was sequentially stripped of all liturgical vestments and instruments that pertained to his order. The stripping occurred in such a manner that a priest was degraded first as a priest, then as a deacon, a subdeacon, and so on. Were he a priest, then in addition the flesh was removed from his consecrated fingers with a knife or glass shard. To conclude, the tonsure was scraped off, as in scalping, with tongs, shears, a shard, or a cutting edge. Afterward, the degraded cleric was handed over to the attending civil judge for final judgment. In doing so, the degradator was supposed to ask the judge neither to kill nor to maim the degraded cleric. But because most degraded clerics were heretics, for whom Gregory IX had already fixed death by burning, this request was a mere formality. The possibility of restitution for a cleric who had been degraded remained for the most part theoretical because it was customary that execution immediately follow the degradation.

BIBLIOGRAPHY

Stephen W. Findlay, *Canonical Norms Governing the Deposition and Degradation of Clerics* (1941); Jean-Louis Gazzaniga, "Les clercs criminels devant le parlement de Toulouse, XVᵉ–XVIIIᵉ siècles," in *Mémoires de la société pour l'histoire du droit et des institutions des anciens pays bourgignons, comtois et romands,* 35 (1978); Robert Génestal, *Le privilegium fori en France du Décret de Gratien à la fin de XIVᵉ siècle,* II.1, *La dégradation suivie de livraison au bras séculier* (1924); Bernhard Schimmelpfennig, "Die Absetzung von Klerikern in Recht und Ritus vornehmlich des 13. und 14. Jahrhunderts," in *Proceedings of* the Fifth International Congress of Medieval Canon Law (1980), and "Die Degradation von Klerikern im späten Mittelalter," in *Zeitschrift für Religions- und Geistesgeschichte,* 34 (1982).

BERNHARD SCHIMMELPFENNIG

[See also **Heresy; Law, Canon.**]

DELLA ROBBIA, LUCA, ANDREA, GIOVANNI.
Luca della Robbia (*ca.* 1399/1400–1482) was born in Florence. Nothing is known of his training and career before 1431. After that time he trained in the workshops of the cathedral of Florence and may well have studied with Nanni di Banco. His works include the *cantoria* in the cathedral of Florence (begun 1431); five reliefs for the campanile begun by Andrea Pisano (1437); and the altar in the cathedral. Though best known for his enameled terra-cotta, he also worked in bronze and marble. The exquisite beauty of the glazed terra-cotta technique and the possibilities of colors of all sorts, including the typical della Robbia blue-and-white method, is still famous as seen in contemporary ceramics, porcelain, and pottery.

Andrea della Robbia (1435–1525), a nephew of

Detail from Cantoria. Luca della Robbia, begun 1431. MUSEO DELL' OPERA DEL DUOMO, FLORENCE: ALINARI/ART RESOURCE

Luca, was also born in Florence. He took over Luca's workshop in 1482 and continued to use the glazed terra-cotta technique developed by his uncle, though he added more color. Andrea was active mostly in Florence.

Giovanni della Robbia (1469–1529) was the son of Andrea and grandnephew of Luca. Little is known of his activity before his work on the lavabo of the sacristy of S. Maria Novella in Florence, commissioned in 1497. He inherited the della Robbia workshop.

BIBLIOGRAPHY

Luca della Robbia. Giulia Brunetti, "Note su Luca della Robbia," in *Scritti di Storia dell'Arte in onore di Mario Salmi,* II (1962), 263–272; Gino Corti and Frederick Hartt, "New Documents Concerning Donatello, Luca and Andrea della Robbia, Desiderio, Mino, Uccello, Pollaiuolo, Filippo Lippi, Baldovinetti and Others," in *Art Bulletin,* 44 (1962); Charles Seymour, Jr., "The Young Luca della Robbia," in *Bulletin of the Dudley Peter Allen Memorial Art Museum of Oberlin College,* 20 (1963).

Andrea della Robbia. Gino Corti, "New Andrea della Robbia Documents," in *Burlington Magazine,* 112 (1970); Allan Marquand, *Andrea della Robbia and His Atelier,* 2 vols. (1922).

Giovanni della Robbia. Allan Marquand, *Giovanni della Robbia* (1920); I. B. Supino, "Giovanni della Robbia," in Ulrich Thieme and Felix Becker, *Allgemeines Lexikon der bildenden Künstler,* XXVIII (1934), 414–415.

SANDRA CANDEE SUSMAN

[See also **Ceramics.**]

DEMES. The demes or circus parties, originally militia for the defense of Constantinople, were political organizations centered on the Hippodrome that involved every sphere of life. Originally there were four parties, but only the Greens and the Blues survived to play a central role in the Nika Revolt of 532, when they joined together against the emperor. Their leaders (demarchs) were imperial officials who continued to exist for court functions even after the demes themselves disappeared in the seventh century. Although it is difficult to categorize the two factions, the Greens were Monophysites, the Blues were of a higher class and Orthodox. Their numbers were not large, but members of the population tended to identify with one side or the other, giving them additional support.

BIBLIOGRAPHY
Alan Cameron, *Circus Factions: Blues and Greens at Rome and Byzantium* (1976).

LINDA ROSE

[See also **Constantinople.**]

DEMETRIOS KYDONES (*ca.* 1324–*ca.* 1398), Byzantine scholar and statesman, was born in Thessaloniki and died in Crete. He enjoyed a long political career in Constantinople, serving emperors John VI Kantakouzenos and John V Palaiologos. To implement his policy of resistance to the Ottoman Turks, he attempted to secure a military alliance with the Catholic powers of western Europe.

Kydones learned Latin and translated into Greek the works of many Latin theologians, including Augustine, Anselm of Canterbury, and Thomas Aquinas. After translating Aquinas' *Summa contra gentiles* and *Summa theologiae,* he became a defender of Aquinas' system of theology along with his brother, the monk Prochoros. He converted to Roman Catholicism about 1357 and later supported the conversion of John V Palaiologos (1369). Kydones opposed the theology of Gregory Palamas and was influential in Byzantine anti-Palamite and pro-Latin circles.

Kydones was a prolific writer whose works include political speeches, religious sermons, and theological treatises of a polemical nature. Most important for his own life and for the history of Byzantium in the fourteenth century is his voluminous correspondence.

BIBLIOGRAPHY
Sources. The complete edition of the letters is *Démétrius Cydonès Correspondance,* R. J. Loenertz, ed., 2 vols. (1956–1960). A partial edition of fifty letters with French translation is *Démétrius Cydonès Correspondance,* G. Cammelli, ed. and trans. (1930). A complete German trans., with commentary, has been undertaken by F. Tinnefeld, *Demetrios Kydones Briefe* (1981–).

Studies. Frances Kianka, "The *Apology* of Demetrius Cydones: A Fourteenth-century Autobiographical Source," in *Byzantine Studies* (Arizona), 7 (1980), and "Demetrius Cydones and Thomas Aquinas," in *Byzantion* (Brussels), 52 (1982); R. J. Loenertz, "Démétrius Cydonès," in *Orientalia christiana periodica,* 36–37 (1970–1971).

FRANCES KIANKA

[See also **Byzantine Church; Byzantine History.**]

DEMETRIOS PRESBYTER, a scribal entry, in gold rustic capitals, on the first page of Luke's Gospel in the Coronation Gospels (Vienna, Weltliche und Geistliche Schatzkammer) produced for Charlemagne by the palace school around 800. The Greek name, though written in Latin letters, has been taken to indicate that Greek artists were responsible for the illusionistic miniatures of the manuscript. In fact, the signature is associated with the text rather than with the pictures and is apparently a later addition.

BIBLIOGRAPHY

Wilhelm Köhler, *Die karolingischen Miniaturen,* III, *Die Gruppe des Wiener Krönungs-Evangeliars-Metzer Handschriften* (1960), 49–51; Florentine Mütherich and Joachim E. Gaehde, *Carolingian Painting* (1976), 51.

LESLIE BRUBAKER

[See also **Pre-Romanesque Art.**]

DEMOGRAPHY. Historical demography is one of the youngest ancillary disciplines in medieval studies, but also one of the most cultivated. Its late development reflects the long-held assumption that medieval documentation, while it allowed occasional estimates of the total size of communities, did not permit a close reconstruction of demographic movements. Civil registrations of vital events—births, marriages, and deaths—are the basis of modern demographic analysis, and these are not available for any medieval community. Still, as many studies now show, medieval data can illuminate demographic trends and behavior, even if they do not support the full panoply of statistical techniques employed in the study of modern populations. Moreover, the current lively interest in social history has given strong stimulus to demographic inquiries. Almost every study of a medieval society—in manor, village, town, region, or kingdom—today includes a section or chapter devoted to population, its size, structure, and movements.

An appreciation of the possibilities and limits of medieval demography requires at least a brief description of the surviving data. The article will then track, on the basis of recent research, the population through its long-term trends of growth and decline. Finally, it will examine certain salient demographic characteristics that marked medieval communities and their small constituent units, the households and families.

SOURCES

The sources illuminating medieval populations may be divided into two large groups: "field" (that is, geographical or archaeological) data and written records. Each set of sources offers both direct and indirect information (the latter often called proxy data) on demographic movements and behavior.

The data on populations from field investigations are almost always indirect, but also extremely varied. The physical size of medieval settlements, often readily apparent from surrounding fortifications, was necessarily a function of the human numbers they contained. The Centro Internazionale per lo Studio delle Cerchie Urbane in Lucca, Italy, sponsors and coordinates work on the spatial aspects of medieval settlements, especially those girded by walls. Historians such as Ferdinand Lot and Edith Ennen have noted, for example, that medieval Western towns having classical origins did not enlarge their typically small circles of walls between the third and the eleventh centuries. This strongly implies that population was small and stagnant during the early Middle Ages—at least within towns.

Field data also illuminate population movements in rural areas through the appearance of new settlements and, even more dramatically, through their abandonment. Deserted villages and fields—called *Wüstungen* in the German literature—were particularly numerous in the fourteenth and fifteenth centuries and have attracted the close attention of geographers, archaeologists, and historians, including Wilhelm Abel, and Maurice Beresford and John Hurst. They give evidence of a precipitous contraction in settled areas—and presumably in human numbers—in the late medieval countryside. In England a society called the Deserted Medieval Village Research Group promotes the systematic study of this fundamental movement and publishes an annual report.

Besides reflecting aggregate movements, field data record the demographic experiences of individuals and small groups. Thus, the excavation of cemeteries and churchyards and the examination of skeletal remains cast light on sex ratios in the community, physical types, robustness, usual age at death, and common causes of death. Although largely uncoordinated and reported in widely scattered publications, the study of skeletal remains is one of the most promising areas of paleodemography. The archaeological investigation of medieval houses offers precious information on domestic relations.

Although nondocumentary evidence looms large in medieval demography, certain obstructions limit its use. First, it is often difficult to assign precise dates to excavated sites and materials. Second, the artifacts and remains do not speak with the fullness and explicitness of written records, and even experts differ as to their true import and meaning. Third, the largest medieval sites are still occupied and cannot be systematically excavated. Field data tend to give disproportionate prominence to the marginal areas of medieval settlement. For these reasons field data have proved especially valuable for places and periods where and when the documentary record is defective or altogether lacking: western Europe during the barbarian migrations; pre-Viking and Viking Scandinavia; Iceland and Greenland; central and eastern Europe, especially in preliterate periods. The demography of the core areas of medieval Europe has been, for the most part, reconstructed on the basis of written documents.

These documents are readily distinguished into two large families: descriptive accounts and administrative records. The chroniclers who produced most descriptive accounts occasionally cite figures with demographic implications—the sizes of armies and fleets; participants in a collective oath; victims of a war, famine, or plague. An entire genre of medieval literature is given over to the praise (laudatio) of cities, and even a moderately enthusiastic laudatio will boast about the number of churches, monasteries, hospitals, or schools; the goods imported; food consumed; taxes raised and moneys spent. The chronicler Giovanni Villani included in his narrative a lengthy description, overflowing with numbers, of Florence in about 1338, and his figures have withstood repeated critical assaults. On the other hand, the numbers contained in descriptive or narrative accounts are often fabulous and ought never to be accepted in the absence of independent supporting evidence.

The basis of the most substantial work in medieval demography has been administrative records. Their great value is objectivity and accuracy: the clerks who redacted them did not seek to influence later opinions, and they usually recorded what they saw. These records can be divided for closer scrutiny into two categories: surveys and serial documents. Surveys record observations taken over a large space—an estate or even a principality—on a fixed date. Serial records preserve observations made over

a small space or limited range of activities for a continuous, and sometimes lengthy, period of time.

The earliest surviving surveys are inventories of great estates or manors, which typically included a count of the peasants living on them. They first appear in number with the formation of the Carolingian empire—from the late eighth century. Almost all of them are ecclesiastical in provenance, and most derive from the northern regions of the empire. Nearly all of them take as their basic unit the single family farm (the mansus or, in German lands, the Hufe; the English equivalent was the hide). The largest of them identify all the members of the dependent families; one of them, from the abbey of St. Victor of Marseilles, states the ages of children younger than sixteen years and identifies the baccularii and baccularie, the unmarried men and women, in the adult population.

By far the largest and most detailed of these Carolingian surveys is the "polyptych" (the word means "many panels" or "many pages") that Irminon, abbot of St. Germain-des-Prés near Paris, redacted sometime between 806 and 829. It scrutinizes twenty-five manors (apparently about half of the monastery's possessions) in the vicinity of Paris and offers a detailed census of more than 4,700 dependent households. This one document has profoundly shaped our conceptions of human settlement and of the manorial economy in early medieval Europe.

Manorial surveys remained common in Europe for as long as the great estate worked by a dependent peasantry survived as a fundamental and widespread institution of agrarian life. For the thirteenth and early fourteenth centuries the richest run of manorial surveys, commonly called extents, is preserved from England, where the great property was exceptionally well organized. During the late Middle Ages, both in England and on the Continent, manorial surveys diminished in number as serfdom and the classical manor were vanishing from the medieval countryside.

Fiscal surveys are of more recent origin. In the eleventh century effectively governed feudal principalities began to appear in Europe, and counts, dukes, and kings took an early interest in the number of vassals they could marshal and in the fiefs that supported them. Lists of fiefs and vassals proliferated, especially from the twelfth century. The most famous of these feudal and fiscal surveys is the English Domesday Book—so called because its entries, like the judgments to be made on the Last Day, were inalterable. William the Conqueror ordered its redaction in 1086, to assess the resources of his newly acquired land. This inquiry went beyond a list of principal vassals, to record the fields and farms that supported them. It is unique in design, scope, and age. It includes most of the Norman realm of England (London and the northern counties are missing), and even for England a survey of comparable range does not survive until the poll tax of 1377.

As the monetary needs of medieval rulers grew, so also did their interest in recording all taxpayers, not only principal vassals. On the Continent comprehensive lists of hearths *(foci)* proliferated from the mid thirteenth century on. Among the oldest to survive is the Book of Hearths from the countryside near Pistoia, Italy. Dated about 1244, it gives the names of 7,312 household heads. Many regions possess runs of hearth lists, beginning in the late thirteenth and continuing into the fourteenth centuries. Among them are Normandy, Brabant, Provence, Toulouse, and Aragon and Valencia. The largest of these early fiscal surveys, in aggregate totals though not in detailed descriptions, is the enumeration of French parishes and hearths redacted in 1328 and subsequently published by Ferdinand Lot (1929). Covering about half the kingdom of France, it includes nearly 25,000 parishes and records the presence of nearly 2.5 million hearths.

These fiscal surveys improve progressively in number, quality, and detail across the late Middle Ages. The expensive wars of the epoch and the radical fall in population beginning in the mid fourteenth century forced governments repeatedly to count the number of surviving hearths. Moreover, in their desperate search for money, governments experimented with more refined methods of taxation. In setting assessments they had regard for individuals as well as hearths—for the size of the family, and consumers of salt or able-bodied males within it. Thus the fiscal surveys allow us to look into, as well as at, the medieval hearth. Among many late medieval surveys the most impressive is the *catasto* (census) that the commune of Florence redacted in 1427–1430. It scrutinized nearly the entirety of the modern province of Tuscany, registered 60,000 households, recorded the names and ages of the 260,000 persons contained within them, and listed their possessions. It is a unique census, the like of which cannot be found elsewhere in Europe (or even at Florence) until the eighteenth and nineteenth centuries.

Surveys, both manorial and fiscal, must be used critically. Most of them omitted some members of the population—ecclesiastics, the privileged nobles, the miserable poor, foreigners, or migrants. Some "fiscal" hearths were entirely fictional. Unwilling to allow revenues to decline, governments were prone to impose taxes according to traditional hearth counts, even when the true number had fallen. To estimate total population, the researcher must choose an appropriate "multiplier"—that is, he must determine the mean number of members in the hearths or households. This is rarely easy. Nevertheless, methods of documentary criticism, carefully applied, are usually able to overcome even these formidable obstacles; most surveys do permit approximate estimates of population size.

The surveys provide something like a series of still photographs of medieval communities at discrete moments in time. They rarely survive in continuous series, and thus they poorly reflect demographic movements—births, deaths, marriages, migrations. To judge change over time, historians rely primarily on the second type of administrative document, serial records. The oldest of them, appearing in volume from the late eighth century, are land conveyances (sales, exchanges, donations, leases, and the like), recorded on charters or in collections of charters (cartularies). Those predating 1200 are counted in the tens of thousands, and later ones are even more plentiful.

Among kinds of serial records with particular relevance to demographic analysis are necrologies of religious institutions (surviving from as early as the Carolingian period), lay Books of the Dead (appearing, though sporadically, from the late fourteenth century), and baptismal registrations (dating from the same period). The cartularies of urban notaries have survived in considerable numbers at Genoa from the mid twelfth century, and from many southern cities from the mid thirteenth century. They include marriage agreements, wills, and other documents reflective of vital movements.

In England the records of manorial courts have proved especially valuable in demographic research. The manorial court met frequently—sessions were often only weeks apart—and transacted a great variety of business. They regularly took "view of frankpledge"—that is, they recorded the names of those males over age twelve who, forming "tithing" groups, were responsible for one another's lawful conduct. They made inquiry into the deaths of tenants and admitted heirs into their tenures; registered land conveyances; and imposed a large number of fines for various infractions of laws and customs.

Also in England, by the mid fifteenth century, the registration of probated wills was full enough to support the construction of statistical series giving insight into mortality fluctuations and "replacement ratios." The latter figure gives the ratio of adult male heirs to male decedents and roughly indicates trends of population growth or decline.

Serial records are often dense enough to permit the tracking of individuals across them; they thus allow the partial reconstruction of life and career cycles for periods as early as the ninth and tenth centuries. Through extraordinary effort and patience a French scholar, Arlette Higounet-Nadal, has tracked every personal reference appearing in every source from the town of Périgueux in the fourteenth and fifteenth centuries. Scholars associated with the Pontifical Institute at Toronto—Edward Britton, Edwin Dewindt, J. A. Raftis—have used comparable methods in the study of several English villages in the thirteenth and later centuries.

The reconstruction of life and career patterns on the basis of serial records is not easy. The work is tedious, and the tedium grows as the number of documents multiplies. The spellings of names shift, and it is often difficult to link with certainty all references to the same person. It is questionable whether individuals who appear most frequently in the documents are typical of the community as a whole. The researcher must remain alert to these difficulties and biases, yet recourse to tracking efficiently exploits a large documentary fund that hitherto has made no substantial contribution to demographic research. Today the computer promises to reduce the time and tedium involved in linking references, and machine-assisted analyses of medieval records are sure to become more frequent and fruitful.

Serial records also provide proxy data reflective of demographic movements. Death dues or heriots, returns from tithes and other imposts, commodity prices, and levels of rent have all supported demographic inferences. For example, high rents and cereal prices in the thirteenth century suggest dense rural settlement and great demand for food; conversely, the collapse of both rents and cereal prices beginning in the late fourteenth century is almost certainly related to the shrinking population of the late Middle Ages.

In summary, medieval documentation bearing on population and its movements shows numerous gaps and is often difficult to interpret. And yet the different types of records are, in part at least, complementary. Surveys permit reliable estimates of total numbers but poorly record movements over time and say little about behavior. Serial records register change but do not illuminate the aggregate size and broad characteristics of the community. Proxy data, while always the product of complex factors, can help confirm inferences drawn from direct evidence. Together the sources provide a sufficiently rounded picture of the demographic experiences of medieval people—how as individuals they passed their lives, and how together they gave form and structure to their communities.

AGGREGATE MOVEMENTS

Crudely delineated, the major trends of population movement during the Middle Ages appear to have been the following: stability at very low levels from about 400 to 1000; vigorous expansion from about 1000 to 1250; stability at very high levels from about 1250 to 1350; precipitous decline from about 1350 to 1420; stability again at low levels from about 1420 to 1470; and renewed expansion beginning slowly about 1470 and gaining momentum in the early sixteenth century.

Although no exact figures can be cited, the transition from the ancient world to the Middle Ages was certainly accompanied by low or falling population. The evidence for this, while indirect, is compelling: the extension of deserted fields, *agri deserti*, over the Roman Empire, which in some provinces, such as North Africa, claimed a third of the land; the imperial policy of settling barbarians on abandoned lands; and the strenuous efforts of the Roman state, from the time of Augustus Caesar, to encourage marriage and procreation. It is likely that the late ancient population reached its low point not long after 540, when bubonic plague cut a murderous swath across the imperial territories. The plague then mysteriously disappeared from western Europe, not to return for nearly 800 years. But the western population gives no indication of vigorous growth until the eleventh century. It may be that the Carolingian epoch (*ca.* 750–850) witnessed a small increment in human numbers, but even this is doubtful; and growth, if it was then initiated, was not long sustained.

Estimates of the absolute size of early medieval populations are highly speculative. Still, fragmentary data and comparisons with the later Domesday Book support the inference that about 800 the entire British Isles may have contained 1.5 million people. Manorial surveys and some allusions to provincial hearth taxes suggest a population of 5 million for

Carolingian France. Presumed densities of settlement support estimates of 4 million each for Italy, Iberia, and German lands (including Scandinavia); 6 million for Slavic lands; and perhaps 2 million for Greece and the southern Balkans. The total for all Europe at the time of Charlemagne would be 25 million or 26 million—a conjecture that at best indicates an order of magnitude.

Although few in absolute number, the population of Carolingian Europe was not distributed evenly across the countryside. Ferdinand Lot, one of the first historians to investigate medieval demography, in 1921 calculated the density of settlement on the estates of St. Germain-des-Prés and projected the figure over the whole of Carolingian France. He arrived at the extraordinary conclusion that the population then numbered 14 million to 15.5 million. If his assumptions were correct, France under Charlemagne would have been as populous as France under Louis XIV.

But Lot was surely wrong in assuming that all of Charlemagne's kingdom shared the density of settlement found on the lands of St. Germain. On the contrary, although areas of dispersed habitation have been noted, most inhabitants lived in highly clustered settlements—population islands that were separated by extensive wilderness. (Geographers estimate that in 800 as much as three-quarters of the land surface of Europe was still forested.) From the early ninth century these clustered settlements give evidence of acute and worsening crowding and overpopulation. Tenures meant to support one family were frequently divided among many, and a constant trading in detached plots of land suggests that cultivators were having difficulty maintaining workable holdings.

Several factors—sometimes called internal constraints—kept these early medieval cultivators packed together in their settlement islands. Serfdom tied many to their places of birth. Facing a violent world, even free peasants hesitated to abandon the security of a large community. The bonds of kinship also discouraged departure to remote areas. And the surrounding wilderness was frightening in its real or imagined dangers. The pattern of settlement visible in ninth- and tenth-century sources is thus singularly paradoxical: large, crowded, impacted communities existed within vast stretches of uncultivated lands.

In the demographic and economic history of medieval Europe, the eleventh century marks a watershed. In about 1000 the population began to move outward from the settlement islands that had hitherto contained it. In a movement traditionally known as the "great clearances," peasants launched a vigorous attack on the forests, wastes, and marshes of Europe. During the central Middle Ages (*ca.* 1000–1250) a larger area of land was won for cultivation than in any other comparable epoch of European history. Simultaneously Europeans were pushing beyond the old frontiers of the Carolingian empire. Germans and Flemings moved across the Elbe River along the southern littoral of the Baltic Sea, and beyond Bavaria down the Danube Valley.

By about 1250 this "push to the east" had tripled the area of German settlement over what it had been in Carolingian times. In Iberia Christian kings and colonists gradually reclaimed and partially resettled nearly the entire peninsula; by 1212 only the small principality of Granada remained under Moorish rule. By about 1016 knights from Normandy were coming in large numbers into southern Italy, and by 1124 a Norman state was established in both southern Italy and Sicily. The crusades are a dramatic, though perhaps not the most significant, example of the expanding frontiers of medieval Europe.

The constraints that kept Carolingian settlers packed into overcrowded communities were clearly loosening. Several factors contributed. Perhaps an improving climate—paleoclimatologists speak of a "little optimum" prevailing in the eleventh and twelfth centuries—eased the labor of colonization. From about the mid tenth century Norsemen, Magyars, and Saracens were no longer mounting frequent and destructive incursions into Europe. Within Europe the great reform of the Western church in the eleventh century and the simultaneous rise of strong feudal governments lent a new stability to social life. Both prelates and princes repressed domestic violence, promoted internal colonization, and organized expansion along the external frontiers. As violence subsided, individuals no longer needed to look to tight kinship networks and to large communities for protection, and they gained a new mobility. The trammels of serfdom also loosened, for complex reasons. Perhaps most fundamentally, with growing numbers of cultivators seeking tenures, landlords no longer perceived an advantage in binding cultivators permanently to the soil. The opening of new lands and, equally, the willingness to colonize them encouraged marriage and procreation; the expansion of the medieval frontier was sustained by, and itself stimulated, substantial growth in human numbers.

Although exact figures remain rare, much indirect

evidence shows the impressive dimensions of this rise in population. New place names identifying parishes, villages, and castles proliferate in the documents. As counted by the German economic historian Karl Lamprecht, the villages in the Moselle valley mentioned in the documents numbered 340 before 800, and by 1237 reached 1,380. To be sure, the fund of documents was itself growing larger, and the numbers have no absolute value. But the multiplying place names indicate that the European countryside was filling up with human settlements.

Towns offer particularly dramatic evidence of this population boom. Inhabitants lived comfortably within their Roman enclosures until the eleventh century; between about 1000 and 1300 most principal towns added two successive circles of walls to contain their obviously burgeoning populations. The enclosed area—and presumably the inhabitants—increased in most towns by a factor of five or six between about 1100 and about 1300. Some towns achieved truly extraordinary growth. At Florence, for example, the Roman enclosure included about 30 hectares; the new circle laid out in the late twelfth century, 100 hectares; and the final medieval enclosure, constructed about 1300, more than 500 hectares.

The largest medieval city seems to have been Paris. Although the estimate is much disputed, the 61,000 hearths attributed to it in the survey of 1328 indicate a population of at least 210,000 persons. The other large cities of northern Europe had populations clustering about 50,000 (Bruges) or 40,000 (London, Ghent, Liège, Ypres). In Italy, Florence about 1338 contained probably 120,000 inhabitants; Venice and Milan were even bigger, with populations perhaps as large as 180,000. Cities of some 30,000 inhabitants were numerous in Italy: Bologna, Cremona, Ferrara, Lucca, Naples, Padua, Pisa, Siena. In northern Italy and Flanders—the most heavily urbanized regions of Europe—about 25 percent of the population was living in towns by 1300. Within regions there may have been a uniform distribution of urban centers according to size and rank, but this intriguing thesis is only now capturing the attention of historians.

By about 1300 Europe had become very crowded—some scholars would now say overpopulated. Estimates of aggregate population remain conjectural, but even the partial evidence shows high densities of settlement in numerous regions. In England, according to J. C. Russell's 1948 estimates, the population grew from about 1.1 million in 1086

to 3.7 million in the early fourteenth century. But this latter figure was based on the size of the population according to the poll tax of 1377 and on questionable assumptions concerning mortalities in 1349; today it appears much too conservative. Estimates of England's population at its medieval height now range as high as 7 million.

On the Continent the county of Beaumont-le-Roger in Normandy contained 6,093 hearths in 1313, distributed over 23 rural communes. Its population of probably 30,000 persons in the early fourteenth century was not much less than its numbers today. The village of Givry in Burgundy counted 310 hearths in 1360—after the Black Death had carried off one-third of its inhabitants. In spite of these losses its population of probably 1,500 persons was close to its present size of about 2,000. For France as a whole the population, according to the hearth count of 1328, certainly surpassed 15 million—a number it would not again attain until the eighteenth century.

In Italy the region of San Gimignano in Tuscany was more densely settled about 1300 than it is today. The population of the entire province of Tuscany may have then surpassed 2 million people—a level the region would not reach again until after 1850.

These high estimates of regional populations—the fruit of recent research—cast doubt on older conjectures concerning aggregate European population in the early fourteenth century. Karl Beloch believed that the population then attained 51.9 million, and Russell in 1958 suggested 54.7 million. Today it seems likely that the population of western Europe about 1300, at its medieval peak, reached levels as high as 100 million.

Population growth in the period of the central Middle Ages was exuberant, but it may also have been the community's nemesis; it may have been, in other words, a principal factor in the demographic disasters of the fourteenth century. Population growth was already visibly slowing, or had altogether halted, in the closing decades of the thirteenth century. The external frontiers had ceased to expand or were already contracting, and internal colonization had all but ended. Replacement ratios on English manors show a downward drift beginning in the late thirteenth century, and some fall below unity (that is, some deceased individuals were not being replaced) in the early fourteenth century. In Italy the populations, both urban and rural, of many regions—San Gimignano, Prato, Pistoia, Volterra, Imola—reached their peak size about 1300 and were stable or even slightly falling in the early 1300's.

Nevertheless, the European population remained remarkably high when, in the fourteenth century, a series of unprecedented catastrophes drastically reduced its numbers. The dread horsemen of the Apocalypse—war, famine, plague, and death—wrought havoc across the land. The Hundred Years War, the best-known of many late-medieval conflicts, spread desolation over large stretches of the French countryside; travelers could journey for miles and never hear the crow of a cock. From 1315 to 1317 harvests in northern Europe failed, provoking famine of unprecedented severity. Years of hunger—and the epoch had many—characteristically came in strings; the starving people ate their seed grain and thus diminished the subsequent harvest. Only a year of exceptional plenty broke the sinister sequence. But by far the most awesome killer of the late Middle Ages was pestilence.

The first of the great plagues of the epoch was the Black Death. The malady initially appeared at Caffa, a Genoese colony in the Crimea, in 1347 and spread to Sicily and the extreme south of France before December. In 1348, growing in power in the spring and summer, it overran all of Italy and Spain and most of France, and penetrated into southwest England. The following year it swept over all the British Isles and broke across Germany; in 1350 it attacked the Baltic countries; and in 1351 it struck deep into Russia, thus nearly closing a circle of death around Europe. Contemporaries report, and most historians concur, that it claimed about one-third of the people. And it was only the first of many epidemics; after 1348, in almost every year, in some European region, plague was raging.

Struck by these ferocious blows, the number of Europeans plummeted; the years from about 1340 to 1420 witnessed the heaviest losses. In German lands about 40 percent of named habitations disappeared. The villages that survived the wave of *Wüstungen* doubtless shrank in size. The population of Provence was 400,000 in 1310; it was half that size a century later and did not register even a modest recovery until after 1470. In some Italian regions, such as Pistoia and San Gimignano in Tuscany, by about 1420 the population had dropped below 30 percent of what it had been a century before. Pini's study of Imola in the Romagna gives the following estimates of its urban population: 11,500 in 1312; 8,800 in 1336; 5,250 in 1371. The town had lost more than half its numbers in sixty years, and in 1371 the pop-

ulation was still declining. For Europe as a whole, in the most recent view, the accumulated losses over this epoch of disasters probably amounted to two-thirds of the population.

The nature and course of these late-medieval epidemics present many mysteries. The symptoms of the victims, occasionally described in contemporary accounts, indicate that bubonic plague was frequently present—a malady absent from the West since the sixth century. However, bubonic plague as observed today is not highly contagious. It is more truly a disease of rats and of small mammals than of human beings, and must be transmitted through flea vectors from rats to human hosts; it cannot pass directly from the sick to the well. Moreover, recovery from a bubonic infection is not unusual for an otherwise healthy person. To account for the high contagion and virulence of the medieval epidemics, scholars have proposed several explanations. The geographic expansion of the central Middle Ages brought Europeans into eastern regions where plague was endemic. It thus introduced them into a large and unfamiliar "disease pool," exposing them to an infection against which they had no hereditary defenses. But Europeans had been visiting the East in large numbers since at least the eleventh century, which makes the belated appearance of plague in the West puzzling.

It has been argued that the true killer was not bubonic but pneumonic plague, a form of pneumonia triggered by a bubonic infection and then able to spread as an independent disease. As an illness of the respiratory tract it could pass directly among humans, and in an age without antibiotics infection was almost always fatal. Yet pneumonia, like all respiratory diseases, spreads most easily in winter, when people are subject to chills and confined to small, poorly ventilated quarters. But the medieval plagues characteristically took their greatest tolls in summer, and their strength quickly dissipated with the cooler weather of fall and winter. Today it appears likely that the great epidemics were not one disease but many. Prominent among them were gastrointestinal disturbances and diarrhea, which desiccated their victims during the summer heat. The chief victims were infants and children, who died by the thousands.

There is, in sum, no entirely satisfactory, purely medical explanation for the staggering mortalities of the late Middle Ages. Historians have in consequence searched for social factors that may have rendered Europeans more vulnerable to the great killers of the epoch—to wars, famines, and social disturbances as well as pestilence. In recent years there has emerged an essentially Malthusian explanation for the late-medieval population plunge. Briefly rehearsed, the argument is the following. Europe about 1300 had become crowded, even glutted, with people. Thousands, millions even, had to be fed without the aid of chemical fertilizers, agricultural machinery, or cheap transport. Large numbers eked out their livelihood from marginal soils. Even in good years they clung to the edges of subsistence. For example, M. M. Postan and J. Titow found that even small spurts in cereal prices visibly affected the number of deaths on the estates of the bishop of Winchester in the period before the plague. Widely over Europe a pervasive malnutrition lowered resistance to diseases. Competing for a diminished social surplus, lords and kings took quickly to arms. The catastrophes of the fourteenth century were, in sum, Malthusian checks working against a population that had grown too large for its resources to support.

Today this interpretation provokes a continuing scholarly debate. Many critics, Marxists prominent among them, contend that the Malthusian model is excessively simplistic and mechanical. It ignores the structure of classes and the distribution of property and power within the community, which, for Marxists at least, are the chief motors of social history. At all events the observed movements of the late-medieval population correspond rather poorly with the patterns to be expected in a classical Malthusian crisis.

The disasters did not strike an exuberantly expanding population but one already stable, or even declining, for a half-century or more before 1348. The pressure of numbers was already intense about 1300 or even 1250. If Europe was even then overpopulated, the long delay of the Malthusian reckoning is puzzling. So too are the persistence of the fall of the late-medieval population and the great size of the cumulative losses. In theory the huge diminution of human numbers should have endowed the survivors with greatly increased resources; this in turn should have stimulated the quick recovery of the population to former levels. No such resiliency is evident in late-medieval Europe. The population continued to decline well into the fifteenth century, then remained stagnant at low levels from about 1420 to 1470. Other factors besides the balance of population and resources were affecting these movements of sharp decline and belated recovery.

Classical Malthusian theory does not, in sum,

offer an entirely convincing explanation for late-medieval demographic swings. One important consideration missing from the analysis is birth rates. These are assumed to have been high and stable. In fact, even within individual communities birth rates were sensitive to social conditions. Poverty in particular limited the opportunity to marry and discouraged reproduction within marriage; it also reduced the chances of survival for infants and children. For any understanding of late-medieval population movements, this crucial factor demands attention.

Here, then, is the most likely, though still tentative, explanation of demographic swings across the late Middle Ages. By 1250 the population had attained high levels, and this intensified competition for both land and jobs. Rents soared and wages sank, and the terms of tenancy and employment shifted in the interests of landlord and employer. The distribution of income thus came to favor, ever more sharply and unfairly, the propertied classes. Both landlords and entrepreneurs enjoyed apparent prosperity in the late thirteenth century, but their good fortune rested in appalling measure on the deprivation of the lowest orders of society. These responded to their misery by failing to reproduce themselves in adequate numbers. This would seem to explain the apparent equilibrium of births and deaths, and the resultant stability of the population, for the fifty and more years preceding 1348.

These bad social conditions aggravated the impact of the great epidemics but cannot entirely account for their appearance. Medical and epidemiological factors played a role, even if their exact nature is not understood. At all events this skewed distribution of income long obstructed the efforts of the community to rebound from its great losses. Recovery required in the long run a redistribution of social benefits—better treatment, in other words, of the lower social orders. Wages did tend to rise, and rents to fall, as the population declined; individual landlords and employers also offered better terms of tenure and employment. But collectively the dominant classes long resisted these tendencies and sought through legislation to freeze both wages and prices at preplague levels.

This is one reason why the late Middle Ages was an epoch of social tumult. Not until the fifteenth century did the situation stabilize, and only then did the lower orders of society gain secure hold over the benefits that their reduced numbers promised them. This in turn encouraged demographic recovery. The period of stability at low levels, lasting from about

1420 to 1470, gave way to one of renewed growth, which continued without interruption into the sixteenth century.

At the close of the Middle Ages, about 1500, the number of Europeans remained substantially below what it had been two centuries before. But the common people seem to have enjoyed higher incomes and to have lived under more favorable social conditions than previously. Presumably they also enjoyed a higher standard of living and consumed a healthier diet. Physically, and perhaps also psychologically, they were prepared for the great expansion—demographic, geographic, and economic—of the early modern age.

GENERAL CHARACTERISTICS

Although a traditional society, the medieval world in its demographic behavior did not consistently follow the patterns expected of preindustrial communities. Insofar as can be judged, the birth rate always ranged much below the biological maximum and was not stable over space and time. Rather, births (and marriages and deaths as well) were sensitive to a variety of socioeconomic influences.

Among the factors that influenced vital events, residence in city or countryside was one of the most powerful. The urban environment obstructed and delayed marriages, especially for men, and almost certainly dampened the fertility of the family. Urban males had to wait until they were established in a craft or profession before they were able to take a wife. In the countryside the peasant needed the help of a wife as soon as he gained possession of a farm. In towns marriage was a reward for economic achievement; in the countryside it was the prerequisite for it.

The status of children was analogous to that of a wife. They were needed and welcome helpers on farms but were less essential in the pursuit of most urban careers. Moreover, the training of an urban child was often long and costly. These conditions discouraged the procreation of large families within the cities. In the late Middle Ages outspoken preachers such as Bernardino of Siena (1380–1444) condemned contraceptive practices, which they equated with the sin of sodomy. Bernardino once claimed that for reason of this sin, out of every 1,000 marriages, 999 were of the devil. Clearly he believed that contraception was a common practice in the urban congregations to which he preached. It has been shown by David Herlihy and Christiane Klapisch-Zuber that at Florence in 1427 the fertility of married women declined sharply from the time they reached their late twenties. This strongly implies that statistically significant numbers of urban wives were somehow limiting their fertility from the middle years of their marriages.

Death rates too were doubtless higher in large cities than in rural areas. The big medieval town, in other words, was, like traditional European cities before the nineteenth century, a sink of humanity.

Social environment or access to wealth and resources also strongly influenced demographic behavior. As has already been observed, the poor were the least prolific members of society. The misery of the destitute obstructed marriages, dampened their fertility, and raised levels of infant mortality. Consistently in surveys, from the Carolingian period on, the rich families have proportionately larger numbers of offspring. This phenomenon had important social repercussions. Because the upper levels of the social pyramid reproduced themselves more successfully than the lower, the offspring of the privileged faced an uncertain future. They might have to accept a position in society lower than that of their parents; the dominant direction of social mobility in medieval society seems to have been downward. This threat of social slippage encouraged the sons of the wealthy to adopt an entrepreneurial stance at home or to emigrate to new lands in hopes of repairing their fortunes. Demographic pressures thus in part explain the remarkable displays of effort and energy—and the turbulence—characteristic of medieval social history.

The long-range economic trend also affected behavior. As has been noted, the scarcity of land and jobs in the late thirteenth century braked the demographic expansion of the central Middle Ages. Conversely, enlarged resources (measured in per capita terms) and a fairer system of distributing income sustained the demographic recovery from the late fifteenth century on.

The model of demographic behavior to which the medieval community most closely corresponds is that of an equilibrium system, in which population and resources were kept in balance. The population tended to reproduce itself up to, but not beyond, the limits imposed by available resources. When the volume of resources fluctuated across the social pyramid or over time, so did the reproductive performance of the population. The regulating mechanisms worked imperfectly and were at times overwhelmed by external shocks—notably by the great epidemics of the fourteenth century—yet the medieval community did not reproduce itself blindly, solely in response to biological urges.

A basic tool of modern demographic analysis is the life table, which records the number of deaths for each sex at every age in the population and permits a calculation of "expectation of life." Through a variety of strategies (the examination of skeletal remains, the tracking of individual careers in the documentary record, the examination of death lists) historians have developed certain crude estimates of the duration of life in medieval times. Average duration of life from birth appears to have been about thirty years, but it also shows substantial shifts over time. In the plague-free period of the early and central Middle Ages, to about 1300, it seems to have reached as high as forty years—at least for certain favored and visible groups, such as English princes and Florentine merchants. With the onslaught of plague the average duration of life from birth dropped below twenty years, and thereafter it slowly rose as the ferocity of the epidemics gradually waned.

The distribution of the population according to age also shifted over time, in response both to changes in longevity and, still more, to variations in fertility. In the thirteenth century, under conditions of comparatively extended expectation of life and restrained fertility, the population contained proportionately high numbers of active adults. The "dependency ratio"—the balance between economically productive adults and young and old dependents—was consequently favorable. With the coming of the great epidemics life expectancy fell and fertility increased, as the community sought to maintain its numbers in the face of devastating losses.

The age pyramid thus came to carry large numbers of young children. In Florence in 1427 more than 15 percent of the population was age four or younger; the city swarmed with babies. Curiously, the community also accumulated large numbers of the very old. In 1427, 11.7 percent of Florentines were age sixty or older, a proportion to be expected in a modern, "aging" population. The plague seems to have attacked children and young adults mercilessly but to have spared the aged; those who lived through one epidemic were likely to survive the next. Under plague conditions the community thus came to support large numbers of economically inactive members. This shift in age distribution across the Middle Ages seems also to have influenced the style of medieval life and culture.

Historians have also paid close attention to the small units of medieval society, the family and the household. They have investigated how the family was formed through marriage, its usual size, and its ordinary structure.

Marriage patterns are difficult to investigate, particularly in the early Middle Ages. It is known that Roman girls were young at first marriage, seventeen or eighteen years of age, and that their grooms were typically mature men, some nine years older. On the other hand, the Roman historian Tacitus reports that among the barbarian Germans both women and men were mature, and presumably of a like age, when they first married. This Germanic, rather than Roman, pattern of marriage seems to have prevailed in early-medieval society.

The survey of the peasants of St. Victor of Marseilles from the early ninth century gives the ages of children (to fifteen) and the marriage status of adults. It is unique in offering a view of marriage patterns within an early-medieval peasant community. Out of a total population of 1,027, unmarried males over age fifteen numbered 127 and females 120. This suggests that both men and women married late—probably in their late twenties—and were of comparable age.

Although evidence remains sketchy, it would appear that this pattern changed in approximately the twelfth century. The change is most visible, and was doubtless most pronounced, within two social groups: the nobility and the townsmen. The age of first marriage for women fell to very low levels—below twenty years. Men were still in their late twenties, or even older, when they married. Some males remained bachelors, but all women either married or entered the religious life.

Several significant results flowed from this changing marriage pattern. In the early Middle Ages women entered marriage on favorable terms, probably because grooms had to compete for scarce mates. Usually the marriage gifts and assignments to the bride exceeded the dowry that she brought to her husband. But when the age of first marriage for women fell, the financial balance tipped in favor of the males. Girls in their late teens—now the usual age of marriage—outnumbered men in their late twenties. They, or their families, had to bid for scarce spouses through offering better terms. The flow of property in the making of a marriage reversed, and the groom, rather than the bride, gained the advantage. Dowries paid by brides (or their families) to the grooms inflated continuously during the middle and late Middle Ages. Dante noted how the birth of a daughter struck terror into her father's heart. Competition to settle a daughter's future, he affirmed, drove the age of female marriage down, and the size of the dowry up, to unreasonable levels (*Paradiso*, XV, 103–105).

Because of the shrinking of the age pyramid at its higher levels, girls at the usual age of marriage, between fifteen and twenty, inevitably outnumbered men between twenty-five and thirty; it was statistically certain that some girls would not find a husband. And the wide age difference between bride and groom assured that despite the risks of childbearing, the wife had a good chance of surviving her older husband. Medieval society, especially in towns and among the nobles, contained numerous unmarriageable girls and young widows. These unattached women gave impetus to the formation of irregular and unauthorized religious communities (such as the Beguines) and aggravated the *Frauenfrage* (the woman question) that profoundly troubled society.

Demographers today speak of a "modern west-European marriage pattern" that displays the following characteristics: both men and women marry late, at comparable ages, and large numbers of both sexes do not marry at all. The pattern prevailing in medieval society from the twelfth century on was thus quite distinctive: men were modern in their behavior, while women distinctly were not—at least, not among the nobles and the bourgeoisie. Women were very young at first marriage, and those who could not marry entered the religious life; spinsters seem to have been virtually unknown in medieval society. When and why the modern marriage pattern emerged are still not known, but it was not established over the course of the Middle Ages.

The medieval household seems always to have been small in size and simple in structure. The average number of members fluctuated between three and six, with four and a half apparently the usual mean. Most households included only husband, wife, and children; they were based, in sum, on the nuclear family. Medieval data thus lend support to the "small family hypothesis," the argument that in all known societies the nuclear family has predominated.

Nevertheless, the size and structure of medieval households did vary over space, time, and society. Peasant families, for example, were characteristically larger than those of the city, reflecting younger marriages and greater fertility within them. Peasant families were also more complex in their structure and frequently contained more than one married couple.

Often the eldest son of a peasant couple would be allowed to marry while his parents still lived. This generational extension of the household approximates the structure of what modern sociologists call the stem family. But sometimes more than one son married; there was no dominant, rigorously respected pattern. Inheritance customs, and perhaps cultural values, had strong influence.

Wealth, too, influenced household structure. Wealthy families tended to be complex, while the nuclear family enjoyed an overwhelming predominance among the less affluent. Characteristically the wealthy household contained more children, more collateral relatives (unmarried siblings of the head), and more servants than its poorer neighbor.

Finally, the household varied according to its own developmental cycle, which was usually linked to the age of its head. As the head aged, his household usually grew larger. Daughters departed in marriage, but a son often brought a wife into the parents' household, which would then be further enlarged through grandchildren. At the death of the head the several male heirs might decide to keep their patrimony undivided. They then formed a laterally extended joint-family household. These joint-family households were common at this particular point in the developmental cycle but rarely proved durable. The straw that broke their fraternal unity was usually the maturation of the offspring of the joint heads. The question arose of how much of the common patrimony should be used to endow the daughter of a single member or to establish a son in business. Such issues caused contention, and the heads were then prone to divide the common patrimony and allocate to each an equal share. The joint-family household thus rather quickly dissolved into nuclear families; at this moment, for each of them, the developmental cycle began anew. The medieval household, in sum, was not stable and enduring; it was sensitive both to external forces and to the pressures emanating from its internal life.

The study of medieval population is always difficult, sometimes frustrating, but indisputably rewarding. Much is known about the size and structure of medieval communities, and it can be discerned rather clearly how medieval people lived out their lives. Historical demography now makes an essential contribution to the understanding of medieval society and culture. It is fundamental too in any examination of populations in the modern West. It illuminates how Western communities have evolved over time and displays the deep roots of modern behavior.

BIBLIOGRAPHY

Wilhelm Abel, *Die Wüstungen des ausgehenden Mittelalters*, 2nd ed. (1955); Édouard Baratier, *La démographie provençale du XIIIᵉ au XVIᵉ siècle* (1961); Karl Julius Beloch, *Bevölkerungsgeschichte Italiens*, 3 vols. (1937–1961); Maurice W. Beresford, *New Towns of the Middle Ages* (1967); Maurice W. Beresford and John G. Hurst, *Deserted Medieval Villages* (1971); Jean-Nöel Biraben, ed., *Les hommes et la peste en France et dans les pays européens et méditerranéens*, 2 vols. (1975–1976); Guy Bois, *Crise du féodalisme* (1976); William M. Bowsky, "The Impact of the Black Death Upon Sienese Government and Society," in *Speculum*, 39 (1964); Robert Brenner, "Agrarian Class Structure and Economic Development in Pre-industrial Europe," in *Past and Present*, 70 (1976); Edward Britton, *The Community of the Vill: A Study in the History of the Family and Village Life in Fourteenth-century England* (1977); D. Brothwell, "British Palaeodemography and Earlier British Populations," in *World Archaeology*, 4 (1972); J. D. Chambers, *Population, Economy, and Society in Pre-industrial England* (1972); Emily R. Coleman, "Infanticide in the Early Middle Ages," in Susan Mosher Stuard, ed., *Women in Medieval Society* (1976), 47–70; Joseph Cuvelier, *Les dénombrements de foyers à Brabant* (1912); P. Desportes, "La population de Reims au XVᵉ siècle," in *Le moyen-âge*, 72 (1966); Edwin B. Dewindt, *Land and People in Holywell-cum-Needingworth* (1972); Phillippe Dollinger, "Le chiffre de population de Paris au XIVᵉ siècle: 210,000 ou 80,000 habitants," in *Revue historique*, 216 (1956); Edith Ennen, *Frühgeschichte der europäischen Stadt* (1953), and *Die europäische Stadt des Mittelalters* (1972), trans. by Natalie Fryde as *The Medieval Town* (1979); Enrico Fiumi, "Il computo della popolazione di Volterra nel medioevo secondo il 'sal delle bocche,'" in *Archivio storico italiano*, 107 (1949), "La demografia fiorentina nelle pagine di Giovanni Villani," *ibid.*, 108 (1950), "Economia e vita privata dei Fiorentini nelle rilevazioni statistiche di Giovanni Villani," *ibid.*, 111 (1953); *Storia economica e sociale di San Gimignano* (1961); "La popolazione del territorio volterrano-sangimignanese ed il problema demografico dell'età communale," in *Studi in onore di Amintore Fanfani*, I (1962), 248–290, and *Demografia, movimento urbanistico e classi sociali in Prato dall'età communale ai tempi moderni* (1968); Lucie Fossier, André Vauchez, and Cinzio Violante, *Informatique et histoire médiévale* (1977); Robert Fossier, *La terre et les hommes en Picardie jusqu'à la fin du XIIIᵉ siècle*, 2 vols. (1968); Guy Fourquin, "La population de la région parisienne aux environs de 1328," in *Le moyen-âge*, 62 (1956); Nils Gejvall, *Westerhus: Medieval Population and Church in the Light of Skeletal Remains* (1960); Léopold Genicot, "Sur les témoinages d'accroissement de la population en Occident du XIᵉ au XIIIᵉ siècle," in *Cahiers d'histoire mondiale*, 1 (1953), trans. as "On the Growth of Population in the West from the Eleventh to the Thirteenth Centuries," in Sylvia L. Thrupps, ed., *Change in Medieval Society* (1964); Irena Gieysztorowa, "Research Into the Demographic History of Poland: A Provisional Summing-up," in *Acta Poloniae historica*, 18 (1968); Robert S. Gottfried, *Epidemic Disease in Fifteenth Century England* (1978); P. Gras, "Le registre paroissial de Givry (1334–1357)," in *Bibliothèque de l'École des chartes*, 100 (1939); Benjamin Guérard, ed., *Polyptyque de l'abbé Irminon* (1844), and *Cartulaire de l'abbaye de Saint-Victor de Marseille*, 2 vols. (1857); John Hatcher, *Plague, Population, and the English Economy* (1977); Jacques Heers, *Gênes au XVᵉ siècle: Activité économique et problèmes sociaux* (1961), "Les limites des méthodes statistiques pour les recherches de démographie médiévale," in *Annales de démographie historique* (1968), and *Le clan familial au moyen-âge* (1974), trans. by Barry Herbert as *Family Clans in the Middle Ages* (1977); Louis Henry, *Manuel de démographie historique* (1967); David Herlihy, "The Agrarian Revolution in Southern France and Italy, 810–1150," in *Speculum*, 33 (1958), "The Carolingian *Mansus*," in *The Economic History Review*, 2nd ser. 13 (1960), "The Generation in Medieval History," in *Viator*, 5 (1974), *Medieval and Renaissance Pistoia: The Social History of an Italian Town* (1967), "The Medieval Marriage Market," in *Medieval and Renaissance Studies*, 6 (1976), and *The Social History of Italy and Western Europe, 700–1500* (1978); David Herlihy and Christiane Klapisch-Zuber, *Les Toscans et leurs familles* (1978); Arlette Higounet-Nadal, *Les comptes de la taille et les sources de l'histoire démographique de Périgueux au XIVᵉ siècle* (1965), and *Périgueux aux XIVᵉ et XVᵉ siècles* (1978); Thomas H. Hollingsworth, *Historical Demography* (1969); George C. Homans, *English Villagers of the Thirteenth Century* (1960); David Jacoby, *Société et démographie à Byzance et en Romanie latine* (1975); Karl Lamprecht, *Deutsches Wirtschaftsleben im Mittelalter*, 3 vols. (1885–1886); Auguste Longnon, ed., *Polyptyque de l'abbaye de Saint-Germain des Prés*, 2 vols. (1886–1895); Ferdinand Lot, "Conjectures démographiques sur la France au IXᵉ siècle," in *Le moyen-âge*, 32 (1921), "L'état des paroisses et des feux de 1328," in *Bibliothèque de l'École des chartes*, 90 (1929), and *Recherches sur la population et la superficie des cités remontant à la période gallo-romaine*, 3 vols. (1945–1946); Henry S. Lucas, "The Great European Famine of 1315, 1316, and 1317," in *Speculum*, 5 (1930); William H. McNeill, *Plagues and Peoples* (1976); Roger Mols, *Introduction à la démographie historique des villes d'Europe*, 3 vols. (1954–1956); C. E. Perrin, "Observations sur le manse dans la région parisienne au début du IXᵉ siècle," in *Annales d'histoire sociale, Hommages à Marc Bloch*, II (1945); Henri Pirenne, "Les dénombrements de la population d'Ypres au XVe siècle (1412–1506)," in his *Histoire économique de l'Occident médiéval* (1951), 458–489; Antonio Ivan Pini, *La popolazione di Imola e del suo ter-*

ritorio nel XIII e XIV secolo (1976); M. M. Postan, "England," in *The Cambridge Economic History of Europe,* I, *The Agrarian Life of the Middle Ages,* 2nd ed. (1966), 549–632, and *Essays on Medieval Agriculture and General Problems of the Medieval Economy* (1973); Norman J. G. Pounds, "Northwest Europe in the Ninth Century: Its Geography in Light of the Polyptyques," in *Annals of the Association of American Geographers,* 57 (1967), and *An Historical Geography of Europe, 450 B.C.–A.D. 1330* (1973); J. Ambrose Raftis, *The Estates of Ramsey Abbey* (1957), *Tenure and Mobility: Studies in the Social History of the Medieval English Village* (1964), and *Warboys: Two Hundred Years in the Life of a Mediaeval English Village* (1974); Richard R. Ring, "Early Medieval Peasant Households in Central Italy," in *Journal of Family History,* 4 (Spring 1979); Josiah C. Russell, *British Medieval Population* (1948), *Late Ancient and Medieval Populations* (1958), "The Medieval Monedatge of Aragon and Valencia," in *Proceedings of the American Philosophical Society,* 106 (1962), "Recent Advances in Medieval Demography," in *Speculum,* 40 (1965), and *Medieval Cities and Their Regions* (1972); Quinto Sàntoli, ed., *Liber focorum districtus Pistorii (a. 1226); Liber finium districtus Pistorii (a. 1255)* (1956); Joseph R. Strayer, "Economic Conditions in the County of Beaumont-le-Roger, 1261–1313," in *Speculum,* 26 (1951); Sylvia L. Thrupp, *Society and History* (1977); Pierre Toubert, *Les structures du Latium médiéval,* 2 vols. (1973); *Villages désertés et histoire économique, XIe–XVIIIe siècle* (1965); Philippe Wolff, *Les estimes toulousaines des XIVe et XVe siècles* (1956); E. A. Wrigley, *Identifying People in the Past* (1973); Philip Ziegler, *The Black Death* (1969).

DAVID HERLIHY

[See also **Barbarians, Invasions of; Black Death; Class Structure, Western European; Contraception, European; Family, Western European; Famine in Western Europe; Urbanism, Western European.**]

DĒNKARD (Acts of the Religion), the longest extant Pahlavi work, exists only in mutilated form, its surviving books being numbered III–IX. It constitutes a vast storehouse of Zoroastrian knowledge, in which materials from diverse epochs and of varied origins have been rehandled by successive priestly authors. The final redaction belongs to the ninth century. The manuscript tradition is poor and the style often tortuous, so that with the added difficulties of the script much still remains obscure. There is no complete, up-to-date translation, but there are many studies of individual passages and some of whole books.

Much of the first part is apologetic, compiled in an epoch dominated by Islam. Most of the second is devoted to preserving knowledge from or about the Avesta. The early books contain collections of answers to questions about doctrine, ethics, and practices. These vary greatly in length and are often set out without any particular connecting links. There are also sets of admonitions and lists of virtues and their opposing vices, emphasizing the importance of balance or the mean. There is a long chapter on medicine and an important account of the transmission of the Zoroastrian scriptures. The sixth book, written in a relatively clear, straightforward style, is an anthology of wise sayings attributed to the ancients or to various Sasanian sages. Book VII, which contains translations of many lost Avestan passages, with paraphrases and glosses, sets out a universal history, from the First Man to Judgment Day, with Zoroaster at its central point. This is one of the chief sources for traditions about the prophet's life. The eighth book gives invaluable summaries of nineteen *nasks* of the great Sasanian Avesta; and the ninth deals with three of the holiest of these through detailed and difficult commentaries.

BIBLIOGRAPHY

A complete text and translation are in P. B. Sanjana and D. P. Sanjana, *The Dinkard,* 19 vols. (1874–1928). Partial texts and translations include Jean Pierre de Menasce, *Le troisième livre du Denkart,* vol. III of *Travaux de l'Institut d'études iraniennes de l'Université de Paris* (1973); Marijan Molé, *La légende de Zoroastre selon les textes pehlevis* (1967), 2–115, 139–237 (from Books V and VII); Shaul Shaked, *The Wisdom of the Sasanian Sages (Dēnkard VI)* (1979). See also Jean Pierre de Menasce, *Une encyclopédie mazdéenne: Le Dēnkart* (1958).

MARY BOYCE

[See also **Avesta; Zoroastrianism.**]

DENMARK

LAND AND PEOPLE

"Water unites, but land divides" could be called the theme of the first millennium of Danish history. Consisting of peninsulas and innumerable islands, the country was originally settled by people who inhabited the coastlines, used the sounds, bays, and inlets for transportation and communication, and only slowly penetrated the forests. Consequently the moors and swamps north of the Eider River in Germany and the forests and mountains south of the Göta River in Sweden became impassable boundaries. Efforts dating back to the mid thirteenth century by the nobility of Holstein and Slesvig to merge the Danish with the German principality effectively moved the southern boundary north to the Kongeå River, but the northeastern boundary held firm until the mid seventeenth century, making the present-day southern Swedish provinces of Halland, Skåne, and Blekinge important parts of medieval Denmark. In addition to effecting the unification of the Danish kingdom, the sea provided the foci of the expansion, first across the North Sea to England and later into the Baltic, incorporating northern Germany, Poland, and Estonia.

Although the ubiquitous water furnished ample supplies of fish, thus sustaining an early primitive society, the Danish countryside with its flat terrain and gently rolling hills was easy to farm, in contrast with the rest of Scandinavia. The relatively fertile soil made agriculture the most important economic activity. The village was the key feature and owed its origin to the introduction of the heavy iron plow. The expense of the plow and the draft animals necessitated the communal features of the village; the peasants worked the fields together and acted as a council in all community matters.

This system led earlier historians to postulate a society of free, equal farmers, but the existence of a distinct class of great property owners and nobles by the mid thirteenth century makes it probable that social distinctions were pronounced already in the Viking period. These great property owners characteristically possessed several villages, each supervised by a bailiff and inhabited by peasants in various degrees of economic and personal dependence. The land was exploited in a wide variety of patterns of crop rotation known elsewhere in Europe, but the efficient three-field system was probably not introduced until about 1300. Crops consisted primarily of rye, with barley and oats ranking second, and wheat very rare.

After agriculture, trading was the second most important economic endeavor, closely allied to piracy in the Viking period. Two towns, Hedeby (later renamed Slesvig, modern German name Schleswig) and Ribe, appeared at least by the eighth century. Coins and evidence of imported finery show that these places were centers of mercantile activity and owed their existence to the long-distance international trade. This trade, in turn, stimulated local commerce, which soon became centered in new towns that enjoyed royal protection. By the middle of the thirteenth century more than eighty towns, mainly situated on royal land, can be identified. This number is more than twice that found at the same time in the rest of Scandinavia. Besides catering to local needs, the towns exported grain and butter.

The greatest export was, however, herring from Skåne. From the end of the twelfth century and for the next 300 years, the herring appeared yearly from August to October in such quantities that at times it was difficult to row through them. The fish could even be caught with bare hands, though the normal method was by net. By the end of the thirteenth century the catch was six times that at the beginning of the twentieth century. The herring were cleaned, salted, and packed in barrels—jobs handled largely by women—and shipped to the rest of Europe, where they became an important staple on meatless Fridays and during Lent. Since Hanseatic merchants, particularly from Lübeck, brought the necessary salt from Lüneburg and in addition contributed capital investments, they dominated the export trade. Because of the frenzy of human activity stirred up by the herring, the area became a lively trading center for northern Europe, similar to the fairs of Champagne, with seasonal concentration in Skanør and Falsterbo.

These economic activities sustained a population that reached a peak of 1 million, estimated from a survey partially preserved in *Waldemar's Land Book* (1231). The economy was not able to maintain this population by the end of the thirteenth century, and a decline set in, accentuated, as elsewhere in Europe, by the Black Death in the following century. The medieval figure was not attained again until the nineteenth century.

RELIGION

With the rest of the Scandinavian-Germanic world the Danes shared the Nordic mythology and religion. Odin and Thor were the most prominent gods, whose importance can be gauged not only from the mythological texts preserved in Iceland but also, more significantly, from numerous place names. Holding its rituals out of doors, the pagan cult was led by male chieftains but also may have allowed roles for women. There were large cult centers in Viborg, Odense, and Leire where human sacrifices were performed. Of more importance for

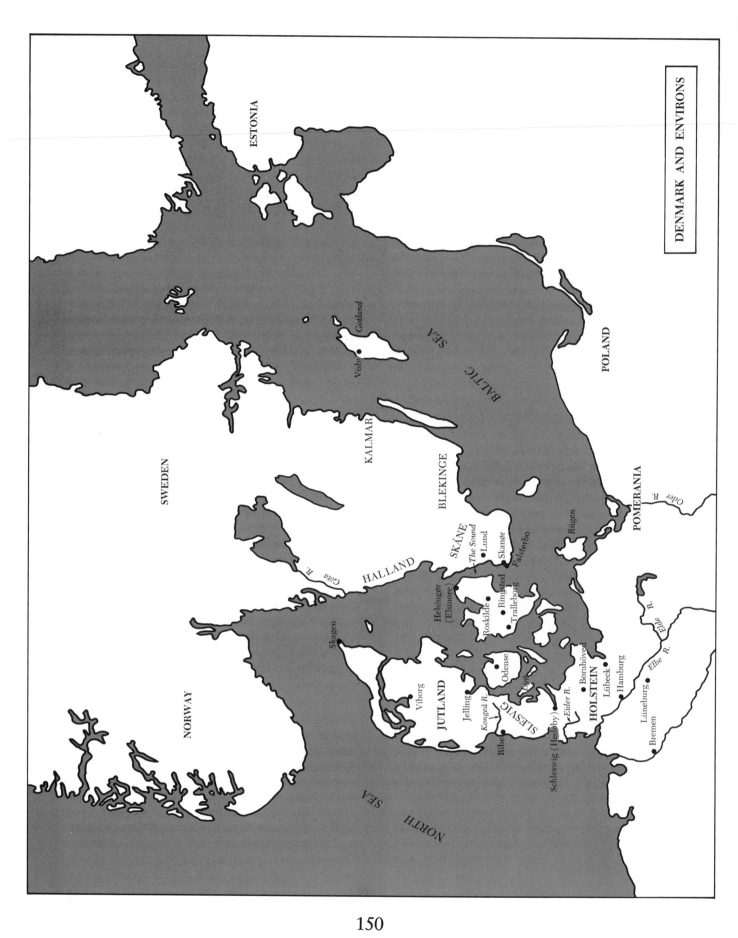

DENMARK AND ENVIRONS

ordinary people was the worship of minor deities, including trolls and dwarfs, and the veneration of nonpersonified powers in nature. The purpose of religion at all levels was to protect life and ensure the harvest by propitiating hostile powers. This purpose remained the same for centuries in the popular religion, though the outer forms changed from paganism to Christianity. During the late Middle Ages an important ceremony in village life was to carry the cross or images of saints around the village and over the fields in the same way that Tacitus reported the Germanic tribes acted with their pagan idols.

The conversion of the Danish people, therefore, cannot be dated precisely, but officially Denmark became Christian about 960, after 250 years of aggressive activity by the church and increased receptivity among the Danish leaders, many of whom had been exposed to the new religion on their Viking journeys. In the first half of the eighth century the Anglo-Saxon missionary Willibrord took time from his labors among the Frisians to launch a preliminary expedition among the Danes. It was not until Saxony had been conquered and Christianized by the Franks, however, that the church was able to focus its attention on Scandinavia. In 823 Archbishop Ebo of Rheims, the northernmost metropolitan see in the Frankish empire, journeyed to southern Denmark with the expressed desire to convert the Nordic world. This wish was realized in a small way a few years later, when one of the pretenders to the Danish throne, Harald Klak, came with his wife and children to the court of Louis the Pious to ask for help against his enemies. He was baptized and returned to Denmark accompanied by two monks, of whom one, Ansgar, has been called the Apostle of the North.

Ansgar's achievements, however, were only modest in Denmark, where he established churches in Slesvig and Ribe, but he had more success in Sweden. He was nonetheless able to bring Denmark into the orbit of the church when he obtained a papal letter establishing a new archbishopric at Hamburg and appointing him as its first occupant. The prime purpose of this new see was the conversion of the Nordic world. A century later—about 960 according to tradition—Harald Bluetooth, one of the first kings of the united monarchy, was so impressed with the hot-iron ordeal performed by a Christian priest named Poppo that he accepted baptism and attempted to induce his people to follow his lead. Apparently he felt that he had succeeded, because he identified himself as "the Harald who won for him-

self all Denmark and Norway and made the Danes Christians" on a magnificent runic stone erected at Jelling to commemorate his parents.

The period of conversion lasted at least until the middle of the next century and resulted in an incipient Danish church. It was less influenced by the mother church in Hamburg-Bremen than by English Christianity, because renewed Viking attacks brought the Danes into contact with the English. The subsequent history of the church will be examined in the context of political development.

POLITICAL HISTORY

The Viking period: 800–1042. Denmark entered the historical period about 800, when Carolingian sources report frontier skirmishes with a Danish king named Godfred. At one time historians dealt extensively with a more remote past, centered on the so-called Leire monarchy. Because of important discoveries since the 1920's, archaeologists dominate this field today. The two outstanding features of the historical period—besides the Christianization—are the Viking expeditions and the unification of the country under a single monarch.

Spurred by land hunger and avid in the search for both international and domestic trade, the Vikings started out in smallish groups, each headed by a chieftain. When Gorm the Old and his son Harald Bluetooth, the first of the Jelling dynasty, achieved prominence over other war leaders, they profited from this position by staging large-scale attacks and expeditions beyond the North Sea and the Baltic. In the 980's Harald's son, Sweyn (Svend) Forkbeard, embarked on a systematic conquest of England, where he was accepted as king in 1014. The organization and impact of this Viking monarchy can be judged from the massive, circular fortified camps, four of which have been discovered in Denmark. (They are often called Trelleborgs from the name of the first one, uncovered in the 1930's.) While earlier they were seen as training camps to ready soldiers for attacks on England, they are now generally recognized as impressive fortifications intended to subdue a recalcitrant people.

The Viking monarchy culminated with Cnut (Canute, Knud), Sweyn's son, who was accepted as English king after his father's death in 1014. Cnut (Knud) was the first Danish king to spend considerable time in England. His contact with the superior English civilization encouraged him not only to continue Anglo-Saxon customs in England but also to imitate them in Denmark. On the English pattern, for example, he initiated the regular minting of coins. With the death of Cnut, however, Denmark and England went their separate ways. For the Danes this period of playing a leading role on the north European stage had come to an end. Their goal was henceforth reduced to the more modest ambition of bringing the country abreast of the general European development.

Growing pains: 1042–1157. A good sign of Denmark's increased absorption into the mainstream of European culture is the greater availability of historical sources beginning in the middle of the eleventh century. Foreigners showed more interest in the Nordic scene, as is evidenced by Adam of Bremen's *History of the Bishops of the Church of Hamburg* from the 1070's, in which Denmark figures prominently in the bishopric's mission field. A native group of historians also emerged, among whom Saxo Grammaticus was outstanding. His massive *Gesta Danorum,* written about 1200, was a national history similar to Bede's *Ecclesiastical History of the English People,* covering the period from the origin of the Danish monarchy to about 1185.

Impressive by literary standards, Saxo provided detailed knowledge both of his own period, the Waldemar age, and of the preceding century. His account was taken at face value until the early twentieth century, but historians now realize that Saxo, deeply inspired by—indeed, perhaps responsible for—the ideology of the victorious Waldemar monarchy, tried to give it a suitable past by tailoring the history of the previous century according to this view. Recent historians, therefore, shy away from Saxo and prefer other narrative sources, which are often in opposition to his history. More reliable evidence is contained in letters and charters, which, however, are far less abundant than in the rest of western Europe. The oldest royal charter of which the text is known dates from 1085 (the only one before 1100), and the oldest royal letter preserved in the original is from 1135.

The period from the mid eleventh to the mid twelfth century may be characterized by attempts to create identities by the monarchy and the church, the two powers that dominated the next several centuries. At home the monarchy sought to define its authority over the local chieftains. In particular this involved striking a balance between the older, elective principle, by which the aristocracy participated in choosing the king from a pool of throneworthy candidates, and the newer ideal of lineage, by which the kingship devolved through hereditary succes-

sion. Abroad the kings reluctantly gave up their marauding Viking activities, but toward the end of the period their relations with the German emperors threatened their independence. The church attempted to shake off dependency on Hamburg-Bremen and to obtain a Danish archbishopric in direct communication with the papacy.

The monarchy. The most important of the kings was the first, Sweyn (Svend) Estridsen, son of Cnut's sister and an Anglo-Saxon earl. From his uncle's vast North Sea empire he secured Denmark in 1042 and ruled there until his death in 1074. Working hand in hand with the archbishop of Hamburg, he reorganized the church and by about 1060 had eight bishoprics. Despite his unorthodox sexual life he seems to have impressed the papacy, because the reform pope Gregory VII sent him a series of friendly letters.

During the next sixty years five of Sweyn's sons were elected king in succession, which both avoided dividing the kingdom and prepared for the later principle of hereditary succession through primogeniture. Two of the five, Cnut IV (1080–1086) and Eric I (1095–1103), were particularly noteworthy. Cnut entertained such exalted ideas concerning the monarch's prerogatives that he caused an uprising. Seeking refuge in a church in Odense, he was killed. When Eric in turn became king, he capitalized both on the years of bad harvest following Cnut's murder and the alleged miracles at his tomb to have Cnut declared a saint by the papacy. When Eric and his wife Bodil made a pilgrimage to Jerusalem, he designated his son regent. This scheme was intended to endow his own family with royal dignity by hereditary right and to strengthen the dynasty with a native saint. When he died on Cyprus, however, the nobles overlooked this arrangement and elected Niels, Sweyn's last son, as king (1104–1134). Unlike those of his predecessors, his long reign was largely peaceful.

Eventually, though, the problem of succession required a solution. In theory all sons of the last five kings could claim the royal title, but in fact a contest resulted between Magnus, son of Niels, and Eric's son, Cnut Lavard (Bread Giver), whom Niels had made duke of Slesvig. In addition Cnut obtained the contiguous area north of the Elbe as a fief from the German king after a successful campaign against the Wends. In 1131 Magnus, jealous of his rival's accumulation of power, treacherously killed him. The German king Lothair took the murder of his vassal as an opportunity to interfere in Danish affairs, and in 1134 he forced Magnus to accept him as overlord. The same year Magnus died in battle against Eric II, who had taken up the cause of his brother Cnut Lavard, and Niels was assassinated.

The next quarter of a century brought to fruition the worst tendencies in the electoral monarchy. After the murder of one king and the withdrawal to a monastery of another, the rivalry between the pretenders resulted in a dual election of Sweyn and Cnut, sons of Eric II and of Magnus, respectively. Following a period of civil war they both appealed to the German emperor. In 1152 Frederick Barbarossa gave Denmark to Sweyn as a fief of the empire; Cnut received smaller territories; and a third candidate, Waldemar, son of Cnut Lavard, obtained his father's position as duke of Slesvig. A few years later these three attempted a more equitable division of the monarchy, but in 1157 the rivalry among them surfaced again, causing Sweyn to kill Cnut. Sweyn died later that year in battle near Viborg, thus making possible the single rule of Waldemar, during whose reign the monarchy finally came of age.

The church. The goal of an independent Danish archbishopric was already envisioned by Sweyn Estridsen, but it was not achieved until 1103/1104, when Lund was transformed into an archbishopric by direct negotiations between Eric I and Pope Pascal II. Asser, who as bishop of Lund since 1089 had brought his wealthy family's prestige to the hierarchy of the church, now as archbishop became the leader not only of the Danish church but also of the whole Scandinavian province, including Iceland and Greenland. In return the pope obtained the establishment of the tithe, which gave the church an improved economic base. A monument to Asser's tenure is the splendid cathedral at Lund, built in an Anglo-Norman and Italian style and consecrated in 1145, only eight years after Asser's death.

How far the Danish church was still removed from the European norm, however, can be seen from the king's request in 1117 that the pope have the requirement for clerical celibacy relaxed. Only with Eskil, Asser's nephew and successor as archbishop, did the Gregorian reform movement gain entry into the Danish church. An impressive sign, however, of the church's popular strength is found in the 2,000 stone and brick Romanesque parish churches that were erected from the middle of the eleventh century. Still in use today, they testify to the control of Danish society and its resources by the political and ecclesiastical regimes.

The glory of the Waldemar age: 1157–1241. The period of nearly a century that is called the Waldemar age represents the high point in Danish medieval history. Victimized by the civil wars resulting from the elective principle, the monarchy now became hereditary, thereby enabling the kings, in close collaboration with the church, to reinforce their position within the country and to pursue an active policy abroad. Initially securing independence from the German emperor, they subsequently created a vast Baltic empire, but only of short duration. The architects of this development were three kings—Waldemar I (1157–1182), his sons Cnut VI (1182–1202) and Waldemar II (1202–1241), and three successive archbishops of Lund: Eskil, Absalon, and Anders Sunesøn.

Eskil's support of the Gregorian ideals at Rome inevitably brought him into conflict with a monarch determined to increase royal power. Siding with Pope Alexander III against the antipope Victor IV supported by the German emperor, Eskil expected Waldemar I to follow his example. When the king, obeying political necessity, supported the choice of the emperor, an impasse resulted. In 1161 Eskil exiled himself to France for six years. When Alexander's position improved during this period, Waldemar saw the need for reconciliation with Eskil. In 1170 the archbishop officiated at a splendid ceremony in the church at Ringsted, where Waldemar's father, Cnut Lavard, was canonized and his young son Cnut crowned.

During Eskil's absence the leading figure next to the king was Absalon, the bishop of Roskilde, who succeeded Eskil as archbishop. Like Eskil, he had studied abroad, but was less influenced by the extreme Gregorian theory of ecclesiastical superiority over monarchy and more inspired by the ideal of cooperation between the two powers, expressed in the *Polycraticus* of his contemporary, John of Salisbury. Such a program suited the young monarchy perfectly. Leading the royal party, Absalon crushed a threatening rebellion. He and the king summoned nobles and peasants to yearly expeditions against the Slavs. Disguised as crusades, these wars were conducted sometimes in collaboration, at other times in conflict, with Henry the Lion, duke of Saxony and a rival to imperial leadership in Germany. They were possible only because Emperor Frederick Barbarossa was preoccupied with Italian affairs, and later because the premature death of his son, Henry VI, caused strife between the Welfs and the Hohenstaufens.

Three phases can be distinguished in this Baltic

expansion. From 1160 until the 1190's the areas immediately south of the Danish isles and the Swedish provinces were attacked, resulting in the conquest of Rügen in 1169 and the coast of Germany to the mouth of the Oder by the 1180's. The 1190's saw the conquest of Holstein to the Elbe and Elde rivers, including important cities such as Hamburg and Lübeck. The third period, comprising the first two decades of the thirteenth century, resulted in the acquisition of distant Estonia, an achievement that Waldemar II and Archbishop Anders Sunesøn shared. The archbishop, however, was less of a warrior than his predecessor, and more adept at scholarly and literary pursuits.

The significance of these conquests can best be illustrated by the changing relations between Denmark and the German empire. While Waldemar I had been obliged to swear an oath of allegiance to Frederick Barbarossa, Cnut had refused to do so, and in 1214 his brother Waldemar II obtained a golden bull from Frederick II, formally granting him all the conquered territories. Waldemar II exhibited the self-confidence of the monarchy in 1218 when he personally crowned his nine-year-old son. As hereditary monarch he also felt free to grant his other sons sizable territories on the feudal pattern known elsewhere in Europe, thus laying the basis for the fratricidal wars of the following era.

The Baltic empire, however, was jerry-built, as became clear in 1223, when King Waldemar and his son were captured by a German count during a hunting expedition at Lyø in Denmark and imprisoned in Germany. Forced to pay a huge ransom and to return all German territories granted by the emperor, the king was not released for two years. When Waldemar tried to reverse this decision by military action, he suffered another serious defeat at Bornhöved in 1227. Of the vast Baltic territories only Estonia remained. A more ominous sign for the future was the marriage between his son Abel, duke of Slesvig, and the daughter of the count of Holstein, which initiated a union between the Danish and the German principalities and brought repercussions far beyond the Middle Ages.

The rise of the aristocracy and the dissolution of the monarchy: 1241–1340. Although the monarchy made advances in the judicial field during this century, it encountered serious problems, which sapped its vitality and resulted in a constitutional monarchy that offered Danish nobles an important role in the government. In the long run, however, they were un-

able to maintain their participation, losing out to German nobles. The kings were forced to mortgage the country piecemeal to the latter as a consequence of an expensive foreign policy, for which the resources, depleted by a concomitant agrarian crisis, were not sufficient. These German nobles became the virtual rulers of the country and eventually did not even deign to appoint a king.

Among four noteworthy problems that of the succession was the most persistent. Waldemar II's habit of distributing important provinces to his younger sons had set a dangerous precedent and created a new brood of potential royal candidates, always ready whenever the succession failed to proceed smoothly. Three of Waldemar's sons succeeded him: Eric (1241–1250), Abel (1250–1252), and Christopher I (1252–1259); Abel probably murdered Eric, and Christopher ignored Abel's sons. Christopher was followed by his son Eric V, who was murdered in 1286; and he, in turn, was succeeded by his two sons, of whom the younger, Christopher II, was elected to the position in 1320. Thus the elective principle had returned in full force.

Previously, hereditary succession was possible largely through the prestige lent by the church to the coronation ceremonies. Though requested, such support was refused in this period. The earlier cooperation between church and state, best exemplified by Absalon, was replaced by serious conflicts between the kings and the archbishops, of which the most dramatic episodes involved the archbishops Jakob Erlandsen in the 1250's and Jens Grand in the 1290's. Both prelates appealed to the papacy. When the popes did not respond with as serious sanctions against the kings as might have been expected, given the royal transgressions in both cases involving imprisonment, their actions can only be explained by the fact that the papacy preferred the alliance of the distant Danish king over the freedom of the local church.

The third problem, encompassing the nobles' dissatisfaction, is the most interesting because it resulted in new ways of governing the country. Resenting the civil wars involving the three first kings, the nobles had been disturbed by the vicious struggle between Christopher I and Jakob Erlandsen. In 1214, when Eric V wanted his infant son crowned immediately in order to secure the succession, certain nobles demurred. The coronation did take place two years later, but when dissatisfied nobles further conspired with the large group of pretenders, Eric acceded to their demands. The result was a Danish Magna Carta, the *handfæstning* signed in 1282, which limited the king's juridical authority and curtailed excessive taxation. It also stipulated yearly meetings of the Danehof, a parliamentary body that had emerged by the middle of the century. (About this time a council of state was also created that became a permanent feature of royal administration.)

During the next few years the aristocracy and the king worked together on important legislation. Eric's murder in 1286 brought this fruitful cooperation to an end. The group responsible for the charter was unjustly accused of the crime and outlawed, and a royal autocratic reaction set in during the reign of Eric VI. Since he did not have a son, the nobles were able in 1320, at his death in 1319, to write a new charter as their condition for electing his brother Christopher II. But this *handfæstning* went so far in curtailing the king's power that it made his job virtually impossible.

Foreign policy, however, and not restrictions imposed by the nobles, eventually brought the monarchy down. Considering the internal difficulties, the monarchy was surprisingly aggressive and showed interest in both Norwegian and Swedish affairs that would be of importance in the following period, and in the traditional Waldemar policy of expanding along the Baltic. The kings maintained peaceful relations with Lübeck, thereby wisely fostering the mercantile elements of Denmark. By relying, however, on mercenary troops against the other north German cities and by constructing expensive stone castles to maintain internal peace, they overtaxed the resources of the country. After having borrowed heavily, they could solve their financial difficulties only by handing over castles and whole provinces to their creditors, the German princes, who became the real rulers. When Christopher II died in 1332, the country had already been divided between Count Gerhard of Holstein in the west and Count John the Mild of Holstein in the east, and no new king was appointed. The monarchial idea was kept alive only in Skåne, which Magnus VII joined to his holdings as king of Norway and Sweden by paying off the mortgage to Count John. Gerhard fared worse. In 1340 he was killed by Niels Ebbesen, the leader of a rebellion in Jutland that had been brewing for a decade.

From Danish monarchy to Nordic Union: 1340–1523. In the late-medieval period Denmark regained its national independence. Abandoning the earlier fixation on German affairs and turning to the other Nordic countries, Danish leaders were instrumental in creating a Scandinavian union.

The difficult task of reuniting the kingdom was accomplished under the leadership of Waldemar IV, the youngest son of Christopher II, who in 1340 was accepted as king by the German creditors. Raised at the German imperial court, he was restless and ruthlessly ambitious, and held much in common with the new type of Renaissance ruler appearing in Italy at this time. During the first twenty years of his reign Waldemar reunited Denmark west of the Sound by peacefully redeeming some castles and provinces and by conquering others outright. The money came from heavy taxation and the sale of Estonia to the Teutonic Knights. Throughout the period he enjoyed the support of the church and most of the nobles, though the traditional resentment of the monarchy grew as Waldemar's strength increased. Rallying the country behind him in 1360, Waldemar conquered the remaining provinces of Skåne, Halland, and Blekinge, thus achieving his goal of reunification. But by proceeding one step further and taking the island of Gotland with the important Hanseatic stronghold of Visby, he alienated his former Hanseatic allies. This resulted in an anti-Danish coalition consisting of Sweden, most of the Hanseatic cities, Slesvig, and Holstein.

Able at first to defeat his enemies, Waldemar stood at the pinnacle of his power in the early 1360's. When he continued to increase tolls and confiscate the cities' merchandise, the Hanseatic League enlisted all its members, traditionally numbered at seventy-seven, and declared an all-out war against Denmark. Waldemar responded by leaving the country and letting the council of state manage the government. After two years in which cities and castles were systematically destroyed, the council was forced to sign a treaty with the Hansa, relinquishing control over castles on the western shore of Skåne and thereby allowing them access to the lucrative herring market. When Waldemar finally returned to Denmark, he faced a situation almost identical to the one he had encountered more than twenty years earlier, replete with local uprisings and foreign occupation. Before his death in 1375, however, he had once again brought the country, with the exception of Slesvig, back under control.

His heir was a daughter, Margaret, married to the Norwegian king Haakon VI. Their son Olaf was accepted by the Danish nobles as king. When Haakon died in 1380, Olaf became king of both countries, thereby starting a union that lasted more than four centuries. Since Olaf was only a child, the real ruler was his mother. Margaret promoted the idea of incorporating Sweden within the dynastic net of her family. Here Olaf claimed hereditary rights through his grandfather. When the Swedish nobility became disillusioned with their German king, Albert of Mecklenburg, Margaret persuaded them to accept her son in 1386. Olaf died the following year, and Margaret became regent in all three countries. The nobility, moreover, promised to take as common king whomever she suggested.

At a meeting in Kalmar in 1397 Margaret's grand-nephew, Eric of Pomerania, was accepted as king in all three countries. At the same time she attempted to formalize the Nordic Union, which lasted intermittently until 1523. By origin the union was dynastic, and the leadership remained with Denmark, the most fully developed among the Nordic countries. It was supported, nonetheless, by large groups of the aristocracy from all three nations, who through intermarriage often held land in more than one country and therefore found the blurring of national boundaries to their advantage. The union represented an effort by the Scandinavian ruling classes to present a solid front against the overwhelming German economic and political infiltration that had threatened Denmark, Norway, and Sweden throughout the fourteenth century.

The union functioned reasonably well during Margaret's able reign, but Eric managed to alienate the Swedes to such a degree that both they and the Danes deposed him in 1439. His cousin, Christopher of Bavaria, was accepted as king of the union from 1440 to 1448. The following three kings, of the new Oldenburg dynasty—Christian I (1448–1481), John (1481–1513), and Christian II (1513–1523)—fought for their position in Sweden. Noble resentment against Danes and other foreigners in prominent positions in Sweden, as well as intense nationalism among the lower classes, especially the miners, rendered the union impossible. It was further made obsolete by the decrease of German economic influence under competition from Dutch and English merchants, who went around Skagen to get to the Scandinavian markets, thereby providing a lucrative source of income for Danish kings, who levied a toll at Helsingør (Elsinore). In 1520, after having conquered Sweden, Christian was the last ruler of a united Scandinavia. When he subsequently staged the infamous Stockholm Bloodbath, in which more than eighty prominent Swedes were executed, this brutal act caused an uproar in Sweden and resulted in his dismissal as king of Denmark and Norway as well. His uncle, Frederick I, followed him as king in Denmark and Norway only, while Sweden chose a native king, Gustavus I.

BIBLIOGRAPHY

Sources. Primary sources in the form of chronicles, letters and charters, laws, and so on, exist in modern editions in Latin and medieval Danish, often with translation into modern Danish.

Studies. The most recent comprehensive treatment in Danish is Inge Skovgaard-Petersen, E. Christensen, and H. Paludan, eds., *Danmarks historie* (1977–). Other comprehensive works include Erik Arup, *Danmarks historie*, 3 vols. (1925–1955); John Danstrup and Hal Koch, eds., *Danmarks historie*, 3rd ed., 14 vols. (1977); Aage Friis *et al.,* eds., *Schultz Danmarks historie*, 2nd ed., 6 vols. (1941–1943); Niels Skyum-Nielsen, *Kvinde og Slave, Danmarks-historie uden retouche*, III (1971).

Comprehensive works in other languages include John H. S. Birch, *Denmark in History* (1938); John Danstrup, *A History of Denmark*, 2nd ed. (1949); Ludvig Krabbe, *Histoire de Danemark* (1950); Palle Lauring, *A History of the Kingdom of Denmark*, D. Hohnen, trans., 2nd ed. (1963); Stewart Oakley, *A Short History of Denmark* (1972).

The history of the church is treated in Leslie S. Hunter, ed., *Scandinavian Churches* (1965); Hal Koch and B. Kornerup, eds., *Den danske kirkes historie*, 8 vols. (1950–1966); Hubert Krins, *Die frühen Steinkirchen Dänemarks* (1968).

Special topics treated in non-Scandinavian languages include Sidney Cohen, *Viking Fortresses of the Trelleborg Type* (1965); Hilda R. E. Davidson, *Pagan Scandinavia* (1967); Oscar Eggert, *Die Wendenzüge Waldemars I und Knuts VI von Dänemark nach Pommern und Mecklenburg* (1927); Peter G. Foote and D. M. Wilson, *The Viking Achievement* (1970); Vilhelm Grønbech, *The Culture of the Teutons*, W. Worster, trans., 3 vols., (1932); Adolf Hofmeister, *Der Kampf um die Ostsee von 9. bis 12. Jahrhundert*, 3rd ed. (1960); Archibald R. Lewis, *The Northern Seas* (1958, repr. 1978); Vilho Niitemaa, *Der Kaiser und die Nordische Union bis zu den Burgunderkriegen* (1960); Thomas Riis, *Les institutions politiques centrales du Danemark, 1100–1332* (1977); Klaus von See, *Das skandinavische Königstum des frühen und hohen Mittelalters* (1953); E. O. G. Turville-Petre, *Myth and Religion of the North* (1964, repr. 1975).

Important articles in major European languages appear in *Mediaeval Scandinavia; Scandinavian Economic History Review; Scandinavian Journal of History.*

JENNY M. JOCHENS

[See also **Cnut the Great; Hanseatic League; Saxo Grammaticus; Vikings.**]

Deposition from the Cross. Austria, first half of the 11th century. THE PIERPONT MORGAN LIBRARY, MS 781, fol. 223v

DEPOSITION FROM THE CROSS. The removal of Christ's body from the cross by Joseph of Arimathea, who then wrapped the corpse in linen and placed it in his own tomb, is described in Matthew 27:57–61, Mark 15:42–47, Luke 23:50–55, and John 19:38–42. According to John, Nicodemus brought spices to anoint Christ's body; the remaining Gospels note that two women were present. The Deposition appears as an independent image by the ninth century. Joseph removes Christ's dead body with or without the aid of Nicodemus, usually in the presence of the onlookers—especially St. John and the Virgin—who had been present at the Crucifixion. From the tenth century on, Byzantine artists gave increasing importance to the Virgin's role and stressed the pathos of the episode; in this they were followed by Italian artists of the thirteenth and fourteenth centuries.

BIBLIOGRAPHY

Elizabeth Parker, *The Descent from the Cross* (1978); Gertrud Schiller, *Iconography of Christian Art,* Janet Seligman, trans., II (1972), 164–168; Kurt Weitzmann, "The Origin of the Threnos," in Millard Meiss, ed., *De artibus opuscula XL: Essays in Honor of Erwin Panofsky* (1961), 476–490.

LESLIE BRUBAKER

[See also **Crucifixion; Lamentation; Pietà.**]

DEPOSITION OF RULERS, THEORIES OF. At the beginning of the Middle Ages the sources of political theory, of which theories of the deposition of rulers are a part, consisted of Roman theories of the office of emperor, of subordinate administrative offices in Roman government, and Roman military command; the definitions and images of ruler and community in Scripture and in the writings of the church fathers; and the customs of the Celtic, Germanic, and Slavic peoples of transalpine Europe. These sources constituted a large and diverse, but not a coherent or systematic, political theory.

The history of medieval deposition theory is the history of the ways by which European peoples after the end of the Roman Empire drew upon these sources during a period in which both the theory and the character of political society and of rulership changed drastically. As the theory and practice of the office of ruler and the features of the ruled polity changed, traditional sources of deposition theory were often used in novel ways and new sources were developed. A final, but no less important, feature of medieval deposition theory is the character of the circumstances surrounding each case of deposition and each expression of deposition theory, regardless of whether that theory was ever applied.

With the end of Roman imperial power in the western parts of the empire at the end of the fifth century, the political structure of Europe consisted of new kingdoms carved by ambitious, warlike kings and migrating peoples from the ruins of Roman and non-Roman Europe. These peoples' experience of migration and conquest had transformed older tribal institutions and bonds, as well as the office of tribal ruler. In the first century the Roman historian Tacitus had described these early Germanic societies as tribes ruled by kings who were chosen by virtue of their descent within a kingly family, and occasionally as ruled by dukes chosen for their warlike abilities. In these societies kings were sacral, that is, they were links between their people and the gods. They were expected to guarantee their people's safety, good fortune, agricultural prosperity, and victory in battle. When the tribe was defeated in battle or the fields lost their fertility, the king may originally have been ritually sacrificed, shamed, abandoned, or simply assassinated and replaced by another.

Between the first and the sixth centuries, the character of both the Germanic tribe and its leader changed. Tacitus mentioned more than fifty tribes in the *Germania,* but very few of these survived intact the great period of folk migrations and military encounters and conquests that filled both Roman and Germanic history from the third to the seventh centuries. Successful leaders of war bands who carved territorial conquests out of the Roman Empire and the territory of neighboring peoples imposed many of the features of the war band on the older, largely familial tribal structures.

Military organization and successful conquest made kings of war leaders, active and ambitious rulers of new peoples formed from parts of older tribes that were mobilized and reshaped for war and conquest. When they had established themselves, the new kings modeled their office on older tribal offices, that is, they attempted to transform the basis of their power from war leadership to blood right. In addition, they borrowed elements of Roman office and of earlier Christian theories of rulership as many of them converted to Christianity. These elements changed the office of the ruler, the character of the polity, and the theory of deposition.

A striking example of the transformed character of both ruler and ruled in Germanic Christian society is the Merovingian dynasty of the Frankish people. Originally, the family of its greatest representative, Clovis (466–511), had ruled a small Frankish tribe by virtue of its alleged descent from the remote ancestor Merovech. At the end of the fifth century these kings by blood right increased their military adventurousness, conquered more land and subjects, and transformed themselves into successful war kings. When Clovis converted to Christianity and was recognized by Roman rulers, his kingship and that of his successors created a new phenomenon in the early medieval world. Although Clovis and his successors to 751 continued to exploit their blood right to the Frankish kingship, they also adopted new forms of legitimacy.

Blood right, war leadership, and Roman recognition were joined in Clovis' case by ideas of Christian kingship modeled on those of the Old Testament as revised and elaborated by the work of the church fathers, especially Augustine, Gregory the Great, and Isidore of Seville. These thinkers had adopted the scriptural view that both good and evil rulers are God's anointed and that God alone can judge them (Prov. 8:15), and that no subject may act against the king (1 Sam. 24:7)—an idea echoed in St. Paul's observation that the powers that be are ordained by God (Rom. 13:1–7), and in the writings of other fathers of the church. In the seventh century Isidore of Seville observed that "the name of king comes from rightly ruling," and he cited an old

Roman proverb to the effect that "You shall be a king if you act rightly; if you do not, you will not be king." But Isidore offered no more extensive a deposition theory than this. In general, ecclesiastical writers supported the sacrosanctity of kings and denied to mere mortals the right of deposing them.

The unstable new kingships of the sixth and seventh centuries inevitably attracted usurpers. In seventh-century Visigothic Spain a few kings were murdered or deposed, usually by rivals and relatives, with very little attention given to deposition theory. The Fifth Council of Toledo (636) stated that no one might aspire to the kingship who had not been acclaimed by the people or could prove that he was the choice of the nobility. By implication the nobles might indicate the deposition of a ruler simply by electing another to take his place or by using the excuse of such a choice subsequent to the fact of an actual abandonment, deposition, or assassination. Churchmen might rationalize that by the new election God had signaled the withdrawal of his favor from the deposed ruler. These ideas imply strongly that kings individually lost their kingliness by their acts even before they were formally or informally eliminated.

By the middle of the eighth century the unstable combination of war leadership and blood right no longer sufficed to keep a king on the Frankish throne. The growth of a powerful nobility, led by the family of the mayors of the palace of the Frankish kings, placed heavy strains on the archaic Merovingian kingship. In 751 Pepin, the father of Charlemagne, enunciated the most elaborate deposition theory yet developed in early medieval Europe. Having allied himself with a substantial faction of the Frankish aristocracy and prominent members of the Frankish church, Pepin issued a series of statements, including a letter to the pope, in which he claimed that the last Merovingian ruler, Childeric III, had lost all power, wealth, dignity, and usefulness as a Christian king. This claim led the pope to answer that the person possessing power ought to be king, "so as not to disturb the order of things," that Childeric III should be tonsured and placed in a monastery, and that Pepin should be elected king.

Tonsuring the old king meant removing the long hair that was a symbol of the Frankish kingship. Making the king a formal penitent in a monastery liturgically deprived him of the right to participate in worldly affairs. By focusing on the novel criterion of "uselessness," Pepin and the pope dismissed all earlier claims to rule by blood right and substituted for them the criteria of vigorous rule, adequate wealth, and the active defense and governance of a Christian people as the supreme standards of royal legitimacy. Explicitly, any ruler who failed to meet these standards might expect legitimate opposition and deposition, though Pepin was attempting to put his own dynasty on the Frankish throne and remove the old one, surely not setting out broad criteria for future constitutional policy. He most emphasized his winning of God's favor and Childeric's loss of it when he began to use the phrase *gratia Dei* (by the favor of God) in his designation of himself as king.

Pepin's construction of new criteria for legitimate Christian kingship played an important role in later deposition theory, being cited again and again by political opponents of kings and by popes. The deposition of Childeric III became the starting point for subsequent discussions of deposition theory.

With the brief deposition of Pepin's grandson Louis the Pious in 833, Frankish kings found that those criteria could be employed even against Pepin's own dynasty. The criteria that Pepin and his supporters established were incorporated into later coronation ceremonies, particularly in the wording and interpretation of coronation oaths, and led to a general ninth-century sense that, as J. M. Wallace-Hadrill observed, "the Church could thus control the actions of kings, at least in so far as a king chose to abide by the undertakings at his inauguration and have his actions reviewed by churchmen in the light of them" (*Early Germanic Kingship*, p. 134). The ninth-century church could thus lend support to certain kinds of opposition to a king far more effectively than could the Fifth Council of Toledo two centuries earlier.

Between 1075 and 1085 Pope Gregory VII created another deposition theory in his conflict with Emperor Henry IV. Gregory claimed for the papacy, especially in the case of the emperor, the rights that Frankish churchmen had earlier claimed for churchmen generally. Gregory sharply distinguished between the just king, the *rex justus,* and the tyrant, the *tyrannus.* Although the classical meaning of tyranny was royal power acquired illegally, Gregory sharpened the Christian idea of tyranny as sin, and instead of relying on earlier ideas that a wicked ruler was God's punishment of a people and had to be removed by God alone, Gregory claimed that a tyrant was a sinner and might be removed by the pope in the interests of justice.

The basis for Gregory VII's claim was his and his supporters' theory that God's will was reflected in

the church and the clergy, at the head of which was the pope. Gregory interpreted even the deposition of Childeric III in 751 as a papal deposition exclusively. But Gregory's deposition theory was biblical and liturgical, not juridical or constitutional, and he and his supporters failed to make precise the conditions and steps necessary in the process. Twelfth- and thirteenth-century canon lawyers, however, made these papal claims far more precise and juridical.

Gregory also insisted on the pope's right to release a king's subjects from the oaths of loyalty they had made to him. He encouraged the subjects of a sinful king to regard the ruler as having lost any right to their loyalty, thereby echoing an older Germanic right of resistance to an unjust lord. These two theories of deposition greatly weakened the sacrosanctity and ecclesiastical character of late Carolingian kingship. Twelfth-century kings sought new bases for their power and legitimacy that might prove impervious to the claims of the Gregorians and their rebellious subjects. To a large extent they were successful.

In 1159 John of Salisbury wrote a tract called the *Policraticus,* the most influential expression of political theory in the twelfth century. In this work John appreciated the vast new powers of twelfth-century kings, but he greatly feared their misuse. He preserved both the older and the more recent definitions of tyranny: that of illegal seizure of power and that of sinful misuse of the power necessary for a good king to rule well. John even propounded a doctrine of legitimate tyrannicide, the right of certain individuals to assassinate a tyrant. The canon lawyer Rufinus, a contemporary of John of Salisbury, insisted that "legitimate institution and moderation of justice," that is, legitimate acquisition of royal power and its just use, separated the just king from the tyrant.

In works such as those of John of Salisbury and Rufinus and other canon lawyers, deposition theory slowly acquired a philosophical, theological, and juridical basis. Even strong kings were unable to deny parts of these deposition theories. Kings themselves acknowledged that it was wrong for a king to break his coronation oath or fail to defend the church (for example, by permitting heresy to flourish or actively supporting it). In twelfth-century deposition theory the moral condition of the ruler became a secondary cause of deposition, the juridical character of his rule coming more to the foreground.

The deposition theory of the twelfth and thirteenth centuries worked most effectively on behalf of the papacy and against the Roman emperors, who were considered bound to the popes in special juridical relationships and dependency. But extreme papalists also applied this deposition theory to kings as well. In 1245, at the First Council of Lyons, Pope Innocent IV brought the two traditions together in two important depositions. He suspended the king of Portugal, Sancho II, from the right to rule (but did not deprive him of the royal dignity) and appointed Sancho's brother, Alfonso III, as keeper of the kingdom, on the grounds that Sancho was useless. Thus, Innocent echoed the juridical development of the old case against Childeric III in 751. Innocent also deposed the Roman emperor Frederick II on the grounds of heresy, tyranny, oath breaking, and attacks on the church. These two actions in the same year illustrate the highest development of papal rights to depose temporal rulers.

The problem of the deposition of a pope was treated far less extensively during this period. Although Carolingian kings and later emperors had claimed the right to dismiss a wicked or erring pope, their claims were countered by those of later canon lawyers, who focused exclusively on the somewhat unlikely question of papal heresy. The chief text in canon law on this subject stated flatly, but vaguely, that "[The pope] who is to judge all is to be judged by no one, unless he is found straying from the faith." Such a narrow basis did not provide for much elaboration of theories of deposing a pope. Not until the abdication of Pope Celestine V in 1294 was the question of terminating a pontificate within the lifetime of a pope even discussed; Celestine's case led to a doctrine of limited reasons justifying papal abdication but to no doctrine of deposing a pope. Popes, of course, might depose ecclesiastical subordinates, even great prelates, and their right to depose kings and emperors was considered analogous to their rights over lower clergy.

During the Great Schism (1378–1417) first two, then three, men claimed to be the legitimate pope at the same time. Some representatives of the movement known as conciliarism claimed that a universal church council could depose a pope whose legitimacy was doubtful, especially in cases of grave and immediate scandal to the faithful. At the Council of Constance in 1415, two papal claimants were in fact deposed, and one resigned. No later popes recognized this extraordinary conciliar authority, and papal deposition remained virtually a dead letter in Christian constitutional law.

Between the thirteenth and the sixteenth centuries the deposition theories of philosophers, theologians, and canon lawyers influenced movements of resistance to kings in territorial monarchies. In this period one may speak of the beginnings of national constitutional deposition theory. In addition, political resistance to many rulers grew, and political opposition joined general deposition theory as a potentially powerful force with which to reform or remove a weak or illegitimately oppressive ruler.

A series of five depositions in England between 1327 and 1485 constitutes the best example of this process, because these events forced the English clergy, nobility, lawyers, and others to think, write, and act against royal power and to justify its legal termination. These events, in the words of Charles T. Wood and William H. Dunham, Jr., "created a doctrine of restraint upon the regal power that eventually became part of England's constitutional, or public, law." Magnates and clergy alike had already challenged the unbridled royal power in 1215, when they forced King John to confirm Magna Carta, and again in 1265, when they revolted against King Henry III. The depositions of Edward II in 1327 and Richard II in 1399 linked personal incapacity of the kings to specific acts against their subjects, oaths, the church, and the inalienable rights of their crowns. These depositions claimed for "the people," sometimes designated "the estates of the realm," the right to act against an evil or incompetent king. They also insisted on the king's abdication, as if this act were an essential part of the deposition process.

These and other deposition processes contained longer and longer lists of specific crimes the kings were alleged to have committed, as if the cumulative criminality of rulers had come to possess constitutional significance. In several fifteenth-century depositions, chiefly that of Edward V in 1483, specific claims against the king's legal right to inherit the throne were added.

From blood kings and war leaders abandoned by their subjects or assassinated to the later medieval rulers deposed by specifically juridical theories and strong political opposition, medieval deposition theory reflects the changing nature of medieval kingship and the medieval political community on their complicated route from tribe and war band to the early modern constitutional state.

BIBLIOGRAPHY

Edward Peters, *The Shadow King: 'Rex Inutilis' in Medieval Law and Literature, 751–1327* (1970), sums up most of the relevant theory and recent scholarship. For the earlier period see John M. Wallace-Hadrill, *The Long-Haired Kings* (1962), and *Early Germanic Kingship in England and on the Continent* (1971). An older work still very useful is Fritz Kern, *Kingship and Law in the Middle Ages*, Stanley B. Chrimes, trans. (1948, repr. 1956). Brian Tierney, *The Crisis of Church and State, 1050–1300* (1964), prints most of the important documentary sources in translation and comments ably on them. Other texts are in Ewart Lewis, *Medieval Political Ideas*, 2 vols. (1954, repr. 1973).

Much work on canonist political theory is cited and discussed in J. A. Watt, "The Theory of Papal Monarchy in the Thirteenth Century: The Contribution of the Canonists," in *Traditio*, 20 (1964). On Gregory VII see Gerd Tellenbach, *Church, State, and Christian Society at the Time of the Investiture Contest*, R. F. Bennett, trans. (1948).

The conjunction of political opposition and learned theory is illustrated in Reginald F. Treharne, comp., *Documents of the Baronial Movement of Reform and Rebellion*, I. J. Sanders, ed. (1973). An excellent general view of deposition theory and practice in fourteenth- and fifteenth-century England is William Huse Dunham, Jr., and Charles T. Wood, "The Right to Rule in England: Depositions and the Kingdom's Authority, 1327–1485," in *American Historical Review*, 81 (1976). For a single case see Charles T. Wood, "The Deposition of Edward V," in *Traditio*, 31 (1975). Documents are in Stanley B. Chrimes and A. L. Brown, eds., *Select Documents of English Constitutional History, 1307–1485* (1961). Many of these documents are translated in Alec R. Myers, *English Historical Documents*, IV (1969).

The best and most interesting study of medieval rulership generally, and one that says much about deposition, is Ernst H. Kantorowicz, *The King's Two Bodies* (1957). There is also much important material in Gaines Post, *Studies in Medieval Legal Thought* (1964).

EDWARD PETERS

[See also **Clovis; Edward II of England; Germany; Gregory VII, Pope; Innocent IV, Pope; Isidore of Seville, St.; John of Salisbury; Kingship, Theories of: Western European; Pepin; Political Theory, Western European; Richard II of England; Richard III of England.**]

DER VON KÜRENBERG, the earliest known lyric poet (minnesinger) writing in Middle High German, was active around 1160, probably in the Danube Valley of Austria. His thirteen poems, which are preserved only in the famous Heidelberg (Manesse) manuscript of minnesong, are in the main mono-

strophic and employ a variation of a four-line stanza related to that used in the *Nibelungenlied*.

Unlike the poems of the later minnesingers, Der von Kürenberg's songs appear to be untouched by the influence of the Provençal troubadours, though they are nonetheless clearly written by a knight for an aristocratic audience. Thus one does not find the typical motifs of the knight in the service of a lady, love as the hoped-for reward of such service, and the lament of the knight because his wooing has been in vain. Instead of the distant lady who seems uninterested in the attentions of the knight, there is a woman in love. Where there are lamentations, they come from the loving woman; and in the poems in which the man appears as the wooer, he does not act as the humble servant of his lady, but often with the boldness (and at times even haughtiness) of a man confident of his irresistibility. In one song a man almost audaciously propositions the woman with the words, "Beautiful woman, now come with me," and in another the speaker claims it is easy to woo a woman successfully, since women, like birds, are easy to tame: if one knows the right bait to use, they will seek out the male. Conversely, in another poem a knight reveals his independence of spirit when he is courted by an aggressive female determined to possess him: he calls for his horse and his armor, for he would rather leave the country than be forced to love her.

The nine poems in which a loving woman speaks reveal a wide range of feelings and themes: the woman's fear of losing her beloved; admonitions to her lover to be faithful; complaints about the destructive influence of her guardians; annoyance at the timidity of the lover who dared not wake her; aggressive determination to take possession of an attractive knight; intimate remembrances of her beloved that cause her to blush; and pain at the realization that she cannot have what she desires. In the best-known and most discussed poem of Der von Kürenberg, his "Falcon Song," a woman tells how she had tamed a falcon, but when she thought she had trained and adorned it as she had wanted it to be, it flew away. Later, when she sees it flying, still splendidly adorned, she expresses the wish that God bring together those who would like to be lovers. Although there have been many interpretations of this puzzling song, the most widely accepted approach considers the falcon as representing the woman's lover, a knight, who leaves her—whether temporarily or permanently is not clear—in order to seek a wider sphere of activity.

161

BIBLIOGRAPHY

The critical edition is Carl von Kraus, ed., *Des Minnesangs Frühling*, 36th ed., rev. by Hugo Moser and Helmut Tervooren (1977), 24–27. See also Helmut de Boor, *Die höfische Literatur*, vol. II of Helmut de Boor and Richard Newald, *Geschichte der deutschen Literatur*, 5th ed. (1962), 241–244, 249, 447 (with bibliography); Stephen J. Kaplowitt, "A Note on the 'Falcon Song' of Der von Kürenberg," in *German Quarterly*, 44 (1971); Peter Wapnewski, "Des Kürenbergers Falkenlied," in *Euphorion*, 53 (1959).

STEPHEN J. KAPLOWITT

[See also **Courtly Love; German Lyric; Middle High German Literature; Minnesingers.**]

DERBENT (Persian: Darband; Armenian: Pahak Honac^c, Pahak, or Kapan Čoray; Georgian: Darubanda; Greek: Viratarrak; Arabic: Sul, then Al-Bāb waʾl-Abwāb, later Bāb al-Abwāb or simply Al-Bāb; Osmanli Turkish: Gapugh; New Turkish: Demir Gapi; Mongol: Qahulga), a fortified town on the western coast of the Caspian Sea defending the littoral pass from northern to southern Caucasia at its narrowest point and serving as the bastion of the civilized world against the predatory nomads of the steppes beyond. Perhaps the Albana of Ptolemy and certainly the Albanian Gates of other classical authors, Derbent was probably fortified as early as the Achaemenid period (ca. 550–330 B.C.). The present fortifications, attributed to the Sasanian shah Xusrō I Anōšarwān (531–579), were much repaired and extended in later centuries.

The Arabs reached Derbent in 643, taking the town from a Persian garrison and making it a bastion against the Khazar state to the north. Derbent suffered severely as a result of Khazar invasions, the last of which occurred in 799. From the ninth century the town was held by the Hashimids, an Arab dynasty that became greatly involved with the politics of the neighboring mountain tribes and was closely connected with the shahs of Shirvan. Under the Hashimids, Derbent became the most important Caspian port, exporting slaves, linen cloth, and saffron, serving as a port of call for ships bearing furs from Astrakhan, and flourishing as a transit point in the trade of sheep and hides. Larger than Ardabīl, it was dominated by a commercial aristocracy that virtually confined the power of its ruler to the citadel.

The territory of Derbent, which was never much more than a city-state, did not extend far beyond its walls. These were surrounded by orchards and vineyards in which excavations have revealed the remains of an elaborate irrigation system testifying to a highly developed technology. In the eleventh century Derbent was taken by the Seljuk Turks and in 1222 by the Mongols; in 1275 it was still strong and prosperous. Its emirs intermarried with the Bagratids of Georgia and frequently warred with the shahs of Shirvan. In 1466 Derbent appears to have been a vassal of Shirvan, but it later became a Persian khanate (1747) until being ultimately acquired by Russia in 1806.

The famed fortifications of Derbent consist of two walls extending from the citadel into the sea, with the town and the harbor between them. A middle wall, demolished in 1824, joined the other two from north to south, cutting the town in two. Beyond the citadel a single wall continues some twenty-five miles (forty kilometers) into the mountains, with additional forts and blockhouses guarding the inner passes that might be used to outflank the wall. The area of the city-state was about 251 square miles (650 square kilometers).

BIBLIOGRAPHY

M. Artomonov, "Drevnii Derbent," in *Sovetskaya arkheologiya*, 7 (1946); Selim O. Khan-Magomedov, *Derbent* (1973); E. I. Kozubski, *Istoriya goroda Derbenta* (1906); Vladimir Minorsky, ed. and trans., *A History of Sharvān and Darband in the 10th–11th Centuries*, (1958); Michael Perreira, *Across the Caucasus* (1973), 245–253; Kamilla V. Trever, *Ocherki po istorii i kul'ture kavkazskoi Albanii* (1959), 179–182, 271–273, 275–287, 346–352.

ROBERT H. HEWSEN

[See also **Albania (Caucasian); Shirvan; Xusrō I Anōšarwān.**]

DEREHAM, ELIAS OF. See Nicholas of Ely.

DERVISH (*darwīsh*, pl. *darāwīsh*), from Persian *dar* (door), a mendicant; hence *darwīshī*, poverty, the religious life. Etymologically "dervish" should mean "seeking door(s)," but a variant form, *daryōsh*, does not support this view. Although dervish connotes a member of some religious fraternity (*ṭarīqa*), in Turkey, Persia, Pakistan, and India the term usually signifies an itinerant dervish (*qalandarī*, calender), what in Arabic would be termed a *faqīr* (fakir), who solicits alms with a begging-bowl and puts up at religious hospices. In Arabic-speaking countries *darwīsh* denotes any member of a fraternity.

Man is *faqīr,* whereas God is *ghanī* (self-sufficient) as stated in Koran 35:15. Obedient to the principle of reliance on God (*tawakkul*) as Provider (*ar-Rāziq,* one of the ninety-nine names), a *faqīr* abjures personal wealth and takes to the road to "live for the Lord alone." As al-Shiblī says, "The *faqīr* does not rest content with anything except God."

Islamic monasticism is both cenobitic and eremitical. A hermit *(rābiṭ)* retreats to a hermitage *(rābiṭa)* or cave to mortify the flesh in solitude. In Egypt, Mt. Muqaṭṭam behind Cairo was favored for this purpose, and in Spain the mountains to the west of Almería, on account of their many caves. It was more usual to live as part of a community in a monastery (*khānaqāh, takiyya, zāwiya, dargāh, ribāṭ*) under rule, with a master (*shaykh, murshid, pīr*) who undertook the spiritual formation of the neophyte (*murīd*), who aspired to gnosis (*maᶜrifa*). Most, perhaps, were content with the status of tertiary (*muḥibb*), only being required to reside in the monastery periodically before participating in the ritual (*dhikr, âyin, ḥaḍra*) of the order, in which case celibacy was not required. Investiture with a *khirqa* (dervish cloak), varying in color and design according to the order, signified the admission of the candidate after he had bound himself by oath *(baiᶜa)* to obey his *shaykh* in all things. In this way the influence of the mystical system of Islam known as Sufism came to pervade Islamic society. Although the practice of ascetic Sufism goes back to earliest times, these institutionalized forms did not emerge until the twelfth century.

The impact of the orders on the cultural and political life of the Islamic community is difficult to overestimate. The Mawlawīya order, popularly known as the whirling dervishes, was closely linked to the Ottoman regime, whereas others had a history of dissent. An organic relationship between the trade guilds (*ḥiraf*) and the orders obtained throughout Islamic societies, certain trades being traditionally linked to certain orders. The teaching of the order constituted the spiritual basis of the craftsman's inspiration, accounting in part for the high level of the industrial arts in Islam.

BIBLIOGRAPHY

John P. Browne, *The Dervishes,* Horace A. Rose, ed. (1927).

JAMES DICKIE

[See also **Ribāṭ; Sufism.**]

DES CHAMPS, JEAN. See **Jean des Champs.**

DES CHAMPS, PIERRE. See **Pierre des Champs.**

DESCENT INTO LIMBO. See **Anastasis.**

DESCHAMPS, EUSTACHE (*ca.* 1346–*ca.* 1406), French poet, also known as Eustache Morel (the Moor) on account of his dark complexion, was born in Vertus, Champagne. He was the pupil and quite probably the nephew of the poet-musician Guillaume de Machaut, with whom he studied at Rheims. Deschamps studied law at the University of Orléans, where he translated the Latin comedy *Geta* of Vital de Blois. He was in the service of the family of the duke of Orléans and held a number of public offices under Charles V and Charles VI. In 1367 he became a royal messenger (*chevaucheur*), a post that took him all over Europe, often under trying conditions, and realistic details of these experiences are scattered throughout his writings. An even greater suffering came from the burning of his family home, Les Champs, by the English in 1380, after which he called himself Brûlé des Champs, that is, the burned-out dweller of Les Champs.

The poetic work of Deschamps contains about 1,500 pieces (82,000 verses), most of which are fixed-form poems: 1,032 ballades, 170 rondeaux, 142 *chants royaux,* 14 lais, 84 virelais. He also wrote the *Farce de Maître Trubert et d'Antroignart* and several treatises in verse, including *La fiction du lion* (1382), which traces allegorically his duties on behalf of the young king Charles VI, and the strongly antifeminist satire *Le miroir de mariage.* His treatise on versification, *L'art de dictier et de fere chançons, balades, virelais, et rondeaux* (1392), is the first

French poetics to develop both a general theory of poetry and detailed rules for the various fixed forms.

While his love poetry is highly conventional, Deschamps displays his talents best in satire. Because the author's own personality, thoughts, and opinions appear constantly throughout his works, they have unusual documentary value for understanding the life, manners, and people of the late fourteenth century.

BIBLIOGRAPHY

Source. *Oeuvres complètes d'Eustache Deschamps*, Queux de Saint-Hilaire, ed., 10 vols. (1878–1903, repr. 1966).

Studies. Monique Dufournaud-Engel, *Le miroir de mariage d'Eustache Deschamps*, also contains a critical edition of his work (diss. McGill Univ., 1975); John Livingston Lowes, "Illustrations of Chaucer. Drawn Chiefly from Deschamps," in *Romanic Review*, 2 (1911); Christopher Page, "Machaut's 'Pupil' Deschamps on the Performance of Music," in *Early Music, 5* (1977); Jean C. E. Rault, *Eustache Deschamps, poète bourgeois* (diss. Univ. of Toronto, 1973); Friedrich Wolfzettel, "La poésie lyrique en France comme mode d'appréhension de la réalité: Remarques sur l'invention du sens visuel chez Machaut, Froissart, Deschamps et Charles d'Orléans," in *Mélanges Foulon* (1980), 409–419.

THOMAS KELLY

[See also **French Literature; Machaut, Guillaume de.**]

DESCORT, a musical-poetical form of the late twelfth to early fourteenth centuries. Unlike other such genres, which consist of patterned verse and rhyme schemes that recur in several stanzas, the ideal of the descort (discord) is irregularity. Each stanza is different in its verse structure (syllable count), rhyme scheme, and melody. This "discordant" formal scheme mirrors the disharmonious state of the poet's mind: an unhappy lover sings of his lady's unfairness toward him or of his lack of success in wooing her.

The form described here is identical to that of the *lai lyrique*. The term "descort" was generally preferred by the troubadours, while "lai" was preferred by the trouvères, though there are some French descorts and some Provençal lais. Attempts to differentiate the forms have been unconvincing.

BIBLIOGRAPHY

A complete list of descorts is in Jean Maillard, *Évolution et esthétique du lai lyrique dès origines à la fin du XIVe siècle* (1963), 119–127. Maillard's list is slightly larger than that of István Frank, *Répertoire métrique de la poésie des troubadours*, I (1953), 183–195; II (1957), 71–72. Both Maillard and Frank indicate modern editions. A readily available example of a descort, with translation into modern French and a discussion of the structure, is in Pierre Bec, ed., *Nouvelle anthologie de la lyrique occitaine du moyen âge* (1970), 255–261.

LAWRENCE M. EARP

[See also **Courtly Love; Lai, Lay; Troubadours, Trouvères, Trovadores.**]

DESIDERIUS OF MONTE CASSINO (1027–1087). Born with the name Dauferius to a noble Lombard family of Benevento, about 1047 he became a monk at La Cava, against the wishes of his family, and later adopted the name Desiderius. In 1054 he became a Benedictine at Monte Cassino, where he succeeded Frederick of Lorraine as abbot in 1058; in the following year he was made cardinal priest of S. Cecilia by Pope Nicholas II. As abbot, Desiderius renovated the monastery and made it a scholarly center. Between 1076 and 1079 he wrote the partially extant *Dialogue on the Miracles of St. Benedict* in four books. In May 1086 he was forcibly consecrated as Victor III to succeed Gregory VII, but he did not finally accept the office until March 1087.

Throughout his lifetime Desiderius was much involved in politics, and he served several times as a mediator between the Normans and the popes (Leo IX in 1053, Nicholas II in 1059, Gregory VII in 1080); in 1082 he attempted to reconcile Gregory VII and Henry IV. As pope, however, Desiderius himself was opposed by the partisans of Gregory and accused of being a Norman puppet. At a synod at Benevento in August 1087, he excommunicated his opponents, though he did support Gregory's policy on lay investiture. He died on 16 September 1087.

BIBLIOGRAPHY

The text of the *Dialogus de miraculis S. Benedicti* is in *Monumenta Germaniae historica, Scriptores*, XXX, pt. 2, 1111–1151. A study is F. Hirsch, "Desiderius von Monte Cassino als Papst Victor III," in *Forschungen zur deutschen Geschichte*, 7 (1867).

RALPH WHITNEY MATHISEN

[See also **Gregory VII, Pope; Monte Cassino; Papacy, Origins and Development of.**]

The consecration of St. Anianus by St. Mark. Ramón Destorrents, central panel of St. Mark's Altarpiece, Barcelona, late 14th century. ORONOZ

DESPOT, an imperial title that became a separate dignity, the first in the Byzantine hierarchy, most probably under Manuel I Komnenos (1143–1180). Bestowed mainly on sons-in-law and later on sons of the emperor, it was also granted to foreign princes (beginning in the thirteenth century). Addressed as *paneutychestatos,* the despot wore a costume similar to the emperor's and had vast prerogatives. His wife was called *basilissa.* In the fourteenth and fifteenth centuries several Byzantine despots were semiautonomous rulers of parts of the empire, the best known of which is the despotate of Morea.

BIBLIOGRAPHY

Rodolphe Guilland, "Le despote," in *Revue des études byzantines,* **17** (1959), repr. in his *Recherches sur les institutions byzantines,* II (1967), 1–24; Božidar Ferjančić, *Despoti u Vizantii i južnoslovenskim zemeljama* (1960); A. P. Každan, "Sevastokratori i despoti v Vizantii XII v.," in *Zbornik radova Viz. Inst.,* **14–15** (1973); B. Ferjančić, "Još

jednom o počecima titule despota," *ibid.* (with French summary).

NICOLAS OIKONOMIDES

[See also **Basileus; Byzantine Empire: Bureaucracy.**]

DESTORRENTS, RAMÓN (*fl.* 1351–1391), the most important Italo-Gothic artist in Barcelona during the second half of the fourteenth century. Both miniaturist and panel painter, he worked for the court of Peter IV as well as for ecclesiastical patrons. Formerly known as the Master of St. Mark, he derived his style from the Sienese painter Simone Martini. His son, Rafael, became the leading miniaturist in Barcelona.

MARY GRIZZARD

[See also **Martini, Simone.**]

DEUSDEDIT, CARDINAL (*d.* 1100), canonist and one of the most fervent adherents of the Gregorian reform. He is famous for two works. His enormous *Collectio canonum* (1087) is an ambitious, if ultimately unsuccessful, attempt to rationalize, by means of topical organization and cross-references, exceedingly diverse canonical materials, particularly with regard to the categories of papal primacy, the temporalities of churches, and relations between ecclesiastical and secular powers. Also noteworthy is Deusdedit's use of the original register of Pope Gregory VII as a canonical source. The *Libellus contra invasores et symoniacos* (1097) passionately denounces those "who say that Christ's church is subject to royal power," utterly rejects lay investiture, and denies the validity of the sacraments of simoniacs. This work also attacks the party of Archibishop Guibert of Ravenna, who was installed by Emperor Henry IV as the antipope Clement III.

BIBLIOGRAPHY

Sources. Die Kanonensammlung des Kardinals Deusdedit, Victor Wolf von Glanvell, ed. (1905, repr. 1967); "Deusdedit presbyteri cardinalis Libellus contra invasores et symoniacos et reliquos schismaticos," Ernst Sackur, ed., in *Monumenta Germaniae historica, Libelli de Lite,* II (1892, repr. 1956), 292–365.

Studies. Paul Fournier, "Les collections canoniques romaines de l'époque de Grégoire VII," in *Mémoires de l'In-*

stitut national de France: Académie des inscriptions et belles-lettres, 41 (1920); Paul Fournier and Gabriel Le Bras, Histoire des collections canoniques en occident, II (1932), 37–54; Walther Holtzmann, "Kardinal Deusdedit als Dichter," in Historisches Jahrbuch, 57 (1937); Ernst Sackur, "Der Dictatus papae und die Canonsammlung des Deusdedit," in Neues Archiv, 18 (1893). See also the informative introductions by Wolf von Glanvell and Sackur to their editions cited above.

ELAINE GOLDEN ROBISON

[See also Dictatus Papae; Gregory VII, Pope; Law, Canon.]

DEVOTIO MODERNA, a movement beginning in the late fourteenth century in the IJssel Valley of Holland that sought to renew piety and spiritual life through semimonastic communities of devout clerics and lay persons. This "current" or "modern" devotion was inspired by Geert Groote (1340–1384), the orphaned son of a Deventer cloth merchant and city councilman. After studies in Paris, Groote experienced a radical conversion sometime after 1372. He made his spacious house in Deventer available as a home for poor, pious women (1374), renounced his prebends, and spent several years at the Carthusian monastery of Monnikhuizen near Arnhem. After 1380, having been ordained a deacon, Groote became known as an itinerant preacher of repentance and conversion to a life in imitation of Christ, campaigning vigorously against heresy, simony, and clerical concubinage. He was opposed by members of the mendicant orders, some civic leaders, and portions of the secular clergy.

Under the guidance of one of Groote's disciples, Florens Radewijns (ca. 1350–1400), the group of students and other persons, some in minor orders, who were living in his vicarage at Deventer initiated a community of property about the time of Groote's death. A similar community emerged at Zwolle. Earning their own living, especially by copying manuscripts, community members followed monastic patterns, including observance of the canonical hours and an emphasis on silence, obedience, fraternal correction, and frequent meditation and examination of conscience. They made no binding or solemn vows. These Brethren of the Common Life provided pastoral care for the occupants of the houses of the Sisters of the Common Life, which had emerged in similar manner from the community of devout women living in Groote's house (statutes by Groote, 1379). The Brethren shared Groote's concern for the welfare of schoolboys attending the renowned schools of Deventer and other cities, providing lodging, counseling, and, eventually, some aid with lessons. In isolated instances in the later fifteenth century, Brethren taught in and administered schools.

Living in community without binding vows or strict claustration brought condemnation, especially from the mendicant orders. Groote's second outstanding disciple, Gerard Zerbolt of Zutphen (1367–1398), defended the new establishments in the Libellus de modo vivendi hominum simul commorantium, arguing, as had Groote, that the designation religio was not to be limited to monastic orders. (The main works of Zerbolt, one of the most fertile of the Devotio Moderna writers, were the widely disseminated De reformatione virium animae and De spiritualibus ascensionibus.) Despite episcopal approval (1401), opposition to the communities of Brethren and Sisters resurfaced, culminating in the attacks of the Dominican Matthaeus of Grabow, who was silenced at the Council of Constance.

Partly in response to opposition the communities gradually adopted more characteristics of traditional monastic orders. The Brethren of the Common Life received their first constitutions about 1415. Some houses placed themselves under the Rule of the Third Order of St. Francis or the Rule of St. Augustine. In other cases individuals transferred to houses of regular canons, such as the one built at Windesheim near Zwolle in 1387 by friends of the new movement who were carrying out Groote's wishes. Here they lived under the Rule of St. Augustine, protected against charges of having violated the Fourth Lateran Council's prohibition of new orders in 1215. In 1394/1395 four such houses formed what became the Windesheim Congregation, the monastic branch of the Devotio Moderna.

The Windesheim Congregation paralleled efforts by Benedictines and other orders to restore and standardize monastic observance and to renew monastic spirituality. Leading writers from Windesheim circles included Gerlach Peters (1378–1411) and Hendrik Mande (1360–1431), whose works reveal a rich, practical contemplative spirituality. Thomas à Kempis (1380–1471), the best known of all writers from the Devotio Moderna, was a canon of Mount St. Agnes near Zwolle. In addition to a chronicle of his cloister, biographies of Groote, Zerbolt, and Radewijns, and sermons, he compiled the Imitatio

Christi, one of the world's most popular spiritual treatises. Earlier versions have been ascribed to Zerbolt or Groote, but in its most common form, with its strong contemplative and interiorizing monastic flavor, the book is generally accepted as the work of Thomas. The *Rosetum exercitiorum spiritualium et sacrarum meditationum* of Jan Mombaer (or Mauburnus) (*ca.* 1460–1501) was widely transmitted, especially in Catholic reform circles in France and Spain.

In the mid fifteenth century the Brethren and Sisters of the Common Life had expanded to about 100 houses in the Low Countries and Germany. The Windesheim Congregation also grew rapidly, drawing many of its novices from the brotherhouses. By 1464 John Busch (1399–1479/1480), the historian of the congregation, reported more than eighty houses of men and women.

The impact of the Devotio Moderna has been assessed variously. It has been claimed as a source for northern European humanism and pedagogical innovation, and for the Protestant and Catholic reformations. Even Zwinglian Sacramentarianism and modern individualism, nonconformity, or liberalism have been given Devotio Moderna pedigrees. Among the many fifteenth- and sixteenth-century personages linked to the movement are Johann Wessel Gansfort (*ca.* 1419–1489), Nicholas of Cusa (1401–1464), Gabriel Biel (*ca.* 1412–1495), and Erasmus (1466/1469–1536). Recent scholarship has cast doubt on most of the above-mentioned claims for Devotio Moderna influence, though the widespread impact of Devotio Moderna writings in fifteenth-century monastic circles is beyond question.

The first adherents of the Devotio Moderna, drawing on traditional monastic literature and practice, attempted to live a practical, devout life without the legal and formal structures of monastic vows and orders. The movement may have been an unconscious attempt to meet the needs of an increasingly self-conscious and literate bourgeoisie that preferred the practical, down-to-earth, and moral to the speculative and metaphysical. Yet the Devotio Moderna moved gradually toward increased monasticization. In Protestant areas the Devotio Moderna institutions did not survive the urban transformations of the sixteenth century that removed monastic establishments from their privileged position. In Catholic areas some houses of the Windesheim Congregation survived until the secularizations of the eighteenth century.

BIBLIOGRAPHY

Stephaan G. Axters, *Geschiedenis van de vroomheid in de Nederlanden,* III, *De moderne devotie 1380–1550* (1956); Émile Brouette and Reinhold Makrosch, "Devotio Moderna," in Gerhard Krause and Gerhard Müller, eds., *Theologische Realenzyklopädie,* VIII (1981), 605–619; Erwin Iserloh, "The Devotio Moderna," in Hubert Jedin and John Dolan, eds., *Handbook of Church History,* III, *From the High Middle Ages to the Eve of the Reformation,* Anselm Biggs, trans. (1970), 426–443, 723–727; H. J. Janowski, *Geert Groote, Thomas von Kempen, und die Devotio Moderna* (1978); M. Josef Pohl, ed., *Thomae Hemerken a Kempis Opera Omnia,* 7 vols. (1902–1922), used as text for five vols. of translations issued as *The Works of Thomas a Kempis* (1903–1908); Regnerus R. Post, *The Modern Devotion* (1968), the standard study; Theodore P. van Zijl, *Gerard Groote: Ascetic and Reformer, 1340–1384* (1963); Gerard Zerbolt van Zutphen, *The Spiritual Ascent,* J. P. Arthur, trans. (1908).

DENNIS D. MARTIN

[See also **Biel, Gabriel; Brethren of the Common Life; Groote, Geert; Thomas à Kempis.**]

DIABOLUS IN MUSICA. In all recent literature this phrase ("the devil in music") is said to refer to the musical interval of the tritone between the notes *B* natural and *F*; this interval created theoretical and practical difficulties, and was certainly avoided. However, there seems to be no justification in medieval sources for the use of the word *diabolus* in this context.

ANDREW HUGHES

DIACONICON, the Greek equivalent of a sacristy, a small room used as a church archive, vestry, and library. In the early Christian period the offerings of the congregation were received in the diaconicon, but by about 700 (earlier in Syria) the room was liturgically most important as the library where the Gospel was kept. Diaconica are normally found on the south side of the church, flanking the apse, encased in or extending from the transept or narthex, or enclosed in the easternmost bay of a side aisle.

BIBLIOGRAPHY

Richard Krautheimer, *Early Christian and Byzantine Architecture* (1975), 99, 108, 124, 127, 152, 312–313; Jean Lassus, *Sanctuaires chrétiens de Syrie* (1947), 194ff.

LESLIE BRUBAKER

[See also **Early Christian and Byzantine Architecture.**]

DIAGONAL ARCH. See **Arch.**

DIALECT conventionally designates the sum of linguistic peculiarities proper to a given region. Dialectal boundaries cannot be absolute, since any linguistic feature may overlap across the frontiers that have been arbitrarily imposed by the linguist. Nevertheless, the notion that a set of regional peculiarities effectively constitutes a linguistic entity was a medieval as well as a modern one. Guernes de Pont-Sainte-Maxence (late twelfth century) claimed his dialect was "good" because he was born in the Île-de-France ("Mis lengages est bons car en France fui nez") and a century later Jean de Meun apologized for his dialect because he was not born in that region ("Si m'escuse de mon langage / Car nes ne sui de Paris").

Politics, not literary expressivity, was ultimately responsible for the success or failure of a dialect. Thus the Francien dialect mentioned in the examples above triumphed over more productive literary dialects like Provençal or Picard because of the strength of the centralized monarchy in Paris. Indeed, Francien finally became the accepted standard for all of France, at least in bureaucratic matters.

JEANETTE M. A. BEER

DIALECTIC. The medieval understanding of dialectic was shaped by thinkers of antiquity. For Plato it was "the coping-stone of the sciences" (*Republic*, 534E); truth would come to light through Socrates' technique of questioning, and classification could be used to show what things have in common and where they differ (*Sophist*, 253E). Aristotle claims to have written the first systematic study of reasoning (*De sophisticis elenchis*, 34, 184b2–4). His treatment of dialectic in the *Topica* limits its scope to arguing from generally accepted opinions (*Topica*, I.1, 100a30–b19); he reserves to the *Analytica posteriora* the account of arguments demonstrating truth from statements that are certain. Fragments of Stoic writings indicate that dialectic for Chrysippus, as for Plato, was a discovery of truth and not merely, as for Aristotle, a matter of arguing well on either side of a question. It studied utterances and their meanings in order to resolve the inherent ambiguities of language; it also established conditions under which various kinds of propositions are true, particularly those affected by time, and formulated schemes for validly inferring conclusions when constructing arguments.

Stoic influence is evident in the unfinished *De dialectica*, not judged to be a genuine work of St. Augustine, composed at Milan in 387. It opens with a definition of dialectic as knowing how to dispute well: "Dialectica est bene disputandi scientia." The treatment progresses from simple words through combinations forming complete expressions to simple judgments and their combinations in arguments. The thought content of what is said (*dicibile*) is distinguished from its meaningful expression (*dictio*) and the thing (*res*) that is meant. Finally, Augustine treats obscure utterances and ambiguous expressions, carefully noting the forms of equivocity, in which language has several senses that the dialectician must resolve in the pursuit of truth.

Augustine's elementary work was widely read down to the twelfth century with that of another North African, Martianus Capella. In book IV of his *De nuptiis Philologiae at Mercurii*, written sometime before 439, he provided a compendium of dialectic within an allegory of the liberal arts. It drew on Porphyry's *Isagoge* for the predicables, the five universals (genus, species, difference, property, and accident) that characterize ways of saying something about an individual; on the *Categoriae decem*, a Latin paraphrase of Aristotle by a follower of the Greek commentator Themistius, later attributed to Augustine, for the ten categories (substance, quantity, relation, quality, where, when, position, state, action, and passion) that characterize the kinds of things that can be said about an individual; on Aristotle's *De interpretatione* for an account of the noun and verb, the complete sentence, and the oppositions between contrary and contradictory propositions. The *Peri hermeneias* of Apuleius of Madaura (*ca.* 125–*ca.* 171) may have supplied some part of Aristotle's teaching on the syllogism in the *Analytica priora* with various patterns of argument in which a conclusion is drawn from two premises, one a general statement and the other less general. The forms of the hypothetical syllogism, patterns of argument involving conditional statements, largely agree with those in Cicero's *Topica.*

The eight books of Aristotle's *Topica,* on the "places" in which the dialectician will find arguments, are organized according to the predicables. Early in the sixth century the *Topica* was translated into Latin by Boethius, but his version did not become current until the first half of the twelfth century. In the early Middle Ages knowledge of the topics was derived mainly from Boethius' commentary *In Topica Ciceronis* and a more advanced treatise, *De topicis differentiis.* The latter compares the accounts of Themistius and Cicero, devoting three books to the topics used by the dialectician and a fourth to a comparison with those used by the rhetorician.

Both works are concerned with dialectic in the restricted sense of a technique for finding arguments that will be accepted in disputation. Boethius identifies the topics *(loci),* the "places" in which arguments are to be found, with general statements *(maximae propositiones)* that will validate arguments, such as "What inheres in the parts inheres in the whole." The search for an intermediate term (M) that will link a given subject (S) and predicate (P) in constructing an argument of the form "If every M is P and every S is M, then every S is P" is pursued through twenty-eight classes of intermediate terms *(differentiae)* such as definition, description, explanation, genus, species, whole, and part.

In the mid sixth and early seventh centuries the encyclopedists included in their works, under the rubric *dialectica,* short surveys of logic without originality. Cassiodorus *(Institutiones,* II.3) uses Boethius for the *Isagoge, Categoriae,* and *De interpretatione;* Apuleius for the categorical syllogism; and Marius Victorinus for the hypothetical syllogism, topics, and definition. Isidore of Seville covered the same ground in his *Etymologiae* (II.22–31). At the end of the eighth century, with Alcuin's *Dialectica,* a beginner's introduction to logic in the form of a dialogue with Charlemagne, the center of interest was Aristotle's categories, known through the Pseudo-Augustine. From the tenth century on, there are short pieces on dialectic, teaching from the monastery of St. Gall, still at a very elementary level.

Boethius had discovered the possibilities of a dialectical theology using Aristotle's categories in his theological tractates. A similar use of philosophical argumentation in theology is found in John Scottus Eriugena's *Periphyseon* (from the 860's), in which John asks what can be said of God in the various categories. He also attempts, without much success, a dialectical refutation of Gottschalk's predestination theory. In the ninth century, Ratramnus of Corbie subjected the eucharistic theology of Paschasius Radbertus to a philosophical critique.

By the tenth century there was a more comprehensive program of logic teaching. Gerbert of Aurillac, the future Pope Sylvester II, taught dialectic at Rheims between 972 and 991, going through all the works later known as the "old logic": *Isagoge, Categoriae, De interpretatione,* Cicero's *Topica* with the commentaries of Boethius and the Boethian treatises *De topicis differentiis, De categoricis syllogismis, De hypotheticis syllogismis,* and the *Liber divisionum,* and Victorinus' *Liber definitionum.* In the early or mid eleventh century Garlandus compiled a *Dialectica* that used the same sources as Gerbert's course; the most complete synthesis of the old logic, however, is the *Dialectica* of Peter Abelard, which probably assumed its final form in the 1130's. In it all the old texts are powerfully developed, at a time when the resources of logic were being greatly enlarged by the discovery of Boethius' versions of Aristotle's *Topica, De sophisticis elenchis,* and *Analytica priora,* and the translation by James of Venice of the *Analytica posteriora,* the "new logic." In the eleventh and twelfth centuries the applications of logic to theology met with criticism both from those who rejected a dialectical theology and from those who claimed to find flaws in the dialectic. St. Peter Damian and Manegold of Lautenbach vehemently opposed any use of dialectic in theology. Lanfranc of Bec, the author of a lost *Dialectica,* was probably more skilled as a grammarian, but in his *Liber de corpore et sanguine Domini*—his refutation of Berengar of Tours, composed in the form of a dialogue in the 1060's—his opposition is to the use of bad logic in the exposition of the Eucharist. Apart from a fragment, St. Anselm of Canterbury, Lanfranc's student, is known as the author of only one logical work, *De grammatico.* Nevertheless, his theological treatises written between 1076 and 1108 show him as an able dialectician applying logic to the discussion of the divine existence and attributes, the theology of incarnation and redemption, predestination, and grace. In the spirit of faith seeking understanding ("fides quaerens intellectum," *Proslogion,* 1.227), he sought a rational understanding of Christian belief. In this he was more successful than

Abelard and Gilbert of Poitiers, whose ambiguous language with regard to the Trinity led to the condemnations of Abelard in 1121 and 1140 and of Gilbert in 1147.

The dialectical approach to theology in the first half of the twelfth century is well illustrated by Abelard's *Sic et non,* which presents opposing texts on 158 current questions. There the questions are unresolved; but the canon lawyer Gratian, in his *Decretum* (*ca.* 1140), attempts to reconcile conflicting canons, and Peter Lombard's *Sentences* (*ca.* 1150) proved a durable synthesis of theological authorities. As late as 1177–1178, Walter of St. Victor's *Contra quattuor labyrinthos Franciae* attacked Abelard, Lombard, Peter of Poitiers, and Gilbert of Poitiers as representatives of an Aristotelian spirit leading to heresy. But by the end of the twelfth century, at the University of Paris, logic flourished and its applications in Scholastic theology had won general acceptance.

Adam of Balsham made limited use of Aristotle's *Topica* in his *Ars disserendi* (1132), and John of Salisbury hailed its discovery and reported its contents in 1159 (*Metalogicon,* III.5–10); nevertheless, the study of dialectic in the narrower sense made slow progress, the earliest surviving Latin commentaries on the *Topica* being from the thirteenth century. Altogether there are some sixty commentaries from the Middle Ages, of which fifteen are from the thirteenth century. The earliest, apparently from the 1230's, is that of an unidentified "Robertus" (Lisbon, Biblioteca Nacional, fundo Alcobaça, MS 175). The commentary of Albertus Magnus, *In octos libros Topicorum,* probably dates from the early 1250's; the *Questiones super librum Topicorum* of Boethius of Dacia, from the 1270's. The *Topica* appears in the arts curricula of Paris and Oxford in the thirteenth century but never replaces Boethius' *De topicis differentiis,* the first three books of which were read as logic and the fourth as rhetoric.

The practice of dialectic was fostered in the universities by the use of disputations to investigate the truth of questions. In arts the student first had the task of objecting (*obiciens*) and replying (*respondens*) in logic and grammar (*de sophismatibus*), then in the other branches of philosophy (*de quaestione*). Disputed questions (*quaestiones disputatae*) were settled by the presiding master, who would determine the point at issue on his next lecture day. Bachelors were exercised as determiners before becoming masters. In the higher faculties of theology, law, and medicine, disputations also formed part of the student's training, and at times masters in theology engaged in disputations *de quolibet,* on any question raised by the audience. Later these *quaestiones disputatae* and *quodlibetales* were published in an edited form.

The thirteenth century saw the circulation in the Latin West of new material from other sources. Of the many Arabic works on logic by Avicenna (Ibn Sīnā, 980–1037), only the sections of the *Shifāʾ* (*Sufficientia*) dealing with the *Isagoge* and part of the *Analytica posteriora* were translated at Toledo after 1150. Thence too came the *Logica Algazeli,* based on part of the Maqāṣid of al-Ghazālī (*ca.* 1058–1111). This includes a brief account of dialectical argumentation, in which it is distinguished from demonstration, fallacious reasoning, rhetoric, and poetic discourse. Although Latin versions of the Aristotelian commentaries of Averroës (Ibn Rushd, 1126–1198) began to circulate around 1230, his natural philosophy was more read than the logic, and his expositions of dialectic with regard to the *Topica* appear to have had little influence outside the Islamic world.

Around 1240 Robert Grosseteste translated into Latin, under the title of *Dialectica,* a short Greek work by St. John of Damascus dealing with the predicables and categories. Among the later Greek commentators, Alexander of Aphrodisias around A.D. 200 had written on the *Topica,* and in the eleventh century the text was expounded by the Byzantine writers Michael of Ephesus and Michael Psellos, but these works never reached the West in Latin translations.

Of the logic manuals the most celebrated is that of Petrus Hispanus from the 1230's. His *Tractatus* or *Summulae logicales* opens with a definition echoing the *Topica:* "Dialectica est ars ad omnium methodorum principia viam habens." Within a compendious treatment of logic the fifth tractate, *De locis,* is devoted to the topics. Similarly, William of Sherwood's *Introductiones in Logicam,* Lambert of Auxerre's *Summa,* and Roger Bacon's *Summule dialectices*—other thirteenth-century manuals combining the material of the old and new logic with terminist tracts—have sections on *loci.* There is a strange silence about dialectical reasoning in the *Summa logicae* (1323) of William of Ockham, but the *Topica* is there in rules for the construction and destruction of problems relating to the predicables and the account of induction, arguments from the particular to the general (III.3.18–37). Albert of Saxony, later in the fourteenth century, has six chapters on *loci dialectici* in his *Perutilis logica* (IV.19–24).

Such writings continued to be influential until the end of the Middle Ages, and the practice of disputation was exercised with increasing formality of argument, sharpened by attention to *obligationes*. Here logical consistency was explored by one party obliging himself to hold hypothetical positions while the other attempted to trap him in inconsistencies. A humanist reaction appeared in the first half of the fifteenth century with Lorenzo Valla's *Dialecticae disputationes* (1439), in which the whole inheritance of Aristotelian-Boethian logic is criticized and an effort is made to reduce dialectic to rhetoric. In Germany this tendency is represented by Rodolphus Agricola's *De inventione dialectica* (1479), a work that lay behind the *Dialecticae partitiones* (1543) and *Dialectica* (1555) of Petrus Ramus, with their critique of Aristotle and rejection of the logic of the merely probable, the domain of the *Topica*. Even then the older Aristotelian-Boethian dialectic persisted and found applications in a theology that owed its logical form to medieval scholasticism.

BIBLIOGRAPHY

A comprehensive bibliography of works published since 1836 on the history of logic from the time of Anselm to the end of the seventeenth century is in E. J. Ashworth, *The Tradition of Medieval Logic and Speculative Grammar* (1978).

Since *dialectica* was often synonymous with logic in the Middle Ages, general histories of logic may be consulted with profit, including William C. Kneale and Martha Kneale, *The Development of Logic* (1962), ch. 4. Alfonso Maierù, *Terminologia logica della tarda scolastica* (1972), is a useful guide to medieval logical terminology.

For dialectic in antiquity see Richard Robinson, *Plato's Earlier Dialectic*, 2nd ed. (1953); G. E. L. Owens, ed., *Aristotle on Dialectic* (1968); Benson Mates, *Stoic Logic* (1961). For late antiquity an important study is Mark W. Sullivan, *Apuleian Logic* (1967). William Harris Stahl, ed., *Martianus Capella and the Seven Liberal Arts*, 2 vols. (1971–1977), includes a study of dialectic by E. L. Burge, I, 104–115.

Medieval understanding of the topics before the discovery of Aristotle's *Topica* in the twelfth century was derived from Boethius. Eleonore Stump, *Boethius's "De topicis differentiis"* (1978), has translated his treatise and studied its influence. For the wider influence of Boethius see P. Osmund Lewry, "Boethian Logic in the Medieval West," in Margaret Gibson, ed., *Boethius: His Life, Writings and Influence* (1982). Several important studies of the Boethian tradition have been written by N. J. Green-Pedersen, who is also the author of "On the Interpretation of Aristotle's Topics in the Thirteenth Century," in *Cahiers de l'Institut du moyen âge grec et latin* (Copenhagen), 9 (1973). The applications of dialectic and the origins of the disputation

have been studied by Martin Grabmann, *Die Geschichte der scholastischen Methode,* 2 vols. (1909–1911).

For Arabic dialectic see Nicholas Rescher, *Studies in the History of Arabic Logic* (1963). An account of the later Greek dialecticians is in Herbert Hunger, *Die hochsprachliche profane Literatur der Byzantiner,* I (1978). On the humanist reaction against the Scholastic dialectic see the many studies of Cesare Vosoli, including "Le *Dialecticae disputationes* del Valla e la critica umanistica della logica aristotelica," in *Rivista critica di storia della filosofia,* **12** (1957) and **13** (1958).

P. OSMUND LEWRY, O.P.

[See also **Abelard, Peter; Alcuin of York; Anselm of Canterbury; Aristotle in the Middle Ages; Bacon, Roger; Boethius, Anicius Manlius Severinus; Cassiodorus Senator, Flavius Magnus Aurelius; Isidore of Seville, St.; Lanfranc of Bec; Martianus Capella; Ockham, William of; Peter Lombard; Petrus Hispanus; Quodlibet; Sylvester II, Pope.**]

DIAPER PATTERN, an ornamental surface pattern composed of repeating geometric shapes such as loz-

St. Mark reading. Book of Hours by an unidentified artist (circle of the Master of Guillebert de Mets), northern France or Flanders, *ca.* 1445. THE PIERPONT MORGAN LIBRARY, MS 287, fol. 19

enges or triangles. Diaper patterns were especially popular as background fill in French manuscripts of the late Gothic period (*ca.* 1300).

LESLIE BRUBAKER

[See also **Manuscript Illumination: Western European.**]

DIAPHONIA, in the vocabulary of medieval music theory, is used to mean both dissonance in general and polyphony or, more specifically, two-part organum. The first meaning, based loosely on ancient Greek music theory, through a passage from Isidore of Seville, was used exceptionally as a synonym for dissonance throughout the Middle Ages. The second meaning was restricted to the period from the ninth to the fourteenth centuries. The existence of this double tradition has led some scholars to see references to polyphony where only dissonance or disagreement was meant. The tradition that equates diaphonia with dissonance, disharmony, or disagreement is based firmly on Isidore, who defined it as the opposite of symphonia: "Symphonia est modulationis temperamentum ex gravi et acuti concordantibus sonis. . . . Cuius contraria est diaphonia, id est voces discrepantes vel dissone" (Symphonia is proportioned modulation from low and high concordant sounds . . . the opposite of which is diaphonia, that is, incompatible or dissonant sounds; *Etymologiae,* III, 20). Variants on this definition, some of which cite Isidore as the source, survive even in Johannes de Tinctoris' *Liber de arte contrapuncti* (1477).

The narrower meaning as polyphony in general, or as the Greek equivalent of discantus in particular, first occurred in the ninth-century *Musica enchiriadis:* "Haec [polyphony] namque est quam diaphoniam cantilenam vel assuete organum nuncupamus. Dictus autem diaphonia, quod non uniformi canore constet, sed concentur concorditer dissonu" (This is what we call diaphonia, cantilena, or usually organum. It is called diaphonia because it does not consist of uniform song, but of concerted dissonant concords). As a name for polyphony in general, "diaphonia" was used more or less interchangeably with "organum" from the ninth to the twelfth centuries, but there is no general agreement as to whether the two terms should be regarded as synonymous, or whether some special meaning—or at least special nuance—is expressed by each.

Beginning in the twelfth century, the term "dis-cantus," which must be regarded as a translation of "diaphonia," is used in contradistinction to "organum" to distinguish between melismatic (organum) and note-against-note (discantus) style. Some scholars have tried to show that organum always emphasized the "harmonious" aspects of polyphony, while diaphonia and discantus emphasized its "contrapuntal" aspect. This meaning can be read into the passage quoted from the *Musica enchiriades,* but in other descriptions the two are simply listed as synonyms: "Diaphonia seu organum" and "diaphonia vel organum."

In the thirteenth and fourteenth centuries discantus virtually replaced diaphonia in the vocabulary of music theory; the latter term was used as a scholarly curiosity requiring etymological explanation rather than as a current term to be defined.

BIBLIOGRAPHY

Hans Heinrich Eggebrecht, "Diaphonia vulgariter organum," in *Report of the Seventh Congress of the International Musicological Society* (1959), 93–97; Fritz Reckow, "Diaphonia," in *Handwörterbuch der musikalischen Terminologie* (1971).

ROBERT FALCK

[See also **Consonance/Dissonance; Discantor; Musical Notation, Western; Neume; Organum.**]

DIAPHRAGM ARCH. See **Arch.**

DIASTEMY (Greek: *diastēma,* "interval") is a term encountered occasionally in the writings of medieval music theorists. Since the late nineteenth century it has been used, usually in the adjectival form (diastemic), to describe the newer notation (beginning in the eleventh century) that, by means of heightening (distinguishing visually between high and low pitches) and, eventually, the lined staff, allowed for the exact location of pitches while retaining the traditional neumes. Older sources are written in so-called chironomic or *in campo aperto* (in a space without ruled horizontal lines) notation in which no attempt at heightening can be discerned. According to Peter Wagner, diastemy was the original basis of neumatic notation, and the chironomic was a later corruption.

BIBLIOGRAPHY

Paléographie musicale, I (1889), 3–50; Peter Wagner, *Einführung in die Gregorianischen Melodien*, II (1912, repr. 1962), 258ff.

ROBERT FALCK

[See also **Musical Notation, Western; Neume.**]

DĪBĀJ is a broadly defined term in Arabic for silk brocade. Often woven with a pattern, it is distinguished from *mulḥam* by having both warp and weft of silk. In medieval Islam *dībāj* occurred in many different colors, sometimes embellished with gold threads and embroidery. The best quality is described as being of fine silk, brilliant in color, and

Silk brocade strip. Purple satin with ogival framework and medallions in gold outlined with white, 16th century Turkish. THE METROPOLITAN MUSEUM OF ART, ANONYMOUS GIFT, 1949 (49.32.79)

heavy in weight. In poetry and literature the word came to signify all that is brilliant, beautiful, and elegant.

The many varieties of *dībāj* are often identified by geographic names indicative of place of manufacture. In the courts of Baghdad and Cairo *dībāj* fabrics were in great demand for cut and sewn garments and for furnishings such as cushions, pillows, curtains, and coverings. They were exported throughout the Islamic world and to the West. Many fragments of medieval Islamic textiles preserved in museum collections probably fall into the generic classification *dībāj*.

BIBLIOGRAPHY

Reinhart Dozy, *Supplément aux dictionnaires arabes* (1927), 421; R. B. Serjeant, *Islamic Textiles: Material for a History up to the Mongol Conquest* (1972), *passim*.

CAROL MANSON BIER

[See also **Silk; Textiles, Islamic.**]

DICTAMEN referred to any type of prose, metrical, or rhythmical composition, but it was used primarily for one kind of prose writing, the composition of letters, one of the most important forms of discourse in the High Middle Ages. The *ars dictaminis* or *ars dictandi* was the medieval art of epistolary composition, a specialized branch of rhetoric found in textbooks that presented highly developed and rigidly formulated doctrines on proper style and the structure of the letter, usually with models and examples of the parts. There were also formularies, or books of form letters, called *dictamina,* which covered persons of all social ranks and included various compilations ranging from church and state correspondence to authentic and fictional personal letters. The manuals and treatises on epistolary *dictamen,* many of them anonymous, number several hundred and are found in a few thousand manuscripts. This vast body of dictaminal material represents a major achievement of medieval civilization and an important link in the history of epistolography extending from the twelfth century into the Renaissance.

Although they had particular features, works on composing letters adhered to a standard format. There were definitions of composition and the letter, which according to formal rules usually consisted of five parts: salutation; introduction, for which the *captatio benevolentiae,* a statement to secure the readers' interest, or a proverb was used; narration; petition; and conclusion. The requirements and duties of the *dictator,* the professional secretary or teacher of *dictamen,* who might also hold the position of chancellor or notary, were described. Of great importance was the use of elegant style, which was achieved by the rhythmical patterns for the end of sentences *(cursus),* and the art of punctuation. Figures of speech and thought, as well as mistakes in writing, were enumerated. For making proper addresses in salutations and correct references to a person's status, detailed catalogs of religious and lay societies (with upper, middle, and lower categories for both) were compiled. In some manuals attention was given to documents, seals, and validation, topics suitable for the notary.

The origin of *dictamen* remains obscure, though there has been an effort to reconstruct the history of its beginnings. In early medieval Italy there was a survival of the notarial profession, and legal documents and letters were composed for public and private needs. Notaries and scribes had access to formularies, but they probably had to depend on an oral tradition for the rules for composing letters. The parts of a letter, except for the salutation, were adapted from the ancient rhetorical doctrine of the parts of an oration.

Extant letters indicate that the rules for the five parts were widely known before they were written in dictaminal manuals. By the eleventh century, in response to the demands of a society experiencing economic growth and the rise of towns and schools along with the emergence of states and the church, partly reflected in the investiture controversy, there appeared in Italy and elsewhere teachers and writers of *dictamen* who filled the growing need for written communication. A few of these earliest writers are known by references in their successors' works and from extant fragments, but the first whose works have survived is Alberic of Monte Cassino, who taught in the monastic school there in the late eleventh century. In his works *Breviarium de dictamine* and *Dictaminum radii* he presented doctrines on letter writing with a few forms, not as an independent discipline but as one bound to grammar and rhetoric.

Dictamen became the sole subject of a manual in Adalbert of Samaria's *Praecepta dictaminum,* written between 1111 and 1115 at Bologna. This textbook was significant not only for the growing im-

portance of letter writing, but also for marking the beginning of an identification of *dictamen* with Bologna, which was to become the most important center for the study of *dictamen* for two centuries. A line of Bolognese *dictatores,* whose fundamental works had influence outside Italy, followed Adalbert in the twelfth century. Characterized by practicality, utility, and contemporary usages, *dictamen* was taught in relation to law and rhetoric at the University of Bologna to future lawyers, notaries, and chancery officials. At the papal curia in Rome in the twelfth century the rules for *cursus* were formulated, and dictaminal works were produced for its use. By the end of the twelfth century larger, detailed textbooks on *dictamen,* usually with epistolary models, appeared in Italy and beyond.

From then into the early thirteenth century, the great contributor to practical *dictamen* was Boncompagno of Signa, the colorful critic of the Orléans school and its classical usages and artificial style in letter writing, which had spread to Italy. His younger rival, Guido Faba, probably the most outstanding *dictator* in the history of the genre, produced authoritative works on *dictamen* and contributed material for secular speeches to the *ars arengandi,* another form of discourse dependent on classical rhetoric, for which Boncompagno produced *Rhetorica novissima* and other *dictatores* wrote. Bene of Florence, Guido's colleague, wrote *Candelabrum,* which examined in detail grammar and *dictamen.* At the imperial court of Frederick II, Peter of Vinea produced *Dictamina,* a much used, model-letter collection with a rich and complex rhetorical style using biblical sources.

In the mid thirteenth century the *ars notaria* became an independent discipline at Bologna when Rolandino Passaggerii wrote *Summa artis notariae* for instruction on the writing of legal documents. The number of dictaminal works produced there declined by the fourteenth century as Giovanni di Bonandrea's *Brevis introductio ad dictamen* (1321) became a standard textbook. As grammar and Latin classical studies increased because of French influence in the later thirteenth century, the Italian *dictatores* combined these subjects and the rhetorical teaching in *dictamen.* The dictaminal works that were then produced at Arezzo, Padua, Siena, Bologna, and elsewhere in Italy thus became part of an expanding Latin culture. Their authors, the later medieval Italian epistolographers with interests in classical Latin literature, grammar, *dictamen,* and secular oratory, hence appear as the forerunners of the Renaissance humanists.

By the mid twelfth century *dictamen* from northern Italy appeared in France, where schools that offered the study of letter writing arose at Tours, Orléans, and Meun. The earliest work to reach France was Bernard of Bologna's *Introductiones prosaici dictaminis,* which underwent several recensions there and in Germany. Since grammar, the first of the liberal arts, had dominated rhetoric in France since Carolingian times, it was inevitable that letter writing should be recognized there as an adjunct to grammar. Also because of the importance of the study of the Latin classics, letters were written with classical literary expressions and in an ornate and artificial style derived from ancient literature.

Achievements in *dictamen* in twelfth-century France include Matthew of Vendôme's *Epistolarium,* a collection of model letters in verse, and Bernard of Meun's *Summa dictaminis* and *Flores dictaminum,* a rich collection of model letters. About 1252 Pons of Provence continued the French interest in grammar in his *Summa dictaminis* and *Epistolarium,* a popular formulary. Dictaminal activity later began to decline, but in 1332 a treatise on *dictamen* by an anonymous Cistercian monk, *Compendium rhetorice,* a work based on ancient rhetorical doctrine and mainly concerning style, appeared at Paris.

Before the end of the twelfth century *dictamen* appeared in England, and was subsequently taught along with grammar, as in France. Peter of Blois, who emigrated from there and became chancellor for the archbishop of Canterbury and archdeacon in Bath, introduced the subject in his *Libellus de arte dictandi rethorice,* written between 1181 and 1185. Like the dictaminal treatises produced in France, this manual presented letter writing in a grammatical context and reflected the literary character of the Orléans school, though the author was familiar with the Bolognese *Rationes dictandi.* He also compiled a very popular letter collection that contained models.

Dictamen advanced when it came to be taught probably as a "business course" at Oxford University, perhaps before 1300. In addition the dictaminal works of Guido Faba and Peter of Vinea became the sources for the style of the foreign correspondence of the royal chancery, beginning about 1250 and reaching its height a century later. In the fourteenth and fifteenth centuries several *dictatores* produced *dictamina* under northern Italian influence. Basi-

cally business communications with little literary quality, their production testified to the practicality of the *ars dictandi.* Probably the first theoretical treatise since Gervase of Melkley's study of poetic and prose composition, written in the early thirteenth century, was Thomas Merke's early-fifteenth-century *De moderno dictamine,* which examined only prose composition.

Spain's role in the history of *dictamen* was established in the thirteenth century by the works of a few *dictatores.* In Castile, Alphonse X the Wise, who was trained in *dictamen,* had as a member of his court Geoffrey of Eversley, an English cleric and *dictator.* Geoffrey, who may have taught at the University of Salamanca, wrote *Ars epistolaris ornatus,* a treatise with model letters that showed northern Italian influence and made references to Boncompagno and Guido Faba. The work was dedicated to King Alphonse and was probably intended for use at Salamanca. About a decade later Juan Gil de Zamora wrote *Dictaminis epithalamium,* a personalized manual for a cleric with literary interests. Although Guido Faba was a source, the work was not intended for use by lawyers and notaries. One *dictator* is known from the kingdom of Portugal. Dominicus Dominici Visentinus (from Viseu) compiled a popular collection of model letters and documents under the title *Summa dictaminis* (*ca.* 1280) for the use of notaries in episcopal and archiepiscopal chanceries.

The northern Italian tradition of *dictamen* also spread across the Alps into German lands by the mid twelfth century. About 1160, at the Cistercian monastery in Viktring, Baldwin composed *Liber dictaminum,* the contents of which reveal a transfer of Bolognese doctrines. Recensions were made of other works imported from France and Italy, and model letter collections indicating a developing interest in notarial activities were compiled. The anonymous *dictator* from Halberstadt produced the first collection of model letters, documents, and secular speeches in Germany, *Libellus dictaminum et privilegiorum* (1193–1194). Other *dictatores* from Zurich, Hildesheim, Heiligenkreuz, and other far-flung places followed suit with treatises usually containing model letters. In the fourteenth and fifteenth centuries works on *dictamen* increased to meet the needs of church and state chanceries and the first universities in Germany. An anonymous compiler at the Cistercian monastery in Baumgartenberg gathered a collection of models for *Formularius de modo prosandi* about 1302. Vincent Grüner of Zwickau, who in 1410 became rector of the recently founded University of Leipzig, wrote *Ars rethorica*, which presented *dictamen* in the context of classical rhetoric.

In the kingdom of Bohemia *dictamen* was introduced in the thirteenth century by Henry of Isernia, who emigrated from southern Italy, where he had studied at Capua. The author of *Epistolare dictamen* (a treatise that used the Latin classics) and the compiler of *Codex epistolaris,* he served as notary in the royal chancery and founded a school in Prague for training in notarial art and rhetoric. In the following century *dictamen* flourished and appeared in classical rhetorical treatises and official letter collections. At the University of Prague, founded in 1348, dictaminal textbooks of Nicholas Dybinus of Dresden, who wrote extensively on grammar, rhetoric, and *dictamen,* were used for instruction. The outstanding career of John of Neumarkt, the leading early humanist in Bohemia, also flourished then. A friend of Petrarch, he was notary and chancellor in the imperial court of Charles IV and later was bishop of Olomouc. He compiled two collections of *dictamina* written in humanistic Latin style. In the fifteenth century *dictamen* continued to be an active discipline, to which Procopius, a royal notary in Prague, contributed.

By the fourteenth century *dictamen* was found in Poland, though mainly in formularies. One of the collections of *dictamina* was compiled in *Liber formularum* by Georgius, notary at Cracow from about 1399 to 1415. Among the limited evidence of *dictamen* in Hungary is an anonymous collection of model letters titled *Summa dictaminis,* concerning ecclesiastical matters in Budapest in the early fourteenth century. *Dictamen* does not appear to have been used beyond the areas mentioned here.

Although the problem of the decline and end of the tradition of *dictamen* is yet to be studied, contributing factors are known. By its inflexible procedures, insistence on elegant style, and demand for brevity, *dictamen* by the late twelfth century probably had thwarted any creative activity in the writing of personal letters and was responsible for the decline of letter collections. It is evident that as the *ars notaria* developed as a discipline, it drew from *dictamen.* The use of Bolognese dialect and Italian in the thirteenth century, and other vernacular languages such as German, Czech, and Polish in the fourteenth and fifteenth centuries, for model letters and parts of the letter (combined with Latin instruction) was followed by vernacular manuals. The elaborate schemata for assembling stock phrases for a letter, as found about 1300 in the tabular works of Lawrence of Aquileia and his followers, came to reduce letter writing to a mechanical process.

The humanists in the Renaissance, successors to the medieval epistolographers, brought letter writing to a higher level of learning by returning to classical models and reviving the writing of personal letters in a modest style. They created the *ars epistolandi,* which replaced *dictamen,* though both coexisted for over a century. Neither the final work on *dictamen* nor the last *dictator* has been identified, though Nicholas Vulpis, a fifteenth-century Bolognese writer, qualifies. Toward the end of its history, *dictamen* appeared in incunabula in the anonymous *Ars rethorica,* which is actually an *ars dictandi,* and in other works by Boncompagno, Dominicus Dominici of Viseu, Pons (not of Provence), Paul Lescherius, Anthony Liporita, Guarino da Verona, and Anthony Haneron. By the early sixteenth century *dictamen* is found in a few manuscripts and among early printed books only in Peter of Vinea's *Dictamina.*

BIBLIOGRAPHY

Sources. Juan Gil de Zamora, *Dictaminis epithalamium,* Charles Faulhaber, ed. (1978); Paul O. Kristeller, "Matteo de' Libri, Bolognese Notary of the Thirteenth Century, and His *Artes Dictaminis,*" in Giovanni Capovilla, ed., *Miscellanea Giovanni Galbiati,* II (1951), 283–320; and "Un *Ars dictaminis* de Giovanni del Virgilio," in *Italia medioevale e umanistica,* 4 (1961), 181–200; E. J. Polak, *A Textual Study of Jacques de Dinant's 'Summa dictaminis'* (1975); Ludwig Rockinger, *Briefsteller und Formelbücher des eilften bis vierzehnten Jahrhunderts,* 2 vols. (1863–1864, repr. 1961), contains excerpts and complete texts of eighteen dictaminal and notarial works; Josef Tříška, "Henricus de Isernia, *Epistolare dictamen,*" in his *Výbor ze starší Pražské Univerzitní lituratury* (1977), 5–8, has an excerpt.

Studies. Robert L. Benson and Giles Constable, eds., with Carol D. Lanham, *Renaissance and Renewal in the Twelfth Century* (1982); Ernst H. Kantorowicz, *Selected Studies* (1965), contains three articles on the *ars dictaminis;* Paul O. Kristeller, *Renaissance Thought and Its Sources,* Michael Mooney, ed. (1979), 232–242 and *passim;* Carol D. Lanham, *'Salutatio' Formulas in Latin Letters to 1200* (1975); James J. Murphy, *Rhetoric in the Middle Ages* (1974), 194–268 and *passim,* and *idem,* ed., *Medieval Eloquence* (1978); William D. Patt, "The Early 'Ars dictaminis' as Response to a Changing Society," in *Viator,* 9 (1978); Hans Martin Schaller, "Die Kanzlei Kaiser Friedrichs II: Ihr Personal und ihr Sprachstil: Zweiter

Teil," in *Archiv für Diplomatik, Schriftgeschichte, Siegel-und Wappenkunde*, **4** (1958); Helene Wieruszowski, *Politics and Culture in Medieval Spain and Italy* (1971), contains eight articles on the *ars dictaminis*; Lidia Winniczuk, *Epistolografia* (1952); Ronald Will, "Medieval 'Ars dictaminis' and the Beginnings of Humanism: A New Construction of the Problem," in *Renaissance Quarterly*, **35** (1982).

E. J. POLAK

[See also **Alberic of Monte Cassino; Bologna, University of; Boncompagno of Signa; Cursus; Grammar; Latin Language; Matthew of Vendôme; Peter of Blois; Rhetoric.**]

DICTATUS PAPAE. In the original manuscript of Gregory VII's register, interposed between Epistle II, 55 (3 March 1075) and Epistle II, 56 (4 March 1075) is a list of twenty-seven numbered propositions beginning "I. That the Roman Church was founded by the Lord alone" and ending "XXVII. That [the pope] may absolve subjects from their fealty to the iniquitous." The title heading this list is "Dictatus Papae," a technical term denoting a document for which the wording was provided by the pope personally, rather than one drafted by a member of the papal chancery working from general instructions. But this particular *dictatus papae* has become so famous that, unless qualification is given, the title refers exclusively to Gregory's II, 55a.

Seen as a whole, the twenty-seven propositions of Gregory's "Dictatus" present a comprehensive outline of the doctrine of papal primacy as it affects three broad areas: first, the implications of Christ's commission to Peter (Matthew 16:18–19), and the role of the popes as sole lawful successors to Peter, in the area of ecclesiology and ritual (nos. 1–2, 8–11, 22–23, 26); second, the administrative and juristic implications of papal primacy vis-à-vis the internal hierarchy of the church (nos. 3–7, 13–21, 24–25); and third, the implications of papal primacy for relations between the pope and secular rulers (nos. 12, 27).

For each of these propositions, scholars have found precedents in canon law and church history, frequently with pedigrees dating back to the early Christian era. But the juxtaposition of all twenty-seven propositions within such a brief compass gives Gregory's "Dictatus" far more revolutionary impact than twenty-seven separate pamphlets could ever attain, and extensive research has been devoted to explaining the precise nature of this composition.

Of the many explanations proposed, only two need careful consideration. The first is that Gregory was outlining the title headings of a canon law text that he wished to have composed. We know from a letter of St. Peter Damian that even before 1059, Gregory (while still Archdeacon Hildebrand) had frequently requested that Damian scan decrees and histories of earlier popes and make excerpts, suitable for inclusion in a "collection of small size," of material which "specially related to the authority of the Apostolic See." If, in the intervening sixteen years, no such compendium had been produced, perhaps Gregory was now preparing the outline that would lead to the realization of his old project.

It has also been argued that the desired compendium had been produced in the interim, and that Gregory was here having its chapter headings entered in his register much in the fashion of a modern aide-mémoire. The compendium itself was then lost, in part, perhaps, because Gregory kept it for his personal use and thus separate from the more assiduously maintained papal register.

Although viewing the "Dictatus" as either a prospective or a retrospective table of contents tells us what it is, the fascination of Gregory's document for historical and canon law researchers has not ended. There remains, for upholders of the retrospective thesis, the task of reconstructing the compendium from its headings, which also raises the question of its authorship—suggested authors include Damian and Cardinal Deusdedit. Then, too, there is the unresolved question of the relation of Gregory's "Dictatus" to a twelfth-century document called the "Dictatus of Avranches." Finally, there will always remain the necessity of assessing and reassessing the place of the "Dictatus" in the history of ideas.

BIBLIOGRAPHY

Source. Erich Caspar, ed., "Das Register Gregors VII.," in *Monumenta Germaniae historica, Epistolae selecta*, II.1 (1920), 201–208.

Studies. Karl Hofmann, "Der 'Dictatus papae' Gregors VIII. als Index einer Kanonessammlung?" in *Studi Gregoriani*, **1** (1974); B. Jacqueline, "À propos des *Dictatus papae*: Les *Auctoritates apostolici sedis* d'Avranches," in *Revue historique de droit français et étranger*, **34** (1956); Stephan Kuttner, "Liber Canonicus: A Note on '*Dictatus papae*' c. 17," in *Studi Gregoriani*, **2** (1947); S. Löwenfeld, "Der Dictatus papae Gregors VII. und eine Ueberarbeitung desselben im XII. Jahrhundert," in *Neues Archiv*, **16** (1891), includes an edition of the "Dictatus of Avranches"; Ernst Sackur, "Der Dictatus papae und die Canonsammlung des Deusdedit," in *Neues Archiv*, **18** (1893); Walter Ullmann, "Romanus Pontifex Indubitanter Efficitur Sanctus: Dictatus papae 23 in Retrospect and Prospect," in *Studi Gregoriani*, **6** (1959–1961).

ELAINE GOLDEN ROBISON

[See also **Deusdedit, Cardinal; Gregory VII, Pope; Peter Damian, St.**]

DICTIONARIES. See **Encyclopedias and Dictionaries.**

DICTIONARIES, HEBREW. See **Hebrew Language, Study of.**

DICUIL (eighth/ninth century), a polymath active in France during the reign of Louis the Pious. Dicuil was born in Ireland and educated by a certain Suibne. He toured the island hermitages surrounding Ireland and Scotland, arriving on the Continent before 810. He wrote works on astronomy, weights and measures, grammar, and geography: *Computus* or *Liber de astronomia* (814–818), *Epistula censuum* (818), *De prima syllaba* (825), and *De mensura orbis terrae* (825). Another treatise, *De questionibus decim artis grammaticae,* is lost. The *Epistula censuum* and the *De prima syllaba* are wholly in verse, and verse (rhythmical and metrical) is interspersed in the remaining works.

BIBLIOGRAPHY

Sources. Several of Dicuil's works may be found in *Monumenta Germaniae historica, Poetae latini aevi carolini:* in II, Ernst Dümmler, ed. (1884, repr. 1978), 666–668, are the Valenciennes text of the *De prima syllaba* and the poetic sections of *De mensura orbis,* and in IV.2–3, Karl Strecker, ed. (1923), 659–660 and 917, are poems from the *Liber de astronomia.* Editions of other works are Mario Esposito, ed., "An Unpublished Astronomical Treatise by the Irish Monk Dicuil," in *Proceedings of the Royal Irish Academy,* **26** (1907), contains *Liber de astronomia*—Esposito added corrections and emendations in *Modern Philology,* **18** (1920); G. T. Heinrich Keil, *Grammatici latini,* 8 vols. plus suppl. (1857–1880), III.390–391, contains the Leiden text of *De prima syllaba;* and James Tierney, ed., *Dicuili Liber de mensura orbis terrae* (1967), contains also a valuable discussion of life, works, and sources.

Study. A. van de Vyver, "Dicuil et Micon de Saint-Riquier," in *Revue belge de philologie et d'histoire,* **14** (1935), is an indispensable guide to the corpus of Dicuil's writings.

MICHAEL HERREN

DIET. See **Representative Assembly.**

DIETARY LAWS, ISLAMIC. Islamic food regulations, like the regulations of many other religious communities, delineate a border between the believer and the unbeliever: what the members of the community of believers eat defines that community. As a token of a special relationship with God, it separates them from those outside the community, from those who do not share in this relationship.

The earliest formulations of dietary regulations in Islamic law are found in the Koran. They define specific rules concerning foods and emphasize, explicitly and implicitly, a symbolic break with the practice of other peoples and earlier Arab tradition. Coming between verses containing general and specific principles concerning food, one passage of the Koran (2:169–171) warns believers against following blindly the practice of their forefathers, who "had neither intelligence nor [divine] guidance." An even clearer indication of the desire for a decisive break with all tokens of the idolatrous past is the inclusion, among foods forbidden in 5:4, of meat slaughtered on stone altars (*nuṣub*), or the dividing of meat into lots to be raffled through the use of divining arrows (*azlām*), practices particularly evocative of pre-Islamic paganism, and associated through proximity with the Koranic prohibition of wine (5:90–91) as well. Most Koranic food laws stress the moderation and leniency of the injunctions, as opposed to those restrictions on diet, apparently common among certain Arab tribes, which are portrayed as based on hypocrisy, superstition, and ignorance rather than on true revelation (see 6:138–145). Concerning Jewish dietary laws, the Koran emphasizes that those restrictions not found in Islam which the Jews observe (no flesh of animals without cloven hooves; no fat except from certain parts) were imposed on them by God for their "conscious disobedience" (6:146), while true believers need not observe such rules.

Four foods are explicitly prohibited by the Koran: carrion (*mayta*), blood, pork, and animals that have been consecrated to other gods. The last three are clear, but *mayta* requires some explanation. Usually translated as carrion, it signifies the flesh of any animal that has died or been killed without the express purpose of using it for food, or any animal, except for fish, that has not been ritually slaughtered in the prescribed manner, which includes pronouncing the name of God over the victim. The use of the flesh of animals that die in unorthodox ways, those strangled, killed in falls, knocked down, or gored, is prohibited (5:4). One exception to the prohibition of *mayta* is that an animal dying of some cause other than ritual slaughter, but still found to have the breath of life, may, before it dies, be ritually slaughtered and thus become permitted. Animals that have been killed and in part eaten by wild beasts are prohibited, but the use of trained animals in hunting is allowed. It is generally accepted that game killed by hunting, which therefore cannot be ritually slaughtered, is nonetheless permitted. It is stipulated that the hunter should invoke the name of God at the moment of releasing the arrow or the hunting beast. An exception is held in the case of those in a state of ritual purity (*iḥrām*) for the pilgrimage, who are prohibited from hunting; they may, however, fish.

The Koran allows the consumption by Muslims of the food of the *ahl al-kitāb* (peoples of the book): Christians, Jews, and, by a few interpretations, Zoroastrians. "The food of those who have received the book is permitted you, and your food is permitted them" (5:6). In addition, those who eat one of the prohibited foods under compulsion, duress, or extreme necessity, are not held culpable for their actions: "Yet whoso is constrained, not desiring nor transgressing, no sin shall be upon him; God is forgiving, all compassionate" (2:173, trans. Arberry).

The copious *ḥadīth* literature, containing sayings or deeds attributed to Muḥammad and regarded as a source of considerable importance in the later formulation of holy law (*sharīᶜa*), elaborates on, and in some cases adds to, what is said in the Koran concerning food. The acceptability of the food of the *ahl al-kitāb;* the evils of slaughtering on stone altars; the necessity of invoking the name of God during slaughter; the proper way to slaughter animals for food; the acceptability of slaughtering sick or dying animals for food before they die and hence become *mayta;* and various rules regarding table manners—all are touched on. The legality of other foods, not specifically mentioned in the Koran, is taken up: horseflesh; the meat of ravens, hyenas, domestic asses, and mules; beasts and birds of prey; carrion eaters; and lizards are all included among the pro-

hibited foods. Concerning many of these foods, however, there are mutually contradictory *ḥadīths.* Dogs are viewed as essentially unclean and hence inedible; nonetheless the acceptability of using them in hunting is confirmed. Finally, the personal preferences of Muḥammad find expression in this literature: on the one hand, he is fond of cucumbers, honey and sweets, dates, and *tharīd,* a sort of bread crumbled in broth. On the other hand, he seems to have had a pronounced distaste for the odor of onions and garlic, particularly when that odor emanated from other people; neither is generally prohibited as food, but the believer is enjoined from entering the mosque after eating them.

The food laws, as they are formulated in later works of practical jurisprudence, incorporate the basic principles set out in Koran and *ḥadīth,* but also seem to draw on other sources, local customs, and the like. The list of prohibited animals was augmented and, with variations from school to school, generally included: beasts and birds of prey; carrion-eating crows (but not those that eat grain) and ravens (magpies, the subject of some debate, are generally prohibited); hyenas (again questionable); lizards; turtles; hornets (because they are harmful); and insects in general. Also prohibited are domestic asses and mules. There is, however, controversy concerning horseflesh: Shāfiᶜī considers it permissible, Mālik considers it prohibited. Hanafi opinion is mixed; Abū Ḥanīfa condemns it, Abū Yūsuf approves it. Similar to the situation in Jewish law, of the aquatic animals, only fish with fins and scales (*samak*) may be eaten, though Mālik disagrees. The origins of this rule in Islam are particularly obscure. At the same time, fish, while requiring no ritual slaughter, could not be consumed if they died of natural causes and floated to the surface, though those killed by accident were permissible.

BIBLIOGRAPHY

Sources. The major primary source for the study of Islamic dietary regulations is the Koran, available in many translations into European languages. Arent J. Wensinck's *A Handbook of Early Muhammadan Tradition* (1960), arranged by subject and with references to the Arabic texts, is the standard starting point for a study of *ḥadīth* on any given subject. Numerous translations into European languages exist of books on practical jurisprudence (*furūᶜ*), in which one can usually find a separate chapter devoted to dietary laws. Among these are: al-Marghīnānī, *Hidāya,* Charles Hamilton, trans., an important Ḥanafī work; Qayrawānī, *Risāla,* Léon Bercher, trans., 3rd ed. (1949); Khalīl ibn Isḥāq, *Mukhtaṣar,* Georges Bousquet, trans., in

Abrégé de la loi musulmane selon le rite de l'imâm Mâlek (1962); Shīrāzī, *al-Tanbīh fī al-fiqh*, Georges Bousquet, trans., 4 vols. (1949–1952); Ibn Qudāma, ͨ*Umdat fī aḥkām al-fiqh*, Henri Laoust, trans., in *Le précis de droit d'Ibn Qudama* (1950).

Studies. By far the best work in this area has been done by Maxime Rodinson: of particular interest are his articles "Ghidhāʾ," in *Encyclopaedia of Islam,* 2nd ed., II (1965), and "Recherches sur les documents arabes relatifs à la cuisine" in *Revue des études islamiques* (1949). As an interesting example of interpretation of the phenomenon of dietary laws in one religious system, Jean Soler's "The Semiotics of Food in the Bible," in Robert Forster and Orest Ranum, eds., *Food and Drink in History* (1979), is highly recommended.

RALPH S. HATTOX

[See also **Agriculture and Nutrition: The Islamic World; Beverages, Islamic; Ḥadith; Hunting and Fowling, Islamic; Koran; Law, Islamic.**]

DIETARY LAWS, JEWISH. The members of every society observe certain rules, formal or informal, regarding what kinds of foodstuffs may be eaten, in what manner they may be consumed, and with whom. Child rearing and education ensure the preservation of those rules. Nonetheless, such traditions are not necessarily static. The Jewish dietary laws developed as religious authorities followed out the implications of certain prohibitions or extended the application of others into new areas. Moreover, as they experienced different cultures in various historical periods and encountered new foodstuffs, varying economic and social constraints, and new means of integrating their knowledge, Jews were influenced in the modification of their dietary laws. At the same time the devotion of the Jews (including Marranos) in their observance, often at the cost of their own lives, ensured the essential integrity of form of those ancient traditions, which are deeply rooted in Old Testament codes. The traditions of the rabbanite Jews, mediated through the Talmudic and halakic literature, will be surveyed here. The rules for agricultural products will be treated first, followed by those for animals and for certain mainly processed foods.

AGRICULTURAL RULES

The agricultural dietary rules are of two types. One governs when the harvest may be consumed and what ritual activities free it for consumption; the other type prohibits certain mixtures. Some agricultural products could be freed for consumption by the payment of a tax; some, by the presentation of a thanksgiving offering or participation in a thanksgiving celebration. The tax was imposed in the form of a taboo placed on any food intended for human consumption that grew from the soil as a result of human cultivation, whether grain, fruit, or, by rabbinic decree, vegetables, as well as wine and oil. Separation of *terumah* (heave offering), to be given to a priest (Num. 18:8, 11–12, 25–32), and *ma* ͨ*aser* (tithe, specifically *ma* ͨ*aser rishon,* first tithe, Num. 18:21–24), to be given to the Levites, freed the food for use. A "second tithe" (*ma* ͨ*aser sheni*), to be consumed by the owner in Jerusalem (Deut. 14:22–27), and a tithe to be given to the poor (*ma* ͨ*aser* ͨ*ani*) were also prescribed (Deut. 26:12–15). *Terumah* and *ma* ͨ*aser* applied in Israel (including Syria) and were extended to the neighboring territories of Ammon and Moab, as well as Babylonia. Following the destruction of the Temple in A.D. 70, priests, unable to undergo ritual purification, could no longer consume their perquisites. As a result it became customary to offer them a token gift, which they would burn or otherwise destroy; such was the manner of this observance in the Middle Ages. Grain from which *terumah* and *ma* ͨ*aser* had not been separated was designated *tevel;* grain from which it was uncertain whether they had been separated was designated *demai.* Both were forbidden until the separation was made.

Dough from the "five species" of grain (wheat, emmer, barley, two-rowed barley, and spelt [Mishnah, Ḥallah, I:2]) was prohibited until a portion ([*terumat*] *ḥalah* [*terumah* of dough]) was separated (Num. 15:17–21). Before the destruction of the Temple it was given to the priests; afterward it was destroyed by the person preparing the dough or baking the bread. *Ḥalah* applied in all places.

Newly harvested grain (*ḥadash*) of the "five species" was prohibited until the ͨ*omer* ([thanksgiving offering of] sheaves) for the new harvest was brought to the Temple (Lev. 23:9–14). This was understood to have taken place on the second day of Passover. The prohibition of *ḥadash* applied everywhere, even when the ͨ*omer* could no longer be offered.

The fruit of new trees was not allowed until the fifth year. The first three years' fruit, designated ͨ*orlah* (foreskin), was prohibited in all places, for any use, while the *neta* ͨ *reva* ͨ*i* (fourth-year produce) was consumed in Jerusalem by the owner, in thanksgiving. ͨ*Orlah* continued to be prohibited everywhere even after the destruction of the Temple, though *neta^c reva^c i*, which applied only within Israel, had to be symbolically redeemed—for example, by casting a small coin into the Dead Sea.

The second type of agricultural prohibition, on certain mixtures, seems to have been based on the assumption that the integrity of a field is violated when more than one type of crop is cultivated in it at the same time. *Kilayim* (mixed seeds) applies to any two species of seeds (Lev. 19:19). *Kile ha-kerem* (*kilayim* of the vineyard) applies to mixed seeds cultivated in a vineyard (Deut. 22:9). The latter prohibition was extended to all places, whereas *kilayim* were prohibited only in Israel. Although mixed fruit trees in an orchard were allowed, grafting one species onto another was not.

RULES FOR ANIMALS

The dietary rules for living creatures may be categorized as follows: those creatures prohibited and those allowed; of those allowed, which sections are prohibited; ritual acts necessary to transform the living creature into permited food; and forbidden mixtures. Permitted products of living creatures have come to be designated "Kosher," from the Hebrew *kāshēr* (fit for eating).

The rules distinguishing permitted living creatures from prohibited ones are in Leviticus 11 and Deuteronomy 14. Of land animals, only those that chew the cud (ruminants) and are cloven-hoofed with two toes may be eaten. Thus cows and sheep are allowed, whereas swine, which are not ruminants, and camels, which lack split hoofs, as well as all carnivores, may not be eaten.

The Torah provides a list of the creatures of the air that are forbidden, but it neither characterizes nor lists permitted ones. According to the Mishnah (Ḥullin III:6) and Talmud (there, 61*a*–62*b*), edible birds must have a crop, a gizzard that may be peeled easily, and an extra talon on each foot. If a morsel is thrown to them, they must not swallow it from the air nor hold it on the ground with one foot while tearing it in pieces, but must catch it, lay it on the ground, and tear it with their bills. These criteria, in line with the biblical listings, would exclude carnivorous birds and carrion feeders, which were seen by medieval codifiers as the primary exclusion of the Torah. When questioned regarding the permissibility of a particular species, some halakists were willing to reason from the four criteria, but many demanded evidence of an authentic tradition as to the birds' permissibility (Jacob ben Asher, *Tur, Yoreh*

De^c ah, siman 82). Local traditions did vary. Among the species universally recognized as permitted were selected members of the following orders: Columbiformes (pigeons and doves), Galliformes (chickens, quail, partridges), Passeriformes (house sparrow), and Anseriformes (ducks and geese). Among swarming creatures of the air certain members of the insect order Orthoptera, families Acrididae and Tettingoniidae, are permitted: specifically, those possessing four front legs of approximately equal length, a pair of longer jumping legs jointed above the foot, and four wings that cover most of the length and surface of the body. Scientists are not certain of the precise identification of permitted grasshoppers.

Permitted denizens of the water must have at least one fin and one easily removable scale. Thus, all cartilaginous fishes, such as sharks, and some bony fishes, such as catfish and eels, are prohibited. Swarming creatures of the water, as well as those of the air and land (reptiles, amphibians, all invertebrates, and any small mammals), with the exception of some grasshoppers mentioned above, are forbidden.

Certain sections of permitted animals could not be consumed. The sciatic nerve (*gid ha-Nasheh; nervus ischiadicus*), in the rear of the thighs, was forbidden in memory of Jacob's laming by the angel (Gen. 32:33). *Ḥelev,* fat attached to the stomach and intestines of sacrificeable animals (cattle, sheep, goats) had to be removed, since the *ḥelev* had originally been reserved for the altar (Lev. 3:17, 7:23–25).

As with agricultural products, so with living creatures: some act was prescribed to transform them into food. With fish and insects "their gathering frees them" (Maimonides, *Mishneh Torah, Hilkhot shehitah,* 1:3), but warm-blooded animals (fowl and mammals) required shehitah (ritual slaughter) to guarantee a swift and painless death. In an uninterrupted movement the trachea, esophagus, jugular veins, and carotid arteries had to be severed rapidly.

Beyond the humanitarian concern for pain, shehitah expressed a deep respect for life and the seriousness of killing a living animal for food. In the biblical conception blood was absolutely forbidden for human consumption, "for blood is the life" (Lev. 17:11, 14; Deut. 12:23); only by returning the lifeblood to the creator of life through shehitah, which was designed to release immediately a major portion of the animal's blood, would the animal be allowed for consumption. Animals that died naturally or were killed by any method other than shehitah were considered *nevelah* (corpse, carrion) and were not allowed (Deut. 14:21). In addition shehitah could not release animals so sick or wounded (even by improper shehitah) that they would die as a result of their condition within one year. Rather, they were considered *terefah* ([animals that would die because they were] torn, Ex. 22:30).

Shehitah was very important in the medieval economy. Through meat taxes the Jewish community was able to subsidize communal government, educational and charitable activities, and the payment of taxes imposed by the Christian or Muslim governments of their domains. To prevent ritual laxity, the office of shohet (slaughterer; plural, shohetim) was made independent of that of the butcher, who actually sold the meat. Many communities demanded that their shohetim undergo an examination in the intricate rules of their profession, which required advanced training in talmudic and halakic sources as well as applied experience, with the result that shohetim became respected, well-paid communal functionaries.

A dietary restriction of far-reaching consequences is the prohibited combination of milk and meat. It first occurs in biblical sources as a ban on cooking a kid in its mother's milk (Ex. 23:19, 34:26; Deut. 24:21). Both Exodus passages occur in the context of seasonal celebrations, which supports the widely held theory that the ban was imposed in opposition to pagan cultic (fertility) rituals. In Deuteronomy it has been affixed to the other meat prohibitions as an additional dietary restriction. Biblically the ban has been related to similar forbidden practices, such as sacrificing (slaughtering) both a cow and her calf on the same day (Lev. 22:28) or taking both a dam and its young from the nest (Deut. 22:6–7), in which case humanitarian (even ecological) motivations may have been at work. The prohibition of milk and meat was understood to apply to any (permitted) meat, extending even to the flesh of fowl (which have no milk) by rabbinic decree. According to rabbinic exegesis, the threefold mention of this ban taught the interdiction of both eating and deriving any benefit, as well as of cooking.

It was necessary to wait up to six hours between consuming meat and milk. Between milk and meat most authorities required little more than rinsing the mouth and eating a piece of bread or fruit. Milk products were included in the interdiction. The separation was strict, with separate pots, plates, and tableware required for milk and meat.

Classical, medieval, and modern authors generally coincide in explaining the various meat prohibitions along four lines, alone or in combination: hygiene, symbolism, idolatry, arbitrary decrees. Both forbidden flesh and the combination of blood or milk with flesh have been considered difficult to digest. Some claimed that spiritual or physical harm, and disease or even death, could result from ingesting them. Alternatively, the animals or the combination of milk and meat might have been forbidden because of associations with pagan sacrifice or cultic worship. Moral considerations could be adduced along both allegorical and physiological lines. Man was forbidden beasts and birds of prey lest he become rapacious like them; blood was strictly forbidden in order to instill a horror of bloodshed. Rabbinically the rules were regarded as *hukkim*, rules for which no reason is given (*Sifra, Aḥare*, 23). The opinion was also expressed that the rules would be reversed in the messianic era, emphasizing the disciplinary purpose of the dietary rules by acknowledging the desirability of the forbidden foods (*Leviticus Rabbah*, 13).

In a related rabbinic formulation from *Leviticus Rabbah*, the purpose of these laws is "to refine mankind." The biblical passages refrain from giving reasons for the various meat prohibitions, but a definite purpose is enjoined: the Israelites, set apart in a special relationship with their Holy God, are to be holy as well. Jacob Milgrom explains that ethics are closely intertwined with ritual in biblical thought (as is the case in later Judaism as well), which is why the injunctions to holiness in Leviticus cluster around both the dietary laws and passages enjoining ethical ideals (among them, sexual laws and laws concerning the spilling of blood).

Applying techniques of structural analysis to locate the biblical symbolism, Mary Douglas understands the underlying conception to be that living creatures that are not "perfectly normal" for their particular realm (land, water, air) are not permissible to a holy people. Land creatures must be like pastoral animals (which the Lord also accepts in sacrifice); water creatures must swim, and not dwell on or crawl along the bottom; denizens of the air must either fly or hop properly, and may not prey on living animals or consume *nevelah* (carrion) from which the blood has not been drained. A small nation insecure in their land (or in the lands of their exile), threatened with assimilation and foreign domination, Jews have always been concerned with preserving boundaries. Bounded in their diet like their God, the Israelites symbolically mirrored through their dietary laws the other restrictions of their culture in order to keep themselves separate from the nations among which they dwelt, holy unto their Lord, and devoted to a life of intertwined purity and integrity.

FOODS PROCESSED BY GENTILES

Separation for the preservation of ethnic identity and ritual integrity motivated various bans on foods handled by non-Jews. They were enacted to regulate the contacts of Jews with gentiles so that idolatry, intermarriage, and the adulteration of Jewish foodstuffs would be prevented (Mishnah, Avodah Zarah, II; Babylonian Talmud there, esp. 35bff.). These bans have roots in the Old Testament and were practiced in the Hellenistic world.

Milk and milk products (cheese, and according to many, butter) produced, handled, or sold by a gentile were prohibited for fear of adulteration with the milk of forbidden animals or other substances. Gentile wine was banned for two reasons: lest it have been devoted to idolatry (yein nesekh, libation wine), all contact with which was shunned by Jews, and lest even "ordinary wine" (setam yeinam) conduce to conviviality, resulting in intermarriage. Since wine was the basic drink of the European Middle Ages, this interdiction had important consequences. Ways were found to allow gentile wine on the grounds that Christians and Muslims were not idolaters. Alternatively, Jews became heavily involved in all aspects of the medieval wine trade (on an international level) and remained so long after social and economic factors had pushed them out of other areas of agriculture.

The basic foodstuff, bread, was banned as well, in order to restrict social contact. As a result, travelers (merchants) were sorely pressed, as were the inhabitants of villages and towns where the one communal oven was controlled, often through feudal privilege, by a gentile. The ban seems to have been widely ignored in Spain and Egypt, and may not have been known in France until the twelfth century. German authorities took it seriously and tried to find ways to restrict its application. Assuming that the ingredients of the dough were acceptable, a Jew could purchase the dough, so that the baker would merely be the Jew's agent in the preparation. The Jew could also participate in the baking in ever so small a manner, as by throwing a splinter onto the fire.

Gentile cooking was also prohibited in order to prevent intermarriage. Where this concern was not relevant, as in the case of gentile servants cooking in Jewish homes, ways were found to avoid the ban. A Jewish householder could make some token contribution to the cooking. Some authorities allowed the assumption of such participation because of the circumstances of the cooking.

The Jewish dietary laws of the Middle Ages, as in previous periods, played an essential role in structuring the Jewish way of life, transforming their separation from the majority Christian and Muslim populations into a source of ethnic pride and spiritual values. The rules may be traced back from rabbinic codes and responsa through the Talmud and to the Torah, though a certain diversity of observance may be discerned.

For example, variant traditions as to the permissibility of certain species of birds or the amount of time one must wait between consuming meat and milk foods were preserved among the widespread Jewish communities in the Middle Ages. There were different levels of observance of the ban on gentile bread, in part due to the unavailability of Jewish bread in some areas, in part because the ban had not always been universally accepted or accepted to the same degree. The dietary laws had social and economic consequences, such as the institutionalization and professionalization of the shohetim. As a result of the ban on gentile wine, Jews became leaders in the wine industry.

Whatever particular strain of interpretation of the value and meaning of the dietary laws any particular Jew may have selected from among the wide range of homiletical, exegetical, philosophical, and medical interpretations available to him, his participation in their unique and widespread observance played a crucial role in preserving his people and their culture throughout this period.

BIBLIOGRAPHY

On the nature and meaning of the dietary laws, see Jacob Cohn, *The Royal Table* (1936, repr. 1970); Mary T. Douglas, *Purity and Danger* (1966), 41–57, and "Deciphering a meal," in her *Implicit Meanings* (1975), 249–275; Isidor Grunfeld, *The Jewish Dietary Laws*, 2 Vols. (1972); Jacob Milgrom, "Biblical Laws as an Ethical System," in *Interpretation*, 17 (1963); Gordon J. Wenham, *The Book of Leviticus* (1979).

On socio-economic aspects of the dietary laws in the Middle Ages, see Salo W. Baron, *The Jewish Community, Its History and Structure, to the American Revolution* (1942), esp. ch. 1, 161–164, 175, 202, ch. 2, 107–110, 157ff., 171, 258, ch. 3, 138; Solomon D. F. Goitein, *A Mediterra-*

nean Society (1967), esp. ch. 2, 104, 114, 224–228, 308; Jacob Katz, *Exclusiveness and Tolerance* (1961), 24–47; on *yein nesekh,* Haym Soloveitchik, "Can Halakhic Texts Talk History?" in *Association for Jewish Studies Review,* 3 (1978).

JAY ROVNER

[See also **Jews in Christian Spain; Jews in Egypt; Jews in Europe: Before 900; Jews in Europe: After 900; Jews in Muslim Spain; Maimonides, Moses.**]

DIETMAR VON AIST (*d. ca.* 1171). There are numerous attestations of the name Ditmarus de Agasta and the like in Lower Austrian documents from about 1139 to 1171. Since many of the forty strophes attributed to Dietmar von Aist in one or several manuscripts do not seem archaic enough to have been created before the late 1170's, the person whose death is reported about 1171 could scarcely have been the author of all the strophes. A relative or retainer with the same name, however, might well have been. Almost all scholars have disputed the attribution of some (or most) strophes to one author; since the late 1970's some (Moser and Tervooren, Schweikle) have declared that they are probably all by Dietmar. There is some merit to the notion, which still surfaces occasionally, that there were two or three Dietmars; according to Helmut Tervooren (1980) the manuscript tradition seems to reflect an older and a younger level. However, the diversity of forms, styles, and approaches to the themes could also be the consequence of a versatile poet's creating in a period of transition.

Of the sixteen songs attributed to Dietmar, four are single-strophe songs, two of which may be fragments of longer ones; but the two archaic woman's monologues that Wapnewski (1975) joins previous scholars in attributing to some earlier poet seem complete in themselves. The twelve multistrophe songs predominantly share men's and women's voices. At least one set of strophes (33, 15–34, 18) is best read as a conglomeration of two or more songs. Most such sets, however, display a considerable degree of coherence, if not unity, in their two or, more commonly, three strophes (Wapnewski, 1980). There seems little reason other than preconceptions about the history of the *Tagelied* to deny Dietmar the well-known "Slâfest du friedal ziere" (39, 18–29). To be

sure, this song contains the only clear dialogue, as opposed to the linked monologues of the *Wechsel,* but such strophes as I, 2 (32, 5) and XIV, 3 (40, 11) seem to contain embryonic dialogue (their authenticity has also been challenged). Thus Dietmar probably did write the first known German dawn song.

The thematic and formal repertoire of Dietmar shows a continuation of the traditions of the Danubian school of *Minnesang* as well as probable echoes of Provençal song. Several affinities are reflected in manuscript attributions to two poets: Reinmar der Alte (von Hagenau) apparently learned from Dietmar; the relationship between Dietmar and Heinrich von Veldeke is less clearly explicable and may stem from the use of similar models and subsequent scribal confusion.

The sixteen songs present a broad and vigorous array of stances and images available to a lover and his beloved. The court is seldom an obtrusive impediment to the fulfillment of their love. A lament about surveillance in I, 1 (32, 1) is not developed; the messengers in II, 1 (32, 13) and XI, 3 (38, 14) are not explicit go-betweens used in order to avoid the attention of society. Reasons for a lack of fulfillment, where there is one, are generally not stated.

In such songs as II (32, 13), IV (34, 19), and XV (40, 19) there is a subtle but clear interaction between the poet/performer and his audience. In none of the songs, however, is this technique as obvious as in the presumably earlier ones by Der von Kürenberg or the later ones by Hartmann von Aue.

BIBLIOGRAPHY

Hugo Moser and Helmut Tervooren, eds., *Des Minnesangs Frühling,* 36th ed. (1977), I, 56–69, and II, 71–73; Günther Schweikle, ed., *Die mittelhochdeutsche Minnelyrik,* I, *Die frühe Minnelyrik* (1977), 136–159, 388–408; Helmut Tervooren, "Dietmar von Aist," in Kurt Ruh *et al,* eds., *Die deutsche Literatur des Mittelalters, Verfasserlexikon,* 2nd ed. (1980), II, 95–98; Peter Wapnewski, *Waz ist minne. Studien zur Mittelhochdeutschen Lyrik* (1975), 9–22; and "Dietmar von Eist XII: 'Nu ist ez an ein ende komen,'" in W. T. H. Jackson, ed., *The Interpretation of Medieval Lyric Poetry* (1980), 163–175.

HUBERT HEINEN

[See also **German Lyric; Middle High German Literature; Minnesingers.**]

DIETRICHS FLUCHT. See **Buch von Bern, Das.**

DIFFERENTIA (difference, *terminatio*), the musical formula ending a psalm tone. The psalm tone is chosen according to the mode of the antiphon that is sung before and after the psalm. The musical incipit of the antiphon, or variatio(n), can begin with any pitch. The end of the psalm tone must link smoothly with the incipit of the antiphon and, to accommodate the different ways in which antiphons begin, several differentiae are normally provided for each tone. Each consists of a short musical phrase of several notes.

Because in the liturgy every psalm ends with the doxology, the last words of which are *et in secula seculorum. Amen.*, the musical formula is associated with the letters EVOVAE (in some areas SEVOVAEN), from the vowels of the last two words. The formulas are given, along with other information about the tones and the modal system, in the Tonary. Because the appropriate formula is needed for every psalm that is sung, however, it also appears in Graduals and Antiphonals at the end of each antiphon or other chant sung with a psalm.

BIBLIOGRAPHY

Terence Bailey, *The Intonation Formulas of Western Chant* (1974); Clyde Brockett, "Saeculorum Amen and Differentia: Practical Versus Theoretical Tradition," in *Musica disciplina,* 30 (1976); Andrew Hughes, *Medieval Manuscripts for Mass and Office* (1982), 111–116.

ANDREW HUGHES

[See also **Antiphon; Antiphonal; Music, Liturgical; Psalm Tones; Tonary.**]

DIGENIS AKRITAS, Byzantine epic poem compiled between the tenth and twelfth centuries. The name Digenis is found widely in modern Greek folk song, often referring to a near superhuman being who yields to *Charos* (Death) only after a heroic fight. When, therefore, six manuscripts of a Byzantine epic *Digenis Akritas* were published between 1875 and 1926, scholarly and nationalist expectations were high. It was called the national epic of modern Greece, a later *Iliad,* an eastern *Roland.* Although these early claims have not been substantiated, we are left with a poem of absorbing general interest and a fascinating puzzle for specialists.

Digenis' father is an Arab emir; his mother, the emir's prisoner, daughter of a Byzantine general.

The emir, defeated by the girl's brothers, chooses Christian baptism in order to marry her. Digenis is thus born of two races (*di-genís*). After showing precocious strength in hunting, he elopes with the daughter of a Byzantine fortress commander, defeating the whole garrison single-handed. Later he lives in domestic happiness, policing the empire's Euphrates border against bands of robbers (*apelatai*), mostly Christians, including the colorful old captain Philopappous and the Amazon Maximo. From this he derives his other name, Akritas or Akritis (borderer). The emperor, in a strangely tense visit, confirms his position. Digenis builds a palace by the Euphrates, reminisces over past exploits, and dies together with his wife, mourned by the whole Middle East.

The poem falls into two halves, centering on the emir and Digenis. The first is rather epic in tone, perhaps deriving from an Arab epic on the ninth-century emir Omar (ᶜAmr ibn ᶜUbayd Allāh) of Melitene (Malatya). The second part seems too romantic and conciliatory for the stern struggles against the Arabs on the Euphrates. One suggestion is that Digenis himself symbolizes a yearning for peace in an age of constant warfare; another is that he predates Islam and reflects the kings of Commagene, a buffer state between Rome and Parthia in the century before and the century after Christ. The terminus ante quem for both halves of the poem is the Turkish invasion of Asia Minor in the late eleventh century. Tenth- to twelfth-century dates have been suggested for the combination of the two halves. The poem is composed in the fifteen-syllable verse of modern Greek folk songs, but at a rather formal linguistic level, especially in manuscript G. Only the language prevents us from calling this poem the earliest work of Modern Greek literature.

Thanks mainly to the Belgian scholar Henri Grégoire, dozens of historical, geographical, and literary references have been seen in the poem, the clearest of which refer to Commagene and to the Paulicians, ninth-century Christian heretics who were driven to join the Arabs. Other suggested connections include Armenian and Arab elements. Recent scholarship has confirmed many of Grégoire's proposals but has cautiously rejected others, particularly those based on Russian versions of *Digenis,* in which Grégoire saw a primitive stage of the poem.

Other studies have dealt with textual problems. There seems to be strong evidence for the surprising hypothesis that one of the three surviving versions of the poem (Z, lost common source of four late manuscripts) is a compilation from texts of the other two versions, those now represented by manuscripts G and E respectively. Future analysis of the original form and early history of the story and the poem will depend largely on the results of comparative study of these two early and primary manuscripts.

BIBLIOGRAPHY

Digenis Akrites, John Mavrogrodato, ed. and trans. (1956). See also H. F. Graham, "The Tale of Devgenij," in *Byzantinoslavica,* **29** (1968); Henri Grégoire, *Autour de l'épopée byzantine* (1975); George Huxley, "Antecedents and Context of *Digenes Akrites,*" in *Greek, Roman, and Byzantine Studies,* **15** (1974); Michael J. Jeffreys, "Digenis Akritas and Kommagene," in *Svenska Forskningsinstitutet i Istanbul: Meddelanden,* **3** (1978); L. Politis, "L'épopée byzantine de Digénis Akritas: Problèmes de la tradition du texte et des rapports avec les chansons akritiques," in Accademia Nazionale dei Lincei, *Atti del Convegno internazionale sul tema: La poesia epica e la sua formazione (1969)* (1970); Erich Trapp, *Digenes Akrites: Synoptische Ausgabe der ältesten Versionen* (1971).

MICHAEL JEFFREYS

[See also **Byzantine Literature.**]

DIGEST. See **Corpus Iuris Civilis.**

DIJON, CHARTREUSE DE CHAMPMOL, Carthusian monastery in Burgundy founded by Philip the Bold to serve as mausoleum for him and his successors. Constructed in 1383–1388 by the French architects Drouet of Dammartin and Jacques de Neuilly, decorated with sculpture by a team of Netherlandish artists under the successive direction of Jean de Marville (1384–1389), Claus Sluter (1389–1406), and Claus de Werve (1406–1439), and provided with a rich array of interior furnishings, the Chartreuse presented one of the most sumptuous and important artistic ensembles of the later Middle Ages. The monastery was largely destroyed in 1793; most of the works of art have been destroyed or dispersed. Among the most important surviving elements are the base of a Calvary group (Well of Moses), a votive group on the church portal, and the duke's tomb (the latter now in the Musée des Beaux-Arts, Dijon).

BIBLIOGRAPHY

Cyprien Monget, *La Chartreuse de Dijon d'après les documents des archives de Bourgogne,* 3 vols., (1898–1905); Musée Municipal de Dijon, *La Chartreuse de Champmol* (1960); H. J. J. Scholtens "De Chartreuse bij Dijon en haar Kunstenaars 1379–1411," in *Oud Holland,* **81** (1966).

J. STEYAERT

[See also **Carthusians; Drouet of Dammartin; Sluter, Claus; Werve, Claus de.**]

DINANDERIE, metalwork, usually of brass, copper, or bronze, produced in the area around Dinant in the Meuse Valley in the fifteenth and first half of the sixteenth centuries. The term usually refers to objects for the household, particularly plates, candlesticks, sconces, chandeliers, and cooking vessels, but it also includes ecclesiastical objects such as lecterns and funerary plaques.

BIBLIOGRAPHY

Suzanne Collon-Gevaert, *Histoire des arts du métal en Belgique* (1951), 248–273; Metropolitan Museum of Art, *The Secular Spirit: Life and Art at the End of the Middle Ages* (1975), 33, 61.

ROBERT G. CALKINS

[See also **Metallurgy.**]

Pelican in her piety. Dinanderie, bronze plate. Low Countries (area of Dinant), *ca.* 1480. THE METROPOLITAN MUSEUM OF ART, GIFT OF IRWIN UNTERMYER, 1964 (64.101.1498)

DINAR, the Islamic unit of gold currency. The Arabic word *dīnār* comes ultimately from the Latin *denarius,* which originally meant a silver coin but later became a common term for the Roman–Byzantine gold solidus. This coin was known and used by the Arabs before Islam and in the Prophet's time, and the word "dinar" appears in the Koran.

The earliest Arab gold coins, probably struck sometime between 691 and 693, were inspired by Byzantine issues of Emperor Heraklios (610–641) with the imperial figures Arabicized, all crosses eliminated, and Arabic religious inscriptions in place of Greek. These were followed by coins, with dates from A.H. 74 to 77 (693 to 697) portraying the caliph standing with his sword and other regalia. Even this Islamic image, however, was unacceptable to pious Muslims, and in A.H. 77 (696–697) the first Islamic dinars were struck at Damascus, with Arabic inscriptions only. The inscriptions included the date and several religious statements. These dinars set the general pattern for all subsequent Muslim gold coinage.

For almost a century all dinars were anonymous. The governor of Egypt was the first to put his name on dinars in 786–787. Within fifty years rulers' names became a standard addition to the inscriptions on all dinars. During the same period, starting in 813–814, mint names came to appear on dinars as a result of the spread of gold coinage from the capital to mints throughout the caliphate.

The Byzantine solidus and its early Arab derivatives weighed about 4.50 grams, but with the introduction of Islamic dinars the standard was changed to 4.25 grams. Most medieval dinars approximate this weight, but there were always minor variations with place and time. For example, in the Umayyad period, while Damascus was striking dinars of 4.25 grams, Egypt weighed imported dinars against precise glass weights of 4.22 grams, and North Africa and Spain struck dinars of about 4.29 grams. Major variant standards include the late North African and Spanish dinar of about 4.65 grams, introduced in 1145, and the Venetian ducat standard of 3.50 grams, adopted in the eastern Mediterranean in the fifteenth century.

Strictly speaking, these standards were for the accounting unit of payment in gold coin. Sometimes mints endeavored to strike dinars precisely to these standards, so that coins could be counted in payment, but more often there was enough variation in the weight of dinars that payments had to be weighed out with a balance. From the eleventh to the fifteenth century, most mints in the eastern Muslim countries made little attempt to regulate the weight of each coin.

Fineness was much more important in determining the value of dinars. Except in time of financial exigency, dinars were as pure as technology allowed, or slightly alloyed for durability. Relative fineness set the basic value of foreign or outdated dinars against current gold issue in each locality, but daily exchange rates were determined by supply and demand, as was the value of coined dinars against gold bullion.

Fractional gold coins—halves and thirds—were struck by the Umayyads, and the quarter dinar (Arabic: *rub*^{c}; Italian: *tari*) was popular in the Mediterranean lands from the ninth to the twelfth centuries. Otherwise, fractions and multiples of the dinar were seldom issued. Nearly all gold coins, whatever their intended value, bear the words "this dinar" until the twelfth to the fourteenth centuries, when they were undenominated.

Medieval documents and texts discriminate among dozens of different kinds of dinars, which are identified by issuing authority, by geographical origin, or by some special feature of appearance. In addition to the many different Muslim dinars, Christians in England, Spain, Sicily, and the crusader states imitated dinars or struck their own with distinctive Arabic legends.

BIBLIOGRAPHY

G. C. Miles has treated the evolution of the first dinars in "The Earliest Arab Gold Coinage," in *American Numismatic Society Museum Notes,* 13 (1967). Data on fineness of dinars are provided by Andrew S. Ehrenkreutz, "Studies in the Monetary History of the Near East in the Middle Ages," in *Journal of the Economic and Social History of the Orient,* 2 (1959) and 6 (1963); and by W. A. Oddy, "The Gold Contents of Fatimid Coins Reconsidered," in D. M. Metcalf and W. A. Oddy, eds., *Metallurgy in Numismatics,* I (1980).

MICHAEL L. BATES

[See also **Mints and Money, Islamic.**]

DĪNAWARĪ, ABŪ ḤANĪFA AḤMAD IBN DĀWŪD AL-, an Arab scholar of the ninth century (*d.* before 903) and a famous philologist in the formative era of Arabic linguistic sciences. Despite his renown and the frequency with which later authors cited his works, little is known of his life. Of Iranian origin, he studied under the famous grammarian Ibn al-Sikkīt in Iraq. He also took up mathematics, geography, and history, and he had a house in Dīnawar that he used as an astronomical observatory.

His best work was his philological writing, the character and scope of which we may assess from the preserved volumes of his *Book of Plants (Kitāb al-nabāt)*, the book for which he was best known to medieval scholars. Here the author offers a systematic critical work of botany and lexicography on the entire range of Arabic vocabulary pertaining to plants and plant life. His purpose is to collect all the relevant learning, both written and oral, on the subject and to arrange it in a systematic fashion. Al-Dīnawarī incorporates into his book the works of his predecessors, but also adds large amounts of material based on his own research into bedouin poetry and dialects, as well as observations on the plants and other topics he discusses. The first part of the work consists of chapters on particular topics that "we considered appropriate to mention before mentioning the plants one after another." These chapters, often only indirectly related to botany, cover such subjects as bows and arrows, rope making, tanning, fire starting, insect pests, and beekeeping. The second part of the work is an alphabetical exposition of individual plants. This presentation is more lexicographical than botanical and includes, for example, numerous observations on words of Persian, Nabataean, and Greek origin.

Al-Dīnawarī is better known to modern scholars as the author of the *Book of Long Narratives (al-Akhbār al-ṭiwāl)*. The only one of his works to survive in its entirety, it is a universal history that places primary emphasis on the history of Persia. It presents synchronous sketches of events in Persia as compared with developments in Yemen, elsewhere in Arabia, and in Byzantium, but it covers only Alexander and the Sasanians in any detail. The prophet Muḥammad appears but momentarily, and the book quickly moves on to the Arab conquest of Iraq, with particularly vivid attention to the battle of Al-Qādisīya. The conflicts of ᶜAlī with Muᶜāwiya and the Kharijites receive considerable attention, but of Umayyad history only such events as the death of al-Ḥusayn and the revolts of the Azāriqa and al-Mukhtār are related at length. The remainder of the book gives a synopsis of the reigns of the caliphs from ᶜAbd al-Malik to al-Muᶜtaṣim—again, with hardly any detailed coverage of events not immediately germane to the affairs of Persia.

This history is essentially a summary based on the works of earlier authors, and al-Dīnawarī, never credited by medieval authorities as a historian, clearly saw it as a work of literature and entertainment rather than historiography. Indeed, while the book does have considerable literary merit, as a work of history it appears to be a series of narratives strung together with little thought for differentiating between sober tradition and popular fable.

Al-Dīnawarī also wrote books on popular dialects, poetry and poets, rhetoric, and law, and he compiled an exegesis of the Koran in thirteen volumes. None of these works has survived.

BIBLIOGRAPHY

On al-Dīnawarī as a philologist and botanist, see Fuat Sezgin, *Geschichte des arabischen Schrifttums*, IV (1971), 338–343, which has a good bibliography. The *Kitāb al-nabāt* has not been translated, but on it see, in particular, B. Silverberg, "Das Pflanzenbuch des ad-Dînawarî: Ein Beitrag zur Geschichte der Botanik bei den Arabern," in *Zeitschrift für Assyriologie*, 24 (1910) and 25 (1911); Ahmed Issa Bey, "Abou Hanifa el Dinawari et son 'Livre des plantes,'" in *Bulletin de l'Institut d'Égypte*, 16 (1934); Muhammad Hamidullah, "Dinawariy's Encyclopedia Botanica (*K. al-nabāt*) in the Light of Fragments in Turkish Libraries," in Ankara, Üniversite, Dil ve Tarih-Coğrafya Fakültesi, *Mélanges Fuad Köprülü* (1953), 195–206; and Bernhard Lewin's English inroductions to his editions of the extant volumes III and V.1 (1974), and V.2 (1953). On his role as a historian, see Carl Brokelmann, *Geschichte der arabischen Literatur*, 2nd ed. (1943–1949), I.127; *Supp.*, I.187; E. L. Petersen, *ᶜAlī and Muᶜāwiya in Early Arabic Tradition* (1964), 159ff.; Franz Rosenthal, *A History of Muslim Historiography*, 2nd ed. (1968), 92, 133; A. A. Duri, *The Rise of Historical Writing Among the Arabs*, Lawrence I. Conrad, ed. and trans. (1983), index. There is no translation of the *Al-Akhbār al-ṭiwāl*.

LAWRENCE I. CONRAD

[See also **Botany; Historiography, Islamic; Science, Islamic.**]

DINDSHENCHAS (alt.: *Dinnshenchas*). The *Dindshenchas* (Lore of places) is a large collection of toponymic legends in Middle Irish verse and prose produced by professional literati between the ninth and twelfth centuries, though a few items may be earlier or later. The name is a compound of *dind* (hillock; eminent or notable place) and *senchas* (ancient and traditional lore); the latter word was almost a synonym for knowledge in early Irish society.

Although toponymic lore must have been part of the learned tradition from preliterate times, it is unlikely that many legends in the *Dindshenchas* are much older than the text itself. They tend to rely on such roughly contemporary texts as the Book of Invasions, which contains poems attributed to some of the same authors, and the scholars of these centuries seem to have seen themselves as antiquarians rediscovering a lost past rather than transcribers of what was commonly known. Even if they invented their own toponymic legends, however, each legend had to be based on some already accepted tradition, or it would have failed to qualify as *senchas* and would therefore have explained nothing. Paradoxically, then, the legends in the *Dindshenchas*, although few can be accepted as traditional, are made of material that does represent genuine tradition, though perhaps distorted in the process of adaptation. Much of that tradition is preserved in other texts, but some stories are known today only because they were used in the *Dindshenchas*.

The earliest form of the text (Collection *A*, represented in the Book of Leinster) consists of poems by various hands, apparently dating from the ninth to the eleventh centuries. A prose extract (Recension *B*) was made from *A* and survives in two versions, one independent and the other combined with the verse in the third and final recension (*C*), probably in the twelfth century. The redactor supplied a brief prose introduction and imposed a geographical pattern, placing Tara first and going on to each of the five ancient provinces (Meath, Leinster, Munster, Connacht, and Ulster) in turn—following the clockwise direction considered auspicious for any roundabout journey. He also standardized the format, in which an onomastic query ("*X*, how was it named?") forms a heading and is answered by the legend in prose, then in verse—one or more versions of each.

This recension became authoritative and popular in the Irish literary world, and it appears in most of the important later medieval miscellanies, including the Books of Ballymote, Uí Máine, and Lecan and the Yellow Book of Lecan. Various scribes added items to the collection on their own initiative. Counting all of these additions, and including the poems and prose from *A* and *B* that were never taken into Recension *C*, the *Dindshenchas* as a whole contains 207 poems and an equal number of prose pieces. This body of legendary material may not always represent the mainstream of earlier tradition reliably, but it contributes much to our knowledge of that tradition, extending it in some places and deepening it in others.

BIBLIOGRAPHY

The *Dindshenchas* has never been completely edited. The prose portions, covering one of the two surviving versions of Recension *B*, were edited and translated in piecemeal fashion by Whitley Stokes: "The Bodleian Dindshenchas," in *Folk-lore*, **3** (1892), and "The Edinburgh Dindshenchas," *ibid.*, **4** (1893). "The Prose Tales in the Rennes Dindshenchas," in *Revue celtique*, **15** (1894), **16** (1895) covers the prose of Recension *C*, adding a few unduplicated items from the other version of *B*, found in the Book of Leinster. A more thorough and systematic edition of the verse is Edward Gwynn, ed., *The Metrical Dindshenchas*, 5 vols. (1903–1935). Gwynn's account of the relationship of the manuscripts and the development of the text, as well as the somewhat different conclusions reached by Rudolf Thurneysen, *Irische Helden- und Königsage* (1921), 36–46, are summarized in Charles Bowen, "A Historical Inventory of the *Dindshenchas*," in *Studia celtica*, **10–11** (1975–1976). A more accurate account of textual development is given in Tomás Ó Concheannáin, "The Three Forms of *Dindschenchas Érenn*," in *Journal of Celtic Studies*, **3** (1981–1982).

CHARLES BOWEN

DINIS (1261–1325), the sixth king of Portugal. Son of Afonso III of Portugal, and through his mother's line grandson of Alfonso X of Castile and León, Dinis came to the throne at the age of eighteen, already skilled in the handling of affairs of state. As a youth he was sent on many embassies to his grandfather's court, one of the most brilliant of the thirteenth century and famed for its international assemblage of translators, scientists, and poets. The common lyric tongue of the troubadours from the central and western portions of the Iberian Peninsula being Galician-Portuguese, poets and poetry flowed freely among the courts of Dinis' father and grandfather, and of his eventual father-in-law Peter III the Great of Aragon, whose daughter Isabel he later wed. Thus Dinis grew up in the company of many of the most accomplished poets of his time and became one of them.

He supported and fostered poetic activity at his court over his entire reign of almost half a century through both personal example and royal largess.

His bastard sons, Afonso Sanches and Pedro, count of Barcelos, were also poets. Dinis collected his own poetry and in all likelihood oversaw the compilation of the *Cancioneiro da Ajuda,* devoted to the *cantiga d'amor* (love song). His collecting activities encouraged his son Pedro to compile a larger selection in which the poetry of Dinis' court and previous eras is amply displayed. These poets included court notables such as Estevam da Guarda (who came from Aragon in the entourage of Isabel) and ranged all the way down to traveling jongleurs and other entertainers.

While the statement of João de Leão in his elegy of Dinis that "never after his death did poets write" may be treated as hyperbole, in fact Dinis advocated and refined a poetic tradition that had enjoyed its moments of greatness in his youth and in the earlier years of his rule. He knew, or knew of, the great masters of the *bailada* (dance) forms: João Zorro, Pero Meogo, and Martim Codax. The luminaries of his father's court and also those of Castile shaped the art practiced at his own court: troubadours such as João Airas de Santiago, João de Aboim, João Soares Coelho, Juyião Bolseiro, Roi Queimado, Airas Nunes, Pedr'Amigo, Paay Gomez Charinho, and João Garcia de Guilhade. Many of them lived to grace the poetic assemblies presided over by Dinis.

This last flowering of courtly style, being at some remove in time from the great twelfth-century practitioners of the Provençal manner, was the culmination of the progressive refinements and transformations effected throughout the thirteenth century. While these are evident in the love poetry, they have even affected the indigenous woman's song, the *cantiga d'amigo,* which, despite its popular origins, acquired a large measure of refinement and stylization during the reign of Dinis. One poet proves this general trend with an exception: Estevam Coelho's "Sedia la fremosa seu sirgo torcendo" retains an air of graceful spontaneity that surpasses in simple charm (the intended effect) the others of its genre.

Dinis' own verse illustrates other poetic trends at his court. He left 138 compositions. Of these, 76 are *cantigas d'amor,* all but a few consisting of three seven-line stanzas. They have a limited thematic range but demonstrate great diversity of rhyme arrangements and use of both verbal and semantic parallelism. The poet concentrates on the pangs and grief love brings, no longer aspiring to the privileged position of *drut,* or successful suitor of his ladylove. The increasingly diminished use of visual images is replaced by a complicated tracery of concepts based

to a large extent on the repeated use of different forms of key verbs intended to project feelings of bewilderment, dejection, hurt, and desperation in the face of unrequited love. The sophistication of thought and feeling permits only irregular use of popular elements such as a refrain.

Dinis' fifty-two *cantigas d'amigo* also treat of love, and typically the tone is lighter, the interlocking stanzas more open to continuous development of the wider thematic spectrum of the genre (lovers meet or part, plan pilgrimages, lament absence, confide their fears and feelings to sisters, mothers, and other confidantes, and so on). The effect of the provençalized vocabulary is evident, but there is a greater sense of music, rhythm, and spontaneity preserved here than in the love songs.

The third major classification of song, the satirical *cantigas d'escarnho e de maldizer,* had little attraction for Dinis: he wrote only ten. These songs had become more popular with time, however, and many of the poets of Dinis' court wrote them with a finely honed wit. Targets were almost anyone: rich and poor, courtiers and tradesmen, clergy and laity, men and women of all classes. Hypocrisy, sexual perversion, miserliness, immorality, cowardice, and other vices, both comic and serious, were frequent targets in the compositions of Afonso Sanches, Pedro, count of Barcelos, Fernan Esquio, Vasco Martins, João de Gaia, João Lobeira, and the most renowned of them all, Estevam da Guarda—all of whom wrote in the tradition of such able satirists of the thirteenth-century courts as Alfonso X, Pero da Ponte, Pedr'Amigo de Sevilha, João Soares de Paiva, and dozens of others. As usual, however, most poets continued to write in all genres, even if they excelled in a particular one.

It is accurate to summarize by stating that the stylized and analytical Provençal love poetry attained its greatest heights in Dinis' day, but that the capacity for regeneration of fresh ideas and flexible forms was winding down. When Dinis, the last royal patron of any consequence, died in 1325, the strongest underpinnings of this poetic achievement were effectively removed. Decline was rapid. Contributing to it were two strong challenges, one from a nascent, vital Castilian hegemony (both political and literary), which ended forever the use of Galician-Portuguese as the principal language of lyric poetry in the central portion of the Iberian Peninsula, and the other from the growing vogue of the new explorations of the vagaries of love in prose form, notably the Arthurian matter which, along with the French pilgrims, traveled the roads through Spain to Galicia's Santiago de Compostela.

BIBLIOGRAPHY

Source. Das Liederbuch des Königs Denis von Portugal, Henry R. Lang, ed. (1894, repr. 1972), with useful introduction, notes, and glossary.

Studies. Sheila Ackerlind, "The Relationship of Alfonso X of Castile to Diniz of Portugal" (Ph.D. diss., Yale, 1972), exploring the example and stimulus Alfonso provided for Dinis' roles as patron and poet; Aubrey F. G. Bell, "King Diniz and the Early Lyric," in his *Studies in Portuguese Literature* (1914), 1–39, an early study with generous examples and translations of the various types of poetry; Arlene T. Lesser, *La pastorela medieval hispánica: Pastorelas y serranas galaico-portuguesas* (1970), treating the popular genre of the encounter of poet and shepherdess.

JOSEPH SNOW

[See also **Alfonso X; Cantigas de Amor, Amigo, and Escarnio; Galician–Portuguese Poetry; Portuguese Literature.**]

DINNSHENCHAS. See **Dindshenchas.**

DIOCESE, ECCLESIASTICAL. "Diocese" and "parish" are derived from *oikos,* the Greek word meaning "house" and, with prefixes, "caring for a house" or "caring for a group of houses." Thus "diocese" became a term meaning "administration," and in the late Roman Empire a diocese could be a very large administrative unit: for example, Spain was a diocese. As the Christian church grew larger, both in territory and in membership, some formal organization became necessary. The leader of a city's clergy became a bishop, with responsibility for the clergy of his area. This included rural districts, which in the Roman administrative system were governed by the city authorities—a natural situation, since rural parishes developed very slowly (Christianity was at first a city religion) and drew their clergy from the towns. The area administered by a bishop was eventually called a diocese, but usage varied for a long time. A parish could be called a diocese, and vice versa. As late as the ninth century, Archbishop Hincmar of Rheims could call his province a diocese and his own diocese a parish.

The early diocese grew up spontaneously around early centers of Christian converts, usually in the larger towns of a province. As the administrative authority of the pope increased, he gained the right to establish new dioceses or to divide old ones that had grown too large.

In the Eastern church the Greek word for "parish" was still used for the equivalent of the Western diocese; sometimes the secular term "eparchy" was also used.

BIBLIOGRAPHY

J. F. Niermeyer, *Mediae Latinitatis lexicon minus* (1976), see *diocesis, parochia* (with English translations); J. R. Palanque, G. Bardy, and P. de Labriolle, *Histoire de l'Église,* III, *De la paix constantinienne à la mort de Théodose* (1936), 437–487.

JOSEPH R. STRAYER

[See also **Church, Latin: Organization; Parishes, Organization and Development of.**]

DIOCESE, SECULAR. The diocese was an administrative unit of the Roman Empire that originated in Diocletian's reorganization of the government in the late third century. Under his plan the old provinces were divided into twelve dioceses that later became fourteen: the prefecture of the East contained five dioceses, that of Illyricum two, Gaul four, and Italy three. Constantine split the empire into four prefectures, each containing from two to five dioceses, which were further subdivided into provinces. The diocesan governor was called *vicarius* except in the East, where he was called *comes orientis.* The diocesan system seems to have fallen into disuse in the East during the fifth century and a bit later in the western part of the empire; it was abolished by Justinian in the sixth century.

BIBLIOGRAPHY

George Ostrogorsky, *History of the Byzantine State,* Joan Hussey, trans. (1957, rev. ed. 1969).

LINDA C. ROSE

[See also **Roman Empire, Late.**]

DIONYSIOS OF FOURNA, author of the *Hermeneia* (Manual of Christian iconography), an eighteenth-century painter's guide that lists biblical subjects in rough chronological order. Each subject is accompanied by the appropriate inscription for the painter to append and a description of the scene; Dionysios also frequently notes the proper location within a church for a particular subject. Although the *Hermeneia* depends heavily on Matthew, interpolating episodes from the remaining Gospels only when Matthew omits them, it attempts to synthesize the diverse accounts of Christ's life relayed in the four Gospels. Because pictorial cycles in churches such as Sant'Angelo in Formis (eleventh century) and the Metropole at Mistra (fourteenth century) present synthesized versions of Christ's life that presuppose a "harmonized chronology," it is generally believed that the *Hermeneia* relies on medieval sources, though the descriptions of individual scenes were probably added by Dionysios himself.

BIBLIOGRAPHY

Ἑρμηνεία τῆς ζωγραφικῆς τέχνης, A. Papadopoulos-Kerameus, ed. (1909); A. N. Didron, ed., *Manuel d'iconographie chrétienne grecque et latine,* P. Durand, trans. (1845). Gabriel Millet, *Recherches sur l'iconographie de l'évangile aux XIVᵉ, XVᵉ et XVIᵉ siècles* (1916), *passim;* Paul A. Underwood, "Some Problems in Programs and Iconography of Ministry Cycles," in the work he edited, *The Kariye Djami,* IV (1975).

LESLIE BRUBAKER

[See also **Byzantine Art.**]

Detail from fresco of the Last Judgment. Dionysios the Greek together with his sons, Feodosy and Vladimir, 1500–1502. Church of the Birth of the Virgin, Ferapontov Monastery. REPRODUCED WITH PERMISSION FROM PHAIDON PRESS LIMITED, OXFORD

BIBLIOGRAPHY

Valentin Bulkin, *Dionysius* (1982); Viktor Lazarev, *Old Russian Murals and Mosaics* (1966).

LESLIE BRUBAKER

[See also **Russian and Slavic Art.**]

DIONYSIOS THE PSEUDO-AREOPAGITE. See Pseudo-Dionysius the Areopagite.

DIONYSIOS THE GREEK (*ca.* 1440/1450–*ca.* 1505), the preeminent Muscovite icon and fresco painter after Andrei Rublev, probably was born of a privileged family and was last documented in 1503. He is first mentioned as working in Mitrophones' shop at the Cathedral of the Nativity in the Pafnutyev-Borovsk Monastery near Moscow in 1467. Dionysios seems to have caught Czar Ivan III's attention, and he was commissioned in 1481 to paint the iconostasis at the newly built Cathedral of the Dormition in the Kremlin. Other major works are at the Pavlov-Obnorsky Monastery and St. Therapont Monastery, Vologda. Dionysios favored bright colors and delicate, elongated figures with small heads. His frescoes are compositions beautifully coordinated with their architectural confines. Though never radical, Dionysios did not hesitate to present his own, subtly different interpretations of standard subjects.

DIONYSIUS EXIGUUS, or Denis the Little, a monk of Scythian origin, important as a canonist, computist, and translator from Greek into Latin. He came to Rome around 497, when he was already a recognized scholar, and was still writing in 526. Cassiodorus knew him well (*Institutiones,* 1.23). His compilation of conciliar canons and papal decretals, known as the *Collectio Dionysiana,* came to enjoy semiofficial status in the Roman church and formed the basis of the *Collectio Dionysio-Hadriana,* which Pope Hadrian I gave to Charlemagne in 774. In computus Dionysius is best known for introducing the custom of numbering years from the birth of Christ, though he dated this event four to seven years too late. His translations include, besides the canons, several hagiographical writings, some anti-Nestorian tracts, and Gregory of Nyssa's *De opificio hominis.*

BIBLIOGRAPHY

Dionysius Exiguus, *Opera omnia,* in *Patrologia latina,* LXVII (1848), 9–520; Alphonsus van Hove, *Prolegomena ad codicem iuris canonici,* 2nd ed. (1945), 154–161; Gabriel Le Bras, "Un moment décisif dans l'histoire de l'église et du droit canon: La renaissance gélasienne," in *Revue historique de droit français et étranger,* 4th ser., 9 (1930); Hubert Wurm, *Studien und Texte zur Dekretalensammlung des Dionysius Exiguus* (1939, repr. 1964).

JAMES J. JOHN

[See also **Calendars and Reckoning of Time; Computus; Translations and Translators, Western European.**]

DIONYSIUS OF TEL-MAHRÉ, historian of the first half of the ninth century. Some question exists about whether Dionysius (or Denis), a Syrian Jacobite patriarch, actually wrote the history that is attributed to him. The book continues the works of earlier historians such as Eusebius and Socrates Scholasticus, and it adds fresh material as well. There were two versions of the *Annals:* a longer one, now lost, and a shorter one called the *Chronicle.* The latter consists of four parts, the first three of which cover the period from the Creation to the mid sixth century and depend heavily on earlier historians. The fourth part is original and extends to 774/775. It includes chronologies and biographies of various ecclesiastical dignitaries, as well as considerable information about the Arabs and other topics. The author states that it is based on written documents, oral interviews of elders, and his own observations.

BIBLIOGRAPHY

J. B. Chabot, ed. and trans., *Chronique de Denys de Tell-Mahré, quatrième partie* (1895).

LINDA C. ROSE

[See also **Historiography.**]

Church of S. Sepolcro. Pisa, 12th century. ALINARI/ART RESOURCE

DIOTISALVI (DEOTISALVI) (*fl. ca.* 1150–1165), architect in Pisa. Inscriptions credit him with the church of S. Sepolcro and with the grander and more famous Baptistery (*Deotisalvi magister huius opis*), begun in 1153. He may also have worked in Lucca. His works evidence unusual structural expertise and familiarity with foreign architecture, including the Holy Sepulcher.

BIBLIOGRAPHY

Christine Smith, *The Baptistery of Pisa* (1978), 220–226 and *passim;* Ulrich Thieme and Felix Becker, eds., *Allgemeines Lexikon der bildenden Künstler von der Antike bis zur Gegenwart,* IX (1913), 321.

DALE KINNEY

DIPLOMACY, BYZANTINE. Diplomacy was a fundamental factor in the survival of the Byzantine Empire and made as great a contribution to the defense of the state as the military services. Because of the cost and vicissitudes of war, the government of the empire held a long-standing preference for diplomatic initiatives rather than military action. The Byzantine state was involved in a very large number of wars, but, given the basic attitudes and assumptions of its leaders, war was really a continuation of foreign policy by less satisfactory means. Diplomats fulfilled functions fundamentally similar to those performed by the army and navy—that is, the defense of the empire and its interests among foreign nations. At all times the Byzantine government kept a very subtle diplomacy at work, a long and unbroken succession of negotiations seeking to regularize its relations with foreign powers and to reduce the threat of war.

This pragmatic approach, which recognized the cost of war in manpower and resources, was founded on a remarkably unrealistic perception of the world and the position of the emperor. The emperor claimed supremacy over all other rulers; just as there was one God in heaven, so there could be only one emperor on earth (the imperium and the world were coterminous). The emperor was the leader of all the world, the protector and guardian of the Christian faith; his rule was legitimate because he had been chosen by God and was the successor of the Roman emperors.

From these basic principles came the foundations for a Byzantine ideology that should have made, but did not make, foreign relations impossible. Theoretically, the emperor was only issuing orders to his natural subordinates or chastising rebels against universal imperial authority. To sustain the appearances of these claims, the government at Constantinople developed and promoted an artificial system of relations with other states and peoples called the family of the kings. In this system, the emperor was the basileus or ruler of the world; all other rulers were his subordinates and stood in a quasi-family relationship as his honorary cousins, nephews, or brothers, the degrees of real and diplomatic intimacy varying according to their level of civilization, their religion, and their power. To a surprising degree, medieval rulers, both Christian and non-Christian, recognized the theoretical supremacy of the empire and, for both practical and sentimental reasons, wished to be incorporated within this hierarchy of states.

The formalization of this system can be seen in the court at Constantinople, where titles and offices were bestowed and foreign rulers or their representatives were exposed to the ceremonials that glorified the emperor and the empire. Byzantine treaties asserted imperial claims as unilateral documents bestowed by the emperor on an inferior: burdensome or humiliating terms were defined as privileges granted by the emperor, and tribute was a gift to for-

eigners. In all of these matters, the emperor was bound by the formalities of court protocol to diplomatic traditions that were founded on long experience with different peoples and states. These traditions, as codified in the *De ceremoniis* of Constantine VII Porphyrogenitos (tenth century), served to enhance the prestige of the emperor and the empire.

While maintaining the illusion of world dominion, the theories of sovereignty and superiority of the emperor were not allowed to interfere with the implementation of a pragmatic foreign policy. However artificial or intransigent the imperial ideology, the diplomacy of the empire was eminently practical. Concessions, compromises, and modifications of the formal system were frequent, and often irreversible in their effects; but these discrepancies were always regarded as temporary arrangements, no matter how permanent they might become.

Diplomatic initiatives were intended to defend the frontiers of the state by preventing or deflecting foreign attacks, as well as to extend Byzantine political and cultural influence as far as possible by creating a chain of subordinate states beyond the frontiers. Diplomacy was thus treated as an intricate science, even a fine art, in which military intimidation, political intelligence, economic concessions, and missionary propaganda were combined into a powerful defensive instrument.

In diplomacy, as in all governmental affairs, the ultimate decisions were made by the emperor. In the conduct of diplomacy he could call on the services of numerous administrative agencies, but there was no central administrative office that supervised the conduct of foreign plicy (that is, no ministry for foreign affairs). The logothete of the drome (post) was the imperial officer most intimately concerned with diplomacy. As defined in the late ninth and early tenth centuries the logothete was responsible for the functioning of the imperial post, the supervision of imperial diplomatic officers within the empire, the reception of foreign envoys and their formal introduction to the emperor and his court, and the internal security of the empire.The logothete was not an ambassador but a bureaucrat.

The two most important diplomatic agencies subordinate to the logothete were the *scrinium barbarorum* and the corps of interpreters. The *scrinium barbarorum* had existed since the fifth century and was responsible for the direction and coordination of the housing, feeding, supervision, and surveillance of foreign envoys in Constantinople. Its activities were limited to the capital; the transportation of these foreigners to and from the Byzantine frontiers, and their care during transit, were the responsibility of the imperial post.

Because reliable and abundant intelligence was the cornerstone of any rational and effective foreign policy, the Byzantine government gave careful consideration and encouragement to the gathering of information on foreign states and peoples. Together and individually two agencies (the *scrinium barbarorum* and the drome) were responsible for the collection and analysis of information on the states and peoples whose activities might affect the security of the empire. Neither of these agencies acted as a foreign service; their actions were confined within the frontiers of the empire (that is, they did not provide trained diplomatic officers). Their findings were, on occasion, collected into general statements on foreign policy, such as that formulated by Constantine VII in his *De administrando imperio.* Intelligence was gathered by merchants, frontiersmen, and diplomats, who had a special responsibility as citizens of the empire, as well as from immigrants, refugees, and allies. These same groups served as a reservoir of linguists available to the corps of interpreters. Byzantine diplomacy was dependent on loyal and competent translators and interpreters to communicate with the diverse states and peoples of the known world.

In addition to all of his administrative duties, the logothete of the drome was the most significant figure, next to the emperor, at the formal receptions of foreign envoys and guests in Constantinople. These ceremonies, as described by Constantine VII, followed a carefully orchestrated etiquette that was intended to impress foreigners with the power, prestige, and splendor of the emperor. The formalities of the reception were predetermined by the status, within the imperial hierarchy of states, of the foreigners' own countries. In general the foreigners were led into the imperial audience hall past the massed members of the imperial guard and throngs of dignitaries. At the end of this procession a curtain was drawn aside to reveal the emperor, attired in the robes of state and seated on the imperial throne. At the same time, in a display of mechanical genius, golden lions roared and birds sang in gilded trees. While the foreigners made the three obligatory prostrations, the imperial throne was raised hydraulically to emphasize the unapproachability of the emperor. At this first reception the emperor was silent: the logothete of the drome and the foreigners communi-

cated in words carefully determined by protocol. Every aspect of the reception was meticulously planned, as was the calculated generosity of the emperor at subsequent receptions, where he might even dine with the foreign envoys or guests. Although the whole ceremonial system might appear childish, it nonetheless seems to have consistently impressed its audiences with the power and grandeur of the empire and its leader.

During their stay at Constantinople, the foreign envoys or guests were closely watched by agents of the logothete. The Byzantine goverment expected its own envoys to collect information while abroad, and it therefore took care to ensure that foreigners in the capital did not see or hear more than the government wished. All Byzantine travelers, whether merchants, envoys, or missionaries, were instructed to gather foreign intelligence, especially vital details on the internal affairs of other states. Within the empire, frontier officers were responsible for watchng neighboring states and peoples, and in some cases they had the power to initiate relations. The empire sought information and diplomatic contacts in order to extend Byzantine influence and prestige, to secure its territories from attack, to spread Christianity and Byzantine culture, and above all to gain peace and order in the world.

The emperor had the duties of defending the territory of the empire and of bringing peace. The securing of peace was seen as more easily obtainable by diplomacy than by military means, given the expense and uncertainties of war. The sign of success and the goal of Byzantine diplomacy was "peace and a treaty." Treaties served to bind a foreign people or state to certain duties and responsibilities. The Byzantines did not negotiate separate commercial, political, or peace treaties. Instead, they sought to regularize all relations between the empire and the foreign power, which meant that the treaties included political, military, commercial, legal, religious, tributary, and refugee clauses. All treaties were secured by oaths in an attempt to bind the other side to carry out its terms. Here the Byzantines displayed substantial flexibiity and realism with non-Christian powers; these peoples swore their oaths by their own gods while the Byzantines swore on the cross and by the Trinity. The Byzantines did not hesitate to hold the barbarians directly accountable to their own gods for their behavior.

The Byzantines usually observed their treaty obligations; but they never considered it wrong, nor did they hesitate, to incite some third party against their enemies or even their allies to secure immediate relief or benefits for the empire. In fact, in the *De administrando imperio,* Constantine VII advocated and justified the positive advantages of such a calculated attitude toward one's allies. According to Constantine, responsible leadersip meant making adequate preparations and taking timely preventive action against a present or potential enemy, even if that enemy were temporarily a friend or ally. Such an approach often cost the empire heavily when foreign rulers accused it of duplicity in foreign relations, but such accusations were regarded as trivial when compared with the advantages gained for the empire.

Carrying out this diplomacy required envoys who were flexible and competent. Because there was no foreign service as such, the Byzantine government drew on individuals with a diversity of backgrounds and experiences in the military, the church, and the bureaucracy. Rarely did there emerge anyone who could be called a professional diplomat; exceptions were Valentinios, on the steppe (second half of the sixth century), and Leo Choerosphactes, with the Bulgars and Arabs (*ca.* 900). In general, although it did not matter whether the envoy was a military or civil official or even a cleric (as in the case of Constantine/Cyril in the ninth century), great care was taken in the selection of an ambassador. Beyond matters of temperament, rank, language skill, and acceptability to a foreign ruler, an envoy had to be willing to sacrifice himself for the interests of the empire.

In the matter of influencing foreign peoples, missionaries were often as valuable as diplomats. Conversions were planned and carried out as part of a calculated effort to control or influence foreign states or peoples through Christianization. Missionaries, as much as diplomats, were agents of the Byzantine state, not only because their activities served the interests of the state but also because the state financed and organized nearly all missionary endeavors that originated within the empire.

No matter how diplomacy was carried out, it was expensive. Byzantine embassies and their ambassadors and entourages, along with the numerous and luxurious presents, were costly, as was the reception of foreign envoys, but these costs were minor compared with the payments made to foreign rulers to ensure peace. The recipients considered these payments to be tribute, but the Byzantines believed them to be part of a wise government policy and the sign of a diplomatic victory. Payments to gain peace or military allies were not held to diminish the prestige

of the empire; they were only a necessary diplomatic lubricant in a world filled with greedy and fickle barbarians. If money would not restrain a foreign power, then in some cases diplomatic marriages were arranged (for example, Princess Anna to Vladimir I of Kiev). Such marriages became especially frequent after the thirteenth century, when the Palaiologoi substituted diplomatic marriages for military strength as the underpinning of their foreign relations.

Throughout their history the Byzantines preferred clever diplomacy to the cruder methods of violence; they had a penchant for ingenious and subtle maneuverings that required finesse, foresight, and adroitness. Through a combination of skillful diplomacy and missionary activities, imperial statesmen hoped to forestall the enemies of the empire and extend the influence of the emperor without bloodshed. To Byzantine diplomats, the simplest way of influencing foreign nations was money; a basic tenet of Byzantine diplomacy was that every man had his price, whether in money or in flattery. Through appeals to greed and vanity, they secured peace and protected the state. By careful distribution of money and favors, Byzantine diplomats sought to divide their enemies, or to neutralize them by playing one against another or by encouraging jealousies, grudges, and wars between them. The Byzantines did not shrink from questionable methods if these were considered necessary to the safety of the empire. Emperor Anastasios wrote in 515: "There is a law that orders the emperor to lie and to violate his oath if it is necessary for the well-being of the empire."

Despite some notable mistakes and an apparently intransigent ideology, Byzantine diplomats displayed remarkable flexibility in carrying out the foreign policy of the empire, and their accumulated experience was frequently used to good advantage. As a consequence, diplomacy was a source of strength and vital to the survival of the Byzantine Empire

BIBLIOGRAPHY

Sources. Constantine VII Porphyrogenitos, *De administrando imperio,* Gyula Moravcsik, ed., R. J. H. Jenkins, trans., 2 vols. (1949–1962), an excellent translation with commentary of the best Byzantine source that deals directly and intimately with diplomacy; Liutprand of Cremona, *Antapodosis,* F. A. Wright, trans. (1930), tenth-century Byzantine diplomacy as seen from outside the empire.

Studies. Louis Bréhier, *Les institutions de l'empire byzantin* (1949), 229–262, a brief, general account; Francis Dvornik, "Byzantine Intelligence Service," in *Origins of*

Intelligence Services (1974), 121–187; C. D. Gordon, *The Age of Attila* (1960), a good translation, with commentary, of the Byzantine authors who discussed relations with barbarians in the fifth century, especially valuable for the translation of Priscus; D. A. Miller, "The Logothete of the Drome in the Middle Byzantine Period," in *Byzantion,* 36 (1966); Dimitri Obolensky, "The Principles and Methods of Byzantine Diplomacy," in *Actes du XIIᵉ Congrès international d'études byzantines* (1964), 43–61, a good examination of the nature of Byzantine diplomacy despite its limited focus on the steppe tribes.

FRANK E. WOZNIAK

[See also **Byzantine Empire: History; Constantine VII Porphyrogenitos; Cyril and Methodios, Sts.; Logothete; Scrinium.**]

DIPLOMACY, ISLAMIC. In order to reconstruct the Islamic system of diplomacy and international relations, it should be recalled that Islam is not merely a set of religious ideas and practices, but also a political community (Arabic: *umma,* nation-state) endowed with a social order designed to organize the internal affairs of the community of believers as well as its foreign relations. The basic assumption underlying Islam's relations with other nations is the doctrine of the jihad (popularly called "holy war"), which was devised partly to protect the interests of believers within the political community but mainly to establish Islam as an ecumenical state in the world. In theory, the ultimate objective of Islam was to establish peace and order within its dominion and to extend its territory to encompass the whole world. But the Islamic state, not unlike other universal states, could not possibly expand ad infinitum. Outside it there remained political communities with which Islam had to deal permanently by war or diplomacy and had to enter into peaceful relations in accordance with principles and practices agreeable to Muslims and non-Muslims.

From the Islamic viewpoint the world was divided into two blocs: *Dār al-Islām* (Abode of Islam), which may be called *Pax Islamica,* comprising Islamic and non-Islamic communities that had accepted Islamic sovereignty, and the rest of mankind, called *Dār al-Ḥarb* (Abode of War). The first included the community of believers as well as those who entered into an alliance with Islam. The inhabitants of those territories were Muslims, forming the community of believers (the *umma*), and non-Muslims of the tolerated religious communities called the People of the Book or *dhimmī*s (Christians, Jews, and others known to have possessed scriptures), who preferred to hold fast to their own religion and law at the price of paying a poll tax *(jizya)* to Islamic authority. The Muslims enjoyed full rights of citizenship, whereas non-Muslims enjoyed restricted civil rights, but all possessed full status as subjects of the caliph or imam, the head of the state, in their claims to internal security and protection from foreign dangers. The imam, in the discharge of his responsibilities, spoke in the name of all subjects, Muslims and non-Muslims alike. The relations between Muslims and non-Muslims within the Islamic superstructure were regulated in accordance with special charters, originally issued by the imam, recognizing the canon law of each tolerated religious community bearing on matters of personal status.

The world surrounding the Islamic state was collectively called *Dār al-Ḥarb* because it remained beyond the pale of *Pax Islamica.* Muslim publicists, especially *Shāfiᶜī* jurists, devised a third temporary division of the world, called *Dār al-Ṣulḥ* (Abode of Truce) or *Dār al-ᶜAhd* (Abode of Covenant), giving qualified recognition to non-Islamic communities whenever they entered into peaceful arrangements with Islam on conditions agreed on between the two parties, including the payment of an annual tribute to Muslim authorities. The Hanafite school of law, however, did not recognize the third division, arguing that if the inhabitants of a territory conclude a peace treaty with Islam and pay a tribute, that territory becomes part of *Dār al-Islām* and its people are entitled to the protection of Muslim authorities.

In theory, *Dār al-Islām* was in a state of war with *Dār al-Ḥarb,* for the ultimate objective of Islam was the world. If *Dār al-Ḥarb* were reduced by Islam, the public order of *Pax Islamica* would supersede all others, and non-Muslim communities would either become part of the Islamic territory or submit to Islam's sovereignty as non-Islamic communities or autonomous entities within the Islamic superstructure. Even in this permanent state of war, however, relations between *Dār al-Ḥarb* and *Dār al-Islām* were regulated in accordance with the principles of Islamic law and the diplomatic practices recognized in the international relationships of the time. The Muslim was under obligation to respect the rights of non-Muslims, both combatants and civilians, whenever fighting was in progress. During the short intervals of peace, when hostilities were suspended, Islam took cognizance of the authority or authorities that existed in the countries with which it had to deal. But this cognizance did not constitute recognition in the modern sense of the term, as recognition would have implied Islam's acceptance of non-Muslim sovereignties as equal states. Cognizance of non-Islamic sovereignties merely meant that some form of authority was by nature necessary in other territories even though they professed a religion different from Islam, and that Islam had to maintain hostile or peaceful relations with these authorities.

The state of war existing between *Dār al-Islām* and *Dār al-Ḥarb* did not necessarily involve actual warfare. Whenever fighting came to an end, the state of war was construed to mean what is called today a state of nonrecognition. But nonrecognition did not mean that no diplomatic relations existed; on the contrary, Muslims and non-Muslims crossed frontiers with relative ease by safe-conduct *(amān)* on the unofficial level and by diplomacy on the official level.

The state of war that existed in theory between *Dār al-Islām* and *Dār al-Ḥarb* was envisaged to come to an end when the latter was absorbed by the former. At such a stage *Dār al-Islām*, the *Pax Islamica,* would provide peace for the world. In theory, therefore, the ultimate objective of Islam was the achievement of permanent peace rather than permanent war. Thus the jihad, a temporary device designed to realize Islam's ideal social order, would come to an end when *Dār al-Ḥarb* had become part of *Dār al-Islām.* In practice, however, *Dār al-Islām* and *Dār al-Ḥarb* proved more permanent than was expected, and the Muslims became more accustomed to a state of dormant jihad than a state of open hostility. Contacts between the two areas, on official and unofficial levels, were conducted by peaceful means, the most important being the granting of safe-conduct *(amān)*, the signing of peace treaties, and the exchange of emissaries.

The *amān* was a pledge of security that entitled non-Muslims who entered Islamic lands to protection by Muslim authorities during their visit. It could be granted by the authorities or by individual Muslims. The first type, called the official *amān,* was granted by the imam (or his representative) to a few persons or to the entire population of a territory or a city whose ruler had signed an agreement or a peace treaty with Muslim authorities. The other type, the unofficial *amān,* could be given on request by any adult. The procedure was very simple: once the non-Muslim's request to enter an Islamic land was known, a word or a sign of approval was enough to constitute the granting of it.

If the non-Muslim entered *Dār al-Islām* without *amān,* or was unable to obtain one, he would be liable to punishment. Some publicists (in accordance with the *Shāfiᶜī* school of law) were in favor of giving him a period of four months, at the end of which he had either to leave (conducted safely to the frontiers), to pay a poll tax and acquire the status of a member of the tolerated religious communities (Christians, Jews, and others), or to become a Muslim. Others held that he should be expelled, provided he was given protection until he reached the frontier of *Dār al-Ḥarb.* If the non-Muslim claimed that he was on a mission carrying a message to the imam, he was permitted to proceed without *amān,* but if the imam found that the messenger lacked letters of credence or that he had no message to deliver, he was liable to be killed. If the non-Muslim entered *Dār al-Islām* by mistake or as a result of shipwreck and found himself among Muslims without *amān,* the Muslim authorities would act on the merit of the case—either to set him free, to release him by ransom, or to order his execution.

Once the non-Muslim was admitted to *Dār al-Islām* with an *amān,* he could bring his family with him, visit any city except the holy cities of Mecca and Medina, and reside permanently if he became a *dhimmī* or adopted Islam. While in residence in *Dār al-Islām,* he was allowed to carry on his business in accordance with Islamic law and practice, but he was not permitted to engage in the purchase of weapons or carry back with him instruments useful in war. During this visit the non-Muslim was expected to respect the religious beliefs and practices of Islam, and his activities could in no way hurt or endanger Islam's interests. If he turned out to be a spy, he would be liable to be executed. If the non-Muslim failed to observe the law or committed a crime, his *amān* remained valid, but he would be liable for punishment in accordance with Islamic law.

The *amān* was normally considered terminated when its period (not exceeding a year) expired or when the non-Muslim left *Dār al-Islām.* If he wanted to return, he had to obtain another *amān.* The *amān* might be canceled and the non-Muslim expelled if his activities proved harmful to Islam. The imam might even punish the Muslim who had granted him the *amān.* If the non-Muslim, after his return to *Dār al-Ḥarb,* suddenly died, any property he had left in *Dār al-Islām* could not be recovered by his heirs and was liable to confiscation by the state. But if he died while in *Dār al-Islām,* the *amān* granted him would be still valid for his property and his heirs, who could therefore take it out of *Dār al-Islām.*

The *amān* served the useful purpose of permitting Muslims and non-Muslims to cross frontiers and travel in one another's territory on the basis of reciprocity. The imam would not grant the *amān* to non-Muslims whose authorities denied permits to Muslims desiring to enter *Dār al-Ḥarb.* Thus the *amān* was like a modern passport. Without it, travel abroad and exchange of goods between *Dār al-Islām* and *Dār al-Ḥarb* would have been impossible, since the normal relation between Islam and other states was considered to be a state of war.

In the same way that the non-Muslims entered Muslim lands by *amān,* the conditions of which required certain limitations on their freedom and conduct, so the Muslims often entered non-Muslim lands with similar limitations in mind even if they were not specifically stated. It was taken for granted that the Muslim who entered *Dār al-Ḥarb* was obliged to abstain from doing any harm or injury to non-Muslims as long as he enjoyed the benefits of an *amān.* Moreover, he had to observe the rules of his own law and morality in such matters as prayer, the practice of usury, or the sale of wine or pork, because Islamic law was binding on the Muslim regardless of the country in which he resided. He was also under obligation to fulfill his promises and all other arrangements even after he had returned to *Dār al-Islām.* For instance, if he borrowed or stole property, it had to be returned before or after he left *Dār al-Ḥarb.* The Muslim would be liable for punishment after he returned to *Dār al-Islām* if he had violated the rights of another Muslim or committed a crime against him.

If a Muslim entered *Dār al-Ḥarb* without *amān,* he was under no obligation to observe the laws of that territory. True, he would be in a country in a state of war with Islam; but he would not be expected to engage in hostile actions unless he was ordered by the imam to do so. If he was captured, he would be treated as a prisoner of war. In accordance with Islamic law, he was liable to be executed or to be set free for ransom, provided the Muslim authorities were prepared to fulfill an agreement for setting him free.

The practice of diplomacy as a means of intercourse among nations dates from antiquity, and it has been used for both hostile and peaceful purposes. Its adoption by Islam to conduct relations between *Dār al-Islām* and *Dār al-Ḥarb* was not necessarily for pacific ends until the jihad became dormant and Islam agreed to maintain peaceful liaisons with other nations.

In early Islam, diplomacy was used as an auxiliary or a substitute for war. It served either as a herald to deliver the message of Islam before fighting began or as a means to exchange prisoners of war after the termination of fighting. To be sure, certain peaceful purposes, such as negotiation of truces or peace agreements, were achieved; but it was not until the Abbasid period (750–1258), when relations between Islamic and Christian states reached an equilibrium, that meaningful diplomatic negotiations were resorted to.

Diplomacy was understood in the broad sense of statecraft, not as an instrument to maintain long-term relationships; it was used to achieve certain immediate peaceful objectives. The right of legation was therefore designed to secure temporary and not permanent representation of the head of state in the court of foreign monarchs. The emissaries, once they had delivered their messages, returned to their chiefs to report success or failure. Though often received with ceremonies and lavish entertainments, the emissaries were almost always regarded as official spies. True, they were taken to visit the court and other public institutions, and they talked with whomever they met; they were, however, carefully watched and denied access to valuable sources of information or contact with civilians.

Muslim emissaries (called *rasūl*s or *safīr*s), representing caliphs or sultans as heads of state, were normally chosen from among confidants known for their knowledge, adroitness, and reliability. But they also were often chosen for their physical appearance, courage, charm, and presence of mind when such qualities might be needed in delicate negotiations. They were instructed to refrain from drinking in accordance with Islamic law, even though it might be permitted in foreign lands, and to keep away from women—two possible means to compromise secrecy. Not infrequently the imams, unable to find a single person with the necessary qualifications, sent two or three emissaries, one of them a man of the sword, another a man of learning, and the third a scribe who acted as a secretary. The emissaries were supplied with official letters of credence and messages indicating that the secret information was to be delivered orally by the chief emissary.

Foreign emissaries entered *Dār al-Islām* without *amān,* for from the moment they declared themselves to be on a mission, they were clothed with immunity and allowed to proceed to the capital, accompanied by an official who acted as a guide. The right to enter *Dār al-Islām* without *amān* was in accordance with an ancient custom that entitled emissaries to security during their temporary mission, provided they abstained from such prohibited acts as spying and acquiring war material. Although such immunity was not always strictly observed, in particular at times of ill feeling between heads of state, both Muslim and non-Muslim rulers found it mutually advantageous to observe on the grounds of reciprocity.

From early Islam, emissaries were sent abroad for either religious or political purposes. According to Muslim chronicles, the Prophet sent emissaries to Byzantium, Egypt, Persia, and Ethiopia, inviting these nations to accept Islam. The emperor of Ethiopia and the *muqawqis* (governor) of Egypt, according to Muslim traditions, accepted the invitation; the Byzantine emperor replied that his people were not of the opinion of adopting Islam; and the king of Persia tore up the letter and dismissed the emissaries. When the Prophet learned about the action of the Persian king, he is said to have remarked: "His kingdom will be torn." The character of such missions was essentially religious.

Under the early caliphs, especially during the Umayyad period (661–750), negotiations were often conducted with the Byzantine Empire, mainly for the purpose of signing peace treaties. During civil wars, especially under Muᶜāwiya (*d.* 680) and ᶜAbd al-Malik ibn Marwān (*d.* 705), peace treaties were negotiated and annual tributes were paid in order to avoid Byzantine attacks, but when the caliphs felt strong enough, they refused to pay the tribute.

The Abbasid caliphs, who came to power in the middle of the eighth century, inherited the legacy of the Umayyads in dealing with their Byzantine neighbors. The almost annual campaigns at the Byzantine borders required the negotiation of treaties for the exchange of prisoners of war and the payment of ransom. Emissaries were also frequently sent to non-Muslim rulers for various political, economic, or social purposes.

Foreign emissaries were met by representatives of the imam and received with pomp. They entered the capital in a procession, marching through streets lined with soldiers and decorations; they resided as guests in houses reserved for such occasions and were lavishly entertained. Most chroniclers give detailed descriptions of the visits of Byzantine emissaries to Baghdad. Perhaps the most profusely described

is the Byzantine delegation to Caliph al-Muqtadir in 918, which was lavishly treated to the splendors of the capital of Islam. While engaged in the fulfillment of their missions, the emissaries were entertained and given presents and robes as symbols of hospitality and examples of the excellent crafts of Baghdad. Gifts were exchanged by both sides as part of the diplomatic ceremonies. When the emissaries had accomplished their mission, they requested leave, and they were often accorded ceremonies similar to those at their reception. If the mission proved to be a failure, the emissaries were dismissed with obvious coolness; and if hostilities broke out while the emissaries were still in Islamic lands, they were often slighted, imprisoned, or even killed.

One of the most intriguing tales known in medieval diplomacy was the exchange of missions between Charlemagne and Hārūn al-Rashīd—concerning which the Muslim chronicles are completely silent, at least in the form reported in the Latin chronicles. (F. W. Buckler maintains that this diplomatic intercourse resulted in a "transaction of the nature of a transfer to Charles of some form of authority over Jerusalem," and Louis Bréhier states that Charlemagne attained a protectorate over Palestine, but there is little evidence to substantiate these views.) According to Latin sources, diplomatic relations between the Frankish and Abbasid rulers were initiated in 765 by Pepin, who sent the first of a series of missions to al-Manṣūr, the second Abbasid caliph, then at war with the Byzantine emperor. After three years the mission returned, accompanied by an emissary from the caliph and gifts. Pepin seems to have received the Muslim emissaries honorably, and subsequently permitted them to return.

Charlemagne, son of Pepin, dispatched several missions. Two were sent to the court of Hārūn al-Rashīd (in 797 and 802) and one to the patriarch of Jerusalem (799). In 797 two Franks and a Jewish interpreter were sent; the Franks died in the East, and the interpreter returned with an elephant after two years. In 802 Charlemagne sent a second mission to Baghdad. It is alleged that this mission attained "what was requested to be done" and that Charlemagne was granted the "sacred and salutory place he assigned to his power." But no evidence exists to indicate the nature of that power. In 799 the patriarch of Jerusalem sent a mission to Charlemagne, and the latter sent a return mission with alms and offerings. In 800 another mission was sent by the patriarch, carrying to Charlemagne, by way of a blessing, the keys of the Holy Sepulcher and of the place of Calvary, together with a banner.

If the reports of the Latin sources are to be accepted, the purpose of these diplomatic missions could hardly have gone beyond the desire to establish friendly relations between the two great monarchs. Hārūn al-Rashīd and Charlemagne, then the greatest rulers in Islam and Christendom, might have wanted an understanding vis-à-vis their enemies in Córdoba and Constantinople. But it is unlikely that Hārūn, at the height of Muslim power, surrendered control over Palestine to Charlemagne, for when the Crusaders attempted to take the Holy Land, at a time when Muslim power had declined, they were obstinately resisted.

As to the correspondence of the patriarch with Charlemagne, its purpose must have been purely religious rather than political. Having heard of the friendly relations between Hārūn and Charlemagne, the patriarch perhaps sought to take advantage of this opportunity to enhance his spiritual position by establishing relations with a great Christian monarch. The keys and the banner were symbolic gifts of friendship and could not be regarded as a surrender of political privileges beyond his power to transfer to a foreign ruler.

Like the *amān,* which made possible the movement of persons across frontiers, diplomacy served as a means to establish official relations between Muslim and non-Muslim rulers, even though they had been in a state of war with each other. Moreover, the prosecution and suspension of the jihad, which required an invitation before fighting should begin and negotiation preceding the signing of a truce or peace treaty, could not be carried out without diplomatic channels. Before negotiation for peace, emissaries were often sent to discuss the terms of a peace treaty. Thus, diplomacy, as an auxiliary to the jihad, was regarded as an integral part of the law of war.

At a time when means of communication were still primitive, the exchange of missions was necessary to facilitate commercial and cultural contacts. Emissaries, in addition to functioning as diplomats, were often commissioned to obtain books and manuscripts from countries known to have a rich cultural heritage. Caliph al-Maʾmūn (*d.* 813), renowned for his encouragement of learning, sent missions to Byzantium to translate the classics into Arabic. Emissaries carried back with them information and rarities from such distant places as central and eastern Asia, specimens of culture and art from foreign lands. Above all, since there were no permanent missions, emissaries tried to keep Muslim rulers informed about foreign countries, to alert them to possible threats or dangers, and to seek foreign support against their enemies.

BIBLIOGRAPHY

Sources. Abū ᶜAlī al-Ḥusayn ibn al-Farra, *Kitāb rusul al-mulūk,* Ṣalāḥ al-Dīn al-Munajjid, ed. (1947); Shams al-Dīn al-Sarakhsī, *Sharḥ al-Siyar al-Kabīr of Shaybānī,* Ṣalāḥ al-Dīn al-Munajjid, ed. (1957); Muḥammad ibn Idrīs al-Shāfiᶜī, *Kitāb al-umm,* VII (1907); Muḥammad ibn al-Ḥasan al-Shaybānī, "Abwāb al-Siyar," in Majid Khadduri, trans., *The Islamic Law of Nations* (1966); Muḥammad ibn Jarīr al-Ṭabarī, *Kitāb al-jihād wa al-jizya wa ahkam al-muḥāribīn,* Joseph Schacht, ed. (1933).

Studies. Ibrāhīm al-ᶜAwaḍī, *al-Safaret al-Islamīya ila awruba* (1957); Najib Armanazi, *L'Islam et le droit international* (1929); Louis Bréhier, "Charlemagne et la Palestine," in *Revue historique,* 157 (1928); F. W. Buckler, *Harunu'l-Rashid and Charles the Great* (1931); Muhammad Hamidullah, *Documents sur la diplomatie musulmane à l'époque du prophète et des khalifes orthodoxes* (1935), and *Muslim Conduct of State,* 5th ed. (1968); Majid Khadduri, *al-ᶜAlāqāt al-diplomatiqīya bayn Hārūn al-Rashīd and Charlemagne* (1939), *War and Peace in the Law of Islam* (1955), and "The Islamic Theory of International Relations and Its Contemporary Relevance," in Jesse H. Proctor, ed., *Islam and International Relations* (1965, repr. 1981), 24–39.

MAJID KHADDURI

[See also **Abode of Islam—Abode of War; Charlemagne; Hārūn al-Rashid; Islamic Administration; Jihad.**]

DIPLOMACY, WESTERN EUROPEAN. In the early Middle Ages, when diplomacy was a much more occasional activity than it later became, summit meetings of heads of states or of peoples loomed very large. Kings or other rulers met, often at a neutral site—for example, at the middle of a bridge over a stream dividing their territories—to settle their differences. Still, even then, not all communications between rulers could be handled personally.

THE NUNCIUS

Since the dim and distant past when war and diplomacy were born twins and primitive societies communicated with one another by means of messengers, these envoys have been invested with diverse names and different ceremonial trappings. Their basic function, however, has remained the same.

In the Merovingian age *legatus* was a commonly used title, but by the thirteenth century the word *nuncius* (nuncio, classical Latin: *nuntius*) had taken prominence among the terms given to message bearers, although the titles *missus* and *message* are also found in the documents. The variety of terminology has no real significance, however, for all were message bearers. Venetian senatorial decrees demonstrate the broad scope of the title *nuncius,* which is used to refer to all diplomatic envoys. In fact, the definition of *nuncius* given by Guillaume Durand in the thirteenth century specified that it was a broad term meaning simply someone sent from another, and medieval legists and canonists agreed that the legal effect was equivalent to sending a letter. Like a magpie, according to Azo, the *nuncius* recited the words of his principal.

Why, then, should a *nuncius* be sent instead of a written message borne by any traveler? The Venetian Great Council, appointing an envoy to Genoa in 1306, pointed out the advantages of this "living letter," whose attitude, intonation and wording of the message, and response to questions represented a much more flexible means of communication. Added security was also important.

The freedom of the *nuncius,* however, was very limited. He could not declare anything on his own initiative and possessed no will of his own, but was simply a means of transmission of the will of another. He could be employed to make treaties, truces, marriage alliances, and other pacts, but in entering into a covenant he was no more flexible an instrument than a letter, being able to conclude an act only on terms already specifically accepted by his principal.

A *nuncius* did not exist as a distinct legal person, because he fully represented the person of his principal. This totality of representation distinguishes the *nuncius* from the procurator. It was as if the principal were speaking through him. It followed from this representation that all honors due to the principal should be paid to the *nuncius,* and that one who harmed a *nuncius* was considered to have harmed his principal.

Much nonsense has been written about the *droit d'ambassade,* the right of sending and receiving diplomatic agents, and it is often claimed that this privilege belonged only to the sovereign, who alone could make war and treat for peace. The concept of sovereignty, however, is not very useful in dealing with medieval diplomacy. In the Middle Ages all sorts of principals sent diplomatic agents, as needed, to all sorts of recipients.

Between 1066 and 1453 English and French envoys were frequently exchanged on affairs that touched the English ruler, not as king of England or sovereign, but as vassal of the king of France. By the mid fifteenth century in Italy, considerable numbers of *nuncii* were sent and received by condottieri, many of whom had no status in public law but freely exercised rights of war and diplomacy. Such instances demonstrate the pragmatic way in which envoys were sent and received in an age when public and private status were hopelessly confused.

The functions that *nuncii* actually performed were, if anything, more varied than the persons who sent and received them. Although the raison d'être of the *nuncius* was to provide a channel of communication between principals, an important and delicate function also entrusted to him was the exploration of possible treaties, alliances, or *condotte.* The *nuncius,* it is true, could not negotiate and conclude without reference to the principal, but it was possible to do both with the latter's specific consent to be bound. Letters empowering a *nuncius ad tractandum* did not constitute full powers, however, and did not authorize him to conclude on the basis of his negotiations. Any agreements had to be referred to the principal for approval before the conventions could be concluded by *nuncii.* If authorized to do so in a sufficiently specific manner, however, a *nuncius* could carry out the most solemn acts, having power to swear on behalf of his principal, for example, and to receive the oaths of others.

Exchange of money was another of the relatively routine tasks of a *nuncius* which, though it required trustworthiness (since large sums might be involved), demanded little exercise of discretion by the envoy. Propagandizing, fomenting revolts, and attempting to break unfriendly alliances could also be among the functions of *nuncii.* In the formation of the League of Friuli (1384), Venice sent *nuncii* to Friuli, towns dependent on that city, and the church of Aquileia, urging them to resist foreign encroachment. A state that felt itself injured might employ *nuncii* to convey a protest, an ultimatum, or even a declaration of war. From the beginning of the Middle Ages *nuncii* were often sent in time of war to an ally in order to coordinate efforts against the enemy.

A considerable number of envoys were sent by medieval rulers in the interests of private persons—

usually but not always merchants. They might be instructed to claim and receive amends for robberies, attacks at sea, and other injuries inflicted on private citizens (though this was frequently also in the public interest, forestalling a general disruption of trade). The Venetian government sent a great many envoys on such missions to defend merchants whose goods had been seized by legal process or otherwise, or who had been required to pay customs or taxes not regarded as customary. Other kinds of citizens, too, often required assistance. In 1295 the king of Serbia dispatched a *nuncius* to Venice to claim a *villanus* of a certain Serbian knight who had fallen into Venetian hands.

The functions of the *nuncius* were as broad as the uses of letters, though as a "living letter" he was a somewhat more flexible instrument. A *nuncius* was allowed only a limited discretion, however, and when he overstepped his authority the consequences could be serious. Lack of restraint could be as minor as the indiscretion of a papal *tabellarius,* bringing a letter concerning the negotiation of a treaty from the pope to Venice, who revealed publicly that he was bearing "good news." This and other rumors brought inquiries from the Milanese and Florentine ambassadors and forced the Senate into a premature publication of the treaty. At the other extreme, a Venetian *nuncius* made a treaty with Aragon for which he had no mandate. The acts of a *nuncius* in excess of his authority could of course be repudiated, but the repudiation of an envoy was an embarrassing and unpleasant measure.

The character and functions of the *nuncius* did not alter significantly over the centuries. The envoys described by François Ganshof for the Merovingian Age do not differ from the *nuncii* of the late fifteenth century. In the High and late Middle Ages, however, a radically different diplomatic representation was introduced with the Roman law *procurator,* and titles such as "ambassador" and "orator" were given to many *nuncii,* especially those of high rank. Whether under the more modern titles of ambassador and orator, or bearing the more modest designation, the *nuncius* remained a vital alternative in diplomacy throughout the Middle Ages.

THE PROCURATOR OR PLENIPOTENTIARY

The limited flexibility of the *nuncius* became more of a handicap as the power, wealth, and governmental efficiency of some states increased, diplomatic activity became more frequent and less personal, and diplomacy was conducted with more

distant powers. New devices had to be found for carrying on affairs of state.

Through the Roman influence on canon law a new instrumentality became available for diplomatic use in the form of procuration. In an age of poor communications it provided a convenient though risky solution, for a properly empowered procurator could both negotiate and conclude. An expeditious conclusion to negotiations no longer had to be hindered by an interminable succession of messages sent back and forth between principals, who were separated not only by distance but also by primitive means of communication.

Procurators were employed for other than diplomatic purposes from about the mid eleventh century. In the 1060's and 1070's evidence appears of procurations with full powers in the hands of papal *legati, missi,* and *apocrisarii,* though these do not seem to have received diplomatic missions. If procurators could enter into private contracts for their principals, they could also enter into public conventions, and so in 1167 the bishop of Novara concluded an alliance with the Milanese through his procurator. In 1175 the protocol of the Peace of Constance summarized Frederick Barbarossa's letters, typical of subsequent procurations, granting to his so-called *nuncii* (actually procurators) full powers (*plena potestas*) to treat for and to conclude a peace. The emperor promised to hold firm to whatever they swore and to incorporate it in letters sealed with his seal.

Although the evidence is scanty, and in many cases full powers seem tacked onto the letters of credence of the primitive *nuncius, plena potestas* became well known before the end of the twelfth century. Geoffroi de Villehardouin and his colleagues, who were given free rein to negotiate on behalf of the chiefs of the Fourth Crusade in 1201, stand in marked contrast to *nuncii* with their sharply limited discretionary powers.

The nature of the procurator is most easily made clear to American readers by substituting the word "attorney," understood in its broadest significance and not as coterminous with "lawyer." Indeed, a number of diplomatic documents use "procurator" and "attorney" as synonyms. The interchangeability of the two words is further emphasized by the fact that, as in Anglo-American law there are attorneys-at-law and attorneys-in-fact, in Roman law and canon law there are procurators *litis* (mainly for legal representation before a court) and procurators *negotiorum* (for the transaction of business in general).

What was done by a procurator had exactly the status in law as if it had been done by the principal. The crusader-envoys of 1201, sent merely to contract for transportation for the crusading army, had sufficiently broad powers to accept Enrico Dandolo's offer of active Venetian participation in the Fourth Crusade in return for a share of the conquests. They concluded a treaty on this basis, sent it to Rome for confirmation, and borrowed money to carry it out. The principals had no knowledge of what their envoys were doing until their return, nor did they expect any—an early and spectacular example of the conclusive nature of *plena potestas.*

The extreme freedom of the procurator in the thirteenth century was, however, restricted in practice in the fourteenth and fifteenth centuries as diplomatic activity intensified and resident representatives became separated by miles and months from the minds of their principals. Full powers continued to be granted, but the discretion allowed to the envoy was usually more limited.

It is difficult to define the representative character of the procurator because the concept of representation itself is often unclear and the evidence is not entirely consistent. Some authorities describe the procurator as representative and others deny him that description. Since the procurator acted not by the will of another but by his own in the name of the principal, his representative role differed from that of the *nuncius,* who represented the person of the principal and expressed only the principal's will. Clearly the *nuncius* was a more absolute and personal representative, suitable where the immediate and direct role of the principal was to be emphasized, as on ceremonial occasions. The procurator was a more free and flexible representative, more useful in negotiations.

Since anything that a man could do himself could be done by a properly empowered procurator, the diplomatic uses of procuration were legion. Besides the delivery and receipt of official documents—a legally binding act—procurators could pay or collect debts for their principals, though they were usually more concerned with collecting than with paying.

Preeminently, procurators were appointed to negotiate agreements, because for many other tasks *nuncii* were more appropriate. Venice often gave considerable freedom of action to its procurators. Hearing that ten or twelve Catalan galleys might be available under the command of the brother of the king of Aragon, and fearing that the enemies of the republic might obtain them, Venice sent full powers to its envoy to negotiate for them. In the Senate's instructions to him, however, he was authorized to spend only a certain amount, and less if he could— a fairly typical instruction in matters of this sort.

Since procurators could conclude truces and treaties, they could also be authorized to make one or the other at their discretion and as circumstances dictated. Frequently, too, plenipotentiaries were sent "fishing" for allies, so that even the parties with whom they were to deal were not specified. In answer to an inquiry by the count of Hülcrath, Edward I replied that he had no knowledge of the conventions allegedly made by his procurators but would inform the count when he learned.

The most solemn acts, such as contracting and completing—everything, in fact, short of consummating—a marriage alliance, could be done by procurators, who could, moreover, carry out the marriage ceremony *per verba de presenti,* actually standing in for the bride or the groom. Frederick II's famous counselor, Peter della Vigna, fulfilled this role for him in the emperor's marriage in 1235 to Isabella of England, exchanging consent and rings with the bride. In the marriage by proxy of Bona of Savoy to Galeazzo Maria Sforza, the procurator, Tristano Sforza, actually entered the marriage bed and touched her thigh.

Homage was occasionally performed or received by the use of procurators, though it was generally recognized that this constituted an infraction of the highly personal character of the feudal relationship. Royalty, becoming increasingly conscious of its exalted position as the Middle Ages progressed, grew understandably reluctant to bend the knee in homage before a lord, though it was not at all squeamish toward the benefit of vassalage. Procuration could allow a monarch to accept those benefits without personally performing an act of subordination. Richard II made it clear in his instructions to an embassy to France that he was prepared to perform simple homage for Guienne, though he would not perform it personally and would not appear at the court of France except through a procurator.

Freedom to do, and to pay, whatever seemed appropriate was quite common in medieval procurations. Remarkable discretionary powers were allowed to the crusader-envoys of 1201. They received full powers to treat for transportation "in whatever seaport, wherever they should go," and it was the envoys themselves who made all the decisions concerning the treaty. Nevertheless, the procurator was obligated to remain within the limitations of his mandate, whether broad or narrow. Acts of procurators in excess of their instructions (which, unlike mandates, were not legally binding instruments) were rarely repudiated by principals, who were aware that their envoys labored under serious handicaps in attempting to negotiate far from home. It was clear, however, that procurators could not bind their principals beyond the terms of their mandates.

Much confusion has surrounded the distinction between *nuncius* and procurator. Many authors are not clear as to what the differences were or why both terms were often used of the same envoys, while others tend to denigrate both offices. Even Garrett Mattingly, who is so seldom wrong, sees their decline and the rise of a distinct ambassadorial office before that sequence of events actually occurred. It is true that in medieval diplomatic documents the terms *nuncius* and procurator were used without discrimination, although the legal distinction—that a *nuncius* spoke in the person of his principal, whereas the procurator spoke in his own person—was quite clear. The words may have been used confusedly, but as Hostiensis said, as long as the intention of the principal is clear, it does not matter whether the envoy is called "ass."

THE AMBASSADOR

The word "ambassador" is derived from *ambactiare,* "to go on a mission," and the fundamental meaning of "ambassador" until the end of the Middle Ages was precisely "one sent on a mission." He was not necessarily endowed with specific legal powers or status, and his mission was not invariably diplomatic. As Maulde la Clavière pointed out, "the names of ambassador, orator, messenger were applied to every person charged with a temporary mission of a public character having in view a peaceful settlement. . . ." It has been the fault of some writers to make these loose terms and shadowy institutions more precise than the facts allow.

It is generally agreed that the usage of "ambassador" in diplomacy stems from thirteenth-century Italy, and documents dating from 1198 to 1240 show much evidence of this. The close relation of "ambassador" to the term *legatus* led Bernard du Rosier to declare that they differed only in name, for the office was the same. Since "ambassador" and "orator" (a term deemed more elegant) were equivalent to "legate," they were also frequently used synonymously with *nuncius.* A letter of Edward II to James II of Aragon refers first to *nuncii* that the latter was sending to England and later calls them ambassadors.

Two Venetian documents of the fifteenth century refer to the same envoy as "orator" and later as *nuncius.* Sometimes all these titles and others were strung together. English ambassadors to France in 1488, for example, were referred to as *ambassiatoribus, oratoribus, nunciis, legatis, et commissariis* and also received the full powers of a procurator.

By the mid fourteenth century a social distinction between *ambaxator* and *nuncius* had been introduced in Venice, the former title generally reserved for Venetian patricians, whereas governmental notaries or secretaries, who received many diplomatic missions, were called simply *notarius, secretarius,* or *nuncius.* Thus *ambaxator,* not *nuncius,* was the word that took on special meaning in Venice. *Nuncius* remained the generic term for an envoy.

The modern notion that only a sovereign state can be represented by an ambassador was as inchoate in the Middle Ages as the concept of sovereignty itself. Bernard du Rosier, a fifteenth-century authority in the diplomatic field, limited the custom of sending ambassadors to "the greater princes of the age by birth, the commune of any city, and the three estates of a country or kingdom." Garrett Mattingly more cautiously maintained that the usage of "ambassador" was increasingly restricted to the major diplomatic agents of the major diplomatic powers. Although a number of early fifteenth-century documents seem to specify royal emissaries as ambassadors and nonroyal emissaries as something else, a large amount of evidence indicates that this development was extremely rudimentary and that it did not constantly prevail anywhere before the sixteenth century. Ambassadors were sent and received by the very widest variety of persons and corporate bodies, for all sorts of important and trivial affairs.

Cities and other corporate identities subject to another power frequently employed ambassadors. Treviso, which had submitted to Venetian dominion in 1339, sent its own ambassador to the duke of Austria in 1350. In 1301 the monks of St. Edmund's Abbey sent ambassadors to the king to obtain his permission for the election of a new abbot, certainly not an affair of great international significance. Orators from a Dominican convent in Venice appeared before the Council of Ten to discuss strictly domestic matters, and even private citizens exchanged ambassadors.

The German emperor had many dealings with ambassadors of those who were actually his subjects. Some were sent to him by cities within the empire for the confirmation of their privileges. Venice, too, received a large number of orators from dependent cities, requesting a new *podestà* or rector and dealing with minor administrative concerns. In the early fifteenth century Venice refused to accept ambassadors from Zara until the latter had unconditionally submitted. So many ambassadors of subject cities were received, in fact, that the Senate and Council of Ten were forced to limit their number, their salaries, and the frequency of their visits in the interest of the public purses of the subjects.

Just as ambassadors could be sent from nonsovereign bodies, so they were dispached to a wide variety of recipients. In the late thirteenth century a Venetian ambassador negotiating for the security of the roads, in the interest of commerce, was received by various nonsovereign persons as well as the king of Germany. The rise of the condottieri introduced another important factor into the already confused scheme of medieval diplomacy. During Francesco Sforza's career as mercenary chieftain there was perhaps as much diplomatic activity directed toward him as toward any head of state.

The sending of ambassadors to vassals and subjects was not at all uncommon. The German kings sent ambassadors to their subordinates in order to invest them with their rights and receive fealty from them, and the Venetians had an interesting habit of dispatching ambassadors to their newly elected doge if that dignitary happened to be outside the city at the time.

The question that has dominated historical discussion of diplomacy during these centuries of transition to the modern state is the rise of the resident ambassador. The appearance of the resident marks the beginning of the "new diplomacy" of the Renaissance. Identification of the first of this new breed hinges, of course, on what is meant by "resident ambassador." Mattingly, rejecting resident procurators and other candidates as not being diplomats, saw the significant departure in the development of the resident ambassador in his assignment to remain at his diplomatic post, in general charge of the interests of his principal, until recalled. Paolo Selmi further refined the notion by insisting on the concept of an office that continued to exist even if there were no incumbent, such a vacancy creating the necessity for naming a successor.

Some Italian scholars, including Selmi, have claimed to find the origin of the resident ambassador in the Venetian consuls. There is abundant evidence that such resident consuls did engage in diplomatic activity. One man might even be appointed both ambassador and consul. The two offices, however, were distinct. Much evidence leads me to conclude that the consul was an official whose main functions of jurisdiction over his fellow countrymen and representation of their commercial interests before the government of the land in which they dwelt were quite distinct from the diplomatic functions of an ambassador.

In fact, the origin of the resident ambassador is not to be found in the resident procurator or the resident consul but, rather, in the increasing frequency and duration of ad hoc embassies. Diplomatic activity became so intense that it was discovered to be more practical and more economical to appoint an ambassador to remain at a much frequented court. In addition to cost and convenience, another factor that would make the resident embassy preferable was unobtrusiveness. A resident could much more easily carry out his tasks without attracting unwanted attention. Often out of touch with happenings at home and poorly informed by his own government, he was nevertheless wonderfully situated for gathering information from abroad. Since he rarely had the power to negotiate, a resident ambassador functioned chiefly to keep his government informed. Gradually the extended duration of service and a more generalized responsibility came to characterize the office of resident ambassador.

Strictly speaking, the terms *nuncius* and "ambassador" were used synonymously, but new nuances were making an appearance. Like the *nuncius,* the ambassador often served as a "living letter," but a considerable miscellany of public functions exceeding mere message bearing fell to his lot as well. It was also common for ambassadors to receive missions of a somewhat private nature. A fourteenth-century Mantuan ambassador had to make a list of the many little tasks to fulfill for friends—carrying letters, making visits, even buying a new saddle for the bishop's mule.

These functions were not new. It was essentially the gathering of information and the enhancement of ceremonial that acquired a new emphasis with the advent of the resident ambassador and the "new diplomacy." The ad hoc envoy previously had only rather limited opportunities for the systematic gathering of information. His attention was customarily focused on the negotiation or other assignment that was his specific mission.

For the resident ambassador the opportunities for gathering news were excellent, and thus the acquisition and transmission of information became his primary function. The Italian city-states took the lead. In Venice an ambassador who kept the Senate well informed was richly praised; indeed, the reputation of Venetian ambassadors as news gatherers was unsurpassed. Trafficking in news with other diplomats became an important function. By the end of the Middle Ages possession of information was vital to the reputation and success of an orator.

Ambassadors sometimes crossed the nebulous line between the legitimate gathering of information and espionage and other ill-reputed activities. Philippe de Comines declared that ambassadors should be heard and quickly licensed to depart, since it is not safe to keep enemies about; he himself had known much mischief and many intrigues brought about by ambassadors. Bernard du Rosier's admonition that ambassadors should not inquire into the secrets of states and the dispositions of kingdoms, "for this in no way belongs to the office of ambassador," must be regarded as bookish nonsense. The suspicion that an ambassador was a legalized spy was never far from men's minds.

As the danger of spying became more and more apparent, rulers proved less than eager to receive ambassadors. Attempts were made to isolate them and to limit their access to information. In thirteenth- and fourteenth-century England messengers were assigned to accompany foreign envoys, not only to offer respect and to reinforce the king's safe-conduct but also to monitor the envoys' movements and contacts. After 1451, Venetian nobles having a position in the government were forbidden to have any dealings with foreigners, especially ambassadors, touching affairs of state.

Ambassadors were expected to be able to report on such things as the condition of the routes, the locations of streams and bridges, the forces of the state to which they were sent or those through which they passed, and possible adverse alliances. The line between the legitimate gathering of information and espionage is difficult to draw, but diplomatic envoys often became involved in intrigues far from ambiguous. The Venetian secretary and the Milanese *commissarius* at Genoa in 1496, for example, served as intermediaries between their governments and an adventurer who offered to burn two of three French ships either in the port of Villefranche or at Nice.

Bribery also appears to have been a very common activity of ambassadors. Venetian representatives to Pope Martin V and to the king of the Romans were allowed to spend up to 10,000 ducats on those persons they thought most suitable. Ambassadors often complained of the high cost of doing business in Rome because of the necessity to offer great gifts.

Since ambassadors dealt with so much secret information, the revelation of which would be harmful to the state and could cost the lives of informers, precautions had to be taken to prevent ambassadorial records from falling into the wrong hands. Embassy staffs were often ordered to burn all their papers.

The second new emphasis was on the ceremonial function of envoys. The late Middle Ages was a period of "a thousand formalities," and it is not surprising that diplomatic envoys played a ceremonial role. Marriage ceremonies required the presence of ambassadors representing states friendly to those becoming allied through marriage, and a reluctance to send ambassadors or orators to grace a wedding would tend to indicate a coolness toward at least one of the parties. The death of a friendly prince or a member of his family was another of those climactic events surrounded with solemn pageantry and calling for an embassy to share the grief and offer condolences.

Ambassadors nevertheless continued to act as negotiators, but like the *nuncii* they did not necessarily possess the power to conclude. In the course of negotiations it might be demanded of an ambassador whether he had received such authority; the reply often was that he had not and must either go or send to his principal to inform him of the status of the proceedings. This represents a conscious effort on the part of the principal to maintain control over negotiations. Venetian ambassadors were instructed again and again to learn what the other party had to propose and then write to Venice and await instructions. This lack of power provided a valuable protection to the ambassador and was a convenient device for gaining time for consideration or simply for stalling.

Like a *nuncius*, an ambassador might also have received procuratorial powers. Although he was not per se a plenipotentiary, he could be both an ambassador and a plenipotentiary. The effect of full powers, of course, was to authorize the ambassador to conclude. This was quite commonly done in the case of missions to distant places, in consideration of the slowness of communication. An ambassador endowed with full powers could do anything that any other procurator could do.

A few ambassadors, however, were inclined to assume that the lesser powers included the greater, and thus, exceeding their mandates, they introduced a most disrupting factor into diplomacy. Venice had a great name for the efficiency of its administration of diplomacy and for the tight control exercised by the Senate over it, yet the republic had a great deal of trouble with overly ambitious ambassadors. A succession of such problems led the Senate in 1478 to complain of the most harmful customs that had grown up among ambassadors: presuming to undertake matters not committed to them and speaking and responding beyond what they received in their mandates. These abuses were so widespread that the Senate enacted a decree imposing penalties on ambassadors who should dare henceforth to exceed their mandates. Nevertheless, slow communications caused problems for ambassadors, and it was understandable that, insufficiently informed from home and under pressure to act, they tended to do whatever they thought best.

In spite of occasional examples of devious methods in diplomacy, it must be borne in mind that these instances represent aberrations from the norm. Most of the activities of the ambassador were routine, commendable, and appropriate for furthering the objectives of both parties. While Bernard du Rosier may have been overly sanguine concerning the virtues of ambassadors, Niccolò Machiavelli surely was overly cynical.

LETTERS AND REPORTS

The medieval "diplomatic pouch" contained a variety of papers. A letter of credence was accepted as the authorization of an ambassador, without which he should not be believed. The heart of this document was the clause of supplication requesting, as did the letters of Edward II in 1309, that the recipient hear the very voice of the king in the speech of the envoy, or, more frequently, simply that he give evidence to them. These letters, however, could do no more than commend the bearer as a faithful person to be trusted. They contained no authority to obligate the sender to any agreement.

The discovery that envoys could be sent without letters is surprising, albeit the occasion was rare. A reluctance to address letters of credence to a government that was not recognized was one reason for their omission. The count of Charolais was much insulted in 1466 when Louis XI sent him ambassadors with only an oral credence.

Letters of credence would not be essential, however, if the envoy was provided with a procuration or mandate allowing him to conclude a juristic act in the name of his principal. This legal authority to conclude in the name of another by an act of the rep-

resentative's will is called *plena potestas*. The words *plena potestas,* however, do not always appear: the power to conclude could also be conveyed through the grant of a specific power or by *ratihabitio,* a clause promising that whatever was said or done by the procurator would be held firm by the principal. Although a great variety of wording is found in procurations, legal and notarial manuals containing forms for such documents indicate that considerable care was usually taken in their composition. Indeed, procurations were examined for formal adequacy very carefully, for in diplomacy an unclear procuration could lead to endless controversy.

Letters of instruction were not necessary to the medieval diplomat, although they became increasingly common. In fact, not even verbal instructions were essential. In 1383 a Mantuan ambassador informed the council of the emperor "my Lord, when I inquired concerning the things to be done in this court, said to me: 'You are a wise man. I send you to handle my affairs. It is not necesary that I should tell you what is to be done.'" Whether this was merely a case of wily diplomacy is not clear, but it does establish the possibility of an uninstructed envoy.

Letters of instruction in no way obligated the principal and did not grant powers. Where negotiation was the object, instructions provided guidelines for obtaining the greatest possible concessions from the opposite party by means of the slightest possible concessions by the envoy. In general the envoy was instructed as to what he should do or say, and perhaps the manner in which he should do or say it. Instructions might be very specific (one *commissione* of 1480 occupies six pages in a folio register and contains thirty-one separate items) and might supply the exact words that the envoy had to use. On the other hand, considerable latitude might be left to the ambassador.

The diplomatic pouch also often contained, and sometimes bulged with, copies of documents providing evidence in support of the envoy's mission, including records of previous negotiations. Often it was felt necessary that an envoy should have a safe-conduct from the government to which he was accredited or from the countries through which he passed. Bernard du Rosier indicated that safe-conducts were sought when the principals were not on friendly terms and that such assurance should not be denied. By a statute of 1414 Henry V of England declared the violation of safe-conduct an act of high treason against the crown.

The most spectacular documents borne by diplomats were blanks sealed in advance by the principal and left to be filled out by the envoys. Papal legates to Frederick Barbarossa at Besançon in 1157 possessed "blank parchments with seals affixed that were still to be written on at their discretion." In 1253 Countess Margaret of Flanders dispatched to Thomas of Savoy, widower of her sister Countess Jeanne, and to Pope Innocent IV an embassy entrusted with sealed blanks. She later complained to the pope that they had been misused. Henry III gave the bishop of Hereford a document appointing a new royal procurator in Rome with a space left for the bishop to insert the procurator's name. Blanks were thus used in the thirteenth century with incredible freedom and power of discretion on the part of the diplomatic envoy, although in later centuries they were employed in a more limited and conservative manner.

Negotiations of any duration or complexity, especially after the thirteenth century, required correspondence from the ambassador informing his government of developments and new instructions sent from the government to him. Some of the communications directed to the ambassador were obviously not intended to be conveyed to the opposite party. A large part of the art of diplomacy lies in knowing what to reveal and what not to reveal.

Communications, however, had to flow in both directions. Governments repeatedly and strongly urged their ambassadors to write frequently, particularly in a time of crisis. How often an ambassador wrote to his government varied greatly. Venetians sometimes wrote every few days, and sometimes rather infrequently, whereas an English ambassador in 1418 was instructed to write at least once a week. Generally, it seems that ambassadors wrote only when they had something to report. The contents of dispatches were not restricted to a single subject; they ranged across any topics apt to be interesting or useful to the government, and much of the material was repeated in successive dispatches, presumably because of the danger of their not arriving. It was not uncommon to employ a cipher, although most of these would not have been hard to crack.

Written reports on missions became customary in Byzantine diplomacy, and by the late Middle Ages this custom was also common in the West. The Venetian *relazione* became a special kind of report: in its classical form it was not a chronicle of events but a comprehensive political tableau, depicting characters of princes and the strengths and weaknesses of states. The origin of this document goes back to December 1268, when a law of the Great Council required that miscellaneous matter pertaining to the profit and honor of Venice be added to the ambassador's report on the response to his mission. Thus it seems probable that the classical *relazioni* of the sixteenth century evolved from the traditional final report. This evolution was by no means complete by the end of the fifteenth century, for even after a further act of 1425, repeating the requirement that *relazioni* must be given in writing, ambassadors continued to ignore the duty. I previously believed that the verb *referir* had specific reference to a *relazione*, but it turns out that it is a very general word. Although there are extant written *relazioni* dated prior to 1533, they were customarily delivered orally through the thirteenth, fourteenth, and fifteenth centuries. The earliest surviving *relazione* is Zaccaria Contarini's of 1492. No great historical treasure of *relazioni* was destroyed by fires in the sixteenth century, as historians have believed, for such an archive did not exist.

PERSONNEL AND EXPENSES

The manner of selecting diplomatic envoys differed according to the type of government and from one century to another. The ambassadors of monarchies were normally named by the king. Among the Italian republics the process was much more complex. In Venice by the fifteenth century, the Senate usually conducted elections, although the Great Council, the Council of Ten, and sometimes even private citizens possessed some responsibility for electing ambassadors.

The sense of national identity was weak in the Middle Ages, and the feeling that a diplomat ought to be a subject of the state he represented came into being very slowly. Foreigners were frequently used, often having a responsibility to both parties equally. Count Florence of Holland, for example, seems to have represented both sides in negotiating a treaty between Edward I and Adolf of Nassau. Sometimes a mission was entrusted, for the sake of convenience and economy, to foreigners who were already present at the court of the recipient or on their way to it.

More important than the nationality of an envoy was his social status. Bernard du Rosier pointed out that one should not be assigned an embassy if he was not "suitable" (*dignus*) and personally acceptable to the recipient. An embassy of Henry VI to treat of a marriage alliance was headed by a cardinal, the duke of Burgundy, the archbishop of York, a bishop, two earls, and a mere lord. Venetian embassies were replete with the most illustrious names in Venice. Indeed, when a mission required an ambassador of high rank who, at the same time, had to have the complete trust of the principal, princely governments often solved their personnel problem by calling on a member of the ruling house.

The religious aura that surrounded medieval diplomacy called for participation of the clergy, which was an abundant source of educated diplomatic personnel. Envoys were also selected from the various ranks of the lay nobility. The greater nobles offered ceremonial value comparable with that of a bishop or a great abbot, and they were commonly found at the head of an embassy. Men of the middle class grew increasingly important in diplomacy during the period under consideration, usually in less prestigious though often important roles. These were men—such as legists, canonists, notaries, and secretaries—who were educated, trusted, and dependent on the state for their careers.

The sending of an ambassador of insufficient prestige could be construed as disrespectful to the power to which he was sent and, since a lesser man required a smaller retinue, degrading penny pinching on the part of the principal. Edward III and his council took affront at Chrles V's defiance sent by the hands of a kitchen varlet, for wars between great princes ought to be declared by prelates or barons or, at least, by knights. Of course, one could scarcely reject an embassy of defiance.

Trends changed with the rise of monarchy, bureaucracy, and the middle class, which encouraged a progressive tranfer of diplomatic activity from hereditary members of the ancient feudal court to new councillors freely elected by the ruler and to his professional administrators. Toward the end of the thirteenth century in Flanders, for example, the majority of missions were entrusted to professional civil servants. Medieval governments, however, did not evolve a professional and specialized foreign service, though certain men were repeatedly employed in missions arising out of affairs of which they had experience and knowledge. The same names—men such as Geoffroi de Villehardouin and Philippe de Comines—appear again and again in diplomatic affairs. Chancery clerks, because of their familiarity with affairs through the process of copying and enrolling documents, were well suited for diplomatic tasks, especially for secondary roles, and many of them became somewhat specialized in foreign affairs.

Although a few men of middling estate might achieve successful careers in the diplomatic service of lords or communes, there was considerable resistance to undertaking diplomatic missions because of the sacrifices in time and money and the hazards of travel. The Venetian archives are full of documents proving the great difficulty that the government had in trying to coerce patricians to serve the state at the sacrifice of their own interests. Legislation continually attempted to impose penalties and define acceptable exuses.

An appalling lapse of time often occurred between the decision to send an envoy and his departure, largely owing to the reluctance of medieval envoys to set forth on their journeys. Two Venetian ambassadors sent to the emperor complained that they had been captured, robbed, and kept in prison for more than twenty-two and a half months, hungry, thirsty, and subjected to many injuries. Besides, travel was slow. A mission from Flanders to Nuremberg in the late thirteenth century required fourteen days of travel each way. Since medieval courts were peripatetic, ambassadors could not count on finding the lord to whom they were sent at a given place and often had to spend time and effort seeking him out.

From the thirteenth to the fifteenth century, more of the Venetian laws dealing with ambassadors were concerned with expenses and expense accounts than any other matter. The Great Council had complained of the almost intolerable expenses of ambassadors, incurred because of their liberal consciences in spending the wealth of the commune. The other side to this problem, though, was that of the suffering ambassador upon whom the financial burden of the embassy largely rested. Sometimes an envoy was fortunate enough to receive payment for his expenses, at least in part, from the prince or state to which he had been sent. At other times ambassadors were received as guests. Philippe de Comines declared it only honorable that they should be feasted, their expenses paid, and presents given to them. Milanese hospitality to ambassadors was well known, while Venice sometimes furnished houses as well as expenses for visiting ambassadors. For envoys sent abroad, the Great Council had taken precautions at an early date to see that the doge and his councillors and the heads of the Forty fixed the number of servants and horses, the salary (if any), and other expenses that would be permitted. Another persistent problem was that of obtaining accurate and understandable accounts submitted promptly after the conclusion of a mission. An act of the Great Council in 1273 required ambassadors to keep day-by-day expense accounts with justification for each item. Medieval governments were often constrained to resort to loans for the financial needs of their embassies. The Venetians very commonly authorized their envoys to borrow money. Edward I and Edward II made use of the Luccan bankers and of the Bardi of Florence, among others, to support their ambassadors. In some cases, interested private parties, particularly merchants, were required to finance an embassy wholly or in part.

When all the provisions for meeting the cost of an embassy are taken into consideration, they were still usually inadequate. Ambassadors often had to absorb a considerable portion of their expenses, which they might or might not eventually recover, with profit, through the grant of a prebend, fief, or rent, or election to some remunerative office. An embassy to a distant country was regarded by a family of the Venetian patriciate as a great misfortune that many patricians sought frantically to escape.

IMMUNITIES AND CEREMONIES

Authors of treatises on ambassadors, such as Bernard du Rosier, justify the extraordinary security of ambassadors as a necessity for conducting diplomatic intercourse. This protection consisted in the inviolability of the ambassador, his retinue, and his goods. In general, diplomatic immunity was recognized and honored from an early time. These principles eventually gained incorporation in the *De jure belli ac pacis* of Hugo Grotius and thence in modern international law. The immunities of ambassadors, however, represent not merely the lucubrations of lawyers but the practice of princes and communes. When Mongol ambassadors arrived in France to demand of Louis IX earth and water, in sign of subservience to the Khan, the king of course refused, but he entertained them in Paris and sent them in peace to the pope. Many centuries earlier the fierce Attila spared with a mere rebuke a Byzantine ambassador proved to have been sent to murder him.

Ambassadors were not subject to judicial action for criminal or civil offenses of their own, at least not for those committed prior to their missions. Even in a case of homicide, an ambassador might be released. It must be remembered, however, that ambassadors who abused their status to work against the interests of their hosts did not always enjoy the immunity granted to them today.

Although violations of these immunities sometimes occurred, the complaints and retaliations that they evoked prove that immunity was the rule and violation its exception. Perhaps the most famous seizure of diplomatic envoys in medieval history was Frederick II's capture of more than 100 archbishops, bishops, *nuncii,* and procurators of prelates and ambassadors of the rebellious Lombard towns in 1241. An outraged public opinion, represented chiefly by St. Louis, compelled him to release them. Violations of immunities were probably more common than today but very similar in nature. Marino Sannto reports that in 1499 a band of about 800 disguised youths from the best families of Florence brought a cartful of excrement before the house of the Milanese orator and used it to wall up his door. Examples are found, of course, of the murder of ambassadors and the cutting off of their noses and ears. The infamous Vlad the Impaler had the turbans of Turkish ambassadors who refused to uncover in his presence nailed to their heads. These acts of profound violence are different in degree from plastering excrement in 1499 or throwing ink today, but in one degree or another the acts of barbarism against medieval diplomats were not so different from modern-day abuses and were about equally disapproved.

It was generally the rule that not only courtesy but also an exaggerated etiquette were employed in diplomacy. An insulation of elaborate ceremony helped to protect the fragile thread of civilized intercourse against the violence and brutality then prevalent in European society. Not the least of the ceremonial factors involved in an embassy was its size: the greater the number of ambassadors, the more numerous their retinue and baggage, the greater was the honor paid to the recipient and the greater the impression of the wealth and power of the principal. In the thirteenth and fourteenth centuries, embassies usually were relatively modest in size. A thirteenth-century Venetian embassy to Constantinople numbered seventeen persons, excluding the ambassadors. Maulde la Claviére contends, however, that by the late fifteenth century a special embassy to a major court had to number at least 150 horses, although his estimate is somewhat excessive. In Venetian records of the fifteenth century there is no evidence of such enormous retinues. As early as 1371 the Senate began passing a series of decrees attempting to limit the size of all embassies.

The composition as well as the size of the ambassador's retinue is of interest. Wives did not normally accompany their husbands on embassies, but various specialists in chancery practices, accounting, and law were sometimes important members of an ambassador's entourage. A secretary generally wrote the dispatches and kept necessary records other than the financial ones. Only in the case of especially important communications was the ambassador likely to write in his own hand, though he probably signed all dispatches. A chaplain was often included besides a number of persons of more menial status. Many important embassies, especially those of a ceremonial character, included trumpeters, and those of the highest status might be expected to include an orchestra of minstrels, lute players, and trumpeters, as well as a cook, a stableboy, and the usual household servants.

Diplomacy today remains circumscribed by ceremony, and so it was in antiquity, but probably at no other time in history has ceremony been more important, in diplomacy and elsewhere, than at the end of the Middle Ages. Comines stresses the importance of making the visiting ambassador welcome, entertaining him, making presents to him, and always treating him honorably even if there is a cause for suspecting him of enmity toward the government.

The dress of an ambassador had to reflect the solemnity of the occasion and the dignity of his master. Accounts of ambassadors claim expenses for cloth and plumes, and even the stingy Venetians often provided crimson robes for their ambassadors.

As a ceremonial representative of his principal, an ambassador had to be received on his entry with great honor. As early as 1284 Venetian law required that when a *legatus* came to Venice, four *ambaxatores* should be sent to meet him in order to learn the cause of his coming, so that whatever would be suitable might be done. At the court of Milan a codification of 1468 determined the requisite reception according to rank.

Soon after the reception of envoys, they were customarily granted an audience. Contarini in the fifteenth century tells of his first meeting with the king of France: he and his colleagues were presented in a great hall, at the end of which the king sat upon a dais, with the barons of the blood on a bench at his right side. At the other end of the hall was a bench reserved for the ambassadors, upon which the king wished that they should sit and relate to him the purpose of their embassy.

Under the influence of humanism, the opening oration by an ambassador took on great importance as an item of prestige, and skilled orators therefore found themselves much in demand as diplomats. The words of ambassadors, however, were not always po-

lite and sometimes even contained calculated insults. Still, the niceties were generally observed.

The ambassador himself was entitled to various signs of respect. At the papal court, for instance, an envoy was commonly accorded the privilege of bearing the papal train. Occasionally, quite extraordinary honors were bestowed. The son-in-law and envoy of Ludovico il Moro Sforza proudly reported that the French king led him into the apartment where the royal mistresses were kept, took one of them by the hand and presented her to the ambassador, and chose another for himself, whereupon they amused themselves for two hours. The duke of Milan was pleased at the honor shown to his representative.

The conclusion and proclamation of a treaty was an occasion for elaborate diplomatic ceremonies, but ambassadors also played a prominent part on other solemn occasions. At marriage ceremonies, multiple ambassadors with large retinues, richly garbed and bearing fine gifts, were commonly sent by friendly states to grace the solemnities.

The order of precedence of ambassadors were taken very seriously and often caused endless disputes though it was generally accepted that the envoys of the pope had precedence over all Italian diplomats, and after them the Venetians had place. Among the orators of non-Italian powers, those of the emperor naturally had the highest standing, followed by those of France and Spain.

An ambassador departing in peace and with honor was accustomed to receive a gift, such as rich clothing or silver, from his host. This was an ancient and widespread usage, which even the thrifty Venetians recognized. It was generally conceded that the gift made to an ambassador was his own—except in Venice, where such gifts had to be turned over to the state to be sold at public auction. This requirement is indicative of the feeling in Venice that an ambassador ought to concentrate exclusively on the affairs of the commune. By a decree of 1396 ambassadors and others who served outside the city were denied the privilege of doing business, either for themselves or through others, in the places where they served.

As has been shown, the position of the ambassador was hedged about with immunities and ceremonies. His sacrosanctity was recognized almost of necessity, for medieval lawyers and medieval governments understood that only by a free and secure exchange of envoys can diplomatic activity of any degree of intensity and complexity be conducted.

RATIFICATION

Although most modern authorities would disagree, the medieval evidence supports the thesis that under certain common circumstances, subsequent ratification by the principal of the acts of his envoys was not necessary to the conclusion of binding covenants. Indeed, this is only a modern development. Diplomacy in the Middle Ages was conducted under forms of private law where ratification was not obligatory or even customary.

Any agreements made by *nuncii,* legates, ambassadors, or orators without full powers could become binding covenants only on formal approval by the principals. A Milanese ambassador to France in 1446–1447, made covenants with the king, stipulating that those exceeding his powers should be subject to ratification, although the others should be considered binding in any case. Even the treaties negotiated by plenipotentiaries sometimes included the provision that the principals should take an oath personally in support of the conventions. A procurator might sometimes be authorized to promise that the principal would ratify his letters. Other principals would ratify if necessary or if requested, and often by the terms of a treaty an exchange of ratifications was required.

Nevertheless, treaties, truces, and other covenants made by medieval plenipotentiaries were complete and valid without subsequent ratification by the principals. This point is contested by many authorities. Maulde la Clavière regarded the ratification as an indispensable formality. Lucas, writing of fourteenth-century England, declared that it was customary to ratify all agreements or treaties, even those made by plenipotentiaries. Mattingly, with his usual inerrant judgment, found the normal result of ambassadorial negotiations to be a draft requiring subsequent ratification by the principals. No principal could be bound merely by the force of the ambassador's credentials or instructions, but ratification of the acts of a plenipotentiary, though common, was not juridically required.

By the fifteenth century, in Venice at least, and probably throughout Italy, a draft treaty submitted to the principal was the typical result of ambassadorial relations, but this was not invariably the case, and it was certainly less common in the thirteenth and fourteenth centuries. Quite often a mandatory was given reasonably broad authority to conclude and, occasionally, surprisingly sweeping powers, which were in themselves sufficient.

The authority to publish treaties and truces, which was often specifically granted to plenipotentiaries, strengthens the argument that subsequent ratification by the principals was not essential. It is even more conclusive that other measures were taken under the terms of covenants that were to be ratified but had not yet received ratification. The crusader-envoys of 1201 sent their covenants to the pope for confirmation and borrowed money for beginning construction of the desired fleet before reporting to their principals. Only subsequently was the treaty ratified by the barons at Corbie.

Still clearer proofs can also be found. In 1421 the Venetian Senate removed from the draft of a league with Milan a provision that unless it was ratified by both parties within fifteen days, it should be considered null; nevertheless, it promised to ratify the draft within the prescribed time for the sake of greater firmness. At the very end of the period under study here, in 1499, the Venetians still did not consider subsequent ratification of the acts of plenipotentiaries to be necessary.

On a few occasions however, ratification appears to have been required despite the apparent possession of full powers by the envoys, frequently because a *ratihabitio* clause was omitted from the procuration. It must also be remembered that the procuration formed a voluntary relationship between the principal and the procurator, and that the principal might limit his consent in any way he wished. One such limitation might be required referral to the principal of any agreements before he could be bound.

The acts of plenipotentiaries were subsequently ratified in many instances where no juridical necessity for such ratification existed. There may be several reasons why this was sometimes desired. Papal ratification of the grant of Sicily to Henry III's son Edmund indicates one of them, the wish to remedy any unknown defect of the original covenant. The lesser status of some envoys made ratification more important, though not essential, for the acts of an envoy of great estate were more convincing in themselves and had less need of supportive acts by the principal. In the case of treaties, subsequent ratification was intended to give added security to the opposite party. Although diplomacy employs the forms of law, the relations among sovereign and quasi-sovereign states are only superficially subject to law. It is for this reason that various devices in excess of those required by law were used in an effort to en-

213

sure compliance with covenants in a field that is ultimately lawless.

Since the purpose of ratifying the acts of plenipotentiaries was not juridical, but to obtain whatever additional sanction could be obtained from a solemn act of the principal, the ratification of important covenants was given as much publicity and surrounded by as much ceremony as possible. The Milanese ambassador Leonardo Botta recounted the publication of the Franco-Venetian alliance of 1499. Ambassadors and other dignitaries assembled in the Piazza San Marco. A Mass was said, then a procession marched about the piazza to the sound of bells and other instruments, and finally the alliance was proclaimed. Other means of publicity and ceremonial sanction were possible. In 1475 the kings of England and France agreed to meet at the heads of their forces in full battle array and, by means of envoys passing from one to the other, to establish, proclaim, and publish the agreement that had been reached. Ratification was sometimes performed by an assembly, so that knowledge of it would be more widespread and broader acceptance of it might be assured. Lucas gives examples of English treaties ratified in Parliament in 1328 and in 1365.

The form of ratification was relatively simple, consisting in the principal's affirmation of his intent to carry out the conventions made by his envoy. By this act a principal accepted obligations arising from negotiations by an envoy lacking full powers or reaffirmed obligations already accepted for him by a plenipotentiary.

BIBLIOGRAPHY

This essay is based on Donald E. Queller, *The Office of the Ambassador in the Middle Ages* (1967), with some updating. The reader certainly ought to see Garrett Mattingly's *Renaissance Diplomacy* (1955, repr. 1970), and should not miss the old but very learned M. A. R. de Maulde la Clavière, *La diplomatie au temps de Machiavel,* 3 vols. (1892–1893). For a respectable survey, but a less original work, in spite of the distinction of the author, see François L. Ganshof, *Le moyen âge* (1953).

On more limited topics the reader might wish to consult Willy Andreas, *Staatskunst und Diplomatie der Venezianer* (1943); Paolo Selmi, *L'inizio e il primo sviluppo della diplomazia stabile della Repubblica di Venezia* (unpublished thesis, Padua, 1960); Bernard Behrens, "Treatises on the Ambassador Written in the Fifteenth and Early Sixteenth Centuries," in *English Historical Review,* 51 (1936); George P. Cuttino, *English Diplomatic Administration, 1259–1339* (1940, 2nd rev. ed. 1971); Henry S. Lucas, "The Machinery of Diplomatic Intercourse," in James F. Willard and William A. Morris, eds., *The English Government at Work* (1940).

Readers interested in the publication of a single type of archival document should consult Donald E. Queller, ed., *Early Venetian Legislation on Ambassadors* (1966). An excellent sampling of English diplomatic documents is in Thomas Rymer's *Foedera.* I have used the Dutch ed., 10 vols. (1739–1745); and the Record ed., 4 vols. in 7 pts. (1816–1869). Paul M. Kendall and Vincent Ilardi have so far published the first two volumes of *Dispatches with Related Documents of Milanese Ambassadors in France and Burgundy, 1450–1483,* 2 vols. (1970–1971), which have English translations of the documents on facing pages.

To sample treaties on the office of ambassador, see Vladimir E. Hrabar, ed., *De legatis et legationibus tractatus vardii* (1906). A good introduction to the sources on the juristic aspect can be found in Ludwig Wahrmund, ed., *Quellen zur Geschichte des römisch-kanonischen Processes im Mittelalter,* 5 vols. (1905–1931). On papal diplomacy of the late fifteenth and early sixteenth centuries, especially the ceremonial features, see Johannes Burkhard, *Liber notarum de anno MCCCCLXXXIII usque ad annum MDVI,* Enrico Celano, ed., 2 vols. (1906–1911).

For an extensive but by no means exhaustive bibliography, see Queller, *The Office of the Ambassador.*

DONALD E. QUELLER

[See also **Diplomacy, Byzantine; Diplomacy, Islamic; Nuncio; Venice.**]

DIPTYCH, a hinged pair of writing tablets, usually of ivory. The inner sides contain sunken recesses originally filled with wax and written upon; when closed, the wax text would be protected by the cover. Diptychs were particularly popular in the fifth and sixth centuries, and chiefly bore commemorative texts. Secular diptychs were sent as gifts to commemorate important occasions, political or familial; they carried pictures of the donor or the event, or simple decoration, depending on the status of the recipient. Religious diptychs, showing Christian scenes, recorded the names of those to be commemorated during the prayer of intercession or, perhaps, the names of saints recited in individual church litanies. A diptych leaf in some elaborate imperial and religious examples may be formed of five parts with wide horizontal bands at top and bottom sandwiching three vertical plaques, the central of which is largest.

BIBLIOGRAPHY

Richard Delbrueck, *Die Consulardiptychen und verwandte Denkmaler* (1929); Wolfgang F. Volbach, *Elfen-*

Diptych of the consul Justinian. Ivory, from Constantinople, 516 or 521. THE METROPOLITAN MUSEUM OF ART, GIFT OF J. PIERPONT MORGAN, 1917 (17.190.52, 53)

beinarbeiten der Spätantike und das frühen Mittelalters, 3rd ed. (1976); Kurt Weitzmann, ed., *Age of Spirituality: Late Antique and Early Christian Art* (1979).

LESLIE BRUBAKER

[See also **Ivory Carving; Writing Materials.**]

DIPTYCH, CONSULAR, a diptych made to commemorate the consuls who administered the eastern and western capitals of the Roman Empire. Consular diptychs were presented by the newly inaugurated consul as gifts to senators, high-ranking officials and acquaintances. The exterior decoration may be an elaborate portrait or simple ornament, depending on the recipient's rank. The earliest example, the Probus diptych of 406, shows Emperor Honorius; all later consular diptychs with figural decoration show the consul. The latest preserved consular diptych is from 540 and portrays Justin, who abolished the office the following year.

BIBLIOGRAPHY

Richard Delbrueck, *Die Konsulardiptychen und verwandte Denkmäler* (1929); Kurt Weitzmann, ed., *Age of Spirituality: Late Antique and Early Christian Art* (1979), 5–6.

LESLIE BRUBAKER

DIRHAM (or dirhem), the Islamic silver currency unit and a Muslim weight unit. The word "dirham" is from the Greek *drachma,* through the Aramaic and Pahlavi *drahm.* The only silver coin known to the Arabs in the Prophet's time was the Sasanian *drahm,* which was extensively imitated by the Arabs (with added short Arabic inscriptions) after their conquest of the Sasanian empire in the mid seventh century. These imitations were replaced in A.H. 79 (698) by smaller dirhams with Arabic inscriptions only, including the date, the mint name, and religious statements (two such dirhams of A.H. 78 (698) are also known). Coinage of dirhams was introduced in North Africa and Spain about 720 and in Egypt in 787.

Dirhams were struck throughout the Islamic world until the early eleventh century. Aside from some evolution of style, the major change was the addition of the name of the official under whose authority the coin was struck, seen first in 762. From the eighth to the tenth century, Islamic dirhams were exported from Muslim central Asia to Russia, eastern Europe, and Scandinavia, where they are still found in great quantities. This drain of silver coinage may be connected with the disappearance of the classical Islamic dirham in the eleventh century, though the relationship is problematic.

Meanwhile, minting of small, somewhat debased dirhams had begun in Sicily in the ninth century. By the eleventh century such dirhams made up the bulk of the silver currency in Muslim Mediterranean lands from Spain to Syria. They were struck to no precise weight standard but average about half the weight of the classical dirham. In 1145 square silver dirhams weighing about half a dirham (about 1.50 grams) were introduced by the Almohads (Muwaḥḥids) of North Africa and Spain. These became the standard silver coinage of the Muslim West until the sixteenth century and were also imitated by Christian states. In the eastern Islamic lands Saladin reintroduced full-weight good silver dirhams, starting in Damascus in 1175. Minting of dirhams spread throughout the East during the next century, with many different design arrangements and weight standards. Dirhams were struck in large quantities by the thirteenth-century crusaders, at first in close imitation of Syrian Muslim dirhams and then with Christian inscriptions in Arabic.

Medieval Muslim writers on coinage generally agreed that the coined dirham should weigh seven-tenths the weight of the gold dinar. Taking 4.25 grams as a norm for the dinar, this ratio results in a theoretical dirham weight of 2.975 grams. In practice, however, this standard was very seldom observed. The 7:10 ratio was only one of several possible weight relationships between the dinar and the dirham, and the weight standard of the dinar itself varied. It is therefore impossible to generalize, but most of the identified dirham weight standards fall between 2.50 and 3.05 grams. Dirhams, like dinars, were usually paid by weight, not by count.

The fineness of dirhams varied greatly, much more than that of dinars. This explains the wide range of exchange rates between the two currency units. The nominal rates were based on the respective values of the precious metal content of each coin, but actual rates were set daily by the force of supply and demand. Dinars and dirhams were regarded as two separate currencies, each with its own function.

The dirham as a small weight unit for commodities differed from the monetary dirham weight. It ranged from 3.08 to 3.26 grams in different regions.

BIBLIOGRAPHY

G. C. Miles, "Dirham," in *The Encyclopedia of Islam,* 2nd ed., II (1965), is a useful survey. Exchange rates for different times and places are collected in Eliyahu Ashtor, *Les métaux précieux et la balance des payements du Proche-Orient à la basse époque* (1971); and Solomon D. Goitein, *A Mediterranean Society,* I (1967), 368–392, but to understand these correctly it is necessary to know the weight and fineness of the coins in each instance.

MICHAEL L. BATES

[See also **Mints and Money, Islamic.**]

DISCANT. See **Notre Dame School.**

DISCANTOR had two meanings in the Middle Ages: one who, in polyphonic music, devised a second voice, note against note, in contrary motion to the given melody, as in two twelfth-century treatises (Seay, p. 33; Schneider, pp. 116–117); or, as Anonymous IV designates Pérotin *optimus discantor* (Reckow, 1:46), one who composed passages in discant in the thirteenth-century Notre Dame repertory.

BIBLIOGRAPHY

Fritz Reckow, ed., *Der Musiktraktat des Anonymus 4,* 2 vols. (1967); Marius Schneider, ed., *De tractatu tonorum,* in *Geschichte der Mehrstimmigkeit,* II (1935), 106–118; Albert Seay, "An Anonymous Treatise from St. Martial," in *Annales musicologiques, moyen âge et renaissance,* 5 (1957).

JAMES GRIER

[See also **Anonymous IV; Ars Antiqua.**]

DISCIPLINA CLERICALIS, a collection of moralizing but entertaining tales in Latin, written by Petrus Alfonsi, an Aragonese Jew converted to Christianity in 1106, who gained a considerable reputation in astronomy and medicine as well as in theology and literature. The *Disciplina clericalis* (Scholar's guide) was translated into Anglo-Norman French *(Le chastoiement d'un père à son fils)* in the twelfth century and later into Spanish.

BIBLIOGRAPHY

Petrus Alfonsi, *Disciplina clericalis,* Alfons Hilka and W. Söderhjelm, eds. (1911); also Eberhard Hermes, ed., translated from the German by P. R. Quarrie (1977); and *The Scholar's Guide,* Ramon Jones and John Esten Keller, trans. (1969).

BRIAN MERRILEES

[See also **Anglo-Norman Literature.**]

DISPENSATION, a term referring to an act by a competent ecclesiastical authority suspending the obligation of a law in a particular case. It is derived from the Latin *dispensare,* meaning to pay out and, hence, to distribute in equitable fashion or to administer. Among Latin Christian writers *dispensatio* came to have several meanings related to the notion of administration of sacred things, meanings that were equivalent to various senses of *oikonomia* in the Greek Christian tradition. The term was applied to divine interventions, to providence, and to various actions by ecclesiastical superiors. Among the latter was the suspension of the application of a usage or law in a given case for the good of the church; it was with "dispensation" in this sense that canon law was principally concerned.

This sympathetic attitude in circumstances of special need can be observed in the practice of church leaders during the patristic period and the early Middle Ages, though there does not seem to have been serious reflection on the procedure. The first developed analysis of the theory and practice of dispensation began toward the end of the eleventh century in the writings of Bernold of Constance and Ivo of Chartres. The latter examined dispensation in some detail as part of his reflection on law in the prologue to his *Decretum (Patrologia latina,* CLXI, 47–60). Progress continued in the *Decretum* of Gratian and in the writings of the decretists, so that by the end of the twelfth century the main elements of a theory of dispensation, an analysis of its components, and its distinction from several similar procedures had been completed. In this discussion it was made clear that, while dispensation suspended the obligation of a law, that law remained in force. Dispensation was distinguished from actions such as excuse or interpretation, which concluded that a law was not intended to apply in a given case; from abrogation and derogation, involving complete or partial suppression of law; and from tolerance, permission, and privilege.

Dispensations were of two types, those applying to the past and those applying to the future. The former, much the more common type in the early period, not only removed the obligation of a law retroactively but also rectified the consequences of the original act that was against that law. Thus, in the case of a marriage that was invalid because of a legal impediment, a dispensation removed the obligation of the law, thereby rendering the union valid, and also legitimized children that had been born to the couple. The analysis of the dispensation *post factum* would lead to the notion of retroactive validation *(sanatio in radice).* From the Middle Ages to the present the more prevalent form of dispensation has been for acts not yet performed *(in futurum).*

Where the grant of dispensation can be observed in the first millennium, it seems ordinarily to have occurred in cases of grave need that touched the general good of the church. With the passage of time, more personal necessity became an accepted motive, though it was emphasized that wider interests were served as well. Innocent III considered merit or the

dignity of the beneficiary to be sufficient reason. Thus, in the course of the Middle Ages there was a significant shift toward the use of the power to dispense for the benefit of the individual.

The exercise of the power to dispense was examined by canonists and theologians of the twelfth century; it remained a subject of discussion, often of sharp disagreement, until modern times. The bishops of the early church seem to have considered it to belong to their role as head of a diocese, but as the years passed, distinctions began to be made between the powers of bishops, councils, and pope. Bernold of Constance and Ivo of Chartres saw dispensation as an act of legislative authority. As the applicability of the general laws of the church and the regulations of local councils and episcopal synods was clarified, the extent of the bishop's dispensing power came under more careful scrutiny. With the growth of the theory and practice of papal plenitude of power, it became the common opinion that bishops dispensed from the general law of the church only by concession.

This position was to be disputed for centuries, but by the later Middle Ages it was customary to refer such matters to the Holy See, bishops frequently obtaining faculties to dispense from certain impediments in a given number of cases. For example, a bishop might be empowered to dispense from the impediment of consanguinity in ten cases. It was also discussed whether papal dispensing power could be applied to natural law and divine positive law. The general opinion was that the pope's authority did not extend to these areas, though he could interpret and, on the basis of his judgment, declare whether they applied in a given case.

As papal dispensing power was elaborated, it became an instrument for a degree of control over the choice of prelates and minor clergy and over their income. Similarly the grant of marriage dispensations could be the occasion of powerful influence on dynastic policy, for example, the intervention by Innocent III during the first decade of his reign in several marriages uniting Spanish houses, including his refusal to allow the union of Peter II of Aragon and Bianca of Navarre, related in the third degree (1199). This procedure invoked the notion that dispensation was granted for motives wider than the desires of the individual, but many saw in it an unacceptable instrument of papal power; it was much criticized through the fourteenth and fifteenth centuries.

In countries that accepted the Reformation, the rejection of the papacy involved the removal of the principal dispensing authority in the church. It soon became clear that a jurisdiction of this sort was needed; it passed to the heads of the new churches either by national law, as in the case of England, where the archbishop of Canterbury became the final authority by statute in 1534, or by usage associated with the leadership of the various denominations. By and large the systematic exercise of a power of dispensation quickly dwindled among the Reformed churches, though a similar end was often achieved by interpretation or permission. The Council of Trent included a careful overhaul of the procedures of dispensation in its deliberations; with this reform the essential medieval usages have continued in the Roman Catholic church until the present.

BIBLIOGRAPHY

Joseph Brys, *De dispensatione in iure canonico* (1925); R. Naz, "Dispense," in *Dictionnaire de droit canonique,* IV (1949), 1284–1296; W. Rudt de Collenberg, "Les dispenses matrimoniales accordées à l'Ouest latin selon les registres du Vatican d'Honorius III à Clement VII (1223–1385)," in *Mélanges de l'École française de Rome: Moyen âge et temps modernes,* **89** (1977); Maria Albert Stiegler, *Dispensation, Dispensationswesen, und Dispensationsrecht im Kirchenrecht,* I (1901); R. Weigand, "Zur Lehre von der Dispensmöglichkeit des Gelübdes in Raymunds *Summa de poenitentia* und bei ihrer Bearbeitern," in *Escritos del Vedat,* 7 (1977).

MICHAEL M. SHEEHAN

[See also **Decretists; Decretum; Gratian; Law, Canon.**]

DISPUTATIO INTER CLERICUM ET MILITEM, a short tract written in France between 1296 and 1303. It deals mainly with the early phase of the controversy between King Philip the Fair and Pope Boniface VIII. The work was apparently unknown at the time and did not appear until 1378, as the opening section of the royalist *Somnium viridarii.* During the Great Schism the *Disputatio* was utilized in defense of the liberties of the French church. An English translation by John Trevisa was popular in England because of its antipapalism. The Latin text and English translation were printed many times in the sixteenth century.

The anonymous treatise is in the form of a combative dialogue between a *miles* (a nonnoble soldier) and a cleric. The language is simple and direct,

clearly aimed at a wide audience. In translation the *miles* was changed to a knight whose objective is to demonstrate the king's right to tax clerical property for the defense of the realm. Since the pope (and the clergy in general) is limited to spiritual affairs, the knight argues, he cannot interfere with the monarch's administration of temporals. To be sure, the clergy are permitted to administer temporal goods, since it is natural that God's ministers have adequate means of support. But anything beyond these necessities is to be used to help others, especially the poor. If the clergy retain these excess goods for their own enjoyment, they forfeit their control of them. After all, princes have freely granted temporals to churchmen for the purpose of putting them to pious use. The secular prince, who has an indirect concern for the salvation of souls, can legitimately confiscate any "superfluous" wealth that is being squandered by soft-living clerics.

The knight then introduces his main argument. As members of the body politic, the clergy should contribute to its survival and welfare. The king protects the clergy, ecclesiastical holdings, and the Christian faith from rapacious nobles and outside invasion. Out of gratitude the church should willingly offer material support. If it refuses, he can justly seize whatever he needs to protect his regnum. As emperor in his own realm, the king is subject to no one save God. The king has primary responsibility in temporals and secondary responsibility in spirituals. He may tax church lands only in times of necessity, when the realm is endangered. His emergency jurisdiction is conditional on the clergy's misbehavior and/or the internal-external threats to the kingdom—two distinct justifications that the knight never integrates. Presumably the tax ceases with the end of the crisis.

To support this argument the knight summons the New Testament, the Old Testament (when kings ruled priests), public law and Roman law maxims, natural law, and historical precedent. This sharply worded polemic exploits the widespread criticism of clerical wealth and secular involvement. It reveals the increasing acceptance of dualism: the monarch holds casual or incidental jurisdiction over all temporals in the realm because of his obligation to defend the realm and indirectly to serve spirituals. The crude *Disputatio* foreshadows the fourteenth-century royalist arguments based on national sovereignty, the crown's supremacy in temporals, and the church's fall from evangelical poverty.

BIBLIOGRAPHY

N. Erickson, "A Dispute Between a Priest and a Knight," in *Proceedings of the American Philosophical Society*, **111** (1967), critical edition and translation; Melchior Goldast, *Monarchia sancti romani imperii*, I (1612), 13–18; Thomas Renna, "Kingship in the *Disputatio inter clericum et militem*," in *Speculum*, **48** (1973); Jean Rivière, *Le problème de l'église et de l'état au temps de Philippe le Bel* (1926).

THOMAS RENNA

[See also **Boniface VIII, Pope; Kingship, Theories of: Western Europe; Philip IV the Fair; Political Theory, Western European; Trevisa, John.**]

DISPUTATIONS. See **Polemics.**

DISTICHA CATONIS. See **Cato's Distichs (Latin).**

DISTILLED LIQUORS. Wines and beers are limited to an alcoholic content of about 15 percent, for beyond that concentration the fermenting action of yeast is adversely affected. A stronger beverage may be obtained in several ways. Wine gently heated in an animal bladder becomes concentrated because of the greater affinity of animal matter for water. If wine is partially frozen, the ice consists of pure water and the remaining liquid is thus strengthened in alcohol. It remains to be shown that the first method was known before modern times, but the second may have been used in central Asia as early as the seventh century, according to Joseph Needham, who also suggests that the Chinese (and perhaps also the Europeans) were thus introduced to the pleasures of strong drink.

The freezing method, however, had limitations, both geographical and technical. Therefore the history of alcoholic beverages in the Middle Ages correlates with that of the modern method of alcohol concentration, distillation. The process comes into focus only with the introduction of alcohol production through distillation for making wine or beer in the twelfth and thirteenth centuries—even though some historians argue for the greater antiquity of some beverages, such as Irish whiskey, for which the evidence seems to be mainly linguistic.

In a rudimentary form the technique of distillation goes back to Babylonia and the fourth millennium B.C.—if, as has been argued, excavated clay vessels with tops having an internal flange were intended for this purpose. Some distillate would collect in this circular canal, but probably not much alcohol. The vessels are thought to have been used in the extraction of perfumes. More probable as a source of alcohol is the "Mongolian still," a vessel (of uncertain but probably early date) with a dish-shaped lid in which cooling water or ice could be put. The condensate would have formed on the bottom of the lid and dripped from the center into a small collecting vessel suspended below the lid.

Evidence is tenuous that either of these devices was significant in the history of strong beverages, nor do the more sophisticated distillatories described in the Greek alchemical literature of the early Christian era appear to have been significant in the history of alcohol. The literary sources on which our knowledge of this apparatus rests also deal with its uses, which seem to have been exclusively sublimation and the metal-coloring processes so dear to the heart of the alchemist. But the alchemists of Europe ten centuries later were more preoccupied with medical "elixirs" than with making gold, and alcohol was to emerge among these elixirs. It appears as a distinct substance in the mid twelfth century, under the appropriate name *aqua ardens* (burning water), in the *Compendium Salerni*, a collection from the medical school at Salerno. The recipe is given in cipher, suggesting that it was secret, but there is another recipe from about the same time in the artist's recipe book *Mappae clavicula*.

Other recipes followed, but without comprehensible detail on how alcohol was actually made, before the *Consilia medicinalis* of Taddeo Alderotti (*d. ca.* 1295). Alderotti refers to the "serpente," which is taken to be the adequate condensation apparatus lacking in stills described earlier. It was a long tube, straight or coiled, sometimes immersed in water.

Paracelsus (*ca.* 1493–1541) appears to have given alcohol its modern name, taking it from an Arabic word referring to any finely divided material. Alcohol was "finely divided" wine. Paracelsus' test for it was that a spoonful burned away without leaving a residue. More frequently mentioned was that a linen cloth soaked in alcohol burned without damage to the cloth. In either case the alcohol must have been nearly as "pure" as possible, 95.5 percent being the maximum (for the water remaining beyond that cannot be removed by distillation).

But "alcoholic beverages" were common long before Paracelsus. Claims for Irish whiskey become more plausible from the twelfth century and are joined by German claims for *Hausbrand,* a distilled liquor said to have been made and sold by innkeepers from the end of that century. Brandy, the principal liquor distilled from wine, was reputedly an inexpensive beverage sold at Nuremberg in the thirteenth century, a product of the apothecaries.

These beverages would have ranged from 30 percent to 40 percent alcohol, and thus would have required apparatus of a much lower order of efficiency than that required by the chemist-pharmacists who discovered alcohol. The latter were in pursuit of the elixir—or quintessence—a "universal" medicine; and although one recommended alcohol as a remedy for despondent alchemists, in general the substance was but an incident to the medical chemistry of an era replete with new remedies. The economic exploitation of alcohol was largely left to the apothecary.

He did not fail to exploit it. It is believed that a great increase in the consumption of distilled liquors occurred after the mid fourteenth century in consequence of their prescription as remedies for the Black Death. A variety of liquors were available. The production of sweetened and strengthened wines is said to have been an industry in Italy as early as 1320, the favorite being *rosiglio,* which smelled of roses. About 1400 it was found how to distill "spirits" from beer, and "corn" (grain) spirits appeared about that time. Grain yielded almost four times as much alcohol as grapes, per pound of raw material, and many other plant materials could be fermented (including sawdust, which gives a stronger—but probably less tasty—alcohol than grapes). Thus began the development of the "national" drinks of northern Europe, mostly distilled from grain: *genever* (Holland), gin (England), schnapps (Germany), aquavit (Scandinavia), vodka (Russia). The names become evident only in the sixteenth century, but the drinks, differing in the presence or absence of flavoring additives, certainly preceded that time.

The demand exceeded the facilities of the apothecary, who passed the art to another specialist (in Germany, the *Weinbrenner*). Regulations against drunkenness are said to have multiplied from the fourteenth century, though they were already numerous enough, thanks to wine and beer.

BIBLIOGRAPHY
Robert J. Forbes, *Short History of the Art of Distillation* (1948, repr. 1979); Mechthild Krüger, *Zur Geschichte der Elixiere, Essenzen, und Tinkturen* (1968); E. O. von Lippmann, *Beiträge zur Geschichte der Naturwissenschaften und der Technik,* 2 vols. (1923–1953), contains most of his numerous articles on alcohol; Adam Maurizio, *Geschichte der gegorenen Getränke* (1933); Robert P. Multhauf, *The Origins of Chemistry* (1966), reproducing several early accounts of alcohol; Joseph Needham, *Science and Civilization in China,* V, pt. 4 (1980), the most recent, and one of the best, treatments of the history of alcohol in both Western and Chinese history.

ROBERT P. MULTHAUF

[See also **Brewing; Wine, Winemaking.**]

DISTRAINT. See **Distress.**

DISTRESS. Although, according to Theodore Plucknett, "the law of distress still awaits its historian as far as England is concerned," the important role played by distress or distraint in English feudal society and in feudal and royal courts is clear. A society with much law but insufficient established coercive power must authorize a certain amount of self-help; likewise a royal government lacking a police force must find means of forcing men to appear in court or to carry out any other duties. Distress provided the needed leverage by authorizing a lord or the king to seize the chattels (usually beasts) or real property of the defaulting tenant or subject and hold it until he had done his duty.

A feudal lord deprived of services owed him by a tenant could thus seize the man's chattels without any court judgment; he had only to stay carefully within well-known limitations as to what he could seize and to give not the slightest indication that he was treating the distrained property as his own. As soon as the tenant rendered his services or paid his arrears, or even gave gage and pledge that he would contest the lord's claim in a court of law, the distraint must end.

After failure of distraint by chattels a lord could, through a judgment in his own court, play his trump card and "distrain by the fee," that is, temporarily seize the tenant's holding itself. But distraint of chattels was easier and less likely to result in legal action by the tenant (such as an action of novel disseisin), so distraint by the fee tended to fall out of use in the thirteenth century. Still, extralegal distraint was troublesome enough that Simon de Montfort called it "the beginning of all wars," and Bracton wrote, "where gage and pledge fail, peace fails."

So deeply ingrained was the concept of distraint that the Magna Carta barons wrote it into the sanctions clause of the charter; if King John did not fulfill his obligations, they would distrain his castles, lands, and chattels. In the less politically troubled period of Henry III and Edward I, John's son and grandson, the crown tried repeatedly to legislate against abuses of distraint that so easily affected public order, whether the actions were taken by feudal lords or by crown officers. But distraint remained in use as an important if potentially troublesome device throughout the Middle Ages.

BIBLIOGRAPHY

Theodore F. T. Plucknett, *Legislation of Edward I* (1949); Frederick Pollock and Frederic W. Maitland, *The History of English Law Before the Time of Edward I*, 2nd ed. (1968); Donald W. Sutherland, *The Assize of Novel Disseisin* (1973).

RICHARD W. KAEUPER

[See also **Assize, English; Land-Tenure, Western European; Law, English Common; Magna Carta.**]

Dominican nuns in choir. FROM BRITISH LIBRARY, COTTON MS A. XVII, fol. 74v

DIT, a short thirteenth-century verse narrative, without musical accompaniment, treating daily life. Many are moralizing or satirical attacks on contemporary evils. By the fourteenth century, *dits* were longer allegorical visions of an adventure or debate. The *dit* reflects the interplay of didactic and lyric modes from Rutebeuf to Machaut.

BIBLIOGRAPHY

Paul Zumthor, "Le triomphe de la parole," in his *Essai de poétique médiévale* (1972), 405–420.

ROY ROSENSTEIN

[See also **French Literature.**]

DIVINE COMEDY. See Dante Alighieri.

DIVINE OFFICE, the service of prayers, psalms, readings, antiphons, responses, canticles, and hymns said and sung during specific parts of the night and day called the hours of matins, lauds, prime, terce, sext, none, vespers, and compline. The Office was performed primarily by the clergy and members of religious orders, and both its structure and its length could vary enormously depending on the century, the geographical location, the time of year, and the specific needs and obligations of the persons and groups engaged in this liturgical activity. Because the Office came to be said privately in some quarters, there is dispute about its quality in such circumstances as a liturgical act, which generally has been described as the public worship of the church. This article will set forth generalized practices in the performance of the Office while indicating some of the variety that characterizes medieval practice.

SOURCES OF THE OFFICE

Our knowledge of the medieval Office derives primarily from two major types of sources: first, the "external" sources, including rules pertaining to monastic orders and groups of clerics, canon-law prescriptions and collections, and liturgical commentaries or expositions; and second, the formularies themselves, including texts of the prayers, psalms, readings, hymns and so forth, and the liturgical directories.

"External" sources: (1) Rules pertaining to religious orders and groups of clerics. The rules or collections of regulations governing medieval religious and secular houses usually contained prescriptions regarding the Office. In the late patristic period Cassian indicates the diversity of practices saying that he had seen almost as many systems and regulations as the number of monasteries and cells he had visited. Among the earliest monastic rules in the West were the *Ordo monasterii,* which is contained in what has traditionally been called the Rule of St. Augustine; a rule for monks and nuns at Arles drawn up by Caesarius and later augmented and clarified by his successor Aurelian; the Rule of the Irish wandering missionary Columbanus; and most important, in Italy the *Regula magistri* and its derivative, the Rule of Benedict of Nursia, which was to become the norm for later monastic performance and development of the Office.

During the late patristic period clergy attached to cathedrals, be they secular or religious, also had their regulations for the performance of the Office, as we know from the writings of Augustine, Ambrose, Jerome, Nicetas of Remesiana, and Gregory of Tours.

In the early Middle Ages these earlier rules were expanded and modified. Among the most significant of the revisions were those of Chrodegang for the clergy of Metz, Benedict of Aniane for the Benedictine monks of Carolingian times, and the Cluniac customaries.

In the late eleventh and twelfth centuries with the reforms of religious houses, the foundation of new orders such as the Cistercians, and the rise of the clerical movement known as the canons regular (Augustinian canons), new rules appeared that would contain norms governing the performance of the Office. And with the growth of the mendicant orders in the thirteenth century and beyond, a further set of rules was added to the existing layers of older rules.

(2) Canon-law regulations. Closely related to, and often dependent on, the regulations for religious orders and groups of clerics were the rules for the performance of the Office in canon-law compilations. As early as the late fourth century and into the seventh, synods such as those of Toledo, Vannes, Agde, and Braga legislated on the Office, and these synodical pronouncements were augmented with papal and episcopal decrees. These canons, together with those later enacted, were then gathered into canon-law collections that dealt with such topics as the number of hours; the obligation of stipendiary clerics to say the Office; the distribution of the elements of the Office over the year and during the day and night; the use of hymns, psalms, scriptural and non-scriptural readings; and fasting in relation to the hours of the Office. From the earliest historically and systematically arranged collections down to the so-called *Decretum* of Gratian of the mid twelfth century, these canons appear frequently. Thereafter commentators on the *Decretum* further elucidated them.

In the High and later Middle Ages, synods, popes, and bishops continued to legislate on the Office; and, as was the case in the earlier period, this legislation made its way into collections of canonical material and was further commented on by the canonistic specialists.

(3) Liturgical commentaries or expositiones. During patristic antiquity in the West most comments on the Office were made in passing reference to other subjects. But beginning with the late sixth and early seventh centuries the Office became the object of systematic exposition. Isidore of Seville in his *De ecclesiasticis officiis* gathered together older miscellaneous comments to describe the origins and etymological significance of the Office. His description was later very influential because of its systematic treatment and the wide manuscript diffusion of the *De ecclesiasticis officiis.* Not long after Isidore an author known as Pseudo-Germanus seems to have used the Spanish doctor to describe the Office, the first such commentary originating in Gallican-rite territories. And in the eighth century there appeared for the Celtic rite a tract on the Office entitled *Ratio decursus qui fuerunt eius auctores.*

The most extensive and certainly the most important commentaries on the Office in the Carolingian period were written by Amalarius of Metz and his critics, principally those in Lyons, where he had been bishop temporarily. Amalarius' first major work on the Office was book 4 of his *Liber officialis,* and this was followed by his *Liber de ordine anti-*

phonarii, compiled at Lyons. In these he commented on the formulas found in his sources and explained the selection of material that he had made for his own antiphonary. Among the works of the Office ascribed to Amalarius' Lyonese opponents are the *Liber de correctione antiphonarii,* attributed to Agobard, and the *De divina psalmodia,* written either by the deacon Florus or by an anonymous follower of Agobard.

Beyond the work of Amalarius and his Lyonese opponents, other ninth-century liturgiologists commented on aspects of the Office. Hrabanus Maurus in his *De clericorum institutione* was heavily dependent on Isidore. Walafrid Strabo was much more concerned with the origins of the daily *cursus* or round of services and the generic elements of the Office. And finally, some time around 900, an author now known as Pseudo-Alcuin wrote the *Liber de divinis officiis,* depending heavily on Isidore and Amalarius.

With the revival of liturgical commentaries in the late eleventh century the Office again became a focus for liturgical expositors. Among the best known of these are Berno of Reichenau, Peter Damian, John of Avranches, and Bernold of Constance. The foundations of liturgical commentary on the Office of the ninth and eleventh centuries were built upon in the twelfth century by such figures as Rupert of Deutz, Drogo of Laon, and Honorius Augustodunensis. In Rome a group of "rubricists" described the Office as performed there. These include Benedict of St. Peter's, Prior Bernard of the Lateran, and Cencio Savelli (the future Pope Honorius III). From the late twelfth century on, the Office was a regular subject for treatment by commentators, the best known being John Beleth, Sicard of Cremona, and Guillaume Durand.

"Formulaic" sources. Although it is often said that the recitation of the psalms is the heart of the Office, this was originally true only in the monastic setting. Rather, the Office is the prayer of the church, and psalms were simply one type of prayer among many. While the psalms were contained in the format of psalters, the prayers, collects, or orations were entered into a variety of sources.

(1) Sacramentaries. Strangely, some of the first evidence in the West of the prayers for the Office is found in the sacramentaries, generally thought of as containing Mass texts exclusively. But to the sacramentaries, which were originally made up of *libelli* (little books) of Mass prayers, additional *libelli* with

Office prayers could be attached. Thus, in some of the earliest Mass books, such as the Veronese, Gelasian, and Gregorian ones, there are *Orationes matutinales vel vespertinales.*

(2) Collectariums. The prayers in the earliest *libelli precum* and sacramentaries were eventually gathered into a book known as the collectar, which was also known as a *collectaneum, orationale,* or *manuale.* But because these books were basically books of prayer, they might include prayers of the Mass, benedictions, or even prayers for private devotion.

The collectars, which were primarily for monastic use, could contain a variety of material beyond prayers, and it is on this basis that scholars divide them into simple and enriched collectars. Besides the prayers, the collectar might include the capitula (the very short readings for the Office), kalendars, litanies, benedictions, and directories or rituals.

The earliest simple collectars, going back as far as the tenth century, are actually collectar-rituals (that is, with directories), but by the eleventh and twelfth centuries they included not only collects and capitula but also brief verses, responses, litanies, and gradual psalms. Sometimes the various parts are presented in the manuscripts together in one series; sometimes they are ordered according to a mixed sequence according to the liturgical year with its temporal and sanctoral constituents.

Enriched collectars have the services of the Offices used on both Sundays (dominical) and weekdays (ferial). Moreoever, they may have hymns, sequences, antiphons, and so forth, and because of this additional material they resemble the later breviaries. Many of these enriched collectars give only the incipit for the prayer or chant and hence are very close to the original meaning of *breviarium,* a brief order of the Office throughout the year.

(3) Psalters. From the monastic Office the psalms became the heart also of the so-called cathedral or secular Office, and hence one of the most important sources of the Office in both circumstances is the psalter.

In the early Latin churches of North Africa, Italy, Spain, and Gaul there was the old Latin or *Vetus Latina* Psalter for the Office. This psalter, together with the Greek Septuagint Psalter, served as the basis for Jerome's Roman Psalter, used in Rome throughout the Middle Ages. Jerome also translated the psalter from the Origenistic Hexapla, and this translation came to be known as the Gallican Psalter. It had its first success in Ireland, but was also known in Gaul, Africa, and Italy. By the ninth century this psalter had become extremely popular outside Rome as a liturgical text. There are many examples of illustrated Gallican psalters.

Liturgical psalters as a source of the Office are to be carefully distinguished from literary psalters in that the former are set up according to liturgical divisions with special illuminated initials and can have a variety of additions. Among these may be kalendars, invitatories used at the beginning of the night Office, psalter collects or prayers based on the Psalms, and canticles or biblical songs from books other than the Psalms (for example, the Canticle of the Three Children [Benedicite] from Vulgate Dan. 3:52–90, and 56; the Canticle of Hezekiah from Isa. 38:10–20; the Canticle of Isaiah the Prophet from Isa. 12; the Canticle of Hannah from 1 Kings 2:1–10 (1 Sam. 2:1–10), the Canticles of Moses from Exod. 15:1–18 and Deut. 32:1–43; the Canticle of Habakkuk from Hab. 3:2–19; the Canticle of Zechariah [Benedictus] from Luke 1:68–79; the Canticle of Mary [Magnificat] from Luke 1:46–55; and the Canticle of Simeon [Nunc Dimittis] from Luke 2:29–32). Also in liturgical psalters there might be the Te Deum, *Quicunque vult* or Athanasian Creed, the *Trisagion,* litanies, capitula, and hymns. Finally there might be *tituli,* titles for the psalms explaining their Christic or New Testament significance.

All of this material in the psalter could be arranged according to various methods. The *psalterium non feriatum* was basically a biblical psalter with the 150 psalms in order, but there could be signs of liturgical use in that the psalms themselves might be grouped under large initials according to monastic or secular usage. The *psalterium cum ordinario officii* would have contained the psalms like the *Psalterium non feriatum* but with the additional material described above. And in the *psalterium feriatum* or *psalterium per hebdomadam* the psalms were divided according to the feasts and weeks of the liturgical year as reflected in the Office. Here, too, additional material might be added.

(4) Lectionaries. Together with prayers and psalms, the Office contained readings of lessons, and these were gathered in the *lectionarium* or *lectionale.* Because they were used in the night Office they might also be called a *nocturale* or *matutinale.* The readings themselves could be from the Bible, the legends of saints, and the writings of the Fathers. And because they could be very extensive, they were often divided into winter and summer lectionaries.

As with the other books of the Office, the lections could be in separate sections according to the temporale following the *cursus* of the ecclesiastical year, or the sanctorale following the *cursus* of saints' feasts, or they might be mixed. Monastic (especially Benedictine) lectionaries usually arrange the readings in groups of fours for Sundays and feasts, but secular lectionaries (and those for some other religious orders) are usually arranged in groups of threes. Like the collectar, the lectionary might be simple or enriched with such materials as responses, antiphons, capitula, collects, hymns, and so forth.

(5) Passionalia and legendae. Two special types of lectionaries used in the Office were the passional (*passionale* or *liber passionalis*) and the legenda, the former giving accounts of the suffering of the martyrs and the latter the acts of saints, often highly embellished.

(6) Homiliaries. Another special type of lectionary is the *homiliarium.* Because the writings of the Fathers were often in sermonic or homily form, they, together with the other tracts and letters of the Fathers, were read in the Office, and the homiliary would contain these writings.

(7) Hymnaries. Hymns were probably first used in the Eastern church among such heterodox groups as the Gnostics and Arians. But soon the orthodox accepted them in principle and a host of early Westerners composed hymns, including Hilary, Ambrose, Prudentius, Sedulius, and Fortunatus. In Carolingian times and beyond, hymns continued to be composed. Although the church in Rome was chary about their use, the churches outside Rome, especially those in Gallican- and Milanese-rite territories, early used them. If not kept in psalters, the hymns might be found in a separate book called the hymnary. If found in a *psalterium feriatum,* the hymns would be arranged according to the feasts within the body of the psalter.

(8) Antiphonaries and responsories. These books contained the musical antiphons and responses of the Office (not to be confused with the so-called *antiphonalia* or *antiphonaria missarum,* containing music for the Mass). The earliest examples of these books are from the ninth century, but by that time they were well evolved since already the antiphons had been divided according to the liturgical year with temporale and sanctorale mixed. Also they contained commons of the saints, invitatories, canticles, and other material. In the ninth century the antiphonaries could bear musical neumes or not, and Klaus Gamber divides these early antiphonaries on

this basis. But later there was a more practical division: so large did the antiphonaries become that they were separated into diurnals (containing material for the Offices of the daytime) and nocturnals (with material for the night Office). The responses might be kept in separate books called responsorials, which would contain the *Responsoria prolixa* or Great Responses for the night Office, and the *Responsoria brevia* or Short Responses used after the capitulum. Often, however, the responses were simply included in the antiphonary.

(9) Ordines. For the correct use of the texts and music contained in the formulaic sources already described, it was necessary to have directories. The norms laying out the appropriate sequence of the Office and their constituent parts could, as has been noted, be found in the rules for monastic groups and secular clerics. But beyond these were ordines. Although there are several types of these, the most common—such as *Ordines romani* XII–XIV—contained directions for antiphons and lections to be used on specific days.

(10) Liber Ordinarius. Closely related to the *Ordines* is the *liber ordinarius,* called in the manuscripts *breviarium, ordinale, ordo officiorum,* or *ordinarium.* This directory for the Office often begins with a kalendar, which is followed by incipits for the texts to be used throughout the year.

(11) Libelli with complete offices. From the tenth to the twelfth century especially, *libelli* were compiled that presented a complete Office for Sundays and weekdays. Usually they lacked complete lessons, antiphons, and responses, thus showing that the larger books described above had to be consulted with them.

(12) Breviary-missals. These books, which were especially popular in Spain, were in reality breviaries containing material for the Office into which Mass texts were worked, usually after the hour of terce.

(13) Breviaries. Breviaries were the book of the Office and incorporated into one volume material kept separately in the other books. The earliest breviaries, dating from the eleventh century, simply juxtaposed this material with little attempt at integrating it into individual feasts or days but ordered it according to the liturgical year and sequence of saints' feasts. Gradually, however, the texts came to be presented as complete offices. It seems that the breviaries were really collectars to which lessons, antiphons, and responses were added. But because all this material made for an enormous book, the breviaries were often divided into two volumes for win-

ter and summer use. Another way to reduce the size of the volume was to excise the lessons, thereby returning to the earlier practice where several books had to be used in the performance of the Office.

The breviary itself probably was one of the products of the so-called Gregorian reform of the late eleventh century. Not only were monks to perform the Office but also clergy were urged to form houses of canons regular where the Office might be performed. Dom Pierre Salmon suggests that the origins of the breviary can be traced to the impetus seen in the great collections of canon law of the same period, such as those of Ivo of Chartres. That is, there was an attempt to collect, summarize, and harmonize the texts of the Office. The result was perhaps a loss of freedom of choice in the plethora of possible texts, but there was produced a synthesis of the Office.

Once the breviary reached its "mature" form from the thirteenth century on, it would contain the following: (*a*) kalendar noting the number of lessons and the different grades or importances of the feasts in the event of overlap; (*b*) feriated psalter; (*c*) *proprium de tempore*, or proper of time, giving a *cursus* of the daily Offices beginning with Advent; (*d*) *proprium de sanctis*, or proper of saints, beginning with the feast of St. Andrew on 30 November; (*e*) *commune de sanctis*, giving Offices for general types of saints such as bishops, monks, virgins, and so forth; and (*f*) additional material such as the *officium Marianum*.

THE STRUCTURE OF THE OFFICE

From the sources described above, the shape of the Office in the Middle Ages emerges. It must be stressed, however, that there was no single perfect text or structure. The most complete or extensive text was not necessarily the most perfect. Throughout the Middle Ages the performance of the Office varied from church to church and from monastery to monastery. And although there are definite groupings of Office performance according to religious order or geographical and ecclesiastical boundaries, there was for the Office none of the structural stability that was found, for example, in the canon of the Roman Mass. With this caveat in mind it is possible to present a generalized structure of the Office, and the accompanying table giving the elements of the Office, together with the cursus or distribution of the psalms during the Offices, represent the two major types of Office, the Benedictine and the secular. It is to be noted that the lines with arrows signify

DIVINE OFFICE

ELEMENTS OF THE DIVINE OFFICE
MATINS

BENEDICTINE		SECULAR		
Sundays and Feasts	*Ferial*	*Sunday*	*Festal*	*Ferial*
Introduction		Introduction		
vs. Domine labia mea (×3) ———→		vs. Domine labia mea ———→	———→	
Ps. 3 + Gloria				
Invitatory (Ps. 94 + Antiphon) ———→		Invitatory (Ps. 94 + Antiphon) ———→	———→	
Hymn ———→		Hymn ———→	———→	
I. Nocturn		I. Nocturn		
6 Pss. + Antiphons ———→		12 Pss. + Antiphon + Gloria	3 Pss. + Antiphons	12 Pss. + Antiphon after each pair
Versicle ———→		Versicle ———→	———→	———→
Benediction ———→		Pater noster ———→	———→	———→
4 Lessons + Responses + Gloria	3 Lessons + 3 Responses + Gloria (Summer: 1 O.T. Lesson + Responsory)	Benediction ———→	———→	———→
		3 Lessons + Responses ———→	———→	———→
II. Nocturn		II. Nocturn		
6 Pss. + Antiphons	6 Pss. + Alleluia	3 Pss. + Antiphons ———→	———→	
Versicle		Versicle ———→	———→	
Benediction		Benediction ———→	———→	
4 Lessons + Responses + Gloria	Capitulum Versicle Kyrie Pater noster	3 Lessons + Responses ———→	———→	
III. Nocturn		III. Nocturn		
3 Canticles + Alleluia		3 Pss. + Antiphons ———→	———→	
Versicle		Versicle ———→	———→	
Benediction		Benediction ———→	———→	
4 Lessons + Responses + Gloria		Pater noster ———→	———→	
		3 Lessons + 2 Responses ———→	———→	
Conclusion		Conclusion		
Te Deum		Te Deum after Lesson 3 ———→	———→	
Gospel				
Te decet laus				
Hymn				
Benediction				

MATINS CURSUS OF PSALMS

BENEDICTINE		SECULAR
Sun	3, 94, 20–31	94, 1–3, 6–14, 15–20
Mon	32–34, 36–41, 43–44	26–37
Tues	45–49, 51–57, 58	38–41, 43–49, 51
Wed	59–61, 65, 67–72	52, 54–61, 63, 65, 67
Thurs	73–74, 76–84	68–79
Fri	85–86, 88, 92–93, 95	80–88, 93, 95–96
Sat	101–108	97–108

LAUDS

BENEDICTINE	SECULAR		
Sunday and Ferial	*Sunday*	*Festal*	*Ferial*
vs. Deus in adiutorium + Gloria	vs. Deus in adiutorium ———→	———→	
Ps. 66	Ps. 92 + Antiphon ———→	———→	Ps. 50 + Antiphon
Ps. 50 + Alleluia	1 Ps. + Antiphon ———→	———→	
2 Pss. + Antiphons	Pss. 62, 66 + Antiphons ———→	———→	
O.T. Canticle + Antiphon	O.T. Canticle + Antiphon ———→	———→	
Pss. 148–50 + Antiphon	Pss. 148–50 + Antiphon ———→	———→	

DIVINE OFFICE

LAUDS (Continued)

Sunday and Ferial

Capitulum + Response
Hymn
Versicle + Response
Canticle (Benedictus) + Antiphon
Litany
Pater noster

Sunday	Festal	Ferial
Capitulum + Response ———————→	————————→	
Hymn —————	————————→	————————→
Versicle + Response ——————→	————————→	
Canticle (Benedictus) + Antiphon —→	————————→	
Preces ————————→	————————→	

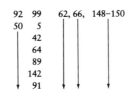

LAUDS CURSUS OF PSALMS

BENEDICTINE

Sun	66, 50	117, 62	148–150
Mon		5, 35	
Tues		42, 56	
Wed		63, 64	
Thurs		87, 89	
Fri		75, 91	
Sat		142, 142	

SECULAR

	92 99	62, 66,	148–150
	50 5		
	42		
	64		
	89		
	142		
	91		

PRIME, TERCE, SEXT, NONE

BENEDICTINE

vs. Deus in adiutorium + Gloria

Hymn
Pss. (4 on Sun; 3 on Ferial) + Antiphon
Capitulum + Response
Versicle
Kyrie
Pater noster

SECULAR

vs. Deus in adiutorium + Gloria
+ Alleluia
Hymn
3 Pss. (9 on Sun)
Quicunque vult (at Prime)
Capitulum + Response
Versicle
Preces
Collect

PRIME, TERCE, SEXT, NONE CURSUS OF PSALMS

BENEDICTINE

	Prime	Terce	Sext	None
Sun	118	118	118	118
Mon	1, 2, 6	118	118	118
Tues	7–9	119–121	122–124	125–127
Wed	9–11			
Thurs	12–14			
Fri	15–17			
Sat	17–19			

SECULAR

Prime	Terce	Sext	None
21–25, 53, 117, 118, 120	118	118	118

VESPERS

BENEDICTINE

vs. Deus in adiutorium + Gloria

4 Pss. + Antiphons
Capitulum + Response
Hymn
Versicle
Canticle (Magnificat) + Antiphon
Preces
Pater noster

SECULAR

vs. Deus in adiutorium + Gloria
+ Alleluia
5 Pss. + Antiphons
Capitulum + Response
Hymn
Versicle
Canticle (Magnificat) + Antiphon
Preces
Pater noster

DIVINE OFFICE

ELEMENTS OF THE DIVINE OFFICE (Continued)
VESPERS CURSUS OF PSALMS

BENEDICTINE		SECULAR
Sun	109–112	109–113
Mon	113–116, 128	114–120
Tues	129–132	121–125
Wed	134–137	126–130
Thurs	138–140	131–132, 134–136
Fri	141, 143–144	137–141
Sat	144–147	143–147

COMPLINE

BENEDICTINE	SECULAR
vs. Deus in adiutorium + Gloria	vs. Deus in adiutorium + Gloria + Alleluia
3 Pss.	4 Pss.
Hymn	Hymn
Capitulum	Capitulum
Versicle	Versicle
Kyrie	Canticle (Nunc Dimittis) + Antiphon
Benediction	Preces
Pater noster	

COMPLINE CURSUS OF PSALMS

BENEDICTINE	SECULAR
Sun 4, 90, 133	4, 30, 90, 133
Mon	
Tues	
Wed	
Thurs	
Fri	
Sat	

the same practice on festal and ferial days and that individual psalm chapters may be broken into a number of sections to be said at different hours or days.

Beginning in patristic times the Office was performed at various times of the day and night, referred to as the hours; as the Office developed in the Middle Ages, the hours came to have their own distinctive sequences of components.

Night Office (matins). The longest of the hours was the night Office, or matins, sometimes called nocturns or vigils. Depending on the season and whether it was performed in southern or northern Europe, matins would have been said at different times. Dom David Knowles, for example, notes that at Monte Cassino matins would have begun about 2:10 A.M. and ended at 3:30 on normal days. In summer it would have lasted approximately from 1:00 to 2:00. Further, the length of matins would vary according to the day, Sundays and feast days having more components than ferial or weekdays.

In both the Benedictine and secular matins there is an introductory and concluding section surrounding the body of the Office consisting of three segments called nocturns. In the introduction and conclusion the major difference between the Benedictine and secular matins is that the former includes an additional psalm and a much longer conclusion on Sundays and feasts. An even greater difference is found in the body of matins. Characteristic of the Benedictine Office is the use of six psalms and antiphons for the first two nocturns, three canticles for the third nocturn, and four lessons in all nocturns. The secular matins, however, has twelve psalms in the first nocturn, three in the second and third, and only three lessons for each nocturn.

Daily office. The day Office consisted of seven hours: *(1) Lauds.* The service of lauds followed matins, sometimes immediately depending on the feasts and seasons. Dom Knowles, again describing the practice at Monte Cassino, notes that in winter lauds would have begun at about 5:00 A.M. and in summer at about 2:15 A.M. After an introductory section, the body of lauds consisted of psalms and antiphons, but to these were added an Old Testament canticle, the capitulum or little chapter (often from the Pauline letters), Benedictus, and prayers. Characteristic of the psalms used in both the Benedictine and secular lauds was the *Alleluiaticum* (psalms 148–150), which Paul Bradshaw argues originated in the monastic vigil of Syria and Palestine, and also psalms 66 and 50.

(2–5) Prime, terce, sext, none. Although lauds technically was the first Office of the day, the first hour of the day was prime, and the liturgical Office of prime was celebrated in winter about 6:00 and in summer much earlier. The other hours of terce, sext, and none corresponded roughly to 9:00 A.M., noon, and 3:00 P.M, though the Office was not necessarily performed exactly at those hours. These four hours are structured very much alike, though there were additional psalms for Sundays, and in the secular Office the Anthanasian Creed or *Quicunque vult* was sung at prime. Characteristic of both the Benedictine and secular Offices was the distribution of sections of Psalm 118 (119) over these hours or over certain days.

(6) Vespers. One of the most ancient hours, known as vespers, would be performed in winter about 4:30 P.M. and in summer about 6–6:30. On Sundays and greater feasts there might be two or a double vespers. The first and more important of the two would be celebrated on the eve of the feast and the second on the day itself. In its structure vespers resembles lauds, the major differences being that lauds lacks the set psalms and Old Testament canticle and replaces the Benedictus with the Magnificat, during which the altars were censed.

(7) Compline. The last hour of the day, originally a monastic Office, might be said as early as 5:00 P.M. in the winter and 7:30 in summer. During most of the year there was very little change in the service, and hence it is at times omitted in manuscripts of the Office. The Benedictine and secular practice is very similar, except that in the latter there are more psalms and the New Testament canticle Nunc Dimittis is used.

THE HISTORICAL DEVELOPMENT OF THE OFFICE

From earliest Christian times the followers of Jesus in the context of contemporary Jewish practice prayed not only privately but publicly at certain times of the day. By the second and third centuries a pattern of daily prayer—morning, noon, evening, and night—had developed, perhaps going back to the beginnings of the church and an ancient Jewish tradition of praying at the cardinal points of the day. In the third century there is a great deal of conflicting evidence regarding the public prayers of the church; but it is not until the fourth that the picture begins to clear, and even here there are two major types of Offices, one that is traditionally called the cathedral Office, and another traditionally called the monastic Office. In the East the witnesses for the cathedral Office are John Chrysostom, who describes the practice in the church of Antioch; the *Apostolic Constitutions,* reflecting Syriac usage; and especially the fourth-century pilgrim from the West, Etheria, who describes the services in Jerusalem of a mixed monastic and cathedral type. For the eastern monastic Office the primary witnesses are Palladius, John Cassian, and Basil. According to Paul Bradshaw the most noticeable difference between the secular and monastic Offices in the East was that the latter was more of a continuation of individual meditation on the word of God and that the prayers following psalms were not so much prayers for the needs of the world but petitions for ascetic growth. The Office of the secular church, by contrast, was more outward-looking with corporate expressions of praise in hymns or canticles, communal response to the psalms (which had been selected for their appropriateness), ceremonial lighting of lamps, and offering of incense.

In the West the cathedral Office is known through references in Augustine, Ambrose, the Gallican and Spanish councils noted earlier, and in the works of Isidore of Seville. Much more extensive is the evidence for the monastic Office in the West because there exist such monastic rules as those of Caesarius, the *Regula magistri,* and the Rule of St. Benedict, all with their extensive description of the monastic Office.

The monastic Office that Benedict developed was actually based on the practices of the *ecclesia romana.* In Rome it seems that the Offices were divided among the various basilicas; each Office was provided for by the more or less regular communities of the basilicas, though not necessarily everywhere at the same time. In the Roman basilicas, if we can judge by Benedict, the psalter would have been sung each week with antiphons, readings, and preces, with the collect or prayer being reserved to the pope or a bishop. Also in Rome at the martyrial cemetery churches vigils and Offices would have been celebrated. But as the relics of saints were brought into the city and all of the churches began to celebrate the saints' feasts, the continuous psalter was interrupted by a sanctorale.

Outside Rome the Office was said in secular churches, but the institution must have been similar. In Spain, for example, there could be a principal church with title churches where the Office was divided. And some cities, like Rome, had stational organizations, according to which parts of the Office would be said in different churches. Such was the case at Angers, Mainz, Cologne, Trier, Metz, Tours, and Augsburg. In these cities the senior basilica would be surrounded by urban basilicas served by clerics or "monks" responsible for the Office, perhaps reciting it by rote.

From the time of Gregory I the Roman Office began to spread northward with missionaries, first to Gaul, then Britain, and finally into Germany with Boniface, under whom the daily *cursus* became obligatory.

At the Council of Clovesho (747) it was laid down that the seven hours according to the *cursus* of the Roman church were obligatory, and not long thereafter Chrodegang of Metz, Pepin the Short, and Charlemagne made the Office obligatory for all clergy, whom they urged to live according to a rule as *canonici*. Because the clerics were to live under a rule, it seemed appropriate for them to perform the Office as the monks did. Hence, there was legislation enjoining clerics to use the complete Office; especially important were the decrees of the Council of Aachen (816) known as the *Institutio canonicorum,* which was given wide broadcast in the manuscripts from the ninth century and beyond.

During the Carolingian period not only were there changes regarding the obligation of clerics to say the Office but changes were also made in the Office itself. First, there appears to have been a revision of the Roman Office under Pope Adrian I because Amalarius early in the ninth century speaks of having compared an antiphonal sent by Gregory IV to Wala with one sent to Metz in 768. Second, not content with these Roman Office books, Amalarius created a synthetic antiphonal in which he distinguished his own creation from the usages in the

Roman books. Third, the rather simple *ordines* of the late patristic period were augmented with complicated directories of reading, antiphons, and the like. Fourth, there developed the *Officium capitula,* an Office that according to the Rule of Chrodegang of Metz was to be said after prime (in Lent after terce) and which consisted of a sermon, spiritual reading, reading of the martyrology, prayer, and confession of fault. Fifth, there was added to the Office a plethora of services, among which were: (1) the recitation of the fifteen gradual psalms *pro defunctis* (Pss. 119–133 [120–134]) in the matins of the dead inserted between matins and lauds or between lauds and prime depending on the season; (2) the seven penitential psalms (Pss. 6, 31 [32], 37 [38], 50 [51], 101 [102], 129 [130], and 142 [143]) recited after prime; and (3) the *trina oratio* said before matins, consisting of the penitential psalms divided into three sections, followed by the gradual psalms divided into three sections.

During the ninth century and beyond, further supererogatory Offices, the origins of which seem to have been in private devotions, were added to both the monastic and secular daily Office: the Offices of the Dead, of the Virgin, of All Saints, and of the Cross, and special commemorations for benefactors, relatives, and others. These Offices were not necessarily restricted to one recitation a day but might be inserted after each hour. Moreover, they could be used privately.

The tenth century, which saw the growth of these supererogatory Offices, also saw the tendency of secular clerics to abandon the canonical or regular life and live by themselves, with the effect of diminishing the celebration of a solemn Office among the clergy. But this situation was to change in the later eleventh century. One of the goals of the reformers was the reestablishment of the regular life among the clergy, and one aspect of this was the recitation of the Office. If one can judge by the canonical legislation and canonical collections, the emphasis was on solemn recitation, but clearly private recitation among clerics was making inroads, especially among absentee clerics. To stem this practice Ivo of Chartres argued that clerical benefices be tied to the recital of the Office in the church. These reforms, associated with the rise of the movement known as the canons regular, were in part successful, though some of the less monastic-oriented groups of canons regular reduced the Office. Also the relatively small size of the groups of canons made it difficult for them to have choir recitals of the Offices.

Among the secular clergy of the twelfth century the recitation of the Office declined even further. In Rome, where the curial clergy were otherwise occupied or absent, and among the clergy in university communities, the solemn recitation of the Office was further reduced.

During the pontificate of Innocent III (1198–1216) an abbreviation of the Roman curial Office was compiled. This shortened the Office for the papal court itself, and so popular did it become that it gradually came to replace the solemn basilican practice. Further, so useful in its brevity was this curial Office that it was accepted by the Franciscans, who in their wandering gave it very wide diffusion, thereby making it quasi-official in Europe.

Like the clerics in the universities, the Franciscans usually found it impossible to say the Office solemnly, except in large houses. Hence, the private recitation of the Office became even more widely spread. Although the ideal remained solemn, public recitation, nevertheless, a number of legal decisions and commentaries from the thirteenth century on allowed private recitation under certain conditions. This was the necessary edge leading to the sweeping practice of private recitation of the Office, which characterized the late Middle Ages.

BIBLIOGRAPHY

Paul F. Bradshaw, *Daily Prayer in the Early Church* (1982); V. Fiala and W. Irtenkauf, "Versuch einer liturgischen Nomenklautur: Zur katalogisierung mittelalterlicher und neuerer Handschriften," in *Zeitschrift für Bibliothekswesen und Bibliographie,* 10 (1963); Klaus Gamber, *Codices luturgici latini antiquiores,* II (1968), 492–500, 576–614; Andrew Hughes, *Medieval Manuscripts for Mass and Office: A Guide to Their Organization and Terminology* (1982), 50–80, 160–244; *International Bibliography of Liturgy,* classes 42–47; David Knowles, *Christian Monasticism* (1969); Aimé G. Martimort, *L'église en prière: Introduction à la liturgie* (1961), 787–843; Richard W. Pfaff, *Medieval Latin Liturgy: A Select Bibliography* (1982), 26–33; Pierre Salmon, *The Breviary Through the Centuries,* Sister David Mary, trans. (1962), and *L'office divin au moyen âge* (1967); *The Study of Liturgy,* Cheslyn Jones, Geoffrey Wainwright, and Edward Yarnold, eds. (1978), 350–389; Erich J. Thiel, "Die liturgischen Bücher des Mittelalters," in *Börsenblatt für den deutschen Buchhandel,* 134 (1967, no. 23), 2379–2395.

ROGER E. REYNOLDS

[See also **Amalarius of Metz; Antiphonal; Benedictine Rule; Book of Hours; Breviary; Canonical Hours; Clergy; Collectarium; Lectionary; Liturgy, Treatises on; Psalter.**]

DIVORCE. See **Family.**

DIYARBAKIR (Greek: Amida), a town situated in Mesopotamia on a plateau on the bank of the Tigris (37° 55′ N. latitude, 40° 14′ E. longitude) and taking its name from the Bakr tribe, Diyarbakir became a Roman colony in 230. In the fourth century it was taken by Shapur II from the Byzantines and often changed hands in the wars between the Byzantines and the Persians. In 638 it was taken by the Arabs, and in 856 Byzantine armies crossed the Euphrates and reached as far as Diyarbakir. The Byzantines took it in 941, but in 973 in a battle near the town, the emir of Mosul defeated them. From the tenth century on, Diyarbakir was successively in the hands of various Muslim dynasties: the Hamdanids, the Marwanids, the Artugids, and finally the Ottomans.

BIBLIOGRAPHY

George Ostrogorsky, *History of the Byzantine State,* Joan Hussey, trans. (1957, rev. ed. 1969).

LINDA C. ROSE

DJVARI, the Georgian term for cross, refers to a monumental wooden cross erected on top of a mountain in the ancient capital of Georgia (Iberia), Mtsxet{^{c}}a, by King Mirian in the first half of the fourth century. In 545–586 King Guaram built a small church next to this cross, and his successor, Stephanos (586/587–604/605), constructed a larger church to house the original cross.

In this tetraconch the conchae alternate with four rectangular compartments that have groin vaults and are connected to the central square by narrow three-quarter circular niches. The elongation of the east-west axis is achieved by adding bemas on either end. The eastern compartments not directly connected to the apse could have been used as pastophoria. The function of the western chambers is not clear; an inscription found in the southwestern chamber suggests that it was used to accommodate women. The eastern apse is accentuated with three windows, a synthronon, and a concha. The central square is surmounted by a semispherical masonry dome with an octagonal drum resting on sustaining walls and squinches. The interior of the church is characterized by clearly defined harmonious proportions that are boldly perceived in the monumentality of its masses. The architectural logic revealed in the formation of the interior is sustained in the exterior structure of the church: in the rhythmic articulation of its exterior walls with niches between the rectangular compartments and projected polygonal conchae the cruciform shape of the church is distinctly emphasized.

In contrast with other Byzantine churches the architectural sculpture adorning the exterior walls of the Djvari church assumes great significance. The windows are surmounted by brows embellished with vegetal motifs; the tympanum of the southern doorway contains the elevation of a green cross by two angels; the eastern apse displays three reliefs composed of the salvation-seeking donors, identified by inscriptions, and Christ in a blessing posture.

BIBLIOGRAPHY

Wachtang Z. Djobadze, "The Sculptures of the Holy Cross of Mtskheta," in *Oriens christianus,* 44 (1960) and 45 (1961); Georg N. Tshubinashvili, *Pamiatniki tipa Djvari* (1948), with French summary 199–210.

WACHTANG DJOBADZE

[See also **Georgian Art and Architecture.**]

DMITRII IVANOVICH DONSKOI (1350–1389), prince of Moscow and grand prince of Vladimir, remembered as one of the great Muscovite military heroes.

When Dmitrii came to the throne at the age of nine, Muscovy's position was an uncertain one. Lithuanian influence was growing to the west, and the favor that had been shown to Muscovite princes by the Mongol Empire was jeopardized. In the early fourteenth century the khans of the Golden Horde had raised Dmitrii's predecessors to a status of preeminence among the principalities of northeastern Russia by granting them letters patent *(yarlyk),* naming them grand princes of Vladimir. By 1359, however, a struggle for supremacy within the Mongol Empire had prompted certain descendants of Genghis Khan, who were competing contenders for leadership of the Golden Horde, to issue letters patent to Moscow's rivals, the princes of Suzdal and Tver. Dmitrii's regency council repressed the Suzdal prince's claim by invading his territory in 1363; and in 1370 Dmitrii himself led his army into Tver, tem-

porarily restoring Muscovite primacy. In 1375 Prince Michael of Tver again obtained a letter patent as well as a promise of military aid from the grand duke of Lithuania; but Dmitrii mustered a large force against him, which encouraged the Lithuanians to break their promise, and Michael was forced to accept a position of momentary subservience to Dmitrii.

With Muscovy's dominant position among the northeastern Russian principalities now confirmed, Dmitrii was ready to challenge the divided Golden Horde in order to assure his primacy as grand prince. To advertise his stance he undertook military actions against Mongol forays into neighboring principalities, thereby enraging Emir Mamai, who had regained control of the steppe for a puppet khan and resolved to reimpose Mongol overlordship in Russia. The two leaders met in a bitterly contested battle in 1380 at Kulikovo Pole, near the Don River in the principality of Ryazan. Mamai's Lithuanian allies never appeared, and the Mongol forces were defeated and fled in disarray. In honor of this, the first Russian victory over a Mongol army, Dmitrii was henceforth known as Donskoi (of the Don).

Muscovite independence was short-lived, however, for in 1382 a briefly united Golden Horde sacked Moscow and reasserted its overlordship. But the khan, Tokhtamîsh, wisely endorsed Dmitrii as grand prince, recognizing that a satisfied Muscovite leader would remain loyal. Thereafter Muscovy's rivals never again sought to challenge its preeminence, and Donskoi even "bequeathed" the grand principality to his eldest son.

BIBLIOGRAPHY

Dmytro Chyzhevs'kyĭ, *History of Russian Literature from the Eleventh Century to the End of the Baroque* (1960), 194–198; C. J. Halperin, "The Russian Land and the Russian Tsar: The Emergence of Muscovite Ideology, 1380–1408," in *Forschungen zur osteuropäischen Geschichte,* 23 (1976), 7–103, deals with the various tales of the battle at Kulikovo Pole and the eulogies of Donskoi—both the dates given for the appearance of these tales and the thesis of the article have been questioned, but this is the only extended discussion of the literature in English. See also Alexander E. Presniakov, *The Formation of the Great Russian State,* A. E. Moorhouse, trans. (1970), 238–269, esp. 262ff.; George Vernadsky, *The Mongols and Russia* (1953), 245–267.

GUSTAVE ALEF

[See also **Golden Horde; Mongols; Muscovy, Rise of; Vladimir-Suzdal.**]

DOCCIONI. See **Gargoyle.**

DOCETISM, the doctrine that holds that the Second Person of the Trinity did not actually become flesh as Jesus Christ but merely took on the appearance of a body. Some evidence for the early existence of this heresy may be found in the New Testament (1 John 4:1–3; 2 John 7). Clement of Alexandria (*Stromateis,* 3.12, 7.17) and Hippolytus (*Refutatio omnium haeresium,* or *Syntagma,* 8.2) seem to be writing against a specific sect, but in general ecclesiastical writers treated Docetism as a tendency or aspect of the systems propounded by Marcion, Valentinus, and other Gnostics. Docetism would be a logical necessity for dualistic systems in which the creator (demiurge) is distinct from the true God, and where the creator and his creation are either contaminated by matter or are an integral part of it. In dualistic systems where Jesus is the savior, he assumes a phantom body. Salvation is not accomplished through the birth, death, and resurrection of Jesus, but through his revelation of saving knowledge (gnosis).

A later third-century docetic tendency is found in Manichaeism. Here, however, the issue is complicated by the fact that there are two figures named Jesus, "Jesus of Light" and the historical Jesus. The former is an emanation of the Father of Greatness and belongs to a World of Light that is uncontaminated by darkness and its offspring, matter. What the relationship of this Jesus to the historical Jesus might be is unclear. Mani counted Jesus with Zoroaster and Buddha as special envoys of the World of Light who foreshadowed Mani's own final and definitive revelation. Some Manichaean texts that do treat Jesus state that he was born without a body but took on the appearance of a man. His death was an illusion. Perhaps Mani was refuting any Christian claims about the efficacy of the redemptive acts attributed to the incarnate Jesus.

After 451 Monophysite splinter groups such as the Gaianites, who taught that Jesus' body was incorruptible before the Resurrection, were accused of Docetism. But there is no evidence that they intended to deny the actual incarnation of Jesus. The charge of Docetism was also leveled against the early Armenian Paulicians, but this group taught an adoptionist Christology. Later ninth-century Paulicians in Byzantium may have had docetic tendencies. The Bogomil sect, which arose in the Balkans in the tenth century and had doctrines resembling those of the Manichaeans, held a docetic view of Jesus and rejected the sacraments. In Italy and France the Albigensians held similar views. Both sects taught that Jesus saved mankind only through the revelation of the true doctrine. Although Albigensianism did not survive after the fourteenth century, Bogomilism still existed in the mid fifteenth century, when it was absorbed into Islam.

BIBLIOGRAPHY

The best general treatment of the early period, with references to all the extant patristic citations, is G. Bareilles, "Docétisme," in *Dictionnaire de théologie catholique,* IV.2 (1939), 1484–1501. Also available are G. Salmon, "Docetae" and "Docetism," in William Smith and Henry Wace, eds., *A Dictionary of Christian Biography, Literature, Sects and Doctrines,* I (1900), 865–870.

D. W. JOHNSON

[See also **Bogomilism; Dualism; Heresy; Manichaeans; Paulicians.**]

DOCTOR (from the Latin *doctus,* past participle of *docere,* to teach) had the basic meaning in the Middle Ages of someone qualified to teach. Doctor, professor, and master (*magister*) were practically equivalent terms. As education became more organized and as universities began to take shape, there were strong pressures to keep unqualified men from teaching. Successful teachers did not wish to face competition from upstarts, and the church wanted to be sure that unorthodox ideas were not being taught. Therefore the would-be teacher had to pass an examination in order to have the right to teach. An advanced student (a bachelor in arts or law, for instance) who had passed preliminary tests might be allowed to teach under the supervision of a master, but full license to teach (*licentia docendi*) came only after a rigorous final examination.

The title given to these teachers varied from place to place and, to some extent, from subject to subject. At Paris, the most prestigious university, leading scholars were called masters. The same was true in England and in Germany. "Doctor" was the more common title in Italy. This may be why teachers of law and medicine were more often called "doctors" than teachers of arts, since advanced study of law and medicine began in Italy. In general, the differences in title meant little; the essential thing was acceptance by other professors as an equal.

BIBLIOGRAPHY

Charles H. Haskins, *The Rise of Universities* (1923, many reprints); Hastings Rashdall, *The Universities of Europe in the Middle Ages,* new ed. by F. M. Powicke and A. B. Emden, 3 vols. (1936), esp. vol. I; Helene Wieruszowski, *The Medieval University* (1966).

JOSEPH R. STRAYER

[See also **Universities.**]

DOCTORS OF THE CHURCH (from the Latin sense of *doctor:* teacher). The Roman Catholic church now recognizes thirty-one doctors of the church. The title may be conferred by decision of an ecumenical council or by papal decree, and acknowledges unusual intellectual distinction, orthodoxy, and holiness of life. A doctor's theological pronouncements are accorded an authority that falls short of infallibility but far exceeds that of other saints and church fathers. Only four doctors were proclaimed during the medieval period (by Boniface VIII in 1298)—St. Ámbrose (*ca.* 340–397), for contributions to the Christian life in his manual of ethics, *De officiis ministrorum;* St. Jerome (*ca.* 347–419/420), translator of the Vulgate, for his biblical scholarship in Hebrew, Greek, and Latin; St. Augustine of Hippo (354–430), "Doctor of Grace," the most influential of Western theologians, particularly for his exaltation of the role of grace in human salvation and for his Christian interpretation of history; and St. Gregory I the Great (*ca.* 540–604), for his contributions to papal supremacy, clarification of the clerical role in Christian life, and hopefulness in depressing times. The Orthodox church recognizes only three "great universal teachers"—St. Basil the Great (*ca.* 330–379), for his doctrine of the Trinity, discussion of the relation of faith to reason, and the idea of monasticism; St. Gregory of Nazianzus (*ca.* 330–390), for his doctrines of the divine nature and of the Trinity; and St. John Chrysostom (*ca.* 349–407), for his brilliant exposition in homilies of the Christian life. These three, along with St. Athanasius of Alexandria (*ca.* 295–373), were acknowledged as doctors in the West by Pope Pius V in 1568.

The other doctors from the late Roman period (all saints) are Ephraim the Syrian, Cyril of Jerusalem, Hilary of Poitiers, Cyril of Alexandria, Peter Chrysologus, Leo the Great, and Isidore of Seville.

For the medieval period one might choose for comment the contributions of the saints John of Da-

mascus (*ca.* 675–*ca.* 749) to the remembrance of the classical period in Greek theology as digested in his *Fountain of Wisdom;* Anselm of Canterbury (1033–1109), "father of the Schoolmen," to discussion of the relationship of faith and reason, arguments for the existence of God, theories of atonement, and the cause of realism over nominalism; Bernard of Clairvaux (1090–1153), "Doctor Mellifluus," to the monastic life, and to the interpretation of Scripture; Albertus Magnus (*ca.* 1200–1280) and Thomas Aquinas (*ca.* 1225–1274) toward a systematic reconciliation of religious and scientific thought; and Bonaventure (*ca.* 1217–1274) to mystical theology. Other medieval doctors are the Venerable Bede, Peter Damian, Anthony of Padua, and Catherine of Siena (with Teresa of Avila the only female doctor, proclaimed in 1970).

The remaining doctors lived after the Middle Ages: Sts. Peter Canisius, Robert Bellarmine, John of the Cross, Francis de Sales, Alphonsus of Liguori, and Lawrence of Brindisi.

BIBLIOGRAPHY

Ernest Simmons, *The Fathers and Doctors of the Church* (1959); John W. C. Wand, *Doctors and Councils* (1962).

G. L. KEYES

[See also **Albertus Magnus; Ambrose, St.; Anselm of Canterbury; Anthony of Padua, St.; Aquinas, St. Thomas; Athanasius of Alexandria, St.; Augustine of Hippo, St.; Basil the Great of Caesarea, St.; Bede; Bernard of Clairvaux, St.; Bonaventure, St.; Chrysostom, John, St.; Church Fathers; Cyril of Alexandria, St.; Gregory I the Great, Pope; Gregory of Nazianzus, St.; Hilary of Poitiers, St.; Isidore of Seville, St.; Jerome, St.; John of Damascus, St.; Peter Damian, St.**]

DOME, a hemispherical vault, usually on a round base, that covers a circular or polygonal space; if the latter, the corners are bridged by pendentives or squinches. The dome is often raised above the space it covers on a curved or polygonal vertical wall called a drum; particularly in Byzantine architecture, the drum is frequently pierced by windows. Additional light may be obtained by opening a round window (oculus) at the summit of the dome; the summit may be topped by a small turret pierced by windows called a lantern.

The dome was fully developed by the Romans, who perfected the use of graded cement to lighten

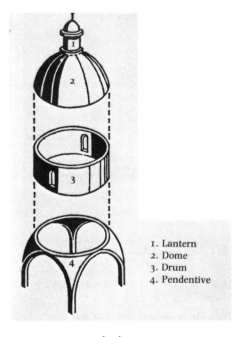

Component parts of a dome. FROM NICHOLAS PEVS-NER, THE PENGUIN DICTIONARY OF ARCHITECTURE (© 1976)

1. Lantern
2. Dome
3. Drum
4. Pendentive

Diagram of a squinch. FROM RICHARD KRAUTHEIMER, EARLY CHRISTIAN AND BYZANTINE ARCHITECTURE (© 1965)

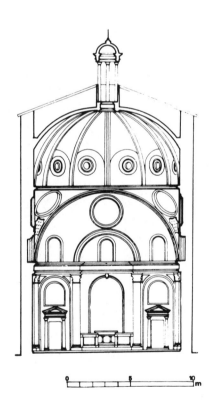

Onion dome. Plan of the Church of St. John the Baptist, Dyakovo. FROM SAMUEL H. CROSS, MEDIAEVAL RUSSIAN CHURCHES, KENNETH J. CONANT, ED. (1949)

Pendentive dome (sail vault) and pumpkin dome (umbrella dome). FROM NICHOLAS PEVSNER, THE PENGUIN DICTIONARY OF ARCHITECTURE (© 1976)

Section plan of a double-shell dome. Filippo Brunelleschi's old sacristy in the Duomo, Florence, 15th century. From Christian Norberg-Schultz, *Meaning in Western Architecture* (1975). ELECTA EDITRICE

235

and solidify the structure; coffers and ribbing were also introduced by the Romans to further reduce the dome's weight. A good example of a Roman coffered cement dome is provided by the Pantheon. After the fourth century, cement was increasingly replaced by stone and, especially, brick, resulting in lighter domes, an achievement furthered by the substitution of hollow, interlocking terra-cotta tubes (*tubi fittili*) for some or all of the solid materials in certain Italian monuments such as S. Vitale in Ravenna (*ca.* 547); empty amphoras might also be inserted among the bricks to lighten the weight.

Double-shell dome. A dome within a dome, wherein the space between the interior ceiling and the exterior roof is hollow, creating a very light dome that is easily accessible. Brunelleschi's fifteenth-century dome on the Duomo in Florence is a highly developed example of the technique, which appears during the early Christian period, such as at S. Lorenzo in Milan (fourth century).

Onion dome (bulbous dome). A dome with bulging sides and a protracted apex characteristic of north Russian architecture. The Russian examples, which first appear in the twelfth century, may have been influenced by earlier Indian or Near Eastern onion domes, or may have developed independently from the native carpentry tradition, in response to the need for a roof that sheds snow and rain quickly.

Pendentive dome (sail vault). The hemispherical curve of the dome continues uninterrupted down through the pendentives, as in the fifth-century Mausoleum of Galla Placidia at Ravenna.

Pumpkin dome (melon dome, umbrella dome). Composed of numerous curved or fluted segments, thus resembling a pumpkin. One variant, as at Sts. Sergios and Bacchos in Constantinople (sixth century), shows alternate curved and flat segments. Pumpkin domes first appear in Roman architecture; their use continued throughout the Middle Ages, particularly in Byzantium, especially to cover irregularly shaped rooms.

Saucer dome. A shallow, segmental dome.

Semidome. Half of a dome: in Byzantine architecture, semidomes often buttress full domes, as at Hagia Sophia in Constantinople (sixth century).

Stilted dome. A dome with a springing point well above its base, as if drum and dome were combined into a single unit; popular in Islamic architecture.

BIBLIOGRAPHY

W. Born, "The Origin and the Distribution of the Bulbous Dome," in *Journal of the American Society of Architectural Historians,* **3,** no. 4 (1943); George H. Hamilton, *The Art and Architecture of Russia,* 3rd ed. (1983), 34, 42–43; Richard Krautheimer, *Early Christian and Byzantine Architecture,* rev. ed. (1975), 534–536 and *passim;* William L. MacDonald, *The Pantheon* (1976).

LESLIE BRUBAKER

[See also **Brunelleschi, Filippo; Early Christian and Byzantine Architecture; Hagia Sophia (Constantinople); Russian Architecture.**]

DOME OF HEAVEN. Following Roman precedents, the domes and semidomes of early Christian and Byzantine churches were often interpreted as images of heaven. The concept of a ceiling representing the sky is ancient, and the specific cosmological significance of Christian vault decoration has its roots in Roman imagery. Early Christian vaults such as that at Albenga often showed a cross against a starry sky; the canonical Middle Byzantine format presents Christ radially ringed by the apostles or prophets, who act as intermediaries between heaven and earth. The earliest, and most explicit, literary expression of the theme of the dome of heaven ap-

Dome mosaic with the Pantocrator in the center. Palazzo dei Normanni, Cappella Palatina, Palermo, 12th century. ALINARI/ART RESOURCE

pears in a sixth-century Syrian description of the Church of Hagia Sophia at Edessa.

BIBLIOGRAPHY

André Grabar, "Le témoinage d'une hymne syriaque sur l'architecture de la cathédrale d'Edesse au VIᵉ siècle," in *Cahiers archéologiques,* 2 (1947); Karl Lehmann, "The Dome of Heaven," in *Art Bulletin,* 27 (1945); Cyril Mango, *The Art of the Byzantine Empire 312–1453* (1972), 57–60.

LESLIE BRUBAKER

DOME OF THE ROCK, a structure near the earlier site of Solomon's Temple in Jerusalem, completed in 691/692 for the Umayyad caliph ᶜAbd al-Malik. The building consists of two octagonal ambulatories around a domed circular center that rises above a large rock. Jewish tradition held that this rock contained Adam's tomb and was the site of Abraham's sacrifice; this association apparently influenced ᶜAbd al-Malik's decision to build a shrine above the rock, for Abraham is especially venerated by the Muslims. The centralized plan of the Dome of the Rock emphasizes its commemorative function by following an established Christian formula for martyria and shrines. By the eighth century the rock within the building was believed to mark the place of Muḥammad's ascension; this belief continues to the present day among the faithful.

The Dome of the Rock is richly decorated with nonfigural mosaics consisting of vegetal motifs interspersed with vases, cornucopias, and jewels. Aside from the jewels, which simulate actual royal gifts to

Dome of the Rock. Jerusalem, 688–692. SCALA/ART RESOURCE

sacred places, the decorative forms are conventional, but the abundance of richly colored mosaics is unusual for the period. The lavish ornament was apparently meant to emphasize the holiness of the site and to respond to Christian architectural decoration in an effort to attract converts to Islam and keep Muslims from straying to Christianity.

BIBLIOGRAPHY

Margaret van Berchem, "The Mosaics of the Dome of the Rock in Jerusalem and of the Great Mosque in Damascus," in K. A. C. Creswell, ed., *Early Muslim Architecture,* I (1932, repr. 1978); Oleg Grabar, "The Umayyad Dome of the Rock," in *Ars orientalis,* 3 (1959); and *The Formation of Islamic Art* (1973), 48–67.

LESLIE BRUBAKER

[See also **Islamic Architecture; Islamic Art; Marwān, ᶜAbd al-Malik ibn.**]

DOMESDAY BOOK is the name popularly given to a two-volume manuscript containing a comprehensive description of England toward the end of the reign of William I. Designed on a grand scale and executed with unrelenting thoroughness, the survey that produced these documents is considered to be the greatest administrative accomplishment achieved by a royal government in the Middle Ages. Domesday has served for centuries as the definitive record of the feudal order introduced into England by its Norman conquerors.

The Great Survey leading to the compilation of Domesday Book was undertaken in 1086 by order of the king and was conducted with extraordinary haste; the documents were completed in their surviving form before William's death in September 1087. With the exception of the extreme northern regions, the entire kingdom was divided into groups of counties, or circuits, each of which was visited by a team of royal commissioners whose duty it was to collect information on the wealth and people of their assigned territory. These *legati* appear to have used whatever sources were available to them: earlier documents, new statements written specially in preparation for the survey, and oral testimony. They initially arranged their information geographically according to shire, hundred, and village. An example of this stage of the survey is preserved in the *Inquisitio comitatus Cantabrigiensis.* Using the forms of the Norman sworn inquest, local jurors were then

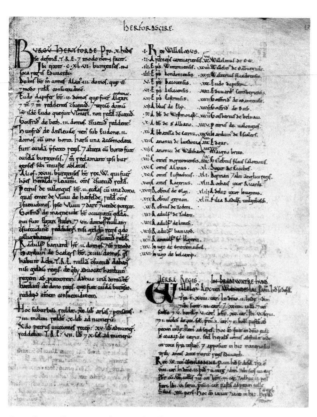

Page from the Domesday Book, showing records for Hertfordshire. 1086–1087. PUBLIC RECORD OFFICE, LONDON, vol. I, fol. 132

summoned to formal court sessions at which they attested to the accuracy of the information. All of this material was then rearranged in feudal order, resulting in a preliminary return for each circuit. The Exon Domesday represents a surviving example of such an early recension.

When the *legati* had completed their local work, a final circuit return was produced and sent to Winchester, where a treasury scribe abbreviated the descriptions of the respective counties and combined them into a single-volume summary, today called Great Domesday. This process was interrupted, however, probably by William's death, leaving one circuit return (that for Essex, Suffolk, and Norfolk) in its original, unabbreviated form; this second volume is called Little Domesday.

The county remained the gross unit of organization for the vast collection of data produced by the survey, but within the county the organizing principle was feudal rather than geographical. The Domesday description of each county includes a numbered list of landholders, beginning with the king and continuing with the names of all tenants in chief who held land of the king. After this initial list comes a detailed description of the king's manors and estates *(terra regis)*, followed by similar descriptions of the manorial holdings of each tenant in chief in the order listed.

For each manor is recorded its holder *modo* (now, that is, in 1086) and its holder at the time of the Conquest twenty years earlier; its size as measured in units of plough capacity; the numbers and classes of people who work on it; its mills, ponds, meadows, woods, and other appurtenances; and its value in pounds *tempore regis Edwardi* (before the Conquest), *quando recepit* (when the present holder received the manor), and *modo* (now). Some information on subtenure also appears.

The treatment of towns is inconsistent. For some counties the chief borough heads the rest of the description; other towns appear within the manorial accounts; still others are missing altogether, including some of the largest (London) and most important (Winchester).

Domesday's organizational structure provides the clue to William's fundamental purpose in ordering the survey. Contrary to speculation by earlier historians, who believed the king's aim was to render the inherited Anglo-Saxon geld collection system more productive, it is clear that Domesday was intended primarily to record and institutionalize the feudal land tenure system introduced by the Normans. It fully embodied the legal concept that all land was held either by the king or of the king, a notion that lay at the heart of the Anglo-Norman kings' considerable success in controlling and governing their large new territory.

As a ready reference to the resources at the command of the king and of his principal tenants, Domesday was useful in administering the Norman system of military taxation *(servicium debitum)*. As a formal record of land tenure, its utility extended to the settlement of disruptive disputes between rival claimants to land. Because it was accepted as an authoritative account of conditions at the end of William's reign, Domesday Book became a bulwark of the new order in post-Conquest England. In modern times it has become an indispensable source for historians who wish to understand eleventh-century England.

BIBLIOGRAPHY
Domesday Book, A. Farley and Henry Ellis, eds., 5 vols. (1783–1816). See also Vivian H. Galbraith, *The Making of*

Domesday Book (1961, repr. 1981); C. Warren Hollister, *The Military Organization of Norman England* (1965); Reginald Lennard, *Rural England, 1086–1135* (1959); Frederic W. Maitland, *Domesday Book and Beyond* (1897); John H. Round, *Feudal England* (1895).

F. F. KREISLER

[See also **Demography; England: Norman-Angevin; William the Conqueror.**]

DOMESTIC, a type of Byzantine military commander whose Latin title originally suggested an intimate member of the imperial household; subsequently it could refer to the highest subordinate of an important commander or official—that is, his adjutant. The commanders of most of the imperial *tagmata,* the mobile elite guard and expeditionary forces, were domestics. The commander of the theme Optimaton was a domestic. In the ninth and tenth centuries the supreme commander of all Byzantine thematic armies in Asia held the title "domestic of the schools in the East." Later there appeared the "domestic of the schools in the West" (for the Balkans). In the reigns of the Komnenoi, the Nicaean emperors, and the Palaiologoi, the supreme military commander was the grand domestic.

BIBLIOGRAPHY

John B. Bury, *The Imperial Administrative System in the Ninth Century* (1911, repr. 1958); Nicolas Oikonomides, *Les listes de préséance byzantines des IXe et Xe siècles* (1972).

WALTER EMIL KAEGI, JR.

[See also **Byzantine Bureaucracy.**]

DOMICAL VAULT. See **Vault.**

DOMINIC, ST. (*ca.* 1171–1221), founder of the Order of Friars Preachers, was born to the possibly noble Guzmán family in the village of Caleruega in Castile, the area of Spain that combined traditions of zealous Christianity and militant opposition to the Muslim invaders. After liberal and scriptural studies at Palencia, he was appointed canon of the cathedral chapter of Osma, his native diocese (*ca.* 1196), which required that he take vows according to the Rule of

St. Augustine. Shortly afterward he was ordained a priest, and about 1201 was elected subprior of the cathedral chapter. In addition to the cultural values of Castile, a deep devotion to Scripture and a special appreciation for the *Conferences* of John Cassian seem to have been the decisive influences on Dominic's intellectual formation.

As part of a royal embassy to Denmark in 1203, Dominic acquired familiarity with religious conditions in northern Europe. In 1206 Bishop Diego de Azevedo of Osma selected Dominic to accompany him on a mission to preach to the Albigensian heretics of Languedoc. The style of simplicity and poverty in which they traveled contrasted sharply with the pomp and display of the papal legates to the Albigensians, and in preaching and public debates Dominic and Diego scored notable successes. They established a convent for women converts at Prouille that became the preachers' first headquarters.

The murder of the legate Cardinal Peter of Castelnau provoked Pope Innocent III in 1208 to proclaim a crusade against the Albigensians. During the violence and civil wars that wracked Languedoc for the next seven years, Dominic and his slowly increasing number of followers continued to try to convert the Albigensians by persuasion, but with modest results; his reputation for personal austerity and theological learning, however, won popular approval.

In 1215 property and gifts from Simon de Montfort and a few other wealthy citizens of Toulouse, and the enthusiasm of several volunteers, provided material support and manpower for the realization of Dominic's desire to found an order of preachers; since the authority to preach belonged exclusively to bishops, the idea of an order of preachers was at the time a novelty. Establishing his headquarters at Toulouse, in 1216 Dominic secured from Pope Honorius III confirmation of his new order; in 1217 the pope approved its name and gave it permission to preach universally. Since its purpose was preaching, Dominic insisted that the brothers of the order receive a strong theological foundation for their ministry and sent them to universities for study. His own preachings to students at Rome, Bologna, Paris, and Montpellier won many able recruits to the new order.

Dominic spent the last years of his life traveling, preaching, and organizing the priories of the order. In 1220 he summoned the first general chapter at Bologna, which drafted constitutions. At Madrid, Rome, and Bologna he established houses of nuns whose work combined educational and apostolic activity with contemplation. He was buried in Bologna and was canonized in 1234. His feast day is 4 August.

Dominic's success as the founder of an order was due to his personal charisma, zeal, and reputation for austerity; his organizational ability; the importance he attached to the help of women in all the order's work; and his insistence on the utilization of the latest learning in the order's preaching ministry.

BIBLIOGRAPHY

Francis C. Lehner, ed., *Saint Dominic: Biographical Documents* (1964), provides an English translation of many contemporary sources. See also François Balme, Paul Lelaidier, and A. I. Collomb, eds., *Cartulaire; ou, Histoire diplomatique de St. Dominique*, 3 vols. (1893–1901). The best modern biographies are William A. Hinnebusch, *The History of the Dominican Order*, I (1966), chaps. 1–3; and Marie Humbert Vicaire, *Saint Dominic and His Times*, K. Pond, trans. (1964). Though pietistic in tone, the following studies are useful: Bede Jarrett, *The Life of St. Dominic*, 2nd ed. (1934); Pierre F. Mandonnet, *St. Dominic and His Work*, M. B. Larkin, trans., (1944). For inconography see Leonard von Matt and Marie Humbert Vicaire, *St. Dominic: A Pictorial Biography*, G. Meath, trans. (1957).

BENNETT D. HILL

[See also **Cathars; Dominicans; Innocent III, Pope; Preaching and Sermon Literature, Western European.**]

DOMINICAN CHANT, the variant form of plainchant used by the Dominicans. For the first two and a half years of its existence the Dominican order, founded in 1215, followed the local liturgical and musical practices of Toulouse. When the order began to spread late in 1217, first to other dioceses in the south of France and then to other countries, its members seem to have continued their original custom of using the liturgical traditions of the areas in which they were working.

Practical considerations, however, soon made it evident that the order needed liturgical uniformity, and a first effort in this direction was made by Jordan of Saxony, who succeeded St. Dominic as head of the order in 1222 and served until 1237. His work, hastily done, soon proved to be unsatisfactory, and at the order's general chapter of 1245 a commission of four friars, from England, France, Germany, and Lombardy, was established and charged with the task of preparing a set of books that would take into account the differing liturgical practices of the many geographic areas from which the order now drew its

membership. The work of these four friars, which comprehensively dealt not only with texts, but also with rubrics and plainchant, was completed early in 1246 and received the mandatory approval from three successive general chapters in 1246, 1247, and 1248. Nevertheless, complaints about the books emerged at the chapter of 1250, and in 1251 the four friars undertook further work on the order's liturgy, finishing in time for it to be approved at the chapter of 1252.

A certain dissatisfaction with the liturgical books persisted despite this additional work by the commission, and in 1254 Humbert of Romans was charged with the task of making further revisions by the same general chapter that elected him the fifth master general of the order. Humbert, who had played a role in the efforts at liturgical uniformity that had been made in 1246 (although it is not certain that he was one of the four friars commissioned to do this) completed his work in 1256. It was accepted by the general chapter of that year and proved to be the final, definitive revision of the order's liturgical books. In all probability Humbert based his work on that of the four friars, but this cannot be proved because no copy of their work has survived. Humbert's work, however, has been preserved in fourteen books that were prepared under his direction and bound together in one huge volume. For many years all Dominican liturgical books were copied directly from this prototype, which until the French Revolution was kept in the Dominican house in Paris and now is preserved in the order's archives in Rome.

Among the fourteen books of Humbert's prototype are three that are essentially musical in nature: an antiphonary, a gradual, and a processional. All three, of course, conform liturgically to the other books, and all reveal that the liturgical revisions characterizing them were based largely on late-twelfth-century practices followed in the Roman basilicas and hardly at all on the usage of Parisian churches, despite the fact that Paris was then the intellectual and cultural center of Christendom and the seat of the principal house of the Dominican order. The version of plainchant found in the three musical books is, however, not that of Rome or its basilicas; rather, it seems to be one that was made specifically for the Dominicans—but whether this was done before or after Humbert was placed in charge is uncertain.

The principles used in preparing these chant books seem to have been much the same as those followed earlier by the monks of Cîteaux in creating the Cistercian version of plainsong. This is suggested by the fact that the Dominican version is more closely related to that of Cîteaux than to any other variant of the time. Whether it was based directly on the Cistercian version, however, is a question not yet definitively answered.

Several characteristics of Dominican chant set it apart from the central tradition of the Middle Ages, which is closely related to that found in modern liturgical books such as the *Graduale romanum,* the *Antiphonale romanum,* and the *Liber usualis.* One is the smaller range of the more elaborate chants such as graduals, alleluias, offertories, and greater responsories. In the Dominican version the range of pieces in these categories rarely exceeds ten notes, whereas in the central tradition some have a range of twelve and, occasionally, even thirteen notes. Dominican chant also has fewer as well as shorter melismas in its more elaborate chants, and makes no use at all of such special notational forms as the *strophicus* and *quilisma.* Finally, in the Dominican tradition many pieces are in a mode other than the one in which they occur in the standard medieval tradition. This results from a variety of factors, one of the most common being the presentation of the last phrase or group of notes of a piece a step higher or lower than in the standard version. Consequently, a piece ending on *G* in the standard tradition, and thus assigned to mode 8, might have its last few notes written a step lower in the Dominican version, thereby making it end on *F* and thus be assigned to mode 6.

The Dominican order continued to use its own version of plainsong until the introduction of vernacular languages into the celebration of the Roman and related rites of the Catholic church. During the more than seven centuries that this tradition was in use, it was transmitted primarily in manuscript books until 1907, when the *Graduale juxta ritum Sacri Ordinis Praedicatorum* was published at Rome. Prior to that time only the order's *Processionale* had appeared in an appreciable number of printed editions, the earliest of which dates from the sixteenth century.

BIBLIOGRAPHY

William R. Bonniwell, *A History of the Dominican Liturgy,* 2nd ed. (1945), definitive; Dominique Delalande, *Le graduel des Prêcheurs* (1949), the most complete study to date of the Dominican chant tradition; *Graduale juxta ritum Sacri Ordinis Praedicatorum* (1907), the Dominican version of the chants used in the Mass throughout the liturgical year; Archdale A. King, *Liturgies of the Religious Orders* (1955), 325–395, a brief history of the Dominican order and a concise description of the distinguishing features of the liturgical rites followed by its members.

ROBERT J. SNOW

[See also **Dominic, St.; Dominicans.**]

DOMINICAN RITE. When St. Dominic's Order of Preachers received the approbation of the Holy See in 1217, becoming thereby an international organization, liturgical uniformity became imperative. The Roman rite of the Middle Ages neither knew nor conceived of exact conformity in text or rubric. Rather, each diocese, church, and monastery adopted its own use. Rubrics tended to be transmitted orally. If the highly mobile friars were to celebrate the liturgy when they gathered for chapters, or as they moved from one house to another, uniform texts, ceremonies, and rubrics were a necessity.

Humbert of Romans, fifth master of the order, notes stages in the development of the uniform liturgy: "From the beginning of the order there was much variety in the office, and therefore one office was compiled so that there should be unity everywhere. In the course of time four friars from four provinces were commissioned to put it in better order, which they did" (*De vita regulari,* II, 152).

Four phases are implied here: (1) a period of diversity in liturgical practice, (2) the introduction of a unified liturgy, (3) the revision of the four friars, and (4) Humbert's final redaction.

Before its approval by Honorius III, the Order of Preachers served the diocese of Toulouse and followed, no doubt, the liturgical use of that church. The period of diversity began on 15 August 1217, when Dominic dispersed his small group to Paris, Bologna, and Spain, while he himself went to Rome. These new foundations observed local customs.

How long this period of diversity lasted is more difficult to ascertain than when it began, because of the scanty documentation available. There are a few liturgical manuscripts and the remarks of chroniclers, but no acts of the general chapters from before 1240. Probably the uniform liturgy was introduced by Dominic himself and completed by his successor, Jordan of Saxony, before 1228. A text in the constitutions, identified as belonging to the period 1221–1228, states: "We confirm the whole office, nocturnal and diurnal, and we ordain that it be uniformly observed by all, so that no one is permitted to add anything new."

Even with a uniform liturgy, however, one must not expect absolute conformity. To avoid friction with seculars, some local customs were tolerated. Even Humbert counsels flexibility in this regard (*De vita regulari,* II, 6–7). This tendency, together with a slowness to correct manuscripts, scribal error, lack of precise written rubrics, and the enthusiasm engendered by the newly revised office of the Roman curia (which the Franciscans had adopted for their own use) led Dominicans to call for a thorough revision of their office.

Accordingly, the 1245 chapter appointed a commission of four friars to study the manuscripts brought from each house and to carry out a complete revision. The first of the three chapter votes required to give their work constitutional force was taken in 1246, before the work was complete. Further complaints, perhaps reflecting the reluctance of the provinces to part with local customs, necessitated further revision, but the constitutional process was interrupted by the death of the master general of the order.

The chapter of 1254 elected Humbert of Romans master of the order, charging him with the task of settling once and for all the liturgical question and giving the first of the three necessary votes. Humbert's revision became definitive. His own copy of the prototype, which he carried with him on visitations, still exists (London, British Library, MS Add. 23935) along with a copy (Rome, Santa Sabina, codex XIV.L 1). Subsequent chapters urged priors to secure copies of the office made from the exemplar lodged at the Convent of St. Jacques in Paris.

To give the office more than merely constitutional force, Humbert's successor, John of Vercelli, petitioned the Holy See for confirmation of the Dominican rite. Pope Clement IV, responding with the bull *Consurgit in nobis* (7 July 1267), approved the Dominican liturgy, forbidding any further change without the express approval of the Holy See.

That the work of the four friars and the work of Humbert consisted of corrections and revisions rather than new compilation has been shown by Philip Gleeson through careful study of manuscripts that predate the time of Humbert. There is thus shown to be a high degree of continuity from the time of St. Dominic to Humbert. This fact is further attested by the numerous religious orders and dioceses that adopted the Dominican rite.

Because so little is known in detail about the rites of the twelfth and thirteenth centuries, or about patterns of influence and borrowing among churches, the question of the sources of the Dominican rite is difficult to answer. Clearly there was Cistercian influence, particularly in the calendar and gradual. There is some evidence to suggest that the Dominican liturgists were strongly influenced by the ritual of the Lateran Basilica in Rome. Final judgment, however, will have to await a more complete knowledge of individual thirteenth-century liturgical rites.

Because of the need to balance the ideal of choral recitation of the office against the needs of study and the care of souls, brevity and simplicity characterize the Dominican liturgy. This is seen, for example, in the calendar that includes only saints of universal significance, thus preserving the integrity of the temporal cycle. Proper feasts are kept to a minimum, as are the commons.

The low mass differs from that of the Tridentine rite in various ways. The chalice is prepared before the confiteor, and the prayers at the foot of the altar are very brief, as is the offertory. Bonniwell points out that the details of the solemn high mass also differ from the Tridentine in many respects.

The only exception to this rule of simplicity is compline, said at the end of the day's labors. With its more elaborate chant, variety of text, and the *Salve Regina* procession in honor of the Virgin, compline won a special place in the friars' affection.

BIBLIOGRAPHY

Sources. Acta capitulorum generalium Ordinis Praedicatorum, B. M. Reichert, ed. (1898); *Constitutiones antiquae Ordinis Fratrum Praedicatorum,* A. H. Thomas, ed., (1965); Humbert of Romans, *Opera de vita regulari,* J. J. Berthier, ed. (1888–1889).

Studies. William R. Bonniwell, *A History of the Dominican Liturgy,* 2nd ed. (1945); Dominique Delalande, *Le graduel des Prêcheurs* (1949); Philip Gleeson, "Dominican Liturgical Manuscripts from Before 1254," in *Archivum fratrum Praedicatorum,* 42 (1972); Archdale A. King, *Liturgies of the Religious Orders* (1955), 325–395.

RONALD JOHN ZAWILLA, O.P.

[See also **Dominican Chant; Dominicans.**]

DOMINICANS. The Dominicans are a religious family, officially known as the Order of Friars Preachers. The order is made up of priests and brothers, nuns, sisters, members of secular institutes (since 1945), and laymen affiliated with the order. The priests and brothers form a religious institute of mendicant friars who pledge themselves under vows, binding for life, to live according to the Rule of St. Augustine and the constitutions of the order. The nuns live a life of prayer and contemplation in a strictly enclosed monastery. The sisters live in community under vows and undertake an active ministry, such as education; they are members of autonomous congregations. The Dominican laity (Third Order of Penance) are layfolk who, in their ordinary walks of life, follow a rule of life embodying the Dominican spirit.

The spirit of the order emerges from the union of the apostolic ministry with the contemplative life of prayer. The contemplative elements of Dominican life include the vows of poverty, chastity, and obedience, living in community, the choral celebration of the Eucharist and Divine Office, monastic observances such as fasting and abstinence, and the assiduous study of sacred truth. The vow of obedience obliges the friar to obey the master general and his other superiors according to the Rule of St. Augustine and the constitutions of the order. Obedience is thus the keystone of Dominican life. The mendicant poverty embraced from the first by the order was stricter than that professed by the older orders and made the friars utterly dependent on divine providence and the generosity of the faithful. Until it adopted the liturgical revisions of Vatican II, the order had its own liturgical rite with distinctive rubrics, missal, breviary, and calendar.

The apostolic element of the order, considered an imitation of the evangelical life of the apostles, involves the propagation and defense of Christian truth, primarily through preaching. Dominic resolved the conflicts that might arise from the simultaneous implementation of the apostolic and contemplative elements by granting superiors power to dispense students and preachers from monastic observances that impede their work. An original feature of the order's law and life that has had an important influence on the Dominican spirit was the decision of St. Dominic that the rule, constitutions, and commands of chapters and superiors would not bind under sin. However, a friar was obliged in conscience to endure any penalty that might be laid upon him for his infractions. The Dominican motto, "to contemplate and give to others the fruits of contemplation," aptly sums up the Dominican spirit.

FOUNDATION AND ORGANIZATION

The order has its roots in the preaching mission inaugurated among the Albigensian heretics in southern France by Innocent III. St. Dominic, the founder of the Dominicans, joined these preachers in 1206 and continued to preach in the area until he founded his order. To aid them in their campaign against the Albigensians, whose leaders practiced voluntary poverty, Dominic and his associates embraced a life of strict evangelical poverty in imitation of the apostles. In April 1215, with the approval of Bishop Fulk of Toulouse, Dominic transformed this voluntary association into a diocesan institute of preachers "for the purpose of stamping out the perversion of heresy, uprooting vice, teaching the rule of faith, and instructing the people in sound morals." Its members proposed "to travel on foot and to preach the word of the Gospel in evangelical poverty as religious."

When Dominic sought papal confirmation of his order in October 1215, Innocent III directed him first to choose one of the traditional rules of religious orders. Accordingly, in the spring of 1216 Dominic and his companions, meeting in a founding chapter, chose the Rule of St. Augustine and drew up statutes embodying the details of their religious life. To implement their determination to live and work in apostolic poverty, they abandoned the ownership of property, though for the time being they retained rental income. On 22 December 1216, Honorius III confirmed the order as a religious institute. On 17 January 1217 he formally approved its name and granted it a preaching mission that was universal in extent.

Dominic began to implement this mission on 15 August 1217. Retaining the existing houses in Toulouse and Prouille, he sent four friars into Spain and seven to Paris. He himself went to Italy to prepare to establish the order in Rome, in Bologna, and in other Italian cities. In 1220, after he had made a visitation of existing foundations and had noted the experience gained by the friars in fulfilling their apostolate, Dominic convened the first general chapter at Bologna. Under his presidency the chapter enacted statutes, supplementary to those passed in 1216, that regulated preaching, studies, poverty, and the governmental machinery of the order. The chapter also adopted strict mendicancy, prohibiting the ownership of both property and fixed revenues. Only the property on which the priories stood might be retained. This measure made the friars dependent on freewill offerings and necessitated the daily quest for alms. The chapter enunciated the preaching mission of the order by inserting a statement of purpose into the prologue of the constitutions: " . . . our order was founded from the beginning for preaching and the salvation of souls."

The 1221 general chapter completed the work of organization. It divided the order into provinces, enacted statutes to provide for their governance, and sent friars to make foundations in projected provinces. Groups of friars were sent to Hungary, Poland, Germany, Denmark, England, and probably Greece. St. Hyacinth led the Polish contingent, while Paul of Hungary went with four friars to found the order in his native land. Friar Christian opened a priory in Cologne, and Solomon of Aarhus founded one in Lund. The English group was the largest, consisting of Gilbert of Fresney and twelve friars. Making their foundation at Oxford in late August, they were soon enrolled as students at the university. About 1224 some provinces were well enough organized to hold their first chapters and to select their first provincials.

The minutes of the general chapters from 1222 to 1227 have been lost. Probably these chapters executed the provisions of the constitutions regarding the life and ministry of the order; founded new priories, organized schools of theology, perfected the governmental machinery of the provinces, and promoted preaching. It was probably the 1225 chapter that decided that general chapters should vary in their composition. Two successive chapters would be composed of an elected delegate (definitor) from each province. The third chapter would be made up of the provincials. The series would then begin again. Elective chapters would consist of the provincial, a delegate, and an elector from each province. Until 1370 the order held a general chapter annually, except when a vacancy in the office of master general necessitated a postponement. Biennial or triennial chapters began in 1372, a change that tended to heighten the influence of the master general.

The general chapter was the supreme Dominican authority and possessed executive, legislative, and judicial powers. It alone could amend the constitutions. Also, it issued executive orders (ordinationes), a right possessed likewise by provincial chapters and all superiors. Until the 1228 chapter adopted a new legislative process, each chapter had been competent to enact laws. The new procedure, which is still followed, required the affirmative action of three successive general chapters in order to add to, modify, replace, or remove any part of the constitutions,

with the exception of certain key elements that were considered irrevocable because of their importance to Dominican life. A proposal that had been introduced by one chapter lapsed should a second or third chapter fail to act favorably upon it. No measure was binding during the first or second stages but could be made operative if an order to that effect were attached. The new process safeguarded the flexibility of the lawmaking procedure but removed the danger of hasty action.

The originality and perfection of the Dominican constitutions caused some of the other mendicant orders to imitate them. In 1241 Raymond of Peñafort, a canonist, revised the primitive constitutions. He cast them in better juridical form but did not substantially alter them. Though subjected to many additions, Raymond's version remained the basic text until 1932.

Dominican provinces were composed of priories and a small number of nonprioral houses. They enjoyed a considerable degree of autonomy and were governed by a provincial and a provincial chapter. The priors of the province and one elected representative from each priory made up the membership of the provincial chapter. Although they could not change the constitutions, provincial chapters held powers in the province similar to those of the general chapter throughout the order. They met every year until 1410 and every two years until 1629, and have met every four years since then. Congregations or vicariates, governed by a vicar and, under certain circumstances, by a chapter, were common in the order after the fourteenth century. They resembled the provinces but were more restricted in their rights and privileges. Some of them had no fixed territory. The first congregation, which brought together under one jurisdiction friars working as missionaries in the Near East and southern Asia, was formed shortly after 1300.

The chapters of the respective jurisdictions, including the priory, elected their superiors, though by exception the master general could appoint a provincial, and the master general or provincial, a prior. The master general appointed vicars of congregations. These superiors presided over the chapters of their area of government, except for elective sessions. During the medieval period superiors remained in office until a higher authority terminated their tenure, which was usually of short duration. Masters general held office until death, though an incumbent might resign and could be removed for misconduct or incompetence. The master general was aided by an assistant and by the procurator general, the liaison officer with the Holy See.

The death of St. Dominic on 6 August 1221 did not interrupt the steady development of the order, for five extremely able men of saintly character succeeded him as master general: Jordan of Saxony, Raymond of Peñafort, John Teutonicus of Wildeshausen, Humbert of Romans, and John of Vercelli. Under their guidance, which covered a period of sixty years, the order increased its membership, established many new priories, and developed its characteristic apostolate and activities. Except for mission countries, the area covered by the twelve provinces established in the 1220's constituted the theater of Dominican activity until 1510, when the first members of the order entered the New World.

However, as the number of priories and their membership increased, it became necessary to divide some of the provinces. Between 1295 and 1303 all of them were divided except England, France, and the smaller provinces of Scandinavia, Hungary, Greece, and the Holy Land, bringing the number to eighteen. Before the end of the Middle Ages, four new provinces were added to the roster: Sicily (1378), Dalmatia (1380), Portugal (1418), and Scotland (1481). Priories also grew in number. In 1277 there were 404; in 1303, 590; in 1358, 635. There were approximately 13,000 friars in 1256 and probably more than 21,000 in 1347. The Black Death occasioned a decline in membership, and there was a chronic shortage of vocations throughout the rest of the Middle Ages.

SCHOLARSHIP

The order's intellectual bent and educational system dveloped from the ideas and experience of St. Dominic. Convinced that the church needed preachers who were well educated, he made study an essential duty of the friars and theological learning an indispensable requirement of the Dominican apostolate. He took steps to ensure that his followers would be trained in theology. During the first year of the order, he enrolled six of his disciples in a lecture course that Alexander of Stavensby was giving at the cathedral school of Toulouse. By "word and example" he insisted that the friars study the Bible. In August of 1217, the year Honorius III confirmed the Dominican preaching mission, Dominic sent friars to Paris to study, preach, and found a priory. In 1220 he engaged John of St. Albans, a master of theology, to teach in the Parisian priory, an act that set up a school of theology and incorporated it into the university. He founded priories in the university cities of Bologna (1218), Palencia (1220), and Montpellier (1221), and sent a contingent of friars to Oxford (1221).

At the first general chapter in 1220, Dominic introduced into the constitutions a provision that forbade the founding of a priory unless its membership included a professor. Other clauses contained instructions for students, student masters, and professors, for disputes, review of lectures, and methods of study. Professors and student friars were accorded various privileges. Superiors were empowered to exempt them from religious exercises so they might give themselves to study. Talented friars might be given the use of a cell and stay up at night to study. Superiors were to single out students who displayed aptitude for teaching and send them on for higher studies.

The first comprehensive code of studies was commissioned by the general chapter that met at Valenciennes in 1259. Occasioned by developments at the University of Paris, which had broadened its philosophical courses in 1255, the code was drawn up by five masters of theology: Albertus Magnus, Thomas Aquinas, Peter of Tarentaise (later Pope Innocent V), Florence of Hesdin, and Bonhomme of Brittany. In a brief and concise document the commissioners regulated many aspects of Dominican studies. Although in some provisions it merely repeated earlier ordinances, in its integration it laid the foundation for an academic organization that lasted for many centuries.

The order constructed an academic system that provided a graduate program of studies and an interlocking series of schools that ranged upward through priory schools of theology and provincial schools of arts, philosophy, and theology, to general houses of studies. The system was crowned by the general house of studies in the priory of St. Jacques at Paris. It obtained its first chair of theology at the university in 1229, its second in 1230. The English Dominicans gained a chair at the University of Oxford before 1248. The general chapter ordered the erection of four additional general houses of studies in 1248. They were founded at Cologne, Bologna, Montpellier, and Oxford, though the English province failed to open the doors of Oxford to foreign friars until 1260. The province of Rome opened a general house of studies at Naples in 1290; the province of Spain, at Barcelona in 1293. In 1304 the general chapter commanded all the major provinces to establish general houses of studies. From the beginning each province was permitted to maintain three friars at the Paris school and two at each of the other general houses of study. The order promoted friars to the mastership in theology at these schools when they were incorporated into a university, as at Paris and Oxford.

Although the intellectual endeavor of the order was intended primarily to prepare the friars for preaching, Dominicans became prominent and wrote books in many fields of knowledge. Constituting the foundation of their theological curriculum, biblical studies first engaged the attention of the friars. To facilitate this study, those at Paris, under the direction of Hugh of St. Cher, the first Dominican cardinal, undertook the correction of the Vulgate text of the Bible and compiled several biblical concordances. Biblical and theological studies and preaching were so intertwined that scarcely a friar who taught or wrote failed to compose one or more commentaries on the sacred books. Thomas Aquinas, who is thought of as a theologian; Nicholas Trevet, as a historian; Meister Eckhart, as a mystic; Juan de Torquemada, as a churchman—all devoted part of their scholastic life to the exposition of the Scriptures. Although most of the commentators followed traditional methods, Roland of Cremona, the first Dominican master of theology at Paris, struck out on new lines. Commenting on the Book of Job, he used astronomy, astrology, and medicine to aid him in expounding the text. In his *Postillae in totam Bibliam,* Hugh of St. Cher commented on all the books of the Bible. His book became an instrument of research that was almost as highly regarded as the *glossa ordinaria.*

Dominican translators, orientalists, and geographers contributed indirectly to biblical studies. Dominicans are associated with many of the earliest French, Catalan, Valencian, Castilian, Armenian, and German translations of the Bible. John Rellach of Constance rendered the entire Bible into German shortly before 1450. Except for the Book of Psalms, his translation was the pioneer German version of the sacred text and one of the earliest to be printed. Peter Schwartz (Nigri) was the most important Hebraist of the late Middle Ages, though he used his knowledge of Hebrew and Aramaic more for controversy with the Jews than for biblical studies. Girolamo Savonarola, whose great sermons could be ranked as popular commentaries on the sacred books, grasped the importance of a philological and critical-historical approach to biblical studies. He

believed that the constant reading of the Bible was the great means of rejuvenating the Christian spirit of the people. He sought to develop in the friars of San Marco a deeper understanding of the Bible and had them study the oriental languages.

In 1283 Burchard of Mount Sion illumined the Bible by writing a description of the Holy Land that was characterized by scientific precision and minute detail. Felix Fabri, a friar of Ulm, followed Burchard eastward 200 years later. He made two pilgrimages to the East and wrote a lengthy and interesting account, rich in detail and originality, of what he saw in Palestine, Arabia, and Egypt.

Dominican devotion to theology produced a lengthy procession of eminent theologians. Richard Fishacre, the first Dominican to graduate as master of theology at Oxford, was probably the first theologian to use Greek learning in theological speculation. His *Commentary on the Sentences of Peter Lombard* was highly regarded by contemporary and later Schoolmen. Albertus Magnus worked at a time when the introduction of Eastern thought into western Europe posed many difficulties for Christian scholars. He proposed the first solutions for these problems and opened the way for the assimilation of Eastern learning. He was also distinguished in other ways, serving as provincial of the German province from 1254 to 1257 and as bishop of Regensburg from 1260 to 1262. Robert Kilwardby was a philosopher and theologian of outstanding merit whose literary legacy is extensive. Provincial of the English province from 1261 to 1272, he was elected archbishop of Canterbury in 1272, and appointed cardinal in 1278.

Thomas Aquinas, the greatest theologian the order produced, graduated as master of theology at the University of Paris in 1256. He continued to teach at Paris until 1259. After then teaching in Italy until 1268, he returned to Paris to face several resolute antagonists—the followers of Gerard of Abbeville, who were attacking the mendicant orders; the radical Aristotelians, who had developed a heretical rationalism; and the theologians of the old school, who opposed his theses. After returning to Italy in 1272, Thomas wrote his final works and taught at Naples until his death in March 1274. The intellectual stature of Thomas and the excellence of his doctrine were recognized during his lifetime. He was primarily a theologian but developed his philosophy as a tool that could be used to explore the problems of theology. His many works, which are still prized and studied, are characterized by progressiveness, originality, and greatness. This is especially true of the *Summa theologiae,* his masterpiece.

The disciples of Thomas carried his system of thought to all the Dominican schools. Outside the order some of the major theses of Thomas were challenged by theologians of the so-called Augustinian school. In 1277 Archbishop Stephen Tempier of Paris and Archbishop Robert Kilwardby of Canterbury condemned some of the Thomistic theses. Archbishop John Peckham of Canterbury issued a further condemnation in 1284. The disciples of Thomas responded to these attacks with vigor. Although a few Dominican theologians, especially Durand de St. Pourçain in the early fourteenth century, developed their own systems and refused to accept the theology of Thomas, the order endorsed his doctrine and commanded that it be taught in Dominican schools. By the end of the first quarter of the fourteenth century, the doctrine of Thomas was generally followed by Dominicans, among whom a Thomistic school of teachers and commentators had developed.

To keep the memory of Thomas alive, his followers wrote his biography, compiled catalogs of his works, and collected his writings. To lighten the labor of studying his books and to facilitate the penetration of his thought, his disciples commented on his works and prepared epitomes, concordances, and indexes of them. John Capreolus (*d.* 1444) was one of the greatest expositors of Thomas. His *Defensiones theologiae divi Thomae* is a comprehensive interpretation of the Thomistic synthesis that refutes opponents of every variety. Capreolus was a link binding the primitive Thomistic school of the thirteenth and early fourteenth centuries to the brilliant commentators of the sixteenth century. After his death a number of exceptional Thomistic scholars in Germany, Spain, Italy, and Flanders prepared the way for the masterly commentaries of Francisco de Vitoria, Cajetan, and Ferrariensis (Francesco Silvestri). During this same period the *Summa theologiae* of Thomas began to replace the *Sentences* of Peter Lombard as the theological text in Dominican schools. The acceptance of the Thomistic synthesis by most Dominicans made it a profoundly unifying and cohesive factor in the order.

It is possible to give here only a sampling of the friars who excelled in literary fields apart from theology. Raymond of Peñafort achieved eminence as a canonist and moralist. While he was in Rome as chaplain and papal penitentiary, Gregory IX commissioned him to gather together the papal decretals. Promulgated in 1234, the *Decretals* are named after Gregory but are the basis for Raymond's lasting fame. As master general (1238–1240) he published a revised version of the order's constitutions. His *Summa de casibus poenitentiae* was intended to give confessors the principles and norms they would need to solve cases of conscience. Raymond's exposition was methodical, clear, detailed, and complete. The way he handled his material manifested the depth and solidity of his knowledge. He also wrote a number of minor works in the field of canon law. The *Summa de vitiis et virtutibus* of William Peraldus (Perault), a treatise on the vices and virtues written for preachers, became one of the most popular books of the Middle Ages. The rapid and enduring success of the work, completed in 1249, is traceable to its well-coordinated structure, rich and practical material, ease of consultation, and response to a need that the speculative theologians of the universities did not fill.

William of Moerbeke, a metaphysician in his own right, made an important contribution to the speculation of Scholastic theologians through his translations of the works of Aristotle, Plotinus, and other Greek writers. Moneta of Cremona's detailed explanation of the beliefs and practices of the Cathars and Waldensians, and the directories that Nicholas Eymeric and Bernard of Gui wrote for inquisitors, were designed to promote the campaign against heresy. With his *Speculum maius,* Vincent of Beauvais provided his contemporaries with an encyclopedic reference book that summarized the learning of both ancient and contemporary times. Jerome of Moravia, who was professor of music at St. Jacques priory in Paris about 1250, wrote a *Tractatus de musica* that aimed to present the musical knowledge of the time. Jerome treated the theory, esthetics, and performance of chant and other forms of music. His book was highly appreciated by the professors of the university. *The Golden Legend* of Jacobus de Voragine, a compilation of saints' lives, influenced not only the sermons of the preachers, for whom it was originally intended, but also the art of the period and the lives of the people.

Theodoric Borgognoni of Lucca was the most progressive surgeon of the Middle Ages. Though a Dominican and ultimately a bishop, he was more interested in medicine and surgery than ecclesiastical subjects. He learned medicine and surgery from his father, Hugh of Lucca, and practiced both as long as he lived. His fame rests on his *Surgery (Chirurgia)*, which gives a complete coverage of general and special surgery in four books. Far in advance of his time, Theodoric taught the theory and practice of aseptic surgery.

In his *Catholicon,* John Balbus (*d. ca.* 1298) wrote a pioneering treatise on, and etymological dictionary of, the Latin language. Bernard of Gui, Ptolemy of Lucca, Nicholas Trevet, Martin of Troppau, and Antoninus of Florence produced influential historical works. Bernard of Gui's works are valuable particularly to the historian of the Dominican order. The *Summa moralis* of Antoninus of Florence was a multivolume work in which moral theology emerged as a discipline in its own right, independent of speculative theology and canon law. A pastoral work, it treats all aspects of moral theology in systematic and comprehensive detail. Antoninus wrote it to assist preachers and parish priests with their work of preaching, hearing confessions, and counseling. It was the most popular text of moral theology for three centuries and even today provides a wealth of material on social morality. Cardinals Juan de Torquemada and John Stojkovic of Ragusa opened a new field of theological research with their treatises on ecclesiology. The Dominican humanist Francis Colonna published his *Dream of Poliphilus (Hypernotomachia Poliphili)* in 1467. This celebrated romance is a curious synthesis of medieval allegory, pagan mysticism, and the knowledge of antiquity.

DOMINICAN MYSTICS

The Dominican contemplative life, aiming at intimate union with God, and its preaching, seeking to carry the fruits of contemplation to the people, bore within them the seeds of mysticism. Dominican preaching forged links between the friars and people—priests, nuns, laymen, and beguines—who thirsted for a life of more perfect union with God. St. Dominic and Jordan of Saxony contributed to the current of Dominican mysticism when they fastened the ties that bound the friars and nuns in a union of service and friendship. Jordan's letters to Diana d'Andalo, a nun of St. Agnes Monastery in Bologna, were the first of the Dominican spiritual classics. Henry of Cologne, Siger of Lille, Walter of Strasbourg, and other friars worked among the devout women of Belgium and Germany. Dominicans supported St. Juliana of Liège when she sought to introduce the feast of Corpus Christi. Henry of Halle was closely associated with St. Gertrude and the two

Mechtilds of the Cistercian monastery of Helfta, where devotion to the Sacred Heart first flowered.

The German mystics of the fourteenth century inherited the tradition of working among people who sought to live a deeply spiritual life. Meister Eckhart and his disciples, Johannes Tauler and Heinrich Suso, led the mystical movement. A wide circle of religious people working and praying for spiritual renewal gathered round these leaders. Their mysticism is called speculative because it sought to probe and record the depths of man's sanctification and union with God. This was especially true of Eckhart. His writings and those of Tauler and Suso are the monuments of German mysticism. Suso's *Little Book of Eternal Wisdom,* one of the best-loved works of the Middle Ages, is a perennial classic. A remarkable series of biographies and chronicles, written in Dominican monasteries, bears witness to the intense mystical life that flowered at that time among Dominican nuns. St. Catherine of Siena (1347–1380), a member of the Third Order, was the greatest of the Dominican mystics. She surpassed the German mystics in personal holiness and outstripped her own countrymen with the excellence of her writings: prayers, letters, and the *Dialogue of Divine Providence.* It was especially this latter work that moved Pope Paul VI to proclaim her a doctor of the church in 1970, a singular honor for one who could neither read nor write, and had no schooling. For her zeal she was compared to St. Paul in that she was not merely gifted with sublime charisms but shared them with others for the good of the church.

APOSTOLIC ACTIVITIES

The Dominican order was founded, in the words of Honorious III, "to preach the word of God and to proclaim the name of the Lord Jesus throughout the world." Established "for preaching and the salvation of souls," in the words of the constitutions, the order was the first in the history of monasticism to incorporate an active ministry and the mission to preach into its religious life as essential ingredients and not as tolerated appendages. Approved by the pope, the universal bishop, the Dominican ministry shared the fundamental duty of bishops to preach the word of God. The order sought to assist the bishops by placing a body of educated and trained preachers at their service. The Fourth Lateran Council had called on bishops to appoint such preachers as a remedy for the long-standing need of the church for regular and competent preaching. Dominic sent his disciples to study theology at Paris and inspired the establishment of the order's academic organization precisely to prepare the friars to become preachers.

As the basic Dominican apostolate, preaching claimed the energy of the greater number of the friars. Dominican priories, erected by preference in the cities or their suburbs, became centers of an organized preaching ministry. Each priory was entrusted with a definite territory in which to evangelize, quest for alms, and recruit new members. Friars might not work in the territory of another priory, except in transit, without the consent of the provincial. If they did so, they were obliged to make restitution to the injured house. Exact fixing of the boundaries was a necessity. The provinces were busying themselves with this problem about the middle of the thirteenth century, when there was a great boom in founding new priories in all the provinces.

To compensate for territory that was taken from them and given to newly founded houses, the friars divided their assigned territories into smaller areas called districts (limites). This enabled them to use their areas to better advantage, preaching to the people, ministering to them, and seeking alms for themselves. Each district was entrusted to a talented preacher, who was responsible for the preaching and questing in that area. He was called a "limiter" (limitator, also terminarius), a term made familiar by Chaucer. In the fifteenth century the priories farmed out each of their districts annually to a friar in return for a stipulated tax. The limiter had exclusive rights to his district, and other friars might not preach or collect alms there without his consent. It was the abuses rising from the collection of alms that attracted Chaucer's attention. In his *Canterbury Tales* his picture of the friar—"a wanton one and merry, a limiter, a very festive fellow"—is not very flattering.

The friar lived in a preaching home while away from his priory. If it had a chapel, he celebrated Mass and heard confessions there. He also preached in the churches and chapels throughout his district. Preaching homes developed before 1270. They were built in remote areas so that the friars could stay for longer periods of preaching and alms collecting, especially during Advent, Lent, and the harvest and vintage periods. The district method of evangelizing provided a more regular ministry and a more certain income for the priory. By constantly moving about his district, the limiter came to know his people and could better fill their spiritual needs. It was when religious discipline declined that abuses appeared.

The order permitted only qualified friars to preach. The more talented preachers were chosen for special occasions and sermons. There were two types of Dominican preacher: the preacher-in-ordinary and the preacher general. The first was required to be at least twenty-five years old and to have studied theology for at least a year (three years after 1313). He also had to be examined as to capability, and licensed by his prior. Previously he must have preached practice sermons to his brethren. These were often delivered in the refectory during meals. When the young friar began to preach to the faithful, he did so under the tutelage of an experienced preacher.

The most honored function among the Friars Preachers was that of preacher general. This office was highly regarded and the friars aspired to it. Before long (1242) preachers general were being named with a lavish hand. Then began a long struggle to keep the number within bounds. Early in the fourteenth century it was decided that there might be but one preacher general for each priory. The preacher general was a skilled preacher of blameless life who had proved himself by years of preaching. He had studied theology for at least three years, knew how to propose the word of God competently, and as an ex officio member of the provincial chapter, he was skilled in the affairs of the order. The preacher general was obligated to reside in the priory for which he had been designated. To maintain his office, though normally it was held for life, he had to preach frequently and be prepared for special sermons.

During the first half century of the order, when the territory of the priories was extensive, the preacher general seems to have been engaged in the kind of itinerant, mendicant preaching that characterized St. Dominic. But this type of roving ministry apparently disappeared when priories became more numerous, and newer houses claimed part of the area of the older ones. About the same time the priories began to divide their territories into districts and entrust them to individual friars. In the face of these two developments, itinerant preaching, except by occasional individuals, probably disappeared.

About the same time, the provinces began to award the office of preacher general to increasing numbers of lectors, priors, provincials, and other dignitaries. Even though these men were qualified and their positions obliged them to preach, they could not devote themselves to preaching full time. Thus the office of preacher general seems gradually to have become honorary, except for attendance at the provincial chapter. However, the connection of the preacher general with preaching was not broken. This is shown by a stipulation of the 1518 general chapter: "Let no one be named a preacher general . . . unless he be one whose preaching is highly esteemed . . . in such wise that for three Lents at least he shall have won great favor for his preaching in one or several large cities or regions."

There have been many outstanding preachers general. Stephen of Bourbon probably exemplifies the office in its earliest form. For forty years during the early part of the thirteenth century he exercised a vigorous preaching ministry throughtout France, especially in the southeast and in Burgundy. His years as preacher and inquisitor made him one of the best-known friars of France, and he came to know many of his famous contemporaries. When he was old in experience, he prepared a handbook of preaching materials for his youthful confreres, recording the anecdotes, stories, and experiences that had given power to his sermons. Generations of preachers drew from this book, and now historians mine its pages.

The so-called penitential preachers, who proclaimed penance and reform of life, preached over a wide area. In 1233 John of Vicenza led a crusade for peace in the cities of Lombardy and the Marches. Venturino of Bergamo preached penance in the fourteenth century; St. Vincent Ferrer and Manfred of Vercelli, in the fifteenth. Savonarola proclaimed reform of life from the pulpits of S. Marco and the cathedral in Florence. The antagonism he aroused led to his execution in May 1498.

To aid its preachers, the order gave them a solid foundation in theology and required priories to stock libraries. The friars acquired reference works, and wrote and collected several kinds of books specifically designed for preachers—books on how to preach (artes praedicandi), sermon collections, and compilations of illustrative material for sermons (exempla). Humbert of Romans, master general from 1254 to 1263, led the way in preparing preaching books. He composed three of them, earning the distinction of being the most productive thirteenth-century author of homiletic works. His De praedicatione crucis contra Saracenos supplied material for friars who were preaching a crusade. De eruditione praedicatorum instructed preachers on every aspect of their office. Its second part presented the preacher with 100 sketches for sermons to men and women of every walk of life, 100 for every kind of occasion, 33 for liturgical seasons, and 25 for feast days. Hum-

bert's De dono timoris is a collection of anecdotes used to point out a moral or illustrate a doctrine. More than twenty other Dominicans made exempla collections, especially John Bromyard (d. ca. 1352), an English Dominican who wrote a Summa praedicantium, a vast repository of homiletic and doctrinal material. It is one of the most celebrated of medieval preaching aids, surpassing its predecessors and contemporaries in scope, size, and the interest it aroused.

Dominicans had preaching in mind when they built their churches. Although they did not develop a distinctive architecture for either their churches or their priories, they built churches with large and spacious naves that were designed to accommodate large congregations. There they preached many times during the year: morning and evening on Sundays, daily during Advent and Lent, on feast days, and on special occasions, such as provincial or general chapters. Except for Latin sermons to the clergy, the friars used the vernacular languages when preaching.

Although the Dominicans normally preached inside churches and chapels, they also delivered sermons outdoors. Often the churchyard pulpit, or preaching cross, served as a preaching place, especially during the warmer months. At Norwich priory in England, a space outside the church long retained the name "preaching yard." Preaching crosses stood in the cemeteries or churchyards of the priories in Bristol, Norwich, London, Brecknock, and the one in Hereford, whose restored cross is the only surviving example in England. We know of outdoor sermons delivered by Peter of Verona to congregations in Florence and Milan, of others preached at the crossroads by the Alleluia preachers in 1233, and of the outdoor sermons of Venturino of Bergamo and Vincent Ferrer. In 1244 a Friar Peter petitioned the podestà and council of Florence to enlarge the square before the Dominican church of S. Maria Novella to accommodate the large crowds that came to hear the sermons.

Since the frequency and success of Dominican preaching depended partly on the congregation, the friars did all they could to attract people to their churches. They abbreviated the divine services to allow more time for the sermons. They obtained the privilege to grant indulgences to those who heard their sermons, to absolve from reserved sins, to hold services during interdicts, to bury the faithful in their churches. They issued letters of fraternity granting the recipient a share in the spiritual goods of the order and allowed the faithful who took the vows of religion on their deathbed to be buried in the Dominican habit. They founded a Third Order for the laity and established various confraternities in their churches. Dominicans sang the evening hour of compline and the *Salve Regina* antiphon that followed it with a solemnity that drew the faithful to their churches. After the middle of the thirteenth century their Marian and flagellant confraternities developed the custom of singing popular vernacular hymns in honor of the Virgin Mary immediately following compline.

Other ministries developed from Dominican preaching. The apostolate to religious women with a contemplative bent led to the rapid growth of monasteries of Dominican nuns. Another facet of this ministry was the apostolate carried on among the beguines and other pious women, especially in the Rhineland and the Netherlands. Preaching to the laity led to the formation of the Dominican Third Order of Penance.

To provide congregations for their preaching and to perpetuate the fruit of their sermons, the friars founded confraternities in their churches. In 1274 Gregory X commissioned the order to preach devotion to the Holy Name. The friars were to exhort the people to bow their heads in reverence when the name of Jesus was mentioned. In the second half of the fifteenth century the friars established confraternities of the Holy Name. The Rosary Confraternity, an offshoot of the earlier Marian confraternities, was founded by Alan de la Roche about 1470 at Douai. The mother confraternity, established at the priory of Cologne in 1475, had soon enrolled members from all over Europe, evidence that Dominicans were actively preaching the rosary. This preaching and the confraternity made the rosary the most popular nonliturgical devotion in the Western church.

The order's first crisis developed out of its preaching mission. It was the expectation of the Dominicans and Franciscans, as of the papacy, that they would cooperate with the secular clergy. Although many bishops and pastors welcomed them, it was not long before animosity toward the friars developed among the secular clergy. In evidence after 1240, it can be related to several factors: the increasing number of friars, their well-organized preaching apostolate, their hearing of confessions, the burial of the faithful in their cemeteries, the exemption of the friars from episcopal control, and mendicant privileges, especially with regard to their preaching ministry. Many of the secular clergy severely hampered the work of the friars and challenged their existence.

The danger became acute when the University of Paris joined the conflict, seeking to limit the teaching of the friars.

The mendicants enjoyed full papal support until 21 November 1254, when Innocent IV, prompted by William of St. Amour and delegates from the university, revoked the privileges of the friars and subjected their ministry to the local clergy. Two weeks later Innocent was dead. Alexander IV, his successor, canceled the bull of Innocent one month after it had been issued. The controversy over hearing confessions went back and forth until 1281, when Martin IV issued the bull *Ad fructus uberes*, explicitly granting friars, licensed by their superiors, power to hear confessions everywhere without further authorization. The bull not only sustained the apostolate of the friars but also, for the first time, officially approved the liberty of the faithful to confess to any priest who had jurisdiction. It was an advance toward greater freedom of conscience and a more fruitful use of the sacrament of penance.

Nevertheless, the controversy continued unabated. In 1300, with the bull *Super cathedram*, Boniface VIII made a statesmanlike compromise that solved some of the pressing problems of the conflict, conceding something to each side. The friars might preach without hindrance, except at the hour when a bishop was preaching or a sermon was being delivered in his presence. For hearing confessions the friar superior must present to the bishop priests capable of administering the sacrament. Should the bishop refuse to accept these friars, they might nevertheless proceed to preach and hear confessions. This uneasy settlement endured until the Council of Trent established that all priests, both secular and religious, should obtain faculties from the local bishop; but conflicts between the two parties were chronic during the rest of the medieval period.

The conflict with the secular clergy produced good results. Resistance to the attempt of the clergy to absorb them into the parochial system made the mendicant orders stronger. Their expanding exemptions gave them an efficiency, mobility, and flexibility that they did not have when they were founded. Under attack a complex of rights and privileges was developed that partly freed the orders from episcopal control and regulation of their ministry. The preaching and confessional work of the friars, and the counsel and help they gave the faithful, were removed beyond the interference of the secular clergy. As ultimately developed, mendicant privileges extended to the following points: direct dependence on the Holy See and total exemption of the internal affairs of the order from episcopal control; the right to erect churches and public oratories; the privilege of burying the faithful in Dominican cemeteries; dispensation from paying imposts and tithes on legacies, funeral fees, and gifts; the right to teach theology in their priories and at the universities; the mission to preach; and the privilege of absolving cases reserved to the bishop.

The controversy served another purpose. The secular clergy acted as a counterweight to the mendicant movement. Without such a balance the new orders might have completely disrupted the ecclesiastical organization. They had to be assimilated, but not in the way the clergy intended. The native strength of the mendicants, together with papal support, was dynamic enough to withstand the assault. By forcing the friars to rely on the papacy, the opposition prevented them from drifting toward the extreme doctrinal positions that had carried other movements, such as the Humiliati, Waldensians, and Fraticelli, into heresy.

The friars performed various tasks for the Holy See. The popes appointed them to reform dioceses and monasteries, to act as officials and clerks in the papal curia, and to go on diplomatic missions. Dominicans served as masters of the Sacred Palace, papal penitentiaries, preachers of the crusade, and collectors of crusading monies. The papal inquisition recruited many, though not all, of its inquisitors among Dominicans, whose doctrinal training especially suited them for this task. Before 1500, two popes, twenty-eight cardinals, and more than two hundred bishops were drawn from the ranks of the order. Some of the kings of France, England, Spain, and Portugal, and various princes and bishops, chose Dominican confessors.

MISSIONS

Considering the evangelization of the pagans an essential part of the order's apostolate, Dominic sent missionaries to the frontiers of Europe: to Sweden, Poland, and Hungary. By 1225 the friars were in touch with the Moors and Jews of Spain and had gone into northern Africa. As a prerequisite for their missionary work they studied the oriental languages. The first to do so were those in the Holy Land. Urged by Raymond of Peñafort, the Spanish province established language schools at Tunis, Murcia, Játiva, and Barcelona, a venture that had the encouragement and support of the master general and general chapters. In 1310 the general chapter urged the

master general to open three schools, for the study of Arabic, Greek, and Hebrew, respectively. Thirteen years later it ordered the appointment of professors of languages at Kaffa and at Pera, near Constantinople. Not only language schools but also books helped the missionaries. Thomas Aquinas wrote his *Summa contra gentiles* partly to assist friars who were preparing for the missions. William of Tripoli, a missionary, wrote about the Muslims in his *On the State of the Saracens*. Raymond Martini, an outstanding orientalist, prepared treatises, especially *Pugio fidei* and *Capistrum Judaeorum*, to aid the friars in their contacts with the Jews. Pablo Cristiani (*d. ca.* 1265), a converted Jew, debated with his former coreligionists.

The Dominicans of the provinces of Scandinavia, Poland, and Germany evangelized the Baltic peoples, the Lithuanians, and the Russians. Soon after their arrival in Hungary in 1221, the friars began to preach to the Cumans. The conversion of Duke Bortz and his son Membrok in 1227 brought many other Cumans to the faith and led to the establishment of a bishopric among them. Theodore, former provincial of Hungary, became their first bishop. Temporarily disrupted by the Tatar invasions of Hungary in 1241, missionary work among the Cumans was resumed after the Tatars had left. Dominicans of the province of Greece worked in the Latin Empire of Constantinople and in the islands off the Greek mainland. When the Latin Empire fell, the friars established themselves in Crete.

The province of the Holy Land labored in Palestine and eastward. After the fall of the crusader states, it retreated to Cyprus. Although they ministered to the Western Christians in those regions, the presence of the friars in the Near East inevitably brought them into contact with Muslims, Jews, and dissident Christians. The friars achieved some early success, but much of it was ephemeral. Philip, provincial of the Holy Land, reported in a letter to Gregory IX in 1237 that the friars had made contact with the Jacobites, Nestorians, and Armenians. Through their efforts the patriarch of the Western Jacobites, the Jacobite patriarch of Alexandria, and a Jacobite and a Nestorian archbishop had submitted to Rome. The Nestorian katholikos of Baghdad, who ruled over a wide territory, had expressed a willingness to return to union. At the invitation of the king of Armenia Minor, four friars had gone there. The friars were also in contact with the Maronites of Lebanon, who had been in union with Rome before the friars had come. Stimulated by these events, Philip ordered all his friars to undertake the study of the oriental languages.

In addition to the missionaries, other friars promoted union of the churches by writing treatises or by serving as legates or messengers between the popes and eastern princes or prelates. Missionary work among the Muslims proceeded side by side with that among the dissident Christians. William of Tripoli claimed that he had baptized 1,000 Arabs. Ricoldo da Montecroce became fluent in Arabic and preached to Nestorians, Jews, and Muslims in the khanate of Persia. His *Itinerary* and *Refutation of the Koran,* William of Tripoli's *On the State of the Saracens,* and Burchard of Mount Sion's *Description of the Holy Land* offered Europeans new knowledge of Islam and the western Asiatic peoples.

The order opened a new missionary phase about 1300 when it established the Congregation of Friars Pilgrims for Christ Among the Gentiles. While enjoying many of the rights of a province, the congregation was more flexible. Eventually it opened a chain of houses that stretched from Greece across the Near East into Mesopotamia. When John XXII established the ecclesiastical province of Sultanieh (Sultaniensis) in 1318, he chose the bishops for the new sees from among the members of the congregation. Its most striking success was the conversion of the dissident monks of Crna (1331). Under Dominican guidance they formed themselves into Unifiers of St. Gregory the Illuminator. Their intention was to work for the reunion of the churches. Placed by Rome under the jurisdiction of the Dominicans, the Unifiers grew rapidly in numbers and were said to have had 700 members in 50 monasteries by about 1370. The hostility of the dissident Christians and the excessive zeal of some of the Unifiers weakened their effectiveness after 1380. In the late sixteenth century the Unifiers joined the Dominican order as the province of Armenia.

DECLINE AND REFORM

Through most of the thirteenth century the leadership of able superiors, the influence of learned and saintly scholars, and the spirit of the friars upheld the ideals of the order, preserved its religious spirit, and maintained its effectiveness. Decline of fervor and relaxation of discipline set in about 1290. There had been difficulty in observing poverty even earlier. The rapid increase in the number of friars and priories and the development of a multiplicity of apostolates created needs that the freewill offerings of the faithful and the quest for alms by the friars could not

fill. Seeking security, priories began to accept property and sign it over to a third party who agreed to provide them with a regular amount of consumer goods in return. Individual friars were granted permission to use funds gained from their own industry or from friends for books or clothing.

Meanwhile, religious observance, no longer supported by the zeal of the friars, weakened under interpretation, compromise, and excessive use of the power of dispensation. Besides reducing the number of friars, the Black Death accentuated these trends, causing a general collapse of observance. Life in common, the heart of a religious order, was extremely weakened and in some places all but disappeared. Friars failed to come to the refectory for meals or to choir for prayers. After the plague was over, unwise recruiting compounded the damage.

About 1300, friars of Tuscany began a movement, of short duration, to renew religious discipline. These friars were called "Spirituals," though they exhibited none of the excesses characteristic of the Franciscan group of that name. In 1367 Stephen Lacombe, vicar of the master general in Italy and provincial of Tuscany, inaugurated a more official reform. However, his adherence to the Avignon obedience when the Great Schism began nullified these efforts.

Elected master general of the Roman obedience in 1380, Raymond of Capua, confessor of Catherine of Siena, assumed leadership of the reform. With papal approval he decreed in 1388 that each province should set aside one priory as a house where religious observance would be maintained. He appointed vicars of observance and founded priories where strict observance was introduced. Friars of the observance reformed many of the monasteries of nuns. As the number of reformed houses multiplied, they were grouped into congregations. The congregations of Holland and Lombardy, the most successful and extensive, practically functioned as provinces. Although the observant congregations enjoyed considerable autonomy, and disagreement existed between them and the nonreformed friars, the reform movement did not divide the order; Dominican insistence on obedience kept both sides loyal to the master general.

Owing to economic and religious changes, even the observants found it extremely difficult to keep the strict poverty the constitutions demanded. Therefore, Master General Bartholomew Texier (*d.* 1449), even though an exponent of reform, obtained authorization from Pope Martin V to permit priories, when there was need, to own property and enjoy fixed income. In 1475 Sixtus IV extended this privilege to all the mendicant orders except the Franciscans. Thus he lifted the yoke of absolute poverty, which had become insupportable, and contributed to the Dominican revival of the sixteenth century. The mitigation introduced by Sixtus led to a lessening of severity among the reformed friars and prepared for a reestablishment of friendly relations with the non-reformed, who in the meantime had tightened their discipline.

The order came to the end of the medieval period renewed in discipline and witnessing the beginning of a Thomistic revival that reached full bloom early in the sixteenth century. Although the rise of Protestantism stripped the order of some of its strength in northern Europe, the Dominicans compensated for this by founding ten new provinces in America and one in the Philippines.

The habit of the Dominican order has four pieces: a white tunic confined at the waist with a leather belt, from which a rosary is suspended; a white scapular; a white cowl (also called a capuce), which is replaced among the nuns and sisters by a black veil; and a black mantle to which (among the fathers and brothers) a black cowl is attached. The mantle is worn only on specified ceremonial occasions and when the friars go outside their priories. This latter circumstance caused Dominicans in England to be called Blackfriars. In the Middle Ages the Dominican laity wore a white tunic and a black mantle. Today the Dominican laity wear a small, white scapular as their habit.

THE NUNS AND SISTERS

The first Dominican monastery of nuns originated at Prouille in 1207, when Bishop Diego de Azevedo of Osma and Dominic gathered a group of women, most of whom were converts from Catharism, into a contemplative religious community. Before his death in 1221 Dominic had founded two additional monasteries, at Rome and Madrid, and had projected a fourth at Bologna. By 1303 the order had 141 monasteries under its jurisdiction. In addition, the nuns of many other monasteries wore the Dominican habit and followed the Dominican constitutions but were under episcopal control. After Dominic had founded his order of friars, he probably gave the nuns of Prouille the Rule of St. Augustine and constitutions modeled on those of the friars. However, considerable diversity characterized the

legal codes followed by the nuns until 1259. In that year Master General Humbert of Romans promulgated uniform constitutions for them and made acceptance of the new code a condition of Dominican affiliation. Since the Council of Trent most monasteries of nuns have been under episcopal jurisdiction. Nevertheless, the nuns live according to the spirit of the order, wear its habit, and follow its constitutions.

Since the nuns lived in strictly enclosed monasteries, they pursued no active ministry. It was their vocation to assist the apostolate of the friars with their prayers and mortified lives. The friars assumed supervision of the monasteries with reluctance. They feared that care of the nuns would absorb all their energies and nullify their primary apostolate—preaching for the salvation of souls. After a period of struggle between them and the nuns, it was agreed in 1267, with the approval of Clement IV, that nuns affiliated with the order would be under its jurisdiction and laws. The friars would guide the nuns spiritually, preach to them, administer the sacraments to them, and supervise the discipline of the monasteries, visiting, correcting, or reforming them if necessary. The friars were not required to manage the temporal affairs of the monasteries or reside as chaplains in them, except at the three founded by Dominic.

The Third Order of Penance of St. Dominic (Dominican laity) was not founded by him, but stemmed from the lay penitential movement of the twelfth century. The brothers and sisters of the movement were lay people who sought to lead a life of Christian perfection and penance in the world while continuing the normal pursuits of the laity. After the founding of the mendicant orders, some of the brothers and sisters and other members of the laity attached themselves for spiritual guidance to one of the various mendicant churches. In 1285 Master General Munio of Zamora organized those who had come to Dominicans for direction, giving them a rule of life that embodied the Dominican spirit. He took those who accepted this rule under his jurisdiction and received them to the benefits of the order. Innocent VII approved the rule in 1405. The most noteworthy members of the Dominican laity were St. Catherine of Siena and St. Rose of Lima.

Convents of Dominican sisters arose when members of the Dominican laity, usually motivated by a pious purpose, such as the care of the sick, began to live in community. The members of some of these communities eventually began to take one or more of the vows of religion. Although at the beginning there were communities of brothers and others of sisters, only communities of sisters have survived. Dominican sisters have flourished in the United States and are represented by over thirty congregations.

BIBLIOGRAPHY

For an overview and bibliography see Ralph F. Bennett, *The Early Dominicans* (1937); William A. Hinnebusch, *The History of the Dominican Order*, 2 vols. to date (1965–1973), and *The Dominicans: A Short History* (1975).

Spirit and spirituality. William R. Bonniwell, *A History of the Dominican Liturgy*, 2nd ed. (1945); William A. Hinnebusch, *Dominican Spirituality* (1965); Pietro Lippini, *La spiritualità domenicana*, 2nd ed. (1958); R. J. Martin, "Le développement historique de la spiritualité dominicaine," in *La vie spirituelle*, 4 (1921), and "Le développement historique de la spiritualité dominicaine pendant la période de la restauration religieuse (1350–1450)," in *L'année dominicaine*, 59 (1923); P. Régamey, "Principles of Dominican Spirituality," in Jean Gautier, ed., *Some Schools of Catholic Spirituality*, K. Sullivan, trans. (1959).

Foundation and organization. Marie Dominique Chapotin, *Histoire des Dominicains de la province de France* (1898); M. A. Coniglione, *La provincia domenicana di Sicilia* (1937); Georgina R. Galbraith, *The Constitution of the Dominican Order, 1216–1360* (1925); William A. Hinnebusch, *The Early English Friars Preachers* (1951); Bede Jarrett, *The English Dominicans*, rev. and abr. by W. Gumbley, 2nd ed. (1938); Daphne D. C. P. Mould, *The Irish Dominicans* (1957); Marie Humbert Vicaire, *Saint Dominic and His Times*, K. Pond, trans. (1964), and *Dominique et ses prêcheurs* (1977).

Scholarship. Yves Congar, "Aspects ecclésiologiques de la querelle entre mendiantes et séculiers dans la seconde moitié du XIIIe siècle et le début du XIVe," in *Archives d'histoire doctrinale et littéraire du moyen âge*, 28 (1961); Célestin Douais, *Essai sur l'organisation des études dans l'ordre des Fréres Prêcheurs au treizième et au quatorzième siècle, 1216–1342* (1884); A. Duval, "L'études dans la législation religieuse de S. Dominique," in *Mélanges offerts à M.-D. Chenu* (1967); H. M. Feret, "Vie intellectuelle et vie scolaire dans l'ordre des Prêcheurs," in *Archives d'histoire dominicaine*, 1 (1936); Frederick J. Roensch, *Early Thomistic School* (1964); Beryl Smalley, *English Friars and Antiquity in the Early Fourteenth Century* (1960); James A. Weisheipl, *Friar Thomas d'Aquino* (1974).

Mystics and mysticism. Jeanne Ancelet-Hustache, *Master Eckhart and the Rhineland Mystics*, H. Graef, trans. (1958); James M. Clark, *The Great German Mystics* (1949); Rufus M. Jones, *The Flowering of Mysticism* (1939).

Apostolic activities. Berthold Altaner, *Die Dominika-nermissionen des 13. Jahrhunderts* (1924); Palémon Glorieux, "Prélats français contre religieux mendiants," in *Revue d'histoire de l'église de France*, 11 (1925); Humbert of Romans, *Treatise on Preaching*, W. M. Conlon, trans. (1951); Albert Lecoy de la Marche, *La chaire française au moyen âge spécialement au XIIIe siècle* (1886); Gordon Leff, *Heresy in the Later Middle Ages*, 2 vols. (1967); Andrew G. Little, "Measures Taken by the Prelates of France Against the Friars in 1289–1290," in *Miscellanea Francesco Ehrle*, III (1924), and "Licence to Hear Confessions Under the Bull *Super cathedram*," in his *Franciscan Papers, Lists, and Documents* (1943); Raymond Loenertz, *La société des frères pérégrinants* (1937); J. T. Welter, *L'exemplum dans la littérature religieuse et didactique du moyen âge* (1927).

The reform movement. A. Barthelmé, *La réforme dominicaine au XVe siècle en Alsace et dans l'ensemble de la province de Teutonie* (1931); Vicente Beltrán de Heredia, *Historia de la reforma de la provincia de España, 1450–1550* (1939); Stephanus Krasić, *Congregatio Ragusina Ordinis Praedicatorum (1487–50)* (1972); Gabriel M. Löhr, *Die Teutonia im 15. Jahrhundert* (1924); G. G. Meersseman, "La réforme des couvents d'Ypres et de Bergues-Saint-Winoc, 1457–1515," in *Archivum fratrum Praedicatorum*, 7 (1937); A. de Meyer, *La congregation de Hollande, ou La réforme dominicaine en territoire Bourguignon, 1465–1515* (1947).

Dominican nuns. Ernest W. McDonnell, *The Beguines and Beghards in Medieval Culture* (1954); G. G. Meersseman, "Les Frères Prêcheurs et le mouvement dévot en Flandre au XIIIe siècle," in *Archivum fratrum Praedicatorum*, 18 (1948); Heironymus Wilms, *Geschichte der deutschen Dominikanerinnen* (1920), and *Das alteste Verzeichnis der deutschen Dominikanerinnenklöster* (1928).

WILLIAM A. HINNEBUSCH

[See also **Albertus Magnus; Aquinas, St. Thomas; Augustinism; Bible; Confession; Dominic, St.; Dominican Chant; Dominican Rite; Durand de St. Pourçain; Eckhart, Meister; Hugh of St. Cher; Inquisition; Kilwardby, Robert; Mendicant Orders; Missions and Missionaries, Christian; Mysticism, European; Peckham, John; Penance, Penitentials; Preaching and Sermon Literature (Western European); Province, Ecclesiastical; Raymond of Peñafort, St. Rosary; Suso (Seuse), H[e]inrich; Tauler, Johannes; Trevet, Nicholas; Vincent of Beauvais; William of Moerbeke.**]

DOMINICUS (*fl.* late eleventh century), the scribe who, with Munnius, his relative, finished writing a Beatus *Commentary* at the Castilian monastery of S. Domingo de Silos in 1091 (London, British Library, MS Add. 11695). In 1109 it received a rich complement of illustration and decoration.

BIBLIOGRAPHY

Meyer Schapiro, "From Mozarabic to Romanesque in Silos," in *Art Bulletin,* **21** (1939).

JOHN WILLIAMS

[See also **Beatus Manuscripts.**]

DOMUS ECCLESIAE (Latin, "house of assembly"), Christian meetinghouse or community center, called an *oikos ekklesias* in Greek and known by the special name of *titulus* in Rome. The *domus ecclesiae* was a utilitarian domestic structure—private, inconspicuous, and unrecognizable from the street—altered inside to fit the religious, administrative, and charitable needs of the congregation. The oldest known *domus ecclesiae* is an ordinary dwelling in Dura Europos converted to Christian use around 230; no examples are known after 400.

BIBLIOGRAPHY

Richard Krautheimer, *Early Christian and Byzantine Architecture* (1975), 27–30.

LESLIE BRUBAKER

DONALD III (DONALDBANE) (*b. ca.* 1033), king of Scotland 1093/1094–1097. Son of Duncan I, Donald is first heard of on the death of his brother Malcolm III at Alnwick in November 1093, when there was a Scottish reaction against English influence on Malcolm; Malcolm's sons were overlooked and the Scots "chose" Donald as king. William II, evidently fearing a renewal of Scottish attacks on England, sent Malcolm's older son, Duncan, north with an army. Donald was defeated and Duncan II became king. His Anglo-Norman following was, however, expelled and Duncan then (May 1094) fell victim to an attack by Donald, who recovered the throne, though apparently at the cost of yielding half the kingdom to Edmund, a son of Malcolm.

In 1097 Edgar, another son of Malcolm, with English support won a hard-fought battle and drove out Donald. Slightly later evidence states that Donald was either blinded and imprisoned for life, or killed by his nephew David I. He was survived by a daughter. The sobriquet "ban" (the fair), whence Shakespeare's Donaldbane, is first found in the last

stanza of Berchan's *Prophecy,* probably composed in the twelfth century.

BIBLIOGRAPHY

A. A. M. Duncan, *Scotland, the Making of the Kingdom* (1975).

A. A. M. DUNCAN

[See also **Duncan I of Scotland; Malcolm III of Scotland; Scotland: History.**]

DONATELLO (Donato di Niccolò di Betto de' Bardi, *ca.* 1386–1466), greatest sculptor of the fifteenth century. Few personal documents survive, but Donatello's large and varied body of work provides a guide to his career. He is first recorded as an assistant in Ghiberti's shop (1404–1407). Ghiberti's stylis-

St. Mark, marble, by Donatello. Or San Michele, Florence, 1411. SCALA/ART RESOURCE

256

tic influence is visible in his early works, such as the marble *David* (Florence, the Bargello), begun in 1408 and completed in 1416. Donatello's marble *St. Mark* (1411, in Or S. Michele) announces his highly innovative style. Complex sources, logical relationships between drapery and anatomy, and planning for the angle from which it would be seen in situ characterize this remarkable work. Also for Or S. Michele Donatello executed a *St. George* (1415–1417), in which Giorgio Vasari noted the alertness and sense of movement imparted to the stone. The exquisite marble base portrays the saint's battle with the dragon in a unified relief surface depending on values of light and shade, made possible by Donatello's invention of a new technique called *rilievo schiacciato*.

Donatello's works of the 1420's include the *Zuccone* (1423–1425), a marble prophet for the campanile in Florence. This powerful ascetic figure, in Roman dress, appears to be filled with Christian spiritual intensity. Significant also is his *St. Louis of Toulouse* and its marble tabernacle for Or S. Michele. The richly textured figure of the saint, the largest fire-gilt bronze of its time, is set in a niche that uses early Renaissance architectural elements. Donatello designed a gilt bronze relief, *The Feast of Herod*, for the baptismal font of *S. Giovanni* in Siena (installed 1427). Its frame functions as a true window; and scientific, one-point perspective is employed for the first time. A dramatic stage set encompasses the dancing Salome, an astounded King Herod, and spectators.

Donatello's bronze *David* (1430–1432) is a freestanding contrapposto figure combining classical images of Mercury with Christian content. Also from the 1430's are his outdoor pulpit in Prato and the *cantoria* in the Duomo of Florence, both decorated with vigorous dancing putti.

By 1444, Donatello was in Padua, where his important commissions are an equestrian statue of Gattamelata and an altar for S. Antonio. *Gattamelata* (1447–1453) is a bronze statue on a stone pedestal that resembles an ancient sarcophagus. However, not its function as a cenotaph but the statue's heroic grandeur impresses the spectator. Donatello dressed Gattamelata in a mixture of ancient and modern armor and designed the face not as a literal portrait but as a type of noble and forceful character. The work equals or surpasses the Roman statue of Marcus Aurelius and represents the first time a general, rather than a ruler, was accorded a freestanding

equestrian monument. Donatello's sculptures for the altar of S. Antonio (1446–1450) are additional examples of his powers of invention. In the four-relief *Miracles of St. Anthony* he composes surging crowds bound together in wavelike motion, anticipating High Renaissance works. A gilt wood *St. Mary Magdalene*, usually believed to have been carved 1454/1455, carries forward the expressionistic aspect of Donatello's work: the emaciated, ascetic figure shocks.

Donatello did not live to complete two bronze pulpits for S. Lorenzo, Florence (begun 1460, completed by Bertoldo di Giovanni and others by 1470), for which he designed relief panels portraying the Passion cycle.

BIBLIOGRAPHY

Frederick Hartt, *Donatello, Prophet of Modern Vision* (1973); Horst W. Janson, *The Sculpture of Donatello*, 2 vols. (1957).

BRUCIA WITTHOFT

[See also **Ghiberti, Lorenzo**.]

DONATION OF CONSTANTINE. The *Constitutum Constantini*, or Donation of Constantine, is an eighth-century document in the form of a constitution or charter, supposedly issued by Emperor Constantine I, who describes in the first person his conversion and confession of faith (lines 1–155, the *Confessio*) and subsequent endowment of the Roman church (lines 158–306, the *Donatio*). These 300-odd lines of Latin text have provoked hundreds of scholarly essays on their authenticity, original purpose, and historical influence.

In 1440, in the context of a resurgent Roman papacy resident once again in central Italy, Lorenzo Valla employed humanist philological techniques to unmask this "forgery," as Nicholas of Cusa had briefly done seven years earlier, both of them doing so in behalf of a more spiritual conception of the church's sovereignty and mission. Protestants seized upon Valla's treatise as sure proof that papal claims rested upon a mass of falsehoods. Catholics frequently defended the authenticity of at least the contents, if not the document itself, until in the nineteenth century all papal claims to temporal sovereignty had become anachronistic. Yet until the 1950's much of the scholarly discussion still betrayed confessional undertones. A new critical text and careful research into its use and transmission have greatly nuanced earlier estimates about the influence of this document on the shaping of Roman papal claims to spiritual and temporal sovereignty.

"Constantine" addressed this constitution to Pope Sylvester I, his successors in Peter's see, and all subject bishops throughout the world, and set out to tell in a "flowing narration" what the Savior had accomplished through his apostles Peter and Paul by means of Sylvester. The account of Constantine's miraculous cure and conversion is based on well-known fifth-century legends regarding Pope Sylvester, here reworked and enriched with a confession of the faith this pope had taught him. Constantine's *Donatio*, though alluded to in the legends, is a more original element. The emperor declares Peter's see, like his own divinely instituted royal power, to be exalted above all other churches and patriarchates; he grants Peter's successors the Lateran Palace ("greatest in the world") and builds there a church dedicated to the Savior; he concedes to them and all Roman clergy the use of numerous imperial insignia and privileges (including the senatorial dignity for the latter); and finally, on moving his own residence to the East, he endows Pope Sylvester with the Lateran Palace, the city of Rome, the province of Italy, and all western regions.

Of many quite fantastic explanations for this document's origin and intent, the one receiving greatest support in the 1960's considered it a "diplomatic forgery" done in the context of the Frankish–papal alliance and designed to sanction Rome's claim to the future papal states. There is, unfortunately, no persuasive evidence whatsoever for any such use of it in the eighth and ninth centuries. Indeed, there is no sure proof of its existence prior to about 850, when it entered the Pseudo-Isidorean collection in northern Frankland, and there are no early Roman copies at all. Close philological analysis nevertheless strongly suggests ascription to a lower cleric at the Church of the Savior (St. John Lateran) and a mid-eighth-century dating, especially the period 754–767.

More recent work is much more inclined to see the document as a "literary fiction" or "hagiographical legend," an essentially private rather than curial effort, reflective perhaps of the mid-eighth-century situation but with no specifically political purpose. This Lateran cleric had in fact prepared a "legend of foundation" in the form of a fictional "foundation charter," which attempted to focus on the Lateran Palace and Church of the Savior all the glory of the first Christian emperor and the apostolic see, with little or no sensitivity to the misreadings possible in the larger political arena. The object of his work was probably the rival church across town, St. Peter's in the Vatican, increasingly the major center of pilgrim traffic, which thus had come to detract from the Church of the Savior, part of the residence of Peter's successors and site of Constantine's conversion. The lands and privileges granted at the end—on which so much attention would later be focused—were in the mid eighth century claims either already well established in precedent or else so vaguely grandiose as to be virtually without concrete meaning.

The chief avenue of transmission of the *Constitutum*—also providing its oldest extant text—is the Pseudo-Isidorean canonistic collection prepared about 850, the longer version of which (A1) includes the complete document at its proper chronological point, while the shorter version (A2) has only the *Confessio*. Frankish visitors to Rome, however, had earlier taken back a version closer to the original (perhaps it was on display in the Lateran for pilgrims), and it yielded several independent copies often bound with the legends of Sylvester.

Around 960, in the context of the Saxon restoration of the Roman Empire, a Roman deacon (*Johannes digitorum mutilus*) prepared a handsome, fictive original, which later (1001) elicited from Otto III's chancellery the only medieval denunciation of this document as an outright forgery. A century later Humbert of Silva Candida, in determined conflict with the Greeks, slightly altered a text also related to the Roman original in order to strengthen the papal position against the Eastern emperor and patriarchs. Apart from a few other references, often not clearly distinguishable from material in the Sylvester legends, these represent the only known uses of the text during its first three centuries of existence (about 750–1050).

The reformed papacy of the later eleventh century and its supporters, determined to win autonomy from the emperor and sovereignty over the papal states, first employed the *Constitutum* to political ends, concentrating exclusively on the concluding *Donatio*—whence arose its modern name, Donation of Constantine. Those close to the Roman curia probably drew on Humbert's text, which eventually entered Gratian's *Decretum* as a palea (D. 96, cc. 13–14) and thus became familiar to all medieval canon lawyers. Initially publicists (such as Honorius Augustodunensis) made much more extravagant use of it than did leading popes (such as Gregory VII and

Innocent III) and canon lawyers. The latter sensed, rightly, that this text could easily be interpreted to mean popes had received much of their sovereignty and privileges from emperors.

Only after one of the greatest lawyer-popes, Innocent IV, had reinterpreted Constantine's "donation" to be a "restitution" of sovereignty originally invested by God in the vicar of Christ did popes and lawyers also make extensive reference to it, particularly on behalf of the papacy's temporal sovereignty. Civil lawyers of the twelfth and thirteenth centuries frequently doubted its authenticity, not on grounds of forgery (as Cusa, Valla, and Pecock would) but, rather, of illegality: emperors could not legally alienate their own authority and property. All this took on political reality once again when French publicists battled Boniface VIII on behalf of Philip IV the Fair and German publicists battled Pope John XXII on behalf of Louis IV the Bavarian. Legal disputes about the interpretation of this document continued with considerable subtlety and force throughout the fourteenth and fifteenth centuries.

In the meantime, radical critics of papal government, most of whom ended up outside the church (such as Waldensians and radical Franciscans), began to cite the Donation of Constantine as marking a turning point in church history, the moment at which political and material concerns had come to outweigh the spiritual. Protestant Reformers were to continue this line of criticism, bolstered by Valla's proof that this fictional "foundation charter" was nothing but a "monstrous forgery."

BIBLIOGRAPHY

Source. Horst Fuhrmann, ed., Constitutum Constantini (1968).

Studies. Christopher B. Coleman, ed. and trans., The Treatise of Lorenzo Valla on the Donation of Constantine (1922, repr. 1971), an English translation; Horst Fuhrmann, "Konstantinische Schenkung und abendländisches Kaisertum," in Deutsches Archiv für Erforschung des Mittelalters, 22 (1966), and "Das frühmittelalterliche Papsttum und die Konstantinische Schenkung," in I problemi dell'occidente nel secolo VIII (1973), 257–292; Nicolas Huyghebaert, "La Donation de Constantin ramenée à ses véritables dimensions," in Revue d'histoire ecclésiastique, 71 (1976), and "Une légende de fondation: Le Constitutum Constantini," in Le Moyen Âge, 85 (1979); Gerhard Laehr, Die konstantinische Schenkung in der abendländischen Literatur des Mittelalters bis zur Mitte des 14. Jahrhunderts (1926), and "Die Konstantinische Schenkung in der abendländischen Literatur des ausgehenden Mittelalters," in Quellen und Forschungen aus italienischen Archiven, 23 (1931–1932); Pietro De Leo, Ricerche sui falsi medioevali, I, Il Constitutum Constantini (1974); Wilhelm Levison, "Konstantinische Schenkung und Silvester-Legende," in his Aus rheinischer und fränkischer Frühzeit (1948), 390–465; Raymond-J. Loenertz, "Constitutum Constantini: Destination, destinataires, auteur, date," in Aevum, 48 (1974), with an additional note in Revue des sciences philosophiques et théologiques, 59 (1975); Wolfram Setz, Lorenzo Vallas Schrift gegen die Konstantinische Schenkung (1975).

JOHN VAN ENGEN

[See also Constantine I, the Great; Decretals, False; Honorius Augustodunensis; Lateran; Nicholas of Cusa; Pecock, Reginald.]

DONATION OF PEPIN. See Pepin III.

DONATISM. The Donatist movement had its origins in problems created by the great persecution of Christians by Emperor Diocletian in 303. In North Africa some Christians tried to save themselves by appearing to cooperate with the authorities—for example, by handing over what appeared to be, but were not always, sacred books. When Constantine first tolerated and then supported the Christian church, the question was raised whether such men could administer the sacraments or hold office in the church. The test came in 312, when a newly elected bishop of Carthage, who had been consecrated by a bishop accused of having been a cooperator, was deposed by a local council and a new bishop was brought in by the dissident faction. The new bishop lived only a short time; he was replaced by Donatus, who had been one of the leaders of the local council. Donatus began to organize a rival church in North Africa, with its own bishops.

Constantine was troubled by this movement, both because he was anxious to preserve the unity of the church and because the division in North Africa tended to follow racial lines. The native Berbers were the largest group in the Donatist church; this brought them into opposition with the Roman settlers and thus weakened imperial government in the region. The emperor called three synods to settle the dispute; the largest was at Arles in 314. These meetings denied the Donatist claim that ordination by an unworthy bishop was invalid: they argued that the sacrament was valid in itself, and did not depend on the character of the minister.

Constantine's efforts to settle the dispute by peaceful means had little effect. He then tried force, imprisoning Donatist bishops and ordering that the churches in their hands be seized, by the army if necessary, thus starting a virtual civil war. The Donatists were also guilty of violence, and in some regions there was no security for many years. Constantine finally issued a sort of edict of toleration (321) that did not end the dispute, though it diminished the disorder. The Donatists remained very numerous; by 400 there were almost as many Donatist bishops in North Africa as there were Catholic bishops.

St. Augustine was troubled by the strength of the sect, and especially by its insistence that the minister was as important as the sacrament. Thus it was useless to be baptized by an unworthy priest (unworthy in the sense of holding the wrong beliefs), and rebaptism would be necessary. The dangers in this doctrine were obvious. How could one be sure that the priest or bishop had never erred in faith, especially if opposing Donatism were accepted as an error? These arguments had some effect, but Donatism, while weakened by external pressure and internal disputes, survived until the Arab conquest in the seventh century. And, as in many parts of the Roman Empire, internal struggles over religious beliefs had weakened the ability of Roman citizens to resist external enemies.

BIBLIOGRAPHY
W. H. C. Frend, *The Donatist Church* (1952); S. L. Greenslade, *Schism in the Early Church* (1953); G. C. Willis, *St. Augustine and the Donatist Controversy* (1950).

JOSEPH R. STRAYER

[See also **Augustine of Hippo, Saint; Constantine I, the Great.**]

DONATUS OF FIESOLE (*ca.* 785/790–*ca.* 876). A native of Ireland, Donatus went on a pilgrimage to Rome about 816 and became one of several contemporary Irish scholars to remain on the continent. After spending time at the courts of the princes Lothair and his son Louis, he set out for home. Around 829, however, he was made bishop of Fiesole, where he remained until his death. Besides teaching grammer, he also wrote two extant poems: a praise of Ireland and his own epitaph.

BIBLIOGRAPHY
Text of the poems is in *Monumenta Germaniae historica, Poetae latini medii aevi*, III (1896), 691–692.

RALPH WHITNEY MATHISEN

DONDI, GIOVANNI DE' (1318–1389), physician and inventor of the "astrarium." Born at Chioggia, he was the son of a physician, Jacopo de' Dondi, and moved to Padua with his family in 1349. In 1350 or 1352 he was appointed professor of medicine at the University of Padua, and in 1359 he received an appointment to the faculties of astrology, philosophy, and logic. He became widely recognized as a scholar of considerable learning, and from early 1367 to 1370 he lectured in medicine at Florence.

For a time de' Dondi enjoyed the favor of Francesco da Carrara, prince of Padua, who sent him as his ambassador to Venice in 1371. In 1372 he served on a committee of five that was to establish the boundaries between Carrara and the Venetian Republic, and in the same year he joined those citizens of Padua voting to wage war on Venice. Following the war between Padua and Venice, de' Dondi appears to have lost the favor of his patron and was subsequently befriended by Duke Gian Galeazzo Visconti of Pavia, who loaded him with benefits and honors. In 1382 he was appointed to the faculty of the University of Pavia, and later in the same year he was provided with living accommodations in the Visconti palace. In 1387 he established his own residence in Pavia.

In 1354 de' Dondi married Giovanna di Reprandino dalle Calze; they had one son and four daughters. He was widowed and in 1379 married Caterina di Gerardo da Tergola; they had four more children. De' Dondi died after an illness contracted during a visit to Venice. He was buried in the family vault in the baptistery of the cathedral of Padua.

De' Dondi's major achievement was the design and construction of a planetary machine that he first described as a "planetarium" and, after revisions, as an "astrarium." He began work on the project in 1348 and completed it sixteen years later, constructing the machine with his own hands. He left several detailed and illustrated manuscripts describing the astrarium, from which several operating reproductions were produced in modern times. The astrarium was operated by clockwork, one of the earliest such mechanisms for which an almost complete and incontestable documentation exists. A mechanized model of the universe, it demonstrated the movements of the five planets then known and the sun and moon, and it was equipped with an horary and other dials.

In 1381 the astrarium was acquired by Duke Gian Galeazzo Visconti and installed in the library of his palace at Pavia. The astrarium was seen and noted by Petrarch, Leonardo da Vinci, Donato Bramante, and Johannes Müller (Regiomontanus), among others. The instrument was last noted in 1529, by which time it had fallen into serious disrepair and after which all trace of it was lost.

BIBLIOGRAPHY

Sources. Antonio Barzon, Enrico Morpurgo, Armando Petrucci, and Giuseppe Francescato, trans., *Giovanni dall'Orlogio, Tractatus astrarii . . . Biblioteca capitolars di Padova Cod. D.39* (1960), a facsimile reproduction of the codex with transcription and commentary, as well as an introduction and glossary by the translators; "Familia nostra in civitate Cremonensi florens es illa factione populari, ut assolet, pulsa fuit anno 1251, ac se Patavium contulit," Padua, Biblioteca del Museo Civico, Archivio Privato Famigliare Dondi dall'Orologio; "Memoria di Monsignor Francesco Scipione Marchese Dondi dall'Orologio: Notizie sopra Jacopo e Giovanni Dondi dall'Orologio," in *Saggi scientifichi e letterari dell'Accademia di Padova,* 2 (1789).

Studies. Granville H. Baillie, "Giovanni de' Dondi and His Planetarium Clock in 1364," in *Horological Journal* (1934); Silvio A. Bedini and Francis R. Maddison, "Mechanical Universe: The Astrarium of Giovanni de' Dondi," in *Transactions of the American Philosophical Society,* n.s. 56, pt. 5 (1966); L. T. Belgrano, "Degli antichi orologi pubblici d'Italia," in *Archivio storico italiano,* 3rd ser., 7 (1868); Andrea Gloria, "I due orologi meravigliosi inventati da Jacopo e Giovanni Dondi," in *Atti del Reale Istituto veneto di scienze, lettere, ed arti,* 7th ser., 7 (1896); Vittorio Lazzarini, "I libri, gli argenti, le vesti di Giovanni dall'Orologio," in *Bollettino del Museo civico di Padova,* 1st ser., 1 (1925); H. Alan Lloyd, "Giovanni de Dondi's Horological Masterpiece 1364," in *La Suisse horlogère,* intl. ed., 2 (1955); Antonio Simoni, "Giovanni de' Dondi e il suo orologio dei pianeti," in *La clessidra,* 8 (1952).

SILVIO A. BEDINI

[See also **Clockwork, Planetary; Visconti.**]

DONIZO (DOMNIZO) (*fl.* 1115, *d. ca.* 1130), Benedictine monk and presbyter of Canossa. He wrote a life of Countess Mathilda of Tuscany (*Vita Mathil-*

dis) in two books of hexameters and leonines. The first book gives an overview of the history of Canossa and Mathilda's life.

BIBLIOGRAPHY

Donizo, *Vita Mathildis,* in *Patrologia latina* CXLVIII, cols. 950–1035; Max Manitius, *Geschichte der lateinischen Literatur des Mittelalters,* III (1931), 662.

EDWARD FRUEH

DONNEI DES AMANTS (or **Amanz**), an anonymous and incomplete Anglo-Norman debate poem written around the end of the twelfth century. The poet overhears a conversation in which a young man attempts to win his lady's favors by recounting various *exempla* concerning famous lovers and less well-known stories such as the *Vilain and the Serpent* (from the *Disciplina clericalis*) and the *Vilain and the Bird*. Three passages deal with the Tristan and Iseut legend, including one not found elsewhere, *Tristan rossignol,* in which Tristan, who has returned to Cornwall from Brittany, imitates a nightingale and various other birds to call Iseut from Mark's bed. King Mark refuses to believe a dwarf who warns him of Tristan's presence and allows his wife to wander in the garden, where she meets her lover.

BIBLIOGRAPHY

Gaston Paris, "Le Donnei des amants," in *Romania,* 25 (1896).

BRIAN MERRILEES

[See also **Anglo-Norman Literature.**]

DONOR PORTRAIT represents the patron or patrons of a commissioned object giving it to its sacred or secular recipient; in some cases, the object itself is not shown, and the patron simply venerates the recipient. Founder portraits show the architectural patron (ktetor in Byzantium) delivering a model of the church to Christ or the Virgin: at the Kariye Camii in Istanbul, Theodore Metochites presents the church to Christ (*ca.* 1320), as Bishop Ecclesius does at S. Vitale in Ravenna (*ca.* 547); in Sicily, William II offers Monreale to the Virgin (before 1183). In other examples—such as a fresco in the Chapel of

SS. Felix and Adauctus in the Commodilla Catacomb of Rome (*ca.* 530) or the apse of SS. Cosmas and Damian, also in Rome (520–530)—the donor simply raises covered hands or a victory wreath. Dedication portraits show the scribe or donor presenting a manuscript, usually to a mundane recipient. The earliest example of a dedication portrait is the picture of Anicia Juliana receiving a copy of the herbal from the citizens of Honoratae in the Vienna Dioscorides (*ca.* 512: Vienna, Österreichisches Nationalbibliothek, MS Med. graec. 1). A later example appears in the Ottonian Egbert Codex, where two scribes present the codex to Egbert. A votive portrait simply shows the donor with a venerated saint, meant to protect the giver. In all cases, the medieval donor portrait is an instrument of salvation, intended to remind the secular or divine recipient—and the viewer—of the donor's good intentions.

Leslie Brubaker

[See also **Byzantine Art (843–1453); Early Christian Art; Egbert of Trier; Theodore Metochites.**]

DONSKOI, DMITRII IVANOVICH. See **Dmitrii Ivanovich Donskoi.**

DORMITION OF THE VIRGIN. See **Koimesis.**

DOUBLE-ENDED CHURCH. See **Church, Types of.**

DOUGLAS, GAVIN (*ca.* 1475–1522), a Scots poet known chiefly for his translation of the *Aeneid.* Douglas' life is well documented, unlike the lives of Henryson and Dunbar, the other two important Middle Scots poets. He was born about 1475, a younger son of Archibald "Bell the Cat," fifth earl of Angus. After graduating from St. Andrews he took orders and became provost of St. Giles' in Edinburgh in or before 1503. As an ambitious member of a powerful family (his position was strenghtened in 1514, when his nephew married Margaret Tudor, the widow of James IV, not long after James's death at Flodden in 1513), he was active in seeking political

power and preferment in the church. Douglas was an important figure, especially after Flodden, but his successes were only partial and intermittent: he may have been briefly chancellor of Scotland, but perhaps this was only by his own styling; he became bishop of Dunkeld but never attained the archbishopric of St. Andrews that he sought. He died in London as an exile in 1522.

Apart from a short and unimportant poem, "Conscience," Douglas' only two surviving works are the *Palice of Honour,* finished probably in 1501, and his translation of the *Aeneid,* finished in 1513. (*King Hart,* an allegorical poem of very considerable merit, was formerly attributed to him, but this attribution is almost certainly incorrect.) The *Palice of Honour* is an interesting and complex dream vision of more than 2,000 lines, written mostly in two varieties of nine-line stanzas. Like Chaucer's *House of Fame,* one of its sources, it describes a supernatural journey to an allegorical building. It is a learned, ironic, and ostentatiously rhetorical poem: the subject of the poem, at least in part, is poetry itself.

Douglas' *Eneados,* his translation of the *Aeneid,* has been widely and deservedly praised: the first translation into English of a classical epic, it remains one of the great English translations. Douglas used the 1501 edition of Vergil by Ascensius (Jodocus Badius) which includes Ascensius' own lengthy commentary as well as the early commentaries of Servius and Donatus; Douglas, an expansive translator, incorporated into his verse a fair amount of, especially, Ascensius' commentary. When one makes allowance for this, and for the fact that Ascensius' text is considerably different from that of any modern edition, Douglas' translation is commendably accurate, as well as forceful and eloquent. He followed Ascensius in including, though without enthusiasm, the thirteenth book written by Maphaeus Vegius, an Italian humanist.

The prologues that are prefixed to each book of the *Aeneid* are perhaps Douglas' best-known poems. While all of his translation is in decasyllabic couplets, the prologues are in a great variety of metrical forms and, indeed, in a number of different genres. The long prologue to book I, which serves as a general introduction, is especially interesting in that it gives Douglas' theories of translation and his views on Vergil. The prologues are usually linked, sometimes in subtle ways, to the books they precede, but their variety and their obtrusive stylistic concerns also enable them to be seen as a set of poems demonstrating Douglas' range.

BIBLIOGRAPHY

D. F. C. Coldwell, ed., *Virgil's Aeneid Translated Into Scottish Verse by Gavin Douglas,* Scottish Text Society, 4 vols. (1957–1964), which however, needs to be used in conjunction with Priscilla Bawcutt's excellent monograph, *Gavin Douglas: A Critical Study* (1976); Priscilla Bawcutt, ed., *The Shorter Poems of Gavin Douglas,* Scottish Text Society (1967). Bibliographies are in Albert E. Hartung, 1180–1204, ed. *A Manual of the Writings in Middle English,* IV (1973), 1180–1204; and George Watson, ed., *The New Cambridge Bibliography of English Literature,* I (1974), 662–664.

DENTON FOX

[See also **Middle English Literature; Translations and Translators, Western European; Vergil in the Middle Ages.**]

DOUKAS, the family that ruled the Byzantine Empire from 1059 to 1078. Constantine X Doukas (1059–1067) was chosen by the antimilitary faction to succeed Isaac I; he did nothing to stem the empire's decline. To protect her children, his widow Eudokia married Romanos IV Diogenes (1068–1071). Upon the latter's capture by the Turks, courtiers elevated Constantine X's son Michael VII (1071–1078), who proved incompetent. Forced to abdicate by Nikephoros III Botaneiates (1078–1081), Michael died (*ca.* 1090) a monk. Alexios I Komnenos owed much of his success to the support of the Doukas family for himself and his wife, a grandniece of Constantine X.

BIBLIOGRAPHY

J. M. Hussey, "The Later Macedonians, the Comneni and the Angeli, 1025–1204," in *Cambridge Medieval History,* 2nd ed., IV, pt. 1 (1966), 858–867; Demetrios I. Polemis, *The Doukai* (1968).

CHARLES M. BRAND

[See also **Byzantine Empire: History (1025–1204).**]

DOWER, DOWRY. See **Family.**

DOWN, ROGER, an early-sixteenth-century English woodcarver from Chittlehampton, Devon. Down is known to have finished, along with John Hyll, the screen at Atherington, Devon, between

Wooden screen by Roger Down. Atherington, Devon, *ca.* 1538–1542. CONWAY LIBRARY, COURTAULD INSTITUTE OF ART

1538 and 1542. Down and Hyll's deft handling of decorative motifs exemplifies the English late-Gothic emphasis on expressive interlace, undulating forms, and plasticity. It is in the west country works of the late 1530's and 1540's, as evidenced by the Atherington screen, that scholars such as Stone first identify a short-lived early-Renaissance style, noting a French influence from Rouen and Brittany in foliage motifs.

BIBLIOGRAPHY

Richard W. Goulding, *Blanchminster Charity Records* (1898), 91; Lawrence Stone, *Sculpture in Britain: The Middle Ages,* 2nd ed. (1972), 224.

JENNIFER E. JONES

[See also **Screen.**]

DRAMA, FRENCH. In France, as in other areas of Europe, the liturgy was one of the principal sources of vernacular drama. By the twelfth century several French monasteries had become centers of dramatic activity and innovation. In addition to a group of unusual liturgical plays from the Benedictine monastery of Fleury (today St. Benoît-sur-Loire), there is a striking *Sponsus* from the abbey of St. Martial at Limoges in which the text alternates between Latin and French. In Paris, Hilarius introduced French refrains into his Latin liturgical dramas, and in Beauvais students at the cathedral school used French refrains in their *Ludus Danielis*. The first play almost entirely in French was the Anglo-Norman *Jeu d'Adam* from the mid twelfth century, though its close connections with the liturgy are still evident in the parts that are sung in Latin. Based on the first chapters of Genesis, the play is a dramatization of the office of Septuagesima and, like the liturgy, was probably performed inside the church, rather than outside, as previously thought.

Judging from the surviving texts, it was in the commercial city of Arras that a purely French non-liturgical drama developed. Greatly enriched by the textile industry, the city and its patricians lavished money on arts and spectacles of all kinds. Around 1200 Jean Bodel wrote a *Jeu de St. Nicolas* that includes comic tavern scenes in an urban setting patterned on the life of Arras. From the same period comes *Courtois d'Arras,* a dramatic adaptation of the parable of the Prodigal Son. Again, the place of the Prodigal's debauchery resembles the taverns of Arras. Three quarters of a century later Adam de la Halle wrote the *Jeu de la feuillée,* a kind of Midsummer Night's dream in which he and other citizens of Arras played themselves. Adam later followed the count of Artois to southern Italy; it was probably there that he wrote the pastoral *Jeu de Robin et Marion* (*ca.* 1282–1288). Two other contemporary plays also came from industrial urban areas: *Le Garçon et l'Aveugle* (the second half of the thirteenth century) from Tournai and Rutebeuf's *Miracle de Théophile* (*ca.* 1261) from Paris. The plays surviving from the thirteenth century are few in number but high in quality.

The fourteenth century saw the beginnings of the Passion play in France. Based largely on a narrative Passion that had long been recited by jongleurs, these plays graphically represented the final week of Christ's life. The earliest such play is the *Passion du Palatinus* (fourteenth century) from eastern France. This, together with several fragments of plays from the same general area, suggests that the Passion plays underwent a significant development in that region. Paris, too, was a center of dramatic activity in the fourteenth century. The *Passion* from the Bibliothèque Ste. Geneviève (*ca.* 1350) foreshadows the licensing of the Confrérie de la Passion at Paris in 1402. This group was accorded exclusive rights to the staging of Passion plays in the city. Also from Paris comes the collection of forty *Miracles de Nostre Dame* that were played, one each year from 1339 to 1382, at the annual assembly of the gold-

smiths' guild. The plays dramatize the stories of people in extreme circumstances who are rescued by the intercession of the Virgin Mary, patron saint of the guild.

By the fifteenth century the French drama had achieved in broad outline the form it would take for the next 150 years. The major genres of Passion play, morality play, and farce had been developed, and the basic techniques of staging had been established. It was principally by the augmentation and elaboration of these traditions that the late medieval drama grew into one of the richest and most prolific expressions of dramatic art in French cultural history. Probably at no time before the advent of television did dramatic spectacle touch the lives of so many people.

The flourishing of drama in late-medieval France led to the development of a variety of new genres. These play types were quite unlike the classical and neoclassical genres of comedy and tragedy in that they freely combined serious and comic matters, as well as high and low styles. Moreover, religious themes and moral lessons were often presented in comic form. Medieval plays may be more aptly classified as either historical or fictional. The first broad genre includes Passion plays, biblical and postbiblical plays, miracle plays, and saints' lives. Although today one might view such plays as including unhistorical material, the medieval audience saw them as true representations of significant past events. The historical plays thus assumed a social function that the other plays did not share. They served to form and to reinforce the spectators' sense of community by showing them where they came from, their place in the cosmos, and their collective destiny. The second broad genre includes morality plays and farces. These are plays with invented plots; their social function was to reinforce the ethical and behavioral ideas of the community by moral teaching or satirical attack.

In the fifteenth century the Passion play grew from a relatively short reenactment of the events of Holy Week to a spectacular representation of the whole of Christ's life. These enormous productions would last for several days and might include 200 or more players. The two most famous Passion plays were those of Arnoul Gréban (Paris, *ca.* 1450) and Jean Michel (Angers, 1486). These were imitated and copied in other productions of Passion plays for more than a century. Among other dramatizations of biblical history were the *Mistere du Viel Testament* and the *Actes des apostres.* The postbiblical destruction of Jerusalem was dramatized in Eustache Mercadé's *La vengeance de Jésus-Christ*. Many towns sponsored plays portraying the lives of their patron saints, among them the *Vie de St. Martin* by André de La Vigne (Seurre, 1496). Secular history was represented in *La destruction de Troye* by Jacques Milet (1450/1452) and the *Mystère du siège d'Orléans* (mid fifteenth century), the first portrayal of Joan of Arc in the theater.

The plays incorporating fictional plots may be divided into two distinct genres based on the antithetical worlds portrayed in the morality play and the farce. Both genres deal with human behavior as exemplified in problems of authority and rationality, but there is a great difference in how these problems are treated. In the world of the morality play, there is always a higher power to reward good and to punish evil. Moreover, the morality hero must use his reason to choose between the two. In the farce world there is no higher authority. Indeed, all authority has been debased, and disorder reigns. Instead of reason, folly rules the actions of farce characters.

Although a few morality plays have survived from the early fifteenth century, most date from between 1450 and 1550. The purpose of the plays was to show the spectators examples of moral behavior to imitate and of immoral behavior to avoid. Two patterns of presentation were possible: plays with two protagonists, one good and one bad, and plays with a single protagonist who is good and bad by turns. The former pattern is found in *Bien Advisé et Mal Advisé* and in *L'Homme Juste et l'Homme Mondain*. In each play the characters are tempted by personified vices; one succumbs to the temptations, whereas the other remains virtuous. The other pattern is exemplified by *L'Homme Pécheur*, in which the protagonist falls into sin, then finally repents. The pattern is mixed in *Les enfants de Maintenant*, in which both youths are initially led into error. In the end one is converted, but the other persists in his sinful ways.

The morality play is a combination of psychomachy and pilgrimage. The former is a battle between personified virtues and vices for influences over the hero; the latter is the hero's progress through life. The earlier morality plays tended to represent the hero's whole life (*Bien Advisé, L'Homme Juste*), while the latter plays tended to represent a segment of life (*L'Enfant Ingrat*) or a single vice (*Les blasphémateurs, Langue Envenimée, La condamnation de Banquet*). In addition to these personal moralities, there were institutional moralities

in which the collective behavior of institutions was criticized (*Les trois états, L'Église et le Commun*). Early Protestants made effective use of this type of play to attack Catholics (*La maladie de Chrétienté, La vérité cachée*).

Among the most popular plays of late medieval France were the farces—short, comic works that served both as entertainment and as social satire. One type of farce is largely domestic and portrays everyday characters, such as cobblers, servants, and schoolboys, in conventional comic situations. A second type deals with personified abstractions, such as Métier and Marchandise, or with representations of folly, such as Mère Folie and Tête Creuse. These plays may be termed allegorical farces. In the texts they are usually called *farces moralisées* or *sotties* and are strongly satirical in nature.

The most celebrated farce of the late medieval period is *Maître Pierre Pathelin* (ca. 1465), which concerns a down-and-out lawyer who cheats a draper out of some cloth, only to be cheated in turn by a simple shepherd. The play thus exemplifies the trickery that is an essential characteristic of the farce world. Another well-known farce is *Le cuvier*, in which a henpecked husband is forced to make a list of all the housework he must do. When his wife falls into the washtub, he refuses to pull her out because that task is not on his list. Most of the surviving farces portray the comic side of conjugal strife or infidelity in order to ridicule weak husbands. Noteworthy examples are *Resjouy d'Amours, Martin de Cambray, Frère Guillebert,* and *Le pâté*. Other objects of ridicule include dull-witted students (*Maître Mimin*), country bumpkins (*Mahuet*), inept and cowardly soldiers (*Colin, fils de Thévot*), and bombastic lovers (*Les trois amoureux de la croix*).

Virulent satire is reserved for the allegorical farces, in which the abuses of the powerful are attacked behind the mask of folly. In *Folle Bobance* the nobility, the bourgeoisie, and the peasantry foolishly debase their ideals for the sake of pleasure and end in ruin. In *Les gens nouveaux* the newly powerful patricians are attacked for abandoning the values of the past. The *Jeu du Prince des Sots* of Pierre Gringore satirizes Pope Julius II in an attempt to rally public support of Louis XII. The *Sottie des copieurs et lardeurs* is a tour de force of verbal play and fantasy, attacking many of the follies of the day.

The staging of late medieval plays was varied and complex. Sometimes performances were put on indoors by guilds, *confréries*, or student groups, but more often they were staged outdoors in public squares, marketplaces, or specially built open theaters. Short plays, such as farces, required few stage properties and were played on trestle stages that were set up in public areas on holidays or at commercial fairs. The longer mystery plays required elaborate staging with many properties and many technical devices or *secrets,* such as trapdoors and unseen cables, to create a realistic dramatic illusion. These stages were constructed in town squares—with spectators on two, three, or four sides—or in circular theaters somewhat resembling Shakespeare's Globe.

There were no professional acting troupes in France before the sixteenth century. The short plays were most often written and staged by amateurs belonging to parish, trade, or professional groups. Members of the society of law clerks, called the Basoche, were especially prolific in writing farces and *sotties.* The long plays, which cost large sums to produce, were at first organized and financed by municipalities. Later, wealthy patricians invested in these plays and made profits from admission fees. The trend toward longer playing times for the Passion plays—in one case twenty-five days—was related to commercial interests, since the plays attracted crowds of visitors to the towns that produced them.

In the turmoil of the Reformation, the medieval biblical plays were perceived as leading to abuses of religious practice. They were banned in Paris in 1548, though they persisted much longer in some remote provinces. Morality plays and farces continued to be played into the seventeenth century. The morality play was not without influence on the development of Renaissance tragedy, and the medieval farce tradition was a rich source of inspiration for Molière.

BIBLIOGRAPHY

Heather Arden, *Fools' Plays* (1980); Jean Claude Aubailly, *Le théâtre médiéval profane et comique* (1975); Barbara Bowen, *Les caractéristiques essentielles de la farce française et leur survivance dans les années 1550–1620* (1964); Grace Frank, *The Medieval French Drama,* 2nd ed. (1960); Alan E. Knight, *Aspects of Genre in Late Medieval French Drama* (1983); Élie Konigson, *L'espace théâtral médiéval* (1975); Louis Petit de Julleville, *Les mystères,* 2 vols. (1880), and *La comédie et les moeurs en France au moyen âge* (1886); Henri Rey-Flaud, *Le cercle magique* (1973); Carl J. Stratman, *Bibliography of Medieval Drama,* 2nd rev. ed., 2 vols. (1972).

ALAN E. KNIGHT

[See also **Adam de la Halle; Bodel, Jean; Drama, Liturgical; Drama, Western European; French Literature: After 1200; Jean Michel; Jeu d'Adam; Morality Play; Passion Cycle; Rutebeuf.**]

DRAMA, GERMAN. As in England and France, medieval drama in Germany, both religious and secular, attained its greatest popularity between about 1450 and the advent of the Reformation. The text corpus preserved is more substantial than those known to us from other European vernaculars: more than 100 religious dramas and about 150 (shorter) texts of nonreligious plays, put on mainly during carnival. Systematic examination of town records such as account books and minute books (Bernd Neumann, 1977, 1985), is beginning to show that, as in England, the surviving texts present a distorted

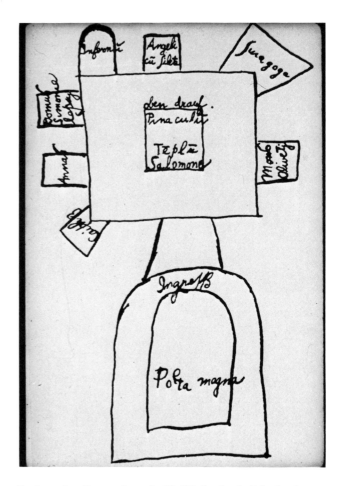

Crude staging diagram drawn by Vigil Raber for the Palm Sunday Play, the first play of a cycle of seven put on in 1514 at Bozen, under his direction. MUSEUM FERDINANDEUM, INNSBRUCK

picture of how many plays were actually staged and in which regions.

Attested performances of religious plays number more than 500. For nonreligious theater there are about 300 references. These show active playmaking not only in centuries (the thirteenth and fourteenth) for which there are few texts, but also in provinces (North Germany, Saxony, the Lower Rhine) where the virtual absence of manuscripts led scholars to posit theatrical blanks. It should be kept in mind that, in medieval times, German was spoken (and hence German plays staged) in regions today no longer associated with the language: as far east as Latvia (Riga) and Transylvania and as far south as northern Italy (Trent).

The first plays in German were written around 1250, a century after the vernacular was first employed in Anglo-Norman England (*Jeu d'Adam*) and Spain (*Auto de los Reyes Magos*). Before that, German verses had, on occasion, been inserted into Latin church plays. Good examples are Mary Magdalene's amorous airs in the Benediktbeuern Passion play (*ca.* 1230/1240) and the hymn "Christ ist erstanden" (Christ is risen), sung by the congregation to conclude Latin Easter plays.

Much of what was thought to be known about the beginnings and development of religious drama (in progressions putting order above facts) has recently been placed in doubt. Because many Easter plays feature Latin passages (sung) followed by verse paraphrases in German, they have always been viewed as exemplifying the emergence of German drama from the matrix of Latin church drama. Yet the chronology (most manuscripts are fifteenth-century) suggests that the opposite is true, that many Easter plays constituted attempts by clerics concerned with the sideshow tendencies of the religious stage around 1500 to return the more sacred subjects to the language and setting of the church.

Judging from the texts, the first plays written in German were not Easter but Passion plays. The Benediktbeuern Passion has a substantial number of German passages. Fragments of a play from the central German monastery of Himmelgarten show that the extended dramatization of Christ's life and death now called a Passion play existed, entirely in German, as early as 1250 (even the Nativity is included). What is emerging is a picture of "several beginnings," play forms that do not always grow larger in ordered series but are subject to reduction as well, a drama more dependent on provincial and local custom.

The aim of religious drama was to instruct in the faith. It was the only form of medieval "literature" heard and seen by large numbers of people. Sermon and pulpit aside, the religious stage was the only "mass medium" available in medieval society before the advent of printing.

Most of the religious plays were written and directed by clerics whose names were not recorded. A similar clerical anonymity pervades much of European drama outside of France, where playwrights seem to have asserted themselves early (Jean Bodel, Adam de la Halle, Jean Michel). Supervision by the church was close to the point of censorship. Rennward Cysat, director of the Lucerne Passion play, routinely submitted all changes he made to the diocese for approval.

German religious dramas may, most conveniently, be divided into five groups: plays of the Easter season, Christmas plays, saints' plays, eschatological plays, and morality plays. Plays of the Easter season (Easter, Passion, and Corpus Christi) constitute by far the largest and most important group. About half of all texts and two-thirds of the performances on record belong to this peak season for religious theater.

The scenes central to the Easter plays, notably the visit of the Marys to Christ's tomb, were taken over from Latin (music) plays first put on in churches in the tenth century. The texts of some twenty-eight German Easter plays survive, a substantial number of which are based on a Latin play in use in west-central Germany in the fourteenth century. Most of them contain the following episodes: braggart soldiers guarding Christ's tomb; Christ harrowing hell; the Resurrection; the Marys approaching the sepulcher; two disciples (Peter and John) running to the tomb to verify the Resurrection; appearances of the risen Christ. On the way to the sepulcher the Marys buy ointments from a spice merchant, an episode that by the fourteenth century had become the major comic scene of religous drama. It involves a plot standard to farce: the stingy husband (merchant), his quarrelsome wife, the equally uncivil but libidinous servant.

Unique to the German Resurrection plays (the oldest, about 1250, is from Muri, Switzerland) is the "gathering of sinners" episode wherein—Christ having released the patriarchs from hell—Lucifer sends out his devils to restock his domains. The sinners, it turns out, are garnered from the kind of small town where the plays were most commonly staged. They include a baker who weighs short, a butcher who sells spoiled meat, a priest given to trysts behind the altar, a servant girl generous with her favors, an old hag fond of witchcraft.

Although centered on Christ's trial and crucifixion, Passion plays normally not only include the Resurrection (Easter play) and episodes of Christ's life, but also often range backward to the Creation in order to establish the link between man's fall and his redemption. Standard is Mary's lament at the foot of the cross, a scene also found as a separate oratorio-like play. In the fifteenth and sixteenth centuries, Passion plays were the most popular form of religious theater. While attested in all regions, the tradition was centered in Hesse (Frankfurt, Alsfeld, Friedberg) and the Tirol (Bozen [Bolzano], Sterzing [Vipiteno], Hall [Solbad Hall]).

Although Corpus Christi plays tend to follow the history of man's salvation to its end in the Last Judgment, they often depict the same scenes as Passion plays. What distinguishes them is that their performance is linked to Corpus Christi day and that it involves a procession of some type. As in England, Corpus Christi plays were commonly put on by the craft guilds and religious confraternities of towns (such as Freiburg im Breisgau, Bozen, Ingolstadt, Eger, Zerbst), but they never achieved the popularity and significance of the great English cycles.

Perhaps because the Nativity constitutes a fairly standard scene in Corpus Christi and Passion plays, the number of independent Nativity or Christmas plays (seven surviving texts) is strikingly small. Although performances attested in the records, starting in the twelfth century, reveal that the regional distribution of Christmas plays is about the same as that of Easter-season drama, the number of such attestations (about thirty-five) is relatively modest. Some of the plays depict scenes found in Latin Nativity plays since the eleventh century: the annunciation to the shepherds, the coming of the Magi, and Herod slaying the innocent children. Unique to the German tradition, however, are plays (the first composed about 1420 at Constance) centering on an intimate scene close to folk custom. Here the infant Jesus is rocked in a cradle (instead of the manger) while those present in the stable, angels included, sing Christmas carols, often dancing around the cradle. In these "cradle plays" Joseph is turned into the stock comic figure of the overanxious old father, complaining about poverty and the cold, fond of the bottle, and beset by slovenly maidservants who appropriate his hose to swaddle the baby and make poor porridge. While no match for the earthy York-

shire lads in the great North English cycles, notably Wakefield (Towneley), the shepherds of the German Nativity plays share the rustic materialism that prompts them to invoke the Christ Child's blessing, mainly on their sheep and vegetables.

In contrast with France, where saints' or miracle plays flourished early (Bodel wrote his *St. Nicholas* around 1200) and had, by the fourteenth century, achieved great popularity (*Miracles de Nostre Dame* of the Paris goldsmiths' guild), the German tradition began late and is sparse in extant texts (about twelve). The earliest of some fifty performances on record is for a St. Catherine play staged at Königsberg (Prussia) in 1323. Aside from St. Catherine (for whom the English, at Dunstable Abbey, had a play as early as 1119), most of the miracle plays dealt with the martyrdom of St. Dorothy, popular in Silesia, and with St. George the dragon slayer, for whom townspeople in the southwestern regions (Rothenburg ob der Tauber, for instance) had a special fondness.

Although miracle plays—characteristically staged in honor of the patron saint of a town—had the smaller scope of local theater, the tradition did produce two documents of dramatic merit: *Spiel von Frau Jutten* (Thuringia, *ca.* 1480), on the rise and fall of the woman cleric who would be pope, and the *Theophilus Miracle* (three fourteenth-century versions in Low German dialect), on the fall of haughty Theophilus, a churchman who, in seeking a bishopric, makes a pact with the devil long before that other medieval figure known to us as Faust.

At a time when people had to live with the knowledge that any day could be Doomsday, plays dealing with the end of the world were naturally popular. These dramas date back to the mid twelfth century, when Gerhoh, the zealous abbot of Reichersberg (Bavaria), inveighed against clerics desecrating churches by staging plays on the advent and reign of the Antichrist. The text from Gerhoh's time, usually assigned to Tegernsee (Bavaria), is part of the twelfth-century revival of letters in which drama flourished no less than the other arts. Yet like other great Christmas-season dramas of that century (the Beauvais *Daniel*, for instance), the Tegernsee *Antichrist*—which in supporting the cause of Emperor Frederick Barbarossa became the first play with a political mission—is written in Latin and must be examined in the context of the pan-European church drama. Of the Antichrist plays written in German (first attested performance at Frankfurt in 1468), none is extant. All that survives is a carnival play from Nuremberg (Des Entkrist vasnacht) that derives from a Swiss Antichrist play attacking political figures prominent around 1350. In Switzerland (the Alemannic provinces) drama depicting the Last Judgment was popular stage fare, and a large body of interrelated texts has survived. Like Antichrist plays, such dramas rehearsed Armageddon on the world scale.

In contrast, the third type of eschatological drama, based on Matthew's parable of the five wise and five foolish maidens, concerns the salvation or damnation of the individual soul. While a minor form (two texts, seven attested performances), the play of the ten virgins is the only one that can be considered a tragedy in the medieval understanding of this term (happy beginning, sad ending). The intercession of the Virgin Mary herself fails to persuade Christ the Judge to pardon the foolish maidens who forgot to do good works in time. The terror this vision held for a medieval spectator is exemplified in the lamentable fate of a count of Thuringia named Friedrich der Freidige, who, after watching a performance of this play at Eisenach on 4 May 1321 (the earliest on record), suffered a stroke and, bedridden, died within two years.

Though popular in France, England (Mankind, The Castle of Perseverance), and the Low Countries (Elkerlijc), the type of allegorical drama known as morality (fall and salvation of a soul in its passage through life) did not gain much of a foothold in the German-speaking regions. A tradition evolved only in Lübeck, where moralities were staged as carnival theater, likely in imitation of practices in the Low Countries, with which Lübeck had trade ties. Little is known about the Lübeck moralities beyond the account books (play titles) of the confraternity of mercers responsible for putting them on. Because it is such a singular and massive effort (about 18,000 verses), the Erfurter Moralität of 1448—allegories on the proper life superimposed on New Testament parables—may have been written not for the stage but for reading or recital.

With few exceptions the plays just surveyed were put on in the open, in town squares mainly, with the stage set either at ground level or on a platform made of posts and boards. Stage locations were marked by open scaffolds seating the players, who were visible at all times to the spectators crowding around the edges of the square. As in France and southern England, the scaffolds (stations, houses) were laid out between heaven (elevated) at the east and the dragon jaws of hell (hellmouth) at the west.

The stations of Christ's antagonists were often lined up to the left of heaven and the Calvary cross, those of his supporters to the right. The world and man in it were thus viewed as suspended between—and watched by—the forces of good (God enthroned) and evil (the devil in hellmouth, with fire, smoke, and din). Since it can also be found in paintings, this practice of having all "scenes" simultaneously in open view, with action in some of them (usually one spoken, the others in dumb show) going on at the same time, appears to correspond to a medieval way of visualizing a chain of historical events.

Adhering to the opening "processional" of church drama, the actors would start the play by marching in procession, accompanied by music, to the scaffolds. Having remained there throughout the performance, they would signal the end of the play by marching out, recessional-style, in the manner they came. An actor "entered" by standing up and starting to play his role, and he simply sat down when his scene was over. Episodes occurring in localities for which no "houses" were built were enacted in the open area at stage center (known as pla-

Beginning of Constance Christmas Play with the play announcer or Prologue with heraldic staff. Probably Augsburg, ca. 1475. HOUGHTON LIBRARY, HARVARD UNIVERSITY, MS GER 74, fol. 22r

tea or "the place" in the English tradition), with protagonists stating in the opening speeches where they are. Although no curtain fell to mark the end of a scene, the spectators would be able to gather that an episode had concluded when the major players marched to the next scaffold. To smooth out the transition and keep the groundlings quiet, the angel choir would intone the *Silete* (be still) song.

As elsewhere in Europe (see the Apollonia miniature in the book of hours of Étienne Chevalier), the play director—comparable with a modern orchestra conductor—would stand in the middle of the open stage, cuing the players with a baton from the prompt copy of the play. Such prompt copies were mainly tall and narrow booklets with the text written verse by verse in one column. In some places (the Frankfurt Passion) scrolls rolled up on sticks were used. Staging the larger cycles, mainly Passion plays, took between two and four days. The lengthiest performance known—the Bozen Passion of 1514, which lasted seven days—is an exception.

Up to the late fifteenth century, scaffolds were simple in design and special effects limited. For the Frankfurt Passion as staged since the early 1300's in the main square of the city, for instance, it was sufficient to represent both mountaintop and temple roof of the Temptation by means of a barrel. Yet by 1500 the desire to foster faith by stirring compassion and hatred had inspired directors—notably in the towns of Hesse and the Tirol, and at Lucerne—to devise naturalistic effects involving the kind of display sadism we know from the Herod, buffeting, and crucifixion pageants of the English cycles. Thus in the Donaueschingen Passion, belonging to the Lucerne branch, Satan not only rips out Judas' bowels after the wretch has hanged himself from a tree (this effect was also used in French plays such as the Arras Passion) but then rides him to hell tied to a pulley running on a rope strung between the tree and hellmouth.

It did not take long for this fondness to startle—reminiscent of Mathias Grünewald's canvases and Tilman Riemenschneider's carvings—to inspire special effects worthy of a Cecil B. de Mille movie. Suffice to describe what happened at the fish market of Lucerne on the Thursday after Easter of 1583, when—under the anxious eye of Rennward Cysat (apothecary, alpinist, town clerk, playwright)—the *Salvator* actor "expired" on the cross. To dirges intoned by several choirs, the curtain in the temple was flung apart, the gilded sun on a tavern façade

was reversed to display its dark-red side, a dove (signaling the soul) alit from a trap box atop the cross, thunder and earthquake were produced by rifle salvos and by boulders rocked in barrels, and the "dead" climbed out of the "common grave" scaffold to circle the square.

In line with the medieval habit of visualizing the past in terms of the present, the actors were dressed in costumes proper to the medieval estate represented. The announcer would don the magnificent gear of a herald, Herod and Pilate appeared as princes, Caiphas and Annas as bishops of the time. Nudity was simulated by means of body stockings. The devils wore the kinds of monster masks and shaggy suits with faces over the genital area used throughout Europe.

As held true in England until the Restoration, women were excluded from acting. All female roles, even Eve in body stocking, were played by men. Only in Tirol—for the Bozen Passion of 1514, for instance—were women allowed to take certain minor roles, with the major ones (Mary Magdalene, the Virgin Mary) still assigned to men.

A religious play required between 100 and 300 actors. The only professionals hired, often from out of town, appear to have been minstrels. In contrast with England, neither the existence of professional actors (a troupe of them put on the *Mankind* morality) nor the engagement of such professionals for religious pageants (fees for players in York) can be attested in central Europe. Recruited from all ranks of the commune—with town officials, clerks, judges, and schoolmasters strongly represented—the players were at best compensated by an "after-theater" supper given by the town. In some cases they actually had to purchase their parts, and usually they laid out money for costumes and props. Acting, like charity, was an act of religious devotion.

Beyond erecting a platform and scaffolds, putting on a play involved the town in expenses for hosting invited dignitaries and feasting the players. Most costly was hiring contingents of guards for protective services as diverse as barring the gates to beggars and sick travelers, policing tavern fees, and sealing off the ghetto in case the play should lead to anti-Semitic mob action, as Passion plays often did.

The Reformation, introduced to German provinces at different times after the early 1520's, did away with religious theater, now considered a remnant of a discredited church. Only in areas remaining Catholic (Lucerne, Tirol, Vienna) were performances carried on until the seventeenth century, at times—as at Lucerne—in conscious affirmation of the old faith.

In contrast with the religious drama, the other major form of medieval theater, plays on secular topics, appears to have been much more of a local affair with less standardization. The church was the communicator and benevolent enforcer of standards in religious drama, but it did not regulate nonreligious playmaking, which was shaped more by local custom, as much of town life was at that time. The only common denominator of the plays about to be surveyed is that they do not deal with religious subjects and were staged mainly during carnival, the week or more preceding Ash Wednesday.

Although the majority of them are sketchlike comedies and farces, some are political or instructional. In fact, documentation from town archives made available by Bernd Neumann suggests that the long-standing habit of regarding secular plays as one genre *(Fastnachtspiele)* is not valid. A more complex picture (diverse forms arising at different times in numerous towns) may emerge from an analysis of the evidence from some sixty towns (starting with Arnheim [Arnhem] in 1395) where secular theatricals existed. Given the uncertain state of research, the best that can be done at this time is to draw a distinction between the typical carnival farce *(Fastnachtspiel)* as it evolved in Nuremberg (from which city stem the vast majority of surviving texts) and other kinds of drama also put on at carnival or Shrovetide. It is known, for instance, that even religious plays such as the *Theophilus Miracle* (Deventer, 1436), the *St. George* (Dortmund, 1497), and morality plays (Lübeck) were sometimes staged at carnival. On the other hand, there is increasing evidence that, in some places, comedies were performed at times other than Shrovetide: in May, June, even August. Although Nuremberg carnival plays were certainly staged inside, the cold weather (carnival is in February or early March) would not exclude outdoor performances in other towns (attested, for instance, for 1426 at Hall in Tirol).

Still, future research will hardly alter the long-established fact that Nuremberg was the performance and dissemination center of Shrovetide theatricals. Beginning their jocular labors about 1440, the people of that city managed to produce the largest corpus (some 100) of carnival farces known. In fact, most of what has, in the past, been said about carnival plays is based on the Nuremberg corpus. From the artisan

class of this city hail the only identifiable playwrights working in this genre before the Reformation: the gunsmith Hans Rosenplüt (*ca.* 1400–after 1460), who specialized in invectives against the corrupt governing estates, and the barber-surgeon Hans Folz (*ca.* 1435/1440–1513), who wrote—and printed—his mostly ribald sketches when not too busy with other forms of short verse literature, lyric song included. (In that sense Folz is the precursor of Hans Sachs and other Meistersingers of the sixteenth century.)

From Nuremberg, carnival theatricals were apparently exported to nearby Eger (now Cheb, Czechoslovakia), where twenty-five performances are attested between 1442 and 1522 (no texts survive), and south into the Tirol, where the plays were substantially modified to accord with dialect and customs of this Alpine region. Between 1510 and 1535 Vigil Raber, shuttling between Sterzing and Bozen, took time to copy twenty-five comedies staged in these towns (not all of Nuremberg origin, however) for the library he kept in his native Sterzing.

Only Lübeck, the fourth major center thus far recognizable, can be said to have developed its Shrovetide dramatics independent of Nuremberg. This helps to explain why the Lübeck plays, attested between 1430 and about 1537, appear to have been so different in scope—judging from what exists, a list of seventy-four titles (only one text is preserved). In contrast with the Nuremberg farces, subjects were drawn from popular stories on classical (Troy, Alexander) and medieval (Charlemagne, Arthur) subjects as well as from the beast epic, traditionally the vehicle for political satire. Also atypical is that a form of religious drama known as the morality plays made up a large portion of Lübeck theater fare at carnival.

Although in Lübeck the plays were the domain of a wealthy confraternity of mercers known as the *Zirkelbrüder*, the group most active in putting on Shrovetide theatricals elsewhere (in Nuremberg especially) was the *gesellen* (journeymen) of craft guilds. It should be noted, however, that in some localities the term *gesellen* meant no more than "young men of the town." Since the records occasionally add *erbare* (honorable), it would seem advisable not to exclude the young men of such wealthier governing classes as merchants.

Taking the Nuremberg tradition to be representative, carnival plays were small sketches between 100 and 600 verses long. They were put on by ad hoc companies of between four and ten amateur players, moving from house to house and using the largest room available. Few props were needed. Most of the playmaking was make-believe aided by the general merriment of the spectators, who rewarded the players with the victuals and wine of Mardi Gras.

In the simplest form of the *Fastnachtspiel* (though not necessarily the oldest), each in a series of stock characters (peasants, artisans of various trades) recites one speech dealing with the same experience (say, the inept wooing of a village lass). A more complex variant employs a court setting, with witnesses speaking against and for the accused. His infraction, however, is usually no more serious than the absurd sentence rendered by jury and judge. The other major type, like the farces of fifteenth-century France, dramatized a story. Featuring intrigue in service to fornication and greed, and character types as old as Plautus (the sly servant, the bumpkin peasant, the matchmaking hag, the libidinous young man), these comedies were frequently patterned on the verse tales (fabliaux) so popular in the later Middle Ages. Verse tales made good models because they were the first to evolve the technique of direct speech exchange now called "dramatic."

Given to extremes in gluttony and lust, the boorish peasant is the most popular figure of carnival plays. Less an attempt by townspeople to vilify country folk, the bumpkin derives from a tradition of parodic literature as old as Neidhart von Reuental, (*fl.* 1230). The medieval rustic is a kind of lusty carnival fool, but one devoid of the wit of Shakespeare's jesters. Aside from belly laughs at human folly, part of the fun of these plays lay in the playwright's linguistic inventiveness. Great stock was placed in devising orgies of words in the manner of Rabelais, whether it was thirty names to call your shrewish wife or a dozen ways to commit profound stupidities in the sex act.

The Reformation marked the end of medieval religious theater, but the late-medieval carnival comedies continued to flourish. In fact, the sixteenth century saw in Hans Sachs and Jakob Ayrer the playwrights most expert and prolific in fashioning drama for Shrovetide—much of it, however, quite serious and instructional.

BIBLIOGRAPHY

Texts. Only four of the hundreds of plays surveyed have been translated into English: *The Redentin Easter Play*, Adolf E. Zucker, trans. (1941, repr. 1966); *The Play of Antichrist*, John Wright, trans. (1967); Hans Folz, "Mirth-ful Peasant Play," in Larry D. Benson and Theodore M. Andersson, eds., *The Literary Context of Chaucer's Fabliaux: Text and Translation* (1971), 46–59; *The Saint Gall Passion Play*, Larry E. West, trans. (1976).

Studies. For those reading German, the only reliable and up-to-date studies are the 100 or so articles, each on one play, in Kurt Ruh *et al.*, eds., *Die deutsche Literatur des Mittelalters: Verfasserlexikon,* 2nd ed. (1977–). See also Werner M. Bauer, "Spiele, mittelalterliche weltliche," in Klaus Kanzog and Achim Masser, eds., *Reallexikon der deutschen Literaturgeschichte,* 2nd ed., IV (1979), 100–105; Rolf Bergmann, "Spiele, mittelalterliche geistliche," *ibid.,* 64–100; Johannes Janota, "Mittelalterlich-frühneuzeitliche Spiele und Dramen," in Walter Hinck, ed., *Handbuch des deutschen Dramas* (1980), 26–34, 529–531; Hansjürgen Linke, "Das volkssprachige Drama und Theater im deutschen und niederländischen Sprachbereich," in *Neues Handbuch der Literaturwissenschaft,* VIII, *Europäisches Spätmittelalter* (1978), 773–763; Bernd Neumann, *Zeugnisse mittelalterlicher Aufführungen im deutschen Sprachraum. Eine Dokumentation zum volkssprachigen geistlichen Schauspiel* (diss., Univ. of Cologne, 1977; to be published in Münchener Texte und Untersuchungen, 2 vols., 1985).

ECKEHARD SIMON

[See also **Drama, Liturgical; Drama, Western European; Everyman; Folz, Hans; Gerhoh of Reichersberg; Morality Play; Neidhart von Reuental; Passion Cycle; Raber, Vigil; Rosenplüt, Hans.**]

DRAMA, LITURGICAL. Liturgical drama is the name given to the dramatizations of particular events in the Old and New Testament that were performed in connection with the liturgy of the Christian church during the Middle Ages. The earliest known example, the *Quem quaeritis* dialogue, is found in manuscripts from the tenth to the sixteenth centuries and involves the resurrection at Christ's tomb on Easter morning. The basic scene is in the form of a three-line dialogue between the three Marys (Mary the mother of James, Mary Salome, and Mary Magdalene) and an angel who tells them Christ has risen (see example 1).

The subject matter of the *Quem quaeritis* dialogue and some of the actual phrases can be found in the accounts of Matthew (28:5–7,10), Mark (16:5–7), and Luke (24:4–6). The actual lines, however, appear to be newly invented.

In its original manuscript location, before the Mass on Easter morning, the three lines of the *Quem quaeritis* are often accompanied by a variety of other lines: exhortations and processional antiphons. Fur-

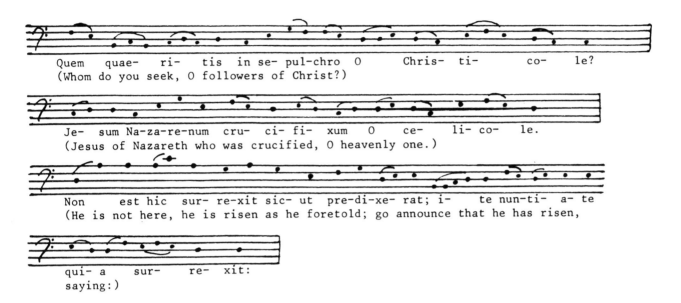

Quem quae- ri- tis in se- pul-chro O Chris- ti- co- le?
(Whom do you seek, O followers of Christ?)

Je- sum Na-za-re-num cru- ci-fi- xum O ce- li-co- le.
(Jesus of Nazareth who was crucified, O heavenly one.)

Non est hic sur- re-xit sic- ut pre-di-xe- rat; i- te nun-ti- a- te
(He is not here, he is risen as he foretold; go announce that he has risen,

qui- a sur- re- xit:
saying:)

Example 1. PARIS, BIBLIOTHÈQUE NATIONALE, FONDS LATIN, MS 12044

ther, the words of the three "core lines" are not ex-actly the same in all manuscripts; variations in one or more words from each of the lines can be found. Helmut de Boor has traced several lines of dissemi-nation of the dialogue by studying the variations in the wording of the core lines and the presence of ac-companying lines. Not all of the accompanying lines are included on the same page of the manuscript as the lines of the dialogue, however, and in many cases they are not even in the same book. The processional antiphons especially were added according to cus-tom from books or sections of processional material.

The section of the book in which the dialogue oc-curs contains materials for the soloist or cantor, and at the end of the dialogue lines there is the direction for the next function of the cantor: to intone the in-troit antiphon for Mass. The soloists' manuscripts often contain only material and directions for the so-loist and usually do not indicate the parts of the cer-emony that do not include the soloist. The presence of items such as prayers or antiphons sung by the choir is not marked, and thus there is some difficulty in reconstructing the ceremony surrounding the drama. The entire sequence is not yet clear.

The first scholarly investigations, in the mid-nine-teenth century, concluded that the liturgical drama began as an introductory trope for the Easter Mass introit, and that it originated at the abbey of St. Mar-tial at Limoges, the source of the earliest known text (931–934). More recent scholars have questioned both the theory of origin and the original function of the dialogue. O. B. Hardison has found elements of the dialogue in the Easter vigil ceremony of the Roman rite and suggests that the drama, or at least the idea of the drama, may have originated in that ceremony. C. Clifford Flanigan has traced elements of the dramatic aspect to the traditions of the Galli-can liturgy and proposes that the idea of dramatiza-tion originated in northern Europe and may have been taken from the Gallican liturgy when that tra-dition was replaced by the liturgy from Rome in the late eighth and ninth centuries. Timothy McGee has produced evidence that the *Quem quaeritis* dialogue was never a part of the liturgy, that the first dramas were instead a part of a paraliturgical ceremony, called the Collecta, that was performed before the introit for the Mass on Easter morning. There is some question as to whether the dialogue was ever a trope. The majority of manuscripts in which it is found are tropers (others are found in processionals and responsories), but the tropers were not exclu-sively devoted to tropes; they also contained other additions to the liturgy.

The actual origin of the idea of the drama, its pur-

273

pose, its placement, and its place of origin are still subjects of controversy and continuing research, but the above three views are not incompatible with one another. The disposition toward personalization of the liturgy in the Gallican tradition and the already existing material in the Roman vigil ceremony both could have been inspirations for the final realization of an actual dramatization of the Resurrection scene. A further model could have been the existence of dialogues in the liturgy of the Byzantine church from as early as the sixth and seventh centuries.

Most recent investigations search for the origin of the dialogue at least a century before the earliest extant evidence, and the court of Charlemagne has been suggested as a likely place of origin. Drama, which had been dormant in the West since the fifth-century suppression by the church, flourished again at Charlemagne's court during the ninth-century Carolingian revival. Amalarius, bishop of Metz (*ca.* 775–*ca.* 850), who wrote tracts encouraging the dramatization of the truths of the liturgy, had been a part of Charlemagne's court and had observed the Byzantine liturgy first hand. The principal court of Charlemagne was situated in Aachen, well within the territory of the old Gallican rite at the time it was being supplanted by the Roman rite under Charlemagne's guidance.

Beginning with the *Regularis concordia*, a customary from Winchester (*ca.* 965–975), manuscripts can be found in which the dialogue is in a new location: at the end of matins, after the the third responsory and before the hymn "Te Deum laudamus." The change of location for the drama may have been in order to coincide more correctly with the traditional belief of the time of Christ's resurrection, at dawn. In the tenth century, reforms in the practice of the monastic office and the Easter vigil ceremony, emanating from the abbey of Cluny, changed the time of matins so that it ended at daybreak. Thus, the placement of the Resurrection drama at the end of that office would be appropriate. Although the change to follow matins began in the late tenth century, the vast majority of tenth- and eleventh-century dialogues are before Mass. Beginning in the twelfth century, however, placement at matins was more frequent, and from the thirteenth century on it is found there almost without exception. In its new placement after matins the *Quem quaeritis* dialogue was no longer surrounded by procession antiphons. New lines were added before and after the three core lines, and the simple dialogue was expanded in many of the manuscripts by

the addition of traditional and newly composed materials. In some cases new scenes were added.

It has been the custom, since the extended study by Karl Young in 1933, to discuss the Easter drama in three stages. This is a convenient way of viewing the different forms of the drama as long as it is accepted as an abstract classification and does not imply evolutionary growth or chronological order.

The first-stage plays are those in which the dialogue is entirely between the three Marys and the angel, the earliest known version regardless of the added lines of exhortation, processionals, or other antiphons. They are found both before the Mass and at the end of the matins.

The second-stage plays are found as early as the twelfth century and involve the apostles Peter and John. The scene is described, in the account of John (20:1–10), as happening on Easter Monday: after being told of the Resurrection by Mary Magdalene, the two apostles run to the tomb to see for themselves. There is some variation in the dramas as to the participation of the apostles; in some they merely run to the tomb and inspect the empty burial cloths, and in others they are given lines to sing.

In the most elaborate second-stage dramas all or some of the lines of the sequence "Victimae pascali laudes" are sung—in some cases as a dialogue between one or more of the Marys and the apostles or the chorus. This elaboration is usually confined to manuscripts from the German-speaking countries, but one of the most dramatic is the drama found in two fourteenth-century manuscripts from Dublin, in which the Marys also sing a lament. Many of the German manuscripts add hymns in the vernacular. "Christ ist erstanden" is found in a number of these, either in addition to or in place of the "Te Deum laudamus." Second- and third-stage dramas are found only at the end of matins.

The third-stage plays include a scene with the risen Christ. Manuscripts with this scene date from as early as the mid twelfth century. A meeting between Christ and one or two of the Marys is given in Matthew (28:9,10), Mark (16:9), and John (20:11–18). The accounts provide the actual words that form the basis of those lines in the various dramas. In its simplest form the new scene is added as an extension of the scene involving the Marys and the angel and excluding the apostles. The more frequently found version includes the sequence "Victimae Pascali laudes" and often the apostles as well. These larger dramas also include additional scenes, such as one involving the merchant from whom the Marys buy spices and ointments, or one in which a group of Roman soldiers guards the tomb.

From its earliest appearance the *Quem quaeritis* dialogue was always sung. The music in the earliest sources cannot be transcribed because it is written in unheightened neumes that indicate the number of notes and relative direction of the melodic line (up or down), but not pitch or interval. It is not until the late eleventh century that there are manuscripts in which the pitches are indicated accurately, and the conformity of the earliest sources in number of notes and relative melodic curve with the more accurately notated versions from later centuries gives evidence of a common melody for all versions. Comparative studies of the melodies of the three core lines of all Easter dramas by Sister Marie Dolores Moore and William Smoldon conclude that a single basic me-

lodic structure was used in all sources, though minor variants can be found from location to location. Exact melodic repetition and even modal properties apparently were not considered to be important. A study by Diane Dolan of the dramas from Normandy and England according to melodic variants has further refined the work of de Boor concerning the dissemination of these manuscripts according to political and monastic affiliations.

There is a further division of the *Quem quaeritis* dialogues into what is usually referred to as the type II text. This group of 116 dramas involves core lines that begin with the words of the original, but after the first two words each lines is concluded differently (see example 2).

The manuscripts containing the type II text are mostly from central and eastern Europe, including

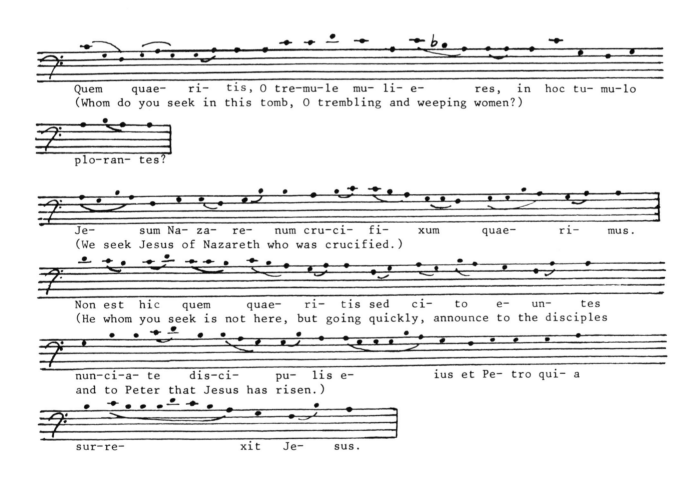

Quem quae- ri- tis, O tre-mu-le mu- li- e- res, in hoc tu- mu-lo
(Whom do you seek in this tomb, O trembling and weeping women?)

plo-ran- tes?

Je- sum Na- za- re- num cru-ci- fi- xum quae- ri- mus.
(We seek Jesus of Nazareth who was crucified.)

Non est hic quem quae- ri- tis sed ci- to e- un- tes
(He whom you seek is not here, but going quickly, announce to the disciples

nun-ci-a-te dis-ci- pu- lis e- ius et Pe- tro qui- a
and to Peter that Jesus has risen.)

sur-re- xit Je- sus.

Example 2. UTRECHT, RIJKSUNIVERSITEIT, MS 406

Germany, Austria, Switzerland, and Czechoslovakia. The core texts have only a small number of added lines; most examples of type II can be classified as stage-two dramas. The lines and music of all type II dramas are quite similar to one another, with very little variation. There has not been much study of this text so far, but it has been suggested that its origin, sometime in the late eleventh century, may have been the result of an incipit copy. Many manuscripts bearing the *Quem quaeritis* drama give only the first two words of each line with the music that accompanies these words. The opening words of each type II line correspond to just the amount given in the incipit manuscripts, and the music for that amount of the first line of the type II text also resembles the type I music. It has therefore been hypothesized that the type II dialogue was developed as the result of an attempt to fill out the lines from an incipit source.

The actual location of the performance of the Easter drama was not the same in all traditions. In its Collecta association it was sometimes performed at an altar in a church separate from that at which the morning Mass would be celebrated, and in other traditions it was performed in the main church either at a side altar or at the main altar. In other churches a separate sepulcher was constructed for the performance.

The lines of the Marys, the angels, and other roles were usually sung by soloists, with varying amounts of participation by the chorus of monks. There is no evidence, however, for the use of musical instruments in any of the liturgical dramas. It is probable that all of the singing was unaccompanied.

No directions for acting out the scene are found in the earliest manuscripts, but ivory plaques from the ninth and tenth centuries show that the monks singing the parts of the Marys wore their cowls on their heads to impersonate women, and the tenth-century *Regularis concordia* states clearly that the Marys carry incense and impersonate women, and that the angel is to be seated at the sepulcher. The implication is that there was probably some degree of acting from the origin of the scene. The existence of the Easter drama in more than 500 manuscripts from the tenth to the sixteenth centuries attests to its popularity throughout the Middle Ages.

In imitation of the Resurrection drama, scenes from other important liturgical feasts were created beginning in the eleventh and twelfth centuries. The earliest and most popular of these imitations was the Christmas play, of which approximately twenty examples survive from the eleventh century alone. The Christmas play was sung before the third Mass on Christmas morning and was closely modeled on the text and the music of the Easter drama (see example 3).

None of the other dramas so closely follow the Easter play. Topics known to be associated with the liturgy include the appearance of Christ to two of the disciples on the road to Emmaus, sung at vespers on Easter Monday; a drama representing the descent of the Holy Ghost, sung after the office of none on

Quem quae- ri- tis in pre- se- pe pas- to- res di-ci-te?
(Whom do you seek in the manger, shepherds, say?)

Sal- va- to- rem Chris-tum do- mi- num in-fan- tem pan- nis
(Our Savior, Christ the Lord, a child wrapped in swaddling clothes, as the angels told.)

in-vo- lu- tum se- cun- dum ser- mo- nem an- ge- li- cum.

Example 3 (pitches are approximate). PARIS, BIBLIOTHÈQUE NATIONALE, FONDS LATIN, MS 1119

Pentecost; and the adoration of the Magi, sung either during the Christmas Mass at the offertory or before the Mass of Epiphany. Other topics from the New and Old Testaments include the slaughter of the innocents, the raising of Lazarus, the procession of the prophets, St. Nicholas, Daniel, and Herod, but their association with any liturgical ceremony is not certain.

The fascination of the liturgical drama for students of liturgics, music, and drama has to do with its position in the history of theater in the Western world. Drama had existed in Europe in early Greek and Roman times, but shortly after the era of Constantine in the fourth century, the newly powerful Christian church forbade drama of all kinds. Although mimes and minstrels flourished throughout the Middle Ages, there is no evidence of drama in Europe from the fifth to the early ninth century, when it is reported once again at the court of Charlemagne. The revival was short-lived, however, and by the late ninth century the church had once again successfully repressed secular drama in the West. All that was left to preserve the dramatic tradition was the three-line Resurrection dialogue that had been made a part of the paraliturgical Collecta ceremony. It was the *Quem quaeritis* dialogue and the other liturgical dramas that carried on the tradition of drama in the West until the advent of extended mystery plays and secular drama in the late thirteenth century.

It is not known when the drama was detached from matins to stand totally independent of a liturgical ceremony. A number of lengthy dramas for Easter and other feasts date from the thirteenth, fourteenth, and fifteenth centuries, involving large casts and many scenes. Some of these were clearly attached to matins, such as the Easter play from the *Carmina burana,* which is explicitly labeled *cantatis matutinis in die Pasche* (sung at matins on the day of Easter). Other plays, such as the ten in the Fleury Play Book (Orleans, Bibliothèque de la Ville, MS 201), end with the hymn "Te Deum laudamus" but were not necessarily performed at the end of matins.

Although at this time a clear separation cannot be made between dramas performed with and without liturgical association, it is clear that by the late thirteenth century dramatic presentations had gained a position of strength apart from those intimately connected with the liturgy. From that point on, until the demise of the liturgical drama as one of the reforms of the Council of Trent, dramatic productions were

a part of both the sacred and the secular lives of the people of Europe.

BIBLIOGRAPHY

Theodore Bogdanos, "Liturgical Drama in Byzantine Literature," in *Comparative Drama,* 10 (1976); Helmut A. W. de Boor, *Die Textgeschichte der lateinischen Osterfeiern* (1967); Diane Dolan, *Le drame liturgique de Pâques en Normandie et en Angleterre au moyen âge* (1975); C. Clifford Flanigan, "The Liturgical Context of the *Quem Quaeritis* Trope," in *Comparative Drama,* 9 (1974), and "The Roman Rite and the Origins of the Liturgical Drama," in *University of Toronto Quarterly,* 43 (1974); O. B. Hardison, Jr., *Christian Rite and Christian Drama in the Middle Ages* (1965), and "Gregorian Easter Vespers and Early Liturgical Drama," in E. Catherine Dunn *et al.,* eds., *The Medieval Drama and Its Claudelian Revival* (1970), 27–40; Carol Heitz, *Recherches sur les rapports entre architecture et liturgie à l'époque carolingienne* (1963); Timothy J. McGee, "The Liturgical Placements of the *Quem quaeritis* Dialogue," in *Journal of the American Musicological Society,* 29 (1976), and "The Role of the *Quem quaeritis* Dialogue in the History of Western Drama," in *Renaissance Drama,* n.s. 7 (1976); Sr. Marie Dolores Moore, R.S.M., *The 'Visitatio sepulchri' of the Medieval Church* (Ph.D. diss., Univ. of Rochester, 1971); J. D. A. Ogilvy, "*Mimi, Scurrae, Histriones:* Entertainers of the Early Middle Ages," in *Speculum,* 38 (1963); William L. Smoldon, "Liturgical Drama," in *New Oxford History of Music,* II (1954), 175–219, and *The Music of the Medieval Church Drama* (1981); Karl Young, *The Drama of the Medieval Church,* 2 vols. (1933, repr. 1967).

TIMOTHY J. MCGEE

[See also **Drama, French; Drama, German; Drama, Western European.**]

DRAMA, WESTERN EUROPEAN

TERMINOLOGY

Medieval writers were conscious of a tradition of dramatic entertainment extending back to classical Latin drama. They knew, and at times imitated, plays by Plautus, Terence, and Menander. They also knew of Christian attacks on the Roman stage, such as Tertullian's *De spectaculis.* They had descriptions of the classical stage, including that in Isidore of Seville's *Etymologiae* (*Patrologia Latina,* LXXXII, 657–658), widely retailed in Vincent of Beauvais's *Speculum maius.* On occasion individuals recognized theater sites, as did Gerald of Wales at Caerleon in 1188 *(loca theatralia)* and Alexander Neckham in his elegy on the ruined amphitheater at Paris in 1211. It has been held that medieval entertainers were the inheritors of traditions of performance disseminated with the closure of the theaters of the Roman Empire, including traditions of impersonation and caricature. The Middle Ages also inherited a terminology for the discussion of dramatic performances and performers that was used by writers, particularly from the twelfth century on.

The extent to which medieval people understood the classical tradition and were accustomed to seeing classical plays performed remains debatable, as does the extent to which they were conscious of drama as a distinct art form in their own society. A ninth- or tenth-century dialogue between Terence and a *delusor* (mocker) seems to be a prelude to a performance of a Terence play; but it also seems that Terence was to read his own work, presumably while the action was mimed. Such separation of text from action is certainly envisaged in the earliest of the medieval lives of Terence and is illustrated in the fifteenth-century *Térence des ducs.* It accords with the description of the *theatrum* and *scena* in Hugo (or Hugutio) of Pisa's *Magnae derivationes,* which suggests that the *scena* is an enclosed place in the *theatrum* in which masked actors wait to mime the substance of the poet's words. Lydgate's *Troy Book* (862ff.) describes such a performance, apparently envisaging drama as an extension of oral narrative and sermon, though critics differ as to whether such performances ever occurred.

Further problems arise in the semantics of the terms employed. *Theatrum* could be applied to any place of entertainment, indoors or outdoors, and even to brothels and crossroads. Yet a ninth-century glossary from Werden, Germany refers to "theatrum de lignis sit ubi ludunt homines et spectacula faciunt" (a theater may be of wooden boards where men play and create spectacular occasions); Caesarius of Heisterbach (1220) says, "in terra nostra in quodam theatro fuminati sunt viginti homines" (in our land in a certain theater twenty men were struck by lightning); and Richard of Devizes' *Chronicon* (*ca.* 1193), purporting to be written by a Jew to a Christian boy about to visit London, begins "Vita talum et tesseram, theatrum et tabernam" (a life of dies and dice, theater and tavern). The early-thirteenth-century *Vision of Thurkill* describes a visit to hell, where sinners enact their earthly sins in a circular theater for an audience of devils and damned, perhaps indicative of a contemporary theater structure.

The performers of the Middle Ages are referred to by a number of Latin terms: *histriones* (actors), *joculatores* (jesters; rare in Latin, but giving the common vernacular *jongleur, jogelour*), *lusores* (players in games or amusements), *mimi* (mime actors or burlesque players), and *scurrae* (buffoons, jesters). The words frequently seem to have little precise meaning, being equivalent designations of versatile entertainers capable of singing, dancing, acrobatics, and juggling. But although such terms convey no sense of a professional actor, they may indicate skilled mimers. Ethelred of Rievaulx in 1141 condemned the delivery of sermons by some priests in terms suggesting dramatic gesture as an accompaniment to oral delivery and indicating the dangerous distractions of its inappropriate use:

Meanwhile the whole body is vibrating with such histrionic movements, the lips twist, they turn, they flex their shoulders, and the movement of their fingers responds to certain individual notes.... Meantime the people standing look on ... not without laughter and derision so that you might think they had attended not at an oratory but at a theater, not for prayer but for spectating.

In the Middle Ages several Latin words were used to refer to dramatic compositions and performances. These included *comedia,* used of the Latin comedies but also more loosely of works with a happy ending, and *repraesentatio* (a showing or exhibiting). More frequent was *miraculum* (wonder, marvel), as in the Fleury play, *The Image of St. Nicholas,* which is described as *aliud miraculum* (another miracle) and concludes *finitur miraculum* (the miracle is ended); from general reference to "illusion," it seems to have been applied to plays on religious subjects, including saints' plays. As such it occurs in the vernacular, as when the Wife of Bath says: "Therefore I made my visitaciouns ... To pleyes of myracles, and to mariages" (Wife of Bath's prologue, in F. N. Robinson, ed., *The Works of Geoffrey Chaucer* (1957), lines 555–558).

But potentially most significant, for a number of reasons, is the extension of *ludus* (public games, plays, spectacles, shows, exhibitions) to lengthy Latin plays such as the Benediktbeuern Passion and Resurrection plays, and hence to religious plays in general. First, liturgical plays had hitherto been alluded to under the nondramatic terms *officium, ordo,* and *processus,* so that *ludus* marks a consciousness of dramatic action as an independent entity. Second, it was a term of activity, not relating to dramatic impersonation solely, suggesting a concept of dramatic action. Third, it carried with it the related idea of jest or joke, of something not serious, hardly appropriate to religious drama unless it carried the idea of the mimetic action against the reality of the historical events portrayed.

It may be significant that vernacular languages similarly employed words signifying "playing" or "jest" to refer to drama: the French *jeu* (Latin: *jocus*, joke), the German *Spiel*, the English "play." V. A. Kolve has assembled usages of "play" and related words such as "game" for the English Corpus Christi plays and, pointing also to the use of game structures within the plays, has advanced a thesis of those dramas as play and game. That writers were aware of the semantic complexities of such words may be inferred from the use of game paradigms in the fourteenth-century Middle English poem *Sir Gawain and the Green Knight*. *Ludus* thus may suggest both the medieval awareness of drama as an art form and the basis of a medieval aesthetic of drama.

Various vernacular terms emerged in the Middle Ages, and critics have attempted to discern finer generic distinctions in their application. Among these may be noted the Old French *mistere*, which first appeared in a Rouen record of 1374—*aucun vrai mistere ou miracle* (a certain true mystery or miracle)—and apparently represents an application to drama of the sense "religious mystery." The term seems to have been unspecific, designating a variety of drama. The *Oxford English Dictionary* notes the dramatic application of "mystery" in English from 1744, arguing that the word has erroneously been associated with a word of different etymology ("mystery" from the Old French *mistere* and Latin *ministerium*, trade guild or company, influenced by the participation of craft guilds in dramatic productions).

The Old French *moralité*, a word of dramatic application, is used beside *farce* and *sottie*, and the boundaries between their meanings are difficult to determine. Technically the *sottie* was performed by the *sot*, the professional fool in motley; being a comic lampoon, it often used allegorical figures. *Farce*, first recorded in dramatic application in 1398, seems to allude to a comic story, often of the *fabliau* type. *Moralité* fits into this spectrum, often containing allegorical figures and comic action, but is essentially didactic in purpose. Other languages did not adopt this range of distinction. Robert Potter has found the first dramatic application of "morality" in English only in a 1741 translation, and then not applied to English drama. The morality form seems to

be comprehended in England under "moral play" or "interlude."

The Latin *interludum* forms part of the title of a fragmentary play, *Interludium de clerico et puella*, a dramatization of *Dame Siriz* from early-fourteenth-century England, and the reference to *laykyng of enterludeȝ* as an accepted courtly activity in the late-fourteenth-century English poem *Sir Gawain and the Green Knight* represents evidence both of the English word and of the currency of courtly dramatic performance. Robert Mannyng of Brunne (*fl.* 1283–1338) classes *entyrludeȝ* with folk games. The use of the term is often compared with the Old French *entre-mets* and with the Spanish *entremés*, a dish served between the main courses of a banquet or an entertainment then performed. In Spanish it was also applied to a platform on which allegorical figures were carried through the streets, and in the sixteenth century *entremés* and *paso* were terms applied to comic subplots within a main action. Although by the sixteenth century it is increasingly possible to apply "interlude" to short dramatic entertainments, it is difficult to limit its reference usefully at any time.

The Middle English *mommynge* corresponds to the Old French *mommerie*. A courtly extension of a folk practice in which people in disguise used a mimed game as a device for presenting gifts, it seems first to have acquired a test spoken by a presenter, and later a set of speeches, leading finally to dramatic action without the giving of presents. Seven texts by John Lydgate, written in 1424–1430 for royal entertainments in England, survive; they are variously titled *mommynge* and "disguising," the latter perhaps further removed from folk practices. Some critics have seen within this development the seeds of the Tudor masque. So far from identifying distinct forms of drama, this plethora of terminology merely serves to indicate the overlapping diversity of medieval dramatic forms and their origins.

Many celebratory occasions have affinities with drama, and much modern criticism of medieval drama has involved the application of an individual definition of "drama" to such activities. An evolutionary thesis, in which medieval drama was a stage in the development toward Renaissance drama, evolving "complex" dramatic forms from "simple" ones, held sway for longer in this branch of literature than in most others and is still influential. Such a view carries with it a number of assumptions, including the "internationalism" of the drama, according to which plays from widely separated regions can be considered together in order to establish a linear development. Since the early 1950's, an alternative approach has been suggested by critics, particularly those with practical theatrical experience, emphasizing the legacy of visual display from nondramatic celebrations in medieval drama and also stressing aspects of production. The most recent products of this concern have been debates on the staging of plays—particularly the processional staging of English cycles and the design of pageant wagons—and concentrated study of the records of drama in limited areas. Both critical viewpoints in effect agree that there is a "medieval" form of theater and drama, and they both direct attention away from the individual text in a quest for general theses.

"Medieval drama" is thus a widely used phrase that has the advantage of inclusiveness but the disadvantage of imprecision. Though ostensibly comprehending all forms of dramatic activity in all countries of medieval Europe, it may be employed within strict chronological limits, or to the exclusion of drama based on classical models, or to exclude or include tableaux and other "nontextual" dramatic forms, or with reference to particular production and casting methods. It is a phrase to be used with caution and with an awareness of underlying assumptions. Yet many modern critics might agree that some features were frequently characteristic of medieval drama.

First, medieval drama was occasional. It marked a seasonal folk rite, a religious feast day, the visit of an important personage.

Second, it was sponsored drama, not dependent on a fee-paying audience. The church, through its local representatives, or the civic authorities and the craft guilds of a town, or wealthy individuals might undertake to provide or raise the money for productions.

Third, it was functional or multifunctional, being an adjunct to worship, to civic order and government, to the religious instruction of the laity, to the education of children, scholars, or noblemen, or to the honor and profit of the sponsoring individual or community.

Fourth, it was performed on temporary staging, if any, in a familiar physical context—a church or its environs, a street or square, a hall owned by an official organization or an individual—and it was presented in conjunction with other celebratory activities: the liturgy, procession, dance, tableau, feast.

Fifth, it was participatory, both in making no sharp physical distinction between acting area and audience area; and in blurring distinctions between the "fictive" world of dramatic illusion and the "real" world of contemporary allusion by a relative lack of disguise, by a direct acknowledgment of the audience's presence, and by "anachronistic" references to contemporary mores and fashions.

Not all of these features may be present in a particular instance, and exceptions may readily be found. Others may wish to include different features, such as the religious nature of the subject matter. But the picture emerging is of a communal drama arising from and answering the needs of a community or class.

RELIGIOUS DRAMA IN LATIN

Recent claims for the harrowing of hell in the early-ninth-century *Book of Cerne* as perhaps the earliest extant liturgical play seem unlikely to disturb the long-held view that, among potentially dramatic ceremonies in the medieval church liturgy, the nexus of the first liturgical play was the troped introit to the Mass of Easter Day: "Quem quaeritis in sepulchro, Christicole? / Jesum Nazarenum crucifixum, o coelicolae. / Non est hic, surrexit. / Alleluia." Moved to the end of matins, before the "Te Deum," it developed as a mimetic action in the form of a dialogue between three priests representing the Marys who proceed toward a fourth cleric, near the altar or Easter sepulcher, representing the angel at the tomb on Easter day. The earliest text of the play (slightly extended from the above trope) with rubrics is found in the tenth-century *Regularis concordia*, where it provides the dramatic conclusion to the mimetic ceremonies of *adoratio*, *depositio*, and *elevatio*. More than 400 texts of the *visitatio sepulchri* are extant.

The play is important for several reasons. First, it provides a catalyst for added episodes of the Resurrection and post-Resurrection period. The sorrowing Marys approaching the tomb may express their grief in extended *planctus* (lamentation). The angel's injunction to announce the Resurrection suggests the additions of the announcement to the disciples and the race to the tomb by Peter and John. The presence of Mary Magdalene suggests the addition of the *hortulanus* (gardener), Christ's appearance to her. Christ's appearance to two disciples on the road to Emmaus forms a related but distinct episode, the *peregrini* (wanderers, travelers). Such developments do not seem to have begun before the eleventh century, and extended texts are comparatively few.

Second, the play provided a model to be imitated

at another focal point of liturgical celebration, Christmas. *Pastores,* a play of the shepherds from the eleventh century, looks directly to the procession-and-dialogue form of the *Quem quaeritis,* with the shepherds being asked by interlocutors—later identified as the apocryphal midwives—"Quem quaeritis in presepe, pastores, dicite?" (What do you seek in the manger, shepherds, say?). The shepherds' trope seems to have arisen in the Mass of Christmas Day and to have been transferred to matins. The play might also include the angel's message. But, perhaps because of considerations of time, the play does not seem to have developed or to have been widely used.

The seminal Christmas episode is a procession and presentation of gifts at the stable by the Magi, the *Stella* (star), which appropriately first appears in connection with the offertory at Mass on Epiphany in the late eleventh century. This play, with its effect of the star, was capable of expansion to include the visit to Herod's court, the angel's warning, the flight of the Holy Family into Egypt, and the massacre of the innocents, concluding with the laments of the representative mother, Rachel *(ordo Rachelis).* On occasion the episode of the shepherds could be included in this action by an unbiblical encounter of Magi and shepherds.

Third, the play suggests the essential features of liturgical drama. It occurs within a liturgy, arising from the service and leading back to it. It is not identified as separate, being termed *ordo* or *officium.* The action is imitative, but there is no question of impersonation or verisimilitude—the Marys and angel are men in clerical vestments, and the Marys carry thuribles of incense, not spices. The "dialogue" is in Latin and is sung. At the conclusion of the action the Marys acknowledge their fellow clerics by spreading the "grave cloth" before them and singing of Christ's resurrection, actions that prompt the prior to begin a hymn of praise, the "Te Deum." The play speaks to and for a congregation of worshiping clerics and takes its significance from the day, the church setting, and the liturgical context. There is a suppression of verisimilitude, of inner life and response by the figures, in order to concentrate on a commemorative event in the manner of other parts of the liturgy.

Liturgical drama is one particular kind of drama. It survived unsuperseded in the form here outlined, but it also developed further forms and influenced and was influenced by other kinds of drama. A new development of drama within the church services is the late and comparatively infrequent prophet play.

Processus prophetarum derives not from tropes but from a *lectio,* a Pseudo-Augustinian sermon *(Sermo contra Judeos, paganos et Arianos de symbolo),* in which the preacher calls a series of Old Testament prophets, New Testament witnesses, and the pagans Vergil, Nebuchadnezzar, and the Erythraean Sybil to attest Christ's messianic mission. When dramatized, clerics represent the witnesses, with identifying properties as appropriate, and deliver the testimonies. The "play" is a series of monologues, thematically directed and ultimately chronologically ordered, without plot, dialogue, or action. The number of prophets could be increased, and individual prophets might be presented in playlets—at Rouen, for instance, of Shadrach, Meshach, and Abednego in the furnace and of Balaam and his ass. This formative and influential play, based on structural and dramatic principles different from those of the other dramas discussed, moves in the direction of demonstration and instruction and away from worship.

A different sort of Latin drama, the extended Latin play, is extant from the twelfth century, evidently independent of the liturgical context, though still performed on an appropriate feast day, using the appointed *lectiones,* and probably acted within a church. Its subjects are outside the scope of normal liturgy and are treated at a length incompatible with normal services. Outstanding among these plays are those of the Passion, a subject not represented in liturgical drama, perhaps because the Mass afforded a sufficient reenactment. The earliest are the incomplete twelfth-century Monte Cassino Passion and long and short plays in the thirteenth-century *Carmina burana* manuscript from Benediktbeuern. Some idea of scope may be gained from the Benediktbeuern longer play, which covers events from the calling of Peter and Andrew and the ministry of Christ to the crucifixion and burial, with an extended section on the sinful life and repentance of Mary Magdalene and the raising of Lazarus.

The thematic and chronological organization of such plays and their concern with motivation are paralleled in other extended plays, such as the Beauvais *Daniel* and the plays of Hilarius. Hilarius, perhaps an Englishman who had studied under Abelard before 1125, was responsible, solely or jointly, for plays on Lazarus, Daniel, and St. Nicholas. He may therefore typify the kind of author and training responsible for these extended dramas.

A unique Latin play seems to have originated at the German imperial court as political propaganda. The *Ludus de adventu et interitu Antichristi* from

Tegernsee, Bavaria, is the forerunner of the Antichrist plays of the fourteenth and fifteenth centuries. It seems to have been written about 1160 in support of Emperor Frederick Barbarossa and to contain a number of allusions to political enmities and ambitions. The play is far removed from normal Latin drama, with a cast of sixty, eight *sedes* (location, stage), and a *platea* (playing area). Some critics have detected a critical reference to it by Gerhoh of Reichersberg, *De investigatione Antichristi* (1161–1162), who objects to drama in general because of the disguises and alludes to a production of a play of Antichrist.

Gerhoh's comments confirm the verisimilitude of such plays, which tend to be termed *ludus* or *miraculum* rather than *ordo, officium,* or *processus.* Yet some interaction between this kind of drama and the liturgical forms may be seen in plays such as the Fleury *Ordo ad repraesentandum Herodem,* in which use of antiphon, Vulgate narrative, and liturgical forms combines with a concern for structural balance and the use of nonliturgical material: the mimic rage of Herod and his son provides an early example of the traditional irate Herod.

Ludi authors already preferred vernacular at certain moments, notably for laments—in German at Benediktbeuern, in Italian at Monte Cassino, in French at Origny and in the plays of Hilarius. A more extensive and deliberately structural preference for vernacular appears in the mid-twelfth-century *Ordo representacionis Adae,* in which the bulk of the text is in Anglo-Norman. But the liturgical element in the play is more prominent in production because the text contains only the incipits for the sung pieces; and the tripartite structure of man's fall, Abel's murder, and the prophets has a liturgical base: the Advent liturgy and the eight responsories in the text provide the basis for the combination of the first two episodes, whereas the third is in basis a *processus prophetarum.*

The liturgical element in the play has therefore been revalued in recent studies, some of which advance a thesis of indoor church performance, though majority critical opinion favors production outside a church. The text also contains extensive directions for staging, costuming, and action, which suggest concern with a degree of verisimilitude, offset and heightened by the choir singing liturgical pieces and by the demons, who do not speak but do react. The structure, though liturgical in basis, has been devised to unite diverse liturgical elements into a literary whole that is chronologically sequential and, more important, thematically and typologically informed.

The *Adam* is closer to the liturgy than other contemporary vernacular plays, such as the Anglo-Normal *La seinte resureccion* or the Spanish *Auto do los Reyes Magos.* But it is not liturgical drama, and, like "Prophets," *ludi,* and *miracula,* it may be considered an adjunct as much to religious education as to worship. The audience, also, may have been secular for at least *ludi* and vernacular drama, and it cannot always be established that performance was within a church. Despite the later date, these plays are not necessarily offshoots of liturgical drama but alternative dramatic forms, looking at times toward the liturgical drama just as liturgical drama might on occasion look toward them. The scale and competence of these texts seem to attest a well-established tradition of extended verisimilar drama in Latin and in the vernacular by the twelfth century. Later vernacular plays show features present in the earlier Latin drama, such as the Passion play, the laments, the *Quem quaeritis* style of dialogue, and the irate Herod.

DRAMA AS AN ADJUNCT OF SCHOLARSHIP

Since a knowledge of Latin was fostered by the study of Latin authors, medieval scholars would usually have studied the plays of Terence as stylistic models, and possibly also those of Plautus. Imitations of these models are found, but it is not clear whether they are merely literary exercises or texts for mime or performance. In the tenth century, roughly contemporary with the *Concordia regularis,* a Benedictine nun named Hrotsvitha (*ca.* 935–*ca.* 1000), from Gandersheim in Lower Saxony, wrote six Latin *comedia* in avowed imitation of Terence, arguing that she wished to extol the life of virginity in a literary form traditionally employed to display female license. Her plays—*Gallicanus, Dulcitius, Calimachus, Abraham, Pafnutius, Sapientia*—were once held to be "the merest literary exercise" (according to Chambers), but emphasis has recently been placed on her use of scene change, dress, facial expression, gestures, and oral misunderstandings to support the plays as acting texts, and her sensitive adaptation of classical comedy has been revalued. Hrotsvitha was a well-educated and possibly well-connected lady, perhaps typical of canonesses in her interests. Her lightly comic, verisimilar actions are very different from the style of liturgical drama.

About the time of the extended Latin *ludi*, other imitations of classical plays began to appear in the Loire valley. The earliest, Vitalis of Blois's *Geta* (ca. 1150), is a reworking of Plautus' *Amphitruo*, but its non-Plautine features—a preliminary dumb show, Birria's walk, a love scene, and Mercury's description of himself as Geta—have been claimed as evidence of the influence of mime actions from a tradition of classical mimic performance. Vitalis also wrote a version of Plautus' *Aulularia;* William of Blois reworked Menander's *Androgynos* as *Alda* (1167–1169); and from the same region and period come the *Lidia* (assigned to Arnulf of Orléans), Matthew of Vendôme's *Milo*, and the anonymous *Panphilus,* a dramatized realization of the teachings of Ovid's *Ara amatoria.*

The authors were scholars capable of original invention, and their influence extended beyond the Loire. *Geta* and *Panphilus* entered the schools, possibly even outside France; the former was later translated into French and Italian, and the latter into Spanish. The influence of such plays on international drama may be gauged from the comedy *Babio,* written in England during the reign of Henry II. The play, despite its reliance on the model of *Geta,* is without direct classical counterpart, being a wholly medieval invention partially suggested by the career of Peter Abelard.

Since no further extensive evidence of classical influence can be found before the Renaissance, such plays are easily dismissed as literary exercises and critics have been reluctant to admit that they may have been acted or may have influenced European dramatic traditions. Certainly their verbal wit, extravagantly verisimilar actions, and explicit bawdiness are far removed from the stylized forms of liturgical drama. But it seems significant that educated men could envisage such drama from a literary text, and it is possibly misleading to regard their authors as having an experience radically different from that of the authors of other Latin plays. The Latin comedies arose at the same time as the *ludi* discussed above, and it is tempting to postulate some connection between the two. Certainly a scholar such as Hilarius, who had studied under Abelard, could well have known classical comedy and perhaps its medieval imitations as well.

DRAMA AS AN ADJUNCT OF CIVIC CELEBRATION

In a village dominated by an agricultural economy, where most people did the same kind of work, the pattern of life was regulated by the seasons. Before Christianity, ancient pagan observances had marked the major points in the year, the equinoxes and the solstices. By the Middle Ages these practices had lost their significance and had changed their character, being transformed into dances and mimetic actions. It is from these and similar observances that the folk play arose. As folk play it is rarely recorded before the eighteenth century and its elements are therefore difficult to discuss, but in the Middle Ages it evidently gave rise to a number of literary and aristocratic variations. The folk play itself is often a play of conflict. A presenter clears space and calls for a champion who fights an enemy, the enemy is killed but is raised by a doctor, and the play ends with a collection and a dance. Some such play may underlie the beheading game of *Sir Gawain and the Green Knight* and suggests the death and revival of the sun at midwinter, though the late texts name the challenger as St. George and the foe as the Turkish Champion or Captain Slasher.

Another formative village custom was maying, with the election of a king and queen of May, a well-attested survival of an ancient fertility rite seen, for example, in Bishop Chanteloup of Worcester's instructions to his clergy in 1240 to stop *ludos . . . de rege et regina.* Rationalizations of such activities in dramatic form seem to include plays of Robin Hood in England, where Robin and Marion derive from the May king and queen (of which the earliest of three surviving English texts is a fragment dating from about 1475), and in France *Jeu de Robin et de Marion* by Adam de la Halle (1282–1288), though the latter was written under strong courtly influence.

Despite the few survivals, it seems very probable that there was a distinctive dramatic form of folk play that contributed to the pattern of European drama. These dramatic activities survived within a village community and might continue if that community grew in independence and importance to become a town. York, for example, which had its riding of St. George on St. George's day, found it necessary to prohibit the riding of Yule and Yule's Wife, "twoo disguysed persons," on St. Thomas' Day in 1572 in order to preserve public order. Evidently the folk celebration of St. George, which took the form of a play in country areas near the city, had in York been acceptably assimilated into the pattern of civic processional, whereas that of Yule, being less institutionalized, had become an occasion of dangerous riot in the large city.

The growth of towns throughout Europe in the later Middle Ages changed the focus of dramatic activity from the monastery and church to the town, and gave it added functions and new forms. Civic ceremonial was a sign of corporate existence, and a model of the hierarchy and order to which a town aspired. The civic year had its own occasions of ceremony, such as the installation of officials, but it also used the opportunities provided by church feasts throughout the liturgical year and by the visits of important people. The guilds would often parade in their appointed order, and there is evidence that on occasion they might adopt disguises and carry appropriate objects, such as the fish images and the image of St. Magnus carried by the London fishmongers in 1298 to mark the triumphal return of Edward I.

Frequently the procession might include tableaux or dumb shows, carried on carts drawn by men or horses, as at Paris in 1313 and Gerona in 1360. Or, instead of the emblems and shows being transported in the procession, the procession might encounter them along its route, mounted on elevated points such as water conduits, market crosses, or town gates, as at London in 1392. Such shows could include religious scenes and characters, and often folk or mythological subjects as well; later, a brief explanatory text or address might be added.

This pattern of civic ceremonial describes much vernacular religious drama in the later Middle Ages. Such drama may be regarded variously as an extension of civic ceremonial with its communal functions, as an act of worship by a civic community on an appropriate day, or as a form of instruction, communicating central tenets of faith to the onlookers. It seems clear, however, that these plays represent an act of cooperation between church and civic authorities, requiring the decorous enactment by the community of a religious subject expressed in a decorous text. The community generally provided the financial support for the venture, determined the venue (usually in major public places within the town), and undertook arrangements for production and casting through its religious or craft guilds. The text, appropriate to the occasion, seems to have been commissioned and approved by the authorities.

Such communal drama took many forms, but most characteristic are extended, multi-episode dramas, involving large casts and often played over a period of days or even years. At Bourges in 1536, it is said to have taken forty days to perform the *Actes des apôtres,* a play of 61,908 lines; more manageably,

it took three days to perform the Chester Whitsun plays, four for the Frankfurt Passion play of 1498, two for the Cornish miracle of St. Meriasek. The English *N*-town envisages a two-part Passion performed in successive years, and French texts such as *Miracles de Nostre Dame* and *Mystère du Vieil Testament* were evidently performed as individual plays or sections, not as complete texts.

Production methods varied, but the use of fixed stages (scaffolds) about an open acting area (*platea,* place) in public places in the town is attested by plans for Alsfeld, Frankfurt, Villingen, Lucerne, Mons, and the much debated Valenciennes. Staging on wagons that stopped for performances at appointed sites on the route (processional production) was a uniquely English method, employed at Chester and Coventry. Arena staging, locating scaffolds in and around a constructed circular playing area, was the method for the Cornish *Ordinalia.* The texts might be by a gifted writer, such as the Greban brothers in France or the anonymous Wakefield Master in England. In France groups known as *confréries* or *puys,* consisting of clergy and laity, might commission and perform plays, and a high degree of professionalism seems to have obtained.

Civic drama might be performed at any time, though great feasts such as Christmas, Easter, and the Assumption often provided the occasion for performance. But the major feast for dramatic production was Corpus Christi, finally instituted in 1311 in honor of the Blessed Sacrament, which was regularly celebrated with civic processions. In England a unique dramatic genre, the Corpus Christi play, seems to have crystallized around the occasion. Some critics have seen the play as the outcome of processional; others have suggested that it was a doctrinally appropriate celebration of the sacrament and have stressed figural interpretations underlying the text.

The play presents the significant interventions by God in human history from the Creation to Doomsday, divided into a series of playlets; one craft guild, or a group of guilds, was responsible for each episode. Such play cycles seem to have been regular—though not annual—events in English towns, particularly in the north, though only a few texts survive: complete cycles from Chester, Wakefield (Towneley), and York; the unlocated cycle variously termed *N*-town, Hegge, or (misleadingly) *Ludus Coventriae;* and individual plays from Coventry, Newcastle, and Norwich. The earliest reference may be from York in 1376, and the genre continued into the second half of the sixteenth century and beyond, falling victim to Protestant Tudor censorship. The performance of such plays was not limited to Corpus Christi Day (the Thursday after Trinity Sunday), but the title tended to be applied regardless of occasion.

Staging of such plays has been much debated, discussion centering on the term "pageant," which was applied to any sort of show (including tableau), to a play episode, or to a movable stage. Whereas some cities (such as Chester and Coventry) used processional production, others (perhaps Lincoln) combined procession with a single-site performance, and others (for instance, London, where a similar play seems to have been performed at Skinners Well by clerks) used fixed-set staging. The function and design of the pageant wagons have been much debated, particularly in the most extensive description of them, in the seventeenth-century *Brevary or Some Fewe Collectiones of the Cittie of Chester,* compiled from the notes of Archdeacon Robert Rogers (*d.* 1595). Probably no single theory will embrace all towns at all periods for all plays.

It also seems that the form of the play was subject to modification. Evidence from city records, lists of plays, and descriptions in the text of the banns (the preliminary announcements of performance) reflects changing content and distribution of material. Some of these alterations resulted from the uncertain economic circumstances of companies, which affected their ability to undertake their allotted dramatic responsibilities, whereas others were textual or theological improvements. Nevertheless, certain episodes of the cycles—such as Cain and Abel, the Flood, Abraham and Isaac—seem to have been recurring features of the form. There is also evidence to suggest that on occasion towns borrowed texts from each other. This uniquely English play form, with its vast chronological sweep, offers a paradigm of order, in which a play on the order of God's creation in honor of a church feast was presented by the hierarchy of craft guilds in a manner befitting the honor of the town.

Although civic drama is immediately associated with extended plays on biblical history, plays on other religious matters, not dependent on the biblical texts, could serve the same purpose. Lucerne had plays of the Last Judgment, the saints, and carnival that might be performed in its wine market square instead of its Easter play. York, in addition to its Corpus Christi play and folk festivals, had a Creed play, associated with a procession and performed once in the middle years of each decade (the earliest reference is 1446); it also had a Paternoster play, first

mentioned about 1378 in Wyclif's *De officio pastorali:* "Herefore freris han tauȝht in englond the paternoster in engliȝsh tunge, as men seyen in the pley of ȝork, and in many othere cuntreys." The former play was the responsibility of the Corpus Christi guild, the latter of the Paternoster guild, but the productions were clearly civic occasions.

Wyclif's reference suggests that other regions may have had plays similar to the Paternoster, but the only other evidence in England is from Beverley in 1441 and 1467, and from Lincoln between 1397 and 1521; both cities supported Corpus Christi plays. The Beverley play was performed by the craftsmen, and since pageants are assigned to each of the Seven Deadly Sins and to Vicious, it has been postulated that such plays were early examples of allegorical drama on a civic scale.

But civic celebration represents either the model for or the extension of drama on a more limited scale. The parishes, in town or village, might also present plays. E. K. Chambers comments: "At London, Kingston, Oxford, Reading, Salisbury, Bath, Tewkesbury, Leicester, Bungay, and Yarmouth, such parochial plays can be traced, sometimes side by side with those provided by craft or other guilds" (II, p. 121). Such plays may well have been on the same subjects, and even the same occasions, as the drama of civic celebration. Possibly the Northampton *Abraham* and the Brome *Abraham and Isaac,* both recorded from places without known Corpus Christi plays, are parish plays, although Chester's cycle episode of the *Sacrifice of Isaac* is related textually to the Brome play. Others were saints' plays—for instance, the play of St. Thomas Becket presented at King's Lynn in 1385. The London clerks, responsible for a Corpus Christi type of play, presented a "pley of seynt Katerine" in 1393.

In a town such plays might be considered distinct from wider civic productions, but there is little to suggest that they were a distinct kind of drama. Yet as the scale of involvement declined, the sense of a drama performed by a few for the edification of an audience may have grown, touching commercialism in the production of a play of St. Olave in 1557 by the London parish of St. Olave to raise money.

DRAMA AS AN ADJUNCT OF RELIGIOUS INSTRUCTION

Worship and instruction were interrelated concerns of the church, and as liturgy provided the basis for the former, so sermon provided the main medium for the latter. The shift in emphasis from a liturgically focused, monastic church to a sermon-focused, evangelizing church is usually marked conveniently by the Fourth Lateran Council of 1215, with its emphasis on penance and on the education of priesthood and laity in the fundamentals of the faith. From such concerns there developed a range of instructional manuals, an emphasis on the *ars praedicandi,* and a new importance for the friars, who fulfilled the church's need for an international organization of instructors. The connection between these movements within the church and the rise of vernacular religious drama has been much debated, as has the possible connection between the friars and the rise of vernacular drama.

Wyclif's reference to the York Paternoster play not only stresses a didactic intent but also links it with the teaching activities of the friars. In 1426 a friar, William Melton, though he was concerned with the difficult timetable of Corpus Christi Day, when York's cycle and procession took place on the same day, nevertheless "in suis sermonibus diversis ludum predictum populo commendavit affirmando quod bonus erat in se et laudabilis valde" (in his various sermons he commended the aforesaid play to the populace by asserting that it was itself good and highly praiseworthy; Reed, *York,* I, p. 43).

Whatever the connection, it seems clear that some plays were performed for audiences—perhaps paying audiences—by acting troupes, probably sponsored by religious houses. The *N*-town cycle, in its final stages, was apparently intended for such performance. The kind of drama presented seems to have been not only didactic and explanatory in intention, but also on occasion defensive. An example is the *Croxton Play of the Sacrament,* which, it has been suggested, was composed about 1461 in the Thetford region of Norfolk and evidently toured the local villages. The play, on the conversion of a Jew through the demonstration of the truth of transubstantiation, seems to require performance both outside and inside a church. But its theme appears to address a latent skepticism among the audience, and it has been suggested that the play may have been a response to Wycliffite questionings of transubstantiation. The legend was dramatized in Italy (1473), the Netherlands (1500), and France (sixteenth century), though no version closely matches the English play, which encompasses liturgical and comic folk elements, culminating in a procession into the church that apparently involved the audience.

In its defensive stance, the play contrasts with the early-fifteenth-century allegorical English play, *The*

Castle of Perseverance, another "toured" play, which required an ambitious arena with scaffolds and a central castle (for which the earliest staging diagram for an English play is appended to the text, as may be seen in vol. 3, p. 142 of this *Dictionary*). In its staging effects, including a detachable hand and an exploding oven, *The Sacrament* contrasts with the tightly structured and functional *Everyman,* extant in sixteenth-century texts. Like *The Sacrament,* however, *Everyman* is a defensive play, affirming the sacramental role of the church; and like it also, *Everyman* has a continental counterpart in the late-fifteenth-century Dutch play *Elckerlijc.* *Everyman* has been seen as a response to contemporary questionings, but there is no evidence of its actors or the circumstances of performance, if it was ever performed.

Although there are many forms of religious didactic play, that using allegory seems most characteristic. The Middle Ages inherited a literary tradition of allegory going back through the battles of Vice and Virtue in Prudentius' *Psychomachia,* as well as a tradition of exegetical allegory by the church fathers in religious exposition, and it is against the context of medieval allegory that allegorical drama in all its forms must be assessed. As religious drama the allegorical play is a play of repentance, presenting debate for the soul of man between Vice and Virtue. Such plays look toward the death and judgment of an Everyman figure and draw on elements in both the *Ars moriendi* and the death cults of the later Middle Ages, including the *Danse macabre.* But the representation of Vice, using the tradition of the Seven Deadly Sins, inevitably leads such drama in the direction of the comic realization of the vicious mores and conduct of contemporary society. The balance between the spiritual goal of perfection and the corruption of contemporary life is held only with difficulty. Moreover, the dramatic impact of fixed allegorical figures dominating a central "human" representative lends a strong sense of determinism to the thesis of such plays.

The dramatic use of allegory is found as early as about 1155 in the *Ordo virtutum.* Allegorical figures are found in the Tegernsee *Antichrist.* In France there are two early-fourteenth-century Walloon texts based on literary allegories: the *Moralité des sept pechés mortels et des sept vertus,* based on Robert de l'Omme's *Le miroir de vie et de mort,* and the *Moralité du pèlerinage de la vie humaine,* a version of Guillaume de Deguilleville's poem. Significantly, the third play in the same collection, *Moralité de l'alliance de foy et de loyalté* is a pastoral morality with social overtones, rather than a drama of sin and repentance. The earliest extant English text is the mid-fourteenth-century *Pride of Life*. But allegorical drama of this kind is found throughout Europe. The religious allegorical play should be seen as a complement to biblical drama and as the microcosm of the Corpus Christi play, in which the historical Fall and Redemption are explored in relation to the contemporary individual. The interaction of the two forms can be seen in, for example, the use of allegorical figures in the *N-town* cycle and John Bale's combination of cycle and allegory in *King Johan.* Both forms contributed to the fifteenth-century English saint's play *Mary Magdalene.*

Allegorical drama, however, can itself be seen as the interaction of religious drama with a device used not only in exegesis and instruction, but also in civic tableaux and disguisings to delight the eye, to divert, and also, on occasion, to admonish a personage on his social duty. This drama had numerous possible variations, many far removed from religious instruction. Thus the "educational morals" of the sixteenth century extol education of the young as a means of eliminating vicious and antisocial tendencies, praise the new learning, and become a mode of instruction for children in their own right. The Youth interludes concentrate on the anarchy of a worldly society and represent moral reform as the vehicle of social order.

Other allegories of social order, such as Sir David Lyndsay's *Satyre of the Thrie Estaitis,* a version of which was played before King James V and Queen Marie of Scotland at Linlithgow Palace in 1540, and John Skelton's *Magnificence,* presumably written for the court of Henry VIII, apply moral standards to the conduct of a ruler. In English interludes the older sins and devils yield to Vice, an anarchic and amoral figure whose comic activities come to dominate the play. In these and other ways the drama of religious instruction merged with less specific admonitory forms or even mere entertainments. At its extreme, allegorical drama, through the disguisings at court, became an element in the masque.

DRAMA AS AN ADJUNCT OF PRIVATE
ENTERTAINMENT

The medieval hall, with its high table, side tables, and screen, offered an enclosed area in which entertainments could be presented during banquets. Some might be courtly elaborations of folk activities. Others might be mimed actions on elaborate sets, such as the presentation of the siege of Troy at the marriage of Charles VI to Isabella of Bavaria in 1389 (described by Froissart), where entertainment and visual appeal were dominant considerations. Still others might include singing by children from the private chapel of the house and an appropriate dialogue or address, as with the scenes at the wedding of Prince Arthur of England and Catherine of Aragon in 1501, thus moving spectacle closer to the concept of drama. Or the entertainment might be a textually controlled drama, such as the *Estoire de Griseldis,* France's first nonreligious play (1395)—perhaps intended for the marriage of Isabella to Richard II of England in 1396—or Henry Medwall's *Fulgens and Lucrece,* apparently intended for production before Cardinal John Morton on the occasion of the visit of the Spanish and Flemish ambassadors to England in 1497.

Private entertainment was not confined to the halls of the nobles. Civic halls might also be used, as well as the halls of universities and schools. The themes of the plays performed were diverse: religious history, mythology, humanist allegory, political and religious controversy. Central to such drama was the professional troupe. Glynne Wickham notes that before 1485 in England, "We hear of players belonging to the King, the Dukes of Buckingham, Exeter, Gloucester, and York, the Earls of Essex, Oxford, Northumberland and Westmorland, the Queen, the Duchess of Norfolk, the Archbishop of Canterbury and the Bishop of Carlisle, and to many lesser lords and knights" (*The Medieval Theatre,* p. 172). Such companies evidently toured widely, performing in city halls, in inns, even in the open air for the public.

It is thus difficult to affirm that drama for private entertainment was distinct from the other forms discussed, or that it was written for a different kind of audience. A play such as the late-fifteenth-century English *Mankind* has the structure of an allegory of religious instruction but highly comic action by the Vices; it has been variously held to be intended for the inn yard, for a hall at an inn, or even for the hall of a nobleman. At Chester in 1529/1530 an interlude of *King Robert of Sicily* (a subject that might have seemed appropriate to a noble audience) was performed at the high cross.

It is possible to establish a paradigm of authority whereby the God of religious drama, presiding over human history, has a counterpart in the earthly lord or king presiding over his realm, and to argue that as the town is microcosm of the realm, so the hierarchy of the hall is microcosm of the town. The hall context gave point to images of the player-king and to dramas of political advice. It also afforded individual writers and producers direct access to figures in authority and made drama an offering to a patron that might ensure personal preferment, rather than an offering to God that might ensure grace. To the extent that the tastes of the patron became determinants of the drama, such plays anticipated the commercial theater, in which plays are designed to attract an audience. In England the first public theaters were built by members of the private professional troupes as a logical extension of their touring activities and a means of escaping the jurisdiction of local authorities. Such developments did not mark the end of the traditions of drama rooted in the Middle Ages, but they do offer a convenient stopping point in their discussion.

BIBLIOGRAPHY

The standard bibliography, Carl J. Stratman, *Bibliography of Medieval Drama*, 2nd rev. ed., 2 vols. (1972), may be supplemented from material in *Research Opportunities in Renaissance Drama* and the *Newsletter* of the *Records of Early English Drama*.

Collections of texts. General: David Bevington, *Medieval Drama* (1975); Cornwall: Edwin Norris, ed., *The Ancient Cornish Drama*, 2 vols. (1859, repr. 1968); England: A. C. Cawley, *Everyman and Medieval Miracle Plays*, rev. ed. (1974); Peter Happé, *Tudor Interludes* (1972), *English Mystery Plays* (1975), and *Four Morality Plays* (1979); John M. Manly, *Specimens of the Pre-Shakespearean Drama*, 2 vols. (1897, repr. 1967); Glynne Wickham, *English Moral Interludes* (1976); France: Richard Axton and John Stevens, trans., *Medieval French Plays* (1971); Germany: Richard Froning, *Das Drama des Mittelalters* (1891–1892, repr. 1964); Spain: Fernando Lázaro Carreter, *Teatro medieval: Textos íntegros en versión* (1958).

Critical surveys. General: Richard Axton, *European Drama of the Early Middle Ages* (1974); Edmund K. Chambers, *The Medieval Stage*, 2 vols. (1903, repr. 1963), standard survey and reference work; William Tydeman, *The Theatre in the Middle Ages* (1978); Glynne Wickham, *The Medieval Theatre* (1974); England: Hardin Craig, *English Religious Drama of the Middle Ages* (1955, repr. 1978); Alfred Harbage, *Annals of English Drama, 975–1700*, rev. S. Schoenbaum (1964), lists recorded productions; Stanley J. Kahrl, *Traditions of Medieval English Drama* (1974); Glynne Wickham, *Early English Stages, I, 1300–1576*, rev. ed. (1963), stresses links with civic ceremonial and courtly celebration, a major study; F. P. Wilson and G. K. Hunter, *The English Drama 1485–1585* (1969). Local records for England have appeared in the volumes of Collections issued by the Malone Society. The series Records of Early English Drama will make local records for England available as part of an ongoing project; first publications are J. J. Anderson, ed., *Newcastle Upon Tyne* (1982); Lawrence M. Clopper, ed., *Chester* (1979); R. W. Ingram, ed., *Coventry* (1981); Alexandra F. Johnston and Margaret Rogerson, eds., *York*, 2 vols. (1979).

France: Gustave Cohen, *Histoire de la mise en scène dans le théâtre réligieux français du moyen âge* (1926, rev. ed. 1951); Grace Frank, *The Medieval French Drama* (1954). Germany: Wilhelm Creiznach, *Geschichte des neueren Dramas*, I (1893, repr. 1965). Italy: Alessandro d'Ancone, *Origini del teatro italiano*, 2 vols. (1892, repr. 1966). Scotland: Anna Jean Mill, *Mediaeval Plays in Scotland* (1927, repr. 1978). Spain: J. P. Wickersham Crawford, *Spanish Drama Before Lope de Vega*, rev. ed. (1967), with bibliographical supplement by Warren T. MacCready.

Drama as an adjunct to worship. Liturgical and Latin drama: O. B. Hardison, Jr., *Christian Rite and Christian Drama in the Middle Ages* (1965); William L. Smoldon, "The origins of the *Quem Quaeritis* Trope and the Easter Sepulchre Music-Dramas, as Demonstrated by Their Musical Settings," in Sandro Sticca, ed., *The Medieval Drama* (1972), 121–154; Sandro Sticca, *The Latin Passion Play* (1970); Karl Young, *The Drama of the Medieval Church*, 2 vols. (1933, repr. 1967), a standard work with texts and discussion. *Ordo representacionis Adae*: Tony Hunt, "The Unity of the Play of Adam (*Ordo Representacionis Adae*)," in *Romania*, 96 (1975); Lynette R. Muir, *Liturgy and Drama in the Anglo-Norman Adam* (1973); William Noomen, "*Le Jeu d'Adam*: Étude descriptive et analytique," in *Romania*, 89 (1968).

Drama as an adjunct to scholarship. Hrotsvitha: Sr. Mary M. Butler, *Hrotsvitha: The Theatricality of Her Plays* (1960); H. J. W. Tillyard, trans., *Plays of Roswitha* (1923). Latin comedy: Keith Bate, "Twelfth-Century Latin Comedies and the Theatre," in *Papers of the Liverpool Latin Seminar, Second Volume 1979* (1978), 249–262; Gustave Cohen, ed., *La comédie latine en France au XIIᵉ siècle*, 2 vols. (1931), standard work, texts, and discussion.

Drama as an adjunct to communal celebration. Folk drama: Alan Brody, *The English Mummers and Their Plays* (1970); E. C. Cawte, Alan Helm, and N. Peacock, *English Ritual Drama: A Geographical Index* (1967). The English Corpus Christi play texts: K. S. Block, ed., *Ludus Coventriae or The Plaie Called Corpus Christi* (1922), the Hegge or *N*-town cycle; A. C. Cawley, ed., *The Wakefield Pageants in the Towneley Cycle* (1958), a good edition of plays assigned to the Wakefield Master; Hardin Craig, *Two Coventry Corpus Christi Plays*, 2nd ed. (1957); Norman Davis, ed., *Non-cycle Plays and Fragments* (1970); George England and Alfred W. Pollard, *The Towneley Cycle* (1897), the Wakefield cycle; R. M. Lumiansky and David Mills, eds., *The Chester Mystery Cycle, I, Text* (1974), and II, *Explanatory Notes, Glossaries, etc.* (at press); Lucy Toulmin Smith, ed., *The York Plays* (1885, repr. 1963). Facsimiles of MSS of Chester, Towneley, *N*-town, and York, and of a miscellany of Non-cycle plays, have appeared in the Medieval Drama Facsimile series of Leeds Texts and Monographs; and a facsimile of a further Chester MS is at press. English Corpus Christi plays, criticism: V. A. Kolve, *The Play Called Corpus Christi* (1966), important theses of structure and aesthetic; Eleanor Prosser, *Drama and Religion in the English Mystery Plays* (1961); Rosemary Woolf, ed., *The English Mystery Plays* (1972).

Discussions of staging respond to, but rarely accept entirely, Alan H. Nelson, *The Medieval English Stage: Corpus Christi Pageants and Plays* (1974). The final years of the cycles are discussed in Harold C. Gardiner, *Mysteries' End: An Investigation of the Last Days of the Medieval Religious Stage* (1946, repr. 1967).

Related drama. Saints' plays: Donald C. Baker, John L. Murphy, and Louis B. Hall, Jr., eds., *The Late Mediaeval Religious Plays of Bodleian Manuscripts Digby 133 and E Museo 160* (1982); E. Catherine Dunn, "The Origin of the Saints' Plays: The Question Reopened," in William A. Selz, ed., *Medieval Drama* (1968), 46–54; David L. Jeffrey, "English Saints Plays," in Neville Denny, ed., *Medieval Drama* (1973), 69–90. Vol. VII of the Medieval Drama Facsimiles series of Leeds Texts and Monographs, Donald C. Baker and John L. Murphy, eds., *The Digby Plays* (1976), contains a facsimile of the manuscript. Cornish trilogy: Neville Denny, "Arena Staging and Dramatic Quality in the Cornish Passion Play," in his *Medieval Drama* (1973); Markham Harris, *The Cornish Ordinalia* (1969), translated text.

Drama as an adjunct of religious instruction. Texts: *The Croxton Play of the Sacrament* is in Davis, *Non-cycle Plays and Fragments*, and the morality *Wisdom* is in Baker et al., *The Late Mediaeval Religious Plays*; A. C. Cawley, ed., *Everyman* (1961); Gustave Cohen, *Nativités et moralités liègeoises du moyen âge* (1953); Mark Eccles, ed., *The Macro Plays* (1969), contains *Castle of Perseverance, Mankind,* and *Wisdom;* Bruce W. Hozeski, "Ordo Virtutum," in *Annuale medievale,* 13 (1972). There is a facsimile edition of the *Macro Plays* by David Bevington (1972). Critical discussion: William O. Harris, *Skelton's Magnifycence and the Cardinal Virtue Tradition* (1965); Robert Potter, *The English Morality Play* (1975), a well-received reappraisal, with a survey of continental traditions; Richard W. Southern, *The Medieval Theatre in the Round,* 2nd ed. (1975), arena staging of the *Castle of Perseverance;* Bernard Spivack, *Shakespeare and the Allegory of Evil* (1958).

Drama as an adjunct of courtly entertainment. Texts of Tudor interludes are published by the Malone Society. Editions are appearing in a new series, Tudor Interludes, of which Marie Axton, ed., *Three Tudor Classical Interludes* (1982); Richard Axton, ed., *Three Rastell Plays* (1979); and Alan H. Nelson, ed., *The Plays of Henry Medwall* (1980) have so far been published. Critical discussion: See especially Wickham, *Early English Stages.* See also Thomas W. Craik, *The Tudor Interlude,* 2nd ed. (1962); L. W. Cushman, *The Devil and the Vice in English Dramatic*

Literature Before Shakespeare (1900, repr. 1970); J. A. B. Somerset, "'Fair Is Foul and Foul Is Fair': Vice-Comedy's Development and Theatrical Effects," in George R. Hibbard, ed., *The Elizabethan Theatre V* (1975), 54–75; Richard W. Southern, *The Staging of Plays Before Shakespeare* (1973); John Stevens, *Music and Poetry in the Early Tudor Court* (1961).

DAVID MILLS

[See also **Castle of Perseverance; Chester Plays; Drama, French; Drama, German; Drama, Liturgical; Everyman; Hrotsvitha of Gandesheim; Jeu d'Adam; Ludus de Antichristo; Morality Play; Mystery Play; Processions; Towneley Plays; York Plays.**]

DRAUMA-JÓNS SAGA is a short narrative preserved in five Icelandic vellum manuscripts, the oldest from around 1400, and in some forty-five manuscripts. It was probably first written down at the beginning of the fourteenth century, but whether it is a translation from a foreign source or a native product employing foreign (including oriental) motifs is not certain. In content, style, and moral tone the tale bears a similarity to the *ævintýri* attributed to Jón Halldórsson and to the learned *Klári saga.*

The story centers on Drauma-Jón, a poor farmer's son who demonstrates for a wealthy landowner his power to interpret dreams. Earl Heinrekr in Saxland, noted for a similar ability, hears of Drauma-Jón, summons him to his court, and uses him to enhance his own renown. He soon becomes envious of Jón's talent for interpreting dreams without even being told their content, and he thinks to obtain Jón's gift by eating his heart. Heinrekr threatens Ingibjörg, his wife and the daughter of the emperor, until she consents to murder Jón in his sleep. Unable at the last moment to do so, she plots with the intended victim to deceive her husband by substituting a dog's heart and by burying a wax image of Jón.

Meanwhile, the emperor of Saxland comes to Heinrekr to discover the meaning of his own dream—in which his capital city is flooded and his subjects stand in different depths of water—and he learns of the earl's deception from Ingibjörg. Jón interprets the dream to reveal an affair between the queen and her Flemish lover, as well as the various degrees of knowledge and complicity among members of the court. Sent as the emperor's envoy to the city, Jón catches the couple in flagrante delicto and has them banished. On returning to his capital, the emperor expels the earl, forgives his contrite subjects, and gives Heinrekr's earldom and wife to the righteous, compassionate Drauma-Jón.

Only two *rímur* versions of the material are extant, one probably from the seventeenth century and the other from the eighteenth century.

BIBLIOGRAPHY

Sources. Hugo Gering, ed., "Drauma-Jóns Saga," in *Zeitschrift für deutsche Philologie,* **26** (1894); R. I. Page, ed., "Drauma-Jóns Saga," in *Nottingham Mediaeval Studies,* **1** (1957).

Studies. Finnur Jónsson, *Den oldnorske og oldislandske litteraturs historie,* 2nd ed., III (1924), 97; Margaret Schlauch, *Romance in Iceland* (1934, repr. 1973), 71–73; Finnur Sigmundsson, *Rímnatal,* I (1966), 105–106; Bjarni Vilhjálmsson, ed., *Riddarasögur,* VI (1961), 147–170.

PETER A. JORGENSEN

DRAUMKVÆDE is a Norwegian ballad, or several closely related ballads, with a visionary motif. It exists in approximately 150 variants, the longest of which contains 74 stanzas and the shortest a single line. The basic form is the four-line stanza with *y a z a* end rhyme.

The amount of extant ballad material that can be classed as *Draumkvæde* is disputed. Only eighteen of the variants contain ten stanzas or more, and since the ballad lacks a clear narrative thread there has been disagreement about how many even of these eighteen are "genuine" *Draumkvæde* variants. What cannot be disputed is the existence of ballad material with a visionary motif and certain clearly defined episodes that reciters or collectors called *Draumkvæde, Draugkveen, Droukveen,* and the like.

This material was written down in Telemark, Norway, between 1842 and the early decades of the twentieth century. It concerns a man called Olav Aasteson or Aakneson (or variations on this name) who fell asleep on Christmas Eve and did not reawaken until Epiphany, whereupon he rode to church and interrupted the service with news of his dreams. He saw heaven and hell and much else beyond the grave, including a narrow bridge across which souls had to pass and a place reminiscent of purgatory. In many variants the visionary makes a series of pronouncements rather like the beatitudes (Matt. 5:3–11), in which rewards are promised for good deeds done in this life and, by implication, punishments threatened for failure to do them. One or two variants have a scene in which a host from the north (representing the forces of darkness) and a host from the south (led by Christ and St. Michael) meet to take part in the judgment of sinful souls.

Draumkvæde is unusual not only in having no clear narrative thread or order of stanzas. Three features distinguish it from the majority of Norwegian ballads: the inclusion in many variants of an "introductory" stanza; the use of the first person singular; the occurrence in one or two variants of several different refrains. These characteristics mark ballads in Denmark and Sweden as late, mainly after 1500. It is uncertain whether the practice of varying the refrain is at all old. The variants that have this feature all look like late reworkings or reconstructions by a reciter or a collector; in each case a selection of refrains from among the seven or so associated with *Draumkvæde* appears to have been made and an appropriate place found for them in the variant.

Draumkvæde was thought by many scholars to have been composed in the thirteenth or early fourteenth century, largely because of alleged similarities to certain medieval visions, notably those of Tundale (1149), Gundelin (1161), Gottskalk (1190), and Thurcill (1206). Even if a connection between these visions and *Draumkvæde* is accepted (and few would now argue that the connection is clear), they only provide a terminus a quo. There is internal evidence to suggest that a number of the stanzas were composed before the Reformation or while the memory of Catholicism was still strong, but beyond that no reliable terminus ante quem has been found.

BIBLIOGRAPHY

Brynjulf Alver, *Draumkvedet: Folkevise eller lærd kopidikting* (1971); Michael Barnes, *Draumkvæde, an Edition and Study* (1974); Karl-Ivar Hildeman, "I marginalen till Draumkvædet," in *Medeltid på vers* (1958); Knut Liestøl, *Draumkvæde, a Norwegian Visionary Poem from the Middle Ages* (1946); Moltke Moe, "Middelalderens visionsdigtning" and "Kommentar," in *Moltke Moes samlede skrifter,* III (1927), 209–345; Dag Strömbäck, "Om Draumkvædet och dess källor," in *Arv,* **2** (1946).

M. P. BARNES

[See also **Visions.**]

DRAWINGS AND MODEL BOOKS. Medieval artists made drawings in various media: ink, paint, charcoal, bister, silverpoint, lead point, and incised wax, ivory, and metal. Unlike later drawings, which

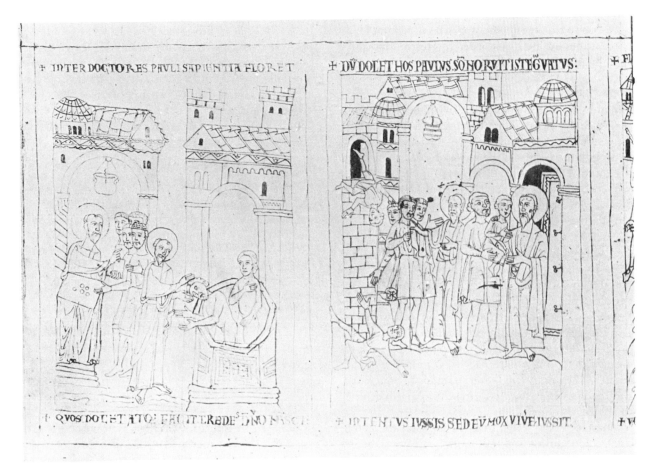

✝ INTER DOCTORES PAVLI SAPIENTIA FLORET   ✝ DV DOLET HOS PAVLVS SO HONORVIT ISTE GVBIT VS: ✝ FL

✝ QVOS DOCET ATO: FACIT EREDE DNO   ✝ INTENTVS IVSSIS SEDEV MOX VIVE IVSSIT.

Rotulus, 13th century. VERCELLI, BIBLIOTECA CAPITOLARE

often were vehicles for experimentation and personal expression, medieval drawings primarily served utilitarian purposes or were used as finished art works in themselves.

Ancient artists had used drawings in preparing works of art (see Pliny, *Natural History,* XXXV, 145), and throughout the Middle Ages artists continued the practice. Fresco painters and mosaicists outlined their compositions on plaster-covered walls before applying color and surface details. Preliminary drawings called sinopias have been discovered beneath many murals (for instance, S. Maria Maggiore, Rome) and are described in artists' manuals (such as Cennino Cennini's *Libro dell'arte,* ch. 67). The creators of smaller-scale works delineated their designs with stylus, metal point, or ink as a first step; the twelfth-century Winchester Bible, for example, contains incomplete historiated initials rendered only in drawings.

To what extent artists also used drawings to develop ideas before turning to the work itself is not certain. The theologian Alexander Neckham (1157–1217) describes a goldsmith who made ornamental designs on a wax tablet, and in an inventory from the Pechersky monastery at Kiev painters' parchment rolls and books are listed. That these were sketches in the modern sense is unlikely. Because of the traditionalism of medieval practices and the costliness of materials, experimental drawings were probably rare.

Parchment exemplars (often gathered into books) recording figures and ornament for continued use within a workshop were undoubtedly the most common form of drawing and still survive in considerable number. In his *Institutiones* Cassiodorus describes a pattern book containing designs for bookbindings used in his monastery, and a thirteenth-century book of drawings in Vienna (Österreichische Nationalbibliothek, Codex 507) includes models for initials, ornament, and animals.

Increased travel by artists during the crusades and the concurrent emergence of individual personalities

291

gave rise to the development of true sketchbooks. In these, itinerant artists recorded interesting motifs to take back to their workshops. The most important surviving sketchbooks are the Wolfenbüttel model book (Biblioteca Augusta, codex ma. Aug. oct. 61/62) and the "Sketchbook" of Villard de Honnecourt (Paris, Bibliothèque Nationale, MS fr. 19093), both from the second quarter of the thirteenth century. Although the former is the work of a Saxon artist on a trip to Venice, while the latter is an architect's workshop handbook, the two are alike in their exclusive concentration on random motifs set down in a disjointed fashion.

Such motifs, when introduced into new works of art, changed identity, as in the Gospel at Goslar (Rathaus) based on the Wolfenbüttel model book. Fourteenth- and fifteenth-century sketchbooks by Giovannino de' Grassi (Bergamo, Biblioteca Civica), Pisanello (Paris, Louvre), and Jacopo Bellini (Paris, Louvre) had the random character of the earlier motif books, but the earlier interest in active figures and exotic forms was replaced by authentic nature studies. The impulse to preserve and distribute workshop models contributed during the fifteenth century to the development of printing techniques.

Some scholars assert that, in addition to sketchbooks containing isolated motifs, medieval artists had access to "pictorial guides" that diagramed extensive series of compositions. The eighth-century *Life of St. Pancratius of Taormina* mentions tablets and papyri used as guides for the decoration of churches, but the sole surviving "pictorial guide" is a thirteenth-century rotulus in Vercelli (Biblioteca Capitolare) depicting eighteen episodes from the Acts of the Apostles. Because special circumstances (the need to record earlier compositions during restoration work) engendered the Vercelli rotulus, the question of "pictorial guides" remains open. In general, when artists sought models for long narrative sequences, they turned to existing cycles in illuminated manuscripts. The frescoes in St. Julien at Tours (based on the Ashburnham Pentateuch), the frescoes in the convent at Sigena (copied from an English psalter), and the mosaics in S. Marco in Venice (taken from the Cotton Genesis) reflect this practice.

Drawing techniques were also used for finished works. The Heracles Papyrus from Oxyrhynchos (London, Egypt Exploration Society) attests the existence during antiquity of manuscripts illustrated with uncolored sketches; the mode became increasingly popular from the Carolingian period. The

Utrecht Psalter (Bibliotheek der Rijksuniversiteit), illustrated exclusively with dramatic drawings, is a masterpiece of ninth-century art. Drawing was especially favored in England, where artists often used tinted inks and delicate washes of color. Because of its inherent austerity, drawing was valued by Cistercian illuminators. Byzantine book illustrators also occasionally used wash drawing techniques.

BIBLIOGRAPHY

Ernst Kitzinger, "The Role of Miniature Painting in Mural Decoration," in Kurt Weitzmann *et al., The Place of Book Illumination in Byzantine Art* (1975), 99ff.; R. W. Scheller, *A Survey of Medieval Model Books* (1963); David Winfield, "Middle and Later Byzantine Wall Painting Methods," in *Dumbarton Oaks Papers,* 22 (1968).

HERBERT L. KESSLER

[See also **Fresco Painting; Model Books and Models.**]

DREAM VISION. See Visions.

DRESDENER HELDENBUCH. The codex Dresden MS 201 (formerly MS 103), also known as *Kaspars von der Roen Heldenbuch,* is an illuminated paper manuscript of 349 leaves that was written in 1472 by Kaspar von Rhön and one or more anonymous scribes. During the eighteenth century the codex was owned first by the Nuremberg archivist Gottfried Thomasius, and then by Johann Christoph Gottsched. The Dresdener Landesbibliothek acquired the manuscript from the Gottsched collection.

Like other late Middle High German *Heldenbücher,* the Dresden manuscript is devoted entirely to narrative material; it differs from other works of its kind (such as the *Ambraser Heldenbuch*) in that several of the poems it contains have been deliberately abridged. All the works preserved in the *Dresdener Heldenbuch* are cast in epic strophes; the rhymed couplet of the classical Middle High German romances occurs nowhere in the codex. Whether the choice of strophic forms should be attributed to the antecedents or to the writers of the codex remains unclear because little is known about the immediate sources from which Kaspar and the others copied.

The Dresden manuscript was probably written for Balthasar of Mecklenburg (1451–1507) before he became duke of that province. Slightly more than half the works in the collection are Kaspar von der Rhön holographs, and the last of these, "Laurin," bears his signature. The remaining poems, which were penned by Kaspar's collaborators, are those that were shortened most radically and suggest the stylistic principle on which the *Heldenbuch* redactions are based. In the closing lines of "Wolfdietrich," the scribe writes that he has, by eliminating "many a useless word" (*manck vnnücz wort*), reduced the older version of the work from 700 to 333 strophes, "so that one can hear both the beginning and the end of the poem in one sitting" (*das man auf einem siczen dick, Müg hörn anfangk vnd ent*).

The indifferent poetic quality of the abridged works caused early investigators of the codex, such as A. F. C. Vilmar and Wilhelm Wackernagel, to assume that it had been written by a *Bänkelsänger* (mountebank) or a *Volkssäger* (popular singer). On the basis of Leipzig matriculation records for the year 1474, however, Friedrich Zarncke established that Kaspar von der Rhön was both a highly educated man and a member of a socially prominent family from Münnerstadt in Lower Franconia.

The *Dresdener Heldenbuch* contains eleven poems, of which six (marked by asterisks) were penned by Kaspar von der Rhön: "Ortnit," "Wolfdietrich *A*," "Ecke,"* "Der Rosengarten zu Worms,"* "Das Meerwunder," "Sigenot,"* "Der Wunderer" ("Etzels Hofhaltung"),* "Herzog Ernst,"* "Laurin,"* "Dietrich und seine Gesellen" ("Virginal"), and "Das [jüngere] Hildebrandslied."

BIBLIOGRAPHY

Sources. F. H. von der Hagen and A. Primisser, eds., *Der Helden Buch in det Ursprache,* 2 pts. (1820–1825), which is vol. II of F. H. von der Hagen and J. G. Büsching, eds., *Deutsche Gedichte des Mittelalters.* For references to published editions of the individual works contained in the codex, see Werner Hoffman, *Mittelhochdeutsche Heldendichtung* (1974); Hermann Schneider and Wolfgang Mohr, "Heldendichtung," in Paul Merker and Wolfgang Stammler, eds., *Reallexikon der deutschen Literaturgeschichte,* 2nd ed. (1958), I, 631–646.

Studies. Karl Goedeke, "Kaspar von der Roen," in *Deutsche Dichtung im Mittelalter* (1854), 530–547, an extremely useful general analysis of the *Dresdener Heldenbuch* that includes plot summaries, comparative literary historical materials, and excerpts from the poems contained in the codex; Joachim Heinzle, "'Heldenbücher,'" in *Verfasserlexikon: Die deutsche Literatur des Mittelalters,* 2nd ed. (1981), III, 947–956. The section of this essay that is devoted to the *Dresdener Heldenbuch* supersedes

much of the earlier scholarship on the codex and provides a good selected bibliography; Friedrich Zarncke, "Kaspar von der Roen," in *Pfeiffer's Germania,* **1** (1856), still the best single source of factual information on the *Dresdener Heldenbuch* and its author, including a detailed description of the codex—the focus is on the manuscript itself rather than on its literary significance.

ELAINE C. TENNANT

[See also **Middle High German Literature.**]

DRESS. See Costume.

DREUX, JEAN. See Jean, Dreux.

Psalter with initial depicting the Trinity and scene of St. Francis, with drolleries in the margins. Region of Cambrai, 13th century. WALTERS ART GALLERY, BALTIMORE

DROLLERY, often called a "grotesque," any lively, fanciful figure, animal or hybrid, represented in the margins of Gothic manuscripts from about 1250 through the fifteenth century. The activities of these figures sometimes refer to the context of the miniature and text on the same page, but frequently they depict humorous or satirical secular themes.

BILBIOGRAPHY
Lilian M. C. Randall, *Images in the Margins of Gothic Manuscripts* (1966).

ROBERT G. CALKINS

[See also **Manuscript Illumination**; illust. p. 293, above.]

DROPLAUGARSONA SAGA. The *Saga of Droplaug's Sons* is one of the briefer family sagas, clear in outline but somewhat intricate in detail. It is prefaced with an account of the widow Droplaug's ancestry, then centers on a feud between her son Helgi and the chieftain Helgi Ásbjarnarson. The feud is precipitated when one of Helgi Ásbjarnarson's freedmen charges Droplaug with having been an adulteress. Her sons retaliate by killing the offender, and Helgi Ásbjarnarson keeps the quarrel alive by exacting a fine. Helgi Droplaugarson subsequently discredits him with a series of legal schemes and maneuvers, but public opinion turns against him when he connives with his mother, now remarried, to murder her unwanted husband. Droplaug leaves Iceland and her son is outlawed by Helgi Ásbjarnarson. Helgi Droplaugarson fails to heed the sentence, and the conflict culminates when he assists his relative Rannveig in a divorce proceeding against her husband. The husband appeals to Helgi Ásbjarnarson, who assembles forces and ambushes Droplaug's sons, Helgi and Grímr. Both fall after a heroic defense, but Grímr is nursed back to life and avenges his brother by invading Helgi Ásbjarnarson's house at night and killing him as he lies in bed. He makes good his escape, is outlawed, and eventually takes refuge in Norway, where he dies of a wound suffered in a duel with the viking Gauss.

Droplaugarsona saga is preserved complete only in the great saga manuscript *Mǫðruvallabók* from the middle of the fourteenth century. Judging from the fragment of another manuscript, *Mǫðruvallabók* is a considerably revised version of the original. The conclusion of the saga dates the fall of Helgi Droplaugarson to 998 and attributes the telling of the saga

to a certain Þorvaldr, who, according to a genealogical calculation, should have lived in the latter part of the twelfth century. Such an early date for the composition of a family saga, however, seems unlikely: the attribution may be corrupt or based on a misunderstanding.

The story must be to some extent traditional, because the death of Helgi Droplaugarson and Grímr's vengeance are referred to in Haukr Valdísarson's *Íslendingadrápa* (*ca.* 1200), but many details are reminiscent of other sagas and suggest conscious literary borrowing. The affinities to *Gísla saga Súrssonar* are particularly palpable (for example, the invasion of Helgi Ásbjarnarson's bedchamber under the cloak of darkness), and though the indexes have been variously interpreted, the author of *Droplaugarsona saga* is more likely to have been the borrower. *Gísla saga* is generally assigned to the first half of the thirteenth century, and *Droplaugarsona saga* must therefore belong to the middle or latter part of that century. A full study of the literary interrelationships is needed. The author of the saga has a taste for narrative mystification in the form of subtle planning and legal chicanery, but his management of scene, dialogue, and psychology is not highly developed and reflects mechanical dependence on his literary models.

BIBLIOGRAPHY
Sources. Jón Jóhannesson, ed., *Austfirðinga sǫgur* (1950), 137–180; M. H. Scargill and Margaret Schlauch, trans., *Three Icelandic Sagas: Gunnlaugs saga ormstungu; Bandamanna saga; Droplaugarsona saga* (1950), 102–135.
Studies. Rolf Heller, "Droplaugarsona saga—Vápnfirðinga saga—Laxdœla saga," in *Arkiv för nordisk filologi,* 78 (1963); Björn K. Thórólfsson, "Droplaugarsonasaga," in *Festskrift til Finnur Jónsson* (1928).

THEODORE M. ANDERSSON

[See also **Family Sagas, Icelandic; Gísla Saga Súrssonar; Haukr Valdísarson (Íslendingadrápa); Helgi Poems.**]

DRÓTTKVÆTT, short for *dróttkvæðr háttr*—the measure fit for the *drótt,* the king's band of retainers—was the chief meter of the Norse skalds. More than 20,000 lines of *dróttkvætt* have survived, attributed to skalds who lived between 850 and 1400.

A *dróttkvætt* stanza (*vísa*) consists of eight lines; a syntactic break after the fourth line divides the whole into two halves, each called a *helmingr*. The basic metrical unit is the couplet (*vísufjórðungr*), the two lines of which each contain three stresses and six syllables. Every line (vísuorð) has a prescribed ending in a long stressed syllable followed by a short unstressed one. The lines of the couplet are linked by alliteration: two initial sounds (stuðlar) in the odd-numbered line alliterate with the first syllable (hǫfuðstafr) of the even-numbered line. In each line the penultimate syllable (viðrhending) rhymes with a stressed or semistressed syllable (frumhending) in the same line. In even-numbered lines there is aðal-hending or full rhyme; odd-numbered lines have skothending or half rhyme, in which different vowels are followed by an identical consonant (for instance, hotly/meaty, rider/leading). Every line has a caesura—falling between the rhyming syllables and (in the odd-numbered line) also between the alliterating syllables—that frequently helps to mark syntactic divisions. In dróttkvætt the sense can be spread over the helmingr in one, two, or three independent clauses. These clauses and the kennings they contain may themselves be broken into segments and dispersed throughout the four lines.

The earliest dróttkvætt stanzas to have survived are assigned to Bragi Boddason (ca. 835–900). Serious attempts have been made to show that the form evolved under the influence of Latin hymnology and Irish poetry.

BIBLIOGRAPHY

Peter G. Foote, "Beginnings and Endings: Some Notes on the Study of Skaldic Poetry," in Régis Boyer, ed., Les vikings et leur civilisation (1976), 179–190; Roberta Frank, Old Norse Court Poetry: The Dróttkvætt Stanza (1978); Hans Kuhn, Das Dróttkvætt (1983); Klaus von See, Germanische Verskunst (1967), 37–47; E. O. G. Turville-Petre, Scaldic Poetry (1976); John Turville-Petre, "The Meter of Icelandic Court Poetry," in Saga-book of the Viking Society, 17 (1969).

ROBERTA FRANK

[See also Skaldic Verse.]

DROUET OF DAMMARTIN (d. 1413), sculptor and architect who worked under the patronage of Jean, duke of Berry. His major works include renovation of the Louvre with Raymond du Temple (ca. 1367–1377), construction of the Hôtel de Nesle in Paris, and construction of the château of Rouves, the Chartreuse de Champmol, and the Ste. Chapelle at Dijon. He also completed the work of his brother,

Guy of Dammartin, on the Ste. Chapelle at Bourges in 1398.

BIBLIOGRAPHY

Paul Gauchery, "L'influence de Jean de France, duc de Berry, sur le développement de l'architecture et des arts à la fin du XIVᵉ siècle et au commencement du XVᵉ siècle," in Congrès archéologique, 65 (1898); Réunion des Musées Nationaux, Les fastes du gothique (1981).

JENNIFER E. JONES

[See also **Dijon, Chartreuse de Champmol; Gothic Architecture; Guy of Dammartin.**]

DRUNGARIOS, a Byzantine military commander, especially in the early and middle Byzantine periods. The word is of Germanic origin, but holders of the post of drungarios may have been of either indigenous Greek or foreign origins. Prominent drungarioi included the drungarios of the watch (Vigla) or tagma (regiment) of the Arithmos, the drungarios tou ploimou or grand drungarios or commander of the imperial fleet (whose title survived as late as the fifteenth century), as well as such shorter-lived naval commands as the drungarios of the Dodecanese, the drungarios tou kolpou (commander of the Gulf and on the staff of the commander of the fleet), and the drungarios of the Cibyrrhaeot theme. Each drungarios had a subordinate staff to assist him in his duties. He was appointed by the emperor and served at his pleasure.

BIBLIOGRAPHY

Rodolphe Guilland, "Études de titulature et de prosopographie byzantines: Les chefs de la marine byzantine," in Byzantinische Zeitschrift 44 (1951); Nicholas Oikonomides, Les listes de préséance byzantines des IXᵉ et Xᵉ siècles (1972).

WALTER EMIL KAEGI, JR.

DRUZES, a sect that originally stemmed from the Ismaili sect of the Shiites and came into existence in Egypt and Syria in the eleventh century. The first person to expound the Druze faith was al-Darazī, a dāᶜī (missionary) of the Ismaili Fatimid caliph al-Hākim bi-Amr Allāh (996–1021). Responding to widespread popular frustration in waiting for the promised coming of the Ismaili Mahdi, and probably with the tacit approval of al-Ḥākim, Darazī in 1017 publicly called for al-Ḥakim's recognition as the Neoplatonic (and Ismaili) Universal Intellect *(al-ʿaql al-kullī)*, an imam above the Prophet. This call was met with riots, and in 1019 Darazī was killed, having been accused of fostering sexual excess and wine drinking. Another *dāʿī*, Ḥamza ibn ʿAlī, took over the movement and developed it into a sophisticated, organized Ḥakim cult, thus becoming the real founder of the Druze faith.

Ḥamza's teachings were more extreme than Darazī's. He, not al-Ḥakim, was the imam, *Mawlāna al-ʿaql* (our Lord the Intellect), Amīr *al-Muʾminīn* (commander of the faithful), *Ṣāḥib al-Zamān* (master of the time), and *al-Nāṭiq* (prophet). Al-Ḥakim, on the other hand, was the last embodiment of the One *(al-Wāḥid*, hence *al-Muwaḥḥidūn)*: the Godhead, the creator of the intellects *(al-Bārī)*, the ever Present, beyond name or position, good or evil, having neither father nor son. From him emanated persons called *ḥudūd* (boundaries, laws), each embodying a cosmic principle: *al-ʿAql* (intellect, Ḥamza); *al-Nafs* (soul, Ismāʿīl ibn Muḥammad al-Tamīmī); *al-Kalima* (word, Muḥammad ibn al-Wahb al-Qurashī; *al-Sābiq* or *al-Janāḥ al-Ayman* (preceder or right wing, Salama ibn ʿAbd al-Wahhāb); *al-Tālī* or *al-Janāḥ al-Aysar* (follower or left wing, ʿAlī Bahāʾ al-Dīn al-Muqtanā). Below these were a number of *dāʿīs*, then *maʾdhūns* (licensed preachers), then *mukāsirs* (persuaders), then *naqībs*. All these were commanded to spread the knowledge of the faith among the believers. No Druze was to be ignorant of the *ḥudūd*; no other religion or *Sharīʿa* was to be accepted.

When al-Ḥakim disappeared in 1021, Ḥamza announced that he would return, with Ḥamza, in full power. That same year Ḥamza gave up his leadership to ʿAlī Bahāʾ al-Dīn al-Muqtanā. The movement had by then died out in Egypt, but it was revived in Syria in the form of peasant revolts. The rebels were accused of tearing down mosques and of moral depravity; consequently, Muqtanā wrote a series of letters to the Druze community in which he laid the foundations of Druze orthodoxy. His letters, together with those of Ḥamza, al-Tamīmī, and supposedly al-Ḥakim (101 letters in all) constituted the Druze scriptures, *Rasāʾil al-ḥikma* (letters of wisdom), which were to serve as the canons of the faith until the return of al-Ḥakim and Ḥamza. Most aspects of these religious formulations were later presented by an anonymous author in *Kitāb al-Taʿlīm* (book of instruction), with extensive quotations from sacred Druze texts. From that time on, the Druze community became secretive about its beliefs,

permitting neither conversion nor apostasy. The Druzes also developed their own aristocracy and cultivated a strange blend of belligerence, harshness, hospitality, and strict moral discipline.

The Druzes practice monogamy, but divorce is possible. They help each other, especially against non-Druzes. In the presence of the latter they adhere to strict secrecy about their faith, but they are allowed to deny this faith publicly if their lives are endangered *(taqīya)*. Furthermore, since they hold that the number of souls of believers has been fixed from the time of creation, they believe in metempsychosis *(tanāsukh)*. They do not, however, deny the Resurrection: in the Last Times al-Ḥakim will return to judge the world and grant the righteous *muwaḥḥidūn* power, the kingdom, gold, silver, and property.

The Druzes follow Ḥamza's and Muqtanā's seven commandments instead of the five pillars of Islam: recognition of al-Ḥakim at all times as "our Lord"; negation of all non-Druze religions and tenets; avoidance of unbelievers; contentment with God's (al-Ḥakim's) orders as transmitted through his *ḥudūd;* submission to those orders; truthfulness (but lying to non-Druzes is permissible); and mutual defense and solidarity among fellow Druzes. The order and number of duties vary in different texts.

The Druzes do not fast during the month of Ramadan, but they celebrate ʿĪd al-Aḍḥā. They do not perform the hegira, but they do make pilgrimages to the sites of holy places. The prophet Shuʿayb (Jethro) has a special place in their tenets, since he is believed to have been an incarnation of the Universal Intellect before Ḥamza.

The Druzes worship in places called *khalawāt* (places of seclusion). The *khalwa* worship is open to all sect members, male and female; however, when prayer, study, and meditation commence, only the *ʿuqqāl* (sages) are allowed to remain, while the *juhhāl* (ignorant) must leave. Attaining the ranks of the *ʿuqqal* requires severe trials. After having been allowed into this privileged circle, the *ʿaqīl* must lead a strict religious life, abstaining from all stimulants, saying daily prayers, and refraining from deceit, stealing, and revenge. They are visually distinguished by their special dress and white turbans. Only they know the innermost secrets of the Druze faith.

It is from the *ʿuqqal* that the *shaykhs* are chosen. Trained in a special school, they work as copiers of religious books and often go into religious retirement. They guide the *juhhāl,* lead the ritual services, and maintain the religious secrets of the sect.

The Druzes are now legally considered a Muslim sect. Their religious, social, and political identities, however, are clearly marked out and give them special standing.

BIBLIOGRAPHY
Because of the sensitivity of the subject and the strict secrecy about the Druze faith, most of the studies on the Druzes have been the work of Orientalists rather than Arabic scholars. Works by Arab Druzes represent the Druze faith as they wish it to appear—see, for instance, Sami Nasib Makarim, *The Druze Faith* (1974). ᶜAbd Allāh al-Najjār, *Madhhab al-Durūz wa-l-Tawhīd* (1965), represents a noncanonical image of the faith, but it was withdrawn from the market shortly after publication. Many Druze documents still exist only in manuscript form.

Much Druze literature, nevertheless, has been published in the West. The most fundamental European work is Antoine I. Silvestre de Sacy, *Exposé de la religion des Druzes, tiré de livres religieux de cette secte*, 2 vols. (1838), containing a list of about 120 manuscripts, with many excerpts. It has been partially translated into German by Philipp Wolff as *Die Drusen und ihre Vorläufer* (1845); see also Silvestre de Sacy's *Chrestomathie arabe*, II (1826), for annotated Druze source writings. Other Druze sources are Pierre-Marie-François-Henri Guys, *Théogonie des Druses* (1863); Bahāʔ al-Dīn ᶜAlī ibn Ahmad, *Die Drusenschrift: Kitāb Alnoqat Waldawāir*, Christian F. Seybold, ed. (1902); M. Sprengling, "The Berlin Druze Lexicon," in *American Journal of Semitic Languages and Literatures*, 56 (1939) and 57 (1940). See also M. G. S. Hodgson, "Al-Darazī and Hamza in the Origin of the Druze Religion," in *Journal of the American Oriental Society*, 82 (1962), and "Durūz," in *Encyclopedia of Islam*, 2nd ed., II (1965).

On the history of the Druzes, see Narcisse Bouron, *Les druzes, histoire du Liban et de la Montagne houranaise*, 2nd ed. (1930), trans. by F. Massey as *Druze History* (1952); H. Z. Hirschberg, "The Druzes," in A. J. Arberry, ed., *Religion in the Middle East*, II (1969); Philip K. Hitti, *The Origins of the Druze People and Religion, with Extracts from Their Sacred Writings* (1928). See also J. N. D. Anderson, "The Personal Law of the Druze Community," in *Die Welt des Islams*, n.s. 2 (1953).

WADĀD AL-QĀDĪ

[See also **Hakim bi-Amr Allāh, al-**; **Islam, Religion**; **Ismāᶜiliya**; **Shiᶜa**.]

DUALISM. The term "dualism" was first employed by historians of ideas in the early eighteenth century and, considered abstractly, indicates the belief that there are two absolute and distinct principles that constitute the basis of all reality. The role of dualism in the medieval intellectual milieu can most easily be assessed by considering it in its two basic forms—theological and philosophical.

Theological dualism asserted that in the realm of the divine there is a principle of goodness and a principle of evil, self-caused and independent of one another, which are the basis of good and evil things in the world generally. In the realm of the human, there are elements of good and evil that are derived from the primary principles and give rise to good and evil in human conduct. This duality in the human sphere was also held to be manifested in the contrast of soul and body, with the obvious ethical implication that the purest life requires the eradication of the influence of the body through asceticism and celibacy.

In late antiquity this form of dualism appeared most strikingly in the Manichaean system, as well as among the followers of Priscillian of Ávila, whose influence in Spain led to the condemnation of such beliefs by the First Council of Toledo (400) and the First Council of Braga (561). In the Middle Ages the resurgence of these ideas among the Albigensians produced the condemnation of the Synod of Toulouse (1119), repeated at the Second Lateran Council (1139) and the Council of Florence (1442).

A different kind of dualism was retained by orthodox Christianity: God the creator as opposed to created beings, such as angelic or human souls and physical bodies. This dualism posited, not two self-caused and independent principles, but a self-caused and independent principle (God) and an externally caused and dependent being (creation). Such a limited dualism was so fundamental to medieval Christianity that the church quickly condemned any thinkers who appeared to undermine it by moving toward a monistic viewpoint. Thus, John Scottus Eriugena and Amalric of Bène had their teachings proscribed by the Council of Paris (1210) and the Fourth Lateran Council (1215).

A special concern with problems of dualism is found in the works of Augustine, who described his own development toward Catholic Christianity as being accompanied by a rejection of the Manichaeanism that detained him in his youth (*Confessions*, 3.6–7). During much of his subsequent career, Augustine engaged in the systematic refutation of his early beliefs; among his most important writings on the subject are *De Genesi contra Manichaeos, De duabus animabus contra Manichaeos, Contra Epistulam Fundamenti*, and *Contra Faustum Manichaeum*. In all these works he rejects the opposition of two self-caused and independent principles in favor of that of a self-caused and independent principle (God) and an externally caused and dependent being (human soul and body).

The rejection of theological dualism is an essential feature of Augustine's thought, but at the same time he allows certain types of philosophical dualism that are not inconsistent with his general aims. First, he reiterates the opposition of the intelligible and the sensible characteristics of Platonism by contrasting the divine ideas and individual things that participate in them (*De diversis quaestionibus LXXXIII,* 46). Second, he employs the contrast of form and matter fundamental to Aristotelianism in his own analysis of two moments in the creation of both spiritual and material things (*De Genesi ad litteram,* I.4–7; *De vera religione,* 18).

Since Augustine's works were studied extensively throughout the Middle Ages, these examples of philosophical dualism easily found their way into the medieval speculative tradition.

One of Boethius' declared philosophical aims was to reconcile the teachings of Plato and Aristotle, so that in *De Trinitate* he not only contrasts God as pure form with individual created things—preserving the Platonic dualism of intelligible and sensible—but, within the created realm itself, he opposes image to substratum—a thinly disguised reference to the Aristotelian dualism of form and matter (*De Trinitate,* II.40–58, Stewart-Rand). The reconciliation of the two principal types of philosophical dualism became a standard feature of medieval speculation thereafter, appearing during the Carolingian period in Pseudo-Eriugena's *Commentum in Boethii De Trinitate* (II, pp. 35.27–38.15, Rand), in Gerbert of Aurillac's *De rationali et de ratione uti* (11, pp. 305–306, Olleris) in the late tenth century, and in Adelard of Bath's *De eodem et diverso* (p. 18.12–23, Willner) and John of Salisbury's *Metalogicon* (IV.35, Webb) during the twelfth century.

In the late Middle Ages this reconciliation ceased to be an explicit aim, since the Aristotelian writings that became available for the first time through new translations from Arabic and Greek—especially the *Metaphysics*—suggested opposition rather than harmony between the two ancient systems. Nevertheless, when Thomas Aquinas implied that if Plato had located his intelligible Forms in the mind of God, Aristotle would not have found it necessary to attack him, he was in fact moving back toward the pre-Scholastic synthesis of the two thinkers. For Aquinas

also, the dualisms of intelligible and sensible and of form and matter were basic philosophical postulates.

BIBLIOGRAPHY

Among the excellent studies in French, Henri-Charles Puech, *Le manichéisme* (1949), is perhaps the best introduction. For the medieval resurgence see Steven Runciman, *The Medieval Manichee* (1947). The most informative treatments of Augustine's relation to Manichaeanism are Peter Brown, *Augustine of Hippo: A Biography* (1967), 46–60; and John J. O'Meara, *The Young Augustine* (1954), 61–91. For the monistic heresies see G. C. Capelle, *Amaury de Bène* (1932).

STEPHEN GERSH

[See also **Adelard of Bath; Amalric of Bène; Aquinas, St. Thomas; Aristotle in the Middle Ages; Augustine of Hippo, Saint; Boethius, Anicius Manlius Severinus; John of Salisbury; John Scottus Eriugena; Manichaeans; Plato in the Middle Ages; Priscillian.**]

DUBIIS NOMINIBUS, DE, an alphabetically arranged list of words whose gender, plural form, or spelling was regarded as uncertain. The anonymous writer attempted to clarify these difficulties in each entry, basing his judgment on citations, some of which are otherwise unattested, from classical and Christian authors. The work seems to have been compiled in the early seventh century, possibly in Bordeaux.

BIBLIOGRAPHY

Franciscus Glorie, ed., *Variae collectiones aenigmatum Merovingicae aetatis (pars altera),* in Corpus Christianorum, Series Latina CXXXIII a (1968), 745–820.

MICHAEL HERREN

DUBLIN. Settlement at Dublin in the early historical period probably occurred at two different sites: beside the ford across the Liffey River, *Áth Cliath* (the ford of the hurdles), from which the city takes the Irish form of its name (Baile Átha Cliath); and in the proximity of the black pool *(Dubh Linn)* formed by the Poddle River, the origin of the city's English name. Viking raids on Ireland in the late eighth and early ninth centuries culminated in 841 in the creation of a ship harbor (*longphort*) by the raiders near the black pool. This formed the core of a Scandinavian settlement, which, though interrupted for fifteen years after the expulsion of the invaders in 902, evolved into the later Hiberno-Norse town.

The most important Viking settlement in Ireland, the kingdom of Dublin stood apart from the rest of the country. Distinguished both ethnically and, by its paganism, religiously, it looked toward northwestern Europe. Like its sister kingdom of York in England, Dublin's development in the tenth century was based on its involvement in international trade, and recent archaeological excavations have confirmed its importance as a European commercial center. Its growing prosperity allowed it to play a prominent role in the politics of the British Isles; but its wealth also attracted the envious attentions of Gaelic Irish neighbors, and, inevitably, Dublin became enmeshed in complex struggles for power between rival Irish kingdoms.

The integration of Hiberno-Norse Dublin into Gaelic Ireland was slow, gradual, and ultimately incomplete. The town was unable to maintain its independence against attack, and after 1052 it was always subject to one or another of the strong Gaelic Irish kingdoms. Yet the inhabitants of Dublin, like those of other Scandinavian coastal towns in Ireland, retained a separate identity and continued, up to the thirteenth century, to be distinguished by the title of *Ostmen* (men from the east). Their general acceptance of Christianity in the early eleventh century removed one of the barriers between themselves and the Gaelic Irish, but even as Christians they continued to look elsewhere for guidance and inspiration—to England, which had been conquered by the Normans in 1066. Throughout the late eleventh and early twelfth centuries a succession of bishops of Dublin sought consecration from the archbishop of Canterbury, the leading figure in the English church, rather than from any Irish bishops. Dublin's naval strength continued to attract the interest of England's kings, who wanted the aid of its fleet in their own struggles. Recent archaeological finds have emphasized the strength of Anglo-Norman influence in Dublin even before the first Anglo-Norman invaders arrived in Ireland in 1169.

The fall of Dublin to these new invaders in September 1170 opened a new phase in the town's history. Large numbers of immigrants from England flooded into Dublin in the late twelfth century, and the *Ostmen* were forced out of the town to the north

of the Liffey. The town now became the center of English power in Ireland, a position it was to hold for the next 750 years. Dublin Castle, built in the early thirteenth century, became the headquarters of an administration that presided over a growing English colony within Ireland. Dublin, once a predominantly Norse town, was now a predominantly English one. The inhabitants gave their loyalty to the English crown and regarded the Gaelic natives as "the Irish enemies."

That loyalty was put to one of its most severe tests in 1317, when the town faced attack by a Scottish army under the command of the brothers Robert and Edward Bruce, who had invaded Ireland in an attempt to overthrow English power in the country. As the Scottish forces neared the town, the inhabitants were thrown into a state of near panic. The bridge across the Liffey was destroyed, buildings were torn down to strengthen the town walls, and parts of the suburbs were set on fire. Much damage was done, but the Scots were deterred by this show of resistance and marched away from the city.

Dublin's English or, as it became, Anglo-Irish population never again encountered such a severe threat during the medieval period. But in the later Middle Ages English power in Ireland declined to the point where it was exercised effectively only in the area known as the Pale—Dublin and its immediate environs. The town, finding itself "on the frontier near the Irish enemies," was determined to maintain its English character. Dublin citizenship or membership in any trade guild was restricted to those of English descent, and attempts were made to curb Irish migration into the town. But Dublin could not stand completely apart from the surrounding Gaelic countryside, and prohibitions against the wearing of Gaelic Irish dress are but one indication of the growing Gaelic influence within the town in the later Middle Ages.

Despite an unfavorable political climate and the recurrent threat of plague, Dublin remained prosperous. Secure behind their walls, the inhabitants continued to engage in the trade and commerce on which the town's livelihood depended. Exports of hides and wool and imports of wine, iron, and salt formed the basis of a busy overseas trade. Although it briefly gave its allegiance to the impostor Lambert Simnel, who was crowned king of England as Edward VI in Christ Church Cathedral, Dublin, in 1487, its overall loyalty to the English crown was not in doubt.

BIBLIOGRAPHY

H. B. Clarke, "The Topographical Development of Early Medieval Dublin," in *Journal of the Royal Society of Antiquaries of Ireland,* **107** (1977), and *Dublin c. 840–c. 1540: The Medieval Town in the Modern City* (1978), map of the medieval town with commentary; B. J. Graham, "The Towns of Medieval Ireland," in R. A. Butlin, ed., *The Development of the Irish Town* (1977), 28–60; L. de Paor, "The Viking Towns of Ireland," in Bo Almqvist and David Greene, eds., *Proceedings of the Seventh Viking Congress* (1976), 29–37; B. O Ríordáin, "The High Street Excavations," *ibid.,* 135–140; *Viking and Medieval Dublin, National Museum Excavations, 1962–73; Catalogue of Exhibition* (1973); Patrick Wallace, "The Origins of Dublin," in B. G. Scott, ed., *Studies in Early Ireland, Essays in Honour of M. V. Duignan* (1982), 129–142.

ART COSGROVE

[See also **Ireland, Early History; Ireland Under English Rule.**]

DUBROVNIK (Latin: Ragusium; Italian: Ragusa), city on the eastern coast of the Adriatic Sea. According to tradition it was founded in the early seventh century, on a rock separated from the mainland by a channel, by refugees from nearby Epidaurus. Well-fortified and under Byzantine domination, it withstood Arab attacks in 866–867. Between 1000 and 1030 Dubrovnik recognized Venetian supremacy, then returned to Byzantine rule and was the seat of a Byzantine theme. In 1022 it became an archbishopric. Normans dominated the city in 1081–1085, 1172, and 1189–1190, and Venetian rule returned in 1205.

After mines opened in Serbia (mid thirteenth century) and Bosnia (early fourteenth century), copper, iron, lead, and large quantities of silver flowed through Dubrovnik onto Western markets. The metal and maritime trade constituted the base of the city's prosperity between the fourteenth and sixteenth centuries. In the thirteenth century the strongly slavicized city was enlarged and encircled by walls. Planned urban growth took place, and social and administrative structures developed toward a patrician city-republic, with a Major Council and a Minor Council, a Senate, and a Venetian count until 1358. After that a local patrician was elected rector for one month at a time.

The Cathedral of St. Mary the Great, built prob-

ably with some financial help from Richard I of England, was completed in the first half of the fourteenth century, and a beautiful rector's palace was built from the thirteenth to the fifteenth century. Physicians and pharmacists were hired by the government from the thirteenth century on. One of the oldest pharmacies in Europe was founded in Dubrovnik in 1317, a hospital for the poor was organized in 1347, and an orphanage was established in 1432. In 1377 quarantine was instituted, but bubonic plague remained frequent. The institution of quarantine in Dubrovnik is the oldest instance of the practice in Europe. Between 1046 and 1414 almost all wooden houses were replaced by stone ones. In 1436 an excellent sewage system was begun, and in 1436–1438 an aqueduct was built; both are still functioning.

A local school of painting flourished, with Nikolas Božidarević (*ca.* 1460–1517) and Mihajlo Hamzić (late fifteenth–early sixteenth centuries) as important artists. A lively literature developed, including increasing numbers of works influenced by Italian models but written in the Slavic language and containing Slavic folk elements. The most famous authors were Marin Držić (1508–1567), who wrote comedies, and the poet Djivo Gundulić (1589–1638).

After Venetian domination ceased in 1358, Dubrovnik accepted the protection of the kings of Hungary, though the city was practically independent. It established contacts with the Ottomans in the late fourteenth century, and from 1478 it paid 12,500 ducats as annual tribute to the sultan. The Hungarian protectorate ended in 1526, when Dubrovnik placed itself under Ottoman protection and enjoyed Spanish friendship in the West.

BIBLIOGRAPHY

The best surveys of Dubrovnik's medieval history are Milan Prelog, in *Historija naroda Jugoslavije,* I (1953), 654–660, and Jorjo Tadić, *ibid.,* 629–654. A voluminous but very unreliable overview is F. W. Carter, *Dubrovnik: The Classic City-state* (1972). See also Bariša Krekić, *Dubrovnik (Raguse) et le Levant au moyen âge* (1961), *Dubrovnik in the 14th and 15th Centuries* (1972), and *Dubrovnik, Italy and the Balkans in the Late Middle Ages* (1980). Another recent work is Vinko Foretić, *Povijest Dubrovnika do 1808,* 2 vols. (1980).

BARIŠA KREKIĆ

[See also **Bosnia; Croatia; Russian and Slavic Art; Serbia; Slavic Language and Literature.**]

Gold Ducat. Venice, 1284–1289. THE AMERICAN NUMISMATIC SOCIETY
Gold Florin. Florence, 1256. THE AMERICAN NUMISMATIC SOCIETY
Gold Nomisma. Constantinople, 545–565. THE AMERICAN NUMISMATIC SOCIETY

DUCAT, a Venetian gold coin, also called a zechin or sequin, first struck and issued in 1284. Consisting of approximately 3.5 grams of pure gold (24 carats), its weight and fineness remained remarkably stable until the end of the Venetian Republic. After 1284 the city magistrates ordered that all payments, including interest on public debt, be made in or be based on the ducat.

Earlier in the thirteenth century Venice had attempted to solve its major currency problem of lacking a sufficiently large coin denomination, coupled with a dwindling supply of silver, by minting a large silver coin called a groat or grosso and equating it to twenty-four denarii or common pennies. Still, silver coinage sufficed mainly for the needs of local trade and proved a hindrance to large-scale merchants and bankers engaged in long-distance transactions. To solve this problem, Venice issued the ducat and valued it at twenty-four groats.

The ducat (*ducato d'oro*) has been called the "dollar of the Middle Ages" by modern numismatic and economic historians, a title bestowed on three other gold coins of the later Middle Ages: the Florentine florin (about 3.5 grams), the Byzantine nomisma or solidus (about 4.5 grams), and the Muslim

dinar (about 4.25 grams). During the fifteenth century it enjoyed its greatest reputation, owing to the phenomenal expansion of the Venetian economy in international commercial relations, and it served at the same time as the standard on which Christian and Muslim rulers throughout the Mediterranean world reformed their coinage; among the most important were the Mamluk *ashrafti,* the Ottoman *altun,* the Portuguese crusado, and the Castilian *ducato.* Its strength for almost two centuries rested principally on its high unitary value, its intrinsic stability in both weight and alloy, and its association with a successful Venetian regional and interregional economy.

On the obverse of the coin was an effigy of the reigning doge kneeling and receiving a banner from St. Mark, the patron saint of Venice. On the reverse was an image of Christ in the marketplace, together with the inscription *Sit tibi, Christe, datus quem tu regis iste ducatus* (May the sovereignty that you exercise be accorded you, O Christ). It is from this last word that the ducat received its name.

BIBLIOGRAPHY

Carlo M. Cipolla, *Money, Prices, and Civilization in the Mediterranean World: Fifth to Seventeenth Century* (1956); Allan Evans, "Some Coinage Systems of the Fourteenth Century," in *Journal of Economic and Business History,* 3 (1931).

RONALD EDWARD ZUPKO

[See also **Mints and Money, Byzantine; Mints and Money, Islamic; Mints and Money, Western European.**]

DUCCIO DI BUONINSEGNA (*ca.* 1255–1260–*ca.* 1318), Sienese painter considered the "father of Sienese painting." His early Rucellai madonna (in the Uffizi, Florence), certainly the one referred to in a document of commission dated 15 April 1285, was famous from the time it was painted for the chapel of the Laudesi in S. Maria Novella, Florence. After a centuries-long attribution of the work to Duccio's Florentine contemporary Cimabue, a debate over that attribution began, to be resolved only in modern times. During much of that time distinctions between Florentine and Sienese painting were obscured. The work is informed with elegance and grace, inspired partly, no doubt, by Duccio's firsthand knowledge of recent French sculpture and il-

The Maestà, front panel, Virgin and Child with Angels and Saints. Duccio, 1308–1311, Museo dell'Opera della Cattedrale, Siena. ALINARI

luminated manuscripts. It typifies Sienese style and is an accurate forecaster of Sienese artistic taste of the next few centuries.

It has been supposed that Duccio traveled to France in his early years; this would explain the French mode already apparent in what may be his earliest extant work, the *Madonna of the Franciscans* (*ca.* 1279–1280). But besides a keen appreciation of French manuscripts and stained glass (even of St. Louis's royal ateliers), the *Madonna of the Franciscans* shows the fundamental importance to Duccio of the Florentine master Cimabue—for instance, in the throne of a type that Cimabue had recently devised for his *Madonna with St. Francis* in the Lower Church of St. Francis of Assisi.

A document of 1302 attests a payment to Duccio for a *Maestà* with a predella for the chapel of the governors in the Palazzo Pubblico, Siena; although this has been lost, the attempts to reconstruct it reveal surprisingly innovative tendencies, especially in comparison with some of the conservative elements found in the later *Maestà*. By contrast, his half-length madonnas—the one formerly in the Stoclet collection at Brussels, the one in the Perugia gallery, and the small enthroned madonna in the National Gallery, London—reveal Duccio's lingering attachment to Byzantine form and, in the bittersweet sentiment of his Virgins' faces, to Byzantine pathos.

The *Maestà* painted for the Siena cathedral between 1308 and 1311 is the last important statement of Duccio's art, made at a distance of a quarter of a century from his Rucellai madonna. In the figure of the Virgin and her assembled court of worshipers, considerable influence of Giotto can be recognized: the full light on the Virgin's knees and thighs, so similar to that in Giotto's contemporary Ognissanti madonna, marks a distinct change from those linear, two-dimensional refinements of his earlier Rucellai madonna. It is almost certain that Duccio and a number of his pupils collaborated on this immense project.

Other works, even some of very high quality often ascribed to Duccio's hand, reveal the participation of the workshop: the tabernacles in Boston and the National Gallery, London; polyptychs no. 28 and no. 47 in the Siena Pinacoteca. The evidence suggests a sizable shop in which most young Sienese painters of the early fourteenth century learned their craft. Some pupils, such as Pietro and Ambrogio Lorenzetti and Simone Martini, revealed their own styles soon after they left the master's shop. Others, including Segna di Bonaventura and Ugolino di Nerio—among the closest and most distinguished of Duccio's followers—always adhered to his artistic language: Segna, sculpturesque in form and somber in tone; Ugolino, more emotionally intense in his

302

Saint Agnes, detail from the front panel of the Maestà. Duccio, 1308–1311, Museo dell'Opera della Cattedrale, Siena. SCALA/ART RESOURCE

distillation of Duccio's art. The amount of Duccio-style painting remaining to us today is considerable. About thirty distinct hands can be isolated before the last traces of Duccio's style died away toward the middle of the fourteenth century.

BIBLIOGRAPHY

Cesare Brandi, *Duccio* (1951); Enzo Carli, *Duccio di Buoninsegna* (1962), with 69 plates; James H. Stubblebine, *Duccio di Buoninsegna and His School*, 2 vols. (1979); Curt H. Weigelt, *Duccio di Buoninsegna. Studien zur Geschichte der frühsienesischen Tafelmalerei* (1911); John White, *Duccio: Tuscan Art and the Medieval Workshop* (1979).

JAMES H. STUBBLEBINE

[See also **Cimabue; Giotto di Bondone; Lorenzetti, Ambrogio; Lorenzetti, Pietro; Segna di Bonaventura; Simone Martini.**]

DUCHY, an aristocratic domain that derived from both Roman and Germanic traditions. In the late Roman Empire, *duces* were military commanders (and from the mid sixth century civilian commanders) of frontier areas. Migration-period Germanic peoples were often led by *duces,* apparently nonroyal military leaders (Byzantine Greek: *reiks*) who, through victory, came in time to acquire royal authority.

In Merovingian Francia dukes, along with patricians *(patricii)* and governors *(rectores),* were leaders of quasi-independent peripheral peoples such as the Gascons, Saxons, Bavarians, and Frisians, and of regions such as Burgundy and Provence. "Service dukes" were important, powerful military leaders sometimes entrusted by Merovingian kings with other administrative and judicial roles. In both cases the title of duke implied the extremely high, quasi-royal status of the bearer. Although initially dukes were apparently appointed by Merovingian kings, in the later seventh century, as royal power waned, dukes and patricians consolidated their power in their regions, which they developed into hereditary petty kingdoms. Gradually other ducal families were defeated and deposed by the Arnulfings, who ultimately replaced the royal family and established the Carolingian dynasty.

As a result of their healthy mistrust of an institution that had aided their own usurpation of royal dignity, the Carolingians largely suppressed the office of duke, using the term only rarely to designate counts with temporary mandates (usually military) over large regions or with command over troops from a number of counties.

The tenth century saw the reappearance of the title, though initially it was a supplemental designation of a count or a marquis. The title was particularly used in the great duchies or territorial units emerging in this period: Bavaria, Aquitaine, Normandy, Lotharingia, Saxony, Swabia, and Franconia. Particularly in the eastern part of the old Frankish empire, the so-called *Stammesherzogtum,* or stem or tribal duchies, of Bavaria, Saxony, Swabia, Lorraine, and Franconia, under the leadership of their dukes, became the essential elements of the formation of the medieval German Empire. These duchies, despite their names, were almost certainly not the continuations of old, pre-Carolingian ethnic or tribal units, but rather regions in which the aristocracy was drawn together and united under particularly powerful families that had been put into place by the Carolingians. In France the title was never given to some very powerful rulers (such as the count of Flanders) and was assumed only slowly by others (Normandy in the late tenth century, Brittany in the thirteenth century). In England the title appeared only in the late fourteenth century and had little territorial significance.

BIBLIOGRAPHY

Karl Brunner, "Der fränkische Fürstentitel im neunten und zehnten Jahrhundert," in Herwig Wolfram, *Intitulatio*, II, *Lateinische Herrscher- und Fürstentitel im neunten und zehnten Jahrhundert* (1973), 211–214; Walther Kienast, *Der Herzogstitel in Frankreich und Deutschland (9. bis 12. Jahrhundert)* (1968); Archibald R. Lewis, "The Dukes in the *Regnum Francorum*, A.D. 550–751," in *Speculum*, 51 (1976); Herwig Wolfram, *Intitulatio*, I, *Lateinische Königs- und Fürstentitel bis zum Ende des 8. Jahrhunderts* (1967).

PATRICK GEARY

[See also **Aquitaine; Bavaria, Brittany; Burgundy; Carolingians and the Carolingian Empire; Dux; Germany: Stem Duchies; Merovingians; Normans and Normandy; Provence; Roman Empire, Late; Saxony, Duchy of; Swabia, Duchy of.**]

DUDO OF ST. QUENTIN (d. ca. 1043), a monk, was commissioned in 994 by Richard I, duke of Normandy, to write a history of the Normans. Dudo completed the chronicle during the reign of Richard II, who then appointed him dean of the monastery of St. Quentin. Dudo's history was used as a source by William of Jumièges.

BIBLIOGRAPHY

Jules Lair, ed., *De moribus et actis primorum Normaniae ducum*, Mémoires de la société des antiquaires de Normandie, XXIII (1865); Max Manitius, *Geschichte der lateinischen Literatur*, II (1923), 257–265; *Monumenta Germaniae historica, Scriptores*, IV (1841), 93–106.

NATHALIE HANLET

[See also **Normans and Normandy; William of Jumièges.**]

DUGENTO (DUECENTO) ART, the art of Italy produced between 1200 and 1300. Economic growth, a spiritual revival (as demonstrated by St. Francis of Assisi), and thriving metropolitan centers all contributed to the emergence of several important schools of Italian painting and sculpture, including those of Pisa, Lucca, Siena, Venice, Rome, and Florence. These centers set the stage for the great flowering of the arts in Trecento Italy; among their notable leaders were Nicola and Giovanni Pisano, sculptors; the painter Berlinghiero Berlinghieri and his sons Bonaventura, Barone, and Marco (all of Lucca), Guido da Siena the painter and his contemporary Coppo di Marcovaldo of Florence, as well as the Florentine sculptor Arnolfo di Cambio.

BIBLIOGRAPHY

John White, *Art and Architecture in Italy, 1250–1400* (1966).

ADELHEID M. GEALT

[See also **Arnolfo di Cambio; Berlinghieri, Bonaventura; Coppo di Marcovaldo; Giovanni Pisano; Guido da Siena; Nicola Pisano.**]

DUKE. See Duchy.

DUKUS HORANT, a poetical fragment, the last and longest of eight items constituting a manuscript written in Ashkenazic script from the Cairo Genizah. The manuscript, written in 1382–1383, is currently part of the Taylor-Schechter Collection of Cambridge University Library and carries the signature T-S. 10. K. 22. Since the first publication of its texts by Lajb Fuks in 1957, it has been the center of lively controversy, in respect to both its language and its place in literary history. There are cogent arguments in favor of an identification of the language of the texts of the manuscript as Old Yiddish as well as "substantially German," that is, Middle High German.

That the narrative matter of *Dukus Horant* emanates from German heroic epic material is beyond question. It is a tale of bridal abduction reminiscent of *Kudrun* and *König Rother*. The hero of the title, Horant, plays a less central, but similar, role in *Kudrun*: in both poems he is sent—by King Etene in *Dukus Horant*, by Hetel in *Kudrun*—to sue for the hand of Hilde, daughter of Hagen (here of Greece, in *Kudrun* of Ireland); his singing is an essential component of the plot to abduct Hilde in both narratives, and the giants Witold and Asprian perform a role similar to that accorded them in *König Rother*. And the *Kudrun* hero Wate turns up in company with the giants in *Dukus Horant*. There is no lack of other parallels, which are discussed in detail in the introduction to the edition by P. F. Ganz, F. Norman, and W. Schwarz. Some motifs that occur neither in *Kudrun* nor in *König Rother* may have originated in a hypothetical Song of Herbort, which in vague outlines is recognizable in the *Þiðreks saga* and in *Biterolf*. The poem is written in a strophic form resembling the "Rabenschlachtstrophe," but without the rhyme in the caesura and with free variation between masculine and feminine rhymes in the second half of the stanza. Irregularities in the rhythm are abundant, and the variety of rhymes as well as of vocabulary is noticeably limited.

The paucity in lexical variation is due to the heavily oral-formulaic style of the poem, which unquestionably originated in the oral tradition, both as a text as well as in terms of its narrative components. Whether the text transmitted in the Genizah manuscript is relatively close to the oral transmission or is based on a number of written antecedents is difficult to say with certainty. The formulaic density and the metrical irregularities of the text, however, make an assumption of its relative closeness to oral transmission justified, though it is extremely unlikely that the transmitted text, as component of a manuscript consisting of a variety of texts, is derived directly from an oral performance. It is probably a copy of an Ashkenazic written text, which may itself have been transcribed from a Middle High German model. Whatever the case, the manuscript testifies to an interest in German heroic narrative on the part of a Jewish public.

BIBLIOGRAPHY

Sources. P. F. Ganz, F. Norman, and W. Schwarz, eds., *Dukus Horant* (1964), with excursus by S. A. Birnbaum; Heikki J. Hakkarainen, *Studien zum Cambridger Codex T-S. 10. K. 22*, I, *Text* (1967), contains a full bibliography to 1967; Eli Katz, "Six Germano-Judaic Poems from the Cairo Genizah" (Ph.D. diss., Univ. of California, Los Angeles, 1963).

Studies. Manfred Caliebe, *"Dukus Horant." Studien zu seiner literarischen Tradition* (1973); Lajb Fuks, *The Oldest Known Literary Documents of Yiddish Literature* (1957); Walter Röll and Christoph Gerhardt, "Zur literarhistorischen Einordnung des sog. *Dukus Horant*," in *Deutsche Vierteljahrsschrift für Literaturwissenschaft und Geistesgeschichte*, **41** (1967).

                                    Franz H. Bauml

[See also **Kudrun; König Rother; Middle High German Literature**.]

DUMA, the designation given to a princely council in medieval Russia. Despite its longevity as an institution, not much is known about the competence and composition of the duma for most of its existence, thereby occasioning conflicting scholarly opinions. A few historians believe that duma sessions were simply ad hoc convocations of people whom the prince trusted; the majority hold that the duma was a permanent institution with defined membership and competence. The narrative sources, always brief and often fragmentary, allude to a wide variety of consultations with influential landholders, close confidants, senior clergy, or military chieftains. Whether all such convocations may be classified as "dumas" is debatable, for a duma would need to have continuity, permanence, and defined authority. While consultation was not a constitutional requirement, it was a practical necessity.

The most important laymen in the many Russian principalities were the ranking servitors, free men in service who were bound to the prince by common interest rather than by contract or law. A tradition, enshrined in treaties between princes, permitted free servitors to transfer to another lord's banner whenever they so desired. Since warfare was frequent and the loyalty of warriors vitally necessary, consultation between a prince and his military chieftains was mandatory. These untitled senior servitors (called boyars) became the permanent members of the duma. The boyars staffed the principal offices of administration. Some looked after the princely domains, others supervised the collection of revenues, while still others became governors of key fortresses and provinces.

Members of the duma, when resident at court, headed commissions to review judicial findings in lower courts and made recommendations to the prince concerning disposition of cases. They were also assigned to see that judgments were executed. The role of councillors became particularly important during the minority of a prince, or when he was feeble or incapacitated.

The greatest evolution of the duma occurred in Muscovy, in connection with its expansion at the expense of neighboring principalities. In the fourteenth and early fifteenth centuries Muscovy was governed as a patrimonial principality. The senior prince consulted with his councillors and with his close relatives. Each of the junior princes inherited a share of his father's possessions and had an interest in protecting the family's interests. Fortunately for Muscovy the number of family princes was small.

This reduced opportunities to challenge the senior prince's councillors.

During the minority of Dmitrii Donskoi in the mid fourteenth century, the boyars fought off external challenges to the authority of Moscow and preserved the young prince's legacy. Their importance waned momentarily when Donskoi died (1389), leaving five sons, but became pivotal when some of the inheritors challenged the seniority of the eldest son. The role of the steadfast servitors who helped to ensure victory for the senior prince in the second quarter of the fifteenth century and the duplicity of a number of the family princes led to the greater authority of the duma.

Thereafter the senior prince consulted almost exclusively with his duma in matters of state. Its boyars commanded the armies of Muscovy. The junior family princes could lead only their own contingents, while watched by members of the council. After the annexation of the extensive territories of Novgorod in 1478, the viceroy was always a boyar.

The expanding business of government no longer permitted councillors to be routinely assigned as governors in lesser jurisdictions. They advised the prince, supervised the expanding departments of government, participated in diplomatic affairs, nominated the governors, and had considerable influence in choosing regimental officers. In effect, they supervised the day-to-day business of government. The social composition of the duma remained aristocratic. When Vasilii II named several lowborn supporters as boyars in the later phases of the dynastic struggle, the aristocratic members stubbornly resisted the precedent and eventually won; but the untitled aristocrats could not keep out servitor princes rewarded for similar services.

Throughout the fifteenth century the ruler sought to ensure the loyalty of the duma by naming as the senior councillor one who was related to him by marriage. In principle, those chosen as members of the duma were the ablest, most experienced, and most loyal; in fact, a number were selected because they came from the most illustrious serving families and others because they were related to sitting members. But almost all had to serve long years of apprenticeship at court—at least twenty-five to thirty years for appointment as boyars and a somewhat shorter time to become *okol'nichie,* the second-level duma members. The number of *okol'nichie* increased during the latter part of the fifteenth century, thereby reducing the number of boyars (when the council averaged only about twelve members).

Okol'nichie were charged with the growing volume of administrative, ceremonial, and judicial functions. They were eligible for promotion to senior rank after ten to twenty years in office.

By 1500 the duma had become the most important Muscovite institution. Its members had great social status and exerted considerable influence upon the careers of the upper service aristocracy, as well as upon those lower in the service order. Their rewards were commensurate with their office and status. But the authority of the duma went only as far as the governing prince allowed. Those who displeased him were disgraced, deposed, stripped of their wealth, and even executed, all without recourse to any judicial process. Ivan III (1462–1505) expelled more councillors in his forty-three years as the ruler of Muscovy than did all the Capetian kings in their three and a half centuries of existence. With the consolidation of Muscovite power and the disappearance of rival principalities, the councillors of the realm no longer possessed the substantive authority to oppose their lord. The duma had become the instrument of an autocratic ruler.

BIBLIOGRAPHY

Gustave Alef, "Reflections on the Boyar Duma in the Reign of Ivan III," in *Slavonic and East European Review,* 45 (1967); Horace W. Dewey, ed. and trans., *Muscovite Judicial Texts, 1488–1556,* Michigan Slavic Materials, VII (1966), 9–21 (see section of the 1497 law code pertaining to boyar involvement in judicial affairs); Ann M. Kleimola, *Justice in Medieval Russia* (1975), 13; Vasilii O. Kliuchevskii, *Boiarskaia duma drevnei Rusi,* 5th ed. (1919); Richard Pipes, *Russia Under the Old Regime* (1974), 106; Vasilii Sergeevich, *Russkiia iuridicheskiia drevnosti,* 2nd ed., II (1900), 337–417.

GUSTAVE ALEF

[See also **Boyar; Muscovy.**]

DUNATOI (or *potentes* or *potentiores* in the legislation of Theodosius II and Justinian I) is found in fourth-century texts and continued to be used through the fifteenth century; its literal meaning is "powerful." In Byzantine usage it had social connotations, designating individuals who had great wealth and/or political power in the countryside or (in the fourth century) in the cities. In the legislation of the Macedonians, the term was used to describe those who were able to oppress economically the bulk of the population. A novella of Romanos I (934) opposes the powerful to the *penetes* and describes the *dunatoi* as those who are *magistri* or patricians, *strategoi* or holders of high civil or military office, members of the senate, high ecclesiastics, or administrators of pious or imperial foundations.

Beginning with Constantine the Great and until the eleventh century, the Byzantine state waged a struggle against the *dunatoi*. In the fifth century the powerful used legal and illegal means to increase their fiscal revenues by extending their lands (through the absorption of lands of peasants who could not pay their taxes) or their immunities. They had their own prisons and their private armies *(bucellarii)*. Justinian I (527–565) was particularly active against them, since their power diminished both the authority and the revenues of the state.

The struggle took its most acute form during the Macedonian period, starting with a novella of Romanos I (922). He and his successors opposed the powerful because, by buying lands that belonged to the peasants, they eroded the economic and fiscal basis of the village community, thus destroying the greatest source of taxes and soldiers. The Macedonians took a series of measures that limited the rights of nonmembers of the community to acquire village lands and annulled any sale of peasant lands that had been made under duress or against the law. In 996 Basil II took the most drastic measures against the powerful, annulling all land sales by the *penetes* to them since 922 and confiscating the property of great magnates. Later he forced them to pay the taxes of poor peasants *(allelengyon)*. After his death the struggle against the *dunatoi*, always a difficult one, was essentially abandoned, since his successors were unable or unwilling to carry it through.

BIBLIOGRAPHY

Alexander P. Každan, *Derevnja i gorod v Vizantii ix–x vv.* (1960); Paul Lemerle, "Esquisse pour une histoire agraire de Byzance," in *Revue historique*, **219** (1958); George Ostrogorsky, *Quelques problèmes d'histoire de la paysannerie byzantine* (1956).

ANGELIKI LAIOU

[See also **Byzantine Economy and Society; Penetes; Romanos I Lekapenos.**]

DUNBAR, WILLIAM, a court poet to James IV of Scotland and, together with Henryson and Douglas, one of the three important Middle Scots poets. Very little is known about his life. He is presumably the

William Dunbar who appears on the list of determinants (B.A.s) at St. Andrews for 1477, and on the list of licentiates for 1479, which might suggest a birth date of about 1455. His name appears more than thirty times in the records between 1500 and 1513 as a priest and, usually, as the recipient of a pension from James: all of his poems that can be dated from internal evidence (about a third of the eighty or so that survive) fall within this period. He disappears from the records after 1513, the year James died at the Battle of Flodden.

Dunbar's poems are mostly short (the surviving corpus amounts to only about 6,000 lines) and are remarkable for the extreme heterogeneity of their genres and stylistic levels. Two of his longest and most famous poems, "The Tretis of the Tua Mariit Wemen and the Wedo" and "The Flyting of Dunbar and Kennedie," are filled with scurrilous invective and bawdry, and some of his other poems vigorously describe the seamier side of court life. There is a group of moral lyrics in what might be called a middle style; the best known of these is the "Lament for the Makaris." Then there are a few fine and lofty religious poems, as well as a compressed and ornate love allegory, "The Goldyn Targe," and some bejeweled courtly poems. But this list gives only a sampling of his variety: Dunbar is, for instance, one of the great masters of the petitionary poem and the author of some brilliant comic poems.

While Dunbar has sometimes been called a "Scottish Chaucerian," this label is very misleading. It is true that his metrics, diction, and rhetoric are in part descended from Chaucer (often by way of Lydgate); it is true, too, that he sometimes writes in Chaucerian genres. But as poets Chaucer and Dunbar could hardly be more different. Where Chaucer typically uses a bumbling, involved, and anxiously seeking persona, Dunbar's poetry is essentially impersonal: when he does use a persona, it tends to be a conventional and simple one. The resulting ambiguities, uncertainties, and complexities of Chaucer's verse are absent in Dunbar, whose verse is clear, precise, and static, a poetry of statement. Dunbar seems to have been a court poet par excellence, someone who could turn out a perfectly fashioned poem in any mode and on any subject. His poetry has undoubted limitations, but his craftsmanship has hardly been surpassed by later English or Scottish poets.

BIBLIOGRAPHY

The best edition is now James Kinsley, ed., *The Poems of William Dunbar* (1979). It does not include the numerous poems, some of them excellent, that have been attributed to Dunbar on little or no evidence. For a more literary approach, see C. S. Lewis, *English Literature in the Sixteenth Century* (1954), 90–98; and Edwin Morgan, "Dunbar and the Language of Poetry," in *Essays in Criticism*, **2** (1952). Bibliographies are in Albert E. Hartung, ed., *A Manual of the Writings in Middle English*, IV (1973), 1005–1060, and 1204–1284; and George Watson, ed., *The New Cambridge Bibliography of English Literature*, I (1974), 660–662.

DENTON FOX

[See also **Middle English Literature.**]

DUNCAN I OF SCOTLAND (*ca.* 1010/1020–1040). According to John of Fordun (possibly using a lost early source), Duncan's grandfather, Malcolm II, made him king of Cumbria (Strathclyde). There is some twelfth-century confirmation of this. Malcolm also killed—though not necessarily in person—other male members of the royal family so that Duncan, son of Malcolm's daughter Bethoc and of Crinan, abbot of Dunkeld, might succeed—a remarkable breach in succession from kindred in the male line. Duncan was thus the first ruler of all mainland Scotland as now understood. In 1039 he led a great raid to besiege Durham but was heavily defeated. In the following year, while Duncan was still a young man, Macbeth, mormaer (provincial ruler) of Moray, had him killed at Elgin. Shakespeare's old Duncan is derived ultimately from the fanciful history of Scotland by Hector Boece (1526).

BIBLIOGRAPHY

A. A. M. Duncan, *Scotland: The Making of the Kingdom* (1975).

A. A. M. DUNCAN

[See also **Macbeth; Scotland.**]

DUNGEON, from the French *donjon,* the strongest, and in the early Middle Ages the only, tower of a castle. It was sometimes also called the keep. There were no windows in the lower part of the tower because they would have weakened the walls. The dungeon was a safe, if uncomfortable, place to keep prisoners, and came to be used primarily for this purpose

as more luxurious quarters for the lord and his retinue were added to the castle complex.

JOSEPH R. STRAYER

[See also **Castles and Fortifications.**]

DUNS SCOTUS, JOHN (*ca.* 1266–1308), Franciscan friar, philosopher, and theologian. Born in Duns, Scotland, the future *doctor subtilis* began his education with his uncle, Elias Duns, a Franciscan, at the friary of Dumfries, and entered the Franciscan order at the age of fifteen. Some nine years later he was ordained a priest at Northampton (1291), having begun his studies at Oxford the previous year. Following his ordination Duns Scotus went to Paris to study for the *magister* in theology. A student of Gonsalvus of Spain between 1293 and 1296, he did not take the degree but returned to Oxford and commented on the *Sentences* of Peter Lombard from 1297 to 1301. The following year he returned to Paris, where he commented on the *Sentences* for either a second or a third time, but had to leave in 1303 when he sided with Pope Boniface VIII in his quarrel with Philip IV the Fair. His exile, however, was short-lived, and Duns Scotus returned to his studies the next year, completing them in 1305 and occupying the Franciscan chair at the university until 1307. He then went to Cologne, where he lectured until his death on 8 November 1308, at the age of forty-two.

Of all Duns Scotus' works the commentaries on the *Sentences,* available today in various forms, are the most important. The earlier commentary done at Oxford, known as the *Lectura prima,* was later reworked into the *Ordinatio* (or, as it was formerly known, the *Opus Oxoniense*). It seems probable that there is also an earlier version produced at Cambridge sometime before 1300 and therefore known as the *Reportatio Cantabrigiensis.* There is also the *Reportata Parisiensia,* based on the *Ordinatio* and produced in the course of Duns Scotus' Paris lectures. To these commentaries may be added the *Theoremata,* the *Tractatus de primo principio* (but not the *De rerum principio quaestiones XXVI*), some *Quaestiones disputatae* and *Quaestiones quodlibetales,* and some commentaries on the works of Aristotle—the *Super Perihermeneias,* the *Super libros elenchorum,* the *De praedicamentis,* the *De anima* and *Metaphysica* (books I–IX)—and the *Quaestiones super universalia* of Porphyry.

An Aristotelian at heart and frankly skeptical of much of the Augustinian philosophical paraphernalia (he was the first of the Franciscans to discard the Augustinian teaching on the need for a special divine illumination in order to know genuine and certain truth), Duns Scotus found himself in a difficult position in light of the condemnation of certain forms of Aristotelianism in 1277. Propositions attributed not just to Aristotle and Averroës (Ibn Rushd) but even to Thomas Aquinas having been condemned, Duns Scotus had to exercise the utmost discretion and care in developing his unique solutions to the philosophical and theological problems confronting him. The problems were a legacy of his predecessors, especially Henry of Ghent, principal architect of the attempt to restore Augustinianism to its favored position at the University of Paris during his sojourn there from 1276 to 1292.

The solutions of Duns Scotus could leave nothing to chance, nothing to presumption. Everything philosophical had to be explained in the minutest detail; every point had to be defended; every conceivable objection had to be dealt with on the spot. The result is a wealth of tortuous detail at almost every point in his thought. Every simplification, no matter how innocent or inconspicuous, runs the risk of being an oversimplification; even the most tested generalization admits almost as many exceptions as cases covered. If ever a medieval title was deserved, *doctor subtilis* was deserved by Duns Scotus.

In both philosophy and theology, however, certain central and indispensable features of his thought can be pointed out. Being, says Duns Scotus, must be predicated univocally of all that is. This is so because the primary object of the human intellect cannot be God, as the Augustinian tradition would have it (though admittedly God is its highest object), nor can it be the essences of material things, as the Aristotelians would have it. To opt for either is in fact to exclude some being from its right to be known and is to begin philosophy with an unwarranted and arbitrary restriction on the powers of the human intellect.

The proper and per se object of the human intellect must, therefore, be being in its widest extension. Being is universal, but not a genus, for, as Parmenides had stated, there is nothing but being that could be added to being. Any differences in being must come from within being after the fashion of *for-*

malitates or intrinsic modes. God and creatures are intrinsic modes of being, though being is predicated univocally of both. The transcendentals (the one, the true, the good, and so forth) are formalities of being. Since we are dealing here with the predication of being, Duns Scotus cannot be accused of some variety of pantheism or emanationism. His followers, however, were often at a loss to explain the presence of *formalitates* and modalities in being.

In a more Augustinian and less Aristotelian vein, Duns Scotus' metaphysics allows a positive status to prime matter that permits it to be spoken of not as pure potentiality but, rather, as a definite something in its own right that is capable of having further perfections added to it. He avoids the trap of an infinite regress of forms, establishing unity in the composite of positive matter and its forms by maintaining that matter and form are in the very first instance essentially, and not just accidentally, ordered to each other. The union of matter and form is such that one substance results, and not a substance and an accident.

Holding, as did Avicenna (Ibn Sīnā), that being is indifferent to all its further modifications *(equinitas est tantum equinitas)*, Duns Scotus maintained that a being is neither universal nor singular in itself, but only in virtue of something added to it. Thus, in every being there is a common nature *(natura communis)*—and being itself is often treated by Scotus as though it were a common nature—that is made either singular or universal by an appropriate principle that, like prime matter and every other reality in Duns Scotus, must be a positive something. This modality of being whereby a common nature is turned into an individual is frequently referred to in the literature on Duns Scotus as "thisness" *(haecceitas)*, though it must be admitted that this terminology is found but infrequently in his work. More often than not he speaks only of the principle of individuation.

This individuation of the common nature takes place through the form of the entity (or, rather, through several forms) progressively actualizing the entity and making it to be more and more individually what it is. Thus, matter has as its first form that of corporeity *(forma corporeitatis)*, making it into a physical body. Corporeity is used by Duns Scotus to account for the corpse of the dead person maintaining for a time its likeness to the living individual. The form of corporeity prepares matter to receive another form, called soul, which further actualizes the common nature of humanity—for instance, as this individual man—and it remains when the soul has departed the body.

The metaphysics of Duns Scotus, then, allows for a great deal of diversity and multiplicity within the unity of the being in question. Unity is not necessarily destroyed by distinction, though Duns Scotus of course recognizes the situation in which two realities are in fact distinct as thing and thing. He recognizes, that is, a real distinction. He also acknowledges the situation in which unity is left totally undisturbed, where a distinction of reason alone prevails and the two supposed "realities" differ in name only. But between these two types of distinction, Duns Scotus locates a third, called the formal distinction (distinctio formalis a parte rei), which obtains between different formalitates within the unified object.

It is as difficult to account for the functioning of the formal distinction in Duns Scotus as it is to account for the functioning of a Platonic Idea or Form. It seems that the most that can be said is that a formalitas has enough reality to keep it from being simply a being of reason and just enough of the being of reason about it to keep it from being a concretely existing thing. There are similar problems with the intentional distinction and the intentiones of Henry of Ghent.

Inasmuch as the chief area of application of the formal distinction is to the human soul and its powers, and to the powers of the soul in relation to each other (the soul is distinct from its powers by virtue of a formal distinction; those powers are distinct from each other in virtue of the same kind of distinction), it may be surmised that Duns Scotus affirmed the formal distinction with a view toward preserving the unity of man, at the same time acknowledging the diversity of his operations (e.g. sensing, understanding, and willing).

Indeed, the metaphysics of Duns Scotus may fairly be characterized as dominated throughout by this passion for unity. It was evident from the outset, when Duns Scotus opted for the univocity of being. It is still further evident in his insistence that the transcendentals of being, like the soul and its powers, are distinct from being and from each other by a formal distinction only. The pluralism of Aristotelian metaphysics, in its strained tension with the thrust toward unity so evident in Augustinian metaphysics, is sharply captured in Duns Scotus' formal distinction. The condemnation of 1277 is not far in the background.

It is evident that Duns Scotus is concerned, first and foremost, with the metaphysical essences of things. This concern is perhaps nowhere more evident than in his exceedingly complex proof for the existence of God, in which he clearly inclines more toward the wisdom of Augustine and Anselm than toward the more existence-oriented approach of Aquinas. From the intrinsic possibility of all being that is other than that which can be at least postulated as necessary, he moves to the possible-to-be of a first efficient cause. The source of the possible being of creatures cannot be nothing, for this is to say that there is no cause at all and that possible-to-be is prior to being—clearly a contradiction. Nor can the possible being itself account for its own possibility, for then it would have to be actual before it is actual—just as clearly a contradiction.

Therefore, there must be a being that is the source of this possibility in all other being. Ultimately there must actually exist one being that is the source of its own possibility and the cause of all other possibility, for there cannot be an actually infinite series of caused causes. The argument proceeds from possibility to possibility, the First Being being actual of necessity because there is no other way of accounting for its possibility (Duns Scotus rules out self-causation on the ground that it is "absurd"). Infinity, Duns Scotus then argues, is the first and most important essential trait of this being.

Against Averroës, Duns Scotus argues that there is nothing necessary about the conduct of God. He is absolutely free in his will, though at the same time Duns Scotus insists that the divine essence, from which the divine will is formally distinct, is completely rational; and the divine law, the objective foundation of human moral law, is willed to be what it is by God, not arbitrarily but in accordance with the absolute rationality of his divine nature. Thus, what is moral for man can be changed as the divine will changes. This flexibility of the divine will cannot extend, however, to what is contradictory to the divine nature.

The primacy of the will is a cardinal feature of the moral philosophy of Duns Scotus. This does not violate the principle that something must be known in order to be desired, but it does mean that whether something is known depends on an act of the will. The will dominates the intellect and moves it to know that which it knows. The will is man's highest faculty and power, according to the "subtle doctor." In this he differs markedly from Aquinas and puts himself once again into an Augustinian tradition that remains characteristic of Scotistic thought down to the present day.

The exceedingly complex nature of Duns Scotus' philosophy and theology was bound to produce different results in different quarters. Some, like William of Ockham, became even more cautious than Duns Scotus himself about the possibilities of philosophy when used as a tool for theological speculation. Others, infuriated perhaps by his labyrinthine argumentation, took his name and gave to the English-speaking world the word "dunce," as a reflection of his supposed stupidity! There was also, however, the Duns Scotus who wrote so magnificently in defense of Mary, the mother of God, and in particular of her Immaculate Conception. The promulgation of that doctrine on 8 December 1854 by the Roman Catholic church certainly depended in no small measure on the emphasis placed by the followers of Duns Scotus on his Marian theology.

BIBLIOGRAPHY

Sources. Joannes Duns Scotus, *Opera omnia*, Commissio Scotisticae, ed., under the direction of Father Carlo Balić (1950–); *God and Creatures: The Quodlibetal Questions*, Felix Alluntis and Allan B. Wolter, eds. and trans. (1975); *Philosophical Writings: A Selection*, Allan B. Wolter, ed. and trans. (1962).

Studies. Timotheus Barth, "Individualität und Allgemeinheit bei J. Duns Skotus. Eine ontologische Untersuchung," in *Wissenschaft und Weisheit*, **16–20** (1953–1957), in seven parts; Efrem Bettoni, *Duns Scotus: The Basic Principles of His Philosophy*, Bernardine Bonansea, trans. (1961); Donald A. Cress, "Toward a Bibliography on Duns Scotus on the Existence of God," in *Franciscan Studies*, n.s. 35 (1975); Étienne Gilson, *Jean Duns Scot: Introduction à ses positions fondamentales* (1952); Joseph Owens, "Common Nature: A Point of Comparison Between Thomistic and Scotistic Metaphysics," in *Mediaeval Studies*, 19 (1957); Faustino A. Prezioso, *La critica di Duns Scoto all'ontologismo di Enrico di Gand* (1961); Father Odulf Schäfer, *Bibliographia de vita, operibus et doctrina Iohannis Duns Scoti, doctoris subtilis ac Mariani, saec. XIX–XX* (1955); Michael Schmaus, *Zur Diskussion über des Problem der Univozität im Umkreis des Johannes Duns Skotus* (1957); Father Uriel Smeets, on behalf of the Commissio Scotisticae, *Lineamenta bibliographiae Scotisticae* (1942).

JEROME V. BROWN

[See also **Aristotle in the Middle Ages; Henry of Ghent; Ockham, William of; Philosophy-Theology, Western European; Rushd, Ibn (Averroës); Sīnā, Ibn (Avicenna).**]

DUNSTAN, LIFE OF, the record of the life and works of St. Dunstan (909–988), one of the major Benedictine reformers of the late-tenth-century monastic revival in England. It was written about 1000 by a Saxon priest, possibly Byrhtferth, living at Ramsey. The work was later versified by Abbo of Fleury, Dunstan's friend and Byrhtferth's teacher.

BIBLIOGRAPHY

Peter H. Blair, *An Introduction to Anglo-Saxon England*, 2nd ed. (1977), 173–177; C. J. Godfrey, *The Church in Anglo-Saxon England* (1962), 297–308, 344–345; John A. Robinson, *The Times of St. Dunstan* (1923, repr. 1969), 81–103, 132.

THOMAS H. OHLGREN

[See also **Dunstanus Saga.**]

DUNSTANUS SAGA, an Icelandic life of St. Dunstan (909–988), written in the first half of the fourteenth century by the priest Árni Laurentiusson, son of Bishop Laurentius of Hólar (whose biography is related in *Laurentius saga*). The saga is known in one fifteenth-century vellum manuscript and in a later copy.

St. Dunstan, an important English churchman, was quite a popular saint in Scandinavia and Iceland. With St. Thomas à Becket (the subject of *Thómas saga erkibiskups*) and some other English saints he exemplifies the close connection between the British Isles and Norway and Iceland from the time of the Norse conversion to Christianity (*ca.* 1000) on.

Dunstanus saga is a compilation from various sources. The author/compiler's main source was Adelard of Ghent's *Vita Dunstani*, written shortly after 1000, supplemented by information from the thirteenth-century *Speculum historiale* of Vincent of Beauvais and other works. The author was obviously, as Christine Fell wrote, "a selective and imaginative borrower."

The saga is not one of the more exciting of the numerous saints' lives in Old Norse, but it is fairly typical in style and outlook of Icelandic-Norwegian hagiography of the fourteenth century. Little is known of the author, but it is likely that he acquired his taste for hagiography while a monk at Thingeyrar, where he was a contemporary of Bergr Sokkason (*d.* 1350), one of the foremost hagiographic writers of the time.

BIBLIOGRAPHY

An edition is Christine Elizabeth Fell, ed., *Dunstanus saga* (1963). See also Eyvind Fjeld Halvorsen, "Dunstanus saga," in *Kulturhistorisk leksikon for nordisk middelalder*, III (1958), 370; Ole Widdig, Hans Bekker-Nielsen, and L. K. Shook, C.S.B. "The Lives of the Saints in Old Norse Prose: A Handlist," in *Mediaeval Studies*, 25 (1963).

HANS BEKKER-NIELSEN

[See also **Dunstan, Life of.**]

DUODECIM ABUSIVIS SAECULI, DE, a treatise on social and political morality that condemns the following twelve abuses: *sapiens sine operibus* (the wise man without works); *senex sine religione* (the old man without religion); *adolescens sine oboedientia* (the young man without obedience); *dives sine elemosyna* (the rich man without almsgiving); *femina sine pudicitia* (the woman without modesty); *dominus sine virtute* (the nobleman without virtue); *Christianus contentiosus* (the quarrelsome Christian); *pauper superbus* (the proud pauper); *rex iniquus* (the unjust king); *episcopus neglegens* (the neglectful bishop); *plebs sine disciplina* (the community without [ecclesiastical] discipline); *populus sine lege* (the nation without law).

During the Middle Ages this work enjoyed enormous popularity, as evidenced by more than 200 manuscripts containing it. It was variously attributed to St. Patrick, St. Augustine of Hippo, and St. Cyprian of Carthage, attributions that facilitated its widespread acceptance and propagation. *De duodecim*, however, as Hellmann (1909) showed, was written by an anonymous Irishman between 630 and 700. (Most scholars suggest a more precise data of *ca.* 630–650.) In the eighth century the work was propagated throughout Europe by Irish missionaries and scholars.

Structurally, *De duodecim* is modeled on the twelve grades of humility elaborated in St. Benedict's Rule (ch. 7). Other sources include Isidore of Seville's *Etymologiae*, Jerome's commentary on St. Matthew, and probably Augustine's sermons. For biblical quotations the author used the Vulgate, which was well known in southern Ireland at this date. Though clearly inspired by and dependent on Christian and patristic ideas, *De duodecim* draws as well on native, secular Irish concepts of morality, some of them pre-Christian. Three of the abuses it describes—*rex iniquus, episcopus neglegens,* and *dominus sine vir-*

tute—are likewise castigated in the *Senchas Már* (a compilation of secular Irish law made about the beginning of the eighth century), which decrees loss of honor price (Irish: *díre*) for their agents. The section of *De duodecim* on *rex iniquus*, establishing the relationship between the natural prosperity of a kingdom and the adherence of its king to moral maxims, was inspired by the Irish concept of *fír flathemon* (the justice of the ruler) and has much in common with the seventh-century *Audacht Morainn* (Testament of Morann) and other Old Irish *specula principum* ("mirrors" for princes).

Stylistically, *De duodecim* has analogies with two seventh-century Old Irish ecclesiastical texts, the *Apgitir Chrábaid* (The alphabet of piety) and the Cambrai Homily, in its use of the technique of *contradictio in adiecto* (contradiction implied in the adjective or phrase added as qualifier of a noun) and in the sententious, gnomic quality of its phrasing.

Even more closely linked to the *De duodecim* is the *Collectio canonum hibernensis*, a compilation of Irish ecclesiastical legislation made about 720. Both use the same sources, frequently employ homoeoteleuton as a stylistic device, and share the same pro-Roman bias on the question of dating Easter. On the basis of these similarities Hellmann suggests that *De duodecim* may have originated in the same milieu as the *Collectio,* in southern (or southeastern) Ireland. His suggestion, though hypothetical, finds support in the evidence that *De ordine creaturarum* (ca. 680–700), the first work to borrow from *De duodecim*, probably also comes from southern Ireland.

BIBLIOGRAPHY

The standard edition is Siegmund Hellmann, ed., *Pseudo-Cyprianus de XII abusivis saeculi* (1909). On the manuscript tradition see Eligius Dekkers, *Clavis patrum latinorum,* 2nd ed. (1961), 244, no. 1106. See also Fergus Kelly, ed., *Audacht Morainn* (1976), xv–xvi; Manuel C. Díaz y Díaz, ed., *Liber de ordine creaturum* (1972), 25, 37–38; James F. Kenney, ed., *The Sources for the Early History of Ireland* (1929, repr. with addenda by Ludwig Bieler 1966).

PÁDRAIG P. Ó'NÉILL

[See also **Irish Literature: Religious; Mirror of Princes.**]

DUPLUM, in the thirteenth-century repertory of polyphonic music from Notre Dame, the voice above the tenor. Anonymous IV also used the term to denote a two-voice piece. In the thirteenth-century motet repertory, the term was superseded by *motetus* (from the French *mot*) because the voice was texted.

BIBLIOGRAPHY

Fritz Reckow, ed., *Der Musiktraktat des Anonymous 4,* 2 vols. (1967), esp. 1.70, 77, 79, 80, 82, and 83.

JAMES GRIER

[See also **Anonymous IV; Motet; Notre Dame School.**]

DURA EUROPOS. Built by Macedonian Greeks as a Syrian outpost on the Euphrates at the end of the fourth century B.C., Dura Europos served later as a Parthian fortification, and then as a Roman garrison town, until it fell in 256 to the Sasanians. Little known until it was excavated between 1922 and 1937, Dura became a "third-century Pompeii," preserving extraordinary buildings, fresco decorations, and other archaeological materials (all removed to the National Museum, Damascus, and to Yale University). The synagogue and the Christian chapel are of greatest historical interest.

The synagogue (245) comprises residential quarters around a courtyard that served as a hospice, a colonnaded forecourt, and a house of assembly. The latter has on its west wall an aedicula for the Torah scrolls and is decorated with three tiers of narrative frescoes around all four walls. Episodes from various Old Testament books were selected to emphasize the history of the chosen people and God's promise to reestablish their nation in a new messianic era. Violating the Second Commandment, which forbids images, the synagogue frescoes reflect the assimilation of Hellenistic culture by third-century Jews and suggest that Christian art may have been based, in part, on Jewish precedents.

The Christian chapel (*ca.* 244) is the best surviving example of a *domus ecclesiae,* a modified house that served as a permanent Christian cult building before Constantine's recognition of the church. It includes an assembly hall, an unction room, and a baptistery (now at Yale University). The last is decorated with a painting of the Good Shepherd and scenes from the Old and New Testaments. Though based on local, pagan schemes of decoration, the baptistery uses images found in Christian buildings elsewhere in the Roman Empire. In style the art of Dura Europos resembles that of Palmyra, 145 miles to the west.

BIBLIOGRAPHY

Ann Perkins, *The Art of Dura-Europos* (1973); Yale University, *The Excavations at Dura-Europos: Final Reports, 4–5–6–8* (1943–1969).

HERBERT L. KESSLER

[See also **Domus Ecclesiae; Early Christian and Byzantine Architecture; Early Christian Art; Jewish Art.**]

DURAND OF ST. POURÇAIN (*ca.* 1275–1334) belongs to the avant-garde of the *via moderna* (hence one of his titles, *Doctor modernus*). A Dominican of the Clermont priory, in 1303 he transferred to St. Jacques for theological studies at the University of Paris.

His *Commentaria in quattuor libros Sententiarum* (1307–1308) opposed the teachings of Thomas Aquinas. It was highly controversial, and in its first condemnation (1314) ninety-one articles were censured by Hervaeus Natalis (Harvey Nedellec) on behalf of the Dominican Order. Especially important is that Durand allowed no connection between subject and object of knowledge: impressed species (*species impressae*) and agent intellect (*intellectus agens*) were unnecessary. He also rejected the need for a principle of individuation (*principium individuationis*). Around 1316 Durand was promoted away from the heat of doctrinal strife. Pope John XXII called him to diplomatic affairs and as a reward he was appointed bishop of Limoux (1317). He later became bishop of Le Puy en Velay (1318) and of Meaux (1326).

Durand's difficult doctrinal position is illustrated by the fact that as bishop of Meaux he helped to censure Ockham's commentary on the *Sentences,* but was himself again censured (1333), this time by a papal commission, for his views on the beatific vision (*De visione Dei*). Influenced more strongly by Augustine and Bonaventure than by Aristotle and Thomism, he anticipated the revival of Augustine later in the fourteenth century.

In the controversy between Pope John XXII and Philip VI of France, Durand wrote *De origine potestatum et jurisdictionum,* which shows little innovation on the matter being debated, but in a novel way discusses men as Christians and as citizens. John Gerson used it for his *De jurisdictione spirituali et temporale* (1405), and it was translated into French by Laurens Pignon, confessor of Philip the Good of Burgundy (*ca.* 1430).

BIBLIOGRAPHY

Editions. De origine potestatum et jurisdictionum, quibus populus regitur (1506) was published by Jean Barbier under the name of Petrus Bertrand; a more available edition is in Marguerin de La Bigne, ed., *Maxima bibliotheca veterum patrum,* XXVI (1677), 127–135, also under the name of Petrus Bertrand—the first three chapters are Durand's. *Commentaria in quattuor libros Sententiarum* was printed twelve times between 1508 and 1586.

Studies. Josef Koch, *Durandus de S. Porciano, O.P.* (1927); Jacques Quétif and Jacques Échard, *Scriptores ordinis Praedicatorum,* I (1719), 586–587; P. T. Stella, "Le 'Quaestiones de libero arbitrio' di Durando da S. Porciano," in *Salesianum,* 24 (1962). On *De origine potestatum* see Guillaume H. M. Posthumus Meyjes, *Jean Gerson et l'assemblée de Vincennes (1329)* (1978); and Arjo Vanderjagt, ed., *Laurens Pignon, Confessor of Philip the Good* (1984), contains both the Latin text and the French translation.

ARJO VANDERJAGT

[See also **Thomism and Its Opponents; Via Moderna.**]

DURAND, GUILLAUME (*ca.* 1230–1 November 1296). Even in his own day Guillaume Durand enjoyed a distinguished reputation as a learned canonist and liturgist, an able judge and administrator, and a conscientious bishop. Through his extensive writings he continued to exercise considerable influence even after his death.

Born at Puymisson, a village near Béziers, Durand entered the service of the diocese of Narbonne and became a canon regular of Maguelonne. About 1255 he went to Italy to study law, earning his doctorate at Bologna and then teaching at Bologna and Modena.

Clement IV (1265–1268) appointed Durand an *auditor causarum sacri palatii,* one of the judges who heard cases appealed to Rome. He attended the conclave of 1268 and helped frame the legislation that Gregory X promulgated at the Second Council of Lyons (1274). Holding numerous high offices after 1278, he served, from about 1283, as papal governor of Bologna and the Romagna.

In 1285 the cathedral chapter of Mende elected Durand bishop. Though consecrated in the autumn of 1286, he did not take possession of his see until 1291. Having declined the archbishopric of Ravenna in 1295, he was called once again to the Romagna that same year to pacify the region, where he remained until his death.

The inscription carved on the tomb made for Durand in Rome by Giovanni Cosmati lists his works: the *Speculum iudiciale,* which earned Durand the nickname "Speculator"; the *Repertorium iuris canonici,* a digest of canon law; a book of instructions and statutes for the clergy of his diocese; a revision of the Roman Pontifical; and the *Rationale divinorum officiorum.*

The *Speculum iudiciale,* first published in 1271–1276 and revised about 1289–1291, was highly esteemed for many generations because of its scope and the clarity of its organization. Incorporating the works of others along with much substantive law and the author's broad experience as a presiding judge, the *Speculum* is arranged in four books covering the persons involved in litigation, general procedure, criminal procedure, and the precedents for pleadings.

Durand included his *Speculum legatorum* in the revised edition of the *Speculum iudiciale,* and it was further enlarged by the *Additiones* of Johannes Andreae in the fourteenth century. Remaining authoritative for centuries in civil and ecclesiastical courts, the *Speculum* was printed some fifty times between 1473 and 1678.

Besides the *Repertorium iuris canonici,* which was widely used, Durand wrote a commentary on the decrees of the Second Council of Lyons and glosses on the *Decretum* of Gratian, the decretals, and a constitution of Nicholas III. These last three are presumed lost.

The instructions and statutes that Durand composed for his diocese were also presumed lost until a manuscript was discovered in the late nineteenth century by M. J. Berthelé in the archives of Cessenon, a village of the Languedoc near Puymisson. The manuscript, which Berthelé published, was apparently Durand's own copy, because it is annotated in his hand. The book is divided into two parts. The first deals with the mode of life appropriate to the clerical state and the duties incumbent on those in the pastoral office. Included as well are short instructions on the essentials of the sacraments, with emphasis on penance and the Eucharist. The second part contains the statutes enacted by Durand while he was bishop of Mende. This work, intended as a handbook for priests, was to be a companion piece to the revision of the Roman Pontifical undertaken by Durand. The instructions and statutes were probably completed by 1292, shortly after his arrival in Mende; the pontifical, begun soon thereafter, was completed between 1293 and 1295.

In his revision of the Roman Pontifical, Durand set out to restore authentic Roman tradition and custom, incorporating some elements of the newly revised pontifical of the curia and giving the whole a better organization. He included many references to local tradition, especially from his own diocese, and pronounced on the value of these customs.

That he intended his work for more than merely personal use is shown by the fact that Durand included among the ceremonies the rite of the ordination of the pope, the coronation of the emperor, and the investiture of the counts palatine. The work did, in fact, have an extensive influence. It was used together with the pontifical of the curia both at Avignon and at Rome, finally serving as the model for the authoritative text of the Roman Pontifical produced in 1485.

Durand composed his *Rationale divinorum officiorum* before the pontifical and the statutes, probably between 1285 and 1292. Like the *Speculum* it is a massive and encyclopedic work. As its title suggests, the eight books of this work cover all aspects of the public worship of the church: the meaning of the church building and its parts and ornamentation, the orders of the clergy and the symbolism of their vesture, the liturgy of the Eucharist, the hours of the Divine Office, the temporal cycle of the church year, the feasts celebrated in honor of the saints, and the method of computing time.

The *Rationale* is, indeed, a summa of the long tradition of liturgical commentary. Durand explains the liturgy from symbolic, canonical, theological, and moral viewpoints. He explains the symbolism of texts, objects, and actions in the liturgy. He is also concerned with the correct rubrics of celebration, discussing both Roman tradition and local customs. Where relevant, Durand includes chapters of theology and relates theological principles to practical pastoral issues. Finally, he brings out the moral and spiritual meanings implicit in the liturgical actions.

BIBLIOGRAPHY

Sources. Rationale divinorum officiorum, in a French trans. by Charles Barthélemy, 6 vols. (1854); also in English as *Sacred Vestments,* T. H. Passmore, ed. and trans. (1899), and as *The Symbolism of Churches and Church Ornaments,* John Mason Neale and Benjamin Webb, eds. and trans. (1906); M. J. Berthelé and M. Valmary, eds., "Les instructions et constitutions de Guillaume Durand . . . ," in *Mémoires de l'Académie des sciences et lettres de Montpellier,* 2nd ser., 3 (1900), also published separately; Michel Andrieu, ed., *Le pontifical romain au moyen âge,* III, *Le pontifical de Guillaume Durand* (1940).

Studies. L. Falletti, "Guillaume Durand," in *Dictionnaire du droit canonique,* V (1953), 1014–1075; John Ashton Clarence Smith, *Medieval Law Teachers and Writers: Civilian and Canonist* (1975), 54–55.

RONALD JOHN ZAWILLA, O.P.

[See also **Law, Canon; Pontificals.**]

DURANDUS (*d.* 1071), bishop of Toulouse and first Cluniac abbot of Moissac (from 1047 until his death), where he dedicated a new church in 1063. Durandus is represented as a half-life-sized figure on one of the ten relief plaques in the cloister at Moissac Abbey. These reliefs, dated about 1100–1105, are the earliest known examples of medieval sculpture on the exterior of a structure. The remaining nine plaques show apostles; though the abbot is frontal while the apostles turn their heads, he clearly forms part of the same sculptural ensemble. Apparently, the equation of the Cluniac Durandus and the apostles pictorially expresses the contemporary idea that monasticism continued the apostolic tradition.

BIBLIOGRAPHY

Millard F. Hearn, *Romanesque Sculpture: The Revival of Monumental Stone Sculpture in the Eleventh and Twelfth Centuries* (1981), 125–126; Meyer Schapiro, "The Romanesque Sculpture of Moissac I," in *Art Bulletin,* **13** (1931), repr. in his *Romanesque Art* (1977), 131–200.

LESLIE BRUBAKER

[See also **Moissac, Church of St. Pierre; Romanesque Architecture.**]

DURHAM CATHEDRAL. Situated on a steep hill above the river Wear, Durham is perhaps the most imposing Romanesque cathedral in Britain. Constructed between 1093 and 1133, it has been regarded as the first European church to be covered completely with rib vaults, a harbinger of the later Gothic style. The massiveness of the architecture is relieved inside by the delicate chevron patterning on the arches and piers, a motif of Islamic origin. The church culminates in the spectacular eastern transept called the Chapel of the Nine Altars, an addition in the Early English style of the thirteenth century. The cathedral was also a monastery and houses the shrine of St. Cuthbert.

Durham Cathedral, west view. 1093–1133. From Billings, *Illustrations of Architectural Antiquities of the County of Durham.* THE NEW YORK PUBLIC LIBRARY

BIBLIOGRAPHY

Robert W. Billings, *Architectural Illustrations and Description of the Cathedral Church at Durham* (1843); William Greenwell, *Durham Cathedral,* 9th ed. (1932).

STEPHEN GARDNER

[See also **Romanesque Architecture.**]

DURHAM, TREATIES OF. When Stephen succeeded Henry I in 1135, David I of Scotland responded by occupying Carlisle and Newcastle, besieging Durham to promote long-cherished Scottish regnal and territorial claims in England. In the treaty of February 1136, David permitted his son Henry to perform homage for the earldom of Huntingdon, hitherto held by David in right of his wife. Stephen undertook to consider Henry's ancestral claim to the earldom of Northumbria. David refused homage, having previously recognized the legitimacy of the empress' claim to the English throne, but he was forced to surrender Northumberland and Newcastle while retaining Cumbria.

Two years later David invaded Northumbria allegedly on behalf of his niece the empress. Despite defeat at the battle of the Standard on 22 August 1138, the Scots secured Carlisle and Wark Castle. In the second treaty of Durham on 9 April 1139, Stephen supplemented the settlement of 1136 by granting Henry the earldom of Northumbria. He insisted on retaining Newcastle and Bamborough Castle, vaguely promising to cede two southern English cities as compensation. The Northumbrian magnates were to acknowledge Henry's title, while the Scots agreed to adhere to the laws established by Henry I. Possibly as a further condition of the treaty, Henry married a member of the powerful de Warenne family later that year. David handed over five hostages as surety—the sons of the earls of Strathearn, Atholl, and Dunbar, as well as the sons of Fergus Lord of Galloway and Hugh de Moreville. The agreement was sworn in the presence of Stephen's queen, Matilda, who was also David's niece.

Through subsequent intervention on behalf of the empress, Henry lost the earldom of Huntingdon. His early death in 1152 ruined his father's carefully wrought design. Some details of the treaties remain obscure since both are documented only in competing chronicle accounts.

BIBLIOGRAPHY

Alan O. Anderson, *Scottish Annals from English Chroniclers A.D. 500 to 1286* (1908), 170–174; John T. Appleby, *The Troubled Reign of King Stephen* (1969), 26, 63; Geoffrey W. S. Barrow, *Kingship and Unity: Scotland 1000–1306* (1981), 35–39; Ralph H. C. Davis, *King Stephen* (1967), 21, 49; Archibald A. M. Duncan, *Scotland: The Making of the Kingdom* (1975), 216–224.

EDWARD J. COWAN

[See also **David I of Scotland; Henry I of England; Scotland, History of.**]

DURROW, BOOK OF, the earliest of the richly decorated Hiberno-Saxon Gospelbooks, usually dated between 675 and 680; it was at the Columban monastery at Durrow until about 1661, when it was transferred to Trinity College Library, Dublin (MS 57 [formerly A.IV.5]). The prefatory material includes elements found in numerous later insular manuscripts such as carpet pages, a page with the four evangelist symbols, and framed canon tables with a gap in the upper left corner of each table; the spiral decoration of one of the carpet pages (fol. 3v),

Opening of the Book of Matthew. The Book of Durrow, *ca.* 675–680, fol. 21v. COURTESY OF THE BOARD OF TRINITY COLLEGE, DUBLIN

Many of the formal motifs of the Book of Durrow have precedents in manuscripts produced in the British Isles or in books written by Irish monks living on the Continent (especially at Bobbio, Italy). Initials of decreasing sizes, decorated with borders of dots and projecting spirals, are found in earlier Irish and Northumbrian manuscripts (for instance, Dublin, Trinity College Library, MS 55 [formerly A.IV.55]; Durham, Cathedral Library, MS A.II.10), and carpet pages are known by the early seventh century (for example, Milan, Biblioteca Ambrosiana, codex D.23. Sup). Stronger German influence is found in the Book of Durrow than in earlier preserved insular manuscripts, but the Teutonic elements are known in earlier metalwork (such as the Sutton Hoo treasure of *ca.* 625–650), suggesting the impact of metal shops on the scriptorium that produced the Book of Durrow. The flattened and patternized symbols of the evangelists may also be descended from metalwork exemplars, though similar animal forms are found in Pictish relief sculpture.

Although the Book of Durrow anticipates later insular illustrated Gospelbooks in many respects, it

Carpet page. The Book of Durrow, *ca.* 675–680, fol. 30v. COURTESY OF THE BOARD OF TRINITY COLLEGE, DUBLIN

the order of the evangelist symbols, and the rectangular form of the canon tables are rare in later Gospelbooks produced in the British Isles. Each of the four Gospels is preceded by three decorated pages. The book of Matthew opens with a representation of Matthew's symbol (the winged man) and two pages with enlarged decorated initials, including the earliest known example (fol. 23r) of elaborated chi-rho initials; the books of Mark, Luke, and John are each introduced by the evangelist's symbol according to Irenaeus (Mark = eagle; Luke = calf; John = lion), a carpet page, and a page with enlarged initials (*Initium* for Mark, *Quoniuam* for Luke, *In principio* for John). The final page of the Book of Durrow (fol. 248r) is decorated with an interlace pattern; decorated initials are scattered throughout the text, often embellished with unusual triangular protuberances (as in the Book of Armagh).

is unusual in the relatively large forms of its decorative motifs, the preponderance of black and absence of blue, and the lack of plant and animal motifs in its initials. The latter characteristic, along with the abstract and patternized evangelist symbols, has suggested to many scholars that the Book of Durrow was produced before the incursion of Mediterranean influence evident in the Lindisfarne Gospels (London, British Library, MS Cotton Nero D.IV) of about 700; since the Book of Durrow presupposes various works of the mid seventh century, the manuscript is usually dated in the 670's. The Book of Durrow has been inconclusively assigned to both Irish and Northumbrian scriptoria: proponents of an Irish origin point to the provenance of the manuscript, its (later) colophon, and the Irish prefatory texts; a Northumbrian source is argued on the basis of the orderly script, influence of Northumbrian text recensions, and the infiltration of northern decorative elements known to have been current in Northumbria by the second quarter of the seventh century.

BIBLIOGRAPHY

Jonathan J. G. Alexander, *Insular Manuscripts 6th to the 9th Century* (1978), 30–32; A. A. Luce, G. O. Simms, Paul Meyer, and Ludwig Bieler, eds., *Evangeliorum quattuor Codex Durmachensis,* 2 vols. (1960), facsimile and commentary; Carl Nordenfalk, *Celtic and Anglo-Saxon Painting: Book Illumination in the British Isles 600–800* (1977), 34–47.

LESLIE BRUBAKER

[See also **Gospelbook; Manuscript Illumination**.]

DUTCH LITERATURE. Dutch language and literature in the Middle Ages are surrounded by linguistic, geographical, and political problems that often make generalizations difficult. For clarity the Flemish-speaking part of what is today Belgium will be referred to as "Flanders," while "the Low Countries" includes both the Netherlands and Belgium. "Dutch" means "the language of the Low Countries." Some scholars believe that a literature in the vernacular existed before the appearance of the first Dutch texts in the twelfth century. Although the vernacular was beginning to replace Latin in official documents, there was still no common Dutch language. Hendrik van Veldeke, for example, wrote the *Leven van Sint Servaes* (Life of St. Servatius, before 1170) and the *Eneide* (Aeneid, ca. 1185) in the Maas-

land-Old Limburg dialect of the Meuse region. Since his *Eneide* and *minneliederen* (courtly lyrics) have survived only in Middle High German versions, the Germans also claim him as one of their poets, under the name of Heinrich von Veldeke.

The romances of chivalry, written in rhymed verse, are mainly translations or adaptations of French originals. The first such romances appeared in the second half of the twelfth century, and celebrate the deeds of Karel de Grote (Charlemagne). With the advent of the Crusades, Eastern adventures entered medieval Dutch literature. Classical sources provided additional new material, and the British Arthurian legends were blended with Christian tradition. This combination gave rise to the courtly epics of Parsifal and the Holy Grail, which have a depth and idealism not apparent in the earlier epics.

The Trier *Floyris* proves the existence of poetry in the Maasland dialect even before Veldeke. One of the oldest adaptations of a French original is *Aiol,* written in the Limburg dialect around the end of the twelfth century. There is also a fragment of a translation of the very popular *Renout van Montalbaen,* which tells of the rebellion of Haymijn (Aymon) against Charlemagne and of the adventures of Haymijn's four sons and the horse Beyart. One of the best Charlemagne romances is *Karel ende Elegast* (Charles and the king of the elves), which may be an original work.

Jacob van Maerlant (*ca.* 1235–*ca.* 1291), a West Fleming who was born near Bruges, began with *Alexanders geesten* (Heroic deeds of Alexander, *ca.* 1258), an adaptation of a Latin original; reworked two British romances, one of them being *Merlijns boeck* (Merlin's book, 1261); and then produced his *Historie van Troyen* (History of Troy, *ca.* 1263). The most important of the few Eastern romances is *Floris ende Blanchefloer,* translated from the French by Diederic van Assenede.

The *Reis van Sinte Brandaen* (Voyage of St. Brendan) contains Irish motifs. It may go back as far as the twelfth century and is thus two centuries older than the English *Life of Saint Brandan.* The British romance *Ferguut,* an adaptation of the French *Fergus,* tells how a peasant becomes a perfect knight through love. A few other Arthurian romances, such as *Walewein* and *Moriaen,* having no immediate models, are considered originals. *Walewein,* written by Penninc and Vostaert (*ca.* 1210), is one of the oldest and most important of Arthurian romances. The brave Walewein sets off for the strange realm of King Wonder, in search of a floating chessboard that drifted into Arthur's castle and then disappeared. *Moriaen*, dating from about the middle of the thirteenth century, is a tale by a West Fleming about Walewijn, Lancelot, Perchevael, and the Black Knight (Moriaen). *Die wrake van Ragisel* (Vengeance for Ragisel) is a thirteenth-century Middle Dutch adaptation of the Old French *Vengeance Raguidel*, in which Walewijn avenges the death of Ragisel.

Hein van Aken, a Flemish priest who wrote about the end of the thirteenth century and the beginning of the fourteenth, produced the didactic poem *Van den Coninc Saladijn ende van Hughen van Tabaryen* (King Saladin and Hugh of Tiberias), based on a French original, which presents the knight as a model of moral behavior and explains the ways of chivalry and the significance of the knighting ceremonies.

The courtly romance was still widely imitated in the fourteenth century, when there was also a middle-class audience and a new interest in allegory. Van Aken made this a dominant characteristic with *Die rose,* his popular adaptation of the *Roman de la Rose.* The Dutch version, which retained the allegory of love from the first part of the French original and the information on nature and medieval science in the second, became a significant and popular work. Around 1290 a West Flemish writer, who was a better poet than van Aken, produced another adaptation, the *Tweede rose* (Second rose), and reduced the allegorical content.

The most famous beast epic in Western European literature is *Van den Vos Reinaerde,* written in Flemish verse by Willem, and possibly another author, around 1270. While there are earlier versions of this story of Renard the Fox in French and one in German, Willem's masterpiece is now regarded as an almost entirely original work. The animals in this satire on courtly life still retain, in Western literature and culture, the personality traits that Willem's characterizations gave them. *Reinaert* enjoyed tremendous popularity, and by the fifteenth century the material had been reworked into a prose chapbook, a translation of which was published by Caxton in 1481.

The first Dutch writer to introduce mysticism into the literature of the Low Countries and, moreover, to use prose was Beatrijs van Nazareth, a nun of the thirteenth century. In *Van zeven manieren van heiliger minnen* (On the seven ways of holy love, *ca.* 1236) she describes seven stages in the purification and transformation of the love that came from

God before it can return to him. Very little is known about the life of Hadewijch (*ca.* 1200–*ca.* 1269), but she was one of the most gifted and remarkable poets of the Low Countries in the Middle Ages. Although her *Strophische gedichten* (Strophic poems) are related in form to those of the French troubadours and the German minnesingers, they also contain a note of mysticism. In her prose *Brieven* (Letters) she sees the soul as coming from God and created in his image. The soul will find its way back to God through submission to divine love *(minne),* a love that is sometimes tinged with sensuality, and yet asceticism plays a role in achieving this mystical love. In the prose *Visioenen* (Visions) the exercise of virtue, guided by reason, leads the soul to God. Hadewijch's ideals are those of chivalry, such as loyalty and courtly love. Her extraordinary prose is animated by her passion and imagery.

Jacob van Maerlant eventually rejected the courtly romance and turned to didactic works that would satisfy the thirst for knowledge and information of the rising middle class, such as his compendium of natural history, *Der naturen bloeme* (The best of Nature); adaptations of historical accounts in the Bible (such as *Rijmbijbel:* Verse Bible), in Josephus (*Die wracke van Jherusalem:* The avenging of Jerusalem), and in Vincent of Beauvais (*Spieghel historiael,* Mirror of history). Although these works were more prose than poetry, van Maerlant did reveal his poetical talent in his *Strophische gedichten* (Strophic poems) and a work attributed to him, *Der kerken claghe* (Complaint of the church), an outcry against ecclesiastical abuses.

The medieval chroniclers recorded the historical, political, and economic events of their age, and frequently wrote in praise of a particular prince or region. The *Rijmkroniek van Holland* (Rhymed chronicle of Holland, 1305), at one time attributed to Melis Stoke, reveals the author's admiration for the counts of Holland, particularly Floris V. Jan van Boendale (*ca.* 1280–*ca.* 1350), a follower of van Maerlant, wrote *Die Brabantsche yeesten* (History of Brabant). His chief work, however, written between 1325 and 1333, is *Der leken spieghel* (Laymen's mirror), a compendium for the layman on God, this world and the next, history, morals, the various kinds of love, and the end of the world. Included in this long poem is the first example of a medieval Dutch *ars poetica.*

In the fourteenth century the role of the Netherlands in literature became more important. Storytellers recited *sproken,* short tales in verse, for the upper classes. Although they were often based on older classical or oriental sources, these tales were frequently allegorical. The *boerden,* on the other hand, were comic tales making use of indigenous material. While the *sproken* were mostly set in a courtly milieu, the *boerden* took their material from the lower and middle classes, and both generally revealed a moral purpose.

The best-known of the storytellers was Willem van Hildegaersberch (*ca.* 1350–*ca.* 1408), one of the first Dutch writers, who came from Hillegersberg, near Rotterdam. Didacticism pervades all of his poetry, even his comic verse. Dirc Potter (*ca.* 1370–1428), a Dutch courtier, wrote *Der minnen loep* (The course of love), a didactic poem describing the four kinds of love. He borrowed much of his material from classical writers, especially Ovid, some from the Bible, and some from medieval romances. Although *Der minnen loep* is a moralistic warning against foolish and illicit love relationships, Potter included some sixty tales of love and proved to be a master storyteller.

There is not always a clear line of demarcation between religious and secular poetry. Van Veldeke's *Leven van Sint Servaes* is the oldest life of a saint in the vernacular, but it is of more historical and cultural, than literary, value. In the thirteenth century, Latin lives of the saints were recast in Dutch verse. The *Leven van Sinte Lutgart* (Life of St. Lutgardis), a hagiology of a holy woman from Tongeren (Tongres), is a good example. Its description of the soul's love for God contains notes of mysticism, and it may be the work of Willem van Afflighem (1210–1297). Both the author and date of *Vanden levene ons Heren* (From the life of Our Lord) are unknown. It is a popular verse account of the life and sufferings of Jesus. The *Limburgse leven van Jezus* (Limburg life of Jesus), a prose work of a very different kind, goes back at least to 1271. It is an adaptation of an old Latin text that included almost all of Tatian's *Evangelienharmonie (Diatessaron).*

Marian legends include the *Beatrijs,* a masterpiece of uncertain origin. The only surviving manuscript originated about 1374, but it is possible that an earlier version goes back to the thirteenth century. In this moving poem Beatrijs leaves the convent to live with her lover for seven happy years. When he leaves her, she enters a life of sin and misery in order to support herself and her children. After seven years of this life, she returns to the convent as a penitent, and finds that Mary had taken her place in order to protect her. The fourteenth-century

Theophilus is the story of a priest who falls into disgrace with his bishop because of evil tongues. In order to regain his honor, he makes a pact with the devil, but is saved by Mary's intervention.

In the fourteenth century religious literature reached its peak in South Brabant, where Jan van Ruusbroec (1293–1381) continued and developed the tradition of Hadewijch. Ruusbroec was both systematic and didactic in setting forth his ideas in prose treatises. Unlike Hadewijch, he was not a passionate poet with a lyrical gift. His most important work is *Die chierheit der gheestelijker brulocht* (The adornment of the spiritual wedding), which bases mystical ideas on the analysis of a biblical text. He also contributed to the development of Dutch prose with *Vanden blinckenden steen* (On the sparkling stone), in which the sparkling stone is a symbol of Christ. The German mystics Tauler and Suso admired Ruusbroec, and Geert Groote translated *Die chierheit der gheestelijker brulocht* into Latin. Groote became the leader of the Devotio Moderna, a spiritual revival aimed at penetrating practical everyday life and a reaction against metaphysical speculation.

Under the influence of mysticism the entire Bible and many books of Christian literature were translated into Dutch, but the writers of the Devotio Moderna usually used Latin, which promoted the spread of their ideas. The renowned Latin work by Thomas à Kempis, *De imitatione Christi,* arose from the Devotio Moderna. The practical side of this movement is evident from the various religious groups known as Brethren of the Common Life, which were interested in education, the copying of manuscripts, and later the printing of books. They paved the way for such Dutch humanists as Agricola and Erasmus.

Very little popular poetry has been preserved. One of the great collections of secular poetry, along with the Hulthem and Hague manuscripts, is the Gruuthuse manuscript. It contains the famous "Egidiuslied" (Song for Egidius), an elegy for the poet's dead friend; another lament for the same Egidius, probably by the same poet; "Aloeëtte, voghel clein" (Alouette, little bird), a poem to a skylark; "Dune laets mi rustn, dach no nacht" (You do not let me rest, day or night), a modern-sounding rondeau in which the author complains of thoughts that have been tormenting him; and a "Kerelslied" (Song of the churls), which reflects the antagonism of the nobles toward the peasants. The last poem—like "Cheraert van Velzen," which blames the death of Count Floris V on Floris' assault on the honor of van Velzen's wife—is an example of lyrical poetry based on historical events.

Of particular significance however are the popular ballads and courtly romances, which drew their material in part from fairy tales, legends, the German heroic epics, and chivalry. *Van Heer Halewijn,* for example, tells of a medieval Bluebeard who lures young girls to their death with a song, until one of them, who is cleverer than he, chops off his head. In *Van 't kind van twalef jaren,* a twelve-year-old child, condemned by the cruel lord of the manor for some minor transgression, keeps looking round while climbing the steps of the gallows, hoping that help will appear. As chivalry declined, there were also drinking songs, the songs of riders, and songs of middle-class social and domestic life. The oldest printed collection of secular songs is *Een schoon liedekens boeck* (A beautiful book of songs), the so-called *Antwerp Songbook* of 1544.

Although she did not produce very much, the best-known of the religious poets of this period was Zuster Bertken (*ca.* 1426–1514), who for fifty-seven years shut herself up in a church cell in Utrecht, where she wrote some sensitive prose and a number of lyrics that recall the symbolism of thirteenth-century mysticism. Her work is more careful but less passionate than that of Hadewijch.

The sources of the medieval drama in the Low Countries are both secular and ecclesiastical. The beginnings of the secular drama have been sought in the nature worship of the Germanic tribes, which led to dramatizations of the change of seasons, dramatic dialogues in the recitations of minstrels and the tales of wandering storytellers, and the acting of the storytellers themselves. In any case there is very little definite information available on the origin of the four secular dramas in the Hulthem manuscript: *Esmoreit, Gloriant, Lanseloet van Denemarken,* and *Vanden winter en vanden somer.* These *abele spelen* (beautiful plays) date from the middle of the fourteenth century, and although they are based on themes that were international common property, they are the oldest serious secular dramas in western European literature. They are all based on the problems of love, and with the exception of *Vanden winter en vanden somer,* are dramatized motifs from the courtly romances.

Esmoreit is about the son of the king of Sicily, who was stolen as a child and sold to the Saracens. He falls in love with Damiët, the daughter of the king of Damascus, at whose court he grew up, but he resists marriage because he is not sure that she belongs to the same royal class. *Gloriant* concerns a proud Christian prince's love for an equally proud Muslim princess, whose father is an enemy of Gloriant's father. Their love conquers treachery and violence, however, and she becomes a Christian.

Lanseloet van Denemarken portrays the love of Lanseloet (Lancelot), a young prince of Denmark, for Sanderijn, a poor girl of the lower nobility who is one of his mother's servants. His downfall comes when, on the advice of his mother, he satisfies his desire for Sanderijn, then mistreats and insults her in a most unchivalrous manner. Sanderijn leaves him forever, and finds happiness with a knight in another country. Lanseloet dies repentant, of a broken heart. The popularity of *Lanseloet* may be judged from the fact that it was the only one of the four *abele spelen* to be published as a chapbook (*ca.* 1486) and later to be printed at Cologne in German translation. In spite of the naive intrigue, the *abele spelen* differ from each other, and there is considerable variety in the problems of love that arise in these plays. *Vanden winter ende vanden somer* (Of winter and of summer) is the old debate between the two seasons on which is of the greater benefit to mankind. Love appears as a problem here, too, for Venus is one of the characters in the play.

A farce *(sotternie)* usually followed each *abel spel,* depicting a humorous but realistic domestic anecdote quite different from the courtly life of the serious plays. The Hulthem manuscript, for example, which contains several farces, also includes the *Buskenblaser* (The man who blew into the little box), in which an old man seeks rejuvenation from a charlatan, who has him blow into a box filled with soot. His face is blackened, and his young wife rewards him with a beating. Both the *abele spelen* and the *sotternieën* were probably written in South Brabant.

The medieval religious drama originated within the church, but secular elements gradually entered the genre. Laymen were among the actors now, and the dramatic action had been expanded so that it could no longer be included in the liturgy, though it was still performed in or near the church. By the thirteenth century the spoken word was more important than the music, and the language was no longer Latin but Dutch. There were comic and even realistic elements in the religious drama, and performances were no longer confined to the church or its precincts. The most important of the mystery plays were the seven based on the joys of Mary, but only the first and the last of the seven have survived. Beginning in 1448, one of these plays was performed each year by *rederijkers* (rhetoricians) in Brussels. *De eerste bliscap van Maria* (The first joy of Mary) is based on Mary's life up to the Annunciation, while *De sevenste bliscap* covers her last days up to the Assumption. There is considerable development in technique between the two plays.

The oldest known Dutch miracle play is *Het spel vanden heilighen sacramente vander Nyeuwervaert* (Play of the holy sacrament of Nieuwervaart, before 1500). Although the play is allegorical, there are some realistic scenes. In it a consecrated wafer that has been found in the bog exerts magical powers in spite of the clownish devils. Such comic figures as the latter eventually became important characters, representing human vices and even coming to determine the action and comment on it.

The outstanding example of the miracle play is *Mariken van Nieumeghen* (between 1485 and 1510). Mariken is enticed by the devil and leaves Nijmegen with him on what becomes a journey of seven years, until a performance of the wagon play of Masscheroen, portraying the struggle between Christ and the devil for the soul of man, moves her to repentance and penance; eventually her sins are forgiven. Mariken is neither a type nor an allegorical figure, but a living human being, and in this masterpiece of poetic form and dramatic technique the notes of a new age are heard—that of the *rederijkers* and the Renaissance.

In addition to miracle plays, mystery plays, and plays about saints' lives, the religious drama also includes the morality plays, which were often allegorical and didactic. The best-known of the morality plays is *Elckerlijc* (ca. 1475) by an author whose identity is still a subject of debate. The play was widely translated and has gained a world reputation in its English version, *Everyman*. When Death comes for Elckerlijc in the play, he calls in vain on such figures as Society, Friends, and Property to accompany him on his last journey, but they are unable to help him. While other figures, such as Knowledge (of God), Virtue, Wisdom, and Beauty, come to his assistance, only Virtue goes with him to the grave.

The *rederijkers* were a remarkable literary and social phenomenon of the early fifteenth century. Members of the urban middle class, they organized themselves into *kamers* (chambers), often under clerical leadership, where they could practice acting, recitation, and writing. There had been groups of *rhétoriqueurs* in northern France in the twelfth century, but the first use of the designation *camer van rhetorica* occurred in Oudenaarde, Flanders, in 1441.

By that time chambers of rhetoric were also appearing in the Netherlands. Like the guilds, they had a hierarchical organization. The head of the chamber, who was usually a man of high social rank, was called the prince; the man in charge of all the literary activities was the factor. These activities reached their height in the competition, which became a feast that sometimes lasted for days.

The most important poet who belonged to a chamber of rhetoric was Anthonis de Roovere of Bruges (*ca.* 1430–1482). His *Rhetoricale wercken* (Rhetorical works) were published posthumously in 1562, but he achieved fame in his own time with the religious poem *Lof vanden Heilighen Sacramente* (Praise of the Holy Sacrament), which hangs in the Cathedral of Bruges to this day. His lyrical poetry, which is charged with emotion, his satires, and his erotic verse have greater appeal to the modern reader. *Vander Mollenfeeste* (Feast of the moles) is a well-known humorous poem in which Death is sent as a messenger to invite everyone, of all classes and including the ladies, to the feast of the moles in their underground realm. It is related to the medieval literature of the Dance of Death.

Mathys Casteleyn (1485–1550) was one of the most famous and versatile *rederijkers* of his day. His *De conste van rhetoriken* (Art of rhetoric), written in 1548 but only published posthumously in 1555, was the first comprehensive *ars poetica* in Dutch. Although his views on poetry were largely traditional and he was a follower of de Roovere, he was the first *rederijker* to hold up the classical writers as models. Later *rederijkers* include such followers of Erasmus as Cornelis Crul and Cornelis Everaert (1485–1566), both of whom believed in reform within the church and remained aloof from the religious conflicts of the Reformation. The serious allegorical and didactic plays and the *esbattementen* (realistic medieval farces) flourished at this time, and are best exemplified in the work of Everaert, the last of the *rederijkers* to work entirely within the medieval tradition. Late writers in the *rederijker* tradition include Colijn van Rijssele of Brussels, author of *Spiegel der minnen* (Mirror of love) in the first half of the sixteenth century; Jan Baptist Houwaert, author of allegorical plays and the didactic peom *Pegasides pleyn ende den lust-hof der maeghden* (Pegasus' plain and the pleasure garden of the maidens, 1583); Jan van den Berghe (*d*. 1559), author of the *esbattement* (literally "frolic") *Hanneken Leckertant* (Little Hannah Sweet-tooth) and probably the allegorical *De wellustige mensch* (The hedonist); and Anna Bijns (1493–

1575), an Antwerp writer of love lyrics and polemical verse opposing the Reformation.

BIBLIOGRAPHY

Johan Huizinga, *Herfsttij der Middeleeuwen* (1919, repr. 1963); Gerrit Kalff, *Geschiedenis der Nederlandsche Letterkunde* (1906–1912), III; Gerard P. M. Knuvelder, *Handboek tot de geschiedenis der Nederlandse letterkunde*, 2nd ed., I (1976); Reinder P. Meijer, *Literature of the Low Countries* (1978); Jozef van Mierlo, *Geschiedenis van de Oud- en Middelnederlandsche letterkunde* (1928), and his volumes in Frank Baur *et al.*, *Geschiedenis van de letterkunde der Nederlanden*, I, *De letterkunde van de Middeleeuwen tot omstreeks 1300* (1939) and II, *De Middelnederlandsche letterkunde van omstreeks 1300 tot de Renaissance* (1940); Jan te Winkel, *De ontwikkelingsgang der Nederlandsche letterkunde*, 2 vols., 2nd ed. (1922–1927).

SEYMOUR L. FLAXMAN

[See also **Arthurian Literature; Beast Epic; Devotio Moderna; Drama, Liturgical; Drama, Western European; Elckerlijc; Flanders and the Low Countries; Groote, Geert; Hadewijch; Mysticism, European; Renard the Fox; Ruusbroec, Jan van.**]

DUX, Roman military commander of the provinces. In the Byzantine Empire the term was used by the ninth century to indicate the heads of ethnic minorities living in the themes; it was also used as an alternative name for *domesticus scholae* (the head of the imperial heavy cavalry). Under Nikephoros Phokas (963–969) and through the eleventh century the term *dux* designated a high provincial commander with attributes similar to those of the *katepano*. *Duces* are attested in many frontier districts, such as Antioch, Mesopotamia, Chaldea, Thessaloniki, and Italy. Beginning in the twelfth century, the *dux* lost prestige and became simply the governor of a Byzantine theme, with increasing fiscal responsibilities. Starting with Alexios I Komnenos (1081–1118) and until the fifteenth century the term *dux* (and, later, *megas dux*) was used to refer to the commander in chief of the Byzantine fleet.

BIBLIOGRAPHY

Hélène Ahrweiler, *Recherches sur l'administration de l'empire byzantin aux IXᵉ–XIᵉ siècles* (1960), 52ff., and *Byzance et la mer* (1966), *passim*; Nicolas Oikonomides, *Les listes de préséance byzantines des IXᵉ et Xᵉ siècles* (1972), 344, 354, and "L'évolution de l'organisation administrative de l'empire byzantin au XIᵉ siècle (1025–1118)," in *Travaux et mémoires,* 6 (1976).

NICOLAS OIKONOMIDES

[See also **Domestic; Duchy.**]

DWIN (Greek: Doubios; Arabic: Dabil, al-Duwil), 40°00′N by 44°41′E. Dwin was the early medieval capital of Armenia, some twenty kilometers south southeast of present-day Erevan and ten kilometers northeast of Artašat, the earlier capital.

The city was founded in the second quarter of the fourth century A.D. by the Arsacid Armenian king Xosrov II on the left bank of the Azat River as a healthier residence than the nearby Artašat, located in the marshlands of the Araks. Dwin may immediately have replaced Artašat as the capital of Armenia, but it is more probable that this shift took place after the partition of Armenia between Byzantium and Sasanian Persia in A.D. 387. In any case, Dwin was the residence of the rulers of eastern Armenia by the fifth century as against Karin/Theodosiopolis, the capital of Byzantine Armenia. As a result of the new partition of Armenia in 591, the frontier between the two realms ran past Dwin along the Azat, leaving the city in Persian territory. After the end of the Armenian Arsacid dynasty, Dwin became the seat of the Persian governor or *marzpan,* probably in the 670's. Because of its importance and border position, the city was continually attacked by Armenian rebels, as in 571/572, and by the Byzantines, as in 623, when it was sacked by Emperor Heraklios, and in 652–653, when Emperor Constans II established his winter quarters there.

The first Arab attack against Dwin occurred in 640, and in 654 the city capitulated to Ḥabīb ibn Maslama, who granted it his protection on payment of a required tribute. An Arab garrison was quartered in the city and, like their Persian predecessors, the Arab governors *(ostikans)* took it over as their official residence until at least 789, when the *ostikan* Sulayman moved to Partaw (Bardhaᶜa) in Azerbaijan. According to some Soviet scholars, Dwin ceased to be an administrative center at that time, but it is more likely that it remained alongside Partaw as the alternate capital of Arab Armenia and occasional residence of the *ostikan* until late in the ninth century.

Through most of the period of its political importance, Dwin also played a central religious role as the seat of the Armenian *katᶜołikos* from the late fifth to the early tenth century, when the *katᶜołikos* moved to Vaspurakan. Numerous councils of the Armenian church were held there between A.D. 505 and 719, primarily against Nestorians, Chalcedonians and Paulicians. During the schism of the sixth and seventh centuries Dwin's location on Persian territory made it the seat of the national Armenian *katᶜołikos* as against his Chalcedonian rival residing over the border at Awan in Byzantine Armenia.

With the end of the ninth century, the political role of Dwin altered radically. The Bagratid kings of Armenia never considered it their capital; its position became increasingly uncertain and chaotic, and our information as to its status is often imprecise or altogether lacking. As early as the second decade of the ninth century, Arab Jahhafid emirs tried to establish themselves there, and though the Bagratids— Ašot I (862–890), Ašot II in the 920's, possibly Ašot III (957–966), and especially Gagik I (990–1020/1021)—recognized its importance and attempted to control it, they never held it for long or made it their primary residence.

In 893/894 the city was ravaged by an earthquake that destroyed the cathedral and the palace of the *katᶜołikos* (who moved from the city), and took between 70,000 and 150,000 lives, according to contemporary sources. Immediately thereafter the city was captured by Afshin ibn Abū'l Sāj, the Turkish *ostikan* of Azerbaijan, who rebuilt it and probably founded its major mosque. Under his brother Yūsuf and his lieutenants it became the headquarters of the Sajid emirs, especially in their struggle against King Smbat I, who was martyred at Dwin in 914. From then on, though Dwin was still occasionally held by Bagratid rulers and menaced by the Byzantines, who attacked it in 921 and 928, it became primarily a Muslim emirate.

The position of Dwin became more chaotic as it entered what Vladimir Minorsky called the "Iranian Interlude" of the tenth and eleventh centuries; the chronology of the entire later period is by no means certain. With the exception of the rule of Gagik I and intrusions by the nearby Arab emir of Goltᶜn (982–987, 989–990), the city was passed back and forth among Kurdish and Daylamite emirs of Iranian descent coming from Azerbaijan: Daysam ibn Ibrahim al-Kurdi (937–942, 948/950–951), the Sallarids or Musafirids (941/942–948, 954–957, 966–982), the Rawwadids (987–989), and, most important, the Shaddadids, who held it for the better part of a century (951–954, 1022–1105, *ca.* 1125–*ca.* 1130). Yet

another Kurdish Rawwadid clan, the ancestors of Saladin, resided near Dwin during this period.

The Iranian interlude was followed by an equally anarchic century of Turkish domination under the *atabeg* Kĭzĭl Arslan (1105–*ca.* 1118), the emirs of Arzen and Bitlis (1118–*ca.* 1162), and the Ildiguizids (1163–1203). A last period of prosperity came to Dwin under the overlordship of the Georgian Bagratids, who had briefly seized the city in August 1162/1163. The Armenian Zakarid viceroys of the Georgian crown controlled, rebuilt, and adorned the city (1203–1225, ca. 1228), and queen Tᶜamar used it as her winter residence. The final decline of the city began with its sack by the khwarazmshah Jalal al-Dīn in 1225 and the Mongol invasion of 1286.

The importance of Dwin in the Middle Ages derived as much from its economic as from its political status. Commanding the same transit routes as its predecessor Artašat, it soon replaced it as a center of international trade. As early as the sixth century it was known to the Byzantine historian Procopius as a transit market for goods from India as well as from Georgia, and the lucrative trade in raw silk coming from China to Byzantium via Persia increased the wealth of the city. In the tenth century Dwin was familiar to Arab geographers as a major trade and manufacturing center famous for its textile industries including rugs, saddle blankets, cushions, hangings, fine woolens, and especially the flowered embroidered silks dyed in nearby Artašat. Recent archaeological excavations have revealed the presence of important ceramic works and metalworks.

Very little is known of the internal administration of Dwin, though in later times the city seems to have been laid out like contemporary Muslim cities with an inner walled town containing the citadel, and considerable suburbs. "Elders" and "nobles" of the city are mentioned by Armenian and Muslim sources as occasionally taking action in defense of their city alongside the governors and emirs. The large population of Dwin was increasingly mixed— Armenian, possibly Jewish, Arab, Kurdish, and Daylamite—though the Armenians remained in the majority through the tenth century, according to al-Muqaddasī. The international and commercial character of the city is indicated by the references to its bazaar alongside the citadel and to administrative buildings, to its gates controlling routes in all directions, to the mercantile villages surrounding it, and to the presence of a mint that operated until at least 941/942.

Dwin retained its position as the most important

manufacturing and trade center of Armenia until the end of the tenth century, when it was partially superseded by the northern capital of Ani. Even so, it continued to flourish until the thirteenth century, despite the political chaos and repeated sacks, and enjoyed a final burst of prosperity marked by considerable building activity under the Zakᶜarids and even into the early Mongol period. Only with the southward shift of the trade routes in the fourteenth century did the city share the decline of other Armenian trade centers and cease to be mentioned by Muslim and Western travelers such as al-Qazwīnī and Pegolotti.

BIBLIOGRAPHY

Hakob Manandyan, *The Trade and Cities of Armenia in Relation to Ancient World Trade,* Nina G. Garsoïan, trans. (1965), 81–82, 87, 133, 143–144, 149, 152, 154, 158–161, 169–170, 198; Vladimir Minorsky, "Vicissitudes of Dvin," in *Studies in Caucasian History* (1953), 116–124; Aram Ter-Ghevondian, "Duin (Dvine) sous les Salarides," in *Revue des études arméniennes,* n.s. 1 (1964), "Chronologie de la ville de Dvin (Duin) aux 9ᵉ et 11ᵉ siècles," *ibid.,* n.s. 2 (1965), and *The Arab Emirates in Bagratid Armenia,* Nina G. Garsoïan, trans. (1976), 9, 13–14, 21, 35–37, 39–40, 54–55, 58–66, 70–79, 82, 93–104, 106–107, 111, 119–124, 125–131, 134, 137–142, 145–147, 179–180.

NINA G. GARSOÏAN

[See also **Armenia, geography; Armenia: History of; Artašat; Ašot I Mec (the Great); Ašot II Erkatᶜ; Ašot III Oɫormac (the Merciful); Bagratids, Armenian; Gagik I.**]

DYES AND DYEING. The love of bright colors is primordial. Cave paintings are virtually the oldest evidence of human intellectual activity. "Savages" often color themselves—the Romans supposedly found the Picts dyeing themselves blue—and the working of dyed bones into utensils and ornaments was one of mankind's most primitive occupations. In the material remains of ancient civilizations, this preoccupation with color manifests itself more often in paintings and glazed ceramic objects than in dyeing, but only because the fabrics and dyes were so perishable. The materials of painting and glazing were almost exclusively of mineral origin, and though sometimes used in dyeing, mineral colors were found very early to be inferior for this purpose to colors derived from vegetable and animal materials.

On the evidence of mineral pigments it would ap-

Dyeing cloth. English manuscript, 15th century. THE BRITISH LIBRARY, MS ROYAL 15 EIII, fol. 269

pear that the Babylonians were ahead of the Egyptians in the range of colors used and in the techniques of applying them. A few surviving Babylonian textiles suggest that shades from red to purple were particularly popular, though green and a reddish-yellow approaching gold have also been found. Egyptian fabrics survive in a much larger quantity, preserved by a hot, dry climate, and the colors used by dyers are also approximated in tomb paintings. Together they show a full range of colors by late antiquity, so extensive that it has been claimed that the art of dyeing remained essentially static from the end of the pre-Christian era to the sixteenth century. Dyeing, however, did have a history in the Middle Ages.

The blue with which the Britons dyed themselves was woad *(Isatis tinctoria),* derived from a plant known in the Middle East and common in Europe. The leaves were dampened, allowed to ferment, dried, and pulverized, then were ready for use in dyeing. The same pigment, in a purer form, existed in the oriental plant indigo *(Indigofera tinctoria),* but it appears that indigo was barely known, if at all, in medieval Europe. The preparation of indigo involved an additional step, in which the fermented leaves were steeped, with constant stirring, until the pigment oxidized and precipitated out.

The process for producing henna *(Lawsonia inermis),* an orange-red color, was as simple as that for woad and had been popular among sophisticated Egyptians as a cosmetic, for coloring the nails and other parts of the body. Red-haired people often owed their color to henna. It was supposed to be therapeutic as well as decorative; indeed, most of the ancient dyestuffs were assigned medicinal properties and were included in the pharmacopoeia.

Saffron *(Crocus sativus),* an autumn-blooming flower, was the source of a yellow dye derived from the stamens of the flowers, which were carefully picked out, dried, and powdered. The saffron-dyed mantle of an early Irish king survives, and the popularity of the dye in medieval Europe is certified by a long series of edicts against its adulteration.

Although green is nature's favorite color, plants failed to yield a green dye of any permanence, and the color was usually achieved by successively dyeing a cloth with yellow and blue. Black dye came from "gallnuts," excrescences caused by insects, particularly on oak trees. Long thought to be of vegetable origin, gallnuts had a pleasing symmetry that made them popular as ornaments. Pulverized, they were used in medicine, for darkening hair, as well as for black dye. The dried oak-gall is from one-quarter to three-quarters tannin, a complex, water-soluble organic compound so important in leather preparation that it has given rise to the term "tanning."

Dyes were also derived from foodstuffs. The major use of saffron has been as a spice. The root of the turmeric plant *(Curcuma longa),* native to southern Asia, was used as a condiment (it is an ingredient of curry powder) and as a dye, giving, with the addition of an alkali such as natron (sodium carbonate) or decomposed urine, a reddish brown color suitable for dyeing. Also native to southern Asia was safflower *(Catharmus tinctorius),* the source of a yellow dye obtained by digesting the flower in an alkaline solution. When applied to cloth, the dye was fixed by adding an acid, such as vinegar or a vegetable juice.

Thus, the production of a dye was usually more than a matter of extracting it with water. Dyestuffs within plants are rarely soluble. They can be rendered soluble in various ways—for instance, by allowing the plant to decompose through fermentation. Experience also taught the dyer that some colors could be extracted by adding various substances during the process such as table salt, natron, vegetable and fruit juices, urine, vitriol, or alum, all of which had been discovered very early because of

their distinctive tastes and mildly corrosive action. They were fixtures in the pharmacopoeia and were also used in embalming and leather working. In chemical terms they provided an acid or alkaline environment that facilitated the decomposition of the plant and extraction of the dye.

The most common color was red. Henna was used as a red dye in Egypt, as was archil or orseille *(Rocella tinctoria),* obtained from several varieties of lichen, which was ground up and fermented with urine, yielding a purple-red dye. Archil was unknown in medieval Europe until reintroduced (probably from the Orient) in thirteenth-century Florence.

Another red dye, known in Egypt from about 1000 B.C., was kermes, obtained from a scale insect that inhabits plants. Having laid her eggs, the female dies, forming a ball about the size of a pea, which dries up and contains a red powder. It is soluble in water and has only to be dried and separated with a sieve. The color is scarlet, that word being derived from the Persian word for kermes.

A fourth red dye was madder *(Rubia tinctorum).* Apparently unknown much before the end of the pre-Christian era, the madder plant flourished in medieval Europe. The dye was obtained from the root

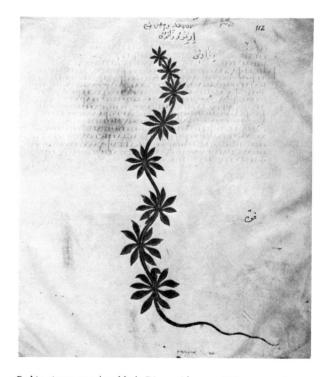

Rubia tinctorum (madder). Dioscorides, *ca.* 512. VIENNA, ÖSTER-REICHISCHE NATIONALBIBLIOTHEK, COD. MED. GRAEC. 1, fol. 112

by grinding and fermenting it over an extended period, followed by solution in water.

The process seems simple enough, but madder exemplifies a large number of dyes that cannot be "fixed" (permanently attached to the fabric) without a mordant. Just as the dye must be made soluble in order to extract it from the plant, so it must be made insoluble if it is to remain on the fabric. This is the role of the mordant, which may be one or more of the salts already mentioned. The most effective mordant was found very early to be alum, and the production of that substance (actually a family of related substances), through the weathering of certain rocks, was for centuries of great economic importance. As the production of madder became an agricultural industry, the production of alum became a chemical industry. Alum was imported from the eastern Mediterranean in the Middle Ages, a trade controlled by the Genoese from about 1275, when they secured a monopoly on the principal alum works at Phocaea in Asia Minor. Shortly after the loss of that monopoly in the fifteenth century, a Genoese expert, Giovanni di Castro, discovered an Italian source at Tolfa in the Papal States, and from the 1460's alum became a papal monopoly.

One ancient dye was esteemed beyond all others, perhaps originally because of its extraordinary resistance to fading. This was purple, which takes its name from *Purpura,* a genus of mollusks from which the dye was obtained. The dye is supposed to have been discovered in Phoenicia in the fifteenth century B.C. A pigment-containing gland was extracted from large shells, or small shells were crushed. Steeped in salt water for several days, the mass was then boiled and next heated by introducing steam through tubes for ten days, during which solid impurities were removed and the solution evaporated to about a sixth of its original volume. Two species of mollusks, *Purpurea* and *Murex,* gave varieties of red and violet; when the two were combined, by dyeing first with one and then with the other, the color was Tyrian purple (a dye which actually ranged from bright red to nearly black), the most expensive, and hence the most highly esteemed, ancient dye.

The long Phoenician monopoly on the purple dye industry was in part a consequence of the necessity of using fresh mollusks. But in the course of time "purple factories" appeared in other places where the mollusks were available: North Africa, Spain, and Italy. "Purple"—fabrics colored red to violet with these dyes—became the symbol of power and

Carthamus tinctorius (safflower). Dioscorides, *ca.* 512. VIENNA, ÖS-TERREICHISCHE NATIONALBIBLIOTHEK, COD. MED. GRAEC. 1, fol. 198v

luxury throughout the ancient Mediterranean. There were attempts to confine the use of the color to courts and favorites, but many were born (or reborn) to the purple, despite continuous increases in the price of purple cloth, which by the time of Diocletian (*ca.* 300) had reached nearly $700 (according to 1890 monetary values) per pound. The Western Christians vigorously opposed such luxury, using purple principally for book illustrations and for coloring the parchment covers of books. Purple clothing remained common in Byzantium, where in the fourth century a method was discovered for the preservation of mollusks for shipment, and a factory for producing royal purple was established.

In the West the purple industry disappeared with the Roman Empire; a shipment from Taranto to Ravenna about 500 is the last heard of it. But the Arabs took over factories in the lands they conquered, including Sicily, and a factory at Palermo came into the possession of the Normans in the eleventh century. The quarrel over this luxurious pigment then resumed within the church, to be ended, more or less, in 1464, when Pope Paul II introduced "cardinal's purple," a cheaper red dye made from kermes.

The art of dyeing passed, with the Roman Empire, from the awareness of western Europe. The northern peoples obtained some chromatic variety by taking advantage of the natural differences in colors of wool, and they occasionally dyed with woad, madder, and various plants yielding colors that quickly faded, such as whortleberry, currant, and the bark of apple trees. A mixture of soot and egg white was used to blacken leather, an important article of clothing in northern Europe.

Such folk recipes were enshrined in the *Allerly Matkel* (1532), the earliest printed book on dyeing (and spot removal, which was, not surprisingly, an equally important problem). But the products of the still-flourishing dye industry of the East were not totally unknown. The body of a woman buried in the crypt of St. Denis, near Paris, about 570 (possibly Queen Arnegunde) was found lying on a bright red blanket; she was wearing a fine linen shift, a violet silk tunic, an ankle-length dark red silk gown, and a red satin veil. The garments were almost certainly imported, for trade in precious materials never entirely ceased. The Vikings imported fabrics: the remains of the Oseberg ship of about 800 (found in 1904) included cloth dyed with woad and madder.

The dye industry began to revive with Charlemagne. In his *Capitulare de villis* (812) he tried to promote domestic cultivation of dye plants, including woad, madder, and "vermillian," the latter possibly signifying kermes, a dye with which some of Charlemagne's own garments were colored. About the same time there appeared in Italy a recipe book, *Compositiones ad tinguenda* (or *Compositiones variae*), which gives seventeen recipes for "dyes and colors": yellow, red, green, blue, azure, and purple.

In the tenth century Lucca boasted a silk-dyeing industry, apparently founded by Jewish immigrants: in the 1160's Benjamin of Tudela claimed that all 200 Jews in Jerusalem were dyers. By the twelfth century dyestuffs as well as dyed fabrics were being imported, including brazilwood, an East Indian plant yielding a red dye—a dye so important that it was to give its name to a country. Some dye plants were domesticated, saffron being grown in Spain from the twelfth century. Venice was famous from the thirteenth century for violet dyes, and Florence, where immigrants from Lucca established the industry, for scarlet dyes from kermes. By 1338 there were nearly 200 dye "factories" in Florence. Southern France became famous for red, blue, and rose-colored dyes.

At the same time the nobility began to appear in tunics, mantles, hose, and shoes of bright blue, yellow, crimson, purple, and green—more colorful, if less tasteful, than the garments in which the reputed Queen Arnegunde had been laid to rest. In Germany the most popular colors were blue, green, and red; the clothes were usually made of wool. Much remained to be learned about dyeing, however, for wool, linen, and silk often required different dyes, which in some cases could be applied only to the unwoven threads.

The crusades broadened European knowledge of dyed fabrics and increased the demand for them. On his return from the Holy Land, King Louis IX of France appointed Etienne Boileau to the post of provost of the guilds (*prévôt des marchands*), with the duty, among others, of improving the dye industry. In 1268 Boileau issued a *Livre des métiers*, which reveals the existence of three grades of dyers: those working in "simple" colors, those working in "high" colors, and those dyeing silk. The simple colors were those obtained with dyes from walnut root, the bark of oak and alder, yellowwood, gallnuts, and vitriol, typical dyes of the early Middle Ages. The high colors included woad, kermes, and madder. Brazilwood, for some reason, was included in both categories (perhaps because it lacked a tradition).

Although it is alleged that a dyers' guild existed in Germany in the tenth century, the vast majority of dyers there and elsewhere remained for centuries subject to other guilds, notably those of the weavers. The dyers of Florence were organized from the beginning of the twelfth century into a religious brotherhood, since they were not allowed to form a guild. Subjected to harsh conditions by the weavers' and cloth merchants' guilds, many dyers emigrated. The same conditions existed in Flanders and most of northern Europe. In Paris, where there were sixteen dyers in 1287 and thirty-five by 1300, they were allowed to dye only wool and linen. Tapestry weavers did their own dyeing; and silk, the use of which was largely limited to ribbons, was dyed by haberdashers.

The grades of dyers and their production were carefully controlled, but it was exceedingly difficult to do so, especially because of the difficulty of detecting "illegal" colors. Yellow, red, and green, for example, could be derived from the inferior yellowwood, which gave a pale yellow color when dissolved in water, red when potash (potassium carbonate) or urine was added, and green when soluble sulfur compounds were added. The complexity of the art finally forced authorities to elevate the status of the dyer. The specialty was recognized at Paris in

1375, when the weavers were prohibited from dyeing (although only later were the dyers allowed a guild). The dyers at Florence dated their guild from 1429. Their charter included dye recipes that served as the basis for the first important dye recipe book of the sixteenth century, the *Plictho* of Gioanventura Rosetti (1548), a work that, according to S. M. Edelstein, ranks with Vannoccio Biringuccio's *Pirotechnia* and Agricola's *De re metallica* as a landmark in the history of technology.

BIBLIOGRAPHY

Johann Beckmann, *Beyträge zur Geschichte der Erfindungen*, 5 vols. (1783–1805), has articles on archil, saffron, madder, indigo, and alum; Franco Brunello, *The Art of Dyeing in the History of Mankind* (1973); Charlemagne, *Capitulare de villis*, in *Monumenta Germaniae historica, Legum*, I (1835), 181–187—also (with copious notes) in M. Guérard, "Explication du *Capitulare de villis*," in *Mémoires de l'Institut impérial de France*, 21 (1857), dyes mentioned in ch. 43. *Ciba Review* is replete with short pieces on dyeing in the Middle Ages, in particular, "Medieval Dyeing," in 1 (1937), "Purple in the Middle Ages," in 4 (1937), "Scarlet," in 7 (1938), "Trade Routes of the Middle Ages" and "Medieval Dye Markets in Europe," in 10 (1938), "Dyeing in France Before Colbert," in 18 (1939), and "Madder and Turkey Red," in 39 (1941). H. O. Clark and Rex Wailes,"The Preparation of Woad in England," in *Transactions of the Newcomen Society*, 16 (1936), primarily a description of the processes, machinery, and costs of the last surviving woad factory in England; S. M. Edelstein, "The Allerly Matkel, 1532," in *Technology and Culture*, 5 (1964); Rozelle P. Johnson, *Compositiones variae* (1939); Mary P. Merrifield, *Original Treatises on the Arts of Painting*, 2 vols. (1849, repr. 1967); E. E. Ploss, *Ein Buch von alten Farben* (1962); Gioanventura Rosetti, *Plictho*, S. M. Edelstein and H. C. Borghetty, trans. and eds. (1969); Charles Singer, *The Earliest Chemical Industry* (1948), a history of alum.

ROBERT P. MULTHAUF

[See also **Linen; Scarlet; Silk; Textiles; Wool.**]

DYFED derived its name from the Demetae, a Celtic tribe identified in the mid second century A.D. by Ptolemy of Alexandria as inhabitants of southwestern Wales—roughly the modern counties of Pembroke, Carmarthen, and Cardigan.

About the fourth century an Irish dynasty from Munster, the Déisi, migrated there and formed an Irish-speaking aristocracy. Inscriptions in the Irish ogham alphabet found on the numerous standing stones in the area that date from the fifth and sixth centuries bear ample witness to this Irish dominance.

Although Dyfed gradually became subsumed into Welsh culture, its Irish elements color the group of eleventh-century Welsh tales known as the *Mabinogion*. Genealogies in the British Library, MS Harley 3859 and various annal entries confirm that Dyfed's Irish dynasty managed to survive until the tenth century. During that time, however, Dyfed's borders shrank. Its northern part, bounded by the Teifi and Tywy rivers, became the kingdom of Ceredigion (Cardigan) sometime in the fifth century. Early in the eighth century King Rhain ap Cadwgan lost the land north of Carmarthen to the Welsh conqueror Seisyll.

Llywarch, son of King Hyfaidd, was the last king of Dyfed. On his death in 904, Hywel Dda (Howell the Good) annexed Dyfed through his marriage (892) to Elen, Llywarch's daughter. Beginning about 1090, the Normans overran Dyfed, establishing for themselves the lordships of Pembroke and Carmarthen.

Throughout much of the Middle Ages Dyfed was an important spiritual and cultural center. St. David, patron saint of Wales, founded his mother church of Mynyw (Menevia) in the Hodnant Valley of Dyfed. By the late eighth and early ninth centuries scholarship began to flourish there.

BIBLIOGRAPHY

Myles Dillon, "The Irish Settlements in Wales," in *Celtica*, 12 (1977); Myles Dillon and Nora K. Chadwick, *The Celtic Realms* (1967); J. E. Lloyd, *A History of Wales from the Earliest Times to the Edwardian Conquest*, 3rd ed., I (1939, repr. 1948).

MARILYN KAY KENNEY

[See also **Celtic Church; Wales, Early History.**]

DYRRACHIUM (Greek: Epidamnos; Serbo-Croatian: Drač; Italian: Durazzo; Albanian: Durrës), city and harbor on the eastern coast of the Adriatic Sea. Founded as a Greek colony in 627 B.C., under Roman protection from 229 B.C., it became an important economic, military, and administrative center. The Via Egnatia, which connected the Adriatic with Thessaloniki and eastern portions of the Roman Empire, began in Dyrrachium. In the second half of the fifth century the city was briefly held by the Ostrogoths, then returned to Byzantine rule. Except for brief periods of Bulgarian (late tenth to early eleventh centuries) and Norman (1082–1085) domination, Dyrrachium was the main Byzantine base on the Adriatic between the seventh and twelfth centuries.

In 1205 the city was conquered by Venice but it was taken in 1212 by Michael I of Epiros. In 1258 it was given as dowry to Manfred, king of Sicily (1258–1266). Reconquered by the Epirotes in 1266, Dyrrachium fell in 1272 to Charles I of Anjou, king of Naples (1266–1285), and became capital of his "kingdom of Albania," only to be retaken briefly by the Byzantines and then occupied in 1296 by the Serbian king Stefan Milutin (1282–1321). Reconquered briefly by the Byzantines at the beginning of the fourteenth century, Dyrrachium was held mostly by the Neapolitan Angevins with the help of Albanian chieftains until 1368. After that year it was conquered and lost several times by the Albanian prince Karl Topia (1359–1388). In 1379 Robert of Artois took the city, and after 1382 the Serb Balša Balšić held it briefly. Reconquered by the Topias, Dyrrachium was ceded to Venice by 1392 and remained Venetian until 1501, when the Ottomans conquered it. A flourishing commercial center through all its troubles, Dyrrachium began decaying in the fifteenth century, and after the Ottoman conquest it sank to the position of a minor provincial city.

BIBLIOGRAPHY

J. Ferluga, "Drač i dračka oblast pred kraj X i početkom XI veka," in *Mélanges G. Ostrogorsky*, II, published in the series Zbornik radova Vizant. instituta, VIII (1964); K. Jireček, "Položaj i prošlost grada Drača," in *Glasnik Srpskog geografskog društva*, 2 (1912); Milan von Šufflay, *Staedte und Burgen Albaniens hauptsächlich während des Mittelalters* (1924).

BARIŠA KREKIĆ

E. S., MASTER (*d. ca.* 1467), the most important of the second generation of artists using the engraving medium. He is the first engraver to have left a large body of work—more than 300 surviving prints, with others known from copies. Some of his most famous works are the *Einsiedeln Madonna, Hortus conclusus,* a Nativity, and a figural alphabet. First active about 1450, he worked in the region of Strasbourg, Constance, and Basel, and possibly further down the Rhine Valley. The more systematic engraving technique of E. S. permitted a wider range of modeling and the printing of more impressions from each plate than had that of his predecessors. While E. S.

Master E. S., letter "B." Engraving, before 1452. COURTESY OF THE ART INSTITUTE OF CHICAGO, CLARENCE BUCKINGHAM COLLECTION

was probably trained as a goldsmith, he based many of his prints on designs in a variety of media, including painting and sculpture. His prints were widely copied. To date, efforts to identify the engraver's monogram and oeuvre with a documented artist have been unconvincing.

BIBLIOGRAPHY

Lilli Fischel, "Werk und Name des 'Meisters von 1445'" in *Zeitschrift für Kunstgeschichte*, **13** (1950); Max Geisberg, *Die Kupferstiche des Meisters E.S.* (1924); Max Lehrs, *Geschichte und kritischer Katalog des deutschen, niederländischen und französischen Kupferstichs im XV. Jahrhundert*, II (1910); Alan Schestack, *Master E. S.: Five Hundredth Anniversary Exhibition* (1967).

MARTHA WOLFF

[See also **Engraving.**]

EADMER OF CANTERBURY (*ca.* 1060–*ca.* 1130), Benedictine historian and hagiographer. Chaplain and secretary to St. Anselm, he wrote a biography of him, drawing on notes made of the saint's actions and conversations from 1093 to 1100, when Anselm discovered the work and ordered Eadmer to abandon it. After Anselm's death in 1109, Eadmer revised and completed the work, relying on his memory for the period after 1100 and adding a section on the saint's posthumous miracles. He also composed a history of contemporary events, the *Historia novorum*, describing Anselm's public life. Important thematic concerns are the relation between church and state under William Rufus and Henry I, and the dispute between Canterbury and York. The influence of Eadmer's work can be seen in the writings of the Worcester chronicler and William of Malmesbury.

BIBLIOGRAPHY

The texts may be found in *Eadmeri Historia novorum in Anglia*, M. Rule, ed. (1884); *Eadmer's History of Recent Events in England*, G. Bosanquet, trans. (1964); and *The Life of St. Anselm, Archbishop of Canterbury*, Richard W. Southern, ed. and trans. (1962). Studies are Antonia Gransden, *Historical Writing in England: C. 550 to c. 1307* (1974), 129–142; and Richard W. Southern, *Saint Anselm and His Biographer* (1963).

Mary Lynn Rampolla

[See also **Anselm of Canterbury; Hagiography, Western European; Historiography, Western European.**]

EARLY CHRISTIAN AND BYZANTINE ARCHITECTURE. As applied to architecture, the term "early Christian" refers to the interval between the advent of Constantine and that of Charlemagne in the West (312–768), or between the advent of Constantine and that of iconoclasm in the East (312–726). The term "Byzantine," on the other hand, is a political designation tied to the limits and influence of the Byzantine state. While earlier historians tended to restrict "Byzantine" to a period starting after iconoclasm, more recent scholars, acknowledging the strong cultural continuity of the Eastern empire, have used the term to refer to the entire life of that state from the founding of the new capital of Constantinople in 330 to the Turkish conquest of the city in 1453. Byzantine architecture, then, is defined as the architecture of Constantinople and its empire, and of the realms that came under its sphere of influence. The two terms, therefore, overlap considerably, and for this reason it makes sense to treat the two categories together.

The emergence of a new, distinctive Christian architecture, like the process of conversion of the nations of the ancient world to the new faith, was

gradual. As far as materials and techniques are concerned, early Christian and Byzantine architecture represents a continuous development of the usages of the late Roman Empire. In Constantinople building materials consisted of local variations of those in use earlier in Rome. Lacking the ingredients of Italian concrete (the volcanic pozzolana), architects around the Aegean and in Asia Minor employed a rougher concrete with a large measure of rubble fill; this core material was faced with brick, or with alternating courses of brick and stone having occasional bonding courses of brick to hold the mass more firmly together. Vaults were executed in pure brick, often in a "pitched" brick technique that allowed the masons to cover an area quickly without centering; the vault, once dry, was made secure with a covering of concrete. For revetments and finer details Constantinople had at hand the marble quarries of Proconessus in the Sea of Marmara, which produced abundant supplies of a fine, gray-veined marble; colored marbles for more brilliant effects were imported from quarries around the Mediterranean, as they had been in Rome.

The spirit that reshaped these materials into something new was intensely concerned with the geometry of spaces. The limited, sober repertoire of Roman vaulted forms was multiplied with a wide range of forms, some imported from the East and some newly invented; severe Roman trabeated colonnades were transformed into arcades, then bent into curves and circles; the massiveness of Roman architecture gave way to ever lighter and more daring engineering feats to which the Byzantine mind attached a theological importance bordering on mysticism.

CITY PLANNING

The gradual transformation of older forms is evident in city planning from the outset. In his planning of the new capital in Constantinople (324–330), Emperor Constantine was most anxious that the New Rome should be in no way inferior to the old. Within a fortified perimeter he provided broad colonnaded avenues, forums, and public baths. The senate was housed in a basilica facing onto the civic center, the Augusteion. The hippodrome (420–440 meters, 1,378–1,443 feet long) was built on the scale of the Circus Maximus in Rome (609.6 meters, 1,999 feet), and, as in Rome, the imperial palace lay along one flank and provided the emperor with direct communication to his private box. But while many individual units of the plan remained purposefully

The walls of Constantinople, moat and double enceinte. Begun 412. COURTESY OF R. VAN NICE, DUMBARTON OAKS

conservative, important innovations were being introduced. The principal forum, named for Constantine and having his statue on a grand column of porphyry in the center, was laid out on an unprecedented elliptical plan. In the heart of the civic center, the placement of the cathedral and episcopal residence across the Augusteion from the palace of the emperor reflected very graphically the new role the Christian religion was to play in Constantine's empire. In addition the erection of the cruciform Church of the Holy Apostles to serve as Constantine's personal mausoleum gave expression not only to the emperor's piety but also to his extraordinary pretension to rank among the apostles.

In other cities in which substantial redesigning took place, a marked new imprint was evident in the fourth century. In Antioch a great church known as the Golden Octagon was erected alongside the emperor's palace, which, as in Constantinople, stood beside the hippodrome. In Jerusalem the colonnaded city that was laid out in Hadrian's time was given a new focus with a monumental building program at Golgotha, the site of Christ's death. In Rome, on the other hand, the Christian replanning of the city was much less conspicuous. The Lateran Cathedral was placed far from the city center at the east, and the largest basilicas were erected outside the walls at Christian burial sites (St. Peter's, S. Lorenzo, S. Agnese, and SS. Marcellino e Pietro). In the center of the city Constantine was concerned with secular architecture. He added a new public bath on the south slope of the Quirinal and completed the enormous civil basilica begun by Maxentius adjoining the Forum Romanorum. This situation did not change until the fifth century, when a majority of the population could be counted Christian and Pope Sixtus III began to erect large, fine basilicas, such as S. Maria Maggiore, in the very center of Rome.

Meanwhile, in border provinces, where military concerns were always uppermost, the Roman square castrum plan continued to dominate the design of cities well into the sixth century. By this time, however, the urban economy of the ancient Roman world was crumbling before invasions from without and depopulation from within. The subsequent shape of the city was substantially medieval, modeled on new patterns of life. The decline in the importance of the ancient cultural centers of hippodrome, theater, and bath coincided with the gradual proliferation of churches and monasteries that transformed the fabric of the city. The public services of hospital, school, and relief for the poor were incorporated into the monasteries. The development of a stational liturgy, moreover, brought Christian cult into the streets of the city, establishing a very visible web of links from shrine to shrine. In Constantinople, for example, feasts of the Virgin were celebrated at three stations: matins would be held in the cathedral of Hagia Sophia, litanies would be chanted in the forum, and finally Mass would be celebrated at the Chalkoprateia or Blachernai basilica of the Virgin. The city, in effect, was transformed into a kind of miniature Holy Land, dotted with holy places that took turns as the focus of attention.

At the same time the multiplication of ecclesiastical foundations (there were more than 500 in medieval Constantinople) had a private dimension as well; privately founded, they offered places for the personal devotion and burial of the patrons and their extended families. The consequent loss of a clearly defined center in medieval Byzantine cities (for example, Kastoria and Athens) was therefore a sociological phenomenon as much as a phenomenon of planning. In addition, the needs of defense became more and more important in the greatly diminished empire. The planning of the late Byzantine city of Mistra, Greece, was governed by the need to cluster the city under the steep slopes of an impregnable citadel. At the same time, in Constantinople the emperor abandoned his great palace on the sea for a fortress-palace along the city walls, where his guard could double as defenders of the city.

Perhaps the greatest contribution of early Christian and Byzantine architecture to city planning is not found in the secular city but in the "ideal" city of the monastery. Often located on sites unencumbered by earlier buildings, erected for a controlled population, and not complicated by commercial needs, monasteries offered the architect wide scope for site development. At Qalᶜat Simᶜan in Syria, the column on which St. Simeon Stylites endured his extraordinary feat of asceticism determined the situation of the subsequent monastery, along the spine of a barren mountaintop. Around this column in the late fifth century was built a great cruciform church measuring 100 meters (328 feet) from east to west. In the southeast angle of the cross lay the monastic enclosure, organized around a rectangular courtyard and consisting of a smaller church for the monks' private use, refectory, storerooms, and a U-shaped block of monastic cells rising three stories high. Farther to the south lay a baptistery and hostelry, and farther still lay the *via sacra* that permitted approach to this acropolis from the valley below.

The pilgrimage character of Qalᶜat Simᶜan required the development of a town (anc. Telanissus, mod. Deir Simᶜan) to provide accommodations in the valley, but this was not the rule in Byzantine monasteries, which were often places of remote seclusion. While a plan as formal as that of St. Gall in the West was never worked out, Byzantine architects seem to have arrived at a loose formula capable of free accommodation to the site. The monasteries that ringed Mt. Athos from the tenth century on are the best examples. A defensible eminence was usually chosen for the site, and its shape determined the overall plan of the fortified perimeter, defended by one or more towers. (The chief enemies were not invading armies but marauding pirates.) A single gate controlled entrance to the courtyard, within which, often freestanding in the center of the enclosure, was the principal church (*katholikon*) of the monastery. The refectory (*trapeza*) either flanked the church or, more commonly, faced it, and between them stood a fountain (*phiale*) for washing. The cells (*kellia*) of the individual monks were generally inserted in several stories into the perimeter wall of the monastery, facing onto the courtyard from a succession of balconies. Compared with monasteries of the West, Byzantine monasteries are much more compact, and in their irregularity they convey an impression of organically growing out of the site.

SECULAR ARCHITECTURE

Very incomplete evidence remains to assess the contribution of early Christian and Byzantine secular architecture. The continuous occupation of many sites down to modern times has covered the traces of earlier architecture and prevented its excavation; the sites that are best preserved are those in Syria that were abandoned after the Arab occupation of the country, but they contain a village architecture that is probably not representative of secular building in the rest of the empire. In all parts of the empire the architecture of fortifications has survived best, and it is clear that the Byzantines possessed considerable skill in this area. The land walls of Constantinople are the most impressive example and constitute the earliest introduction of the fully developed double-enceinte system of fortification, unknown in the West until the end of the Middle Ages. The principal wall, 10 to 15 meters (33 to 49 feet) high, with a projecting tower every 60 meters (197 feet), was preceded by a wall 20 meters (66 feet) forward, 8 to 10 meters (26 to 33 feet) high which had its own string of projecting towers. This forward wall was de-

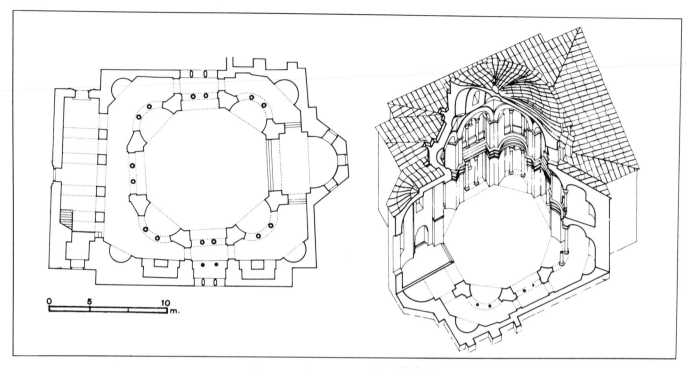

Hagioi Sergios and Bakchos. Ground plan and isometric drawing. Constantinople, begun *ca. 525*. From Christian Norberg-Schulz, *Meaning in Western Architecture* (1974). ELECTA EDITRICE, MILAN

fended by a moat some 18 meters (59 feet) broad. Stretching for six kilometers (almost four miles) from the Sea of Marmara to the Golden Horn, this mighty defense was erected by Constantine, prefect of the Orient under Theodosius II between 412 and 415, and it successfully defended the city for a thousand years, until Mehmed II brought modern European cannons to assault it in 1453.

The defense of the empire was a major concern of Justinian (527–565), who attempted to stabilize the eastern border with a string of fortified outposts from the Black Sea to the Sinai Peninsula. The greatest builder since Hadrian, he invested an enormous share of the income of the empire in public building projects of all kinds. Procopius produced a minute record of this work—stoae and forums, roads and bridges, harbors and markets, aqueducts and cisterns. Beyond the fortresses a meager sampling of this architecture remains to give some inkling of its accomplishment. Built to assure ease of communication between Constantinople and central Asia Minor, one of Justinian's bridges arches seven times to cross the Sangarius (Sakarya) River in Bithynia, a total distance of some 368 meters (1,207 feet). In Constantinople the largest of the cisterns that Justinian built still remain, known by their Turkish names of Yerebatan and Binbirdirek (formerly the Basilica and Philoxenos cisterns). These underground reservoirs are vast columnar halls covered with repeated pendentive domical vaults of brick; their combined capacity was more than 100,000 cubic meters (more than 3.5 million cubic feet).

Palace architecture, so often referred to in literary sources, is perhaps the greatest loss of all in the realm of Byzantine secular architecture. The Great Palace of Constantinople was simultaneously the residence of the emperor, the seat of government, and the center of the social life of the city. Literary sources would have the reader see something on the order of Hadrian's villa near Tivoli, a sprawling succession of gardens, courtyards, reception halls, and chapels, added to continuously by successive emperors from the time of Constantine to the Latin conquest of 1204. Practically nothing remains of it. The Byzantine palaces that are best preserved (the Tekfur Saray of the Blachernai Palace in Constantinople, and the palaces of Nymphaion, Mistra, and Trebizond) all date to the late Byzantine period and owe much to contemporary Western architecture.

334

EARLY CHRISTIAN CHURCHES: ORIGINS AND USES

Regrettable as the losses of early Christian and Byzantine secular architecture are, the higher survival rate for church architecture is not without meaning. The church building enjoyed an undisputed preeminence among the art forms of Byzantine society. Sheltering what was regarded as the most exalted of human experiences—the performance of the Divine Liturgy—it was the object of the most attentive concern. It demanded the best materials, the most costly furnishings, and the finest workmanship available; but most important, it required the greatest virtuosity of design. The church building is therefore the fairest measure of the achievement of the Byzantine architect; on this must stand or fall his place in history.

From the beginning the sponsorship of the newly converted Emperor Constantine gave an impetus to church building that influenced its direction for centuries. In the era before the "Peace of the Church" (311), church building, as in the *domus ecclesiae* discovered at Dura Europos, was as private and unobtrusive as possible. Constantine initiated an era of imperial patronage, the aim of which was to place the church on a par with the most expensive and imposing structures of public architecture. Almost as soon as he had taken Rome, work was begun on a new cathedral on imperial property at the Lateran. A grand, timber-roofed nave, 75 meters (246 feet) long and 55 meters (180 feet) wide, was supported on either side by two rows of fifteen monolithic columns of colored marble. On each side of the nave a pair of aisles repeated the width of the nave at a lower height, making a total of five long, parallel corridors of space. The floors and walls were covered with rich marble, but the focus of attention was on the altar at the end of the nave, which stood under a silver canopy in front of the gold-vaulted apse.

Similar works were undertaken under imperial sponsorship at St. Peter's and other sites in Rome, and in the East at Jerusalem, Bethlehem, and Mambre (Ramat-el-khalil). In some the aisles were reduced to two, and in others a gallery story was added above the aisles, but the overall effect was the same. The church was a variant on the form of the civil basilica. Its basic elements of aisles and nave, its classical vocabulary of decoration, and its overall proportions could be encountered in Roman forums all over the empire. The basic difference was in the orientation—the axis was turned ninety degrees. The principal entrances to a civil basilica were on the long side and the apse (for judge or magistrate) would be found opposite, across the nave. The reorientation of the basilica for Christian use must be attributed to its functional adaptation to the liturgy: the longitudinal plan made the processional movement of the liturgy more effective.

The basilica proved to be an eminently practical form of church building, for while it was suitable for lavish embellishment under imperial sponsorship, it could also be erected very simply and modestly by communities with lesser means. Local building materials could be employed: limestone in Syria, columns salvaged from older ruins in Rome. In addition, the basilica required no special technical expertise on the part of the workmen but could be erected under the direction of a master builder (*architekton*), without the services of the skilled architect or engineer (*mechanikos*). Sometimes unskilled parishioners joined the work force.

The flexibility of the basilica helped to ensure its popularity, for with minor adaptations it could be suited to local variations in the liturgy. The place of the altar, somewhat in front of the apse, was usual almost everywhere, and the place of the clergy was generally a semicircular bench (synthronon) in the apse, with the bishop's throne in the center. The bishop preached from his throne. Arrangements for readings differed from place to place. In Constantinople an elevated pulpit for reading (ambo) was placed near the center of the church; in Syria a large U-shaped platform (bema) in the center of the nave accommodated the clergy during the readings, chants, and litanies—that is, for the first half of the liturgy.

Variations in the offertory rite also dictated modifications in the plan in the basilica. In Rome bread and wine were brought forward by men and women during the liturgy to reserved areas—the *senatorium* and *matroneum*—at the east end of either aisle. In Constantinople the bread and wine were prepared privately by the clergy before the liturgy, in a separate little building called the treasury (*skeuophylakion*); from there, at the appropriate time, they were carried into the church by the deacons in a solemn procession called the Great Entrance. Syria had still a different arrangement, in which the elements were prepared in a sacristy (pastophorium) immediately adjoining the sanctuary and then brought out at the anaphora.

Early Christian architecture was eminently practical. Not only were local variations in liturgy reflected in the layout of the church, but separate functions tended to be housed in separate structures.

San Vitale, Ravenna, 546–548. PHOTOGRAPH BY G. E. KIDDER SMITH

Thus the baptistery developed as a separate structure to house the piscina, or font. The plan was usually centrally designed; circular and polygonal plans were common, but the octagon was the preferred shape, following a pattern established at the Lateran in Rome and at St. Ambrose's Church of S. Tecla in Milan. Like the basilica, the baptistery carried overtones of its pre-Christian origins, but in this case the reminiscences were, appropriately, of the bath and the mausoleum. Paul had described baptism as death with Christ (Rom. 6:3–4), and Ambrose saw the number eight of the octagonal plan as symbolic of Christ's resurrection, since he rose on the eighth day of the week.

Other functions required different kinds of structures. In Rome and North Africa the funeral banquets for the dead *(refrigeria)* were given separate architectural treatment. Over the earlier catacombs on the outskirts of Rome (S. Agnese and S. Sebastiano, for example), spacious ambulatory basilicas arose with floors virtually paved with tombs. However, much more important as an early Christian architectural type was the shrine, whether erected at a martyr's tomb or at the site of a special event in the history of salvation. In modern scholarship this type of shrine has been called a martyrium. The term has given rise to considerable confusion, since in early Christian sources it seems to have referred to any church dedicated to a martyr, whether or not it was the site of his death and/or burial; on the other hand, shrines over holy sites, such as the octagon erected by Constantine over the cave of the Nativity in Bethlehem, were not called martyria in early Christian literature.

In this category of shrines the most important was certainly the Holy Sepulcher in Jerusalem, the holiest of all pilgrimage goals. When Constantine completed the basilica of Jerusalem, about 335, the shrine of Christ's tomb consisted of an aediculum that stood free in an open court beyond the apse of the basilica. Before the end of the century, however, this aediculum was housed within a great rotunda called the Anastasis (the Resurrection). Its plan did not differ essentially from the mausoleum that Constantine built for his daughter, S. Costanza in Rome. The circular rotunda of the Anastasis was supported

336

by paired piers on the cardinal axes with sets of three columns (7.15 meters [23.5 feet] high) in between; an ambulatory ringed the rotunda with niches on three axes and a great entrance porch on the fourth.

Shrines could take a wide variety of forms. The shrine of the Nativity in Bethlehem consisted of an octagon joined to a basilica, while the shrine of St. Peter in the Vatican consisted of a transverse hall, or transept, joined to the basilica. According to literary sources, the fourth-century shrine that contained the tomb of St. Euphemia in Chalcedon repeated the rotunda and ambulatory plan of the Holy Sepulcher, with a gallery added. In Constantinople the shrines of St. Polycarp and of Sts. Martha, Mary, and Lazarus were also said to be rotundas in imitation of the Holy Sepulcher. In other words, among the variety of forms available for the building of such shrines, the preferred choice seemed to be the rotunda with its obvious overtones of mausoleum.

Palace churches erected for the personal use of the emperor may have constituted, even in this period, a separate type of structure, for which a galleried octagon was preferred. Constantine's Golden Octagon of Antioch may have set the pattern which was soon followed by that of his son, Constantius, in his church of S. Lorenzo in Milan. In Justinian's reign the type was taken up at the churches of Hagioi Sergios and Bakchos and St. John of Hebdomon in Constantinople.

THE FIFTH CENTURY

At the end of the fourth century Emperor Theodosius I (379–395) made Christianity no longer simply a licit religion but the only approved religion of the state, and the following century witnessed unprecedented church-building activity. The building types introduced in the fourth century became standardized by use and could be found in virtually every corner of the empire. At this point regional differences began to appear that went beyond the differences of local liturgical practices and constituted regional styles. These differences may have been less pronounced in metropolitan centers that were in contact with the capital and were frequently the beneficiaries of imperial building projects, but where local builders were left to their own devices, regional differences asserted themselves.

In the Near East, from southern Anatolia to Syria and Palestine, the preference for cut stone architecture, generally with little or no mortar, gave rise to a fairly homogeneous style of considerable distinction. Broad arches on short piers formed the main nave arcade or, especially in southern Syria, were used transversely to span the entire nave. Doors were crowned with monolithic lintels, and roofs often were made of broad slabs of stone. Stone skeletons were even used to frame dwellings rising in blocks three of four stories high. The decoration also was suited to the medium: wall surfaces were rarely frescoed, the chief ornament being a rich range of stone sculptural decoration. Classical moldings were transformed into flowing ribbons; applied colonnettes articulated the walls; squinch arches encircled turrets or octagonal units. On this virtuosity in stone the architects forged a regional style of considerable vitality that survived through the sixth century, at which time it served as the point of departure for the development of a native Armenian architecture before succumbing to the cultural upheaval of the Arab invasions.

Around the Aegean quite a different style appeared, with Constantinople setting the pace. Copious supplies of marble columns and timber for roofs made possible spacious interiors of much grander dimension than generally found in the Near East. In Constantinople square basilicas were popular, with galleries for catechumens on three sides, as at the St. John Studios and Chalkoprateia basilicas of the mid fifth century. In Greece basilicas with a transept area enlarging the space around the sanctuary were more popular. But in either case there was lavish use of marble and mosaic on floors, walls, and vaults. Sculptural ornament began to break decisively with the classical past. Leaves were swept into wind-blown patterns, rinceaux were treated as abstract patterns of light and shade, and double-zoned capitals were loaded with birds and beasts. Manufactured in the quarries of the Marmora, this ornament was exported in large quantities around the Aegean, and in diminishing supply even farther around the Mediterranean.

Although the imperial administrative center for the West was Ravenna, leadership in ecclesiastical matters, and more and more in political affairs as well, lay with the papacy. The regional style in the Latin West is somewhat plainer both in planning and in decoration. The aisled basilica without transept or galleries was the rule, and the decoration even of the grandest monuments, such as S. Maria Maggiore in Rome (432–440), consisted of reused columns, capitals, and architraves. Yet it is in the West that one finds the earliest examples of nave decoration with mosaics of narrative illustrations of the Old and New Testaments. At S. Maria Maggiore

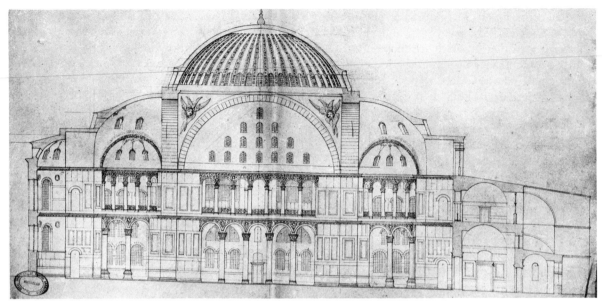

Hagia Sophia, Istanbul, 532–537. Cross-section drawing by Charles Texier, 1834, Royal Institute of British Architects, London. PHOTO COURTESY OF DUMBARTON OAKS CENTER FOR BYZANTINE STUDIES, WASHINGTON, D.C.

this consisted of discrete, framed panels, but at S. Paolo fuori le Mura and at St. Peter's, which was decorated in the fifth century, the entire clerestory wall was covered with narrative material transforming the nave into an enormous gallery of sacred history. Both the simple lines of the Latin basilica and the taste for narration were to have an enormous impact on the architecture of the later Middle Ages.

CHURCHES OF THE JUSTINIANIC PERIOD

The extraordinary energies that Justinian channeled into reconstructing the civil architecture of the empire were more than matched by his achievement in ecclesiastical architecture. Had he built only Hagia Sophia, his place in the history of architecture would be guaranteed; but in fact he left many monuments of startling originality that had a decisive impact on the history of architecture. Justinian's contribution, however, was not so much a new style—for the buildings are much too diverse to constitute a homogeneous style—as a new conception of church architecture. Whereas formerly church building was for the most part contained within the larger category of basilica architecture, now it created new categories of vaulted architecture all its own; whereas formerly it was largely the work of contracting foremen planning varieties of a standard design, it now became the work of professional architects of a speculative bent who delighted in new inventions; whereas formerly church architecture

followed the innovations made in other genres, now it took the lead, dragging the others in its train. The problem of church planning now became an exercise in geometry, a problem of the kaleidoscopic transmutations possible within the symmetry of stars, octagons, crosses, and flowers.

The sources of Justinianic architecture were many, but they cannot account for the inventiveness of the monuments. Martyrs' shrines have been alleged as sources for the Church of Hagioi Sergios and Bakchos in Constantinople, but nothing could be further from the heavy, mausoleum quality of such shrines. The building can be described as a play between an octagon and a square. The outer shell of the building is a square, but it tends toward an octagonal shape inside through an arrangement of diagonal niches in the four corners; the inner unit in turn, though octagonal, tends toward a square in that its diagonal sides have been expanded with semicircular niches. These two contrasting forms interact through graceful colonnades on both ground-floor and gallery levels. Above is a dome of sixteen segments, alternately flat and concave, lightened by eight windows. The original wall decoration in marble and mosaic has disappeared, but the marble columns in dark green and rose and the lacy carving of capitals and entablature give a hint of what the rest must have looked like.

The challenge of this idea evidently fascinated Justinian's architects. According to Procopius two

338

additional variants of the plan were built in the suburbs of Constantinople, while in Philippi remains of another have been excavated, the inner octagon of which was much more regular, with straight colonnades on all sides and columns replacing the corner piers. At S. Vitale in Ravenna (546–548) the plan went through another mutation; this time it is an octagon within an octagon, and each face of the inner octagon expands into a niche. Precedents for this sort of architecture seem not to have been found in mausoleums but in palace architecture, whether in the Golden Octagon of Antioch or in its predecessors—the pavilions of Hadrian's villa in Tivoli and the Minerva Medica in Rome.

A second group of buildings of the Justinianic period seem to have had their inspiration in the grand interior spaces of Roman bath architecture. But instead of the heavy groin vaults of the baths, these churches were crowned with windowed domes. The basic unit was a square with sides consisting of four broad arches or barrel vaults; in the intervals between the four arches the architects introduced four monumental pendentives, in the shape of spherical triangles, to form the transition from the square of the four arches to the circle of the dome above. A church might consist of a single unit of this kind, as at Hagia Irene in Constantinople, St. Titus at Gortyna in Crete, or Church B at Philippi. Or the unit might be multiplied five or six times in a cruciform pattern, as at the enormous Church of the Holy Apostles in Constantinople, or the Church of St. John the Evangelist in Ephesus. The effect was as bold and powerful as Hagioi Sergios and Bakchos was subtle and delicate.

Hagia Sophia stands in a class by itself. It is the largest of all Byzantine churches, and for length and breadth of space enclosed within a single span it easily surpasses all the vaulted interiors of antiquity and the Middle Ages. From the nave entrance to the bishop's throne in the apse the interior measures 80 meters (262 feet) while from side to side it spans 32.6 meters (107 feet). This enormous monument was raised in five years (532–537) to replace the earlier basilica on the same site, which had been destroyed in the Nika insurrection. A mathematician-geometrician, Anthemios of Tralles, and a mathematician who had written commentaries on works by Archimedes and Hero, Isidoros of Miletos, were the architects, and their firm grasp of vaulting theory is evident everywhere in the monument.

The central unit is a square resting on four enormous stone piers (the rest of the building is brick);

four broad arches link the piers, and four enormous pendentives link the arches. On the rim of these pendentives is a shallow ribbed dome 32.6 meters (107 feet) in diameter. The thrusts of this powerful dome required buttressing on all sides. To the north and south four buttress towers were erected, arching over the aisles and galleries, while to the east and west a uniquely modern solution was found by transferring the thrust to abutting half domes. The half domes in turn each rested on two smaller half domes containing niches to the right and left, and on barrel vaults on the main axis.

The inventiveness of the design as a whole was matched by inventiveness in details. In architectural sculpture the advances of the fifth century culminated in a new style during Justinianic times that was characterized by sharply undercut surfaces; vine and leaf motifs were made to stand free of the stone behind them, creating a lacy effect of the utmost delicacy. Covered with gold leaf, the stone was transformed in a way sculpture had never before achieved. Capitals took on a basket shape that eliminated previous divisions into zones, and the carving of the capital spilled over into spandrels and archivolts. Elsewhere inlaid work achieved the same effects of dematerialization, shining with colored marbles and mother-of-pearl.

Sheathed in marble and gold and furnished with a sanctuary of silver, Hagia Sophia became an unfailing source of inspiration to later architects. Countless "copies" were attempted, and although the design itself was not imitated, the concern with the subtleties of geometry and opulence of decoration exerted an irresistible attraction. It was a monument worthy of its destiny as the heart of Eastern Christendom for nine centuries.

MIDDLE BYZANTINE CHURCH ARCHITECTURE

In the years following Justinian his grand reconstruction of the empire proved far too ambitious. The territories claimed were too vast for the resources of the state to hold together, and while in the East the war with Persia dragged on, the Slavs overran the Balkans and claimed the very core of the empire in the late sixth century. The seventh century marked the nadir of the Byzantine state; even Heraklios' stunning defeat of the Persians in 628 did more to facilitate the eventual Arab conquests of the Near East than to reestablish Byzantine hegemony in that area; it was only with great difficulty that the Arabs were thrown back from the walls of Constantinople in 678.

Hagia Sophia, Istanbul, 532–537. Guillaume Joseph Grelot, *Relation d'un voyage de Constantinople* (1680).
PHOTOGRAPH COURTESY OF DUMBARTON OAKS

The period of iconoclasm that followed saw a reorganization of government that prepared for a new flowering of Byzantine civilization. The civilization that emerged, however, was very different from what had flourished in early Christian times. The changed shape of cities was only one symptom of the transformation. In territory the empire was greatly reduced; the loss of Rome, Alexandria, and Antioch gave greater importance to Constantinople. In population, too, the empire was very different, for it now sought to extend its influence by war and diplomacy to the newer settlers in eastern Europe—the Slavs, the Serbs, the Bulgars, the Russians. In its religious life the conflict of iconoclasm had given images an unparalleled importance in Orthodoxy and broadened the chasm between Constantinople and the West.

The churches built during the seventh and eighth centuries, such as Hagia Sophia of Thessaloniki and Hagia Sofia of Bizye, Thrace, retained the standard domed-cross unit that had been popularized in the Justinianic period. In the ninth and tenth centuries, however, new architectural types appeared that became the foundation for middle and late Byzantine architecture. An understanding of these types is essential to any discussion of Byzantine architecture. Three families of building types can be distinguished, and within each family numerous subtypes developed.

The simplest group of designs is that of the Greek-cross type, the vaulting consisting of four converging barrel vaults supporting drum and dome on pendentives. This element is clearly derived from the vaulting system of Justinian's domed-cross unit, but it has been scaled down to much more modest dimensions and a new symmetry governs the plan. Instead of the pseudo-basilican lines of Justinian's floor plans, the four arms of the cross are of nearly equal length, and the corner bays between the arms of the cross are symmetrical little squares of space. The earliest example of the type in Constantinople seems to be the Atik Mustafa Pasha Camii, probably of the ninth century. This type enjoyed an enormous popularity in Russia, where many varieties were developed. At times the four corner bays opened through wide arches into the cross element of the plan, while at other times they were clearly segregated from it into separate chambers; at Spaso Preobrazhenski in the Mirozshki monastery (before 1156) the corner bays are much lower than the cross element, while at the Church of the Savior at Nereditsa, Novgorod (1198), they match the height of the cross and include gallery chapels in the west corners. The three great cathedrals of Kiev (begun 1037), Novgorod (begun 1045), and Vladimir (begun 1158) should really be classified with this type. In these instances the Greek cross is enveloped on all sides by aisles and galleries, creating a complex and mysterious interior broken into a succession of separate, darker compartments grouped around the larger, lighter well of space in the center of the church. On the exterior the addition of domes over the corner bays creates a colorful and picturesque profile.

A second family of designs belongs to a type that has been variously referred to as a cross-in-square, inscribed cross, quincunx, or four-column plan. The plan consists of a neatly layered succession of geometric shapes. The first layer is cubical with four columns defining, but not shutting off, small corners of the cube. These four columns support a cruciform space on the next layer; and the cross in turn supports on pendentives a third, cylindrical layer consisting of the drum and dome. The Byzantine fascination with geometry is evident in one of the earliest surviving cross-in-square monuments, the Myrelaion Church in Constantinople, built by Emperor Romanos Lekapenos in 920–922. Each successive layer is marked off with a cornice; the first cornice is exactly half the height of the third cornice, while the second cornice is twice as high as the nave is wide. The cupola exhibits an even more intricate geometry: an umbrella dome of eight gored segments was planned by laying out a ring of eight tangent semicircles, the diameter of each semicircle being one-third the diameter of the dome. A subtle complex of proportions thus governed the design of the whole church.

Because it depended for its effect on the use of marble columns, the cross-in-square proved most popular around the Aegean, where spoils from ancient monuments provided plenty of columns. Like the simpler Greek-cross type, the cross-in-square could be developed by the addition of corner cupolas, as in Basil I's New Church (Nea) in Constantinople (880) or in the Church of the Mother-of-God of Constantine Lips in Constantinople (907). In the monasteries of Mt. Athos, on the other hand, the plan was often expanded laterally by the addition of apses to the north and south arms of the cross, a variation that became popular in Serbian architecture.

The third family of designs is referred to at times as the domed octagon, at times as the squinch type. It includes fewer monuments than the two other families, but the variations within it are still very numerous. One of the most elegant examples is the Church of Nea Moni, Chios, erected by Constantine IX Monomachos between 1042 and 1056. On the ground floor the body of the church is perfectly square; in a second zone the square is reshaped into eight niches—four deep niches in the corners and four broader, shallow niches on the axes. In the vaulting zone the corner niches are modified into squinches that support the drum on a corona vault, an inverted crown shape consisting of eight pseudopendentives.

Variations on this type were especially popular in the eleventh century. In the Kamariotissa Church in Constantinople the diagonal niches reach from the floor to the vault, and the axial niches are developed into a cross plan with apses in all four directions. At Hosios Lukas in Phocis, Greece, the cubical lines of the nave are retained right up to the vaulting, where squinches are placed in the angles; to this cubical unit are added cross arms and auxiliary spaces ringing the interior on ground and gallery levels.

What all of these Middle Byzantine church designs have in common is a preoccupation with the symmetrical development of a centralized space. The architect proved himself above all in the realm of solid geometry—in the design of interior spaces of exquisite harmony. At the same time, however, he did not neglect the decoration of the monument. Integral to the sophisticated effect of the churches was the refinement of their finish. When the means were available, floors were paved with marble that was often inlaid with geometric and figurative designs. Multicolored marbles covered the walls, arranged in mirror patterns in which panels on one side echoed the placement of panels on the other. Capitals and cornices were worked in precious metals, and the vaults above were covered with mosaics in which figures floated against rich gold backgrounds. In

Hagia Sophia, Istanbul, 532–537. Interior view looking into vaulting. From Christian Norberg-Schulz, *Meaning in Western Architecture* (1974). ELECTA EDITRICE, MILAN. PHOTOGRAPH BY BRUNO BALESTRINI

churches where such splendor could not be afforded, the interior was colorfully frescoed, and often the lower zones were painted to imitate marble.

SOURCES AND INTERPRETATION OF MIDDLE BYZANTINE DESIGNS

More difficult than cataloging the types of Middle Byzantine architecture is the task of interpreting its extraordinary development of forms. It must be asked where the impulse for these central-plan types came from and why they should have become so all-pervasive in posticonoclast times. The basilica, which proved so adaptable a form in early Christian times, virtually disappeared in this period and, more surprisingly, even the solutions of Justinianic architecture were abandoned. The new fascination with the geometric possibilities of the three basic types described above had its roots in larger cultural phenomena. Several interpretations of the data have been advanced, and while none is entirely satisfactory, each sheds light on some aspect of the development.

The reduced dimensions of Middle Byzantine architecture and the fact that some of the first examples of the cross-in-square appeared in a monastic setting have suggested that the impetus for Middle Byzantine church design was basically monastic. Clearly monasticism dominated medieval Byzantine spirituality, and generally monasteries required smaller churches than bishoprics. Nevertheless, the fact remains that Middle Byzantine church plans, whatever their type, were interchangeable as far as their ecclesiastical status was concerned. A cross-in-square building might serve as a cathedral, a monastery, or a private family chapel.

Palace architecture has also been advanced as a mainspring of Middle Byzantine church designs. Literary sources often describe the chambers of the Great Palace of Constantinople in terms that are interchangeable with church architecture: four-column bedrooms and triple-apsed reception halls are mentioned. On the other hand, churches of the Middle Byzantine period are frequently described as palace halls of the Lord, and the iconography of the church tended to reinforce the imperial associations. The figure of Christ Pantokrator that occupied the dome of the Kauleas Church in Constantinople (893–901) was described by Leo VI as representing the Governor of the Universe surrounded by his imperial court of angels. The preponderant role of imperial patronage in architectural commissions adds weight to this "palace theory" of the origins of Middle Byz-

antine designs. Nothing would be more natural than that the style and forms that had evolved in imperial domestic architecture should be adopted for church use. The theory remains in the realm of speculation, however, for the decisive evidence was lost with the destruction of the Great Palace.

Others have proposed Syrian or Armenian origins for Middle Byzantine architecture. Archaeological evidence for this theory has survived, and in Armenia it is both plentiful and convincing. The seventh century witnessed a brilliant flowering of central-plan structures in Armenia, including each of the three types that appeared later in Byzantium. The medium is somewhat different and the result achieved has a different feeling. In Armenia a fine, stone-faced masonry was used instead of the brick-faced or marble-covered work of Constantinople; stone piers served where columns would stand in Constantinople. Nevertheless, the similarity of plans is striking. Standing as a buffer nation between the Byzantine Empire and its Arab rivals, Armenia supplied the empire with a large corps of military and civil servants as well as several emperors of the Middle Byzantine period. Connections were frequent and far-reaching, thus making Armenian origins for Middle Byzantine architecture very plausible.

At the same time other forces were at work that might predispose Byzantine architecture to this kind of "orientalizing." The liturgy underwent a kind of orientalizing in the Middle Byzantine period, and the changes in its form are reflected in the changes in church design. The public processional character of the early liturgy was sharply curtailed in medieval times. Neither the First Entrance nor the Great Entrance was any longer an entrance in the true sense of the word—that is, from outside the church; both were abbreviated to "appearances" in which the clergy emerged from the sanctuary and returned to it, in a fashion somewhat similar to the usage in early Christian Syria.

As in Syria the activities of vesting and of preparing the bread and wine were now consolidated in a triple sanctuary at the east end of the church. To the right of the sanctuary proper (the bema in Byzantine use of that term) was the diaconicon (vestry); to the left, the prothesis chamber for preparing the bread and wine. The readings, too, were curtailed and the ambo in the nave was eliminated. At the same time the barrier (templon) separating the sacred functions of the sanctuary from the lay spaces of the church became more pronounced and was hung with curtains and decorated with icons, the starting point in the evolution of the wall-like iconostasis of later Byzantine churches. Curtains, too, are a feature first mentioned in Syria.

All of these changes point to a general withdrawal of liturgical action from the nave of the church in medieval times and its consolidation within the restricted sanctuary area. The sacred became ever more remote, untouchable, inaccessible, and invisible. The liturgy became strictly a performance of the clergy, with lay participation restricted more and more to their response in song.

In the final analysis the formation of Middle Byzantine architecture must be attributed to the convergence of a series of developments in Byzantine culture. The proliferation of monasteries called for a multiplication of churches of much reduced scale, since their congregations were smaller than the early Christian congregations. Imperial patronage and the development of an iconographic program with imperial overtones may have popularized designs and styles of decoration that had been introduced in the Great Palace. Meanwhile, changes in the form of the liturgy eliminating the processional requirements of early Byzantine church designs left the architects free to turn for their models to central-plan types that had been explored earlier in Armenia and Syria.

THE KOMNENIAN PERIOD (1081–1204)

The accession of Alexios Komnenos (1081–1118) followed half a century of internal disintegration in Byzantine government and a series of disastrous setbacks in its external affairs culminating in the invasion of Anatolia by the Seljuk Turks and the Battle of Manazkert (1071). The passage of the First Crusade through Anatolia (1097–1098) restored many of the lost cities to Byzantium for a time, and reorganization of government ushered in a new period of prosperity in twelfth-century Byzantium. The new prosperity is reflected in the building and endowment of the great Pantokrator monastery in Constantinople (1118–1136). The monastery included cells for eighty monks, a fifty-bed hospital, a home for the aged, and three spacious churches. The south church was the *katholikon* of the monastery, dedicated to Christ Pantokrator; the north church was the semipublic Church of the Mother of God Eleousa (the Merciful); the middle church served as mausoleum, replacing the Church of the Holy Apostles as the traditional burial place of the imperial family. In the design of the churches the cross-in-square was reemployed, with a narthex gallery added for the private use of the emperor.

Hagia Sophia, Istanbul, 532–537. Detail of capital. HIRMER FOTOARCHIV

Only decorative details mark the Pantokrator churches as twelfth-century. The domes are divided into twelve, sixteen, and twenty-four segments; the apses are composed of many facets and enlivened with repeated niches in several tiers; the brickwork introduces chevron and recessed brick patterns; and the sculptural decoration exhibits a vigorous vine-and-pomegranate motif inhabited by various species of birds.

Other twelfth-century Constantinople churches turn back to different building types. The Gül Camii and the Kalenderhane Camii are of the cross-domed type with added galleries, and show a similar interest in spacious interior dimensions along with the new style of handling such details as the segmented dome or the multifaceted apse. The period may not have been one of extraordinary inventiveness, but it was a century of considerable accomplishment within the established building types.

PALAIOLOGAN ARCHITECTURE (1261–1453)

The spread of Byzantine culture in this period can almost be said to have operated in inverse proportion to the size of the empire. In the period following the Latin occupation of Constantinople (1204–1261) the empire was a mere shadow of its former self, consisting chiefly of three cities—Constantinople, Thessaloniki, and Mistra—with varying amounts of the country surrounding them. On the other hand, with the spread of Eastern Orthodoxy across eastern Europe, all the nations from the Balkans to the Baltic owed spiritual allegiance to Byzantium. All the principal forms of their cultural life—their creed, their ritual, their imagery, their alphabet, and their learning—came from the contact with Byzantium. Hence, while Byzantine architecture, strictly defined as the architecture of the empire, would present an ever narrowing scope of investigation, the architecture of the broad sweep of Byzantine civilization covers an ever-widening geographical sweep from Bulgaria to the farthest reaches of Russia, not to mention its more remote impact on the West.

During the interval of Latin occupation the continuity of Byzantine cultural institutions was provided principally by the Laskarid dynasty that remained in possession of Nicaea and a stretch of northwestern Anatolia. A handful of churches bear witness to the architectural continuity of this interregnum. The Church of Panagia (Mother of God) at Krina on Chios (ca. 1225–1240) repeats the plan of Nea Moni on Chios, while Church E at Sardis (ca. 1250) repeats cross-in-square plans of Constantinople with surprising refinement of proportions. What is new in these buildings is an increased interest in the decorative handling of exteriors and a new freedom of exterior design from interior structure. Both of these features became pronounced characteristics of the Palaiologan period.

This is not to say that new types of plans were not being invented in the late Byzantine period. The inventions, however, were more in the nature of recombinations of older elements than fresh designs. At Mistra a two-column type combines the eastern half of a Greek-cross type with the western half of a cross-in-square type. More startling in effect is the Mistra invention of a type that places a five-dome cross-in-square on top of what is essentially a galleried basilica. This type, which appeared first at the Church of the Hodegitria of Aphendiko in Mistra (ca. 1310), was repeated in the remodeling of Mistra's cathedral and later in the Pantanassa monastery church of 1428. The interior effect is quite novel, for the visibility of the corner domes from the nave below makes for interesting lighting. Another new combination consists of adding narthexes and outer aisles, sometimes domed, to an inner cross-in-square unit, as at the Holy Apostles and Hagia Katherini in Thessaloniki.

In general, however, Palaiologan architecture achieved its effects not through new plans but through recasting older types in new proportions. At the Parigoritissa (1282–1289) in Arta, Greece, the architect revised the squinch plan by markedly heightening the proportions. The steepness was further ac-

centuated by articulating the wall surface with eight sets of superimposed colonnettes running up three stories to support the vaults. A similar shift in proportions can be observed in the best-preserved Palaiologan church in Constantinople, the *parekklesion,* or side church, of Pammakaristos (1310). Here, dealing with the cross-in-square type, the architect has stretched the proportions of the middle layer of the design to a point where the ratio between the height and the floor area is almost twice that of the tenth-century Myrelaion church. There is the effect, when entering the nave of a Palaiologan church, of standing at the bottom of a well.

In spite of such subtleties in the interior design of Palaiologan churches, it was on the exterior that they achieved their most characteristic effects: a predilection for the colorful, the rich, and the variegated. This preference showed itself in several ways. First, the growing independence of exterior design from interior structure, which was noted in the Laskarid period, gave the architect freedom to develop the facade as a design in its own right. The south facade of the Pammakaristos masks rather than reveals its interior disposition. There are three successive zones of arches of varying spans, including an ogee arch and a pair of roundels in the top zone; the windows are set within single-, double-, and triple-recessed arches; niches are sometimes flat, sometimes concave; voussoirs alternate red brick with white stone, while other surfaces are decorated with areas of chevron, checker, or lozenge patterns. This is Palaiologan surface decoration at its richest.

The same love of the colorful animated the exterior profile of the building. The multiplication of steep domes gave a jagged line to the exterior. Campaniles, an importation from the Latin West, were added usually to the west facade, increasing the vertical emphasis. And an interest in sculpture, both interior and exterior, increased. By the time of the Turkish conquest the city of Constantinople must have presented an appearance substantially different from that of the Middle Byzantine city.

BYZANTINE ARCHITECTURE AND THE MEDIEVAL WEST

The diffusion of Byzantine architectural concepts in the medieval West went forward in uneven stages. Byzantine political authority in the West was marked by a series of irreversible losses—of the exarchate of Ravenna to the Lombards in 751; of Sicily to the Arabs during the ninth century, completed with the conquest of Taormina in 902; of southern

Mother-of-God Pammakaristos. The parekklesion from the southwest. Constantinople, after 1310. PHOTOGRAPH BY THE AUTHOR

Italy to the Normans, ending in the conquest of Bari in 1071. Yet the prestige of Byzantine culture suffered no real eclipse, and as late as Abbot Suger's rebuilding of St. Denis in 1135–1144 the abbot was eager to learn from travelers how his church compared with Hagia Sophia in Constantinople.

Northern Italy, ever in contact with Constantinople through Venetian trade, was especially receptive to Byzantine designs. The cross-in-square S. Satiro in Milan (868) and the squinch-plan S. Fosca in Torcello (*ca.* 1000) are among the earliest and most subtle examples of their respective types. But when the new S. Marco was begun in Venice (*ca.* 1063–1071) the architects rejected Middle Byzantine types in favor of the grand scheme of Justinian's cruciform, five-domed Holy Apostles in Constantinople. Venice chose to assert its own apostolic origins by copying the most revered apostles' church of Byzantium. The result was that a building type long archaic in Constantinople enjoyed a new popularity in the West in the twelfth century. The repetition of dome-on-pendentive units served as the design principle for a series of Romanesque churches in southwestern France.

At approximately the same time the newly established Norman kingdom in Sicily looked to Byzantium for its inspiration in architecture, but with different results. Pure cross-in-square plans were adopted in Ssma. Trinità di Delia at Castelvetrano (late eleventh century) and the Church of the Martorana in Palermo (1143–1151); but builders may well have been Arab, using slightly pointed arches, coursed stone masonry, and squinches where pendentives had been standard. In the larger cathedral-building enterprises the Normans worked out a fusion of Romanesque facades from their native Normandy, early Christian basilica naves, and Middle Byzantine cupolas and sanctuaries. This was the hybrid formula for Cefalù (begun 1131), the Cappella Palatina of Palermo (1129–1143), and Monreale (1174–1182).

In northern Europe the penetration of Byzantine influence was more sporadic or indirect. Occasionally early Byzantine designs were seized upon for the special association they carried. Charlemagne copied the octagonal S. Vitale in Ravenna for his palace chapel in Aachen for the imperial association he saw in it, while Romanesque architects in Fulda, Paderborn, and Cambridge copied the Holy Sepulcher in Jerusalem for churches dedicated to the Holy Sepulcher. Middle Byzantine designs may have had a less direct impact. The Carolingian St. Germigny-des-Prés, near Orléans, reproduced the cross-in-square floor plan but significantly transformed the dome into a square tower. The crossing tower at the intersection of nave and transept in Romanesque architecture, sometimes square and sometimes octagonal, may represent a distant evocation of the central dome of the Middle Byzantine church. The concept of a central tower of light at the entrance to the sanctuary seems too close to be an accidental parallel.

SERBIAN ARCHITECTURE

Serbian architecture represents still another kind of fusion of Byzantine and Western styles, for while the preceding examples are Latin borrowings of Byzantine concepts, the Serbian churches are Byzantine borrowings of Latin ideas. When Stefan Nemanja declared independence for Serbia, he carved his state out of Byzantine territory in present-day southern Yugoslavia. Although the Serbian church declared itself autocephalous, it had received all its traditions from Byzantium, including its architecture. The new state, however, had strong economic ties with the Western states around the Adriatic, and the new architecture had very much the appearance, especially on the exterior, of the Italian Romanesque. At Studenica (before 1183), Sopocani (*ca.* 1250), and Dečani (1327–1335), the plan raises a Byzantine cupola on pendentives but attaches a barrel-vaulted nave and low transepts to this unit. The exterior, at Studenica and Dečani, is covered in bright marble, corbel friezes define all the rooflines, and portals are framed in deep Romanesque moldings. Only the dome and the decoration of the interior remain faithful to the Byzantine tradition.

Other Serbian churches, however, stand much more securely within the development of Byzantine architecture. King Milutin's marriage to the sister of Emperor Andronikos II (1299) brought a large dowry of Byzantine territory in Macedonia and an intensive Byzantinization of the Serbian court. The churches erected by Milutin at Prizren, Staro Nagoričino and Gračanica were erected on an elongated cross-in-square plan with steep corner cupolas

enlivening the profile. On the exterior the Palaiologan taste for colorful patterns was exploited to the full. In the lower zones bricks enframe stones in a cloisonné pattern; chevron, fan pattern, and cruciform tiles decorate the window areas; and the rooflines are broken with repeated arches. The motifs come from Constantinople, but the freedom with which they are employed is a new development.

The last phase of Serbian architecture prior to the Turkish conquest, the Morava phase (1355–1459), turned to Mt. Athos for its standard plan. The core of the building might be a steep cross-domed unit or a cross-in-square, but the north and south arms were invariably expanded with apses, making a triconch plan. Rich sculpture surrounded the windows, often designed in Gothic lancets; twisted colonnettes articulated the apses; red-and-white checker patterns in brick and stone covered the upper parts of the building. In churches at Kruševac (1377–1378), Ljubostinja (1394), and Kalenić (1413–1417), the architects achieved a sumptuous effect far beyond anything the impoverished Constantinople could afford in its declining years.

BIBLIOGRAPHY

Howard C. Butler, *Early Churches in Syria* (1929); John W. Crowfoot, *Early Churches in Palestine* (1941); Friedrich W. Deichmann, *Ravenna: Haupstadt des spätantiken Abendlandes, Geschichte und Monumente,* 2 vols. (1969–1976); André Grabar, *Martyrium: Recherches sur le culte des reliques et l'art chrétien antique,* 2 vols. (1943–1946); Heinz Kähler and Cyril Mango, *Hagia Sophia,* E. Childs, trans. (1967); Armen Khatchatrian, *Les baptistères paléochrétiens* (1962); Richard Krautheimer, *Corpus basilicarum christianarum Romae,* 5 vols. (1939–1977), and *Early Christian and Byzantine Architecture,* 2nd ed. (1975); Cyril Mango, *The Art of the Byzantine Empire 312–1453* (1972); and *Byzantine Architecture* (1974); Thomas F. Mathews, *The Early Churches of Constantinople* (1971), and *The Byzantine Churches of Istanbul* (1976); Gabriel Millet, *L'école grecque dans l'architecture byzantine* (1916); and *L'ancien art serbe: Les églises* (1919); Wolfgang Müler-Wiener, *Bildlexikon zur Topographie Istanbuls* (1977); Asher Ovadiah, *Corpus of the Byzantine Churches in the Holy Land* (1970); Josef Strzygowski, *Die Baukunst der Armenier und Europa,* 2 vols. (1918); Emerson H. Swift, *Hagia Sophia* (1940); Georges Tchalenko, *Villages antiques de la Syrie du nord,* 3 vols. (1953–1958); Alexander van Millingen, *Byzantine Churches in Constantinople* (1912).

THOMAS F. MATHEWS

[See also **Architecture, Liturgical Aspects; Armenian Art; Basilica; Catacombs; Church, Latin: To 1054; Church,**

Types of; Constantinople; Dura Europos; Hagia Sophia; Hosios Lukas; Iconostasis; Lateran; Martyrium; Monasticism, Byzantine; Roman Empire, Late; Rome; Serbian Art; Urbanism, Byzantine; Urbanism, Western European.]

EARLY CHRISTIAN ART. The New Testament asserts a suspicion of art inherited by Christians from Judaism: "Claiming to be wise, they [wicked men] became fools, and exchanged the glory of immortal God for images resembling mortal man or birds or animals or reptiles" (Rom. 1:22–23). Certain Christians did reject art, and the propriety of images remained an issue throughout the early Christian period. Nevertheless, most Christians embraced art as an effective instrument of their religion. The opinion, promulgated since the Renaissance, that early adherents to Christianity disrupted the artistic culture of classical antiquity, is erroneous.

Distinctly Christian depictions survive from about 200. From then until the seventh to early eighth centuries, when Arab conquests and Byzantine iconoclasm halted the production of art in the East and new, decorative styles totally transformed it in the Latin West, the foundations of a rich Christian tradition were laid throughout the Mediterranean littoral. Christian artists adopted the basic forms of Roman art—symbol, effigy, narrative, and ornament—and they mastered the major crafts—painting, mosaic making, carving and casting, and fine metalwork.

No simple evolution can be plotted for this formative period. Roman art was heterogeneous, and the Christian forms it engendered acquired its diversity. Nonetheless, broad phases can be described. The first, paleo-Christian, phase lasted until the conversion of Constantine in 312; its art is distinctly plebeian and betrays, in the preference for symbols, a lingering hesitancy toward images. The second phase, comprising art produced during the fourth and fifth centuries, reflects the shift of patronage to the aristocratic class following the Edict of Milan (313). It is marked by a new refinement and luxuriousness and by the transferral of imperial formulas to Christian depictions. The third phase, known as the first golden age, is associated with the reign of Justinian (527–565). Classical ideals were reasserted during this period, and at the same time innovative forms were devised to represent the Christian hierarchy. Conflicting currents—perennial classicism, strong tendencies toward abstraction, and emphatic local styles—reflected the fragmentation of the beleaguered empire during the final phase.

In the hybrid culture of Rome, the idealized naturalism inherited from Greece had existed alongside more abstract modes of expression, and local peculiarities had penetrated the Greco-Roman veneer to produce regional styles in captured provinces. The same diversity is evident in early Christian art. The emperor and aristocrats generally favored classical forms, which as a result came to dominate art produced in Rome and Constantinople. In other centers regional traditions prevailed. An expressive style employing hot colors, vivid gestures, and free, loose painting invigorated the depiction of Christian narratives in Syria and northern Mesopotamia. The importance of holy sites (*loca sancta*) in Palestine created a market for portable objects—reliquaries and ampullae—decorated with images of events and saints associated with those sites. In Egypt an impressive local tradition of art and the doctrines of the church of Alexandria combined to produce a separate school of Coptic art. The decorative styles of the migratory tribes gradually replaced classical forms as vehicles of Christian expression in transalpine Europe.

Theme and function also affected the style of depictions and created variety in early Christian art. In general, artists were willing to apply the conventions of antique naturalism to secular subjects and biblical narratives; but to differentiate levels of sanctity in theological images, they adapted the anticlassical system that had been developed for imperial portraits.

Although Christians worked comfortably within the artistic framework of Greco-Roman culture, special Christian emphases and requirements gradually transformed art during the formative period. Because of their wariness of idolatry, for instance, Christians generally avoided freestanding sculpture, which had been a principal vehicle of artistic expression. On the other hand, they elevated book illumination to a major art form because, unlike the pagans', their religion centered on a sacred text. The unprecedented importance of congregational buildings, such as baptisteries and churches, necessitated new forms of mural decoration and liturgical art, while concern with transcendental matters led ultimately to the abandonment of such purely mundane genres as landscape painting and to the development of elaborate schemes for portraying theological hierarchies. Drastic geopolitical changes also reshaped art. The capital of the empire was removed from

Baptistery of the Christian chapel, reconstruction. Dura Europos, mid 3rd century. YALE UNIVERSITY ART GALLERY, DURA-EUROPOS COLLECTION

Rome to Constantinople; barbarian tribes disrupted the Christian empire in Latin Europe; and Islamic incursions terminated dominion in Africa and Asia Minor. By the end of the period, a fundamental shift in art had taken place. Although the ancient traditions persisted in certain spheres, a new, more spiritual style had emerged.

By synthesizing Greco-Roman forms with Christian concepts, early Christian artists effected a transition between late antique and medieval culture. They also established the basis of many later developments. Particularly during periods of renaissance, such as the Byzantine, the Carolingian, and the Trecento, artists turned for inspiration to the early Christian heritage, where they found Christian themes rendered in a genuine classical style.

PALEO-CHRISTIAN BEGINNINGS

No work of certain Christian origin survives from the first two centuries following the birth of Christ. At the start some Christians may have rejected "graven images" because they associated art with paganism or because they considered depictions to be antithetical to the fundamental spirituality of their faith. Such early theologians as Tertullian attacked all religious pictures as idols and went so far as to argue that no Christian could work as an artist. As late as about 300, long after most Christians had accepted artistic expression, the Council of Elvira prohibited images in churches.

The more tolerant attitude toward art expressed by Clement of Alexandria reflects the prevailing view of art more accurately than do the extreme postures of Tertullian and other iconophobes. Addressing his coreligionists, Clement advocated a flexible approach to art and recommended that Christians select neutral images from the contemporary picto-

rial repertory: "Let the seals of your rings be of a dove or fish or ship in full sail or of a musical lyre or of a ship anchor, or if anyone be a fisherman, let him make an image of the children drawn out of the water. No representation of an idol may be impressed on the ring for we are forbidden to possess such an image" (*Paedagogus*, 3).

Though current also in pagan art, the subjects inventoried by Clement had special meaning for Christians. The anchor, for instance, is used metaphorically in the New Testament, where faith is likened to "an anchor for our lives, an anchor safe and true" (Heb. 6:19), and it also resembles the cross. The Greek word for fish (*ichthus*) was interpreted as an acronym of "Jesus Christ, Son of God and Savior." Christian meanings were extended to other pagan images in the same fashion. For example, Christians adopted the popular bucolic figure of a shepherd tending his flock as a surrogate for portraits of Christ because they associated it with Christ the Good Shepherd (John 10:11).

The interpretation of symbols such as these lay entirely with the beholder. Consequently, when modern archaeologists uncover a gem, terra-cotta lamp, or other object adorned with doves, fish, or a shepherd, they can determine only from its context whether it is pagan or Christian. The very earliest works of Christian art may, as a result, still be unidentified. The adapted symbols remained popular even after overtly Christian themes began to appear. The Good Shepherd is the focus of the baptistery decorations in the Christian chapel at Dura Europos (before 256), for example, and he is depicted in the third-century mosaics in the Vatican grottoes, where Christ is also represented in the guise of *Sol invictus*, the Roman sun god, rising in his chariot.

Expressly Christian images first appeared toward

349

the beginning of the third century. Their invention and popularity coincided with a period of religious tolerance under the Severan dynasty (193–235). Old and New Testament themes, on wall paintings, gold glass, gems, stone carvings, and ceramic lamps, are preserved from this period, primarily in subterranean burial chambers known as catacombs. The S. Callistus catacomb outside Rome contains typical examples of the early forms of decoration. The walls and ceilings of its small rooms (cubicula) are painted with symbols and scenes set in a delicate matrix against a white ground. Identical with that of contemporary pagan murals, the light, airy style is well suited to the underground setting. Biblical episodes, such as Daniel in the lions' den, Jonah and the whale, and Christ reviving Lazarus, are represented with a minimum of detail and with virtually no interest in action or setting. Rendered in a cursive style and randomly juxtaposed, these scenes were not intended to portray the actual Bible narrative; they were merely meant to recall to the faithful examples of God's intervention on behalf of pious men.

The catacomb paintings parallel the prayers recited during the funeral liturgy in their chambers: "As thou raised the dead, gave sight to the blind, and cleanliness to the lepers, so do to thy servants who with all the power of their souls do believe in thee and that the son who suffered shall come to judge the quick and the dead" (Commendatio animae). The high proportion of Old Testament subjects in catacomb art (approximately three for each New Testament scene) raises the possibility that the motifs may have been adopted from a preexistent Jewish tradition. Jewish seals and coins with analogous depictions do survive from the third century; however, the more elaborate versions of certain episodes painted on the baptistery walls at Dura Europos suggest that the symbol-scenes may actually be abbreviated excerpts from a genuine narrative tradition of Bible illustration. The Dura baptistery also establishes that, as early as 256, artists were capable of constructing programs of decoration for an ecclesiastic building. The scenes depicted on its lateral walls were intelligently selected to relate to the baptismal function of the chamber.

Where required by the narrative action, Christ was portrayed in these depictions either as a child or as a beardless young man in a toga. Where the context invited idolatry, however, the cryptic effigies (such as the Good Shepherd) were used. During the third century the repertory of themes was expanded to include not only emblems of salvation but also

scenes of Christ's infancy and passion and representations of the apostles and other saints. At the same time, to suit the tastes of wealthy converts to Christianity, the subjects were often rendered in materials and techniques of the very highest quality. The paleo-Christian system persisted in such fourth-century monuments as the mausoleum of S. Costanza, Rome (ca. 350), the sarcophagus of Junius Bassus (Vatican, 359), and the Via Latina catacomb, Rome (350–375); but in these the vocabulary of images is greatly enriched and the style of representation is explicitly aristocratic.

THE CLASSICAL HERITAGE

Constantine's conversion and the subsequent Christianization of the empire did not result in a radical transformation of Christian art or in an abrupt termination of pagan production. Diehard pagans continued to portray their gods and illustrate their mythology; in fact, the entrenched Roman aristocracy, faced with increasingly intolerant Christian authorities, revived the classical tradition in an attempt to reassert its heritage. The exquisite ivory diptych (now in the Victoria and Albert Museum, London and the Musée de Cluny, Paris) carved to commemorate the marriage of members of the Symmachi and Nichomachi families around 400, and the richly illustrated volume of Vergil's writings in the Vatican (Biblioteca Apostolica Vaticana, Codex lat. 3225) are

David fighting Goliath. Silver plate, Cyprus, *ca.* 610–630. THE METROPOLITAN MUSEUM OF ART, GIFT OF J. PIERPONT MORGAN, 1917

among the most impressive documents of this "pagan revival."

Even after heathen statues were banned in 408 and the pagan cliques finally succumbed to the new religion, the classical tradition was maintained surprisingly intact. While some zealots destroyed pagan works, most Christians valued ancient art as an important part of their heritage. Constantine and his successors, for instance, raided neighboring territories for Greek sculpture to adorn the new capital of Constantinople. And even so ardent a defender of Christianity as Prudentius could distinguish the artistic worth of statues from their function as idols: "Let your statues, the works of great artists, be allowed to rest clean; be these our country's finest ornament; and let no debased usage pollute the monuments of art and turn it into sin." (*Contra Symmachum*, I, 502–505).

Christians not only treasured the Greco-Roman legacy, they perpetuated it in new works. Throughout the early Christian period, Christian artists continued to illustrate mythological subjects, especially in luxury works of ivory, precious metal, and fabric intended for the private pleasure of aristocratic patrons. The fourth-century silver hoard found on the Esquiline Hill in Rome (now in the British Museum, London), though made for a Christian bride, features pagan themes; the epic illustrations of the Milan *Iliad* (Biblioteca Ambrosiana, codex F. 205 inf.) were copied from old sources for a fifth-century resident of Constantinople; Isis and Bacchus were still subjects on sixth-century ivories (now in the Cathedral, Aachen); and as late as the seventh century deceptively authentic representations of Meleager and Atalanta and of Silenus dancing with a maenad were embossed on Byzantine silver plates (the Hermitage, Leningrad).

Pagan traditions continued to inspire Christian artists long after the Edict of Milan. Heathen motifs were sometimes incorporated directly into Christian works: Hercules reviving Alcestis was painted in the Via Latina catacomb as an emblem of resurrection; Caelus, the Roman god of heaven, was portrayed beneath Christ's throne on the Junius Bassus sarcophagus to indicate the celestial setting of the *traditio legis* (Christ Giving the New Law to Sts. Peter and Paul); and an antique river god suggests the site of David's encounter with Goliath (1 Sam. 17:40) on a seventh-century silver plate from Cyprus. Christian artists also effectively transformed the inherited traditions to serve their own needs. They refashioned the likenesses of Greco-Roman gods and philosophers into portraits of Christ and his saints. The beardless, youthful type of Christ depicted on an ivory plaque produced in Rome around 400 (Bayerisches Nationalmuseum, Munich) recalls Apollo, while the more imposing, bearded figure in such monuments as the apse mosaic of S. Pudenziana, Rome (*ca.* 410), resembles representations of Jupiter. St. Paul's features were patterned after those of Plotinus, and the portraits of the evangelists were fashioned after various philosophers. Angels and many other "Christian" elements were likewise adapted from classical sources.

To illustrate Bible stories, artists used the expressive postures and compositional schemes developed in classical art. The gestures, poses, and settings used to depict the history of King Saul in a fragmentary Book of Kings in Berlin (Staatsbibliothek, Codex theol. lat., fol. 485), for example, are identical with those in the Vatican Vergil. The sequence of scenes representing the creation of Adam in the Cotton Genesis (London, British Library, Codex Cotton, Otho B. VI) was patterned after classical renderings of the Prometheus legend. And the scene of David slaying the lion on one of the Cyprus silver plates (the Metropolitan Museum of Art, New York) follows portrayals of Hercules fighting the Nemean lion. By adapting well-known compositions to their own narrative needs, Christian artists not only took advantage of a convenient resource but also transferred to the biblical account much of the expressive richness of classical art.

At first Christian artists had worked primarily in the rude, cursive styles of plebeian art; increasingly during the fourth century, as the emperor and aristocrats came to commission works, Christian art became more refined and luxurious. The marble sarcophagus of Junius Bassus repeats motifs common in funereal art more than a century earlier, but it presents them in a delicate, naturalistic manner in which details of anatomy and setting convey physical and psychological interactions. The late-fourth-century Sarigüzel sarcophagus (İstanbul) represents two angels bearing a wreathed cross with such crystalline elegance that it calls to mind reliefs of the fourth century B.C.

These works, reflecting the taste of aristocratic patrons, introduced a new function into Christian art. Pictures no longer served only to recall the significance of history; they were now reenactments of sacred events intended to engage and to affect the beholder. A group of ivories carved in Rome around the turn of the fifth century provides the fullest testimony to the regeneration of classical form within the Christian context. The group includes the Brescia reliquary chest (*lipsanotheca:* Museo civico cristiano, Brescia), the Carrand diptych (Museo Nazionale, Florence), plaques from two chests (the British Museum, London), and the Munich *Ascension.* As in the best Roman art, a total confidence in the harmony of the physical and spiritual worlds governs these works. Biblical events are presented as graceful human dramas enacted by well-articulated figures in an environment controlled by natural laws. Overtly miraculous elements are suppressed; to enter heaven, for example, even Christ must scale a mountain. The mood of these works is lyrical, evoking the idealized realm of antique art.

Although the late-fourth-century revival of classical forms is often referred to as the "Theodosian renaissance," it was not limited to Theodosius' reign (379–395) or to his patronage. An elegant classicism also characterizes such Roman monuments as the apse mosaic of S. Pudenziana, the carved doors of S. Sabina, and the lost frescoes of St. Peter's and of St. Paul's Outside the Walls, Rome, all of which were papal commissions of the fifth century. The influence of the revival was felt outside the two capital cities in the Chapel of S. Aquilino in the Church of S. Lorenzo Maggiore, Milan (*ca.* 390), the mausoleum of Empress Galla Placidia, Ravenna (*ca.* 450), the Church of St. George, Thessaloniki (*ca.* 450), and the Baptistery of the Orthodox, Ravenna (*ca.* 458). The acceptance and strengthening of classical form by Christian artists reflect the willingness of a triumphant church to embrace the entire legacy of Roman culture, especially the achievements of its gifted artists.

The removal of the capital to Constantinople and repeated barbarian incursions gradually sapped the artistic strength of Italy. By the end of the fifth century, the classical impulse had largely been spent. The mosaics in the Baptistery of the Arians, Ravenna (*ca.* 500), though patterned after those in the Baptistery of the Orthodox, lack the grace and subtlety of the earlier work. The figures are stiff and angular; gradated modeling is reduced to line; and a gold background emphasizes the architectural surface at the cost of spatial illusion. An even stronger tendency toward convention and abstraction is evident in Roman monuments of the sixth and seventh centuries, such as the mosaics of Sts. Cosmas and Damian (*ca.* 525), S. Lorenzo Outside the Walls (579–590), and S. Agnese (625–638). The flat, motionless figures isolated against spaceless backgrounds in these mo-

The three Marys at the tomb and Christ's Ascension. Ivory, late 4th or early 5th century. MUNICH, HIRMER FOTOARCHIV

saics suggest the insubstantiality and spiritual power traditionally associated with medieval art.

With the decline of Rome, Constantinople became the guardian of classical art. Pervasive, local styles affected the art of other centers, but in the new city on the Bosporus imperial interests preserved antique currents. The few works remaining from the fourth and fifth centuries, such as a fragment of a historiated column erected by Theodosius, a relief from the Ayvan Saray gate, and the bust of an evangelist (all in the Archaeological Museum, İstanbul), indicate that at first Constantinopolitan artists were not entirely successful in their attempt to emulate Roman works. By the beginning of the sixth century, however, classical traditions had been fully instated in the new capital. The heroic paintings in the Milan *Iliad* and the naturalistic representations of plants, birds, insects, and reptiles in the edition of Dioscorides' *De materia medica* (Vienna, National-bibliothek, Codex med. gr. 1), illustrated for Princess Anicia Juliana in 512, recapture the style of their ancient models. An ivory plaque portraying the archangel Michael (the British Museum, London), carved in Constantinople during the second or third decade of the sixth century, is so subtle and refined that for many years scholars assigned it to the late fourth century.

Whether these works represent a continuous classical tradition of Constantinopolitan art, now largely lost, or are the products of a revival at the start of the sixth century, is impossible to determine. No doubt can exist, however, that the classical tendencies of the capital were greatly reinforced by the active patronage of Justinian. Justinian's political aim was the restoration of Roman hegemony; to assert that goal, he sought to revive Greco-Roman art. Silver plates bearing Justinian's control stamps (Dumbarton Oaks, Washington and the Hermitage, Leningrad) portray mythological and pastoral subjects in a manner that suggests the finest ancient reliefs; the great cathedra (bishop's throne) in S. Vitale, Ravenna, constructed of historiated ivory plaques for Maximian around 547, combines statuesque portraits, vivid narrative sequences from the Old and New Testaments, and richly detailed "inhabited scrolls"; and the ivory diptych in the Staatliche Museum, Berlin (*ca.* 550) portrays Christ and the Virgin in a remarkably secular manner. Even icon painting, usually highly transcendental in aspect, was infused with classical character during the Justinianic age.

The antique impulse diminished during the second half of the sixth century but was restored during the reign of Heraklios (610–641), a usurper who used art to link his authority to Theodosius and Justinian. The embossed pieces of silver produced during his lifetime present a distinctly retrospective quality. A bucket (Kunsthistorisches Museum, Vienna) and two plates (the Hermitage, Leningrad) portraying mythological images fully recapture the subtle naturalism of fourth-century art, while the set of nine plates found on Cyprus (Cyprus Museum, Nicosia and the Metropolitan Museum of Art, New York), depicting events from the life of King David, is an extraordinary witness to the vitality of classical forms as late as the seventh century. A silver jug showing a nereid riding a sea monster (the Hermitage, Leningrad), dated 641–651, indicates that antique subjects rendered in a classical style continued even after Heraklios' death; and written documents from the period

of iconoclasm confirm that secular art remained of interest even when religious images were banned.

Whether classicism was a perennial aspect of Byzantine art or, instead, the recurring result of periodic revivals is the subject of debate. While the fashion for Greco-Roman art did not remain constant, it seems always to have existed. Even during the second half of the sixth century, when artists generally favored more abstract forms, robust figures of an ancient mien were portrayed on the mosaic pavement in the palace of the Byzantine emperors (İstanbul) and on a silver plate depicting Abundance of about 577 (location unknown). Constantinople became a supplier of classical forms to other cultures. The animated, fully modeled figures in the seventh- and eighth-century frescoes of S. Maria Antiqua, Rome, for instance, derive from Byzantium, as do the later paintings of S. Salvatore, Brescia, and S. Maria, Castelseprio.

THE LEGACY OF IMPERIAL ART

To distinguish the emperor from other figures, Roman artists had employed not only costume and attributes but also a subtle system of gestures and compositional devices that interrupted illusionistic consistency to signal the status of each figure in the representation. These imperial schemes, which by the fourth century had become abstract and highly conventionalized, were applied to Christian emperors after Constantine's conversion. On the large silver plate (*missorium*) issued in 388 to commemorate Theodosius' anniversary (Academia de la Historia, Madrid), for instance, classical naturalism was abandoned altogether and was replaced by formulas of gesture, position, and relative size that indicate the political station of each man. Size, proximity to the center of the circular field, and the degree of physical involvement are indexes of rank. The emperor is a huge, immobile figure enthroned in the middle; his heirs, smaller and more casual, sit to his left and right; and a tiny court official, shown in profile, accepts an edict from his hand.

Court portraits on the stone base of the obelisk in Constantinople (*ca.* 390) and on numerous fifth- and sixth-century ivory diptychs issued by Roman consuls are structured according to similar conventions. In the Vienna Dioscorides, the imperial mode applied to the dedication miniature contrasts starkly with the naturalistic rendering of author portraits and biological specimens; the princess dominates the hexagonal field, an aloof, unmoving giant surrounded by subordinate figures. Of the surviving

Woad (Isatis tinctoria). From Dioscorides, *De materia medica, ca.* 512. VIENNA, ÖSTERREICHISCHES NATIONALBIBLIOTHEK, CODEX MED. GRAEC. 1, fol. 160v

imperial portraits, the mosaic panel in S. Vitale, Ravenna (*ca.* 547), representing Justinian and his entourage, is perhaps the most impressive. Although it depicts the First Entrance procession, an actual liturgical ritual, the mosaic is composed so that the social status of each participant is revealed by his size, placement within the frame, spatial overlapping, and movement. On the Barberini diptych (Louvre, Paris), which may also portray Justinian, a variant system is employed to distinguish the emperor from the barbarians on the one hand and from Christ on the other.

Christian artists adapted many of the imperial devices to their religious themes. They conceived Christ as the celestial ruler; in St. Peter's Rome, and in other churches they portrayed him dressed in royal garb and majestically enthroned in the apse. Attracted especially to themes of victory, they patterned the entry into Jerusalem after the imperial *adventus* and Christ trampling the beasts (Psalm 91:13) after depictions of the emperor conquering the bar-

barians. Even such a characteristically Christian feature as the nimbus (halo) originated in imperial imagery, and the icon was derived from the devotional effigy *(lauraton)* of the Roman emperor. Christian illustrators also applied the imperial mode of representation to appropriate biblical themes. The depiction of David appearing before Saul on one of the Cyprus plates (the Metropolitan Museum of Art, New York) recalls the *Missorium* of Theodosius, and two miniatures depicting Christ before Pilate in the Rossano cathedral Gospels are composed as authentic Roman court scenes.

The most significant contribution of imperial art to Christian imagery was the system of hierarchical ranking. Independent of actual appearance, this system was perfect for the presentation of theological hierarchies as well. Ranks of sanctity—pious laymen, saints, apostles, Mary, Christ, orders of angels—could be differentiated from one another in the same manner that political status had been distinguished. On the so-called sarcophagus of St. Ambrose (S. Ambrogio, Milan), for example, Christ is shown in frontal view, elevated above symmetrical files of apostles shown in three-quarter position; at his feet two minuscule donor figures bow in profile.

Semidomes with their diminishing fields were especially well suited to hierarchical compositions, and many early Christian apses accommodate appropriate images. S. Vitale, Ravenna, is a good example: Christ, robed in imperial blue and gold, is enthroned at the center of the apse; he is flanked by two angels who, like imperial bodyguards, usher S. Apollinaris and Bishop Ecclesius into his celestial court. In the slightly later Basilica Eufrasiana at Parenzo (Poreč, Yugoslavia), a queenly Virgin Mary dominates the apse and two angel guards introduce saints and living church officials into her presence. A more abstract portrayal in the apse of Hosios David, Thessaloniki, presents Christ enthroned in a mandorla borne by angels, while in the cloisters at Bawiti the ascension of Christ is arranged hierarchically, with Christ and the angels in a celestial zone and Mary and the apostles below on earth.

Of all the apse compositions, that in the mid-sixth-century church of the monastery of St. Catherine, Sinai, is the most remarkable. Designed by Constantinopolitan mosaicists sent by Justinian, the Sinai apse adjusts the rendering of individual figures and transforms the action of the Transfiguration to display the divine hierarchy. Christ, an imposing, static figure wrapped in an aureole, dominates the center, his impassive body seemingly dematerialized

Missorium of Emperor Theodosius. Byzantine, 388. MADRID, REAL ACADEMIA DE LA HISTORIA

in light. Moses and Elijah, the Old Testament witnesses, are slightly smaller, statuesque figures shown in three-quarter view, while the apostles on the ground are comparatively tiny but react with genuine movement and human emotion.

To represent hierarchical themes on rectangular icons, painters often employed even more subtle means to distinguish rank. A magnificent encaustic panel at St. Catherine's monastery on Mt. Sinai, for instance, not only uses size and position to indicate theological status but also manipulates the degree of physical reality suggested by the forms. In this case the lowest echelon, occupied by Sts. Theodore and George, is the most abstract; the figures are flat and rigid, and stare impassively toward the viewer. In contrast Christ and Mary are robust, naturalistic figures firmly modeled to assert their physical presence; and the angels above them are painted so fluently they seem to dissolve in the light that emanates from above. A variant of the same theme on an icon in S. Maria in Trastevere, Rome, is conceived in the more schematic style of early-eighth-century Rome; Mary and Christ are rigidly hieratic and totally dwarf the cramped donor who kneels at their feet, and only the angels retain something of the antique style that elevates them above the more mundane beings.

The conventions developed for imperial images provided Christian artists with a system well suited to the presentation of theological hierarchies. Fun-

damentally different from classical naturalism, it aimed not at the representation of actual appearance but, rather, at the portrayal of an immutable order. Different versions of the system were used; sometimes position and size, other times degree of physical involvement, were the variable elements, and often both. Whatever the version, the hierarchical system offered an alternative to strict illusionism and enabled artists to represent transcendental concepts.

MANUSCRIPT ILLUMINATION

No book occupied a place in pagan culture comparable to that held by the Bible in Christianity; and whereas the Greeks and Romans had illustrated epic poems and other narrative texts, manuscript illumination had remained for them a secondary art form compared with monumental painting and sculpture. As the source of sacred history and as an object of veneration, the Bible played a central role in Christian religion; consequently book illumination became a major focus of artistic expression. Early Christian artists did not abandon the ancient traditions altogether; the Vienna Dioscorides (512) with its biological depictions, the diagrams and landscapes in a sixth-century compilation of land-surveying treatises (Wolfenböttel, Landesbibliothek, Codex 36.23), and a calendar containing portraits and personifications (Vatican, Biblioteca Vaticana, Codex Barb. lat. 2154) attest to the continuing interest in secular illustration, especially scientific material. Early Christian artists were, in fact, largely responsible for transmitting much of classical illustration to the later Middle Ages. From the start, however, they focused on religious texts.

Even the earliest papyri fragments manifest the Christian willingness to adorn the Bible text with *nomina sacra* (abbreviations of holy names) and with such rudimentary symbols as the staurogram. The vellum codex, which Christians quickly adopted after it was introduced at the start of the second century, provided a stouter matrix than papyrus rolls and was better suited to painted decorations. Even though St. Jerome and other authorities admonished them not to corrupt the sacred words with embellishments, scribes enlarged important initials in their codices, composed letters in the shapes of birds, fish, and other creatures, and filled letter stems and openings with decorative patterns. They also began to mark the beginnings and closings of books with ornaments. A modest cross with the alpha and omega decorates the frontispiece of an Italian Gospel of John (Paris, Bibliothèque Nationale, Codex lat.

355

The Transfiguration. Apse mosaic, monastery of St. Catherine, Mt. Sinai, *ca.* 548–565. REPRODUCED THROUGH THE COURTESY OF THE MICHIGAN-PRINCETON-ALEXANDRIA EXPEDITION TO MOUNT SINAI

10439, *ca.* 500), while in a fifth-century Book of Acts (New York, Morgan Library, Glazer Codex 67), a cross filled with interlace pattern and flanked by peacocks concludes the manuscript.

Tables of contents also were adorned. In the Ashburnham Pentateuch (Paris, Bibliothèque Nationale, Codex N.a. lat. 2334) the titles of the five books of Moses are framed by a curtained arch, and in the *Formularium spiritualis* of Eucherius of Lyons (Paris, Bibliothèque Nationale, Codex lat. 2769), the contents page is enclosed by an arch on columns. An important variant of these framed tables of contents was the canon table, a chart developed in the fourth century to correlate passages in the Gospels. A sixth-century manuscript in Vienna (Nationalbibliothek, Codex 847) preserves the basic system, in which a large arch encompasses smaller ones separating columns of numbers. The extensive set of nineteen canons in the Rabula Gospels of about 586 (Florence, Biblioteca Laurenziana, Plut. I, 56) is embellished with portraits and an extensive series of narrative pictures, while a lavish seventh-century fragment on gold-stained vellum now in London (British Library, Codex Add. 5111) is decorated with rich vegetal ornament and busts of the apostles.

Portraits of the author and sometimes of the patron had been included in luxurious books produced in antiquity; the classical tradition is preserved in the land-surveying manual in Wolfenbüttel and in the Roman Vergil (Vatican, Biblioteca Apostolica Vaticana, Codex lat. 3867); the Vienna Dioscorides contains full-page miniatures of the patron, of the au-

thor composing his text in the presence of an artist painting one of the plants, and of seven botanists together. Following ancient precedent, Christian illuminators often included author portraits in their manuscripts. In the sixth-century Syriac Bible in Paris (Bibliothèque Nationale, Codex syr. 341), depictions of Old Testament prophets precede the texts they wrote, while in the Rossano cathedral Gospels and the Gospels of St. Augustine (Cambridge, Corpus Christi College, Codex 286), evangelists are shown seated like ancient philosophers before the backdrop of a theater.

Artists also illustrated the biblical narrative. Again they adopted an ancient system wherein the columns of text were interrupted by numerous little scenes that traced the action step by step. The result was an extraordinarily rich form of illustration. The sixth-century Cotton Genesis, for example, largely destroyed by fire in 1731, once contained some 330 miniatures within the Book of Genesis alone, while in the Vienna Genesis (Vienna, Nationalbibliothek, codex theol. gr. 31) nearly 200 episodes were rendered in a lively fashion at the bottoms of the pages. Some illuminators adapted this system, which had originated in papyri rolls, to the codex format by gathering the pictures onto separate folios, as in the fifth-century fragmentary Book of Kings and the seventh-century Ashburnham Pentateuch; but even that did not destroy the dense, literal aspect of the narrative form. Because the same basic story is repeated in the Gospels four times, artists found it more convenient to construct New Testament cycles apart from the text. In the sixth-century Rossano Gospels, for example, scenes selected from the four texts are arranged according to liturgical use, while in the Rabula Gospels a harmonized cycle of pictures illustrating events from Christ's life decorates the canon tables. Twelve tiny pictures fill one page of the Gospels of St. Augustine, and an equal number are squeezed onto the portrait page.

The Pentateuch, Books of Kings, and Gospels were not the only books of the Bible illustrated by early Christian artists, but the illuminated editions of Joshua, Judges, Psalms, Prophets, Acts, and Revelation they produced are known today only from copies in other media and from later replicas. Illuminators seem never to have attempted to illustrate the entire Bible with the same sort of dense sequences of miniatures they invented for individual books and small compilations. The Syriac Bible contains only portraits and selected scenes, and Cassiodorus' *Codex grandior* was illustrated with a few frontispieces and diagrams.

Illuminators sometimes copied monumental paintings onto the pages of their codices; the Rossano and Rabula Gospels both include full-page illustrations taken from mural decorations. By and large it was the illuminated manuscript, however, that served as a source, supplying models for artists working in other media. The mosaics in S. Maria Maggiore, Rome, and in the basilica at Misis (Mopsuestia) seem to have been copied from illustrated texts; biblical scenes on some ivories may replicate lost manuscript illuminations; and the depictions of David's life on the Cyprus silver plates were certainly based on an illustrated Book of Kings. Manuscripts produced during the early Christian period not only provided models for contemporary works of art but also supplied prototypes for the later Middle Ages. Carolingian and Middle Byzantine artists copied early cycles of Genesis, Joshua, Acts, and Revelation onto the pages of their own manuscripts, while later muralists in Tours and Venice used early Christian books as models for frescoes and mosaics.

DECORATION AND FURNISHING OF
ECCLESIASTICAL STRUCTURES

Most early Christian churches have been destroyed, and of those that remain, none preserves its furnishings and original decoration intact. Iconoclasts dismantled all figural ornament in churches under Byzantine control during the eighth century, while natural and human disasters took heavy tolls elsewhere. Pilgrims' accounts describe numerous

Christ. Icon, monastery of St. Catherine, Mt. Sinai, 6th or 7th century. REPRODUCED THROUGH THE COURTESY OF THE MICHIGAN-PRINCETON-ALEXANDRIA EXPEDITION TO MOUNT SINAI

shrines in the Holy Land adorned with images appropriate to their sites, but these have all disappeared; ecclesiastical implements of precious metals, ivory, and cloth have suffered equal devastation. While generally leaving the exteriors plain, Christians lavished attention on the interiors of their churches, where the rituals of their faith were performed. They sought to impress visitors with the wealth and power of Christianity, and they recognized that church art could be an effective pedagogic instrument, particularly for pagans and illiterates. Pope Gregory the Great, for instance, asserted, "If you wish to have images in church in order to gain from them the instruction for which they were formerly made, I freely permit them to be made and placed there" (Epistle 13).

To judge from the Dura Europos baptistery, pre-Constantinian church decoration did not differ essentially from that of contemporary pagan cult rooms. The deity (in the baptistery represented by the Good Shepherd) was portrayed on the focal wall, and depictions of his deeds (healing the lame, calling Peter) were painted on the lateral surfaces. After the Edict of Milan the ad hoc systems of decoration developed in the catacombs and the more organized programs of congregational buildings such as the Dura chapel were expanded and translated into luxurious materials. The mosaic (now lost) in the dome of the mausoleum of S. Costanza, Rome (*ca.* 350), perpetuated the scenes of salvation and bucolic images known from catacomb art. In the tomb of Galla Placidia, Ravenna (425–450) the Good Shepherd is still featured. The mosaics in S. Giovanni in Fonte, Naples (*ca.* 400), belong stylistically to the revival at the end of the fourth century, but are thematically akin to the frescoes of the Dura baptistery.

Pre-Constantinian art offered no sufficient precedent, however, for decorating the enormous structures erected for congregational purposes after the Peace of the Church. Most of the new buildings were basilicas, which provided long, flat surfaces well suited for painting between the nave colonnades and clerestory windows and also focal areas at the apse and triumphal arch. By the beginning of the fifth century, the standard practice was to represent narrative cycles from the Bible in basilican naves.

Writing around 405, Paulinus of Nola described

Nave, with mosaic decoration. S. Apollinare Nuovo, Ravenna, *ca.* 556–569. ART RESOURCE

Old Testament frescoes in the new church at Nola; in general form these must have resembled the oldest surviving basilica decorations, the mosaics in S. Maria Maggiore, Rome (*ca.* 432), which in forty-two nave panels portrayed episodes from the lives of Abraham, Jacob, Moses, and Joshua. The style of the S. Maria Maggiore mosaics recalls contemporary manuscript illumination (Vatican Vergil and Berlin Kings); the Old Testament scenes may have been copied from a book. Prudentius recorded a somewhat different arrangement wherein Old and New Testament scenes were on opposite walls of the nave of an unidentified Roman church; this system of complementary scenes was also adopted in the churches of St. Peter and of St. Paul's Outside the Walls, Rome, the destroyed fifth-century paintings of which are preserved in seventeenth-century copies.

Elpidius Rusticus records the earliest known attempt to correlate individual pairs of biblical pictures—for example, the Tower of Babel with the apostles speaking in various languages, Joseph sold by his brothers with Judas selling Christ, and the sacrifice of Isaac with the Crucifixion. The nave of S. Apollinare Nuovo, Ravenna (*ca.* 500), presents another variant of basilica decoration; scenes from the life of Christ are depicted in registers just below the nave ceiling, prophets and apostles are portrayed between the clerestory windows, and the adoration of the Magi and Christ enthroned are represented above the arcade (the processions of saints are additions of *ca.* 560). New Testament cycles also adorn the presbytery of S. Maria Antiqua, Rome (705–707).

As an analogue to the ruler who appeared enthroned in the apse of secular basilicas, Christ majestically seated on a throne was often depicted in church apses. In S. Aquilino, Milan, and S. Pudenziana, Rome, Christ is enthroned among the apostles; in S. Constanza and in St. Peter's, Rome, he is shown giving the roll of the New Law to Sts. Peter and Paul; in St. Theodore's Rome, and in Sts. Cosmas and Damian, Rome, Christ is depicted with other saints; while in Hosios David, Thessaloniki, he is shown in majesty. The Virgin and Child are featured in other church apses (Basilica Eufrasiana, Parenzo; Bawiti; and Panagia Kanakria, in Lythrankomi, Cyprus), and in still others are found hieratic renderings of the Ascension (Bawiti) or Transfiguration (St. Catherine's, Sinai; S. Apollinare in Classe, Ravenna).

The flat, arcuated wall in front of the apse, known as the triumphal arch, also received the special attention of early Christian decorators. In S. Maria

Maggiore eight scenes from the infancy of Christ, arranged in registers, present the fulfillment of the Old Testament history portrayed in the nave. In the church of the monastery of St. Catherine, panels show Moses on Mt. Sinai. In most cases the well-known theme of Christ and his saints or a subject drawn from the Apocalypse was pictured on the triumphal arch (S. Lorenzo Outside the Walls, Sts. Cosmas and Damian, and St. Paul's Outside the Walls, Rome).

Domed buildings—baptisteries, mausoleums, and centrally planned churches—required forms of decoration different from those in basilicas. They offered no continuous walls for narrative cycles and no main axial focus. In certain domical buildings, among them S. Vitale, Ravenna, figural decoration is confined to the apse area. The chancel of S. Vitale preserves a heterogeneous program of mosaics that ascends from the altar, through depictions of Old Testament types of the Eucharist (Abel, Abraham, Melchizedek) and portraits of prophets and evangelists, and culminates in a celestial image of the Agnus Dei in the ceiling; a similar hierarchical arrangement in the apse comprises portraits of Emperor Justinian and Empress Theodora below a depiction of Christ and his saints in the heavenly court.

In some small, centrally planned structures the dome was treated as the main focus of the decoration. In the Baptistery of the Orthodox (*ca.* 458) and in the Arian Baptistery (*ca.* 500), both in Ravenna, the main cupola is filled with depictions of Christ's baptism encircled by files of apostles; in the rotunda of St. George, Thessaloniki (*ca.* 450), the Parousia was represented by angels bearing a wreath in which Christ stood, and saints or patrons ringed the main image. In large churches the dome usually contained no figural ornament. The ceiling of Hagia Sophia, Constantinople (532–537), for example, was covered with plain, gold mosaics broken only at the center by a simple cross. Church domes connoted the "dome of heaven," or celestial vault, and this connotation was often made explicit in their decorations. The dome mosaics in the mausoleum of Galla Placidia and in the later Archbishop's Chapel in Ravenna, for instance, feature a cross and evangelist symbols set against starry heavens.

Even the light-reflecting gold mosaics of unadorned domes may have had referential significance. A sixth-century hymn describing the church at Edessa identifies the golden dome mosaic as "the firmament with shining stars." Cosmological significance may have extended to other surfaces as well;

Apse, with mosaic decoration. S. Vitale, Ravenna, *ca.* 525–550. ART RESOURCE

in Hagia Sophia and in the Dome of the Rock, Jerusalem (691–692), supporting arches and walls were covered with vegetal ornament, perhaps indicating that the vertical elements were to be understood as terrestrial areas. This interpretation is supported by the Edessa hymn, which refers to the arches as "the four sides of the world" and as "outcrops of rock on the top of a mountain."

Floors in most churches consisted of simple revetments; those of others were covered by mosaic carpets. Because the depictions would be trod upon, religious themes generally were avoided on floors. The mosaics in the Church of Karoussie, Antioch (late fourth century), the Church of the Nativity, Bethlehem (fifth century), and the Chapel of Dominus Flevit, Jerusalem (*ca.* 600), consist of geometric or simple vegetal patterns, borrowed from domestic buildings, that assert the essential flatness of the floor. More elaborate designs incorporating animals are found in the Church of Sts. Cosmas and Damian, Gerasa (or Jerash, 533) and the Armenian Chapel, Jerusalem (sixth century). By including specific references to the physical world—maps (Madaba, sixth

Detail of wooden doors. West Portal of S. Sabina, Rome, *ca.* 430. MUNICH, HIRMER FOTOARCHIV

century), landscapes (Tabgha or Heptapegron, fifth century), of zodiacs (Beth Shan, late sixth century)—some floors may have been conceived as elements in the cosmological plan that governed the decoration of ceilings and walls.

Two basic systems can be discerned in the interior decorations of early Christian churches: the first, essentially historical, was adapted from pagan cult rooms and applied to basilicas; the second, in which cosmological elements were organized to create a hierarchy from floor to ceiling, was fitted to centrally planned structures.

Exteriors of early Christian buildings were not normally decorated. St. Peter's, Rome, was an exception; during the second quarter of the fifth century the scene of the twenty-four elders of the Apocalypse adoring the Lamb of God was depicted on its facade. Portals, on the other hand, were frequently embellished. Sixth-century wood doors with ornamental carvings are still in place in the church of St. Catherine's, Sinai, and fragments of a door from S. Ambrogio, Milan (*ca.* 385) with carvings of the life of King David are preserved. The enormous cypress doors of the Church of S. Sabina, Rome (*ca.* 431–433), are the most impressive examples still surviving; eighteen of the original twenty-eight relief panels representing episodes from the Old and New Testaments remain. Interior doors of ivory are recorded in documents, and it has been suggested that a group of plaques (Castello Sforzesco, Milan and the Victoria and Albert Museum, London) depicting scenes from the life of St. Mark and other subjects might have come from such an ivory portal. Decorated lintels (Al-Mᵓallaqa or Muallaqa, Cairo) and ceiling beams (St. Catherine's, Sinai) also survive.

Artistry and great wealth were lavished on church furnishings, especially on implements used in the church service. Shortly after the Lateran basilica in Rome was completed, for example, Constantine donated to it "a ciborium of hammered silver, which has on its front the Savior seated upon a chair, in height 5 feet, weighing 120 pounds ... 7 altars of purest silver weighing each 200 pounds, 7 golden patens, weighing each 30 pounds, 16 silver patens, 7 goblets of purest gold, 20 silver goblets," and other treasures. In the fifth century Princess Pulcheria gave to Hagia Sophia, Constantinople, "a holy table ... a marvelous object of gold and precious stones"; similar extravagant benefaction is recorded throughout the period.

Time has greatly reduced these church treasures,

but vast quantities of ecclesiastical implements still provide a clear impression of early Christian church furnishings. A hoard of liturgical silver (565–575) unearthed near Antalya, Turkey (the Archaeological Museum, İstanbul, and Dumbarton Oaks, Washington), includes enormous patens, candlesticks and lampstands, book covers, and spoons for dispensing the Eucharist, finely wrought and decorated with crosses and ornamental patterns, all destined for a single church. Smaller collections and individual pieces from diverse centers and periods attest further to the special importance of liturgical art. Among the most interesting of these are a gilt silver chalice of about 450 from Antioch (the Metropolitan Museum of Art, New York) covered with openwork reliefs of Christ and the apostles seated in a grapevine, two patens (the Archaeological Museum, İstanbul, and Dumbarton Oaks, Washington) with appropriate images of Christ administering Communion to the apostles rendered in gilt silver, oil phials (Walters Art Gallery, Baltimore) with full-length portraits of saints, liturgical fans (*flabella*) adorned with tetramorphs (the Archaeological Museum, İstanbul, and Dumbarton Oaks, Washington), numerous ivory receptacles for eucharistic wafers (pyxes) carved with depictions of suitable biblical scenes, an ivory comb (Coptic Museum, Cairo), and ivory book covers with scenes of Christ's miracles (Cathedral Treasury, Milan).

A magnificent marble ambo made for Archbishop Agnellus (556–569) and decorated with birds, fish, and animals remains in place in the cathedral of Ravenna, and elegantly carved marble transennae are preserved in S. Vitale and S. Apollinare Nuovo, Ravenna. Relics of saints and mementos from the *loca sancta* were often provided with elaborate containers. The Brescia *lipsanotheca,* for instance, is decorated on five surfaces with elegant ivory carvings, and a tiny silver chest, unearthed near Thessaloniki, presents handsome pictures of Moses receiving the laws, the *traditio legis,* and other popular themes. Among the most interesting of the early Christian reliquaries is a seventh-century wood box (Sancta Sanctorum, Vatican) containing bits of stone gathered at the holy sites in Palestine and decorated with replicas of paintings that once adorned those sites. Of all the luxurious furnishings surviving from early Christian churches, perhaps the most unusual is the cathedra made around 547 for Maximian of Ravenna and covered with ivory plaques depicting saints and events from the Old and New Testaments (Ravenna).

Folio from the Ashburnham Pentateuch. Probably Italy, late 6th or 7th century. PARIS, BIBLIOTHÈQUE NATIONALE, MS N.A.L. 2334, fol. 6r

ART FOR PRIVATE USE

Like their Roman predecessors, Christians decorated their dwellings, delighted in finely crafted jewelry, and acquired religious works for private contemplation. In character and quality these personal objects reflect a wide range of need and patronage. The exquisite silver plates from Cyprus (Cyprus Museum, Nicosia, and the Metropolitan Museum of Art, New York), for instance, were probably made for Emperor Heraklios (the episodes from the life of David may allude to Heraklios' battle with the Persians), while the mass-produced ceramic bowls (terra sigillata) and lead vials (ampullae), embossed with rude biblical depictions, served a different class of patron. Among the notable aristocratic objects surviving from the period are gold and niello wedding rings on which scenes from the New Testament are depicted (Dumbarton Oaks, Washington and the Walters Art Gallery, Baltimore), silver-gilt flasks, plates and cosmetic caskets from the fourth-century Esquiline Treasure (British Museum, London), and gold marriage belts (Dumbarton Oaks, Washington and the Metropolitan Museum of Art, New York).

Quantities of mosaics dating from the fourth through sixth centuries have been uncovered in pri-

vate houses in North Africa and Antioch. These perpetuate a variety of formats and themes—geometric and vegetal patterns, hunts, and mythological depictions—inherited from antiquity. The mosaic pavement uncovered in the Imperial Palace, Constantinople (late sixth century), represents bucolic subjects on a white ground. More fragile forms of personal art, such as textiles, have largely been destroyed; but even these are well represented. Large holdings of Coptic textiles, decorated with ornament, mythological depictions, and biblical scenes, were preserved in Egypt; and fragments of silk cloth decorated with imperial portraits (Musée de Cluny, Paris) and with episodes from the life of Joseph (in the cathedral treasure at Sens) also remain.

Personal objects constituted a realm of early Christian art that was largely unaffected by ecclesiastical developments. Antique traditions remained alive and remarkably intact in this realm; secular works, especially, often owed more to ancient models than they did to contemporary church art. Silver plates embossed with mythological subjects and dated by stamps—for example, a plate from the time of Justinian showing Venus in the tent of Anchises (the Hermitage, Leningrad) and a seventh-century plate depicting Meleager (the Hermitage, Leningrad)—reflect the strength and endurance of classical forms within the private sphere.

One form of private art, the icon, stands apart from other types of personal objects. Though rooted in traditions of imperial portraits and pagan cult images, the depiction of holy persons on early Christian icons was a special development, stimulated by the incarnate aspect of the Christian God and the important role assigned his saints as intermediaries of the faithful. Afforded the status of relics, icons were treasured, venerated, and copied. To some, such as the *mandylion* of Edessa, believed to have been produced when a piece of cloth was pressed against Christ's face, a divine origin was ascribed; to many, magical qualities were attributed. Anagogic concepts introduced into Christian thought by sixth-century Neoplatonic theologians provided a powerful impetus to the development of icons. According to these concepts, icons could serve as vehicles of communication between the physical and spiritual worlds, and were effective, in particular, for the uneducated.

Because of the miraculous powers attributed to them, icons were the special targets of iconoclasts; early examples survive only in non-Byzantine areas such as Rome and Sinai. The unique, metaphysical

Man milking a goat. Mosaic floor of the Great Palace, Constantinople, second half of 6th century. SCALA/ ART RESOURCE

function of icons is apparent in their styles. Several of the extant examples—for example, icons of the Virgin and Child in Sinai and Rome—are overtly hierarchical so that they would lead the viewer through successive stages of reality. Others, such as the Sinai Christ icon (*ca.* 600), are distinctly human and empathetic so that they would engage the viewer and create a devotional feeling.

CONCLUSION

The welter of styles, modes, and functions discernible in early Christian art permits few generalizations; even a distinctive name such as "Byzantine" or "Gothic" has not been devised to characterize its heterogeneous manifestations. Had more works survived, greater consistency might be evident in the culture, but probably not. Whenever major new discoveries are made, such as the Via Latina catacomb or the Sinai icons, the history of early Christian art appears richer and more complicated, not clearer. Like the religion that engendered it, early Christian art originated in no single event; it sprang from a complex cultural situation replete with contradictions and tensions. Greco-Roman art and its provincial variations contributed to the new tradition, as did Jewish art, the art of the mystery cults, and images of imperial propaganda. Theologians and laymen of differing attitudes, inheritance, and purpose also affected its course.

The achievement of early Christian art, taken as a whole, was enormous. During the first seven cen-turies following Christ's death, Christians selected from the antique legacy what was useful to them, thereby preserving and transmitting much of the classical heritage to later ages. In Roman territories conquered by Germanic tribes or Muslims, the classical tradition ceased; in areas retained by Christians, it survived. Christian artists also transformed the Greco-Roman forms into a channel of communication suited to their religious beliefs. Overcoming an initial hostility toward images, they devised defenses for art in which they argued that pictures could help to educate the illiterate and to bridge the gulf between the physical and spiritual worlds. Although the admissibility of images continued to be questioned, the artistic edifice constructed during the early Christian period remained unassailable. Early Christian artists bequeathed to later eras major forms of expression, including narrative and complex theological programs, realized with such skill and sophistication that their legacy remained a source of inspiration through the Middle Ages.

BIBLIOGRAPHY

Documents. Caecilia Davis-Weyer, *Early Medieval Art: 300–1150* (1971); Cyril Mango, *The Art of the Byzantine Empire: 312–1453* (1972).

Theory of images. A. Bryer and J. Herrin, eds., *Iconoclasm* (1977); Paul C. Finney, "Antecedents of Byzantine Iconoclasm: Christian Evidence Before Constantine," in Joseph Gutmann, ed., *The Image and the Word* (1977), 27–47; Ernst Kitzinger, "The Cult of Images in the Age Before

Iconoclasm," in *Dumbarton Oaks Papers*, **8** (1954), repr. in Ernst Kitzinger, *The Art of Byzantium and the Medieval West*, W. E. Kleinbauer, ed. (1976), 90–156; Sister Charles Murray, *Rebirth and Afterlife* (1981).

General works. John Beckwith, *Early Christian and Byzantine Art* (1970); Beat Brenk et al., *Spätantike und frühes Christentum* (1977); Michael Gough, *The Early Christians* (1961); André Grabar, *Byzantium: From the Death of Theodosius to the Rise of Islam*, S. Gilbert and J. Emmons, trans. (1966), *The Beginnings of Christian Art*, S. Gilbert and J. Emmons, trans. (1967), and *Christian Iconography* (1968); Ernst Kitzinger, *Early Medieval Art*, 2nd ed. (1964); *The Art of Byzantium and the Medieval West*, W. E. Kleinbauer, ed. (1976), and *Byzantine Art in the Making* (1977); Metropolitan Museum of Art, *Age of Spirituality* (1979); Arnold Toynbee, ed., *The Crucible of Christianity* (1969); Wolfgang Volbach, *Early Christian Art* (1962); Wolfgang Volbach and Jacqueline Lafontaine-Dosogne, *Byzanz und der christliche Osten* (1968).

The classical and imperial heritage. Dmitrii V. Ainalov, *The Hellenistic Origins of Byzantine Art*, E. Sobolevitch and S. Sobolevitch, trans. (1961); André Grabar, *L'empereur dans l'art byzantin* (1936); Kurt Weitzmann, "The Survival of Mythological Representations in Early Christian and Byzantine Art," in *Dumbarton Oaks Papers*, **14** (1960), and "The Classical in Byzantine Art as a Mode of Individual Expression," in *Byzantine Art; an European Art*, 2nd ed. (1964), 149–177, repr. in his *Studies in Classical and Byzantine Manuscript Illumination*, Herbert Kessler, ed. (1971), 151–175, which also contains Weitzmann's "The Classical Heritage in the Art of Constantinople," 126–150.

Paleo-Christian art. Pierre Du Bourguet, *Early Christian Painting*, S. W. Taylor, trans. (1966); André Grabar, "Recherches sur les sources juives de l'art paléochrétien," in *Cahiers archéologiques*, **11** (1960); Ludwig Hertling and Engelbert Kirschbaum, *The Roman Catacombs and Their Martyrs*, M. J. Costelloe, trans., rev. ed. (1960); Theodor Klauser, "Studien zur Entstehungsgeschichte der christlichen Kunst," in *Jahrbuch für Antike und Christentum*, **1** (1958ff.); Carl Kraeling, *The Christian Building* (1967); Paul Styger, *Die römischen Katakomben* (1933); Josef Wilpert, *Pittura della catacombe romane* (1903), and *I sarcofagi cristiani antichi*, 3 vols. (1929–1936).

Manuscript illumination. Albert M. Friend, Jr., "The Portraits of the Evangelists in Greek and Latin Manuscripts," in *Art Studies*, **5** (1927), and **7** (1929); Carl Nordenfalk, *Die spätantiken Kanontafeln* (1938), and *Die spätantiken Zierbuchstaben* (1970); Kurt Weitzmann, *Illustrations in Roll and Codex*, 2nd ed. (1970), and *Late Antique and Early Christian Book Illumination* (1977).

Church decoration. Giuseppe Bovini, *Chiese di Ravenna* (1957); Friedrich W. Deichmann, *Frühchristliche Bauten und Mosaiken von Ravenna* (1958); Christa Ihm, *Die programme der christlichen Apsismalerei vom vierten Jahrhundert bis zur Mitte des achten Jahrhunderts* (1960); Walter Oakeshott, *The Mosaics of Rome* (1967); Stephan

Waetzoldt, *Die Kopien des 17. Jahrhunderts nach Mosaiken und Malereien in Rom* (1964); Josef Wilpert, *Die römischen Mosaiken und Malereien der kirchlichen Bauten vom IV bis XIII Jahrhundert* (1916).

Other art forms. Erica Cruikshank Dodd, *Byzantine Silver Stamps* (1961); André Grabar, *Sculptures byzantines de Constantinople* (1963); J. P. C. Kent and K. S. Painter, eds., *Wealth of the Roman World* (1967); Wolfgang Volbach, *Elfenbeinarbeiten der Spätantike und des frühen Mittelalters,* 2nd ed. (1976); Kurt Weitzmann, *The Icon* (1978).

HERBERT L. KESSLER

[See also **Agnus Dei; Ampulla; Baptism of Christ; Baptistery; Byzantine Art; Canon Table; Catacombs; Constantinople; Coptic Art; Dome of Heaven; Evangelist Symbols; Flabellum; Hosios Lukas; Iconoclasm, Christian; Justinian I; Lipsanotheca; Locus Sanctus; Mandorla; Mandylion; Manuscript Illumination, Western European; Migration and Hiberno-Saxon Art; Missorium; Nimbus; Nomen Sacrum; Parousia; Pyx; Ravenna; Reliquary; Roman Empire, Late; Rome; Staurogram; Terra Sigillata; Theodosius; Traditio Legis; Transfiguration; Visigothic Art.**]

EAST SYRIAN RITES. See Syrian Rites.

EASTER. Easter is the English name for the day, the week, and the entire season in which the Christian church commemorates the resurrection of Jesus of Nazareth from the dead. A festival of joy and hope, Easter served as the controlling center of the medieval Christian calendar.

NAME

In most tongues the celebration of Jesus' resurrection is named from the Hebrew word for "passover," *pesaḥ;* it is not named, as once thought, from the Greek word "to suffer," *paschein.* In Latin it was known as *pascha* and as *dominica resurrectionis* (the Sunday of the Resurrection). The English name has more doubtful and less edifying origins. In the early view of the Venerable Bede, the Christians' spring festival stole the name, and thus the power, of the Anglo-Saxon goddess of spring, Eastre. In recent years a different and more complex derivation has been suggested. Early Latin sources called the week of Easter *hebdomada alba* (white week) and the Sunday after Easter day *dominica in albis,* from the white robes of those newly baptized. Since *alba* is also the Latin word for "dawn," Old High German then mistakenly furnished its own (plural) word for "dawn," *ōstarun*, to form the name Ostern and, thus, Easter.

DATE

Earliest Christian tradition, including the New Testament, records little commemoration of the death and Resurrection of Jesus on an annual basis. The primary Christian cycle was not the year but the week, which observed the Resurrection every first day, namely Sunday. The controversies caused by the emergence of an annual commemoration were largely limited to the early church. Yet the determination of the actual date of Easter in a given year remained a complex issue well into the Middle Ages.

The occasion for Jesus' fatal trip to Jerusalem was the Jewish Passover. An early attempt by churches in Asia Minor to mark the Resurrection according to the actual date of Passover (14 Nisan, dubbing its advocates "Quartodecimans") failed before the conviction, championed by the churches in Rome and Alexandria, that the proper day is always a Sunday. Thus the First Council of Nicaea (325) fixed Easter as the Sunday after the first full moon of spring, that is, after the vernal equinox. Determined by the relative positions of the sun, the moon, and the earth, plus the Judeo-Christian week, this computation then became independent of the Jewish Passover. Some differences between the Roman and Alexandrian computation remained until the latter was successfully advocated in Rome by Dionysius Exiguus (*ca.* 500). The modern difference between the dates of Easter in the West and the East resulted from the Western adoption of the Gregorian calendar in 1582.

DURATION

For several centuries the duration of Easter steadily expanded from one night to three days to a week and to a season. In the early church the core observances took place in the vigil during the night until Easter dawn. The Easter vigil marked the death, burial, and resurrection of Jesus, and eventually encompassed the three days from Good Friday to Easter Sunday. These three days were known as the "triduum." Holy Week and the forty fasting days of Lent were well established before the Middle Ages, though not identical in the East and West. The sixth and seventh centuries saw further expansions of the preparatory period to Quinquagesima (fifty days), Sexagesima (sixty days), and Septuagesima (seventy days), the latter two lasting into the week after Easter Sunday.

Easter included not only this week as an octave, a week-long observance culminating on the following Sunday, but also an "octave of octaves," a week of weeks, the fifty days leading up to Pentecost, the next major festival. This maximal duration of Easter as a season was also present at the time of Christ, the Christian feast of Pentecost falling on the Jewish feast of Shavuoth. After that first "Easter" the apostles were gathered together on the feast following Passover—namely, Pentecost—when they received the Holy Spirit and founded the church, according to Christian tradition. The festival of Pentecost thus marked the conclusion of the medieval season of Easter.

MEANING

For lay people in the Middle Ages, the meaning of Easter was inextricably tied to the specific ceremonies and social customs of their various traditions, whether Christian or pagan. Yet for the ecclesiastical authorities the inner meaning of Easter was the very basis of Christianity. Regarding the nature and significance of the Resurrection, there were countless sermons but virtually no important debates among medieval theologians. The central Christian belief was largely assumed, except for comprehensive works treating every theological topic and the biblical commentaries treating every chapter and verse.

The basis for the assumption, the sermons, and the commentaries was the New Testament. At least for the theologians, Easter was the exposition—in sermon, song, dramatic rite, and visual symbol—of the biblical testimony to a triumph over the grave. Earliest scriptural tradition claimed that Christ "was raised on the third day in accordance with the scriptures" (1 Cor. 15:4). What the New Testament actually meant by this phrase was open to interpretation, which it generously received. On the one hand, Jesus was raised in a bodily form that his disciples recognized, wounds and all (Luke 24:39, John 20:20). On the other hand, this was no mere resuscitation and temporary return from the dead, as in the raising of Lazarus (John 11:38–44), for Jesus could appear in a closed room in Jerusalem, remain unrecognized on the road to Emmaus (Luke 24:13–43), and finally "ascend" into heaven (Acts 1:1–11).

The Resurrection was considered a victory over

death, and thus a vindication of Jesus as the Messiah and an event of universal significance. So it was that Thomas Aquinas could discuss not only the nature of Jesus' raised body—true and glorious, yet fully integral and retaining the wounds—but also the significance of the Resurrection as the efficient cause of the eventual resurrection of each believer (*Summa theologiae*, III, 54–56). The link between the resurrection of Jesus and that of a believer was baptism, again based on St. Paul: "We were buried therefore with him by baptism into death, so that as Christ was raised from the dead by the glory of the Father, we too might walk in newness of life" (Rom. 6:4).

RITES

Because Easter in its entirety included the triduum of Friday through Sunday, and since a Judeo-Christian day began at sundown, the rites of a medieval Easter actually began on Thursday evening. Holy Thursday, the commemoration of Jesus' last supper with his disciples, was called Maundy Thursday in English, probably from the *mandatum novum* (new commandment) to love one another, which Jesus illustrated that night by washing his disciples' feet (John 13). Appropriately, the ceremonies of Holy Thursday emphasized both the original institution of the Lord's Supper, or Eucharist, considered a preview of Jesus' sacrificial death the next day, and the example of the foot washing. The ceremony of humbly washing another's feet does not appear in the Roman liturgy until the eleventh or twelfth century, though it had been practiced elsewhere much earlier, notably in Milan. The Seventeenth Council of Toledo decreed this annual rite for all the churches of Spain and Gaul as early as 694. Other observances on this day in the thirteenth-century cathedral of Salisbury, for example, included the gradual extinction of twenty-four candles (tenebrae); the ceremonial reconciliation of penitents; the blessing of oils used throughout the year on catechumens, confirmands, and the sick; and the stripping and washing of the altars.

Good Friday (perhaps a form of "God's Friday") first received dramatic-liturgical observance at its original location, Jerusalem. From these local, fourth-century beginnings, the Good Friday liturgy spread to the entire medieval hurch. Even the supposed hour of death, 3:00 P.M., was carefully noted, at least until the very late Middle Ages, when the entire liturgy was celebrated earlier in the day. Based in part on Jesus' words that when the bridegroom was taken away, the disciples would fast (Mark 2:20),

total fasting and mourning marked a medieval Good Friday and the full forty hours of the entombed bridegroom's absence from the living. Bells were silent and the cross was veiled. Even the Eucharist was not celebrated on this day, though there eventually developed a "Mass of the presanctified," meaning that the bread and wine reserved from the Holy Thursday Mass were distributed on Good Friday.

Throughout Good Friday the cross was a central theme and symbol; churches thought to possess a relic of the true cross received special attention. In seventh-century Rome, for example, barefoot popes annually carried a relic of the cross from the Lateran basilica to the Church of the Holy Cross for general veneration. The Western Good Friday rite of the veneration of the cross included the "reproaches," supposedly addressed by Jesus on the cross to his ungrateful people, the Jews. The anti-Semitism fueled by this fiction is also apparent in the conciliar edicts that forbade Jews to appear in public during parts of the Easter festivities: Orléans (538), Mâcon (581), Fourth Lateran (1215). English churches in the later Middle Ages added the "burial" of a cross and of a portion of the consecrated bread in representation of Christ's burial.

The principal service of the triduum was the Easter vigil. Originally this liturgy lasted from Saturday night to Sunday morning, so that Sunday saw no separate service. The vigil *was* Easter. By the sixth century it ended before midnight and Sunday had its own liturgy. In the ninth-century Einsiedeln ordo the vigil began as early as 3:00 P.M. In subsequent centuries Western churches permitted even earlier services, while the East retained the evening hour. The latter was certainly more suited to the occasion, for several reasons: Jesus was believed to have been raised during the night; the Passover, considered fulfilled in the Passion of Christ, was celebrated at night; the vigil itself made great use of light amid darkness.

In the West the full Easter vigil began outside the church with the kindling and blessing of the fire from which the large, processional paschal candle was lit. As often happened in medieval liturgical rites, a simple function—in this case the lighting of a candle—acquired an eleborate ritual and a symbolic meaning. The practice of a "new fire" as the first rite of spring seems to have originated in pagan Germany, where Christian kindling and blessing are attested in the eighth and tenth centuries, respectively. The fire was struck from a flintstone, which led a thirteenth-century interpreter and perhaps inventor of liturgical symbols, Guillaume Durand, to identify the stone as Christ, the biblical cornerstone.

Usually the height of a human form (though the Salisbury rite mentions a candle thirty-six feet high), the candle symbolized Christ in his paschal triumph over darkness. Yet its origins probably lie in the standard, nightly ritual of *Lucernarium,* a ceremonial elaboration of the practical function of illuminating a dark church. The paschal candle is mentioned by some early church fathers, but does not appear in the papal liturgical documents until the twelfth century. The inscription of a cross, the current year, and the Greek letters alpha and omega (Rev. 22:13) seem to date from Gallic and Frankish customs of the ninth and tenth centuries. Also pressed into the wax were five grains of incense, taken to indicate the five wounds of Jesus, but perhaps deriving from a confusion of the word "incense" with the designation of the candle as "lit" (*incensus*).

The deacon then carried this candle through the nave, announcing "the light of Christ" and providing the flame for all other candles. Reaching the front of the church, he sang a hymn in praise of the candle and what it symbolized. This "Easter proclamation" (*praeconium paschale*) was originally left to local authors, such as St. Augustine and possibly St. Jerome. Eventually one standard version emerged, "Exsultet iam angelica turba" (Now let the angelic host exult), perhaps by St. Ambrose. As the climax of the opening ritual of light, this hymn summed up the entire Easter message; portions of it were originally addressed to the candle, including praises of the bees that made the wax. The hymn survives in elaborate illustrated scrolls, which must have given the worshipers a visual aid as it was read.

In Jerusalem, its birthplace, the medieval paschal vigil was introduced by a lighting of the lamps during the chanting of Psalm 112. This ritual slowly received increased prominence, with elaborations such as triple processions with incense in the eighth century, until some observers ascribed magical properties to the fire and its miraculous kindling. The *Lucernarium* thus came to overshadow the vigil proper, which, in Jerusalem at least, consisted of ten Old Testament readings, baptism, and the eucharistic liturgy.

The historical core of the vigil began with several Scripture readings, separated by psalms and prayers. In Jerusalem there were always as many as ten lessons, whereas the early Roman practice of six readings was later expanded to twelve. The majority of the readings came from the Old Testament—such as the accounts of the Creation and the Flood in Genesis 1 and 6–8 and the crossing of the Red Sea in Exodus 14—and were generally related to baptism. In the early church the Easter vigil was considered the principal occasion for baptism, since the immersion and emersion of the initiates bound them to the death/burial and resurrection of Christ.

Through the Carolingian period baptisms and their anniversary observances characterized the Easter vigil. Although this annual event was undermined by the later medieval practice of baptizing infants within days of birth, the vigil retained a yearly blessing of the baptismal font. As the symbol of Christ, the paschal candle was plunged into the waters of the font, the womb of the church, now able to bear her spiritual children. The Holy Spirit sanctified the waters in the pouring of the holy chrism, especially if a baptism were to take place at that service. The paschal candle was then placed on its prominent stand, ready to be lit at every Mass until its removal forty days later on Ascension Day, the anniversary of Christ's departure.

Portions of the vigil—such as the delay of baptisms until this one evening when the fire was "new" and the font renewed, and the implication that all of salvation history was represented in one particular night—suggest that this conjunction of the earth, moon, and sun was seen as a sacred moment with special power. Medieval theology never attempted a biblical justification, but this sort of liturgical astrology seemed to thrive just below the surface of popular piety.

The vigil reached its presumed climax with the Eucharist. The fast was over and the joyous feast began: the bells were heard again at the *Gloria in excelsis,* the Alleluia returned in triplicate after its long Lenten absence (in the West), and the faithful received Communion. The Fourth Lateran Council (1215) decreed that every believer of the age of reason should receive the sacraments of penance and the Eucharist at least once a year, at Easter. Fasting and kneeling were banished throughout the season as the church celebrated the festival of new life.

The general renewal of nature in the spring season was already inherent in Easter's Passover context. This timing led many to associate with Easter some common spring symbols for fertility, such as the egg and the hare. The rebirth of drama in the Middle Ages also owed much to the Easter liturgy. A tenth-century manuscript from St. Gall in Switzerland documents a choir's antiphonal singing of the biblical dialogue at the empty tomb among Jesus, an angel, and the women (John 20:11–17). *Quem quaeritis* ("Whom do you seek?") led to fuller dramatizations of the Easter story and, by the thirteenth century, of other scriptural events as well. In fact, the biblical basis of Easter stimulated great creativity in every medieval art form.

BIBLIOGRAPHY

Adolf Adam, *The Liturgical Year,* M. O'Connell, trans. (1981); Gabriel Bertonière, *The Historical Development of the Easter Vigil and Related Services in the Greek Church* (1972); John Gordon Davies, *Holy Week: A Short History* (1963); O. B. Hardison, Jr., *Christian Rite and Christian Drama in the Middle Ages* (1965).

PAUL ROREM

[See also **Computus; Corpus Christi, Feast of; Drama, Liturgical; Feasts and Festivals, European; Lent.**]

EASTERN ORTHODOX CHURCH. See **Byzantine Church.**

EBARCIUS OF ST. AMAND (late eighth/early ninth century), a deacon and monk at the monastery of St. Amand. His only known work, dedicated as an act of piety to St. Amand, is the *Scripturarum claves iuxta traditionem seniorum* (Keys to writings according to the tradition of the ancients). It is a compendious lexicon, basically in alphabetical order, that draws on earlier glossaries and commentaries, both pagan and Christian. The work has never been published.

BIBLIOGRAPHY

Max Manitius, *Geschichte der lateinischen Literatur des Mittelalters,* II (1923), 641–646.

W. T. H. JACKSON

EBO OF RHEIMS (or Ebbo, *fl.* first half of ninth century). Son of a royal serf freed by Charlemagne and childhood companion of Louis the Pious, Ebo rose to become archbishop of Rheims (816–835). One of the most important Carolingian manuscripts done after Charlemagne's death in 814, the Gospelbook of Épernay (Bibliothèque Municipale 1), was

St. Matthew. From the Gospelbook of Ebo of Rheims, Hautvillers, before 823. ÉPERNAY, BIBLIOTHÈQUE MUNICIPALE, MS 1, fol. 18v

made for Ebo at Hautvillers near Rheims. Because Abbot Peter, in the dedicatory poem of the Gospel, praised the archbishop as patron and donor, the style found in the pictures—an agitated and expressive linearity—is habitually identified with the school of Rheims. Peter calls Ebo archbishop but does not mention his missionary activities among the Danes; hence the Gospelbook is dated between 816, the year he became archbishop, and 823, the year of his mission. The other major books associated with the Ebo Gospels are the Utrecht Psalter, perhaps the most spectacular of all Carolingian manuscripts, and the Bern *Physiologus,* the earliest Latin edition of this Christian allegorical text on animals. The style of these manuscripts was probably the most influential of all Carolingian styles; elements of it linger on into the Romanesque period.

BIBLIOGRAPHY

Florentine Mütherich and Joachim Gaehde, *Carolingian Painting* (1976), 19–20, 25, 56–65.

LESLIE BRUBAKER

[See also **Manuscript Illumination: Western European; Pre-Romanesque Art; Utrecht Psalter.**]

ECBASIS CAPTIVI (full title: *Ecbasis cuiusdam captivi per tropologiam,* Escape of a certain captive told in a figurative manner), an animal epic of the tenth or eleventh century in 1,175 mostly leonine hexameters. It consists of an inner tale (392–1,097) told by a wolf to an otter and a hedgehog, relating the Aesopic fable of the sick lion (with passing reference to a *vita Malchi,* perhaps by St. Jerome), and an outer tale of a calf left alone in its stall, its escape and capture by the wolf, and its rescue by its herd, led by a fox and a bull and guided by a dog.

Two manuscripts, both written at Trier and now in the Bibliothèque Royale, Brussels (MS 10615–10729, fols. 187r–191v, *ca.* 1250, and MS 9799–9809, fols. 130r–134v, somewhat later), were first published in 1838 by their discoverer, Jacob Grimm, who reconstructed the generally accepted title from HEC.BASIS . . . TOPOLOGIAM, found in the earlier manuscript only.

The French or German author, from the Vosges, was a monk in Toul, probably at St. Èvre. He mentions Trier (417, 733, 738), the Black Forest (1,073), and the Moselle and Meuse rivers (171), though the inner fable is located in Romance lands: Bordeaux and the Gironde River are named.

The time of composition has been set as possibly 912 by Ross and others, based on dates for emperors Henry I and Conrad I, calendar data in the poem (69), and political references. Previously Grimm and Voigt had favored 936; and Langosch, Zeydel, and others suggest 1043–1046.

A cento, the poem makes extensive use of quotations from Horace; cites Vergil, Ovid, Prudentius, Juvencus, Sedulius, Marcellus Empiricus, and Venantius Fortunatus; and uses literary topoi ("poetry writing as a cure for sloth" in the introduction, and the poet ends "because he is tired").

For Jauss, the *Ecbasis,* perhaps written in the late-antique enigma tradition, is the first substantial medieval poem emphasizing the wolf–fox antagonism. Voigt calls it "the oldest beast epic in the Middle Ages," based on its frame-tale format with a sick-lion fable as the inner tale, the feudal structure of the animal world, the motif of a threefold summons issued to the fox, and the erection of a gallows for the fox by the wolf. Yet the animals have no epic roles, but represent *figurae* according to their heterogenous literary derivations. For instance, the hedgehog, the sole character to sing epic songs, who is adapted from the *miles gloriosus,* also has the task of transporting fruit, which derives from the *Physiologus,* where he is a *figura diaboli.* The mixture of monastic and feudal milieus produces ambivalence, especially in the fox–wolf relationship, for which the *Physiologus* has no parallel, according to Jauss.

For Ross the monastic-school situation explains the poem's backdrop. *Ecbasis* (literary digression) is desired by an idled, melancholic schoolmaster who, like a "fettered calf" (66)—a scribe's formula (according to Bischoff) and a monastic topos (according to Ross, 278f.)—is tied up with metric intricacies when he would rather romp through the fields like the Muses (28). His poem, dealing with the flight and return of a prisoner, thus reflects the actual and fictive senses in its tropology of a tale "woven not without complexity" (68), which may also be a reference to the many citations. Ross notes that an emendator added eighty verses of theological content to the nightingale's song. The stichic dialogues of the work indicate its function as a monastic Easter entertainment, a point further developed by Gompf on the basis of grammatical evidence that indicates it was read by several speakers. Gühlich interprets the "tropologia" of the caption theologically (de Lubac) as a threefold *moralis explanatio* (moral clarification) given by the calf's experiences, the wolf's fate, and the speeches of parrot and nightingale.

Future research is likely to center on the ironical sense of the many quotations, which define the work as a satire with an as yet unrecognized focus.

BIBLIOGRAPHY

Sources. Jacob Grimm and [Johann] Andreas Schmeller, eds., *Lateinische Gedichte des X. und XI. Jahrhunderts* (1838), ix–xi, 241–330, the first edition of the poem based on MS (*A*) only; Karl Strecker, ed., *Ecbasis cuiusdam captivi per tropologiam* (1935), the definitive edition; Winfried Trillitzsch and Siegfried Hoyer, eds. and trans., *Ecbasis cuiusdam captivi per tropologiam. Die Flucht eines Gefangenen (tropologisch), Text und Übersetzung* (1964), with German trans.; Ernst Voigt, ed., *Ecbasis captivi, das älteste Thierepos des Mittelalters* (1975), based on (*A*) and (*B*), since he assumed them to be independent [actually (*B*) is copied from (*A*)]. An English translation is in Edwin H. Zeydel, ed. and trans., *Ecbasis cuiusdam captivi per tropologiam: Escape of a Certain Captive Told in a Figurative Manner* (1964), a bilingual edition.

Studies. Margarethe Billerbeck, "Die Horaz-Zitate in der 'Ecbasis cuiusdam captivi,'" in *Mittellateinisches Jahrbuch,* **11** (1976); Bernhard Bischoff, "Elementarunterricht und *probationes pennae* in der ersten Hälfte des Mittelalters," in Leslie W. Jones, ed., *Classical and Mediaeval Studies in Honor of Edward Kennard Rand* (1938, repr. 1968), proves the "calf" formula to be a school exercise; Ernst R. Curtius, *Europäische Literatur und lateinisches*

Mittelalter, 3rd ed. (1961), 99 n. 2, 432, 463; English trans. of 2nd ed. by Willard R. Trask, *European Literature and the Latin Middle Ages* (1953): offers a methodology by which to evaluate *cento* features; Werner Fechter, "Die Zitate aus der antiken Dichtung in der 'Ecbasis captivi,'" in *Der altsprachliche Unterricht,* 12, no. 4 (1969); Ludwig Gompf, "Die 'Ecbasis cuiusdam captivi' und ihr Publikum," in *Mittellateinisches Jahrbuch,* 8 (1973); Elisabeth Gühlich, "Die Bedeutung der Tropologia in der 'Ecbasis cuiusdam captivi,'" in *Mittellateinisches Jahrbuch,* 4 (1967), has noteworthy commentary and annotated bibliographic material in a careful apparatus; Hans R. Jauss, *Untersuchungen zur mittelalterlichen Tierdichtung* (1959), is basic; Henri de Lubac, *Exégèse médiévale, les quatre sens de l'écriture,* 4 vols. (1959), is a standard work on the reading of Scripture during the Middle Ages; Werner Ross, "Die 'Ecbasis captivi' und die Anfänge der mittelalterlichen Tierdichtung," in *Germanisch-Romanische Monatsschrift,* 35 (n.s. 4) (1954), regards the poem as a premature attempt to give the animal jest literary form; Karl Strecker, "'Ecbasis captivi,'" in Wolfgang Stammler *et al.,* eds., *Die deutsche Literatur des Mittelalters: Verfasserlexikon,* I (1933), cols. 484–490; in the same work, V (1955), cols. 161–162, Karl Langosch summarizes literature and research through 1953, and his work is updated by Udo Kindermann in the 2nd ed., II (1978), cols. 315–321; Karl Strecker, "Ecbasisfragen," in *Historische Vierteljahresschrift,* 29 (1934), still useful regarding the value of (*B*), location and date written, and some prosody; Heinz Thomas, "Die Ecbasis captivi: Eine Trierer Dichtung aus der Zeit Heinrichs IV," in *Deutsches Archiv* (Münster), 20 (1964), emphasizes ironical sense of Horace citations; Winfried Trillitzsch, "Die 'Ecbasis captivi' im Lichte der Forschung," in *Forschungen und Funde,* 35 (1961), comprehensive; F. Zarncke, "Beiträge zur Ecbasis captivi," in *Sitzungsberichte der sächsischen Gesellschaft der Wissenschaften zu Leipzig, phil. hist. Klasse,* 42 (1890); Edwin H. Zeydel, "Betrachtungen über die 'Ecbasis captivi,'" in *Mittellateinisches Jahrbuch,* 2 (1965).

FRANK RAINER JACOBY

[See also **Beast Epic.**]

ECCE HOMO. A visual image based on the Gospel of John (19:4–15), this scene captures the moment of the Passion where Christ, tormented and mocked, is presented by Pilate to the people, who collectively deny him mercy. In later medieval art, excerpted from the Gospel sequence and pictured with rich descriptive detail, it sharply contrasts the suffering Christ and the vicious rabble, particularly in art after 1500.

Ecce Homo. Hieronymous Bosch, Flemish, early 16th century. COURTESY OF THE MUSEUM OF FINE ARTS, BOSTON: RICHARDS, EDWARDS, AND WARREN FUNDS

BIBLIOGRAPHY

A. Legner, "Ecce Homo," in *Lexikon der Christlichen Ikonographie* (1968), 557–561; Erwin Panofsky, "Jean Hey's *Ecce Homo,*" in *Bulletin des Musées Royaux des Beaux-Arts de Belgique,* 5 (1956); Karl-August Wirth and Gert von der Osten, "Ecce Homo," in O. Schmitt, ed., *Reallexikon zur deutschen kunstgeschichte,* IV (1958), 674–700.

LARRY SILVER

[See also **Flemish Painting; Gothic Art: Painting and Manuscript Illumination; Iconography.**]

ECCLESIA AND SYNAGOGA. The theme of Ecclesia coupled with Synagoga was already extant at the beginning of Christianity, since the Easter liturgy had disseminated the oracle of the new covenant in Jeremiah (31:31–34). Thus, a contrast arose between the old and new covenants; and the figures used in personifying it were those of Ecclesia and Synagoga. The latter was endowed with the spiritual traits of the Queen of Lamentations; the church was personified as the Bride of Christ.

The antithesis was sustained by the church fathers. Augustine took from Paul the theme of Ecclesia as wife and Synagoga as disowned, and in the early fifth century the theme was revived by the poet Sedulius in his *Carmen paschale.* Eventually a true and clear confrontation emerged, as in Augustine's *De altercatione ecclesiae et synagogae dialogus,* which had become an integral part of the Easter liturgy in France by the ninth century. In *Contra Iudaeos, paganos et Arianos sermo de symbolo,* also attributed to Augustine, Synagoga personifies blindness, madness, and crime.

But voices absolving Synagoga are also heard; for Gregory of Tours she is the companion of Ecclesia and has the same rights. Gregory the Great, in comparing Ecclesia to Rachel and Synagoga to Leah, makes them a couple with equal rights, and his *Libri*

Ecclesia and Synagoga. From the portal of Strasbourg Cathedral, 1276–1365. MUNICH, HIRMER FOTOARCHIV

dialogorum were important to the medieval definition of the two churches.

With the First Crusade (1095–1099) animosity toward the Jews, who were considered enemies to be persecuted even at home, influenced the conception of the theme. In Carolingian miniatures Synagoga still held the same rank as Ecclesia—she could even wear a halo; now she shared the fate of the conquered Jew and assumed a defeated aspect. She was not the personification of the people who had condemned Christ to death but, rather, a neutral image. Sometimes she was only the symbol of the Hebrew world and the old law, as an old, white-haired man—for instance, in the ninth-century sacramentary of Bishop Drogo of Metz. The two figures are first identified in writing, as Holy Church and Jerusalem, in the diptych of St. Nicasius.

The fixed attributes of Ecclesia are a crown, a chalice containing the blood of Christ, a halo, a sumptuous gown, and a banner. Synagoga's banner is torn, her crown is falling, her gown is shabby, and she sometimes holds a knife or goat's head—an allusion to blood sacrifices but also, perhaps, the symbol of depravity.

An important turning point is embodied in those portrayals in which Synagoga holds the instruments of the Passion, indicating the active responsibility of the entire people who condemned Christ to death (window of the cathedral at Châlons sur Marne). In a twelfth-century paten (at Witten) Synagoga is brought firmly into the contemporary world. The inscription "Synagoga" is depicted by a group of Jews on their way to hell. A message of hope, suggesting that even at the end of the world there is a chance for all—even the Jews—to understand the preaching of Christ is shown in a miniature in the twelfth-century sacramentary in the municipal library at Tours, in which Christ lifts the veil from Synagoga's eyes, a theme sometimes found later in England.

The pair Ecclesia–Synagoga disappeared with the Counter-Reformation, when the Jew yielded to the Protestant as the infidel to be conquered. In Rome, Pierre II Legros was commissioned in the eighteenth century to sculpt a pair of female figures for the church of the Gesù; but they were not—as they might have been in the Middle Ages—the church against the synagogue but, rather, Faith defeating Heresy.

BIBLIOGRAPHY

Bernhard Blumenkranz, "Géographie historique d'un thème de l'iconographie religieuse: Les représentation de

Synagoga en France," in *Mélanges offerts à René Crozet*, II (1966), and "La représentation de Synagoga dans les Bibles moralisées françaises du XIIIe au XVe siècle," in *Proceedings of the Israel Academy of Sciences and Humanities*, 5 (1970); Wolfgang S. Seiferth, *Synagoge und Kirche im Mittelalter* (1964); Hélène Toubert, "Une fresque de San Pedro de Sorpe (Catalogne) et le thème iconographique de l' *Arbor bona-Ecclesia, Arbor mala-Synagoga*," in *Cahiers archéologiques*, **19** (1969); Paul Weber, *Geistliches Schauspiel und kirchliche Kunst in ihrem Verhältnis erläutert an einer Ikonographie der Kirche und Synagoge* (1894).

CHIARA FRUGONI

ECCLESIA PRIMITIVA. See **Primitive Church, Concept of.**

ECCLESIOLOGY

PATRISTIC HERITAGE

Medieval ecclesiology was dominated by theological ideas inherited chiefly from Augustine, Leo the Great, and Gregory the Great, as well as by political problems concerning relations among bishops, popes, emperors, and kings. Evolving interpretations of these ideas and the political interplay of temporal and spiritual powers entailed geographic and successive differences in ecclesiology.

In the transition between the patristic and the Carolingian periods, the church *(ecclesia)*, which had survived the transformation of the Western Empire into a multiplicity of more or less ephemeral kingdoms of Germanic origin, was seen as both a spiritual and a temporal body. As a spiritual entity it was closely related to, though not identical with, St. Augustine's City of God—the universal and everlasting assembly of the elect, the inner structure of which, invisible to human reason, is known to faith, and the outer structure the visible organization of the baptized. As universal the church was the *catholica*, distinguished from separatist or heretical groups, from local gatherings such as that of the Donatists, from any community claiming to be exclusively the church of the saints; as such it could only be one throughout the world. As everlasting, the church appeared on earth with "Abel the Just" and would last until the end of the world; this implied its continuity with the apostles. Under both aspects the

ecclesia is a mixed body containing in itself both saints and sinners, those struggling for holiness and those still entangled in the original sinfulness of humanity. This mixed body was the outer garment of the invisible church of the saints, whose names are known only to God.

The spiritual dimension of the church was closely connected with Christ, for it was Christ's body in the world. The scriptural metaphors of the body and the spouse, which led Augustine to identify the church as *totus christus*, the head and members, engendered a double view of the church as a "communion of saints" and a "communion of holy gifts" through which the communion of saints took shape. These gifts were the sacraments, understood strictly as the sacraments of Christian initiation (baptism, sealing, Eucharist) and broadly as all the signs of the gift of divine grace and the presence of the Kingdom of God.

The church had a visible structure. The keystone was the bishop, who served the community by witnessing exemplarily to the faith of Peter, "Thou art the Christ." The church as a whole was a communion of local churches headed by bishops. From Cyprian and Augustine the early Middle Ages inherited the conviction that the bishop of Rome and his church hold a special place in the communion of all the bishops and their churches, as well as an ambiguity as to the exact nature and implications of this place. The Roman tradition itself, exemplified by St. Leo the Great, was that the bishop of Rome inherited the charism of St. Peter as head of the apostolic body, as a result of which he had responsibilities for preserving the faith of all the churches. As mediated through Gregory the Great, the patristic view of the church was interpreted in a moralistic direction influenced by the monastic tradition of St. Benedict. The church was the family of God, the people of God, the gathering of the faithful, in which each had a rightful place—whether bishop, priest, or deacon, whether cleric, monk, or laity, whether male or female, each contributing to the welfare of all.

This view of the church, somewhat slanted in an institutional direction in the works of Isidore of Seville, is embodied in early postpatristic writings, such as the works of Bede in England and Ambrosius Autpertus in Italy. Filled with the Holy Spirit and his seven gifts, the church, the body of Christ, struggled against the "body of the devil"; it educated its members in the practice of virtues and the shunning of vices.

THE CAROLINGIAN AGE

The reign of Charlemagne, who reorganized schools in a restored empire, further advanced the conception of the church as the new Eve, bride of Christ, mother of the faithful. The church was a true body, of which Christ was the head. The faithful participated in this true body through communion with the mystical body of Christ, the Eucharist. This view was closely bound to liturgical debates between followers of Amalarius of Metz and of Florus of Lyons. It enhanced spiritual and sacramental aspects of the church and stressed its dependence on Christ and the Holy Spirit. Each faithful soul was the church, yet the church was not limited to human beings. The ambiguities of patristic angelology having been overcome, Christ was seen as the head of both angels and humanity. The church comprised the faithful angels and faithful humanity. This enlarged universalism underlined the oneness of the church, despite the breakup of the Carolingian Empire and the growing misunderstanding between East and West. The description of the church as a body (corpus) led to further investigation of the lineaments of that body, the several senses of corpus being inseparable.

Charlemagne and his successors were intent on order and organization. The first collections of canons (including Dionysiana and Dionysio-Hadriana) constituted canon law as a systematic study, with doctrinal implications, of conciliar and papal decisions. Ecclesiology thus developed institutional and juridical dimensions. Since canonical sources were sometimes interpreted differently, rival conceptions of ecclesial structures arose.

These controversies were muddied by several collections of false decretals. The Symmachan forgeries (early sixth century) coined the principle that "The first see is judged by no one," and the Donation of Constantine (eighth century) asserted the temporal authority of the bishop of Rome. Following these precedents, a team of forgers in France (ca. 850) produced spurious conciliar decrees to protect bishops from temporal rulers and from archbishops. Because these forgeries appealed to the bishop of Rome, they promoted Roman centralism, which happened to fit the Petrine ideology of the Roman tradition. Introduced to Rome in 864 by Rothad of Soissons, the False Decretals of "Isidorus Mercator" were used to fight the ecclesiology of Hincmar. They reinforced a canonical interpretation of the Roman primacy that was implied in the presence of the canons of Sardica (ca. 343) in the Dionysio-Hadriana.

Hincmar, archbishop of Rheims, was the chief spokesman for an ecclesial structure based on the earlier councils. While the diocese remained the central unit of the church, the archbishop or metropolitan had considerable authority over his province. All bishops were successors to all the apostles. The bishops of Rome succeeded Peter. Yet the words addressed to Peter in Matthew 16:19 were spoken, through him, to all the apostles. Consequently the privilege of the keys belonged to all bishops. In order to lead the Christian people in harmony, the bishops made laws collegially, in both regional and universal councils. Such laws were catholic once they had been received by the local churches.

Hincmar repudiated the Second Council of Nicaea (787) as not having been submitted to the Western bishops (though signed by papal legates). He also opposed the popes of his time—especially Nicholas I, Adrian II, and John VIII—for trying to impose new decrees inconsistent with the old laws. Episcopal consensus was required, since the universal church was a communion of local churches. Hincmar did not deny the Roman primacy, but he saw it as a primacy of example, piety, and devotion to authentic doctrinal and legal tradition. He also favored the relative independence of temporal rulers. Emperors and kings had been entrusted by God with the governance of this world. While bishops ruled the spiritual society, the emperors and kings ruled temporal society. For certain temporal affairs they had power over the goods of the church, yet in the area of religious and moral conscience they came under the bishops. Because of their wider spiritual authority, metropolitans should work in close cooperation with kings.

On most of these points Hincmar was at odds with Roman ecclesiology. He saw the communion of local churches as a moral unanimity reached by consensus through discussion in provincial councils. Regional primates were essential to secure the consensus of the bishops. All contributed to universal consensus under the bishop of Rome. As seen in Rome, however, the process was reversed: decisions were to be made by the bishop of Rome and imposed on metropolitans and bishops, who owed obedience to Roman decrees. The Roman view was based on the canons of Sardica, the Petrine theology of popes Siricius and Leo I, which interpreted Matthew 16:19 as spoken exclusively to Peter and held that Peter himself acts through the bishop of Rome, his vicar on earth. From the notion of vicarius Petri (vicar of Peter) the Roman tradition began to pass to that of *vicarius Christi* (vicar of Christ). Although all bishops were bound to the canons, the bishop of Rome might promulgate new canons for the good of the Christian people, just as he might create new regional primates. The Roman conception of ecclesial structure conflicted with both Byzantine theology and the theology of the Franks.

In relations between church and empire, the Carolingians inherited the principle of Pope Gelasius I that God had given primacy in this world both to "the sacred authority of bishops and to the royal power." This duality was strongly maintained in Rome against royal interventions in spiritual affairs. Through Alcuin it was incorporated into Charlemagne's conception of authority. Yet it became a source of conflict when kings wanted to dispose of temporal properties belonging to the church, to bring bishops to trial before civil courts, or, as Charlemagne himself did through the Frankish councils, to intervene in liturgical or doctrinal questions. The difficulty of limiting each power to a neatly defined sphere derived from the general conviction that the *respublica* was one body with a temporal and a spiritual aspect.

FROM THE TENTH TO THE TWELFTH CENTURY

Several factors contributed to ecclesiological developments. Monastic reforms, especially at Cluny (founded 910), fostered the ideal of a church that was spiritual, freed from lay power, and centered on papal monarchy. Canonical developments through Gratian's *Decretum* (*ca.* 1140), with its commentaries, and growing collections of decretals focused attention on the institutions and legal aspects of the church. The struggle between lay power and clerical freedom in regard to investitures produced several conceptions of the "two swords" of temporal and spiritual authority. Some maintained duality of authority, the two powers being equal in separate domains. Others, with a more unitive conception, subordinated one power to the other. The rivalry between pope and emperor turned into a struggle between pope and kings when the latter began to claim imperial power in their realms.

The Roman conception was strengthened by these movements. With St. Leo IX and his legate Humbert of Silva Candida, monastic reform shaped Roman theology and practice of authority. To the Byzantine prelates Humbert opposed a monarchic, though deeply spiritual, view of the church. This re-sulted in the excommunications of 1054 and the ensuing schism between Rome and Constantinople. Given the centralism of Cluny and its geographic spread, the Cluniac reform enhanced the ideal of a supranational church functioning under one head. With Gregory VII, a former Cluniac monk, the trend to papal monarchy was reinforced, along with the institutional and juridical aspects of the church. Embodied in the *Dictatus papae* (1075), this ideal saw Peter as the origin of episcopal authority and the bishop of Rome as the one through whom authority was given to all bishops. Gregory triumphed over Emperor Henry IV after excommunicating him, but the ecclesial freedom thus gained was accompanied by a wave of legalism based on conciliar decrees and papal decretals. This entailed a loss of the patristic sense of the church as eschatological community: the intermediate primacies of metropolitans lost their former importance; the bishops became more immediately subject to the pope. Innocent III called himself successor of Peter, vicar of Christ, and vicar of God, instead of the older expression, vicar of Peter.

Disagreement with this centralist-unitary conception took several forms. On the side of the emperor, theologians and canonists affirmed the independence of the temporal order. Within ecclesial institutions the cardinals—originally mere deacons but later priests and bishops, and sole electors of the pope since 1059—claimed authority as the senate of the church: not the bishop of Rome alone, but the see of Rome, governed the church. Some even affirmed that the pope was nothing without the cardinals.

There were also reactions among the laity. Many lay movements with evangelical orientations emerged in the eleventh century in connection with popular enthusiasm for the crusades. Some were quite orthodox, such as the one initiated by Robert d'Arbrissel, the founder of Fontevrault, in 1096. Others condemned the institutional and sacramental aspects of the church: Peter de Bruys (*ca.* 1112), Arnold of Brescia (*d.* 1155), and the Waldensian movement, originating at Lyons about 1173 from the preaching of Peter Valdo (sometimes called Waldes). The Cathars spread in southern France in the eleventh and twelfth centuries, becoming, for all practical purposes, a new church with a Manichaean doctrine and provoking the Albigensian Crusade and the Fourth Lateran Council (1215).

At a more theological level a revolutionary ecclesiology was formulated by the "Norman Anonymous" (Anonymous of York) around 1100. Composed by, or in circles connected with, the archbishop of Rouen, William Bona Anima, these writings describe the church as purely spiritual, identified only with the believers united in faith, hope, and love, living under priests and bishops as spiritual leaders, and ruled by divinely empowered kings. The Norman Anonymous had no following, but the ecclesiology of Joachim of Fiore gained considerable popularity: he held that the present was in transition between the Age of the Son (the New Testament) and the Age of the Spirit, yet to come. The latter would be heralded by a new religious order, and the eternal Gospel would be preached. As reformulated and applied to St. Francis and the Franciscan order by Gerard of Borgo S. Donnino in 1245, Joachimism was counterbalanced by St. Bonaventure after 1258, but it survived in the Fraticelli.

The theologians of the period reflected deeply on the nature of the church. St. Peter Damian emphasized the priesthood of the laity and, at the same time, regarded the pope as the only universal bishop. By and large, however, monastic theologians viewed the church essentially as the sacrament of the Kingdom of God, patterned on, yet containing and dispensing, the traditional sacraments. In the process the heavenly dimension of the Church tended to be lost. Rather than made of angels and men, the church was militant on earth, serving the people through sacramental activity. It was the bride of Christ, the mother of the faithful, but also the teacher (*magistra*).

One of the first tractates on the church was the *Contra haereticos* of Archbishop Hugh of Rouen, written about 1150 (*Patrologia latina*, CXCII, 1255–1298). Hugh's treatise, directed against some lay spiritualist movements of Brittany, has three parts. First, spiritually, the church is the spouse of Christ, the gateway to the heavenly Jerusalem, the tower of David. She exercises her motherhood in the sacraments, especially baptism and the Eucharist. Second, the church is also the Kingdom of God, a house built on seven columns—that is, the seven orders of the clerical hierarchy (from porter to priest), which correspond to the seven gifts of the Holy Spirit and the seven beatitudes. Christ himself is the supreme porter, lector, exorcist, acolyte, subdeacon, deacon, and priest, as well as the supreme bishop. Third, there are three orders of laity: virgins, continents, married. Each is nurtured by "the justice of faith," in keeping with the "image" of God in the soul, and this image

is destined to become "similitude" by resurrection. The unity of the church is trinitarian.

THE THIRTEENTH CENTURY

Though not set forth in systematic treatises, reflections on the church pervade all Scholastic theology, tied as it is to Christology, to the sacraments, to eschatology. Yet there are differences of accent between Franciscan and Thomist lines of thought. Early Franciscan theology reached its high point in St. Bonaventure, whose ecclesiology was patterned on the "intelligible cross" of a vertical and a horizontal dimension. Vertically the church imaged the heavenly hierarchy of angels and, higher still, the Trinity, a notion inspired by the hierarchies of Denys. Horizontally the church derives from the historical institution and development of ecclesial functions under the guidance of the Holy Spirit. Both dimensions highlighted the supremacy on earth of the bishop of Rome as representative of Christ the Head in his mystical body, the church, which was seen as a communion of believers in his true, or eucharistic, body. Pope Honorius III's support of St. Francis and Alexander IV's approval of Franciscan poverty in opposition to William of St. Amour (1256) encouraged this view of papal authority. Although the word "infallibility" was not yet in use in this sense, Bonaventure affirmed the supreme doctrinal authority of the pope as vicar of Christ, just as he affirmed that the church cannot fail in its teaching.

Thomas Aquinas reached similar conclusions, without the Dionysian slant. His ecclesiology, spread through his major works, is strongly christocentric and soteriological. Christ is the head of his body, which is the church. As head he is the owner and giver of divine grace though the whole body. This is done chiefly through the sacraments, which therefore work *ex opere operato* (by virtue of the work done) and not by virtue of the minister's holiness. The church is at the same time a gathering (*congregatio*) of the faithful, with all the visibility that this entails, and a spiritual unity of angels and saints in heaven with struggling believers on earth.

Hierarchic organization follows from the sacramentality of the church. It is stratified like the medieval guilds, for the good of the whole body. If the church draws its life from the grace-giving Holy Spirit, it lives, corporately, as a body politic. In this body only the bishop of Rome can formulate articles of faith. This amounts to an assertion of papal infallibility, but in spiritual matters. Thomist principles entail the independence of temporal authority in its own domain, the consequences of which were fully drawn by John of Paris in *De potestate regia et papali* (*ca.* 1304).

The growth of the universities established the authority of "doctors" speaking in the name of knowledge (*studium*), while bishops represented sacred power (*sacerdotium*), and emperor and kings, temporal power (*imperium*). Yet Roman ecclesiology, bolstered by many canon lawyers, pursued its own course. The victory of Innocent III and the Fourth Lateran Council (1215) over the Albigensian heresy was instrumental in creating the tribunals of the Inquisition and orienting Roman thought toward ecclesiastical theocracy. But the king of France's political triumph over Albigensian power helped to shape the concept of the king's imperial authority, equal and perhaps superior to that of the pope—and implying that bishops, as spiritual leaders in the political realm, owe allegiance to the king even in spiritual affairs. Through Gregory IX and Innocent IV papal theocracy, strengthened by the struggle against Latin Averroism, climaxed with the bull *Unam sanctam* (1302) of Boniface VIII. Against the theocratic claims of King Philip IV the Fair, Boniface proclaimed that submission to the Roman pontiff was necessary to salvation.

THE AVIGNON PAPACY AND THE FOURTEENTH CENTURY

In 1309 Clement V transferred the papal residence to Avignon, where it remained until 1377. Along with *Unam Sanctam* and its sequel (the imprisonment of Boniface VIII at Anagni), this move sparked polemics on theories of power and jurisdiction. At least forty treatises *De ecclesia* (On the nature of the church) appeared during the Avignon papacy. They slanted ecclesiology toward institutional questions and the extent of papal jurisdiction. The spiritual and sacramental aspects of the church took second place. Yet it was chiefly the moral authority of two women, St. Brigid of Sweden and St. Catherine of Siena, which brought the popes back to Rome.

There were many rival theories. For Boniface VIII the temporal sword was under the spiritual one (*imperium* under *sacerdotum*). Spiritual power, dispersed among the bishops, was concentrated in the pope, heir to the divine authority committed to St. Peter and his successors. The pope had authority over every human creature.

For Philip IV the Fair's lawyers the church did not reside only in the clergy but, first of all, in the Christian people. King and people formed one community that was also one church, over which the pope had only spiritual authority.

For supporters of papal theocracy, some of whom (such as Egidius Colonna and Jacobus of Viterbo) interpreted St. Thomas in this sense, the pope was, on earth, the head of the mystical body of Christ. All authority in the church and the world derived from Christ through the pope.

For moderate Thomists, like John of Paris, who brought reflections on the kingship of Christ to bear on the matter, temporal authority had its own origin and integrity independent of spiritual authority; yet it should respect and assist the church in pursuit of its spiritual goals.

For the Ghibelline party in Italy (Dante in *De monarchia* and even in the *Divine Comedy*) the church, which should be purely spiritual, was subject to imperial power for its temporalities. Imperial authority came directly from God.

For Marsilius of Padua (*Defensor pacis,* 1324) the church was the universal gathering of the faithful, over which the pope had no primacy. Supreme authority was vested in general councils.

For the Franciscan Fraticelli the true church, which is spiritual and directly ruled by Christ, was distinguished from the carnal church, led by the pope.

For William of Ockham, John XXII, who in 1323 rejected the decree of Nicholas III (1279) on Franciscan poverty, was a heretic; yet a nonheretical pope had a spiritual authority that was more service than power.

For Wyclif the authority of bishops and priests not only was purely spiritual, but also depended on their personal faith and holiness. A bad pope was not a pope, and the faithful should reject him. Wyclif also denied the necessity of sacraments. Similar positions were held by the Lollards in England and by the Brethren of the Free Spirit in the Netherlands and the Rhineland.

The arguments of the French royal lawyers were opposed by Boniface VIII. Although the Avignon papacy had to reach a compromise with the kings of France, John XXII condemned the doctrines of Marsilius in 1327. Wyclif was anathematized by Gregory XI in 1377 and at synods of London in 1382 and 1398. Dante and Ockham, never condemned, were often interpreted mildly. Ockham's position served to bring back to the fore the evangelical conception of authority as service without implying an opposition between the church and the faith.

Yet in the course of the controversies arising from the actions of John XXII, the question of the infallibility of the church and the pope was raised as never before. John XXII asserted, against Nicholas III, that Jesus Christ had not practiced the Franciscan type of poverty, in which there is use, but no ownership, of worldly goods. Against the Fraticelli he upheld the right of the church to own property. In keeping with the legal principle "Equals have no authority over one another," he repealed the nondogmatic decree of Nicholas III on poverty. But his opponents claimed that this decree was indeed dogmatic, and that, being heretical by rejecting it, John XXII was not a true pope but Antichrist. The term "infallible," already applied to Christ by Peter Olivi (who was ambiguous on whether it could apply, in some sense, to the pope), was used in regard to the pope by Agostino Trionfo in 1320 and, somewhat later, by Guido Terreni, and was applied to Nicholas III by some of John XXII's opponents. In these cases the term presupposed both the infallibility of the church and the dependence of the pope on Christ.

THE GREAT SCHISM AND THE FIFTEENTH CENTURY

The Great Schism began in 1378, when rival factions of cardinals elected two different popes; it worsened in 1409 when a third pope was elected at the Council of Pisa; and it ended in 1417 through the Council of Constance. The schism raised questions of the oneness of the church, the function and even the existence of the papacy, the role of cardinals, the authority of general councils, the right of nations to choose between rival popes, and, generally, the structure of the church. Treatises on the unity of the church and on the power of the pope abounded. The chief theological result was the emergence of conciliarism.

Ecclesiological questions were also raised by the Hussite movement in Moravia, especially through John Hus's *De ecclesia* (1412–1413). Hus revived and sharpened Wyclif's theology, stressing the internal, spiritual dimension of the church. He admitted papal primacy but only as a primacy of faith and holiness, example rather than jurisdiction. Though opposed by some theologians and bishops of Moravia, the Hussite movement thrived on the theological confusion of the times and on anti-German nationalist feelings. Condemned at the Council of Constance, where Hus was burned at the stake in 1415, the movement led to the first break in the institutional unity of the church since the schism between Constantinople and Rome.

The Council of Constance (1414–1418), called to end the Great Schism, was a crossroads of ecclesiologies and a ferment of further ecclesiological reflection. It weakened the power of the papacy by removing the reigning popes, but it also strengthened that power by electing Martin V the sole pope.

There were three main factions among the theologians of Constance. One group held that the council had authority because it represented the Christian people, in whom full authority is vested; it was therefore superior to any individual bishop or pope. This was the view of Conrad of Gelnhausen and Dietrich of Nieheim, who were influenced by Ockham and Marsilius. According to a second group, the church resided essentially in the faith of the people. It had features of aristocracy and of monarchy: the pope succeeds Peter; bishops succeed the apostles generally; cardinals succeed the apostles particularly, as a small group around Peter; and priests succeed the seventy-two disciples. The council represented all the faithful, but especially the bishops; it had authority from Christ and could depose an unworthy pope. This was roughly the position of the University of Paris (Pierre d'Ailly and John Gerson, the latter with more spiritual and pastoral concerns). A strict papalist position was maintained by several bishops and theologians, who insisted that no council was superior to the pope and that the pope had a mandate from Christ that resided neither in the church at large nor in the episcopal college nor in the college of cardinals. This was the position adopted, against the Council of Basel, by Eugenius IV, who succeeded Martin V in 1431.

The heart of the ecclesiology of Constance, which was illustrated in its condemnation of Wyclif and Hus, was expressed in the decrees *Haec sancta* (1415) and *Frequens* (1417). Against Hus, Constance rejected the notion of a purely spiritual church; in its two chief decrees it endorsed a moderate conciliarism as normative ecclesiology. *Haec sancta* teaches that the general council represents the whole church on earth, has its authority directly from Christ, and must be obeyed by the pope. *Frequens* orders a general council to be held five years after the end of

Constance, the next one twelve years after Constance, and all subsequent councils at ten-year intervals. Historians have debated whether *Haec sancta* was endorsed by Martin V and Eugenius IV, but it is certain that there was no unequivocal endorsement of it by Martin V and that Eugenius IV eventually rejected it. As for *Frequens,* the Council of Basel (1431–1449), which tried to enforce it, petered out when the Council of Ferrara-Florence, called by Eugenius IV, adopted a papalist doctrine (decree *Laetentur coeli,* 1439): "The Roman pontiff is successor of Peter, vicar of Christ, head of the whole Church, father and doctor of all Christians"; he had received from Christ "in St. Peter full authority to rule and govern the universal church." The lasting influence of conciliarism was felt in the Pragmatic Sanction of Bourges (1438), which laid the foundation for later Gallicanism.

Several theological works are especially important to ecclesiology. The writings of Nicholas of Cusa, related to mystical currents of the fourteenth and fifteenth centuries, emphasize the unity of the church in plurality, on the model of the Trinity, and the influence of the Holy Spirit in keeping the "concordance" of its many members and levels. Nicholas affirms a limited primacy of the pope in the context of a patriarchal pentarchy and the conciliarity of the whole church. But the major contribution arising from the controversies about conciliarism is Juan de Torquemada's *Summa de ecclesia* (1448–1449), a systematic application of Thomism to ecclesiology. While looking closely at the institutional structures of the church, it reemphasizes the internal dimensions of faith, worship, and eschatological preparation to glory, along with the spiritual meaning of the four marks of the church. In four books the author studies the church as mystery, the Roman primacy, the councils, and the nature of schism and heresy.

In the last decades of the fifteenth century, the popes brought a new luster to the papacy through their encouragement of the arts. But their involvement in Italian politics drew them into numerous local conflicts. Although Savonarola, in Florence, had no original ecclesiology, he was led to denounce Alexander VI as Antichrist. Condemned for heresy and burned in 1498, he had contributed to a theme that had been widely discussed throughout the Middle Ages: the possibility of the pope being a heretic. Thus the medieval period, in ecclesiology, closed on an ambiguous note that would have consequences for the Reformation.

BIBLIOGRAPHY

Yves Congar, *L'ecclésiologie du haut moyen âge* (1968), and *L'église, de saint Augustin à l'époque moderne* (1970); Ernest H. Davenport, *The False Decretals* (1916); Jean Devisse, *Hincmar, archévêque de Reims,* 3 vols. (1976); Ernest Fortin, *Dissidence et philosophie au moyen âge* (1981); Trevor G. Jalland, *The Church and the Papacy* (1946); Ernst H. Kantorowicz, *The King's Two Bodies* (1957); Hans Küng, *Structures of the Church* (1964); Jean Leclercq, *Jean de Paris et l'ecclésiologie du XIIIᵉ siècle* (1942); Henri de Lubac, *Corpus Mysticum: L'eucharistie et l'eglise au moyen âge* (1942); Michele Maccarone, *Vicarius Christi: Storia del titolo papale* (1952); Karl F. Morrison, *The Two Kingdoms: Ecclesiology in Carolingian Political Thought* (1964), and *Authority and Tradition in the Western Church* (1969); Francis Oakley, *The Western Church in the Later Middle Ages* (1979); Marcel Pacaut, *La théocratie, l'église et le pouvoir au moyen âge* (1957); Henry E. Symonds, *The Church Universal and the See of Rome* (1939); George H. Tavard, "Episcopacy and Apostolic Succession According to Hincmar of Reims," in *Theological Studies,* 34 (1973), "The Bull *Unam Sanctam* of Boniface VIII," in Paul Empie and Austin Murphy, eds., *Papal Primacy and the Universal Church* (1974), 105–119, "The Papacy in the Middle Ages," *ibid.,* 98–105, and "Succession et ordre dans la structure de l'église," in Jacques Guy Bougerol, ed., *S. Bonaventura, 1274–1974,* IV (1974), 421–446; Brian Tierney, *Foundations of the Conciliar Theory* (1955, repr. 1968), and *Origins of Papal Infallibility, 1150–1350* (1973); Walter Ullmann, *The Origins of the Great Schism* (1948, repr. 1976), *The Growth of Papal Government in the Middle Ages* (1955), and *Principles of Government and Politics in the Middle Ages* (1961).

GEORGE H. TAVARD

[See also **Ailly, Pierre d'**; **Aquinas, St. Thomas**; **Augustine of Hippo, St.**; **Bonaventure, St.**; **Boniface VIII, Pope**; **Conciliar Theory**; **Councils, Western (869–1274)**; **Decretals, False**; **Donation of Constantine**; **Franciscans**; **Gerson, John**; **Hincmar of Rheims**; **Hus, John**; **John of Paris**; **Joachim of Fiore**; **Marsilius (Marsiglio) of Padua**; **Ockham, William of**; **Papacy, Origin and Development of**; **Wyclif, John.**]

ÉCHEVIN. Members of the courts and councils of medieval towns in the Low Countries and northern France were called *échevins.* Their counterparts in Italy, southern France, and some regions in Germany were called *consules;* in other parts of the Continent, *jurés;* and in England, aldermen or councillors.

The medieval Latin word for *échevin* is *scabinus.*

During the Carolingian period (eighth and ninth centuries) and in the feudal states that replaced the Carolingian state in the late ninth century, *scabini,* often called *rachimburgi,* were members of the public courts of the administrative circumscriptions. In Flanders, for example, each administrative district known as a *châtellenie* (castellany) had a group of *échevins* comprising a court presided over by a comital officer, generally the *châtelain* (castellan), and meeting at his castle. During the late tenth and eleventh centuries, when towns developed next to such castles and at other strategic points, these *échevinages* dispensed justice for both the feudal territory and the new urban community. Perhaps as early as the late eleventh century and definitely by the twelfth, in the Low Countries and northern France, territorial princes permitted towns to have their own bodies of *échevins,* generally twelve in number, to serve as courts for the townspeople. Meanwhile, the older bodies of *échevins* continued to assemble under the *châtelains* or their successors, the bailiffs, to dispense justice for castle functionaries and for the rest of the *châtellenie.*

During the early twelfth century the *échevinages* of the large towns assumed the administrative functions of the comital officials and became town councils. This change occurred when these towns acquired political rights and self-government, which made the councils responsible not only for urban justice but also for taxation, supervision of local markets and trade, regulation of guilds, construction and maintenance of walls and public works, and organization of militia, police, schools, and hospitals. *Échevins* were then appointed or elected by the townspeople rather than by the territorial prince.

By the thirteenth century the larger Flemish towns limited tenure of office generally to one year, but the office became a monopoly of the rich and powerful bourgeois families. Working people were forbidden to be *échevins,* and even wealth and power were insufficient qualifications for this office in such towns as Ghent, where certain older, entrenched families reserved it for themselves. In the thirteenth century there developed at Ghent the *échevinage* of the thirty-nine individuals from a few families, thirteen of whom served each year as *échevins* while the other twenty-six were judges and advisers. Rotation provided that the same group of thirteen served as *échevins* every three years.

Royal power in northern France was too great to permit the large towns to win the political independence of the Italian communes and the Rhenish

towns, but comital authority in Flanders became so weak in the thirteenth and fourteenth centuries that the *échevinages* of Bruges and Ghent almost achieved the autonomy of their Italian and German counterparts. Only an alliance of the counts with the craft guilds blocked such an occurrence. Through their blatant disregard for the rights of citizens outside their class, the *échevins* provoked social tensions and revolts among the unprivileged classes in the late thirteenth and fourteenth centuries. Occasionally large craft guilds, such as that of the weavers, gained control of the *échevinage,* but not for long: medieval *échevinages* were never democratic. Late in the fourteenth century the Burgundian dukes became the rulers of Flanders and broke the power of the urban *échevinages,* placing them under close princely surveillance.

Motivated by civic pride during the twelfth and thirteenth centuries, the *échevins* fulfilled their functions admirably. Only when the office became restricted and, in practice, heritable did most townsmen come to regard *échevins* as selfish and oppressive tyrants. Though modified through the centuries, the modern office of *échevin* in Belgian cities and towns is indebted to its medieval ancestor.

BIBLIOGRAPHY

There is no book devoted solely to the medieval *échevin;* the development and function of the office must be pieced together from studies devoted to medieval urban institutions. See G. Espinas, *La vie urbaine de Douai au moyen âge,* 4 vols. (1913); Jean Lestocquoy, *Les villes de Flandre et d'Italie sous le gouvernement des patriciens (XIᵉ–XVᵉ siècles)* (1952); Charles E. Petit-Dutaillis, *Les communes françaises* (1947)—also in English, *The French Communes in the Middle Ages* (1978); Henri Pirenne, *Belgian Democracy: Its Early History,* J. V. Saunders, trans. (1915, repr. 1970), and *Medieval Cities,* Frank D. Halsey, trans. (1925, repr. 1948).

BRYCE LYON

[See also **Flanders and the Low Countries; Urbanism, 1000–1300; Urbanism, 1300–1500.**]

ÉCHOPPE, French for "graver." An early etching needle, large in diameter, with the point cut to form an oval cutting edge.

LESLIE BRUBAKER

[See also **Engraving.**]

ECKENLIED is one of the Middle High German Dietrich epics known as *märchenhaft* (like a fairy tale) or *aventiurehaft* (like a knightly quest). It survives in seven manuscript and eleven printed versions, of which the most important are a long manuscript fragment from the thirteenth century, a complete manuscript version from the *Dresdener Heldenbuch* of 1472, and a complete printed version of 1559 from Strasbourg. All versions are composed in the thirteen-line *Eckenstrophe* or *Bernerton* strophe, but individual versions vary considerably in the order, number, and wording of the strophes, as well as in details of the plot. Although the composition and transmission were quite fluid, the important versions are more or less in agreement through the Fasold episode.

Ecke, a young knight of gigantic stature, is eager to prove himself by fighting Dietrich von Bern. Seburg, the noblest of the three queens at Castle Jochgrimm, dispatches Ecke to bring Dietrich to her. Dietrich and Ecke duel until Dietrich mortally wounds Ecke. Lamenting Ecke's death, he dons Ecke's armor and takes his sword, binding Ecke's head to his saddle. Dietrich then encounters a maiden who is being pursued by Ecke's brother, the giant Fasold, whom Dietrich vanquishes.

At this point the texts diverge substantially, though all append further duels between Dietrich and giants. In the complete versions Dietrich journeys to Castle Jochgrimm, where he defeats two armed statues. In the *Dresdener Heldenbuch* he then confronts Seburg, reproaches her for sending Ecke to his death, throws Ecke's head at her feet, and walks out. In the printed version the queens are grateful that the threat of marriage to Ecke and Fasold no longer exists, and they honor Dietrich with a feast. Both versions conclude with Dietrich's return to Bern.

The *Eckenlied* probably originated as an etymological explanation for Dietrich's sword, *Eckesachs*, though the name actually means only "sharp-edged sword." References to Tirolean geography and folklore and the early transmission of one strophe in the Benediktbeuern *Carmina burana* manuscript suggest that the epic originated in the southern part of the German-speaking realm, but it soon became popular over a wide area. The closely related Ecca episode in the Old Norse *Þiðreks saga* shows that it was known as far north as Scandinavia at an early date.

The *Eckenlied* could have achieved its preserved form only through contact with courtly literature. Its strophes have the complexity of courtly lyric; its

similarity to an episode in the French Arthurian prose novel *Chevalier du Papagau* is too strong to be coincidental; the plot is set in motion by a quest in the service of a noble lady. The narrative's juxtaposition of courtly and folkloristic elements and the fluid transmission of the story make it a typical example of the kind of poetry intended for the casual entertainment of a mixed audience.

BIBLIOGRAPHY

Sources. MS *L,* the thirteenth-century fragment: Julius Zupitza, ed., *Deutsches Heldenbuch,* V (1870, repr. 1968), 219–264; MS *d,* the version of Kaspar von der Rhön's *Dresdener Heldenbuch* of 1472: Friedrich Heinrich von der Hagen and Alois Primisser, eds., *Der Helden Buch in der Ursprache,* pt. 2, in F. H. von der Hagen and J. G. G. Büsching, eds., *Deutsche Gedichte des Mittelalters,* II (1825), 74–116; the printed version from Strasbourg, *s:* Oskar Schade, ed., *Ecken Auszfart: Nach dem alten Strassburger Drucke von MDLIX* (1854).

Studies. A brief outline of the present state of research is in Joachim Heinzle, "Eckenlied," in *Verfasserlexikon,* 2nd ed., II (1978), cols. 323–327. The basic, indispensable guide to the fairy-tale Dietrich epics is Joachim Heinzle, *Mittelhochdeutsche Dietrichepik* (1978), the detailed listing of all texts (pp. 290–298) being of particular interest.

RUTH H. FIRESTONE

[See also **Alpharts Tod; Buch von Bern, Das; Dresdener Heldenbuch; Middle High German Literature; Þiðreks Saga.**]

ECKHART, MEISTER (ECKHART VON HOCHHEIM) (*ca.* 1260–*ca.* 1328), the most important German mystic of the Middle Ages and one of the most original religious thinkers of the late thirteenth and early fourteenth centuries. Eckhart's impact on contemporaries was primarily as a teacher and preacher, and his extant sermons in Middle High German are powerful monuments to a high-flying poetic spirit and linguistic genius. No one before Martin Luther expanded the possibilities of religious expression in the vernacular as much as Eckhart, and no other mystic described the experience of the mystical union in such intellectual terms as he did.

Not much is known about Eckhart's early life. He is first documented as a member of the Dominican Order and a student of the arts at Paris in 1277. He was born probably about 1260 in one of the two

Hochheims in Thuringia. In 1280 he was a student at the *studium generale* of the Dominicans in Cologne, where he most likely met Albertus Magnus. In 1293 Eckhart lectured at St. Jacques in Paris, and from 1294 to 1298 he held the posts of prior of the Dominican convent in Erfurt and vicar of the Dominican vicariate of Thuringia. He had become an important administrator and a leading intellectual personality in his order while still in his thirties.

Later, in 1302–1303 and again in 1311–1313, he held the only chair reserved for non-French professors at the University of Paris, where he obtained the honorific title *magister sacrae theologiae*, which in German was translated into *Meister*. He was also elected provincial of the Dominican province of Saxony (1303), vicar-general of Bohemia (1307), and head of the Dominican *studium generale* (1322).

During the last years of his life, Eckhart came into serious conflict with the Roman curia; in fact, he became the first Dominican friar to be accused of heresy. His trials in Cologne (1326) and Avignon (1327) have been the subject of much scholarly discussion, most of it colored by denominational bias. The papal bull *In agro dominico* (27 March 1329) condemned as potentially heretical *(prout verba sonant)* twenty-eight sentences in Eckhart's writings and noted that Eckhart recanted these statements before his death. (Since he is elsewhere mentioned as being still alive early in 1327, the year of his death can be approximated.)

Although the papal condemnation cast a shadow on Eckhart's reputation immediately after his death, he inspired the sermons and writings of such popular religious figures as Tauler and Suso (who were students at the *studium generale* in Cologne) and numerous nuns and layfolk who heard him speak. Eckhart's influence extended to Nicholas of Cusa, Martin Luther, Jakob Boehme, Hegel, Fichte, and the existentialist philosophers. Recent comparative studies have pointed out similarities between Eckhart's mystical doctrines and certain aspects of Hinduism and Zen Buddhism.

The bulk of Eckhart's German works consists of fifty-nine authenticated sermons. He may have dictated some of these sermons to followers, but most were probably written down from memory by listeners. The only signed sermon is "Vom edlen Menschen" (On noble men), composed in 1313 in conjunction with Eckhart's most beautiful work, the *Buch der göttlichen Tröstung* (Book of divine consolation). He also wrote two German tractates: *Reden der Unterscheidung* (Talks of instruction)

(1289) and *Von Abegescheidenheit* (On emptiness) *(ca. 1290)*.

Eckhart's Latin work was conceived on a grand scale, probably during his first professorship in Paris; but apparently the master did not find time to execute his plan of presenting to posterity the sum of his theology. What remains of his *Opus tripartitum* is an introduction to the first part, the *Opus propositionum,* and nearly all of the third part, the *Opus expositionum,* but nothing of the second part, the *Opus quaestionum.* Thus the *Opus expositionum,* the expository part, constitutes Eckhart's principal Latin work. Because of its precise vocabulary and clear syntax, it contains many valuable clues to the interpretation of some of his German sermons. Of considerable importance is the *Rechtfertigungsschrift* (Writ of justification, 1327), in which Eckhart adamantly rejects the accusation of heresy. His minor Latin works include a commentary on the *Sentences* of Peter Lombard (1293/1294), a *collatio,* or inaugural lecture *(ca.* 1297), and three disputations (1302/1303).

Eckhart's Latin works, though helpful to the modern scholar, would not secure his reputation as a great mystic or innovative theologian. The German works, by contrast, bear witness to his brilliance. There is little in Middle High German prose that can bear comparison with Eckhart's style and diction. His sermons are filled with unique images and metaphors; his use of paradox, abstraction, hyperbole, asyndeton, and circumscription appears exaggerated by modern standards, but it must be kept in mind that there was no ready-made working German vocabulary for complex theological matters, and that it was primarily Eckhart who created one. The *doctor extaticus,* as he was called by a contemporary, was a "God-intoxicated" mystic who addressed believers eager to share his experience of the mystical union.

Eckhart's early training was as a Scholastic, and there is much in his writings that he learned from Peter Lombard's *Sentences* and Thomas Aquinas' *Summa contra gentiles,* both staples of Scholasticism. Later, though, as his mysticism crystallized, he leaned more on the writings of St. Augustine, Proclus, Pseudo-Dionysius the Areopagite, Plotinus, and the Jewish philosopher Maimonides, whose *Guide of the Perplexed* seems to have had a special impact on Eckhart. Although he built his theology on Scholastic (that is Aristotelian-Thomist) foundations, the spirit that permeates his ideas and makes him a mystic is Neoplatonic. Eckhart's greatest achievement as a religious innovator was to solve the contradiction between divine transcendence and divine immanence, though in doing so he made himself vulnerable to charges of pantheism and heresy.

The central idea in all of Eckhart's teachings is the *Gottesgeburt in der Seele* (birth of God in the soul): God can fill the soul with himself; he can be born, or "generated," in the "empty" soul. The human soul is a mirror that "absorbs" the divine light and reflects it back to God without losing its identity. The point at which God and the soul "touch" is the very depth of the soul, at the *Seelengrund*. From there emanates a spark *(Seelenfünklein)*, a part of the soul and of God, yet external to both. It "leaps" spontaneously from one to the other, connects them but leaves them separate and differentiated.

How does a person prepare for the leap of the *Seelenfünklein?* Eckhart says that just as God ultimately is nothingness, so man must rid himself of all physical and spiritual desires that remind him of created things; in other words, his aim should be to approximate God's nothingness as much as possible. When the individual has become "nothing," has achieved poverty in spirit, then the attraction between God and the soul is so great that the spark of the soul "ignites" and the mystical union takes place. Thus Eckhart in his sermons emphasizes again and again that the only purpose of life in the physical world is to engage in a spiritual cleansing process, an asceticism that allows the soul to realize its *Adel*, the nobility with which God endowed it on its creation. In one of his most famous sermons there is the following passage:

> When I preach, I usually speak of "emptiness," of the need for man to rid himself of his self and of all things. Then, I also preach the possibility that one can be molded into the uniform goodness that is God. And third, [I preach] that one should think of the great nobility that God has given to the soul so that man might use it as a miraculous link with God. (Quint, ed., *Meister Eckhart. Die deutschen Werke*, I, 528; my trans.)

Eckhart advocates not renunciation of all worldly activity, but rather a state of nonvolition, an existence that is void of ambition and nonspiritual desire. It is not surprising, then, that Eckhart ascribes little importance to good works. In fact, he considers good works in themselves worthless as far as the relation between the soul and God is concerned: what really matters is the attitude of the individual. "Goodness" is obtained through the grace of God, and even a life led in close imitation of Christ would not avail an individual who lacked inner nobility. In this attitude there are clearly germinal elements of Luther's doctrine of salvation.

Eckhart also has little to say about the historical Christ. He is much more interested in the "role" or "function" of the Son in the triune God, and in such eternal Trinitarian processes as the begetting of the Son by the Father and the procession of the Holy Spirit from the Father and the Son. He is also very much concerned with the manner in which the birth of Christ takes place in the soul, a process that, in his opinion, constitutes the most vital aspect of human existence.

BIBLIOGRAPHY

Sources. Meister Eckhart. Die deutschen Werke, Joseph Quint, ed., I–III, V (1958–1976)—IV still in preparation—the only critical ed. of Eckhart's German works; *Meister Eckhart. Die Lateinischen Werke,* Joseph Koch et al., eds., 5 vols. (1936–1964), the only critical ed. of Eckhart's complete Latin works; Franz Pfeiffer, ed., *Die deutschen Mystiker des 14. Jahrhunderts,* II, *Meister Eckhart* (1857, repr. 1966), not critical and unreliable.

Modern German translations are H. Büttner, *Meister Eckhart's Schriften und Predigten,* 2 vols. (1903); Joseph Quint, *Meister Eckhart, deutsche Predigten und Traktate* (1955, repr. 1963).

English translations are J. M. Clark, ed. and trans., *Meister Eckhart: An Introduction to the Study of His Works* (1957); J. M. Clark and J. V. Skinner, eds. and trans., *Meister Eckhart, Selected Treatises and Sermons . . . from Latin and German* (1958).

Studies. J. Ancelet-Hustache, *Maître Eckhart et la mystique rhénane* (1956); I. Degenhardt, *Studien zum Wandel des Eckhartbildes* (1967); Alois Dempf, *Meister Eckhart* (1960); Dietmar Mieth, *Meister Eckhart* (1979); Ernst H. Soudek, *Meister Eckhart* (1973); F. W. Wentzlaff-Eggebert, *Deutsche Mystik zwischen Mittelalter und Neuzeit,* 2nd ed. (1969), 301–307.

ERNST H. SOUDEK

[See also **Dominicans; Maimonides, Moses; Middle High German Literature; Mysticism, Western European; Neoplatonism.**]

ECLOGA THEODULI. See Latin Literature.

ECLOGUE (Greek: *Ekloga*), a code of law in eighteen titles, issued in 726 by the Byzantine emperor Leo III the Isaurian and by his son and coemperor Constantine V. A committee of three lawyers (including the *quaestor sacri palatii*) was appointed to examine preexisting legislation and to summarize the essential and frequently used rulings in a short code of law convenient for everyone, particularly provincials. Mainly concerned with civil, family, inheritance, and penal law, the *Eclogue* is based on Justinian's legislation but seems to have taken into consideration a number of now lost Novels of later emperors, including Leo III himself. It also attests a strong influence of canon law and of customary law, which sometimes goes back to Hellenistic times. In a deliberate effort to infuse an element of humanity (*philanthropoteron*) into the law, capital punishment is often replaced by mutilation, which does not endanger the salvation of the criminal's soul.

Being the work of iconoclasts, the *Eclogue* was denounced in the ninth century as a "perversion of the law" and formally abrogated. Nevertheless, it remained in use, mainly in the provinces but even in the capital, and influenced legislation in southern Italy and especially the Slavic lands.

BIBLIOGRAPHY

The most available edition is P. Zepos and I. Zepos, eds., *Jus Graecoromanum*, II (1931), 1–62. See also E. H. Freshfield, trans., *A Manual of Roman Law, the Ecloga* (1926); C. A. Spulber, trans., *L'Eclogue des Isauriens* (1929). For the date see V. Grumel, "La date de l'Eclogue des Isauriens: L'année et le jour," in *Revue des études byzantines*, 21 (1963).

NICOLAS OIKONOMIDES

[See also **Byzantine Empire: History (330–1025); Law, Byzantine; Leo III the Isaurian.**]

ECTHESIS. See Ekthesis.

ECUMENICAL PATRIARCH, a title assumed by the archbishop of Constantinople in the sixth century and reflecting primarily his position as bishop of the new capital of the Roman Empire. The word "ecumenical," referring to the *oikoumene* (inhabited world), was also used to designate other institutions and functions of "imperial" importance. Pope Gregory I objected to the use of the title by Patriarch John IV the Faster (582–595), but the latter's successors continued to use it despite repeated papal objections, as in the letters of Adrian I to Patriarch Tarasius (784–806). Apparently, by calling himself "ecumeni-

cal," the patriarch of Constantinople intended not to deny the "primacy of honor" that the Byzantines accorded to the bishop of "Old Rome" but rather to describe his own position in the Byzantine Empire, as defined by the councils.

According to canon 28 of the Council of Chalcedon (451), the archbishop of the new capital was granted "equal privileges" with the Roman pope because Constantinople was the residence "of the emperor and the Senate." A later legal text, known as the *Epanagoge* (ninth century), describes the patriarch as the "living image of Christ" in the affairs of the empire, so that he and the emperor are "the most exalted and the most necessary members of society."

From the fifth century the archbishop of Constantinople exercised patriarchal jurisdiction (which involved ordination of all "provincial" metropolitans) in the imperial "dioceses" of Asia, Pontus, and Thrace, which included most of Asia Minor and the eastern part of the Balkan Peninsula. In the eighth century the emperors added Illyricum, previously under Rome, to the patriarch's jurisdiction. In the ninth and tenth centuries, with the conversion of the Slavs by Byzantine missionaries, the powers of the ecumenical patriarch extended over most of eastern Europe, including particularly Russia (from 988). In the tenth and eleventh centuries, as relations with the Latin West turned into a permanent state of schism, the ecumenical patriarchate was at the zenith of its prestige. The liturgical usages of its cathedral—the "Great Church" of Hagia Sophia—were accepted by half of Christendom, as the other patriarchal sees of the East—Alexandria, Antioch, and Jerusalem—were only shadows of their glorious pasts.

Elected by a synod of metropolitans and "invested" by the emperor, the ecumenical patriarch was generally, but not always, dependent on imperial power. The weak Palaiologoi emperors (1261–1453) did not succeed in imposing on him a union with Rome, which they were pursuing for political reasons. In the late Byzantine period the patriarchate was often exercising greater powers and prestige than the diminished Byzantine state. After the capture of Constantinople by the Turks in 1453, it was the patriarch who was invested by the Muslim authorities with both civil and ecclesiastical powers over all the Christians of the Ottoman Empire.

BIBLIOGRAPHY

Hans-Georg Beck, *Kirche und theologische Literatur im byzantinischen Reich* (1959), 60–92; Louis Bréhier, *Les institutions de l'empire byzantin* (1949), 461–506; John Meyendorff, *Byzantine Theology* (1974), 83–88.

JOHN MEYENDORFF

[See also **Byzantine Church; Epanagoge.**]

EDDIC METERS. The two chief measures of eddic poetry are *fornyrðislag* (old-lore meter) and *ljóð-aháttr* (chant meter). *Málaháttr* (speech meter) is a heavier variant of *fornyrðislag*, and *galdralag* (magic-spell meter) is an augmented variant of *ljóð-aháttr*.

Fornyrðislag and *málaháttr* do not differ radically from the meter of Old English, Old Saxon, or Old High German alliterative poetry. The basic metrical unit is the couplet, whose lines, each containing two stressed syllables and two or more unstressed syllables, are linked in pairs by alliteration. The old line has one or two alliterating syllables, usually stressed; the even line has only one alliterating word, regularly the first stressed syllable of the line (alliterating words are given below in italics):

> Ár vas *alda*
> þáts *ekki* var,
> vara *sandr* ne *sær*
> né *svalar* unnir. (*Vǫluspá*, stanza 3)

All vowel sounds alliterate with each other and with words beginning with *j*; a single consonant alliterates with itself, as does each of the consonant groups *sk*, *sp*, and *st*. *Fornyrðislag* occurs both with and without a fixed number of syllables. The quotation from *Vǫluspá* above illustrates the syllable-counting variety with four syllables to the line; two short syllables, like *vara* or *Ymir*, count as a long one in the practice known as "resolution."

Málaháttr differs from *fornyrðislag* only in that it allows a greater number of syllables—five in its regularized form:

> Lito, es lýsti,
> létoz þeir fúsir
> allir upp rísa—
> ǫnnur þau lǫtto. (*Atlamál*, stanza 27)

Ljóðaháttr and *galdralag* appear to be native Norse creations: nothing comparable is known from other Germanic poetry. In *ljóðaháttr*, the basic metrical unit is the alliterating couplet, which is followed by a third single line (called the full line) that alliterates internally, has two, two and a half, or three stresses, and ends in a distinctive cadence that is never a trochee:

> Ganga skal,
> skala gestr vesa
> ey i einom stað. (*Hávamál*, stanza 35)

After this third line the pattern is repeated, creating a stanza of six rather than eight lines. *Galdralag* is an adaptation of *ljóðaháttr* in which the full line is repeated with variation.

Some differentiation in the use of *fornyrðislag* and *ljóðaháttr* for various types of eddic poetry is apparent. *Fornyrðislag* is frequent in epic narrative poems (such as *Vǫluspá, Helreið Brynhildar, Atlakviða*). *Ljóðaháttr* is used for somebody's words, often a god's or a giant's (as in *Hávamál, Vafþrúð-nismál, Grímnismál*). A mixture of *ljóðaháttr* and *fornyrðislag* is found in certain eddic poems that consist of dialogue joined by prose narrative passages (for instance, *Helgakviða Hjǫrvarðssonar, Sigrdrí-fumál, Fáfnismál, Reginsmál*). All eddic meters are strophic, the chief characteristic distinguishing Norse alliterative verse from its West Germanic stichic counterpart. The earliest eddic poetry (such as *Vǫlundarkviða, Hamðismál, Atlakviða*) shows much metrical variety and has stanzas varying in length from two to fourteen lines. The strict regularization of line and stanza length found in later eddic poetry may reflect the influence of skaldic poetry.

BIBLIOGRAPHY

Peter Foote and David Wilson, *The Viking Achievement* (1980), 319–326; Jóhann S. Hannesson, *Bibliography of the Eddas, a Supplement* (1955); Halldór Hermannsson, *Bibliography of the Eddas* (1920); Gustav Neckel, ed., *Edda: Die Lieder des Codex Regius*, I, 4th rev. ed. by Hans Kuhn (1962); Klaus von See, *Germanische Verskunst* (1967), 52–60.

ROBERTA FRANK

[See also **Eddic Poetry.**]

EDDIC POETRY. The generic concept "Eddic poetry," applied to a widely scattered corpus in Old Norse, is based on similarities with a central group of poems in the *Poetic Edda* proper. This diverse anthology is found in two Icelandic manuscripts of the thirteenth century.

POETIC EDDA AND PROSE EDDA

The Codex Regius was discovered by Bishop Brynjólfr Sveinsson in 1643, during the revival of scholarly interest in the past of Iceland. The manuscript was sent to King Frederick III of Denmark in 1662 and joined the "Old Royal Collection" as Gml. kgl. saml. 2365, 4°. The bishop's present was part of a massive export of medieval manuscripts from Iceland, then a Danish colony; in the 1970's these manuscripts began to be returned, and the Codex Regius is now in the Arnamagnaean Manuscript Institute in Reykjavik, Iceland. The plain vellum book, a so-called small quarto, contains twenty-nine poems, according to the conventional division, about Norse gods and Scandinavian and Germanic heroes, and is dated paleographically to about 1270. The name *Poetic Edda* derives from an early error. Snorri Sturluson had written a treatise on poetics and mythology (*ca.* 1223); this book, called *Edda* in one manuscript, was well known in Iceland down to the seventeenth century, and Icelandic scholars of that period had concluded that Snorri must have had a lost poetic source.

When Bishop Brynjólfr's manuscript turned up, it was hailed as the lost source and attributed to one of Snorri's predecessors among the scholars of medieval Iceland, Sæmundr Sigfússon the Learned (*d.* 1133). *Sæmundr's Edda* was thus established as its title, in contrast to *Snorri's Edda*. In time the attribution to Sæmundr (with the dating it implied) was rejected, but the designation *(Poetic) Edda* remains in contrast with Snorri's *(Prose) Edda*. (The name *Elder Edda* was also current but is perhaps less popular today because of its obvious assumptions about chronology.) The meaning and etymology of *edda* have long constituted a special puzzle; the most recent solution is a jokingly deprecating hypocoristic formulation from the Latin *edere* (to write, publish), analogous to *kredda* (a little credo, from *credere*), according to Faulkes.

Another manuscript, the fragmentary Arnamagnaean 748 I 4°, contains seven complete or partial poems. One of these, *Baldrs draumar* (Baldr's dreams), is not in Codex Regius, and the rest are in what appears to be a random order that agrees with Codex Regius in only one point: *Vafþrúðnismál* (Lay of Vafþrúðnir) precedes *Grímnismál* (Lay of Grímnir) in both. Arnamagnaean 748 I 4° is dated about 1300. The textual agreements of these two manuscripts are due to a common written, not oral, source. Snorri's *Prose Edda* draws on the same written versions of *Vafþrúðnismál* and *Grímnismál;* to-

gether these clues constitute evidence for the existence of a pamphlet containing only these two poems before about 1220. Lindblad, whose statistical studies of spelling variations uncovered traces of separate pamphlets underlying Codex Regius, established this current standard view. With other scholars he believes further that a collection of prose and verse, a *Sigurðar saga*, that served as the source of part of the section of Codex Regius dealing with Sigurd was in existence by about 1200, and other pamphlets with heroic poems seem to have had a separate existence. However, it was due to the stimulus of Snorri's treatise that other mythological poems were written down in the period from about 1225 to 1240. The unordered collection mirrored in Arnamagnaean 748 I 4° represents a stage before the ordered (and perhaps selected) direct ancestor of Codex Regius was finally created about the middle of the thirteenth century.

In this arrangement the mythological poems precede the heroic, with a rather sharp paleographical boundary between the two parts. The boundary is further emphasized by the oversize initial of the first heroic poem, a capital matched only by the initial of the first mythological poem. In general the heroic poems are ordered according to the "saga principle"—that is, in supposed chronological order of the events narrated, and linked by the family relationships of the main characters. However, the first poems of the heroic section violate this principle: their order is *Helgakviða Hundingsbana I* (HHI; First lay of Helgi Hunding's-slayer), *Helgakviða Hjǫrvarðssonar* (HHv; Lay of Helgi Hjǫrvarð's son), *Helgakviða Hundingsbana II* (HHII; Second lay of Helgi Hunding's-slayer). The hero of *HHv* and his guardian-lover, the Valkyrie Sváva, were "reborn" as Helgi Hunding's-slayer and his Valkyrie Sigrún, and must have preceded them in time. But *HH* tells of the birth and youth of the later Helgi, and no thoroughly convincing explanation has been offered. With Helgi Hjǫrvarðsson the saga principle is stretched to include relationship by rebirth; but oral tradition had made Helgi Hunding's-slayer into a genuine son of Sigmund, consolidating his story with those about the Vǫlsung clan.

Thus, following the Helgi poems a prose passage lists the sons of Sigmund and narrates the death of another of them: *Frá dauða Sinfjǫtla* (The Death of Sinfjǫtli). Next *Grípisspá* (Prophecy of Grípir) introduces the story of Sigurd, another son of Sigmund, with a prophetic overview. There follows a long stretch of prose and verse dealing with Sigurd's youth; modern editors divide this into *Reginsmál* (Lay of Reginn), *Fáfnismál* (Lay of Fáfnir), and *Sigrdrífumál* (Lay of Sigrdrífa). After a lacuna the history of Sigurd continues in *Brot af Sigurðarkviðu* (*Brot;* fragmentary Lay of Sigurd); the surviving portion recounts the aftermath of Sigurd's murder by his brothers-in-law, at the instigation of the jealous Brynhild. The grief of Sigurd's widow is the subject of *Guðrúnarkviða I* (First lay of Guðrún), the next poem; the following *Sigurðarkviða in skamma* (Short lay of Sigurd) doubles back to cover much the same ground as *Brot;* and *Helreið Brynhildar* (Brynhild's ride to Hel), the next poem, shows Brynhild joining Sigurd in death.

A new phase of the story of the Vǫlsungs begins with the prose *Dráp Niflunga* (Slaughter of the Niflungs); the following poems work out the fate of Sigurd's relatives. *Guðrúnarkviða II* (Second lay of Guðrún) tells how Guðrún came to be married to King Atli (Attila) in the land of the Huns, and *Guðrúnarkviða III* (Third lay of Guðrún) concerns an incident in the married life of Atli and Guðrún; *Oddrúnargrátr* (Lament of Oddrún) deals with tragic events in the lives of Sigurd's brother-in-law Gunnarr and of Atli's sister Oddrún. The mainstream story resumes in *Atlakviða* and *Atlamál* ([Old] Lay of Atli, [Greenlandic] Lay of Atli), both of which narrate the death of Gunnarr at Atli's hands and Guðrún's barbaric revenge on Atli. The final group of poems depicts the extinction of the family: Guðrún again remarries and produces sons; Svanhildr, her daughter by Sigurd, is murdered by her own husband Jǫrmunrekkr (the historical Gothic king Ermanaric); in *Guðrúnarhvǫt* (Guðrún's incitement) and *Hamðismál* (Lay of Hamðir), the last poem of the anthology, Guðrún drives her sons into a suicidal revenge for their half sister.

The organization of the mythological poems is not quite so perspicacious. The manuscript opens with *Vǫluspá* (Sibyl's prophecy), probably because of its connection with the origins of the universe and the gods and because as a vision it surveys (like *Grípisspá*) the chronological field of the poems that follow. *Hávamál* (Sayings of the High One), the second poem, purports to be advice and precepts straight from the mouth of Odin. The next two poems, *Vafþrúðnismál* and *Grímnismál*, incorporate collections of esoteric lore into Odin's encounters with a giant and a cruel king. An isolated poem about Freyr (*Skírnismál*) follows, narrating his proxy wooing of a giant's daughter; then come four comic poems grouped together because in each Thor is a central

character: *Hárbarðsljóð* (Lay of Hárbarðr), *Hymiskviða* (Lay of Hymir), *Lokasenna* (Insolence of Loki), and *Þrymskviða* (Lay of Þrymr). The ordering of the mythological poems to this point may have been dictated by a combination of the survey principle and the order of the death of the major gods at Ragnarǫk (*Vǫluspá*, 53–56): Odin, Freyr, Thor.

The last two mythological poems—*Vǫlundarkviða* (Lay of Vǫlundr) and *Alvíssmál* (Words of Allwise)—however, constitute a problem. *Alvíssmál,* telling of Thor's wisdom contest, would seem to belong with the Thor poems, while *Vǫlundarkviða* seems to belong with the heroic poems: it tells of Vǫlundr's captivity by King Níðuðr and of his gruesome revenge and escape. Perhaps *Vǫlundarkviða* is merely misplaced, but many students now accept that the arranger of Codex Regius regarded it as a mythological poem. *Vǫlundarkviða* and *Alvíssmál* may be grouped together as poems that feature "lower divinities," for Vǫlundr is a prince of "elves" and Alvíss is a wise dwarf; possibly, too, the "lower divinities" are intended as a transition to the human heroes. Placing the mythological poems first may be intended to provide an impressive background and, in some way, a divine genealogy of the heroes. Klingenberg has demonstrated corresponding passages in the two parts of Codex Regius and finds the overall theme of the book, the evil of intrafamilial violence, to be an expression of national concerns of mid-thirteenth-century Iceland.

The Codex Regius is composed of five gatherings of eight leaves each and one of only five leaves. The total of forty-five surviving pages, however, is only a part of the original, which had a seventh gathering of eight leaves, now lost except as reconstructed. The lacuna begins near the original end of *Sigrdrífumál* and terminates in the middle of *Brot*. No copy of Codex Regius antedates the loss, but the contents of the lost poems can be determined from a thirteenth-century paraphrase in prose (with some verse quotations) in *Vǫlsunga saga*. According to the classic view established by Heusler, the lacuna contained, in addition to the end of *Sigrdrífumál* and the beginning of *Brot*, three poems: *Falkenlied* (Lay of the falcon), *Traumlied* (Dream lay), and *Sigurðarkviða in meiri* (Longer Sigurd lay); Andersson has argued with probability that the three poems all belonged to one very full lost Sigurd lay.

Another Icelandic manuscript, *Hauksbók* (relevant leaves in Arnamagnaean 544, 4°, from about 1350), contained a copy of one Eddic poem, *Vǫluspá*, in a variant form that seems a little closer to the one used by Snorri than to the version in Codex Regius. Oral variants seem to be behind these three texts of *Vǫluspá*. This constitutes the Eddic inner group, the *Poetic Edda* proper.

OTHER EDDIC MANUSCRIPTS

Other poems and fragments regularly appear alongside them in editions and translations as the "Eddic appendix." *Rígsþula* (Lay of Rígr) is preserved on the last page of a late-fourteenth-century manuscript (Wormianus) of Snorri's *Edda;* fragmentary but fully intelligible, it traces the classes of medieval Norse society to visitations by the god Rígr (perhaps identical with Heimdall). Thirteen additional individual stanzas or fragments of otherwise lost mythological poems are preserved, worked into the main manuscripts of Snorri's *Prose Edda.* Among the most important are two stanzas spoken by the god Njǫrðr and his giant wife Skaði, capping the story of their marriage; a close parallel in Saxo Grammaticus' Latin history of the Danes (*ca.* 1200) adds some literary-historical potential. The title of one of the important lost poems (only two lines remain) is preserved as *Heimdalargaldr* (Spell of Heimdall). The lost poems underlying Snorri's account of Baldr's death and Hermóðr's ride to Hel to attempt his delivery can be recognized in the alliterative prose of these passages in Snorri.

Three titled fragments are mnemonic lists (*þulur*) of mythological names. The complete *Hyndluljóð* (Song of Hyndla) is preserved along with genealogical matter near the beginning of *Flateyjarbók,* a huge compilation mainly of saga histories, dating from the late fourteenth century; the poem records the lineage of Óttarr Innsteinsson within the mythic framework of a dialogue between the goddess Freyja and the giantess Hyndla. Interpolated into Óttarr's genealogy are some sixteen stanzas of a fragmentary poem on the origins and destinies of the gods and their opponents, *Vǫluspá in skamma* (Short sibyl's prophecy). This title derives from Snorri, in whose time this poem must still have existed in independent form. *Grógaldr* and *Fjǫlsvinnsmál* are two separate poems (collectively *Svipdagsmál* [Lay of Svipdag]) that fit together to form a single story about a stepmother's curse and the hero's quest for his destined princess; the extant paper manuscripts of this fairy tale with Norse mythological trappings are very late, but according to Sveinsson there seems to have been a lost vellum.

Such are the mythological poems of the "Eddic appendix." The heroic poems usually collected there include *Grottasǫngr* (Mill song), in which, however, the distinction between mythological and heroic is not readily applicable; preserved as an editorial addition in Codex Regius of the *Prose Edda* (Gml. kgl. saml. 2367, 4°) from the early fourteenth century (and also in the *T* redaction), it is (in part) the work song of two giantesses as they turn the mill that grinds out gold and peace for a Danish king of the heroic age. *Hlǫðskviða* (Battle of the Goths and Huns), one of the oldest heroic poems, is preserved in fragmentary form with prose transitions in the *Hervarar saga ok Heiðreks konungs,* a romantic-mythological composition of about 1250; it presents the story of the tragic clash of half brothers over their royal patrimony, against the historical background of the battles between the Goths and the Huns in southeastern Europe, probably in the second half of the fifth century. The "death-song" or last words of Hildibrandr is also in a late *fornaldar saga* but preserves in a confused form poetic fragments from early south Germanic material best known from the German *Hildebrandslied* (in manuscript before 840); the tale is again of tragic killing within a family.

These last two poems are also included in the influential collection *Eddica minora,* in which Heusler and Ranisch brought together "poems of the Eddic type," mainly from *fornaldar sǫgur.* The remainder of these works are attributed to "Eddic poetry" but definitely not to the *Poetic Edda* or its conventional appendix. *Hervarar saga* further contributes a poem in which the woman warrior Hervǫr, braving the terrors of the dead, awakens her father in his funeral mound to demand from him the cursed family sword, and a poetic wisdom (riddle) contest between Odin (Gestumblindi) and the wise king Heiðrekr, a situation resembling that in *Vafþrúðnismál.* The *Bjarkamál* (Lay of Bjarki) is an important (probably Danish) dialogue poem set at the last battle of King Hrólf Kraki. The poem is known only through three groups of fragmentary survivals (eight stanzas in all) in various Icelandic sources, through Saxo Grammaticus' Latin reworking of about 1200, and through a prose paraphrase in the late medieval Icelandic *Hrólfs saga kraka.*

The other verses of the *Eddica minora* share many of the characteristics of these most important examples, especially late transmission; there are "death-songs" and retrospective life stories, "flytings" and related dialogue forms, prophecies, curses, and catalogs. In general the contents are at least as varied as in the inner groups of Eddic poetry. However, the *Eddica minora* does not contain all the poetry of "Eddic type" found in sagas, but only that judged older and artistically more valuable by the editors.

METER

The clearest criterion for the generic category "Eddic poetry" is metrical. All Eddic meters are based on principles derived from Old Germanic metrics in which the metrical unit was the "half-line"; half-lines were linked into lines (or "long lines") by alliteration, the rules for which included the alliteration of any vowel with any other. Each normal half-line had two major stresses; the alliteration had to fall on one or both of the stresses in the first half-line and on the first only in the second half-line. Stressed syllables or "lifts" alternated in a variety of patterns with unstressed or lightly stressed syllables of the "dips." Sievers showed that Old Germanic had had five major patterns (*A–E*) of distribution of syllables in the dips and lifts, but half-lines of different types were combined without any restrictions (*A* + *B*, *B* + *C*, and so on).

In Old Norse there are two basic meters and two major variants. *Fornyrðislag* (old-lore meter) remains closest to the Common Germanic (*Gemeingermanisch*) principles; phonological developments in Scandinavia dictated, however, that *j* alliterate as a vowel, and a short type of half-line came into being in which one or both of the dips were missing (originally three of the five types had two dips). The most obvious difference, however, between *fornyrðislag* verse and the closely comparable poetry in West Germanic languages is that the Old Norse is always stanzaic while the Old English, Old Saxon, and Old High German are almost always stichic; as a rule the *fornyrðislag* stanza consists of four long lines, but the older poetry (such as *Vǫlundarkviða*) presents stanzas of unequal length.

Peculiar to Old Norse is *ljóðaháttr* (chant meter), which was used almost entirely for speeches, as opposed to third-person narrative. In it the four-line stanza consisted of first and third long lines in *fornyrðislag* and second and fourth "full lines" (*Vollzeile*) with two or three lifts separated by two or even only one dip; certain rules governed the pattern of stress on the final syllables of the full line. The old problem of whether the norm called for two or three (or two and a half) lifts seems still unresolved; in any case the full line alliterates only internally. The variant form of *ljóðaháttr* called *galdralag* (charm or

magic spell meter) simply adds one or more similar or identical full lines after line two or four, giving a stanza of five or more lines; *galdralag* is thought to have originated in magical verse like the elaborate curse in *Skírnismál*.

The variant form of *fornyrðislag* is called *málaháttr* (speech meter). In Old Norse *fornyrðislag* had developed in the direction of smooth, short lines, very often with four syllables and regular alternation of lifts and dips; *málaháttr* appears to have developed in the opposite direction: toward a longer line with more syllables in the dips; sometimes there are secondary stresses that approach the weight of a third main stress. *Fornyrðislag*, preeminently the meter of the poems on southern Germanic legends, and *málaháttr* were employed for both third-person narrative and speech. The analysis and history of *málaháttr* are still unclear, especially whether it is the somewhat systematized heir of older occasional heavy lines or perhaps a late import from West Germanic languages (see von See).

The stylistic concept "Eddic" stands in contrast with "skaldic," which is used in a technical sense to refer to a large group of complicated metrical forms developed only in Scandinavia and to typical poetry in those meters. Whereas Eddic verse is anonymous, traditional, broadly narrative, and impossible to link to specific times and places, skaldic verse stems from poets who are (on the whole) known by name, attempts more originality, is not usually a narrative medium, and is often composed for a public occasion. This contrast, traditional in Old Norse literary history, is easy to overstate. Influence from the intricate diction of skaldic poetry can be detected with certainty in several Eddic poems, such as *Helgakviða Hundingsbana I* and *Hymiskviða,* and named skalds knew and exploited Eddic poems.

With the Eddic–skaldic distinction, however, the outermost circle in the inventory of Eddic verse, transitional forms, is reached. *Haraldskvæði* (early tenth century), *Eiríksmál* (just after 954), and *Hákonarmál* (about 961) share a typical skaldic occasion, praise of a king, yet they are written in a mixture of Eddic meters and employ motifs from the Eddic repertory. The author of *Eiríksmál* is unknown, and the poet of *Hákonarmál* is intimately familiar with certain extant Eddic poems. Many other "skaldic" poems, such as *Hugsvinnsmál*, are anonymous and, to some extent, Eddic in manner. A special case is *Sólarljóð* (Song of the sun), a brilliant fusion of Christian thought with pre-Christian gnomic style.

Two notable twelfth-century skalds, Gísl Illugason and Ívarr Ingimundarson, adopted *fornyrðislag* and drew on Eddic diction in poems with a typically skaldic purpose.

DATING AND PROVENANCE

The closely related problems of age and provenance have long been the most important questions in Eddic studies. Criteria for assigning a date to Eddic poems include the following. First, language: Primitive Norse (second through seventh centuries) underwent a period of radical loss of unstressed medial and final vowels, becoming Old Norse (eighth through eleventh centuries). When pre-syncope forms are inserted into lines of Eddic verse, the meter is usually destroyed; this metrical test has long been accepted as setting the terminus a quo for Eddic poetry in general. Other linguistic criteria provide only probabilistic evidence for deciding on a date within the range of time between syncope and the manuscripts; some important criteria are the suffixed definite article (very late), contractions (such as *blám* for the earlier *bláum*), and the percentage of occurrences of the prefix substitute *of/um*. Historical semantics can provide some indications.

Second, archaeology and history: references to realia and institutions can be given an approximate date. However, since the memory of ring-hilted swords or a slave class, for example, can survive in tradition or be imitated by archaizing poets, such criteria provide only a terminus a quo and perhaps some hints.

Third, Christianity: Norway and Iceland were converted between 995 and 1030. Mythological poetry should antedate this period unless it is transitional or else nonreligious antiquarianism from a century or two later.

Fourth, citations: the authors of skaldic verse are datable persons; if a skald borrows from an Eddic poem, it provides a firm terminus ad quem. In a few cases other historically fixed quotations (for instance, by King Sverrir of Norway) may be useful, and a relative chronology can be worked out on the basis of citations of one Eddic poem by another. Citation in Snorri's *Edda* sets an extreme limit, but absence of citation there has also been interpreted as evidence of very late origin.

Fifth, relation to foreign poetry and heroic legend: many of the heroic poems treat stories with a historical core from the period of the Germanic migrations (*ca.* 300–600), especially from Gothic and Burgundian historical tradition. Since the legends grew more and more complex and elaborately linked together, it is sometimes possible to assign a relative order to poems on the basis of the form of the legend they embody. The poems based on foreign legends (*Fremdstofflieder*) also carry some linguistic clues to their earlier poetic forms.

Until well into the nineteenth century, the poems were considered very ancient and of common Scandinavian genesis; the texts of editions tended to reflect early dating with systematic restoration of old forms, but more recent editions (Helgason, Kuhn, Dronke) tend to normalize to the usage of the manuscripts. A turning point in scholarly opinion was Jessen's 1871 paper arguing for a late (mostly eleventh- or twelfth-century) date and an Icelandic origin. The present standard view is represented by that of Jan de Vries and is built on a long line of continental scholars (including Sijmons, Heusler, Kuhn, and Mohr). The dates range from before 850 well into the thirteenth century, with most of the texts belonging to a smaller early group (850–1030) or to a larger late group (1150–1300); a few belong to a middle group (1030–1150).

The "old" mythological poems are chiefly *Vafþrúðnismál* (900–950), *Grímnismál*, *Hárbarðsljóð*, and *Vǫluspá* (950–1000); *Hávamál* is made up of elements of various ages though the major components are "old." The chief "old" heroic poems are *Hlǫðskviða* and *Hamðismál* (*ca.* 850), *Atlakviða* (*ca.* 873), *Vǫlundarkviða* (900's), and *Bjarkamál* (well before 1030); *Grottasǫngr* may just belong with this group (900's, surviving version 1050–1100). The "late" mythological poems are a product of the renaissance of interest in antiquity in late-twelfth and thirteenth-century Iceland; they include *Baldrs draumar*, *Skírnismál*, *Hyndluljóð*, *Alvíssmál*, *Hymiskviða*, and *Þrymskviða*. Heroic texts of this "late" period include the four poems about Guðrún and *Helreið Brynhildar*, *Sigurðarkviða in skamma*, *Atlamál*, and *Grípisspá*. The small "middle" group contains no mythological poems (except perhaps *Darraðarljóð*, *ca.* 1015–1020): *Helgakviða Hundingsbana I* (*ca.* 1070), *Helgakviða Hjǫrvarðssonar*, *Helgakviða Hundingsbana II*, and *Brot* (all twelfth century).

HISTORY AND GENRES

Stylistic and chronological differences within Eddic poetry can be integrated (following chiefly Heusler, *Die altgermanische Dichtung;* and de Vries) into a developmental history. The major poetic form common to all the Germanic groups, the heroic lay of mixed narrative and speeches (*doppelseitiges Ereignislied*), is represented in the "old" heroic group (which for Heusler included *Brot*). This form of poem may be called the *kviða* (pl., *kviður*); the subject matter of leading examples points to the Gothic southeast as the probable point of origin, perhaps in contacts of the Germanic migration with other peoples. Continental legends embodied in *kviður* arrived in Scandinavia before 800 in a first wave of continental influence and, still in the pagan period, inspired formal imitations with mythological subject matter; however, the surviving mythological *kviður*, *Þrymskviða* and *Hymiskviða*, may be of late date. More direct generic derivatives are the "middle" and "late" heroic poems that mix narrative and speeches (*jüngere doppelseitige Ereignislieder*); to some extent these are formal imitations using native heroic legends (such as the parts of *Helgakviða Hundingsbana II* called "Vǫlsungakviða in forna" [Old lay of the Vǫlsungs] and perhaps *Grottasǫngr*) and to some extent they embody continental material from a second wave of German influence (*Guðrúnarkviða III*). Special Scandinavian developments from the imported *kviða* tended in two new directions: drama and lyric. The tendency to drama produced heroic poems composed entirely of speeches (*einseitiges Ereignislied*), beginning in the "old" and "middle," but especially characteristic of the "late," period; their distinctive feature, whether dialogues (*Bjarkamál*; the "Hortlied" reconstructed from *Reginsmál* and *Fáfnismál*; and numbers II and IV of *Eddica minora*) or the speech of a single character (Starcatherus' incitement of Ingellus in Saxo Grammaticus), is that they portray action through speech alone. The most brilliant member of the group is the only mythological poem of this kind: *Skírnismál* (however, the meter here, *ljóðaháttr*, belongs to the native Scandinavian tradition [see the qualifications on dating below]).

The lyric tendency produced contemplative heroic poetry of two types. The first are still "action" poems of mixed narrative and speeches, but in these "young" poems—*Atlamál, Sigurðarkviða in skamma,* and the reconstructed *Sigurðarkviða in meiri*—the poets focus on psychological states and expand the depiction of the inner life of their heroes far beyond the limits of the old *kviður*. The second lyric type generated late romantic poems in which little or nothing happens, but a heroic story is told or alluded to in retrospect; these can be distinguished

as focusing more on a present scene (such as the grieving women beside the corpse of Sigurd in *Guðrúnarkviða I*) or more on the retrospective (as in *Guðrúnarkviða II*). Five are associated with and partly spoken by women; seven more are retrospectives by men, especially at the moment of their death (the "death songs" of Hildibrandr, Hjálmarr, Ǫrvar-Oddr, and Starkaðr in *Eddica minora*). One group of these lyrics is regarded as elegies and shows special affinities of motif, vocabulary, and meter with West Germanic alliterative verse and Danish ballads (Mohr). The second wave of German influence in the "late" period coincided with the flourishing of minstrel narrative poetry (*Spielmannsepik*) in Germany and can often be distinguished in story form, versification, and vocabulary (Mohr).

This evolution from a single starting point does not take in the *ljóðaháttr* poems; Heusler accounts for them as artistic developments from varieties of Common Germanic primitive poetry (*niedere Dichtung*). Much of *Hávamál* derives from simple sapiential verse, including proverbs (*Spruchdichtung*); *Hárbarðsljóð* and *Lokasenna* go back to verbal abuse in real life; and the large group of mythological poems embodying lists may be traced, very generally, to mnemonic verse. The oldest of the didactic mythological poetry in *ljóðaháttr*, *Vafþrúðnismál* and *Grímnismál,* manifests a genuine heathen religious sensibility in quasi-dramatic verse. *Vǫluspá* may be an expression of dying heathenism, already given new moral and historical perspectives by familiarity with Christianity, according to de Vries, or may stem from the beginning of the Christian period in Iceland, according to Heusler; in any case it and its imitator *Vǫluspá in skamma* are unconnected with the main lines of development from the *kviða* (despite the characteristic *fornyrðislag* of prophecy) and from primitive poetry and *ljóðaháttr* verse.

The hiatus in the production of mythological poetry between the conversion period and the mid-twelfth-century beginning of the "late" revival reflects the insecurity of the new religion: poems about the gods could not be allowed, just as kennings (metaphorical periphrases traditional in Eddic, but especially in skaldic, verse—for instance, "deer of the waves" is "ship") with a mythological component seem almost to have vanished during this period.

With the "late" period came an Icelandic renaissance of interest in antiquity and a new confidence that allowed Christians to treat the old myths—often, however, humorously or critically. Hence the comic touch of *Skírnismál, Hymiskviða,* and *Þryms-*

kviða, and the satire of *Lokasenna,* according to de Vries (Heusler was of a different opinon about some details of this picture). These late Icelandic mythologists, poetic forerunners of Snorri Sturluson's prose, were interested in collecting old lore *(Alvíssmál, Lokasenna, Hyndluljóð),* and they imitated earlier poems; but in some cases their poems may have been reworkings of older pieces *(Baldrs draumar, Skírnismál).*

Important qualifications of these standard views should be mentioned. In Finnur Jónsson's account (1920) almost all the mythological poems are dated before the conversion, and very few poems are as late as the twelfth century. He also disagreed with the standard view on provenance; most of the poems, he argued, are from Norway, and only a handful from Greenland and Iceland. Einar Ólafur Sveinsson's "old" group matches de Vries's in the heroic poems but includes *Skírnismál, Þrymskviða, Rígsþula,* and perhaps *Baldrs draumar* among the "old" mythological poems, with *Lokasenna* and *Vǫluspá* as expressions of the conversion period (1962). Sveinsson's "middle" group of heroic poems adds *Guðrúnarkviða II* and *Atlamál* toward the end (50–100 years earlier than de Vries); *Alvíssmál* and *Hymiskviða* belong in that group in the eleventh century (late twelfth in de Vries), and perhaps *Hyndluljóð.* The heroic poems of the "late" period are almost the same *(Guðrúnarkviða I* may be "middle"), and only *Vǫluspá in skamma* is reckoned by Sveinsson (as by Jónsson) as decidedly "late" among the main mythological poems.

Sveinsson interprets many of the dating tests differently from de Vries, putting more emphasis on direct contacts between the Goths and their relatives in the Scandinavian homeland; the Gothic heroic lays may have come by the "east way" through modern Russia, and West Germanicisms are less prominent. Still, German influence in both waves is undeniable. Hofmann has revived (in very cautious and persuasive forms) earlier ideas associating the Helgi lays with the mixed Scandinavian–English culture in northern Britain, and Butt has convincingly placed *Vǫluspá,* too, in this milieu around 1000.

Although the positive evidence is slight, Eddic poetry must be assumed to be, like skaldic poetry, an oral, not a written, literary medium. *Norna-Gests þáttr* depicts performances at court in a situation not very unlike those firmly attested for skaldic verse. Skalds may well have been active in the transmission and recomposition of Eddic poems, and at least three Eddic poems have plausibly been attributed to particular skalds. Poetry in Eddic meters is also attested from noncourtly situations (an Icelandic wedding); a historical skald is said to have recited the *Bjarkamál* to encourage troops before a battle, and a Saxon singer recited a poem from the Nibelung-Vǫlsung cycle as a warning to a Danish king. The harp figures little in the sparse references to performance (in contrast with West Germanic poetry), and there has been little analysis of the verse in terms of "oral formulas." The axiom (chiefly from Heusler) that legends *(Sagen)* were transmitted only as embodied in poems *(Lieder)* has been effectively challenged by Genzmer and by Kuhn, and mythological material in particular may have been regularly transmitted by oral tradition in a mixture of prose and verse.

BIBLIOGRAPHY

Theodore M. Andersson, *The Legend of Brynhild* (1980), and "The Lays of the Lacuna of *Codex Regius,*" in Ursula Dronke *et al.,* eds., *Speculum Norrænum: Norse Studies in Memory of Gabriel Turville-Petre* (1981); Helmut de Boor, "Die religiöse Sprache der Voluspá und verwandter Denkmäler," in Walther H. Vogt, ed., *Deutsche Islandforschung,* I (1930); Wolfgang Butt, "Zur Herkunft der Vǫluspá," in *Beiträge zur Geschichte der deutschen Sprache und Literatur,* 91 (1969); Ursula Dronke, ed., *The Poetic Edda,* I, *Heroic Poems* (1969); Einar Ólafur Sveinsson, *Íslenzkar bókmenntir í fornöld,* I (1962); Felix Genzmer, "Vorzeitsaga and Heldenlied," in *Festschrift Paul Kluckhohn und Hermann Schneider gewidmet zu ihrem 60. Geburtstag* (1948), and "Das eddische Preislied," in *Beiträge zur Geschichte der deutschen Sprache und Literatur,* 44 (1919); Jóhann S. Hannesson, *Bibliography of the Eddas: A Supplement to Bibliography of the Eddas (Islandica XIII)* (1955); Heinrich M. Heinrichs, *Stilbedeutung des Adjektivs im eddischen Heldenlied* (1938); Halldór Hermannsson, *Bibliography of the Eddas,* Islandica XIII (1920, repr. 1966); Andreas Heusler, *Die altgermanische Dichtung,* 2nd rev. ed. (1943, repr. 1967), "Heimat und Alter der eddischen Gedichte: Das isländische Sondergut," in *Archiv für das Studium der neueren Sprachen und Literaturen,* 116 (1906), repr. in his *Kleine Schriften,* Helga Reuschel and Stefan Sonderegger, eds., II (1969), and "Die Lieder der Lücke im Codex Regius," in *Germanistische Abhandlungen Hermann Paul zum 17. März 1902 dargebracht* (1902); idem and Wilhelm Ranisch, eds., *Eddica minora: Dichtungen eddischer Art aus den Fornaldarsögur und anderen Prosawerken* (1903); Dietrich Hofmann, *Nordisch-Englische Lehnbeziehungen der Wikingerzeit* (1955); Lee M. Hollander, ed. and trans., *The Poetic Edda* (1928, 2nd ed. 1962); Edwin Jessen, "Über die Eddalieder: Heimat, Alter, Character," in *Zeitschrift für deutsche Philologie,* 3 (1871); Finnur Jónsson, *Lexicon poeticum antiquæ linguæ septentrionalis: Ordbog over det norsk-islandske skjaldesprog,* 2nd ed. (1931, repr. 1966), and *Den oldnorske og oldislandske litteraturs historie,* 2nd rev. ed., I (1920); Heinz Klingenberg, *Edda—Sammlung und Dichtung* (1974); Hans Kuhn, "Heldensage vor und ausserhalb der Dichtung," in Hermann Schneider, ed., *Edda, Skalden, Saga: Festschrift zum 70. Geburtstag von Felix Genzmer* (1952); Gustaf Lindblad, "Centrala eddaproblem i 1970-talets forskningsläge," in *Scripta Islandica* (Lund), **28** (1978), "Poetiska Eddans förhistoria och skrivskicket i Codex regius," in *Arkiv för nordisk filologi,* **95** (1980), and *Studier i Codex Regius av äldre Eddan* (1954); Wolfgang Mohr, "Entstehungsgeschichte und Heimat der jüngeren Eddalieder südgermanischen Stoffes," in *Zeitschrift für deutsches Altertum,* 75 (1938–1939), and "Wortschatz und Motive der jüngeren Eddalieder mit südgermanischem Stoff," in *Zeitschrift für deutsches Altertum,* 76 (1939–1940); Gustav Neckel, ed., *Edda: Die Lieder Des Codex Regius nebst verwandten Denkmälern,* 3rd ed. rev. by Hans Kuhn, 2 vols. (1962–1968); Marius Nygaard, *Eddasprogets Syntax fremstillet,* 2 vols. (1865–1867); Klaus von See, *Germanische Verskunst* (1967); Eduard Sievers, *Altgermanische Metrik* (1893); Barend Sijmons and Hugo Gering, eds., *Die Lieder der Edda,* 3 vols. (1903–1931); Patricia A. Terry, trans., *Poems of the Vikings: The Elder Edda* (1969); Jan de Vries, *Altnordische Literaturgeschichte,* 2 vols., 2nd rev. ed. (1964–1967).

JOSEPH HARRIS

[See also **Alvíssmál; Atlakviða; Atlamál; Baldrs Draumar; Bjarkamál; Darraðarljóð; Eddic Meters; Eiríksmál and Hákonarmál; Grímnismál; Grípisspá; Grottasǫngr; Guðrúnarhvǫt; Hamðismál; Haraldskvæði; Hárbarðsljóð; Hávamál; Helreið Brynhildar; Hervarar Saga ok Heiðreks Konungs; Hlǫðskviða; Hrólfs Saga Kraka; Hyndluljóð; Lokasenna; Norna-Gests Þáttr; Oddrúnargrátr; Reginsmál and Fáfnismál; Rígsþula; Sigrdrífumál; Sigurðarkviða in Meiri; Sigurðarkviða in skamma; Skaldic Verse; Skírnismál; Snorri Sturluson; Sólarljóð; Svipdagsmál; Þrymskviða; Vafþrúþnismál; Vǫlsunga saga; Vǫlundarkviða; Vǫluspá.**]

EDESSA (Turkish: Urfa), an important strategic and economic center in Mesopotamia, at latitude 37°08′ N, longitude 38°45′E. Edessa was a center of Nestorian Christianity and the home of a Nestorian school that was closed, after accusations of heresy, in 489. During the Persian–Byzantine wars the city changed hands several times and was finally taken by the Arabs in 638. Edessa also possessed a famous image of Christ, the Mandylion, said to have been sent by Christ to Abgar, the ruler of Edessa. When the Byzantines beseiged the city in 944, the inhabitants agreed to the removal of the sacred image to Constantinople.

Edessa, which had a large Armenian population, was held briefly, from 1077 to 1098, by an Armenian chieftain, from whom it was taken by Baldwin during the First Crusade. Baldwin set up the county of Edessa, the first Latin state in the East and a vassal of the Latin Kingdom of Jerusalem. In 1144 Edessa was reconquered by the Muslims under Zangi, retaken briefly by the Christians after his death, and finally captured by Nūr al-Dīn. He massacred the Christian men, sold the women and children into slavery, and almost entirely destroyed the city in 1146.

BIBLIOGRAPHY

George Ostrogorsky, *History of the Byzantine State,* Joan Hussey, trans. (1957, rev. ed. 1969); 277–278, 322, 364.

LINDA C. ROSE

[See also **Crusades and Crusader States: To 1192; Mandylion; Nestorianism.**]

EDINBURGH. The site of a rock crag with a ridge to the east, there was probably in Roman times a natural fort at Din Eidyn, the hill fort of Edin. It overlooked Deer Street, the Roman route north to the Firth of Forth at Cramond. The controversial collection of Welsh verses known as the *Gododdin* of Aneirin includes a number of stanzas about a great feast at Edin, whose host of the Gododdin (Votadini, a British tribe) attacked the men of Deira. These verses may have been written around 600. The "siege of Edin" of 638 perhaps records the Anglian conquest that doubtless led to the English translation of the name as Edinburgh. In the twelfth century the fanciful etymology "Edwin'sburgh" appears. Equally fanciful was the name Castrum Puellarum, a translation of Maidens' Castle, either a misapprehension of *Mai-dyn,* or drawn from Arthurian legend. (The name of the nearby volcanic plug, Arthur's Seat, is not found in the Middle Ages.)

Probably during the Anglian occupation the Church of St. Cuthbert was founded in the western shadow of the rock, and beside a route from the northwest curving round the rock to the highest ground to the south (the later Grassmarket). It joined a route from the south, and from that junction ascent of the ridge at its neck and access to the rock was possible. It is likely that the earliest trading settlement grew up on this neck in the tenth or eleventh century, after Edinburgh had passed under the political control of the king of Scotland (*ca.* 900–970).

There is no reason to doubt John of Fordun's claim (*ca.* 1360) that Queen Margaret died at Edinburgh (1093). The castle still contains a tiny early chapel that in Fordun's time was said to be of her foundation. Her youngest son, David I, founded the Augustinian Abbey of the Holy Cross (Holyrood) at the lower end of the ridge. The royal castle and *Eigenkloster* are reminiscent of the Tower of London and Westminster Abbey. There are no other surviving remains at the castle earlier than the mid fourteenth century, by which time a stone curtain wall surrounded a few wooden buildings, the chapel, and possibly one other stone building, a royal treasury.

After 1357 a new gatehouse tower was built, the foot of which survives within the Half-moon Battery. The English took the castle several times during the Wars of Independence, Edward I requiring three days of intensive bombardment in 1296. In 1314 the Scots retook it in a night attack, having been shown where to climb the crag and wall. The English took the castle again in 1333, but in 1341 it was again retaken by the Scots, and the English garrison of 115 men was slaughtered. English sieges in 1385 (possibly) and in 1400 and 1482 (certainly) were unsuccessful. James II was kept there while a minor and witnessed the execution of the earl of Douglas and his brother in 1440; he later besieged the castle (1445). James III was taken there after his arrest at Lauder in 1482, and the castle was again besieged. James IV kept his ordnance there, including the surviving huge cannon *Mons Meg,* and developed gunpowder and cannonball manufacture therein.

Kings resided in the castle from the twelfth century. In 1174 it and the town were handed over to the English garrison, but both were restored to the Scottish king in 1186, and he began to deposit his archives in a treasury there. The development of Edinburgh as a capital was reversed in 1296, when Lothian was vulnerable to English attack, and resumed only after 1357. David II (*d.* 1371) undoubtedly used it as his center of government, but his successors did so much less until James III (1460–1488), who, during his adult rule, rarely left the town except to hunt during the summer. The Council sat regularly in Edinburgh, which in 1454 had been recognized as the chief burgh in the realm, and James IV began building a palace near Holyrood Abbey that would provide more spacious quarters than the castle. In his reign the section of the Council that functioned as a supreme civil court (the Session) settled in Edinburgh.

David I gave the town of Edinburgh near the castle the status of a burgh by about 1130 and allowed the canons of Holyrood to found their own burgh (the Canongate) on the lower half of the ridge. A new urban parish was carved from St. Cuthbert's and the Edinburgh church dedicated to St. Giles. The church's situation and its elaborate Romanesque doorway show that the burgh was already well developed and wealthy by about 1170, whereas the position of the Blackfriars, founded about 1230, suggests serious urban repletion.

The names of early inhabitants are English and Flemish, indicating substantial immigration in the twelfth century. Edinburgh lacked a port, but during the thirteenth century Inverlieth, eight kilometers (five miles) distant, was developed. No doubt the town became more prosperous, but most records of this period and region were destroyed during the English Wars. In 1329 Edinburgh, with its port of Leith, became the third Scottish town to be given feu-ferme (fixed-rent) status after Berwick and Aberdeen, but with a much lower annual ferme (£34 3s. 4d.) than theirs, so that it was clearly of less economic importance.

Nonetheless, the customs returns for 1327 show that the exports of Edinburgh were not far behind those of Berwick, and the loss of that town to the English in 1333 meant a shift of trade to Edinburgh. The latter suffered badly in the war, being "waste" in 1341 and burned in 1385. But recovery seems to have been rapid: the crown gave land for the building of a new tolbooth in 1386, and a new street, the Cowgate, lying parallel to the High Street on the ridge and turning south in the hollow, developed in the fourteenth century. Local merchants probably flourished through financing the ransom of David II after 1357, and the early fifteenth century shows a steady shift of Scottish overseas trade to Edinburgh. By the 1480's Edinburgh merchants had close links with the government and exercised a controlling influence over the commerce of the kingdom.

The records of the town council begin in 1449, when strife between merchants and crafts was probably long-standing. In 1469 and later, acts of Parliament consolidated the hold of the merchant oligarchy on the town council, but the crafts were allowed a share of power. Conflict between the two groups therefore continued and was recorded in the acts of the council.

There is no evidence indicating when Edinburgh was provided with a stone wall, but it is unlikely to have been before the fifteenth century, since invading armies had no trouble occupying the town. A "King's Wall" is referred to as a boundary of property in 1427, and royal authority to build a wall was given in 1450 and 1472. It is likely that the project took many years; hence, in 1513–1514, a new wall to enclose an exposed southern suburb was begun. To the north of the ridge a small stream had been dammed, and in the fifteenth century the Nor' Loch was formed where Princes Street Gardens now lie, hemming in the town. Population growth was accommodated by building in gardens and by building upwards, so that density was high and the consequent filth and disease appalling, as the poetry of William Dunbar (ca. 1510) testifies. The only surviving medieval house is that on the High Street known as John Knox's house.

BIBLIOGRAPHY
The Book of the Old Edinburgh Club (1908–1974); Royal Commission on the Ancient Monuments of Scotland, *An Inventory of the Ancient Historical Monuments of Edinburgh* (1951), with plans.

A. A. M. DUNCAN

[See also **Scotland: History**.]

EDMUND, ST. See **Passiun Seint Edmund, La; Vie Seint Edmund le Rei, La**.

EDOUARD LE CONFESSEUR, VIE D'. See **Vie d'Edouard le Confesseur**.

EDUCATION. See **Schools; Universities**.

EDWARD THE CONFESSOR, ST. (ca. 1005–1066). Edward the Confessor was probably born in 1005 at Islip, the son of Ethelred II the Unready and Emma of Normandy, who was later the wife of Cnut. When, on 8 June 1042, his half brother Hardecnut fell dead while "standing at his drink, . . . all the people then received Edward as king, as was his natural right" (*Anglo-Saxon Chronicle*, C and D versions). Because he was then in exile in Normandy, his crowning at Canterbury did not take place until Easter Sunday, 3 April 1043. He died at London on 5 January 1066 and was buried the next day at Westminster Abbey, which he had just finished building.

Not an especially able king, Edward had to rule amid constant struggles over the right to succeed him, struggles that set the scene for the Norman Conquest, which began ten months after his death. Nevertheless, memories of the Conquest and of the dynastic questions it raised, combined with legends of Edward's sanctity, later transformed him into an archetype for the holy king as lawgiver and judge, a model even for the French royal mythology surrounding Charlemagne and Louis IX.

Edward appears to have spent his early years at the monastery of Ely, but when the Danish king Sweyn Forkbeard invaded England in 1013 and momentarily succeeded in supplanting Ethelred, Edward, his brother Alfred, and their mother fled to the court of Emma's brother, Duke Richard the Good of Normandy. Sweyn's death in 1014 allowed a brief return to England, but in 1016, with the death of Ethelred and the rise of Cnut, Edward and Alfred went back to the Norman court, where they were raised and received their education.

At Cnut's death in 1035, the succession was uncertain but ultimately fell to Hardecnut, who, as the son of the Scandinavian king and Ethelred's widow, could claim to represent a union of both royal lines. Edward reappeared in England the following year, probably in a bid for the throne, but when Alfred was killed on his way to London, Edward fled back to Normandy, convinced that his brother had been murdered by Godwin, earl of Wessex and a supporter of Danish claims. He next crossed the English Channel in 1041, probably at the invitation of Hardecnut, who, ill and childless, was beginning to think of his half brother as a potential heir. Though back in Normandy when the king died, Edward found himself proclaimed the true successor. He then entered into negotiations with Godwin, reputedly over the extent of permissible Norman influence, and, after the successful completion of these talks, the earl brought him back to England for his formal installation at Canterbury.

Though king in name, Edward found that true power tended to rest in the hands of three of his earls: Godwin of Wessex, Leofric of Mercia, and Siward of Northumbria. In the fall of 1043, for example, they advised action against Edward's mother, whose continuing Danish sympathies appeared greater than her loyalty to her son. Emma's treasure was seized; Stigand, her chaplain, was deprived of his bishopric; and various Danes in her retinue were banished. The three earls then effectively divided England among themselves, but Godwin evidently enjoyed a marked superiority over the other two, as suggested by Edward's marriage to Edith, his daughter, on 23 January 1045.

This marriage brought difficulties in its train, for soon there were rumors that it had never been consummated and, indeed, that Edward had sworn vows of perpetual chastity. Though unverifiable, these rumors seem plausible and testify either to the Confessor's piety or to his continuing hostility to Godwin. Whatever the case, Edith remained childless and, over time, her barrenness intensified the conflicts over immediate power and ultimate succession.

The most obvious threats to Edward's authority came from two sources, the Scandinavian claimants to Cnut's legacy and the house of Godwin. By the mid 1040's King Magnus I of Norway had conquered Denmark and claimed England as well. His death in 1047 put an end to a planned invasion, but the next few years were clouded by the threat of Norse raids. In 1066, following Edward's death, the claims of the North were again pressed, this time by Harold III Hardrada, then king of Norway, whose ambitious pretensions were ended when he fell at Stamford Bridge on 25 September.

More insidious, because ever present and less explicit, were the designs of Earl Godwin and his clan. Just how far the earl was prepared to go is uncertain, but that he hoped to graft his line onto that of the royal house is clear from Edith's marriage to Edward, and it must surely have surprised no one when Godwin's son Harold claimed the throne on Edward's demise, arguing both a royal deathbed designation and election by the Witenagemot, the Anglo-Saxon council of notables.

Edward struggled against these twin threats, especially the continuing one of Godwin, largely by searching out alternatives, though seldom with much success. By 1050 he was turning to Norman advisers to reduce Godwin's influence, and it is likely that Duke William of Normandy visited England at his invitation in 1051, at which time Edward may have made him his heir. These developments led to outlawry and exile for Godwin and his sons, but when they stormed back and threatened civil war in 1052, the Normans were forced to flee.

When Godwin's death led to the rise of his son Harold, the king turned in 1054 to his nephew Edward the Atheling, son of Edmund Ironside and the closest royal heir, inviting him home from exile in Hungary. Understandably hesitant, he did not return until 1057—and died immediately. Thus with the succession still in doubt, Harold remained the strongest contender.

In Edward's final years his thoughts were increasingly devoted to Westminster Abbey, in which he was eventually buried and where so many of his miracles occurred. Pope Alexander III canonized him in 1161.

BIBLIOGRAPHY

G. N. Garmonsway, ed. and trans. *The Anglo-Saxon Chronicle,* (1953); Timothy Baker, *The Normans* (1966), 37–96; Frank Barlow, *Edward the Confessor* (1970); *idem,* ed. and trans., *The Life of King Edward, Who Rests at Westminster* (1962); David C. Douglas, *William the Conqueror* (1964), 159–207; David C. Douglas and George W. Greenaway, eds., *English Historical Documents: 1042–1189,* 2nd ed. (1981); H. R. Luard, ed., *The Lives of Edward the Confessor,* 3 vols. (1858); F. M. Stenton, *Anglo-Saxon England,* 2nd ed. (1947)

CHARLES T. WOOD

[See also **England: Anglo-Saxon; Vie d'Edouard le Confesseur.**]

EDWARD I OF ENGLAND (1239–1307). Edward I was born at Westminster during the night of 17/18 June 1239, the son of Henry III and Eleanor of Provence. Though not in England when Henry III died (16 November 1272), he was nevertheless declared king immediately after his father's burial on 20 November. His coronation, deferred until his return, took place in 1274. He died near Carlisle, at Burgh-upon-the-Sands, on 7 July 1307. Through campaigns both at home and in the Holy Land, Edward gained prominence first as a warrior and a crusader, but history remembers him more as a shaper of Parliament and the law.

Edward began to achieve political prominence in the late 1250's, largely as a result of Henry III's quarrels with his barons. By 1258 his importance was such that he was made to swear "an oath personally taken" to uphold the baronial reforms that, when enacted later that year, became known as the Provisions of Oxford. Edward appears to have supported his father initially, but when, during 1259, he found himself increasingly sympathetic to the views of Simon de Montfort the Younger, the principal baronial leader, he solved the problem of divided allegiance by largely withdrawing from the fray. He reemerged only after Henry's disastrous defeat at Lewes (14 May 1264), at which point he was made a baronial hostage to guarantee Henry's good behavior. A year later he escaped and formed a new army that defeated and killed Simon at Evesham (4 August 1265). The final settlement of the Barons' War was the Dictum of Kenilworth (31 October 1266), theoretically an arbitral judgment but largely of Edward's design.

During his early career, Edward had several times met and come to admire his uncle Louis IX, the saintly king of France. Responding to Louis's appeal for what became the Eighth Crusade, against Carthage, he took the cross on 24 June 1268 but arrived in North Africa only after Louis's death at Tunis in 1270. Edward refused to accept the peace terms already made and early in the spring of 1271 transferred his military operations to Syria, staying there until 15 August 1272. Hearing of Henry III's death while on his way home, he decided to defer his return in order to quell a series of revolts in Aquitaine. As a result he reached Dover only on 2 August 1274. His coronation followed on 19 August.

At that ceremony Llewelyn ap Gruffudd, the leading Welsh prince, refused to pay Edward the homage he had done to his father, so a Welsh war became inevitable. Edward began his campaigns in 1277, though the heaviest fighting did not occur until 1282–1284; at the end of that period, with Llewelyn dead, Wales lay prostrate. Edward then consolidated his gains by constructing protective castles; by issuing, in 1284, the Statute of Wales, which incorporated most of the principality into the English shire system; and, in 1301, by declaring his son prince of Wales.

Edward met greater frustration in his conflicts with Scotland and France. Unlike Llewelyn, the Scots king Alexander III had done homage at Edward's coronation, but after Alexander's death in 1286 was followed in 1290 by that of his granddaughter and sole heir, Margaret, the Maid of Norway, a succession crisis arose. Edward attempted to mediate among the thirteen aspirants to the crown, finding for John de Baliol on 17 November 1292. Although Baliol, like Alexander, recognized an English overlordship at first, he quickly renounced it. Edward could not respond immediately, however, for in the following year naval engagements with the French in the English Channel fully occupied his attention. Those battles led, in 1294, to a French seizure of Gascony.

It was only in 1296 that Edward was able to invade Scotland, whence he brought back from Scone the Scottish coronation stone now at Westminster Abbey. Still, because his victory proved inconclusive, he was forced to campaign again in 1298, following

a French truce, this time crushing Sir William Wallace and the Scots at Falkirk (22 July). The French truce was converted to a permanent peace on 20 May 1303, at which point Gascony was restored (though it was lost again in the following reign). Although Wallace was captured and executed in 1305, Robert Bruce began a new revolt in 1306, one that Edward was still trying to quell at the time of his death.

Edward achieved more lasting success in legal matters. Within months of his coronation, he ordered inquiries into royal rights and private franchises, a process that culminated in the Statute of Gloucester (1278), which required all holders of private franchises or courts to demonstrate that they enjoyed them by virtue of specific royal grants. The principle that all justice emanated from the king was thereby established. Further statutes limited the right of the church to acquire real property (Mortmain, 1279); regulated commercial transactions (Merchants or Acton Burnell, 1283); reformed criminal justice (Winchester, 1285); recognized entails (Second Westminster, 1285); and forbade the subinfeudation of fiefs (*Quia emptores,* 1290), a law that eventually broke down the feudal hierarchy by making most landholders tenants-in-chief of the crown. For such legislation, Edward used to be called "the English Justinian."

Like Justinian, Edward may frequently have been autocratic but, unlike him, he never held that "the will of the prince has the force of law." Rather, he argued that "what touches all must be approved by all," and to achieve that end he made frequent use of meetings called parliaments. Because the whole "community of the realm" was deemed to be present at these meetings, they had the power, with the king's approval, to levy taxes and (as in the statutes mentioned or in the handling of innumerable petitions) to decide how the law should cover unprecedented situations. Simply put, Edward's parliaments were seen as the most solemn form of his council and court; and their members were considered his representatives. No one yet thought of Parliament as a legislative body, and no one was about to argue that it had the authority to challenge the king.

BIBLIOGRAPHY

Theodore F. T. Plucknett, *The Legislation of Edward I* (1949), and *Edward I and Criminal Law* (1960); Frederick M. Powicke, *King Henry III and the Lord Edward*, 2 vols. (1947), and *The Thirteenth Century, 1216–1307* (1953), 227–719; Michael Prestwich, *War, Politics and Finance*

Under Edward I (1972); George O. Sayles, *The King's Parliament of England* (1974), 70–93; Geoffrey Templeman, "The History of Parliament to 1400 in the Light of Modern Research," in *University of Birmingham Historical Journal*, **1** (1948), and "Edward I and the Historians," in *Cambridge Historical Journal*, **10** (1950); Charles T. Wood, "The English Crisis of 1297 in the Light of French Experience," in *Journal of British Studies*, **18** (1979).

CHARLES T. WOOD

[See also **Barons' War; England: Norman-Angevin; England: 1272–1485; Henry III of England; Llewelyn ap Gruffudd; Mortmain; Parliament; Robert I of Scotland; Scotland: History; Simon de Montfort the Younger; Wales: Later History.**]

EDWARD II OF ENGLAND (1284–1327). Edward II, son of Edward I and Eleanor of Castile, was born at Caernarvon on 25 April 1284 and became the first English prince of Wales in 1301. He succeeded his father on 7 July 1307 but was deposed in January 1327, after twenty years of military disaster and misrule through favorites had amply demonstrated his incompetence. Kept a prisoner thereafter, he was probably murdered at Berkeley Castle on 21 September 1327, though a recent theory holds that he may in fact have escaped.

Most historians have accepted the view, common among Edward's contemporaries, that his talents ran less to government than to "digging ditches and thatching roofs, to working at blacksmithing at night with his associates, and to other mechanical occupations" (*Chronicon de Lanercost*). In truth, though, the problems he faced were not entirely of his own making, for his father's legacy to him included not just the crown but also restless barons, a depleted treasury, towering debts, and a foreign policy with objectives attainable only through war. Such an inheritance would have taxed the skills of a ruler far abler than he, and the difficulties of his reign were compounded by the first signs of those hard times that for more than a century aggravated political and social unrest even as they diminished the resources needed to deal with it.

Nevertheless, Edward had a true genius for making bad situations worse. Once he had become king, he not only recalled Piers Gaveston, his exiled favorite, but also showered him with gifts and followed his advice. An outraged baronage responded in 1312 by having Gaveston executed, but Edward's later favorites, Hugh le Despenser the elder and the younger, were scarcely better. In foreign affairs, Edward's crushing defeat at Bannockburn (24 June 1314) ended all hope of English influence in Scotland, and the Gascon campaign of 1324 lost him a part of France that even King John had been able to retain.

Yet the political skills of Edward's opponents were scarcely greater than his. Their declaration of 1308—that homage was owed more to the crown than to the person of the king—may have had later constitutional significance, but it had no immediate impact; and the Ordinances of 1311, another attempt to manage Edward, this time through baronial control of the royal bureaucracy, had little more success. They served mainly to enrage the king, who, after defeating Thomas of Lancaster at Boroughbridge (16 March 1322), had the Ordinances quashed in the Statute of York less than two months later.

Edward's downfall began in 1325, when he sent his wife, Isabella of France, to Paris to negotiate a Gascon settlement. She there became the lover of Roger Mortimer, later earl of March, and in the following year the two of them invaded England, capturing the king on 16 November. The archbishop of Canterbury preached his deposition before a so-called parliament on 15 January 1327, at which point Edward was forced to abdicate. This deposition, based on earlier French attempts to depose Pope Boniface VIII, became the model for all subsequent English depositions.

BIBLIOGRAPHY

G. P. Cuttino and Thomas W. Lyman, "Where Is Edward II?" in *Speculum*, **53** (1978); William Huse Dunham, Jr., and Charles T. Wood, "The Right to Rule in England: Depositions and the Kingdom's Authority, 1327–1485," in *American Historical Review*, **81** (1976); T. F. Tout, *The Place of the Reign of Edward II in English History*, 2nd ed. (1936); Charles T. Wood, "Personality, Politics, and Constitutional Progress: The Lessons of Edward II," in *Studia Gratiana (post scripta)*, **15** (1972).

"Queens, Queans, and Kingship: An Inquiry Into Theories of Royal Legitimacy in Late Medieval England and France," in William Chester Jordan, Bruce McNab, and Teofilo F. Ruiz, eds., *Order and Innovation in the Middle Ages: Essays in Honor of Joseph R. Strayer* (1976), 385–400, 562–566, and "Celestine V, Boniface VIII and the Authority of Parliament," in *Journal of Medieval History*, **8** (1982).

CHARLES T. WOOD

[See also **England: 1216–1485.**]

EDWARD III OF ENGLAND (1312–1377). Edward III, son of Edward II and Isabella of France, was born at Windsor Castle on 13 November 1312 and died at Sheen, Surrey, on 21 June 1377. Following the deposition of his father, Edward II, he became king on 25 January 1327 and was crowned a week later. His reign is noted mainly for its wars, the Black Death, and the rise of Parliament as a major force in government.

Only fourteen at the time of his accession, Edward found his own authority superseded by that of his mother and Roger Mortimer, her lover. Their rule came to an end only in 1330, when the young king had Mortimer seized and executed on charges that, among other things, he had "falsely and maliciously caused discord between the father of our lord the king and the queen his wife." Isabella was persuaded to take the veil.

The success of government during much of Edward's reign depended on a tacit agreement whereby the king allowed his barons to participate in royal administration and policy decisions, provided that they refrain from interfering with the estate of the crown. Edward took little interest in governmental routine, preferring to leave it to others so that he could pursue his true love, fighting. His legendary devotion to chivalry found expression in the creation of the Order of the Garter (1348). Although his martial ardor attracted early support, his wars proved a long-term failure.

Edward began his military career with victories in Scotland, but initial success gave way to increasing difficulty, especially after 1337, when he turned his attention to France and began what became the Hundred Years War. By 1341 Scotland had regained its independence. In France, though English arms proved decisive at Sluys (1340) and Crécy (1346), Edward lacked the resources for lasting conquest. Even Poitiers (1356), where Edward the Black Prince defeated and captured the French king, John II the Good, failed to change the situation more than temporarily. By 1377 English domains in France had been reduced to coastal areas surrounding such places as Calais and Bordeaux.

To finance his wars, Edward was increasingly forced to seek money from Parliament, a body quick to learn that taxes could be exchanged for practical political concessions. As a result Parliament—and especially the Commons—became more powerful. The "Good Parliament" of 1376 even claimed the right to impeach two of the king's ministers. Although that action was quickly reversed following the death of its crucial supporter, the Black Prince, a notable precedent had been set.

The first onslaught of the Black Death in 1348–1350 killed up to 40 percent of the population. By the 1370's the English people were thoroughly battered by recurring war and plague, neither of which would go away. It is said that Edward III died alone, with rings stripped from his fingers by Alice Perrers, his fleeing mistress, and only a simple priest remaining behind to administer the last rites of the church.

BIBLIOGRAPHY

Jean Froissart, *Chronicles*, Geoffrey Brereton, trans. (1968); Gerald L. Harriss, "War and the Emergence of the English Parliament, 1297–1360," in *Journal of Medieval History*, 2 (1976); Herbert J. Hewitt, *The Organization of War Under Edward III, 1338–62* (1966); May McKisack, *The Fourteenth Century, 1307–1399* (1959); Edouard Perroy, *The Hundred Years War*, W. B. Wells, trans. (1951), 34–174; Bertie Wilkinson, *Studies in the Constitutional History of the Thirteenth and Fourteenth Centuries* (1937).

CHARLES T. WOOD

[See also **England: 1216–1485; Hundred Years War.**]

EDWARD THE BLACK PRINCE (1330–1376). Edward the Black Prince was born at Woodstock on 15 June 1330, the eldest son of Edward III and Philippa of Hainault. He was created prince of Wales on 12 May 1343 and died at Westminster on 8 July 1376, a year before his father. Contemporaries praised him as the perfect knight, a model of the successful military commander, but his reputation for chivalry appears to have reflected his prowess in tournaments rather than his conduct in battle. Nevertheless, he was a hero to his age, and his shield and armor were hung above his tomb at Canterbury, where their replicas may still be viewed.

As heir to the English crown, Edward found himself loaded with honors and symbolic duties from an early age. Made earl of Chester before he was three, he became duke of Cornwall while still only six. In 1338 his father left him as guardian of the realm during the king's first invasion of France, and he again held that title under similar circumstances in 1340 and 1342. Edward's own involvement with the Hundred Years War began in 1345, and he achieved distinction the following year when he led a *chevauchée* through the Cotentin, burning and pillaging as he went. It was, as a chronicler put it, "a right good beginning." He came fully into his own at the Battle of Crécy (26 August 1346), where he commanded the van of the English army. It is often claimed, though with no real proof, that he acquired his sobriquet because he had worn black armor in that victory.

Edward gained his greatest fame in 1356, at the Battle of Poitiers. Tradition assigns an inflated figure of 50,000 men to the French and only 7,500 to the English. On 19 September the Black Prince's archers met repeated French charges with a withering hail of arrows, at the end of which 11,000 French lay dead. More than 2,000 were captured, among them their king, John II the Good. It is part of the legend that the prince helped John to remove his armor and then waited on him at supper, refusing even to join "so valiant a man" at table.

Unskilled as a ruler, Edward was never able to master the restless Gascon nobility. When his Spanish expedition of 1367 led not just to the victory at Navarrete (or Nájera, 3 April), but also to harsh taxation to pay for it, their response was revolt and an appeal to the king of France. Charles V replied on 23 January 1369 by summoning the Black Prince to Paris. Edward's answer—that he would come, but "with helm on head and sixty thousand men in our company"—is famous, but it was pure bravado: he was too ill to ride, suffering from dysentery and dropsy acquired in Spain. In 1370 he was forced to lead his last campaign from a litter, and though successful, its savagery, especially at Limoges, does little to enhance his chivalrous reputation, at least for a person of modern sensibilities.

Returning to England in 1371, Edward spent his final years leading the opposition to the Lancastrian party of his brother, John of Gaunt. He also became the Commons' chief supporter in 1376 when, just before his death, they impeached the crown's chief ministers, Richard Lyons and William Latimer.

BIBLIOGRAPHY

Sir John Chandos' herald, *Life of the Black Prince,* Mildred K. Hope and Eleanor C. Lodge, eds. (1974); Jean Froissart, *Chronicles,* Geoffrey Brereton, trans. (1968); Herbert J. Hewitt, *The Black Prince's Expedition of 1355-1357* (1958), and *The Organization of War Under Edward III, 1338-62,* (1966); Edouard Perroy, *The Hundred Years War,* W. B. Wells, trans. (1951), 112–180.

CHARLES T. WOOD

[See also **England: 1216–1485; Hundred Years War.**]

EGBERT OF LIÈGE (*fl. ca.* 1024) taught at the cathedral school of Liège, and, for the benefit of his students, he composed the *Fecunda ratis* (Richly laden ship). This work is divided into two sections and consists of 2,373 Latin hexameters: 1,768 in the *Prora* (Prow) and 605 in the *Puppis* (Stern). Much of his material consisted of standard classical and biblical maxims, but Egbert also included many translations of contemporary vernacular proverbs. These last make the *Fecunda ratis* a treasure trove for students of medieval folklore.

BIBLIOGRAPHY

Ernst Voigt, ed., *Egberts von Lüttich Fecunda Ratis* (1889), contains both the text and a valuable introduction. See also Gaston Paris, review article in *Journal de savants* (September 1890).

ELAINE GOLDEN ROBISON

[See also **Magic and Folklore, Western Europeans.**]

EGBERT OF TRIER (*fl.* late tenth century), son of a Dutch count, trained at Egmond Abbey in Freisland (founded by his grandfather), imperial chancellor from 976 to 977 and archbishop of Trier from 977 to 993. Egbert was one of the great patrons of Ottonian art and seems to have generated flourishing schools of metalwork and manuscript illumination at Trier. His name is particularly associated with the "Ruodpreht Group," so called after a scribe of one of the manuscripts, because two books in the group contain dedicatory pictures and inscriptions specifying him as recipient. Of these, the Egbert Codex (Trier, Stadtbibliothek, cod. 24), a book of pericopes, is one of the finest and most lavishly illustrated Ottonian manuscripts preserved. In addition to the dedication picture, it contains evangelist portraits and fifty illustrations from the New Testament, five of them by the famous Gregory Master.

BIBLIOGRAPHY

Charles R. Dodwell, *Painting in Europe 800 to 1200* (1971), 53–60; Charles R. Dodwell and D. H. Turner, *Reichenau Reconsidered* (1965), 13–28; Franz J. Ronig, *Codex Egberti* (1977); Hubert Schiel, ed., Der *Codex Egberti der Stadtbibliothek Trier* (1960).

LESLIE BRUBAKER

[See also **Manuscript Illumination: Western European; Pre-Romanesque Art.**]

EGIDIUS COLONNA (*ca.* 1247–1316), also known as Aegidius Romanus and Giles of Rome, was born in Rome. After joining the Hermits of St. Augustine, he studied theology at the University of Paris, where he probably attended the lectures of Thomas Aquinas. Included in the condemnation of 1277 was the Thomist proposition that each being contains but a single substantial form, a view Egidius vigorously defended. When he refused to retract, the bishop of Paris expelled him from the city. Egidius resided for a time at Bayeux, then returned to Rome, where he became vicar general of his order in 1285. The pope soon reinstated him at Paris, where he received the first Augustinian chair in theology.

King Philip III of France (1270–1285) appointed Egidius tutor to his son, Philip (IV), for whom he wrote the *De regimine principum*. In 1287 a general chapter made his teachings binding on all teachers in the order. He soon became prior general of his order (1292) and archbishop of Bourges (1295). Egidius defended Pope Boniface VIII by writing a treatise in support of the validity of Celestine V's disputed resignation. About 1301, Egidius penned the most vigorous defense of papalist claims during the Philip IV–Boniface VIII controversy, his *De ecclesiastica potestate*. He attended the Council of Vienne (1311) and died at Avignon.

Egidius wrote commentaries on many works of Aristotle, including the *Physics, Metaphysics, De anima,* and *Posterior Analytics.* The influence of Aquinas is apparent in most of his work, though Neoplatonism often serves to modify Aquinas' doctrines. Egidius was particularly original in his distinction between essence and existence. Unlike Aquinas, he held that *esse* and *essentia* were completely distinct *res.* But he also espoused the doctrines of Augustine and warned contemporaries against the uncritical adoption of the errors contained in Aristotle and his non-Christian commentators.

Egidius had much to say about basic scientific problems, such as those concerning time, gravity, and the dual nature of quantity. He even speculated on bodies falling in a vacuum.

Egidius' ecclesiology centers on the lordship (*dominium*) of the church over temporal things. The pope as the vicar of Christ is conceded virtually all authority in both spirituals and temporals. Since temporals are subject to spirituals, secular princes derive their authority from the church, which alone can sacramentally absolve them and grant them legitimate authority over temporal affairs. Princes possess lordship in their own right, but it is inferior to the superior and universal lordship of the church. Should the church decide that a secular prince is not using his material sword to defend the church, the latter may deprive him of his lordship and transfer it to another, more worthy ruler.

In his Aristotelian–Thomist theory of kingship Egidius proposes a strong monarchy. While the king is partially limited by customary law and feudal counsel, he possesses broad powers when the common good is threatened. Going beyond Aquinas, Egidius makes the king above positive law, yet below natural law. But in certain circumstances he legislates and rules without constraint. While in his *De regimine principum* Egidius ignored the relation of the monarchy to the church, Philip the Fair's publicists applied his theory of extraordinary jurisdiction to a two-power theory tilted in favor of the king. Egidius demonstrated that Aristotle's common good could be marshaled in defense of strong Christian monarchy.

BIBLIOGRAPHY

De ecclesiastica potestate, R. Scholz, ed. (1929); *Errores philosophorum,* Josef Koch, ed., and John Riedl, trans. (1944); P. Mandonnet, "La carrière scolaire de Gilles de Rome (1276–91)," in *Revue des sciences philosophiques,* **4** (1910); N. Merlin, "Gilles de Rome," in *Dictionnaire de théologie catholique,* VI (1358–1366); B. Nardi, "Egidio Romano e l'avverismo," in *Rivista di storia della filosofia,* 3 (1947) and 4 (1948); P. W. Nash, "Giles of Rome: Auditor and Critic of St. Thomas," in *Modern Schoolman,* 28 (1950); R. Scholz, *Die Publizistik zur Zeit Philipps des Schönen und Bonifaz VIII* (1903).

THOMAS RENNA

[See also **Aristotle in the Middle Ages; Ecclesiology; Kingship, Theories of: Western Europe; Thomism and Its Opponents.**]

EGILL SKALLAGRÍMSSON (*ca.* 910–990), Icelandic chieftain and skald whose life is told in *Egils saga Skallagrímssonar.* Three long poems have been preserved under his name—*Hǫfuðlausn, Sonatorrek,* and *Arinbjarnarkviða*—as well as some forty-six *lausavísur,* a pair of opening stanzas from two shield poems, and one stanza and a refrain from a *drápa* composed for King Athelstan of England. Egill is the most personal-seeming of the skalds, a quality that has inspired commentators to trace the poet's emotional development from his first *dróttkvætt* efforts at the age of three to the final, rueful poems of his old age.

Sonatorrek (Loss of sons), composed about 960, according to the chronology of *Egils saga,* is a memorial poem in honor of the poet's sons, Gunnarr and Boðvarr. The poem, in swift-moving *kviðuháttr,* describes the speaker's sense of desolation and his uneasy relationship with Odin: he is very angry with the treacherous god, but cannot forget to whom he owes the "flawless art of poetry." The twenty-four stanzas and one couplet of *Sonatorrek* that have survived contain some twenty allusions to gods and myths: at least half have to do with Odin. The text of the poem is quite corrupt, extant in its present incomplete state only in two seventeenth-century transcripts *(Ketilsbók)* of a fifteenth-century vellum. The first stanza is preserved in *Moðruvallabók* (fourteenth century) and in a group of seventeenth-century paper manuscripts; stanza 23 and the first half of 24 are found in manuscripts of *Snorra Edda.*

Twenty-five stanzas of *Arinbjarnarkviða,* a praise poem in honor of Egill's friend and patron Arinbjǫrn hersir Þórisson, survive on a partially illegible page in *Moðruvallabók,* added to the end of *Egils saga* by a different hand. Like *Sonatorrek, Arinbjarnarkviða* is composed in *kviðuháttr;* and, like the earlier poem, it says more about the skald himself—his deeds, aspirations, and poetic genius—than about the man he intends to honor. Egill boasts in the final stanza that he has raised a "praise pile" that will long stand, a skaldic monument more enduring than bronze.

Arinbjarnarkviða tells how Arinbjǫrn played a decisive role in preserving Egill's life at the court of Eiríkr Bloodaxe in York. *Hǫfuðlausn* (Head ransom) was the praise poem offered to Eiríkr by Egill, composed—says the saga—in the course of a single night. It has survived complete (twenty stanzas; refrains in stanzas 6, 9, 12, and 15) in two of the chief manuscripts of *Egils saga; Snorra Edda* cites some of its stanzas as well. Egill's praise of Eiríkr is general and conventional; the poem's chief claim to fame is its form: if it is by Egill, it is the first Norse poem to employ end rhyme *(runhent). Hǫfuðlausn* is also the first skaldic composition to have been printed (Ole Worm, *Runir seu Danica literatura antiqvissima,* 1636).

Egill's *dróttkvætt* stanzas include some of the most brilliant skaldic verse that has survived. In his *lausavísur* the poet laments the death of a brother, covets gold, curses his enemies, describes a drunken brawl and a fierce storm at sea, and mourns his cold

heels. The authenticity of some of the occasional verse attributed to Egill is very doubtful. Nevertheless, many of the best appear to be the work of one poet.

BIBLIOGRAPHY

Jón Helgason, "Höfuðlausnarhjal," in *Einarsbók: Afmæliskveðja til Einars Ól. Sveinssonar* (1969); Dietrich Hofmann, "Das Reimwort *giǫr* in Egill Skallagrímssons *Hǫfuðlausn,*" in *Mediaeval Scandinavia,* 6 (1973); Sigurður Nordal, ed., *Egils saga* (1933); E. O. G. Turville-Petre, *Scaldic Poetry* (1976); Jan de Vries, *Altnordische Literaturgeschichte,* 2 vols., 2nd rev. ed. I (1964), 158–171.

ROBERTA FRANK

[See also **Eddic Poetry; Egils Saga Skallagrímssonar.**]

EGILS SAGA EINHENDA OK ÁSMUNDAR BERSERKJABANA (Story of Egill One-hand and Ásmundr the Berserks' Killer), one of the heroic sagas *(fornaldarsögur),* was composed in Iceland about 1300 and survives in three vellum manuscripts of the fifteenth century. The major quest in this Viking romance is the rescue of two Russian princesses, whose abduction by a giant vulture and another monstrous creature is described at the outset.

The quest is undertaken by two young Scandinavian princes, who first meet as enemies fighting a deadly duel and then become blood brothers and friends for life. The search for the missing girls takes Egill and Ásmundr north to Jǫtunheimar (Realms of the giants). There they meet a friendly giantess called Arinnefja (Eagle Beak), who tells them that the princesses had been carried off to Jǫtunheimar by her brothers and that the wedding is to take place at Christmas. She offers the blood brothers hospitality, and while they are waiting for the meal to be prepared, each of the three in turn tells his or her life story. These flashbacks constitute a significant part of the tale, revealing not only the character and previous experiences of each but also the interesting detail that Egill One-hand and Arinnefja had met fleetingly once before: she had been present when he lost his hand. Now she produces the hand, carefully wrapped in life-preserving herbs, "still warm and steaming," and grafts it onto the arm.

One of the adventures described by Egill in his autobiographical account bears a striking resemblance to the Polyphemus story in the *Odyssey.* Other analogues of that tale, which probably reached Iceland in a Latin form, are found in *Hrólfs saga Gautreks-sonar* and *Maríu saga.*

In his life story, Ásmundr describes how he had met a stranger called Arán, "the son of King Róðíán of Tartary," and become his blood brother, each swearing to avenge the other and sharing equally the other's money. "It was also a part of their pact that the one who lived the longer should raise a burial mound over the one who was dead, and place in it as much money as he thought fit. And the survivor was to sit in the mound over the dead for three nights." Arán died and Ásmundr joined him in the burial mound. During the first night Arán got up, killed his hawk and hound, and ate them. On the second night he treated his horse in the same fashion, and on the third night he set on Ásmundr, tearing his ears off. But Ásmundr sliced off Arán's head and burned him to ashes.

The blood brothers, Egill and Ásmundr, and the giantess go to the wedding, which is a grand affair celebrated in a large cave. It ends predictably with the bridegrooms and most of the other giants being killed and the princesses brought home to their father's palace, where they marry their rescuers at a splendid feast. Egill becomes king of Tartary and Ásmundr ruler of Hálogaland, succeeding his father. Ásmundr was killed off Hlésey and over three thousand men with him. It is said that Odin ran him through with a spear and that Ásmundr jumped overboard.

BIBLIOGRAPHY

Editions are Åke Lagerholm, ed., in *Drei Lygisögur* (1927), xviii–li and 1–83; and Hermann Pálsson and Paul Edwards, trans., in *Gautrek's Saga and Other Medieval Tales* (1968), 91–120. See also Donald K. Fry, "Polyphemus in Iceland," in *The Fourteenth Century, Acta,* IV (1977), 65–86.

HERMANN PÁLSSON

[See also **Fornaldarsögur.**]

EGILS SAGA SKALLAGRÍMSSONAR

EGILS SAGA SKALLAGRÍMSSONAR (Saga of Egill Skallagrímsson, or *Egla,* to use its less formal Icelandic title) is one of the greatest of the Icelandic sagas. Its greatness lies partly in the brilliant portrait presented of its principal hero—killer, drunkard, miser, poet, wanderer, and farmer, as well as devoted husband and father—and partly in the powerful impressions it offers of the northern world in the ninth and tenth centuries. The narrative spans several generations, opening in Norway in pagan times with an account of the hero's grandfather, Kveldúlfr, a berserk who "used to go off on Viking trips looking for plunder," and closing with the exhumation of the hero's bones after Iceland had been converted to Christianity and with a brief mention of his immediate descendants, including two of his grandchildren, the tragic heroine of *Gunnlaugs saga ormstungu* and the central character of *Laxdæla saga.*

More so than any other saga of its kind, *Egla* is a work of history, and in that respect it resembles the kings' sagas *(konungasögur).* With a few bold strokes, executed with the sureness of a true master, it sketches the emergence of Norway as a unified state through the ruthless efforts of Haraldr Hárfagri, who subjected several independent kingdoms under his sole authority late in the ninth century. A detailed though highly stylized account of a major clash of arms between the Scots and the English has been identified with the historical Battle of Brunanburh, fought in 937. The settlement of Iceland is another important event figuring in the saga, the hero's father being one of the leading settlers. The scene changes constantly in *Egla,* moving from the opening chapters set in Norway to Sweden, Finland, and Lapland, south to the Low Countries, and west to Britain and Iceland, suggesting that the author was no less informed in geography than in history.

The principal interest in *Egla,* however, lies in its delineation of the character of Egill, whose fictional life story is related in vivid detail, partly by means of memorable poetry attributed to him from early childhood to old age. The first appearance of Egill, at the age of three, serves as a key to his character and conduct later in life. His grandfather, living several miles away, invites the family to a party, but Egill's father refuses to let the boy come with them, on the grounds that "you don't know how to behave yourself when there's company gathered and a lot of drinking going on. You're difficult enough to cope with when you're sober." But, stubborn and self-willed—as he continues to be throughout his long and eventful life—the three-year-old Egill does not let this hold him back: after the others have gone, he mounts one of his father's cart horses and makes his way over difficult terrain to the party.

Egill's numerous adventures include Viking expeditions to the Baltic Sea and Friesland, duels with berserks in Norway, a perilous winter journey to hostile Sweden, and a deadly battle in England, where his beloved brother is killed (Egill soon marries his widow). Motivated by greed as well as by a primitive sense of justice, he keeps fighting, against heavy odds, for the property and good name of the family of his wife, whose parents had eloped from Norway to Iceland because of strong opposition to their marriage. Characteristically, when Egill is a blind old man, he asks to be taken to the Althing, where he intends to scatter a great deal of silver among the crowd, in the hope that "the whole assembly will start fighting." But he is refused his last wish, as he was his first. Instead, he has two slaves help him bury his silver hoard in a secret place, "but neither the slaves nor the two coffers were ever seen again, and there have been plenty of guesses where Egill hid his money."

In addition to numerous incidental verses in which Egill describes his actions and thoughts, the saga contains three important poems: the *Hǫfuðlausn* (Head ransom), *Sonatorrek* (Lament for my sons), and *Arinbjarnarkviða*. The first is a poem in praise of his vengeful enemy, King Eiríkr Bloodaxe, whose son and friends Egill had killed; nevertheless, the king rewards him for the poem by sparing his life. The second describes Egill's grief at the deaths of his two young sons, one of them, his favorite, having drowned. Here Egill complains that he has not the strength to fight the seagod Ægir and thus avenge his son's death. He blames Odin for his irreparable loss, but admits that his poetic skill, which helps alleviate his sufferings, was a gift from Odin. The third poem describes the unswerving loyalty of his friend, Arinbjǫrn, who risks the king's enmity by helping Egill.

There is no medieval evidence as to the authorship of *Egils saga,* but it is now generally assumed that it was written by Snorri Sturluson, whose other works, *Heimskringla* and *Edda,* share some striking features with it, including a keen interest in and an appreciation of skaldic poetry, and also an unmistakable affinity of style. Like *Heimskringla, Egla* offers an informed vision of early Scandinavian and English history, an understanding and subtle illustration of human motives, and a narrative design giving a panoramic view of the Viking world from the middle of the ninth century to the end of the tenth. The claim for Snorri's authorship of *Egla* is supported by the fact that he lived for a while at Borg, where Egill farmed, and spent most of his adult life in the district of Borgarfjörður.

The precise date of *Egla* is a matter for speculation. Earlier scholars assumed that it was written

about 1230 and thus was older than *Heimskringla,* but it has recently been argued that it dates from the last years of Snorri's life.

Egils saga Skallagrímssonar survives in a number of manuscripts, the principal being *Mǫðruvallabók,* written toward the middle of the fourteenth century. A defective manuscript, *Wolfenbüttelbók,* dates from about the same time. In addition there are several fragments on vellum, the earliest written about the middle of the thirteenth century. Finally, there are several paper manuscripts, of which the seventeenth-century *Ketilsbók* is the most important.

BIBLIOGRAPHY

A. Bley, *Eigla-Studien* (1909); Bjarni Einarsson, *Litterære forudsætninger for Egils saga* (1975); Jón Helgason, "Athuganir um nokkur handrit Egils sögu," in *Nordæla. Afmælisrit til Sigurðar Nordals 14 September 1956* (1956); Sigurður Nordal, ed., *Egils saga* (1933).

HERMANN PÁLSSON

[See also **Egill Skallagrímsson; Snorri Sturluson.**]

EGLA. See **Egils Saga Skallagrímssonar.**

EGRISI. See **Georgia: Geography.**

EGYPT IN THE LATE EMPIRE. See **Roman Egypt, Late.**

EGYPT, ISLAMIC. In 639 the Arab general ᶜAmr ibn al-ᶜĀṣ led his Muslim army into Egypt and initiated a new era in Egyptian history. The following year he decisively defeated the Byzantine army at Heliopolis; afterward, the Byzantines abandoned all of Egypt except for the main fortified cities, which held out a little longer. The citadel of Babylon, at the apex of the Nile Delta, fell in April 641, and Alexandria, the capital, was surrendered to the Arabs and occupied by them in September 642. In the following winter ᶜAmr undertook an expedition against neighboring Pentapolis (Barqa); subsequently a brief Byzantine reoccupation of Alexandria from the sea was repulsed in the summer of 646. The last step in

the conquest of the land was to secure the ill-defined southern frontier. Egypt has on the whole clear natural boundaries—the sea on the north, the Libyan Desert on the west, and the Red Sea on the east. In 651–652 an expeditionary force advanced against the Christian kingdom of Nubia and reached Dongola, where a treaty with the ruler was concluded. Down to the Mamluk period Philae (Bilāq) formed the southern frontier of Islamic Egypt.

The conquest of Egypt safeguarded the recent Arab conquests in Syria-Palestine, and Arabia itself, from Byzantine counteroffensives. Aside from the prestige that was added to the nascent Islamic empire, the acquisition of Egypt provided substantial revenues, and regular wheat shipments were sent from Egypt to the Hejaz soon after the conquest. In addition, the occupied Egypt served as a base for further conquest and missionary activity in Africa and the Mediterranean littoral.

Until the mid seventh century Egypt was an integral part of the classical Mediterranean world; Alexandria, particularly, had been a vital center of Hellenistic civilization, and later of Christianity and Byzantine culture. The Arab conquest reoriented Egypt toward the East; its chief ties—political, commercial, and cultural—were to be with the Islamic heartlands in southwest Asia. The introduction of Islam, especially, created barriers of faith, language, and law with Greek and Latin Christendom. These important processes, however, were only gradual, for considerable continuity can be seen between the Byzantine and early Islamic periods—for instance, in the highly complex administration and its civilian personnel.

Islam, its language, and its way of life were introduced into Egypt by the Arab conquerors and later Arab colonization; during the eighth and ninth centuries large numbers of Arab tribesmen, mainly of Yemenite origin, migrated to Egypt. Unlike the earlier Greeks and Byzantines, who were concentrated in the cities, the Arab tribesmen settled in the countryside; consequently, the racial assimilation and cultural impact of the Arabs was far greater and more durable than the preceding Hellenism. The Arab elite, however, settled in the cities, where they fostered the use of the Arabic language from the early eighth century, so that Arabic gradually became the language of communication, culture, and government.

The replacement of Greek by Arabic can be clearly traced in the administrative papyri that have survived; the Greek papyri decrease in number and disappear in the second half of the eighth century. The first purely Arabic papyrus dates from 709, after which Arabic rapidly became the principal language. This language change did not prompt a cultural reaction by the native Coptic-speaking Christians and the retention of a separate Egyptian identity after their conversion to Islam, as occurred in Persia. The native Egyptians—even those who rejected Islam—abandoned their ancient language, except for liturgical purposes, and adopted Arabic while the Arab settlers were absorbed into the age-old pattern of life of the Nile Valley.

Conversion to Islam in Egypt began during the conquest; coercion was rare, and the adoption of Islam by the native Christians proceeded gradually. The crucial period of conversion appears to have been the ninth century, by the end of which the conversion process may have passed the halfway point. Yet a very substantial Christian population persisted; the eclipse of Egyptian Christianity was largely the result of the crusades. Throughout the medieval period the Christian and Jewish populations were protected by the government, but it was occasionally forced to make concessions to Muslim fanaticism by enforcing sumptuary laws against minorities. In any case, the subjection of Arab and Egyptian alike to the imperial rule of the Abbasids in the ninth century removed the distinction between Egyptianized Arabs and Arabized Egyptians.

Egypt became a province of the Islamic empire as a result of the conquest. The capital was transferred from Alexandria to Al-Fusṭāṭ, a move symbolic of the reorientation of the country. Al-Fusṭāṭ was initially a garrison encampment adjacent to the Byzantine fort of Babylon; it developed into a major city. Successive dynasties created a series of planned cities stretching northward from Al-Fusṭāṭ along the Nile; they slowly fused during the medieval period to form an elongated urban settlement. From Al-Fusṭāṭ, Egypt was ruled by a series of Arab governors appointed by the caliphs who reigned, successively, at the imperial capitals in Medina, Damascus, and Baghdad.

A new phase in the political history of Islamic Egypt began with the appointment of Aḥmad ibn Ṭūlūn as governor on 15 September 868. Within a few years he achieved virtual independence of Abbasid control. He reinvigorated the Egyptian economy and attained full financial autonomy; he also created a strong army and added much of Syria to his dominion. On his death in 884, Ibn Ṭūlūn was succeeded by his son, but the dynasty was short-lived. Imperial hegemony was reasserted in January 905 and Egypt was restored to the direct authority of Baghdad. In 935 Muḥammad ibn Ṭughj was appointed governor with considerable autonomy to defend the country and was given the title of *ikhshīd* by the caliph in 937.

The *ikhshīd* resumed the policies of Ibn Ṭūlūn. He was nominally succeeded in 946 by his two sons but the real ruler was their tutor, a brilliant and able eunuch of Nubian or Abyssinian origin known as Abū 'l-Misk Kāfūr. He was preoccupied with defending Egypt against dangerous external pressures, especially the new threat from the west—the Fatimid caliphate, which was established in Tunisia at the beginning of the tenth century.

Following Kāfūr's death in 968, the Fatimid armies began their conquest of Egypt. In retrospect, the Tulunid and Ikhshidid dynasties had not aimed at complete separation from the Abbasid caliphate; their objective was an autonomous principality under loose caliphal suzerainty. Nor were they backed by any national revival; Ibn Ṭūlūn and the *ikhshīd* were central Asian Turks, and Kāfūr was an African. Their armies consisted of Turkish, Sudanese, and Greek slaves; their art and architecture reflected the imperial style of Baghdad and Samarra. Under these two dynasties, however, Egypt became, for the first time since the Ptolemies, the seat of a separate military and political power.

The independent role of Egypt in the Middle East was greatly increased by the advent of the Fatimids, who conquered Egypt in 969 and founded their new imperial capital of Cairo. The Fatimid caliph was the head of a rival religious sect, the Ismaili Shīᶜa, which repudiated the authority of the Sunni Abbasid caliph in Baghdad. Under the Fatimids Egypt became the center of a vast empire that at its peak included North Africa, Sicily, Syria-Palestine, the African Red Sea coast, the Hejaz, and the Yemen. Despite their successes, the Fatimids failed to overthrow the Abbasid caliphate or even to establish the Shiite creed firmly in Egypt. From the late eleventh century the Fatimid state declined and real power was usurped by the Turkish and other foreign soldiery. Finally, in 1171, Saladin brought the Fatimid caliphate to an end and restored Egypt to Sunni orthodoxy and Abbasid suzerainty. He created a united Syro-Egyptian kingdom and founded the Ayyubid dynasty, which ruled Egypt as nominal vassals of the caliph in Baghdad until the middle of the thirteenth century.

Although Saladin was a Kurd, he introduced into Egypt a regime of the Turkish type that was characteristic of Seljuk rule in the rest of the Middle East. The most significant feature of the Ayyubid regime was the elite corps of Turkish *mamlūks* or freedmen, whose great virtue was their intense loyalty to their manumitter. Reliance on such alien cavalrymen as the backbone of the army can be traced back to Abbasid practice in the ninth century; from that time the *mamlūk* institution and its Turkish personnel were major characteristics of Islamic polity until modern times. The fullest development of this military system occurred in Egypt, where the *mamlūks* wrested power from the Ayyubids in 1250 and established a thoroughly military oligarchy without any pretense of civilian leadership. The extension of the military land grant *(iqṭāᶜ),* as a means of supporting the *mamlūks,* instead of the ancient system of tax farming, gave an entirely military character to the government.

During the Mamluk sultanate (1250–1517) any

adept *mamlūk* could aspire to being the sultan; the strength of the regime was the advancement of forceful and able leaders, though at the expense of considerable strife and human suffering—virtually a government by coup d'état. Each sultan possessed his praetorian corps of *mamlūks;* they were bought slaves who were converted to Islam, trained in the palace school, and manumitted by the sultan. They formed a separate, privileged, yet nonhereditary ruling class. The Mamluk sultanate is traditionally divided into the Baḥrī (1250–1382) and Burjī (1382–1517) periods; in the first the *mamlūks* were primarily Qipchaq Turks, and a loose hereditary succession of sultans was followed. In the second period the *mamlūks* were predominantly Circassians, and the hereditary principle was abandoned.

The militarization of the Egyptian government from the eleventh century on is comparable to that of the Roman Empire from the third century; both were caused primarily by external threats to their survival. Beginning in the eleventh century, the Middle East was subjected to a series of shattering invasions: crusaders from the West, Turks and Mongols from the East, bedouin and Berbers from the unsubjugated interior. As a result Egypt acquired a new leadership in the diminished but still important Arab world. It served as base for the wars of reconquest that eventually ejected the crusaders from Syria-Palestine and provided the resources for the *mamlūks* to halt the Mongol armies. The defeat of the Mongol army at the battle of ᶜAyn Jālūt in 1260 bestowed great prestige on the *mamlūk* adventurers, who thereby saved Egypt from massive destruction. In addition, formal legitimation of the sultanate was provided by a line of puppet caliphs, descended from an Abbasid refugee from Baghdad, who lived in Cairo as powerless protégés of the sultans. Thus, Egypt's role in the later Middle Ages was one of retrenchment and conservation of classical Islamic culture; in some ways it was analogous to that of Byzantium in the Christian world.

The Mamluk sultanate eventually declined for a number of reasons. The Black Death, the great plague pandemic of the mid fourteenth century, initiated a sustained decline in population, especially of the costly *mamlūks,* with a concomitant contraction of the economy. Diminished agricultural revenue prompted increasingly oppressive economic policies by the Mamluk sultans in the fifteenth century. At the same time the Italian city-states displaced Egyptian industries, such as textile and sugar manufacture, and the Portuguese discovery of a direct sea route to India seriously damaged Egypt's valuable transit trade. Militarily, the invasions of Tamerlane and the decay of the *mamlūk* institution weakened the empire. Moreover, the *mamlūks* were unwilling to adopt the use of firearms, so that Egypt was an easy victim for the Ottoman Sultan Selīm I, who in a swift campaign in 1516–1517 finally destroyed the tottering Mamluk sultanate and brought all its territories under Ottoman rule.

From the conquest of Egypt in the mid seventh century until the demise of the Mamluk sultanate in the early sixteenth century, Egypt made distinctive contributions to Islamic culture. The first religious figure of major importance in Egypt was the great jurist al-Shāfiᶜī (767–820), founder of one of the four orthodox schools of Islamic law, and the pioneer of theoretical jurisprudence in Islam. The Shāfiᶜī school of law spread throughout the Muslim world in the medieval period, and Cairo became a center of legal scholarship. Legal education in Egypt also included, from the late eighth century, the school of Mālik ibn Anas; from Egypt the Malikite school spread to the Sudan, to most of Muslim North Africa and western Africa, and to Muslim Sicily and Spain. During the Fatimid period a series of distinguished jurists and theologians formulated and expounded the law and doctrine of the Ismailis. To train their missionaries and propagandists, the Fatimids established important colleges, the most famous of which was al-Azhar; with the Sunni reaction under Saladin, al-Azhar was converted into a major institution of orthodox learning.

A new feature of post-Fatimid Egypt was the growth and proliferation of Sufi brotherhoods. This institutionalization of Islamic mysticism had a venerable history in Egypt; one of the earliest and most famous of Muslim mystics was Dhu 'l-Nūn al-Miṣrī (*ca.* 796–861). He was among the first to expound and systematize what became characteristic Sufi teaching. In the later Middle Ages a number of Sufi orders were founded or received their distinctive form in Egypt, and numerous Sufi convents (*khānqāhs*) were established by the *mamlūks*. The best known of these orders is the Aḥmadīya or Babawīya confraternity, founded by Aḥmad al-Badawī (*d.* 1276).

The Egyptian contribution to classical Arabic poetry and belles-lettres was relatively small. More important was the contribution to popular narrative literature, particularly the anonymous romances, such as those of Antar and the Banū Hilāl, that were written largely in semicolloquial language. These are sagas of Arab chivalry and Muslim holy war that contained old Arabian material and gradually developed during the wars against the Byzantines and crusaders. The best known of these works in the West is the collection of tales known as *Alf layla wa layla* (Thousand and one nights). From diverse sources the final version of the work, on which all modern translations are based, was written down in Egypt in the fourteenth century. Many of the individual stories are obviously Egyptian, such as Aladdin and the wonderful lamp. Related to this literature was the development of the popular Egyptian shadow theater.

In philology and history Egyptian authors made significant additions to Arabic literature. In the writings of history Egyptian scholarship appears to have made its greatest and most characteristic contribution. From the beginning of the Islamic era, the history of Egypt had a particular interest for Muslims because Egypt is mentioned several times in the Koran; Miryam al-Qibṭīya, one of the wives of the Prophet, came from Egypt, and Jesus' stay in Egypt was well known through Muslim traditions. The first great historian of Islamic Egypt was Ibn ᶜAbd al-Ḥakam (*d.* 871); his pioneer work on the Muslim conquest of Egypt and its aftermath inaugurated the long and rich tradition of Arabic historiography in Egypt.

In the Mamluk period Egyptian historiography achieved its fullest development, in the long series of authors whose numerous works make late medieval Egypt potentially one of the best-known regions of premodern Islamic history. Many of these historians were also government officials. Some, such as the Tunisian Ibn Khaldūn (1332–1406) and the Turk al-ᶜAynī (1361–1451), were immigrants who settled in Egypt; most were of Egyptian birth, such as al-Maqrīzī (1346–1442), Ibn Taghrībirdī (*d.* 1474), and Ibn Iyās (1448–1524). Linked with the historical literature is a large body of writings of biographical, topographical, geographical, and administrative content that deal primarily with medieval Egypt.

In science as in letters, Egypt attracted many scientists from other countries who found a home and a career in Egypt. Representative of such men are the Iraqi physicist and mathematician Ibn al-Haytham (*d. ca.* 1039), who wrote a famous work on optics; the Spanish-Jewish physician and philosopher Ibn Maymūn or Maimonides (1135–1204); and the Syrian physician Ibn al-Nafīs (*ca.* 1210–1288), who gave the earliest account of the lesser (pulmonary) circulation of the blood. Native Egyptians played a not inconsiderable part in the development of Greek science and medicine. The two major classical Arabic works on the history of science are both of Egyptian provenance; a biographical dictionary of physicians, scientists, and philosophers by Ibn al-Qiftī (d. 1248) and one of physicians only by the Syrian-born Ibn Abī Uṣaybiʿa (d. 1270).

In art and architecture there was a blending of native techniques and styles with increasingly Eastern, particularly Persian, influence. The earliest surviving mosque was founded in Al-Fusṭāṭ by ʿAmr ibn al-ʿĀṣ soon after the conquest; much rebuilding has left little of the original structure. More remarkable is the well-preserved Mosque of Ibn Ṭūlūn, which reflects the imperial Abbasid style. The early Fatimid period was the high-water mark of medieval Egypt in the patronage of the arts. In the Ayyubid period military architecture was strongly influenced by European models as a result of the crusades. Other Ayyubid changes reflect the conservative nature of the regime: the replacement of Kufic by Naskhī writing for decoration, and the establishment of the *khānqāh* and the *madrasa* (legal college).

The *īwān* plan, referring to four large vaulted halls walled on three sides and opening on the fourth side directly to a central courtyard, was introduced from the East. The *īwān* plan was frequently used for these new structures, as well as for mosques, hospitals, and caravansaries. Eastern tilework, however, was never popular in Egypt. Stone construction became common during the Mamluk sultanate, and most of the surviving Islamic monuments in Egypt date from this period. The domed tomb *(turba)* was a conspicuous feature of Mamluk architecture, often combined with a mosque and *madrasa*; a good example of such a complex is that of Sultan Ḥasan (1356) in Cairo. The surviving art and architecture are striking evidence of the rich and cosmopolitan nature of medieval Egyptian society.

BIBLIOGRAPHY:
Janet L. Abu-Lughod, *Cairo: 1001 Years of the City Victorious* (1971); Richard W. Bulliet, *Conversion to Islam in the Medieval Period* (1979), ch. 8; Albert J. Butler, *The Arab Conquest of Egypt*, 2nd ed. (1978); *Colloque international sur l'histoire du Caire* (1972); K. A. C. Creswell, *The Muslim Architecture of Egypt*, 2 vols. (1952–1959); Michael W. Dols, *The Black Death in the Middle East* (1977); *idem* and A. S. Gamal, *Medieval Islamic Medicine* (1984); Solomon D. Goitein, *A Mediterranean Society,* (1967–1983); W. Kubiak, *Al-Fusṭāṭ: Its Foundation and Early Urban Development* (1982); S. Y. Labib, *Handelsgeschichte Ägyptens im Spätmittelalter (1171–1517),*

(1965); Stanley Lane-Poole, *The Art of the Saracens* (1886, repr. 1971), and *History of Egypt in the Middle Ages,* 4th ed. (1925, repr. 1968); Ira M. Lapidus, *Muslim Cities in the Later Middle Ages* (1967); Bernard Lewis, "Egypt and Syria," in P. M. Holt *et al.*, eds., *The Cambridge History of Islam,* 1A (1970), 175–230, and "The Contribution to Islam," in *The Legacy of Egypt,* 2nd ed. (1971), 456–477; Otto Meinardus, *Christian Egypt, Ancient and Modern,* 2nd ed. (1977); Carl F. Petry, *The Civilian Elite of Cairo in the Later Middle Ages* (1981); H. Rabie, *The Financial System of Egypt* (1972); Susan J. Staffa, *Conquest and Fusion: The Social Evolution of Cairo A.D. 642–1850* (1977); A. L. Udovitch, ed., *The Islamic Middle East, 700–1900* (1981); Gaston Wiet, *L'Égypte arabe,* vol. 4 of G. Hanotaux, ed., *Histoire de la nation égyptienne* (1937).

MICHAEL W. DOLS

[See also **Abbasids; ʿAmr ibn al-ʿĀṣ; Arabic Literature, Prose; Ayyubids; Cairo; Fatimids; Ikhshidids; Islam, Conquests of; Islam, Religion; Law, Islamic; Mamluks; Saladin; Sufism; Tuluids.**]

EIGEL (*ca.* 750–822), abbot and hagiographer, was born to a Bavarian aristocratic family. He entered the monastery at Fulda as a child and was educated by his kinsman, the abbot Sturmi. About 817 Eigel (or Agilus) became abbot, succeeding the deposed Ratger. He composed a life of Sturmi that emphasized the privileges of the monastery, a dedicatory letter to the virgin in Angildruth, and his own epitaph. He also received poems from his eventual successor, Hrabanus Maurus. Eigel's biography was written about 840 by Candidus (or Bruun), a teacher at the monastery.

BIBLIOGRAPHY
The following texts are all in the series *Monumenta Germaniae historica:* Poetry and epitaph in *Poetae latini medii aevi,* Ernst Dümmler, ed., II (1884), 96–117; *Vita Sturmi,* in *Scriptores* II, Georg H. Pertz, ed. (1829, repr. 1963), 365–377; *Vita Egilis,* in *Scriptores* XV, Georg Waitz, ed. (1887, repr. 1963), 221–233.

RALPH WHITNEY MATHISEN

[See also **Candidus of Fulda; Fulda; Hrabanus Maurus.**]

EIKE VON REPGOWE (1180/1190–after 1233) was the author of the *Sachsenspiegel,* the greatest medieval German lawbook. He was born to a family of minor nobility in the hamlet of Reppichau in Anhalt and appears as a witness in six documents between 1209 and 1233; otherwise all that is known about his life is what can be deduced from his writings. Undoubtedly he obtained an excellent education for a layman, for it is clear that his working method was to draft passages of the *Sachsenspiegel* in Latin before rewriting them in his native Low German. Certainly too he had much practical experience in East Saxon law courts, because his work is based on his intimate knowledge of contemporary law and judicial procedure.

Parts of the *Sachsenspiegel* appear to have been written between 1221 and 1224, but it is clear that Eike wrote the entire work over a much longer period—probably between about 1220 and 1235—by a process of continual revision and enlargement. Until recently it was thought that he also wrote the *Sächsische Weltchronik,* the first world chronicle in the German vernacular, but the trend of current scholarship is to deny this.

The *Sachsenspiegel* was the first comprehensive treatise on any legal subject in a European vernacular. It displays no knowledge of Roman law and only a little familiarity with canon law. Although Eike often employs biblical formulations, the Sachsenspiegel does not draw on any other written sources and is based exclusively on practical experience. Its preeminence in medieval German legal literature rests on its creation of a German legal vocabulary and on its achievements in systematization. Eike does not merely report the law but attempts to explain in an orderly fashion the historical origins and the concepts behind legal principles and practices.

The *Sachsenspiegel* is of great historical interest because of the many political and social arguments it expresses. Eike espoused the right of resistance to unjust rulers, declaring that "a man must resist and hinder in every way his king and his judge if such a ruler does wrong." He also was opposed to slavery even though he knew it was a practice of long standing: in his opinion even age-old custom did not make an unlawful practice lawful. In regard to the contemporary struggle between the papacy and the German emperor, Eike was a strong partisan of the latter, and in internal German constitutional matters he favored a strong monarchy as opposed to the sovereignty of the territorial princes.

The *Sachsenspiegel* exerted an enormous influence on the subsequent development of the German legal language and the structure of later German lawbooks, but the particular lines of argument it es-

poused were sometimes repudiated. Above all, the anticlerical positions it took on matters concerning the relationships between secular and spiritual powers were frequently attacked by papal partisans; indeed, fourteen extracts were condemned as heretical by Pope Gregory XI in 1374.

BIBLIOGRAPHY

Eike von Repgowe, *Sachsenspiegel: Landrecht und Lehnrecht,* K. A. Eckhardt, ed., 2 vols., rev. ed. (1973); H. Fehr, "Die Staatsauffassung Eikes von Repgau," in *Zeitschrift der Savigny-Stiftung für Rechtsgeschichte, Ger. Abt.,* **37** (1916); Guido Kirsch, *Repertorium fontium historiae medii aevi,* **4** (1976), 291–293, bibliography; Ruth Schmidt-Wiegand, "Eike von Repgow," in *Die deutsche Literatur des Mittelalters: Verfasserlexikon,* 2nd ed., II (1978), 400–409.

ROBERT E. LERNER

[See also **Law, German: After the Carolingians; Sachsenspiegel.**]

EILHART VON OBERG. See **Tristrant.**

EILÍFR GOÐRÚNARSON. Manuscripts of *Snorra Edda* preserve nineteen whole and two half-stanzas from Eilífr's *Þórsdrápa,* widely reputed to be the most difficult *dróttkvætt* poem extant. The *drápa* relates how Þórr (Thor), minus his hammer and belt of strength, journeys with his servant Þjálfi to the hall of the giant Geirrøðr, a dwelling later portrayed by Saxo Grammaticus as the Norse underworld. The god repels all evil plots against him, including a swollen river fed by a squatting giantess; he breaks the backs of Geirrøðr's two daughters and spears Geirrøðr with a glowing ingot that the giant had hurled at him. Eilífr's kennings turn this culminating scene into kitchen comedy, with the host offering his guest fortified food and drink. Þórr survives by swallowing the "heavy red bits of the seaweed of the tongs" (the pieces of glowing iron) with his "mouth of the lower arm" (hand) before regurgitating the morsels most effectively. Snorri's *Skáldskaparmál* tells a slightly different version of this presumably very popular adventure.

Almost nothing is known about Eilífr's life, not even whether he was Icelandic or Norwegian. *Skáldatal* lists him among the skalds who composed for the archpagan Earl Hákon (Haakon) the Great (*ca.*

409

970–995) of Norway, yet among the verses cited as Eilífr's in *Snorra Edda* is an indisputably Christian half-stanza. Scholars differ over whether *Þórsdrápa* is a last gasp of heathen fervor or high parody. Eilífr's treatment of the red-bearded god is certainly more in the comic mode of *Þrymskviða* than in the reverent tones of the other fragmentary Þórr odes of the late tenth century, such as the strophes by Vetrliði, Þórbjǫrn Dísarskáld, Eysteinn Valdason, and Gamli Gnævaðaskáld.

The kennings in *Þórsdrápa* consistently demythologize the god and his opponents, reducing rather than magnifying their dimensions. There is even some xenophobia: giants are called Gandvík-Scots, cave-Welsh, mountain-Britons, battle-Swedes, rock-Danes, and mountain-Rogalanders. A giantess' backbone is called "the very old keel of the laughter-ship" (breast), a kenning that makes a rather modern impression. Þórr and his companion are called Vikings of Odin's seat, giantess-seducer, and lady-killer. In one stanza (17), the god and his giant opponent are four times defined by their passions for various women.

One reason why Eilífr's poem is so hard to interpret is that many of his kennings, which are numerous and often very long, appear either to be completely original (such as his circumlocution for backbone) or to transgress customary bounds. The skald sometimes seems to be pushing inherited kenning systems to their logical limits, even to the point of absurdity. A mild example is his transformation of the kenning type "Odin's mead" (poetry) into "Odin's whiskers" (stream), a suggestion that the god was a bit sloppy in his cups. A traditional kenning for sea is "blood of the giant," recalling the myth of Ymir's dismemberment; Eilífr appears to call a river "blood of the giantess."

Perhaps the nearest thing to panegyric in the *drápa* is its refrain, twice repeated in the surviving stanzas: "The stone of strength [heart] of Þórr and Þjálfi shook not with fear." Yet even here the linkage of the god with his servant involves some reduction in the former's stature. Despite the difficulty in determining whether *Þórsdrápa* is a heathen rally or a Christian burlesque, Eilífr Goðrúnarson comes through as a skilled and sophisticated wordsmith.

BIBLIOGRAPHY

Finnur Jónsson, ed., *Den norsk-islandske skjaldedigtning*, 4 vols. (1912–1915), AI (1912), 148–152, and BI (1915), 139–144; Ernst A. Kock, ed., *Den norsk-isländska skaldediktningen*, I (1946), 76–79; Hallvard Lie, "Þórs-drapa," in *Kulturhistorisk leksikon for nordisk middelalder*, XX (1976); Konstantin Reichardt, "Die *Thórsdrápa* des Eilífr Godrúnarson: Textinterpretation," in *PMLA*, 63 (1948); Margaret Clunies Ross, "An Interpretation of the Myth of Þórr's Encounter with Geirrøðr and His Daughters," in *Speculum Norroenum: Norse Studies in Memory of Gabriel Turville-Petre* (1981), 370–391.

ROBERTA FRANK

[See also **Snorra Edda; Thor.**]

EINARR HELGASON SKÁLAGLAMM (*ca.* 945–995), younger contemporary and friend of Egill Skallagrímsson, was one of the outstanding Norse skalds of the tenth century; his *Vellekla* is perhaps the most important *dróttkvætt* poem from the pagan period. It was composed probably between 980 and 990 in honor of Earl Hákon (Haakon) the Great (ruler of Norway *ca.* 970–995), the pagan leader who drove out the sons of Eiríkr Bloodaxe and whose court attracted a multitude of skalds. The poem survives, piecemeal, in three texts: *Heimskringla, Fagrskinna,* and *Snorra Edda.*

Probably not all thirty-seven stanzas (twenty whole and seventeen half) making up *Vellekla* in modern editions actually belong to the poem. Stanzas 7–9, 14–17, 22–32, and 37 are said by Snorri to come from *Vellekla;* stanzas 10–12, attributed to Einarr by Snorri, are also likely to come from the poem. Stanzas 13 and 18–21 survive only in *Fagrskinna* and may belong to *Vellekla.* More doubtful are the half-stanzas (1–6, 33–36) preserved only in *Snorra Edda* under Einarr's name; the most doubtful of these is stanza 34, which has to do with the famous battle between Earl Hákon and the Jómsvíkings at Hjǫrungavágr (*ca.* 985), a battle that may have taken place after *Vellekla* was composed. The sources call *Vellekla* a *drápa,* though no refrain has survived. The order of the stanzas varies in the different saga collections.

Vellekla provides precious glimpses into what was believed to constitute a pagan leader's strength, what gave him his mandate to rule. One group of stanzas describes Hákon's revenge against the sons of Eiríkr; another section extols his reestablishment of pagan temples and worship; then comes a description of an attack by his enemies, followed by their resounding defeat and Hákon's rejection of Danish overlordship for Norway. Einarr depicts a *do ut des* reciprocity existing between the ideal king, his skalds, his warriors, and his gods. Hákon tended the sanctuaries, pleasing the land spirits who let the ground grow again; he killed his enemies, charming Odin with the increase in warriors for Valhǫll. The precipitation that brings fertility in an Odin-approved reign is transmuted—through Einarr's kennings—into the ruler's successful downpour of spears in Odin's gale (battle). His exploits bring the earl glory (*tírr*), the inclination to victory that only a god can bestow and a poet confirm.

There are more than thirty god names in *Vellekla*. The kind of praise poem represented by this *drápa* has analogues in other early Indo-European poetry, such as that of the Hindus, where an essential part of a prince's election to the kingship was his eulogy by the bards, in which they expounded his ability to procure the favor of the divine powers.

Einarr's nickname and the name of his poem remain puzzles. *Vellekla* (perhaps "lack of gold") has been explained as a reference to the skald's poverty, while *skálaglamm* (perhaps "scales' tinkle") is supposed by *Jómsvíkinga saga* to derive from a pair of scales once given to the poet by his king. Neither explanation is persuasive; both names may derive from kennings that were in a now lost stanza or refrain of Einarr's poem.

BIBLIOGRAPHY

Finnur Jónsson, ed., *Den norsk-islandske skjaldedigtning*, 4 vols. (1912–1915), AI (1912), 122–131, and BI (1915), 117–124; Ernst A. Kock, ed., *Den norsk-isländska skaldediktningen*, I (1946), 66–69; Hallvard Lie, "Vellekla," in *Kulturhistorisk leksikon for nordisk middelalder*, XIX (1975); Jan de Vries, *Altnordische Literaturgeschichte*, 2nd rev. ed., I (1964), 174–176.

ROBERTA FRANK

[See also **Dróttkvætt; Skaldic Verse; Snorra Edda.**]

EINARR SKÚLASON, the most significant twelfth-century Icelandic poet, is mentioned among priests of western Iceland in 1143 but served both before and after that year as a court poet to several Norwegian kings, beginning with Sigurðr I Jerusalem Farer (*d.* 1130). Some of his independent single verses (*lausavísur*) and fragments of longer encomiums survive, and Snorri Sturluson quotes from these frequently in *Heimskringla* and *Skaldskaparmál*.

Einarr's reputation rests largely on his only complete surviving *drápa, Geisli* (The ray), or *Ólafs-drápa* as it is called in *Heimskringla* and *Morkinskinna*. It is a poem honoring St. Ólafr. In 1152 a papal legate established the first Norwegian archiepiscopal see in Niðarós (Trondheim). Some months later, in 1153 (possibly on St. Ólafr's feast, 29 July), Einarr recited *Geisli* in Christ's Church before an audience including the archbiship, Jón Birgisson, and the coregent kings, Eysteinn (who commissioned the poem), Sigurðr, and Ingi.

Composed in *dróttkvætt* meter, *Geisli* is in tripartite *drápa* form: prologue (*upphaf*), refrain section (*stefjabálkr*), and conclusion (*slœmr*). Einarr begins the prologue (stanzas 1–17) by dedicating his poem to Ólafr, "the battle-mighty ray [hence the title] of the Sun of Mercy [Christ]," and, using light imagery throughout, recounts the birth, passion, resurrection, and ascension of Christ. He then appeals to each dignitary and all Norsemen for attention. Since Ólafr's earthly deeds had been sung by the contemporary skalds Sigvatr and Óttarr, Einarr mentions only two details from the end of the saint's life: his vision of a heavenly ladder and (in the refrain section) the solar eclipse at his death; both touch on figural correspondences between the saint's life and Christ's.

As the refrain praising Ólafr's intercessory powers recurs ten times, the *stefjabálkr* (stanzas 18–45) enumerates the saint's widely accepted miracles: the radiance of his body, restoration of sight to the blind and speech to men whose tongues had been cut out (three times), aid in battle, and the ruining of the loaves of a Danish woman who dared bake on his feast. The *stefjabálkr* ends in the midst of a miracle involving Ólafr's sword in Constantinople (Einarr cites a certain Eindriði as his oral source).

The *slœmr* (stanzas 46–71) continues this account and adds further recent miracles: aid to the Varangian guard and the healing of a maimed priest. The poet concludes by hinting broadly at reward and seeking Eysteinn's opinion of the poem.

In deference to his Christian subject matter, Einarr eschews mythological kennings in *Geisli* (in contrast with their heavy use in his *Øxarflokkr*), with a few exceptions such as compounds involving Huginn (Odin's raven) and Hildr (a Valkyrie name), and a sword kenning that alludes obliquely to the slaying of Fenrir. Instead of diction rooted in paganism, he adapts kenninglike rotes from ecclesiastical Latin, such as *réttlætis sunna* (*sol justitiae*, "Sun of Justice" = Christ), *flæðar stjarna* (*maris stella*, "Star of the Sea" = Mary), and *friðar sýn* (*visio pacis*, "Vision of Peace" = etymology of Jerusalem).

Considering the royal subject and commission, *Geisli* may well have political overtones in the context of the ongoing church–state debate of the period.

BIBLIOGRAPHY

Sources. Finnur Jónsson, ed., *Den norsk-islandske Skjaldedigtning,* 4 vols. (1912–1915), AI (1912), 455–458, and BI (1915), 423–457; Martin Chase, *Einar Skúlason's "Geisli": A Critical Edition* (diss., Univ. of Toronto, 1981), with translation.

Studies. Wolfgang Lange, *Studien zur christlichen Dichtung der Nordgermanen 1000–1200* (1958), 120–143; Fredrik Paasche, *Kristendom og Kvad* (1914), 72–84; George S. Tate, "The Cross as Ladder: *Geisli* 15–16 and *Líknarbraut* 34," in *Mediaeval Scandinavia,* **11** (1978–1979); Jan de Vries, *Altnordische Literaturgeschichte,* 2 vols., 2nd ed. (1964–1967), I, 15–23.

GEORGE S. TATE

[See also **Dróttkvætt; Skaldic Verse.**]

EINHARD (*ca.* 770–840; variant spellings: Einhartus, Ainhardus, Heinhardus, Agenardus, or Eginhartus) was born in the region around the Main River. The scion of a noble Upper Franconian family, he was educated in the monastery of Fulda. Walafrid Strabo called him "a tiny man" (*homuncio*) of "ridiculously small stature" (*statura despicabilis*), and one of his nicknames was Nardulus, the diminutive of his name. Abbot Baugulf of Fulda recommended his intelligent and well-read pupil to the court of Charlemagne. Einhard came to the famous palace school at Aachen in the early 790's, while Alcuin still directed it. When the latter retired to Tours, Einhard probably succeeded him.

Early on, Einhard had been placed in charge of Charlemagne's literary and mathematical studies. Apart from being a poet, he was also known as an expert in architecture, the arts, and the crafts; he was, for instance, supervisor of new constructions (especially the basilica in Aachen). His nickname Bezaleel (see Exod. 31:2) bears witness to his mastery of all types of workmanship. In later years Charlemagne sent him on ambassadorial missions: in 806 he secured from Pope Leo III the approval of Charlemagne's plan for partitioning the empire; in 813 he was the successful spokesman for the Frankish nobles to have Louis the Pious recognized as coemperor.

After Charlemagne's death Einhard became the private secretary of Louis, who rewarded his faithful services by appointing him lay abbot and by presenting him with a number of abbeys, such as St. Cloud near Paris, St. Servatius in Maastricht, and St. Pierre and St. Bavo near Ghent. Among land grants, he received in 815 Mühlheim (later Seligenstadt) on the Main River; in 828 he had a church and monastery erected there for the bones of the martyrs St. Marcellinus and St. Peter. These precious reliquaries had been illegally secured for him in Rome by Ratleic, his notary and emissary, in the previous year.

After Einhard was appointed tutor to Lothair in 817, his attitude toward Louis the Pious' narrow, monkish attitudes in ecclesiastical matters seems to have become increasingly negative. He started to spend a great deal of time away from the court. In 830 Empress Judith's influence reached its zenith and an open family quarrel broke out between Louis and his sons; at this time Einhard retired with his wife Imma (since the twelfth century confused with Charlemagne's daughter Bertha) to his monastery in Seligenstadt. There he spent the rest of his life as a monk. Imma, who had become abbess, died in 836, and Einhard on 14 March 840, after he had managed to effect a reconciliation between Lothair and Louis. Einhard's epitaph was written by Hrabanus Maurus, the abbot of Fulda.

Einhard produced several works in Latin, mostly religious in nature: *Libellus de adoranda cruce* written for his friend Lupus of Ferrières; *Translatio et miracula SS. Marcellini et Petri* (*ca.* 830); *Passio martyrum Marcellini et Petri;* and a lost treatise on the Psalms. In addition there are more than sixty letters dating from 823 to 836, which deal chiefly with political events during Louis's reign.

But Einhard's most important work is the *Vita Caroli Magni,* written probably at Seligenstadt between 830 and 833. It is the first and probably the best secular biography written in the Middle Ages and a significant contribution to the history of German language, literature, and culture. In chapter 29 Einhard describes the codification of the Germanic tribal laws under Charlemagne, the now-lost collection of the old Germanic heroic lays, the attempt at a German grammar, and the German names for the months and winds coined by Charlemagne.

The influence of Suetonius is evident throughout, but Caesar, Livy, Orosius, Ovid, Cicero, and Tacitus also left their mark. Even though the *Vita* contains a number of factual errors and Einhard never personally participated in Charlemagne's numerous military campaigns, it remains the only extant eyewitness account of the life and works of Charlemagne by someone who knew him well. It was very popular during the Middle Ages, and more than eighty manuscripts and fragments survive. Shortly after 840 Walafrid Strabo added the chapter divisions and headings and also a prologue in which he gives important details about Einhard's life. The *Vita* was translated into Middle High German in the thirteenth century, but only small fragments of this version remain.

BIBLIOGRAPHY

Sources. The following works by Einhard are in *Monumenta Germaniae historica:* the letters, Karl Hampe, ed., in *Epistolae Karolini aevi,* V (1899, repr. 1978), 105–149 and 286, no. 14; the *Libellus,* in *Epistolae Karolini aevi,* V, 146ff.; the *Passio,* Ernst L. Dümmler, ed., in *Poetae latini medii aevi,* II (1884), 125–135; the *Translatio,* in *Scriptores,* XV (1887, repr. 1963), 238–264; the *Vita,* G. H. Pertz, Georg Waitz, and Oswald Holder-Egger, eds., in *Scriptores rerum Germanicarum,* VI (1911). Also available are *Einhard's Life of Charlemagne,* Latin text ed. by Heathcote W. Garrod and Robert B. Mowat (1915); and *Einhard: Vita Caroli Magni. The Life of Charlemagne,* Latin text with a new English trans., intro., and notes by Evelyn Scherabon Firchow and Edwin H. Zeydel (1972).

Studies. Helmut Beumann, *Ideengeschichtliche Studien zu Einhard und anderen Geschichtsschreibern des früheren Mittelalters* (1962); Max Buchner, *Einhards Künstler- und Gelehrtenleben* (1922); Karl Esselborn, "Einhards Leben und Werke," in *Archiv für hessische Geschichte und Altertumskunde,* n.s. **15** (1928); Arthur J. Kleinclausz, *Eginhard* (1942); Peter Munz, *Life in the Age of Charlemagne* (1969).

EVELYN SCHERABON FIRCHOW

[See also **Biography, Secular; Carolingians and the Carolingian Empire; Charlemagne; Walafrid Strabo.**]

EINON AP GWALCHMAI (*fl.* 1203–1223), one of the court poets of the Welsh princes. He was a member of the only bardic family for which there is firm evidence in Wales: his father Gwalchmai is traditionally assumed to be Gwalchmai, court poet to Owain Gwynedd and son of Meilyr, the court poet of Gruffudd ap Cynan. Einon's period of activity may be determined by his family connections—he was brother to Meilyr ap Gwalchmai and probably to Elidir Sais—and by a few lines in an ode to Llywelyn ap Iorwerth the Great (1173–1240), in which he refers to the latter's heroism against the English. One of Einon's finest poems is an elegy on Nest, the

daughter of Hywel of Towyn, Merionethshire. This poem and his three odes *(awdlau)* to God are indicative of a change from the court poets' traditional themes of praising secular lords for their warlike qualities.

Like Elidir Sais, and perhaps under his influence, Einon seems to have decided that it was better to use his poetic gifts to praise God rather than men, and he hankered after the monastic life even if he did not embrace it. Like his grandfather Meilyr, he expressed the wish to end his life among the religious community on Bardsey Island.

Einon had the unusual distinction of becoming the hero of a folk tale.

BIBLIOGRAPHY

John Gwenogvryn Evans, ed., *The Poetry in the Red Book of Hergest* (1911), 1177–1181; Owen Jones, Edward Williams, and William Owen Pughe, eds., *The Myvyrian Archaiology of Wales,* 2nd ed. (1870), 230–232; John Lloyd-Jones, "The Court Poets of the Welsh Princes," in *Proceedings of the British Academy,* **34** (1948), also published as a monograph; Rhiannon Morris-Jones, John Morris-Jones, and Thomas H. Parry-Williams, eds., *Llawysgrif Hendregadredd* (1933, repr. 1971), 33–42.

J. E. CAERWYN WILLIAMS

[See also **Elidir Sais; Welsh Literature: Poetry.**]

EIRÍKR ODDSSON was a twelfth-century historian, a pioneer in Icelandic saga writing of whom practically nothing is known except that he wrote a book called *Hryggjarstykki.* Scholars do not know what the title means: the most probable translation is "a calfskin" and therefore "a book written on a piece of calfskin." This implies that *Hryggjarstykki* was a very short saga and did not cover more than two folios (some 6,000–7,000 words). Since *Hryggjarstykki* was in all likelihood the first saga to be written in the vernacular, this brevity is not surprising.

Hrggjarstykki is not extant as an independent work. The text is found in three Icelandic compendia dealing with the Norwegian kings: *Morkinskinna, Fagrskinna,* and *Heimskringla.* Scholars consequently hold different views on the historical setting, time of composition, and purpose of the work, but a comparison of the compendia reveals that they are independent descendants of Eiríkr's book, and this implies that it is possible to formulate a relatively clear conception of the saga.

The saga covers only the years 1136–1139, and its main character is Sigurðr Slembidjákn (sham deacon), a warrior who claimed to be the son of Magnús Bareleg, king of Norway. Sigurðr killed King Harald Gilli in 1136 and fell into the hands of Harald's sons in 1139. He was subjected to agonizing tortures and died a martyr's death, singing psalms and praying for his enemies. Sigurðr had spent a winter in Iceland and many Icelanders were in his retinue, but his main support came from Denmark, where he found shelter and amassed troops to harry the coasts of Norway.

The sources of Eiríkr Oddsson's saga were almost exclusively oral. He based his story partly on what he had seen or heard, naming clerical as well as lay informants of high rank. Eiríkr used the style and structure of native oral accounts, as well as foreign biographies of martyrs, as models. The *Vita sancti Magni*, the biography of Magnús, earl of Orkney, who was canonized in 1137, was used as a source and a particular model for the saga.

Hryggjarstykki is a contemporary history probably written in support of Sigurðr's case for canonization. In the twelfth century Scandinavian kings and princes were acclaimed as saints for political reasons, especially if they had lost their lives in a gruesome manner. The Danish historian Saxo Grammaticus used the saga as a source for his *Gesta Danorum,* and his narrative lends support to this theory.

Hryggjarstykki was composed about 1150 and marks the beginning of historical writing in Iceland. It is a vital link between foreign literary models and native storytelling. Furthermore, it indicates that the kings' sagas, as a literary genre, have their roots at least partly in hagiographic literature. *Hryggjarstykki* had such a highly developed style that Snorri Sturluson saw no reason to change it to any great extent when he incorporated it into *Heimskringla,* which substantiates the view that the saga style is essentially a product of the art of native storytelling.

BIBLIOGRAPHY

Bjarni Aðalbjarnarson, *Om de norske kongers sagaer* (1937), 159–169; Bjarni Guðnason, *Fyrsta sagan* (1978); Finn Hødnebø, "Hryggjarstykki," in *Kulturhistorisk leksikon for nordisk middelader,* VII (1962), cols. 25–26; Sigurður Nordal, "Sagalitteraturen," in *Litteraturhistorie: B, Norge og Island* (1953), 195–197; Jan de Vries, *Altnordische Literaturgeschichte,* 2nd ed. (1967), II, 233–235.

BJARNI GUÐNASON

[See also **Snorri Sturluson.**]

EIRÍKS SAGA RAUDA. See **Vinland Sagas.**

EIRÍKSMÁL AND HÁKONARMÁL. Eiríkr blóð-øx (Bloodaxe) was among the older sons of Haraldr inn hárfagri (the Fairhaired), who brought Norway under a single kingship; he succeeded his father about 930 and earned his sobriquet by killing four fraternal rivals for the throne. About 935 Hákon I the Good, a younger son of Haraldr, returned from fosterage at the court of Athelstan of England and expelled Eiríkr. Eiríkr next appears about 948 in northern England, where he served intermittently as an underking of Northumbria until he was killed in 954.

Eiríksmál (Lay of Erik) and *Hákonarmál* (Lay of Hákon), two tenth-century poems depicting the entry of these royal brothers into Valhalla, are thus closely linked by history and poetic conception. With *Haraldskvæði* they comprise the Eddic praise poems, occupying a middle ground between the anonymous, traditional Eddic poem and the personal, occasionally skaldic praise poem. All three employ a mixture of Eddic meters and a mythological framework for royal encomium.

Eiríksmál consists entirely of speeches, beginning abruptly with a soliloquy by Odin: he awakens from a dream of preparing Valhalla for guests, new armies of the dead. The poet-god Bragi hears a thunderous sound, as if Baldr were returning at Ragnarǫk, but Odin realizes that it announces Eiríkr's approach. Odin orders the heroes Sigmund and Sinfjǫtli to receive him; Sigmund asks Odin why he has deprived Eiríkr of victory, and Odin implies that Eiríkr will be needed in the coming battle against the monsters. Then Sigmund welcomes Eiríkr, asking about his following; the poem breaks off with Eiríkr's reply that it comprises five kings.

Hákonarmál begins with narrative. Odin sends out Valkyries to choose a king for Valhalla; they find Hákon preparing for battle. Four stanzas of intensely skaldic diction describe the battle; then the Valkyries address Hákon among the gloomy dead (5–10). He asks why Odin has deprived him of victory, and the Valkyries ride to Valhalla (11–13). Odin sends two gods, Hermóðr and Bragi, to greet Hákon, who arrives bloody and cautious; Bragi assures him of safety, but Hákon retains his weapons (14–17). The poet directly praises Hákon: no better king will come until Ragnarǫk, and since Hákon's death the land has suffered (18–21).

The *Prose Edda* gives a few stanzas of both poems, and *Heimskringla* quotes all of *Hákonarmál*. The text of *Eiríksmál* is preserved in a fourteenth-century Norwegian manuscript of kings' sagas, *Fagrskinna*, which also outlines the literary history of the two poems: Queen Gunnhild commissioned *Eiríksmál* in honor of her husband (after 954), and the Norwegian poet Eyvindr Finnsson composed *Hákonarmál* in imitation (961 or later). Eyvindr was a well-known poet of Hákon's court, and his epithet *skáldaspillir* is usually interpreted, with reference to his penchant for imitation, as "the plagiarist" or "despoiler of poets."

Each poem is, in its own way, brilliantly executed, but *Eiríksmál* is fragmentary. Its "five kings" have been variously identified. *Hákonarmál* is complete, but there is reason to believe its last stanza is a later addition, according to de Vries. Both poems are of great importance as historical sources for tenth-century conceptions of kingship and afterlife, but their images of Valhalla differ. *Hákonarmál* preserves an older, gloomier Valhalla alongside features that may be specific to late Norwegian paganism, whereas *Eiríksmál* may be closer to a Danish or Anglo-Danish tradition.

BIBLIOGRAPHY

Felix Genzmer, "Das eddische Preislied," in *Beiträge zur Geschichte der deutschen Sprache und Literatur,* **44** (1919), 146–168; Jón Helgason, ed., *Skjaldevers,* 2nd ed. (1962); Lee M. Hollander, trans., *Old Norse Poems: The Most Important Non-skaldic Verse Not Included in the Poetic Edda* (1936); Ludvig Holm-Olsen, "Øyvind Skaldaspillir," in *Edda,* 53 (1953); Edith Marold, "Das Walhallbild in den Eiríksmál und den Hákonarmál," in *Mediaeval Scandinavia,* 5 (1972); Klaus von See, "Zwei eddische Preislieder: Eiríksmál und Hákonarmál," in Werner Simon, Wolfgang Bachofer, and Wolfgang Dittmann, eds., *Festgabe für Ulrich Pretzel zum 65. Geburtstag dargebracht von Freunden und Schülern,* (1963), 107–117; Jan de Vries, Altnordische Literaturgeschichte, 2nd rev. ed., I (1964), 140–146; Alois Wolf, "Zitat und Polemik in den 'Hákonarmál' Eyvinds," in Johannes Erben and Eugen Thurnher, eds., *Germanistische Studien* (1969), 9–32.

JOSEPH HARRIS

[See also **Eddic Poetry; Ragnarǫk; Skaldic Verse; Valhalla.**]

EISTEDDFOD (Welsh, "session" or "assembly"), the term used from the fifteenth century on to signify an assembly of poets and musicians. The modern eisteddfod includes extensive exhibitions and concerts in addition to musical and bardic competitions, but the medieval eisteddfod was primarily a conference at which the complex rules of Welsh poetry were laid down and the regulations for the organization and governance of the bardic order were established. Although the name was not used, such conferences clearly took place during the period of the court poets (1100–1282). Gruffudd ap Cynan (d. 1137) is said to have instituted a poetic reform about 1100. Sixteenth-century eisteddfodau based their organization and authority on the so-called *Statute of Gruffudd ap Cynan,* but the earliest version of this text survives from the sixteenth century, so its authenticity is very uncertain.

The first such conference for which the sources are clear was held at Cardigan Castle at Christmas 1176, sponsored by Lord Rhys ap Gruffudd. A full description is given in the *Brut y Tywysogion* (The chronicle of the princes); competitions were held between "bards and poets, harpers, crwth-players, and pipers, and various kinds of musical craft." Much like the modern eisteddfod, this gathering was announced for a year throughout the British Isles.

The first eisteddfod named as such was held at Carmarthen in the early 1450's, sponsored by Gruffudd ap Nicolas (d. 1461). In addition to musical and bardic competitions, this assembly codified the metrics of Welsh poetry under the guidance of Dafydd ap Edmẃnt.

Two eisteddfodau documented from the sixteenth century, both held at Caerwys, Flintshire, one in 1523, the other in 1568, and both under the authority of the *Statute of Gruffudd ap Cynan.* Both were principally concerned with the bardic order and its organization, which by this time had so declined that the 1568 eisteddfod had to deal with a commission from Elizabeth I to purge the bardic order of the "intollerable multitude . . . [of] vagraunt and idle persons, naming theim selfes mynstrelles Rithmers, and barthes."

BIBLIOGRAPHY

Brut y Tywysogion, Thomas Jones, ed. (1955), 166–167; Thomas Parry, *A History of Welsh Literature,* H. Idris Bell, trans. (1955), 133–136.

DAVID N. KLAUSNER

[See also **Bard; Gruffudd ap Cynan; Welsh Literature.**]

EIXIMENIS, FRANCESC (*ca.* 1326–1409), Catalan friar minor, ordained deacon in 1351 (variant spellings: Examenis, Eximenis, Ximenis). He is traditionally thought to have been educated in Gerona. Recent research, however, suggests he may have been born there but probably spent his early years in Barcelona, where his family were wealthy merchants closely associated with the house of friars minor. Nothing is known about his life until the date of his ordination; and from then until he took up residence in Valencia in 1383, only a few references indicate the scope of his activities. In 1352 he was still in Barcelona; in 1357 he attended a conventual chapter in the Franciscan house in Gerona; and in 1367 he probably resided in the Majorcan house where his name appears on a document with the designation *bachiller*. From references in his works we know that he visited England, Germany, and Italy, presumably between 1371 (when he appears as custodian of the Barcelona house) and 1383.

Eiximenis witnessed the condemnation of the *Revelations* of Friar Peter of Aragon at the papal court of Avignon in 1365; he examined the Jewish quarters in Valencia; and he had a close connection with the royal family of Aragon, even advising Martin I the Humane on ruling Sicily. His association with the royal family helped him to obtain his degree of master of theology, which must have served him in his duties in Valencia as professor of the Holy Scriptures (1394–1395). He also undertook a number of official functions, such as preaching at royal funerals (including that of Peter III the Ceremonious in 1387), intervening in social disputes (1391), and participating in an arbitration sentence concerning St. Vincent Ferrer (1406). In addition he was one of the junta of seven theologians to put an end to the Great Schism. Shortly before his death he was called to the papal court at Avignon by Benedict XIII (1408) and consecrated bishop of Elna and patriarch of Jerusalem.

Eiximenis' very active social and political life did not prevent him from completing a vast corpus of works on Christian life in his times. His most important work was *Lo Crestià* (The Christian), a vast encyclopedia that was printed in many editions in the fourteenth and fifteenth centuries. It was to have been divided into thirteen books—reflecting the life and activities of Christ and his twelve disciples—but only the first three and the twelfth are extant. Eiximenis probably never completed the other nine, though the first book gives the plan for the entire work.

The first volume was dedicated to Peter III, and it shows how the practice of Christianity differs from that of Judaism and Islam. The period of composition (*ca.* 1378–1391) coincides with an outbreak of anti-Jewish massacres, but no mention is made of them: the references to Judaism are purely theoretical and have no bearing on the contemporary situation. Eiximenis, however, does describe other sectors of society as he knew them in his lifetime. His works are among the most valuable documents of fourteenth-century life and customs. The second volume of the *Crestià* emphasizes the temptations the Christian has to face throughout life and the benefits he will obtain if he remains faithful to the Christian code of ethics. The third book enumerates very carefully the sins besetting the Christian, thus giving Eiximenis an opportunity to indicate the failings of his contemporaries.

Eiximenis probably interrupted his work at this point, possibly at the request of the rulers of Valencia, at whose behest he wrote *El regiment de la cosa pública*, later incorporated into the twelfth and last extant volume of the *Crestià*. This treatise and the twelfth book as a whole deal with the duties and functions of a ruler. Court officials such as the chancellor, treasurer, and majordomo are all described, with heavy reliance on the *Ordenacions* of Peter III and many other sources—classical, patristic, legal, and contemporary. Eiximenis' original contribution lay in his commentary on his society and the fact that most of this works were written in Catalan.

His other Catalan works include the *Libre dels angels* (1392), the *Libre de les dones* (1936), and the *Vida de Jesucrist* (*ca.* 1400). The first two achieved a measure of popularity at the time and were translated into various languages. They too contain valuable information on contemporary customs and rely on numerous sources. Eiximenis also wrote the *Cercapou*, a devotional tract; the *Doctrina compendiosa* (similar to the twelfth book of the *Crestià* in subject matter); and three works in Latin: *Scala Dei, Ars praedicandi populo*, and the *Pastorale*. He is also thought to have at least begun a *Summa theologica*, of which a fragment has been found, and some sermons. In all, his known literary output fills several large volumes, and he was one of the most prolific authors of medieval times. Unfortunately much of his work remains unedited.

BIBLIOGRAPHY

Two recent editions are *Lo Crestià*, Albert Hauf, ed. (1983), selections; and *La societat catalana al segle XIV*,

Jill R. Webster, ed., 2nd ed. (1980). A bibliography is David J. Viera, *Bibliografia anotada de la vida i obra de Francesc Eiximenis* (1980). Among the useful studies are Martín de Riquer, *Història de la literatura catalana*, II (1964), 133–196; and Jill R. Webster, "Nuevas aportaciones a los estudios Examenianos—Francesc Examenis—su familia y su vida," in *Archivo Ibero-Americano*, jul.-dic. (1980).

JILL R. WEBSTER

[See also **Catalan Literature; Peter III the Ceremonious, Literary Court of.**]

EJMIACIN. The monastery of Holy Ējmiacin (the descent of the Only Begotten) is the spiritual center of the Armenian church and the seat of the katⁱolikos of all Armenians. It is located in the city of Ējmiacin (Soviet Armenia)—the ancient Vałaršapat. The oldest building in the complex is the cathedral, which is dedicated to the *Theotokos*.

According to the tradition transmitted by the fifth-century Armenian historian Agatⁱangełos, the cathedral of Ējmiacin was founded by St. Gregory the Illuminator in the early fourth century. In a vision Gregory witnessed Christ descending from heaven and striking the ground with a "hammer of gold." On that site, which was near the royal palace, Gregory saw "a circular base of gold" and on it "an exceedingly tall column of fire." Soon thereafter Gregory, assisted by the King Trdat III/IV and the Armenian people, enclosed this area "with a high wall and secured it with doors and bolts." The fifth-century historian Pⁱawstos Buzand refers to this structure as *naχekełecⁱi* (protochurch) to distinguish it from the "first church" that Gregory built a little later in Aštišat in the district of Tarōn.

The nature of Gregory's structure is not clear. According to tradition, the site of Gregory's vision is marked by a shrine located in the center of the cathedral. Some scholars have suggested that the original building serves as a prototype for the subsequent cruciform churches with a central plan, whereas others have argued more recently in favor of a basilican church. The historical evidence suggests that Ējmiacin became the patriarchal residence only after the middle of the fourth century, Aštišat being the first seat of the early bishops of Armenia. Eznak the Priest, a seventh-century author, informs us that Katⁱolikos Sahak the Parthian (387–439) rebuilt the church. The Zoroastrian fire altar discovered by archaeologists under the present main altar in the 1950's predates Sahak's structure, since the Persians invaded Armenia in the 360's and destroyed many churches.

About 483 Vahan Mamikonean, the general of the Armenian forces in Persarmenia, built the present cathedral on the earlier site, even though the patriarchal see had already been transferred to Dwin in the 470's. At the end of the fifth century the historian Łazar Pⁱarpecⁱi was the prior of the monastery of Ējmiacin. The place was still thriving with activity in the early seventh century, but from the eighth to the fourteenth century we know nothing about its fate.

Toward the end of the thirteenth century Stepⁱanos Orbelean, the archbishop of Siwnikⁱ (Sisakan), in his *Lamentation on the Holy Cathedral of Vałaršapat,* wrote of the deplorable condition of the church. In 1441, however, the altered political situation in eastern Armenia allowed the Armenian church fathers to end the peregrination of the patriarchal see and transfer it from Cilicia back to Vałaršapat. The association of Vałaršapat with the patriarchal see was part and parcel of the accepted tradition, so much so that one of the patriarchs, Constantine VI (1430–1439), residing in Cilicia, called himself "katⁱolikos of Vałaršapat" in an official letter.

Most of the buildings in the present-day monastery—including the bell tower—date from the seventeenth, eighteenth, and nineteenth centuries, but Ējmiacin was and remains the national symbol of the Armenian people.

BIBLIOGRAPHY

Agathangelos, History of the Armenians, trans. and commentary by R. W. Thomson (1976), 277, 309–311; Pⁱawstosi Buzandacⁱwoy Patmutⁱiwn Hayocⁱ (1889); Eznak Erēcⁱ, "Nšanagir kargacⁱ banicⁱ," in *Yišatakakarankⁱ jeʰagracⁱ,* compiled by Catholicos Garegin Yovsēpⁱean, I (1951); Alexandre Sahinian, "Recherches scientifiques sous les voûtes de la cathédrale d'Étchmiadzine," in *Revue des études arméniennes,* n.s. 3 (1966).

KRIKOR H. MAKSOUDIAN

[See also **Agatⁱangełos; Armenian Church, Doctrines and Councils; Gregory the Illuminator, St.; Sahak, St.**]

EKKEHARD OF AURA (*d. ca.* 1126), abbot of Aura from 1108, updated the important world chronicle of Frutolf of Michelsberg. His continuations have independent worth as accounts of German history between 1098 and 1125 and the early history of the crusading movement, especially because Ekkehard was a participant in the crusade of 1101. In his account of the investiture controversy he sided vigorously with the papacy.

ROBERT E. LERNER

[See also Chronicles; Frutolf of Michelsberg.]

EKKEHARD I OF ST. GALL (*ca.* 910–973), liturgical poet born into a family with close connections to the Swiss Abbey of St. Gall. Two nephews who were also namesakes account for the seemingly dynastic series of Ekkehards at St. Gall. Ekkehard II Palatinus ("the Courtier," *d.* 990) was prominent at the court of Emperor Otto I. Ekkehard III was a dean of St. Gall. The first Ekkehard was an accomplished poet, but he has always been most famous for the statement in the chronicle of St. Gall (written by Ekkehard IV *ca.* 1031) that he authored a *Vita Waltharii manufortis,* long identified with the epic poem *Waltharius.* Modern historians have rejected this identification, and an enormous literature on the "Waltharius problem" has been produced since 1941.

BIBLIOGRAPHY

The chief biographical source is Ekkehard IV, *Casuum S. Galli continuatio,* Ildephonsus ab Arx, ed., in *Monumenta Germaniae historica, Scriptores,* II (1963), 75–147. Ekkehard I's religious poems are analyzed and printed in Wolfram von den Steinen, *Notker der Dichter und seine geistige Welt* (1948), I, 439–457, and II, 134. See also Hans F. Haefele, "Vita Waltharii manufortis," in Johanne Autenrieth and Franz Brunhölzl, eds., *Festschrift Bernhard Bischoff zu seinem 65. Geburtstag* (1971), 260–276; Rudolf Schieffer, "Zu neuen Thesen uber den 'Waltharius,'" in *Deutsches Archiv für Erforschung des Mittelalters,* **36** (1980).

ELAINE GOLDEN ROBISON

[See also Ekkehard IV of St. Gall; Waltharius.]

EKKEHARD IV OF ST. GALL (*ca.* 980–*ca.* 1060), historian and composer. Brought up in St. Gall, he was director of the cathedral school at Mainz (1022–1031), where he wrote the *Liber benedictionum.* He then returned to St. Gall as head of the abbey school.

There he embarked on the continuation of the *Casus sancti Galli,* the official history of the monastery. The initial author, Ratpert, had gotten as far as 833; Ekkehard brought the account forward to 972. Whereas Ratpert had been interested mainly in legal and political affairs, Ekkehard concerned himself with St. Gall's cultural and literary history, the intellectual achievements and writings of its various monks. In this context he mentioned Ekkehard I's authorship of *Vita Waltharii manufortis* and so planted the seeds of the modern "Waltharius problem."

BIBLIOGRAPHY

Sources. Casuum S. Galli continuatio, Ildephonsus ab Arx, ed., in *Monumenta Germaniae historica, Scriptores,* II (1963), 75–147; *Liber benedictionum,* Johannes Egli, ed. (1909).

Studies. Hans F. Haefele, "Wolo cecidit: Zur Deutung einer Ekkehard-Erzählung," in *Deutsches Archiv,* **35** (1979), and "Tu dixisti: Zitate und Reminiszenzen in Ekkehards Casus sancti Galli," in Otto P. Clavadetscher, Helmut Maurer, and Stefan Sonderegger, eds., *Florilegium Sangallense: Festschrift für Johannes Duft* (1980).

ELAINE GOLDEN ROBISON

[See also Ekkehard I of St. Gall; Ratpert of St. Gall.]

EKTHESIS, a document promulgated in 638 by Emperor Heraklios as part of a series of attempts to effect a compromise between Orthodoxy and Monophysitism. Drafted by the patriarch Sergios, this so-called Monothelite formula put forth the doctrine of two natures but a single will in Christ. The compromise, however, satisfied neither of the contending groups and ultimately failed in its purpose of reconciliation, despite its acceptance by Pope Honorius I. The leading opponent of the *Ekthesis* was Sophronios, the Monophysite patriarch of Jerusalem.

The issue became moot when, shortly after the promulgation of the *Ekthesis,* the Arabs conquered the Monophysite provinces of Syria and Palestine. In 648 Emperor Constans II promulgated the *Type,* which ordered the removal of the *Ekthesis* from the narthex of Hagia Sophia and forbade any discussion of divine will or divine energy. In 680 the sixth ecumenical council condemned the document.

BIBLIOGRAPHY

The text is in Giovanni Mansi, ed., *Collectio conciliorum,* X (1764), 991–998. See also George Ostrogorsky,

History of the Byzantine State, Joan Hussey, trans. (1957, rev. ed. 1969).

LINDA C. ROSE

[See also **Monophysitism; Monothelitism; Sergios, Patriarch.**]

ELCKERLIJC, written by Petrus van Diest in the second half of the fifteenth century, is an outstanding morality play. It was widely translated, and was adapted in an English version, *Everyman,* which has become world famous. In this allegory, Death, Society, and Property appear as figures in the play, but only Virtue is able to help Everyman save his soul.

BIBLIOGRAPHY

W. Asselbergs, *De stijl van Elkerlijk* (1968); H. de Vocht, *Everyman: A Comparative Study* (1947).

SEYMOUR L. FLAXMAN

[See also **Dutch Literature; Everyman.**]

ELDIGÜZIDS. See Ildegizids.

ELEANOR OF AQUITAINE (*ca.* 1122–1204), successively queen of France and of England and the mother of two English kings. The granddaughter of Guillaume IX (count of Poitou, duke of Aquitaine, and one of the early troubadours), she inherited his lands and so became the most magnificent and coveted heiress in Europe. Her territories, stretching from the Pyrenees to the Loire, were larger than those held directly by the king of France. In a shrewd political maneuver Louis VI of France arranged for the marriage of his sixteen-year-old son Louis to Eleanor in 1137. A year later, after the decease of Louis VI, the two were crowned king and queen of France.

Louis had been brought up for the church, and his austerity and timid personality were hard to bear for the lively Eleanor. In 1146, after the birth of her first child, Marie (1145), St. Bernard preached the Second Crusade at Vézelay. Louis strongly believed in his duty to take the cross. Eleanor's participation in the crusade gave rise to many unpleasant rumors as well as to fantastic legends of Eleanor and her ladies as Amazons. On their way to the Holy Land the crusaders stopped in Constantinople and Antioch, where Raymond of Antioch (Eleanor's uncle) welcomed his guests with oriental splendor. This expedition brought a taste for the marvelous and the exotic to French literature, but the crusade itself ended in a disaster at Damascus, though Louis and Eleanor did see Jerusalem as pilgrims.

Despite the birth of a second daughter, Alix, the tensions between Louis and Eleanor finally led to a divorce in 1152 on grounds of consanguinity. For political reasons the divorce had been strongly opposed by Abbot Suger.

Only two months later Eleanor married Henry Plantagenet, having evaded two clever traps laid for her by other suitors. Since Henry was duke of Normandy and count of Anjou and Eleanor held Poitou and Aquitaine, the whole west of France was controlled by the couple. Eleanor became queen of England in 1154, when Henry (not without many difficulties) succeeded Stephen of Blois on the English throne.

Eight children issued from their marriage: they included two future kings, Richard (*b.* 1157) and John (*b.* 1166), and two queens, Eleanor of Castile (*b.* 1161) and Joanna of Sicily (*b.* 1165). Two other sons, Henry (*b.* 1155) and Geoffrey (*b.* 1158), died in the midst of plots or insurrections against their father.

The itinerary of Eleanor reveals constant displacements of her court, spanning the vast territories of the Angevin kingdom. But it was in Poitiers, where a brilliant circle of poets and courtiers gathered, that Eleanor held her famous court most often. The period before 1174 saw the "courts of love" and the rise of vernacular literature, of which both Eleanor and Henry were active patrons. The name of one of the greatest troubadours of the time, Bernart de Ventadorn, is linked to hers; her influence is visible in the epic *Girart de Rousillon.* Northern French literature as well flourished under the protection of Eleanor: Wace dedicated his *Roman de Brut* to her. Other romances, especially the romances of antiquity, show Angevin influence: the *Roman de Troie* by Benoît de Sainte-Maure, for example, contains an explicit reference to Eleanor. The Tristan legend also benefited from her interest in Thomas of Britain. Eleanor and especially her eldest daughter, Marie of Champagne, encouraged and favored the greatest of all French romancers, Chrétien de Troyes. One of the most controversial contributions of Eleanor's court to twelfth-century culture were the debates of love as formulated by Andreas Capellanus (*De amore*). This discussion of courtly love and its relation to religion, marriage, and adultery has not ceased to be a subject of intense scholarly debate.

Henry had many political problems during this period, most notably a failed plan to dominate the church in England that culminated in the scandalous murder of Becket in 1170. His authoritarianism also alienated the barons, especially in Aquitaine. His sons rebelled when Henry gave them empty titles without any powers attached. The strife within the family reached such a point that a contemporary chronicler, Richard of Devizes, likened Henry's affairs to "the troubled house of Oedipus." Eleanor sided with her sons against her husband and was promptly imprisoned (1174); she regained complete freedom only in 1189, after Henry's death. In the intervening years she was allowed short periods of liberty, during which she was used as a pawn in Henry's complicated political maneuvers. A campaign led by his sons and the French king, Philip Augustus, against Henry ended with the English king's death in 1189.

Richard the Lionhearted became king in 1189, and for Eleanor a period of renewed political activity began. Reestablished in all her rights and former glory by her favorite son, she proved herself to be a sovereign of grand stature. She arranged for the marriage of Richard and Berengaria of Navarre, and when her son was captured by the duke of Austria on his return from the Third Crusade (1192) Eleanor almost singlehandedly governed the vast Angevin realm. One of her most difficult tasks was raising the enormous ransom that the Holy Roman emperor demanded. On delivery of a huge sum of money Richard was finally freed, but he died a few years later during a pointless siege at Châlus (1199).

Even in her old age Eleanor knew no rest. John Lackland, whom Richard had designated as his successor, had to struggle against Arthur of Brittany, the son of John's elder brother Geoffrey and the favorite of the Poitevin barons. Eleanor made a last grand effort at fortifying the dynastic edifice that her family had built in Europe: the French king desired to marry his son Louis to Eleanor's granddaughter Blanche of Castile, and it was the aged queen, now about seventy-seven years old, who crossed the Pyrenees in winter in order to fetch the prospective bride. This successful mission was the last of her many accomplishments. In 1202 she retired to Fontevrault, where she died a quiet death in 1204.

BIBLIOGRAPHY

Reto Bezzola, *Les origines et la formation de la littérature courtoise en Occident*, 3 vols. in 5 (1944–1963); Frank Chambers, "Some Legends Concerning Eleanor of Aquitaine," in *Speculum*, **16** (1941); Charles H. Haskins, "Henry II as a Patron of Literature," in Andrew G. Little and Frederic M. Powicke, eds., *Essays in Medieval History Presented to Thomas Frederick Tout* (1925), 71–77; Amy Kelly, *Eleanor of Aquitaine and the Four Kings* (1950); William W. Kibler, ed., *Eleanor of Aquitaine* (1976); Regine Pernoud, *Aliénor d'Aquitaine* (1965); Wilfred L. Warren, *Henry II* (1973).

RENATE BLUMENFELD-KOSINSKI

[See also Angevins; Aquitaine; Courtly Love; Crusades and Crusader States: To 1192; French Literature; Henry II of England; Louis VI of France; Richard I the Lionhearted.]

ELEAZAR BEN JUDAH OF WORMS (*ca.* 1165–*ca.* 1230): a descendant of the aristocratic Qalonimide dynasty that emigrated from Italy to Germany in the tenth century and helped found the Jewish community of Mainz, where Eleazar ben Judah ben Qualonimos was born. He studied there, in Speyer, and in Metz and mastered the esoteric theology of his relative Rabbi Judah the Pietist in Regensburg. He married Dulcie, the daughter of another prominent member of the Mainz community, and in the 1190's they moved to Worms, where he became one of the rabbinic authorities of the community and she became known as a learned woman. In 1196 his wife and two daughters were brutally murdered in an attack on his home, which he describes in elegies modeled after Proverbs 31 ("A woman of valor"). Eleazar and his son were wounded, his son mortally. In the 1220's he participated in the intercommunal Jewish synods held in Mainz and Speyer.

Eleazar wrote extensive commentaries on the Bible and the liturgy as well as liturgical poetry, but he is especially known as the author of a collection of Rhenish Jewish customary law, *Sefer ha-Roqeaḥ* (Book of the perfumer). His role in preserving Judah the Pietist's traditions of esoteric theology and ascetic pietism are of primary significance. Lacking an heir, Eleazar wrote down or edited a library of formerly esoteric oral and written lore, which still remains largely unedited and even unpublished. This corpus is an important link between ancient Jewish mysticism and the development of theosophical mysticism (Kabbalah) in twelfth-century Provence and thirteenth-century Spain.

Above all Eleazar adapted, and thereby preserved, his teacher's program for a new kind of ascetic, spiritualized pietism—Hasidism. When Judah's socioreligious program, designed for a sectarian fellowship led by charismatic sages, failed to win acceptance, Eleazar offered a personalist mode designed to bring salvation to the individual, rather than to Jewish society as a whole. By incorporating an epitome of his revisionist reformulation of pietism into his book of Jewish law, he legitimated pietism and enabled all Jews in Germany to be pietists simply by being pious Jews.

BIBLIOGRAPHY

Avigdor (Victor) Aptowitzer, *Mavo le-Sefer raviah* (Introduction to *Sefer raviah*) (1938), 316–318; Joseph Dan, *Torat ha-sod shel ḥasidut Ashkenaz* (The esoteric theology of Ashkenazi Hasidism) (1968); Israel Kamelhar, *Rabenu Eleazar ben Yehudah mi-Germaiza* (1930); Ivan G. Marcus, *Piety and Society: The Jewish Pietists of Medieval Germany* (1981).

IVAN G. MARCUS

[See also **Cabala; Hasidei Ashkenaz.**]

ELECTIONS, CHURCH. From the councils of the fourth century on, the church held that election and consecration were the two principal acts in the making of a bishop. For some centuries active participation in an episcopal election was not confined to a close body of electors, but was the business of a wide group of people. In the fifth century the bishops of each province were primarily responsible for the election of a new colleague, though, as Pope Celestine I put it, "a bishop should not be given to those who are unwilling [to receive him]. The consent and wishes of the clergy, the people, and the nobility are required." This comment was reinforced by Pope Leo I's dictum that "He who governs all should be elected by all." A bishop was thus mainly chosen through election by the clergy and the people, the bishops of the province acting together with the clergy and citizens of the diocese, and with the consent of the metropolitan.

These theoretical ideals were difficult to put into operation because of the growing pressure that a prince could bring to bear on the process of election, especially when the Western church fell under the dominance of Germanic kings. The Twelfth Council of Toledo (681), for instance, explicitly spoke of the "prince's free choice of bishops," adding that the archbishop of Toledo should raise to the episcopate "whomever the royal power chooses." To an ever-increasing extent, the appointment of bishops in the early Middle Ages became a prerogative of the ruling prince.

Heads of monasteries were appointed in a similar fashion, though the Rule of St. Benedict, based on an even earlier tradition, had insisted that the abbot should be elected by monks from their own number. St. Benedict Biscop secured for the Northumbrian monasteries of Jarrow and Wearmouth a papal privilege adumbrating a right of free election. But the practice that became general in pre-Conquest England, as on the Continent, was laid down in the *Regularis concordia,* which asserted that abbots should be elected in accordance with the Benedictine rule but with the advice and consent of the king. Although the king might consult the monks, the appointment virtually rested with him.

In Carolingian and Capetian France most bishoprics were in the gift and under the suzerainty of either the king or the more important magnates. Elections were at their nomination and virtually under their control. License to elect a new bishop or abbot had to be obtained from the king, and royal commissioners presided over the election, which was in effect a confirmation by the electors of a candidate nominated by the crown.

In the eleventh century one of the main concerns of the ecclesiastical reformers was to seek to ensure that free election, by clergy and people, to bishoprics, and by monks to abbacies, should be an essential ingredient in the liberation of the church from corrupt secular influence. At the reforming synod of the French clergy that Leo IX called in 1049, the first canon decreed that no one should accept ecclesiastical office without free election. Such canonical election of bishops implied the participation of the canons of the cathedral chapter, cathedral and monastic clergy, nobles, *ministeriales,* and citizens.

The principle received classical definition in the *Decretum* of Gratian (1140) in *distinctio* 63, where the canonist strongly asserted the right of the church to freedom from all lay intervention in the election of bishops, though acknowledging that the lay ruler's approval must be sought for the bishop-elect. "By all these authorities," he observed, "laymen are excluded from the election of bishops, and even the necessity of obedience, not the freedom of command, is enjoined upon them." Gratian recognized that an election needed to be confirmed by the higher ecclesiastical dignitaries as well as by the lay power, but provided that in case of a dispute, the issue should be decided by the metropolitan. The Third Lateran Council (1179) laid down the conditions, including the requisite age (thirty for a bishop), for valid election to ecclesiastical office.

The claim to free elections was intended to remove abuses characteristic of a proprietary church, such as simony and nepotism, but was seen in its implications as an encroachment on the traditional powers of the secular ruler and gave rise to the prolonged investiture controversy. Under Nicholas II, Alexander II, and especially Gregory VII, measures were taken not merely to keep papal elections free from secular influence but also to secure free canonical elections to all high ecclesiastical offices. The reformers taught that only after election, consecration and investiture with ring and staff by the metropolitan, and enthronement should the king give whatever rights there remained for the crown to confer.

In the eleventh and twelfth centuries an election sometimes preceded the investiture; sometimes an election followed the investiture, confirming the royal choice of a bishop; and occasionally the election was dispensed with altogether. The reformers strongly opposed the lay investiture of a new bishop with the episcopal ring and staff. The bitter struggle that followed was resolved by a series of compromises: the Compromise of Bec (the Westminster Agreement of 1107) with Henry I of England and the Concordat of Worms in imperial Germany (1122), where Emperor Henry V renounced "investiture with ring and crozier," promising canonical election and free consecration for the bishops and abbots of his empire. Those who received ecclesiastical preferment and did homage to the king could be consecrated, provided they had not received investiture with the sacred symbols of their office at his hands. The Concordat of Worms provided for elections to take place in the imperial court. If there was a dispute among the electors, the emperor was entitled to support whom he construed to be the "sounder part" (*sanior pars*) of the electors. Emperor Frederick Barbarossa asserted his rights to confirm an election and to settle a disputed election, if need be, by nominating a third party.

In his *Summa decretorum* (*ca.* 1158) the late-twelfth-century canonist Rufinus, later bishop of Assisi and archbishop of Sorrento, posited the continuing ecclesiastical ideal: "In the election of a bishop, these five things are especially to be considered: the wishes of the citizens, the testimony of the people,

the choice of those in high positions and of the regular clergy, the election of the clerics, the confirmation of the metropolitan and of the comprovincial bishops." This was the foundation of decretalistic and canonical thought for some time to come.

In theory a bishop should normally be chosen from the clergy of the diocese, as a responsible man who had won the regard of the clergy and the people, not excluding—supposing that he possessed the best qualities as a pastor—even a layman; in such a case postulation would be made to the pope, *aliud est postulari, aliud eligere* (in one place by postulation, in another by election). The vagueness implicit in Gratian's discussion was made clear in subsequent works, such as the *Quinque compilationes antiquae* (1187–1226) and the *Decretals* of Gregory IX (1234). In the latter's chapter *De electione et electi potestate*, the right of making the bishop was declared to belong to the cathedral clergy and three valid forms of election were admitted: *quasi per inspirationem* (inspired unanimity), scrutiny, and the way of compromise. There were many other commentaries or glosses that endeavored to provide greater academic exactness in the interpretation of such terms as *major et sanior pars* (weightier and sounder part) including the *Tractatus seu summa de electionibus episcoporum* of Laurence of Somercote (*ca.* 1254) and *De jure electionis novorum prelatorum* by Cardinal William of Mandagout (*ca.* 1285).

In practice, even though the right to a free election was generally admitted, the part of the clergy or chapter in such elections to bishoprics and abbacies was greatly restricted and only very intermittently applied. The Compromise of Bec provided for the presence of the king at the election, and though some lip service was paid to the right of the chapter to participate in such elections, in reality nomination to high ecclesiastical office remained the perquisite of the secular ruler. The chapter notified the crown of the impending vacancy and requested permission to proceed to an election, followed by the granting of a permission to elect (*congé d'élire*); but the subsequent election was habitually made in the king's chapel.

Article 12 of the *Constitutions of Clarendon* (1164) declared that when a vacancy occurred in a bishopric, abbey, or priory of which the crown was patron, the king was to summon the principal members of the body concerned in order that they might fill the vacancy by an election in the king's chapel "with the assent of the lord king and the advice of the dignitaries of the kingdom whom he had summoned for this purpose." The bishop-elect or abbot-elect was to do homage and fealty to the king as his liege lord before he was consecrated. For instance, in 1173 Henry II nominated Richard of Ilchester to the electors of the see of Winchester in a writ that stated, "I order you to hold a free election, but forbid you to elect anyone but Richard my clerk." Henry II and his two sons, Richard I and John, used the machinery to secure the election of their own nominees and to exclude candidates they did not like. They normally persuaded a chapter to elect one out of two or three royal nominees, or invited them to present two or three names for the king's choice. The English kings claimed the same right in their territories overseas.

The results of such royal intervention were not necessarily disastrous. Peter of Blois wrote of Henry II that "while according to the custom of the kingdom, he plays a very powerful and influential part in elections, he has nevertheless always kept his hands clean and unsoiled by venality," a verdict borne out by the king's selection of Hugh of Avalon, the Carthusian prior of Witham, as bishop of Lincoln in 1186.

Although the king acted according to custom, he was not bound by canonistic rules. In 1200 King John of England wrote to the dean and chapter of Lisieux, forbidding them to presume to "elect anyone as pastor of your church without our will and assent, action which we could not allow." Such action caused Innocent III in 1203 to rebuke John for "attempting to impede elections, and by your unlawful persecution you are forcing the rightful electors to choose in accordance with your arbitrary will, as you are known to have done in the church of Lincoln." In 1206 Innocent quashed the elections to the archbishopric of Canterbury of both the subprior, Reginald, the nominee of some of the younger monks of Christ Church, and the king's candidate, John de Grey, obliging the monks to elect his own candidate, Stephen Langton. Langton's eventual occupation of the see in 1213 testified to the success of Innocent's efforts to secure free canonical election.

In 1214 John issued a charter guaranteeing freedom of election to all cathedral churches and monasteries. The king no longer insisted on the custom of election in the royal chapel, but he retained his custody over the temporalities and the right to grant a license or to plead legitimate exceptions against the bishop-elect in an ecclesiastical court. John's charter was confirmed by Innocent III in 1215 and later by Gregory IX. The charter was formally observed, but

the freedom of conventual churches to elect their pastors according to canonical procedure was nonetheless restricted by the king's admitted right to delay or withhold his assent to the election.

When, in 1237, King Henry III tried to procure the see of Durham for his own protégé and half-brother, William of Valence, he opposed the election of Thomas of Melsanby by taking his case through his proctor, Master Simon, to the court of the archbishop of York. There he alleged that the bishop-elect was guilty of numerous charges, including treachery to the king, which disqualified him on grounds of character for such high office.

In practice the chapter's right to free election was largely thwarted by the action of the secular ruler or by the intervention of the pope or his legate. Chapters were permitted to carry out free elections if the bishop-elect was likely to have royal approval. So, in Henry III's reign it has been reckoned that in fifteen out of seventy-six episcopal elections the cathedral chapters enjoyed the right of "free election" without undue external influence being brought to bear on their proceedings. Yet in most countries the right of the clergy and people dwindled to a mere formality. In Castile, for instance, both Gregory IX and Innocent IV allowed Ferdinand III to exercise to the full the right to intervene in episcopal elections as lord of the land and defender of the true faith.

The rights claimed by cathedral chapters to proceed to a free election were diminished further by increased papal control, both by reason of appeals for papal decision in disputed elections and by the growth in the papal rights of reservation and provision. The difficulties in procuring a free election were promoted both by the uncertainties of canon law and by the disputes to which such elections frequently gave rise. Such irregularities could be resolved effectively only by reference to the pope. The see of Coventry and Lichfield, for instance, was a bishopric with two cathedral chapters, one a monastic society and the other a chapter of secular canons, often at loggerheads with each other. At Winchester the archdeacons claimed a part with the monks of St. Swithin's. At Canterbury the suffragan bishops asserted a right to share in the election with the monks of Christ Church. If a candidate for the episcopate required dispensation because of an irregularity—for instance, in 1199 Mauger, the bishop-elect of Worcester, was disqualified by reason of bastardy—his choice by the cathedral chapter was regarded not as an election but as a postulation that the pope had to authorize. Appeals in episcopal elections were referred more and more to the pope. When Innocent III gave judgment on the Canterbury election in 1208, it was asserted that judgment in such disputes was reserved to the apostolic see.

Apart from disputes arising out of contention in cathedral chapters or other irregularities that evoked papal interference, the pope's claim to be the universal ordinary of the church led to the assumption that he had oversight over all episcopal appointments. Although the *Decretum* provided for the confirmation and consecration of an archbishop-elect by his suffragans, the custom arose whereby the pope confirmed the election of the metropolitan. The growth of the papal right of reservation and provision to ecclesiastical benefices, greatly strengthened under the Avignon popes, led to a further diminution in the rights of the cathedral chapter.

In practice, nomination to bishoprics passed either to the king or to the pope, though the theory and ceremonial of free canonical election persisted. Strong kings continued to make appointments to bishoprics, though they did not challenge the papal right of provision. A bishop or archbishop was in normal circumstances elected by the chapter and provided by the pope; the king gave permission to the chapter to elect, normally indicating his choice and requesting the pope to provide the successful candidate. "If a bishop dies," Nicholas of Clamanges wrote of the French church in 1564, "or a dean, or a prior or some other ecclesiastical personage, whoever, seeking to be appointed to the place of the deceased does not go first to the king rather than the pope; indeed, who is crazy enough to approach the pope as a petitioner without royal letters?" The system worked reasonably well, for while it gave national sovereigns control over such appointments, the pope retained his theoretical powers and the financial advantages of nomination.

The situation in Italy was somewhat different from that of France or England. Although chapters occasionally sought to insist on their right of capitular election, they were normally overridden by the pope, who had the right to fill all Italian sees by provision. For example, at Verona in 1453 the canons, supported by the local commune and Venice, elected Gregorio Correr as bishop, but Nicholas V had already translated Ermolao Barbaro the elder from Treviso and insisted on his nomination.

The history of elections to English abbacies and priories followed a similar development, though for practical reasons monasteries enjoyed a freedom of election in the late Middle Ages that cathedral chap-

ters did not. In Anglo-Saxon England the monastic revival of the late tenth century made appointments to abbacies through nominations by either the ecclesiastical reformers or the king and the Witan. The Anglo-Norman kings paid little or no attention to the monks' claim to elect their heads, but between 1140 and 1154, during the comparatively weak rule of King Stephen, many English monasteries, especially those of the Cistercians, enjoyed a substantial measure of freedom in this respect. In the early years of the reign of Henry II, there was a steady reversion to earlier practice. Monasteries tried to secure the final election of the candidate of their choice by holding a previous election and stating that they would abide by their decision, in the hope that the king could be persuaded to accept their candidate. Such was the case in 1182, when he accepted Samson as abbot of Bury St. Edmunds.

More often, in England as on the Continent, the monks had to accept a royal nomination, especially in those houses patronized by the crown. Between 1208 and 1213 the interdict imposed by Innocent III on England held up all elections, but at its termination John claimed his old rights—refusing, for instance, to accept Hugh, whom the monks of Bury had elected as their abbot. Eventually Innocent agreed to guarantee full canonical election, reserving to himself only the rights of granting *congé d'élire* and of giving his approval to the new abbot.

In fact, in the later Middle Ages English monasteries enjoyed substantial freedom of election. They were better situated than cathedral chapters in this respect, partly because the monastic body had a more permanent and continuous existence and partly because, apart from major abbacies, the abbot, unlike the bishop, had less political importance. Although the English king might interfere in an election to an influential abbey, such as Westminster, he was content to allow the monks to proceed with the election of their head. In the case of monastic houses that ranked as baronies, the community had to get permission from the king to elect and to secure confirmation of their choice.

In most monasteries, election became a domestic affair, though a canon lawyer or notary public might be present to ensure that the procedure was regular. The professed members of the community had three methods of electing their head: by "inspiration" (of the Holy Spirit), by scrutiny, and by compromise. In the first instance a name would be suggested and instantly acclaimed. In the second the issue was determined by the scrutiny of individual votes, though in practice the verdict of a mere majority was regarded with some suspicion. St. Benedict had proposed election by what was described in Gratian's *Decretum* as the "weightier and sounder portion." The Fourth Lateran Council (1215) provided for a two-thirds majority; the Second Council of Lyons (1274), for a mere majority.

The way of compromise became the usual manner of electing to a monastic headship. The community selected a group of representatives from among their number, usually seven, who were entrusted with the choice of a future abbot. Their corporate decision would then be approved by the full chapter. If the abbot-elect accepted nomination, he had, unless royal or papal interests were involved, only to receive benediction at the hands of his diocesan bishop, followed by installation and a celebratory feast.

Continental monasteries—for instance, in France—still often remained under the patronage of secular rulers who used abbacies to reward their civil servants, thus making the process of election a pure formality.

BIBLIOGRAPHY

Geoffrey Barraclough, "The Making of a Bishop in the Middle Ages," in *Catholic Historical Review,* **19** (1933–1934); Robert L. Benson, *The Bishop-elect* (1968); Christopher R. Cheney, *Pope Innocent III and England* (1976), 121–178; André Desprairies, *L'élection des évêques par les chapitres au XIIIᵉ siècle* (1922); Marion Gibbs and Jane Lang, *Bishops and Reform, 1215–1272* (1934, repr. 1962), 53–93; Marcel Pacaut, *Louis VII et les élections épiscopales dans le royaume de France* (1957); Anscar J. Parsons, *Canonical Elections* (1939).

VIVIAN H. H. GREEN

[See also **Clarendon, Constitutions of; Clergy; Congé d'Élire; Innocent III, Pope; Investiture and Investiture Controversy; Langton, Stephen; Worms, Concordat of.**]

ELECTIONS, ROYAL. Strictly speaking, the double election of Philip of Swabia and of Otto IV in 1198 was the first royal election in German history. Until that date the election, defined as the selection of one from among several candidates, was merely one step in the elevation of a king to the throne. This sequence of events could include (not necessarily in this order) paternal designation, election, homage by the magnates, acclamation by the people, enthronement, and a ceremonial banquet; and could extend over a long period of time. Conrad II designated his son Henry as his successor, for example, at the request of the magnates in 1026; Henry III was crowned in 1028, but the magnates paid homage to him and enthroned him only after his father's death in 1039. The selection of every king before 1198 was thus an improvisation.

Innocent III's intervention after the election of Philip and Otto separated it from the other events, transformed it into a legal act with carefully prescribed procedures, and raised the question of the precise connection between the election and the other steps that elevated a man to the German and imperial thrones. By the middle of the thirteenth century, the right to elect the king had been restricted to the seven electors; their rights were formally recognized in 1356 in the Golden Bull, the basic constitutional document of the Holy Roman Empire until the end of its existence in 1806. The gaps in the documentation, the often contradictory accounts of chroniclers, and the ambiguity of terminology (such as the use of *electio* to refer to both the selection of the candidate and the sequence of events that elevated the king to the throne) make it impossible to trace with complete certainty the evolution of electoral procedures.

Before 1198 the selection of a king involved two complementary principles: election and blood right. The Germanic tribes believed in a charisma possessed by all members of a royal clan, each of whom was equally entitled to the throne. This belief explains why the Merovingians and Carolingians customarily divided the Frankish kingdom among all the king's sons. Blood right should not be confused with hereditary succession, which recognized the eldest son's substantive right to the crown. The history of England between 1087 and 1199, when only one monarch, Richard, succeeded to the throne in accordance with the modern rules of succession, reveals the difference between the two concepts. Hereditary succession eventually became the norm in Plantagenet England and, above all, in Capetian France; but the failure of successive German dynasties to produce a male heir strengthened the electoral principle in that country.

Even when the Merovingians and Carolingians were at the height of their power, some form of election was required to activate an heir's right to the throne and to select among possible claimants to the crown. For instance, Charlemagne and Louis the Pious decreed in 806 and 817, respectively, that if one of their sons died, his brothers would inherit his subkingdom unless the people elected the son of the dead king as their ruler. The repeated feuds among the Carolingians increased the role played by the magnates in the selection of the monarch.

Louis the German divided the East Frankish kingdom among his three sons in 865, but paid some attention to stem divisions. In 879 Louis III forced the Bavarian magnates to accept him rather than the dying Carloman's illegitimate son, Arnulf. After Louis's death in 882, the Bavarian and Frankish magnates paid homage to the last surviving brother, Charles III; but in 887 the magnates rebelled against him and invited Arnulf to accept the crown.

According to Widukind of Corvey, the East Franks and Saxons offered the crown to Duke Otto of Saxony after the death of the last German Carolingian, Louis the Child, in 911; when Otto rejected the offer, they anointed Duke Conrad of Franconia as king at Otto's recommendation. In fact, Widukind's account is a later attempt to justify the accession of the Saxon dynasty, and Conrad was probably elected, as the *Annales Alamannici* report, by all the tribes. As a Frank and as the leader of the dominant clan during the minority of Louis the Child, he was the obvious candidate. Conrad was the first German king to be anointed, a ceremony first employed in 751, when the Carolingians replaced the Merovingians as kings. Unction was an ecclesiastical substitute for the royal charisma that Pepin the Short and Conrad lacked.

The chroniclers agree that Conrad designated Otto's son, Duke Henry of Saxony, as his successor, but they disagree about the circumstances under which this occurred. According to Widukind, Conrad's brother, Eberhard, made peace with Henry and gave him the royal insignia. In May 919, five months after Conrad's death, the Frankish magnates assembled at Fritzlar, and Eberhard designated Henry king in the presence of the Frankish and Saxon people. Archbishop Heriger of Mainz offered to anoint and crown Henry, but the latter refused; thereupon the assembled multitude acclaimed Henry.

Widukind's report may be true, but Conrad's designation of Henry was at best a recommendation without binding power. Moreover, the Swabians refused at first to accept Henry, and the Bavarians elected their own duke, Arnulf the Bad, as king. It is not known what happened in the five months after Conrad's death, and it is possible that Arnulf was actually elected before Henry. It is thus conceivable that the story of Conrad's designation of Henry was a later attempt to justify Henry's election, while

Henry's rejection of Heriger's offer may have been a gesture to indicate his abandonment of Conrad's alliance with the church against the dukes.

Henry designated his eldest son, Otto I the Great, as his successor in 929. Since Henry could have divided the kingdom among his sons only by dispossessing the dukes, he procured the magnates' consent by accepting the indivisibility of the realm and the existence of the separate stem duchies. The kingdom was never again divided among a king's sons. After Henry's death on 2 July 936, the Franks and Saxons elected Otto as their ruler. The formal election occurred at Aachen on 7 August. On this occasion the lay princes paid homage to Otto after placing him on a specially constructed throne in the portico of the Church of St. Mary. He was received inside the church by Archbishop Hildebert of Mainz, who asked the people to approve Otto's election by their acclamation. Hildebert, assisted by Archbishop Wikfried of Cologne, then anointed and crowned Otto and placed him on the throne of Charlemagne. The festivites ended with a banquet in the palace, during which the dukes performed the ceremonial court offices.

This carefully planned ceremony was, as the choice of Aachen shows, a programmatic revival of the Carolingian legacy, which may have been designed to win the permanent allegiance of the recently annexed duchy of Lorraine. Aachen was until the end of the Middle Ages the coronation city of the German kings. Otto II and Otto III were designated by their fathers and subsequently elected and crowned during their fathers' lifetimes (Otto II was already dead when Otto III was crowned, but this was not known at the time).

Otto III, the last male member of the senior branch of the Saxon dynasty, died in 1002; he was succeeded by his nearest agnate kinsman, Duke Henry of Bavaria, the grandson of Otto's brother. Two princes who were not of royal blood had been serious candidates, and Henry II won the support of the Saxons by promising to respect their rights. His promise was the first in a long series of electoral capitulations that later transformed the election of a German king into an auction. The circumstances surrounding Henry's accession suggest that while royal blood was a major factor in the choice of a king, the final decision lay with the magnates.

The same situation can be observed following Henry's death without an heir in 1024. According to Wipo, Conrad II's biographer, the princes had initially considered a number of candidates; but their choice narrowed to Conrad II the Salian and Conrad of Carinthia, who were descended on the distaff side from Otto I. The impasse ended when the latter Conrad deferred to the founder of the Salian dynasty. A formal election was then held, in which Archbishop Aribo of Mainz cast the first vote, and Conrad exercised his royal authority immediately after his election. Wipo's report offers the earliest evidence for the casting of individual votes in what became known in the thirteenth century as the *Kur.* This was the public, and originally unanimous, election of the previously selected candidate. The *Kur* gradually replaced homage as the decisive electoral act that initiated a king's reign. It is generally believed that the Germans borrowed this procedure from France, but recent research indicates that the reverse may be true.

The *Kur* was employed in the Salian period only during a free election—that is, when the candidate was not the king's son. Conrad procured Henry III's succession without difficulty, but there was some opposition to Henry IV's elevation, reflecting the growing discontent with the Salians' assertion of royal authority. This opposition reached its climax with the election of the antiking, Rudolf of Rheinfelden (also known as Rudolf of Swabia), at Forchheim in March 1077. Rudolf promised that his son, no matter how worthy, would have no claim to the throne; instead, the magnates would be free to elect the worthiest candidate. This rejection of blood right and the introduction of the principle of suitability, derived from canon law, into the electoral proceedings were harbingers of later developments.

The election of Lothair II in 1125 was another milestone in the triumph of the elective principle. Duke Frederick II of Swabia, the son of the sister of the last Salian king, Henry V, was the leading candidate. When Frederick refused to promise in advance to obey whoever was elected—that is to renounce his blood claims to the crown—Archbishop Adalbert of Mainz secured Lothair's selection.

The pendulum seemed to swing back in favor of blood right with the election of the first of the Hohenstaufen kings, Conrad III, but his selection bears many of the attributes of a coup aimed against Lothair's son-in-law, Henry the Proud, who would have been a powerful king. Moreover, Conrad, the younger brother of Duke Frederick II, was succeeded by his nephew Frederick Barbarossa rather than by his son, and Henry VI may have been Barbarossa's second son. The princes thus asserted their

electoral rights even when they elected a Hohenstaufen. The *Kur,* which had previously been used only in a free election, became the customary form in all elections during the Hohenstaufen period.

After Pope Adrian IV suggested, in a letter read at the Diet of Besançon (1157), that the empire was a papal fief, Frederick Barbarossa replied that he owed his imperial crown, which he held in fief from God, to his election by the princes. Frederick's acknowledgment of the princes' electoral rights was the first official declaration that election as king of Germany created a substantive claim to the imperial dignity. He also indicated that the archbishop of Mainz had cast the first vote and that the archbishop of Cologne had crowned the king, a privilege first recognized by Pope Leo IX in 1052. Frederick's son Henry VI tried to transform Germany into a hereditary monarchy to assure the permanent union of the empire with Sicily, but in 1196 princely and papal opposition forced him to abandon the proposal and to accept as a partial compensation the election of his two-year-old son, Frederick II.

Innocent III's intervention after the election of Philip of Swabia and Otto IV was a direct response to this Hohenstaufen conception of the imperial dignity and to the threat that the unification of Italy under a single ruler posed to papal independence. Innocent expressed his views in the *Deliberatio,* a memorandum presented to the papal consistory at the end of 1200, and in *Venerabilem* (1202), a decretal that became part of canon law. Since the papacy had conferred on the princes the right to elect the future emperor when it transferred the empire from the Greeks in the East to the Franks in the West, Innocent argued that the pope had the right to judge the suitability of the candidate he crowned as emperor.

This was especially true in the case of a disputed election. To justify his recognition of Otto, who had been elected by a minority of the princes, Innocent adopted the argument of the Welf party that the right to elect the king belonged to certain princes in particular. Innocent mentioned by name only Otto's chief supporter, the archbishop of Cologne, but he appears also to have had in mind the two other Rhenish archbishops (of Trier and Cologne) and the count palatine of the Rhine. Since Philip had ignored the electoral rights of these princes by his premature election, this election was invalid. The pope's insistence that the validity of an election was dependent on the participation of certain electors at a specified time and place was a deliberate application of the procedures used in an episcopal election to the election of a German king.

Although in the *Sachsenspiegel,* the codification of Saxon law written about 1220, Eike von Repgowe recognized the right of all the princes to be consulted in the selection of the candidate, he stated that the actual *Kur* belonged to only six princes: the archbishops of Cologne, Mainz, and Trier, the count palatine of the Rhine, the duke of Saxony, and the margrave of Brandenburg. The archbishops' votes were founded in the traditional role they played in the elevation of a monarch, but it is less apparent why Eike regarded the participation of the three lay electors as crucial. He linked the presence of the lay electors to their ceremonial court offices, though the connection is far from clear, but excluded the king of Bohemia, the imperial butler, because he was a non-German. Eike's Saxon pride may provide the best explanation for the inclusion of the two most powerful north German princes.

The procedure Eike described was employed in the election of Conrad IV in 1237, the first election that occurred after the composition of the *Sachsenspiegel.* Eleven princes participated the first time that all nonprinces were excluded; but only the votes of the four electors present were considered to be of decisive importance.

There was general agreement by the middle of the thirteenth century that a candidate required the votes of at least four electors, but the identity of the potential electors was not yet fixed. Henry Raspe, the landgrave of Thuringia, provided the fourth vote at his own election in 1246, while the duke of Brabant joined the three archbishops in electing William of Holland in 1247. The Saxon cities refused to recognize William as king until the duke of Saxony and the margrave of Brandenburg had given him their votes in a supplementary election in 1252, but both William and Innocent IV regarded William's initial election as valid.

In the double election of 1257, the archbishops of Cologne and Mainz and the count palatine voted for Richard of Cornwall, while Trier, Saxony, and Brandenburg elected Alfonso X of Castile; Ottokar II of Bohemia voted for both. This double election is of constitutional significance because it marked the first time that the right to elect a king was restricted to the seven princes who formed the college of electors (*Kurkollegium* in German) until 1648. It appears that the *Kur* was restricted to these seven electors because they were the most powerful German princes in the middle of the thirteenth century. The identity of the

seventh elector remained, however, in dispute. Duke Henry of Bavaria cast the seventh vote at the election of Rudolf I of Habsburg in 1273, but in 1289 Rudolf confirmed the electoral rights of the king of Bohemia because the recognition of the Bavarian claim would have given two votes to the Wittelsbachs, who were also the counts palatine.

The double election of 1314 occurred because the Saxon and Bohemian votes were in dispute. After Louis the Bavarian had defeated his rival, Frederick the Fair of Austria, in 1322, Pope John XXII threatened to excommunicate Louis for assuming the royal title without papal approbation after a divided election and for exercising royal authority in Italy as well as Germany. Louis responded in a series of appeals that a king who had been elected by a majority of the electors was fully empowered to govern. The electors, whose own rights were threatened by the pope, supported Louis's position in the Declaration of Rhens (16 July 1338). Louis went a step further, and in the imperial law *Licet iuris,* promulgated on 6 August, proclaimed that the duly elected German king required no papal confirmation to exercise all imperial rights.

To prevent any further controversies, Charles IV codified the traditional electoral procedures in the Golden Bull of 1356. The archbishop of Mainz was to summon the electors to Frankfurt, which had become the customary site for elections in the twelfth century, and was to preside at the proceedings. A majority was required for election, and votes could be cast by proctors. The electors' special privileges and territorial supremacy were recognized, and the lay electorates were declared to be indivisible principalities inherited by primogeniture. The latter provision was designed to stop the type of argument about electoral votes that had led to the double election of 1314. The Golden Bull did not mention the pope's right of approbation or the king's imperial authority, but the stipulation that the king was to confirm the electors' privileges immediately after his election implied that his reign began with his election. Once the electors' rights had been firmly established, they could accept a son's succession without endangering their own position, and Germany became in fact, though not in law, a hereditary monarchy.

BIBLIOGRAPHY

Charles C. Bayley, *The Formation of the German College of Electors in the Mid-thirteenth Century* (1949, repr. 1980); *Die Goldene Bulle Kaiser Karls IV. vom Jahre 1356,*

Wolfgang D. Fritz, ed., in *Monumenta Germaniae historica, Fontes iuris Germanici antiqui in usum scholarum,* XI (1972); Eduard Hlawitschka, ed., *Königswahl und Thronfolge in ottonisch-frühdeutscher Zeit* (1971) and *Königswahl und Thronfolge in fränkisch-karolingischer Zeit* (1975); Hellmut Kämpf, ed., *Die Entstehung des deutschen Reiches (Deutschland um 900)* (1956); Heinrich Mitteis, *Die deutsche Königswahl,* 2nd ed. (1944, repr. 1965); Roswitha Reisinger, *Die römisch-deutschen Könige und ihre Wähler 1198–1273* (1977); Ulrich Reuling, "Die Kur in Deutschland und Frankreich," in *Veröffentlichungen des Max-Planck-Instituts für Geschichte,* 64 (1979).

JOHN B. FREED

[See also **Carolingians and the Carolingian Empire; Eike von Repgowe; Frederick I Barbarossa; Germany; Hohenstaufen Dynasty; Innocent III, Pope; Otto I the Great; Otto III of Germany; Sachsenspiegel.**]

ELEONORE OF AUSTRIA (1433–1480), the daughter of James I of Scotland, was raised in France, married Duke Siegmund of Tyrol in 1448, and was regent in his absence (1455–1458 and 1467). With her husband she shared an interest in literary matters (and little else). George of Ehingen reports of the splendor of her court, Hermann von Sachsenheim refers to her, and Heinrich Steinhöwel dedicated his version of Boccaccio's *De mulieribus claris* to her in 1473.

Of the two German translations of *Ponthus et la belle Sidoyne* (ascribed to Geoffrey de La Tour Landry), a late-fourteenth-century prose reworking of the twelfth-century Anglo-Norman chanson de geste *Horn et Rimenhild,* hers (*ca.* 1456) was the only successful one. It was first printed in 1483 in Augsburg and was printed three more times in the fifteenth century, nine times in the sixteenth, six in the seventeenth, and twice in the eighteenth. *Pontus und Sidonia* has more affinities to the courtly romances that became popular in prose versions in the fifteenth and sixteenth centuries than to the sparse, rather crude prose renditions of chansons de geste also popular in France and Germany. Eleonore may have been moved to make her translation by the example of Elisabeth of Nassau-Saarbrücken, but her style and the elegance of the work she selected suggest more refined sensibilities.

The approach that Norbert Thomas chooses for discussing motifs and narrative structures uncovers basic similarities between the works of the two women and other comparable early novels (such as *Die schöne Magelone*); its limitations become evident when *Pontus und Sidonia* is compared with *Herpin* or *Hug Schapler.* Thomas is following the lead of the Romanists in downplaying distinctions between epic and romance (for instance, mass actions versus individual fates), but an acknowledgment that *Pontus und Sidonia* should not be equated blindly with the narrative of Elisabeth is also pertinent to a discussion of these works (and, for example, Thüring von Ringoltingen's *Melusine*) as chapbooks (*Volksbücher*). The popularity of a chapbook was clearly not determined by its proximity to the aspirations and problems of a newly prominent middle class. The authors were, of course, writing for their own courtly audience. The posthumous early editions of *Pontus und Sidonia* were not intended for a large general audience but rather for the wealthy and discriminating. A comparison of the manuscripts of Eleonore's translation with the French original remains to be done.

BIBLIOGRAPHY

Heinz Kindermann, ed., *Volksbücher vom sterbenden Rittertum* (1928), 115–236; M. Köfler, *Eleonore von Schotland: Versuch einer Biographie* (diss. Univ. Innsbruck, 1968); Norbert Thomas, *Handlungsstruktur und dominante Motivik im deutschen Prosaroman des 15. und frühen 16. Jahrhunderts* (1971); Hans-Hugo Steinhoff, "Eleonore von Österreich (Eleonore Stuart, Eleonore von Schottland)," in *Die deutsche Literatur des Mittelalters: Verfasserlexikon,* 2nd ed., II (1978), 470–473.

HUBERT HEINEN

[See also **Elisabeth of Nassau-Saarbrücken; German Romance.**]

ELEOUSA (Greek, "merciful" or "compassionate"), an image of the Virgin Mary holding the Christ child on her right arm, gesturing toward him with her left, and inclining her head to him. Christ grasps his mother around her neck and presses his cheek to hers. The Eleousa developed in Byzantium from the Hodegetria and was popular from the eleventh century on; by the twelfth century the type had spread throughout Europe. Originally, the Virgin was apparently shown full-length (as at the Kariye Camii in Istanbul), either seated or standing, but half-length figures are also common: one outstanding example is the Virgin of Vladimir, a Constantinopolitan product of 1131. In some late examples (often Italian), Christ stands on his seated mother's knee.

Eleousa. The Virgin of Vladimir, Constantinople, early 12th century (now in the Dormition Cathedral, Moscow Kremlin). SOVFOTO 1970/23/1

BIBLIOGRAPHY

Victor Lasareff, "Studies in the Iconography of the Virgin," in *Art Bulletin,* **20** (1938).

LESLIE BRUBAKER

ELEVATION OF THE HOLY CROSS, a major Byzantine liturgical feast, celebrated at Hagia Sophia on 14 September and preceded by at least four days of preliminary activities, which honored the relic of the True Cross found by St. Helena. The patriarch mounted the ambo with the relic, knelt before it, then raised the cross before the congregation three times. Pictures of the ceremony, showing the patriarch raising the cross on the ambo or, more fancifully, above the cavern where Helena was supposed to have discovered it, appear from the eleventh century on, reflecting the increased interest in liturgi-

Elevation of the Holy Cross. The menologion of Basil II, late 10th century. BIBLIOTECA APOSTOLICA VATICANA, CODEX GRAEC. 1613, p. 35

cally inspired art during the Middle Byzantine period.

BIBLIOGRAPHY

Juan Mateos, *Le typicon de la Grande Église,* I (1962), 24–33; Kurt Weitzmann, "Byzantine Miniature and Icon Painting in the Eleventh Century," in *Proceedings of the XIIIth International Congress of Byzantine Studies* (1967), 218–219, repr. in his *Studies in Classical and Byzantine Manuscript Illumination* (1971), 294–295.

LESLIE BRUBAKER

[See also **Liturgy, Byzantine Church.**]

ELIAS OF DEREHAM. See **Nicholas of Ely.**

ELIDIR SAIS (*fl.* 1195–1246), Welsh poet. His floruit is determined by the fact that he composed elegies on prince Rhodri ab Owain Gwynedd (*d.* 1195) and Ednyfed Fychan (*d.* 1246). Elidir belonged to the great school of Welsh poets sometimes called the Poets of Princes because they flourished during the revival of Welsh independence under the native princes after the initial attacks of the Normans had been beaten back. The school is also called the *Gogynfeirdd* (sing.: *Gogynfardd*), that is, the poets who succeed the *Cynfeirdd* or the poets of the earliest period of Welsh literature. The second designation is more apt because the *Gogynfeirdd* consciously modeled their work on that of their predecessors. Although they were primarily learned craftsmen whose intense conservatism apparently led them to eschew all originality of theme and treatment, the *Gogynfeirdd,* by taking the vocabulary and themes of the *Cynfeirdd* as material that they had to rework, elaborate, and refine, succeeded in tightening and developing bardic technique. They also achieved poetic effects not found elsewhere except in the work of similar schools of poetry such as that of the Icelandic skalds. All this is reflected in the way Elidir is praised by a later *Gogynfardd* who tells us that he was a true standard *(iawn ganon),* a phrase in itself evocative of the school's ideal. That Elidir Sais was at one stage a typical court poet is proved by the poems he composed for the noblemen mentioned above. He must have composed many others that are now lost. It has been assumed that he was the son of the court poet Gwalchmai and the brother of the poets Meilyr and Einon ap Gwalchmai; the latter seems to be corroborated by the description of him as "one of the wise men of Anglesey." But he was atypical in some respects. He was called "Sais," Englishman. This suggests that he knew English or that he had spent some time in England. Such a foreign sojourn, especially for a court poet, presupposes banishment. We know that Elidir displeased Llywelyn the Great, for he wrote a reconciliation or appeasement *(dadolwch),* a poem to appease that prince. It is not difficult to guess the reason for Llywelyn's displeasure. The poet disapproved of his sovereign's expansionist policies, which seems to exclude the assumption that he may have earned the epithet "Sais" by serving as an emissary to the English court. A period of residence in England would, however, explain two features displayed in his poetry. He gives the impression that he is much better informed than his fellow poets: he is the first to quote the name of a hero found in Geoffrey of Monmouth's *Historia regum Britanniae,* and he compares the confiscation of Dafydd ab Owain Gwynedd's land to the rape of Jerusalem by Saladin. Moreover, if we take literally his words, "I shall be a poet to God while I am a man," he seems deliberately to have broken with the tradition of composing panegyrics to the nobility. He may have come under the influence of the English devotional lyric that began to flourish in the thirteenth century, for unlike the religious poetry of some of his contemporaries who modeled their praise of God on that of the princes, Elidir's work exhibits a truly religious and

devotional feeling. In one poem *(I'r Grawys)* he seems to have structured a Lenten meditation on the days of the week.

BIBLIOGRAPHY

John Gwenogvryn Evans, ed., *The Poetry in the Red Book of Hergest* (1911), 1143–1146; Owen Jones, Edward Williams, William Owen Pughe, eds., *The Myvyrian Archaiology of Wales,* 2nd ed. (1870), 240*b*–245*b*; Henry Lewis, ed., *Hen Gerddi Crefyddol* (1931), xxvii–xxxii. Also J. Lloyd-Jones, "The Court Poets of the Welsh Princes," in *Proceedings of the British Academy,* 34 (1948).

J. E. CAERWYN WILLIAMS

[See also **Welsh Literature.**]

ELIS SAGA OK ROSAMUNDU. The tale of Elis and Rosamunda is a translated *riddarasaga* (tale of chivalry) dating from around the second quarter of the thirteenth century. At the request of King Hákon (or Haakon) Hákonarson of Norway (1217–1263), a certain Abbot Robert translated *Élie de St. Gille,* a French chanson de geste, into Norwegian. Abbot Robert is thought to have been the same person as the Brother Robert who had translated Thomas' Anglo-Norman *Tristan* (as *Tristrams saga ok Ísöndar*) in the year 1226, also at the behest of King Hákon.

The content of the Norwegian *Elis saga* is as follows: At a festive banquet the aging and mighty Duke Julien of France publicly chides his son Elis for behavior that is more becoming to a monk in a cloister than to a young man old enough to be knighted. Aroused to anger, Elis jousts admirably and is dubbed knight, but then he refuses to accept the honors his father now wants to bestow on him. Instead, Elis leaves the court and soon enters on a career of warfare against heathen forces. He is captured by King Malkabrez, who is impressed enough by Elis' bearing and good looks to promise him his daughter Rosamunda in marriage, provided Elis renounces the Christian faith. This Elis refuses to do, and he miraculously manages to escape in full view of the king and his men. Nonetheless, Elis later finds himself once more in the environs of his enemy's stronghold, where he is attacked and left wounded. He is secretly taken by Rosamunda to her quarters, and there he is granted rest, healing, and her love. In the end Elis triumphs. As Rosamunda's champion he vanquishes the old King Juben, the archenemy of Malkabrez.

The manuscript from which Abbot Robert translated was defective. The translation ends with Rosamunda's promise to become a Christian. The translator informs us, however, that Elis and Rosamunda had yet to endure a number of tribulations before they could begin their journey home to France, but that his source is silent in this regard.

Elis saga is found in nine pre-Reformation manuscripts or fragments and in over thirty paper manuscripts, some as recent as the nineteenth century. The oldest and most important manuscript is the Norwegian codex De la Gardie 4–7 (*ca.* 1250) preserved in the University Library at Uppsala. This manuscript also contains the *Strengleikar*, a Norwegian translation of a group of lais, some of which have been attributed to Marie de France. There are three primary Icelandic manuscripts: Codex Holm. perg. 6, quarto; Codex Holm. perg. 7, fol.; and AM 533, quarto. The first two date from the beginning of the fifteenth century and are in the Royal Library in Stockholm; the third dates from after 1450 and is in the Arnamagnaean Institute, Copenhagen.

Although Abbot Robert's translation concludes with chapter 50 in DG 4–7, the Icelandic manuscripts contain a continuation that deviates considerably from the conclusion of the chanson de geste. In the latter, Elis is not permitted to marry Rosamunda because he became her godfather when she was baptized. In the Icelandic continuation all ends well. The lovers marry, and in typical saga fashion the tale concludes with a brief report about the couple's children. The continuation is an invention of an Icelandic redactor. It was not unusual for Icelandic scribes either to abridge or to expand texts they were supposed to be copying. Here the Icelandic redactor went so far as to repeat almost verbatim passages from the Norwegian translation, such as the description of Rosamunda's garments.

Elis saga ok Rosamundu is characterized by a repetitiveness with variation that derives in part from its source but is in part also a stylistic characteristic of most of the works translated during Hákon's time. On the whole, the Old Norse-Icelandic versions of longer French works are characterized by considerable condensation, the result primarily of excision of reduplicative passages. *Elis saga* departs somewhat from this practice in that the translator follows the pattern of the *laisses similaires* of his source by repeating with variation similar material

in subsequent chapters. Not infrequently, alliterating clusters result in a stately, rhythmic language, the effect of which is not unlike that of verse.

BIBLIOGRAPHY

For the text of *Elis saga*, see Eugen Kölbing, ed., *Elis saga ok Rosamundu* (1881); Mattias Tveitane, ed., *Elis saga, Strengleikar and Other Texts* (1972); Bjarni Vilhjálmsson, ed., "Elis saga og Rósamundu," in *Riddarasögur*, IV (1954).

The translations are: "La saga d'Elie," Eugen Kölbing, trans., in Gaston Raynaud, ed., *Élie de Saint Gille: Chanson de geste* (1879), and "Die Geschichte von Elis und Rosamunda," Eugen Kölbing, trans., in Eugen Kölbing, ed., *Elis saga ok Rosamundu* (1881).

MARIANNE E. KALINKE

[See also **Chansons de Geste; Riddarasögur.**]

ELISABETH OF NASSAU-SAARBRÜCKEN (*ca.* 1397–1456). The daughter of Frederick V of Lorraine and Margaret of Vaudémont and Joinville, Elisabeth married Philip I of Nassau-Saarbrücken in 1412 and after his death in 1429 was regent until her sons succeeded her (Philip II in 1438; John in 1442). She had literary connections with Nancy through her uncle Charles I of Lorraine, with Paris through her brother Anton (an associate of Charles of Orléans) and her son John, and with Heidelberg through Mechthild of Rottenburg. Her mother had had four chansons de geste copied in 1405, and in the mid 1430's Elisabeth followed contemporary fashion by retelling these in prose—but in German rather than in French.

The first of her works was a translation of *Lion de Bourges* with some deletions and a tendency to downplay erotic scenes, a reticence also found in her other retellings. Several manuscripts of this work exist, and some six printings. In the nineteenth century it acquired the title *Herpin*. *Sibille* is a prose reworking of *Reine Sebile* based on an original that has been transmitted only in fragments. *Loher und Maller* is based on a lost chanson of the fourteenth century; a Middle Dutch version also exists. *Sibille* did not become a chapbook (*Volksbuch*), and *Loher und Maller* seems to have been rapidly forgotten, but the fourth of Elisabeth's prose renditions was quite popular, though it is arguably inferior as a narrative to *Herpin* and *Sibille*. *Huge Scheppel* (as a chapbook,

Hug Schapler) retells *Huges Capet* fairly freely, though there are echoes of the laisses of the original, and Elisabeth apparently tried to give her audience the flavor of the courtly original.

In the first translation there is a strange comment that Herpin's son is really called Löw in order for the song to rhyme better. Perhaps this was intended as an "in" joke for those at court with enough French to catch the point *(lion : chanson)*. In part, at least, Elisabeth would have been writing for a listening audience, and the frequent references to what they will hear or have heard need not be considered clumsy relics of an oral original inappropriate to a written text. To be sure, even the original, for her, was primarily a written text. She apparently revised her translations shortly before her death, using new texts of the chansons brought from Paris.

These four texts are important not only as products of French literary tradition but also as a part of the development of the *Volksbuch*.

BIBLIOGRAPHY

Sources. Marie-Luise Linn, ed., *Hug Schapler. Ein liepliches lesen und ein warhafftige Hystorij* (1974); Hermann Tiemann, ed., *Der Roman von der Königin Sibille in drei Prosafassungen des 14. und 15. Jahrhunderts* (1977).

Studies. Hans-Hugo Steinhoff, "Elisabeth von Nassau-Saarbrücken," in *Die deutsche Literatur des Mittelalters. Verfasserlexikon,* 2nd ed., II (1978), 482–488; Norbert Thomas, *Handlungsstruktur und dominante Motivik im deutschen Prosaroman des 15. und frühen 16. Jahrhunderts* (1971).

HUBERT HEINEN

[See also **German Lyric; German Romance**.]

EŁIŠĒ (probably *fl.* late fifth century). To Ełišē is attributed the *History of Vardan and the Armenian War,* one of the great classics of Armenian literature. The hero of this work remains a prominent figure in Armenian tradition to the present time. The *History of Vardan* describes the revolt for religious freedom in 450–451 of those Armenians living in the Iranian sector of Armenia. Although Vardan and many of his supporters were killed in the final battle of the war (at Avarayr on the day before Pentecost in 451), the Armenian resistance led the shah to accord tolerance for Christianity.

There has been much debate about the authorship of this *History* and the date of its composition. Ełišē claims to have been an eyewitness to the events he describes, but such claims are common in early Armenian historical writing. The text quotes Armenian translations of various foreign writers, including Philo, whose works were translated later than the fifth century. Nersēs Akinean thought that this *History* was the reworking of a (now lost) description of the revolt of 571–574, also led by a Vardan of the Mamikonean family. But no evidence for a shorter, earlier text has ever come to light.

The revolt of 450 is also described in the *History* of Łazar Pcarpecci, but Ełišē's account is longer and different in many respects. It shows significant use of the Armenian text of the Books of Maccabees, both as a general model and as the specific source of numerous details. Also important for Ełišē was the Armenian version of Syriac texts describing the martyrdoms of several fourth-century Syrian Christians in Iran. Like Łazar, Ełišē appends to his *History* the story of Armenian prisoners exiled to eastern Iran and the martyrdom of several clergymen there.

Ełišē's work is unique in Armenian literature for the use of letters and speeches in the classical mold. It is not so much a straightforward description of events as an exposition of moral and religious choices set in the framework of an epic struggle wherein idealized portraits of patriots and religious heroes are contrasted with those of apostates and traitors.

Also attributed to Ełišē are various homilies; these have no proved connection with the *History* and their author, who may or may not be the same as the author of the *History*, remains unknown.

BIBLIOGRAPHY

The *History* of Ełišē was first printed in Constantinople in 1764. Since then there have been numerous editions, but the only critical one is by Eruand Ter-Minasean, *Elishēi, Vasn Vardanay ew Hayocc Paterazmin* (1957). This contains a full bibliography of previous editions, translations, and studies. For those homilies attributed to Ełišē that have been printed see *Elishēi Vardapeti Matenagrut'iwnk'* (1859).

The most recent translation is by Robert W. Thomson, *Eḷishē: History of Vardan and the Armenian War* (1982). The introduction contains a full discussion of Eḷišē's sources and of his historical methods.

For general studies of the *History* see Babgen Kiwleserean, *Eḷišē* (1909), and Nersēs Akinean, *Elisäus Vardapet und seine Geschichte des armenischen Krieges,* 3 vols. (1932–1960), with summaries in German for vols. I and II.

For the homilies attributed to Ełišē see *Elisée Vardapet: Questions et réponses sur la Génèse,* S. Kogian, trans. (1928), and the bibliography in Stanislas Lyonnet, *Les origines de la version arménienne et le Diatessaron* (1950).

R. W. THOMSON

[See also Łazar P^carpec^ci; Vardan Mamikonean, St.]

ELUCIDARIUM AND SPANISH LUCIDARIO.

Consisting of three books composed in Latin around the beginning of the twelfth century and generally attributed to Honorius Augustodunensis (*fl.* first half of twelfth century), the *Elucidarium* is a virtual compendium of popular medieval thought. Structured as a dialogue between a master and his pupil, the principal aim of this text was not to address major philosophical and theological issues but to provide simple and reassuring answers to the most basic and common questions that might arise among Christian clergy and laity. Its tone and content therefore tend to be oversimplified, dogmatic, and doctrinaire. Questions posed by the pupil are summarily dispatched by the master with concise and easily understood explanations that reflect the basic duality of medieval logic. Most medievals were quite capable of visually constructing and mentally accepting two diametrically opposed points of view because they knew that all phenomena could be explained either by the terrestrial laws of nature, the *lex naturalis,* or by the spiritual laws of God, the *lex theologiae.*

The *Elucidarium* was a highly effective catechistic tool. Its vast popularity is confirmed by its translation into all major European languages, and it survives in hundreds of manuscripts, most of them as yet unedited. Between the twelfth and fifteenth centuries this little treatise set the standards of Christian orthodoxy for those confronted by such questions as "What is the nature of the sun and the moon?" "Where was God before he made Heaven and Earth?" "How could the Virgin Mary have remained a virgin after giving birth to Christ?" "Why did Christ wish to die at age thirty-three?" "Will the Antichrist have a guardian angel?" and "Why did God make the world if he wanted it to end one day?" These and similar queries pertaining to cosmogony, cosmography, or Christology were more efficaciously resolved by referring to the *Elucidarium* than by reading one of the intricate and convoluted explanations found in the more elaborate scientific tomes of the Scholastics. The *Elucidarium* was pop-

ular precisely because it avoided ambiguity and the need for critical acumen. It was conventional, dogmatic, direct, and always undemanding of its audience.

With its encyclopedic, digestlike approach to knowledge, the *Elucidarium* soon expanded its contents through successive translations in the vernacular and, in time, covered not only theology but also natural history, zoology, and biology. At this point the original *Elucidarium* became the *Lucydary, Lucidaire,* or *Lucidario,* enlarged with topics derived from the works of Aristotle, Pliny, Solinus, and early medievals such as Isidore of Seville, Bede, and Albertus Magnus. Questions now ranged from "How does the spider spin its web?" and "Why are all men different?" to the more commonplace and often entertaining answers given to "Why do the flea and the louse, which are small, have many legs while large animals, such as the horse and elephant, have only four?" and "How was the whale able to swallow Jonah if its mouth is so small?" Some questions reveal uniquely national concerns: in the Castilian translation composed around 1293 under the auspices of Sancho IV are questions germane to the Iberian Peninsula, such as "Why does it damage trees to strip off their bark but not the cork tree?"

The evolutionary process that radically expanded and enriched the original Latin *Elucidarium* was equally visible throughout the vernacular translations, which, over time, added chapters of national and ethnic information, including matters of interest to those who reproduced the work, so that very few manuscripts are exact copies. The Castilian translations of the *Elucidarium,* four from the fifteenth century and one from the early sixteenth century, provide a succinct overview of the evolutionary process described by Yves Lefèvre, showing that neither the original order of the Latin text nor the questions themselves were respected by patron or scribe. When Sancho IV commissioned the original thirteenth-century translation of the Latin *Elucidarium,* he clearly felt no qualms about supplementing its contents with chapters on topics of interest to his audience. Thus, at this juncture the title *Lucidario* must have become synonymous with the act of elucidation; every example that might shed light on questions of natural or spiritual import was now a legitimate subject for inclusion in the text.

If the character of an age may be best assessed through a study of its minor works—those reflecting the concerns of the masses as opposed to the lasting, transcendent works of the period—then a study of the *Elucidarium* is certainly justified, for it faithfully profiles those questions that concerned the common man. For that same reason the *Elucidarium* dropped from sight with the coming of the Renaissance and the Reformation, in which the new emphasis on individual research and analysis was contrary to the spirit and doctrines of this essentially medieval exposition. The simplicity and dogmatism of the *Elucidarium* and its vernacular progeny militated against them in an age of middle-class values and greater intellectual sophistication.

BIBLIOGRAPHY

The best critical edition and study of the history and influence of the *Elucidarium* is Yves Lefèvre, *L'Elucidarium et les lucidaires* (1954). For a review of work on the French *Elucidaire,* with a current bibliography since Lefèvre, see Henning Düwell, ed., *Eine altfranzösische Übersetzung des Elucidarium* (1974). A valuable related study prior to Lefèvre is Karl Schorbach, *Studien über das deutsche Volksbuch Lucidarius* (1894). On Honorius see P. Rousset, "À propos de l'Elucidarium d'Honorius Augustodunensis: Quelques problèmes d'histoire ecclésiastique," in *Zeitschrift für schweizer Kirchengeschichte,* 52 (1958). For a critical edition and study of the Spanish *Lucidarios,* see Richard P. Kinkade, *Los "Lucidarios" españoles* (1968).

R. P. KINKADE

[See also **Encyclopedias and Dictionaries, Western European; Honorius Augustodunensis.**]

Reliquary of the True Cross. Wood and copper, engraved, enameled, and gilded, with silver repoussé and émail brun work; Mosan region, ca. 1200. BRUSSELS, MUSÉES ROYAUX D'ART ET D'HISTOIRE

ÉMAIL BRUN, a metalworking technique described by Theophilus (*De diversis artibus,* III, 71) and favored by Mosan artisans wherein a coat of linseed oil is heated on a copper sheet until it turns deep brown or black, a design is scraped away, and the revealed copper is gilded. The design, usually a floral pattern, thus stands out against the dark brown ground.

BIBLIOGRAPHY

Theophilus, *On Divers Arts,* John G. Hawthorne and Cyril S. Smith, trans. (1963), 147–148.

LESLIE BRUBAKER

[See also **Metalworkers; Theophilus.**]

EMBER DAYS. The current practice of designating the Wednesdays, Fridays, and Saturdays following the first Sunday in Lent, Pentecost, the feast of the Holy Cross (14 September), and St. Lucy's Day (13 December) as days of fasting, almsgiving, and prayer was established for the Western church as a whole by Gregory VII in 1078.

The custom of observing the *quattuor temporum* was, however, much older in Rome, England, and France. Perhaps the most general consensus of recent scholars is that the origins of these four annual fasts are not known, but that similar seasonal observances in both Jewish and pagan antiquity may have provided the ground from which the Christian practice grew. The spirit of penitential purification and the connection of the fasts with the agricultural year seem to be common elements in both ancient non-

Christian and early Christian practices. In the fifth century Pope Leo I, who preached a number of sermons for these seasons of fasting, described the practice as ancient. He urged the faithful to observe these seasons of spiritual renewal with fasting, prayer, and alms.

It is probable that Leo I considered Lent itself, and not a separate ember week during Lent, as the fourth period of fasting, since he does not seem to have preached a distinct series of sermons for a Lenten ember week. Other early documents, such as the *Liber pontificalis,* mention three, not four, festivals. At any rate, by the late sixth century there were four ember seasons, and the practice had been established of ordaining priests and deacons during those weeks.

The multiple purposes of ember weeks, and the fact that three of them fall within major festivals of the church—Advent, Lent, and the octave of Pentecost—have led to some variation in both dates of observance and liturgical practice. At first ember weeks were calculated according to the calendar. Even after Gregory VII established the modern practice, the older custom continued in some places.

Originally the observance of ember days was confined to the church in Rome, but gradually the practice was extended to other parts of Europe. St. Augustine of Canterbury brought the Roman practice to England. English monks introduced ember days into France during Carolingian times. The observance of ember days, or the "four seasons," continued to spread until it was established throughout most of the Western church in the eleventh century.

Throughout the Middle Ages the ember days retained their dual importance as times for purification and for ordination. Aelfric lists the Sundays after ember fasts among the sixteen times during the year when Christians of sufficiently righteous lives can take Communion.

It is not clear how the fasts called *quattuor temporum* in Latin and *quatre-temps* in French came to be called *Quatember* in German and *Ymbrenfæstenum* in Old English. John Mirk, writing early in the fifteenth century, says the term *ymbren* (embers) comes from the old custom of observing the fast by eating bread baked in ashes, reminding us that we never know when we will return to ashes.

BIBLIOGRAPHY

The most useful modern English discussion of ember days is by Geoffrey G. Willis in *Essays in Early Roman Liturgy* (1964), 51–97. See also Ludwig Fischer, *Die kirchlichen Quatember* (1914); Henri Leclercq, "Quatre-temps," in *Dictionnaire d'archéologie chrétienne et de liturgie,* XIV, pt. 2 (1948), 2014–2016; Gustave Morin, "L'origine des quatre-temps," in *Revue bénédictine,* **14** (1897); Thomas J. Talley, "The Development of Ember Days to the Time of Gregory VII" (diss., unpubl., General Theological Seminary, 1969).

KATHLEEN GREENFIELD

[See also **Fasting, Christian; Penance and Penitentials.**]

EMBRICHO OF MAINZ (*ca.* 1010–1077) was born at Mainz. As a cleric he soon distinguished himself by his erudition in many fields, and in 1064 he became bishop of Augsburg. As a young man Embricho was encouraged by a certain Godebald to write on the origins and early years of Islam. The result was the poem *Vita Mahumeti,* a 1,148-line work in distichs. It is perhaps the most stylistically polished of the numerous treatments of Islamic figures in the Middle Ages.

BIBLIOGRAPHY

Embricho of Mainz, *La vie de Mahomet,* Guy Cambier, ed. (1962); Max Manitius, *Geschichte der lateinischen Literatur des Mittelalters,* II (1923), 582–587. *Vita Mahumeti* is edited in *Patrologia latina,* CLXXI (1854), 1347.

EDWARD FRUEH

EMBROIDERY. See **Tapestry; Textiles.**

EMETERIUS OF TÁBARA, a scribe and/or illuminator who contributed to the Beatus commentaries executed at Tábara (León, Spain). The first was finished in 970 (Madrid, Archivo Histórico Nacional, Codex 1097B) and includes a depiction of the scriptorium of Tábara. The second, one of the outstanding manuscripts of the Mozarabic school, was completed in 975 and is in the archives of the cathedral of Gerona.

BIBLIOGRAPHY

Jesús Domínguez Bordona, *Spanish Illumination,* I (1930, repr. 1969); John Williams, *Early Spanish Manuscript Illumination* (1977), 92–99.

JOHN WILLIAMS

[See also Apocalypse, Illustration of; Beatus Manuscripts; Manuscript Illumination.]

EMHAIN MACHA. See Ulster.

EMIR, an Arabic term (sing., *amīr;* pl., *umarāʾ*) denoting a commander or military leader. Later it also designated a prince, governor, or tribal leader. Its initial meaning in the early Islamic community was army commander, and usually also the governor of the territory he conquered. In theory the caliph was the *amīr al-muʾmīnīn* (commander of the faithful).

Under the Abbasids (750–1258) the Persianization of the state machinery, the Turkicization of the military, and the growing autonomy of the provinces changed the emirate. Increasingly emirs (such as the Samanids of Transoxiana and the Ikhshidids of Egypt) became de facto independent rulers of large states while still bearing only this modest title.

In Turkic times "emir" was virtually interchangeable with "beg."

BIBLIOGRAPHY

Niẓām al-Mulk, *Siyāsat-nāma,* M. Qazvīnī and M. M. Chahārdihī, eds. (1956), trans. by Hubert Darke as *The Book of Government or Rules for Kings* (1960, rev. ed. 1978); Ann K. S. Lambton, "The Internal Structure of the Saljuq Empire," in John A. Boyle, ed., *The Cambridge History of Iran,* V (1968); Reuben Levy, *The Social Structure of Islam* (1957).

PETER B. GOLDEN

[See also Islamic Administration.]

EMMANUEL (Hebrew for "God is with us"), in art a youthful, beardless type of Christ derived from Isa. 7:14, "Behold, a virgin shall conceive and bear a son, and shall call his name Emmanuel." Isaiah's prophecy was connected with the description of the Logos from John 1:1; hence Christ Emmanuel signified the preexisting Logos or, at times, the incarnate Logos. With Christ Pantokrator and the Ancient of Days, the other two visual manifestations of Christ promoted in Byzantium, Christ Emmanuel was a representation of eternity.

BIBLIOGRAPHY

"Christus-Sondertypen," in *Lexikon der christlichen Ikonographie,* I (1968); André Grabar, "La représentation de l'intelligible dans l'art byzantin du moyen âge," in his *L'art de la fin de l'antiquité et du moyen âge,* I (1968), 51–62.

LESLIE BRUBAKER

[See also Ancient of Days; Pantokrator.]

ENAMEL (from late Latin *smaltum,* Frankish *smalt,* derived from Germanic *smaltjan* [modern German *schmelzen,* smelt]), applies to a variety of glass, a pulverized flux made of silica, borates, and alkalies, to which metallic oxides are added. It is fused by heat onto a base of gold, copper, or silver.

There were two main families of medieval enamel. Cloisonné enamels were the first form to appear, adapting the Byzantine cloisonné technique, culminating in masterpieces produced in the middle of the tenth century. In cloisonné, enamel pastes, which become translucent after firing, are poured into compartments separated by a pattern of gold strips soldered on a gold base. Cloisonné enamels were derived from "cold enamels," vitreous pastes held in fillets of gold and subsequently fused on a base. In Merovingian times they were called *opus sancti Eligii,* after St. Eligius (*ca.* 588–656). The principal work in this "cold" technique was Eligius' cross, destroyed in 1794 but formerly at St. Denis.

The connections between Byzantine and Western cloisonné enamel were complex. Early adaptation was evidenced by a round fibula from Comacchio, in Lombard territory near Byzantine Ravenna (now in Baltimore, Walters Art Gallery), and by the Frankish medallion of Christ from the Guelph Treasure (now in the Cleveland Museum of Art), a rare example of cloisonné on copper. The ewer of Charlemagne in the church treasure at St. Maurice d'Agaune, Switzerland, incorporated Byzantine enamels from an Avar scepter. Enamelers fleeing iconoclasm made the Beresford Hope cross (now in London, Victoria and Albert Museum) and, for Pope Paschal I (817–824), the reliquary cross now in the Vatican. The crown in Budapest was a gift from Emperor Michael VII to the wife of the Hungarian king Geza I (1074–1077). This Greek crown was subsequently transformed into a Latin crown of the Germanic closed type by the addition of two bands crossing above the diadem.

A reliquary of the true cross now in the Metropolitan Museum, New York (the Fieschi-Morgan Staurotheca), and enamels on the frame of a painted icon of the Virgin, now in S. Marco, Venice, were stolen during the looting of Constantinople by the participants in the Fourth Crusade of 1204, as was the reliquary of the true cross now in the cathedral at Limburg an der Lahn, a masterpiece of the imperial workshop dating from about 963. The Byzantine enameled reliquaries of the true cross, either imported during the tenth century or looted by the Franks in the thirteenth century, were copied in the West in triptychs. The Pala D'Oro in S. Marco, Venice, sums up the story of the fascination exerted by Byzantine cloisonné enamels. Its 137 enamels are partitioned in a bejeweled frame 2.10 meters (6.9 feet) by 3.5 meters (11.5 feet) made between 1343 and 1354. They were part of the altar commissioned at Constantinople in the early twelfth century, with additions of earlier enamels and of spoils brought after 1204 that entailed the restoration of the altar.

The second family of enamels was champlevé, obtained by scooping out of a bronze base compartments separated by strips. Opaque enamel was fused in the cavities. Enameling on bronze was first practiced by Celts in Britain and Gauls in Belgium. It was revived in the Mosan region of Lotharingia in the eleventh and twelfth centuries. Mosan produced a mixed technique that included cloisonné opaque enamel in champlevé areas. Occasionally the plaque was entirely covered with enamel: champlevé *en plein.*

Two other techniques of enameling were later used. In basse-taille (as of the second half of the thirteenth century), translucent enamel was fused on a silver or silver-gilt (rarely gold) base that had been chased in shallow relief and engraved. Various degrees of chromatic intensity were obtained by light refracting from a slightly undulating ground. In the second technique, encrusted enameling (as of the last quarter of the fourteenth century), white opaque enamel and semitranslucent or translucent enamels coated gold objects in the round.

Finally, there was a return to enamel painted on copper. Painted enamels are applied like pigments to a slightly domed plaque on which divisions are replaced by an underlying drawing.

Plite or plique-à-jour enamels were restricted to court art around 1300, but the technique was employed until the sixteenth century. They were difficult to execute, each tiny element of opaque enamel being self-contained within a cloison and held only by the ground of translucent enamel on gold. Benvenuto Cellini described the technique in his *Trattato dell'oreficeria.*

In his treatise *De diversis artibus* the German Benedictine monk Theophilus described the methods used in the early twelfth century for preparing *electrum,* a medieval term for *smaltum* (enamel). The enamels described by Theophilus, being of small dimensions, alternated with gems set between two pairs of pearls. A similar arrangement is found on the first cross of Matilda (*ca.* 973–982), now at Essen.

Some larger cloisonné enamels of the eleventh century have been preserved. In Lombardy they show a dependence on Regensburg as a center of precious arts: for instance, a book binding made for Aribert, archbishop of Milan. Elsewhere, Byzantine patterns were followed as in a pax at S. Lorenzo, Chiavenna, or completely assimilated together with their iconography, as in a cross in the cathedral at Velletri.

There was an extraordinary flowering of champlevé enamel during the twelfth century in the duchy of Aquitaine and in Lotharingia around Liège. The presence of works of considerable dimensions, such as the enameled tomb of S. Domingo of Silos and the altar of S. Miguel in Estella, Navarre, led to the contention that the champlevé enamels historically known as *opus lemovicense* were not *oeuvre de Limoges* but were created in northern Spain. That theory led to the more balanced view that before enamelers settled in Limoges around the end of the twelfth century, itinerant workshops moved among Le Mans, Conques, northern Spain, Italy, and Sicily. They were staffed by laymen rather than monks. One such atelier was active at Grandmont in the Limousin, a priory that was protected by Henry II and Richard I the Lionhearted. Plaques from the altar at Grandmont survive in the Musée de Cluny, Paris, and two crosses are in the Metropolitan Museum, New York, and the Cleveland Museum of Art. Until the destruction of the workshops by the Black Prince in 1371, the production of Limoges enamels remained considerable: more than 7,000 pieces have been assembled, the best being *à fond vermiculé* (a background marked with irregular fine lines or wavy palmette-like patterns) of 1190–1220.

Mosan enamels were also produced by laymen working by invitation in various ecclesiastical centers. The head of an itinerant workshop, Godefroid de Claire, worked at Stavelot for Abbot Wibald, at St. Denis for Abbot Suger, at St. Vanne of Verdun, in Germany, and in England. The St. Denis inventory records that the enameled pillar supporting a gold Christ crucified was covered with sixty-eight plaques representing the "types" symbolically announcing the Crucifixion in the Old Testament. The Klosterneuburg altar by Nicholas of Verdun (1181) survives as a monument of such "typological" iconography: fifteen enameled "antitypes" from the Annunciation to Pentecost are bracketed between fifteen "types" of the Old Testament before Moses and fifteen "types" after Moses.

After a short-lived attempt at enameling in champlevé on silver, Tuscany introduced a new goldsmith's art characterized by Giorgio Vasari as "a mixture of painting and sculpture," in which small enamels, set in the ground and along the frame of silver relief sculpture, pick up light and color. When silver was used as a foil under enamel, basse-taille (shallow relief) was born. A chalice made in that medium by the Sienese Guccio de Manmaia, now at S. Francesco in Assisi, is dated about 1290. In Paris enamelers came into contact with illuminators, as shown by a triptych at the Cloisters, New York, in the style of Jean Pucelle (d. 1334). Some basse-taile pieces are dated: a chalice made at Paris in 1333, now in Copenhagen, the National Museum; the statuette of the Virgin and its enameled base (1339) from St. Denis, now in the Louvre; the reliquary of the miraculous corporal of Bolsena by Ugolino de Vieri, now in the Orvieto cathedral (1338), which measures 1.39 meters (4.66 feet) by .63 meter (2.07 feet). The royal gold cup with scenes from the life of St. Agnes, made in 1381 for Charles V of France and now in the British Museum, and four medallions in the Louvre represent basse-taille enameling on gold in the last quarter of the fourteenth century.

Encrusted enamels made for the French and Burgundian courts include the reliquary of the Order of the Holy Ghost, now in the Louvre; a triptych from the collection of the duke of Berry, now in the British Museum; and many pieces in Italian church treasuries.

Very little survives of the so-called Netherlandish enamels from 1400–1450. These enamels are painted in thin camaïeu (monochrome) enamel and gilding on a silver ground covered with slate blue enamel. A masterpiece of this technique from the Medici treasure is the "monkey cup" at the Cloisters in New York. The Netherlandish technique was continued in the self-portrait of Jean Fouquet (ca. 1450), now in the Louvre, and in Venetian enameling of the second half of the fifteenth century.

A renaissance of enameling started at Limoges in the last quarter of the fifteenth century with the Monvaerni Master, other anonymous masters, and the founders of the Pénicaud dynasty. Limoges-painted enamels were obtained by applying various colored enamels on a previously fired layer of black enamel covered with a layer of white powdered enamel. The black design of the figures was delineated by enlevage, scraping through the white layer with a spatula handle or needle. Retouching could be done by means of black hatchings with a brush on the white layer, after the latter had been fired. Limoges enamels of this period are studded with "jewels," drops of translucent enamel on tiny foils. Their use indicates that the crafts of goldsmith and enameler were not distinct.

In northern Italy around 1500, goldsmiths were commissioned to make liturgical objects of translucent enamels that let the silver background shine through. They had figures modeled in opaque enamel applied with a brush in an impasto method akin to brushwork in painting.

BIBLIOGRAPHY

A complete bibliography on medieval enamels will be found in Marie-Madeleine Gauthier, *Émaux du moyen âge occidental* (1972, 2nd ed. 1973); the following nos. in the 1972 edition are of particular importance: 12, 16, 21, 28, 100, 177, 207, 222, 512, 547, and 552. Erich Steingräber, "Email," in *Reallexikon zur deutschen Kunstgeschichte*, V (1967); Klaus Wessel, *Die Byzantinische Emailkunst, vom 5. bis 13. Jahrhundert* (1964), trans. by Irene R. Gibbons as *Byzantine Enamels, from the Fifth to the Thirteenth Century* (1969).

See also Helmut Buschhausen, *Der Verduner Altar. Das Emailwerk des Nikolaus von Verdun* (1980); Jean-René Gaborit, "L'autel majeur de Grandmont," in *Cahiers de civilisation médiévale*, 19 (1976), esp. 239–246; Marie-Madeleine Gauthier, G. François, and N. Stratford, eds., *Medieval Enamels: Masterpieces from the Keir Collection* (1981); W. L. Hildburgh, *Medieval Spanish Enamels* (1936); Angelo Lipinsky, *Oro, argento, gemme e smalti: Tecnologia delle arti dalle origini alla fine del medioevo* (1975); Luigi Mallè, *Cloisonnés bizantini, con una introduzione all'arte dello smalto medioevale* (1973); Nigel Morgan, "The Iconography of Twelfth Century Mosan Enamels," in *Rhein und Maas*, II (1973); H. Vierck, "Werke des Eligius," in *Festschrift J. Werner* (1974), 309–380.

PHILIPPE VERDIER

[See also **Enamel, Basse-taille; Enamel, Champlevé; Enamel, Cloisonné; Enamel, Limoges; Enamel, Millefiori; Enamel, Vermiculé.**]

Basse-taille enamel. Silver-gilt pendant reliquary, France, 15th century. THE METROPOLITAN MUSEUM OF ART, GIFT OF J. PIERPONT MOR-GAN, 1917 (17.190.983)

Cloisonné enamel. Gold reliquary cross, Saloniki, late 12th or early 13th century. COURTESY OF THE DUMBARTON OAKS COLLECTION, WASHINGTON, D.C.

Champlevé enamel. St. Étienne de Muret and his disciple, Hugo Lacerta: plaque from the altar of Grandmont, Limoges, 1189. MUSÉE DE CLUNY, PARIS

Limoges enamel. Plaque of the Virgin and Child, Italian, 13th cen-tury. THE METROPOLITAN MUSEUM OF ART, ROBERT LEHMAN COLLEC-TION, 1975 (1975.1.1222)

ENAMEL, BASSE-TAILLE, a technique developed in the late thirteenth century in Tuscany, popular and practiced throughout Europe in the fourteenth and fifteenth centuries. An incised or engraved plaque (silver, gold, or copper coated with silver foil) is covered with a transparent enamel, level with the uncarved part of the plate. The engraved design shows through and the incised relief lines accumulate more enamel, darkening the color and creating the effect of shading. The basse-taille technique paralleled, and was probably inspired by, a new emphasis on modeling in painting.

LESLIE BRUBAKER

ENAMEL, CHAMPLEVÉ, a technique in which molten glass is poured into recesses depressed in a thick metal base; the portions of metal that remain between the individual depressions, which may be quite large, thus frame sections of enamel. Champlevé enamel was apparently invented by the Romans and continued to be the most popular enameling technique in the Latin West throughout the medieval period.

LESLIE BRUBAKER

ENAMEL, CLOISONNÉ, a technique in which narrow gold strips, called cloisons, are soldered to a thin base plate of gold or electrum; liquid glass is poured into each small compartment, or cell. The cloisonné technique permits much greater and more delicate detail than champlevé. Additional details can be included by extending gold strips into individual cells, a method used primarily to indicate drapery folds. Cloisonné was apparently known to the Mycenaeans, though it did not become popular until the Roman period. The technique was not common in the medieval West, but was the dominant enameling technique used in Byzantium, where the form reached its highest state of refinement. Byzantine cloisonné enamels, especially of the tenth to twelfth centuries, were avidly sought throughout the Christian world; many are still prized possessions of Western church treasuries.

BIBLIOGRAPHY
Klaus Wessel, *Byzantine Enamels from the Fifth to the Thirteenth Century,* Irene R. Gibbons, trans. (1969).

LESLIE BRUBAKER

ENAMEL, LIMOGES, a technique invented in late-fifteenth-century Limoges, probably by the Pénicaud family, in which enamel covers the entire surface of a plaque without protruding metal partitions. Layers of translucent and opaque enamel are painted on an opaque white enamel or silver foil base supported by a copper plaque.

LESLIE BRUBAKER

ENAMEL, MILLEFIORI (Italian, "thousand flowers"). Long, slender, colored glass rods are grouped into a decorative pattern; the bundle is fused together, then sliced into thin medallions, which are set into metalwork. Millefiori was a Roman technique perfected during the Migration Period in the British Isles; it is particularly associated with the Celts.

LESLIE BRUBAKER

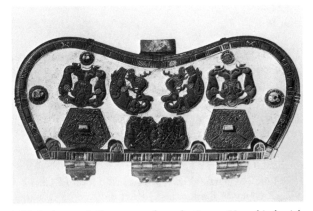

Millefiori enamel. Purse cover from the Sutton Hoo ship burial, Celtic, *ca.* 655. BRITISH MUSEUM, LONDON

ENAMEL, VERMICULÉ, enamels with rinceau ornamentation filling all background space. The rinceau is left in reserve with the ground incised and, normally, left plain. The figures or objects of the

Vermiculé enamel. Scenes from the life of St. Martial on an enameled reliquary from the Limoges workshops, late 12th century. MUSÉE DU LOUVRE, PARIS

foreground are usually rendered in the champlevé technique. Most vermiculé enamel was done around 1200 in the Limoges region.

BIBLIOGRAPHY

Marie-Madeleine Gauthier, *Émaux limousins champlevés des XIIe, XIIIe et XIVe siècles* (1950), 30–31; Jean-Joseph Marquet de Vasselot, *Les émaux limousins à fond vermiculé (XIIe et XIIIe siècles)* (1906).

LESLIE BRUBAKER

[See also **Enamel, Champlevé; Enamel, Limoges.**]

ENCAUSTIC, an ancient technique of painting with colored wax. The wax is heated, mixed with pigments, and applied in semifluid state. The encaustic technique was described by Pliny in his *Natural History* (35.149) and was used by Christian artists until the seventh century, especially for icons.

BIBLIOGRAPHY

Manolis Chatzidakis, "An Encaustic Icon of Christ at Sinai," Gerry Walters, trans., in *Art Bulletin,* **49** (1967); K. Parlasca, *Mumienporträts und verwandte Denkmäler* (1966), 225ff., 293; A. F. Shore, *Portrait Painting from Roman Egypt* (1962), 20–25.

LESLIE BRUBAKER

ENCOLPIUM (ENCOLPION), a medallion worn on a chain around the neck, generally restricted to the clergy, particularly in the Greek East. Normally, encolpia were decorated on both sides; they often functioned as miniature reliquaries.

LESLIE BRUBAKER

ENCYCLOPEDIAS AND DICTIONARIES, ARABIC AND PERSIAN

DICTIONARIES

Lexicography was an important branch of Arabic linguistics within the cultural boundaries of the medieval Muslim world. Its origins may be traced back as far as the seventh century, to the *amthāl* (parable) books that appeared in the circle of Muḥammad's companions. The books are known through later, sometimes extensive quotations. It is assumed that the earliest commentaries on the Koran, which were at least partially lexical, are from the same period.

The first tract containing lexical explanations (about 1,000 entries) was transmitted in a commentary *(tafsīr)* by ᶜAlī ibn Abī Ṭalḥah al-Hāshimī (d. 738), which, in turn, was part of a large Koran commentary, *Jāmiᶜ al-bayān fī tafsīr al-Qurᵓān*, by Muḥammad ibn Jarīr al-Ṭabarī (839–923). A second collection, known as *Masāᵓil Nāfiᶜ ibn al-Azraq* (Problems of Nāfiᶜ ibn al-Azraq), contains 200 words from the Koran with explanations. Both works have been attributed to ᶜAbd Allāh ibn al-ᶜAbbās (d. ca. 688), a cousin of the Prophet. This type of Koranic lexicology had its adherents among Ibn al-ᶜAbbās' disciples, whose work later gave birth to the literary form known as *gharīb al-Qurᵓān* (rare expressions in the Koran), in which theological interpretation parted from philological explanation.

Secular lexicography seems to have begun around the same time, as many poetical texts needed some kind of explanation. A popular genre of didactic poems, *qaṣāᵓid fī-al-gharīb* (poems with rare expressions from the Koran), arose that were later used for memorizing the lexica of such sciences as medicine and alchemy. Earlier works known as *nawādir* (anecdotes) were collections of poetical materials without any apparent systematization; they were often compiled by philologists who spent considerable time with the bedouins, who were considered arbiters in linguistic questions. The *Kitāb al-jīm* (Book of the letter jim), by Abū ᶜAmr al-Shaybānī (728–ca. 820), is both the earliest source on the earlier philologists and a subject lexicon arranged by the first radical.

Around the mid eighth century Arab scholars in various branches of knowledge turned their attention to subject classification. It has been suggested that the semantic principle of entry arrangement antedates the onomasiologic one. Abū ʿUbayd (*ca. 773–ca. 837*) used the semantic principle in each of twenty-five books compiled under the title *al-Gharīb al-muṣannaf* or *Kitāb al-muṣannaf* (Sorted rarities). They present mainly antiquated lexica of pre-Islamic poetry, in the following order: man's body structure, women, clothes, food, diseases, structures and locations, horses, weapons, birds and insects, vessels and pots, mountains, trees and plants, waters and streams, palms, clouds and rain, seasons and winds, and so on. Each of the books is divided into chapters (about 900 in all) structured along narrower topics. The compendium, full of quotations from both named and anonymous poets, enjoyed great popularity and was followed by additions, commentaries, and supracommentaries.

Thematic dictionaries centered on one subject gained prominence about the same time. The most industrious authors of smaller dictionaries were Abū ʿUbayda (728–822/828, credited with almost 100 titles), Abū Zayd al-Anṣārī (738–830, forty works), and al-Asmaʿī (740–828, twenty-six works). The latter begins his *Kitāb al-khalq al-insān* (Book of Creatures), which is considered the best on the subject, with lists of words in this order: pregnancy, childbirth, human development (agewise), a description of the human body and the functions of all body parts, and body types (such as tall, short, lean, fat). It ends with a section on human nature.

Large dictionaries of the same period seem to lack any strict logic in presentation. Thus, the *Kitāb al-alfāẓ* (Book of expressions or words) of Ibn al-Sikkīt (802–*ca.* 857) discusses wealth and abundance, poverty and indigence, then (briefly) camels, valor and cowardice, wine, women, sun, moon, time, water, numbers, grief, sympathy, sleep, hunger, food, weapons, jewelry, clothes, and words in which the hamza may be omitted. Later, Muḥammad ibn ʿAbd Allāh al-Iskāfī (d. 1029) classified his short dictionary *Mabādiʾ al-lugha* (Principles of philology) in a more consistent manner: stars and constellations, time, clothes, utensils, food, beverages, weapons, horses, camels, lions, other animals, birds, agricultural tools, trees, plants, trade, diseases, and rare words illustrated with poetical quotations.

The most famous and complete among semantically oriented dictionaries was the *Mukhaṣṣaṣ* (Categorized) of Ibn Sīda (d. 1066), a blind philologist from Murcia. This *catalogus mundi* starts with six books devoted to human nature, human physiology and psychology, women, clothes, food, and weapons. Seven books on the animal realm follow, then the author turns to celestial bodies, time, meteorological phenomena, waters and everything connected with them (such as ships, wells, bridges), land, and plants. Four more books cover philological problems. In addition, a large number of concrete and abstract aspects of everyday life appear under more general headings. Thus, kings, slaves, and the right of assault are featured in the book of instincts, utensils such as mirrors and combs in the book on women, uncleanliness in the book on clothes, and death and burial in the section on weapons. The book is known as the most complete dictionary of Arabic synonyms. Curiously, it does not include any specifically Spanish features.

Thematic dictionaries were usually prepared for writers, scribes, and poets; hence, they aimed at defining nuances. Grammatical and lexico-semantic matters were often treated in special sections attached, without any obvious reason, to a dictionary. There were dictionaries based on certain lexico-semantic groups: for instance, dictionaries of homonyms (*al-Mushtarak al-lafẓī*) by al-Asmaʿī, and dictionaries of words that, according to Arab philologists, have two opposite meanings, such as *Kitāb al-aḍdād* by Ibn al-Sikkīt. There were also dictionaries of borrowings from other languages, such as the *Kitāb al-muʿarrab* of al-Jawāliqī (1073–1144), which strove to refine the "pure" language in the aftermath of the Seljuq domination, collecting words of foreign origin.

Somewhat off the traditional path is *Asās al-balāgha* (Fundamentals of eloquence) by al-Zamakhsharī (1075–1144), who was interested in the word as part of a word construction. Although he explained particular meanings, his main concern was phraseological unity, which was illustrated by contextual usage in prose and poetry. Each word was shown in its primary meaning (*al-maʿnā al-ḥaqīqī*) and its metaphorical meaning (*al-maʿnā al-majāzī*). The dictionary does not record all derivatives, and it also omits rare roots. The entries are presented according to the main part of the phraseological unit, by its first radical. Sources for the dictionary are traditional: pre-Islamic poetry, the Koran, the *ḥadīth*, and proverbs.

The conventional alphabetical dictionary seems to have had its prototype in the *Kitāb al-ʿain* (The book of the letter ʿain) by the grammarian al-Khalīl ibn Aḥmad (d. ca. 791). Strictly speaking, that work is arranged not alphabetically but by certain groups of sounds following the "order of al-Khalīl": ʿ, ḥ, h, kh, gh, q, k, j, sh, ḍ, ṣ, s, z, ṭ, d, t, ẓ, dh, th, r, l, n, f, b, m, w, alif, y, ʾ. The phonetic-permutative principle of al-Khalīl is attributed to Sanskrit influence. The individual letter section is subdivided into chapters in accordance with the number of radicals of the word: first biliterals, then triliterals, and so on. The compiler used a complex system of letter transposition (taqlīb al-ḥurūf) that lumped all variants of the set of letters together: for instance, under the letter h are all its roots except those that also have either ʿ or ḥ and hence had been collected in the two preceding sections. As a result the earlier sections are considerably larger.

The dictionary Kitāb al-Jamhara (Collection) of Ibn Durayd (837–933) made use of the Kitāb al-ʿain but included only commonly used words, which were presented in conventional alphabetical order modified by the transpositional principle. Rare words appeared together in a separate chapter.

The introduction of the most common method of word arrangement is usually credited to al-Jauharī (d. by 1007), in his dictionary Tāj al-lugha wa ṣihāh al-ʿarabiya (The crown of philology and correct Arabic). The roots are arranged under the last radical, subdivided by the initial radical, and further subdivided by the middle radical. The "weak roots" (bāb al-wāw wa-al-yāʾ) are separated into one chapter, and the earlier subdivision by the number of radicals is eliminated. The arrangement by the last radical is traditionally explained as an aid to poets searching for rhyme words, but it may equally be attributed to the influence of Sanskrit lexicography.

The same method is used by Ibn Manẓūr (1233–1311) in his voluminous Lisān al-ʿArab (Language of the Arabs), which is considered the most complete and authoritative dictionary of Arabic. It contains about 80,000 entries and has an encyclopedic scope. A much smaller dictionary by al-Fīrūzābādī (1329–1415), al-Qāmūs al-muḥīṭ (The surrounding ocean), gained unprecedented popularity, circulating in just under 8,000 manuscript copies when its first printed edition appeared in 1817. Its initial title word became generic.

Although Persian lexicography can be traced as far back as the eleventh century, solely Persian dictionaries of the twelfth and thirteenth centuries have not been preserved. The gap may be filled by a number of contemporary Arabic–Persian dictionaries,

which contain earlier Persian words, their semantic explanations, and archaic grammatical forms. Among the earlier extant Arabic–Persian dictionaries is al-Sāmī fī-al-asāmī (The lofty among the equals) by Aḥmad ibn Muḥammad Abū al-Faẓl Maydānī Nīshāpūrī (d. 1124), which contains thematic sections on religion, animals, celestial bodies and astronomy, and geography. Another popular dictionary, the Muqaddimat al-adab (Introduction to knowledge) of the above-mentioned al-Zamakhsharī, has sections on nouns, verbs, particles, declension of nouns, and conjugation of verbs. The extant manuscripts of the work display its intended multilingual nature and add two more languages, Turkic and Khwarazmian.

The earliest entirely Persian dictionary to have survived is Lughat-i Furs (Language of the Persians) by Asadī al-Ṭūsī (eleventh century), containing rare words from Persian poetry. There was also an imitation of al-Jauharī's dictionary: in 1327/1328 Shams-i-Munshī compiled his own Ṣihāḥ al-Furs (Correct expressions of the Persians).

ENCYCLOPEDIAS

The first Arabic works that can be considered encyclopedias, in a broad sense, were manuals produced in the ninth century for the use of various categories of professionals and guides for public officials composed within the framework of traditionally acquired knowledge (adab). The latter gave birth to branches of knowledge apart from religious and purely scientific disciplines. The scribes (kuttāb) who actually ran the Islamic empire, had to master a number of disciplines and sciences, among them the art of writing, as well as source books of general knowledge. Ibn Qutayba (828–889) composed the first such manual, known as Adab al-kātib (The book of knowledge), with sections on philology, applied sciences (such as arithmetic and practical astronomy), techniques of public works, basics of jurisprudence, history, and ethics. The author rearranged the classification for the education of specialists in particular fields: the ʿālim (Ibn Qutayba undoubtedly means a theologian) should be versed in religion, philology, ethics, and philosophy (a Greek discipline, hence learned only so that it could be refuted). Still another classification is provided in the ʿUyūn al-akhbār (The quintessence of [profane] traditions) for the use of the adīb, a sophisticated man of letters who should know a bit about everything: the sovereign (his qualities and rules of conduct), warfare, loftiness in this world, prime qualities and defects, rhetoric, austerity and piety, choice of friends, how to achieve aims, table manners, and women.

Eventually the *kātib* (scribe) became an *adīb* and began to write new guides, mostly practical handbooks that are real treasure troves of cultural data. Ibn ᶜAbd Rabbih (860–940) compiled his ᶜIqd (The jeweled necklace) of twenty-five chapters, providing a nuanced and complete table of "musts" for the civilized person. Five centuries later the list had grown to eighty-four chapters in a similar work by al-Ibshīhī (*d. ca.* 1446), *al-Mustaṭraf* (Spiritual discoveries).

The genre developed in a totally different direction under the influence of Aristotelian thought. Al-Fārābī (*d.* 950) composed his short *Iḥsāʾ al-ᶜulūm* (Survey of the sciences) in five chapters: philology; logic; mathematics; physics and metaphysics; and political science, law, and theology. His impact was rather limited, however.

In the same century a clandestine group of scholars, known as Ikhwān al-Ṣafā (the Brethren of Purity or Sincerity) and thought to be Ismāᶜīlī in persuasion, produced the first collective encyclopedia in fifty-two epistles. The authors possessed a high degree of intellectual curiosity but displayed no conformity between their own work's classification and the one proposed in the seventh of their epistles: mathematics and logic (epistles 1–14); natural sciences, including philosophy (15–30); metaphysics (31–42); religion, mysticism, astrology, and magic versus the sciences of *adab*, the sciences of Islamic law, and the pure philosophical sciences (43–52). Significantly, they stated that "the *sharīᶜa* [Islamic law] is soiled with ignorance and replete with errors that only philosophy is capable of washing and purifying" and that "the perfection will be attained when Greek philosophy and the *sharīᶜa* are combined in harmony." In reality the Brethren proposed an eclectic doctrine making use of Christian, Persian, and Hindu wisdom as well as the Hellenic (mainly Neoplatonic) heritage. In view of the prevalence of traditional, orthodox education, it is not surprising that the Brethren elicited a positive response from only a limited circle of philosophers and some Shiites.

A century later orthodoxy struck back. The theologian al-Ghazālī (1058–1111) classified sciences into two opposing groups in his voluminous work *Iḥyāʾ ᶜulūm al-dīn* (Revival of religious sciences). The obligatory religious sciences comprised the traditional Koranic disciplines, law, and propaedeutics;

theology, philosophy, and geometry were put aside. The facultative nonreligious sciences were subdivided into the recommended (such as medicine and calculus), the blamable (such as magic), and the permissible (such as poetry and history). This essentially religious work was intended to help the individual Muslim find the path to the hereafter. From a certain perspective, however, the colossal work by al-Qalqashandī (*d.* 1418) known as Ṣubḥ al-aᶜshāʾ (Dawn of the sightless [at night]) continued the work of the Brethren in order to provide scribes with a survey of all that a good secretary should know: adab (here philology in the largest sense), the Koran, ḥadīth, Islamic law, physical sciences, geometry (including weaponry), astronomy, arithmetic, and practical sciences such as politics and ethics.

In Persian encyclopedias, as in Persian dictionaries, the Arabic model was eagerly followed. In many cases the authors were bilingual. The earliest encyclopedia of philosophical and exact sciences is considered to be the *Dānishnāma-i* ᶜAlāʾī (Book of knowledge for ᶜAlāʾ al-Dawla), begun by Ibn Sīnā (*d.* 1037) and completed by Jūzjānī (dates unknown). A work by Fakhr al-Dīn al-Rāzī (1149–1209), Ḥadāʾiqu'l-anvār fī ḥaqāʾiqi'l-asrār (Flowery gardens in the realities of secrets), is much larger in scope: one manuscript contains short summaries of sixty sciences. Soon after that book was written, Abū Bakr al-Muṭahhar Jamālī (twelfth century) compiled the *Farahnāma* (Book of joy), which dealt mainly with the natural sciences, including the properties of human and animal bodies, plants, minerals, drugs, and oils.

About 1340, Muḥammad ibn Maḥmūd al-Āmūlī compiled the *Nafāʾis al-funūn fī ᶜarāʾis al-ᶜuyūn* (Treasures of the sciences in the brides of the springs), which is divided into two parts: the "new sciences" (such as philology, theology, Sufism, history) and the "sciences of the ancients" (such as philosophy, pure sciences, medicine).

The power of religion in Islamic society tended to subordinate the individual to authority and to restrict imagination in favor of erudition: hence the proliferation of dictionaries and encyclopedias. They included memory aids and practical guides for men of letters who were willing to conform to prescribed rules in this world in order to enjoy the hereafter; dictionaries for the use of doctors of religion and traditionally educated writers; and refined encyclopedias destined for an elite of scholars and statesmen receptive to knowledge and conscious of the possibility of losing their national heritage in an age of decline.

BIBLIOGRAPHY

Sources. As a biobibliographical survey, Carl Brockelmann, *Geschichte der arabischen Literatur,* 5 vols. (1937–1949), is indispensable, even though partially superseded by Fuat Sezgin, *Geschichte des arabischen Schrifttums,* VIII (1982). Both academic and popular editions of most dictionaries can be traced in these works and, to a lesser extent, in Muḥammad Hassan Bakalla, *Bibliography of Arabic Linguistics* (1975), which also lists Arabic and Western studies. For Persian works the collective volume edited and mainly written by Jan Rypka, *History of Iranian Literature,* P. van Popta-Hope, trans. (1968), provides the best available coverage. Only one encyclopedia has been translated in full, into French: Muḥammad ibn Ahmad al-Ibshīhī, *al-Mostaṭraf,* Gustave Rat, trans., 2 vols. (1899–1902). Philosophical epistles of the Brethren of Purity were translated into German by Suzanne Diwald, *Arabische Philosophie und Wissenschaft in der Enzyklopädie Kitāb Iḫwān aṣ-Ṣafāʾ,* III, *Die Lehre von Seele und Intellekt* (1975). Al-Ghazālī's *Iḥyāʾ* has been partially translated into English, French, German, and Russian.

Studies. The only monographic study of dictionaries in English is John A. Haywood, *Arabic Lexicography* (1960); see also a review by A. Spitaler in *Orientalistische Literaturzeitung,* 63 (1968). In German, an important article is Jörg Kraemer, "Studien zur altarabischen Lexikographie," in *Oriens,* 6 (1953); in Russian, Vladimir M. Belkin, *Arabskaia lekskologia* (1975), provides a separate chapter on lexicology.

A pioneering survey of encyclopedias is Iu. Iu. Krachkovskii, "Arabskie entsiklopedii Srednevekovia," in *Trudy Instituta knigi, dokumenta, pisma,* 2 (1932). In French, see Gaston Wiet, "Les classiques du scribe égyptien au XVe siècle," in *Studia islamica,* 18 (1963); Charles Pellat, "Les encyclopédies dans le monde arabe," in *Cahiers d'histoire mondiale,* 9 (1966); Roger Paret, "Contribution à l'étude des milieux culturels dans le Proche-Orient médiéval," in *Revue historique,* 235 (1966); and Régis Blachère, "Quelques réflexions sur les formes de l'encyclopédisme en Égypte et en Syrie du viiie/xive siècle à la fin du ixe/xve siècle," in *Bulletin d'études orientales,* 23 (1970). In English, Franz Rosenthal, *Knowledge Triumphant* (1970), ch. 8, provides a useful background. Among authors only the Brethren have received monographic treatment: Adel Awa, *L'esprit critique des Frères de la pureté* (1948); Yves Marquet, *La philosophie des Iḫwān al-Ṣafāʾ* (1975); A. Bausani, *L'enciclopedia dei Fratelli della purità* (1978); and Ian R. Netton, *Muslim Neoplatonists* (1982).

SERGEI SHUISKII

[See also **Arabic Literature, Prose; Fārābi, al-; Ghazāli, al-; Rāzi, al-; Sinā, Ibn; Tabari, al-.**]

ENCYCLOPEDIAS AND DICTIONARIES, BYZANTINE.

A book not intended by the author as a work of reference but frequently used as one was the ninth-century *Bibliotheke* of Patriarch Photios, a collection of 279 notes on books that he had read—mainly prose works by Christian and pagan authors from the fifth century B.C. to the ninth century of the Christian era. Some notes are very brief; others present a detailed summary of the book read; others consist mainly of excerpts. Almost half of the books read by Photios no longer survive.

The tenth century saw both the apogee of Byzantine power and a resurgence of classical literary culture. Many encylopedic works compiled under the patronage of Emperor Constantine VII were designed both to summarize the heritage of antiquity and to make it accessible to those who could not or would not read the original texts. They include the following:

The *Constantinian Excerpts,* a series of lengthy extracts from Greek historians from the fifth century B.C. to the ninth century of the Christian era, arranged by subject matter in fifty-three volumes, of which only a small part survives.

De administrando imperio, a handbook on relations with foreign peoples compiled by Constantine VII for his son Romanos II. It contains priceless information on the empire's neighbors, particularly those north and east of the Black Sea.

De thematibus, a similar handbook on the provinces of the empire. It does not reflect faithfully the conditions of Constantine's time, since it draws largely on much earlier sources.

De ceremoniis, a compilation of documents on court ceremonial from the fifth century on, including protocols of coronations, appointments to high offices, and receptions of ambassadors. An appendix contains documents on the organization and order of battle of the Byzantine army in the mid tenth century.

The *Geoponica,* an agricultural encyclopedia, based largely on lost treatises of the fourth through sixth centuries, contains much incidental information on popular superstitions and magic.

The *Iatrika* of Theophanes Nonnos, a medical encyclopedia compiled from Oreibasios, Aetios of Amida, Alexander of Tralles, and Paul of Aegina, has a pharmacological rather than physiological emphasis.

The *Hippiatrika,* a veterinary encyclopedia including many excerpts from earlier authorities, probably was illustrated, as is suggested by the many pictures in surviving manuscripts.

A collection of zoological excerpts, largely from Aristotle, Aelian, St. Basil, and Timotheos of Gaza, treats man and the elephant at greatest length. Only half of the work survives.

The *Suda*, a combination of lexicon, biographical and historical dictionary, and handbook of literature, is also from the tenth century, though there is no direct evidence to link it with Constantine VII. Alphabetically arranged, it is a compilation from lexica and etymological dictionaries, anthologies of excerpts, commentaries on texts, lists of proverbs, and a biographical dictionary of writers by Hesychios the Illustrious of Miletos (*ca.* 500). The *Suda* is a mine of information, but it must be used critically because it is a compilation from compilations, using material torn from its context.

Handbooks of military strategy and tactics were written throughout the Byzantine period. Some reflect contemporary practice, whereas others are antiquarian compilations. The most noteworthy are the *Strategikon* of Maurice (*ca.* 600), the *Taktika* of Leo VI (*ca.* 900), the *Strategikon* of Nikephoros Phokas (late tenth century), and the *Taktika* of Nikephoros Uranos (eleventh century). Shorter treatises on naval warfare also were written.

There are many Byzantine lists of offices and handbooks of precedence, such as the *Taktikon Uspenski* of 842–843, the *Kleterologion* of Philotheos (899), and the Pseudo-Kodinos (fourteenth century). Much information can be derived from these works on the changing administrative structure of the empire.

The enduring Byzantine taste for such compilations suggests the existence of a wide (in medieval terms) reading public needing quick and easy access to information.

BIBLIOGRAPHY

A. Dain, "L'encyclopédisme de Constantin Porphyrogénète," in *Lettres d'humanité*, **12** (1953); Paul Lemerle, *Le premier humanisme byzantin* (1971), 267–300; Arnold J. Toynbee, *Constantine Porphyrogenitos and His World* (1973), 575–605.

Robert Browning

[See also **Byzantine Literature; Geoponica; Photios; Warfare, Byzantine.**]

ENCYCLOPEDIAS AND DICTIONARIES, WESTERN EUROPEAN. Of the three encyclopedists of ancient Rome—Varro, Celsus, and Pliny—only the work of Pliny has survived whole to modern times, and, except for some use of Varro by Isidore of Seville, only he had an influence on medieval encyclopedists. Virtually all the authors treated below knew his *Natural History* (A.D. 77): they not only drew details from it but also imitated its organization, beginning with the heavens, then moving to earth, man and other animals, plants, and minerals—that is, down the chain of being.

There is a major development from Varro to Pliny that is central to the history of encyclopedias. The word "encyclopedia," as originally used, had a close link with the training of youth—a "well-rounded education"—and Varro's *Disciplines* (*ca.* 50 B.C.) had been well within this propaedeutic tradition. His nine books treated the "seven liberal arts" (grammar, dialectic, rhetoric, geometry, arithmetic, astronomy, and music), plus medicine and architecture. Pliny, who was not an academic but a public servant and amateur scholar—a "spare-time anthologist," in Robert D. Collison's phrase—collected information about the physical world (until he died from the effects of taking notes on the eruption of Vesuvius at too close range) and arranged it in an order that made sense to him. The distinction between their works is roughly the distinction made today between the liberal arts and the natural sciences—but with a further contrast superimposed, between Varro's academic traditionalism and Pliny's freer, more experiential approach. The history of Western encyclopedias is one of movement from a concentration on the liberal arts toward all-inclusiveness. (A final encyclopedic product of the classical period is Martianus Capella's *De nuptiis Philologiae et Mercurii* [*ca.* 425], which treats the seven liberal arts only.)

St. Augustine in his *On Christian Doctrine* expressed the need for a Christian encyclopedia, one that would facilitate explication of the symbols in the Bible. Cassiodorus' *Institutiones* (*ca.* 560) and Isidore of Seville's *Etymologiae* (unfinished when he died in 636; completed soon after by his secretary Braulio) are the first attempts to fill that need. Cassiodorus aimed to give the monks of his monastery Vivarium a summary of both sacred and humane learning. He followed Pliny's design broadly, in that he treated divine subjects (Scripture, Christian history, but also cosmology) before human and in the eclecticism that marks his first book (of "divine readings"). His second book, while still Augustinian, is in the tradition of Varro and Martianus: its seven chapters treat the seven liberal arts.

Isidore's *Etymologies* is the most extensive, important, and influential early medieval encyclopedia. It goes well beyond Pliny's natural science and Cassiodorus' divinity, adding such subjects as cities, food, tools, furniture, public games, and ships. With Isidore encyclopedias moved beyond the liberal arts for good. As his title implies, Isidore regarded the names of things as revealing their nature, either directly or through their root associations. Although the sober researches of modern philologists have exposed most of his etymologies as erroneous, they often had an imaginative aptness that induced readers to accept them for centuries. Isidore was also interested in the origins, not merely of words, but of customs, institutions, skills, and experiences. Thus, his account of cities deals with their founding; his account of marriage describes not only the sources of various customs but also the characteristics in each sex that move the opposite sex to love. The reader learns that nations arise from languages, not languages from nations, as well as the inventors of various arts and sciences.

Between Isidore and the thirteenth century there is no truly original encyclopedia and only one book that deserves the name at all. That is *De rerum naturis* (The natures of things) of Hrabanus Maurus (after 842), largely a rearrangement of Isidore's text, with allegorizations. While Isidore included some doctrinal materials, the *Etymologiae* remains largely a product of classical Roman civilization; Hrabanus' encyclopedia is fully medieval. Isidore had himself produced a brief *Natures of Things,* based largely on Ambrose's *Hexaemeron* (*ca.* 375)—the major repositories of cosmography and natural history in early Christianity were the hexaemeral works. Isidore's book deals with time and the four elements, moving downward from fire to earth. It inspired Bede's similarly organized but more ambitious work of the same name, and his temporal books as well.

The *Image of the World* of Honorius Augustodunensis (*ca.* 1110), the first of a number of embryonic quasi-encyclopedias of the twelfth century that foreshadow the thirteenth-century explosion, draws heavily on Bede's writings. Honorius' first book, on the physical world, is largely a rearrangement and simplification of Bede's *Natures of Things.* His second and third books, on time and human history, respectively, rely chiefly on the material in Bede's temporal works. Lambert of St. Omer's *Liber floridus*

(*ca.* 1120) and the *Hortus deliciarum* of Herrad, abbess of Hohenburg (late twelfth century) are illustrated encyclopedias with a strong religious purpose; both are somewhat eccentric creations. Hugh of St. Victor's *Didascalicon* (*ca.* 1130) is a work in the liberal arts tradition, a survey of learning lacking detail, a curriculum rather than a course. Similarly schematic is Richard of St. Victor's *Book of Excerpts* (*ca.* 1140); both Hugh and Richard, however, include speculative philosophy and history. Finally there is the *Natures of Things* of Alexander Neckham (*ca.* 1195). Although only the first two of five books treat nature, although Neckham was a humanist who would rather cite Ovid than Pliny, although he was too anecdotal and moralistic, he made a clear advance beyond Honorius in the direction of inclusiveness and specificity. His division of birds, fish, animals, plants, and minerals into their species, however haphazard, is a product of a truly encyclopedic urge.

The great period of the medieval encyclopedia is the thirteenth century. Compilers began to take Arabic and Aristotelian learning fully into account; Scholasticism placed a new value on the understanding of parts; and advances in the format of books such as paragraph marks, chapter titles, marginal rubrication, and tables of contents engendered new advances in the art of compilation. Consequently, other kinds of reference books also made their appearance: concordances of the Bible, alphabetical indexes, and catalogs of libraries.

Many of these, encyclopedias included, were meant to help the itinerant preachers of the new mendicant orders prepare sermons. Bartholomaeus Anglicus, the author of *De proprietatibus rerum* (*ca.* 1240), was a Franciscan friar, and Thomas of Cantimpré, the author of *De natura rerum* (*ca.* 1245), was a Dominican friar. Thomas says in his preface that he wrote to provide a "handbook of digression" for preachers, to enable them to lead people to God through his creation, and Bartholomaeus had a similar audience in mind. Of the two books Bartholomaeus' was the more complete and influential. It was translated into six languages and was printed several times, the last edition in 1601; it was the most widely read and quoted of all late-medieval encyclopedias. Bartholomaeus' conception of the properties of things includes the operation of cause and effect: he shares Isidore's interest in origins and a notable interest of his own in results. His nineteen books are far better organized, better informed, and more thorough than those of his predecessors or Thomas of

Cantimpré, whose book is more than half zoology. Bartholomaeus quotes extensively from Aristotle and the Arab savants and is particularly good on medicine and geography.

The late-medieval encyclopedic urge reached its peak in the work of the Dominican Vincent of Beauvais, whose three-part *Speculum maius* (*ca.* 1245–*ca.* 1260) was, in its day, the most ambitious attempt yet to gather all knowledge into one book. It contains more than three million words. Few are Vincent's, however: he compiled authorities, and he spoke on his own as little as he could. The *Speculum naturale* is in the hexaemeral tradition, treating nature according to the six days of creation. The *Speculum doctrinale* is divided, following Hugh and Richard of St. Victor, into four parts: linguistic arts, mechanical arts, practical sciences, and theoretical sciences. In the *Speculum historiale* Vincent treats human history (from Adam to 1254) far more systematically than any encyclopedist before him.

Serge Lusignan points out a striking antinomy between the two most ambitious medieval encyclopedias, Isidore's and Vincent's. Isidore collected the remains of a dying Roman culture; Vincent lived in an age of intellectual abundance, a flood of new knowledge. He wrote because there were "so many books"; Isidore, it seems, wrote because there were too few. Owing to its bulk the *Speculum maius* seems to have circulated less than Bartholomaeus' *Properties,* but it has survived in eighty manuscripts. It was the first book printed at Strasbourg and had five other printings, the last in 1624.

The thirteenth century was an age of "encyclopedic" works: poems like the *Romance of the Rose* and the *Divine Comedy,* reflecting a broad range of learning, or the summae of the great philosophers and theologians. Even cathedrals manifested the "encyclopedic" desire to be at once vast and detailed. This century saw the publication of a quasi-encyclopedic French poem, *L'ymage du monde* (*ca.* 1250), and the first vernacular encyclopedia, Brunetto Latini's *Li livres dou trésor* (*ca.* 1265), which was also the first medieval encyclopedia clearly aimed at a lay audience.

In the fourteenth and fifteenth centuries fewer influential encyclopedias were produced than in the thirteenth. Mention should be made, however, of a brief but sophisticated anonymous *Compendium philosophiae* (*ca.* 1300), devoted to Aristotle's teachings; Pierre Bersuire's *Reductorium morale de proprietatibus rerum* (*ca.* 1340), a moral exposition of Bartholomaeus' work; Domenico Bandini's *Fons me-*

morabilium universa (*ca.* 1415), which reached a wide audience in Italy; and Gregor Reisch's *Margarita philosophica* (1496), a small but thorough and popular survey of knowledge.

The story of dictionaries can be told more briefly. The wellhead of medieval Latin lexicography is the *De verborum significatu* (*ca.* 5 B.C.) of Verrius Flaccus—twice epitomized, first by Pompeius Festus in the first century and by Paul the Deacon in the eighth. Early medieval glossaries—lists made from the marginal glosses of manuscripts—added to this base; they culminated in the early-ninth-century *Liber glossarum.* From this in turn (and from Isidore, Priscian, and numerous other sources) emerged the first medieval dictionary: the *Elementarium erudimentum doctrine* (Rudiments of learning, *ca.* 1053) of the Lombard Papias. Papias had an encyclopedist's urge to convey general information as well as a grammarian's interest in words. His entries are in alphabetical order through the first three letters of each word, but he treats many word families and topically related words in groups regardless of their alphabetical place. Such etymologies as appear are mostly traditional.

Osbern of Gloucester's *Liber derivationum* (*ca.* 1150) shows a shift of interest away from general information and toward etymology as a science. For every letter Osbern lists the word families, emphasizing derivation; then he defines rarer words, generally without attempting etymology. Osbern focuses on words as grammatical entities; he avoids Papias' tendency to bring together words related by subject only. His aims were carried further by Huguccio of Pisa, who replaced his relatively inchoate materials with a complete etymological system. In Huguccio's *Liber derivationum* (of uncertain date, last quarter of the twelfth century) very few words stand alone: almost every one finds its place in the etymological system—often, apparently, by sheer invention on Huguccio's part. Huguccio shows a far stronger interest in words as such than in factual information, yet there is plenty of information scattered through the work: even this most systematically philological of dictionaries is still very much a book about the world.

Huguccio treated almost all words as members of related groups, regardless of alphabetical order, which in any case does not go beyond the initial letter. The Dominican Giovanni Balbi of Genoa rectified this shortcoming in the dictionary portion of his *Catholicon* (1286), a book that covers the whole field of grammar. John rearranged Huguc-

449

cio's materials in absolutely alphabetical order, thus creating a far more usable work of reference (also quite usable, for the same reason, is a Bible dictionary of 2,500 entries, the *Summa Britonis* by the Franciscan William Brito [*ca.* 1260].)

But John by no means drove Huguccio from the field, as Huguccio had driven Papias and Osbern. Their Latin dicionaries were standard reference works until the end of the fifteenth century. About 200 manuscripts of the *Liber derivationum* survive, and as many might be found of the *Catholicon,* which has been less studied. The former was never printed, but the latter was among the first books set in movable type—in 1460, perhaps by Gutenberg—and was reprinted several times.

Near the end of the fifteenth century modern dictionaries began to appear. There was more interest in the vernacular languages and, in Latin, a humanistic revulsion against etymology and a passion for more precise knowledge of words. The result was a rash of vocabularies that appeared in the last quarter of the century, including one by Johann Reuchlin (*Breviloquus,* 1475), followed shortly thereafter by the massive dictionary of Ambrogio Calepino (1502) and, preeminently, by Robert Estienne's monumental *Thesaurus linguae Latine* (1531).

BIBLIOGRAPHY

Bartholomaeus Anglicus, *On the Properties of Body and Soul,* R. James Long, ed. (1979); *Cahiers d'histoire mondiale,* 9 (1966), a special number entitled "Encyclopédies et civilisations," containing six essays on medieval encyclopedias; Robert D. Collison, *Encyclopaedias: Their History Throughout the Ages,* 2nd ed. (1966), 21–81; Lloyd W. Daly and B. A. Daly, "Some Techniques in Mediaeval Latin Lexicography," in *Speculum,* 39 (1964); Klaus Grubmüller, "Überblick über die lateinische lexikographische Tradition bis zum Ende des 14. Jahrhunderts," in his *Vocabularius ex quo* (1967); Richard W. Hunt, "The 'Lost' Preface to the *Liber derivationum* of Osbern of Gloucester," in *Mediaeval and Renaissance Studies,* 4 (1958); Roswitha Klinck, *Die lateinische Etymologie des Mittelalters* (1970); Serge Lusignan, *Préface au Speculum maius de Vincent de Beauvais* (1979); Malcolm B. Parkes, "The Influence of the Concepts of *Ordinatio* and *Compilatio* on the Development of the Book," in J. J. G. Alexander and M. T. Gibson, eds., *Medieval Learning and Literature: Essays Presented to Richard William Hunt* (1976); Claus Riessner, *Die "Magnae derivationes" des Uguccione da Pisa, und ihre Bedeutung für die romanische Philologie* (1965); Richard Rouse, "La diffusion en Occident au xiiie siècle des out-

ils de travail facilitant l'accès aux textes autoritatifs," in *Revue des études islamiques,* 44 (1976).

TRAUGOTT LAWLER

[See also **Bede; Cassiodorus; French Literature: After 1200; Honorius Augustodunensis; Hrabanus Maurus; Hugh of St. Victor; Huguccio; Isidore of Seville; Martianus Capella; Papias; Richard of St. Victor; Romance of the Rose; Thomas of Cantimpré; Vincent of Beauvais.**]

ENDE, perhaps a nun, is cited as "painter and servant of God" in the colophon of the Beatus commentary of 975 (in the archives of the cathedral of Gerona, Spain), the most richly illuminated of the Spanish manuscripts of the Mozarabic school. It probably was executed at the Leonese monastery of Tábara.

BIBLIOGRAPHY

Jaime Marqués y Casanovas *et al., Sancti Beati Liebana in Apocalipsin: Codex Gerundensis* (1962), facsimile; John Williams, *Early Spanish Manuscript Illumination* (1977), 92–99.

JOHN WILLIAMS

[See also **Apocalypse, Illustration of; Beatus Manuscripts; Manuscript Illumination.**]

The triumphant Christian warrior. Ende, Beatus Commentary, Gerona, 975. Archivo Catedralicio de Gerona, Beatus, fol. 134v. ORONOZ

ENDELECHIUS, Latin poet and rhetorician. A native of Gaul and a Christian, his full name was Severus Sanctus qui et Enedelechius. He taught rhetoric at Rome in 395 and was a friend of Paulinus of Nola. His poem *On the Deaths of Oxen,* in thirty-three asclepiadean strophes, is modeled on the *Eclogues* of Vergil. In it three shepherds, Aegon, Bucolus, and Tityrus, discuss how Tityrus' herd escaped the plague by being marked with the sign of the cross.

BIBLIOGRAPHY

Text of the *De mortibus boum* is in *Patrologia latina,* XIX (1846), 797–803; and *Anthologia latina,* 2nd ed., I, pt. 2 (1906), no. 893, 334–339. See also Eleanor S. Duckett, *Latin Writers of the Fifth Century* (1930), 93–95; Martin von Schanz, Carl Hosius, and Gustav Krüger, *Geschichte der römischen Litteratur,* IV, pt. 2 (1920), 360–361.

RALPH WHITNEY MATHISEN

[See also **Latin Literature.**]

ENDOWMENTS. See **Waqf.**

ENÉAS, ROMAN D', a mid-twelfth-century adaptation of Vergil's *Aeneid* into 10,156 Old French octosyllables. Without betraying totally the ethos of antiquity, a Norman cleric, under the influence of Ovidian love rhetoric and numerous other sources, created a new type of courtly romance hero (Enéas) and heroine (Lavine) noted for their reciprocal love.

BIBLIOGRAPHY

Raymond J. Cormier, *One Heart, One Mind* (1973); R. Jones, "The *État présent* of Research on the *Romans antiques,*" in *Encomia,* 1 (1976); J.-J. Salverda de Grave, ed., *Enéas: Roman du XIIᵉ siècle,* 2 vols. (1925–1929); John A. Yunck, trans., *Eneas: A Twelfth-century French Romance* (1974).

RAYMOND J. CORMIER

[See also **Vergil in the Middle Ages.**]

ENECHELON PLAN. See **Apse Echelon.**

ENGELBERT OF ADMONT (*ca.* 1250–1331) was born in Austria and about 1267 entered the Benedictine abbey of Admont. He studied at Prague from 1271 to 1274 and in Italy from 1278 to 1287, spending the last four years at the Dominican school in Padua, where he received a thorough grounding in Thomism. He spent 1288–1297 as abbot of St. Peter's in Salzburg. In 1297 the archbishop of Salzburg appointed him abbot of Admont in a move designed to end the archbishop's feud with Duke Albert of Austria, to whom Engelbert was an acceptable candidate. After an abbacy of thirty years, Engelbert retired because of his advanced age.

It was as a scholar and writer that Engelbert made his mark. Though not one of the greatest thinkers of his generation, he was nevertheless a man of subtle intelligence and many interests. His bibliography of some forty-four works includes writings on theology, political theory, natural and moral philosophy, and music. Engelbert must have been highly esteemed as a theologian by his contemporaries, for he was commissioned, probably about 1304, to write the official church refutation of John of Paris' doctrine of impanation. John taught that, during the Eucharist, the *suppositum* of the bread *(panis)* changes while the *substantia* remains. In his *Tractatus de corpore domini,* a highly technical philosophical work, Engelbert both refuted John of Paris and exhaustively analyzed many difficult points of eucharistic doctrine.

Most of the scholarly attention given Engelbert today is directed to his political theory. Although he was a convinced imperialist, his treatise *De ortu . . . et fine romani imperii* offers no confident vision of a triumphant empire. Rather it opens in a hauntingly elegiac tone:

> Once when some friends of mine—prudent and mature men—were sitting and talking with me, . . . [we spoke] of the Roman empire or kingdom and its condition; some asserting that, inasmuch as this empire or kingdom had weakened in right and might, which seemed to be true, it must in a short time fail and vanish altogether. (Ewart Lewis, *Medieval Political Ideas* [1954], II, 473)

Engelbert's Scholasticism is clearly reflected as he proceeds to elaborate a positive theory of good government in agreement with Aristotelian (and Augustinian) criteria, and carefully reviews arguments that the Roman Empire either cannot provide this good government or that such government could be as well provided by individual kingdoms. Although he is able to refute these arguments, his discussion remains mostly defensive. For example, in answer to the argument that the empire exists in vain because it cannot attain its own end of keeping peace, he responds that the empire need not succeed in keeping peace, but only strive to keep peace, in order to attain its end. Indeed, his only positive argument is that one empire is better than several kingdoms because the unity of the Christian people is better reflected by a single empire than by a multitude of kingdoms.

The subject of the unity of the Christian people approaches the heart of Engelbert's political theory—his (mostly unanalyzed) conviction that no institution can equal the empire in providing for the defense of Christendom. It is precisely because he sees the empire as Christendom's best bulwark against "the pagan world" that he believes its possible demise to be so fraught with doom.

BIBLIOGRAPHY

Lists of works and editions are in George B. Fowler, *Intellectual Interests of Engelbert of Admont* (1947), 183–221. Editions since 1947 (all edited by Fowler) are "Engelbert of Admont's *Tractatus de officiis et abusionibus eorum*," in John H. Mundy *et al.*, eds., *Essays in Mediaeval Life and Thought: Festschrift A. P. Evans* (1955); "Letter of Abbot Engelbert of Admont to Master Ulrich of Vienna," in *Recherches de théologie ancienne et médiévale*, **29** (1962); "Engelberti Admontensis Tractatus de fascinatione," in *ibid.*, **37** (1970). See also Fowler's "A Chronology of the Writings of Englebert of Admont O.S.B.," in H. G. Fletcher III and M. B. Schulte, eds., *Paradosis: Studies in Memory of Edwin A. Quain* (1976), 121–134; and Ewart Lewis, *Medieval Political Ideas*, 2 vols. (1954), 444–447, 472–484.

ELAINE GOLDEN ROBISON

[See also **Eucharist; John of Paris; Political Theory, Western European.**]

ENGELMODUS, after serving as a priest at Corbie, became bishop of Soissons in 862, following the removal of Bishop Rothad. Aside from his involvement in this affair, Engelmodus is known primarily for his three extant panegyrics in the form of metrical letters addressed to Agius, bishop of Orléans; Drogo, bishop of Metz; and Paschasius Radbertus, abbot of Corbie. Others of his poems are lost. His models include Vergil and Venantius Fortunatus. He was dead by 864/865, when Pope Nicholas I allowed Rothad to return to Soissons.

BIBLIOGRAPHY

The text of the poems is in *Monumenta Germaniae historica: Poetae latini medii aevi*, Ludwig Traube, ed., III (1896), 54–66.

RALPH WHITNEY MATHISEN

ENGLAND. The history of England is covered in a series of articles: **England: Anglo-Saxon; England: Norman-Angevin;** and **England: 1216–1485.**

ENGLAND: ANGLO-SAXON. The political history of England during the Anglo-Saxon period presents a simple central theme of movement toward unification, the creation of a true and permanent kingdom of England. By 1066, the date of the Norman conquest, the process was almost complete, though there were difficulties on the fringes. The northern border fluctuated with the fortunes of the rulers of the relatively new Scottish kingdom. To the west, political pressures were making the established Welsh boundary of Offa's Dyke unsatisfactory. But by and large the mass of historic England was fully formed and governed in the name of Edward the Confessor, king of the English. His ill-starred successor, Harold, earl of Wessex, though dismissed by the Norman conquerors as a usurper, in fact exercised unitary authority over the whole of England from the tip of Cornwall to Dover, from Southampton to the precarious Scottish border.

EARLY POLITICAL DIVISIONS

The stages by which political unity was achieved are easy to identify. In the course of the sixth century, Germanic immigrants and settlers sorted themselves out into kingdoms that reflected their beliefs concerning their origins and the geographical realities of their positions within the newly won territories. Four principal groupings emerged from among those that had made the Thames estuary or the south coast their main point of entry.

Kent, which took its name from the Roman Cantium, was the most complicated and the most prosperous of these units. Settled by Jutes and Frisians, among others, and bearing traditions and some tan-

ANGLO-SAXON ENGLAND

gible evidence of federate enterprise and native survival, the Kentish kingdom was the least isolated of the new communities. King Ethelbert (*ca.* 560–616), who was overlord of all English people south of the Humber, had close contacts with the Frankish courts, had married a Christian Frankish princess named Bertha, and had permitted her to observe her religion and to bring a Christian bishop, Liudhard, to Canterbury. The little Church of St. Martin, just outside the walls of Canterbury, stands on the site of the church they set up even before St. Augustine's mission in 597.

453

Another group of migrants, more solidly Saxon in composition, made their home to the west of Kent in the area that came to be known as the land of the South Saxons, or Sussex. They rose to prominence in the later fifth century under a military ruler named Ælle, the first to be recognized as overlord by a substantial federation of German peoples in England; but thereafter they sank back into obscurity. They were the last organized English kingdom to accept Christianity, well into the late seventh century.

North of the Thames another predominantly Saxon group established itself in the territory known as the land of the East Saxons, or Essex. Their political fortunes were much bound up with control of the site of London and jockeying for position with other groups, such as the Middle Saxons (Middlesex), the men of the "southern district" (Surrey), settlers to the northwest of London, or, most of all, with the kingdom of Kent.

The last of the kingdoms to be set up by those who were attracted to the Thames Valley was in many respects the most important. Afforced by migrants who moved southwest from the Wash along Icknield Way, and brought to cohesion by a ruling kindred whose traditions spoke of entry through Portsmouth and Hampshire, the settlers in the middle Thames—the modern counties of Berkshire and Oxfordshire—became known historically as the West Saxons. As the community flourished, the kingdom of the West Saxons, or Wessex, expanded toward the southwest, into Somerset and Devon, but it is important to recognize that its people were originally Thames Valley folk.

The Thames and the southern shores are the best-chronicled entry points of early Anglo-Saxon migration, but there were other important routes. The Wash, with its navigable rivers, provided good access for many of the lesser folk of early Anglo-Saxon England, including a constituent element of the historic West Saxon people. Politically they formed themselves into one major kingdom, that of the East Angles (Norfolk and Suffolk), and many minor peoples who preserved awareness of their integrity into historic times, the most important being the Middle Angles, centered around the Leicester area.

The Humber was also a major point of entry for migrants, with its waterways leading north to the Vale of York and south along the Trent, deep into the heart of the Midlands. In the north the early settlers in the kingdom of Deira around York combined in uneasy partnership with others who had set up hamlets and villages still farther north around Bamborough, to form the kingdom of Bernicia. Together they were known as the dwellers north of the Humber, the Northumbrians, and in the course of the seventh century their kingdom came to be among the most powerful in England. South and west along the Trent, an early kingdom of Lindsey failed to achieve first rank, but settlers who moved to the middle Trent, around the historic centers of Tamworth, Repton, and Lichfield, formed the nucleus of the kingdom of Mercia. By attracting and subordinating smaller groups, the Mercians came to be reckoned among the most prominent of the English nations.

The term "heptarchy" is sometimes applied to England at the beginning of the age of conversion to Christianity. No new kingdoms were created after that period, and the political experience of the English peoples depended on the fate and fortunes of the seven principal kingdoms: Kent, Sussex, Essex, and Wessex in the south, Mercia and East Anglia across the Midland belt, and Northumbria in the north.

The age of conversion, roughly the period from the arrival of St. Augustine in 597 to the death of Bede in 735, saw a further consolidation of political power. Bede's brilliant analysis of the shifting fortunes of the English kings in his *Ecclesiastical History of the English People* (completed in 731) provides good information on the politics of the seventh century. One general truth emerges firmly from the welter of detailed information: by the end of the century, hope of English unification rested with the three *gentes* or *nationes* capable of further colonization and expansion against Celtic peoples. Kent had subsided into a prosperous but subordinate position, as had East Anglia, isolated behind its fenland barriers. The future rested with Northumbria, Mercia, or Wessex.

For a generation after the Battle of Winwæd (654), in which Penda, the heathen creator of greater Mercia, was killed, dominance rested with the Northumbrians. The victorious King Oswy presided over the Synod of Whitby, which resolved to follow the Roman observance in the northern Christian kingdom, a decision that later extended to all the English kingdoms and the Celtic world. Then, with the disastrous military defeat at the hands of the Picts in 685 and the reopening of ancient rivalries between settled, agrarian Deira and more backward, pastoral Bernicia, overlordship passed from the north. Northumbria remained an important cultural center throughout the eighth century. Exquisite illuminated gospel books and stone crosses, the work of the great scholars Bede and (later) Alcuin, and the reputation of the school at York all testify to the vitality of the "Northumbrian renaissance." But politically Northumbria was increasingly a backwater. In 793 it suffered the first of the formidable Viking raids that were to transform the whole area.

Eighth-century politics in England were dominated by Mercia. The West Saxons enjoyed a brief period of strength under the lawgiver Ine (688–726), but their constructive efforts were directed toward the colonization of the southwest. Two Mercian military rulers, Ethelbald (716–757) and Offa (757–796), established themselves as the most powerful rulers in England.

Offa, the not unworthy contemporary of Charlemagne, left a lasting memorial in the great earthwork, Offa's Dyke, that drew the boundary between the English and the Welsh. Modern historians increasingly recognize his positive institutional contribution to the unification of England. He was more than a mere military overlord: he aimed consciously at dominating the ancient smaller kingdoms that surrounded Mercia. Great councils were held that brought together leading churchmen from the other kingdoms of England. Offa operated on an international stage, negotiating with the pope, setting up a short-lived archbishopric at Lichfield in despite of Canterbury, treating with Charlemagne as an equal on marriage alliances and trade. Indeed, a quarrel with Charlemagne over the quality of goods shipped to Francia (among other things) led to the first recorded formal trade dispute in English history.

Offa's ruthlessness bred hostility among subject peoples, notably in East Anglia (where young King Ethelbert had been the victim of a particularly outrageous assassination) and in Kent. Attempts to ensure the easy acceptance of his son Ecgfrith by recognition in Offa's lifetime and an adoption of a formal anointing to the kingship were only partially successful. Ecgfrith died a few months after his father, and the kinsmen who succeeded him and held the Mercian kingdom together for a generation never acquired the prestige of Offa. In 802 Egbert, the West Saxon prince, returned to Wessex from a profitable period of exile at the court of Charlemagne and slowly built up the power that was to displace Mercian supremacy.

WEST SAXON SUPREMACY

The reign of Egbert (802–839) is an important landmark in English history, but there are many ob-

scurities connected with it. The Anglo-Saxon Chronicle gives the impression of a long, quiet period of consolidation followed by swift and decisive campaigns against the Mercians as the direct Mercian dynasty died out and subject peoples rebelled. In 825 Egbert won a great victory at Ellandun (now Nether) Wroughton, and he was said to have conquered Mercia and everything south of the Humber in 829, thus becoming the "eighth king who was 'Bretwalda.'" The chronicler thus linked Egbert with the seven strong rulers singled out for special mention by Bede as men who held an *imperium* over much or all of England: Ælle of the South Saxons, Ceawlin of the West Saxons, Ethelbert of Kent, Rædwald of East Anglia, and the Northumbrians Edwin, Oswald, and Oswy. Whether by design or by accident the chronicler made no mention of the Mercian rulers, not even of Offa. In any event Mercia quickly recovered its independence, but Egbert's victories marked the first step toward West Saxon supremacy. His last recorded campaigns were directed successfully against an alliance of Cornishmen and Danish pirates at Hingston Down in 838.

The fact that Egbert laid the foundations of West Saxon hegemony has led many to consider the possibility that there was some special virtue in Wessex that permitted its ultimate triumph. Undoubtedly a greater mixture of races was present in the West Saxon kingdom, the indigenous Celtic folk enjoying a substantial role in social life. Communications were easier in the south than in the Midlands. Kent acquiesced more readily to West Saxon overlordship after its miserable experience with the Mercians, and with Kent came support from the archbishops of Canterbury. Access to the wealth of Francia, and ultimately of the Mediterranean, was also simpler for those in command of the south and southeast coasts.

For a political answer to a political question, however, immediate practical advantages rather than theoretical virtues should be considered. For two centuries and more after the death of Egbert, the Scandinavian menace threatened settled Christian English life; and Wessex, though ravaged, was farthest from the areas of greatest interest to the Danish migrants and colonizers in the northeast and eastern Midlands. The other advantage possessed by the West Saxons turned out to be the personal qualities of their rulers. For more than a century, up to the death of Edgar in 975, the dynasty provided a succession of able kings, of whom four—Alfred the Great (871–899), his son Edward (899–924), his grandson Athelstan (924–939), and Edgar (959–975)—must rank among the ablest men ever to occupy an English throne.

The Scandinavian menace, manifested in a series of piratic raids dating from the sack of the Northumbrian monastery at Lindisfarne in 793, intensified and altered its nature in the mid ninth century. In 850–851 the Danes first spent the winter in England. In 865 they opened a devastating campaign. Northumbria and East Anglia were overrun and the last native East Anglian king, Edmund, was martyred (869) in savage circumstances that were remembered for generations. A cult of Edmund, king and martyr, quickly sprang up, and his memory was honored even in the still-pagan North. Mercia and Wessex were under desperate threat when in 871, the "year of battles," the young prince Alfred succeeded his brother, virtually while on campaign, as king of the West Saxons.

Alfred, the only English king known to historians as "the Great," was by any criterion a remarkable man. More is known about him than about most early medieval figures thanks to his biographer, Asser, and the Anglo-Saxon Chronicle, which was put together in the form familiar to later generations during the later part of his reign. Those contemporaries or near contemporaries who wrote about him wrote from a West Saxon viewpoint, and a note of adulation was struck, sometimes amplified by medieval and modern commentators. It may be wondered if contemporary Northumbrians, East Angles, or East Mercians, governed by pagan or newly converted Scandinavians, held him in quite such high esteem.

Even so, his achievements were considerable, just as the perils that faced him were great and at one point, in 878, almost overwhelming. The Scandinavians, especially the Danes, were out for territory to settle. In 876 their leader, Healfdene (or Halfdan), shared out the land of Northumbria, and "they proceeded to plough and support themselves." In the following year the Danes partitioned Mercia with the native ruler, Ceolwulf, described by the Chronicle as "a foolish king's thegn." The concerted move against Alfred came in 878. Taken by surprise at midwinter, he fled with a few companions to the marshy fastness of Athelney in Somerset, but, keeping his nerve, he was able to rally the West Saxons and to force peace on the Danish leader Guthrum.

The terms of the peace proved curiously permanent socially, even though politically they may be read merely as an incident in the train of events leading to the unification of England. Alfred's sphere of influence was confined to the south and west of a line drawn along the Thames estuary, up the Lea River (immediately east of London) to its source, then straight to Bedford, up the Ouse to Watling Street, with an ultimate extension along Watling Street toward Chester. In other words, all England except Wessex and Western Mercia passed under the control of the Scandinavians, some of whom, including Guthrum, accepted Christianity.

When Alfred occupied London in 886 he very intelligently entrusted the city to the care of a Mercian nobleman, Ethelred, who became his son-in-law. To the north and east, within an area later known as the Danelaw, Scandinavian settlement intensified. Between 892 and 896 a last great effort was made to overcome Wessex, but the attempt failed. All the English people not subject to the Danes now more than ever looked to Alfred as their lord. By his conscious and systematic support of the church and by active concentration on what was essentially a program of Christian education, Alfred raised the kingship of the West Saxons to new heights. His royal line, the "kin that went [back] to Cerdic" as the Chronicle described it, was the sole ancient dynasty to survive the Danish attacks, and as such, with its strong Christian emphasis, it became the natural focal point for English nationalism.

Alfred's successors proved worthy of their heritage. Edward, helped by his sister Æthelflæd, lady of the Mercians, and her husband Ethelred, began the slow process of reconquering the Danelaw and (equally important) broke down the ancient animosities between West Saxons and Mercians. Athelstan completed the process, reabsorbing rather than conquering much of the Danelaw and finally even Northumbria. The situation was still fluid: a Scandinavian kingdom again emerged at York in the 940's, when for a brief time the possibility of a political unit based on the Viking communities of York and Dublin seemed far from unrealistic. But after the flight and subsequent death of Eric (Eiríkr) Bloodaxe (954), the last Scandinavian king of York, the way was open to completion of the West Saxon conquest.

Again the right man was there for the occasion. After a few years of uncertainty, Edgar succeeded as sole ruler of the Anglo Saxons in 959. He was perhaps lucky in the timing of his reign—a period of rare freedom from Scandinavian pressure—and he took full advantage of his opportunity. In the secular field Edgar was known for the good peace he kept and for his laws, which applied to both Danish and Anglo-Saxon England. In the ecclesiastical field he gave full support to the great movement for monastic reform associated with Dunstan, his archbishop of Canterbury, and bishops Ethelwold of Winchester and Oswald of Worcester. Edgar's splendid coronation at Bath in 973, followed by a ceremonial rowing on the Dee by Celtic, as well as Anglo-Scandinavian princes, testifies to the majesty and range of his Christian kingship.

A massive reform of the currency late in Edgar's reign, which made Anglo-Saxon silver coinage preeminent in Europe, gave evidence of the integrity and practical efficiency of his administration. The only coin to be minted as a matter of routine was (as in the rest of western Europe during the early medieval period) the silver penny, but standards of consistency of weight and craftmanship were high. Central control was maintained by savage legal penalties for false or inferior coinage and by the issue of dies from recognized centers only. At regular intervals—six years at first and two or three at the end of the Anglo-Saxon period—the coinage was recalled and fresh coins minted at sixty or more accredited mints throughout the realm. The legal claims of earlier kings, such as Athelstan, that "one coinage should run throughout the realm" were made reality by Edgar's reforms.

975–1066

The last century of Anglo-Saxon England was a time of political and dynastic turbulence. Edgar died young in 975, and the murder of his eldest son, Edward the Martyr, at Corfe Castle in 978, followed by the long and substantially unhappy reign of the younger son, Ethelred (978–1016), laid the kingdom open to renewed troubles. Scandinavian attacks were pressed hard in the later years of the century, with national leaders, Norwegian as well as Danish, taking part. English defeat in 991 at the Battle of Maldon was followed by the first payment of danegeld, and the Danish armies under the control of King Sweyn Forkbeard and then of his son, Cnut, eventually proved triumphant. Cnut governed England as part of a Danish empire for almost twenty years (1016–1035). The old dynasty was restored under Edward the Confessor, Ethelred's son (1042–1066), a much more capable ruler than reputation and legend would have him. Edward's death, and the succession of the strongest man in the kingdom, Harold, earl of

Wessex (regarded by the Normans as a usurper and oath breaker), paved the way for the Norman conquest.

It should be recognized that throughout this period of dynastic change the basic integrity of the kingdom remained inviolate. Halfhearted attempts at partition or asserting the independence of great regional earldoms failed. Cnut was as much a king of England as Edgar had been, and he was proud to rule in the same legal and religious tradition. The earls under Cnut and his successors were strong, but they were subject to formal appointment from above by the king (with the advice of his council) and to pressures from below by the thanes and powerful men of the shires. The territorial structure of government was firmly established in shires, hundreds, wapentakes, and boroughs, with their distinctive system of courts. The pattern of medieval local government was fully formed by the time of the conquest, needing only the military discipline of the Normans and the reinforced strength of their sheriffs to mold it into final shape.

The outstanding achievement of the Anglo-Saxon period may, therefore, be held to be the creation of a unified kingdom out of a hodgepodge of minor political units and a variety of peoples. The dominant stock and the dominant language were Germanic: West Germanic reinforced by a strong admixture of North Germanic from the Scandinavian invaders and settlers in the latter half of the period. Political unity was coupled with the steady and ultimately effective development of the economy. The Anglo-Saxons and the Scandinavians were the first to exploit fully the agrarian capacity of England. Plowmen and cereal growers, but also masters of mixed farming, they built up the pattern of settlement in English villages and hamlets that was to remain familiar well into modern times. Whole tracts of prosperous and fertile land from Wiltshire to the Vale of York, from East Anglia to Dorset, had as many villages in 1066 as they were to have in 1700—and in favored areas as heavy and concentrated a population.

The last century and a half before the conquest was a period of urban growth. In the seventh century there were already some centers, notably London, that deserved to be called towns. It was not until after the reign of Alfred, however, that urban activity became widespread throughout England south of the Humber and at York. Defensive fortifications known as *burhs*, set up by Alfred and his immediate successors, developed where conditions were favorable into recognizable boroughs, enjoying their own legal customs and organization, dependent on trade and the mobile world of the merchant as well as on the agrarian economy.

In the Danelaw similar growth took place. Unlike the Anglo-Saxons, the Danes retained their skill at sea, and the towns of the east and north, supremely York but also the Five Boroughs (Lincoln, Nottingham, Derby, Leicester, and Stamford), as well as Thetford and Cambridge, thrived during the last century of Anglo-Saxon England. There is evidence of more intensive economic activity, notably connected with sheep rearing and wool production. The wealth of eleventh-century England was famous throughout western Europe.

RELIGIOUS AND CULTURAL ACTIVITY

Modern knowledge of seventh-century England is dominated by the story of Christianization. Pope Gregory I the Great (590–604) was the driving force behind the initial conversion, and the arrival of St. Augustine in 597 coincided with the first moves toward consolidation of the kingdoms. Christianity was a universal religion that had much to offer to pagan settlers from the intrinsic value of its message. The Christian church in western Europe was the direct heir of Rome, and acceptance of the faith brought direct contact with the civilized world of the Mediterranean and Francia. Christianity fostered a keen sense of law and of the responsibility of office, and it provided the English kings with literate servants, allowing the establishment of permanent institutions of government, law codes, charters, and (late in the period) formal wills and writs.

The actual course of the conversion is clear in general outline, partly because its story has been transmitted by one master historian, the Venerable Bede, who wrote his account at a time when memory of many of the events was still fresh. In the first generation (597–633) the initiative rested with the missionaries, St. Augustine and his successors, who came directly from Rome. Their approach was slow and cautious, depending essentially on the conversion of kings and royal courts. Their achievement in the southeast was permanent: the conversion of Kent, the establishment of an archbishopric at Canterbury and bishoprics at London and Rochester, and the further extension of Christianity to Essex and the peoples surrounding London. They also (627–632) planted the seeds of the Christian message at the court of King Edwin of Northumbria. The

second generation (633–663) saw the great breakthrough, with Celtic missionaries joining the Romans to spread Christianity throughout England, even through Mercia after the death of the obdurate heathen King Penda in 654.

In the last decades of the seventh century, after differences of custom and usage between Romans and Celts had been resolved at the Synod of Whitby in 663, the church was consolidated and put on a firm institutional basis under the direction of Archbishop Theodore of Tarsus (668–690), one of the greatest archbishops of Canterbury. Men of outstanding ability, such as Abbot Adrian of Canterbury, St. Wilfrid of Ripon and York, St. Cuthbert of Lindisfarne, and St. Benedict Biscop, founder of the monasteries of Jarrow and Wearmouth, flourished in this consolidating generation of the conversion. Sussex, the last of the organized Anglo-Saxon kingdoms to succumb, accepted the new faith, thanks largely to the efforts of St. Wilfrid in the early 680's. The creation of an organized church with diocesan bishops, powerful monasteries, synods, councils, and written legislation on customs and procedures relating to services, baptism, confirmation, and penance foreshadowed the later unity of England itself.

Two immediate consequences of the conversion deserve attention. A cultural revival of importance to the whole of western Europe took place in England, and supremely in Northumbria, in the late seventh and early eighth centuries, expressing itself above all in literature (the work of Bede and Aldhelm) and in the production of superb illuminated manuscripts such as the Lindisfarne Gospels. The other consequence was of even more importance. A reverse movement of missionaries back to the Continent took place and was largely instrumental in effecting the conversion of the Germans east of the Rhine. St. Boniface (Winfrid from Crediton in Devon) was the driving force behind this movement; he was the first archbishop of Mainz and active beyond the Frankish border until his martyrdom at the hands of the Frisians in 754. The church continued to flourish in spite of the political troubles of the eighth century, and Charlemagne was content to draw one of his principal ecclesiastical and cultural advisers from Northumbria: the great scholar Alcuin, who had been trained in the school at York.

Much of the ninth century, owing to the dislocations caused by the Scandinavian invasions, was a time of tribulation for the church, but toward the end of the century Alfred emerged as its energetic supporter. His program of translating useful literature into Old English helped to make the West Saxon monarchy a true basis for a Christian kingship of England.

His successors carried on the good work. Edgar's support of the monastic revival in the mid tenth century proved vastly important in politics as well as in culture. The new monasteries—some, such as Ramsey, Peterborough, and Ely (later Bury St. Edmunds), firmly planted in the Danelaw—were well endowed and provided permanent bases of strength to the English church and state. Their educational work in the vernacular has yet to be fully appreciated, and they sent out a steady stream of well-educated, powerful men to serve as bishops. In spite of the turbulence of the reign of Ethelred and the subsequent Danish conquest, the inner social stability of England was preserved in large part by the efforts of men trained in these Benedictine monasteries.

On the eve of the Norman conquest there were abuses in the English church. The archbishop of Canterbury, Stigand, was a political figure, pluralism was a common fault, particularly among the higher clergy, and, as in the Germanic world, the lower clergy were, to say the least, ambivalent toward celibacy. But overall the Anglo-Saxon church (like the Anglo-Saxon state) had much to be proud of in its stable organization and its educational activities. The works of the great scholars Ælfric and Wulfstan were widely known and disseminated. Churchmen were active in the inner workings of the royal household and government. Encouragement of vernacular literacy, initially for religious purposes, helped to preserve the finest Anglo-Saxon poetry and prose. There were imperfections in the Anglo-Saxon polity, but it was an essentially Christian and potentially integrated society that William of Normandy came to rule in 1066.

BIBLIOGRAPHY

Sources. English Historical Documents, I, *c. 500–1042*, Dorothy Whitelock, ed. (1955, 2nd ed. 1979) is indispensable not only for the vast amount of material in dependable translation but for the detailed bibliography and indications of best modern editions to use such as the great edition of Anglo-Saxon laws by Felix Liebermann, *Die Gesetze der Angelsachsen*, 3 vols. (1903–1916).

Studies. The outstanding modern history of England in this period remains Frank M. Stenton, *Anglo-Saxon England* (1943, 3rd ed. 1971). Other studies of value are: Frank Barlow, *The English Church, 1000–1066* (1963, 2nd ed. 1979), and *Edward the Confessor* (1970); P. Hunter Blair, *An Introduction to Anglo-Saxon England* (1956, 2nd ed. 1978); Christopher N. L. Brooke, *The Saxon and Nor-*

man Kings (1963); James Campbell, ed., *The Anglo-Saxons* (1982); R. H. N. Dolley, *Anglo-Saxon Pennies* (1964); David Hill, *An Atlas of Anglo-Saxon England* (1981); Charles W. Hollister, ed., *The Making of England 55 B.C.– 1399*, 2nd ed. (1971); David Knowles, *The Monastic Order in England* (1940, 2nd ed. 1963); Wilhelm Levison, *England and the Continent in the Eighth Century* (1946); Henry R. Loyn, *Anglo-Saxon England and the Norman Conquest* (1962), and *The Vikings in Britain* (1977); Bryce D. Lyon, *A Constitutional and Legal History of Medieval England* (1960); P. H. Sawyer, *From Roman Britain to Norman England* (1978); Frank M. Stenton, *Preparatory to Anglo-Saxon England*, Doris M. Stenton, ed. (1970); John M. Wallace-Hadrill, *Early Germanic Kingship in England and on the Continent* (1971); Dorothy Whitelock, *The Beginnings of English Society* (1952).

H. R. Loyn

[See also **Alcuin of York; Aldhelm; Alfred the Great; Anglo-Saxons, Origins and Migration; Augustine of Canterbury; Bede; Benedict Biscop, St.; Boniface, St.; Borough (England–Wales); Canterbury; Cnut the Great; Danegeld; Danelaw; Edward the Confessor of England, St.; Ethelred II the Unready; Ethelwold and the Benedictine Rule; Hundred (Land Division); Lindisfarne Gospels; Mints and Money, Western European; Oswald, St.: Epics; Shire; Urbanism, Western European: To 1000; Vikings; Whitby, Synod of.**]

ENGLAND: NORMAN-ANGEVIN. Until 1066 the history of the British Isles was dominated by the political, institutional, religious, and cultural achievements of the Anglo-Saxon state. After the middle of the tenth century this state stretched north from the English Channel to the southern border of the kingdom of Scotland, which ran southwest from the Tweed to the Irish Sea, and west to that squarish peninsula known as Wales, which was never incorporated into the Anglo-Saxon kingdom but was held by a number of Welsh chiefs descended from the Celts. Also outside the Anglo-Saxon orbit was Ireland, the eastern part of which, however, had succumbed to bands of Norwegians after 850.

In 1066 this long period of Anglo-Saxon ascendancy was terminated by a political regime that wrought change so fundamental historians have considered this year a major watershed in the history of England. It was then that the Normans crossed the English Channel to conquer Anglo-Saxon England and to build what soon became the most remarkable political structure of western Europe. The Normans ruled England from 1066 to 1154, and

SCOTLAND

Tweed R.

IRELAND

Irish Sea

Lancaster
•York

Lincoln

WALES

•Shrewsbury

Norwich•

Northampton• •Cambridge
Ipswich•

Gloucester
•Oxford
Cardiff
London•
•Bristol
Windsor• •Runnymede Canterbury•
Thames R.
Dover•
Salisbury• Winchester• Hastings•
Exeter•
Boulogne•
FLANDERS

HOLY ROMAN
EMPIRE

•Bouvines

English Channel

Rouen•
Rheims•

NORMANDY
Mantes• *Seine* Paris
•Tinchebray
•Mortain
CHAMPAGNE
Chartres•
ÎLE-DE-FRANCE

BRITTANY
MAINE
Orléans•

BLOIS
Loire *R.*
TOURAINE
BERRY
BURGUNDY
ANJOU Chinon•
POITOU
Poitiers•
Lusignan•

Châlus•
AUVERGNE
Angoulême• LIMOUSIN

ENGLISH TERRITORIES
at the End of the 12th Century

Dordogne *R.*
Bordeaux•

English lands in France

AQUITAINE
DAUPHINÉ

Lands ruled by the French king

GASCONY

Lands held by vassals of the French king

LANGUEDOC

TOULOUSE

their descendants, the Angevins, from 1154 to 1216. These two exceptionally able dynasties laid the foundation for political and legal institutions, unique in western Europe, that with modification still function today. After 1066 England became part of a complex of lands encompassing much of northwest France that has sometimes been called the Angevin Empire. Although England may well have been the richest possession of the Norman-Angevin kings until 1216, it was but one of their holdings and was generally regarded as second to their continental interests. Inevitably, therefore, after 1066 England became more involved in the major historical developments on the Continent.

WILLIAM THE CONQUEROR (1066–1087)

When the ineffective Anglo-Saxon king Edward the Confessor (1042–1066) died without an heir, the leading men of the realm offered the crown to Harold, the powerful earl of Wessex, who had actually ruled England in the last years of Edward's reign. Able and energetic, Harold was king for only nine months before losing his kingdom and his life to Duke William of Normandy, a claimant to the English throne. A ruthless adventurer, William had no legitimate rights but made three spurious claims: he was a distant relative of Edward the Confessor by marriage, Edward had promised him the throne, and Harold, when shipwrecked on the Norman coast, had agreed to support his claim. Convincing the pope that the Anglo-Saxon church deviated from various continental practices and that he would support church reform, he secured papal blessing for the conquest of England as a kind of crusade.

With fighters recruited from Normandy and northern France, William assembled a fleet and sailed with the first favorable wind, landing in southern England on 28 September 1066. He marched inland to Hastings, where he prepared to meet Harold, who had just subdued a rebellion of his brother Tostig in northern England. The two forces met on 14 October. In a battle that could have gone either way, Harold was defeated and killed. The mounted Norman knights prevailed over the Anglo-Saxon foot soldiers. With effective Anglo-Saxon resistance soon ended, William occupied London and became the acknowledged lawful ruler of England by assent of the assembled Anglo-Saxons and Normans at his coronation in Westminister Abbey on Christmas Day. By the following March his hold over England was so secure that he returned to Normandy, remaining there until December.

Had William the Conqueror and his immediate successors not been talented rulers, the Norman Conquest might have been transitory. Instead, their rule of almost a century fundamentally transformed English society. Superb fighters, energetic, ruthless, and greedy, they exhibited that special Norman talent for readily adapting to foreign customs and institutions, retaining those that were effective, introducing their own, and then making a fusion that resulted in even better ones. For this reason the period between 1066 and 1154 is known as that of Anglo-Norman institutions.

As conqueror of England, William was occasionally confronted with rebellions and attempts at invasion from the Danes and Norwegians, threats he easily thwarted while also maintaining his authority in the duchy of Normandy and adroitly holding his own against both his Capetian overlord, Philip I of France, and the neighboring counts of Flanders and Anjou. As a defense against the Welsh he established a group of earldoms in western England. In 1072 a show of force against Scotland induced the Scottish king, Malcolm III, to do homage to William. The unchallenged master of England by 1086, William was secure enough to display his strength by two acts. He ordered an inquest that produced the famous *Domesday Book,* an amazing record that provided an accurate account of the resources of his kingdom and of his annual income, and is proof of the efficient government he had constructed. He also assembled a great council of his magnates at Salisbury, where he received their oaths of fealty. He then demanded an oath of fealty from all lesser aristocrats and freemen with whom he had no direct tenurial relations. That he could enforce this oath demonstrated that he had become a ruler to whom all free subjects owed their supreme loyalty.

William's last months were spent in Normandy, where he was injured while watching the burning of Mantes, and died at Rouen on 9 September 1087. Before dying he provided for his three sons. According to the feudal custom of primogeniture, Normandy went to his eldest son, Robert Curthose. William Rufus, his second son, received England, with which William could do as he wished, since it had been acquired by conquest. The third son, Henry, received only a large grant of money and treasure. A testament to William's ability is that even the anti-Norman Anglo-Saxon Chronicle admitted his accomplishments. Noting his power, wisdom, and dignity, it concluded that "the good security he made in his country is not to be forgotten—so that any honest man could travel over his kingdom without injury with his bosom full of gold."

WILLIAM RUFUS (1087–1100)

In William Rufus, England acquired a king with all the bad qualities of his family and none of the good save for his prowess as a fighter and hunter. His reign was characterized by the extortion of money from his subjects and the church, most of which he lavished in bribes and on mercenaries to wrest Normandy from his brother, an incompetent ruler who was unpopular with the Norman aristocracy. William forced some concessions of land from Robert and in 1096 temporarily acquired Normandy from his brother. Anxious to go on the First Crusade but penniless, Robert pawned his duchy to William for three years for 10,000 marks of silver. During Robert's absence William received all the income from Normandy and on Robert's return in 1100 was not inclined to return the pawn.

Robert regained his duchy only by William's untimely death. Toward sunset on 2 August 1100 William, engrossed in pursuing a deer he had wounded while hunting in the New Forest near Winchester, was killed by Walter Tirel, a hunting companion who took aim at the deer but instead pierced the king's heart. It may have been an accident, but the fact that Walter was a friend of William's brother Henry, who was also in the royal hunting party, makes it appear more likely to have been a deliberate act. The king's death elicited no grief, Walter sought immediate safety in Normandy, and Henry galloped off to Winchester to secure the royal treasure. No one was punished for William's death.

HENRY I (1100–1135)

With the speed and determination that characterized his fruitful reign, Henry had himself elected king by a small group of barons the day after William's death and on 5 August was crowned as Henry I at Westminster Abbey. With no time to lose in consolidating his position in England, Henry issued a coronation charter promising an end to the wrongs of William Rufus and a future government according to the principles of justice and the established laws of England. He also achieved at least temporarily better relations with the church. Simply bidding for support, Henry never fulfilled most of the promises of the charter and yet, curiously, it later came to be regarded as a precedent for good government and a model for Magna Carta. By easily suppressing a revolt favoring his brother Robert in 1101 and then

buying Robert's recognition of his royal title with a grant of money, Henry gained firm control of England within a year of his accession.

Two objectives dominated Henry—the conquest and pacification of Normandy and the provision for peaceful succession to his Anglo-Norman realm. Bribing Norman barons and concluding alliances with the counts of Flanders, Anjou, and Brittany, he launched his campaign against the hapless Robert in 1104. With many of the key towns and castles occupied by 1105, he proceeded to inflict a crushing defeat on Robert outside the castle of Tinchebrai on 28 September 1106. Captured and sent to Cardiff Castle, Robert languished there for the remaining twenty-eight years of his life.

Although Henry promptly restored orderly government to Normandy, and although it remained part of the Norman-Angevin possessions for the next century, the reuniting of one of the strongest states of France with England was resented by Louis VI of France and by the counts of Flanders and Anjou. Their repeated attempts to weaken Henry's grip on the duchy succeeded only in forcing him to spend more than half of his reign on the Continent, where he so adroitly played off his opponents against each other that he gained even firmer control over Normandy.

More worrisome than Normandy was the task of providing for a successor. Henry had children in abundance—twenty-two, to be precise—but only two were legitimate. His hopes were centered on his son William, but one stormy night in November 1120 William drowned while crossing the Channel from Normandy to England when the *White Ship* hit a rock and all passengers but one were lost. This disaster deprived Henry of his sole male heir and eventually led to a war of succession and twenty years of discord. Henry's only other legal offspring was his daughter Matilda, who was married to King Henry V of Germany. When her husband died in 1125, she returned to England; in 1127 Henry forced his barons to recognize her as the next lawful ruler. By marrying Matilda to Geoffrey, son of Count Fulk of Anjou, in 1128, Henry detached Anjou from its alliance with Louis VI of France and provided Matilda with a husband who could champion her cause. This union begot Henry Plantagenet, future heir of England and founder of the Angevin dynasty. Henry went to Normandy in August 1133 to see his grandson and never returned to England.

When he died in December 1135, this last of the great Norman kings had assembled a rich collection of lands. The centralized government he had nurtured in England provided the springboard for the institutional innovations of the future Henry II. Fate would have it that this industrious monarch should leave this heritage to a woman incapable of ruling it and deprived of baronial support.

MATILDA AND STEPHEN (1135–1154)

Though forced by Henry to acknowledge Matilda as his successor, few of the English barons abided by their oath after his death. Disdainful of the rule of a woman, especially one who alienated them with her haughty behavior, most promptly supported Stephen, count of Boulogne and Mortain and lord of English estates in Lancaster and Eye, despite the tenuousness of his heritable claim as the son of Adela, William the Conqueror's daughter. With Matilda's Angevin supporters initially overcome by surprise, Stephen rallied most of England to his side. Like Henry I he issued a coronation charter confirming all the good and lawful usages of England, and made concessions to both the church and the baronage in return for their support.

Stephen's reign was, however, disastrous because he lacked those qualities that had made his predecessors successful. A talented warrior, he was too chivalrous to his opponents. Loath to make decisions, he temporized and compromised. Matilda was soon able to win considerable baronial support, and civil war broke out in England and Normandy. During almost twenty years when the victories of neither Stephen nor Matilda were decisive enough to give either of them mastery over England and Normandy, royal government weakened and lost much of its authority to the barons, who illegally exercised legal, administrative, and fiscal powers. Many constructed unauthorized (adulterine) castles, took control of large areas of England, and shamelessly shifted their support back and forth to secure even more concessions. Not until the mid fifteenth century would England again know such disorder and the breakdown of central government.

By 1150 the Angevins had secured control over Normandy, and Matilda's son Henry then became duke. When his father Geoffrey died in 1151, he succeeded him as count of Anjou. His wedding in 1152 to Eleanor of Aquitaine, then divorced from Louis VII of France, secured for Henry the duchy of Aquitaine, the largest feudal state in southwest France. Henry was now prepared to invade England, which he did in 1153. Meanwhile, Stephen's wife, Matilda, had died, and with the death of his son Eustace, to

whom he had looked as his successor, Stephen lost any incentive for continuing the struggle. Through the intermediary of the church a truce was arranged, and the Treaty of Winchester (November 1153) stated that Stephen would rule England until his death, whereupon Henry would succeed him. Less than a year later, on 25 October 1154, Stephen died. The twenty years of strife and drift that had concluded the Norman period were to be followed by one of the most dynamic epochs in the history of medieval England.

NORMAN INSTITUTIONS AND LAW

England's association with a group of continental possessions made the Norman kings the most powerful princes of western Europe and fostered the development of unique and effective political institutions. The most fundamental change was the rapid feudalization of England, which prior to 1066 had known the social and economic system of manorialism, with its estates tilled by peasants under the lordship of a landed aristocracy, but had not known feudal institutions as they had developed on the Continent.

Under William the Conqueror the Norman system of feudalism was introduced. By virtue of his conquest William was the supreme lord of his new realm, able to dispose of it as he saw fit. Much of the land (royal domain) he kept for the support of himself, his family, and his government. He also granted much land in fief to the leading ecclesiastics and some land in free alms to ecclesiastical institutions, such as abbeys, in return for spiritual services. The rest he granted out in fiefs of land as rewards to those French warriors who had come with him to England and who in turn granted out parts of their fiefs to some of their followers. Soon virtually all the Anglo-Saxon landholders were replaced by the French feudal aristocracy, all of whom were the direct vassals or subvassals of William. In return for their fiefs these vassals owed military, political, and legal services to the king. By the feudal system William and his successors governed their realm.

The daily entourage of the king consisted of some of the great vassals, who, along with such functionaries of the royal household as the chancellor, chamberlains, marshal, and constable, constituted a small council for attending to routine business. Only on extraordinary occasions, when the king desired counsel on some political or military problem, needed a special grant of money, or had to render justice for an important case, did he supplement this semipermanent cadre of govenment by summoning his immediate vassals, known as tenants in chief or barons, to a great council to meet and discuss common concerns of the realm. All tasks requiring a knowledge of Latin were performed by the clergy. The chancellor, for example, who guarded the great seal and headed the writing office, was ordinarily a bishop who, assisted by a staff of clerics, was responsible for drawing up and keeping documents.

Royal valuables such as the crown, jewels, plate, and money were kept in the chamber, under the custody of the two chamberlains. They received the royal income and disbursed it when so ordered. As more money came into circulation and as the royal income and government expanded, financial administration was gradually modified. To store the increased amounts of money, a permanent treasury was established at Winchester, but it had to keep the chamber supplied with money as it moved about with the king. In the reign of Henry I this system was replaced by a new financial office, known as the Exchequer, which was responsible for storing the royal income, auditing the accounts of royal officials (such as the sheriffs who collected revenues), disbursing the money, and recording these transactions on what is known as a pipe roll. The head of this new system was a treasurer, assisted by a staff of professionals who kept the records and even tested the quality of the silver coins. Thus began the Exchequer, which is still the English treasury.

By the eleventh century Anglo-Saxon England had developed a system of law that, in spite of being highly Germanic, was in most respects advanced over those on the Continent. So far as we know, the Norman legal system lagged behind the Anglo-Saxon. In a few respects, however, it was more developed and showed the influence of the more rational and sophisticated Roman law that was in the midst of its revival during the eleventh century. Such advance was probably due to certain churchmen (such as Lanfranc) who had studied in Italy and were prominent advisers of William.

To obtain information for settling cases, the Normans had developed the inquest system, whereby a group of men was empaneled and asked certain questions under oath. Such a system merely provided information; it did not produce a verdict. The inquest, which seems to have been a Carolingian institution that the Normans adopted and introduced into England, was to become a fundamental part of the amazing legal system that developed between 1066 and 1216. The Normans also brought with them feu-

dal custom that governed the relations of the aristocracy and used trial by combat to settle disputes. This trial was added to the traditional ones of ordeal and compurgation. Rarely in the Norman period was the evidence of the written charter presented in a court.

At first it appeared that William might favor two laws—Anglo-Saxon for the native population and Norman for the conquerors. With intermarriage and the increased mixing of the two populations, this proved unworkable. By the reign of Henry I any distinction separating the two laws had been blotted out. It is correct, however, to call the law of England in the Norman period Anglo-Norman law because the best of the Anglo-Saxon was retained and blended with the Norman. This was the law enforced at the king's great and small councils and by the shire (county) and hundred courts that came to be regarded as public courts for all freemen. Feudal law was administered in feudal courts and manorial law in the manorial courts.

Another important legal change wrought by the Normans was the separation of church and secular courts. Prior to 1066 cases that fell under canon law had been tried in shire courts at which the bishop and important churchmen were in attendance. By an ordinance of 1072 William proclaimed that henceforth all canon law cases should be settled in proper ecclesiastical courts. This reform brought usage into accordance with that on the Continent. The Normans, it should be emphasized, took over a legal system that had been spread throughout the realm rather than a group of localized legal systems, and by means of their strong and centralized government they ensured that Anglo-Norman law would prosper and become even more common to all the realm.

Although William the Conqueror had governed in Normandy by using his feudal vassals for local administration and for holding ducal castles, in England he retained the nonfeudal system of local Anglo-Saxon government. For some time England had been divided into districts called shires that were administered by sheriffs responsible for administration, security, justice, and collection of the royal revenues. Under the Normans the shires, now called counties, continued to be administered by sheriffs appointed and dismissed at the royal will. Never was the office of sheriff feudalized. The counties were divided into smaller districts, called hundreds, that were administered by nonfeudal officers known as hundred reeves. In a few cases the Norman kings granted large fiefs along the Welsh and Scottish borders to great vassals called earls, who had the arduous military responsibility of defending these frontier areas and, as a reward, were permitted to exercise all the functions of a sheriff. Such privileged districts were called palatinates.

ECONOMIC REVIVAL AND THE BOROUGH

In 1066 England, like most of the Continent, was essentially sustained by an agrarian economy. The economic revival of the late tenth and eleventh centuries had not yet progressed enough to make more than minor transformations in the economy. During the eleventh century, however, the commercial revival affected some of the strategically situated boroughs—of which London, Dover, Bristol, York, and Lincoln were typical—most of which had been administrative, military, and ecclesiastical centers. Increasingly they became centers of both local and overseas commerce, and a few saw industries develop. In the process some differentiated themselves from the agrarian countryside and became much more urban. Their inhabitants, who continued to fulfill the traditional military, administrative, and ecclesiastical functions, came to be outnumbered by merchants and craftsmen.

Under the Normans this process quickened because their conquest of England put it more in touch with economic development on the Continent, which, in such areas as Flanders and northern Italy, was more advanced. During the Norman period the boroughs became commercial and industrial centers whose inhabitants, the burgesses, were primarily occupied with economic affairs. Because of their different occupations and way of life, they received special social, economic and legal privileges. Unlike the peasants they were free, could buy and sell land, could go wherever they desired, and were tried in borough courts under a law that fulfilled their mercantile and industrial needs. The law merchant of these courts provided for the settlement of debts and contracts, and levied penalities on those who sold shoddy products or who did not fulfill their obligations. Such law was totally different from feudal and manorial custom.

In most boroughs the burgesses organized economic associations, called guilds, that gave them economic solidarity, greater buying power, and some leverage in negotiating with royal officers. The guilds regulated prices, quality of goods, and local trade. Some had their own halls, which served them as meeting places and also, at times, as borough halls, where meetings were held to deal with problems such as defense and taxation. Because of economic experience and knowledge gained in their travels, the guildsmen assumed leadership of the boroughs and by the 1130's were bargaining for the privileges of self-government. In London, where this objective was achieved, the burgesses assumed the functions of the sheriffs and other local royal officers, taking responsibility for administration, for collection of royal taxes, and for presiding over the borough court. Although not all boroughs became self-governing, the leading boroughs went in this direction. The more populous and affluent they became, the more concessions the king had to grant them.

The economic and political development of the borough in this period inevitably affected the countryside. The borough became a market for agrarian produce and a place of escape for the peasants, who increasingly fled from the manor to the borough to find employment and, in so doing, transformed their lives. They exchanged the unfreedom of the countryside, with its fetters and peasant obligations, for the freedom of the borough. They became burgesses. So the peasantry of England came to emancipate itself. To retain their labor force the lords had to compete, and thus began to commute peasant obligations, which essentially meant emancipation and the establishment between lord and peasant of a tenurial relation that entitled the peasant to a plot of land in return for an annual rent.

CHURCH REFORM AND CHURCH-STATE RELATIONS

William the Conqueror had received the support of Pope Alexander II for his invasion of England because of his promise to reform the English church, which actually did not deviate much from church ritual and government elsewhere. But William was dedicated to reform and earnestly supported it, although he failed to go as far as the reform Pope Gregory VII (1073–1085) could have wished. William never lost his tight control over the English church and never surrendered his practice of appointing clerics to their spiritual offices; but in attempting to appoint qualified clerics and in generally supporting the principles of Gregorian reform, he avoided the bitter confrontation over investiture that made Gregory's battle with Henry IV of Germany the cause célèbre of Western Christendom.

To accomplish the needed reforms, William promptly staffed the church with Norman and Lotharingian clergy sympathetic to the reform ideals.

In 1070 he appointed Lanfranc as archbishop of Canterbury, an exceptionally wise appointment because Lanfranc was a renowned theologian also learned in canon and Roman law and experienced in ecclesiastical administration. Lanfranc quickly moved to stamp out simony, plurality of offices, and the custom of married clergy. By 1080 all the Anglo-Saxon bishops had been replaced save one. Meanwhile a church council established the primacy of the archbishopric of Canterbury over that of York, which helped to alleviate the chronic quarrels between the respective archbishops and to establish a more sensible chain of command. Dioceses with cathedrals in small villages or towns had their headquarters moved to larger boroughs. Lanfranc also reformed the diocesan clergy down to the humblest parish priest. Although the secular clergy bore the brunt of the reform, Lanfranc also worked to see that English monasteries conformed with those on the Continent.

Because of the good sense with which William the Conqueror and Lanfranc pushed reform, England was spared the acrimonious church–state relations characteristic of Germany, Italy, and France. But all changed under William Rufus, who ignored the rights of the church, appointed unworthy clerics, held church offices vacant for long periods, and despoiled church possessions. Only in 1093, when he thought he was dying, did he consent to appoint an archbishop of Canterbury to fill a four-year vacancy. His choice was the renowned theologian Anselm of Bec, a choice quickly regretted because Anselm lacked the administrative experience of Lanfranc, was passionately dedicated to reform, and was basically a scholar. Refusing to acknowledge the authority of William Rufus over the English church, Anselm was soon engaged in a quarrel over lay investiture, the feudal service due from his lay fiefs, and the proper jurisdiction of spiritual and secular courts.

In 1097 Anselm defied William Rufus and went to Rome to consult with the pope; he remained on the Continent until Henry I became king. At first these two were able to cooperate, but soon Anselm's distaste for lay investiture and the homage performed by churchmen to lay lords led to a break. Refusing to do homage to Henry for his fiefs, Anselm returned to exile in 1103.

In 1106, under threat of excommunication, Henry decided to compromise. An agreement stipulated that henceforth there should be free ecclesiastical elections for offices and that lay investiture of clergy to their offices should end. Henry insisted, however, that such elections be held under royal supervision and that clergy must do homage for their lay fiefs before spiritual investiture occurred. This compromise, while smoothing over the major differences between Henry I and Anselm, did not end the problems associated with the proper authority of church and state. Generally Henry I prevailed, and not until the conflict between Stephen and Matilda were concessions made to the church by Stephen that undermined royal authority over the English church.

CULTURAL ACHIEVEMENT

Though never attaining the intellectual and artistic achievements of France and Italy that were spawned by the intellectual revival of western Europe, Norman England did participate in the general cultural movements of the age. Respected theologians whose works supported the philosophical position of realism, Lanfranc and Anselm both came from the Continent but brought renown to England and encouraged intellectual endeavor at the cathedrals, with the result that canon law came to be better understood and taught. In the twelfth century the principles of Roman law were also taught by such masters as Vacarius, who had served the archbishop of Canterbury, taught at the rising school at Oxford, and written a textbook on Roman law for students. The Normans were also renowned for construction of simple but powerful churches and sturdy stone castles. Even a few of the chroniclers bear comparison with some of the best in France. The English cathedral schools, however, did not equal those in France, nor did intellectual life produce the exciting achievements so characteristic of northern Italy.

HENRY II (1154–1189)

No description of a ruler's accession to the throne is more apt than that of the chronicler Gerald of Wales, who wrote that Henry II, crowned king on 19 December 1154, was smiled upon by the "admirable favor of fortune." Strong and robust, Henry was also singularly intelligent and possessed a good princely education. Keen for the chase yet equally intrigued by legal intricacies, good literature, and the sophisticated talk of cultured companions, this king, who spoke, wrote, and read Latin and French, concentrated feverishly on whatever business was at hand, whether war, diplomacy, or hawking. Surely the greatest of English medieval kings, he left the deepest imprint upon medieval institutions. Within six months after his coronation he brought order to war-torn England. Stephen's supporters were quashed and all adulterine castles were leveled or surrendered to royal officers. Henry made peace with all who wished it; he refrained from the vindictiveness of his mother. By 1155, with the government again operating efficiently, he could turn to other than domestic problems.

Like his Norman predecessors Henry was fundamentally a French prince who considered his continental possessions of paramount importance. Almost twenty of his thirty-four years as king were spent on the Continent. When in England he worked to stabilize its frontiers and guarantee their security. Along the Welsh border he retook lands lost during the civil war and forced the chief Welsh lords to do homage to him. With Scotland it was less easy. A settlement with the Scottish king in 1157 brought temporary peace, but in 1173–1174, when Henry's sons revolted, the Scottish king, William the Lion, supported them. He was captured, however, and had to surrender his five strongest castles on the frontier and to take Scotland in fief from Henry. He even had to permit Henry to take homage from his vassals.

Henry also became involved in Ireland. Some English barons had gone to Ireland in the 1160's to fight in a civil war with the hope of winning some land, which they did. Fearing that these barons might establish independent states, Henry went to Ireland in 1171 and forced both the English and the Irish lords to do homage for their lands. He returned to England in 1172, and the pope confirmed his lordship over Ireland. This brief adventure gave Henry control over the eastern third of Ireland.

Henry's continental problems were insolvable, and in fact never ended. In each possession, the totality of which comprised at least a third of France, he was repeatedly forced to subdue revolts or to outmaneuver alliances formed against him by the French kings Louis VII and Philip II Augustus. Almost to the end of his reign Henry was nevertheless extraordinarily successful. By 1173 he began to arrange for the inheritance of his lands. His eldest son, the Young Henry, was to inherit England, Normandy, and Anjou; his second son, Richard, would inherit Aquitaine. He married his third son, Geoffrey, to Constance, the heiress of the county of Brittany, and his fourth son, John, to Isabella of Angoulême. His eldest daughter, Matilda, married Duke Henry the Lion of Saxony and Bavaria, a union that established the Welf–Angevin alliance, which lasted to the end of John's reign; his two other daughters, Joan and Eleanor, married William II of Sicily and Alphonse VIII of Castile, respectively.

In 1173–1174 the Young Henry, resentful of certain landed concessions to John, revolted with the support of his mother, Eleanor of Aquitaine. Henry quickly subdued this revolt, sending his wife to a castle at Salisbury for safekeeping and reducing the Young Henry to occupying himself in tournaments until he died in 1183. Richard then became heir apparent and Henry had little trouble in France until 1186, when, showing signs of age, he could not get along with his jealous sons, who were being persuaded to revolt by the crafty Philip Augustus. When revolt came in 1187, Henry, old and sick, suffered the first serious military setback of his reign. Shortly before his death at Chinon in 1189, he had to surrender Auvergne and Berry to Philip and to pay an indemnity. Henry's sons had finally gained the upper hand, but in so doing had opened the door to Philip Augustus, whose ultimate objective was seizure of all the Angevin possessions. A blind trust in his sons and a favoritism for John, the worst of the lot, finally defeated Henry, who otherwise was realistic about men and their motives, and brought to a sad end what had been a brilliant reign.

RICHARD I (1189–1199)

Richard I the Lionhearted was quite unlike his father. Where Henry was businesslike, Richard was a chivalrous adventurer. Only as a warrior did he surpass his father. Bored by the responsibilities of ruling, he abandoned them to functionaries and devoted himself to the Third Crusade, tournaments, and war against Philip II Augustus. Exclusively a French prince, he visited England only twice for a total of six months, on both occasions to secure money for his wars. After making a few concessions to Philip Augustus, he gained recognition as Henry's heir and then, eager to go on the Third Crusade (1189–1192), made arrangements for the governance of the realm. To his credit as a warrior, he was the only Western leader to bring any glory to Christian arms. The German king Frederick I Barbarossa died before reaching the Holy Land, and Philip Augustus, perhaps suffering an illness, soon returned to France to conspire with John against Richard. Informed of this treachery, Richard embarked for home in the autumn of 1192. Fearful of crossing France, he returned through central Europe, but was detected by Duke Leopold II of Austria and imprisoned. Handed over early in 1193 to Leopold's Hohenstaufen overlord, King Henry VI of Germany (an ally of Philip), he was held for ransom and had to pay 150,000 marks for his freedom. Liberated in 1194, he departed for England but stayed only long enough to obtain money and forces for revenge against Philip. In the spring of 1194 he crossed to Normandy and never again saw England.

Militarily Richard was more than a match for Philip. During the next five years he repeatedly defeated him, almost captured him, and restored all the lost Angevin possessions. In 1199, while besieging the castle of Châlus in Limousin, which belonged to a disloyal vassal, Richard received an arrow in the shoulder. The wound became infected and within ten days he died, leaving behind a glorious military reputation but little else, not even an heir from his marriage to Berengaria of Navarre, a situation that led to a disputed succession.

JOHN (1199–1216)

Deciding that it would be better to leave his possessions to a man rather than a boy, Richard had designated his treacherous brother John as successor instead of his young nephew Arthur, the son of his elder brother Geoffrey of Brittany. According to the feudal custom of primogeniture, Arthur had the better claim, but John was supported by his mother, Eleanor of Aquitaine, by most of the English and Norman baronage, and by the church. Arthur had the support of Maine, Touraine, and Brittany, plus Philip Augustus, who, continuing to play his divisive game, shrewdly recognized him as heir to the Angevin lands. John finally secured recognition in 1200, after handing over some Norman territory to Philip, and it was agreed that Arthur was to hold Brittany in fief from John.

The good mind and administrative ability of John were nullified by lack of drive and moral character, inconsistency, greed, cruelty, a deficiency in military leadership, and poor relations with his vassals. He was so inept a ruler that he is considered one of England's worst kings. His troubles were mainly self-engendered. Obtaining an annulment in 1200 of his childless marriage to Isabel of Gloucester, he then married Isabella of Angoulême, who had been promised to Count Hugh of La Marche, one of his vassals. Hugh immediately appealed for justice to John's lord, Philip Augustus, who summoned John in 1202 to appear before his court at Paris. When John ignored this and repeated summonses, Philip declared him a traitor and condemned to forfeiture all his French fiefs.

Philip then invaded John's lands. During the ensuing war, John's forces captured Arthur of Brittany,

who died in captivity in 1203. Accused of murdering Arthur and repeatedly failing to provide leadership to his supporters, John was an easy target for Philip. By 1206 John had lost all his possessions except Aquitaine and part of Poitou, and his military setbacks spelled disaster for the Angevin Empire. John thereafter concentrated upon governing England, which, severed politically from Normandy and the other French lands, now entered upon the stage of development that was to differentiate its institutions and law from the other states of western Europe. Also at this point the inhabitants of England began to consider themselves different from the French; they were becoming Englishmen.

John became immersed in three overriding preoccupations—a bitter dispute with Pope Innocent III and the church, an attempt to regain his lost French possessions, and the growing opposition of the English baronage that was to culminate in Magna Carta. When Hubert Walter, archbishop of Canterbury, died in 1205, the monks of Christ Church, Canterbury, ignoring John's order to elect his candidate, secretly elected their subprior, Reginald. Angry, John forced the monks to elect his man, John de Gray, bishop of Norwich. Innocent III quashed both elections in 1206 and incurred John's fury by proposing Stephen Langton as archbishop and consecrating him in 1207. John's refusal to accept Langton led to a six-year struggle, during which England was placed under interdict and John was excommunicated. John appropriated almost all the church lands and drove most of the leading ecclesiastics into exile.

Again the door was open for Philip Augustus, who supported Innocent III with the understanding that his son Louis would invade England. This threat forced John to negotiate. In 1213 he agreed to accept Langton, to reinstate the exiled clergy, to compensate the church for its losses, to take England and Ireland in fief from Innocent III, and to pay an annual tribute to the Holy See. These concessions, though humiliating, saved England from invasion and secured Innocent III as a kind of protector.

On numerous occasions when John was about to lead an expedition to Normandy to recover his lands, lack of money or support from his distrustful vassals blocked him. He finally managed to form a military alliance of German and Low Country princes to move against Philip Augustus. Early in 1214 plans called for the Low Country and German forces, led by the Welf king of Germany, Otto IV, to invade France from Flanders while John was to strike northward from southwestern France. All went awry. John's campaign in Poitou was a complete failure, and on 27 July 1214 Otto and his allies were routed in a decisive battle with Philip Augustus at Bouvines in Flanders, a victory that gave France political ascendancy in western Europe for the next century. Under the weight of this ignominious failure John had to return to face a hostile kingdom unhappy about his military incapacity, sick of his frequent taxes, and disgusted with his performance as king. His arbitrary flouting of feudal custom and of the laws of the realm proved to most of the baronage that his goal was despotism, that he desired to destroy them and dispossess them of their lands.

Signs of baronial discontent had been smoldering. At one meeting of protest the barons declared that they would fight for the provisions of the coronation charter of Henry I. Flames erupted in 1215 when the barons, refusing to pay a tax John demanded from those who had not fought in France, finally revolted, with the aim of forcing John to put his seal to a document that would stipulate in specific terms the laws and customs by which he would govern. With Stephen Langton as both leader and intermediary, meetings held in late May and early June resulted in an agreement acceptable to both parties. On 15 June 1215 the barons met John at Runnymede meadow, on the Thames River near Windsor, where John put his seal to a document in rough draft called the Articles of the Barons. On 19 June a formal draft and revision called Magna Carta was issued under the great seal, with both John and the barons swearing to uphold its provisions.

Neither side intended to keep the agreement, and war broke out. The barons received support from Philip Augustus' son Louis, who made plans to invade England, while John benefited from papal support. Becoming ill in October 1216, John provided for the protection of his infant son, who would succeed him as Henry III, then died on 18 October, a dismal end for a man who had the intelligence of Henry II but was as much a failure as Henry was a success. With John's death the conflict became pointless. Louis renounced his claim to the English throne in 1217, and there was general acceptance of the young Henry III as king.

ANGEVIN GOVERNMENT

Under Henry II institutional and legal development continued the course set by the Norman kings. As government became more efficient and central-

ized, and as royal common law and procedure grew and proved to be effective, feudal and local custom rapidly retreated. As the pipe rolls reveal, under Henry II the Exchequer expanded its fiscal responsibilities. Richard Fitzneale (fitz Nigel), one of its treasurers, gives a good description of its operations in a book entitled *Dialogue of the Exchequer*. Assisting the Exchequer was the household chamber and its subdepartment, the wardrobe, which moved about with the king and provided his daily financial needs. To increase his income Henry II experimented with new taxes. He encouraged his vassals to commute their military service for a payment of money called scutage. Taxes known as tallages enabled him to tap the growing wealth of the boroughs. The most innovative tax was a percentage of the total value of an individual's movable property. This fractional tax was to become the principal form of taxation in later medieval England. Occasionally under Richard a land tax called a carucage was levied.

Like the Normans, Henry II used the great and small councils for advice, consent to taxes, and approval of laws, but often he did what he wished without consulting either. Increasingly the household staff took over the functions of the small council, while the chancellor and writing office became almost a separate department like the Exchequer. Under John began the remarkable Chancery enrollments that provided a copy of all documents issued from this busy office. Henry II wielded tight control over his local officers. He investigated the performance of the sheriffs and in 1170 removed all of them, replacing them with more efficient men. To keep an eye on local government, he regularized a procedure begun by Henry I, whereby royal itinerant justices went out on circuits of the counties not only to try cases but also to investigate local abuses and report back to the king.

Henry II was loath to concede self-government to the boroughs. He punished London for supporting Stephen by depriving it of self-government, a privilege it did not regain until the reign of Richard. By the reign of John, however, Northampton, Ipswich, Gloucester, Lincoln, and Shrewsbury had also become self-governing. Smaller boroughs meanwhile obtained elementary bourgeois privileges, and in the thirteenth century many became self-governing. Urban government was, however, in no sense democratic but oligarchic, dominated by the wealthiest and most influential burgesses, the leading members of the guilds, who occupied all the offices and controlled the appointments.

DECLINE OF MANORIALISM AND FEUDALISM

As royal government expanded, as the economy developed, and as boroughs grew, feudalism and manorialism waned. Emancipation of the peasantry accelerated; the landed estates were increasingly tilled by rent-paying peasants, and began to specialize in crops and produce for the borough markets. In many areas sheep raising increased to profit from the demand for raw wool by manufacturing towns in England, especially eastern England, and those in Flanders. Commerce spread, with English merchants regularly attending the famous Champagne fairs. These activities necessitated the development of more sophisticated banking techniques to facilitate business. As more money came into circulation and the kings could hire more and more of their military and political service, feudalism declined and caused a weakening of the traditional power of the aristocracy. In the last half of the twelfth century, feudal aristocrats struggled to retain their political and economic power as royal government grew and wealth came to the burgesses.

THE COMMON LAW

During the reign of Henry II, the English common law system came of age and developed the legal procedures that still exist in the Anglo-American world. In the first text on the common law, *Treatise on the Laws and Customs of England,* the justice Ranulf de Glanville, an able servant of Henry II, clearly describes the legal system and explains why Roman law had no fundamental influence on English law. As royal justice expanded, the great and small councils that had served as courts of justice for both feudal and common law cases could no longer handle the increasing load, and the litigants found it time-consuming and costly to seek out the king and his court as they moved constantly throughout the Angevin lands. Henry's solution was to create more royal courts.

To settle financial cases connected with the royal income, he established the court of the Exchequer, the first of the central common law courts. To help settle cases between private citizens, he established the court of common pleas, which sat regularly at Westminster. Eventually the court of the King's Bench arose to handle cases between the king and his subjects. Staffing these courts were members of the small council and experienced justices like Glan-

ville. Although the great and small councils continued to hear important and difficult cases, increasingly they heard cases that demanded equity not provided by the common law. To make royal justice more easily obtainable, Henry regularized the use of itinerant justices who went on judicial circuits (eyres) of the counties to hear certain categories of cases. This system helped to make royal law common to all the realm.

The use of more rational procedures, many based on the inquest system, popularized royal justice. Under a system of possessory assizes, disputes over the possession of land and rights were settled by answers given by a jury of men empaneled to answer under oath certain questions put to them. Eventually this procedure also determined the question of ultimate ownership. It may thus be said that trial by jury for civil cases began under Henry II. Disgusted with the system for apprehending and bringing to trial those suspected of crime, he initiated what is known as the presentment or grand jury. The itinerant justices on their eyres would ask empaneled juries under oath to present or to indict anyone suspected of certain categories of crimes. Those indicted were then tried in royal courts by means of the ordeal. Jury trial for criminal cases was not yet used, and would not be until the thirteenth century.

The system of law that arose under Henry II was marvelously just and efficient for the twelfth century, but under John it was quickly converted into a means of coercing and destroying the royal subjects. He capriciously overturned decisions, unjustly accused people of crimes, brought actions against them so as to dispossess them of their land, arbitrarily seized their possessions and punished them, and interpreted the law to his benefit. Such behavior largely explains the baronial discontent, their feudal revolt, and Magna Carta. It is no wonder that many provisions of Magna Carta were intended to force John to respect and uphold the law. It has been said that its greatest contribution to constitutional government and the rule of law was the enunciation of the principle that "the king is, and shall be, below the law."

CHURCH–STATE RELATIONS

Although the settlement between Henry I and Anselm in 1106 established reasonably amicable church–state relations for the rest of Henry's reign, during the civil war that followed, the church usurped or laid claim to powers hitherto not exercised and became more independent of royal authority. Determined to reestablish control over the church, Henry II restricted the jurisdiction of the spiritual courts and exerted a tighter surveillance over clerics tried for crime. In 1162 he appointed Thomas Becket archbishop of Canterbury because Becket not only had served him loyally in many capacities but also, as chancellor, had vigorously carried out his will vis-à-vis the church. As archbishop, however, Becket became the devoted servant of the church and a champion of all its rights.

An acrimonious struggle began in 1164 when Henry II issued the Constitutions of Clarendon, purportedly defining the customs governing the rights of church and state under Henry I. Becket was furious at this document, which he regarded as a distortion of justice, and particularly enraged by the provisions that criminous clergy had the right to be tried in spiritual courts but that the trials had to be witnessed by royal officers, and that clerics found guilty should be turned over to the secular arm and receive secular punishment. Henry II was adamant about this provision because the church courts had been too lenient with those clerics found guilty, permitting many of them to go unpunished.

Becket went into exile in France until the summer of 1170, when he and Henry finally settled their differences. Once in England, however, he immediately fulminated against Henry and those bishops who had supported the royal position. When news of Becket's behavior reached Henry in Normandy, he was incensed and asked publicly why he had to endure this man. Four of his knights took him at his word, went to England, and murdered Becket while he was saying Mass in Canterbury Cathedral on 29 December 1170. This rash act shocked western Christendom and forced Henry to retreat from various positions, including that on criminous clergy, with the result that benefit of clergy remained in England until the nineteenth century. In 1173 the pope canonized Becket and there subsequently arose the cult of Saint Thomas. This was one of the few setbacks that Henry had to accept.

Under Richard and John the church increased its authority. Richard was an absentee king in no position to quarrel with the clergy because he relied upon some to govern the kingdom in his absence. Obviously church–state relations also depended upon the character of the leading clergy. With Hubert Walter, a gifted royal administrator and archbishop of Canterbury under Richard and both archbishop and chancellor under John, relations were reasonably amicable because Hubert was practical

and realistic, able to see both sides of a question. After his death John's relations with the church were disastrous because John was simply outmatched by the very able and politic Innocent III. At John's death in 1216, his infant son Henry III was placed under the protection of the papal legate Gualo. At no time in the Middle Ages was the authority of the church higher than during the reign of Henry III (1216–1272).

CULTURE AND LEARNING

What has been called the "renaissance of the twelfth century" is reflected in the cultural achievements of England during the last half of the century. The study of Roman and canon law, begun under the Normans, increasingly attracted to the schools of northern Italy Englishmen who then returned to England to teach these subjects or to enter the service of the church or the king. Clearly the textbook of Glanville could not have been written without the Roman law texts as models. A new appreciation of the Latin classics emerged in the works of English writers and scholars, many of whom studied in the well-known French cathedral schools. Both Henry II and Archbishop Theobald of Canterbury patronized chroniclers, philosophers, theologians, and poets. Eleanor of Aquitaine was celebrated for the literary ambience of her court, especially for the troubadours and their poetry.

Although educated in France and eventually becoming bishop of Chartres, the celebrated John of Salisbury was English and a member, for a time, of the household of Archbishop Theobald. He was equal in humanistic learning to the best French scholars. His *Policraticus* was one of the first medieval treatises on secular government and political thought, and his *Metalogicus* was a competent discussion of logic. In this period there also appeared some good chronicles and histories, as well as miscellaneous works. Walter Map wrote a fascinating account of life at Henry II's court, and Gerald of Wales composed a tract on the proper education of a prince. Just before Henry II's accession Geoffrey of Monmouth had completed the immensely popular *History of the British Kings*.

The English cathedral schools lagged behind the French. At Oxford, Roman and canon law were taught along with philosophy and theology, but no university developed there until the thirteenth century. The cathedral schools at Lincoln, Winchester, and Exeter were active, and the schools at Northampton were preeminent under Henry II. Dominated by the Benedictines, Canterbury stimulated some commendable literary activity, but strangely no notable cathedral schools arose at either Canterbury or London, where the ingredients for their formation were present. In architecture England followed the tastes of the Continent. The Romanesque architecture of the Normans was generally superseded before the close of the twelfth century by the form of Gothic called Early English, its chief characteristic being the pointed arch, frequently introduced only for decorative effect. An especially fine example of pointed-arch construction is Lincoln Cathedral. The finest Gothic construction, however, did not come until later in the thirteenth and fourteenth centuries.

The period between 1066 and 1216 was notable for the development of a strong kingdom with extremely effective central and local institutions that were closely connected and worked well in tandem. The precocious institutional growth in this period undoubtedly nurtured the remarkable common law and legal procedures found throughout the realm. But all could have been undone in John's reign had not the baronage of the realm been strong enough to unite and collectively force him to issue Magna Carta, a document clearly stating that royal authority was not arbitrary; that the machinery of government and law was not to be used for the selfish interests of the king; that kings, like their subjects, were below the law. In the following centuries royal power declined as institutions and procedures kept developing to control it. With the loss of its French possessions England became more insular and began to develop those institutions and that culture so uniquely English. But the path England trod was ever under the shadow of the achievements of the energetic Norman and Angevin kings.

BIBLIOGRAPHY

For references to the sources and studies on the Norman-Angevin period Edgar B. Graves, *A Bibliography of English History to 1485* (1975); and Bryce Lyon, "From Hengist and Horsa to Edward of Caernarvon: Recent Writing on English History," in Elizabeth C. Furber, ed., *Changing Views on British History* (1966), 1–57. The most comprehensive survey is Austin L. Poole, *From Domesday Book to Magna Carta, 1087–1216*, 2nd ed. (1955). Excellent short histories and good studies on the reigns of kings are Frank Barlow, *The Feudal Kingdom of England: 1042–1216* (2nd ed. 1961, 3rd ed. 1972); Reginald A. Brown, *The Normans and the Norman Conquest* (1969); Ralph H. C. Davis, *King Stephen* (1967); David C. Douglas, *William the Conqueror: The Norman Impact Upon England* (1964);
John B. Gillingham, *The Life and Times of Richard I* (1973); Sidney Painter, *The Reign of King John* (1949); George O. Sayles, *The Medieval Foundations of England*, rev. ed. (1950); Wilfred L. Warren, *King John* (1961), and *Henry II* (1973). For constitutional and legal developments see Raoul C. van Caenegem, *The Birth of the English Common Law* (1973); James C. Holt, *Magna Carta* (1965); John E. A. Jolliffe, *Angevin Kingship*, 2nd ed. (1963); Bryce Lyon, *A Constitutional and Legal History of Medieval England*, 2nd ed. (1980); Frederick Pollock and Frederic W. Maitland, *The History of English Law Before the Time of Edward I*, 2 vols., 2nd rev. ed. (1968), with introduction and select bibliography by Stroud F. C. Milsom; and Henry G. Richardson and George O. Sayles, *The Governance of Mediaeval England from the Conquest to Magna Carta* (1963). For church history see Zachary N. Brooke, *The English Church and the Papacy from the Conquest to the Reign of John* (1931); Christopher R. Cheney, *From Becket to Langton: English Church Government 1170–1213* (1956).

BRYCE LYON

[See also **Angevins: France, England, Sicily; Anglo-Norman Art; Anglo-Norman Literature; Anselm of Canterbury; Assize, English; Becket, Thomas, St.; Borough (England–Wales); Chancery; Clarendon, Constitutions of; Common Pleas, Court of; Domesday Book; Edward the Confessor of England, St.; Eleanor of Aquitaine; England, Anglo-Saxon; Exchequer; Exchequer, Court of; Feudalism; Geoffrey of Monmouth; Glanville, Ranulf de; Guilds and Métiers; Henry I of England; Henry II of England; Innocent III, Pope; John, King of England; John of Salisbury; Lanfranc of Bec; Langton, Stephen; Law, English Common; Magna Carta; Map (Mapes), Walter; Normans and Normandy; Philip II Augustus; Richard I the Lionhearted; Sheriff; Shire; Urbanism, Western European; Walter, Hubert; William the Conqueror.**]

ENGLAND: 1216–1485. In both 1216 and 1485 England welcomed a new ruler, but their differences were striking. Although Henry III was only nine years old, he was the dead king's son, whereas Henry VII was no more than an obscure and long-exiled Welsh cousin of the house of Lancaster, a man who gained the crown by killing his fellow usurper Richard III in battle. Moreover, even though the minor Henry III ascended the throne as son of the hated John, he was also a sixth-generation descendant of William the Conqueror and a boy who could further trace his lineage back through St. Margaret of Scotland to Edmund Ironside, half brother of St. Edward the Confessor, last of the true line of Anglo-Saxon kings. In comparison the seventh Henry's hereditary claims seem almost ludicrous, for his rights, such as they were, sprang from illegitimate descent through the female line from John of Gaunt, fourth son of Edward III, to which he added the genealogically irrelevant fact that he was also the grandson of a secret unison between Owen Tudor and Catherine of Valois, the French widow of Henry V.

These differences explain the differences so apparent in their modes of accession. Although John's barons had invited Prince Louis of France to become their king after Innocent III had quashed Magna Carta, support for Louis melted with John's death. As a result, Henry was able to receive the crown with surprisingly little difficulty, and this in spite of all the rancor and fighting to which minorities traditionally gave rise. In his case, then, blood was enough to still the opposition.

The case proved strikingly different for Henry VII. Although he found himself king, it was not primarily for dynastic reasons. Rather, the first half of his reign was to be plagued by pretenders claiming a better blood right than his, and even though his victory at Bosworth allowed him to argue that the English kingship had first come to him by a judgment of God, the fact remains that his title had little legal meaning until eleven weeks later when, on 7 November 1485, parliament approved without explanation a simple declarative statement announcing that henceforth the royal inheritance was to "be, rest, remain, and abide in the most royal person of our now sovereign lord, King Harry the VIIth, and in the heirs of his body lawfully coming, perpetually with the grace of God so to endure, and in none other." Only with acceptance of that declaration did Henry Tudor truly become king.

As suggested by the above, England in the period 1216–1485 experienced a profound transformation, and not just in the character of its kingship. Society underwent far-reaching alteration, and as it did, the frame of government changed to meet the new challenges, not always successfully. The lessons and precedents of the past were seldom abandoned in their entirety, but seeming continuity often served to hide the extent of the changes, ones that prepared the way for the emergence of a world that was no longer medieval.

THE EVOLUTION OF KINGSHIP

Possibly the clearest shift, though seldom stressed in modern scholarship, came in the concept of kingship. To the medieval mind, kings owed their authority to three sources: the grace or will of God,

heredity, and election or designation by the people they governed. Potentially in conflict though these three may have been, they appeared at the time as no more than three strands in the same theory, one ever dependent on the creative powers of God. Thus, for example, even though succession owed not a little to blood and kinship, the twelfth-century lawyer Ranulf de Glanville could argue that "only God can make an heir." Similarly, though people came together at times to elect their king, they could do so largely because they spoke with a voice greater than their own. As the archbishop of Canterbury put it in 1199 when explaining the choice of John over his nephew Arthur, those assembled had been able to resolve the dispute only because "after invoking the grace of the Holy Spirit, we are unanimous in electing him." With God both choosing the heir and ensuring his election, coronation and its holy oil often appeared to be little more than a quasi-sacramental confirmation of a divine selection already twice expressed.

In practice, however, the balance between and among these three strands was ever changing. Because the Anglo-Saxons had lacked a clear system of primogeniture, all relatives of a king—however distant, legitimate or illegitimate—were deemed to have a "throne-worthiness" making them eligible for succession. As a result, heredity bulked less large than did election by the Witenagemot and subsequent coronation. Under the Normans, moreover, the situation remained equally fluid. Though claiming kinship, William became king primarily through conquest, and to study his successors down through the accession of John is to appreciate the extent to which the crown often fell to men other than those whom a more modern theory of hereditary succession would designate.

At the same time changes were coming. The reforms of Pope Gregory VII had had the effect of placing greater emphasis on the sacraments, among them marriage, and as these reforms gradually took hold, they tended not only to clarify the distinction between legitimate and illegitimate but also to give increasing prominence to children of a canonical union. Moreover, even as such children began to acquire rights of succession greater than those of more distant heirs, the church insisted that marriage was a sacrament in which biblical incest taboos had to obtain. Because that meant, as then interpreted, that none could marry within the sixth degree of relationship, one practical if unexpected consequence was that, to prevent incest, rulers and others were

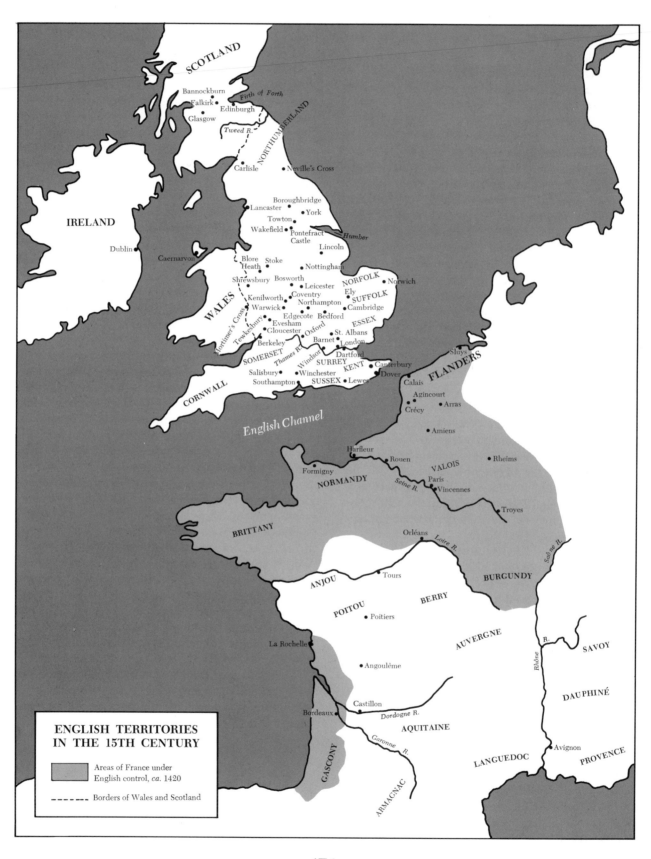

ENGLISH TERRITORIES IN THE 15TH CENTURY

Areas of France under English control, *ca.* 1420

- - - - - - Borders of Wales and Scotland

forced to look to their family trees, stressing their antecedents and thereby fostering the rise of dynastic concerns.

In England these tendencies began to emerge with the accession of Henry II, a grandson of Henry I who had used that fact to argue successfully the legitimacy of his royal rights to the detriment of those possessed by his cousin Stephen. Not content with that, he further encouraged suggestive connections with the British and Anglo-Saxon past. For example, he insisted that his first-born grandson be named Arthur in honor of the legendary Celtic king, and after his own death it was alleged that he had learned in a dream where the grave of Arthur and Guinevere was to be found. Indeed, monks at Glastonbury claimed they had found it in 1191, complete with a leaden identification tag stating: "Here lies the famous King Arthur, buried in the Isle of Avalon." So real did these remains become that in 1278 Edward I found it desirable to give them sumptuous reburial as proof to the Welsh he was about to conquer that this Celtic hero was truly dead, no longer able to save them.

In addition, because Henry II was ever mindful that his grandmother Matilda of Scotland could provide a genealogically useful link to pre-Norman rulers, he took the lead in urging the canonization of Edward the Confessor, whose collateral heir he was. With Pope Alexander III's proclamation of that sainthood in 1161, the fusion of Saxon with Norman seemed confirmed in the creation of a sacred dynasty, succession to which appeared increasingly dependent on a right of blood that promised, in time, to take precedence over those of election and crowning. Thus, though John's hereditary claims were clouded by the existence of Arthur, such was not the case with his son. For in 1216 the nine-year-old Henry had to contend with no one whose blood right could compare with his, and it is in that context that the relative peacefulness of his accession and minority at last becomes comprehensible.

Small wonder, then, that Henry III should have so greatly venerated the Confessor or that he should have given his firstborn their ancestor's holy name. And the seeming triumph of heredity became even clearer with the accession in 1272 of that son, Edward I. On a fruitless crusade at the time of Henry's death, Edward did not return to England for almost two years. Nevertheless, that he was fully king was recognized immediately, even though his coronation did not take place until 19 August 1274.

In short, Edward I ascended the throne almost by right of birth alone, and since England was about to be ruled by more than a century of succeeding Edwards, a line broken only by the Black Prince's premature death, scholars have often assumed that heredity and primogeniture had finally come to dominate the rules of succession. Such was, after all, the apparent position of the second of those Edwards in 1307 when, shortly before his coronation, he wrote to Pope Clement V to assure him that precisely because he governed "in the hereditary kingdom of England," he was understandably anxious to preserve "the rights . . . of our crown and royal dignity."

Yet, even to mention Edward II is to suggest the extent to which strictly applied rules had failed to gain a total victory. For, led by his wife, Isabella of France, Edward's subjects were ultimately to depose him, and deposition is an unthinkable act in kingdoms where heredity prevails, if only because its rules of inheritance can provide no truly legitimate alternative to a king who was himself the unique and legal heir. Given the problems of the reign, it is scarcely surprising that long before its troubled end, Edward himself should have sought other ways to increase his stature and authority, ways that involved a shift in emphasis away from hereditary right and back to traditional, more explicitly divine sources of power, notably unction. Most strikingly, perhaps, in 1318 he acquired a newly discovered oil that the Virgin had given to St. Thomas Becket and, with it in hand, he immediately applied to Pope John XXII for permission to undergo a second coronation. The Virgin had assured Thomas, he said, that the fifth king after Henry II—that is, Edward II—would prove "a man of integrity and champion of the church." Doubtful the pope may have been, but permission was granted, and with renewed unction Edward went forth to battle his barons, authority momentarily buttressed by claims transcending those purely of blood.

Nevertheless, Edward's ploy failed to prevent his deposition, another blow against the unfettered rule of heredity. On balance, though, the nature of kingship then underwent fewer immediate changes than might have been expected, given the possible import of these events. Edward III was, after all, the anticipated heir, so the normal succession had been preserved, albeit accelerated. Similarly, though his coronation received unusual emphasis, that appears to have been more a consequence of his age—not yet fifteen—than of any argument that, owing to the unusual circumstances surrounding his accession, he had acquired the right to rule only with reception of the crown.

The government deemed that Edward's first regnal year had begun on 25 January 1327, a week before his coronation, and the first document of the reign insisted that though "Sire Edward, recently king of England," had freely abdicated, he had also granted "that the government of the realm should devolve upon his eldest son and heir." In short, Mortimer and Isabella, the powers behind the throne, found it expedient to mask the potential implications of their coup with an emphasis on continuity and inheritance. That others may have drawn a different conclusion is suggested only by a contemporary draft for a new coronation order that specified a lay assembly was to elect the king prior to his crowning and that the archbishop of Canterbury could proceed with the ceremony only after "the people" had affirmed the assembly's choice.

Yet that draft seems no more than the exception that proves the rule, for the rest of the fourteenth century proceeded almost as though the deposition of Edward II had never occurred. The fifty years of Edward III's reign gave way in 1377 to the rule of his minor grandson Richard II, without serious challenge even from overmighty uncles whose own ambitions might have tempted them to seek the crown in his stead, if only they had been able to devise justifications persuasive enough to attract the requisite political support. That they—and especially John of Gaunt—were unable to do so demonstrates the extent to which England was again on the road to a purely hereditary monarchy whose divine mission and sacred powers were amply proved by the royal saints who so proudly adorned the family tree.

Nowhere did this vision find greater favor than with Richard II. When, in the 1390's, he ordered a suitable altarpiece for his private chapel, the result was the Wilton Diptych, the iconography of which expresses the theme perfectly. On the right, in heaven, Virgin and Child stand surrounded by angels, all of whom wear the collar and badge of Richard II. One holds the banner of St. George, but from his gestures and those of the Child it is clear that the banner is about to be passed to the left, where, on earth, a kneeling Richard prepares to receive it, in age and dress as he would have appeared on his coronation day. Behind Richard stand three saints, two of them crowned. At one level of interpretation they are John the Baptist and two of Richard's Anglo-Saxon forebears, Kings Edmund the Martyr and Edward the Confessor. At another they are his immediate ancestors, Edward II (as sainted and martyred as Edmund, patron against the plague); Edward III (yet another namesake of the Confessor, whose traditional feast came the day before the 6 January celebration of Richard's own birth, "the day of the kings"); and last, the uncrowned precursor and father, Edward the Black Prince (in later life as emaciated with illness as the Baptist himself, whose feast so nearly coincided with the date of Edward III's death, the event that had brought Richard to the throne). Such symbolism can leave little doubt that in his own mind he ruled the realm of the English solely by virtue of God's grace and hereditary right.

But then came 1399. Suddenly Richard found himself deposed, his place taken not by the closest blood heir but by Henry of Bolingbroke, John of Gaunt's son and a disinherited exile whose right to the crown was anything but certain. No one was more troubled by that fact than Henry himself. Initially he tried to argue that his descent from Henry III was genealogically preferable to Richard's, but when that claim was rejected even by the commission he had established to confirm it, he began hastily to search for alternatives. In particular he ordered supporters to study the precedents created by Edward II, whose deposition now began to have an impact on the nature of kingship.

On 30 September an assembly claiming to speak for and be "the estates and the people" used the authority of the kingdom to sanction Richard's removal, after which Henry set forth his case for the crown, one based on "right lyne of the blode ... [and] that ryght that God of his grace hath sent me, with the helpe of my kyn and of my frendes, to recover it." Once the assembly had accepted the legal truth of these assertions, Henry was recognized as king, his coronation set for 13 October, the feast of the translation of St. Edward the Confessor. Nevertheless, still not satisfied with the strength of his title, Henry made sure at that ceremony that he was anointed with the holy oil, serendipitously rediscovered, that the Blessed Virgin had given to Thomas Becket.

Facts to the contrary notwithstanding, Henry IV continued to insist that he enjoyed the kingship "as by right of birth," but he was realistic and honest enough to add that his title had further come to him "by the unanimous consent of the lords and commons." Others, undoubtedly moved by the divine approval seemingly bestowed on the new king both in battle and in the oil of coronation, asserted with pious acceptance that he was a monarch "chosen by God." Still others, however, were balder in their interpretation: in 1403, for example, the Percys could find no better justification for their impending revolt than the simple observation to Henry that "you crowned yourself king." In short, men's understanding of the deposition of 1399 posed a challenge to purely hereditary kingship in ways unimagined in 1327, for inevitably they saw Henry IV's right to rule as founded not so much on inheritance as on God's will, popular election, and, be it added, the naked use of force.

Thus, if the crown lay uneasy on Henry's head, it testified (as Shakespeare well knew) to the uncertainty of his title. Over time, Henry's line could hope to reinvigorate the hereditary principle through renewed observance of it, but for the moment the weakness of the first Lancastrian's position was amply demonstrated by the continued unrest of his reign. His son Henry V was to obscure the issue, his victories in France a perfect cover for the dubiety of his descent, and it was only with accession of the grandson, nine-month-old Henry VI, that hereditary right began to reassert itself as the sine qua non of legitimate kingship. Crowned and anointed with the Becket oil on 6 November 1429 in order to meet the exigencies of a deteriorating French situation, Henry found, though still short of eight, that his council of regency had gone to considerable lengths to ensure that all would see that the crowns of England and France had come to him solely by blood—and not by some title conferred only by election, crowning, or treaty.

At the coronation banquet the courses were introduced by paraded pastry tableaux, each symbolically designed to amplify the dynastic and religious arguments of the Wilton Diptych, now made as applicable to France as to England. The first course saw Sts. Edward the Confessor and Louis IX joining Henry himself, "the branche borne of hyr blode." As if that were insufficient, after the third there appeared

> Owre Lady syttynge, and hyr Chylde in hyr lappe, holdyng in every honde a crowne, Syn Gorge knelyng on that one syde and Synt Denys in that othyr syde, and they ij presentyng the kynge to owre Lady whythe thys reson:
> "O blessyd lady, Crystys modyr dyre,
> And Syn Gorge callyd hyr owne knyght;
> Hooly Syn Denys, O martyr, most entere,
> To the here vjᵗᵉ Harry we present the in youre syghte.

> Shedythe youre grace on hym,
> Hys tendyr youth whythe vertu avaunce,
> Borne by dyscent and tytylle of ryght
> Justely to raygne in Ingelonde and yn Fraunce."
> (Gairdner, ed., "William Gregory's Chronicle")

Despite such sentiments, in practice the emerging Lancastrian hereditary principle had to contend with the reality of Henry's reign, one torn by internal division, recriminations over the disaster in France, and by the problems created by the king's wavering competence, whether lucid or mad. After a series of protectorships served only to make matters worse, in 1460 Richard of York attempted to cut the Gordian knot by claiming the crown at the October parliament. On the surface the duke based his case on inheritance, for he argued that his descent from the third and fifth sons of Edward III should be preferred to Henry's title, one genealogically dependent on descent from John of Gaunt, merely the fourth son. When compared to such a lineage, he said, the Lancastrians' case surely must fail, since in no way could their sixty-year tenure as kings be taken as granting them a prescriptive right preferable to the imperishable one of blood.

In point of fact, though, York's dynastic case was less firmly grounded than first appeared. Its descent from the third son of Edward III depended on a genealogy that passed through two generations of women, and it was unclear whether the crown could legally descend in such an indirect and unprecedented way. A Lancastrian statute of December 1406 had recognized the possibility of female inheritance, but it was silent on whether women could transmit a right to the throne that they had never directly possessed themselves. In short, there were no rules, and since this act had entailed the royal succession quite specifically on Henry IV, his sons, and the heirs of their bodies, it was hardly one that York could comfortably cite. On the contrary, his own hereditary needs forced him to deny the act's validity because, as he put it, "yf he [Henry of Bolingbroke] myght have obteigned and rejoysed the seid Corones, etc. by title of enheritaunce, discent, or succession, he neither neded nor wold have desired or made thaym to bee graunted to hym in suche wise."

Given the inscrutability of the issues, not to mention a balance of forces that threatened civil war, the October parliament understandably tried to evade the question that Richard of York had placed so squarely before it. Henry VI's judges and lawyers refused to address it, averring that it was a "matter . . . which is above the law and passed their learning," a "matter . . . above his [the king's] authority, wherein they might not meddle." As a result the lords of parliament were ultimately forced to deal with it themselves, patching together a compromise that left Henry the crown for the rest of his "life natural," but recognized the duke of York as his heir. Unsurprisingly, however, the proposed solution failed to work, and by December, Richard lay dead on the field of battle, his paper-crowned head dispatched as a grisly adornment for the gates of the city of York. Thus, if his son was militarily to turn the tide in the following March, coming to the throne as Edward IV, his victory was scarcely one of inheritance. Rather, and in spite of continued dynastic claims, his was a title by conquest. Although it was later to gain some measure of legitimacy, that was largely because, in words first used in 1399 at Bagot's case heard in the House of Commons, "the crown was entailed on him by parliament."

In short, with the rise of the Yorkists, England found itself placed under a kingship having conceptual foundations that little resembled those of Edward I. Much as Edward IV might stress the impeccable genealogy of his line, hereditary rights were of no value unless and until he could get them recognized by those with an authority high enough to ensure their legal and political acceptance. And since, in practice, it was parliament alone that could decide "as of record" where the legal truth lay, the Yorkist monarchy presents an ambiguous spectacle to those believing that constitutional theory should always be neat, precise, and orderly.

Practically speaking, Edward IV owed the crown to the political and military support of towns like London and of nobles like Warwick, but at a more theoretical level his title had first come to him in a judgment of God rendered in battle. Yet to that theory must be added the fact that Edward had fought for the throne but had claimed he had done so out of an abiding faith in the legitimacy of his hereditary right. The legal validity of his right could, however, be determined only in a parliament composed of, and speaking for, the three estates of the realm.

No one theory can possibly cover all these competing claims; at best they reflect little more than the jagged realities of power politics as smoothed out and justified by not entirely disingenuous appeals to all three of those sources for royal authority with which this essay began. What can be said, though, is that of the three—blood, election, and God's

grace—blood was becoming the least important. As England's history after 1399 was amply proving, he who could seize the crown was usually able to invent reasons for so doing in which hereditary elements were but a cover for political support transformed into legal acceptance.

There is an exception to this rule worth mentioning: Edward IV's brother, Richard III. For Richard appears almost totally to have lacked the imagination and skills needed to rationalize his usurpation and to change his brute application of force into a clear and unchallenged right to rule, and the very way in which he failed was to complete the evolution of England's medieval kingship, thereby setting the scene for the accession and title of Henry VII. The story is not, however, quite that of Shakespeare.

On 9 April 1483 the death of Edward IV brought his minor son Edward V to the throne; his uncle Richard, duke of Gloucester, was named as protector. The struggles of the next two months then demonstrated the extent to which Richard was incapable of mastering the political opposition with which he was faced, notably that of the Woodville faction, the leader of which, Elizabeth the queen mother, had sought sanctuary in Westminister, whence she continued to rally the forces of those defying his protectorship. Richard's response, understandably, was to seize the crown himself, but he failed utterly in his attempts to develop plausible reasons for his action. On 22 June a friar, Ralph Shaw, told a crowd assembling for Edward V's expected coronation that the boy's father had in fact been the illegitimate product of an adulterous union—and hence that Edward V had no right to the crown. Two days later, however, the duke of Buckingham assured a hastily gathered group at the Guildhall that if the youth could never be king, it was really because Edward IV had once entered into a proxy marriage with an unnamed lady "on the Continent," thus making his Woodville marriage bigamous and its children bastards.

Richard may have begun his official reign on 26 June, his coronation and anointing with the Becket oil coming on 6 July, but few appear to have accepted his right to rule. Elizabeth Woodville, still defiant, remained in sanctuary, and when it began to be rumored that "Edward bastard, late called King Edward V," had met an untimely end with his younger brother in the Tower, an unholy alliance started to form, one composed of Woodvilles, of Richard's former ally the duke of Buckingham, and, most unlikely of all, of Henry Tudor, the exiled earl of Richmond and possible Lancastrian claimant. In

478

the fall Richard was able to capture Buckingham, executing him immediately, and storms in the Channel put an end to Henry's abortive invasion, but Richard still remained unaccepted as king.

It is of no small significance, then, that when parliament met in January 1484, the act of succession it passed seems finally to have granted Richard the legally and politically viable title he had sought for so long. The specifics alleged were as implausible as those of the previous June—that, for example, Edward IV's marriage to Elizabeth Woodville had been bigamous because he had earlier entered into a precontract of matrimony with one Eleanor Butler, now safely dead—but once parliament had used its authority to declare this preposterous story the legal truth, the political opposition began to waver. Elizabeth Woodville came out of sanctuary and was royally pensioned off; her daughters were received at court; and she even wrote her son the marquess of Dorset, telling him to abandon Henry Tudor and to return to England.

In short, Richard III seemed on the verge of winning his gamble, and that he failed to do so seems largely the result of three imponderable factors: continuing horror over the presumed fate of the "innocent princes"; the death of his only legitimate son; and the death of his wife, Anne Neville, an event that deprived him of the possibility of producing another heir while at the same time leading to rumors, probably justified, that he was planning to remedy this defect through an incestuous marriage with his niece, Elizabeth of York. No act of parliament could prevail against such disasters. Political support melted rapidly; Henry Tudor began making new plans; and the verdict of Bosworth on 22 August 1485 was greeted with general, though not universal, relief.

The uncertainties of Richard III's reign prepared the way for Henry VII's success. Richard may have tried, and tried desperately, to place his title on a hereditary footing, and he may also have assured the doubtful that "since we attained this royal dignity by favor of the divine clemency, we have thought nothing more laudable and more worthy of our princely dignity than to benefit our subjects." Still, the virtues and support provided by blood and grace seem in his case to pale in comparison to those conferred by election. As his act of succession explained:

Albeit that the Right, Title, and Estate, whiche oure Souveraine Lord the Kyng Richard the Third hath to and in the Crown and Roiall Dignite of this Reame of

Englond . . . been juste and lawefull, . . . nevertheless, forasmoche as . . . the moste parte of the people of this Lande is not suffisantly lerned in the abovesaide Laws and Customes, . . . the Courte of Parliament is of suche auctorite, and the people of this Lande of suche nature and disposicion, . . . that manifestacion and declaration of any trueth or right, made by the Three Estates of this Reame assembled in Parliament, and by auctorite of the same, maketh, before all other thyngs, moost feith and certaynte; and, quietyng mens myndes, remoeveth the oocasion of all doubts and seditious langage.

So, briefly, it proved for Richard III; and so, more lastingly, was it to prove for Henry VII. Perhaps no contemporary saw the point better than did the captured earl of Surrey when he defended his support of the fallen tyrant to the victorious Tudor after the Battle of Bosworth: "He was my crowned king, and if the parliament authority of England set the crown upon a stock, I will fight for that stock. And as I fought for him, I will fight for you, when you are established by the same authority." Henry was, and Surrey did—along with the bulk of God's Englishmen.

THE RISE OF PARLIAMENT

That observation made, however, the extent to which the story of the transformation of England involves more than kingship alone becomes apparent. At best, crowned heads are but the pinnacle of the iceberg of government, and in the present instance the evolution of monarchy would remain incomprehensible unless linked to an examination of the gradual emergence of parliament as a body having sufficient authority to challenge, to limit, and possibly even to select, the king. Moreover, since government is seldom more than a murky reflection of forces and values arising from the experience of society—and especially since parliament claimed that its decisions represented nothing less than the considered judgments of the community (or, later, the three estates) of the realm—no review of the rise of parliament would be complete without discussion of the probable relationship between that phenomenon and the historical vicissitudes of English society at the end of the Middle Ages.

Historians have discerned almost as many origins for parliament as there have been scholars of the subject. Nineteenth-century romantics, mystically inclined, thought they had found them in the forests of Germany, dark places where the "Germanic idea of freedom" emerged. Others, more pragmatic and recent, have argued that parliament came into being in response to a new royal need to gain consent for taxes—and thereafter gained in authority as it learned to grant money only in return for political concessions. Still others have urged the importance of so-called military feudalism and of its need for some kind of body where the reciprocal duties of the lord–vassal contract, and particularly those of aid and counsel, could comfortably be performed. Last, though probably most reflective of the consensus today, many allege that parliament began as a court, the highest form of the king's council, a place where cases could be heard, petitions decided, and political questions of the highest importance discussed.

Disparate as these theories may seem, none of them is really wrong, only incomplete. Each has significant evidence in its favor, and to dismiss even one of them would be to distort what was, after all, a very complicated development. The problem resembles nothing so much as the story of the blind men and the proverbial elephant, for while each approach conveys a partial truth, it claims to be the full explanation. In the present instance, however, the difficulty arises not from blindness but more from a failing all too often found in history, the conscious or unconscious tendency to assume that modern concepts and categories can be usefully applied even to the study of places and times that were ignorant of them. Unfortunately, such is seldom the case, and the perfect illustration is parliament, an institution having origins and growth that were at all times intimately related to changing conceptions of law.

In the early Middle Ages legislation in any modern sense was almost unknown. Instead, law was overwhelmingly customary. In theory, custom was held to be God's law, his earthly arrangements for a humanity that he himself had created. Because God does not deign to speak to mere mortals on a daily basis, knowledge of his law depended in practice on recollection of precedent; on their memory of what people in the past had done; or, in short, on knowledge of a law that earlier generations had made. Thus, the source of the law appeared to be both divine and human, and its content was equally ambiguous. In the most general sense laws are universally recognized rules that bind every member of a community, but insofar as custom depended on the memory of precedent, discovery of its rules proved far from easy. For memory is unique to the individual, not to the group, and since its accuracy tends to vary enormously from person to person and interest to interest, a community could know its binding precedents—and hence the content of its enforceable

law—only if its individual members had some way of coming together to express what they found to be their collective judgments and will. This they did either in moots (that is, courts) or informally.

Potentially more confusing still, at least to the modern mind, custom was all-embracing. Societies today would find it hard to function without making certain basic distinctions: among the various branches of government, for example, or between public and private, political and social, habit and law. Yet, for much of the Middle Ages, similar distinctions did not exist, a situation that makes it difficult to tell just where one subject leaves off and another begins. Indeed, given the long-continuing medieval failure to develop a good vocabulary for expressing these kinds of concepts and categories, it is somewhat misleading and even a bit anachronistic to talk about such disjunctive boundaries before their verbal appearance. Silence is a presumptive proof that they did not yet exist.

Since early medieval law was little more than custom based on precedent, it was inevitable that the whole of life would quickly take on a legal cast. In the twentieth century, always to do something in a particular way is considered merely a habit and surely not binding on others. But in the tenth, if most people had a habit, their actions were likely to form a precedent that was, as a result, always potentially applicable to the whole community. Similarly, if kings were to govern with any consistency, as tradition required, then knowing the precedents became the key to every policy decision: rulers both had to know the past and were condemned to repeat it, since to have done otherwise would probably have been judged illegal.

In short, these realities make it clear why sociologists have classified the Middle Ages as a "tradition-directed society" and why nineteenth-century historians were inclined to find the roots of parliament in the forests of Germany. The nature of early medieval society and of its customary law dictated that people would often have to consult with each other in quasi-judicial fashion and that, in this regard, kings would appear little different from their subjects. For if a ruler could decide important political questions only after receiving the advice and counsel of his leading men, the whole process significantly took place in the Curia Regis, the royal *court*. Varied though the meanings of that term may now have become, in pre-twelfth-century Europe it had but one. In effect, even matters that an observer today would consider purely administrative were legal in character, an outlook that helps to explain how the full range of later parliamentary activities could have arisen from a single source, the attitudes so pervasively engendered by the rule of customary or common law.

During the reign of Henry III, chroniclers began occasionally to use the word "parliament" to describe meetings of the king with his magnates. Just why they did so remains a mystery, but for all the needless ink already wasted on the subject, it seems likely that no more was involved than a new term for a traditional practice. No new institution had suddenly come into being, almost ex nihilo; rather, Henry's intentions appear to have been little different from those of his ancestors. At most they took on a more formal character, both because of the increasing formalism of the age and because of the need, thanks to the unfortunate experiences of John, to reassure the mighty that their opinions were at all times being properly weighed and considered.

Nevertheless, in the course of the reign there were increasing signs that people were beginning to think of parliament not just as a new word for a traditional kind of meeting, but more concretely, as an especially solemn occasion at which grievances could be both aired and settled. Here, of course, Henry III's disputes with his barons were crucial, for although, in 1258, the opposition sought reform through the Provisions of Oxford, that document envisaged a system of government in which partial baronial control of the king's ministers was to be coupled with parliaments meeting three times a year "in order to examine the state of the kingdom and to consider the common needs of the kingdom and likewise of the king."

Even more striking were Simon de Montfort's two parliaments (1264 and 1265), gatherings clearly intended to rally popular support for the baronial cause, but also ones that were, in words put into Henry's mouth, "to deliberate with our prelates, magnates, and other faithful men concerning our affairs and those of our kingdom" (1264) or to "hold a deliberation with our prelates and magnates to make salutary provision for his [the Lord Edward's] release, . . . and to consider certain other affairs of our kingdom which we are unwilling to settle without your counsel" (1265). Without doubt, then, parliaments were gaining in stature, though the principles upon which they operated appear to have undergone remarkably little change.

Most important, those principles rested on the belief that there could, and did, exist a community at the national level that was similar to, because the apex of, those local ones so crucial to the discovery and enunciation of customary law. As early as Magna Carta the barons had claimed to be "the community of the entire country," and in the Provisions of Oxford the oath of the baronial party carried the explanatory rubric "Thus swore the community of England at Oxford." Further, and crucially, this rather mystical group was always deemed to be present at meetings of parliament. As the Statute of York put it in 1322, its clauses had legal force because they had been "agreed and established . . . by our lord the king, by the said prelates, earls, and barons, and by the whole community of the realm assembled in this parliament." With the national community thus present and accounted for, parliaments found themselves potentially vested with the kind of omnicompetent authority so characteristic of earlier, typically more local, assemblies and courts.

It was this potential that first led Henry III's recalcitrant barons to see parliament as the most promising forum for redress of grievances. For at bottom their problems were almost entirely legal, at least within the medieval understanding of that term. If God and the community were the source of all law, with near inevitability the king came to be viewed less as a sovereign and more as a judge whose highest duty, to uphold justice, meant that his principle function was simply to carry out the intent of the law, not to make or amend it. As the aphorism then had it: *Lex regem facit, non rex legem* (The law makes the king, not the king the law). If, therefore, the barons judged that Henry had violated this highly judicial conception of office, parliaments were the logical place for the community to render that verdict.

There is, however, another side to the story, one that sheds considerable light on why Edward I should have chosen to place a growing reliance on this nascent institution, which had so recently displayed such antiroyalist proclivities, and against his father at that. Parliament was in large measure a court, and while courts today need judges as well as juries, under normal circumstances it seemed clear that in parliament the king was the judge, all others the jury. Subjects were summoned solely to declare the facts and thereby, with royal instruction and final assent, to transform history into law by granting community recognition to what was taken to be, like guilt or innocence, a preexisting truth. That being the case, parliament was able to function only with the presence and full participation of the king; it was his court, its members his representatives.

Possibly even more to the point, Edward I was no Henry III. Able, forceful, and domineering, he inherited few of the failings that had brought Henry so often to grief. He was not, in short, a man to challenge lightly, and his awesome reputation for rage was of obvious assistance in helping him rapidly transform what had been his father's uncertain relations with parliament. Moreover, insofar as Edward was an anointed monarch, a ruler by grace and blood, he enjoyed a station in life inherently different from those of his subjects. As a result he was soon to discover that, when endowed with his abilities, royal status could be used to seize the initiative: the combination gave his opinions such a presumption of truth that, in the absence of strong evidence to the contrary, his subjects were apt to accept them. Thus, far from being limited by parliaments, he was usually able to dominate their meetings and achieve his objectives.

Nevertheless, if those objectives are thought of as being the king's only in the most limited sense, that would be to miss the extent to which Edward's parliamentary activities often arose not out of selfishness, but out of the need to respond to broader and more fundamental developments taking place in society at large. For England was changing. In particular the twelfth and thirteenth centuries had experienced rapid economic expansion: agriculture had become vastly more efficient; population had doubled; and cities filled with the bustle of commerce and industry had seemed almost to mushroom overnight.

Exciting as these changes were, they also meant that Englsh society was more and more faced with a host of vexing new problems for which the customary law had no remedy. Magnates lost both revenues and personal services as lands were increasingly subinfeudated, mortgaged, sold, or, in return for prayers, given to the church. Bankers found no rules to guide them in their debt collections, and the laws of an agricultural society proved of little use to merchants trying to resolve their contract disputes. Ranging from problems in criminal justice to questions of baronial jurisdiction, the list of such difficulties seemed not only endless but growing.

When viewed in this context, the principal activities of Edward I's and later parliaments begin to make sense. Because times were changing, each session received a flood of petitions, statements from individuals that set forth the peculiar circumstances in which they found themselves; explained how the common law either did not apply or would lead to pernicious results if observed; and then requested parliamentary relief. If, after investigation, a petition was judged to have merit, the desired relief was usually forthcoming in either of two forms. When circumstances seemed truly unique—the usual case—the normal remedy was the grant of individual exceptions to existing law. Not infrequently, however, a number of petitions might raise the same issue, or the government might recognize without prodding that a general problem existed for which existing custom provided inadequate remedy.

To deal with such instances—for example, the problems of change just cited—individual responses were patently insufficient. For them a different and more universal solution was needed, and though the one devised, statutes, was to prove instrumental in bringing the Middle Ages to a close, that was far from Edward I's initial intent. Rather, he, his contemporaries, and centuries of their successors saw the question in a different and fundamentally nonlegislative light. To their minds the issue was complexly simple: how to discover and continue to implement God's eternal plan, his legal arrangements, under conditions of change the very novelty of which denied humanity that knowledge of precedent which had hitherto served as its guide. The challenge, then, was not to innovate, but merely to preserve and realize divine intentions even as society broke free from the constraints of the past. In other words, statute law was at first profoundly conservative in intent and hence was framed less as legislation, as new law, than as a declaration of what that law had always been (though it had previously been unknown to Englishmen because the circumstances for which it was needed had not earlier existed).

Here, of course, the real presence of the community of the realm was of crucial importance. From a practical point of view, that presence made possible all the political negotiations on which the formulation of law so frequently depends, but at a more theoretical level it also ensured that those declaring the statute law were doing so by means of an authority and process remarkably similar to those they had long used in their discovery of custom. Moreover, because statutes claimed to declare, and hence to recognize, only the truths that had always been true, it is scarcely surprising to find that they were enforceable not only without prior publicity but even, in some instances, retroactively. As Chief Justice Thorpe explained in 1365, once the king had assented to a statute, " ... everyone is immediately held to know it when it is made in parliament, for as soon as it has concluded anything, the law understands that each person has knowledge thereof; for the parliament represents the body of the whole realm; and thus it is not necessary to have a proclamation [about it] before the statute takes its effect."

In short, Edward I took what had been a meeting, an occasional event, and transformed it, through use, into a regular institution of government, the highest court in the realm. By the opening of the fourteenth century, it had become the recognized place for addressing problems of law and, in particular, for making whatever adjustments in England's legal system the new needs of society seemed to require. At the same time, though, because meetings were both time-consuming and expensive, no more than a handful of subjects would willingly have attended had it not been for the vigor of Edward's dominating leadership. In the 1290's the jurist Fleta observed that the king had "his court in his council in his parliaments," and by the end of the thirteenth century few would have quarreled with that judgment. For, despite long-standing (though typically inchoate) community claims to an independent existence, parliaments were fast becoming the king's court and their members his representatives.

That parliament failed to develop into a purely royal instrument owes much to the reign and deposition of Edward II. As frequent disasters and rule through questionable favorites made his incompetence ever more manifest, mutinous barons tended increasingly to return to the kinds of remedies first advanced under Henry III. In the Ordinances of 1311, for example, control of the king's household and public officials was again coupled with a reliance on a process for redress of grievances that depended on "the counsel and assent of the baronage, and that in parliament." Still, because these attempts to check the king proved ultimately unsuccessful, the end result was deposition, a deposition which, over time, significantly altered the royal foundations upon which Edward I had so carefully established the authority of his parliaments.

In 1326, Mortimer and Isabella used force to invade England and capture the king. That accomplished, they were understandably anxious to legitimize their coup. Because Edward's forced abdication, though obtained, seemed insufficient justification, in January 1327 they turned to a quasi-parliamentary body for ratification of their deed, one having intellectual origins not found solely in an English or parliamentary tradition. Rather, the victors and their clerical advisers relied much more on theoretical arguments generated by Celestine V's renunciation of the papacy in 1294 and by French attempts to remove Boniface VIII for alleged heresy in 1303.

As canonists had analyzed these events, a pope had the right to resign, but one could also be removed involuntarily if a heretic. In such a case, they argued, he would cease to be pope from the moment and very fact of his heresy, so those deposing him (preferably a general council) would not be removing him as much as simply recognizing in law that, through loss of faith, he had already deposed himself. To this argument John of Paris added one more: that just as a pope could renounce his office if, like Celestine V, he felt incapable of filling it, so others could depose him (or, more precisely, recognize he had deposed himself) if they found that the duty of safeguarding the interests of the church was a challenge beyond his capacities. This a general council could do, said the canonists, because (in the words of *Sacrosancta,* a fifteenth-century conciliar decree) it was "lawfully assembled in the Holy Spirit, ... and ... therefore has its authority immediately from Christ."

Awkwardly fitting these arguments to England, Isabella and Mortimer proceeded to depose their king. Because Edward II was a captive, there could be no parliament, but this proved no probelm: as the Lichfield Chronicle assured its readers, those assembled had been "a general council of the whole clergy and people." The archbishop of Canterbury and two bishops gravely preached on the charges, which made clear not only Edward's incompetence but also the extent to which his violations of the coronation oath had made him an offender against God's law—in other words, someone very close to a heretic. The duty of the "council" was therefore clear. It accepted the king's abdication while also declaring him deposed, and lest anyone wonder about the nature of the powers by which it had acted, the archbishop of Canterbury, Walter Reynolds, was quick to supply an answer: *Vox populi, vox Dei* (The voice of the people is the voice of God). Cliché though that pronouncement may now have become, in 1327 Reynolds was really arguing that, as in ecclesiastical bodies, the Holy Spirit would speak through those gathered at Westminister, animating their recognition of preexisting truth with its mystic authority.

Potentially, then, 1327 marked a turning point, one in which men of politics and law had discovered theoretical underpinnings for the view that parliament was more "the people's" court than the king's, a body in which the community of the realm could judge in God's stead even in opposition to the express wishes of a reigning monarch. For if, as in the case of Edward II, the community were to find that the king had flagrantly broken the law, that was no more than to recognize that from the moment of infraction, he had deposed himself.

Nevertheless, no such radical transformation occurred, at least not immediately—and never completely, except during the eleven-year interregnum of the seventeenth century. It was, after all, a fearful thing to remove one of those whom God had anointed, and just as men had found it desirable to accept the sources of Edward III's kingship as being little different from those of his father, so they returned to, and made more explicit, the earlier view of parliament as the king's high court. Thus, though parliament continued to evolve, the explanation and causes relate not so much to matters of high constitutional principle as they do to the practical politics of trying to cope with the Hundred Years War, economic depression, and the Black Death.

Above all, military needs after 1337 brought questions of taxation and representation to the fore. Under Edward I taxes in any form other than traditional aids and reliefs were a relatively new development, and since they could never be levied without consent, parliament became the logical place to seek them. Nevertheless, though in keeping with the overwhelmingly judicial character of parliament, as late as 1441 a chief baron of the Exchequer still found it proper to call its taxes "a profit of court."

Be that as it may, taxation quickly became entangled with issues of representation. In its beginnings parliament had been primarily an assembly of magnates, of those who had long called themselves "the community of the entire country." Still, because baronial wealth consisted largely of land, not money, that lack of liquidity made it desirable for the king to turn ever more insistently to the ready cash of the merchants and bankers of the new cities for fiscal supply. As a result representatives of the towns began occasionally to be summoned to parliament, and even though the first two Edwards treated them more as observers than as voting members, their mere presence must have had a significant impact both on the course of debates and on their outcome. With the onset of the Hundred Years War, however, Edward III's financial needs became so great that the occasional turned into the regular. After 1340 every

session had its urban representatives, and by 1414 they could tell Henry V that "the commons of your land, who now are and ever have been a member of your parliament, have the power of assenting as well as of petitioning."

Moreover, just as the war refused to end, always costing money and seldom realizing the profits expected of it, so economic conditions turned rapidly worse. Then in 1348 came the plague. Its initial ravages killed more than 35 percent of the English people and its periodic returns made population levels continue to fall at least until the last decades of the fifteenth century. These were the conditions that gave rise to the Peasants' Revolt of 1381; to a continuing series of other disturbances, including the so-called Wars of the Roses; and to a general crisis in confidence expressed in such religious phenomena as a growing mysticism, flagellation or other mortifications of the flesh, and the rise of Lollardry. Finally, though more narrowly, as Edward III continued stubbornly to demand taxes for an unpopular war, his parliaments gradually learned how to grant them only in return for practical political concessions. Hard bargaining replaced constitutional conflict as the main vehicle for the growing powers of parliament, and the one sign that men still remembered it might also have nonroyal sources for its authority came solely in such occasional episodes as the impeachments of William Latimer and Lord Lyons in 1376.

But, to repeat, then came 1399. Once again a quasi-parliamentary body deposed the king, though this time with lasting effects. The Great Schism had revived and amplified all the theories that had earlier justified the renunciation of Celestine V and the attempts to remove Boniface VIII. And in a world that so vigorously debated how best to restore unity to the church—whether by councils, by withdrawal of obedience, or by way of cession—the ideas of the conciliar movement provided a natural context for understanding how those claiming to be "the estates and the people" could use the authority of both God and the kingdom to replace Richard II with Henry IV.

The consequences of 1399 were to prove more durable and wide-ranging than those of 1327, and a major reason lay in the fact that, unlike Edward III, Henry IV was not the deposed king's heir. Because men could reasonably question whether he—or any of those who came to the throne in the fifteenth century—was truly the chosen instrument of God, one practical effect was that he and his successors were forced to give greater prominence to parliament as the one body through which God and the kingdom unerringly spoke. Under the Lancastrians, for example, there was a sudden concern with all aspects of the electoral process, to which they and the Yorkists later added attempts to define more precisely just who, by right, were entitled to sit with the lords spiritual and temporal. In these developments the principal issue lay in representation, for at a time when parliament was supposed to be acting with the authority of the kingdom, care had to be taken to ensure that the whole of its community—what was now called the three estates of the realm—was fully and properly present. Similarly, whereas parliaments under Edward III had opened their sessions with straightforward, highly practical speeches, occasionally from war heroes though more typically from the lord chief justice, those in the fifteenth century began with sermons by the lord chancellor, who was always a bishop. Using an appropriate biblical passage as his text, he would show how it provided the perfect model for present action. Thus, through imitation of God's holy writ parliament gave proof that it acted by his authority.

To put the matter a bit differently, the groups that had deposed two kings were not parliamentary, and neither was the authority by which they had acted. On the other hand, by 1399 parliament had experienced almost a century and a half of development, and the capacities it had come to possess had always depended on general acceptance of the belief that at its every meeting the entire community of the realm had somehow participated. Thus the shapers of Richard II's deposition went to considerable trouble to identify their estates and the people with the membership of one parliament, intended to be Richard's last, while at the same time making equally sure that the record of what they had done was entered on the rolls of another, Henry IV's first. In so doing, the stage managers of these events, no fools, showed that they grasped an essential point: that for success they needed to demonstrate that those involved in their scheme were the same men who had been summoned to parliament under Richard and had then actually served under Henry—and hence that this identity in membership proved that the deposers, the estates and the people, had represented the kingdom and enjoyed its Godly powers, just as fully as did a parliament, the absence of valid writs and royal presence to the contrary notwithstanding.

An unlooked-for result was that parliament soon began to claim as its own all the authority that had earlier belonged to God and the kingdom. Because Henry's supporters in 1399 had had to appeal to the kinds of representation found only in parliament, it seems almost inevitable that men came rapidly to assume that it alone should have the right to speak with the highest authority. Although phraseology to that potential effect had appeared as early as 1398, the true change began only with the October parliament of 1460. For if Henry VI's reluctant lords there made Richard of York the royal heir, silently disinheriting young Edward of Lancaster in the process, they did so not through appeals to the alleged wishes of God or the kingdom; rather, they based their decision entirely on what they called, with deceptive simplicity, "the authority of parliament."

The next and nearly final step came in 1484 when, in Richard III's act of succession, parliament admitted that at Buckingham's Guildhall assembly of the previous June, the three estates had not been gathered "in fourme of Parliament." Therefore, to remedy this acknowledged defect by speaking "to the perpetuall memorie of the trouth, and declaration of th'same," it further specified that everything declared in June was to "bee of like effect, vertue and force, as if all the same things had ben so said . . . in a full Parliament, and by auctorite of the same accepted and approved." With recognition of these views it became legally clear at last that only things done "in a full Parliament, and by auctorite of the same" could be taken as statements of the highest truth in England. The way was thereby prepared not merely for the accession of Henry VII but also (insofar as the authority thus exercised included a newfound capacity for judging the spiritual value of a sacrament, Edward IV's "bigamous" marriage) for that parliamentary break from Rome with which, to English eyes, Henry VIII would usher in the modern world.

On a hot August day in 1485, as the tired victors at Bosworth contemptuously readied the naked corpse of Richard III for its final journey to Leicester, few among them would have paused to reflect on the transformation two and a half centuries had brought. Yet if they had, they would have found it a remarkable story, the twin tale of an ever changing kingship intertwined with an equally changing community, a tale in which parliament had come at the last to be the chief place for judging and resolving the differences between them. England had moved from a stress on sacred heredity to Henry VII's less Godly title, but that title remained one which even a former foe like the earl of Surrey was prepared to accept and defend, once "the parliament authority of England [had] set the crown upon [his] stock." Nevertheless, the central theme of the story lay more in the evolving community, and especially in the final coming together of Norman with Saxon. For that union expressed itself not merely in the newly minted English that Henry of Bolingbroke had used to claim the crown, but even more profoundly in the fresh literary voice that poets like Chaucer were giving their tongue, a language that, for the first time, all Englishmen could share. In spite of future strife that those victors would never know, these bequests from the Middle Ages would remain forever a part of England's heritage.

BIBLIOGRAPHY

H.-X. Arquillière, "L'appel au concile sous Philippe le Bel et la genèse des théories conciliaires," in *Revue des questions historiques,* **89** (1911); Thomas N. Bisson, ed., *Medieval Representative Institutions* (1973); Marc Bloch, *The Royal Touch,* J. E. Anderson, trans. (1973); Stanley B. Chrimes, *English Constitutional Ideas in the Fifteenth Century* (1936); Stanley B. Chrimes and Alfred L. Brown, eds., *Select Documents of English Constitutional History, 1307–1485* (1961); R. G. Davies and J. H. Denton, eds., *The English Parliament in the Middle Ages* (1981); Georges Duby, *Medieval Marriage: Two Models from Twelfth-Century France,* Elborg Forster, trans. (1978); William Huse Dunham, Jr., *The Fane Fragment of the 1461 Lords' Journal* (1935), and "'The Books of the Parliament' and 'The Old Record,' 1396–1504," in *Speculum,* **51** (1976); William Huse Dunham, Jr. and Charles T. Wood, "The Right to Rule in England: Depositions and the Kingdom's Authority, 1327–1485," in *American Historical Review,* **81** (1976).

Geoffrey R. Elton, *The Body of the Whole Realm: Parliament and Representation in Medieval and Tudor England* (1969), and "The Early Journals of the House of Lords," in *English Historical Review,* **89** (1974); Sumner J. Ferris, "The Iconography of the Wilton Diptych," in *The Minnesota Review,* **7** (1967); James Gairdner, ed., "William Gregory's Chronicle of London," in his *The Historical Collections of a Citizen of London in the Fifteenth Century* (1876), 57–239; Ernest F. Jacob, *The Fifteenth Century, 1399–1485* (1961); Ernst H. Kantorowicz, *The King's Two Bodies: A Study in Medieval Political Theology* (1957); Fritz Kern, *Kingship and Law in the Middle Ages,* Stanley B. Chrimes, trans. (1939); Gaillard Lapsley, *Crown, Community, and Parliament in the Later Middle Ages* (1951); Jean Leclercq, "La renonciation de Célestin V et l'opinion théologique en France du vivant de Boniface VIII," in *Revue d'histoire de l'église de France,* **25** (1939), abridged English trans. in Charles T. Wood, ed. and trans., *Philip the Fair and Boniface VIII,* 2nd ed. (1971, repr. 1976), 35–39; Alexander Luders, *et al., Statutes of the Realm,* 2 vols. (Public Records Office, London, 1810–1828); Bryce Lyon, *A Constitutional and Legal History of Medieval England,* 2nd ed. (1980).

May McKisack, *The Fourteenth Century, 1307–1399* (1959); Alex C. Myers, *England in the Late Middle Ages (1307–1536)* (1952, rev. ed. 1956), and idem, ed., *English Historical Documents,* IV, *1327–1485* (1969); Francis Palgrave, ed., *The Parliamentary Writs and Writs of Military Summons,* 2 vols. (1827–1934); Edouard Perroy, *The Hundred Years War,* W. B. Wells, trans. (1951); Edward Peters, *The Shadow King: Rex inutilis in Medieval Law and Literature* (1970); Frederick M. Powicke, *The Thirteenth Century, 1216–1307* (1953, 2nd ed. 1962), and *King Henry III and the Lord Edward,* 2 vols. (1947); Harry Rothwell, ed., *English Historical Documents,* III, *1189–1327* (1975); Thomas Rymer, ed., *Foedera, conventiones, literae, et . . . acta publica . . . ,* 29 vols. (1704–1735); Peter Saccio, *Shakespeare's English Kings* (1977); George O. Sayles, *The King's Parliament of England* (1974); J. Stachey, ed., *Rotuli parliamentorum,* 6 vols. (Public Records Office, London, 1776–1777); Carl Stephenson and Frederick George Marcham, *Sources of English Constitutional History,* 2 vols. rev. ed. (1972); Sylvia L. Thrupp, *Society and History,* Raymond Grew and Nicholas H. Steneck, eds. (1977); Brian Tierney, *Foundations of the Conciliar Theory* (1955).

Bertie Wilkinson, *The Constitutional History of Medieval England, 1216–1399,* 3 vols. (1948–1958), and *Constitutional History of England in the Fifteenth Century (1399–1485)* (1964); Charles T. Wood, "Personality, Politics, and Constitutional Progress: The Lessons of Edward II," in *Studia gratiana,* XV, *Post scripta: Essays on Medieval Law and the Emergence of the European State* (1972), "The Deposition of Edward V," in *Traditio,* **31** (1975), "Queens, Queans, and Kingship: An Inquiry into Theories of Royal Legitimacy in Late Medieval England and France," in William C. Jordan, Bruce McNab, and Teofilo F. Ruiz, eds., *Order and Innovation in the Middle Ages* (1976), 385–400, 562–566; "The English Crisis of 1297 in the Light of French Experience," in *Journal of British Studies,* **18** (1979), and "Celestine V, Boniface VIII, and the Authority of Parliament," in *Journal of Medieval History,* **8** (1982).

CHARLES T. WOOD

[See also **Barons' War; Black Death; Edward I of England; Edward II of England; Edward III of England; Fleta; Glanville, Ranulf de; Henry III of England; Henry IV of England; Henry V of England; Hundred Years War; Kingship, Theories of: Western Europe; Law, English Common; Parliament; Provisions of Oxford; Richard II; Richard III; Roses, Wars of the; Simon de Montfort the Younger.**]

ENGLISH LANGUAGE AND LITERATURE. See Anglo-Saxon; Middle English.

ENGLISHRY, PRESENTMENT OF. From the eleventh century it was law in England that if a foreigner was killed and his slayer escaped, then the hundred where it happened must pay a "murder fine." William the Conqueror may have imposed the law to discourage the English from murdering his French followers, for the law was later said to be for the protection of Frenchmen. But every victim of homicide was presumed to be French unless shown to be English. For an unpunished homicide the hundred could escape the fine only if "presentment" was made of the "Englishry" of the slain.

The *Leges Henrici* (*ca.* 1115) say that Englishry could be shown by the oath of twelve leading men of the hundred, by the ordeal of hot iron, or "according to circumstances." By the thirteenth century the universal practice was to accept the testimony of the nearest kinsmen of the victim, usually one on the father's side and one on the mother's. It is not clear what they had to affirm. Perhaps they said that they and the slain were serfs, for by this time it may have been presumed that all freemen had French blood. But their witness may have been merely that they were close kin, so that a murder fine need fall only where the victim of homicide was a stranger to the area.

The fine was originally forty-six marks. During the twelfth century it became variable and much lighter, sometimes as little as ten shillings. In the thirteenth century it came to be imposed on the hundred only once each time an eyre was held, regardless of the number of unpunished homicides. Since the hundred was hardly allowed to escape what was in effect a recurrent tax, presentment of Englishry in the individual case accomplished nothing. By 1300 it was seldom made.

The law of murder fine and Englishry never applied in Shropshire, Cheshire, or north of the Humber, and a statute of 1340 abolished it altogether.

BIBLIOGRAPHY

Charles E. H. Chadwyck Healey, ed., *Somersetshire Pleas*, XI (1897), lviii–lxii, lxxvii–lxxx; Frederick C. Hamil, "Presentment of Englishry and the Murder Fine," in *Speculum*, **12** (1937); R. F. Hunnisett, *The Medieval Coroner* (1961), 27–29; Cecil A. F. Meekings, ed., *Crown Pleas of the Wiltshire Eyre, 1249* (1961), 61–65; Doris M. Stenton, ed., *The Earliest Northamptonshire Assize Rolls* (1930), no. 55.

DONALD W. SUTHERLAND

[See also **England: Norman-Angevin; Law, English Common.**]

ENGRAVING. The printing of impressions from engraved and inked copperplates began in the second quarter of the fifteenth century in northern Europe, and developed very rapidly during the course of the century. The first engravings were rather awkward images, apparently produced by goldsmiths to record decorative motifs or designs used by illuminators, painters, and sculptors. The potential influence of these cheap and easily distributed images was great, and as the expressive possibilities of the engraving technique were improved, the medium became a vehicle for painters such as Martin Schongauer, the Housebook Master (who used the allied medium of drypoint), Andrea Mantegna, and Albrecht Dürer.

Only a small proportion of engravings made in the fifteenth century survive, frequently in unique or rare impressions. Such impressions as survive may be from worn or reworked plates. Early engraving techniques did not permit the taking of many good impressions, and the prints themselves were frequently used as patterns or subjected to other kinds of hard wear.

Very little is known about the earliest engravers and the circumstances in which they worked. Since engraving was not a distinct branch of artistic activity, its practitioners are not listed separately in guild records. Very few fifteenth-century engravers signed their works, though a number used monograms. Meticulous observation of style and graphic technique is the chief means of separating the surviving examples into the work of individuals. Scholars reassembling the oeuvre of these engravers have assigned them names based on the most salient features of their work, often their most important print or series of prints. However, it is sometimes not possible to link an engraving convincingly with a particular printmaker or body of work. That a print may be known in only one impression from a plate that was heavily reworked by a second hand makes judgment more difficult, and it is not surprising that the prints

The Nativity. Engraving by Martin Schongauer, *ca.* 1480–1490.
NATIONAL GALLERY OF ART, ROSENWALD COLLECTION

attributed to some of the earliest engravers are, in some cases, most notably that of the Master of the Power of Women, a grouping of heterogeneous works sharing a similar graphic technique.

In spite of these limitations on our knowledge of the earliest engravers, it can be surmised that most were goldsmiths. The use of the burin, the engraver's tool, and the skill required to guide it through the metal were part of a goldsmith's craft. The decoration of early-fifteenth-century German metalwork included a wealth of engraved ornament, and the taking of trial proofs or patterns from engraved designs decorating metal objects was almost certainly a preliminary stage in the development of copperplate engraving. An example of such a record or trial proof is the fifteenth-century impression, now in the Biblioteka Jagiellónska, Krakow, taken from the inked design on a contemporary cross (Fritz, *Gestochene Bilder*, fig. 324).

However, the shift from this goldsmith's workshop procedure to designs engraved on copperplates for the purpose of making multiple images implies a new intention to market and disseminate the designs. This change cannot be precisely dated and localized, and probably occurred at about the same time in several centers in northern Europe. The Master of the Death of the Virgin must have been among the very earliest engravers because he employs a

drapery convention of broad, soft folds that is a vestige of the International Gothic. In general, early engravings can be dated on the basis of relationships to contemporary paintings and the existence of datable copies of the prints. Thus, after about 1440 there are numerous copies in datable manuscripts of the engraved cards made by the Master of the Playing Cards, and the playing cards were evidently not the first prints this engraver produced.

Although engravings were probably made from about 1430, the first surviving engraving bearing a date is the *Flagellation* dated 1446 by the Master of 1446 (Lehrs I.216.2.; pl.14, no. 37). Engraving developed later in Italy, where it was also an outgrowth of metalworking techniques. The first Italian engravings were probably made in Florence shortly after midcentury, stimulated by Maso Finiguerra's printing of impressions from sulfur casts of his nielli.

Many of the earliest northern European engravings are surprisingly pictorial in effect. The Master of the Playing Cards, the Master of the Nuremberg Passion, the Master of the Berlin Passion, and others among the first generation of engravers shared a technique of strong contours and fine parallel hatching strokes or flecks, which, in the best of their prints, gives the effect of shimmering light. The fine hatching strokes soon wore out with repeated printing of the plate.

Master E. S. moved toward a solution of this problem in his mature prints, executed in the 1450's, in which longer and deeper hatching strokes and cross-hatching, as well as a variety of dashes and hyphens, give a richer range of texture. E. S.'s engraving technique increased the number of good impressions, enabled him to expresss three-dimensional form when desired, and more adequately conveyed the fact of the burin cutting metal. Martin Schongauer, active from about 1470, further rationalized E. S.'s technique, making cross-hatching, hatching, and shorter strokes follow form consistently and endowing his line with a rhythmic swelling and tapering expressive of the motion of the burin.

While the innovations of Upper Rhenish engravers, especially Master E. S. and Schongauer, were especially important for the later history of the medium, engravers in other centers also developed graphic conventions taking into account the demands of the printing process. The Lower Rhenish engraver and goldsmith Israhel van Meckenem (*ca.* 1445–1503), apparently the son of the Master of the Berlin Passion, and the most prolific fifteenth-century engraver, was evidently in contact with Master E. S., for he copied many of that master's engravings and acquired some of his plates, reworking and reissuing them. Yet his technique placed a greater emphasis on space and atmosphere than did that of his Upper Rhenish contemporaries. Especially in his later prints, Van Meckenem employed large areas of long, straight hatching strokes in superimposed layers that suggest complex interiors or link his figures in a veil of atmosphere.

The earliest Italian engravings are comparable to the first northern efforts in that they employ relatively strong contour with fine parallel hatching and cross-hatching. They too presented the problem of rapid wear to the plate. The so-called Broad Manner, probably developed by the Florentine miniaturist and engraver Francesco Rosselli in the 1470's, extended the life of the plate through the use of broader, longer, parallel hatching lines. Rosselli's straight hatching strokes, all arranged in the same direction, imitate the effect of a drawing, with the parallel hatching approximating areas of wash. Antonio Pollaiuolo and Mantegna and his followers developed this technique into a system of expressive contours, straight parallel hatching strokes of varying lengths, and parallel return strokes to achieve tonal effects of great range and sophistication. However, from the early 1490's on, in Italy as throughout northern Europe, Schongauer's graphic convention gained ascendancy through the brilliant use to which it was put by the young Albrecht Dürer.

There is little evidence of how early engravings were bought and sold, yet they seem to have been aimed in part at connoisseurs and collectors, in distinction to the larger, more popular market for woodcuts. This can be deduced from their closeness to the main artistic currents of their time and from the prominence of secular subjects—of courtly, learned, or satirical themes. The tendency of early engravers to issue their works in series—of Passion scenes, scenes from daily life, coats of arms, or playing cards—may have been directed at collectors.

Engravings also undoubtedly served a very important function as patterns or as substitutes for works of art in other media. Only rarely were such patterns useful specifically for goldsmiths. Ornament prints, playing cards, and coats of arms provided a flexible decorative vocabulary used by artists in a variety of media. In the Lower Rhine several engravers, including the Master of the Berlin Passion, the Master of St. Erasmus, and the Master of the Floral Borders

produced numerous series of religious scenes in which the framing elements and small scale imitate manuscript illumination. These prints often survive pasted into devotional books in place of miniatures.

Some of the very earliest engravings seem to copy paintings in their scale, conception, and number of figures, though this can rarely be demonstrated from surviving works—an exception being the *Annunciation* by the Master of the Nuremberg Passion and the painting, now in Winterthur, of the same composition by the Master of the Frankfurt *Paradise Garden*. In the case of Master E. S., a dependence on diverse painted or sculptural sources seems to account for abrupt stylistic changes in the engraver's work. The relationship of source, engraving, and copy is usually highly complex. Yet it seems that many early prints were intended to serve as models for other artists. The role of intermediary was natural to the engraving medium, and must have accounted in part for its rapid development in the fifteenth century and for the acceleration of exchanges between artists during this period.

The Betrayal of Christ. Engraving by the Master of the Playing Cards, *ca.* 1425–1440. MUSÉE DU LOUVRE, CABINET DES DESSINS, COLL. ROTHSCHILD

Whereas the earliest engravers seem to have been goldsmiths using the images of the major painters, sculptors, and miniaturists of their day as inspiration, toward the end of the fifteenth century painters began to engrave their own designs. This shift was probably spurred by the development of engraving techniques that yielded a greater number of good impressions and produced a range of effects of space, form, and texture, as well as by the growth of an audience of collectors and artists in need of patterns. A painter such as Martin Schongauer no doubt sought a wider audience for his designs; indeed, he is the first engraver whose prints survive in numerous impressions. Mantegna, in his engravings beginning probably in the late 1460's, produced effects of sculptural solidity and luminosity parallel to those of his paintings. He also made designs to be carefully reproduced by engravers using a burin technique based on his own.

The experiments of artists who also worked in other, more monumental media led to more richly pictorial prints. Thus the Housebook Master chose the drypoint needle to make prints having a spontaneity of execution and lively texture even surpassing those of his paintings. Master LCz, identifiable as the painter Lorenz Katzheimer of Bamberg, achieved an extraordinary range of textures in his engravings. The painter and engraver Mair von Landshut, active in Bavaria shortly before 1500, printed on colored paper with added heightening in colors, thus anticipating the effect of chiaroscuro woodcuts. This aspect of the painter-printmaker reached an early high point in the inventiveness and technical brilliance of Albrecht Dürer, whose first engravings were made in the mid 1490's.

An indispensable basis for study of fifteenth-century engraving is provided by the catalogs compiled by Max Lehrs, Max Geisberg, and Arthur M. Hind, with their division of works according to hands. In addition to producing monographs on individual artists, recent studies have concentrated on the relationship of engravings to work in other media and on the forward-looking subjects, especially secular ones, treated in engravings.

BIBLIOGRAPHY

Lilli Fischel, "Oberrheinische Malerei im Spiegel des frühen Kupferstichs," in *Zeitschrift für Kunstwissenschaft*, 1 (1947); Johann Michael Fritz, *Gestochene Bilder* (1966); Max Geisberg, *Die Anfänge des deutschen Kupferstiches*, 2nd ed. (1924); Arthur M. Hind, *Early Italian Engraving*, 7 vols. (1938–1948); Fritz Koreny, "Der frühe Kupferstich und die Anfänge der Reproduktionsgraphik nordlich der Alpen," in *Kunstgeschichtliche Gesellschaft zu Berlin, Sitzungsberichte*, n.s. 20 (1971–1972); Max Lehrs, *Geschichte und kritischer Katalog des deutschen, niederländischen, und französischen Kupferstichs im XV. Jahrhundert*, 10 vols. (1908–1934); Jay A. Levenson, Konrad Oberhuber, and Jacquelyn L. Sheehan, *Early Italian Engravings from the National Gallery of Art* (1973); James Marrow, "A Book of Hours from the Circle of the Master of the Berlin Passion," in *Art Bulletin*, 60 (1978); Alan Shestack, *Fifteenth-century Engravings of Northern Europe from the National Gallery of Art, Washington, D.C.* (1967).

MARTHA WOLFF

[See also **Burin; E. S., Master; Housebook, Master of the; Israhel van Meckenem; Playing Cards, Master of the; Schongauer, Martin.**]

ENGUERRAND VII OF COUCY (1340–1397) was the last of a prominent line of great lords of Picardy in northern France. His father, Enguerrand VI, died in 1346; his mother, Catherine of Austria, in 1349. Enguerrand VII seems to have participated in the Hundred Years War as early as 1355, and two years later he was associated with the partisans of Charles II the Bad, king of Navarre and leader of the French faction that opposed the ruling house of Valois.

After John II of France was captured by the English at Poitiers in 1356, the French had to raise a large ransom that was guaranteed by the sending of hostages to England. Enguerrand de Coucy was among them, but during his honorable confinement he so ingratiated himself with his English captor-host that he won the hand of Edward III's daughter Isabella.

When Anglo-French hostilities resumed in 1369, Coucy faced a problem of divided loyalties. His first obligation was to the king of France, but he avoided taking arms against the English for a few years by participating in other activities, such as aiding the count of Savoy in a campaign against the Visconti of Milan. Only in 1376, when Edward III was senile and no longer in full control of English policy, did Coucy join actively in the French war effort.

From 1376 on, Enguerrand VII was one of the most prominent French military commanders. Like many northern nobles he had, in his youth, been linked with Charles the Bad and the anti-Valois faction and would, in later life, be linked with Louis of Orléans and the anti-Burgundian faction at the

French court. Yet he avoided close affiliation with either of these groups, and his lack of strong partisanship, coupled with his distinguished lineage, made him a prestigious figure whom all parties were willing to trust. He chose not to accept the position of constable in 1380, but he remained active as a conciliator, mediating among the quarrelsome French princes during the minority of Charles VI.

Enguerrand was involved in most of the famous events in late-fourteenth-century Europe. He helped suppress the antinoble uprising known as the Jacquerie in 1358. He was in England at the time of the Peasants' Revolt of 1381. In 1390 he accompanied Duke Louis II of Bourbon to Tunisia on a crusading expedition. In 1394–1395 he was back in Italy, this time leading an expedition to advance the ambitions of Louis of Orléans, who had married a Visconti.

Enguerrand of Coucy's last great adventure was also the final chapter in the medieval crusading movement. He joined a distinguished group of French lords in responding to the request of the king of Hungary for assistance in checking the advance of the Ottoman Turks. This campaign, in 1396, ended disastrously at Nicopolis, where Enguerrand was among those captured by the enemy. He was now an old man by medieval standards and his health deteriorated in captivity. While his ransom was being arranged he died at Brusa in Asia Minor, in February 1397. With his death the male line of the great seigneurial house of Coucy came to an end. His eldest daughter, Marie de Bar, subsequently sold the barony to the duke of Orléans.

BIBLIOGRAPHY

On the military career of Coucy and other leading commanders of the period, see Philippe Contamine, *Guerre, état et société à la fin du moyen âge* (1972); John Bell Henneman, "The Military Class and the French Monarchy in the Late Middle Ages," in *American Historical Review*, 83 (1978). For Coucy's role in the broader context of the fourteenth century, see Barbara W. Tuchman, *A Distant Mirror* (1978).

JOHN BELL HENNEMAN

[See also **Crusades of the Later Middle Ages; France: 1314–1494; Hundred Years War; Jacquerie; Nicopolis; Peasants' Rebellion.**]

ENGUERRAND QUARTON. See **Charonton, Enguerrand.**

ENNODIUS, MAGNUS FELIX (*ca.* 473–521), bishop and rhetorician. Born of a noble family at Arles, he moved, following the death of his parents when he was about fifteen, to Pavia in northern Italy, where he entered the clergy about 493. After serving as a deacon at Milan, he returned to Pavia, where he became bishop about 514. He was educated in both classical and religious literature and composed many surviving works in a highly rhetorical style, including 297 personal letters; 172 poems, including twelve hymns; a panegyric on the Ostrogothic king Theodoric; biographies of the bishop Epiphanius of Pavia and the monk Antonius of Lérins; a short autobiography; a praise of rhetoric; and 28 speeches. His letters in particular are a valuable source for the history and culture of the time. He was a strong supporter of the primacy of the see of Rome and was one of the first to reserve the title of "pope" to the bishop of Rome. In 515 and 517 he traveled to Constantinople on papal delegations in unsuccessful attempts to heal the Acacian schism.

BIBLIOGRAPHY

Corpus scriptorum ecclesiasticorum latinorum, C. Hartel, ed., VI (1882); *Monumenta Germaniae historica: Auctores antiquissimi,* Friedrich Vogel, ed., VII (1885). See also John Martindale, *The Prosopography of the Later Roman Empire,* II (1980), 393–394; Martin von Schanz, Carl Hosius, and Gustav Krüger, *Geschichte der römische Literatur,* IV, pt. 2 (1920), 131–148.

RALPH WHITNEY MATHISEN

[See also **Latin Literature; Papacy, Origins and Development of; Rhetoric, Western European; Theodoric the Ostrogoth.**]

ENTRY INTO JERUSALEM, Christ's arrival in Jerusalem riding an ass, significant as the first time he was publicly hailed as the Messiah (Matthew 21:1–11, Mark 11:1–10, Luke 19:29–40, John 12:12–19). The episode attained liturgical importance as Palm Sunday by the fourth century in the East and by the seventh in the West. Because the Entry into Jerusalem was equated with the entry into Heavenly Jerusalem, and hence taken as a symbol of Christian victory over death, artistic representations stress its triumphal nature and follow Roman formulas for an imperial *adventus,* or triumphal procession. Christ either straddles the donkey or, as in many Byzantine examples, sits sidesaddle; he is often followed by dis-

Christ's entry into Jerusalem. Byzantine ivory, central panel of an altar, 10th century. STAATLICHE MUSEEN PREUSSISCHER KULTURBESITZ, BERLIN, PHOTOGRAPH BY DORE BARLEBEN

ciples and greeted by crowds. Palm branches and garments are normally spread on the ground before the ass, and Zacchaeus or children may hail Christ from the treetops. The traditional iconography was elaborated in tenth-century Germany by the *Palmesel,* a special type of sculpture that was wheeled through the streets on Palm Sunday to simulate the procession into Jerusalem.

BIBLIOGRAPHY

Gertrud Schiller, *Iconography of Christian Art,* II (1972), 18–23.

LESLIE BRUBAKER

[See also **Easter; Heavenly Jerusalem.**]

ENVOI, in French poetry of the fourteenth and fifteenth centuries a short stanza that ends certain poems of fixed form such as the ballade or chant royal. The envoi repeats the rhyme and meter of the previous stanza as well as the refrain. Typically it be-gins with a dedication to the poet's lady or to an important person, such as a prince or the god of love.

BIBLIOGRAPHY

A contemporary description of the envoi is found in Eustace Deschamps's *Art de ditier* in Gaston Raynaud, ed., *Oeuvres completes de Eustache Descamps,* VII (1891), 278.

RICHARD O'GORMAN

[See also **Ballade; Chant Royal.**]

EÓGANACHT, an Irish ruling dynasty. In their genealogical legends the Eóganacht claim descent from Eógan Már, variously taken to be an ancestor deity or a genuine ancestor. The legendary founder of the Eóganacht kingship of Munster is Conall Corc, from whom all the historical dynastic segments of the Eóganacht are said to descend. The earliest historical and genealogical material is associated with Óengus mac Nad Froích, grandson of Corc, who is placed in the fifth century by genealogical writers. But the dominant position of the Eóganacht was by no means as ancient as their hard-pressed propagandists would have us believe.

In the seventh and eighth centuries the Eóganacht were divided into two great and hostile branches, the western Eóganacht, which comprised the kingdom of Loch Léin and Raithliu, and the eastern Eóganacht, which included the kingdoms of Cashel, Áine Cliach, Airther Cliach, and Glendamain. There were other more scattered branches of the Eóganacht, but these had declined into obscurity by the beginning of the eighth century. The Eóganacht Locha Léin were settled about Killarney and at first were successful contenders for the kingship of Munster against their cousins to the east. A text written about 700 preserves the bitterest memories of the struggles. By about 800 Eóganacht Locha Léin were effectively excluded from the kingship of Munster and had become a local kingdom of little importance. Eóganacht Raithlind took their name from their dynastic center at Raithliu, in south Cork. They were early, if largely unsuccessful, contenders for the kingship of Munster and they remained a powerful local kingdom at least until the early eleventh century.

The eastern Eóganacht, located in some of the richest lands in Munster, began to dominate the dynastic confederation from the seventh century. The Eóganacht Glendamnach produced some of the greatest Munster kings of the seventh century, and in the person of Cathal mac Finguine (*d.* 742) they appeared to be about to monopolize the kingship of Munster and extend their political authority outside its boundaries. However, after the reign of Artrí mac Cathail (*d.* 821) this branch of the Eóganacht passed into decline. Eóganacht Áine supplied a number of early kings of Munster, but they too passed into obscurity in the course of the eighth century.

In the second half of the ninth century and in the first half of the tenth century the Eóganacht of Cashel were dominant in Munster, and under the rule of the able Feidlimid mac Crimthainn they appeared to be about to extend their power. However, after the death of Feidlimid (847), Eóganacht power declined dramatically. The Uí Néill used their growing power to intervene to their benefit in Munster, and the weakened Eóganacht kings were unable to defend their province against Viking attack. Cormac mac Cuilennáin, king-bishop of Munster (902–908) was decisively defeated and killed by a combination of the Laigin and Uí Néill, and after the death of Cellachán of Cashel in 954 the Eóganacht kingship of Munster went under to Dál Cais attack.

The later ruling families sprung from the Eóganacht—Mac Carthaig, Ó Cellacháin, Ó Caím, and others—remained important Munster nobility, but apart from the brief reign of Cormac Mac Carthaig (*d.* 1138) they were effectively excluded henceforth from the kingship of Munster. In the early twelfth century, the king of Connacht succeeded in dividing Munster between Dál Cais and the Eóganacht, and Munster declined greatly in political importance.

BIBLIOGRAPHY

Francis J. Byrne, *Irish Kings and High-kings* (1973); Myles Dillon, "The Story of the Finding of Cashel," in *Ériu*, **16** (1952); Vernam Hull, "Conall Corc and the Corco Luigde," in *PMLA*, **62** (1947); Liam Ó Buachalla, "Contributions Towards the Political History of Munster, 480–800 A.D.," in *Journal of the Cork Historical and Archaeological Society*, **56** (1951), **57** (1952), **59** (1954), and **61** (1956).

DONNCHADH Ó CORRÁIN

[See also **Cormac Mac Cuilennáin; Ireland; Munster.**]

EPANAGOGE, a code of civil law in forty chapters, issued by the Byzantine emperor Basil I and by his sons and coemperors Leo VI and Alexander between 879 and 886. Though largely reproducing the *Pro-*

cheiros Nomos, the *Epanagoge* never enjoyed the same widespread use. Still, it is of particular interest because of its chapters (perhaps inspired by Photios) concerning the official political theory about the emperor and the patriarch and their respective positions as lay and spiritual leaders of the universe, closely collaborating for the earthly and heavenly well-being of all the emperor's subjects.

BIBLIOGRAPHY

Text in Panagiōtēs Zepos and Iōannēs Zepos, *Jus graecoromanum,* II (1931), 229–368. See also J. Scharf, "Photios und die Epanagoge," in *Byzantinische Zeitschrift,* **49** (1956), and "Quellenstudien zum Prooimion der Epanagoge," in *ibid.,* **52** (1959).

NICOLAS OIKONOMIDES

[See also **Basil I the Macedonian; Law, Byzantine; Photios; Political Theory, Byzantine; Procheiros Nomos.**]

EPARCH, the prefect of the city of Constantinople. He was the governor of the city and had almost unlimited authority within its limits. It was his task to maintain public order and security, and to carry this out he had a large body of officials known as the *secretum* of the eparch. He also had sole jurisdiction over the guilds and tradesmen. In effect he controlled the whole economic life of Constantinople, as well as the courts of justice and the provisioning of the city. The police and the fire brigade were under his command; he kept watch over foreigners and saw that the sabbath was observed. He presided over the Imperial Court of Justice when the emperor was not present. Being ex officio a member of the imperial council, the eparch ranked high in the imperial hierarchy. In time many of his functions passed to others until, under the Palaiologoi, only a court title survived, devoid of power.

LINDA C. ROSE

[See also **Byzantine Empire: Bureaucracy; Constantinople.**]

EPARCH, BOOK OF THE (*To eparchikon biblion),* a collection of regulations of trade and industrial activity in medieval Constantinople. The entire text is preserved only in a manuscript of the fourteenth century (MS of Geneva, no 23); the title and preamble are also an İstanbul manuscript (Metochion Taphou N 25). The *Book of the Eparch* contains a preamble and twenty-two chapters, most of them dedicated to individual guilds or crafts or to officials connected with trade activity (notaries, middlemen). The guilds dealt with the manufacturing and trade of silk textiles (chs. 4–8) and linen (ch. 9); with the trade of meat, fish, bread, and wine (chs. 15–19); with groceries including spices, candles, salted meat, smoked fish, oil, and pottery (chs. 10–13); and with the jeweler's art and the exchange of money (chs. 2–3); as well as with housing (ch. 22). Some important handicraft professions (pottery makers, ironmongers, tailors, cobblers, barbers) are not mentioned. The title of the İstanbul manuscript supplies a precise attribution: according to it, the *Book* was issued by Leo VI in 911–912, when a certain Philotheos was serving as eparch. However, the *Book* refers several times to the *tetarteron*, a coin introduced by Emperor Nikephoros Phokas (963–969). Thus the questions of the completeness and date of the existing text remain uncertain.

The *Book of the Eparch* is the most valuable source on the Byzantine guild system, especially for the tenth century. The regulations were intended primarily for the protection of the guilds (called *systemata* in the text, *somateia* in a longer version of the title) from the competition of both the unorganized craftsmen and peddlers and the noble owners of ateliers. However, the *Book* also restricted competition between guilds by its precise definition of the limits of their activity. It also regulated internal guild affairs by establishing price ceilings, the number of hired workers, the dimensions of the workshop *(ergasterion)*, and so on. It arranged for the collective purchase of raw materials and it determined the places for trade. The *Book* prescribed severe controls over the quality of production, prohibited the enticement of hired workers from other masters, forbade the hoarding of raw materials, and impeded the purchase (*Vorkauf*) of such materials outside the city.

The three-tiered hierarchy of master-journeyman-apprentice familiar in the West was not established in Constantinople. Byzantine masters used the labor of slaves and hired workers (*misthotoi*), who worked under contracts that could last no longer than a month at a time. Byzantine apprentices were indistinguishable from journeymen because they too were paid by the master. There were no limitations on entry into a guild. The candidate had to swear his loyalty, prove his professional skill, and pay the entrance fee. The most characteristic trait of Constantinopolitan guilds was government control over trade activity. Although guild aldermen existed, they were subordinated to the eparch and his staff, who in the final account fulfilled the duties of controlling trade regulations. Some crafts served the court and government directly.

BIBLIOGRAPHY

Sources. Jules Nicole, ed. and trans., *Le livre du préfet; ou l'édit de l'empereur Léon le Sage sur les corporations de Constantinople* (1893, repr. with intro. by Ivan Dujčev 1970); M. Ja. Sjuzjumov, *Vizantijskaja kniga eparcha* (1962). An English translation is in Edwin H. Freshfield, *Roman Law in the Later Roman Empire* (1938).

Studies. Robert S. Lopez, *Byzantium and the World Around It* (1978), pts. III and IV; Dieter Simon, "Die byzantinische Seidenzünfte," in *Byzantinische Zeitschrift*, 68 (1975); Albert Stöckle, *Spätrömische und byzantinische Zünfte* (1911).

ALEXANDER P. KAZHDAN

[See also **Byzantine Empire: Bureaucracy; Constantinople; Guilds, Byzantine; Leo VI the Wise, Emperor.**]

EPHESUS, the greatest city of Roman Asia Minor, still flourished in the sixth century as the capital of the important province of Asia. The city was large and rich, with sumptuous public buildings. It had an ancient Christian tradition, in which the names of St. Paul, the Apostle John, and the Seven Sleepers figured prominently; it had also been the seat of an ecumenical council (431). The late antique city, a cosmopolitan port, was a center of administration, trade, and pilgrimage. It had a Jewish community, about which little is known. Justinian adorned Ephesus with its greatest building, the richly decorated Basilica of St. John.

As a result of the destruction wrought by the Persian and Arab invasions of the seventh century, the city was greatly reduced in size and divided into two sites. That around the Church of St. John, surrounded by powerful fortifications, became the medieval center. The Byzantine military government of the Dark Ages made Ephesus one of the cities of the Thracian theme. Contemporary texts call it a *kastron*, or castle, and it gradually assumed the name Theologos (The Theologian) after St. John. The site of a local fair and of a miracle annually performed in the cathedral, the town attracted traders and pilgrims.

Ephesus was occasionally captured, but suffered no lasting damage. The Second Crusade arrived there in 1147 and fought the Turks nearby. After the Fourth Crusade it became a major city of the Laskarid kingdom, and in 1304 it was taken by the Turks. As the capital and major port of the emirate of Aydin, Ephesus, then called Ayasuluk (from Agios Theologos), enjoyed a last period of prosperity. It was the base for relations, peaceful or hostile, with the West, and a great entrepot of trade. At the same time, arts and letters flourished and a great mosque was built, the only monumental structure since Justinian. Taken after complex struggles by the Ottomans in 1424, Ayasuluk fell into decline; when Western travelers seeking antiquity rediscovered it in modern times the town was a mere fortress, almost abandoned.

BIBLIOGRAPHY

Clive Foss, *Ephesus After Antiquity* (1979), with full references.

CLIVE FOSS

[See also **Laskarids; Ottomans; Seljuks of Rum; Seven Sleepers of Ephesus; Themes; Urbanism, Byzantine.**]

EPHESUS, COUNCIL OF. See **Councils (Ecumenical, 325–787).**

EPHREM (EPHRAIM), monk, painter, and mosaicist responsible for most of the mosaics set in the eastern end of the Church of the Nativity in Bethlehem when it was restored under the crusaders in 1169. His name is known from a bilingual inscription in the church. The mosaics showed scenes from the New Testament and a frieze of prophets and apostles. Fragments of the *Doubting Thomas,* the *Ascension,* the *Entry into Jerusalem,* and the *Transfiguration* are preserved; the inscriptions are in Latin, but the pictorial style and the technique used suggest that Ephrem was trained in Byzantium or Syro-Palestine.

BIBLIOGRAPHY

R. W. Hamilton, *The Church of the Nativity, Bethlehem, A Guide,* 2nd ed. (1947), 53–58; T. S. R. Boase, "Mosaic, Painting and the Minor Arts," in Kenneth Setton, ed.,

A History of the Crusades, IV, *The Art and Architecture of the Crusader States* (1977).

LESLIE BRUBAKER

[See also **Crusader Art and Architecture.**]

EPIBOLÉ. The *epibolé* (surcharge), which goes back to Ptolemaic times, evolved as a response to a shortage of agricultural labor that resulted in an increase in fallow land. This land, both state and private, was assigned to private landowners for compulsory cultivation, so that taxes would be paid on it. The *epibolé* was a very important means of increasing land revenues during the reign of Justinian. In the ninth century it was transformed into the *allelengyon,* an indication that the original system had ceased to function properly and more stringent regulations were required.

BIBLIOGRAPHY

George Ostrogorsky, *History of the Byzantine State,* Joan Hussey, trans. (1957, rev. ed. 1969).

LINDA C. ROSE

[See also **Allelengyon; Taxation, Byzantine.**]

EPIC, FRENCH. See **Chansons de Geste.**

EPIC, LATIN. It is harder to define medieval Latin epic than classical epic. Although the tradition of Vergil was dominant, not all Latin epics are imitations of Vergil. New subjects were attempted, and where those subjects are Christian, the *Psychomachia* of Prudentius is the dominant influence.

The narrative poems that can be classified as epics may be divided into the following categories: those clearly based on classical themes, particularly the Trojan War; those which, though not classical in theme, model their style closely on that of Vergil, to the point of borrowing whole lines from his works; those which handle less exalted themes, including the conflict between fox and wolf, but still adapt Vergilian style for their own purposes (with these should be included the epic treatments of the Christian story, the *Messiads);* those poems having themes that are both classical and biblical, and that seek merely to present their story in the most attractive verse form (owing more to Ovid than to Vergil).

The best medieval Latin adaptations of classical themes are the *De excidio Troiae* (The fall of Troy) of Josephus Iscanus (Joseph of Exeter) and the *Alexandreis* of Walter of Châtillon. Josephus wrote his poem about 1200, basing it on the prose account of Dares Phrygius, which stressed the love relationship between Achilles and Polyxena, daughter of Priam. Josephus was concerned to imitate what he regarded as classical style, and his poem is a series of highly colored, sometimes strained, descriptive passages either of incident or of character. Walter uses Vergilian stylistic features but is most interested in presenting Alexander as the perfect pagan king. His epic thus becomes a mirror of princes, not a conflict of great powers. Nevertheless, the *Alexandreis* (1184) is probably the greatest medieval Latin epic because of its narrative power and character analysis.

In vigor it can be matched by the *Waltharius* (*ca.* 930), in which Vergilian language is used to convert an essentially Germanic situation into a Latin epic. Although the language is Vergilian (and Prudentian) to the point of borrowing whole passages, the ethic remains Germanic.

The *Ruodlieb* (*ca.* 1050) is hardly heroic. In it a series of folklore motifs is put in Latin verse to show how a young man acquires experience in life. The work is an interesting transitional piece between classical epic and vernacular romance. Much the same can be said of the *Ecbasis captivi* (perhaps tenth century) and the *Ysengrimus* of Nivardus of Ghent (*ca.* 1160). Each is an account of a contest between fox and wolf, but the former is a loosely knit story, whereas the latter is a carefully constructed and highly rhetorical parody of the epic genre.

The epic form was also used to impart an aura of greatness to historical figures. The *Berengarii imperatoris gesta* (or *Panegyricon Berengarii;* the title is actually in Greek), written between 915 and 924, glorifies the imperial state and the emperor Berengar himself by drawing heavily on Vergil, Statius, and the *Ilias latina.* Less successful was a versification of the *Annales de gestis Caroli Magni* made by the "Poeta Saxo" about 890. Its only claim to being an epic lies in the form used.

Attempts to write the life of Christ in epic form appeared first in the *Evangelorum libri IV* of Juvencus (*ca.* 330) and the *Carmen paschale* of Sedulius (mid fifth century), both of which remained highly influential. The most original work of this genre is

that by "Eupolemius," who describes in epic–allegorical form the freeing of the Jewish people by the Messiah. Conflicts between allegorical figures of good and evil provide the epic element, derived as much from Prudentius as from Vergil.

BIBLIOGRAPHY

There is no comprehensive work on the medieval Latin epic, and general works on epic poetry devote very little attention to it. Information must be sought under the titles of individual works in Max Manitius, *Geschichte der lateinischen Literatur des Mittelalters,* 3 vols. (1911–1931); Frederic J. E. Raby, *A History of Christian Latin Poetry,* 2nd ed. (1953), and *A History of Secular Latin Poetry in the Middle Ages,* 2 vols., 2nd ed. (1957). See also Ernst R. Curtius, *European Literature in the Latin Middle Ages,* Willard R. Trask, trans. (1953, repr. 1963).

W. T. H. JACKSON

[See also **Alexander Romances; Beast Epic; Berengarii Imperatoris Gesta; Ecbasis Captivi; Eupolemius; Latin Literature; Latin Meter; Prudentius; Ruodlieb; Troy Story; Vergil in the Middle Ages; Walter of Châtillon; Waltharius; Ysengrimus.**]

EPIPHANY, FEAST OF. The origins and early evolution of the feast of Epiphany are still disputed. There is agreement that Epiphany, celebrated on 6 January, is older than Christmas. It seems that the feast originated in the East and was taken up in the West, whereas Christmas spread eastward from Rome by the end of the fourth century. Different ideas about the meaning of epiphany prevailed in East and West, reflecting different views on Christology. Although a great deal has been written about Epiphany and Christmas, no final conclusion has been reached about the original content of the feast of Epiphany.

The Armenian church commemorates the birth and baptism of Jesus on 6 January; the Greek church celebrates the nativity of Christ on 25 December and his baptism on 6 January; and the Latin church attaches the adoration of the Magi to the feast of Epiphany (6 January), celebrating the birth of Christ on 25 December (as in the Greek church) and Jesus' baptism the week after Epiphany.

This comparison seems to mirror with some accuracy the development of the feast. It may very well be that the theme of Epiphany, as witnessed by the Armenian church, reflects the oldest form of the feast. Probably there was just one feast originally, the celebration of Epiphany on 6 January, at which Jesus' birth and baptism were solemnly commemorated: Jesus emerges from the river Jordan as the Spirit-filled Son of God. The descent of the Spirit and the heavenly voice saying "You are my son, I this day have begotten thee" (Ps. 2:7; variant reading of Luke 3:22) manifest Jesus' divine sonship. Very soon this original unity of birth and baptism was given up because of the possible Adoptionist connotations.

The Greek church maintained one of the original themes of Epiphany, restricting the commemoration to Jesus' baptism, and introducing the celebration of the nativity on 25 December. The polemic attitude of the Roman pontiffs (beginning with Siricius [384–399]) against any baptismal associations with the feast of Epiphany reflects the Roman attempt to play down as much as possible the earlier joint celebration of nativity and baptism. What was least significant for the East, the adoration of the Magi, became most significant for the West and provided the main imagery for Epiphany there. In addition, the solemn blessing of the water was transferred from Epiphany to the Easter vigil, although the prayer still points toward its original place in the liturgy of Epiphany. There is also evidence that the churches in southern Italy, Spain, Gaul, and Ireland reluctantly followed the Roman idea concerning the theological content of Epiphany.

It seems that the origins and early development of Epiphany can be determined only through a better understanding of the origins of the imageries associated with baptism and a new investigation of Christology (of prime importance is the evidence of Judeo-Christian communities, but also of Syria, and some Armenian material). Recent publications concerning the original concepts of baptism have far-reaching implications for the reassessment of the origins of the feast of Epiphany. In Syria (and in Armenia) baptism was originally conceived as a "birth ritual" (its basis is John 3). For nearly 400 years the Syro-Armenian type of baptism had nothing in common with the "death mysticism" in Paul's theology of baptism (Romans 6). The baptismal water is depicted as a womb (or the Jordan) that gives birth to the baptismal candidates. As the Spirit hovered over the waters at the dawn of creation, likewise he (in Syriac, she) is hovering over the baptismal font in order to bring forth the new Adam, who will live henceforth in the Spirit of Christ.

The model for the Syriac baptismal theology is not an assimilation to Christ's death and resurrection, but Jesus' descent into the river Jordan from which he emerged as the Spirit-filled new Adam and Son of God. The Maronite and Armenian baptismal liturgies are centered exclusively on Jesus' baptism in the Jordan, an event associated with the imageries of being "begotten" and "born" through the life-begetting Spirit of Christ. For example, the hymns of the Armenian baptismal liturgy (which are also sung at Epiphany) imply the Creation story and Jesus' ascent from the Jordan as the Son of God: "You who are co-creator with the Father and the Son, through whom the creatures [are] born unto life in the waters. Today you give birth to sons of God" (Maštocᶜ, ed. Jersualem 1961, pp. 47–48) and "You who by staying over the waters didst fashion the creatures. Descending into the waters of the font you give birth to sons of God" (ibid., pp. 50–51). These hymns reflect the Syriac baptismal theology.

This intimate connection between birth and baptism in early Christian Syria sheds new light on the original theme of Epiphany in the East: the unity of baptism and nativity represents one of the oldest doctrines of Christology, Jesus' spiritual birth in the Jordan. The christological disputes led first to the distinction between the spiritual and physical births of Jesus (which is reflected in the introduction of the feast of the Incarnation in the East on 25 December), and eventually to the obliteration of the "birth imagery" from the context of baptism and from Epiphany, in the West.

BIBLIOGRAPHY

Bernard Botte, *Les origines de la Noël et de l'Épiphanie* (1932); Frederick C. Conybeare, *The Key of Truth: A Manual of the Paulician Church of Armenia* (1898), and "The History of Christmas," in *American Journal of Theology,* 3 (1899); Hermann K. Usener, *Das Weihnachtsfest,* 2nd ed. (1911, repr. 1972); Gabriele Winkler, *Das armenische Initiationsrituale* (1981).

GABRIELE WINKLER

[See also **Baptism; Baptism of Christ; Christmas.**]

EPIPHANY IN ART. The story of the magi (Matthew 2:1–12) does not specify how many wise men worshiped Christ, but as three gifts are mentioned, representations habitually present a trio approaching the Virgin and Christ child. The magi came from the Orient, and are thus frequently shown in Persian dress. Following a sixth-century text that elaborates on Psalm 72 and Isaiah 60, they may also be depicted

Adoration of the Magi. Detail of the pulpit in the Cathedral of Pisa by Giovanni Pisano, 1302–1311. ALI-NARI/ART RESOURCE

as kings, particularly from the tenth century and generally after the eleventh century. They were also sometimes associated with the three continents known during the medieval period (Europe, Africa, Asia); hence, from the twelfth century on, the second magus may be black. The magi seem to have acquired names around the year 500, though the earliest preserved pictures inscribed with the names that ultimately became canonical—Caspar, Melchior, and Balthasar—date to the tenth century (the Gerona *Beatus* of 975, the Codex Egberti of *ca.* 980, and wall paintings in Cappadocia). The magi stand before Christ or, especially after the ninth century, kneel with their gifts of gold, frankincense, and myrrh. From the thirteenth century, they frequently are seen kissing his hand or feet. The star that guided the magi to Christ is always present as a reminder that the Incarnation ushered in a new age and that epiphany was the festival of light. Because of typological connections with the Star of Jacob prophesied by Balaam (Numbers 24:17), Balaam is included in some early images. Relics of the magi were discovered in Milan and translated to Cologne in 1164, resulting in a fresh wave of popularity that continued to the end of the medieval period.

BIBLIOGRAPHY

Gertrud Schiller, *Iconography of Christian Art,* I, Janet Seligman, trans. (1971), 94–114.

LESLIE BRUBAKER

EPIROS, DESPOTATE OF. The despotate of Epiros in northwestern Greece originated after the capture of Constantinople during the Fourth Crusade. From being a center of resistance to the crusaders, it evolved into an independent Byzantine state under its self-appointed ruler, Michael I Doukas. For a while under his successor, Theodore, who captured Thessaloniki in 1224 and was crowned emperor there, it comprised much of Macedonia and Thessaly as well. But the empire of Thessaloniki was soon absorbed into the rival Byzantine empire of Nicaea, which defeated Theodore's nephew, Michael II, at Pelagonia in 1259. Thereafter the despotate was confined to the provinces of Aetolia and Acarnania, Thesprotia, and Ioannina, with its capital at Arta. Michael II was its first despot, a rank second only to that of emperor. The title was not hereditary and could be conferred only by an emperor. The derivative word "despotate" was Latin in origin and more geographical than institutional in significance.

After the restoration of the Byzantine Empire at Constantinople in 1261, the despots of Epiros long refused to recognize the new regime and fought to preserve their autonomy. Michael II found an ally in Manfred of Sicily, to whom he ceded a number of places on the coast of Epiros and Albania. When Manfred was dethroned by Charles of Anjou in 1266, these overseas possessions passed under Angevin rule and the despot of Epiros became a vassal of the now-French king of Sicily. This arrangement, irksome though it was, enabled the despots to defy repeated efforts by the emperors in Constantinople to bring them to heel. In 1318 the last direct descendant of Michael I, Thomas, was murdered by his nephew, Nicholas Orsini, count of Cephalonia, and the despotate was governed by hellenized Italians. In

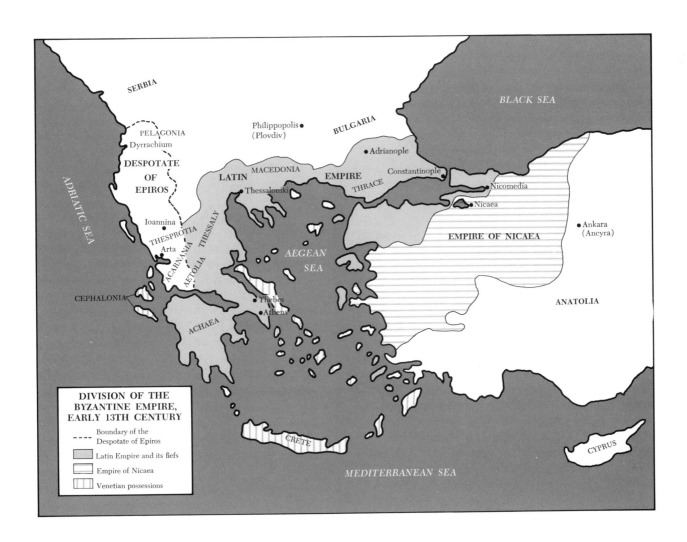

499

1340 the army of Emperor Andronikos III, which had already occupied Ioannina, finally brought the rest of Epiros back into the Byzantine Empire.

Only eight years later the Serbians and Albanians descended on northern Greece. Epiros was appropriated by Symeon Uroš, a half-brother of Stefan Dušan, with the title of despot. He abandoned Arta and the southern area to the Albanians, appointing his son-in-law, Thomas Preljubovič, as despot in Ioannina. There were thus two despotates, Serbian in the north and Albanian in the south, constantly at war. Preljubovič was murdered in 1384 and succeeded in Ioannina by a Florentine, Esau Buondelmonti, who sought to reunite Epiros by marrying an Albanian wife.

When Buondelmonti died in 1411, his nephew Carlo Tocco of Cephalonia was invited to defend Ioannina against the Albanians and the Turks, and for its last few years the despotate was again under Italian rule. The Tocco family had some success against the Albanians, but they could not stem the Turkish tide, and in October 1430 Ioannina surrendered to the Turks. In March 1449 a Turkish army entered Arta, and the despotate of Epiros was swallowed up by the Ottoman Empire. Its surviving monuments include many churches, monasteries, and castles in Arta and the surrounding district, where local architects and artists in the thirteenth and fourteenth centuries evolved provincial versions of the Byzantine style.

BIBLIOGRAPHY

Donald M. Nicol, *The Despotate of Epiros* (1957), *The Last Centuries of Byzantium* (1972), and *The Despotate of Epiros, 1267–1479: A Contribution to the History of Greece in the Middle Ages* (1984).

DONALD M. NICOL

[See also **Byzantine Empire: History; Crusades and Crusader States: Fourth; Sicily, Kingdom of.**]

EPITRAKHIL, Russian term for the stole proper to a Byzantine priest (known in Greek and English as the *epitrachelion*). Originally a long band with crosses on it similar to the Roman stole, the two parts of the band came to be joined permanently with buttons, leaving a loop to be put over the priest's head.

GEORGE P. MAJESKA

[See also **Vestments.**]

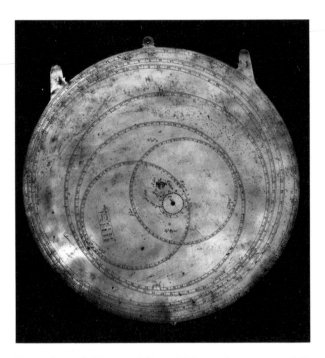

Equatorium of Merton College. Maker unknown, *ca.* 1350. THOMAS-PHOTOS, OXFORD, ENGLAND

EQUATORIUM, an instrument for performing astronomical calculations, in particular for finding the true longitude of a planet by adding a mechanically determined "equation" to the mean longitude (taken from tables). Described by Ibn al-Samḥ and al-Zarquāl in Spain in the eleventh century, it was first described in Latin about 1260 by Campanus of Novara, whose *Theorica planetarum* represented the lines of the Ptolemaic theories by thin threads and the circles by disks of parchment. Later development led to the construction of a single instrument for all the planets, and to the fifteenth-century *volvellae*, in which all moving parts were concentric. The equatorium was popular among astrologers, and many specimens have survived. There are also numerous treatises in Latin and in the vernacular, including one purportedly by Chaucer.

BIBLIOGRAPHY

Emmanuel Poulle, *Les instruments de la théorie des planètes selon Ptolémée* (1980); Derek J. Price, ed., *The Equatorie of the Planetis* (1955), the Middle English text attributed to Chaucer.

OLAF PEDERSON

[See also **Astronomy.**]

EQUITY. Derived from the Greek *epieikeia* and the Latin *aequitas*, the medieval concept of equity incorporated a variety of legal, philosophical, and institutional ideas. The basic meaning of *aequitas* in classical law was "fairness" or, in Ciceronian formulation, "that which demands like law in like cases." A second related Roman idea was that of *aequitas* as an abstract ideal that transcended positive law *(jus)* and confirmed such rights as that of a child to inherit, or that of a landowner to retain any treasure found on his land—whether or not these rights were expressed in written law. The classical texts called on this concept of *aequitas* to offer guidance in filling the inevitable gaps in the established positive law. It was also used to test, by contrast or comparison, the "just spirit" of the enacted rules, the "correspondence between a legal rule or institution and the spirit of civil or natural law" (J. B. Moyle, *Imperatoris Iustiniani Institutionum*, 29, 5th ed. [1964]). See *Digest* 1.1. pr.; 1.1.7.1; 1.1.17; 1.3.25; 2.14.1 pr.; 4.1.7 pr.; 15.1.32 pr.; 16.3.31.1; 37.5.1 pr.; 44.4 pr.; 47.4.1.1; 50.17.90. A final and very distinct element of classical equity jurisprudence was Aristotle's definition of equity as that which corrects "the error that is generated by the unqualified language in which absolute justice must be stated" (*Nicomachean Ethics*, 5.10). In other words, equity is the fair (rather than equal) application of positive law, a principle that may demand that positive laws be applied by exception and exemption rather than by blind obedience. Thus, there were these basic classical ideas about equity: first, the *aequitas* of Cicero that demanded that all laws be justly, in the sense of equally, applied; second, the *aequitas naturalis* of the *Digest* and the *Institutes,* that spirit of natural justice that stands apart from the positive law (*jus*) and guides the discretion of the praetor; and third, the Aristotelian *epieikeia* which, by modification and exception in the light of particular circumstances, corrects the error generated by the unqualified language in which all positive law inevitably must be expressed.

Classical *aequitas* exerted a strong influence on Christian ethical doctrines. Thomas Aquinas particularly seized on both Aristotle's teachings and the classical notion of *aequitas* as an abstract spirit of justice apart from positive law, thus facilitating his great effort to reconcile the law of God, the law of the church, and temporal law. Aquinas thoroughly understood Aristotle's principle of "equitable" construction: "A man who follows the lawmaker's intention is not interpreting the law simply speaking,

as it stands, but setting it in a real situation; there, from the prospect of the damage that would follow, it is evident that the lawmaker would have him act otherwise" (*Summa Theologiae*, 1a2ae.96.6). The notion that "legalism should be ruled by equity" was a fundamental idea of Aquinas. "It seems that human law does not set up an obligation in the court of conscience. An inferior power has no jurisdiction in a superior court" (*Summa Theologiae*, 1a2ae.96.4, 6). It was also largely Aquinas' influence, not classical doctrine, that introduced to Europe the "equity" of Henry Maine's famous definition: "Any body of rules existing by the side of the original civil law, founded on distinct principles and claiming incidentally to supersede the civil law in virtue of a superior sanctity inherent in those principles" (*Ancient Law*, 2nd ed. [1864], 27).

But "distinct principles" more specific than Christian theology itself were slow to emerge. As early as the Frankish kings, and in England after the Conquest, it was accepted that the responsibility for "equity," in the sense of a kind of roughhewn extraordinary justice, lay with the king and his council. In England, the royal council had discretionary powers that enabled it to promote equity, but this discretion was regarded as part and parcel of the common law and the legal constitution, not as a separate system with distinct principles. (See *Glanvill* II, 7, G. D. G. Hall, ed. [1965], 28. See also *Bracton*, vol. 2, 23–24 [fol. 3]; 304 [fol. 107]; 307 [fol. 108], S. E. Thorne, trans. [1968].) Indeed *Bracton* (*ca.* 1230) included the obligation to render decisions "with equity and mercy" as part of the coronation oath of the king, and spoke of the "countenance" from which comes "forth the judgment of equity" when describing the judges who "represent the king's person . . . as they sit in justice" (*Bracton*, 304 [fol. 107]; 307 [fol. 108]).

The king's peculiar responsibility for "equity" was surely assisted by the civil jurists of developing continental and English university law schools and by the canon lawyers of the church. One of the first teachers of law in England was Vacarius, who was teaching at the infant Oxford University, probably earlier than 1149. Vacarius was a follower of continental jurists, such as Irnerius, who regarded the sovereign as both legislatively omnipotent and capable of interpreting and modifying legal rules in specific cases, as he himself could hardly be bound by what was a creation of his own will. According to Vacarius, the king and council could give weight to considerations of "equity," whereas a lower judge was bound by the law. These theories were the seeds of the later special equity jurisdictions of the English conciliar courts.

The growth of humanism among civil law jurists and churchmen during the fourteenth and fifteenth centuries tended to promote the concept of *aequitas*. Jurists such as Lucas de Penna (*d. ca.* 1390) wrote of equity as, first, the source of law, the abstract principle of justice; second, the principle that decides cases concerning which the positive law is silent (*casus omissi*); and third, the criterion of interpretation that safeguards "against the mechanical, literal interpretation of law." The first idea was certainly found in medieval England and known to common lawyers as "reason," the traditional sense of right and wrong that preserved the law from legalistic inconsistency or absurdity. The third idea, the criterion of statutory construction, became equally familiar to English common lawyers as the "equity of statute." Furthermore, through the ecclesiastical courts and through the royal secretariats that they dominated, canonists in England and on the Continent sought to define equity as including Christian ethics—in effect a higher law to be enforced by the sovereign.

In England, the focus of these ideas became the King's Chancellor. Traditionally a cleric and "keeper of the king's conscience," the Chancellor was also a natural representative of the king and council before extraordinary pleas for justice, when ordinary judges and officers either could not or would not "do right." Around this figure developed one of several special courts of equity, together with a distinct and highly developed body of equity law that for centuries was unique to these courts.

There is no doubt that common law and equity originated together: the king ensured justice for all by means of his own prerogative power and his prerogative legal machinery. But differentiations between the royal prerogative powers and the law of equity did eventually occur, and in ways neither required nor anticipated by the classical writers of medieval jurisprudence. This particularly English phenomenon was to have a profound and lasting effect on Anglo-American jurisprudence.

The rationale for this development was more institutional than theoretical, and it is largely explained by the history of English royal courts, particularly the King's Council and the Chancellor. By the time of Edward I, the king's court had gradually evolved into three tribunals: a Common Bench (which sat in Westminster Hall), a King's Bench (which was supposed to follow the king's travels),

and a higher court, which in the days of Edward I we may indifferently call the King in Council or the King in Parliament. The Chancery, by contrast, was not originally a court at all, but a great secretarial bureaucracy and a ministry of justice. As such, it was somewhat similar to the King's Exchequer, an office that was already a curia by the thirteenth century, in that it called the king's debtors before it, issued process, and judged controversies. Both of these royal bureaus were to develop equity jurisdiction apart from the other royal common law courts of Common Bench and King's Bench. Their claim to distinction would be their particular closeness to the King in Council, the "fountainhead" of justice.

At first these institutions did not spawn separate doctrines or bodies of rules. There was, after all, no complete body of written law in England. No one can be absolutely certain when the Chancellor, in addition to his many other duties, began to hear petitions regularly on the "English side" of the Chancery, directed to the king's special justice or equity. Suggestive petitions survive from the latter half of the fourteenth century. Decrees were first issued in the name of the King in Council, but by 1473 at the latest the Chancellor issued decress in his own name.

At least initially, there were four critical differences between this "equity" jurisdiction and the process of the "law" courts. First, the petition was in the form of a simple "bill," not a formal legal writ, alleging some reason why extraordinary justice was required, that is, why the petitioner considered his case to be beyond ordinary procedures. Second, the Chancellor issued a subpoena to the individual defendant, which commenced the action in personam and was good in all counties—a clear advantage over the more restricted common-law process. Third, there was no jury—on the theory that a jury could be misled more easily by faulty pleading than the Chancellor. Fourth, until the 1440's the defendant was verbally examined under oath by the Chancellor, a practice replaced by written answers serving the same purpose. The parties could testify and be examined.

With time English equity evolved special remedies as well as special procedures: the enforcement of "uses," or medieval trusts, wherein the formal legal title of the owner is held to the "use" of a beneficiary; the recognition of copyhold title; the recognition of assignment as a chose in action; relief against inequitable penalties and forfeitures; and specific performance of agreements and injunctive orders, a type of legal remedy that could be substantially more flexible and adaptive than the common-law forms of action.

There is no doubt that these procedures and remedies were derived in part from the procedures of the church courts and the canon law. They were familiar to the chancellors, who were clerics and trained in the civil and canon law traditions of a cosmopolitan church. But as H. D. Hazeltine has shown, many if not most of these special features were borrowed from the older English practices of the justices in eyre and other courts: "The new tribunal . . . simply carried on the work of the older courts by developing in greater fulness and with a different machinery the equity inherent in royal justice" (Hazeltine, in Paul Vinogradoff, ed., *Essays in Legal History* [1913], 285).

Thus the other so-called conciliar courts that split off from the King's Council could be, and were, "courts of equity." One of the most important examples was the Court of Requests, which originated with the official of the King's Council who had the responsibility of dealing with the requests and petitions of the poor. By Tudor times the Court of Requests was a court of conscience that also had many of the "equitable" procedural features of the Chancellor's court. All of these courts, at various times, employed "equitable" procedures and had functions similar to the court of the Chancellor himself. Equity was not the monopoly of the Chancellor. Neither was English equity the special domain of canonists and clerics. Had it been otherwise, the Reformation, Henry VIII's Act of Settlement or Supremacy (1534), and the concurrent suppression of canon-law study in England would have had a disastrous effect.

The ultimate survival and even flourishing of equitable ideas in England, despite the laicization of the Chancery, was due in large part to the intellectual influence of one man, Christopher St. German, an English common lawyer. St. German's great book, *Doctor and Student*, appeared first in a Latin version in 1523. It bridged the gap from a clerical to a lay Chancery with intellectual brilliance. *Doctor and Student*'s success in preserving and reconciling the role of equity in modern English law was one of the first examples of a printed book substantially influencing the course of the law.

Thus, "equitable" law, developed in part from classical and medieval roots, became a permanent part of English law. As such, equity took special notice of fiduciary relationships; gave special relief from fraud or unconscionable dealing; gave relief from strict legal obligation where, through unforeseen events and pure accident, a party was unreasonably prejudiced; and gave special attention to the intentions of parties in the interpretation of wills, settlements, and other formal documents, where a strict legal reading would have perverted the common understanding. Finally, equity took "tutelary jurisdiction" over those who, "through special circumstances, are particularly in need of protection: infants, married women, mariners, borrowers, those who are subject to harsh penalties, and formerly the poor and the insane" (Carleton K. Allen, *Law in the Making,* 2nd ed. [1930], 236). To all these concerns were brought, in principle, the special evidentiary procedures and the special remedies of equitable doctrine, a lasting heritage of classical and medieval thought.

BIBLIOGRAPHY

Equity in medieval jurisprudence. George B. Adams, "The Origin of English Equity," in *Columbia Law Review,* **16** (1916); J. L. Barton, "Equity in the Medieval Common Law," in Ralph A. Newman, ed., *Equity in the World's Legal System* (1973); Charles S. Brice, "Roman *Aequitas* and English Equity," in *Georgetown Law Review,* **2** (1913); William W. Buckland, *Equity in Roman Law* (1911); Frederic W. Maitland, "Canon Law in England," in his *Collected Papers,* III (1911); Frederick Pollock and Frederic W. Maitland, *The History of English Law Before the Time of Edward I,* 2nd ed. by S. F. C. Milsom, I (1968), 189–197, 286–296; S. E. Thorne, "The Equity of a Statute and Heydon's Case," in *Illinois Law Review,* **31** (1936); Paul Vinogradoff, *Roman Law in Mediaeval Europe,* 2nd ed. (1909), 54–58; Walter Ullmann, *The Medieval Idea of Law* (1946, repr. 1969), 41–44; H. E. Yntema, "Equity in the Civil Law and the Common Law," in *The American Journal of Comparative Law,* **15** (1967).

The special English courts and law of equity. Margaret E. Avery, "The History of the Equitable Jurisdiction of the Chancery Before 1460," in *Bulletin of the Institute of Historical Research,* **42** (1969), and "An Evaluation of the Effectiveness of the Court of Chancery Under the Lancastrian Kings," in *Law Quarterly Review,* **86** (1970); William P. Baildon, ed., *Select Cases in Chancery, A.D. 1364 to 1471,* Selden Society, X (1896); John H. Baker, *An Introduction to English Legal History,* 2nd ed. (1979), 83–100; Willard T. Barbour, *The History of Contract in Early English Equity,* Oxford Studies in Social and Legal History, IV (1914); Edgar Bodenheimer, *Jurisprudence,* rev. ed. (1974), 249–251, 363–367; William H. Bryson, *The Equity Side of the Exchequer* (1975); A. D. Hargreaves, "Equity and the Latin Side of the Chances," in *Law Quarterly Review,* **68** (1952); H. D. Hazeltine, "The Early History of English Equity," in Paul Vinogradoff, ed., *Essays in Legal History* (1913); William S. Holdsworth, *A History of*

English Law, I, *History of the Chancery* (1903), 194–263; IV, *Canon Law and Equity*, 3rd ed. (1945), 275–283; and V, *Rules of Equity in the Fifteenth and Sixteenth Centuries*, 3rd ed. (1945), 278–338; Frederic W. Maitland, *Equity* (1909); S. F. C. Milsom, *Historical Foundations of the Common Law* (1969), 74–87; T. F. T. Plucknett, *A Concise History of the Common Law*, 5th ed. (1956), 178–181, 675–694.

DANIEL COQUILLETTE

[See also **Bracton, Henry de; Chancery; Exchequer; Glossators; Kingship, Theories of: Western Europe; Law, Civil; Law, English Common; Vacarius.**]

ERASX. See **Araks River.**

ERCHAMBERT OF FREISING (also called Erchanbert, *d.* 854), grammarian and bishop of Freising from 836. Erchambert taught at Freising, where a school of some importance developed in the ninth century. He wrote a commentary on the *Ars grammatica* of Donatus that was designed to defend "invicta auctoritas Prisciani" against misleading notions of other grammarians.

BIBLIOGRAPHY

Tractatus super Donatum, Wendell V. Claussen, ed. (1948). See also Max Manitius, *Geschichte der lateinischen Literatur des Mittelalters*, I (1911), 490.

EDWARD FRUEH

[See also **Grammar.**]

ERCHENBERT OF MONTE CASSINO (also called Erchempert), a late-ninth-century monk, fled from Monte Cassino during an assault by Saracens in 881. He settled in Capua, where he continued the *History of the Lombards* begun by Paul the Deacon in the eighth century. Erchenbert concludes his part with the events of 889.

BIBLIOGRAPHY

Chronica monasterii sancti Benedicti Casinensis, W. Wattenbach, ed., in *Monumenta Germaniae historica: Scriptores*, VII (1846, repr. 1963), 746; Ernst Dümmler, ed.,

Neues Archiv der Gesellschaft für ältere deutsche Geschichtskunde, VI (1878–1879), 544.

NATHALIE HANLET

[See also **Historiography, Western European; Paul the Deacon.**]

EREROYKᶜ. The Armenian church of Ereroykᶜ near Ani is a large Christian basilica of the fourth or fifth century, with sixth- or seventh-century modifications. Now mostly in ruins, it stands on a six-stepped platform, possibly the remains of a pagan temple, and has a twin-towered facade and porticoes on three sides. The interior, divided by pillars into a high nave and two aisles, has a semicircular east apse and pairs of two-story chambers on the east and west. There is controversy over whether the nave was originally roofed in wood, like Syrian basilicas, or vaulted, like contemporary Armenian examples.

BIBLIOGRAPHY

P. Paboudjian and A. Alpago-Novello, *Ererouk* (1977); Josef Strzygowski, *Die Baukunst der Armenier und Europa*, 2 vols. (1918), 153–158, 397–403.

LUCY DER MANUELIAN

[See also **Armenian Art.**]

EREX SAGA is an Old Norse prose adaptation of the medieval French *Erec* of Chrétien de Troyes. Although there is no indication in the saga, as now preserved, of time or place of origin, the original translation presumably stems from the circle around the Norwegian king Hákon Hákonarson (1217–1263), as does *Ívens saga*, its close counterpart in certain respects. Only later Icelandic copies now exist, however. The oldest, from about 1500, consists of two small vellum fragments that contain only nine lines from the beginning of the saga. The two primary manuscripts are seventeenth-century paper, and it is difficult to say to what extent the preserved text differs from the original translation.

Erex, son of King Ilax, is one of King Arthur's twelve champions. One day, while riding with the queen, Erex (who is unarmed) is forced to suffer insults and even a blow from a dwarf, the servant of an unknown knight. To avenge his disgrace, Erex pursues the knight and defeats him in single combat, thereby winning the hand of the lovely Evida. Now, however, Erex neglects his obligations as a knight, out of love for his wife. When he hears of the reproach circulating at court, he sets out on a series of adventures to restore his honor, taking Evida with him. The adventures include defeating eight robbers, fighting an evil earl, and rescuing various knights and ladies from two giants, a flying dragon, and a band of armed men. The series culminates with the defeat of a knight in an adventure entitled "Joy of the Court." Through the series Erex has advanced from defending himself (and Evida) to rescuing others in distress. His honor now reestablished, Erex returns to Arthur's court, is crowned king—his father has died—and rules his kingdom in peace. He and Evida have two sons, who become distinguished men.

The saga at every stage betrays its derivation from Chrétien's work. Yet some of the most interesting features are the deviations, quite aside from the obvious change from verse to prose. One chapter (10), containing the fights with the dragon and the band of men, is entirely an interpolation. These episodes, however, are not merely inserted for the sake of additional excitement; they are worked into the whole in a very conscious manner. The dragon represents an escalation—from purely human opponents to the giants to this terrible beast of fantasy. The band of men, in turn, forms a clear parallel to the earlier encounter with the robbers, itself a condensation of two episodes in Chrétien. We have here a clear adaptation of the French work to fit structural patterns familiar from the native sagas of the Icelanders. The conclusion, an epilogue not found in Chrétien, likewise conforms to the indigenous model. The changes are not only structural: there are also changes in characterization, motivation, and the role of women, among others. In comparison with *Ívens saga*, *Erex saga* shows considerably more restructuring and is an interesting example of cultural assimilation.

BIBLIOGRAPHY

Foster W. Blaisdell, ed., *Erex saga Artuskappa* (1965); Foster W. Blaisdell and Marianne E. Kalinke, trans., *Erex Saga and Ívens Saga* (1977); Marianne E. Kalinke, "A Structural Comparison of Chrétien de Troyes' *Erec et Enid* and the Norse *Erex saga*," in *Mediaeval Scandinavia*, **4** (1971).

FOSTER W. BLAISDELL

[See also **Chrétien de Troyes; Ívens Saga.**]

ERIGENA. See John Scottus Eriugena.

ERIKSKRÖNIKAN *(EK)* is the earliest of the Scandinavian rhymed chronicles. It was composed in Swedish around 1322/1332 by an anonymous court chronicler, presumably a military person loyal to Duke Erik Magnusson (the title figure of the chronicle) and his brother Valdemar. The text describes seventy years of Swedish history from the rule of Erik Magnusson (1249) to selection of Magnus Eriksson as king in 1319. In its most extensive form it contains 4,545 lines in rhymed couplets *(knittelvers)*.

EK is contained in nineteen manuscripts. The earliest and best of these are: *A*, Cod. Holm. D 2, the "Spegelbergs bok" from about 1470/1480; *B*, "Fru Märetas bok" or Codex Verelianus, written in 1457; and *C*, Cod. Holm. D 3, "Fru Elins bok," written in 1476—all housed in the Royal Library in Stockholm. *A* is closest to the presumed archetype, whereas *B* and *C* represent another tradition, but all three are thought to contain the text in a more original form than is found in the remaining manuscripts. *B* is defective in that it lacks lines 1–82. It has been contested whether or not the text was complete in the form in which it has come down to us, but no better tradition has come to light. The provenience of *EK* has never been determined with complete satisfaction, though it seems very likely that the author was from Uppland.

EK focuses on the feuds between the sons of Magnus Ladulås—Birger, Erik, and Valdemar—as they struggle for supremacy over Sweden. The central episode is a feast at Nyköping Castle. King Birger invites Erik and Valdemar, who are promptly incarcerated and slain by their host, who is often compared to Judas. This episode is thought to have represented the entire account in its earliest version, whereas the preceding and following lines were added later to ensure wider interest in the chronicle as a historical document.

EK is generally regarded as the most artful of the Scandinavian rhymed chronicles and was thought to derive in part from the *Braunschweigische Reimchronik* (1279–1298) and the *Livländische Reimchronik* (ca. 1290). Recent scholarship, however, has shown *EK* to be an independent work not significantly influenced by these earlier Low German chronicles.

ERIST^CAW

BIBLIOGRAPHY

Erikskrönikan, Rolf Pipping, ed. (1921, repr. 1963), is the standard edition. Pipping's *Kommentar till Erikskrönikan* (1926) is the most detailed commentary on any Swedish text. See also Ingwar Andersson, *Erikskrönikans författare* (1958); Gustaf Cederschiöld, *Om Erikskrönikan* (1899); and Sven-Bertil Jansson, *Medeltidens rimkrönikor* (1971).

T. L. MARKEY

[See also **Scandinavian Rhymed Chronicles.**]

ERIST^CAW (pl., *eristavni*), the noble governor of a Georgian province comparable to the western European duke. According to Georgian historical tradition, *eristavni* were originally appointed by the semi-legendary first king of Iberia, P^Carnavaz, in the late fourth century B.C. The *erist^Caw* headed the "people-army" *(eri)* of his province, that is, he commanded the *aznaurni* (nobles) of that area. Parallel to the *naxarar* in Armenia, the *erist^Caw* was less powerful vis-à-vis his monarch than was his Armenian counterpart. Yet the intentions of the Iberian monarchs to keep the "feudal" post of *erist^Caw* noninheritable were ultimately frustrated by the ambitions of the powerful dynasts who held these positions. The class of *eristavni* merged with the class of princes from which its members had originated in about the sixth century when the struggle between the Iberian monarch and his great vassals resulted in the temporary abolition of the Iberian monarchy. During the principate of Iberia (580–888), the leading Georgian political authority was usually referred to as *eristavt-mt^Cavari, eris-mt^Cavari,* or simply *eristavi.*

BIBLIOGRAPHY

Zurab V. Anchabadze, *Iz istorii srednevekovoy Abkhazii* (1959); Georges Charachidzé, *Introduction à l'étude de la féodalité géorgienne* (1971); Cyril Toumanoff, "La noblesse géorgienne: Sa genèse et sa structure," in *Rivista araldica,* 54 (1956), and *Studies in Christian Caucasian History* (1963).

RONALD G. SUNY

[See also **Georgia: Political History.**]

ERMENGAUD, MATFRE, late Provençal poet mentioned in a tax document of Béziers in 1322, is known only through his *Breviari d'amor* (Breviary of love) and two love lyrics. In the preamble of the *Breviari,* Ermengaud gives his origin as the diocese of Béziers and dates the poem 1288. He refers to himself both as a Friar Minor and as a master of laws *(senher de leys),* probably indicating his possession of a degree in civil law.

The *Breviari,* in octosyllabic rhymed couplets, contains nearly 35,000 lines. Twelve manuscripts and ten fragments of it are extant, some of the latter followed by a verse epistle to the poet's sister. The style is familiar and uncomplicated, incorporating numerous Béziers localisms. The *Breviari* belongs to the large medieval genre of the summa (or *tresor,* or *speculum*) and draws liberally from such compendia as those of Honorius Augustodunensis (1120) and Vincent of Beauvais (1256). Ermengaud's vast poem constitutes a compendium of instruction on such varied subjects as religious doctrine, courtly love, manners and etiquette, botany and zoology, the rights of kings and princes, and the knowledge of good and evil. He styles himself expert in all matters of love. His work incorporates numerous Provençal poetic genres: the tenson and partimen (dialogue poems usually involving exchange of opinions on a set topic), the *ensenhamen,* or set of teachings, and the political sirventes, or satire.

A product of the period of decline following the Albigensian persecution of the troubadours (culminating in 1209), the *Breviari* advocates marriage as the proper issue of courtship and defends the honor of ladies against illicit sexual congress. It is, however, a treasure house of citations from earlier and contemporary troubadours, and also from northern French trouvères. Ermengaud categorizes two main kinds of love: the physical attraction between objects and between animate beings, and the human love of God, of fellow man, and of earthly goods. From these forms of love proceeds a complicated amorous hierarchy that culminates in the mystical union of the three persons of the Trinity. The first section of the *Breviari* includes an interpolated prose commentary, anticipating later poetic self-commentaries such as that of Dante in his *Vita nuova.*

BIBLIOGRAPHY

Gabriel Azais, *Le Breviari d'amor de Matfre Ermengaud, suivi de sa lettre à sa soeur,* 2 vols. (1862–1868);

Reinhilt Richter, *Die Troubadourzitate im Breviari d'amor* (1976); Peter T. Ricketts, *Le Breviari d'amor de Matfre Ermengaud* (1976), gives a partial translation from line 27,253 to end of poem.

MARIANNE SHAPIRO

[See also **Provençal Literature.**]

ERMENRICH OF ELLWANGEN (*ca.* 805–874), bishop of Passau, was the author of a life of the Anglo-Saxon monk Salvo, and a life of Hariolf of Langres, the bishop of Ellwangen's mother house. He also wrote a long letter full of derivative information on the *trivium,* ending with a panegyric of his patron Grimald and of St. Gall.

BIBLIOGRAPHY

Texts may be found in *Ermenrici Elwangensis Epistola ad Grimaldum abbatem,* Ernst Dümmler, ed., in *Monumenta Germaniae historica, Epistolae karolini aevi,* III (1899), 534–580; *Vita Harolfi,* in *Monumenta Germaniae historica, Scriptores,* X (1852), 11–15. See also Max Manitius, *Geschichte der lateinischen Literatur des Mittelalters,* I (1911), 493–499.

W. T. H. JACKSON

ERMENRÎKES DÔT, a Middle Low German ballad composed of twenty-four Hildebrand stanzas. Published as a broadside around 1560, the ballad linked the legends of Ermanaric and Dietrich von Bern. Closely resembling the *Hamðismál* of the *Edda,* the story of *Ermenrîkes Dôt* exhibits corruption from centuries of oral transmission. With eleven companions Dietrich undertakes an expedition to Freysack to regain his kingdom from Ermanaric, who had wrested it from him. They ride past a gallows erected by Ermanaric, who boasts that from it he will hang them all. In the ensuing fight Ermanaric and his men are slain.

BIBLIOGRAPHY

Helmut de Boor, "Das niederdeutsche Lied von Koninc Ermenrîkes Dôt," in *Kleine Schriften,* 42–58 (1959); Gustav Ehrismann, *Geschichte der deutschen Literatur bis zum Ausgang des Mittelalters,* VI, pt. 2 (1935), 156; Wolfgang

Stammler and Karl Langosch, eds., *Die deutsche Literatur des Mittelalters,* II (1979), 611–617.

EDDA SPIELMANN

[See also **Buch von Bern, Das.**]

ERMOLDUS NIGELLUS (*d.* before 835), a Carolingian poet apparently from the region of the Loire. Ermoldus appears first at the court of Louis the Pious, probably as a secular cleric, but after Louis's accession he became attached to the court of Prince Pepin and accompanied him on his campaign against the Armoricans in 824. Shortly thereafter, Louis suspected Ermoldus of being a bad influence on his son and banished the poet to Strasbourg and the care of the learned Bishop Bernold. In 826, in an attempt to regain favor, Ermoldus wrote a four-book Latin metrical panegyric, *In Honor of Louis, the Most Christian Caesar Augustus,* which contains much otherwise unknown historical material. When this tactic failed, Ermoldus addressed two shorter metrical panegyrics to Pepin, the first including a dialogue between Pepin and Ermoldus' muse Thalia, the second a more direct appeal for support. What became of Ermoldus afterward is unknown. He is identified by some with an Abbot Hermoldus, whom Louis sent to Pepin in 834, and by others with Pepin's chancellor Hermoldus of 838.

Ermoldus has been called the best Carolingian historical poet. His hunting and battle scenes are especially vivid, though his descriptions of individuals and architecture tend to be classically stereotypical. He also makes use of many nonclassical forms. His three poems are all in elegiac couplets, even the panegyric to Louis, which has something of an epic flavor, with many Vergilian echoes. His attempt to preserve the tradition of Charlemagne's court circle of poets, however, seems not to have been wholly successful. Although his works were appreciated by his contemporaries, they soon fell into obscurity.

BIBLIOGRAPHY

The poems are in *Monumenta Germaniae historica: Scriptores,* II (1829, repr. 1963), 466–523. A French translation is Edmond Faral, ed. and trans., *Ermold le Noir: Poème sur Louis le Pieux et Épîtres au roi Pepin* (1932). See also Edmond Faral, *À propos d'Ermold le Noir* (1934); and

Otto Henkel, *Über den historischen Werth der Gedichte des Ermoldus Nigellus*, 2 vols. (1876–1877).

RALPH WHITNEY MATHISEN

[See also **Carolingian Latin Poetry.**]

ERNST, HERZOG. See Herzog Ernst.

ERNULF (1040–1124), of French origin, held various ecclesiastical positions in England, serving as abbot of Peterborough (1107–1114) and bishop of Rochester (1114–1124). Best known as prior of Canterbury Cathedral (1096–1107) during the archiepiscopacy of Anselm, he instigated construction of the "Glorious Choir" that normally bears the name of his successor, Conrad.

BIBLIOGRAPHY

David Knowles, ed., *The Heads of Religious Houses, England and Wales, 940–1216* (1972), 33, 60; Robert Willis, *The Architectural History of Canterbury Cathedral* (1845), *passim;* Francis Woodman, *The Architectural History of Canterbury Cathedral* (1981), 46.

STEPHEN GARDNER

[See also **Canterbury Cathedral.**]

ERWIN, MASTER, architect of the west facade and chapel of the Virgin of Strasbourg Cathedral from 1275/1277 until his death on 17 January 1318. Strasbourg documents record only "Master Erwin"; the surname "von Steinbach" is entirely legendary. Erwin's fame is due more to Goethe's essay "Von deutscher Baukunst: D[ivis] M[anibus] Ervini a Steinbach" (1773) than to his work at Strasbourg.

BIBLIOGRAPHY

Carl F. Barnes, Jr., "Erwin (von Steinbach?)," in *Macmillan Encyclopedia of Architects*, II (1982), 31–32; Ernst Gall, "Erwin de Steinbach," in *Les architectes célèbres*, II (1959), 38–39; Johann von Goethe, "On German Architecture: To the Divine Spirit of Erwin von Steinbach," trans. in Elizabeth Holt, ed., *A Documentary History of Art,* II (1947, repr. 1958), 360–366.

CARL F. BARNES, JR.

[See also **Strasbourg Cathedral.**]

ERWIN OF MINDEN. See Erwin, Master.

ERZINCAN (ERZINJAN) (Armenian: Erez or Erezawan, later Erznka; Hittite: Urušša; Assyrian: Urusu; probably Ptolemy's Orse and Bressos [read: *Eressos]; Arabic: Arzanjān or Arzinjān), a town and pagan shrine of northwest Armenia (39°30′E. × 39°45′N.). Located on the north bank of the Kara Su (Upper or Western Euphrates) in a fertile plain, Erzincan was the center of the temple state of Anahit or Ekeḷeac^c (Greek: Anaitis or Akilisenē). Following a partition of Armenia between Persia and Byzantium, it came under Byzantine rule in 387 and served as the local capital. According to Armenian sources, it passed to the Arabs around 655; the town was ruled by various Muslim emirs until taken by the Seljuks of Rūm in 1228. Erzincan was captured by the Mongols in 1243 and passed to their Ilkhanid successors; it was seized by Tamerlane in 1387. Under Turkoman rule until incorporated into the Ottoman Empire in 1514, it has been Turkish ever since. Erzincan has been repeatedly devastated by earthquakes, but its location on the caravan road from Erzurum (Theodosiopolis) to Anatolia has guaranteed its recovery. In Marco Polo's time (*ca.* 1300), it was, along with Erzurum and Arčēš, one of the three chief cities of Armenia.

BIBLIOGRAPHY

Vital Cuinet, *La Turquie d'Asie,* I (1890), 210ff.; Sowrem T. Eremyan, *Haystanĕ ĕst "Ašxarhac^{c}oyc^c"-i* (1963); Richard Hartmann [F. Taeschner], "Erzindjan," in *Encyclopedia of Islam,* 2nd ed., II (1965); Heinrich Hübschmann, *Die altarmenischen Ortsnamen* (1904, repr. 1969), 286.

ROBERT H. HEWSEN

[See also **Arčēš; Armenia: Geography; Theodosiopolis.**]

ERZURUM. See Theodosiopolis.

ESCHEAT, ESCHEATOR. Despite a tendency for vassals to view their fiefs as held by hereditary right, the feudal lord continued to enjoy profitable rights deriving from the feudal relationship. These were the so-called feudal incidents, of which the right of escheat was one. If a tenant died without heir or if he committed a felony, the fief reverted to the lord—or, rather, the lord took it back after the king of England, as feudal suzerain, held the land for a year and a day (by right of primer seisin).

Since the king was always lord and never tenant, the crown took a close interest in its feudal rights and the revenues to be derived from them. From the twelfth century on, as the fiscal elements in feudalism grew in importance, the crown paid increasing attention to the administration of these windfall revenues. The task was for some time entrusted to the itinerant justices and the sheriffs; during the twelfth and early thirteenth centuries the justices made sure the king received all due feudal rights, and the sheriffs collected the money and accounted at the Exchequer. But this arrangement came to appear cumbersome, especially as a growing governmental machine weighed more and more heavily on both the sheriffs and the justices. The king clearly needed a new official with a specific responsibility for feudal revenues. Although the official took the name "escheator," he was probably more often concerned with other feudal incidents, such as wardship and marriage, and primer seisin.

Experiments early in the reign of Henry III (1216–1272) paved the way for the escheator. Responsibility for escheats and wardships was lifted from the itinerant justices, and in 1232 pairs of escheators were named for the individual counties. Soon the overall supervision was given to one escheator for the counties north of the Trent and one for those to the south. Despite periodic and rather brief alterations (particularly in time of political troubles), this system of county escheators under the control of an escheator on either side of the Trent lasted until the middle of the fourteenth century. For the remainder of the Middle Ages, the crown relied on individual county escheators who accounted at the Exchequer, with no regional grouping of counties and no superior officer intervening.

Whatever the particulars in the administrative scheme, the escheator appears to have been a relatively efficient officer. Upon learning of the death of a tenant, he was authorized to hold an inquisition *post mortem* to learn what lands the tenant held, their value, and whether the king had any rights in them. He seized into the king's hands any lands in which the king had rights until the government in Westminster could send instructions; thus no chance for royal revenue was lost through the delay

or oversight that had plagued the system based on itinerant justices and sheriffs.

His efficiency made the escheator a focus of concern for landowners. They were particularly unhappy over the two great escheators north and south of the Trent because of their broad authority and the delays in arranging for the inquisitions that had to precede taking possession of inherited lands. However, the arrangement dating from the mid fourteenth century, based on local county escheators, seems to have worked as a satisfactory compromise between crown and landlords.

BIBLIOGRAPHY

John M. W. Bean, *The Decline of English Feudalism, 1215–1540* (1968); S. T. Gibson, "The Escheatries, 1327–1341," in *English Historical Review*, 36 (1921); E. R. Stevenson, "The Escheator," in William A. Morris and Joseph R. Strayer, eds., *The English Government at Work*, II, *Fiscal Administration* (1947), 109–167.

RICHARD W. KAEUPER

[See also **Exchequer; Seisin, Disseisin; Sheriff.**]

ESPURGATOIRE ST. PATRICE is the general title of the French versions of the legend of St. Patrick's purgatory, associated with a cavern on Station Island in Lough Derg (County Donegal) and recounted around 1180 by the Cistercian monk H. (often interpreted as Henry, but probably Hugh) of Saltrey in his *Tractatus de purgatorio sancti Patricii*. This text, telling of the knight Owein's descent into the otherworld, was exploited in the vernacular both as an adventure story and for its homiletic properties. The earliest of five extant Anglo-Norman accounts, which vary considerably in length, is a faithful rendering by Marie (perhaps Marie de France). Two thirteenth-century continental French versions and several prose adaptations exist.

BIBLIOGRAPHY

Sources. Editions of Marie's text are by Thomas Atkinson Jenkins (1894, repr. 1974); and by Karl Warnke (1938). Editions of other versions are by Marianne Mörner (1917, repr. 1920); Prosper Tarbé (1842); P. Johan Vising (1916); and Cornelis van der Zanden (1927).

Studies. Lucien Foulet, "Marie de France et la légende du Purgatoire de Saint Patrice," in *Romanische Forschungen*, 22 (1908); George P. Krapp, *The Legend of St. Patrick's Purgatory* (1900); Shane Leslie, *St. Patrick's Purgatory*

(1932); Kurt Ringger, "Die altfranzösischen Verspurgatorien," in *Zeitschrift für romanische Philologie,* **88** (1972).

GLYN S. BURGESS

[See also **Anglo-Norman Literature; Irish Literature: Voyage Tales; Marie de France; Purgatory, Western Concept of.**]

ESSENCE AND EXISTENCE. Aristotle was the first philosopher who formally asked two questions about an object: What is its nature? and Does it exist? (*Analytica posteriora, B* 89*b*23ff.), and in so doing he was concerned with a purely logical distinction. In the Middle Ages, however, Thomas Aquinas taught that the possibility of asking these questions is grounded in an ontological distinction between the essence of an object and its existence.

For Aquinas all beings except God embody a composition of potency and act. Intellectual substances, the essences of which are pure form, have a single composition of form and existence. Substances having essences that consist of matter and form, however, reveal a twofold composition: first, the composition of matter and form in the substance itself, and second, the composition of that substance already composite with existence (*Summa contra Gentiles,* II.54). The application of this principle established the radical contingency of created being, since in God essence and existence are identical, so that he exists necessarily, whereas in all other beings—both the intellectual and those composed of matter and form—essence and existence are distinct, their existence being dependent on the first principle (*ibid.,* I.22).

This doctrine of the composition of created things is explored at length in *De ente et essentia,* and seems to have varied little during the course of Aquinas' career. It is established by several arguments. In the argument from perception, every essence can be conceived without requiring it to exist; thus, existence is added externally to essence (*In I librum Sententiarum,* 8.4.2). In the argument from the nature of God, the being in which essence and existence are identical must be unique, for it is not subject to differentiation (and, therefore, multiplication); thus, there must be a distinction of essence and existence in creatures (*ibid.,* 8.5.2). In the argument from the nature of created being, created things have their existence not from themselves but through de-

pendence on their creator; thus, their existence is something conferred on their essence (*ibid.,* 8.4.2).

The question of this doctrine's sources has been extensively discussed, and any investigation must begin with the ancient authorities cited by Aquinas himself. The first is Boethius, whose distinction between *id quod est,* and *esse* (*Quomodo substantiae,* II.28, Stewart and Rand, trans.) is interpreted by Aquinas as equivalent to his own distinction of essence and existence. Second, Aquinas appeals to the pseudo-Aristotelian *Liber de causis,* in which the terms "finite" and "infinite" are applied to a pair of principles constituting being itself (*De causis,* IV.42). However, since Boethius probably intended simply to contrast concrete being and form, and the *De causis,* though undeniably concerned with potential and actual elements in the constitution of intellectual being, understands the latter strictly in relation to essence, the real origin of Aquinas' distinction must be sought elsewhere. In fact, the evidence points to Ibn Sīnā (Avicenna) as the first philosopher to explore this question systematically, although he was perhaps influenced by earlier Arabic writers.

A distinction similar to Aquinas' occurs in certain other Schoolmen, such as William of Auvergne and Albertus Magnus. After Aquinas' formulation it became a topic of extensive philosophical controversy.

BIBLIOGRAPHY

Aquinas' treatise *De ente et essentia* is most conveniently available for the English reader in Armand C. Maurer, trans., *St. Thomas Aquinas, On Being and Essence,* 2nd rev. ed. (1968). For thorough historical discussion see M.-D. Roland-Gosselin, ed., *Le "De ente et essentia" de S. Thomas d'Aquin, texte établi d'après les manuscrits parisiens* (1926). Joseph Bobik, *Aquinas on Being and Essence, a Translation and Interpretation* (1965), provides a philosophical discussion of the doctrine.

STEPHEN GERSH

[See also **Aquinas, St. Thomas; Aristotle in the Middle Ages.**]

ESSEX, JOHN, a "marbler" of London who was important enough to have been summoned to make Henry VI's tomb at Westminster Abbey in 1448, though the job fell through. He was also involved with other major London artists in Richard de Beauchamp's monument at St. Mary's, Warwick, in the 1450's, and may have designed the base.

BIBLIOGRAPHY

Robin Emmerson, "Monumental Brasses: London Design *c.* 1420–85," in *Journal of the British Archaeological Association,* **131** (1978); John H. Harvey, *English Mediaeval Architects* (1954), 101; Lawrence Stone, *Sculpture in Britain: The Middle Ages,* 2nd ed. (1972), 207–209.

BARRIE SINGLETON

ESTAMPIE. See Dance.

ESTATE MANAGEMENT. Our knowledge of estate management in the Middle Ages is fairly ample for some periods and some locations, while it is virtually nonexistent for others. Information on this subject depends almost entirely on the survival of contemporary written sources, and that survival is extremely patchy. A narrow interpretation of estate management would limit our knowledge to the years between the twelfth and fifteenth centuries, but taking a broader view, we know of estate management a little in the Roman Empire between the fourth and the sixth centuries; rather more about parts of the Carolingian Empire in the ninth and tenth centuries; a considerable amount about England in the thirteenth century, from treatises on estate management and from the documentation that English estates generated from around 1200; very much about England from around 1250 to 1500, from estate documentation and other sources; and rather less about the continent of Europe during this same period, because of the absence of certain types of documentation.

LATER ROMAN EMPIRE AND EARLY MIDDLE AGES

The poet Rutilius Namatianus (*ca.* 420) provides evidence of large estates *(latifundia)* in Etruria, and Rutilius Taurus Aemilianus Palladius (writing *ca.* 350) throws a little light on the management of such an estate, as do a later compilation known as the *Geoponica* (agricultural treatises) and the legal codes and the writings of jurists. The owner's lands were cultivated by nominally free tenants *(coloni)* who were, as sermon evidence shows (St. John Chrysostom, *d.* 407), often mercilessly exploited. On these large estates, the owner held a portion *(fundus)* in hand, and the tenants had to perform labor services on it.

Such estates did not disappear at the beginning of the medieval period, and as H. P. R. Finberg has shown, even in Britain continuity of estates and of estate management was probably more widespread than scholars previously averred. These large estates became almost self-sufficient units, providing not only grain, meat, fruit, and vegetables, but also iron and cloth; the extant sources, however, do not indicate how agents managed them.

THE CAROLINGIAN EMPIRE

For the early years of the ninth century a number of documents illustrate the management of both royal-imperial and monastic estates. The capitulary *De villis,* dated between 800 and 833, concerns the administration of the royal demesnes. It throws little light on estate management, but it discusses (as do the thirteenth-century treatises) the qualities essential to a good estate manager—who should not be a powerful lord but rather a man of middling condition who would be faithful to the emperor. Models of extents and stock accounts designed to guide administrators have also survived. These documents are fragmentary, but enough remain to demonstrate that estate managers were advised to list the buildings, tools, grain, and livestock on the estate and record what labor services were due.

From ecclesiastical estates, documents known as *polyptycha* have survived. That drawn up by Irminon, abbot of St. Germain-des-Prés, sometime between 806 and 829 is the most complete of the inventories analyzing the constituent parts of each *villa* (estate or manor). There are also *polyptycha* for St. Bertin (844–848), St. Remi of Rheims (861), Lobbes (868), Lorsch in the Rhineland, and Prüm (after 892). These documents were often real deeds used in lawsuits to defend the rights of the lord. They were basically extents that listed the house, the church, and the duties of the tenants both free and unfree. On one estate at Nully, one of the peasants managed the estate for the abbey of St. Germain; in return for his services he received half a holding (manse) and reduced labor services on the lord's demesne. The *polyptycha* describe the kind of grain sown and the rotational system of cultivation.

There is evidence for a two- and, in a few places, a three-field system as early as the ninth and tenth centuries. More important, the *polyptycha* reveal the way in which the cultivation of that part of the estate reserved to the lord (the demesne) was undertaken in part by dependent tenants (whether their status was free or unfree is not in this context significant) in exchange for larger plots *(mansi)* or smaller ones *(hospicia, manselli, curtiles)*. By the early ninth century, the practice of working the demesne by tenant labor, which had grown up in the late Roman Empire and which was to continue in some areas of Europe throughout most of the Middle Ages, was well established. That fact does not mean that working of the demesne by slave labor ceased to exist, although it was rapidly diminishing, or that hired labor was unknown as the occasion demanded. The Edict of Pitres (864) ensured the continued enforcement of manual labor where it was due and aimed to prevent tenants from destroying demesnes by selling parcels of land.

The statutes of Adalard, abbot of Corbie in the Somme valley (822), reveal that individual obedientaries received foodstuffs and money from tenants, but they also make it apparent that individual monastic officers were not yet endowed with separate estates. In sum, however, it is general principles rather than details of estate management that emerge from these ninth-century documents.

ENGLAND IN THE TWELFTH AND THIRTEENTH CENTURIES

One of the main considerations in estate management was whether the lord or his agents should lease out the estate or hold it in hand. Signs of leasing can be glimpsed in the early twelfth century on the Continent, where manual services were replaced by money rents, but the clearest evidence comes from twelfth-century England. From 1066 until about 1180 the prevailing method of estate management was to lease or farm the demesnes for a money rent and to commute or convert the labor services of the peasantry into money payments rather than to cultivate the demesnes directly. Officers were appointed to supervise the working of the demesne and to sell the surplus produce on the open market for a cash income. Policy was determined by the size of the estate and the nature of the household. A small estate with a household that could consume most of its produce would not usually lease out the demesne, nor would a large monastic house lease nearby demesnes from which it could economically acquire the considerable produce that it required; but a large landowner whose family could not consume all the grain produced on his many demesnes usually leased some of them.

By the twelfth century, economic and political considerations were also taken into account. When prices of agricultural products (principally grain) were low, or when labor costs (for there was always some wage labor) were high, or when political instability made supervision of distant estates difficult, then the tendency was to lease. A lack of expertise in estate management in this period may have been the most cogent reason for leasing. Our evidence for leasing policy comes entirely from ecclesiastical documents. Surveys of the estates of St. Paul's Cathedral (a lease of 1152), Glastonbury Abbey (*ca.* 1135, 1176, 1189, and 1201), the bishopric of Durham (Boldon Book, 1183), Peterborough Abbey, Ramsey Abbey, and others demonstrate this policy, but there is every justification for thinking that great lay landowners pursued a similar one.

From about 1180 political and economic circumstances began to make it more profitable for lords to exploit their demesnes directly rather than to lease them. From about 1180 to 1225 prices of agricultural products rose fast and continued to rise, though less rapidly, until the second or third decade of the fourteenth century. Population increase provided more abundant supplies of labor, and while wages remained stable, real wages fell. Lords therefore were persuaded to repossess their demesnes and to produce grain for the expanding market.

Despite the fact that wages were stable, it was more advantageous for lords to cultivate the demesnes with the compulsory labor of villein-serfs, as economic historians once called them. Manual labor, which might have been commuted for a money payment for many years, was again demanded from these customary tenants. Those who held their tenements conditionally on the performance of labor services were employed perhaps one or two days a week on the lord's demesne, and at harvest time they had to do extra work known as boon works. The obligation of customary tenants varied, usually according to the size of their holdings. Those who held a full virgate usually had to perform more labor than those who held only fractions and were called cottars or bordars.

On nearly every estate or manor there were free tenants as well as customary ones. The lord's estate did not benefit much from their presence, but they helped with estate management at critical times in the farming year. Although freeholders were usually not obligated to perform week work on the lord's demesne, they commonly did boon works at harvest time.

The shift to compulsory labor services at the end of the twelfth century did not generally occur on the Continent. Here, between the eleventh and the thirteenth centuries, labor services became insignificant. This decline was brought about principally by enfeoffments and by usurpation by agents *(avoués)*, both of which had broken the relations between the demesne *(réserve)* and the holdings charged with labor services. Also, the resistance of tenants, who did not want to sacrifice the cultivation of their own holdings to work on the lord's fields, was a potent factor. During the eleventh and twelfth centuries, lords, especially ecclesiastical ones, wanted fixed revenues and therefore encouraged commutation of labor services for rents in kind or in money, which, owing to the growth of an exchange economy, tenants were able to pay. As a document of the Abbey of Marmoutier (Alsace) from 1117 records, hired labor made labor services superfluous or "useless." Lords were still entitled to labor services such as mowing, fencing, haymaking, and hay carrying by virtue of the *bannum*—the authority derived from their judicial and administrative functions. But labor services attached to landholdings, which on some estates had involved three days a week in Carolingian times, sank to between two and ten days a year by the late eleventh century, as documented for Thiais, an estate of St. Germain-des-Prés.

Leasing for a fixed term was well under way between 1150 and 1200, and by the thirteenth century it was the common means of cultivating an estate. The leases themselves were verbal, so that no trace of the details survives, but a thirteenth-century rental for Mont-Saint-Michel lists more than 200 leases in two localities alone, and rent books *(censiers)* of the lords of Pamele-Oudenaarde from around 1275 also survive. In the county of Namur only the count's lands were leased out in 1200, but by the end of the century the abbeys had followed suit. Fixed-term leases of the demesne farms came first, then whole demesnes, meadowlands, and woods were leased. Lords in northwestern Germany were enfranchising their semifree tenants during the thirteenth and early fourteenth centuries; even rights and dues such as tithes and rectories were leased. Where the rent was paid from the harvest (frequently half the annual produce), the lessee *(métayer, Halfmann)* had a *bail à part des fruits,* while a tenant who paid a fixed amount of goods or money had a *bail à ferme.*

In order to gain advantage from the expanding economy, English lords had reverted to direct exploitation of the demesnes; continental lords tended, in the thirteenth century, to shorten the term of the leases as they began to understand the movement of prices and output more clearly. But the duration of leases was as much influenced by regional factors as by an appreciation of prices and costs: in the Chartres region twenty years was common, in Normandy one to fifteen years, in Hainault three to eighteen years, and in Lower Saxony three to twelve years. The trend toward a more frequent adjustment of rents was a slow one. In the main, then, in France, the Low Countries, Germany, and also in Italy, estate management was a matter of collecting rents, and thus the documentation consists almost solely of surveys *(cadastres)* and rent rolls. The additional English documentation of court rolls and account rolls *(compoti)* scarcely exists on the European continent.

TREATISES ON ESTATE MANAGEMENT

Because English lords took a greater personal interest in the cultivation of their estates and did not, at least before the late fourteenth century, become mere rentiers, they needed guidance on estate management. Hence it is England that produced treatises on estate management rather than treatises on agriculture, like that of Petrus de Crescentiis, or on the care of sheep, like the one written by Jehan de Brie in 1379. Between 1240 and 1242 Robert Grosseteste, bishop of Lincoln, wrote for the countess of Lincoln two sets of *Rules:* one for the management of an estate, the other for the management of a seignorial household. A treatise known as the *Seneschaucy* was written sometime before 1276 and revised around 1290 by a lawyer incarcerated in the Fleet prison, who incorporated it into the extensive legal compilation known as *Fleta* along with Walter of Henley's treatise on husbandry, written sometime in the thirteenth century. An anonymous treatise on the audit and the keeping of accounts—the *Husbandry*—dates from the last third of the thirteenth century. In addition, a document known as the *Forma compoti* instructed stewards of moderate-sized estates on drafting accounts, and documents drawn up for St. Peter's Gloucester and for Canterbury Cathedral Priory throw further light on estate management. To these treatises must be added thousands of documents produced for individual English manors.

The most important advance in rationalizing estate management was the introduction of accounts. The earliest account rolls are those of the bishop of

Winchester's bailiffs, which date from 1208/1209, but by the middle of the thirteenth century *compoti* (account rolls) are common, at least on large estates. Without them estate management could not have been efficient.

Two forms of accounting existed: the so-called Winchester form and the Westminster or Common form. Basically the principle was that of accounting by charge and discharge. The bailiff was "charged" with the revenues due under the most recent survey, and the payments he made out were the discharge of his liabilities. In the Common form the bailiff's arrears, including bad debts, cash in hand, or working capital carried forward, were listed first; to them were added rents and other receipts. Arrears and receipts were then totaled, along with expenses such as acquittances and liveries, and the balance carried forward was struck.

Both treatises and manorial documents describe the officials managing a large estate. The reeve, chosen by the villagers usually from among the wealthiest customary tenants, saw that the labor services were performed and that seignorial dues and rents were paid. Although the reeve received a money payment or a relaxation of services and was chosen for a year only, his was a thankless task, and an unfree tenant sometimes paid cash to be excused from the office. Above the reeve was a bailiff or sergeant *(serviens)* who often controlled two or more manors. He was a free layman or a clerk in minor orders, a professional farm overseer who was both an instigator and a product of the managerial revolution of the thirteenth century. The salaried bailiffs of Canterbury swore to hold courts, to familiarize themselves with the property, to survey repairs, to fill tenancies, to oversee sales of wood, to check the health and numbers of livestock, to levy debts, and to support the archbishop's tenants against outsiders. The bailiff was usually responsible for drawing up the accounts, which were written by a scribe.

On large estates comprising many manors a steward was necessary. He was often of knightly rank, learned in the law, and frequently dispensed justice: presumably he was the reader for whom Walter of Henley and the anonymous author of the *Seneschaucy* had written. Large landholders usually had their accounts audited; the anonymous *Husbandry* enumerates the duties of the auditors. Very large landowners, both lay and ecclesiastical, had their estates managed by an honorial-baronial or episcopal-abbatial council.

In thirteenth-century England, estate manage-ment became professionalized. Various treatises show that common lawyers, estate stewards and bailiffs, conveyancing clerks, and accounting clerks had much in common and perhaps followed two or more of these professions. Estate management was influenced by legislation, for lords lacked speedy legal redress against fraudulent or negligent officers before the Statute of Westminster II (1285), and such legislation made it essential for stewards and bailiffs to have legal knowledge. Also, they had to have practical knowledge of farming: to know the amount of seed corn required per acre and probable yields, the numbers of stock that could be kept, and the amount of ploughing that could be done by a team. All this knowledge was used so that the lord could make the profits that came not only from grain and stock farming, but also from rents, fines, and perquisites of the manorial court. Between about 1180 to about 1325 in England, the period of "high farming," the clearest picture of estate management in the Middle Ages emerges.

LATE FOURTEENTH AND FIFTEENTH CENTURIES

Even before the first attack of the Black Death (1347–1350) some changes were occurring in estate management in England, but from the 1380's direct exploitation became less common, and widespread leasing took place. The long-term trend in prices and wages made direct exploitation less profitable; declining population and the changing attitudes of customary tenants made it impossible to enforce labor services. Consequently, the demesnes were leased for longer and longer terms, and the obligations of customary tenants were converted from labor services to money rents. Lords usually retained an income from courts and other perquisites connected with their judicial and administrative rights. Small peasant farmers with customary holdings and perhaps leases of parts of the demesne and a few other customary or freehold strips were acquiring estates of up to 100 acres, but these have left little documentation. Thus, a pattern of estate management that had reached many parts of the Continent by the late eleventh century became usual in England from the late fourteenth century.

BIBLIOGRAPHY

Dorothea Oschinsky, ed., *Walter of Henley and Other Treatises on Estate Management and Accounting* (1971); Noël Denholm-Young, *Seignorial Administration in England* (1937); Henry S. Bennett, *Life on the English Manor* (1937); M. M. Postan, ed., *The Agrarian Life of the Middle Ages* (vol. I of *The Cambridge Economic History of Europe*), 2nd ed. (1966); Georges Duby, *Rural Economy and Country Life in the Medieval West,* Cynthia Postan, trans. (1968); J. L. Bolton, *The Medieval English Economy 1150–1500* (1980); F. R. H. Du Boulay, *The Lordship of Canterbury* (1966); T. F. T. Plucknett, *The Mediaeval Bailiff* (1954); Frances M. Page, *The Estates of Crowland Abbey* (1934), 29–52; Edward Miller, *The Abbey and Bishopric of Ely* (1951), 247–279; A. Elizabeth Levett, "Baronial Councils and Their Relation to Manorial Courts," in *Mélanges d'histoire du moyen âge; Offerts à M. Ferdinand Lot* (1925); A. J. Pollard, "Estate Management in the Later Middle Ages: The Talbots and Whitechurch, 1383–1525," in *Economic History Review,* 2nd ser. 25 (1972); E. Stone, "Profit-and-loss Accountancy at Norwich Cathedral Priory," in *Transactions of the Royal Historical Society,* 5th ser. 12 (1962); H. P. R. Finberg, *Roman and Saxon Withington: A Study in Continuity* (1955).

GERALD A. J. HODGETT

[See also **Accounting; Agriculture and Nutrition; Bailiff; Feudalism; Fief; Fief, Money; Field Systems; Geoponica; Land Tenure, Western European; Reeve; Serfdom, Western European; Sergeant.**]

ESTATES, LEGAL AND SOCIAL. See **Class Structure.**

ESTATES, POLITICAL. See **Representative Assembly.**

ESTRABOT, French lyric of mockery and insult mentioned only by Benoît de Sainte-Maure, Guillaume de Machaut, and perhaps Clément Marot. The two Occitan monorhymed alexandrine *estribotz,* from which *estrabot* is probably derived, suggest that it was fixed in form. Its satirical nature has disappeared in the subsequent Spanish *estrambote* and Italian *strambotto.*

BIBLIOGRAPHY

Peter T. Ricketts, "L'estribot: forme et fond," in *Actes du VIIe Congrès international de langue et littérature d'oc et d'études franco-provençales* (in press).

ROY ROSENSTEIN

ÉTABLISSEMENTS DE ST. LOUIS, an anonymous thirteenth-century French legal compilation.

In the oldest manuscripts it is untitled; the presence in a group of manuscripts from the late thirteenth and early fourteenth centuries of a prologue attributing the work to St. Louis and a (spurious) formula of promulgation led to the title by which it is now known. It was composed between November 1272 and June 1273 by someone who probably came from or worked in the region of Orléans. For book I, chapters 1–9, he used a royal ordonnance against judicial duels and a set of royal regulations governing judicial procedure in the Châtelet of Paris. For chapters 10–175 he used a mid-thirteenth-century collection of customs of Touraine and Anjou. At least twenty-four of the thirty-eight chapters of book II (and probably all of them) were based on a text called "Usages of the Orléanais," no longer extant. Into these texts the redactor inserted references to the *Corpus iuris civilis* and *Decretals,* in somewhat the same way that the glossators of Roman and canon law texts inserted cross-references in their comments.

The work appears to have gone through several versions in rapid succession, each of which went a little further toward unifying a text made up of disparate, and occasionally contradictory, elements. It is one of several early French attempts at legal syncretism, seeking in a primitive way both to harmonize divergent customs and to fit the rules of customary law with those of the "written law" (*cf. Livre de jostice et de plet).* In the fourteenth and fifteenth centuries the *Établissements* had a wide diffusion in France: a copy was in the municipal archives of Beauvais early in the fourteenth century, and soon afterward a summary of it was written in Champagne. It was used by the redactors of the *Très ancienne coutume de Bretagne,* by the author of a Poitevan *Livre des droiz* and of the *Anciens usages d'Artois,* by the Maucraux brothers for their Parisian *Style,* and in the late fourteenth century by Boutillier for his *Somme rurale.*

The spurious attribution to St. Louis, which occurred soon after the collection was composed, suggests either an effort to enhance its value by attributing it to the revered monarch or a belief that law, to be valid, had to be promulgated by an authority.

BIBLIOGRAPHY

Les établissements de Saint Louis, Paul Viollet, ed., 4 vols. (1881–1886).

FREDRIC L. CHEYETTE

[See also **Châtelet; Law, French: In North.**]

ETCHING. Etching, like engraving, is a copperplate printing technique. The design or ink lies in lines below the original surface of the plate. Whereas the lines of the engraving originated with the goldsmith's burin, the lines of the etching were obtained with the armorer's acid. The etcher utilizes a needle to scratch through a resistant varnish, exposing the copper beneath. When the plate is placed in an acid bath, the exposed lines are bitten into the copper. The printing of an etching is rather like that of an engraving, though the tendency, even as early as Dürer's time, was to leave some ink on the surface of the plate to produce a slight tone.

As was the case with other printing techniques,

Woman washing her feet. Etching by Urs Graf, 1513. KUPFER-STICHKABINETT, KUNSTMUSEUM BASEL

etching evolved from a preexisting craft: that of the armorer and the jeweler, who both used acid to etch designs into metal. The idea to print such motifs undoubtedly was provided by the engraving, but it does not seem to have been practiced until around 1500. Although the earliest dated etching is Urs Graf's *A Woman Washing Her Feet* of 1513, it is quite likely that the Hopfer family, armorers of Augsburg, were regularly printing from etched iron plates a decade earlier.

During the second decade of the sixteenth century, the etching gained limited acceptance by such consummate engravers as Albrecht Dürer, Lucas van Leyden, Albrecht Altdorfer, Dirk Vellert, and Hans Burgkmair. These artists exploited the gritty, uneven, somewhat coarse and atmospheric qualities of etched line, as well as its greater potential for chiaroscuro. The absence of etchings earlier than 1500 may possibly be explained by the looser and more individualized or autographic qualities of the medium, concerns not particularly encouraged during the fifteenth century.

BIBLIOGRAPHY

André Béguin, *Dictionnaire technique de l'estampe*, 3 vols. (1977); Arthur M. Hind, *A Short History of Engraving and Etching*, 3rd ed. (1923); Pierette Jean-Richard, *Maîtres de l'eau forte des XVIᵉ et XVIIᵉ siècles* (1980); E. S. Lumsden, *The Art of Etching* (1922); Gustav Pauli, *Inkunabeln der deutschen und niederländischen Radierung* (1908).

R. S. FIELD

[See also **Burin; Engraving.**]

ETHELRED OF RIEVAULX, ST. (*ca.* 1110–12 January 1167) was born at Hexham in Northumberland, the son and grandson of married priests. He was educated at the court of King David I of Scotland and later served in his administration. While on royal business with Archbishop Thurstan of York, Ethelred heard of the Cistercians and, after a serious inner struggle, decided in 1134 to enter Rievaulx. He became a monk of exceptional piety and devotion. In 1142 he represented the interests of his monastery at Rome in connection with the disputed York election, served two years (1142–1143) as novice master at Rievaulx, and then became abbot of Revesby, Rievaulx's foundation in Lincolnshire. In 1147 he was

516

elected abbot of Rievaulx, then the dominant Cistercian foundation in England.

The abbacy involved a great deal of public business for the monastery, for the Cistercian order, for the papacy, and with the English crown. Ethelred's recommendation probably persuaded Henry II to support Alexander III rather than the antipope Victor IV in the disputed papal election of 1159. He also arbitrated several ecclesiastical disputes and settled the conflict between two Cistercian houses, Savigny and Furness, for authority over a third, Byland. In these capacities he was known for his great judiciousness. As a recognized "national" and spiritual leader, Ethelred preached the sermon at Westminster Abbey on the occasion of the translation of the relics of Edward the Confessor (1163). As abbot of a very large community (perhaps 600 monks), he was a warm, gentle, and sympathetic superior and a mild disciplinarian. Because, or in spite of, these personal qualities, Rievaulx maintained a reputation for a high standard of monastic observance. Although Ethelred suffered from kidney stones throughout his adult life and was badly afflicted with arthritis in his last years, he led a life of great austerity.

Ethelred's writing enjoyed enormous popularity in the twelfth century and earned him the title "the Bernard of the North." His spiritual treatises include *The Mirror of Charity,* which was influenced by and dedicated to St. Bernard; and *On the Soul,* which is heavily infused with Augustinian doctrine. His most famous work, *On Spiritual Friendship,* which explores the relation between spiritual and human friendship in a monastic context, reveals his own conscious homosexual orientation and gives love between persons of the same gender its most profound expression in Christian theology. The beautiful sermon "When Jesus Was Twelve Years Old" reflects the strong Christocentric devotion of twelfth-century monastic humanism, and *A Rule of Life for a Recluse,* written for his sister, shows Ethelred's appreciation of the eremitic life. Two historical works, *Genealogy of the Kings of England* and *The Life of Edward the Confessor,* suggest his admiration for his old patron, King David of Scotland, and for his contemporary, Henry II.

After Ethelred's death a cult soon developed around his memory. Although the evidence for his formal canonization has been lost, in 1476 the Cistercian general chapter declared that his feast day (12 January, 3 March) should be kept with special celebration.

BIBLIOGRAPHY

Aelredi Rievallensis opera omnia, Dom A. Hoste and C. H. Talbot, eds., Corpus Christianorum, Continuatio medievalis, I (1971) is the best scholarly ed. of all his extant writings. For biographical information see *The Life of Ailred of Rievaulx by Walter Daniel,* Frederick M. Powicke, trans. (1951); and John Boswell, *Christianity, Social Tolerance, and Homosexuality* (1980), 163, 221–226, 303. His most famous work is *Spiritual Friendship,* Mary Eugenia Laker, S.S.N.D., trans. (1974). The best general treatment of Ethelred's thought is Amédée Hallier, O.C.S.O., *The Monastic Theology of Aelred of Rievaulx* (1969).

BENNETT D. HILL

[See also **Cistercian Order.**]

ETHELRED THE UNREADY (Unræd, "without counsel"; 968/969–1016) had a long, disastrous reign as King of England (978–1016). Renewed Scandinavian attacks led to a series of heavy defeats, and payments of Danegeld proved only temporary expedients. He was forced into exile in Normandy in 1013, returned in 1014, but died facing defeat at London in 1016. His reign was not without its achievements. The Benedictine revival reached its full stature during this period, which in terms of language and learning is regarded as the golden age of Anglo-Saxon prose. In government and administration the law codes, charters, coins, and methods of assessing and levying Danegeld speak of an efficiency unusual for the age.

BIBLIOGRAPHY

D. Hill, ed., *Ethelred the Unready,* in British Archaeological Reports British series, LIX (1978); Simon Keynes, *The Diplomas of King Æthelred the Unready, 978–1016* (1980).

H. R. LOYN

[See also **Danegeld; England: Anglo-Saxon.**]

ETHELWOLD AND THE BENEDICTINE RULE. Ethelwold (*ca.* 908–984), born of noble parents at Winchester, lived at King Athelstan's court. Later, with Dunstan, he was ordained a priest by Elfheah, bishop of Winchester, and subsequently continued his studies at Glastonbury. When he proposed to leave England, presumably for Fleury, to study continental monastic reforms, King Eadred persuaded him instead, in 954, to assume charge of the derelict abbey of Abingdon. With followers from Glastonbury and elsewhere, Ethelwold restored the abbey and sent Osgar, one of his disciples, to observe the practice at Fleury, some of which he later introduced to Abingdon.

In 963 Ethelwold was made bishop of Winchester, a post he held until his death. Supported by King Edgar, he expelled the canons from Winchester cathedral, replacing them with Abingdon monks. His episcopacy, coupled with the reform programs of Dunstan, archbishop of Canterbury, and Oswald, bishop of Worcester, gave English monastic life a surge of power and momentum, and ushered in its golden age. By the Norman Conquest, England had nearly forty-six monasteries. Ethelwold's energy was prodigious: he undertook a large-scale reconstruction of the Old Minster; founded monasteries at Peterborough, Ely, and Thorney; and in Winchester restored New Minster and Nunnaminster, then Milton (Dorset), and perhaps Croyland, Chertsey, and St. Neots.

If his charter for the endowment of Peterborough is at all representative, Ethelwold was extraordinarily generous to his foundations, despite his reputed personal austerity and excessive self-abnegation. Ironically, the epithet *Boanerges* (son of thunder), given him by Godeman, the scribe of his *Benedictional,* came to underline his intransigence.

Ethelwold's interest in translation—both of his biographers report that he used to explain Latin books in English to his students—made Winchester the center of language reform. At the request of King Edgar and his wife, he translated (*ca.* 970) into English the *Regula Scanti Benedicti,* which may have reached England by the mid seventh century. Of its twenty-three manuscripts surviving in England, ten date from the period 900–1100 and thirteen from 1110–1400. Of these twenty-three manuscripts, five are bilingual copies; the Latin text of a sixth contains an Old English interlinear gloss; and two more contain the Old English version only, one of which is a fragment. Evidence suggests that the Latin and Old English texts were combined from the time that copies of Ethelwold's translation began to circulate. (Oxford, Corpus Christi College, MS 197 [*ca.* 980–990] is the earliest bilingual copy preserved.) Whereas all the preserved Old English texts were meant for monks, the early Middle English "Winteney Version" (thirteenth century) was adapted for nuns. Ethelwold's translation, along with other Old

English works, constitutes key evidence in recent studies concerning the development at Winchester of a literary language, and argues convincingly for a Winchester origin of standard Old English.

Under Ethelwold, Winchester became a center of cultural reform as well. The Winchester style of illumination, though soon practiced elsewhere, originated there; the *Winchester Troper* is the earliest extant evidence of English polyphony; and the *Regularis concordia,* the first English document regulating monastic life, was drafted at Winchester. These are startling facts, considering that Canterbury—not Winchester—was England's oldest monastery and the seat of the English primates.

BIBLIOGRAPHY

Sources. Wulfstan, *Vita Æthelwoldi,* in *Acta sanctorum,* Aug. 1 (1733), 83–101; Ælfric, *Vita Æthelwoldi,* in Joseph Stevenson, ed., *Chronicon monasterii de Abingdon,* 2 vols. (1858). Both Lives are also in Michael Winterbottom, ed., *Three Lives of English Saints* (1972); see also his "Three Lives of Saint Ethelwold," in *Medium ævum,* 41 (1972).

Studies. Helmut Gneuss, "The Origin of Standard Old English and Æthelwold's School at Winchester," in *Anglo-Saxon England,* 1 (1972); Mechthild Gretsch, "Æthelwold's translation of the *Regula sancti Benedicti* and Its Latin Exemplar," in *Anglo-Saxon England,* 3 (1974), and "Die Winteney-Version der *Regula sancti Benedicti:* Eine frühmittelenglische Bearbeitung der altenglischen Prosaübersetzung der Benediktinerregel," in *Anglia,* 96 (1978).

M.-C. BODDEN

[See also **Benedictine Rule; Dunstan, Life of; Winchester Troper.**]

ETHIOPIA. See **Abyssinia.**

EUCHARIST. See **Mass.**

EUDES OF MONTREUIL, a Parisian master mason listed in a document of September 1285 as "master of the king's [Philip III the Bold's] works." Possibly a son of Pierre de Montreuil, Eudes died in 1287 and was buried in the Church of the Cordeliers in Paris. He may have been an architect at Aigues Mortes, and is said to have accompanied Louis IX on crusade and to have built the fortifications at Jaffa (*ca.* 1250), but no works can be associated with him by documentation.

BIBLIOGRAPHY
Carl F. Barnes, Jr., "Pierre and Eudes de Montreuil," in *Macmillan Encyclopedia of Architects,* III (1982), 228–229.

CARL F. BARNES, JR.

EUDES RIGAUD, Odo Rigaldus (*d.* 2 July 1275), a Franciscan, was elected archbishop of Rouen in March 1248 and served until his death. Little is known about the events leading to his election to the archiepiscopate at a time when it was still a matter of much dispute within the Franciscan order whether such worldly tasks were consonant with its rule. It is presumed (given the unique importance of Rouen) that Eudes knew Louis IX of France prior to this time, but there is no direct evidence of their acquaintanceship. It has been suggested—and this too seems plausible—that Eudes had served as an *enquêteur du roi* in the investigations of the kingdom of France in 1247–1248, on the eve of Louis's first crusade.

What is known with certainty about Eudes's early life is that he was born in the north of France and came from a devout family of knightly status. Several close relatives, including his sister, entered religious orders. By about 1236 he had joined the Franciscan order, and soon after, assuredly by 1240, he was studying theology at the University of Paris. By 1245 Eudes was permitted to comment on the *Sentences* of Peter Lombard; and it is in the manuscripts of this commentary (or the part of it that is identifiable as Eudes's), as well as in his coauthorship of an exposition of the Franciscan rule, that he shows himself to be a first-rate theologian.

As archbishop of Rouen, Eudes was sometimes in conflict with the crown over jurisdictional privileges, but on the whole he worked closely with the king and served repeatedly in the Parlement of Paris. In matters of state the king sought his advice—for example, in the negotiation of the Treaty of Paris (1259), which recognized the Plantagenet loss of Normandy to the Capetians. But Eudes was more than an adviser to Louis IX; he was a dear friend. In

illness the king would seek the comfort of the Franciscan.

As an administrator of his archdiocese Eudes was extremely conscientious. His "visitations" are the records of his systematic inquiries into the life of churchmen and nuns in the see for the years 1248–1269, and they preserve some of the most telling anecdotes of the wide discrepancy between the ideal and the reality of life among ecclesiastics in the High Middle Ages. The visitations are much more than this; they are a sort of diary of clerical life revealing the jurisdictional squabbles plaguing Eudes and the relation of his church to the social and political movements of the time. They constitute one of the most reliable sources, for instance, concerning the Pastoureaux, who in 1251 descended on Rouen and attacked a diocesan synod presided over by the archbishop.

BIBLIOGRAPHY
Pierre Andrieu-Guitrancourt, *L'archevêque Eudes Rigaud et la vie de l'église au XIIIe siècle* (1938); Pierre Aubry, *La musique et les musiciens d'église en Normandie au XIIIe siècle d'après le journal des visites pastorales d'Odon Rigaud* (1906); Sydney Brown and Jeremiah F. O'Sullivan, eds. and trans., *The Register of Eudes of Rouen* (1964); Oscar Darlington, *The Travels of Odo Rigaud, Archbishop of Rouen* (1940); Walter Principe, "Odo Rigaldus, a Precursor of St. Bonaventure on the Holy Spirit as *effectus formalis* in the Mutual Love of the Father and Son," in *Medieval Studies,* **39** (1977); Williell Thomson, *Friars in the Cathedral* (1975), 77–91.

WILLIAM CHESTER JORDAN

[See also **France: 1223–1328; Franciscans; Louis IX of France; Pastoureaux; Rouen.**]

EUFEMIAVISOR is the collective name given to three metrical romances—*Herr Ivan Lejonriddaren, Hertig Fredrik av Normandie,* and *Flores och Blanzeflor*—that appeared in Swedish in the early fourteenth century. Based on continental romances, the translations were made, according to the evidence of the manuscripts, at the behest of the German-born Norwegian queen Eufemia, wife of King Hákon Magnússon. They are of interest and importance for their linguistic information and because they mark the introduction of both the continental courtly material into Sweden and the popular German rhymed couplet verse into Scandinavia.

The past hundred years has produced a considerable literature reflecting the disagreement among scholars on such interdependent problems as the sources, chronology, and authorship of these three poems. Scholars have argued whether the verse translations were first made into Swedish. *Hertig Fredrik* states that the work was translated *aff thyzko och j swänskä thungo* (from German into Swedish), and *Herr Ivan* says more generally, *aff valske tungo ok a vart maal* (from French into our language).

If this information is to be trusted, why would the translations be commissioned by a German-born Norwegian queen? Eufemia was from northern Germany, daughter of Günther von Arnstein and granddaughter of Prince Vitslav of Rügen; she was married in 1299 to Hákon Magnússon, whose father and grandfather had brought continental literature into Norway. Although some scholars have suggested that the poems originated in Norwegian and were translated into Swedish at a later date, the simplest and most likely explanation is that Eufemia ordered the translations in honor of her daughter Ingeborg's engagement to the Swedish duke Erik Magnusson. The sources of *Herr Ivan* and *Flores* were both French verse romances (respectively Chrétien's *Chevalier au lion* and the anonymous *Floyris et Blanchefleur*) and Norwegian prose sagas. Especially in the case of *Flores,* it seems likely that the translator relied heavily on the Norwegian prose saga. Although the text of *Hertig Fredrik* states that the poem was translated from German into Swedish, no French or German verse original is extant, nor is there any evidence of a Norwegian prose saga.

The manuscript evidence has also been doubted on the question of chronology; however, the consensus today is that the dates given in the texts are accurate. *Herr Ivan* was completed in 1303, a suitable time for a gift from the Norwegian court to Duke Erik to celebrate the couple's engagement in 1302. *Hertig Fredrik* is dated to 1308, although in one manuscript the date is 1301. This was a time when the relationship between Norway and Sweden was recovering from a brief rift, and the engagement, which had been broken, was renewed. The date of *Flores,* 1312, corresponds to the date of the marriage of Ingeborg and Erik.

The translator's name is unknown. Because the source material for the translations is so diverse, some scholars have suggested several translators. However, the latest stylistic studies argue in favor of one person, probably from western Sweden, for all three poems.

BIBLIOGRAPHY

Flores och Blanzeflor, Emil Olsson, ed. (1921); *Herr Ivan,* Erik Noreen, ed. (1931); *Hertig Fredrik av Normandie,* Erik Noreen, ed. (1927). See also Valter Jansson, *Eufemiavisorna* (1945); Erik Noreen, "Undersökningar rörande det inbördes förhållandet mellan de så kallade eufemiavisorna," in *Samlaren,* **11** (1930); Stanislaw Sawicki, *Die Eufemiavisor* (1939).

KAAREN GRIMSTAD

[See also **Chrétien de Troyes; Floyris; Riddarasögur; Translations and Translators, Western European.**]

EUGENIUS II OF TOLEDO (*d.* 657), a noble Goth who served as a cleric first at Toledo and then under his uncle, the bishop Braulio, at Saragossa. In 647 the Visigothic king Chindaswinth made him archbishop of Toledo. At Chindaswinth's urging Eugenius revised two of the works of Dracontius, *Praises of the Lord,* which he converted into *Six Days of Creation,* and *Satisfaction.* His short poems and two letters have also survived, but prose works including *On the Trinity* are lost. Eugenius has been called the best seventh-century Spanish poet, and his works achieved a good deal of popularity after his death.

BIBLIOGRAPHY

For the texts of the poems, see *Monumenta Germaniae historica, Auctores antiquissimi,* XIV (1905), 27–69, 115–129, 231–270.

RALPH WHITNEY MATHISEN

[See also **Spanish Latin Literature; Spanish Lost Literature.**]

EUGENIUS VULGARIUS (*d. ca.* 928). Having been educated in grammar and dialectic, probably at the episcopal school of Naples, Eugenius was ordained a priest in the early 890's by Pope Formosus. As a result he became involved in the subsequent Formosan controversy, during which succeeding popes alternately invalidated and reinstated Formosus' acts and ordinations. Both Eugenius and his friend Auxilius defended Formosus' ordinations, and in 907 Eugenius wrote his *Pamphlet on the Case of Formosus.* In response Pope Sergius III had him incarcerated at Monte Cassino. Later, however, Eugenius was called to Rome, and made amends by dedicating to the pope flattering verses, including some striking *carmina figurata* (for instance, one in the shape of an organ).

Eugenius also had close ties to the Byzantines in southern Italy, and he addressed several poems to Emperor Leo VI, including one in the shape of a pyramid. Indeed, his poetry is notable for its shift of emphasis away from the Carolingian concept of *renovatio* and back to the golden age of Rome. Eugenius' extant poems are characterized by their use of such contrivances as acrostics, mesostichs, and telestichs, as well as of wordplay, etymology, and obscurity.

BIBLIOGRAPHY

Thirty-eight poems and letters are in *Monumenta Germaniae historica: Poetae latini medii aevi,* IV, pt. 1, Paul von Winterfeld, ed. (1899), 413–440. See also Ernst Dümmler, *Auxilius und Vulgarius* (1866).

RALPH WHITNEY MATHISEN

[See also **Auxilius; Latin Literature; Papacy, Origins and Development of.**]

EUGIPPIUS (*d.* after 533), a pupil of St. Severinus of Noricum, fled to Italy after the saint's death (*ca.* 482). By 511 he had become abbot of the monastery at Luculanum, near Naples. His surviving works include two letters; *Excerpts from the Works of St. Augustine,* which enjoyed popularity in the Middle Ages; and his best-known work, a biography of Severinus, which is one of the few surviving sources for the history of the Danubian provinces in the late fifth century.

BIBLIOGRAPHY

Texts of the *Epistulae, Excerpta ex operibus S. Augustini,* and *De vita S. Severini* are in Pius Knöll, ed., *Corpus scriptorum ecclesiasticorum latinorum,* IX, pt. 2 (1886). Translations are Ludwig Bieler, *The Life of Saint Severin* (1965); and George W. Robinson, *The Life of St. Severinus by Eugippius* (1914).

RALPH WHITNEY MATHISEN

EULALIE, LA SÉQUENCE DE STE. St. Eulalia, born at Mérida, Spain, died a martyr during Diocletian's repression of Christianity around 304. The legend of her martyrdom is preserved both in a Latin hymn by Prudentius and in the French *Séquence de Ste. Eulalie,* the content of which derives for the

most part from Prudentius. The French sequence is the earliest surviving piece of French hagiography and one of the earliest extant vernacular writings. It was composed two or three years after the discovery at Barcelona in 878 of bones supposed to be those of the saint. The twenty-nine lines were intended to be sung on the saint's day, 10 December. They narrate Eulalia's resistance to pagan threats, to bribery, and to tortures instigated by the pagan emperor Maximian. Her survival of burning at the stake is followed (in the French version) by her decapitation and her ascent to heaven in the form of a dove.

BIBLIOGRAPHY

F. J. Barnett, "Some Notes to the *Sequence of St. Eulalia,*" in *Studies in Medieval French Presented to A. Ewert* (1961).

JEANETTE M. A. BEER

[See also **Cantilène; French Literature: To 1200; Hagiography.**]

EULOGIUS OF CÓRDOBA (*d.* 859). A scion of a prominent Córdoban family, a student of the celebrated abbot Speraindeo, and a Mozarab clergyman during the reigns of ᶜAbd al-Raḥmān II (822–852) and Muḥammad I (852–886), Eulogius has been described as the most important Mozarab figure of the ninth century. When, around the mid ninth century, some Mozarabs in Córdoba sought to gain martyrdom by provoking the Muslim authorities, Eulogius described and incited their voluntary sacrifice in his *Memoriale sanctorum* and *Apologeticus martyrum* and met a similar fate shortly afterward. Eulogius' letters, describing his early travels to Pamplona, Saragossa, and other places in northern Spain, are still a useful source for the study of the Mozarab church of the ninth century.

BIBLIOGRAPHY

Wolf W. F. von Baudissin, *Eulogius und Alvar. Ein Abschnitt Spanischer Kirchengeschichte aus der Zeit der Maurenherrschaft* (1872).

TEOFILO F. RUIZ

EUPHRATES RIVER, the longest river in southwestern Asia, extending about 1,800 miles through Asia Minor and Mesopotamia to the Persian Gulf. It

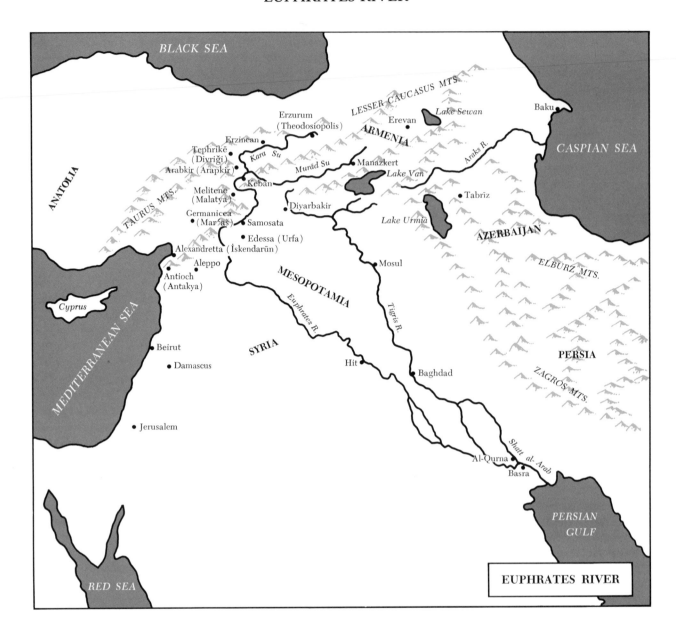

EUPHRATES RIVER

has three parts: the first ends at Samosata (modern Samsat), the second at Hit, and the third at Al-Qurna, where it joins with the Tigris and the two rivers flow together to the Persian Gulf as the Shatt al-Arab.

The upper Euphrates unites two branches, the Kara Su and the Murād Su; these originate in the Bingöl plateau in Armenia, join at Keban, east of Arabkir (modern Arapkir), and from there flow through the Taurus mountains and down from the foothills of Mesopotamia. The Murād Su is the longer and bigger of the two; at their junction it is 415 miles long, while the Kara Su is 275 miles long.

The middle Euphrates, which is about 700 miles long, flows largely through open country. Historically it served to divide the Assyrian and Hittite Empires as well as the eastern and western satrapies of the Persian Empire. At various times it also formed the eastern boundary of the Roman Empire. The lower Euphrates, which flows southeast across a plain from Hit to its junction with the Tigris, supplied the water for the huge network of irrigation canals in the plain of Mesopotamia.

The Euphrates has been an extremely important waterway throughout history. It provided a line of communication between northern Persia and the

West and served as an invasion route for Turks and Mongols. It was for some time the eastern frontier of the Byzantine empire; Emperor Michael III reached and crossed the Euphrates in the course of his triumph over the Arabs in 859. The Paulicians, who threatened the empire in the ninth century, lived on its banks in the north at Tephrikē (Divriği) and near Samosata. In 873 Emperor Basil I seized Samosata, a move that initiated a series of Byzantine advances along the empire's eastern frontiers. In 952 the Byzantines again crossed the Euphrates, but they were defeated the following year near Germanicea (modern Mar^caš) by the Hamdanid Sayf al-Dawla, and it was not until 958 that they again took Samosata on their advance toward the East.

BIBLIOGRAPHY

Raoul Blanchard, *Asie occidentale,* in Paul Vidal de La Blache, ed., *Géographie universelle,* VIII (1921); George Ostrogorsky, *History of the Byzantine State,* Joan Hussey, trans. (1957, rev. ed. 1969).

LINDA C. ROSE

EUPOLEMIUS. The name "Eupolemius" is a pseudonym for the otherwise unknown author of an extant biblical epic in 1,463 hexameters, written probably in the late eleventh or early twelfth century. Nothing whatever is known of his life or personality, although it has been suggested that he was a German cleric; the name is merely derived from the many battles described in the poem.

The work, which lacks a title, is usually referred to as the *Messiad;* it portrays the conflict between good and evil from the time of Adam to Christ, although the action is compressed to fit within a single generation. It draws heavily on the classical tradition, and half the characters in it are not biblical at all. The author uses Vergil, Ovid, and Lucan in particular as models. The work had little subsequent literary influence.

BIBLIOGRAPHY

Max Manitius, "Die Messias des sogenannten Eupolemius, aus Cod. Dresd. D. C. 171 herausgaben," in *Römische Forschungen,* 6 (1891); A. Schlatter, "Eupolemius als Chronolog und seine Beziehungen zu Josephus und Manetho," in *Theologische Studien und Kritiken,* 64 (1891).

RALPH WHITNEY MATHISEN

[See also **Epic, Latin.**]

EUSEBIUS BRUNO (*d.* 1081), bishop of Angers, active in church and political affairs in the mid eleventh century. His sole extant work, *Epistola ad Berengarium magistrum,* was written to clear his own name, which had been damaged by association with Berengar and the eucharistic controversy.

BIBLIOGRAPHY

The *Epistola* is edited in *Patrologia latina,* CXLVII, cols. 1199–1204; see also Max Manitius, *Geschichte der lateinischen Literatur des Mittelalters,* II (1923), 120.

EDWARD FRUEH

[See also **Berengar of Tours.**]

EUSEBIUS OF CAESAREA (*ca.* 263–*ca.* 340), a bishop of the provincial capital in Palestine and church historian. Although he participated in the First Council of Nicaea (325), he later rejected its doctrinal definition and sided with the Arian majority of the Eastern episcopate. His numerous writings include the ten-volume *Ecclesiastical History,* covering the period from apostolic times to 324 and representing the single major source of information about the first three centuries of Christian history. Eusebius also wrote a *Life of Constantine,* in which he blends Christian messianism with the Hellenistic conception of divine kingship, and this line of thought had a profound influence on the imperial ideology of medieval Byzantium.

BIBLIOGRAPHY

A critical ed. of the *Life of Constantine* by I. A. Heikel appears in *Griechische christliche Schriftsteller,* VII (1902); of the *Ecclesiastical History,* E. Schwartz, ed., in *ibid.,* IX (1903–1904).

JOHN MEYENDORFF

[See also **Nicaea, Councils of.**]

EUSTACHE DESCHAMPS. See **Deschamps, Eustache.**

EUTYCHES (mid fourth century–*ca.* 454), the father of the extreme Monophysite movement called, after him, Eutychianism. He was the archimandrite (superior) of a monastery on the outskirts of Constantinople; when he was accused of heresy in 448, he had been archimandrite for at least thirty years and a monk for seventy years. An ardent supporter of Cyril of Alexandria and a foe of Nestorianism, he taught that after the Incarnation there was only one nature in Christ. To his opponents, he appeared to teach that the human nature was totally absorbed by the divine one, and thus to deny that Christ was truly and fully human and consubstantial with humanity.

On 8 November 448 a synod was assembled at Constantinople by Patriarch Flavian to hear the charges brought against Eutyches. In the ensuing discussions Eutyches came off not so much the challenging heretic as a confused, uneducated, possibly senile but nevertheless stubborn old man who simply reiterated his objection to the "two natures." After seven sessions without any concessions from Eutyches, the synod excluded him from his priestly and monastic functions, and excommunicated him. Eutyches was not without support from the monks and from the court, where his godson, the eunuch Chrysaphius, was chamberlain. He also wrote to Pope Leo I, hoping to win his support against what he perceived to be a Nestorian offensive against orthodoxy.

Matters came to head a year later when a council was called at Ephesus by Theodosius II. The emperor appointed Dioscorus, patriarch of Alexandria, a staunch defender of the "one nature" Christology and, in the Alexandrian tradition, a foe of the see of Constantinople, to preside over the council. Supported by imperial troops, Dioscorus set about undoing Flavian's condemnation of Eutyches and condemned Flavian himself, together with other supporters of a "two nature" Christology. The *Tome of Leo,* which backed Flavian against Eutyches, was ignored, and Eutyches was reinstated. Because of the violence used by Dioscorus to secure the support of the bishops, this council came to be known as the Robber Synod *(Latrocinium).*

Theodosius II died in 450 and was succeeded by his sister, Pulcheria, and her consort, Marcian, both supporters of the doctrine of "two natures" as taught by Pope Leo. Chrysaphius, an enemy of Pulcheria, was executed, and without his support at court, Eutyches' position was suddenly eroded. At the Council of Chalcedon (451) the doctrine of two natures was affirmed, and Eutyches' chief supporter, Dioscorus of Alexandria, was stripped of his office and exiled. Eutyches was again condemned and sentenced to exile but may have died before the sentence was carried out. After 454 he vanishes from history. His writings and those of his supporters were confiscated and burned, and the monks of his monastery were dispersed to the West.

In the later development of Monophysite theology, especially that of Severus of Antioch (*ca.* 465–538), Eutyches' teachings were consistently repudiated. They survived for a while among extreme Monophysite sects such as the Gaianites and Julianists, but these groups were gradually converted to Severus' position, which became normative for the churches that repudiated the doctrine of Chalcedon.

BIBLIOGRAPHY

René Draguet, "La christologie d'Eutychès d'après les Actes du synode de Flavien (448)," in *Byzantion,* 6 (1931); J. M. Fuller, "Eutyches and Eutychianism," in *Dictionary of Christian Biography,* II (1880, repr. 1965); M. Jugie, "Eutychès et Eutychianisme," in *Dictionnaire de théologie catholique,* V, pt. 2 (1939), 1582–1609.

D. W. JOHNSON

[See also **Leo I, Pope; Monophysitism; Theodosius II the Calligrapher.**]

EUTYCHIOS (EUTIHIJE), a painter active in Macedonia and Serbia between about 1295, when he signed the frescoes at the Church of the Virgin Peribleptos (now St. Clement), Ochrid, and 1321, when his signature appears at Gračanica in Bosnia. Eutychios worked with Michael Astrapas; they probably came from Thessaloniki, and ultimately became the court painters for King Milutin. Eutychios created massive, volumetric figures clad in drapery with heavy, brittle folds; his work belongs to the "heavy" or "cubic" phase of Palaiologan style. Other fresco cycles attributed to Eutychios and Michael include those at St. Niketas at Skoplje (*ca.* 1310), Staro Nagoričino (1316–1318), and the Protaton and Vatopedi at Mount Athos.

BIBLIOGRAPHY

Otto Demus, "The Style of the Kariye Djami and Its Place in the Development of Palaeologan Art," in Paul Underwood, ed., *The Kariye Djami,* IV (1975), 146–149.

LESLIE BRUBAKER

[See also **Byzantine Art.**]

EUTYCHIOS THE MELCHITE (887–940), the Melchite (Chalcedonian) patriarch of Alexandria from 933 to 940, historian, and theological controversialist. He was born Sa⁻īd ibn Birtrīq (or Batrīq) Al-Fustāt (Old Cairo). Nothing is known about his youth, but he studied medicine and practiced as a physician before entering the monastic life. On 7 February 933 he was consecrated patriarch of Alexandria and took the name Eutychios. The beginning of his episcopate coincided with that of Makarios I, the Coptic Monophysite patriarch (933–953).

Following the Arab conquest of Egypt in 642, the Melchites, who adhered to the decrees of the Council of Chalcedon (451) and remained in communion with the Byzantine church, were greatly reduced in numbers. Between 651 and 742 they were without a patriarch. By the tenth century they were a precarious minority among the dwindling Christian population of Monophysites. The ascendancy of Islamic culture and the widespread use of Arabic as the Egyptian vernacular forced Christian writers to abandon Greek and Coptic. This transition is clearly attested in a preface to the Arabic *History of the Patriarchs of Alexandria* written by Sawīrus ibn al-Muqaffa⁻ (Severus of Ashmunein, *fl.* late tenth century), a Monophysite theologian and Eutychios' chief opponent.

All of Eutychios' writings seem to have been composed in Arabic. His most notable work is *Nazm al-jawhar* (Chaplet of pearls, or simply Annals), a history of the world from the creation to 938 that imitates the form of the Byzantine chronicle. The work is very uneven. Although it lacks any critical evaluation of the sources used, it still contains information about the Egyptian Melchite church that is found nowhere else—for example, a list of his patriarchal predecessors. Eutychios provides the Melchite viewpoint on events surrounding Chalcedon and subsequent Egyptian church history, and his work serves as a control when dealing with Monophysite historical works. Yahyā ibn Sa⁻īd of Antioch, a relative, continued the history to 1027.

Eutychios' history served as a source for several later historians: for William of Tyre (twelfth century), for the Copt al-Makīn (thirteenth century), and for the Muslim al-Maqrīzī (fourteenth century). The seventeenth-century Puritan divine John Selden used excerpts from Eutychios' work in his *Eutychii Aegyptii, patriarchae orthodoxorum Alexandrini . . . ecclesiae suae origines* (1642) to advance the notion that there was no distinction between bishops and priests in the early Alexandrian church. He was answered by the Maronite Abraham Ecchellensis in his *Eutychius, patriarcha Alexandrinus, vindicatus* (1661), in which the author disputes Selden's rendering of the relevant Arabic passages. Selden's interest led Edward Pococke to translate Selden's Arabic edition of the extant portions of the *Nazm* into Latin (1658–1659).

Eutychios also composed a treatise on medicine as well as works of theological controversy. The best known of the latter is the *Kitab al-burhān* (Book of demonstrations), which was attributed to St. Athanasius but probably belongs to Eutychios. The first section deals with the Creation, human destiny, the perfections of God, and the Incarnation; the remaining three sections contain biblical texts mustered in support of the themes discussed. According to his own testimony, Eutychios composed a *Discussion Between the Heretic and the Christian* (that is, between a Monophysite and a Melchite), which defends Chalcedonian orthodoxy. He is probably the author of the *Book on the Creation of the Angels* referred to in the *Kitab al-burhān.* None of Eutychios' works have survived in complete form. From what is extant, it appears that he was preoccupied with challenging the Monophysites and not with polemic against Islam. Nevertheless, like his adversary Ibn al-Muqaffa⁻, his theological language reflects the mutual influence of Christianity and Islam on each other.

BIBLIOGRAPHY

For a complete bibliography and discussion of the authenticity of the works attributed to Eutychios, see Georg Graf, *Geschichte der christlichen arabischen Literatur,* II (1947), 32–38. The critical ed. of the *Nazm al-jawhar,* without a translation, is Louis Cheikho, ed., *Eutychii patriarchae Alexandrini annales,* 2 vols. (1906–1090); for a Latin translation by Edward Pococke, see John Selden, *Contextio gemmarum,* 2 vols. (1658–1659). For the *Kitāb al-burhān,* see the ed. by Pierre Cachia, 2 vols. (1960–1961), and the English translation by W. Montgomery Watt, *The Book of Demonstration,* 2 vols. (1960–1961). For biography and added bibliographical information, see F. Nau, "Eutychios," in *Dictionnaire de théologie catholique,* V, pt. 2 (1913), 1609–1611.

D. W. JOHNSON

[See also **Monophysitism.**]

EVANGELIARY, a book containing the complete text of the four Gospels or, usually, selected readings (lections, pericopes) from the Gospels read during the eucharistic liturgy, arranged according to their use in the liturgical year. Technically, therefore, an evangeliary is an extract from a full lectionary, wherein lections for the entire liturgy are set forth, but in practice the two terms are used interchangeably. Illustrations, arranged in liturgical sequence rather than following the chronological progression of Christ's life, emphasize the major ecclesiastical feasts.

LESLIE BRUBAKER

[See also **Lectionary**.]

EVANGELIST SYMBOLS, the symbolic representations of Matthew, Mark, Luke, and John as respectively a man, lion, ox, and eagle, based on the descriptions of the four creatures in Rev. 4:6–8 and the tetramorph in Ezek. 1:10. The association was established in the second century by Irenaeus, bishop of Lyons, who, however, connected Mark with the eagle and John with the lion. Jerome expressed the now-standard equations around the year 400. The earliest images, such as the ivory plaque in Milan showing the Marys at Christ's tomb (*ca.* 400) and the apse mosaic at S. Pudenziana, Rome (*ca.* 417), depict winged half-figures without attributes floating about in a cloudy sky. Shortly thereafter, as on a five-part ivory book cover in Milan and the apse mosaic at Hosios David in Thessaloniki, the symbols are found holding closed books (or, occasionally, scrolls); open books appear in the eighth century. Full-length symbols are preserved in the bema mosaics at S. Vitale, Ravenna (*ca.* 547), after which time they are common in the Latin West. Until the twelfth century, the symbols rarely appear in Byzantium except as part of a theophany (as at Hosios David in Thessaloniki).

From the earliest period, evangelist symbols most commonly accompany evangelist portraits, where they serve to identify the author, establish his eschatological prestige, and, sometimes, provide divine inspiration for his writings. The symbols also frequently surround the Majestas Domini or Christ of the Last Judgment, following the text of Revelation; they may also be grouped around a cross, apparently with apotropaic intent.

BIBLIOGRAPHY

Ernst Kitzinger, *The Coffin of Saint Cuthbert* (1950); Lawrence Nees, "A Fifth-century Book Cover and the Or-

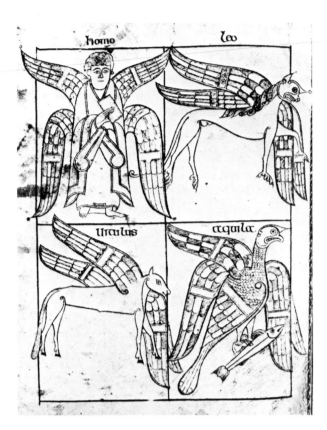

Symbols of the four evangelists. Book of Armagh, fol. 32v: Irish, early 9th century. COURTESY OF THE BOARD OF TRINITY COLLEGE, DUBLIN

igin of the Four Evangelist Symbols Page in the Book of Durrow," in *Gesta*, **17** (1978); Martin Werner, "The Four Evangelist Symbols Page in the Book of Durrow," in *Gesta* **8** (1969).

LESLIE BRUBAKER

[See also **Iconography**.]

EVERYMAN is probably the best, and certainly the best-known, of the English morality plays. Its popularity, while due primarily to its intrinsic quality, owes something to its stage revival in 1901 by the English director William Poel. His imaginative production was an immediate success, and it went on to tour both England and the United States. In the religious and moral climate of the early years of the twentieth century, it gave offense to many people. In particular the appearance of God on the stage was an outrage sternly condemned by some of the re-

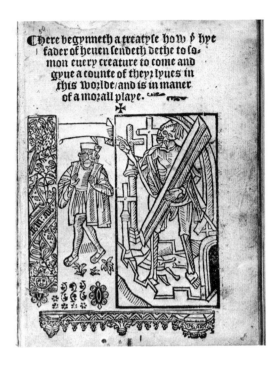

Frontispiece to the earliest printed version of *Everyman*. London, published by John Scott, 1530's. REPRODUCED BY PERMISSION OF THE HUNTINGTON LIBRARY, SAN MARINO, CALIFORNIA

viewers. No evidence has yet been found for a performance of *Everyman* before Poel's production; but since its revival the play has proved perennially popular.

Everyman is probably a translation of the Dutch play *Elckerlijk,* printed at Delft about 1518, although an earlier edition had been printed at Antwerp in 1495. However, there has been considerable controversy about the relationship between the two plays, some scholars arguing for the priority of the Dutch play and others for the English. Many of the arguments have centered on the alleged superiority of one play in diction, meter, theology, or didactic effectiveness—the unwarranted assumption being that such superiority implies priority. The only arguments that have not been turned inside out are ones based on factual evidence, and these point to *Elckerlijk* as the original and to *Everyman* as the translation. E. R. Tigg has shown that a pair of rhyme words in *Elckerlijk* is sometimes found in the corresponding lines of the English play, where each word is followed by a tag that completes the line and provides a new rhyme word. Tigg finds it incredible—

and most people will agree with him—that the Dutch playwright should have found his rhyme words ready-made for him in the lines of the English play. On the other hand it is perfectly credible that an English translator should have added a rhyming tag to each of a pair of words that rhyme in Dutch but not in English.

The two earliest complete copies of *Everyman* were printed at London by John Scott in the third decade of the sixteenth century. (One of these is now in the Huntington Library, San Marino, California; the other in the British Library, London.) The title page of each copy has a woodcut of Everyman and Death, and above this woodcut are the words that serve as the title of the play: "Here begynneth a treatyse how the hye fader of heuen sendeth dethe to somon euery creature to come and gyue a-counte of theyr lyues in this worlde, and is maner of a morall playe." Apart from two other early-sixteenth-century editions printed by Richard Pynson, of which only fragments remain, *Everyman* was not printed again until the Thomas Hawkins edition of 1773.

The typical morality, which flourished in England during the fifteenth and sixteenth centuries, dramatizes the conflict between good and evil in Everyman and shows him the way to salvation through Christ's church. *Everyman* is a salvation play concerned with a representative Catholic Christian on the point of death. God sends Death, his "mighty messenger," to summon Everyman. The sick and dying man is abandoned by all his worldly friends in turn, and in the end is left with only Knowledge and Good Deeds to bring him to salvation. At first Good Deeds is ineffectual, but Knowledge (representing knowledge of the Christian doctrine necessary for salvation) prepares Everyman for a Christian death by persuading him to go to confession and afterward to receive the viaticum and extreme unction. When Everyman is dying, Knowledge neither deserts him nor goes with him into the grave. Instead, she watches over him during his last moments on earth and speaks confidently of his soul's salvation, now made sure by the revived Good Deeds.

Much of the theological, Catholic doctrine in the play is also found in medieval treatises such as the *Ars moriendi* (translated into English as the *Book of the Craft of Dying*), written during the fifteenth century for the purpose of preparing men and women to die a Christian death. For example a close parallel is provided by Wynkyn de Worde's version (1507) of "a lytel treatyse of the dyenge creature enfected with sykenes vncurable." This treatise is in dialogue form, and the situation it presents is similar to that of *Everyman,* although the dramatis personae are different (Faith, Hope, and Charity take the place of Good Deeds and Knowledge). The dying man is warned of his approaching death by "a sergeaunt of armes" whose name is Cruelty (the counterpart of Death in Everyman), who summons him to render an account of "the gyftes of nature, the gyftes of fortune, and the gyftes of grace" bestowed on him by God. The dying man is forsaken in turn by his Good Angel and his earthly faculties, including his "fyue wyttes," and is left "destytute and allone" by everyone but Faith, Hope, and Charity. He first has to lay aside his trust in worldly things, and then these three promise not to fail him in his extremity: "and therfore," they tell him, "putte your soule in comforte, and arme you with the armure of a sure and a hole confessyon."

Shorn of its doctrine, the story of *Everyman* has many counterparts in European nondramatic literature: there are several versions of the Faithful Friend tale, which is the basic story of the play. The earliest European version of this tale is found in *Barlaam and Josaphat,* a collection of Christianized Eastern tales much used as a source book by the medieval preacher in search of moral anecdotes. Ultimately the tale may be of Buddhist origin; indeed, it has been claimed that the source is found in a collection of Buddhist parables, *The Miscellaneous Agama* (no. 101), in which a man is visited by a messenger of Death and commanded to prepare for his last journey. He is deserted in turn by his three favorite wives (Body, Wealth, Knowledge and Family), and only his fourth, neglected wife (Will or Intention) consents to go with him all the way.

The appeal of *Everyman* is no doubt many-sided, varying from reader to reader and from spectator to spectator. As a Catholic play its doctrine concerning holy dying will appeal to any devout Catholic for whom the sacraments of penance and the Eucharist are essential parts of the preparation for death. Moreover, its lesson that holy dying must be prepared for by holy living will be welcomed by anyone with a well-developed moral sense. ✓

Some will admire its fable—the story of a man's desertion by his worldly friends in his hour of need. Some will admire the personification of his gifts of fortune (Fellowship, Kindred, and Goods), his gifts of nature (Strength and Beauty), and his gift of grace (Good Deeds). While *Everyman* is, as a whole, a somber play, the playwright allows himself an occasional touch of humor in describing the evasive antics of Everyman's worldly friends—for example

when Cousin excuses himself for refusing to go with Everyman on his last journey:

Eueryman. My cosyn, wyll you not with me go?
Cosyn. No, by our Lady, I haue the crampe in my to[e].

It takes little imagination to realize that an allegorical character like Cousin is a vivid projection of one aspect of Everyman's dependence on the world. Everyman has to learn, with increasing self-knowledge, that death means the loss not only of his friends, relatives, and possessions but also of all the personal qualities he holds dear. He is *l'homme moyen sensuel,* neither very good nor very bad, a man with whom a reader or spectator can easily identify.

Another thing to admire is the simplicity of the staging, which is completely at one with the action of the play and was probably designed for presentation indoors (in contrast with the multitudinous action of the early-fifteenth-century morality play *The Castle of Perseverance,* performed outdoors in an "epic form of theater" with several scaffolds or acting stations, and reinforced by music, spectacle, and symbolic costume). Apart from the "house of salvation" there are no elaborate scenic effects. Most of the action is unlocalized: it could be happening anywhere in the Christian world to any representative Catholic Christian.

The diction and meter of *Everyman* impress many as being well suited to their purpose. The diction is dignified or colloquial as occasion demands. It is keyed exactly to the subject matter, and seldom comes between the spectator and the spectacle of a man's last hours in this world. The meter (mostly couplets and quatrains, but with many other stanza forms) is freely rhythmical and unobtrusive.

Perhaps the deepest source of the play's appeal is the universal fear of death that it exploits, as well as the desire to control this fear and come to terms with death. "In the midst of life we are in death": it is the duty of any minister of religion to remind the people of this, as it is the duty of any Christian church to teach that Christ is the wellspring of eternal life.

When Death comes, he takes Everyman by surprise, and Everyman can think of nothing better than to offer Death a bribe to stay away (119–130):

Eueryman. O Deth, thou comest when I had the[e] leest in mynde!
In thy power it lyeth me to saue;
Yet of my good wyl I gyue the, yf thou wyl be kynde—
Ye[a], a thousande pounde shalte thou haue—
And dyfferre this mater tyll an other daye.

Dethe. Eueryman, it may not be by no waye.
I set not by golde, syluer, nor rychesse,
Ne by pope, emperour, kynge, duke, ne prynces;
For, and I wolde receyue gyftes grete,
All the worlde I myght gete;
But my custome is clene contrary.
I gyue the[e] no respyte. Come hens, and not tary!

What happens to Everyman afterward is both the story and the moral of the play.

BIBLIOGRAPHY

Everyman, A. C. Cawley, ed. (1961). A full bibliography is in Walter W. Greg, *A Bibliography of the English Printed Drama to the Restoration,* I (1939), 82–84; and Carl J. Stratman, *Bibliography of Medieval Drama,* 2nd ed., I (1972), nos. 5501–5655. See especially Nancy L. Beaty, *The Craft of Dying* (1970); David M. Bevington, *From "Mankind" to Marlowe* (1962); Sumiko Miyajima, *The Theatre of Man* (1977); Robert Potter, *The English Morality Play* (1975); Lawrence V. Ryan, "Doctrine and Dramatic Structure in *Everyman,*" in *Speculum,* 32 (1957); Genji Takahashi, *A Study of "Everyman" with Special Reference to the Source of Its Plot* (1953), 33–39; E. R. Tigg, "Is *Elckerlijc* Prior to *Everyman?*" in *Journal of English and Germanic Philology,* 38 (1939); Reinard W. Zandvoort, "*Everyman–Elckerlijc,*" in *Études anglaises,* 6 (1953), also in his *Collected Papers* (1954).

A. C. CAWLEY

[See also **Ars Moriendi; Barlaam and Josaphat; Drama, Western European; Elckerlijk; Middle English Literature; Morality Play.**]

EVOVAE (or **EUOUAE**), an abbreviation formed with the vowels of the last words (*seculorum amen*) of the *Gloria patri* sung at the conclusion of virtually all psalms in the liturgy. In tonaries, and frequently in the musical service books, the EUOUAE formula with musical notation is given with the antiphon, in order to indicate the correct cadence (called the *differentia*) to be fitted to the final syllables of each psalm verse. The initial inflection (*initium*) and the median cadence (*mediatio*) could easily be ascertained from the mode of the antiphon to be sung with the psalm, but the *differentia* varied, and had to be indicated specifically.

TERENCE BAILEY

[See also **Differentia; Psalm Tones.**]

EX VOTO, an offering—image, object, church, or even a city—made in fulfillment or pursuance of a vow. If Krautheimer is correct, ex voto churches (the Lateran in Rome) and cities (Constantinople) were initiated by Constantine concurrently with the establishment of Christianity as the official state religion. The most famous medieval ex voto images are the seventh-century mosaics at Hagios Demetrios in Thessaloniki, which show the saints responsible for miraculous cures flanked by the grateful recipient donors and St. Demetrios flanked by the two church founders, apparently in response to the rescue of Thessaloniki from the 617 Slavic invasion.

BIBLIOGRAPHY

Ernst Kitzinger, "Byzantine Art in the Period Between Justinian and Iconoclasm," in *Berichte zum XI. Internationalen Byzantinisten-Kongress,* IV, pt. 1 (1958), repr. in his *The Art of Byzantium and the Medieval West* (1976); Richard Krautheimer, *Three Christian Capitals, Topography and Politics* (1982), 12, 42.

LESLIE BRUBAKER

EXARCHATE. *Exarchos* was a Byzantine term that could designate a commander or an official in general, especially in the early Byzantine period; for example, the rebel and later emperor Phokas was hailed as *exarchos* by his fellow mutineers in 602. Yet the principal importance of the term for Byzantine administrative history concerns the exarchates of Ravenna and Africa, both of which appeared during the reign of Emperor Maurice. A 584 letter from Pope Pelagius II to his *apocrisarius* in Constantinople provides the first mention of an exarch, probably Smaragdus, in Italy, while the earliest reference to an exarch in Africa, Gennadios, appears in 591. No archives survive from either exarchate, but there are a few documents from Ravenna.

The exarchs united civilian and military authority in their respective jurisdictions, but these cases should not be considered the earliest examples of such unions of authority; civil and military authority in the late Roman period overlapped and blurred more often than has hitherto been supposed. The exarchate of Ravenna survived until the end of Byzantine authority in northern and central Italy in 751. Ravenna was its administrative seat, but it included parts of Liguria, Venetia, Istria, Aemilia, Pentapolis, the duchy of Rome, Perugia, Naples, Calabria, and Apulia, even though not all of these were contiguous, after the loss of Byzantine control of much Italian territory to the Lombards. Its exarch served at the pleasure of the emperor.

The seat of the exarch of Africa was Carthage, and the exarchate of Africa lasted until the Arabs overran all of its territory at the end of the seventh century. Presumably the uniting of powers under the exarch of Africa was intended to create, as in Ravenna, a more effective authority to resist a military threat, in this case the Berbers, though the *magister militum per Africam* had already enjoyed dual authority. Some scholars believe that the exarchates were a precedent for the later Byzantine themes.

BIBLIOGRAPHY

Charles Diehl, *L'Afrique Byzantine* (1896), and *Études sur l'administration byzantine dans l'Exarchat de Ravenne (568-751)* (1888).

WALTER EMIL KAEGI, JR.

[See also **Byzantine Empire: Bureaucracy; Themes.**]

EXCALIBUR, King Arthur's great sword, is said in Geoffrey of Monmouth's *Historia regum Britanniae* to have come from Avalon. In French romance it sometimes gives off light and occasionally is wielded by Gawain. It also becomes a symbol of kingship, hence its first miraculous appearance in an anvil from which only Arthur can draw it. At Arthur's death it is cast into a lake, where it is received by a mysterious hand. That Excalibur is derived from the weapon named Caladbolg in Irish legend and Caledvwlch (from *calet bwlch*, hard notch) in Welsh is widely accepted, though reservations have been expressed.

BIBLIOGRAPHY

Roger Sherman Loomis, *Arthurian Tradition and Chrétien de Troyes* (1949), 421–425; John S. P. Tatlock, *The Legendary History of Britain* (1950), 202; Eugène Vinaver, "King Arthur's Sword," in *Bulletin of the John Rylands Library*, **40** (1958).

ROBERT W. ACKERMAN

[See also **Arthurian Literature; Arthurian Literature, Welsh.**]

EXCHEQUER. From the Saxon kings of England, William I the Conqueror (1066–1087) inherited a relatively advanced financial system. The royal household chamber, now more than a domestic treasury and storage place for precious documents and possessions, received most of the royal income collected by the sheriffs of the shires. A storehouse or stationary treasury had been established at Winchester to hold surplus money and valuables and to keep the itinerant chamber supplied with money. Early in the reign of Henry I (1100–1135) this treasury, enlarging its role, began to assume administration of the royal finances. It received and disbursed most of the income, kept accounts that were audited by specially designated barons, and supplied the chamber with money. It had in effect superseded the chamber as the chief financial office, and was soon to father the Exchequer.

Except for name and method of financial computation, the Exchequer resembled the treasury. It was probably functioning by the middle of Henry I's reign, or perhaps earlier, but until about 1115 there are no references to the Exchequer, a name derived, because of its system of computation, from the Latin *scaccarium* (chessboard). The Exchequer became and remains today the principal treasury of England. From the pipe rolls and other Exchequer records, such as the receipt rolls, and from *The Dialogue of the Exchequer,* written about 1180 by Richard Fitzneale, formerly treasurer of the Exchequer, there emerges a clear picture of its organization and operations.

Located permanently in London, the Exchequer had two divisions—the lower and the upper. Its treasury of the realm formed the division known as the Exchequer of Receipt or Lower Exchequer, which functioned throughout the year with a staff composed of the treasurer, two chamberlains, and some subordinates. Besides routine clerical work this staff annually compiled the pipe roll, received and disbursed money, transported money for the royal use, and performed special functions during the auditing sessions held at Easter and Michaelmas (29 September). At these sessions the staff received the money from the accountable officials such as the sheriffs, counted it, placed it in bags with appropriate labels, and issued receipts in the form of tallies (wooden sticks with notches representing various sums of money). These wooden receipts were then split lengthwise in half, through the notches, one part being kept by the Lower Exchequer and the other by the accountable official to serve as evidence of his payment. As early as Henry II's reign (1154–1189) written records of receipt also began to be kept and written receipts given to the accountable officials.

By the reign of Henry II the Lower Exchequer had devised a number of techniques to ensure better control over the quality of coins received. In the twelfth century the only coin in circulation was the silver penny, 12 of which made a shilling and 240 a pound. Only later were shilling and pound coins minted. The aim of the Exchequer was to receive for every pound owed 240 good pennies—that is, pennies meeting the standard of those struck by the royal mint. Content for a time merely to count the coins, the Lower Exchequer soon observed that all sorts of clipped, damaged, and counterfeited pennies were being received. A system of payment by weight was then introduced, whereby the 240 pennies of the pound received were placed on one side of a scale and those of a royal pound on the other. If the scales failed to balance, the accountable official had to add the number of pennies needed for balancing, and to pay that same number of pennies for each pound owed.

Later the official automatically paid so many extra pennies per pound, generally six, to ensure a good pound. Under Henry II all money admitted at the Exchequer had to be paid in tested bullion or in specie reduced to that condition. The latter operation was done by an assay. Two hundred and forty pennies were dumped into a melting pot and reduced to a molten state with the dross skimmed off by the assayer. Devoid of impurities, the bullion was then placed in a vessel and weighed against 240 good royal pennies. Any loss of weight required the addition of the necessary pennies.

The Upper Exchequer, essentially a part of the king's small council sitting in a financial capacity, was a board of accountability that assembled at Easter and Michaelmas; it ensured that the king received everything due him and that all disbursements on his behalf were proper. Its members, known as the barons of the Exchequer, included not only the treasurer and two chamberlains of the Exchequer but also the chancellor or his representative, the justiciar, a few notable barons, and various functionaries such as constables, marshals, and clerks, who occupied themselves with the records, the tallies, the accounting, and the ushering in and out of officials rendering their accounts. It sat around a large table about five feet by ten feet at which the officials ac-

counted for the money owed and disbursed. The table was covered with a dark cloth marked off in vertical lines forming columns, each standing for a numerical value: for pennies, shillings, pounds, 20 pounds, 100 pounds, 1,000 pounds, and 10,000 pounds. Counters were placed and moved about on these columns, signifying by their position and number a value such as 9 pennies, 6 shillings, 4 pounds, and so forth.

In essence this device for computations was an adaptation of the abacus or suan pan. By rearranging the counters on the columns, an official known as the calculator computed the accounts as they were audited. This system enabled the uneducated layman, as were most sheriffs and other accountable officials, to follow the addition and subtraction, the only mathematical operations required. Also, because only Roman numerals were used throughout most of the Middle Ages, the abacus simplified the calculations involved. It had come into western Europe by way of Islamic Spain, and though it was probably known in England during the late eleventh century, whether it was first used as a calculating device in the reign of Henry I or that of Henry II is uncertain.

Prior to the auditing sessions at Easter and Michaelmas, the staff of the Exchequer made meticulous preparations. It drew up and entered upon a pipe roll all the known revenues and disbursements for each county, and left blanks to be filled in after the accounting for revenues and disbursements that were unknown. It assembled all the writs authorizing disbursements by the sheriffs and other documents pertinent to the auditing, including the tallies that had been issued and had to be matched with the half given to the sheriff or some other royal creditor. The Exchequer customarily provided individuals at the auditing sessions to serve as witnesses for receipts and disbursements of money and, in lieu of tallies and written documents, the sheriffs were expected to do likewise. At the Easter session the sheriff accounted for half of what was due from his county; the other half was accounted for at the Michaelmas session, at which a final auditing was made for the fiscal year that began and ended on Michaelmas.

The auditing began when the treasurer called out the name of the accountant (sheriff) appearing before the barons of the Exchequer, and it then proceeded item by item. Accounted for first were the annual fixed payments from the revenues of the county, such as alms, tithes, and disbursements to various people and institutions. Next came the value in money of royal lands granted by the king to various individuals, followed by those casual payments that varied yearly. The sheriff then accounted for various fines assessed on individuals, incomes from fiefs that had escheated to the king, the profits from royal justice, and sums of money paid to the king by individuals to obtain the royal favor or feudal concessions. Finally the sheriff accounted for such taxes as the Danegeld and miscellaneous sums owed by various individuals and institutions, such as boroughs and monasteries.

With the auditing completed, the total sum of money paid by the sheriff was entered on the pipe roll across from his name, which was inscribed below the name of the county. If he rendered the exact amount due, it was noted that he was acquitted; if he owed money, it was noted that he owed so much; if he paid more than owed, it was noted that there was a surplus. Throughout the twelfth century the pipe rolls adequately recorded the annual royal income and expenses, but as the developing economy generated new revenues, they had to be supplemented by the receipt rolls and issue rolls, which recorded income and expenses outside the purview of the sheriffs.

In the twelfth century the English Exchequer was the most efficient financial system in Europe; only that of the Norman kingdom of Sicily may be compared with it. There is some evidence that treasury officials from Sicily came to work for Henry II to improve the operations of his Exchequer. The Norman Exchequer at Caen had procedures much like the English, but its records—the great rolls of the Norman exchequer—are both meager and extant only for certain years in the late twelfth and early thirteenth centuries. The financial system of the county of Flanders, though similar, was less sophisticated and is much less well documented. Capetian France had no such institution as an exchequer, but many of the Norman financial procedures were adopted by the royal treasury at Paris after Philip II Augustus acquired Normandy in the early thirteenth century.

By the early thirteenth century the Upper Exchequer, though still the small council tending to financial affairs, had become a financial department with a relatively permanent and skilled staff with its own procedures and customs. By the end of John's reign (1216) it was a department so specialized and independent, and staffed so largely by deputies of the

chief barons of the Exchequer, that its connection with the small council was in practice ended. The chancellor no longer attended the auditing sessions, being represented by his clerk, who came to be called the chancellor of the Exchequer and who ultimately superseded the treasurer as the head of the Exchequer.

The Exchequer remained an important financial department until the end of the Middle Ages, but at times surrendered much of its authority and many of its functions to the chamber or the wardrobe. Because the chamber and wardrobe were a part of the royal household and were always with the king as he moved about, they were in a better position to keep him supplied with money and to make the necessary disbursements. In the late twelfth and early thirteenth centuries the chamber received large sums from the Exchequer or collected revenues that ordinarily would have been paid into the Exchequer. When the wardrobe superseded the chamber as the king's preferred household treasury, the same procedures were followed.

Under Edward I (1272–1307) and Edward III (1327–1377) the wardrobe assumed most of the functions of the Exchequer and became the principal treasury for financing their wars. It nevertheless had to account yearly, in records called wardrobe books, for all the money received from the exchequer and other sources and for all its disbursements. The kings turned to the chamber and wardrobe because their use not only was more efficient, especially during campaigns, but also enabled the kings to circumvent the barons, who during the thirteenth and fourteenth centuries attempted to secure some control over the royal expenditures by placing their own men in the Exchequer and keeping a close surveillance over its operations. The kings resented these baronial actions as a challenge to their prerogative rights, and therefore increasingly bypassed the Exchequer by means of their household treasuries, which were less accessible to the barons.

The kings, however, lost the ability to escape baronial control over royal finance when, in the fourteenth century, parliament developed and acquired the power to grant the kings their most important taxes. Parliament stipulated that the Exchequer should collect and disburse parliamentary taxes, and it developed procedures for auditing the Exchequer and checking on the misuse of the taxes granted. Under such controls the Exchequer functioned as the chief treasury for the rest of the Middle Ages.

Change came with the accession in 1485 of Henry Tudor, who reformed financial administration through a system constructed around the chamber.

BIBLIOGRAPHY

For the development and operation of the Exchequer see especially Richard Fitzneale, *The Course of the Exchequer (Dialogus de scaccario)*, Charles Johnson, ed. and trans. (1950); Hubert Hall, *Court Life Under the Plantagenets* (1902), 114–142; Reginald Lane Poole, *The Exchequer in the Twelfth Century* (1912). Although Thomas F. Tout, *Chapters in Mediaeval Administrative History*, 6 vols. (1920–1933), concentrates on household administration, he also discusses the Exchequer and its relations with the chamber and wardrobe. For the Exchequer in the fourteenth century see *The English Government at Work, 1327–1336*, I, *Central and Prerogative Administration*, James F. Willard and William A. Morris, eds. (1940), and II, *Fiscal Administration*, William A. Morris and Joseph R. Strayer, eds. (1947). For a comparison of the English Exchequer with the financial systems of Normandy, France, and Flanders see Bryce Lyon and Adriaan E. Verhulst, *Medieval Finance* (1967). A translation of *The Dialogue of the Exchequer* is in *The Course of the Exchequer*, cited above, and translations of the pipe rolls are in David C. Douglas and George W. Greenway, eds., *English Historical Documents 1042–1189*, 2nd ed. (1981), 609–623. For references to other studies, see Edgar B. Graves, ed., *A Bibliography of English History to 1485* (1975).

BRYCE LYON

[See also **Accounting; England; Mints and Money, Western European; Pipe Rolls; Taxation, English.**]

EXCHEQUER, COURT OF. Soon after the Conquest the Norman kings established the central treasury of England at Westminster. Beginning in the reign of Henry I (1100–1135), disputes regarding dues owed to the king were decided there by reference to the *Domesday Book* as evidence of tenure. Registration, or enrollment, of payments was recorded as early as the beginning of the twelfth century. In 1118 the word *scaccarium*, later anglicized as "Exchequer," emerged as the name of the financial department of the court A precise system of reckoning with counters on a "checkered" table was based on the novel principle of the abacus, and the results of the calculations were carefully recorded in the pipe rolls.

Money was received and tested in the lower division of the Exchequer, the Exchequer of Receipt.

Accounts between the king and his debtors, or accountants (chief among whom was the sheriff), and legal disputes regarding payments were settled in the upper division, the Exchequer of Account. It is the upper division, the plea side of the *scaccarium*, that became a court of law in the Middle Ages, alongside the King's Bench, the court of common pleas, and the courts of the itinerant justices. By the sixteenth century the three main offices of the upper division—the king's remembrancer's office, the lord treasurer's remembrancer's office, and the office of pleas—had become courts of law with jurisdiction to decide legal disputes arising out of the financial affairs of the crown.

The earliest expositions of the common law, Bracton's *On the Laws and Customs of England* (before 1260) and Ranulf de Glanville's *On the Laws and Customs of the Kingdom of England* (ca. 1187) do not recognize a court at the Exchequer. The *Fleta* (1290–1300), however, did so. The justices of that court, *Fleta* says, are called barons. In certain circumstances they hear complaints against officials, sheriffs, escheators, bailiffs, and other royal ministers.

Britton (ca. 1290) says that it is the king's will that "at our Exchequer at Westminster and elsewhere our treasurers and our barons have jurisdiction and record of things which concern their office, to hear and determine all causes relating to our debts and seignories and things incident thereto; . . . and that they have cognizance of debts owing by our debtors, by means whereof we the more speedily recover our own" (bk. V, chs. 1, 9). *The Mirror of Justices,* written about the same time, tells of a court "established solely for the king's profit, where two knights and two clerks, or two literate men, are assigned to hear and determine wrongs done to the king and his crown in respect of his fees and franchises . . . under the supervision of a chief who is treasurer of England" (bk. I, ch. 14). In a further section, "Of Abuses," *The Mirror of Justices* mentions that the officers of the Exchequer "take jurisdiction in matters other than debts due to the King and his fees and franchises, without original writ from the chancery under white wax" (bk. V, ch. 1, sec. 27).

Thus, from the reign of Edward I (1272–1307) a court with extensive jurisdiction in financial matters and "in matters other than debts due to the king" sat at the Exchequer. Each Easter and Michaelmas term it held special sessions, devoted to the supervision of the king's financial interests and the work of the king's bookkeeping. The medieval Exchequer had jurisdiction over all of England, Wales, and the town of Berwick-on-Tweed.

The barons of the Exchequer numbered the great officials of the realm. The justiciar presided until the disuse of the office in 1234, then was replaced by the treasurer. The treasurer kept the rolls, or records, which were at first duplicates of those kept by the chancellor. During the chancellorship of Hubert Walter, in the reign of Richard I (1189–1199), the chancery became a department distinct from the Exchequer, with a separate set of records. The barons of the exchequer became a distinct class of officials by the thirteenth century and, for the most part, professional lawyers by the middle of the fourteenth century.

A separate branch of the Exchequer, known as the Exchequer of the Jews, with its own chancellor and barons, functioned from the end of the reign of Richard I to the latter part of the reign of Edward I. In 1198 "guardians of Jews" were appointed to exercise jurisdiction over the accounts of the Jews, over pleas upon contracts made with Jews, and over causes touching their lands or chattels, their tallages, fines, forfeitures, and the like. The rolls of pleas heard in the Exchequer of the Jews were kept separately from 1220.

The gradual evolution of the court of the Exchequer out of a purely revenue-gathering agency can be traced in the series of rolls produced in the Exchequer. The first roll, the great roll of the pipe, contains financial accounts. When disputes arose that were put over for further consideration, records were entered on a series called the memoranda rolls. One of the memoranda rolls has survived from the first year of John (1199–1200), though there are hints of earlier rolls under Henry II (1154–1189) and they are known to have existed under Richard I (1189–1199). The first roll of the Exchequer of Pleas, beginning in 1236–1237, and practically continuous after 1267–1268, containing matters that call for judicial treatment, clearly shows the working of a well-established revenue court. This court was a common-law court using common-law procedures. It won great popularity, not only because of its remarkable promptness and efficiency but also because it permitted the king's subjects to bring proceedings against officials, especially sheriffs and customs officers, who had abused their offices.

By statute in 1300 (23 Edw. I, c. 4) Edward I prohibited the Exchequer from hearing common pleas, the first indication of competition between the common-law courts. In 1376 Parliament authorized wager of law in the Exchequer, except in cases to which the king was party, on the ground that jury trial was to the great damage of the people and the impoverishment of the jurors, and caused much delay (*Rot. Parl.* ii, 337, no. 92).

With time, however, common pleas, or nonrevenue cases, developed into a major part of the business of the Court of Exchequer. This occurred in several ways. First, officials of the Exchequer and their servants by privilege could compel their adversaries to answer in the Exchequer, and as defendants they could refuse to answer except in the Exchequer. Second, the affairs of merchants, and in some cases friars or other favored persons, were frequently heard in the Exchequer on the king's command. Furthermore, parties could compel litigation in the Exchequer by the simple expedient of enrolling cognizances of debt on the Exchequer rolls. Finally, parties in debt to the king could use the procedures of the court against their own debtors by alleging that they would be unable to discharge their debt to the crown unless their own debtors paid them. Anyone who owed money to the crown could avail himself of this privilege.

The twofold assertion of a plaintiff—to be a debtor of the king, and to be less able to satisfy the king—was deemed justification enough for the court of Exchequer to intervene by issuing a writ of quominus. The king could sue his debtors' debtors, and so it was reasonable to extend his prerogative to allow his debtors to sue their debtors for his ultimate gain. The writ of quominus was later turned into a mere form to allow anyone with a claim for liquidated or unliquidated damages a choice to sue in the Exchequer.

In 1357 Edward II established a court of appeal to hear errors in the Exchequer, called the Exchequer Chamber (31 Edw. III, stat. 1, c. 12). The chancellor and the treasurer alone were the judges, though they could convene the justices of the common-law courts as assessors. This was unsuccessfully petitioned against in the Commons in 1378. Another and more significant assembly of judges and serjeants began to meet informally after 1400 to consider legal questions of unusual importance or difficulty. This meeting was called the "court" of the Exchequer Chamber, because the meetings were held in a large room in the Exchequer building.

The equity side of the court of Exchequer developed gradually as cases involving uses, trusts, wills, decedents' estates, and personal remedies, such as injuctions and contributions, found their way before the court in the late fifteenth and early sixteenth centuries. The court acted as a court of equity until 1842 and was finally abolished in 1875.

BIBLIOGRAPHY

Sources. Richard Fitzneale, *The Course of the Exchequer (Dialogus de scaccario),* Charles Johnson, ed. and trans. (1950); Mary Hemmant, *Select Cases in the Exchequer Chamber Before All the Justices of England,* 2 vols. (1933–1948); C. Hilary Jenkinson and Beryl E. R. Formoy, eds. *Select Cases in the Exchequer of Pleas* (1932); James M. Rigg, *Select Pleas, Starrs, and Other Records from the Rolls of the Exchequer of the Jews, A.D. 1220–1284* (1902).

Studies. William H. Bryson, *The Equity Side of the Exchequer* (1975); Reginald Lane Poole, *The Exchequer in the Twelfth Century* (1912); Henry G. Richardson, "Richard fitz Neal and the *Dialogus de scaccario,*" in *English Historical Review,* 43 (1928).

Wᴉʟʟɪᴀᴍ W. Bᴀssᴇᴛᴛ

[See also **Escheat; Law, English Common; Sheriff.**]

EXCHEQUER OF THE JEWS, a department within the English royal administration with a particular, though not exclusive, responsibility for matters connected with the Jewish community. It came into existence toward the end of the twelfth century and ceased to operate when the Jews were expelled from England in 1290.

The Exchequer of the Jews exercised both administrative and judicial functions. It supervised the system of local chirograph chests *(arche)* established in 1194. All debts owed to Jews had to be recorded on chirographs written by specially appointed clerks, and one part of each chirograph was deposited in the appropriate chest. There were two Jewish and two Christian chirographers for each chest who were responsible for all documents deposited in it or withdrawn from it on payment or pardoning of the debt.

The permission of the Exchequer of the Jews was required for any Jew wishing to change his place of residence. It also exercised jurisdiction over property and trespass suits where either of the parties was Jewish and in some criminal cases involving Jews.

Its main function was to enforce the payment of the debts recorded in the chirographs (plus the appropriate interest) against the original debtors or (if they were insolvent or dead) against the current holders of their lands. It performed this function both for creditors named in chirographs and for others, both Christian and Jewish, to whom their assets subsequently passed. The king sometimes pardoned an individual debtor or allowed him to pay off his Jewish debts by installments. The Exchequer of the Jews ensured that creditors observed the terms of these grants.

The Exchequer of the Jews was normally run by two or three justices of the Jews. Its clerical staff was mainly Christian but also included Jews. Most of its records were kept in Latin, but in the mid thirteenth century a Hebrew plea roll was also compiled. The *presbyter Judaeorum,* the officially recognized head of the Jewish community, was not an official of the Exchequer of the Jews but played a role in its work.

For brief periods in the 1230's and 1260's the Exchequer of the Jews came under the control of a single individual, but normally external supervision was by the main Exchequer. The justices were required to account there for any monies received and for the levying of Jewish debts that had passed to the king. After 1267 the main Exchequer acted as a court of appeal for cases from the Exchequer of the Jews; in 1272 and 1286 justices of the Jews were tried there for official misconduct.

The Exchequer of the Jews was not responsible for the assessment or the collection of Jewish taxation, and even some Jewish debts were levied through the main Exchequer. The Chancery, not the Exchequer of the Jews, became responsible for issuing licenses for the sale of debts (necessary after 1269) and licenses for the disposal of real property (necessary after 1275).

BIBLIOGRAPHY

Many plea rolls survive in the Public Record Office, London. Those prior to 1277 have been published in James M. Rigg and Hilary Jenkinson with H. G. Richardson, eds., *Calendar of the Plea Rolls of the Exchequer of the Jews,* 4 vols. (1905–1977). Individual cases are also in James M. Rigg, ed., *Select Pleas, Starrs, and Other Records from the Rolls of the Exchequer of the Jews, A.D. 1220–1284* (1902). See also Charles Gross, "The Exchequer of the Jews of England," in *Papers Read at the Anglo-Jewish Historical Exhibition* (1888), 170–230; C. A. F. Meekings, "Justices of the Jews, 1218–68: A Provisional List," in *Bulletin of the Institute of Historical Research,* 28 (1955); Henry G. Richardson, *The English Jewry Under Angevin Kings* (1960), 135–160.

Pᴀᴜʟ A. Bʀᴀɴᴅ

[See also **Exchequer, Court of; Jews in Europe; Taxation, English.**]

EXCIDIO ET CONQUESTU BRITTANIAE, DE. See **Gildas.**

EXCOMMUNICATION refers both to the *sentence* whereby a Christian was excluded from the Christian community and to the *state* of exclusion itself. The exclusion of a person from normal society was a penalty inflicted in medieval Europe by both secular and ecclesiastical authorities. Excommunication was akin to the ban in the German empire and outlawry in England: Frederick W. Maitland recognized this when he called excommunication "ecclesiastical outlawry." By excommunication a Christian was cut off from the body of the church as a scandalizing member. This exclusion was a separation from the community of the faithful *(separatio a communione fidelium).*

There were three phases in the development of excommunication. Until about 400 excommunication simply meant that a person had severed himself from the fellowship of believing Christians. The emphasis lay clearly on the *state* of excommunication rather than on the sentence, which was merely a statement of fact.

Then, during the early Middle Ages—roughly from the fifth to the eleventh century—the *sentence* of excommunication was emphasized: it was imposed always after the crime and always on an individual. Contumacy characterized the excommunicate: he had obstinately opposed not merely specific mandates of the church but, more significantly, the very power of the keys. By this time the spread of private penance had led to a clear distinction between public sins, to be remitted publicly, and private sins, to be remitted privately. A corollary distinction was made between the external forum of public order and the internal forum of private conscience. A crime was a public sin subject to the external forum and excommunication was a penalty used in that forum to constrain the criminal to reconciliation and penance. Lists of excommunicable crimes were circulated, yet the commission of those crimes did not automatically incur the penalty but merely left the offending person liable to the sentence of excommunication.

The beginning of the third phase coincided with the Gregorian reform in the last half of the eleventh century. Excommunication was now used not only to reconcile the heretic but also to coerce Christians to obey church decrees. The reformers enforced their decrees by threatening potential violators with excommunication, which, like deposition and interdict, was used as a means of imposing ecclesiastical discipline. Contumacy now meant the refusal to obey a mandate of the church and did not necessarily imply a general rejection of church authority. Excommunication, the severest penalty of the Christian church, became the coercive edge to even routine decrees.

This significant change did not go unnoticed or unopposed. Peter Damian (*d.* 1072) protested in a letter to Pope Alexander II that Pope Gregory the Great and the other Fathers had not annexed excommunications to their decrees unless the matter pertained to the Christian faith itself. Damian was not heeded, and the new use of excommunication became accepted ecclesiastical practice. And so it remained throughout the rest of the medieval period and even into modern times.

It was excommunication in this sense that was described in classical canon law, where medieval canonists distinguished between major and minor excommunication. The latter excluded a person from the Eucharistic body of Christ and mattered little in law, for it could be imposed and removed by any priest with jurisdiction in the internal forum; it simply referred to the consequences of mortal sin. It was major excommunication that separated the individual from the mystical body of Christ, the church. The excommunicate was dispossessed of all religious rights: entry into church, the company of the faithful, pleading in secular and church courts, holding a benefice, and generally all legitimate ecclesiastical acts; after death he could not receive an ecclesiastical burial. He was denied commerce with other Christians and, in some instances, even the company of his own family, although enforcement of this latter prohibition proved difficult. In a unitary Christian society excommunication amounted to social ostracism.

By the thirteenth century the power to excommunicate was clearly restricted to certain prelates who had jurisdiction (bishops, archdeacons, deans of cathedral chapters, and abbots) and to judges acting by their commission. Even clerics or monks not in priest's orders (archdeacons or abbots) could excommunicate, as could laymen—never laywomen—acting as ecclesiastical judges. Excommunications imposed by them on individuals were said to be *ab homine* (by man). An ecclesiastical decree might include a clause excommunicating all violators of the decree: this was excommunication *a iure* (by law). In excommunications *latae sententiae* the mere performance of the forbidden act gave rise, ipso facto, to an excommunication. In excommunications *ferendae sententiae* a positive judgment after the fact of the crime imposed the penalty: a person who contumaciously refused to answer a judicial citation could be declared excommunicate by the judge. So grave were the consequences of major excommunication that previous warnings were required before it could be imposed: for excommunications *latae sententiae* the decree itself contained the warning, but for excommunications *ferendae sententiae* three warnings or one peremptory had first to be issued.

The books of rituals provided a ceremony in which a bishop and twelve priests stood in a circle in the sanctuary of a cathedral church and, amid the pealing of bells and the dashing of candles, cut off "from the body of the church this corrupt and unhealthy member," who was considered henceforth not a Christian but a pagan. This full ceremonial excommunication—the anathema—was rare indeed: a study of over 15,000 persons excommunicated in English ecclesiastical courts did not reveal even one performance of the solemn rite. In most cases a justice merely uttered a judgment in court, for example, "I excommunicate thee" *(excommunico te).* Whether imposed ceremonially or more simply, the sentence of excommunication was next published, generally in the local parish church, but sometimes more widely.

The crimes for which excommunication was imposed ranged from certain kinds of perjury and forgery to striking a cleric and disobeying a papal mandate. Ecclesiastical judges frequently used this penalty to enforce their authority. Nonappearance in court, when cited, could lead to excommunication, as could failure to obey the directives of the court (such as to restore property or marital rights). Lists of excommunicable crimes were published in parish churches four times year.

The imposition and publication of the sentence of excommunication did not imply, even for the medieval canonist, that the "excommunicate" was in fact excommunicated, only that he had been declared excommunicate and should be treated as such. The excommunication might have been issued by a person having no competence (such as a bishop against a person not his subject in a matter not of his cognizance) or by a judge after a legitimate appeal. Moreover, the person might not be guilty of mortal sin, and the dictum at law was "no mortal sin, no crime;

no crime, no penalty." Thus, Robert Grosseteste, though excommunicated in 1243 by the prior and convent of Canterbury cathedral, treated this sentence with justifiable disdain. On the other hand, the response of Emperor Frederick II to his two excommunications by Pope Gregory IX (in 1227 and 1239) reflected disdain not of the sentence itself but of papal authority.

An excommunicate was free to appeal his sentence. Although generally in canon law appeal from a sentence led to automatic suspension of that sentence, this suspension did not apply in the case of excommunication. As Pope Innocent III stated in 1204, the sentence of excommunication and the execution of that sentence were inseparable. Strictly speaking, an excommunicate could not prosecute an appeal, since he had no standing at law. To resolve this dilemma a procedure was devised whereby an excommunicate appealing the validity of an excommunication was absolved as a precaution *(ad cautelam)* by the appellate court. If the appeal was successful, the appellant was cleared; if the appeal failed and the excommunication was adjudged valid, the defendant was excommunicated once again by the appellate court. Since courts of appeal allowed excommunicates a year within which to prosecute an appeal, this procedure of absolution *ad cautelam* was frequently used in the fourteenth and fifteenth centuries, even in a frivolous manner, as a means of postponing the effects of the sentence.

The purpose of excommunication was, in part, "medicinal." Exclusion from the communion of the faithful was intended to induce the excommunicate to seek absolution, reconciliation to the church, and restoration to his place in society. From the twelfth century absolution from excommunication was distinguished from absolution from sin. The full reconciliation of an excommunicate required, in addition to absolution in the internal forum, absolution from excommunication in the external forum. Generally such absolution was given by the official who had imposed the penalty, his successor, or his delegate; the pope, as universal ordinary, could absolve anyone. The solemn form of reconciliation—at the doors of the church by the bishop and twelve priests—was rarely used; usually a simple decree was issued: "I absolve thee" *(Absolvo te).* In either case, an oath of future obedience was exacted. The penance imposed could take the form of pious acts such as almsgiving or a pilgrimage. For example, in 1307 the Englishman William Sampson, a knight who had committed incest with two of his daughters and adultery with two other women, was required to stand before the high altar during Mass on three successive Sundays, clothed only in a tunic, unshod and ungirded, and carrying a three-pound candle. He also had to feed three poor men for a week and, finally, to undertake a pilgrimage to Canterbury. Penances were performed after absolution, and failure to perform them could lead to reimposition of excommunication.

The penalty of excommunication did not, of itself, always have the desired medicinal effect of reconciliation. The church, having used its ultimate weapon, could then turn to the coercive force of the secular arm against the obdurate excommunicate. In the German empire the imperial ban was imposed on those who remained excommunicate for a year and a day, and in Denmark and Italy a similar ban was imposed, whereas in France a person remaining excommunicate for more than a year was guilty of heresy or suspicion of heresy and was subject to confiscation of property and perhaps even arrest. In Aragon fines and, ultimately, the death penalty, could be used by the secular arm. In England a bishop could petition the king to issue a writ to a sheriff for the arrest of a person obdurately excommunicate for more than forty days.

The practice of excommunication survived the Middle Ages in both the Catholic and Reformed churches. Although Martin Luther averred that the Roman church should be severely punished "for blasphemous misuse of excommunication," he allowed for its use where the Bible demanded, as, for example, against those living notoriously in sin. John Calvin fought successfully to grant the Geneva Consistory authority to excommunicate. The Council of Trent, in its twenty-fifth session (December 1563), recognized the damage involved in trivializing this penalty:

> Although the sword of excommunication is the very sinew of church discipline and is extremely useful in holding people to their duties, nonetheless, this penalty should be imposed only with the greatest care and circumspection. Experience shows that, when excommunication is imposed rashly and in slight matters, then the penalty will be more despised than feared and will produce more harm than good.

This canon can stand as a fitting epitaph to the medieval use of excommunication, a penalty at once expressing and undermining the power of the universal church.

BIBLIOGRAPHY

Walter Doskocil, *Der Bann in der Urkirche: Eine Rechtsgeschichtliche Untersuchung* (1958); Jean Gaudemet, "Note sure les formes anciennes de l'excommunication," in *Revue des sciences religieuses*, 23 (1949); Rosalind Hill, "Public Penance: Some Problems of a Thirteenth-century Bishop," in *History*, 36 (1951), and "The Theory and Practice of Excommunication in Medieval England," in *History*, 42 (1957); Paul Hinschius, *Das Kirchenrecht der Katholiken und Protestanten in Deutschland*, 6 vols. (1869–1897), V, 1–492; Peter Huizing, "Doctrina decretistarum de variis speciebus excommunicationis," in *Gregorianum*, 33 (1952), and "The Earliest Development of Excommunication *Latae sententiae* by Gratian and the Early Decretists," in *Studia Gratiana*, 3 (1955); F. Donald Logan, *Excommunication and the Secular Arm in Medieval England* (1968); Maurice Morel, *L'excommunication et le pouvoir civil en France du droit canonique classique au commencement du XVe siècle* (1926); François Russo, "Pénitence et excommunication: Étude historique sur les rapports entre la théologie et le droit canon dans le domaine pénitentiel du IXe au XIIIe siècle," in *Recherches de science religieuse*, 33 (1946); Eugène Vernay, *Le "Liber de excommunicacione" du Cardinal Bérenger Frédol* (1912).

F. Donald Logan

[See also **Law, Canon; Penance, Penitentials.**]

EXEDRA, a large recess or niche opening full-width into a larger space, thereby extending it.

Leslie Brubaker

EXEGESIS, JEWISH. The phenomenon of interpretation and creative adaptation of a text that has achieved recognition and authority is discernible within biblical tradition itself. The closing of the canon and its undisputed acceptance as the seminal text of Jewish civilization expedited the process, and generated a rich, independent, derivative literature in Hebrew, Aramaic, and Greek. The voluminous and multifaceted talmudic writings that had been produced by the year 500 constitute, in essence, biblical exegesis. The Bible was conceived as a harmoniously integrated unit. Hermeneutical norms had been formulated in the introduction to Sifra (1:7). The idea of the multiple sense of Scripture as a cardinal principle of Jewish exegesis had been articulated in Sanhedrin (34*a*).

Yet no systematic, verse-by-verse commentary existed. Grammatical, textual, and historical studies were practically unknown. It was not until the ninth century that Jewish biblical exegesis emerged as a discipline. A combination of many factors was at work. These included the definitive production of the Masoretic apparatus, the impact of the Islamic conquests, the expansion of intellectual horizons, the deepening of linguistic knowledge, the Karaite schism, and the rise of rationalistic criticism to which the works of Ḥiwi al-Balkhī and others testify.

GAONIC EXEGESIS

Systematic exegesis arose in the circles of the geonim. Saadiah ben Joseph (882–942), pioneer grammarian and lexicographer, translated the Bible into Arabic, and appended an Arabic commentary based on sound philology and having a strong philosophical strain. Saadiah's translation and commentary became a model for future exegetes.

Samuel ben Hophni (d. 1013) translated the Pentateuch and composed a commentary to it in Arabic that was widely quoted by later writers. It exhibits rationalistic tendencies, but it is also laced with philosophic and midrashic observations. It was probably this Gaon who formulated the thirty-two exegetical rules commonly ascribed to Rabbi Eliezer ben Yose ha-Gelili.

From Babylon commentary writing spread to Kairouan, North Africa, where the outstanding personality was Hananel ben Hushi'el (d. 1055/1056). Quotations from his Pentateuch commentary indicate a clear and concise style with emphasis on the plain meaning, but a tendency to midrash and anti-Karaite polemics.

KARAITE EXEGESIS

The challenge of the Karaites lay in their rejection of rabbinic tradition and their acceptance of the written text of the entire Bible (not just the Pentateuch) as the valid and sole source of authority for religious law. The movement laid stress on grammar and lexicography, as well as on the plain meaning of the text. Nevertheless, because of its inherently defensive character, its strong polemical trend, and its need to forge an alternative halakic system, Karaite exegesis never reached its full potential.

The ninth and tenth centuries were the period of its greatest efflorescence, when such major exegetes as Benjamin ben Moses Nahāwendī, Daniel ben Moses al-Qūmisī, Jacob al-Qirqisānī, the lexicographer David ben Abraham Alfasi, Salmon ben Jeroham, and Japhet ben Ali ha-Levi were active. Japhet was the most prolific and most original of all Karaite exegetes. In the following century Aaron ben Jeshuah and Jeshuah ben Judah were the outstanding figures. This golden age of Karaite scholarship produced translations of the Bible into Arabic and commentaries. Despite emphasis on the plain meaning of Scripture, Karaites often resorted to allegorical interpretation for theological purposes and to strained exegesis for halakic ends.

The decline of Arabic-speaking centers of Jewish culture led to the rise of new communities in Byzantium, where Hebrew became the cultural medium. The thirteenth century witnessed renewed Karaite creativity in which biblical exegesis enjoyed the greatest popularity. Jacob ben Reuben ha-Sepharadi, Judah ben Elijah Hadassi, and Tobias ben Moses ha-Avel were the most prominent representatives.

THE SPANISH SCHOOL

By the middle of the tenth century the center of Jewish life had shifted to Muslim Spain, where the study of the Hebrew language reached unparalleled scientific maturity. The first known commentary, that of Joseph ben Isaac ibn Abitur (tenth–eleventh centuries) on Psalms, is midrashic and does not yet show the impact, but thereafter, Spanish Jewish exegesis reached a degree of sophistication unsurpassed elsewhere in the Middle Ages. Jonah Abū'l-Walīd Merwān ibn Janāḥ (ca. 985–ca. 1040) wrote no commentaries, but his philological works are replete with invaluable exegetical material. He insisted on using correct manuscripts, employed Semitic cognates, emphasized the importance of context to determine meaning inductively, and propounded theories of ellipsis and verbal substitution that, in effect, constitute textual emendation. The prevailing liberal spirit is illustrated by the suggestion of Isaac Abu Ibrahim ibn Yashush (982–1056) that Genesis 36:31ff. is an interpolation from the late monarchy period. Moses ben Samuel ha-Kohen Gikatilla (Chiguatilla, d. ca. 1080), who based his commentaries on sound philology and rationalized miracles, tried to uncover the historical setting of individual prophecies. He even questioned the unity of the Book of Isaiah and the Davidic authorship of several psalms. Opposition to such theories is evidenced in the commentaries of Judah ben Samuel ibn Balᶜam (d. ca. 1090).

Exegesis of a different type was generated by the devotion of Spanish Jews to philosophy. This resulted in the need both to support the teachings of philosophy by reference to Scripture, and to reconcile reason with revelation. The Neoplatonist Solomon ben Judah ibn Gabirol (*ca.* 1020–*ca.* 1057) seems to have pioneered this system in Spain. Generally its devotees did not write commentaries, but an enormous amount of scriptural exegesis is ensconced in their philosophical works. Such is the case with Baḥya ben Joseph ibn Paquda (*fl. ca.* 1080) in his *Ḥovot ha-Levavot* (Duties of the heart), with Abraham bar Ḥiyya (*d. ca.* 1136) in his *Hegyon ha-Nefesh ha-Aẓuvah* (Meditation of the sad soul), and with Joseph ben Jacob ibn Ẓaddik (*d.* 1149) in his *Sefer ha-Olam ha-Katan* (Book of the microcosm). The philosophic-allegoric school of biblical exegesis found its culmination in the *Moreh Nevukhim* (Guide for the perplexed), of Moses Maimonides (1135–1204), which centered on Aristotelianism. At the heart of the system was the presupposition of the multiple sense of the text, the metaphoric-esoteric alongside the literal-exoteric. A vast erudition in the form of careful linguistic and semantic analysis was invested in this work, which also dealt with substantive issues of biblical theology.

By the thirteenth century the Christian reconquest had engulfed most of Spanish Jewry. Judeo-Arabic scholarship was fast fading; intellectual horizons were narrowing. The salvaging of much of the past scholarship was the work of Abraham ben Meïr ibn Ezra (1089–1164), a stellar exegete and polymath anthologizer and synthesizer. His commentaries, many now lost, display originality, critical acumen, an allusively insinuated rationalism, and Neoplatonic ideas. Written in Hebrew, they had a popularity exceeded only by Rashi's works.

Hebrew was henceforth the literary medium of Spanish Jewry. Biblical studies became less rationalistic and more pietistic, especially under the impact of the advancing mystical movement. Mysticism is first discernible in the commentaries of Rabbi Moses ben Naḥman, also known as Naḥmanides or Ramban (1194–1270), a scholar of immense rabbinic learning. It becomes more pronounced with Baḥya ben Asher ben Ḥlava (thirteenth century) and in the commentary on the Pentateuch of Jacob ben Asher (*ca.* 1270–1340).

The last of the Spanish school was Isaac ben Judah Abrabanel (1437–1508), whose prolixity and discursiveness, as well as his avoidance of philology, tended to obscure the worth of his innovations, such

as attention to the realia of biblical life, to the political system of ancient Israel, and to propaedeutics in the form of introductions to individual books. He opposed both rationalistic and philosophic-allegorical interpretations, and eschewed mysticism. He even utilized Christian commentators.

THE SCHOOL OF NORTHERN FRANCE

More or less contemporaneously with the flowering of biblical scholarship in Muslim Spain, an important school of commentators emerged in northern France. Its intellectual pursuits were far more circumscribed than those in Spain. Neither philosophical speculation nor advanced grammatical and lexicographical achievements were produced. Biblical study was influenced by the methods and techniques locally employed in intensive talmudic learning. The distinguishing mark of this school was the determined effort to recover the plain sense of Scripture.

While the first known commentator in northern France was Menahem ben Ḥelbo (eleventh century), who appears to have dealt only with the Prophets and Hagiographa, the real founder of the school and its most illustrious representative was Rabbi Solomon ben Isaac, known as Rashi (1040–1105). This master exegete commented on practically the entire Bible, employing a style that is a model of lucidity, concision, and simplicity. He struck a harmonious blend of the literal sense with midrashic interpretation but favored the former. The bulk of his comments are drawn from rabbinic literature, yet his genius lay in judicious selectivity and stylistic reworking to produce a uniform style. Like others in France he utilized the vernacular when deemed necessary, thereby indirectly providing an invaluable resource for research into that language. The impact of his commentaries on future generations is incalculable. Rashi's work became a classic in its own right and was studied for its own sake. It greatly influenced such Christian scholars as the Victorines, and especially Nicholas of Lyre.

The descendants and disciples of Rashi in northern France and Germany, known as the Tosaphists (addendors) because of their additions to his talmudic commentaries, also engaged in Bible research. Joseph Kara (*b. ca.* 1060/1070) wrote extensively on the Prophets and Hagiographa. He placed greater emphasis on the plain sense than did Rashi, displayed a certain critical acumen, and was concerned with the inner dynamics of the text. Rabbi Samuel ben Meïr, also known as Rashbam (*ca.* 1085–*ca.*

1174), was by far the most notable after his grandfather Rashi. He rigorously eschewed homiletics, showed a highly refined linguistic sense, had a knowledge of the Vulgate, and initiated polemics against christological interpretations of Scripture. He even gave explanations that opposed rabbinic legal exegesis. Eliezer of Beaugency (*fl.* twelfth century) followed the same path with still greater consistency. Joseph ben Isaac Bekhor Shor (*fl. ca.* 1130) displayed markedly critical proclivities in his commentary on the Pentateuch. He is conscious of varying versions of the same narrative, explains away anthropomorphisms, rationalizes miracles, and opposes allegorical interpretations while also engaging in anti-christological polemics.

The grave deterioration in the position of the Jews of northern France following the widespread massacres perpetrated by the crusaders led to the eclipse of this school.

THE SCHOOL OF SOUTHERN FRANCE

By contrast, Provence was the scene of an efflorescence of Jewish learning in the twelfth century, the Jews interacting with both neighboring Muslim Spain and the local Christian communities. The region became a haven for Spanish Jewish refugees from Almohad persecution. The dynamic community thus emerged as a meeting place of cultures and the gateway through which much of Spanish Jewish scholarship in Arabic was mediated in Hebrew to the Jews of Christian Europe. It is understandable that its scholarship became a creative blend of different exegetical trends. For this the Tibbon and Kimḥi families were largely responsible. The former translated diverse classics from Judeo-Arabic into Hebrew. Samuel ben Judah ibn Tibbon (*ca.* 1160–*ca.* 1230) wrote a philosophical commentary on Ecclesiastes, while his son Moses (*fl.* thirteenth century) composed one on the Pentateuch and Canticles.

The Kimḥis were the true representatives of the Provençal school of exegesis. Joseph Kimḥi (*ca.* 1105–*ca.*1170) set the tone, being the first to use the philological-critical approach, eschewing the midrashi system that characterized the earlier period, as exemplified by the works of Moses ha-Darshan (mid eleventh century). His son David Kimḥi (*ca.* 1160–*ca.* 1235), a synthesizer of much originality, was one of the greatest medieval exegetes. His commentaries are distinguished by their elegant Hebrew style, and by the skill with which text and exposition are interwoven. Philology, a concern for structure and order, a sensitivity to biblical stylistics, philosophical

interpretation, and occasional homiletics are all harmoniously integrated. David Kimḥi's works constitute the high-water mark of Provençal scholarship. After him came Menahem ben Solomon Meiri (1249–1316), the last of the synthesizers. The voluminous commentaries of the encyclopedic Rabbi Levi ben Gershom, also known as Ralbag or Gersonides (1288–1344), are of a different kind, being thoroughly philosophical and moralistic.

ITALY

Italian scholars generally contributed little to the field, being largely attracted to philosophical and mystical interpretations. Shemariah ben Elijah ben Jacob (1275–1355) and Menahem ben Benjamin Recanati (late thirteenth–fourteenth centuries) best represent this school. An exception was Isaiah ben Elijah di Trani "the Younger" (*d. ca.* 1280), who still pursued the plain meaning and philological analysis. His interpretations often tacitly presuppose textual emendation. Also worthy of mention is Immanuel ben Solomon of Rome (*ca.* 1261–after 1328), who composed numerous sober commentaries and a work on biblical hermeneutics.

By the end of the Middle Ages, Jewish biblical scholarship had atrophied. The intense persecutions and expulsions throughout Europe favored the consolidation of past learning more than original creativity. Through the agency of printing, the Hebrew Bible, together with its classical commentaries, gained mass circulation and popularization. At the same time printing became a contributing factor to the loss of much of Jewish exegetical literature of the Middle Ages; what did not attract the attention of the printers was doomed, at best, to a precarious survival, and more often than not to total oblivion.

BIBLIOGRAPHY

Irving A. Agus, "Rashi and His School," in *World History of the Jewish People*, 2nd ser., II, *The Dark Ages*, Cecil Roth, ed. (1966); Eliyahu Ashtor, *The Jews of Moslem Spain*, Aaron Klein and Jenny Machlowitz Klein, trans., 2 vols. (1973–1979); Simḥah Assaf, *Tekufat ha-geonim ve-sifrutah* (The Gaonic period and its literature) (1955); Wilhelm Bacher, "Die Bibelexegese. Vom Anfange des 10. bis zum Ende des 15. Jahrhunderts," in J. Winter and A. Wünsche, *Die jüdische Literatur seit Abschluss des Kanons*, II (1894); Salo W. Baron, *A Social and Religious History of the Jews*, V (1957), 209–285, VI (1958), 235–313; Moshe Gil, *Ḥivi ha-Balkhi ha-kofer me-Ḥurasan* (1965); Solomon D. F. Goitein, *Jews and Arabs, Their Contacts Through the Ages* (1964); Herman Hailperin, *Rashi and the Christian Scholars* (1963); Isaak Heinemann, "Die Wissenschaftliche Allegoristik des jüdischen Mittelalters," in *Hebrew Union College Annual,* 23 (1950–1951); Samuel Poznánski, *The Karaite Literary Opponents of Saadiah Gaon* (1908), and "Mavo ᶜal ḥakhme Tsarefat mefarsche ha-Miḳra" (Introduction to the Bible exegetes of France), in Eliezer of Beaugency, *Perush ᶜal Yeḥezkel ve-Tere ᶜasar* (Commentaries on Ezekiel and the minor prophets) (1913); Erwin I. J. Rosenthal, "Medieval Jewish Exegesis: Its Character and Significance," in *Journal of Semitic Studies,* 9 (1964), and "The Study of the Bible in Medieval Judaism," in G. W. H. Lampe, ed., *The Cambridge History of the Bible,* II (1969); Nahum M. Sarna, "Hebrew and Bible Studies in Medieval Spain," in Richard David Barnett, ed., *The Sephardi Heritage* (1971); Frank Talmage, *David Kimhi, the Man and the Commentaries* (1975); Isadore Twersky, *Rabad of Posquières* (1980); xv–xxv, 1–67; Ephraim E. Urbach, *Ba ᶜalē ha-tosafot* (The Tosaphists) (1955); Meyer Waxman, *A History of Jewish Literature,* 2nd ed., 5 vols. (1960), I, 180–200, 394–415, II, 24–51, 422–446; Israel Zinberg, *A History of Jewish Literature,* B. Martin, trans., 12 vols. (1972–1978), I, 105–162, II, 3–21, 77–131, III, 21–163, 281–189.

NAHUM M. SARNA

[See also **Abraham bar Ḥiyya; Baḥya ben Joseph ibn Paquda; Hebrew Language, Study of; Kara Yusuf; Karaites; Law, Jewish; Levi ben Gerson; Maimonides, Moses; Nahmanides; Pentateuch; Rashi; Saadiah ben Joseph al-Fayyumi; Schools, Jewish; Solomon ben Judah ibn Gabirol; Talmud, Exegesis and Study of.**]

EXEGESIS, LATIN. Medieval Latin exegesis inherited from patristic exegesis both a method of interpreting the Vulgate Bible in accordance with various senses or meanings and a vast number of actual interpretations. Bible study consisted of applying that method and amplifying those interpretations. Theology was the queen of the sciences; the Vulgate was the supreme ruler of the world of books. As the book of books, it could be approached only after extensive training in the liberal arts. As the book of life, it alone offered salvation; unlike other books, it was written by God through the agency of inspired human authors. This double authorship meant double meaning: beyond the literal or historical sense was the spiritual sense, often subdivided into the moral or tropological sense, the allegorical or typological sense, and the anagogical sense. In the early Middle Ages, exegetes focused on the spiritual sense and tended to neglect the literal sense, but by the middle of the thirteenth century the literal sense was at the center of scholarly attention.

MONASTIC EXEGESIS

According to Gregory the Great, the spiritual sense should always be sought beneath the letter of Scripture. Yet in the dedicatory epistle to his *Moralia in Job* he warns against two extremes in interpretation. Certain passages cannot be understood literally because, when the obvious meaning is taken, the reader is led into error, yet on other occasions whoever ignores the literal sense hides the light of truth that has been offered. Gregory transmitted a considerable amount of patristic exegesis to his successors—he had taken much from Augustine, Jerome, and Origen—but his warning against twisting passages into allegorical sense was often ignored.

Among Gregory's successors in the seventh and early eighth centuries the outstanding figures were Isidore of Seville and Bede. Bede produced highly influential commentaries on Mark, Luke, Acts, the Catholic Epistles, and many Old Testament books. Much work remains to be done on the glosses of lesser scholars. The contribution of Irish monastic exegesis is a particularly fruitful area of inquiry. Moreover, there is a vast number of florilegia, collections of "flowers" or extracts from the church fathers strung together, often with little interest in who had said what, to form a continuum of authoritative exegesis.

The theologians of the Carolingian Renaissance remained heavily dependent on such patristic works as they had to hand. The major figures were Alcuin (who had two brilliant pupils in Amalarius of Metz and Hrabanus Maurus), Christian of Stavelot, Smaragdus of St. Mihiel, Claudian of Turin, Walafrid Strabo, Sedulius Scotus, Florus of Lyons, Paschasius Radbertus, and John Scottus Eriugena. The last days of the Carolingians saw the rise of the school of Auxerre under Haimo, then Heiric and his pupil Remigius.

Despite the general preference for allegorical and moral sense, some attention was paid to "the letter." Attempts were made to study Hebrew; Hrabanus undertook a revision of the Vulgate; Eriugena, Remigius, and others had some Greek. Moreover, this period saw the establishment of a more critical method of handling authorities: "questions" were written about problem passages of Scripture. Homiliaries, collections of sermons arranged according to the ecclesiastical calendar, were major repositories of exegesis. One of the best-known examples was composed around 790 by Paul the Deacon, at the request of Charlemagne.

After the death of Remigius early in the tenth century, there was a lull in the history of Bible study, little notable Latin exegesis being produced for more than a century. Cluniac monasticism inclined to the liturgical use of Scripture rather than theological exegesis. In the eleventh century there emerged the first Scholastic commentaries on the Bible. Bruno of Würzburg, Berengar of Tours, and Lanfranc of Bec applied the techniques of the liberal arts to the Bible, producing a more rigorous and economical kind of interpretation, drastically abbreviated in comparison with Carolingian works, with a more effective and lucid arrangement on the manuscript page.

Most of the Latin exegesis produced from the seventh century until the eleventh was specifically monastic, a product of meditation on the sacred text as found in the Bible and the liturgy. Exegesis proceeded through reminiscence, by a play of associations, echoes, similitudes, comparisons and contrasts. The monk learned the Bible by heart; he became a living concordance who, on hearing a scriptural phrase or image, could recall many of the relevant quotations and spiritual senses from elsewhere in Scripture. This profound preoccupation with the words of Scripture was at the root of the monastic love of learning and desire for God.

SCHOLASTIC EXEGESIS

Exegesis through reminiscence continued well into the twelfth century (and beyond), the most outstanding examples being the expositions of the Song of Songs by Bernard of Clairvaux and his friend William of St. Thierry. Without falling into the trap of making large and insupportable distinctions between monasticism and Scholasticism (which had many texts and techniques in common), it is possible to point to basic contrasts between reminiscence and dialectic as interpretative methods, between monks who were living concordances and Schoolmen who resorted to written concordances together with an ever-increasing and gradually improving battery of study aids (including *correctoria,* collections of "sentences," genealogies, and indexes of various kinds). The concomitant development of "distinctions" that linked by theme the interpretations of diverse scriptural passages, and the appearance of such preachers' aids as collections of exemplary stories and treatises on sermon construction, meant that

scriptural exegesis had become more packaged and predigested for the benefit of preachers.

The first great monument of Scholastic exegesis is the *Glossa ordinaria,* a chain of extracts mainly from the church fathers, which was arranged in the form of marginal and interlinear glosses. The marginal glosses were once ascribed to Walafrid Strabo, but now it is accepted that the whole project originated in the school of Laon. Anselm of Laon glossed the Psalter, the Pauline Epistles, and St. John's Gospel; his brother Radulphus was responsible for St. Matthew's Gospel; and his pupil Gilbert the Universal (bishop of London 1128–*ca.* 1134) worked on several Old Testament books. By the middle of the twelfth century the whole Bible was covered, but it should be noted that the *Glossa* did not attain the form found in early printed Bibles until the early thirteenth century.

Anselm's pupils improved on his work. Gilbert of Poitiers refined the gloss on the Pauline Epistles and the Psalter, the latter being corrected by his master Anselm. This commentary became known as the *Media glosatura.* Peter Abelard, who came to regard Anselm as "a barren tree," wrote a brilliant commentary on Romans in which patristic interpretations are sifted in accordance with the dialectical method conveniently summarized in the prologue to his *Sic et non.* Anselm's glosses on the Psalter and St. Paul were soon superseded in the schools by the *Magna glosatura* of Peter Lombard.

The Lombard's *Sententiarum libri quattuor* (written and published 1155–1158) was to become a standard textbook for theologians, in importance second only to the Bible. The first commentaries on the *Sentences* are full of biblical quotations and exegesis, but in the thirteenth and early fourteenth centuries such citation diminished sharply as commentators became preoccupied with philosophy and the science of theology. Another great twelfth-century textbook was the *Historia scholastica* of Peter Comestor, a compendium of sacred history that incorporated much exegesis. It was to exert a considerable influence on vernacular Bible versions.

Once the whole Bible had been glossed, it could be lectured on. The school of Laon had concentrated on certain books of the Bible to the detriment of others; by contrast the school of St. Victor at Paris emphasized the unity of sacred Scripture. Hugh of St. Victor's *Didascalicon* (*ca.* 1127) recommends a program of Bible study in which the student begins with the literal and historical sense (focusing on the historical books of the Bible) and then proceeds to consider the allegorical sense (concentrating on Old Testament prefiguration and its New Testament fulfillment). Two secular masters of the University of Paris, Peter the Chanter and Stephen Langton, both lectured on the greater part of the Bible. Langton's output is impressive: he wrote commentaries on almost every book of the Bible in two to four different versions. Most of his immediate successors at Paris were preoccupied with theological "questions," although Alexander of Hales expounded on a wide range of scriptural books. Langton's only real heir among the seculars was Robert Grosseteste, an ardent defender of the primacy of Bible study.

The new orders of friars redressed the balance by returning to Bible study on a grand scale. Working under the supervision of Hugh of St. Cher, the Dominicans of St. Jacques at Paris produced a commentary on the whole Bible (which draws heavily on earlier exegesis) and a major new study aid, the first verbal concordance to Scripture. In the period 1230–1270 much exegesis was produced and many exegetical aids were devised.

The great Dominican scholars Albert the Great and Thomas Aquinas emphasized the primacy of the literal sense of Scripture, which they defined as the sense intended by the inspired human authors. Aristotelian epistemology, as interpreted in the thirteenth century, gave the human faculties a new dignity; the scriptural exegetes of that period afforded the "body" of Scripture, its literal sense, a corresponding dignity. Moreover, a more rigorous logical method was applied in exegesis. Thomas Aquinas made much of St. Augustine's remark that an argument can be drawn only from the literal sense, and for Thomas "argument" meant strictly logical argument, proceeding by means of premises and syllogism. Allegorical senses, which involve significative "things," are of no use to the logician, who is confined to the literal sense. But there are various kinds of literal sense: sometimes an author may speak plainly, sometimes he may employ figurative expressions. For Aquinas all kinds of figurative language, including metaphors and parables, involve significative "words" and therefore are part of the literal sense.

In the second prologue to his *Postilla litteralis,* the Franciscan scholar Nicholas of Lyra extended St. Thomas' theory of exegesis by suggesting that there is a "double literal sense" in Scripture: the obvious literal sense and the figural literal sense in the Old Testament, which anticipates an obvious literal sense

in the New Testament. Nicholas accused his predecessors of having neglected "the letter" and set about expounding it in detail. He was admirably equipped for the task, having a knowledge of Hebrew and rabbinic exegesis, including Rashi's. Aquinas' theory and Nicholas' practice dealt a powerful blow to the status of allegory as a Scholastic procedure.

But the spiritual sense survived. No late-medieval exegete could conceive of the Bible wiped clean of traditional glosses. Besides, allegorical exegesis continued to be used widely in preaching and in didactic treatises; it was generally held to be of considerable value in teaching morals and sustaining faith. In 1339 Nicholas addressed his moral interpretation of the whole Bible, the *Postilla moralis,* to "preachers of the word of God." In collections of exempla made for preachers, secular and pagan stories were elaborately allegorized to yield moral sense, good examples being the anonymous *Gesta Romanorum* and the *Ovidius moralizatus* of Pierre Bersuire.

Along with this pedagogic interest in pagan myth went an interest in the sapiential books of the Old Testament, which were expounded with many quotations from pagan authors, particularly Aristotle. St. Bonaventure's commentary on Ecclesiastes (written 1254–1257) was a masterpiece of its kind. The English "classicizing friars" of the early fourteenth century—among them Robert Holcot, John Ridevall, and Thomas Waleys—produced popular commentaries on Ecclesiastes, Wisdom, Ecclesiasticus, and Proverbs. John Ridevall commented on Lamentations.

The mid fourteenth century was a lean time for exegesis. When Bible study revived, it was at the hands of the seculars. The literalism of John Wyclif, which encouraged the translation of the Vulgate into English, was an aspect of his realism. He believed that Scripture is true in its every part by virtue of the unique divine style, which he seems to have conceived of as a divine emanation transposed into writing. At Paris another secular, John Gerson, argued against the uninspired rabbinic reading of Scripture in favor of its true literal sense, which may be discovered by reading the words of "our first leaders, the Apostles, the Evangelists and the Prophets." A champion of orthodoxy and tradition, he attacked the Hussite invocation of "Scripture and Scripture's literal sense, which they call 'Scripture alone.'"

Much work remains to be done on Bible study in the fifteenth and early sixteenth centuries. It is important to discover precisely which aspects of late Scholastic exegesis are reflected by the attacks of the reformers, and to see just how medieval they often were.

BIBLIOGRAPHY

The Cambridge History of the Bible, II, *The West from the Fathers to the Reformation,* G. W. H. Lampe, ed. (1962); Margaret T. Gibson, *Lanfranc of Bec* (1978); Jean Leclercq, *The Love of Learning and the Desire for God,* Catharine Misrahi, trans. (1961); Henri de Lubac, *Exégèse médiévale,* 4 vols. (1959–1964); Alastair Minnis, *Medieval Theory of Authorship: Scholastic Literary Attitudes in the Later Middle Ages* (1984); Robert E. McNally, *The Bible in the Early Middle Ages* (1959); Richard H. Rouse and Mary A. Rouse, "The Verbal Concordance to the Scriptures," in *Archivum Fratrum Praedicatorum,* 41 (1974); Beryl Smalley, *The Study of the Bible in the Middle Ages,* 2nd ed. (1952), and *English Friars and Antiquity in the Early Fourteenth Century* (1960); Ceslaus Spicq, *Esquisse d'une histoire de l'exégèse latine au moyen âge* (1944); Friedrich Stegmüller, *Repertorium Biblicum medii aevi,* 11 vols. (1949–1980).

ALASTAIR J. MINNIS

[See also **Abelard, Peter; Albertus Magnus; Alcuin of York; Anselm of Laon; Aquinas, St. Thomas; Bede; Berengar of Tours; Bernard of Clairvaux, St.; Bonaventure, St.; Bruno of Würzburg, St.; Florilegia; Gerson, John; Gilbert of Poitiers; Gloss; Glossators; Gregory I the Great, Pope; Hrabanus Maurus; Hugh of St. Cher; Hugh of St. Victor; Lanfranc of Bec; Langton, Stephen; Nicholas of Lyra; Paul the Deacon; Peter the Chanter; William of St. Thierry; Wyclif, John.**]

EXEGESIS, MIDDLE ENGLISH. Little work has been done on Middle English exegesis considered as a discrete literary phenomenon. We have individual studies of several English works that include scriptural interpretation, but few general trends have emerged to date, save for the great popularity among the English writers of Peter Comestor's *Historia scholastica* (written between 1169 and 1175), a history of mankind that follows the chronology of the Old and New Testaments, incorporating many literal and allegorical explanations of the sacred text.

Most Middle English exegesis (like most Old English exegesis) stems from Medieval Latin exegesis, either by way of close literal translation, or by way of development and expansion, of the Latin material. There are no original Middle English commentaries on the Bible to compare with the full-scale academic commentaries written in Latin, the language of learning in England as elsewhere in medieval Europe. Such Middle English commentaries as we have are translations from either Medieval Latin or Old French originals.

The greater part of Middle English exegesis is found in paraphrases, amplifications, and free renderings of certain books of the Bible. It consists of interpretations and ideas drawn from Medieval Latin exegesis, handled with varying degrees of skill and imagination and intermingled with the personal contributions of the English writers themselves. In passing, one could mention other genres of Middle English literature that may be said to contain some exegesis, such as sermons, didactic treatises, religious allegories like Langland's *Piers Plowman* and the translations of the *Pilgrimage of the Life of Man,* meditations on Christ's life and passion, mystery plays, and morality plays.

What does require emphasis is the pervasive influence of the medievalized Bible, the Latin Vulgate with its medieval apparatus of titles, divisions, glosses, and commentaries, on Middle English literature in general. Works as widely divergent in purpose, content, and style as the anonymous *Pearl* and Chaucer's Monk's Tale are alike at least in their indebtedness to this abundant source. Whenever an author found that a Vulgate passage did not provide all the information he sought, he would turn to the relevant gloss or comment. For example, when Thomas Hoccleve sought clarification of what happened between Pharaoh and Abraham's wife (Gen. 12:11–20), he looked in Nicholas of Lyra's *Postilla litteralis:*

> The bible makiþ no maner of mynde
> Wheþer þat pharao lay by hire oght;
> But looke in lyre, & þere schalt þou fynde,
> ffor to han done it, was he in ful þoght;
> But god preserued hire; he myghte noght; . . .
> *The Regement of Princes (ca.* 1412),
> lines 1,723–1,727

Indeed, a single gloss could have such a wide currency in Middle English writings that it would become a commonplace of the literary tradition. A good case in point is the belief that David, after Nathan had censured him for his sins of murder and adultery, composed *Miserere mei Deus* (Vulgate Psalm 50 [51]) to express his repentance. A statement to this effect is found in Comestor's *Historia scholastica.* It occurs also in a "psalm title" that prefaces the fiftieth psalm in many medieval manuscripts of the psalter, and therefore was reiterated frequently in psalter commentaries, including the *Glossa ordinaria*, Peter Lombard's *Magna glosatura*, and the postils of Hugh of St. Cher and Nicholas of Lyra. In Middle English it is found in the *Cursor mundi*, in a late-fourteenth-century metrical version of the Old Testament (in northern dialect), and in the Cornish miracle play *Origo mundi*.

This example serves also to highlight a procedural difficulty faced by anyone investigating the sources of Middle English exegesis. Medieval Latin exegesis is hieratic and highly repetitive in nature, since each new generation of exegetes would take over many of the interpretations of their teachers and predecessors. Hence, on many occasions it is impossible to say precisely which Latin work provided a detail in question, since it could have come from any one of several possible sources.

The following review will concentrate on the main instances of scriptural interpretation in Middle English as found in three main types of writing: verse Bible versions, prose Bible versions, and Wycliffite exegesis.

EXEGESIS IN VERSE BIBLE VERSIONS

The *Ormulum*, written by an Augustinian canon named Orm in the East Midlands around 1200, is an English verse translation of the Gospel passages in the "massbook" together with an explanation of what they mean and how God-fearing people should respond to them. Its sources include Bede's *In Lucam* and several homilies, which seem to have been consulted in conjunction with a glossed Bible, perhaps some expanded version of the *Glossa ordinaria*. Dr. Morrison has suggested to me that Orm knew a commentary related to Pseudo-Anselm of Laon's *Enarrationes in Evangelium Matthaei*, since this work stands in closer relationship to the *Ormulum* than does the *Glossa* in two main ways: in slight differences of phraseology, and in the presence of substantial information not found in the *Glossa*.

The *Ormulum* indicates some continuity (in terms of intention and technique) with Old English homiletic exegesis, Aelfric's collection of *Catholic Homilies* being the obvious predecessor. Two vast collections of verse homilies in English date from the thirteenth century, the *Northern Homily Cycle* (still largely unedited) and the *South English Legendary*. The former, based on the Mass Gospels, was probably a handbook for the preparation of sermons in English. Lives of the saints were added later. In the case of the latter, the process was exactly the re-

verse: the *South English Legendary* was originally a compilation of saints' lives, the Gospel homilies being a later extension.

La estorie del euangelie (written sometime between 1250 and 1325), a paraphrase of the Gospel narrative with added homiletic materials, makes use of Peter Comestor's *Historia scholastica* and some psalter commentary based on Augustine's. Quite different in design and scope is the so-called Middle English *Genesis and Exodus*, written in rhyming couplets about 1250 in the northern part of Norfolk. This title is misleading, since the poem strings together the narrative sections of the entire Pentateuch, finishing with the death of Moses at the end of Deuteronomy. The influence of Comestor's *Historia* is obvious, but there are many personal touches, some of which indicate a debt to the conventions of romance literature. The romance element is much stronger in a poem of roughly the same date, *Jacob and Joseph*, which has been described by Fowler as "a remarkable example of the minstrel's art." This free adaptation of Genesis 37–46 bears all the hallmarks of oral recitation, and represents a literary genre quite different from the learned homiletic style of *Genesis and Exodus*.

A resounding condemnation of romances is found at the beginning of the *Cursor mundi* (written *ca.* 1300 in the north of England). Nowadays, the poet complains, no one is esteemed unless he has a paramour, but the only true paramour is the Virgin Mary, in honour of whom this work was begun. The poem tells the story of mankind from Creation until Doomsday, dealing at length with all the principal incidents of the Old and New Testaments, which are divided into seven parts in accordance with the seven ages of the world. Its author drew on an unusual variety of French, Latin, and English sources to produce, according to Sarah Horrall, a "well-proportioned compilation of pre-existing material translated into serviceable Midde English verse." Apart from the ubiquitous *Historia scholastica*, he used the Old French Bible of Herman de Valenciennes, an Old French poetic paraphrase of Genesis and Exodus to which was added a poem about the wood of Christ's cross; the Latin *Legende* version of the same story; and two works by Honorius. On occasion, there are brief additions from other sources. Details from these disparate writings are blended with considerable judgment and economy to produce some of the best exegesis in Middle English.

The exegesis in the *Stanzaic Life of Christ,* perhaps written at St. Werburgh's Abbey, Chester, around the middle of the fourteenth century, is drawn from Ranulf Higden's *Polychronicon* (which incorporated much information from the *Historia scholastica*), Jacobus de Voragine's *Legenda aurea,* and Giovanni Balbi's *Catholicon*. This poem considerably influenced the Chester mystery plays, composed sometime around 1375.

Writing in the final quarter of the fourteenth century in the West Midlands, the *Gawain*-poet produced two fine biblical paraphrases, now known as *Patience* and *Cleanness* (or *Purity*). *Patience* follows the Book of Jonah closely, sometimes almost word for word, at other times elaborating considerably. It has been argued that parts of this poem were indebted to the early Latin poem *De Jona et de Ninive* (attributed to Tertullian), but the parallels that have been adduced are inexact. There are occasional echoes of the *Glossa ordinaria. Cleanness* is based on three major examples of God's violent reaction against uncleanness: the flood, the destruction of Sodom and Gomorrah, and Belshazzar's feast. Apart from the Vulgate, the only sources convincingly demonstrated so far are *Mandeville's Travels* and Jean de Meun's *Roman de la Rose*. Certain details may derive from Comestor's *Historia*.

The author of an extended metrical paraphrase of parts of the Old Testament, written toward the end of the fourteenth century in a northern dialect, acknowledges his debt to "the maystur of storyse," that is, Peter Comestor. However, several passages in the poem are taken from the York plays.

EXEGESIS IN PROSE BIBLE VERSIONS

Two complete prose translations of the psalter, the *English Psalter* of Richard Rolle (*d.* 1349) and the *West Midland Prose Psalter,* manifest the influence of exegesis. Rolle's psalter is accompanied by a commentary that translates parts of Peter Lombard's *Magna glosatura,* though the englished psalms themselves owe more to Rolle's personal brand of mysticism. The Lollards produced an interpolated version of this work. The *West Midland Prose Psalter* is based on an Old French psalter. Striking resemblances between the English verse *Surtees Psalter* (written between 1250 and 1300) and Rolle's psalter have been accounted for by the attractive hypothesis that both were indebted to an early Middle English (northern) interlinear gloss on the Vulgate that constituted a partially modernized form of an Old English gloss. Expositions of psalms 91 and 92 (Vulgate) have been attributed to the mystic Walter Hilton (*d.* 1396). A fifteenth-century commentary on the penitential psalms is a translation, by Eleanor Hull, of an Old French original.

There are several prose translations of parts of the New Testament, accompanied by commentaries or glosses in English, and all except one originated in the north of England: (1) The Gospels of St. Mark and St. Luke; text and a commentary (unedited, one MS). (2) The Gospel of St. Matthew; text and a commentary (unedited, two manuscripts). Translations 1 and 2 may be by the same author. (3) The Apocalypse; text and a commentary (Elis Fridner, ed). The prologue is a translation of the Latin Apocalypse prologue of Gilbert of Poitiers; the original Latin version of the actual commentary is elusive. The Lollards produced an interpolated version of this work. (4) The Pauline Epistles; text and brief glosses taken from either the *Glossa ordinaria* or Peter Lombard's *Magna glosatura* (Margaret Powell, ed.). (5) The southern translation of the Pauline Epistles and the Epistles of Sts. James, Peter, and John (Anna C. Paues, ed.). This is introduced by a prologue that defends the translation of the Bible into English. Margaret Deanesly suggests that it is the work of a Wycliffite sympathizer if not an actual Lollard.

In addition, there are two Gospel harmonies in Middle English prose. One is a Lollard translation (made between 1375 and 1400) of Clement of Llanthony's *Unum ex quattuor;* the other, now known as the *Pepysian Gospel Harmony,* is based on an Old French work that its editor was unable to identify. A fifteenth-century *Historye of the Patriarks* is a close translation of the Genesis section in an Old French version of Comestor's *Historia* by Guyart des Moulins.

WYCLIFFITE EXEGESIS

The *Glossed Gospels,* consisting of the Gospel texts in English accompanied by lengthy commentaries in the same language, are Wycliffite in origin, and perhaps the work of John Purvey. The commentaries on Sts. Luke, Mark, and John are extant in two versions; the commentary on Matthew in three. The prologue to "the short exposicioun on Matheu" acknowledges as a source the *Catena aurea* of St. Thomas Aquinas, but there seem to be two or three other sources for each Gospel. For example, while the *Catena aurea* provides the basis for the commentary on Luke, commentaries by Ambrose and Bede were used also. "Taken together," according to Hargreaves, *The Glossed Gospels* make available in English long continuous extracts if not sometimes the entire texts of standard exegetical commentaries of impeccable orthodoxy."

The sources and nature of the glosses designed to accompany the Wycliffite Bible are relatively straightforward. Apart from a few extracts from St. Augustine and the *Glossa ordinaria,* virtually all are attributed to "Lire," that is the *Postilla litteralia* of Nicholas of Lyra. Since Lyra was the "literal" commentator par excellence, the Lollard glosses concentrate on the literal sense of Scripture. Indeed, so pervasive was his influence that, in the later version of the Lollard Bible, the text of the psalter indicates a debt to Lyra's expositions of the Latin text.

The General Prologue (attributed to Purvey), which introduces the later Lollard Bible, derived much of its exegetical theory from the two prologues to the *Postilla litteralis.* Lyra's account of the four senses of Scripture appears in chapter 13; his version of the Tyconian rules of biblical interpretation follows in chapter 14. The latter excursus is colored by the theory of the "double literal sense" of Scripture as defined by Lyra and amplified by Richard FitzRalph in his *Summa in quaestionibus armenorum,* a work mentioned earlier in the General Prologue. In sum, it would seem that Wyclif's followers wished to make available in English not only the Bible but also biblical exegesis, thereby encouraging "symple men of wit" in their attempts to understand Scripture.

BIBLIOGRAPHY

The Cambridge History of the Bible, II, G. W. H. Lampe, ed., *The West from the Fathers to the Reformation* (1969), 362–415; David C. Fowler, *The Bible in Early English Literature* (1976); Elis Fridner, *An English Fourteenth Century Apocalypse Version with a Prose Commentary* (1961); Henry Hargreaves, "Popularizing Biblical Scholarship: The Role of the Wycliffite *Glossed Gospels,*" in W. Lourdaux and D. Verhelst, eds., *The Bible and Medieval Culture* (1979); Sarah M. Horrall, *Cursor Mundi: The Southern Version of Cursor Mundi* (1978); Laurence Muir, "Translations and Paraphrases of the Bible, and Commentaries," in J. Burke Severs, ed., *A Manual of the Writings in Middle English, 1050–1500,* II (1970).

ALASTAIR J. MINNIS

[See also **Bible; Bible, Old and Middle English; Biblical Interpretation; Middle English Literature; Nicholas of Lyra.**]

EXEGESIS, OLD ENGLISH. In the field of scriptural exegesis Anglo-Saxon England is noted as having produced Bede, one of the great authorities of the Western medieval world, and Alcuin, a major figure in Carolingian biblical studies. There were also, however, several important strands of exegetical writing in vernacular literature. These Old English works in no way attempt to emulate the achievements of men like Bede and Alcuin, who were writing in the scholarly language of Latin, but they represent in their various forms a significant extension of teaching of the Bible and its interpretation to a new, less sophisticated audience.

The Old English exegetical writers, closely follow the Latin fathers. Indeed Aelfric (*ca. 955–ca.* 1010), the greatest of them, speaks of himself not as an original writer but as having simply "translated" the Fathers "into our ordinary speech." But he and other Old English writers show considerable flexibility and discretion in their treatment of inherited materials, carefully adapting them to the requirements of their often uneducated audiences. Old English exegetical writings constitute the earliest fairly substantial body of scriptural commentary in any Western vernacular and the first attempt to provide an exposition of the Bible for the unlearned medieval Christian.

GLOSSES AND PROSE TRANSLATIONS OF THE BIBLE

The simplest level of the explication of the text of the Bible in Old English is that found in the interlinear glosses of Latin texts, such as in the Lindisfarne Gospels (glossed in the later tenth century) and in the numerous glossed psalters. These glosses are word-for-word translations into Old English of the Latin text and they seldom move beyond the most basic level of interpretation. It is interesting, however, that in the case of the psalter glosses, particular translations achieve separate lives of their own and are copied into other Latin psalters even though the accompanying Latin text may differ from that used by the original translator. The ninth-century gloss to the Vespasian Psalter is the archetype for one group of psalters. The tenth-century Royal Psalter may be another "germinal" version. Occasionally, brief spiritual glosses appear in the psalters. Usually these are given as an alternative to the literal gloss but sometimes they displace the literal meaning, as when in Psalm 36 (A.V. 37) of the Lambeth Psalter, *terra* is glossed as "the kingdom of heaven" and again as "church."

Like the glosses, the fairly extensive range of prose translations from the later Old English period (tenth and early eleventh centuries) remains for the most part close to the literal meaning of the Latin text; only infrequently are interpretative passages added. Aelfric, in the preface to his translation of the first part of Genesis, is careful to tell his readers that the literal translation he is providing does not give the total meaning of the text. He urges them to be aware also of the deep spiritual meaning that the literal level contains: "I say in advance that this book has a very deep spiritual meaning and I write no more than the naked narrative."

Aelfric had considerable misgivings about translating the Bible into English at all, fearing that the unlearned might be misled by too simplistic a reading of the literal level. His interest in leading the vernacular audience to a deeper appreciation of the meaning of the Bible is seen in his English version of Alcuin's *Interrogationes et responsiones in Genesin* (992–1003) and in his *Letter to Sigeweard,* also known as the *Treatise on the Old and New Testaments* (1005–1010). This latter is Aelfric's own concise exposition of the Bible, stressing the place of each of its books in an overall pattern of unity. Many typological correspondences are briefly pointed out. Aelfric declares indeed, "Every father by word or work plainly gives testimony to the Savior and his coming."

THE PARIS PSALTER AND PSALM 50

The Paris Psalter is a complete translation into Old English of the Book of Psalms, in two parts and by two different authors, both working in the later ninth or the tenth century. The first fifty psalms are translated into prose, the remainder into verse.

The translation of each prose psalm (except the first) is preceded by a short exegetical introduction in Old English, derived from the Latin commentary attributed in the Middle Ages to Bede (*Patrologia latina,* XCIII [1862]). This commentary was itself influenced by the Greek commentary on the Psalms by the Antiochene exegete Theodore of Mopsuestia, but in the Latin work Theodore's historical exposition is combined with a nonliteral interpretation. The Old English author of the introductions has taken over both levels, adapting and reorganizing his Latin material.

The nature of his interpretation may be gauged from the introduction to Psalm 22 (A.V. 23), which may be translated as follows:

David sang this twenty-second psalm when he prophesied concerning the freedom of the people of Israel, how they should be led from the Babylonian captivity and how they should thank God for the favor which they had on the way homewards, and also (he sang it) concerning his own return from exile. And in each of these things which he sings he thanks God for his deliverance from his difficulties. And so did the apostles and all the Christian people at Christ's Resurrection. And also Christian men in this psalm give thanks for their redemption from their sins in baptism.

Thus in its expression of thanksgiving this psalm is applied—in the fourfold method found throughout the prose psalms—to the Israelites, to David, to the apostles singing of Christ, and to every Christian.

The prose translation of the Paris Psalter itself contains brief exegetical additions. The rod and staff of Psalm 22.5 (A.V. 23.4), for example, are explained as "thy correction and thy consolation." It is believed that the translator of the prose psalms was King Alfred and that he was also the author of the introductions.

The verse psalms, composed later than the prose, have found little sympathy among modern scholars, who point to the colorless adverbs and empty phrases with which the lines are filled out. More impressive is the quite separate tenth-century verse translation of Psalm 50 (A.V. 51), the so-called *Kentish Psalm,* found in a different manuscript. This is a very much expanded version of its psalm. The translation proper is preceded by a thirty-line exegesis of the psalm, following the patristic view of Psalm 50 as David's repentance for his sin against Uriah and Bathsheba. The Old English version ends with an epilogue in which the poet expresses his wish that he and his audience may also overcome their sins and earn eternal joy.

AELFRIC'S EXEGETICAL HOMILIES

Earlier Anglo-Saxon homilists, such as the writers of the Blickling and Vercelli collections, make considerable use of exegesis in their work. Aelfric, however, writing in the context of the tenth-century Benedictine Reform, purposely sets out to present exegesis on a much more comprehensive scale and in a more rigorously orthodox way than his predecessors did. Particularly important among his exegetical homilies are his two series of *Catholic Homilies* (989–992), consisting mainly of explications of Gospel passages. As in his other exegetical work Aelfric here distinguishes carefully between the literal sense (*lichamlice andgit*) and the spiritual (*gastlice andgit*), and he concentrates on the latter. The spiritual sense includes typological and tropological (*þeawlic*) aspects, with some additional attention to anagogical meaning. Aelfric's intention is to reveal as fully as he feels appropriate the meaning of the Gospel narrative, following the interpretations of the great patristic authorities, particularly Augustine, Bede, and Gregory the Great. In his reading of the Fathers his major source has been shown to be the existing eighth-century Latin homiliary of Paul the Deacon, a compendious collection of patristic homilies. Aelfric's work involves a thoughtful selection and reshaping of his sources to suit his own interests and needs.

One homily that illustrates the traditional nature of Aelfric's exegesis and at the same time demonstrates his willingness to expand and abridge his sources is that on John 2:1–12, the marriage feast at Cana, closely based on Bede's homily on the same text. Aelfric follows Bede in seeing Christ's attendance at the feast as a mark of his approval of the state of marriage, and in seeing Christ as the bridegroom of the church. He concentrates particularly in this homily on the detail of the six water jars, signifying the six ages of the world. Much of the homily comprises an extended discussion of the meaning of these ages: the typological significance of each of them is explained, and moral and anagogical teaching is occasionally incorporated. Understanding of the spiritual sense, says Aelfric, turns the water of history into pleasant wine to gladden the mind spiritually. He gives this discussion of the six jars proportionately more emphasis than Bede does, seeing it as encapsulating much central Christian teaching. In this homily, as throughout his exegetical writing, he avoids the overly ingenious in favor of what he considers as genuinely helpful to his audience. There is no systematic multileveled discussion in his exegesis, which aims to combine solidity of teaching with clarity.

OLD ENGLISH POETRY

The extent of the influence of exegesis on Old English poetry is still much debated. It is agreed that exegetical references and allusions are found throughout Christian poetry in Old English. It is natural indeed that this should be the case in an age in which rumination on the meaning of the sacred text occupied so central a place in intellectual and spiritual life. But just how systematically Old English

poetry is guided by the influence of exegesis is more controversial.

The first phase of Christian poetry in Old English (seventh and eighth centuries) is noted for the series of scriptural paraphrases in the tradition of the poet Cædmon. Paraphrases such as *Genesis A* and *Daniel* seem more interested in the literal than the allegorical level of their narratives, though some scholars believe that their principles of construction are based on ideas drawn from Latin exegesis. *Exodus,* however, which probably also belongs to this period, encourages spiritual interpretation in a more direct way: the mysteries of Scripture, we hear, are revealed to us with the help of the keys of the Spirit (*Gastes cægon*), and God grants us the rewards of heaven through the teaching of scholars (*boceras*). *Exodus* itself consciously exploits the techniques of prefiguration and fulfillment, presenting the history of the Israelites as a unified and triumphant process. The poem strongly suggests that the events it describes have a significance beyond the purely historical.

In poetry of the ninth and tenth centuries the influence of exegesis is present to varying degrees: *Christ II (The Ascension),* by the ninth-century poet Cynewulf, is based on a homily by Gregory the Great; exegetical material is also employed in *Christ I (Advent Lyrics)*; other poems that include exegetical ideas from Latin tradition are *Christ III* and *The Phoenix.* There are also from this period explanatory elaborations on certain prayers in Old English, most notably *The Lord's Prayer II.*

Versions of biblical and apocryphal material from the ninth and tenth centuries offer the same problems of interpretation as the earlier paraphrases. It has been suggested that the transformation of the story of the Fall in *Genesis B* results from the poet's knowledge of Latin exegesis, but some critics would look to quite different sources to explain this transformation. The Old Testament poem *Judith* is a thoughtful recreation of its biblical text, but it avoids the kind of explicit exegetical elaboration found in the commentaries. It is thus clear that as well as being influenced by the traditions of Latin writing, Old English poets showed considerable variety and individuality in their response to biblical material.

BIBLIOGRAPHY

The Cambridge History of the Bible, II, G. W. H. Lampe, ed., *The West from the Fathers to the Reformation* (1969); J. Douglas Bruce, "The Anglo-Saxon Version of the Book of Psalms Commonly Known as the Paris Psalter," in *PMLA*, **9** (1894); David C. Fowler, *The Bible in Early English Literature* (1976); Milton McC. Gatch, *Preaching and Theology in Anglo-Saxon England: Aelfric and Wulfstan* (1977); Henry Hargreaves, "From Bede to Wyclif: Medieval English Bible Translations," in *Bulletin of the John Rylands Library*, **48** (1965–1966); Bernard F. Huppé, *Doctrine and Poetry; Augustine's Influence on Old English Poetry* (1959); Minnie C. Morrell, *A Manual of Old English Biblical Materials* (1965); Cyril L. Smetana, "Ælfric and the Early Medieval Homiliary," in *Traditio*, **15** (1959).

HUGH MAGENNIS

[See also **Aelfric; Alcuin of York; Anglo-Saxon Literature; Bede; Bible; Bible, Old and Middle English; Cædmon; Church Fathers.**]

EXEMPLUM, an example or cautionary tale. The medieval exemplum, so favored by the church in its teaching and preaching, belonged to a genre of wisdom literature that had long been fashionable in classical and Eastern civilizations. Any story could become an exemplum as long as it contained a moral. There were exempla from Holy Writ, saints' lives, miracles, visions, the confessional, contemporary events, anecdotes, and the experience of the writers, as well as from secular legends, folktales, bestiary lore, literary cycles like the *matière de Bretagne* and *de Troie*, classical literature and history, fables, the *Roman de Renart,* and even the fabliaux, the *Arabian Nights,* and other stories of eastern provenience found originally in the *Panchatantra* and the Buddhist Jatakas. Alphabets of tales—the *Alphabetum narrationum,* for example—facilitated quick reference.

Exempla were used by Ambrose and Augustine in the fourth century and by St. Isidore and Pope Gregory the Great in the seventh. Gregory gave the genre its greatest impetus by using exempla in his *Dialogues* and recommending their use to others. The High Middle Ages brought forth many clerical collections—those of Jacques de Vitry and Caesarius of Heisterbach, for example—as well as repositories of tales of secular origin such as the *Legenda aurea* and the *Gesta Romanorum.*

The pulpit became the greatest disseminator when Franciscans and Dominicans broadcast exempla far and wide in the thirteenth century. In their desire to captivate congregations with fresh stories, however, the friars preached many unseemly tales. A story about an adulterous wife, later to be used in the *Decameron,* was justified by the poorly contrived moral that "women cannot be trusted." Eventually church councils prohibited the use of such tales in the pulpit and threatened to defrock those who disseminated them.

Secular Latin exempla were produced quite early. The eleventh-century *Disciplina clericalis* of Petrus Alfonsi, drawn entirely from Eastern wisdom books and beast tales, may have been the most influential, since its tales appeared in most collections. It is to collections in the vernaculars, however, that the modern short story owes its emergence. Secular authors sought to win audiences through their style and narrative techniques, and their moralizations were more often practical than merely pious.

Spain was very rich in Eastern exempla. Reworked translations from the *Book of Sindibad, Kalīla wa-Dimna,* and *Barlaam and Josaphat* appeared in such literary masterpieces as *El conde Lucanor,* the *Corbacho,* the *Libro de buen amor,* and the only *alphabetum* in medieval Spanish, the *Libro de los exenplos por a.b.c.* by Archdeacon Clemente Sánchez. In England, drawing from Latin and vernacular collections, Gower retold exempla in his *Confessio Amantis,* as did Chaucer in this *Canterbury Tales.* In France *Les quinze joyes de marriage* and *Cent nouvelles nouvelles* owed much to exempla, as did the works of the Catalonian author Ramon Lull.

BIBLIOGRAPHY

Joseph Bédier, *Les Fabliaux, études de littérature populaire et d'histoire littéraire du moyen âge* (1893); Joseph A. Mosher, *The Exemplum in the Early Religious and Didactic Literature of England* (1911); Gaston Paris, *Les Contes orientaux dans la littérature française du moyen âge,* 2nd ser. (1887); Petrus Alfonsi, *Disciplina Clericalis,* Alfons Hilka and Werner Söderhjelm, eds. (1911), in English as *The Scholar's Guide,* Joseph R. Jones and John E. Keller, trans. (1969); Stith Thompson, *The Folktale* (1951); J.-Th. Welter, *L'Exemplu dans la littérature religieuse et didactique du moyen âge* (1927).

JOHN KELLER

[See also, in addition to the individual works and authors, **Preaching and Sermon Literature.**]

EXILARCH (Hebrew: *rosh ha-golah;* Aramaic: *resh galuta*), head of the Jewish diaspora in Babylonia (Iraq). Although the exilarchs claimed descent from King David, through King Jehoiachin, exiled to Babylonia, the office apparently existed only from the middle of the second century until 1401. The first exilarch of the Arab era was Bustanai (d. 670), who founded a new dynasty with his Jewish and Persian wives.

Muslim rulers apparently granted the exilarch the same recognition as the katholikos, head of the Nestorian community in Baghdad, who (according to a twelfth-century letter of appointment) was authorized to mediate disputes, dispense justice, supervise charitable funds, and organize the collection of the poll tax. Anyone disobeying the katholikos was liable to punishment. One can also deduce the usual functions of the exilarch from letters of appointment granted by the Abbasids in 1208, 1247, and 1250 to the heads of the Jewish academies in Baghdad, who then held most of the power formerly enjoyed by the exilarch. These letters describe the exilarch as a judge: members of the Jewish community had to obey his instructions and pay him taxes. He had to enforce the "Covenant of Omar"—the discriminatory regulations of Islam applied to the dhimmis (Jews and Christians)—and follow the orders of the caliph.

Although the position was hereditary, it passed not always to the firstborn, but to the family member who was most suitable and accepted by the academy heads of Sura and Pumbedita and the important merchants. The academy heads and the exilarch were dependent on each other, as the election of each required the confirmation of the other. The appointment of the exilarch was an occasion for glorious ceremony and popular festivity, as described by Nathan ben Isaac ha-Bavli in the tenth century.

The exilarch's income was derived from taxes imposed on every adult under his jurisdiction, fees for the execution of documents, and gifts from abroad. His honor and power were considered the fulfillment of the verse "The scepter shall not depart from Judah, nor the ruler's staff from between his feet" (Gen. 49:10). This verse was used to support rabbinical enactment of his right of penalization—bans, fines, imprisonment, and flogging—as well as his right to appoint judges. In theory the exilarch exercised these prerogatives over all diaspora Jews; in fact he rarely put this theory into practice. His penal authority was restricted by Caliph al-Ma'mūn (813–833), leaving him only the right to proclaim the ban. Later his power was extended to include the right to sentence offenders.

The right to appoint judges was disputed by the heads of the academies in Babylonia. Until the reign of al-Ma'mūn, the exilarchs alone appointed judges, but after 1175 only the heads of the academies did so. The exilarch had at his disposal a tribunal known as bava de-maruta (gate of the master). If he was learned, he headed it himself. He participated in decisions concerning new halakic regulations (takkanoth), which were circulated to communities abroad after being signed by him and by the heads of the academies.

The exilarch often had personal connections with sages and leaders in distant places, such as Spain. As a formality, he gave his consent to the appointment of the nagid—ra'īs al-yahūd—in Egypt in the Fatimid period. During the twelfth century the Jews of Yemen were placed under the formal "authority" of the exilarch, whose name was invoked in synagogues before sermons and before the reading of the Torah. Beginning in the eleventh century some members of exilarchal families (nesi'im) arrived in communities outside Baghdad, such as Mosul, Aleppo, and Damascus, where they either attained positions of leadership or gave formal assent to the authority exercised by local leaders.

BIBLIOGRAPHY

Walter Fischel, "Arabische Quellen zur Geschichte der babylonischen Judenheit im 13. Jahrhundert," in Monatsschrift für Geschichte und Wissenschaft des Judentums, 79 (1935); Louis Ginsberg, Geonica, I (1968), 14–36, 44–46, 54–66; A. Kremer, "Zwei arabische Urkunden," in Zeitschrift der Deutschen Morgenländischen Gesellschaft, 7 (1853, repr. 1966); H. Tykocinski, "Bustanai Rosh ha-Golah," in Devir, 1 (1923).

ELIEZER BASHAN

[See also Jews (various articles).]

EXIMENIS, FRANCESC. See Eiximenis, Francesc.

EXONARTHEX, a transverse vestibule or porch preceding the facade of a church. It may also double as the terminal portico of an atrium. Exonarthexes appear during the early Christian period, as at the church of the Acheiropoietos in Thessaloniki (ca. 470), and are a standard feature of post-iconoclastic Byzantine churches such as Daphni (ca. 1080).

LESLIE BRUBAKER

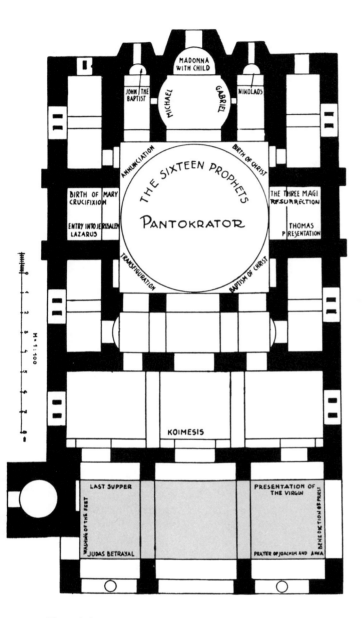

MADONNA WITH CHILD

JOHN THE BAPTIST

MICHAEL

GABRIEL

NIKOLAOS

ANNUNCIATION

BIRTH OF CHRIST

THE SIXTEEN PROPHETS

BIRTH OF MARY
CRUCIFIXION

THE THREE MAGI
RESURRECTION

PANTOKRATOR

ENTRY INTO JERUSALEM
LAZARUS

THOMAS
PRESENTATION

TRANSFIGURATION

BAPTISM OF CHRIST

M = 1:100

KOIMESIS

LAST SUPPER

PRESENTATION OF
THE VIRGIN

WASHING OF THE FEET

BENEDICTION OF PRIEST

JUDAS BETRAYAL

PRAYER OF JOACHIM AND ANNA

Plan of the cathedral at Daphni. The shaded area is the exonarthex. FROM E. DIEZ AND O. DEMUS, BYZANTINE MOSAICS IN GREECE (HARVARD UNIV. PRESS, © 1931)

EXPLORATION BY WESTERN EUROPEANS. For Western Christians, pilgrimages to the holy places played an important role in learning about the rest of the world. At the beginning of the sixth century, Avitus, bishop of Vienne, sent a mission to Je-

rusalem to recover a fragment of the true cross. In the middle of the same century, Saint Radegonde sent a similar mission from Poitiers. About 670 the Frankish bishop Arculf journeyed to the Holy Land by way of Constantinople, Crete, and Syria. He also visited Egypt, where he admired the ancient lighthouse of Alexandria. His account of his travels is lively but inaccurate; he believed that Jerusalem was the center of the earth.

At about the same time, a map drawn at Ravenna showed the earth as far east as the Bay of Bengal. In its depiction of Africa south of a rather fantastic representation of the Nile, the Ravenna map shows a watercourse that does not flow into the ocean; this is probably the last trace of vague and misunderstood knowledge inherited from antiquity. In the eighth century a map drawn by a Spanish monk named Beatus extends to Ceylon, called by its ancient name, "Tabrobane," but even the representation of western Europe is very inaccurate. In the ninth century the Irishman Dicuil claimed that there was a canal between the Mediterranean and the Red Sea, but since his geography is quite wrong in other matters, little importance should be attached to this statement.

Numismatic and archaeological evidence proves that commercial relations between western and eastern Europe did exist. Anglo-Saxon and Frisian sceattas (silver pennies, quite like those of the Frankish kingdom) have been found from southern France to southern Russia; from the valleys of the Rhône and the Meuse through England and Scandinavia and along the Russian rivers. Thus, in the early Middle Ages there was a southern route to eastern Europe and the Middle East—this was the one taken by pilgrims to the Holy Land—and a northern route connecting western and eastern Europe by way of Scandinavia. Trade also flowed in the opposite direction, for all along these routes buried Arab coins have been found.

After an early period in which the northern seas were controlled by Frisian, Anglo-Saxon, and Irish sailors, the Scandinavians took the leading role in relations between East and West. They operated simultaneously as pirates, conquerors, traders, and explorers.

The Scandinavians started their explorations at the beginning of the eighth century. By then the three Scandinavian nations had already begun to take shape. Denmark was formed by the union of the Jutes (who inhabited the Jutland peninsula), the Danish islanders, and the inhabitants of Scania (the south of modern Sweden). "Sweden" at that time was located farther north, around Lake Mälar. "Norway" was the long road of the North (Nordhrvegr). There was little urbanization; society was dominated by wealthy rural landowners who led their men to hunting meets or to war (for which they built ships). Above these chiefs were the jarls (earls), the chiefs of districts. The maritime expansion of the Vikings was led by the clan chiefs and the jarls.

The Vikings, the men of the *vik* (bay), were first pirates and then conquerors. Historians have given this name to all Scandinavians who took part in maritime expeditions. In Russia and the Near East, which the Swedes reached by sea and through the river valleys, however, it would be better to use the term Varangian (in Russian, *varjag*) for these merchants, mercenary soldiers, or adventurers. During the eighth century the Swedes founded settlements in Latvia and Lithuania. The Norwegians conquered the islands north of Scotland. By the end of the century, the northeastern and southwestern coasts of England were being attacked. Ireland was reached in 795 and Gaul, on the Vendée coast, in 799. The Danes first attacked Schleswig and, after 810, all of western Europe.

Each of the Scandinavian peoples had its own forms and areas of expansion. The Norwegians were both pirates and colonizers. Their principal route went from the region of Bergen to the Shetland Islands, where it forked. One branch went along the east coast of England. The other, passing through the Orkneys and the Hebrides, reached Ireland. From Ireland it later went to Gaul, Spain, and the Strait of Gibraltar. In the ninth century the Norwegians sailed northwest from the Shetlands, reached the Faeroes, and then Iceland. From Iceland they took their ships to Greenland and to America in the tenth century.

The Danes usually embarked from Jutland and followed the southern coast of the North Sea. One group then went toward the eastern shore of England, while another, passing through the English Channel, ranged along the Atlantic coast of Gaul. The Varangians of Sweden, starting from the eastern shore of the Baltic, penetrated the Russian interior by following the rivers, portaging from one to another. From the Dvina and the Volkhov they reached the Volga, which they followed to the Caspian Sea. The Dnieper took them to the Black Sea, and by 860 they had reached the Bosporus and Constantinople. All their piratical and conquering expeditions were also voyages of exploration that enlarged knowledge of the European continent.

By the middle of the ninth century, the Norwegians had made extensive conquests. In Ireland they took Dublin in 836. Limerick, at the mouth of the Shannon, was the starting point for their invasion of the interior, but Irish resistance blocked their expansion. They then contented themselves with occupying the best seaports, where they founded city-states: Dublin, Wexford, Waterford, Cork, and Limerick.

In Spain the Norwegians sailed up the Guadalquivir in 844 and sacked Seville. In 859 they reached the coast of Morocco, entered the Mediterranean, went up the Rhône, and pillaged the coast of Italy. To the north they had colonized the Faeroes by the beginning of the ninth century. A tempest drove some of their ships to the shores of Iceland about 860, and settlement of that large island began about ten years later. It was fairly suitable for raising livestock, and attracted leaders of Norwegian clans, some of whom settled there with their followers and slaves (the latter were often Irish). The *Landnámabók,* which is both a sort of land register and an epic poem (composed toward the end of the twelfth century), contains oral traditions about the first settlers. They may have numbered about 20,000 by the end of the tenth century. Iceland soon became the center of Scandinavian literature. It was there that the sagas, collected in the thirteenth-century *Eddas* of Snorri Sturluson, originated, and it is these sagas that contain information on the Norwegian discovery of America.

It was the discovery of Greenland that made possible the voyage from Iceland to America. In 985 a chieftain named Eric the Red was banished from Iceland for three years as a murderer. He sailed west with thirty-five ships, but reached the great central glacier of Greenland with only fourteen. Turning south, he rounded Cape Farewell and found a habitable region on the west coast. He occupied this land and later increased the number of inhabitants by bringing in a group of Norwegian peasants from Iceland, ultimately developing two settled areas with about 300 farms. A temporary warming of the climate made possible the establishment of a dairy industry. Trappers explored the regions to the North, up to about 72°N. latitude. The Greenland settlement prospered until the twelfth century—it even had its own bishop—but a return of cold weather led to its decline. Left to its fate, the colony vanished during the fifteenth century, probably as a result of attacks by the Eskimos.

Snorri Sturluson reports in the *Heimskringla* that in 1001 the first Christian king of Norway, Olaf

Tryggvason, sent Leif, son of Eric the Red, to Greenland to spread Christianity there, but that Leif was driven west by currents and discovered a new land (Vinland), perhaps Nova Scotia. It is not impossible, however, that the Icelander Bjarni Herjulfsson had reached Nova Scotia a few years earlier. Other expeditions came a little later—one by Thorvald Ericsson (brother of Leif) and one by Thorfinn Karlsefni. The latter discovered Helluland (Stoneland), probably Labrador. He saw great flat stones there (hence the name), arctic foxes, and, to the south, forests in which there were bears. Still further south, the land seemed more fertile. This attracted the Icelanders to Newfoundland, which they called Markland (Woodland). From Markland they returned to Vinland. An attempt to colonize this area was ephemeral, and there is no certain archaeological evidence of its location. Nevertheless, the Norwegians of Iceland were the first Europeans to discover America. News of this discovery, however, did not spread through Europe, and the rediscovery of America by Columbus owed nothing to the voyages of the Scandinavians.

The Norwegians also deserve credit for the discovery of the White Sea, beyond the North Cape and the Kola peninsula. It was found at the end of the ninth century by a chieftain named Ottar.

In Russia, probably in the eighth century, the Varangians founded Aldeigjuborg, a fortification surrounding a sanctuary at the mouth of the Volkhov, on Lake Ladoga. The Swedish conquest spread out from this fort. Rurik founded Holmgard—in Slavic it became Novgorod. Of the followers of this chieftain, one occupied Polotsk, another Rostov, and a third Bjelo Osero. Others went as far south as Känugard (Kiev), the limit of the region of Khazar influence, and created a principality there.

Historians of Russia, both Scandinavian and Slavic, have a quite different interpretation of the Swedish impact. It seems, however, that it was contact with the Khazars (a people of Turkish origin who then held the south of Russia) that gave the Swedes the idea of becoming the political heads of the existing Slavic populations. Slavic towns hired, from time to time, Varangian mercenaries whose leaders seized power and founded dynasties. One of these dynasties, that of Kiev, gained primacy over the others and in the end managed to unify the city-states controlled by Varangian princes. It was the Swedish princes of Kiev who sent their Slavic subjects against Constantinople in 860 and again in 941.

From Russia, Swedes reached Byzantium and Baghdad. At Byzantium they formed the Varangian guard that served the Byzantine emperor in the tenth and eleventh centuries, in territories as far as Syria to the east and Sicily and Apulia to the west.

To Baghdad, capital of the Abbasid caliphs and of their successors, the Swedes often came as merchants, and at times as raiders. Muslim Asia was for them the "Sarkland"; they reached the southern shore of the Caspian and Uzbekistan, in the vicinity of Tashkent. Commercial relations with these regions were extensive, as the enormous finds of Muslim silver coins in Sweden, and especially of Iranian dirhams, testify. These deposits are especially numerous on the island of Gotland, a trading center.

While Scandinavian expansion and discoveries were increasing the geographic knowledge of the West, Jewish merchants were playing an important role by assuring relations between East and West through central and southern Europe.

After the fall of the Western Empire, long-distance commerce in the Mediterranean fell into the hands of Syrians, Greeks, and Jews. The Arab invasions of the seventh and eighth centuries turned Syrian merchants toward Asia and made the Byzantines more sedentary. From the ninth century on, the Jews were almost solely responsible for commercial relations among western Europe, Byzantium, the Islamic world, and the East. Small Jewish colonies were established in important commercial centers, and the fact that the Jews were neither Catholic, nor Orthodox, nor Muslim, but were universally recognized, opened many doors to them. To Christians as well as to Muslims they seemed for some time to be the great travelers. An Arab writer of the ninth century, Ibn Khurdadbi, says in *The Book of Roads and Kingdoms*:

These merchants speak Arabic, Persian, Romanian [Byzantine Greek], Frankish, Spanish, and Slavic. They travel from West to East and from East to West, by land and by sea. They bring from the West eunuchs, female slaves, boys, brocade, beaver skins, marten skins, and other furs, and spices. They sail from The Mediterranean coast of France, bound for Al-Farama, on the Strait of Suez. There they load their wares on the backs of camels and cross to the Red Sea. They go to Al-Jar and Jidda in Arabia, to Beluchistan, India, and China. On their return from China, they buy aloe wood, musk, camphor, cinnamon, and other Oriental products, and embark again on the western sea. Some sail to Constantinople to sell their wares to the Byzantines; some go to the palace of the king of the Franks [Aachen] to sell their goods. Sometimes Jewish merchants, sailing from France, travel to Antioch and then to Baghdad, at first by land and then by the Euphrates. From Baghdad they take sail to Oman, Sind, India, and China.

The tenth and eleventh centuries were the golden age of long-distance Jewish commerce. During the eleventh century the riches that they had accumulated aroused envy, and the Jews had to engage in other activities. Meanwhile, the merchants of certain Italian towns had begun to take over the role of the Jews. Venice maintained regular relations with Byzantium (of which it had long been a dependent) as well as with Africa and the Muslim Levant. It imported Oriental luxury goods and exported the products of the West. On the west coast of Italy, Amalfi began its expansion about the same time as Venice. The Amalfitans, like the Venetians, soon established little enclaves or colonies with special privileges in the Byzantine Empire, the Levant, and North Africa. The main axis of Mediterranean trade shifted from a line joining Constantinople and Cairo to one leaving Venice and Amalfi, then splitting into two routes, one to Byzantium and the other to Africa. Italian sailors—first the Venetians and Amalfitans, and shortly afterward the Pisans and Genoese—soon dominated the Mediterranean and took the offensive against the Muslims. The latter were driven out of Corsica and Sardinia, and before the First Crusade a fleet of Genoese, Pisan, and Amalfitan ships took Mahdiya, the capital of Muslim Tunisia. Six years earlier the Venetians had pressured the Byzantine emperor Alexios I Komnenos into giving them a general exemption from taxes in return for naval aid against the Turks.

EXPLORATIONS OF ASIA

The First Crusade, at the very end of the eleventh century, led to the establishment of the Latin Kingdom of Jerusalem, and the Fourth Crusade, in 1204, to the Latin Empire of Constantinople. From there Westerners who had settled in the Levant set out on the great explorations of central and eastern Asia.

The first of these diplomat–explorers, and also the least known, was Baldwin of Hainaut. This knight, who served Baldwin II, the Latin emperor of Constantinople, had married a Cuman princess, daughter of a chief who also served the Latin emperor, in 1239. Until the end of the fourteenth century, the merchants and churchmen who entered central Asia found the Cuman language useful in their travels. Doubtless because, through his marriage, Baldwin of Hainaut had learned this language, he was sent by Emperor Baldwin II in 1243–1244 on an embassy to the Mongols. His mission took him from southern Russia to Karakorum in Mongolia. The purpose of the mission was to gain Mongol support against the Turkish sultan of Konya (in Asia Minor), who was threatening the Latin Empire.

The Franciscan Giovanni of Pian de Carpine was sent on a similar mission in 1245–1247 by Pope Innocent IV, who was seeking the aid of the Mongols against Islam. His account of the journey, while a good source for Mongol ethnology, is not very helpful for geography. The report of William of Rubruck, who was sent to Karakorum by Louis IX of France in 1254, is much more useful.

Like the others William started from southern Russia, but he was the first European to report to the Christian West that the Caspian was a landlocked sea. The Swedish Varangians had doubtless known this, but had not reported the fact to others in the West. William had met Baldwin of Hainaut in Constantinople and had received precious information from him. From the Crimea, William crossed the Don and reached the Volga; he then went toward the Ili Valley, north of the Tien Shan Mountains and south of Lake Balkhash. Then, going by Lake Ebinor, he entered Mongolia and finally reached Karakorum. On his way back he crossed the Volga, exactly a year after his first crossing. William then followed the western shore of the Caspian, crossed Cappadocia, and reached the Gulf of Alexandretta. There he embarked for Cyprus, where he hoped to find Louis IX, but the king had returned to France. William sent his report from Tripoli, Lebanon, where he was living in a house of his order.

The report of William of Rubruck is one of the masterpieces of medieval geographical literature. It is comparable only with the account of Marco Polo, though the two works are quite different. William was not only a good observer; he was also an excellent writer of very clear descriptions. He was curious and asked questions, but he did not take fables for answers. His report was written in Latin, and is therefore not as well known as that of Marco Polo, who wrote in the vernacular.

Moreover, Marco Polo covered more ground and explored regions that were more interesting. Starting from Asia Minor, he crossed Mesopotamia and the Persian Gulf to arrive at Ormuz. He then reached the Pamir plateau by way of Persia and finally arrived at Cambaluc (Peking). There the great khan, Kublai, emperor of China, had his residence. Marco Polo lived in Cathay for seventeen years, and traveled throughout the country. His book is a sort of catalog of the riches of Asia that inspired the medieval and early modern explorers who followed him. (Columbus annotated a copy of Marco Polo's book that is now in the Biblioteca Colombin of Seville.)

Marco Polo returned to Europe by way of southern Asia and India. Like China and Japan, India was, for Westerners, a land of riches and spices. His "Book of Marvels," as it was soon called, has 234 chapters, but the description of his voyage is covered in only eighteen. The rest is a mixture of geographical, historical, physical, economic, botanical, and technical curiosities. It is the work of a great observer, but an observer full of fantasies and imagination. William of Rubruck saw only deserts and a rather monotonous nomad society, which he described as a scholar in a scholar's language. Marco Polo described countries that are among the most picturesque in the world, writing with passion and disorder.

Niccolo and Maffeo Polo, the father and the uncle of Marco, had set up business in the Crimea. From the Crimea they went to the lands of the Volga Tatars, as others had already done; but they were interested in trade, not politics. This journey took place in 1255, about a year after that of William of Rubruck. Like him, they then went to the residence of the great khan, now in China. They returned in 1269, after having made considerable profits. In 1271 they took the road to China again, with young Marco, who was then seventeen. They arrived in Chandu (Xanadu, K'ai-p'ing-fu), the summer residence of the great khan (north of the Great Wall) in May 1275. Marco soon became an important Mongol inspector. His duties took him to southern China, to the frontier of Burma and to Indochina. He visited Kinsai (today Hangchow), capital of southern China, which was much larger than any European city of that time. The return journey began in 1292 and lasted more than two years. Marco embarked at Zayton, the great port of southern China (now Chang-Chou), and after stopping at Sumatra and the East Indies, arrived at Ormuz on the Persian Gulf. From Ormuz he went by land to the Mediterranean and reached Venice in 1295. He dictated his book in Genoa, where he was a prisoner after the naval battle of Curzola, and completed the work in Venice after he was set free.

From that time on, commercial relations with east Asia became more frequent. The Florentine Francesco Pegolotti, in his *Pratica della mercatura* (*ca.* 1340), did not hesitate to assert that the route between Tana (an Italian colony at the mouth of the

Don) and Peking was perfectly safe. Some Genoese even established a warehouse at Zayton, and others traveled to India. This situation lasted, in spite of growing difficulties, until the Ming overthrow of the Mongol dynasty in China in 1368–1370.

WESTWARD EXPLORATIONS

Some time earlier, however, the Turkish advance in the Near East had begun to cut off relations with India. The Italian colonies of the Black Sea—Caffa in the Crimea, Tana on the Sea of Azov—served less and less as points of departure for merchants seeking the riches that Marco Polo had described so seductively. While Venice continued to be concerned especially with the eastern Mediterranean and the Levant, Genoa took increasing interest in the western Mediterranean, particularly the Iberian peninsula, the Atlantic coasts of the rest of Europe, and, to the south, those of Africa.

The Genoese and the Pisans had been trading with Catalonia since the twelfth century. They drew Spain and Portugal into the stream of large-scale international commerce. By the middle of the twelfth century, they had established commercial relations with Muslim Spain: Almería in 1143 at the latest, Valencia in 1149. By 1161 partnership agreements were drawn up in Genoa for trade with Seville, still a Muslim city, and the Pisans had a warehouse there in 1166. To reach Seville, the Genoese and Pisans sailed through the Strait of Gibraltar.

When Seville became Christian in 1248, the Genoese were immediately given extensive privileges. In 1251 Ferdinand III of Castile gave them a district in the city with a warehouse. From that time on, Genoese admirals, such as Ugo Vento and Benedetto Zaccaria, often entered the service of the king of Castile. Merchants of Genoa and Piacenza living in Seville were lending money to the king by the beginning of the fourteenth century. Thus they gradually became bankers of the Castilian state, a role that later enabled them to take an important position in financing the discoveries and the beginnings of commerce in America.

Italian relations with Portugal intensified at the end of the thirteenth century, when Genoese galleys began to go up the Atlantic coast of Europe in order to reach the great international market of Bruges. In the fourteenth and fifteenth centuries, the Italian shipping became important for Portugal as well as for Spain. By then Venice, Genoa, Florence, and the kingdom of Naples were sending regular convoys from the Mediterranean to the North Sea. By 1310

Lagos, in southern Portugal, had become a port of call for Venetian galleys en route to Flanders and England.

In southern Spain—at Jerez, Cádiz, and Puerto de S. Maria—there were many Genoese merchants. They brought their ships with them, and leased them to the king of Castile when they were not using them. Following the examples of Vento and Zaccaria a century earlier, in the fourteenth century the Boccanegras became admirals of Castile, as did the Pessagnos of Portugal. The latter family played an important role in the early Portuguese discoveries.

Spaniards and Portuguese had their own maritime traditions. At the end of the thirteenth century, Portuguese ships appeared from time to time in England and in Flanders. In Spain the ports on the northern coast, such as La Coruña, Bilbao, Santander, and S. Sebastian were noted for their maritime activity. In Andalusia, where Italian influence was very strong in the larger ports, smaller coastal towns, such as Palos and Moguer at the mouth of the Río Tinto, produced hardy seamen and shipowners who were fishermen as well as commercial carriers. Some of these men later became companions of Columbus.

When the Genoese began to lose their colonies in the eastern Mediterranean and the Black Sea, and especially when the Turks closed the Bosporus and the Dardanelles, their businessmen began to take their capital out of the Levant. They transferred it to the Iberian world, where the Spanish and Portuguese kings ruled centralized states with much larger populations than those of the Italian city-states.

The geographical position of Spain and Portugal explains why they were the first to make the discoveries that led to colonization in the modern period. Both countries were closer than other European states to the regions that were first settled: the Atlantic islands, the African coast, and the lands of the Caribbean.

A NEW ROUTE TO INDIA AND CHINA

The missionary–diplomats and merchants who, from the thirteenth century on, had taken the commercial routes to the Far East, told marvelous stories about the lands they had crossed. Little by little, it was realized that the West had certain advantages in armaments and naval technology. It seemed logical, then, to open a new route to the riches of India and China, whence came silk, pearls, gold, precious stones, pepper, and spices. All these goods were costly in the West because Muslim middlemen, who had become indispensable after the collapse of the

Mongol Empire, took large profits for their work. Success would help both the Christian faith and the European merchant.

Little by little the idea arose that a new sea route to the East should be found that would bypass the Muslim countries. Thus the struggle for the riches of the East became a struggle against the ocean. Curiously, Marco Polo's report of the riches of the East, which primarily described land routes, became one of the most influential stimuli toward seeking a sea route to the Orient.

Besides the hope of finding a sea route to the Far East, there was a desire to find allies against Islam. In the thirteenth and fourteenth centuries, it was hoped that the Mongols, who controlled the land routes, would be such allies. Then western Europeans thought of "Prester John," the ruler of Ethiopia, who was known to be a Christian. The problem, however, was to find a sea route to his country. It was vaguely understood that Ethiopia was somewhere on the way to India. Here, as in many other cases, the initiative was taken by Italians. As early as 1291, two Genoese (Vadino and Ugolino Vivaldi) sailed south along the west coast of Africa, hoping to find a passage to the Indian Ocean. They were lost at sea, perhaps in the region of the Canary Islands.

Portugal acquired Lanzarote, and later Gomera (two of the Canary Islands), through the Genoese Lanzarotto Malocello, who was in Portuguese service, about 1336. Malocello was one of the nautical experts on the staff of Manuel Pessagno, whom King Denis of Portugal named admiral of his fleet in 1317. Pessagno was to furnish twenty Genoese captains and pilots for the king's service. He had brought his galleys to serve Portugal, but he also equipped other ships, notably some naos. These ships were larger than the caravel, the other type of vessel used in the Atlantic explorations, and more seaworthy than the galley. Manuel Pessagno remained admiral of Portugal until 1340, and was succeeded by his sons Carlo, Bartolomeo, and, especially, Lanzarote.

In 1341 King Alphonse IV sent two ships and a boat to the Canaries under the command of the Genoese Nicoloso da Recco and the Florentine Angelino del Tegghia. They reached the islands in five days. This accurate and rapid passage was probably due to the fact that Recco had sailed with Malocello in 1336. This time all the islands in the archipelago were sighted, and the most important ones were described in detail in the report sent by Recco to some Italian merchants.

Soon after, the Italians went beyond the Canaries,

for the Medici Atlas of 1351 (preserved in the Biblioteca Laurenziana, Florence) shows the Madeiras. Madeira appears under the Italian name Legname, which means "timber," just as the Portuguese name Madeira does. The island was then well wooded. The rest of the archipelago, Porto Santo and the Desertas, also appeared on the map. Later, when Lanzarote Pessagno was admiral (1365–1385), the Azores were reached. They appear on the maps of the Majorcans Abraham Cresques (1375) and Guillermus Soler (1385). Again, the names given the islands are Italian.

The discovery of the Madeiras and the Azores was made possible by the fact that, when returning from the Canaries, navigators sailed northwest in order to catch the western trade winds that would blow them back to Europe. Shipping to the Canaries grew rapidly during the mid fourteenth century. There were two expeditions from Majorca in 1342, one under Francesco Desvalers and one (which reached the islands) under Domingo Gual. The king of Aragon sent a ship in 1345 and another in 1352, but did not try to take possession. On the other hand, Lanzarotto Malocello, the discoverer (1336), took possession of the island that still bears his name (Lanzarote) in the name of the king of Portugal in 1370. After his death in 1385, Portugal lost interest in the Canaries. Lanzarotto had had difficulties with Martin Ruiz of Avendaño, a Vizcayan serving the king of Castile. Another Castilian expedition took place in 1393. In 1402 the Norman Jean de Béthencourt began the Spanish take-over of the islands, which became more and more effective until the islands were completely conquered by the end of the fifteenth century.

Portugal did not take formal possession of the Madeiras or the Azores until the time of Henry the Navigator (1394–1460). The Madeiras, at first uninhabited, were known to the Genoese serving Portugal in the fourteenth century, and were visited in 1425 by two Portuguese nobles, João Gonçalves Zarco and Tristão Vaz Teixeira, members of the household of Prince Henry. Therefore King Duarte, successor of John I, gave the islands to his brother Henry as a fief in 1433. Colonization began almost at once. On 8 May 1440, Prince Henry gave part of Madeira to Tristão, a knight of his household, very likely the same Tristão who had been a leader of the 1425 expedition. In 1452 Madeira began to produce sugar, a commodity that made the fortune of the island up to the early decades of the sixteenth century.

In the Azores the Flemings collaborated with the Portuguese from the earliest years of the colonization. Henry the Navigator had been given the right to settle the islands by his nephew, Alphonse V, in 1439. In 1447 steps were taken to colonize São Miguel, and by 1450 the first Fleming, Jacques de Bruges, appeared on Terceira. Henry the Navigator gave him the right, as the organizer of the colony, to bring in other Flemings. A second Fleming, Joost de Hurtere, was made captain of the islands of Faial and Pico by Prince Fernando, heir of Henry the Navigator. These Flemings rapidly became members of the Portuguese nobility, and their descendants (whose names soon took on Portuguese forms) continued to play an important role in the Azores throughout the fifteenth century, and in some cases much longer. For example, Willem van der Haegen founded the da Silveira family, which was for centuries active in the economic development of the islands.

CHRISTOPHER COLUMBUS

Full of the inexact knowledge that he had acquired from Marco Polo and the Florentine Paolo del Pozzo Toscannelli, Christopher Columbus, about 1484, asked King John II of Portugal to give him some ships to sail to Cipangu (Japan), which was believed to be near India, and which he proposed to reach by going west. The proposal, after investigation, was rejected. In 1486, however, Fernão Dulmo, a captain at Terceira in the Azores, was appointed by the king to discover the island of the Seven Cities, which was believed to be in the western ocean about halfway between Europe and Japan. Dulmo was actually Ferdinand van Olmen, a Fleming in Portuguese service, whose name had been transliterated as Fernão Dulmo.

For some thirty years the Portuguese had made voyages in the open Atlantic beyond the Madeiras and the Azores. These voyages were individual enterprises; the government merely granted rights in whatever islands were found. In 1475 Fernão Telles had received a royal privilege for the island of the Seven Cities, but nothing indicates that he attempted this voyage, whereas it is certain that van Olmen did.

According to the royal letter of 24 July 1486, Ferdinand van Olmen told King John II that he hoped to find for him "a large island, or a group of islands, or the shore of a continent in the region where the island of the Seven Cities is supposed to be." He promised to do this at his own expense, but asked that he be granted the island, islands, or mainland that he (or someone acting under his orders) found, whether inhabited or not. However, since the cost of the expedition was great, van Olmen gave half of the lordship of the lands to be discovered to Estreito, a rich Portuguese settler in Madeira. In return Estreito promised to provide two good caravels properly supplied, with van Olmen to select the ships and provide them with good pilots and sailors. Everything was to be ready by March 1487; they would sail from Terceira, the island where van Olmen was captain. Each partner would command one of the ships. Van Olmen would sail west for forty days, and Estreito would follow him.

The most striking feature of this contract is the forty-day limit set by van Olmen for reaching his goal. Evidently he expected to find the land granted to him by the king within this period. This figure must have been a compromise between Toscannelli's and Columbus' estimates of the distance to the island of the Seven Cities. Columbus, in fact, took thirty-six days to sail from the Canaries to San Salvador in the Bahamas.

A passage in the *History of the Indies* by Bartolomeo de Las Casas proves that van Olmen actually tried to carry out his plan, but failed. He departed about the end of the winter of 1486/1487, a very unfavorable time of year for an Atlantic crossing, especially for sailing west in two caravels of only fifty to sixty tons' displacement. Moreover, in that season the Azores were too far north as a point of departure. Van Olmen could not use the trade winds, which, at the end of the summer and during the first three weeks of autumn, carried Columbus so smoothly to the Bahamas in 1492. Moreover, van Olmen probably headed straight northwest, as was the tradition for Atlantic navigators from the Azores, from Diego de Teyve in the mid fifteenth century to João Fernandes and the Cortereals at the beginning of the sixteenth century. They all went to the west of Ireland, and some of them to the waters of Newfoundland.

Van Olmen's voyage and other Portuguese expeditions of 1487 influenced the career of Columbus. About the middle of 1485 he went to Spain and made the same proposals that he had made in Portugal, with the same lack of success. Early in 1488 he wrote from Seville to John II, offering his services again, and the king invited him to Lisbon. Van Olmen had sailed ten months earlier—and he had provisions for only six months. It seemed certain that both men and ships had been lost. Columbus may have thought that this was a good time to try his chances in Por-

tugal again. During his stay in Lisbon, however, Bartholomew Dias entered the Tagys (December 1488) with the news of the discovery of the Cape of Good Hope. The king of Portugal now knew that the route to the Indies was open, so the western route no longer interested him. When he thought of it again, Columbus had already found the New World for Spain.

The discoverer of America was at first a rather unimportant member of the large group of Italians in southern Spain. He had little or no money, for he was the son of a poor weaver of Genoa who also kept a small shop. Nevertheless, he had established relations with capitalists as an employee of the powerful Genoese firm of the Centurioni. Columbus had made several voyages—to the Levant, to northwest Europe, and perhaps to Iceland. He had entered the service of Portugal and had sailed as far as the Gold Coast (Ghana) in 1482.

Having married the daughter of the captain of the island of Porto Santo in 1479, Columbus became a man of some standing, and began to seek the support of a king who would make it possible to undertake the voyage of which he had been dreaming—a voyage to Asia by the western route. After setbacks in Portugal and Spain, and after other unsuccessful efforts by his brother Bartholomew in France and in England, Columbus finally succeeded in convincing Isabella, queen of Castile. On 17 April 1492, Columbus signed an agreement with the Crown of Castile. He became hereditary admiral of the Ocean Sea and viceroy of the lands to be discovered. He was to receive a tenth of colonial revenues, and an eighth of profits of commerce, but he had to provide some of the capital needed for his voyage. He managed to do so with the help of some merchants who were his friends.

At Palos, a little seaport that handled some of the trade between Andalusia and the Canaries, Columbus struck a bargain with the shipowner Martin Alonso Pinzón. Two caravels—the *Niña* and the *Pinta*, each about sixty tons—and the *Santa Maria*, 120 tons, left Palos on 3 August 1492. Almost a month was lost in the Canaries, but on 6 September they set sail toward the unknown west. On 12 October a sailor in the *Pinta* spied San Salvador (Watling's Island) in the Bahamas. Columbus took it for one of the islands of Cipangu, Marco Polo's Japan. Sailing south through the Bahamas, he learned from the Indians that there was a rich land nearby. Columbus immediately thought of Cathay—Marco Polo's China. Actually it was Cuba, which he reached on 27 October. For five weeks he explored the northwest coast of the island, and even sent an embassy inland to make contact with the grand khan. Soon afterward Columbus discovered Haiti, which he called Hispaniola (Little Spain). It was there that he built Navidad, the first Spanish settlement in the New World, which was soon destroyed.

THE AFRICAN COAST AND INDIAN OCEAN

The discovery and the colonization of the Canaries, Madeiras, and Azores had prepared the way for the colonization of the Caribbean lands, and later the American continent. This led to a great expansion of western Europe to the west. At the same time, however, another wave of exploration went down the west coast of Africa in an effort to discover a sea route to the Far East.

Whereas the desire for more land pushed the Portuguese toward the Atlantic islands, which were easy to control because of their small area, it was the need for slave labor that made them go down the west African coast. Here, too, only the islands were at first occupied and colonized.

In 1433 Gil Eanes de Lagos, squire of Henry the Navigator, failed in his attempt to round Cape Bojador, but brought back several captives from the Canaries. Not until 1441 was there a real slave raid on the African mainland. In that year Prince Henry sent Antão Gonçalves to get seal skins and oil on the African coast at the mouth of the Rio de Oro; several slaves were also brought back. They were Zanaga (Azànegue) Berbers. Soon regular slaving expeditions were organized at Lagos, on the Algarve coast of Portugal. In 1444 six Lagos caravels reached the Ilha das Garcas (Heron Island), near Arguim, and took 165 men, women, and children. When Dinis Dias reached Guinea, also in 1444, he captured several blacks south of the mouth of the Senegal River.

It was soon realized that, instead of capturing slaves, it was much easier to buy them, profiting from racial or tribal conflicts. Therefore, in 1448 the Portuguese set up a trading post on the island of Arguim, near which caravans of Muslim merchants from the interior ended their journeys. They brought both black slaves and other goods, some of which came from the Orient. These new commercial contacts made the Portuguese anxious to find a sea route that would allow them to dispense with these Muslim middlemen. One of the first results of the Portuguese movement down the African coast was to decrease the importance of the trans-Saharan routes to Tunis or to Barca in Cyrenaica. It was henceforth easier to ship goods directly by sea from Arguim to Lagos or Lisbon.

Meanwhile, the search for island bases further south continued. An Italian, Antonio da Noli, established such a post on the Cape Verde Islands. Antonio, with his brother Bartolomeo and his nephew, Raffael, had come to Portugal with two ships and a pinnace. He received a license from Henry the Navigator and discovered several of the Cape Verde Islands. He was ordered to take possession of part of the archipelago, and to settle and develop it. By 1466 the island of Santiago was prospering, and Antonio was captain there. At that time the island had a population of Moors, blacks (most of them slaves), and whites.

The whites could then go anywhere in Guinea, except to Arguim, where a monopoly of trade had been granted to an Italian from Florence. According to the terms of the grant of 1466, these rules should have remained in effect even if the king granted a monopoly of the commerce with Guinea in return for an annual payment.

In 1469 Alphonse V granted Fernão Gomes, a rich merchant of Lisbon, a five-year monopoly on trade with Guinea. His captains were to explore 100 leagues along the coast every year. From then on, there was very rapid movement down the coast. In 1470 Soeiro da Costa passed Cape Palmas and reached the Ivory Coast. The next year João de Santarem and Pero de Escobar sailed to Elmina on the Gold Coast. This explains why, in 1472, Antonio da Noli and other inhabitants of Santiago in Cape Verde were forbidden to trade freely with Guinea. Fernão Gomes, and after him the Crown, were to have the monopoly of trade in gold from the country of the Wangara, which had just been discovered.

In 1472 Fernão do Po went down the Slave Coast, passed the Niger delta, and discovered the island that bears his name at the eastern end of the Gulf of Guinea. In 1473, the last year of the grant to Gomes, Lopo Gonçalves crossed the equator, and Ruy de Sequeira found the other two islands of the Gulf of Guinea, São Thome and Principe. Finding that the African coast ran south of the equator discouraged the Portuguese, for, on the evidence of erroneous maps from the late Middle Ages, they had believed that the coast curved to the east at those latitudes. Nevertheless, the period of Gomes and his captains was important, for in five years they traveled down the African coast as far as the captains of Henry the Navigator had gone in thirty.

At this time the king of Portugal added to his titles that of "lord of discovery and of Guinea." At the same time the urge to reach India was again stimulated. Meanwhile, the new king of Portugal, John II (1481–1495), wanted to secure the Portuguese hold on Guinea. In 1482 he ordered Diogo de Azambuja to build the fort of São Jorge da Mina (Elmina), which soon became the principal center of trade in gold and in slaves.

Further east, in the Niger delta, Alfonso de Aveiro had founded the trading post of Benin, in an unhealthy location that was soon abandoned. The Portuguese there had been told, however, that the kingdom of "Prester John" (Christian Abyssinia) was a thousand miles to the east. At this time the Portuguese monarchy began to think seriously of establishing relations with "Prester John," by way of the Mediterranean and the Red Sea, or by circumnavigating Africa. John II proposed to try the first route. He sent Pedro da Evora and Gonçalves Eanes to explore the interior of the continent as far as Timbuktu.

At the same time trade with Guinea was a training school for many great explorers. A young, unknown Genoese, Christopher Columbus, sailed to Elmina, and Diogo Cão sailed 1,500 miles to the south along the African coast. In 1482 Cão reached the mouth of the Congo, which he called the Rio do Padrão because he placed there a stone pillar (padrão) marked with the arms of Portugal. He made contact with the local king and lived in his kingdom for several months. This paved the way for the creation of the more or less Christian kingdom of the Congo as a Portuguese protectorate. Cão then continued his journey to thirteen degrees south latitude, where he erected another padrão. On his return journey to Lisbon in 1484 he made much better time because he used the southeast trade winds. At the end of 1485, when the great explorer was again en route to the south, the king told his ambassador to Pope Innocent VIII to announce that the "promontorium Prassum"—according to Ptolemy the southernmost part of Africa—would soon be reached. Cão returned in 1486, but he had only reached Cape Cross (twenty-two degrees south latitude) and not the southern tip of Africa. The king never forgave him.

The year 1487 was one of difficult decisions for King John II. The difficulties experienced by Cão worried him so much that he began to wonder if there was not a better way to reach Asia than by sailing southeast. It was then that, picking up the ideas of Columbus (who had meanwhile gone to Spain), he ordered Ferdinand van Olmen to explore the western route across the Atlantic, starting from the Azores. This attempt, as we have seen, ended in failure.

Meanwhile, in August 1487, Bartholomew Dias left Lisbon with two caravels and a supply ship. His orders were to reach the land of Prester John by sea. Portuguese nautical knowledge had become so considerable that Dias was able to sail directly from Cape Palmas to the Congo without following the coast. He erected pillars at various places, and sent Congo blacks ashore to tell Prester John that the Portuguese were coming. This strange mixture of practical knowledge and traditional ignorance was characteristic of the late Middle Ages.

At Lüderitz (Cape Volta) he erected another pillar. Setting out, he was caught in a tempest and was driven past the Cape of Good Hope without sighting it. He reached land about 200 miles to the east of the cape, at Mossel Bay. He followed the coast eastward to Cape Padrão, and then sailed along the coast of the Indian Ocean as far as the Great Fish River (now in Natal). A mutiny by his crew kept him from going farther, but on his way back he sighted the cape, which he named the Cape of Tempests. King John II changed the name to the Cape of Good Hope in 1488. For the first time in history, the entire west coast of Africa was known to one civilization, that of western Europe.

After 1488 another world was reached, that of the Indian Ocean, a sea dominated for centuries by Muslim sailors. Close relations had developed between the east coast of Africa and India, and navigational techniques were at a high level. The Portuguese now had to learn how to navigate and how to trade in this new world.

The man charged with this task was Pero da Covilhão. He had been a page at court and had learned Arabic in Morocco, where he had been an envoy of the king. He and Afonso de Paiva were ordered to find the land of Prester John, and above all to discover the source of the spices that Italian merchants bought from the Muslims in the Levant. On 7 May 1487 the two explorers left Santarem. They reached Rhodes by way of Lisbon, Valencia, Barcelona, and Naples. At Rhodes they disguised themselves as merchants and sailed to Alexandria. From Cairo they reached Suez, then Tor in Arabia, Souakin on the Egyptian side of the Red Sea, and finally Aden. From Aden, Covilhão went to India, while Paiva headed for Abyssinia. Covilhão traveled in the East for a year. He went first to Cannanore, then to Calicut (which Vasco da Gama reached ten years later), and then to Goa, the future capital of Portuguese India. From Goa he went west to Ormuz on the Persian Gulf. He then went down the east coast of Africa as far as Sofala. At the end of 1491 he returned to Cairo. Two Portuguese Jews, sent by the king, met him there. The information collected by Covilhão had tremendous importance for the voyage of Vasco da Gama.

The voyage of Vasco da Gama was the first important event in the reign of King Manuel (1495–1521). Actually there was little left to discover. Since the northernmost point, reached by Dias at the Great Fish River, and the southernmost point, reached by Covilhão at Sofalo, were separated by only a few hundred miles, all that was needed was to follow the coast to get from one to the other. Of course, there was still the Indian Ocean to cross, but this caused no problem, since, during his journey from Malindi, on the African coast, to Calicut, on the west coast of India, Vasco da Gama had as his pilot Ahmad ibn Majid, the greatest expert on Indian Ocean navigation. Vasco da Gama's task was to establish political and commercial relations. The date of his arrival at Calicut, 20 May 1498, marked the beginning both of Portuguese domination in the Indies and of modern colonization of Asia.

BIBLIOGRAPHY

C. Brochado, *O piloto arabe de Vasco da Gama* (1959); T. A. Chumovsky, *Tres roteiros desconhecidos de Ahmad ibn Madjid, o piloto arabe de Vasco da Gama* (1960); Gomes Eanes de Zurara, *Chronique de Guinée,* L. Bourdon and R. Richard, eds. (1960); Florentino Perez Embid, *Los descubrimientos en el Atlántico y la rivalidad castellano-portuguesa hasta el tratado de Tordesillas* (1948); G. Haman, *Der Eintritt der südlichen Hemisphäre in die europäische Geschichte* (1968); J. Jacobi, "Antwort auf einige Fragen über die Radaniya," in *Der Islam,* 52 (1975); Archibald R. Lewis, *Naval Power and Trade in the Mediterranean A. D. 500–1000* (1951), and *The Northern Seas: Shipping and Commerce in Northern Europe A.D. 300–1100* (1958); Samuel Eliot Morison, *Admiral of the Ocean Sea: A Life of Christopher Columbus,* 2 vols. (1942); Lucien Musset, *Les peuples scandinaves au moyen âge* (1951); Marco Polo, *Il milione,* Luigi Foscolo Benedetto, ed. (1928); William of Rubruck, "Itinerarium," in *Sinica franciscana,* I, *Itinera et relationes fratum minorum saeculi XIII et XIV,* A. A. van den Wijngaert, ed (1929); Haakon Shetelig, *The Viking Ships* (1953).

Relevant works by Charles Verlinden, are "Lanzarotto Malocello et la découverte portugaise des Canaries," in *Revue belge de philologie et d'histoire,* 36 (1958); "Navigateurs, marchands et colons italiens au service de la découverte et de la colonisation portugaise sous Henri le Navigateur," in *Le moyen âge,* 64 (1958); "La signification de l'année 1487 dans l' histoire de la découverte et de l'expansion portugaises," in *Revue d'histoire économique et sociale,* 42 (1964); "Les Génois dans la marine portugaise avant 1385," in *Congresso de Portugal medievo,* III (1966); *idem* and Florentino Perez Embid, *Cristóbal Colón y el descubrimiento de América* (1967); "Antonio da Noli and the Colonization of the Cape Verde Islands" and "A Precursor of Columbus: The Fleming Ferdinand van Olmen (1487)," in his *The Beginnings of Modern Colonization* (1970), and "La découverte des archipels de la 'Méditerranée atlantique' (Canaries, Madères, Açores) et la navigation astronomique primitive," in *Revista portuguesa de historia,* 16 (1978). See also Henry Yule and Henri Cordier, *The Book of Ser Marco Polo,* 2 vols. (1920).

CHARLES VERLINDEN

[See also **Crusades and Crusader States; Crusades of the Later Middle Ages; Iceland; Jews in Russia; Jews in the Middle East; Portugal; Slavery, Slave Trade; Trade, Regulation of; Viking Navigation.**]

EXPULSION OF JEWS. Expulsions were a recurrent feature of medieval Jewish life in western Christendom. A number of banishments are mentioned during the early Middle Ages; they are, however, poorly documented, usually being indicated only in passing by chroniclers. Their circumstances, extent, and impact cannot be reliably ascertained. The latter Middle Ages saw a spate of expulsions, many of which are copiously documented. Some of these involved banishment from individual cities or small principalities; others affected the extensive Jewish populations of large and important states.

The first major late-medieval expulsion took place under the rule of Philip Augustus of France. Assuming the throne at the tender age of fifteen, the new king faced a formidable array of opponents determined to limit decisively the burgeoning power of the monarchy. Desperately in need of financial resources, Philip Augustus exploited the Jewish community that had developed in twelfth-century France. The Jews had no real defenses against royal depredation. After confiscating their goods, the young monarch forgave debts owed to Jews, reserving 20 percent of the sums owed for the royal coffers. In this way Philip Augustus both enhanced his popularity and filled his treasury. The culmination of these steps was the expulsion of Jews from the royal domains in 1182, with immovable goods confiscated by the crown. As a bow in the direction of ecclesiastical sensitivities, synagogues were ceded to the church. Although the king's clerical biographer attempted to portray these actions as pious in nature, they were in fact self-interested measures taken by a crafty statesman.

In actuality, the expulsion of 1182 affected only a limited number of Jews. Indeed, by 1198 Philip Augustus had reversed himself and reintroduced Jews into his domains. Nonetheless, he had established a dangerous precedent.

The next major expulsion involved the Jews of England. Having immigrated after the Norman invasion of 1066, the Jews of England had flourished and had also been heavily exploited by their royal overlords. By the second half of the thirteenth century, the economic health of the Jewish community had been seriously sapped by a combination of ecclesiastical clamor against moneylending and royal cupidity. In a last effort to realize significant sums from his Jews, King Edward I experimented with an expulsion from Gascony, a French province under English control. When the results proved profitable, the king extended this policy to England itself in 1290. Once again royal rhetoric expressed pious intentions, but the reality was despoliation. The expulsion from England lasted until the seventeenth century.

Sixteen years after the expulsion from England, King Philip IV of France emulated his great-great-grandfather and his English contemporary. Searching desperately for new financial resources, Philip decided to maximize his spoils by arresting the Jews and confiscating their goods and business records prior to the edict of banishment of 1306. As soon as the Jews were gone and their real estate and business documents had been safely sequestered, a two-pronged effort was initiated: one group of functionaries involved itself in the sale of Jewish property, the other zealously pursued those in debt to Jews and demanded the monies owed for the royal treasury. Despite serious difficulties, the sums netted were substantial. For a variety of reasons—not the least of which was a desire to realize pre-1306 debts still owed to the Jews—King Louis X readmitted Jews into France in 1315. The fourteenth century saw another expulsion in 1322, readmission in 1359, and final expulsion in 1394.

The most extensive, unanticipated, and devastating expulsion of Jews during the Middle Ages was that of 1492 from Spain, together with the related banishment from Portugal in 1497. Wealthier, more numerous, politically more powerful, and culturally more rooted than their northern coreligionists, the Jews of the Iberian peninsula, despite their difficulties in the late fourteenth and fifteenth centuries, could hardly conceive themselves suffering the fatal blow of expulsion. Yet the seemingly insoluble problem of assimilating large numbers of formerly Jewish New Christians into Spanish society gave rise, by the second half of the fifteenth century, to demands for a dual program of inquisition against recalcitrant New Christians and expulsion of the Jews. The former expedient would address itself directly to the miscreants, and the latter would remove the temptation of relapse to Jewish practice and belief. Ultimately persuaded to adopt this program, King Ferdinand and Queen Isabella exiled the Jews of Spain in 1492 and forced a similar policy on the reluctant King Emanuel I in 1497.

There were a number of motivations behind the expulsion of medieval Jewries. Probably the most common was financial: political leaders strapped for funds could realize significant sums. Others hoped to curry favor with elements antipathetic to the Jews. On rare occasions a yearning to purify the realm by removing a group perceived as harmful played a role as well.

Among the conditioning factors behind these expulsions was the status of the Jews in the eyes of the church, the state, and the populace. Although the (Catholic) church always emphasized the essential right of the Jews to dwell openly as Jews in Christian society, it consistently sought to limit that right by insisting that Jewish behavior should in no way jeopardize the wellbeing of Christendom. This condition offered a convenient rationale for the expulsion of Jews; on occasion it served as an excuse for acts of despoliation.

The fundamental weakness of the medieval Jews in western Christendom thrust them into a dangerous alliance with the political establishment. Here too the stage was set for expulsion—this time following the notion that the guarantor of Jewish safety and security ultimately had the right to abrogate those guarantees. Surely the pervasive popular hostility toward the Jews was yet another precondition for expulsion. In sum the recurrent reality of banishment was a clear index of the basic fragility of Jewish status in medieval western Christendom.

BIBLIOGRAPHY

Yitzhak Baer, A History of the Jews in Christian Spain, Louis Schoffman et al., trans., II (1966), 300–443; Salo W. Baron, A Social and Religious History of the Jews, 2nd ed., XI (1967), 192–283; Robert Chazan, ed., Church, State, and Jew in the Middle Ages (1980), and Medieval Jewry in Northern France (1973), 63–99 and 154–205; Henry G. Richardson, The English Jewry Under Angevin Kings (1960), 213–233; Cecil Roth, A History of the Jews in England, 3rd ed. (1964), 68–80.

ROBERT CHAZAN

[See also Anti-Semitism; Edward I of England; Jews (various articles); Philip II Augustus; Philip IV the Fair.]

EXTREME UNCTION is the Christian liturgical rite of anointing the seriously ill or dying in preparation for death. It is a specialized form of the earlier and originally more widespread practice of unction of the sick. In the late ninth, tenth and eleventh centuries, in the Latin church of western Europe, anointing came to be commonly administered to the dying or seriously ill. Since there was no expectation of physical recovery in such cases, the rite acquired a somewhat different theological interpretation. It was counted as one of the seven sacraments of the Latin church.

Extreme unction was performed with oil of the sick; that is, pure olive oil specially blessed for this purpose by the bishop each year on Maundy Thursday and subsequently distributed to the priests of his diocese. The unction was administered by a priest, usually after the sufferer had made his or her final confession, and just before or after the final reception of Holy Communion, known as the viaticum. These sacramental acts, together with numerous appropriate prayers and chants, constituted the cycle of last rites that were so important for medieval Christians.

Although local usages varied, and the rite sometimes had to be abbreviated in practice, the typical procedure was for the priest, using the oil of the sick, to make a small sign of the cross with his thumb on the eyes, ears, nose, mouth, and hands of the dying person, and often on various other parts of the body, while reciting appropriate Latin formulas. In the late Middle Ages these anointings were interpreted as bringing spiritual purification from the sins committed through the senses. St. Thomas Aquinas wrote that extreme unction "removes the remainder of sin,

and prepares men for final glory," and that, "since the remedy for sin should be applied where sin originates in us first, for that reason the places of the five senses are anointed; the eyes, . . . the ears, etc." (Summa theologiae, 65.1.3 and 32.6. suppl.).

Because extreme unction—the last unction or unction in extremis—could be administered to dying persons no longer able either to make their confessions or to receive the viaticum, it acquired great pastoral importance. A good example of the rite at the end of the Middle Ages is given in the Sarum Manual, a priest's handbook widely used in England. The service is entirely in Latin. In the Christian East unction of the sick was sometimes administered to the dying, but it did not have the special emphasis of extreme unction in the West.

BIBLIOGRAPHY

A. Jefferies Collins, ed., Manuale ad usum percelebris ecclesie Sarisburiensis (1960), 107–114; Paul F. Palmer, ed., Sacraments and Forgiveness, II (1960); H. Boone Porter, "The Rites for the Dying in the Early Middle Ages," pts. 1 and 2, in Journal of Theological Studies, n.s. 10 (1959).

H. BOONE PORTER

[See also Death and Burial, in Europe; Sacramentary; Unction of the Sick.]

EXULTET ROLL, a large liturgical scroll, peculiar to south Italy, containing the illustrated text to the Paschal Proclamation, "Exultet iam angelica turba caelorum . . ." (Let the angelic host of heaven exult), sung by the deacon on Holy Saturday to bless the Paschal candle. The text, written in Beneventan script and accompanied by musical notations, is interspersed with large pictures, mostly of liturgical scenes and usually upside down so that as the text was sung and the scroll unfurled over the ambo, the congregation could see the illustrations right side up. Twenty-eight examples are preserved; all date from the tenth to thirteenth century.

BIBLIOGRAPHY

Myrtilla Avery, The Exultet Rolls of South Italy (1936); Émile Bertaux, L'art dans l'Italie méridionale (1904), 216–240, with supplement, "Iconographie comparée des rouleaux de l'Exultet: Tableaux synoptiques"; Charles Dodwell, Painting in Europe, 800 to 1200 (1971), 126–129.

LESLIE BRUBAKER

Terra. Section of an exultet roll, Italian, 12th century. BIBLIOTECA APOSTOLICA VATICANA, CODEX BARB. LAT. 592, sect. 5

EYCK, JAN VAN and **HUBERT VAN** (Jan, *ca.* 1390–1441; Hubert, *d.* 1426). Jan van Eyck was the leading painter of the early Flemish school in the fifteenth century. He was born about 1390 at Maeseyck, a village near Maastricht in the southeastern Netherlands. His activity is first documented at The Hague, where he served as court painter to John of Bavaria, count of Holland, from 1422 to 1425. Nothing is known of his work there, though some historians believe it may have included a group of miniatures in the Turin-Milan Hours (Hand *G*).

After John's death in 1425, van Eyck was employed by the powerful Burgundian duke, Philip the Good, who had promoted the arts in Flanders by appointing the finest artists and musicians to court positions *(valet de chambre)*.

Van Eyck did not function only as a court painter, however. On at least three occasions between 1426 and 1429 he was a member of diplomatic missions to secret and distant destinations. At least two of these trips were made to negotiate a marriage for Philip. On one trip to Portugal, van Eyck's official duty was to paint a portrait of the infanta Isabella to send to Philip for approval. The Flemings spent nearly a year on their mission, during which time van Eyck traveled extensively in Spain. After his return to Flanders in December 1429, van Eyck moved his residence to Bruges, where he served as painter to Philip's court until his death.

Sometime between 1429 and 1432 the artist took over a monumental project for the completion of the *Ghent Altarpiece of the Lamb,* which (according to an inscription on the frame) was begun by Hubert and finished by Jan in 1432. This "Hubert" is generally believed to be Jan van Eyck's older brother, though there is some controversy regarding the matter. No other works are known to be by Hubert van Eyck, though a panel of *The Three Marys at the Tomb* in Rotterdam is generally attributed to him.

The *Ghent Altarpiece* is a huge polyptych (many-paneled ensemble) with a very complicated iconography. When the altarpiece is closed, an impressive scene of the Annunciation extends across four panels. In the tier below, portraits of the donor, Jodocus Vijt, and his wife appear kneeling before trompe-l'oeil sculptures of John the Baptist and John the Evangelist (the cathedral of St. Bavo, where the altarpiece is today, was originally dedicated to St. John the Baptist). When the panels are opened, a complex ensemble in two tiers is displayed. Above, in the center, are the figures of the Virgin and John the Baptist flanking a sumptuous enthroned Christ. To either side of this group are angelic musicians; on the extremities Adam and Eve stand in niches. The five panels in the lower tier give the altarpiece its name. Here, in a panoramic landscape, processions for the feast of All Saints approach the center where the Lamb appears on the altar of the Heavenly Jerusalem (Rev. 4, 5, 7).

It is not, however, the complex iconography that has made this work one of the most famous monuments in art history. Rather it is the incredible detail displayed in the panels. Van Eyck's style may be called microscopic-telescopic realism. His technique of using glazes of pigment in a matrix of clear oil allowed him to paint with such refinement, and it also gave his paintings a brilliant enamellike effect on the surface.

Another aspect of van Eyck's genius lies in the complex and subtle manner in which he gives everyday objects—which he paints so realistically—several levels of meaning in the form of disguised symbolism. A vase of lilies can allude to purity, a mirror to virginity, a dog to fidelity. Perhaps the most inter-

The three Marys at the Tomb. Jan van Eyck and (probably) Hubert van Eyck, 15th century. MUSEUM BOY-MANS-VAN BEUNINGEN, ROTTERDAM

esting example of this is the *Arnolfini Wedding Portrait* in London's National Gallery (1434). The painting is, at first glance, a double portrait of a man and his wife. But the furnishings of the chamber in which they stand symbolize marriage as one of the sacraments of the church, and, finally, an inscription and a reflection in a mirror indicate that this is actually a pictorial contract (with witnesses) of their marriage in 1434.

Van Eyck's favorite theme is the glorification of the Virgin and Child: the *Madonna in the Church* (*ca.* 1438) in Berlin, the *Ince Hall Madonna* (1433) in Melbourne, the *Lucca Modonna* (*ca.* 1435–1436) in Frankfurt, the *Madonna of Chancellor Rolin* (*ca.* 1434–1436) in Paris, the *Madonna with Canon van der Paele* (1434–1436) in Bruges, the Dresden *Triptych of the Madonna* (1437), and the *Madonna at the Fountain* (1439) in Antwerp. His impressive bust

portraits of leading figures of his day are masterful reconstructions of their facial features. Among the many interesting people that he records so accurately are officials at court (Baudouin de Lannoy), court artists (Gilles Binchois), papal legates (Cardinal Nicolas Albergati), and those closer to him (his wife Margaretha). A *Portrait of a Man in a Red Turban* (1433) in London is thought by many to be a self-portrait of the artist.

BIBLIOGRAPHY

Ludwig von Baldass, *Jan van Eyck* (1952); Max J. Friedländer, *Early Netherlandish Painting,* I (1967); Erwin Panofsky, *Early Netherlandish Painting* (1953); W. H. James Weale, *Hubert and John Van Eyck* (1908).

JAMES SNYDER

[See also **Flemish Painting.**]

EYRBYGGJA SAGA, the "story of the people of Þórsnes, Eyrr, and Álptafjörðr," was probably compiled about 1240 at the Augustinian monastery at Helgafell on Snæfellsnes. The work is preserved complete in two transcripts made from the destroyed codex *Vatnshyrna* and in a fragment of another manuscript. The chief sources were skaldic stanzas (of which thirty-seven are quoted, though not all of them are genuine), genealogical tables (one by Ari Þorgilsson), *Landnámabók,* older sagas, current events, and local anecdotes. Structurally *Eyrbyggja* is unique in that its events are arranged chronologically rather than in cohesive episodes. The topographical descriptions are precise, the narrative is lucid, and the dialogue is pithy. For expository passages the anonymous author employed an involved, even elegant, style.

Eyrbyggja saga sketches the settlement and history of Snæfellsnes, placing emphasis on the conflicts among the Þórsnes, Eyrr, and Álptafjörðr clans from 844 until the death of Snorri goði in 1031. Snorri becomes the leading figure following his dramatic formal introduction in the Helgafell episode, and the dominant hero after slaying his adversary Arnkell goði. Arnkell is depicted as an ideal chieftain who forcefully protects the rights of his followers: "he was in every respect one of the best and wisest men in the ancient faith" (ch. 37). By contrast, his father Þórólfr is a ruthless marauder who brings grief to people even after his death. Snorri has much in common with Arnkell. While inferior as a fighter, he is superior to him in intelligence. Few saga figures excel Snorri as a peacemaker. The most likely model for this character is Þórðr Sturluson (*d.* 1267), a descendant of the historical Snorri goði. Among the other memorable characters is his sister Þuríðr, whose affair with the warrior Björn supplies romantic interest.

The author's antiquarian predilections attracted the attention of Sir Walter Scott, and one of the ghost stories in *Eyrbyggja* inspired Robert Louis Stevenson's "The Waif Woman." One chapter of the saga is devoted to the settlement of Greenland (*ca.* 985) and one to the adoption of Christianity (999). Formerly regarded as authentic, the elaborate descriptions of a pagan temple and pagan rites, borrowed from *Heimskringla,* are probably the imaginative creation of Snorri Sturluson. Although the author delighted in describing customs of former times, he was unaware that the sauna, which plays an essential part in the killing of two berserkers (the episode is borrowed from *Heiðarvíga saga*), was un-

known in Iceland until shortly before 1200. There is more fiction and less fact in *Eyrbyggja* than was once believed. The work can be interpreted as an exemplum extolling moderation and restraint to the ruthless chieftains during the brutal age of the Sturlungs. The generation-gap theme is more fully developed here than in any other saga of native heroes except *Þórðar saga hreðu.*

BIBLIOGRAPHY

Theodore M. Andersson, "The Displacement of the Heroic Ideal in the Family Sagas," in *Speculum,* **45** (1970); *Eyrbyggja Saga,* Paul Edwards and Hermann Pálsson, trans. (1973); Lee M. Hollander, "The Structure of *Eyrbyggja Saga,*" in *Journal of English and Germanic Philology,* **58** (1959).

PAUL SCHACH

[See also **Eddic Poetry; Skaldic Verse; Vinland Sagas.**]

EYSTEINN ÁSGRÍMSSON. *Lilja* (The lily), an Icelandic poem attributed to Eysteinn Ásgrímsson, dates from about 1340–1360. Consisting of 100 *hrynhent* stanzas, the poem is composed in the symmetrical *drápa* form: a prologue (*upphaf* or *inngangr*) of 25 stanzas, a refrain section (*stefjabálkr*) of 50 stanzas divided equally between two refrains (each occurring five times), and a conclusion (*slœmr*) of 25 stanzas. *Lilja* treats the main events of salvation history, focusing on the conflict between good and evil: long passages—one a soliloquy—are devoted to Lucifer's machinations against God. After appealing to God and Mary for inspiration, Eysteinn devotes the prologue to the fall of angels, Creation, the Fall of Man, and the promise of remedy. The first half (*stefjamél*) of the refrain section recounts the Annunciation and the events of Christ's life from the Nativity to the Crucifixion. Eysteinn ends the first refrain and begins the second in successive stanzas (50 and 51)—a unique device—as he continues the passion narrative. The remainder of the second *stefjamél* depicts the conquest of Satan (who is hooked by the bait of the cross), the Harrowing of Hell, the Resurrection, the Ascension, and the Last Judgment. In the *slœmr* Eysteinn confesses his sins, praises Mary, dedicates the poem to her and Christ, justifies his stylistic innovations, and names the poem.

The total number of stanzas places the poem in the tradition of 100-verse Marian poetry based on the number of letters in the thirteenth-century form of Gabriel's greeting. The number, and the repetition of the first stanza as the hundredth, suggest a circular pattern that is reconciled with the tripartite form and emphasis on the number 33 (Nativity, stanza 33; completion of Atonement, stanza 66; and so on). This pattern creates the figure of the "triangular circle," symbol of Mary's mediation of the mysteries of Incarnation and Trinity.

In stanza 4 Eysteinn contrasts his poem with earlier pagan encomia and consciously departs from the use of "obscure archaisms" (kennings), which "hinder understanding," in favor of "clear words" (stanzas 97 and 98). In this context he names the poem "The Lily," a commonplace of Marian iconography, but one that seems also to suggest that the clarity of his style reflects the Lily's purity: he rhymes *Lilja* with *skilja* (to understand). The style is nevertheless quite rhetorical, at times involving elaborate conceits (as in stanzas 92–94): "Even if all things—fish scales, wool, drops, etc.—became tongues they would not be able to praise Mary sufficiently." Occasionally Eysteinn displays metrical tours de force, such as weaving patterns that link the final stem of one line and the initial stem of the following line while rhyming in couplets (stanza 55) or quatrains (stanza 98). The poem was extensively imitated: its meter was renamed *liljulag,* and the saying "All skalds would like to have composed *Lilja*" emerged.

The identity of Eysteinn is disputed. A sixteenth-century manuscript credits a "brother Eysteinn" with the poem, and later sources identify him with Eysteinn Ásgrímsson, a prominent ecclesiastical official whose name appears in annals between 1349 and 1361, the year of his death. But records of 1342–1343 mention a "brother Eysteinn" at Þykkvabœr who was incarcerated for assaulting his abbot. The traditional conflation of these accounts has created colorful biographies but, though there is still disagreement, most scholars now separate the two figures and tend to consider the former as the poet of *Lilja.*

BIBLIOGRAPHY

Eysteinn Ásgrímsson, *Lilja,* Gunnar Finnbogason, ed. (1974); Thomas D. Hill, "Number and Pattern in *Lilja,*" in *Journal of English and Germanic Philology,* **69** (1970); Finnur Jónsson, ed., *Den norskislandske skjaldedigtning,* AII (1912), 363–395 and BII (1915), 390–416; Hans Schottmann, *Die isländische Mariendichtung* (1973), 188–251.

GEORGE S. TATE

[See also **Skaldic Verse.**]

Eyvān. Western side of the Mosque of the Ruler, Isfahan, built under the aegis of Shah ᶜAbbās I, 1612–1638. SEF/ART RESOURCE

EYVĀN (or *īvān, īwān,* also *līwān*), a term used to designate a large, vaulted hall that is walled on three sides and open directly to the outside on the fourth, usually onto a courtyard. The *eyvān* is a distinctive feature of Islamic religious and secular architecture. The form itself, however, is of pre-Islamic origin and is a common feature of Sasanian architecture (third to seventh centuries), which supplied the prototype. Although the *eyvān* can function as an independent unit, it is almost invariably incorporated within a larger architectural entity, of which it becomes the main axis of both plan and elevation. Frequently it serves to emphasize an important section of a building, as in the eighth-century Abbasid palace at Ukhaidir, in which an *eyvān* provides the focus for the throne complex. In Iranian religious architecture an *eyvān* very often precedes the domed area of the *mihrāb,* further stressing the orientation of the mosque toward Mecca.

Perhaps the most significant use of this architectural form is in the "four-*eyvān*" plan, which consists of a courtyard onto which four *eyvān*s open. This plan, also of pre-Islamic origin, first occurred in Islamic secular architecture, as in the eleventh-century Ghaznavid palace at Lashkari Bāzār, though Iranian religious architecture provides the best-known examples. The "four-*eyvān*" mosque was introduced to western Iran in the twelfth century, the classic example being the Masjid-i Jumᶜa at Isfahan. This type of mosque later became the canonical form for almost all such structures in Iran.

In the lands to the west of Iran, the *eyvān* is less commonly associated with the architecture of the mosque. Rather, it is a characteristic feature of the madrasa, the *māristān,* and the *ribāṭ,* where it occurs singly, in pairs, or in groups of four.

BIBLIOGRAPHY

K. A. C. Creswell, *The Muslim Architecture of Egypt,* II (1965), 106ff., 132ff.; Oleg Grabar, "The Visual Arts, 1050–1350," in *The Cambridge History of Iran,* V (1968).

LINDA KOMAROFF

[See also **Islamic Architecture.**]

EYVINDR FINNSSON SKÁLDASPILLIR (ca. 915–990), a descendant of King Haraldr hárfagri (Harald I Fairhair), was one of the last, best, and busiest Norwegian skalds. He worked for three kings: Hákon Aðalsteinsfóstri the Good (*ca.* 933–960), Haraldr gráfeldr (*ca.* 960–970), and Earl Hákon (*ca.* 970–995). Two long poems—*Hákonarmál* and *Háleygjatal*—and fourteen *lausavísur* are attributed to Eyvindr. His nickname, *skáldaspillir* (plagiarist), suggests that Eyvindr borrowed freely from earlier poets: *Hákonarmál,* for example, is probably modeled on *Eiríksmál,* and *Háleygjatal* on *Ynglingatal.*

Hákonarmál commemorates Hákon Aðalsteinsfóstri, who fell, victorious, in the battle of Storð around 960. Twenty-one stanzas are preserved as a unit in *Heimskringla;* stanzas 1–7, 16 (lines 4–6), and 19–21 are also found in *Fagrskinna; Snorra Edda* cites stanzas 1, 4 (lines 5–8), and 14. The meter, like that of *Eiríksmál,* is Eddic: a mixture of *málaháttr* and *fornyrðislag* for the battle scenes, and *ljóðaháttr* for the rest. *Hákonarmál* depicts with brilliant imagery and sound effects the fight in which the king was mortally wounded. Two Valkyries are sent to the battlefield by Odin to escort Hákon to Valhǫll. The central part of the poem is an eight-stanza dialogue involving the Valkyries, Odin, Bragi, and Hákon. The king seems somewhat apprehensive about his reception in Odin's hall; he was, after all, a Christian. Eyvindr must have had good political or personal reasons for stressing that Hákon was royally welcomed by the pagan gods, and that the king never violated the heathen temples of Norway. *Hákonarmál* concludes with the assurance that the world will end before Hákon's equal comes again.

Háleygjatal was composed for Earl Hákon; with some gaps, it traces his ancestry back to Odin or Yngvifreyr. Eyvindr's goal is to give the earls of Lade at least as impressive a family tree as that of the older royal line, the Ynglingar. Nine whole stanzas and seven half-stanzas have survived; some are preserved only in *Heimskringla,* some are only in *Snorra Edda,* and one is found only in *Fagrskinna.* The meter, like that of *Ynglingatal,* is *kviðuháttr.* Eyvindr's sentences often run across the *helmingr* boundary, ignoring the customary syntactic break. *Háleygjatal* tells of the deaths and burials of the earls of Lade. It ends—in its present fragmentary state—with praise of Hákon and his victory over the Jómsvíkings.

The *dróttkvætt* verses attributed to Eyvindr are thought to have been composed between 960 and 970. Five concern the battle at Storð; others complain about a famine, snow in midsummer, and the stinginess of Eiríkr's sons. Eyvindr's kenning style in these *Lausavísur* is distinctively playful and intellectual. One of his finest stanzas is "Bǫrum Ullr um alla," which provides grounds for impeaching Haraldr gráfeldr. Another is "Fengum feldarstinga," which employs the material of heroic legend to confirm that the poet gave his "leaping herring of Egill's palms [arrows, since Egill is the name of a legendary archer] in exchange for the slender arrows of the sea [herring]." The transaction is made rhetorically—if not commercially—satisfying.

BIBLIOGRAPHY

Hallvard Lie, "'Natur' og 'unatur' i skaldekunsten," in *Avhandlinger utgitt av det Norske Videnskaps-Akademi i Oslo,* 2, Hist.-filos. Kl., I (1957); Edith Marold, "Das Walhallbild in den *Eiríksmál* und den *Hákonarmál,*" in *Mediaeval Scandinavia,* 5 (1972); Klaus von See, "Zwei eddische Preislieder: *Eiríksmál* und *Hákonarmál,*" in *Festgabe für U. Pretzel* (1963).

ROBERTA FRANK

[See also **Eddic Poetry; Eiríksmál and Hákonarmál; Snorra Edda; Skaldic Verse.**]

EZNIK OF KOŁB is a fifth-century Armenian writer, translator, and philosopher whose identity and works are known from the fifth-century biography of Maštocᶜ by Koriwn. Eznik was Maštocᶜ's pupil and associate, and assisted him in making Armenian translations of the Bible and many of the works of the early church fathers. He was most probably among the pupils whom Maštocᶜ took to

Edessa to enroll them in Syriac and Greek schools. This may be why at a later date Eznik and Joseph of Pałin were sent to Edessa to translate the works of the Syriac fathers.

From Edessa, Eznik and Joseph went to the "region of the Greeks," where they searched for books in Greek. In Constantinople they were joined by two classmates, Koriwn and Łewond. Eznik and his friends remained there until after the Council of Ephesus (431). On their return to Armenia they brought with them the canons of that council, an authorized Greek version of the Bible, and several other religious works. After his return Eznik assisted Bishop Sahak of Armenia in revising an earlier translation of the Bible and later, biblical commentaries and homilies.

Nothing is known about the life of Eznik besides the fact that he came from the village of Kołb. Certain scholars have tried to identify him with the "Lord Eznik bishop of Bagrewand" who participated in the Armenian Council of Artašat in 449. Identical names, however, do not provide a basis for such an assumption.

Extant in the manuscripts are a number of works attributed to Eznik. All of these are spurious, except a fragment of a letter to Maštoc[C] and a treatise that nineteenth-century scholars chose to call *Ełc ałandoc[C]* (Refutation of sects). The latter, which has survived in a single manuscript, is a mosaic of patristic excerpts that have been skillfully integrated into a single exposition. It is difficult to determine the purpose of this work, since the title page is missing in the original. Earlier scholars thought that it was a treatise refuting Christian heresies, Zoroastrianism, and ancient Greek philosophical schools. Modern scholars have advanced different views: Louis Mariès thought that the book was about God and proposed the title *De Deo;* V. K. Chaloyan suggested that it was a discourse on good and evil. Nikolai Adontz's thesis that it is a treatise on free will is probably the most logical.

BIBLIOGRAPHY

Eznik de Kołb De Deo, Louis Mariès and Charles Mercier, eds. (1959); *Eznik de Kołb De Deo,* Louis Mariès and Charles Mercier, trans. (1959); Louis Mariès, *Le De Deo d'Eznik de Kołb* (1924).

KRIKOR H. MAKSOUDIAN

[See also **Armenian Church, Doctrines and Councils; Armenian Literature; Koriwn.**]

EZRA, IBN. See **Abraham ben Meïr ibn Ezra.**

EZZOLIED, one of the earliest extant Middle High German poems, was written around 1060 by a clergyman named Ezzo at the behest of Bishop Gunther of Bamberg. The song, the music for which was composed by a priest named Wille, may have been commissioned to celebrate the adoption of a monastic life-style by the canons of the Bamberg cathedral. According to a later tradition, however, it was written to be sung on a pilgrimage to the Holy Land led by the same Bishop Gunther in 1065. The complete poem, consisting of thirty-four stanzas (420 verses), is preserved in a somewhat revised form in a twelfth-century manuscript from the monastery of Vorau in Austria.

The beginning (some seventy-six verses) of a version closer to the lost original is in a manuscript from the monastery of Ochsenhausen. In lofty and solemn tones the poet tells the history of the world from the Christian point of view. After singing a hymn of praise to God the Creator, Ezzo narrates concisely the tale of man's creation and fall. After Adam and his descendants had been brought under the sway of the devil, darkness fell upon the world until John the Baptist revealed to mankind the coming of the true light in Christ. The middle portion of the poem is devoted to Christ's life on earth and his death on the cross, which made it possible for man to overcome death and return to his spiritual homeland. At the end Ezzo apostrophizes the holy cross in two stanzas, calling it the best of all woods with which the devil was caught, and then, in an elaborate metaphor, the mast of the ship that, driven by the Holy Ghost, carries man through the sea of the world toward heaven, his ultimate destination.

BIBLIOGRAPHY

Helmut de Boor, *Die deutsche Literatur von Karl dem Grossen bis zum Beginn der höfischen Dichtung (770–1170),* 7th ed. (1966), 145–147; James W. Marchand, "The Ship Allegory in the *Ezzolied* and in Old Icelandic," in *Neophilologus,* 60 (1976); Werner Schröder, ed., *Kleinere deutsche Gedichte des 11. und 12. Jahrhunderts* (1972).

STEPHEN J. KAPLOWITT

[See also **German Lyric; Middle High German Literature.**]

FABLES. "Fable" derives from Latin *fabula,* the special meanings of which include "a fictitious narrative, tale, story" and, within this genre, an apologue—that is, a story intended to convey a moral. Classical writers, church fathers, and medieval philosophers generally emphasize the untrue nature of the fable: Cicero advises us not to attribute authority to fables or to place our faith in "fabricated things" (*De divinatione,* 2.113); in his *Commentaries on the Somnium Scipionis,* Macrobius says of fables that their "name itself proclaims their falsity," yet he goes on to characterize them as useful didactic instruments, doubtless because their roots in popular culture made them accessible to all audiences, as well as vehicles for entertainment (1.2.7).

The source of medieval fable collections is the Greek fable, which by the end of the fifth century B.C. was often associated with the name of Aesop (sixth century B.C.), although the first collection of Aesopic fables was not published until the late fourth century B.C., probably by Demetrius of Phalerum, in a manuscript now lost. Other fable collections are attributed to Babrius and Nicostratus. This last collection was apparently used in rhetorical education. The Greek Aesopic fable gave rise to a Latin verse collection by Phaedrus (*ca.* 15 B.C.–*ca.* 50 A.D.), a freed slave of Augustus. Indebted to Aesop, Phaedrus also added non-Aesopic material to his five books of fables, which he intended to be read for pleasure and instruction. Among later Latin collections are those attributed to Titianus and Avianus, both of whom probably knew Babrius.

Medieval fable collections, or *Isopets* (the Old French for Aesopic compositions) derive for the most part from Phaedrus. According to Bastin, Phaedrus' collection was probably known in the original version until the ninth century, at which time it was lost until the Renaissance. His collection was perpetuated, however, in three Latin redactions: the *Aesop* of the scribe Ademar, the *Aesop* of Wissembourg (both prose, tenth century), and, most importantly for the vernacular fable, the *Romulus.* The latter invents a new prologue, which identifies the author as one Romulus and claims that he translated the fables from Greek.

The *Romulus* exists in prose and verse redactions. The prose redaction is represented, in abbreviated form, in Vincent of Beauvais's *Speculum historiale* and *Speculum doctrinale.* The verse redaction is known most widely in the collection attributed to Walter of England (*ca.* 1175), whose *Romulus* appears in more than 100 manuscripts. It is this collec-

tion which, translated into vernacular French, gives rise to three important texts: the *Isopet* of Lyon, the *Isopet I* and the *Isopet III* of Paris. The Walter of England Latin verse redaction also inspired various Italian collections: those of Per Uno da Siena, Accio Zuccho, Francesco del Tuppo, Riccardiano, Facio Caffarello, and the *Apologhi verseggiati.* Other vernacular versions deriving from the same source are the Portuguese *Ysopet* of Vienna, a Provençal fragment, a Franco-Italian *Ysopet,* the majority of fables in Juan Ruiz' *Libro de buen amor,* a Hebrew *Ysopite,* and the German *Edelstein* of Boner, as well as two manuscript collections at St. Gall and Wolfenbüttel. A second verse redaction of the *Romulus* is ascribed to Walter's contemporary Alexander Neckham, whose less widely disseminated version nonetheless inspired two French collections: the *Isopet II* of Paris and the Chartres *Isopet.* The *Romulus* exists, thirdly, in Latin redactions that combine it with other fable traditions: the Anglo-Latin *Romulus,* for example, when translated into English, was the model for the twelfth-century Anglo-Norman writer Marie de France, whose fables recall both Phaedrus and the *Roman de Renart.*

Vernacular versions derive, to a much lesser degree, from the Latin verse collection of Avianus. Three manuscripts of the French *Isopet I,* of which Phaedrus was the source, include a French translation of eighteen fables from Avianus (*Avionnet*). Twenty-seven of Avianus' fables are found in the fifteenth-century Latin-German edition made by Steinhöwel, and nine appear in French translation in the York fragment.

At least one vernacular *Isopet* does not show the same filiation with Latin intermediate versions. Guillaume Tardif's *Isopet,* composed for Charles VIII, is based on Laurent Valle's contemporary translation of Aesop's fables from Greek to Latin.

The appropriateness of fables to philosophical or theological works and to sermons was much debated in the twelfth and thirteenth centuries. Thomas Aquinas decries the dangers inherent in fabled images (*fabulari similitudine*), whereas twelfth-century Platonists, like William of Conches, defend their value in philosophical discourse. In the thirteenth and fourteenth centuries, despite this debate, exempla collections compiled for sermons include significant numbers of fables.

Fables excited a considerable influence on secular writers, for example, Marie de France, the authors of the fabliaux, and Chaucer.

BIBLIOGRAPHY

Julia Bastin, *Recueil général des Isopets,* I and II (1929–1930); Murray P. Brush, ed., "*Ysopet III* of Paris," in *PMLA,* **24** (1909); Peter Dronke, *Fabula: Explorations into the Uses of Myth in Medieval Platonism* (1974); Léopold Hervieux, *Les fabulistes latins depuis le siècle d'Auguste jusqu'a la fin du moyen âge,* 5 vols. (1893–1899); George C. Keidel, *A Manual of Aesopic Fable Literature* (1896), and "The History of French Fable Manuscripts," in *PMLA,* **24** (1909); Gaston Paris, "Les fabulistes latins," in *Journal des savants* (1884, 1885).

GRACE M. ARMSTRONG

[See also **Avianus; Beast Epic; Marie de France; Neckham, Alexander; Renard the Fox; Romulus; Ruiz, Juan; William of Conches.**]

FABLES, FRENCH. Five principal collections of Old French fables exist, often known as *Isopets (Ysopets),* from the name Aesop, or occasionally as *Avionnets,* from Avianus, the fourth-century composer of a Latin collection.

The oldest extant collection is that of Marie de France, in all probability composed in the third quarter of the twelfth century and consisting of 102 fables plus a fragment (Warnke, LXVb), a prologue, and an epilogue that provide important background details. The existence of twenty-three manuscripts bears witness to the popularity of her collection. Marie claims to have derived her text from an English collection translated from Latin by Alfred the Great, but her source, now lost, must have been composed later than the time of Alfred. Forty of her fables are derived from the *Romulus Nilantii* (the text publishd by Frédéric Nilant under the title *Romuli fabulae Aesopiae* in 1709), and some from the vulgate *Romulus.* Others are of Eastern or unknown origin.

The Lyons *Isopet* is a collection of sixty-one fables translated from the Latin text in elegiac verse composed around 1175 by Gualterus Anglicus, chaplain to Henry II. Gualterus' version was formerly known as the *Romulus Niveleti* (after the editor Isaac Nèvelet, who included it in his *Mythologia Aesopica* of 1610). Written in the thirteenth century, the French version is extant in one manuscript at Lyons, which also contains the Latin text.

Isopet I (or *Isopet-Avionnet*), a second translation of the *Romulus* of Gualterus Anglicus, consists of sixty-four fables, with an additional nineteen fables drawn from Avianus. Consisting of the *Isopet I* and

the *Avionnet,* it is called *Isopet I* or *Isopet-Avionnet.* Extant in six manuscripts, the *Isopet I* by itself has both a prologue and an epilogue. Three manuscripts contain an additional four fables. The *Avionnet* has a prologue and an epilogue that indicates that the existing text was rearranged by a second writer and dedicated to Jeanne of Burgundy, wife of Philip VI (Bastin, II, 199–384).

The *Chartres Isopet,* one of two adaptations of the *Novus Aesopus* of Alexander Neckham, consists of forty fables, thirty-eight of them from Neckham, the final distich of which becomes the moral (called *sentence, essample,* and *exposition* in the text). There is both a prologue and an epilogue. Composed by a cleric, probably from the Île-de-France, in the late thirteenth century, this version is extant in only one manuscript, at Chartres. The fables are generally fairly short (only three exceed sixty lines).

Isopet II, a second adaptation of Alexander Neckham's *Novus Aesopus,* consists of forty fables, a prologue, and an epilogue. Composed by a cleric and extant in one Paris manuscript, the fables in this collection vary from 24 to 102 lines.

A wide range of animals and birds occur in the fables; particularly common are the lion, the wolf, the dog, the ass, the fox, the lamb or sheep, and the eagle. A number contain only humans, and some a mixture of animals and humans. Over and above the castigation of folly, arrogance, envy, and other faults, many fables reflect the ideas, problems, and vocabulary of the feudal world, discussing themes such as disloyalty, honor, and brutality and stressing the misfortunes of serving an evil lord or the consequences of oath breaking. Those fables based on the *Romulus* of Gualterus often go beyond human folly to recommend, in lengthy morals, a life of virtue rather than one of happiness and success.

BIBLIOGRAPHY

Julia Bastin, *Recueil général des Isopets,* 2 vols. (1929–1930), 83–197, 113–181, 199–384; J. Beyer, *Schwank und Moral* (1968); Glyn S. Burgess, *Marie de France; An Analytical Bibliography* (1977); A. Léopold Hervieux, *Les fabulistes latins depuis le siècle d'Auguste jusqu'à la fin du moyen âge,* 2nd ed., 5 vols. (1883–1889, repr. 1964); George C. Keidel, *A Manual of Aesopic Fable Literature* (1895, repr. 1974); Karl Warnke, *Die Fabeln der Marie de France* (1898, repr. 1974).

GLYN S. BURGESS

[See also **Avianus; Fables; Marie de France; Neckham, Alexander.**]

FABLIAU AND COMIC TALE. The term "fabliau," a Picardism, is used conventionally to designate a species of Old French narrative comprising at least 150 texts that date from the close of the twelfth century well into the fourteenth. (Principal manuscript collections of these poems survive from the end of the thirteenth and beginning of the fourteenth century.) Fabliaux are generally quite brief—a few hundred lines of rhyming octosyllabic couplets—but some possess less than 100 and others more than 1,000 lines. Many fabliaux are anonymous, though a number have been attributed to named authors, several of whom—such as Jean Bodel and Rutebeuf—are well known for their works in other genres.

The fabliau was defined by Joseph Bédier as a *conte à rire en vers,* literally "a metrical tale to make [people] laugh." The term itself appears in about sixty surviving poems. However, texts that today would be identified as fabliaux were labeled in medieval times as *fables, lais, romans* (vernacular stories), *dits* (poems, statements), or *exemples.* This state of affairs not only reflects the classificatory looseness of Old French literary terminology but also bespeaks an authentic fluctuation of generic boundaries. Sharply defined, independent genres seldom preoccupied medieval writers and audiences; borrowings between genres and the transformation of them was far more often the rule than not. Nevertheless, despite disagreements over certain borderline cases, modern scholars are fairly unanimous as to which texts make up the corpus of these comic tales.

Identical in form with several other kinds of Old French metrical narrative—the Celtic *Lais* of Marie de France, the *Miracles* of Gautier de Coinci, the *dits* of Rutebeuf—fabliaux may by and large be distinguished from these counterparts by their subject matter and their diction. Their humor is frequently coarse, even obscene. Their mood, which can best be described as resolutely anticourtly and purposefully unrefined, has led several modern scholars to claim that the popularity of fabliaux during the thirteenth century was due to their mirroring of the anti-aristocratic and "realist" tastes of the new middle classes established in the increasingly wealthy towns and cities. This fabliau/bourgeoisie connection was convincingly laid to rest by Per Nykrog, who, following on the brilliant insights of Edmond Faral, argued that since the tone, subject matter, and language of the fabliaux were so systematically opposed to the courtly and aristocratic modes of romance and the love lyric (*grand chant courtois*), familiarity with the latter fashions constitutes virtually a prerequisite for the appreciation of the former. Fabliaux are thus the reverse side of the courtly coin. Coarseness and obscenity do not necessarily imply lack of literary sophistication; in many cases fabliaux evince considerable wit, verbal ingenuity, and intellectual subtlety. Jean Rychner, who studied various manuscript traditions of given fabliaux (some of which provide carefully crafted, "literary" versions of tales furnished by others in a degraded, corrupt, and rather more "oral" state), has described the language of the fabliaux as corresponding to a very conventionalized "low style."

A reader may look in vain in romances by Chrétien de Troyes or Guillaume de Lorris, or in the *lais* of Marie de France, for words designating bluntly the sexual act, male and female genitalia, or such bodily functions as belching, breaking wind, and defecating. A definite preciosity and modesty characterize their vernacular courtly diction. Thus, for instance, the narrator of Chrétien's *Érec et Énide* states his unwillingness to describe the passionate lovemaking of his recently wedded protagonists. Exactly the opposite holds true in the fabliau, where the vernacular becomes vulgar, in both senses of the word. Lusty priests willingly trick, or are tricked by, the wily wives of their parishioners; traveling young men often manage to seduce the (usually cooperative) young daughters of their hosts; clever personages receive their comeuppance at the hands of characters more astute than they; scenes of gluttony and of other sorts of excess abound. The fabliau world is a stylized jungle in which survival and self-betterment belong to the capable and amoral cheat who, because he or she frequently exposes the greed, the sham, and the selfishness of his or her adversary in a funny and "tall story" manner, earns the admiration and even the complicity of the reader. The fabliau theme par excellence is that of the trickster who is finally tricked in turn—usually by a person who pretends to cater to the victim's vanity or principal vice in order to bring off the "sting."

The comedy of these narratives is often boisterous, but not always. There are examples of black humor too. In "L'enfant de neige" (The snow baby) a merchant returns home after two whole years' absence to find that his wife has given birth to a son. She claims that one wintry day, while thinking of her absent husband, she went to her open window and inadvertently swallowed a falling snowflake. This caused her to conceive. The merchant feigns to marvel at this "miracle" and raises the boy to young manhood. When he reaches the age of fifteen, the merchant takes him on a business trip. Upon their arrival in Genoa, he sells the boy into slavery. He returns home alone, and responds to the consternation of his wife by explaining that in Italy the sun burns bright and hot. Since the boy was begotten by a snowflake, he melted in the heat.

Another well-known text, "Le chevalier qui fist parler les cons" (The knight who made cunts speak), amusingly exploits the common clerkly theme of the fickleness of women through the device of a knight who can hear the "spoken confessions" of a socially very wide variety of female sex organs. (This conceit was later utilized by the eighteenth-century encyclopedist and *philosophe,* Denis Diderot, in *Les Bijoux indiscrets* [The indiscreet jewels].) Feminine wiles serve elsewhere to unmask other forms of hypocrisy or weakness, as in the "Lai d'Aristote" (Lay of Aristotle), by Henri d'Andeli, the witty author of the very clerkly "Battle of the Seven Arts." In it Aristotle chides his erstwhile pupil Alexander for having succumbed to the charms of his mistress and no longer behaving as a proper knight should. Alexander recounts the complaint to the lovely courtesan, who decides to take revenge on the philosopher. Barefooted, her legs showing, dressed in a loose-fitting and artfully unbuttoned gown, she appears before Aristotle braiding flowers and singing a pretty song. She flirts with him; he is smitten. She manages to cajole him into going down on all fours; she climbs on his back, and Aristotle carries her about the orchard, trotting like a horse. Delighted, Alexander witnesses the scene from a nearby window. (Antecedents of this story have been traced to ancient India.)

On occasion the morality of the fabliau—each story, incidentally, has its moral—appears to deal directly with, to thematize, the problem of courtly or euphemistic diction. The motif of the young man (a *bachelier*) who benefits from the hospitality of his host only to seduce the latter's young daughter—a medieval avatar of the modern "traveling salesman" story—provides an interesting variant. The girl is delicate, refined to such an extent that she quite literally cannot stand to hear certain uncouth words; if she hears for instance, *foutre* (fuck), she promptly faints. (One is reminded of Jean de Meun's Lover, in the *Romance of the Rose,* who violently objects to Reason's employing the term *coilles* [balls, testicles]; such a word, he avers, has no place in the vocabulary of a well bred young lady.) On the other hand, as

matters turn out, there is apparently nothing the daughter enjoys more than participating in the activity denoted by *foutre;* she becomes a willing partner in the act of lust, though not in its nomenclature. The story, consequently, seems to mock a genre—courtly romance—in which adultery and fornication repeatedly occur (see *Tristan,* "Guigemar," *Lancelot*) but that eschews the vernacular terms pertaining to them. It does not seem too farfetched to see in this particular fabliau tradition a more than oblique reference to the thirteenth-century obsession with the relationship between words and things: the Scholastic debates between realists and nominalists, for example, or the discussions concerning the supposedly inherent mendacity of courtly romance narrative in verse.

Social commentary of diverse sorts can be found as a by-product of many fabliaux; it is usually highly satirical. "Les trois aveugles de Compiègne" (The three blind men from Compiègne), by Cortebarbe, offers a case in point. This tale, narrationally more complex than those referred to above, involves various social classes and types. Yet the characteristic fabliau conventions are scrupulously obeyed.

A young cleric meets three blind men and decides to play a joke on them. He announces that he is going to give them a gold coin (a *besant*). He does nothing of the sort, but each of the blind men believes that one of his companions has the coin. In their collective joy and greed none asks which one has received the money. The three blind men repair to a tavern, order a five-course meal, and reserve a comfortable room for the night. The innkeeper is convinced—perhaps because he wants to be—that they have the wherewithal to pay. Confusion ensues the next morning when no gold piece is discovered and the innkeeper prepares to beat the blind men with a stick. But the cleric appears on the scene and "generously" offers to take care of the bill. The blind men go on their way. The cleric accompanies the innkeeper to church, where, he says, the priest will reimburse him. Mass is about to start, and the cleric explains that he must depart but payment will be made in full as soon as the priest has said Mass. The cleric goes to find the priest and tells him that he has brought the innkeeper to church because he is possessed by demons; he begs the priest to exorcise the innkeeper by reading the Gospel upon his head. The priest promises to do so, and the cleric takes his leave. One easily imagines the scene that follows: the innkeeper demanding his money, the priest (convinced of the man's madness) performing the requested exorcism (helped by the strong arms of his parishioners), the cheated innkeeper slowly reaching the conclusion that he has been duped. The joke (*iocus*), game or play (*jeu*) concludes.

Everything has been staged by the cleric, for his own pleasure as well as for the amusement of Cortebarbe's audience. His (in all probability noble) patron must have been delighted at this gallery of churls being outwitted and fooled, at the mockery of "charity," and perhaps even the more-than-sly dig at the efficacy of certain ecclesiastical practices. The cleric creates illusions, only sardonically to dissipate them—all in the name of fun, for a *conte à rire*.

Much scholarly debate has surrounded the issue of the "origins" of the fabliau. Until Bédier, prevailing opinion held that these tales originated in India and wended their way, over time, through Persia and Muslim lands, via Spain and Sicily, to late-twelfth-century France. This "Oriental hypothesis" tells only a small part of the story, although Bédier's assertion that the fabliau, as it has come down to us, is a purely French (and medieval) invention (possessing, however, counterparts and analogues in other countries and other times) also requires considerable modification. It is probably best to understand the Old French corpus of fabliaux in its thirteenth-century vernacular specificity, but even when so understood, it unites a number of different strands. Arabic and Hebrew collections of stories, some of which bear close resemblance to fabliaux, were known in western Europe, and certain of them recall early Sanskrit prototypes. Eastern wisdom literature, especially as it came to be embodied in texts comprising a frame story and more or less numerous shorter fictions (*romans à tiroir*), helped give shape to very popular Old French compilations (in prose and in verse) like the *Roman des sept sages* and *Dolopathos,* which contain fabliau-style narratives. Such influential Latin works as the twelfth-century *Disciplina clericalis* betray Oriental origins, and surely contributed to the formation of fabliaux. Early troubadour lyrics—such as those of William IX, duke of Aquitaine—at times evince a spirit not too far removed from that of the fabliau.

Nor should the importance of fable and "morality" literature be disregarded; the collection of late-twelfth-century *fables,* often attributed to a Marie "de France" identified conventionally with the author of the *Lais,* resemble in theme, if not always in diction, a goodly number of fabliaux. The same can be—and has been—said for the sometimes ribald and burlesque Latin *comoedia* that flourished in certain clerkly milieus. The entire matter of burlesque and parody deserves mention also. Within the fluidity that characterizes much medieval literature there is the tendency to mock affectionately or otherwise poke fun at those values most cherished and venerated, and to mix styles and tones. Thus, the twelfth-century *Pèlerinage de Charlemagne* treats the beloved emperor's supposed pilgrimage to the Holy Land in a very light vein; the relics he brings to the Byzantine court on his way back to *douce France* save him and his twelve peers from the consequences of their drunken boasts. And Oliver's amazing prowess with their host's beautiful daughter constitutes in and of itself a funny miniature fabliau. (He swears to make love to her more times in one night than is physically possible for him. He fails to accomplish his oath, of course, but his performance is so meritorious that the princess happily testifies that he did what he had promised to do. Her father, the emperor of Constantinople, is duped.) Finally, the fabliau spirit demonstrates obvious kinship with the mood of what is now called goliardic verse—Latin lyrics mainly of the thirteenth century, composed for and by clerks, and often dealing with dicing, drinking, and whoring. (It is surely no accident that Rutebeuf, the Old French poet much of whose work shows considerable affinity with the goliard mode, also composed fabliaux and *Renard*-type fables.)

Before fabliaux as such emerged, then, the resources they would put to use already existed in medieval Latin and French literature: the humor, the coarseness, the motifs, the story models. And the somewhat systematic courtliness of twelfth-century romance (as well as the crisis of confidence undergone by romance diction at the start of the thirteenth century) provided the impetus for what would be the correspondingly systematic anticourtliness of the fabliau. However, even during the thirteenth century, fabliaux belong to a broader literary spectrum. For example, the *Miracles* of Gautier de Coinci celebrate the interventions of the Virgin in the lives of penitent sinners who, frequently, are very humble people; the worth of those helped by Our Lady is often stressed in opposition to the lesser merit of many individuals of higher social rank. And in his didactic writings Gautier sharply criticizes the avarice of the clergy and the false pride of noblemen with extraordinary bluntness and verve. No "ideology," courtly or other, is respected.

Several surviving thirteenth-century plays share features found in goliardic and fabliau texts. The tavern scene in the *Courtois d'Arras* (ca. 1220), for instance, transposes, with its sluttish and dishonest wenches, fabliau elements into this dramatic adaptation of the Prodigal Son parable (Luke 15). Similarly, the *Jeu de la feuillée* (*ca.* 1275), by Adam de la Halle, resembles *Les trois aveugles de Compiègne* in that a character—this time a profiteering monk—is duped into paying for the food and drink consumed by others, to the amusement of the audience and the other characters alike.

By the mid fourteenth century the fabliau as a genre ceased to exist. It was subsumed into other, or into new, forms and consequently lived on in many different guises. Among non-French works, stories in Boccaccio's *Decameron* and in Chaucer's *Canterbury Tales* (such as The Miller's Tale) have been traced to fabliau models. Fabliau diction and themes are present in Villon's *Testament* (*ca.* 1461). The final section of Antoine de la Sale's *Jehan de Saintré* (1456), in which the protagonist takes revenge on his faithless lady and her ignoble new lover (a lubricious and gluttonous abbot), who have tricked him, borrows heavily from the fabliau tradition, as do such collections as the fifteenth-century satirical *Quinze Joies du mariage* and the salaciously comic *Cent nouvelles nouvelles.* Last, *Pathelin* (*ca.* 1470), the best known of medieval French farces, is to all intents and purposes the dramatization of a classic fabliau situation. Later centuries saw the fabliau spirit assimilated into what is often tagged the *esprit gaulois* and/or *esprit libertin.* Passages from the sixteenth-century prose narratives of Rabelais, certain verse *contes* of La Fontaine (seventeenth century), and the *Bijoux indiscrets* of Diderot offer three cases in point. As the fabliau had once surfaced as a fairly definable genre in the thirteenth century from the mix of earlier manifestations of the spirit it came to incarnate, so, in subsequent times, it receded into the mainstream of other, more permanent—or more fashionable—literary kinds.

BIBLIOGRAPHY

Sources. The standard repertory of fabliaux texts remains Anatole de Montaiglon and Gaston Raynaud, *Recueil général et complet des fabliaux des XIIIe et XIVe siècles,* 6 vols. (1872–1890). English translations of twenty-one fabliaux (including the "Lai d'Aristote" and "L'enfant de neige") are in Robert Hellman and Richard O'Gorman, trans., *Fabliaux: Ribald Tales from the Old French* (1965).

Studies. Joseph Bédier, *Les fabliaux* (1893); Edmond Faral, "Les contes," in Joseph Bédier and Paul Hazard, *Histoire de la littérature française illustrée,* I (1923), 58–61; Per Nykrog, *Les fabliaux* (1957); Jean Rychner, *Contribution à l'étude des fabliaux,* 2 vols. (1960), and "Fa-

bliaux," in *Dictionnaire des lettres françaises: Le moyen âge* (1964). Extensive bibliographies, including modern critical editions of various fabliaux, are in Nykrog and in the annual international bibliographies issued by the Modern Language Association of America.

KARL D. UITTI

[See also **Bodel, Jean; Fables, French; French Literature; Goliards; Lai, Lay; Marie de France; Rutebeuf.**]

FACHSCHRIFTTUM, technical, utilitarian, or nonbelletristic secular literature, particularly that of the Middle Ages. The German term is used for want of an exact English equivalent and because the study of utilitarian literature, long neglected by philologists and literary critics, was first raised to an exact discipline by the German scholar Gerhard Eis. For Eis, *Fachschrifttum* includes all specialized works, be they in prose or in verse, that are written for a practical purpose and make no claim to aesthetic value.

The literature of the natural sciences has received little attention even though the natural world was treated, however theocentrically, in medieval encyclopedic works such as Isidore of Seville's *Etymologiae* (seventh century), Hrabanus Maurus' *De rerum naturis* (ninth century), Honorius Augustodunensis' *Imago mundi,* and Hugh of St. Victor's *Didascalicon* (twelfth century), and Thomas of Cantimpré's *Liber de natura rerum* (thirteenth century).

The term *fachprosa* (technical prose), though sometimes used, is too restrictive, since many practical handbooks were in verse. Even after prose had displaced verse for most purposes, verse continued to be used in some manuals for mnemonic reasons.

The chief subjects of medieval *Fachschrifttum* were the seven liberal and the seven mechanical arts, which had been transmitted from ancient Greece to medieval Europe by Latin and Arabic scholars. The seven liberal arts were those the ancients deemed worthy of a freeman, the seven mechanical arts being those delegated to slaves. Of these fourteen arts the medieval clerics naturally favored the liberal ones, which furnished the foundation of their theological training. These were the trivium, consisting of grammar, rhetoric, and dialectic or logic, and the quadrivium, consisting of mathematics, music, geometry, and astronomy/astrology. Grammar was the basis of all writing; rhetoric served in composing

Latin sermons; and dialectic or logic was necessary for Scholastic disputations and legal pleading.

Though less important than the trivium, the quadrivium also aided the clergy: mathematics served in reckoning the church calendar, music served to praise God, and astronomy helped determine the date of Easter. Only geometry had little use, unless perhaps in delimiting church properties. Surprisingly, the church was able to reconcile astrology with Christianity, even though it had developed among the heathen Arabs and was in conflict with free will.

Although churchmen found the mechanical arts less valuable than the liberal ones, abstract knowledge about them remained a clerical monopoly until the late medieval artisans surpassed their ancient predecessors and began to describe their arts in the vernacular. These mechanical, or illiberal, arts were handicraft (opificium); weaponry (armatura), which included military science; navigation (navigatio), which included geography and trade; hunting (venatio), which included forestry and animal husbandry; medicine (medicina); and the court arts (theatrica), which included jousting, fencing, dancing, and spectacles of all kinds. These were followed by the forbidden arts of magic, mantic, and thievery, the last of which dealt with the tricks and jargon of thieves, swindlers, and beggars.

Whereas ancient writers had assigned medicine to the illiberal arts worthy only of slaves, medieval men raised the physician to the social level of the lawyer and theologian, provided he limited himself to traditional knowledge handed down from Hippocrates and Galen and did not dabble in experimentation. As a result, whatever medical progress was made during the Middle Ages was made chiefly by the surgeons, a group despised by the educated classes and lumped together with barbers and tooth pullers. The art of war was, of course, socially acceptable in a society ruled by fighting men. Legal science was limited to Roman and canon law, these being based on classic antecedents and conducted in Latin. It was not concerned with common law, which was merely a body of folk custom handed down orally in the vernacular and could be learned by any spectator at a court of law. Roman law, as codified by Justinian, gradually displaced common law in much of medieval Europe, thereby making lawbooks necessary.

Throughout the Middle Ages the seven liberal arts, as well as law, medicine, and theology, remained the monopoly of the educated classes and

were transmitted in Latin, thus continuing to be international in scope. Some scholars, such as Aelfric in England and Notker Labeo (Teutonicus) of St. Gall, Switzerland, translated works on the liberal arts but they served primarily as keys or teaching aids for understanding the Latin originals. Even when translations did begin to appear in numbers, they were made chiefly to be read to illiterates, because most literates could read Latin and preferred to consult the originals.

Whereas Latin suited the theoretical sciences handed down from antiquity, it was less suitable for the mechanical arts, which made great advances in the late Middle Ages. A Greek medical text based on logic rather than observation, and later translated into Arabic and subjected to astrological thinking before being translated into Latin, could hardly have been as useful as the observations of a surgeon recorded during many years of successful practice. The same would be true of the military theories of Vegetius and other ancient scholars after the invention of firearms revolutionized the art of war. Although the new sciences were first recorded in Latin, it is likely that the innovators were thinking and speaking their vernaculars when they were making their advances; and it is probable that Latin terms like incunabula were translations of vernacular terms such as Wiegendruck, rather than vice versa.

Even though all industrial countries of Europe produced technical vocabularies and literatures, this article will cite mostly German examples because the proper groundwork has not yet been done for the other areas.

Among the best German paraphrases of the great Latin encyclopedias were the Grosse Lucidarius (ca. 1190) and the translation of the Secretum secretorum by the nun Hildgard of Hürnheim (ca. 1282). By the fifteenth century many works on the liberal arts had been translated, mostly anonymously. The writing of chronicles, which was subsumed under the trivium, flourished in the fifteenth century, the greatest example being Hartmann Schedel's Weltkronik, which appeared in both Latin and German in 1493, handsomely illustrated with woodcuts.

Although the mechanical arts were developed and disseminated mostly by men who spoke only the vernacular, there was a parallel Latin tradition. The most frequently treated of the handicrafts were spinning and weaving (ars textrina), and smithing, mining, metallurgy, and architecture (artes fabriles). Since metallurgy was an ars fabrilis, so was alchemy, about which the best-known German text was the *Alchymey teuczsch* (ca. 1425). The first book on mining was the *Bergbüchlein* printed by Ulrich Rülein von Calw in 1500.

By the end of the fifteenth century progress in firearms had made all classic military texts obsolete; handbooks explaining the new techniques were in demand. The best-known of these were the anonymous *Feuerwerksbuch* (ca. 1420) and Philipp von Seldeneck's *Ordenung* (1480).

The science of *navigatio* also advanced during the Middle Ages. The Arthurian knights journeyed in a dream world, in which one could ride a horse from Nantes in France to Caridol in Wales; and even Tristan's trip to Ireland or Siegfried's trip to Iceland cannot be followed on the map. The poet needed to know only the area known to his public: in the *Nibelungenlied*, Siegfried sails right past Xanten on his way to Iceland but does not stop to see his parents, because neither the poet nor his public knew that Xanten lay on the Rhine; but the poet did trace the Burgundians' route carefully from Passau to Vienna, just as the author of the *Cid* took his audience by realistic stages from Burgos to Valencia. The crusades and pilgrimages to Rome, Canterbury, Compostela, and other shrines gradually increased geographic awareness and created a demand for accurate travel books, of which the best German examples were those of Ludolf of Sudheim (mid fourteenth century) and of Georg of Ehingen (mid fifteenth century). The increasing number of harbor guides and sailing instructions also belonged to the science of *navigatio*.

From the thirteenth century on, the most widely read manual on housekeeping was the *De cura et modo rei familiaris*, which was erroneously ascribed to Bernard Silvester. Purportedly addressed to a knight in order to give it respectability, this manual gave practical, almost bourgeois, advice on how to keep house frugally. Also popular among the burghers were cookbooks and guides on table manners, which aimed to help them mimic the customs of the aristocracy. Among the most widespread German best-sellers of the Middle Ages was Gottfried of Franconia's *Pelzbuch*, a thirteenth-century handbook on grafting and other horticultural skills, which spread throughout eastern Europe and was read for centuries.

The ancients had considered *venatio* an illiberal art, yet the medieval gentry, claiming a monopoly on hunting, fostered the writing of hunting manuals, a good example being Hugo Wittenwiller's *Lehre von den Zeichen des Hirsches* (ca. 1410). Whereas south Europeans preferred hunting with falcons, the Germans favored hawks such as the goshawk, which could function better in the forest, with the result that "hawking" was the subject of many texts. Because of dietary restrictions, churchmen required a dependable supply of fish, with the result that many manuals were written on the raising and catching of fish.

Because medieval man depended on animals—the knight on his charger, the peasant on his cattle, the hunter on his hound, the miller on his ass—veterinary science was promoted, even though often mixed with charms and other superstitions. The most famous text on the care of horses was Albrant's *Rossarzneibuch*, presumably written for Emperor Frederick II.

Medical theory remained largely limited to the knowledge handed down from Hippocrates and Galen and was best codified at Salerno, where Arabic, Jewish, and Christian doctors assembled. The most famous treatise from this center was the twelfth-century *De conservanda bona valetudine*, the source of most medieval texts. The best German adaptations of this work were those of Everhard of Wampen, Ortolf of Bayerland, and Arnold Doneldey (fourteenth and fifteenth centuries). There were also specialized tractates on pregnancy and individual ailments. Although surgeons were held in ill repute, their works were read avidly, a good example being the *Cirugia* of Peter of Ulm (ca. 1425).

The courtly entertainments *(theatrica)* included pantomimes, spectacles, sports, and tournaments, for which written directions have survived. Fencing masters also wrote down their instructions. Although the church forbade the magic arts, it did not question their efficacy, as is shown by the fervor with which churchmen hunted witches, an enthusiasm demonstrated in the *Witches' Hammer* (1487), a Dominican handbook on how to detect and punish witches. Many texts were devoted to divining the future through necromancy, geomancy, chiromancy, pyromancy, and dream interpretation.

The neglect of *Fachschrifttum* is reflected in many European dictionaries, which have been based largely on "good" literature and therefore do not truly represent the speech of the populace. A study of *Fachschrifttum* is essential not only for linguistic reasons but also for a correct understanding of medieval belletristic works, which often used technical terms: it is apparent that Chaucer had a textbook on alchemy at hand when he wrote the Canon's Yeoman's Tale, since it would have taken him a lifetime as alchemist to learn all the terminology he flaunts in it.

BIBLIOGRAPHY

Peter Assion, *Altdeutsche Fachliteratur* (1973), with an excellent bibliography according to subject; David Dalby, *Lexicon of the Mediaeval German Hunt* (1965); Gerhard Eis, *Mittelalterliche Fachliteratur* (1967), and *Forschungen zur Fachprosa* (1971); Max Jähns, *Geschichte der Kriegswissenschaften, vornehmlich in Deutschland,* 3 vols. (1889–1891); Gundolf Keil and Peter Assion, eds., *Fachprosaforschung* (1973); Gundolf Keil *et al.,* eds., *Fachliteratur des Mittelalters. Festschrift für Gerhard Eis* (1968); Kurt Lindner, ed., *Quellen und Studien zur Geschichte der Jagd* (1954–1966); Wolfgang Stammler, "Von mittelalterlicher deutscher Prosa: Rechenschaft und Aufgabe," in *Journal of English and Germanic Philology,* 48 (1940); Lynn Thorndike, *A History of Magic and Experimental Science,* 8 vols. (1923–1958).

GEORGE JONES

[See also **Aelfric; Encyclopedias and Dictionaries, Western European; Hunting, Western European; Medicine, History of; Navigation, Western European; Notker Teutonicus; Technology, Treatises on; Translations and Translators, Western European; Trivium.**]

FAḌLĀN, IBN. See **Scandinavia in Arabic Sources.**

FAENZA CODEX (Faenza, Biblioteca Comunale, MS 117), is also known as the Bonadies Codex. The major section, of north Italian origin, was completed about 1420 and contains forty-eight two-part instrumental intabulations; it is one of the earliest known practical sources of medieval ornamentation practices. Eight pieces are elaborations over liturgical *cantus fermi;* others have been identified as secular works of fourteenth-century composers such as Machaut and Landini, and several may be dances. The instrument for which the manuscript was intended may have been organ or harpsichord, or perhaps two separate instruments. The remainder of the manuscript contains vocal works from the late fifteenth century and copies of musical treatises entered about 1470 by Johannes Bonadies.

BIBLIOGRAPHY

A facsimile of the Codex Faenza has been published as *An Early Fifteenth-century Italian Source of Keyboard Music, the Codex Faenza, Biblioteca comunale 117* (1961). See also Dragan Plamenac, ed., *Keyboard Music of the Late Middle Ages in Codex Faenza 117* (1972), and "A Note on the Rearrangement of Faenza Codex 117," in *Journal of the American Musicological Society,* 17 (1964).

TIMOTHY J. MCGEE

[See also **Landini, Francesco; Machaut, Guillaume de.**]

FÆREYINGA SAGA (Saga of the Faroe Islanders), composed by an Icelander around 1220. It focuses on a struggle more than two centuries earlier between two powerful branches of the same family vying for political control of the islands. On one hand there is Þrándr í Gǫtu, a rich and cunning man who holds fast to the old, independent ways of the original settlers, and on the other, his cousins Brestir and Beinir, who, as agents of the Norwegian Earl Hákon, represent a new age of political centralization. Although a plot contrived by Þrándr is successful against the brothers, their sons Sigmundr and Þórir eventually overcome Þrándr, forcing him to pay tribute to Norway.

Later, as liegeman of the new Norwegian king, Óláfr Tryggvason, Sigmundr undertakes the Christianization of the islands, with Þrándr as his chief opponent. Þrándr is again defeated, but not broken, and eventually brings about the destruction of Sigmundr and Þórir. After Sigmundr's death fresh attempts are made to assert Norwegian authority over the islands, this time by Óláfr Tryggvason's successor, King Óláfr Haraldsson. The wily Þrándr seemingly acquiesces to these renewed demands, but the king's tax collectors either mysteriously disappear or are murdered outright. Having frustrated Norwegian efforts to rule the islands, Þrándr and his kinsmen suppress all resistance to their power and enrich themselves at the expense of their countrymen.

Finally, Sigmundr's wife and daughter, Þuríðr and Þóra, with the help of Þóra's husband Leifr Ǫssurarson, succeed in killing Þrándr's chief henchmen, thus avenging Sigmundr's death and breaking Þrándr's grip on the islands. The saga closes in accord with medieval philosophy concerning the rightful sovereignty of kings when Leifr Ǫssurarson travels to Norway to submit the islands to Norwegian royal authority, receiving them back as a fief from the king.

Færeyinga saga did not survive the Middle Ages as an independent work. Today it is known only through the use made of it by later composers and compilers of learned works about the Norwegian kings: *Flateyjarbók, Óláfs saga Tryggvasonar en mesta,* and *Heimskringla* (in *Ólafs saga helga*). In 1832 the Danish scholar C. C. Rafn, relying mainly on *Flateyjarbók,* collected from these sources all the scattered episodes dealing with the Faroe Islands and published them under the title *Færeyingasaga—eller Færøboernes historie i den islandske grundtext med færøisk og dansk oversættelse* (Færeyinga saga—or the history of the inhabitants of the Faroe Islands in the original Icelandic with Faroese and Danish translations). These episodes comprise a coherent whole with regard to both plot and narrative style, so it is reasonably certain that a thirteenth-century *Færeyinga saga* did exist.

The story of Sigmundr Brestisson and Þrándr, as it is found in learned literary sources, inspired more popular compositions—in Iceland, the *ríma* cycle entitled *Þrændlur* and, in the Faroe Islands, the heroic ballads "Sigmundar kvæði," probably derived from *Óláfs saga Tryggvasonar en mesta,* and "Sigmundar kvæði nýggja," composed in the early nineteenth century by Jens Christian Djurhuus of Kollafjørður on the basis of Rafn's edition.

BIBLIOGRAPHY

Færeyinga saga: Den islandske saga om Færeyingerne, Finnur Jónsson, ed. (1927); *The Faeroe Islanders' Saga,* George Johnston, trans. (1975); Peter G. Foote, *On the Saga of the Faroe Islanders* (1965).

PATRICIA L. CONROY

[See also **Faroese Ballads; Riddarasögur.**]

FAEROESE BALLADS. See Faroese Ballads.

FÁFNIR. The *Reginsmál* relate that when Sigurd came to choose a stallion from the herd of King Hjálprekr, there was also at the royal court a smith named Reginn, who took Sigurd into his care and told him of his fate: accompanied by the gods Odin and Hœnir, Loki spies Otr, the brother of Reginn

and Fáfnir, as he sits in the form of an otter on the bank of Andvari's Falls, eating a salmon. Loki sees his chance to get both an otter and a salmon in one blow, and slays Otr. That night Loki, Hœnir, and Odin seek shelter at the house of Hreiðmarr, the father of Otr, Fáfnir, and Reginn. They show Hreiðmarr the pelt of Otr, and he demands compensation for the death of his son. Loki takes the net of the sea goddess, Rán; catches the dwarf Andvari, who dwells beneath the falls in the form of a pike, and takes all of his gold. Andvari places a curse on the hoard as Loki removes it, even to the last ring.

Hreiðmarr orders the gods to stuff the otter pelt with the gold and then to cover up the otter's form. One whisker remains visible, and Odin covers it with the ring Andvaranaut, the last item stolen by Loki from Andvari's hoard. Hreiðmarr vows to possess the gold as long as he lives, but Fáfnir and Reginn demand that Hreiðmarr pay wergild for their brother Otr. Hreiðmarr refuses, and Fáfnir slays his father. Reginn asks Fáfnir for his portion of their inheritance, but Fáfnir declines to give it to him. In recounting this tale Reginn reveals that Fáfnir now lies on Gnita Heath in the form of a serpent and bears the *œgishjálmr,* a helmet of terror that all living beings fear. Reginn makes a sword from the pieces of the broken sword belonging to Sigmund, Sigurd's father. It is so sharp that Sigurd can dip it in the Rhine and cleave a strand of wool that floats against the blade. It is so strong that he splits Reginn's anvil with it.

The *Fáfnismál* continue with the rest of the tale. Sigurd and Reginn ride to Gnita Heath and find the track of Fáfnir where he has gone to water. Sigurd digs a pit there and hides in it. As Fáfnir slides from the hoard of gold and moves over the pit, Sigurd plunges the sword into his heart. In the ensuing dialogue Sigurd seeks knowledge from the dying Fáfnir, who adds his curse to the hoard, prophesying that the gold will be the death of Sigurd and of all who possess it. Reginn comes out of hiding, cuts the heart from Fáfnir, and bids Sigurd roast it for him while he sleeps. When Sigurd thinks it done, he touches the heart, burns his finger, and puts the finger to his mouth. As soon as the blood from Fáfnir's heart comes upon his tongue, he can understand the speech of birds, who reveal treachery planned by Reginn. Sigurd beheads Reginn, eats Fáfnir's heart himself, drinks the blood of both, and seals his fate by taking the hoard.

The legend of Sigurðr Fáfnisbani was known over

the whole of Scandinavia, although it sprang originally from a German source. The rune stone at Ramsundsberg in Södermanland, Sweden, and the door posts of the Hylestad church in Setesdal, Norway, offer striking pictorial evidence for the tale.

BIBLIOGRAPHY

Fafnismol and *Reginsmol,* in Snorri Sturluson, *The Poetic Edda,* Henry Adams Bellows, trans. (1923, repr. 1957). See also H. R. Ellis Davidson, *Gods and Myths of Northern Europe* (1964), 43–44; Eyvind Fjeld Halvorsen, "Fáfnir," in *Kulturhistorisk leksikon for nordisk meddelalder,* IV (1959); E. O. G. Turville-Petre, *Myth and Religion of the North* (1964, repr. 1975), 200; Jan de Vries, *Altnordische Literaturgeschichte,* I (1964), 87–90.

JAMES E. CATHEY

[See also **Hœnir; Loki; Odin; Reginsmál and Fáfnismál; Scandinavian Mythology.**]

FÁFNISMÁL. See **Reginsmál and Fáfnismál.**

FAIENCE (Italian: *faènza,* ceramics) is a term commonly used to describe glazed ceramic ware in general. As applied to Islamic ceramics, frit is the correct term for a man-made glazed ceramic fabric having as its main constituents ground glass (quartz) and white clay. The glazing technique was supposedly invented in ancient Egypt but rediscovered in twelfth-century Seljuk Iran to imitate Chinese porcelain; its manufacture and use are described in a 1301 treatise by Abū'l Qāsim. More versatile than earthenware, this ware is hard and white, and vessels were often pierced for added translucency. Its use spread to Egypt and to the potteries of central and northern Syria in the twelfth and thirteenth centuries.

BIBLIOGRAPHY

J. W. Allan, "Abū'l-Qāsim's Treatise on Ceramics," in *Iran,* **11** (1973); J. W. Allan, L. R. Llewellyn, and F. Schweizer, "The History of So-called Egyptian Faience in Islamic Persia: Investigations into Abū'l-Qāsim's Treatise," in *Archeometry,* **15** (1973).

VENETIA PORTER

[See also **Ceramics, Islamic.**]

Lustered faience vase. Syrian, 12th or 13th century. THE METROPOLITAN MUSEUM OF ART, ROGERS FUND, 1917 (17.74.2)

FAIRS. From the fifth to the fifteenth century fairs were one of the most important forms of activity in Europe. Their history illustrates the general development of the economy in many important ways, for they played a crucial role in assuring a connection, via land routes, between the Mediterranean and the North Sea, and helped to create and sustain early urbanization.

Fairs are a simple way of exchanging goods when both demand and production are low. They solve the problems of distribution by concentrating suppliers and buyers in the same place. These meetings for the exchange of goods took place on neutral territory at a geographic or ethnic frontier, at regular intervals, and often during a holy season. In addition to religious associations they also had social and political functions because they allowed exchange of information among, and collective decisions by, people whose residences were widely scattered.

Medieval fairs were useful for exchange of goods in regions where political authority was fragmented and security lacking. There were few fairs in centralized states, except on the frontiers. The fair lost or gained importance as security increased or declined and as the volume of exchanges grew or diminished. For instance, the Roman conquest of western Europe established regular commerce, while the decline of the empire and the influx of Germanic peoples saw the revival of the old Gallic tradition of fairs. In medieval Europe, after a long period of expansion, the great fairs moved toward the east as governmental authority and urbanization increased in France and the German empire. Thus the fairs of Champagne were succeeded by those of Frankfurt and then those of Leipzig.

A generally accepted definition of "fairs" is "large and organized assemblies, meeting regularly but at rather long intervals, and attended by merchants from distant regions." Sometimes a distinction is made between a "market," held at intervals of a month or less, and a fair, which meets less frequently. There is also the theory that exchanges between merchants, and not simply between sellers and buyers, are the mark of a genuine fair. The characteristics of a "fair" became more precise as forms of exchange developed. At first there were simply periodic markets, but these were already large assemblies meeting at regular intervals, though the degree of organization and the attendance of merchants from distant regions varied from century to century and from country to country.

In the Middle Ages the word "market" was sometimes used to designate a fair. Nevertheless, fairs did

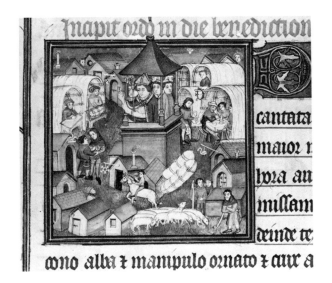

The bishop of Paris blessing the fair at Lendit. French manuscript in Latin, early 15th century. PARIS, BIBLIOTHÈQUE NATIONALE, MS FONDS LATIN 962, fol. 264

not grow out of local markets, any more than markets grew out of fairs. The two forms of exchange are equally old. Markets satisfied local needs and occurred at short intervals, while fairs drew merchants from a distance and the intervals between them were longer, so that the store of goods could be replenished. Fairs usually arose spontaneously, as the result of geographic, economic, and social factors. Changes in place and date, and the founding of new fairs by rulers, were apt to fail, or to be only partially successful. On the other hand, protection of merchants by religious establishments or by rulers, and privileges granted to merchants, favored the growth of fairs. Held at fixed dates and for a period varying from a day to several weeks, fairs generally opened on a religious festival, a connection that assured their continued existence. Many fairs that flourished in the twelfth century had roots that went back to prehistoric times, and endured through the ages to modern times better than those that were founded in the Middle Ages. Fairs were also places for making acquaintances and for amusement. Medieval literature emphasizes this social aspect, which is still evident in fairs that are held today.

Security and mutual trust, necessary for trading, were at first assured by fear of divine vengeance and later by fear of punishments imposed by the police and the judges. Public officials guaranteed respect for regulations and for justice not only within the boundaries of the fair but also along the roads that led to it, either by protecting the caravans with armed guards or by giving written safe-conducts to merchants.

WESTERN EUROPE

The fairs that have left the richest collections of documents and that have been most thoroughly studied are those of the countries where they were most fully developed: France, Flanders, and Germany.

Ancient Italy had had fairs, but the Romans, after their conquests, reached a level of economic development that made fairs unnecessary. In Gaul and in Germany they built monumental forums and warehouses for full-time merchants, but they also tolerated gatherings of native traders. These meetings, for a time overshadowed by the great marketplaces, revived with the decline of the empire and the arrival of the "barbarians," who were accustomed to holding fairs.

In the Latin of the High Middle Ages the yearly

market (*forum* or *mercatum annuale*) was distinguished from the weekly market (*forum* or *mercatum hebdomadale*) as if the only difference was the length of time between meetings. The yearly market, however, was much more important because of the greater amount of buying and selling. At first the larger market was called a *nundinum,* which in classical Latin meant a market held every nine days. But soon *feria* (a feast) became the common term (*foire* in French, *feria* in Spanish, *fiera* in Italian, *feira* in Portuguese, "fair" in English) because fairs were held on Christian festivals, such as saints' days or anniversaries of the dedication of a church. In Germanic languages the usual terms were *messemarkt* or *mismarkt* (from the Latin *missa,* Mass), or *Jahrmarkt,* a yearly market. The Rumanian *iarmaroc* and the Russian *yarmarka* are both derived from the German.

Fairs were at first agricultural, with sales of grain, wool, leather, horses, and other animals. Gradually they began to offer manufactured or imported products: cloth, furs, spices. Finally, in certain places, such as Champagne, they came to involve financial activities: the exchange of currencies, credit. These developments resulted from many factors: population growth, clearing and cultivation of new fields (which increased the income of the rural population), improvement of roads and shipping, increased dealings with Muslim and northern lands, industrial development, and a growing taste for comfort and luxuries.

The legal status of a fair is the surest way to distinguish it from a market. In order to attract merchants, rulers gave them certain privileges, not only at the site of the fair but also on the routes leading to it, for the period of the fair and a certain number of days before its opening and after its close. Taxes and tolls were either waived or reduced. No one could be arrested for debts contracted or offenses committed before the date of the fair; there was also exemption from the laws of reprisal, prosecution, and escheat. The rule of collective liability (which permitted reprisals against any citizen if one of his fellow citizens had incurred debts to or mistreated a citizen of another town) was limited—the person of the merchant and his own goods were not to be touched. The *conductus,* given to merchants by the ruler who controlled the roads to and from the fair, was indispensable: they could now travel without fear.

Often the peace of the town, normally reserved to the inhabitants, was temporarily extended to include the foreign merchants. Champagne had special "guards of the fairs." The "masters of the fairs" or "magistrates of the fairs" in Flanders were selected from the members of the town council, and the town court settled disputes among merchants according to local law, although it speeded up the procedure. In other towns the local agent of the king (as at Montagnac) or the lord's castellan (as at Pézenas) settled disputes. Punishment for offenses such as fraud, theft, or breach of contract could be more severe than usual, since fair privileges had been abused.

Every merchant had his assigned place on the fairground: in huts, in the market halls, on the ground floors of houses, or along the highway. Some of the great fairs had a regular schedule of operations: a period when the merchants moved in, then an exhibition of their goods, a period of sales, a period of removal of goods, and finally a period in which accounts were settled. Because many different currencies were used and because the value of coin was frequently altered, money changers played an important role. They verified the authenticity of coins, weighed them, and estimated their value. In western Europe these money changers were usually Italians or citizens of Cahors. Rarely they were Jews.

The acknowledgment of a debt through a "fair letter" made it unnecessary to carry large sums of money. Such a letter was a promise to pay the sum due on a certain date at a designated fair. Unlike the bill of exchange, which had to be paid in cash, the obligation of a fair letter could be satisfied by a transfer of merchandise or the tendering of services. Such a letter could be turned over to a third party, which made it a useful way of transferring capital. The Italian bill of exchange appeared in Flanders only at the end of the thirteenth century.

The merchants of the same town or same region formed a company (*hansa*) to ensure their safety and increase their profits at fairs. They lived in the same quarters and sold their goods in the same building. They accepted the authority of one or more of their fellows as captains; these leaders protected their interests during and after the fairs, and represented them in the courts.

The role of the fairs in the growth of towns apparently was very important. The early fairs gave rise to commercial and industrial activity in agricultural regions that had limited contact with other areas. Fairs increased consumption and created demands for new products, offered new markets and stimulated new economic activities, encouraged merchants to travel more widely and to find favorable locations for trade, and stimulated an increase in the production of raw materials and of handmade goods by assuring wider distribution of these products. They also brought in scarce materials from distant lands.

In the second stage of the development of fairs, rulers tried to organize and regulate buying and selling, and also to create new fairs on the model of the old ones. By that time fairs were only one of the elements in an established economic activity that could have continued to progress without them. They were great bursts of frantic, episodic activity for which there were all sorts of motives: commercial activities, financial operations, settlement of debts, social gatherings, amusement. Their early role and the need for their existence had long been forgotten; a proliferation of fairs in the fifteenth century was a sign of prosperity and a high level of trade. But the increase in the *number* of fairs was not a mark of their importance; rather the opposite.

The oldest European fair for which there is written evidence is that of St. Denis, mentioned in judgments of 710, 753, and 759—a forgery dated 629 would carry it back to the reign of Dagobert. Like the fairs of Lendit, mentioned in three letters of Gregory VII in 1074, it was held on the plain south of St. Denis. These two fairs were alike in that they were visited by foreign merchants: Saxons, Frisians, Lombards, Spaniards, Provençals, and Italians. They also possessed useful accessories—a mint and an exchange office. The first fair opened on the feast of St. Denis (9 October). In the Merovingian period the commodities sold there were honey, madder from the Orient, and wine. Probably metalwork, horses, and, before long, cloth were also available. The Lendit fair in June had every sort of merchandise from the region, the country, and foreign lands. It opened with a solemn benediction by the bishop of Paris. The two fairs belonged to the abbey of St. Denis, the officials of which supervised their organization, kept order and settled disputes, and received the payments owed to the abbey. But by the fifteenth century these fairs were declining, and the efforts of the king to revive them were unsuccessful.

There were fairs of Champagne and another cycle of fairs in Flanders that is mentioned in early texts: Torhout (1084), Ypres and Lille (1127), Messines (before 1100). The Bruges fair was established in 1200. In the thirteenth century the count of Flanders arranged the fairs so that they covered the entire year. The first fair of Ypres ran from 28 February to 29 March; Bruges was 23 April to 22 May; the second

fair of Ypres, 19 to 26 May; Torhout, 24 June to 24 July; Lille, 15 August to 14 September; and Messines, 1 October to 1 November. At these fairs English wool, and all the materials necessary for cloth making—alum and all kinds of dyes—were available. Also for sale were iron from Spain; lead, tin, and copper from England; and vast quantities of French and Rhine wine. Like the fairs of Champagne, the main Flemish fairs (especially the Ypres fairs) were places for paying debts. The Flemish fairs faded in the fourteenth century as Bruges became a permanent trading center.

Although these two great cycles of fairs began to decline as centers for buying and selling goods in the fourteenth century, they remained important centers of financial operations for some time. In order to simplify settlements, it had become customary to lodge letters of exchange on a single fair and to balance one account against another. Thus the amount of cash to be paid out was minimal. But even in this activity they were supplanted by other fairs, first to the south and later to the east. Northern France and the Low Countries had reached a stage of political, economic, and urban development that enabled business to be carried on throughout the year.

Periodic meetings for buying and selling moved toward Chalon-sur-Saône, Lyons, and Geneva. These three towns had long had fairs: the fair of Chalon is mentioned in 937–938. With the support of the duke of Burgundy it grew, and by the end of the thirteenth century the town had two fairs, the "warm fair" (24 August) and the "cold fair" (the beginning of Lent). These fairs profited from the custom of the papal court at Avignon. The "warm fair" filled the gap in the Champagne cycle between the St. John's fair at Troyes and the St. Ayoul fair at Provins. Merchants from the Low Countries, the Rhineland, Normandy, and Switzerland attended it, and Italians brought silk and spices. The Geneva fairs attracted merchants from Bern and Fribourg from the beginning of the fourteenth century. At their height, in the fifteenth century, there were four Geneva fairs: at Epiphany, at Easter, in August, and at All Saints. When Louis XI established fairs having the same dates at Lyons in the late fifteenth century, the Geneva fairs declined. By that time, however, Geneva had a permanent group of merchants trading on a large scale.

The fairs of Lyons were royal fairs. The dauphin Charles (later Charles VII) gave some privileges in 1420, as did Louis XI in 1463. Louis XI forbade French merchants to go to Geneva, which retaliated by detaining Germans and Italians crossing its territory on the way to Lyons. The advantageous geographic location of Lyons, however, and the favor of the French kings, enabled the town to surpass its rivals. From 1494 the Lyons fairs were held four times a year, and for several decades, between the decline of the Geneva fairs and the rise of the Antwerp fairs, those of Lyons were the most important in Europe for cloth—especially silk—and for spices.

Elsewhere in France there were important regional fairs: Caen, Falaise (fair of Guibray), Avranches, Carentan, and Cherbourg in Normandy; Rennes, Tréguier, and Quimperlé in Brittany; Angers in Anjou; Tours and Chinon in Touraine; and especially in Languedoc. The latter, on some of the main trade routes, saw its fairs expand after it became part of the royal domain in the thirteenth century. The fairs of Nîmes, Narbonne, and the July fair of Beaucaire (already in existence in the eleventh century) were famous, but it was the fairs of Pézenas and Montagnac that acquired an international reputation. By the middle of the fourteenth century the two towns had six fairs running through the year. They reached their peak at that time and remained important for the next century. Their specialties were durable cloth from the region, luxury fabrics from Italy, and haberdashery. Merchants came to these fairs from all parts of France, from Savoy, from north Italy, from Roussillon, and from Catalonia. The fairs also served as centers for settlement of debts. In Languedoc, where economic development had been slower than in the North, it was still necessary to concentrate commercial and financial operations in certain fixed periods.

The fairs of Frankfurt, held in the fall and during Lent, were the best known of the German fairs. They formed a yearly cycle with the two neighboring fairs of Friedberg, and they occupied a key position in trade. They became especially important at the end of the fourteenth century, when the fairs of Champagne were declining and when trade of the south German towns with Venice and of Hanseatic towns with Slavic lands was increasing. Thus, at Frankfurt one could find English cloth, salted herring from Scandinavia, furs from Russia, and goods from the Orient. After a period of prosperity (1330–1400) the Frankfurt fairs declined slightly, but regained all their importance in the second half of the sixteenth century, though they had lost most of their emphasis on exchange of merchandise.

Other German fairs (Nördlingen, Zurzach, Linz, Bolzano) existed by the thirteenth century, but had no great importance until the fifteenth century, during the decline of Frankfurt. It was also in the fifteenth century that the fairs of Leipzig became an important center for exchanging industrial products from the West for raw materials from the East. From the Rhineland, Poland, and Russia merchants came to Leipzig, which was a market for cloth from the Low Countries, furs from the Slavic countries, and, very soon after the invention of printing, for books.

The fairs of the Low Countries—Utrecht, Delft, Valkenburg, Zutphen, Arnhem—go back to the Middle Ages, but only that of Deventer on the IJssel was well attended at the end of the fourteenth century. It had five annual fairs: four lasted two weeks and the fifth, three weeks. These fairs attracted merchants from north Germany and were centers for settling accounts. The four fairs of Brabant—two at Antwerp (Pentecost and St. Bavo) and two at Bergen op Zoom (Easter and St. Martin's in November)—covered most of the year by the fifteenth century. They became the great continental markets for English cloth, which was beginning to replace Flemish cloth in European markets. German, Spanish, Portuguese, and Italian merchants deserted Bruges for Antwerp, which in the sixteenth century became a leading financial center.

In England, as in France, fairs arose spontaneously. After the Norman Conquest new fairs were set up near religious establishments. In the second half of the ninth century, Alfred the Great authorized foreign merchants to come to England to trade at fairs. This privilege, many times renewed, assured the safety of the merchants. The first fairs mentioned are those of London, Winchester, Boston, Northampton, and St. Yves. By the thirteenth century all English fairs used the same seal, weights, and measures. On the Continent, by contrast, variety instead of uniformity was characteristic of the systems of weights and measures. Again in England, during the fair and within the fair ground, justice and order were assured by the piedpoudre court (from *pied,* foot; and *poudre,* dust) an apt description of men who had traveled long distances. This court formed at the fair, was a sort of jury of merchants, and was concerned only with commercial cases.

The most important English fairs were those of St. Bartholomew at Smithfield (London) and Stourbridge. The first was held near a priory founded in 1102 by Rahere, jester of Henry I, who had a vision of St. Bartholomew (though the fair was probably older than the priory). In 1133 Henry I confirmed the privileges of the fair for three days a year. In the cemetery of the priory, surrounded by walls and guarded at night, the merchants built their booths. They sold cloth, leather, livestock, and tin. The success of the fair forced it to expand beyond the limits of the priory, and by the end of the thirteenth century the keeper of the City of London claimed half of its income for the king. With the suppression of the monasteries in 1538–1539, the priory disappeared, but the fair continued to be held into the middle of the nineteenth century.

The origins of the Stourbridge fair are obscure. It was held in mid September on the lands of the leprosarium near the hospital of St. Mary Magdalene. Its privileges were confirmed by King John about 1211, and it reached its peak in the thirteenth century. By the beginning of the fourteenth century it lasted for three weeks. English merchants brought wool, hops, lead, and iron; Venetians and Genoese brought silk, velvet, glassware, and Oriental products; Spaniards, iron; Flemings, linen cloth from Liège and Ghent; Norwegians, pitch and pine tar; the Hanseatic merchants, furs and amber from Slavic lands. Wines came from Gascony, Spain, and occasionally from Greece. The Stourbridge fair was still held at the end of the nineteenth century.

Until the eleventh century Pavia was the capital of the Lombard, Carolingian, and Germanic kingdoms of northern Italy. Located at a point where roads from the Alpine passes converged, it had two great fairs, each lasting two weeks: the first in March/April, and the second beginning on 11 November (St. Martin's day). These fairs were held outside the town, near the monastery of St. Martin. From the ninth to the eleventh century Mediterranean and Oriental goods were exchanged there for products from western and northern Europe. At Pavia metals (tin, copper, iron, silver), weapons, furs, wool, linen, and silk cloth, ivory, spices, and slaves were available. Later, however, the Italians sent most of these goods to the fairs of Champagne and Flanders.

Most of the local fairs of north Italy (Bergamo, Verona, Milan, Mantua, Bolzano, Padua) had only regional importance. Exceptions were those of Ferrara and Lombardy, but these reached their greatest importance only at the end of the fifteenth century. The Venetian fair, the *Sensa* (on Ascension Day), held from the eleventh century in the Piazza S. Marco, first for one week and then for two, attracted only Italians of the north. Venice, in fact, was a perpetual fair with its markets, shops, and highly developed banks.

Andalusia apparently had no fairs either before or during the period of Islamic rule. In the eleventh and twelfth centuries León, with its market and its shops within its walls, was the emporium where products from Islamic Spain and the Christian kingdoms of northern Spain were exchanged. As the Reconquest proceeded, fairs appeared throughout the peninsula. The most famous were those of Burgos, Santiago de Compostela, Alcalá de Henares, Palencia, Toledo, and Madrid. Medina del Campo, Villaleon, and Medina de Rioseco became important only at the end of the fifteenth century, when they attracted buyers of merino wool and ornate weapons from Germany, Russia, and the eastern Mediterranean.

In Scandinavia only the fair of Skanör (near the southern tip of Sweden) gained an international reputation in the thirteenth century. This was a fish fair, held from 15 August to 1 November. Men came there from all parts of Europe to buy herring, which were caught in enormous numbers in the western Baltic. By the end of the fourteenth century more than 200,000 barrels of herring were sold there each year. This trade was dominated by the Hanseatic League, which furnished salt from Lüneburg, barrels for the fish, and capital to buy them. The fair attracted English and Dutch merchants, who sold food products and cloth there. The extension of the herring fishing into the North Sea, the suppression of the Lenten fast in many countries by the Reformation, and, most of all, the increasingly monopolistic practices of the Hanseatic League led to a gradual decline of the fair of Skanör. It disappeared in the second half of the seventeenth century.

THE SLAVIC WORLD

From the eighth century on, the Slavic world was crisscrossed by trade routes between the Byzantine and Muslim worlds and the Scandinavian countries. The numerous finds of Byzantine solidi and Muslim dirhams along the Russian river routes are evidence of this trade. Fairs and towns remained places where trade could be carried on: for example, Kazan, Nizhni Novgorod, Krakow, Prague. The *pogost,* where goods were exchanged between Slavs and foreign merchants, was like the *portus* of the Carolingian West. Surrounded by a ditch and a stockade, the *pogost* became a *gorod,* a fortified town. Of the thirty-five towns in Russian territory at the beginning of the eleventh century, at least twenty-five had this origin. The two largest were Kiev and Novgorod, which had German, Scandinavian, Jewish, and Armenian quarters at an early time.

In the tenth century, the prince of Kiev sent boats

down the Dnieper loaded with tribute in kind that he had collected from his subjects. He used the tribute for trade with Constantinople. The merchants established at Kiev and Cherson in the Crimea served as intermediaries selling to the Byzantines furs, wax, honey, and slaves in exchange for silk, spices, and wine. The coins of the prince of Kiev were imitated in Scandinavia in the eleventh century, and cloth from Ypres is mentioned as an ordinary commodity in a Novgorod document from the period 1130–1136.

Invasions by the Turks at the end of the eleventh century, and the Mongol conquest of 1236–1240, destroyed these early urban settlements in the Dnieper basin and blocked access to the Black Sea. The Mongols controlled Russia for two centuries and isolated it from the rest of Europe. The princes and their vassals *(druzhina)* monopolized the trade in furs and other products of their domains. Novgorod "the Great" was "the one window open to the West," and trade there was carried on year round. The Germans had settlements there (Gotenhof and Peterhof) until after the fall of the city (1478); they were driven out in 1496. Novgorod was then replaced by Moscow as a center of the fur trade. Russian merchants seldom ventured out of their own country; foreign merchants, however, went deep into the provinces and traded at local fairs. Furs were always the most desired commodity, but as Arctic fisheries developed in the fifteenth century, merchants also bought walrus oil and walrus teeth.

Although there was periodic commerce in all the Slavic countries, especially in Poland, no fair gained an international reputation.

BYZANTIUM

Ancient Greece had fairs near the great sanctuaries—Delos, Olympia, Delphos *(panêguris)*. During the Byzantine period regular commerce was reinforced by great international fairs on the frontiers of the empire. At Lamos, on the border between the province of Tarsus and the Byzantine theme of Ctesiphon, Greeks and Muslims at first exchanged their prisoners. Later the Greek merchants bought raw silk, silk cloth, and perfumes. Trebizond (anc. Sinope), capital of an empire founded in 1204, was the site of well-attended fairs. Situated on the southern shore of the Black Sea, it profited from the fall of Baghdad to the Mongols in 1258. Merchants from the Indies then abandoned their route up the Red Sea and took a land route that ended in Trebizond. Genoese and Venetian merchants came to Trebizond in

large numbers. The fairs reached their peak in the early fourteenth century, then declined slowly until the city was taken by the Turks in 1461.

Thessaloniki, which was both a seaport and an important way station on the great road from the Aegean to Albania, held its fair, mentioned early in the twelfth century, in October (St. Demetrius). Jews were very active there. This fair attracted large numbers of merchants until the town was taken by the Turks in 1430.

THE ISLAMIC WORLD

Founded by a city dweller, the Muslim religion and Muslim law have nothing to say about fairs. In most of the Muslim world, trade was conducted in cities, with shops and market places open every day, or at least once a week. Religious ideology had nothing to do with this; it was due to the fact that the Muslim empire was built on highly organized states in which economic activity was already controlled by the bureaucracy. Thus commerce in the Muslim world reached a level of development, of security, of transport facilities, and of monetary circulation that made for permanent instead of intermittent trade relations. Where fairs did exist, they had their roots in an earlier period. This was the case with the pilgrimage fairs, which developed, like those of Europe, from ancient cults.

In pre-Islamic Arabia there had been fairs at which Bedouin tribes assembled, especially in the Hejaz. Fairs combined with pilgrimages at appropriate seasons (whence the Arabic name for such a fair, *mawsim*). Markets *(sūq)* were held in the intervals between religious festivals; they were pauses in the everlasting war that pitted one tribe against another. During the truce of the four holy months, business could be carried on, as could settlement of legal and political disputes, athletic games, and poetry contests. The principal places for such fairs were Mecca and Okaz, an oasis near Al-Tāᵓif.

Muḥammad disrupted these early fairs by adopting a strictly lunar calendar, which upset the old system of the four sacred months. Moreover, Mecca, in becoming the religious capital of the Muslim world, drew hordes of pilgrims and became a sort of permanent pan-Islamic fair. The Koran itself authorized business dealings during the hajj. Trading at first took place at Minā, near Mecca, and then in Mecca itself, where buying and selling continued for a week after the end of religious ceremonies. Ibn Jubayr gives a good description of this fair in the twelfth century. He lists the products sold there—jewels and pearls from India and Abyssinia, goods from Iraq, Yemen, Khorāsān, and the Maghreb: "At this fair enough merchandise is sold in one day so that if it were divided among all the countries of the world it would create well-patronized markets. Everyone gains from trading there."

As far as can be judged from the sources, the Arabs allowed existing fairs to continue in the lands that they conquered. Their sole concern was to suppress the pagan rituals associated with the fairs— very much like the Christian church in the West. At Jerusalem they let themelves be associated in the feast of the Exaltation of the Cross (14 September). Arculf, a Western pilgrim, writing about 680 describes this fair as "an important gathering of different peoples coming from everywhere to trade." In ninth-century Bukhara, where, among other things, Buddhist statues were sold, a mosque replaced the sacred fire that had formerly been venerated by the people. Another example of continuity despite change of religious ceremonies appears at El Muzeirib, about 100 kilometers (60 miles) south of Damascus. William of Tyre reports that around its mineral springs there were, about 1147, yearly fairs at which Arabs and other eastern peoples met and traded. Later this isolated spot became an important place to rest before entering the desert on the way to Mecca. Jews and Christians, as well as Muslims, took part in the trading that went on there.

In North Africa in the middle of the ninth century, fairs were held near *ribāṭ*s (fortified monasteries) on dates when garrisons were relieved. As in the case of the Flemish castles, this raises the question of whether the protection of commerce required a garrison, or whether the presence of a garrison attracted merchants. At Arcila and Cherchell, at Monastir and Sousse, fairs and *ribāṭ*s gave birth to towns. Another center for fairs was Sijilmasa, chief town of the Tafilalt oasis, at the end of the caravan route across the desert, where there had certainly been periodic trade among the Berbers. Leo Africanus described the great fair at Guzzūla, which he visited early in the sixteenth century; he reported that it lasted for two months, that there were no fees or taxes to be paid, and that it attracted crowds from countries of the blacks. There were guards to keep order, and theft was punished by death.

In North Africa there were also many fairs associated with pilgrimages to the tombs of marabouts (*al-murābiṭūn*, saints). The tomb of the saint fixed the place for the meeting and guaranteed peace; the date of his death determined the time. Such meetings

(*moussems*) combining religion and commerce are still held, especially in southern Morocco.

Egypt, which seems to have had no fairs in ancient times, saw a proliferation of the celebrations called *mawālīd*, held to commemorate the birth of the Prophet. These hardly deserve to be called fairs, but two of them, held in the Delta at Tanta and Disūq, were quite important and gave birth to towns.

The Turks used the word *panayir* (from the Greek *panêguris*) to designate a fair. They held annual fairs, called desert markets, far from towns, apparently in places on caravan routes and frontiers where Muslims and Byzantines had exchanged their goods. This was the case of the fair held on the plain of Karahisar (near Caesarea in Cappadocia) for forty days in early spring. These meetings, however, attracted more Jews and Christians (Greeks and Armenians) than Turks.

BIBLIOGRAPHY

General. A. Allix, "Les foires: étude géographique," in *La géographie,* 29 (1923); Paul Huvelin, *Essai historique sur le droit des marchés & des foires* (1897); *Recueils de la Société Jean Bodin,* V, *La foire* (1953), containing essays on the fairs of many lands, including Japan and the Islamic world, brief abstracts in English, and a conclusion by John Gilissen on "La notion de la foire à la lumière de la méthode comparative"; Cornelius Walford, *Fairs, Past and Present: A Chapter in the History of Commerce* (1883); G. Zetter, *Évolution des foires et marchés à travers les siècles* (1923), with bibliography.

Western Europe. E. Cornaert, "Caractères et mouvement des foires internationales au moyen âge et au XVIe siècle," in *Studi in onore di Armando Sapori,* I (1957), 355–372; Charles Verlinden, "Markets and Fairs," in *The Cambridge Economic History of Europe,* III, *Economic Organization and Policies in the Middle Ages* (1963), 119– 153, with bibliography.

Origins. Anne Lombard-Jourdan, "Y a-t-il une protohistoire urbaine en France?" in *Annales: Économies, Sociétés, Civilisations,* 25 (1970); "Foires gauloises et origines urbaines," in *Archéocivilisation,* 11–13 (Dec. 1972–July 1974); and "Les foires aux origines des villes," in *Francia,* 10 (1983); P. Lomry, "Cultes paiens et foires anciennes," in *Annales de l'Institut Archeologique de Luxembourg,* 67 (1936); Michael Mitterauer, "Jahrmärkte in Nachfolge antiker Zentralorte," in *Mitteilungen des Instituts für österreichische Geschichtsforschung,* 75 (1967).

France. Marc Brésard, *Les foires de Lyon aux XVe et XVIe siècles* (1914), with bibliography; Louis Carolus-Barré, "Le Mi-Karesme, foire de Compiègne (1092–1792)," in *Bulletin de la Société historique de Compiègne,* 26 (1979) and 27 (1980); Jean Combes, "Les foires en Languedoc au moyen âge," in *Annales E.S.C.,* 13 (1958); Paul Courteault, "Les origines des foires franches de Bordeaux," in *Revue historique de Bordeaux et du département de la Gironde* (1941–1942); Raphael R. De Soignie, "The Fairs of Nîmes: Evidence of Their Function, Importance, and Demise," in William C. Jordan, Bruce McNab, and Teofilo Ruiz, eds., *Order and Innovation in the Middle Ages* (1976), 195–205; Henri Dubois, "Le commerce de les foires au temps de Philippe Auguste," in *La France de Philippe Auguste: Les temps de mutations, Colloques internationaux du CNRS*, no. 602 (1982); A Fages, *Beaucaire et sa foires à travers les siècles* (1943); Léon Levillain, "Essai sur les origines du Lendit," in *Revue historique*, **155** (1927); and "Études sur l'abbaye de Saint-Denis à l'époque mérovingienne," in *Bibliothèque de l'École des Chartes*, **91** (1930); Lucien Musset, "Foires et marchés en Normandie à l'époque ducale," in *Annales de Normandie*, **10** (1976); Simone Poignant, *La Foire de Lille* (1932), with bibliography; G. Romestan, "Perpignan et les foires de Pézenas et de Montagnac aux XIVe et XVe siècles," in *Fédération historique du Languedoc méditerranéen et du Roussillon, Actes du 48e Congrès: Pézenas, ville et campagne* (1976), 75–103; Paul Toussaint, *Les foires de Chalon-sur-Saône dès origines au XVIe siècle* (1910); Philippe Wolff, "Toulouse et les foires de Pézenas et de Montagnac à la fin du XIVe et au début du XVe siècle," in *Fédération historique du Languedoc, Actes du XXVIème Congres* (1952), 79–83.

Low countries. M. Altschuler, *L'organisation des foires en Luxembourg* (1934); J. A. van Houtte, "La genèse du grand marché international d'Anvers à la fin du moyen âge," in *Revue belge de philologie et d'histoire*, **19** (1940); Henri Laurent, "Les relations économiques des villes brabançonnes avec les foires françaises du XIIe au XVe siècle," in *Actes du premier congrès national des historiens français: Paris, 1927* (1929), 32–33; Jean de Sturler, *Les relations politiques et les échanges commerciaux entre le duché de Brabant et l'Angleterre au moyen âge* (1936); Herman van der Wee, *The Growth of the Antwerp Market and the European Economy* (1963).

England. Eileen E. Power and Michael M. Postan, eds., *Studies in English Trade in the Fifteenth Century* (1933); Elspeth M. Veale, *The English Fur Trade in the Later Middle Ages* (1966).

Germany and Switzerland. Frédéric A. Borel, *Les foires de Genève au quinzième siècle* (1892); Michael Mitterauer, *Markt und Stadt* (1980).

Italy. Filippo Carli, *Storia del commercio italiano: Il mercato nell'alto medio evo* (1934); Giuseppe Mira, *Le fiere lombarde* (1955); Federico Pinna Berchet, *Fiere italiane antiche e moderne* (1936).

Spain and Portugal. Luis Aguirre Prado, *Mercados y ferias* (1955); Cristóbal Espejo, *Las antiguas ferias de Medina del Campo* (1908); Virginia Rau, *Subsídios para o estudo das feiras medievais portuguesas* (1943).

Slavic world. R. Delort, *Le commerce des fourrures en Occident à la fin du moyen âge*, 2 vols. (1978); Alexandre Eck, *Le moyen âge russe* (1933); Leopold-Karl Götz, *Deutsch-Russische Handelsgeschichte des Mittelalters* (1922); Ïosif Kulisher, *Russische Wirtschaftsgeschichte* (1925); A. Vasiliev, "Economic Relations Between Byzantium and Russia," in *Journal of Economic and Business History*, **4** (1931–1932).

ANNE LOMBARD-JOURDAN

[See also **Champagne, County**; **Fairs of Champagne**; **Hanseatic League**; **Markets** (various articles); **Trade** (various articles); **Urbanism, Western European**.]

FAIRS OF CHAMPAGNE. The fairs of Champagne and of Brie are the best examples of this institution in the West. From the mid twelfth century to about 1320 they constituted the international center of European commerce, credit, and exchange of currencies. Their organization and regulation were imitated by other great medieval fairs.

Champagne was a rich region, easily accessible by navigable rivers (the Seine, the Marne, and the Aube) and by the great north–south trade routes from Italy and the Mediterranean to Flanders and the North Sea. This geographic position made possible its precocious economic development. Fairs appeared there very early and were exceptionally well attended. Little is known about their origins; there are about forty references to them before 1150, but the documents often say that the fairs have been held since ancient times or a certain detail proves that they have long been in existence.

Fairs were found near episcopal cities, castles, and monasteries. Though it has been denied, a letter of Apollinaris Sidonius shows that there was a fair at Troyes by the fifth century. There was probably one at Chappes in the ninth century, according to a letter of Lupus of Ferrières dated 862. There was certainly another at Troyes about 1000. There were fairs at Châlons-sur-Marne in the Carolingian period, at Provins and at Lagny by the second half of the eleventh century, and at Bar-sur-Aube by the first years of the twelfth century. Fairs at Épernay, Sézanne, Rebais, Château Porcien, and La Ferté-Gaucher are mentioned at about the same time.

Four of these fairs had considerable success as a result of the economic policies of the counts of Champagne. They tried to shut out the towns of the northeastern part of their county and to direct the flow of trade toward the towns of the southwest, and thus toward the route that led from Burgundy as far as Senlis and Flanders through the valley of the Aube-Seine system. Before 1065 Count Eudes III

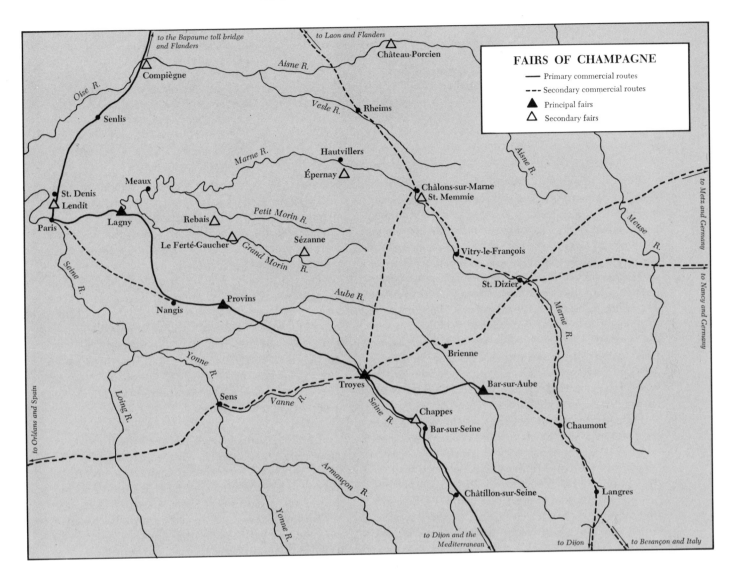

granted the fair held in August near the abbey of St. Memmie to the bishop of Châlons. From then on it declined. The January fair of Épernay was transferred to Troyes between 1130 and 1136, and the fair of Rebais to Sézanne before 1119. In 1095 Count Étienne-Henri had refused to grant a fair to the abbey of Hautvillers at the same time he was granting one to St. Ayoul of Provins.

As a result of this policy, followed systematically by all the counts of Champagne, commercial activity became concentrated in Troyes, Provins, Lagny, and Bar-sur-Aube. Various reasons have been given to explain the success of these fairs: the agricultural richness of the region, its location on main routes, the growth of its cities and population; but these supposed causes are, rather, the results of success. It was the arbitrary choice of the count that enabled the four fairs to succeed. Moreover, the peacefulness of the county of Champagne was in sharp contrast with the disorder in Lorraine and in the Capetian domain, where greedy lords often harassed merchants. However, the counts of Champagne succeeded, by steady pressure, in making everyone respect their safe-conduct.

The golden age of the fairs of Champagne was between the middle of the twelfth century and 1280, when the first signs of their decline appeared. Through adjustments in their dates and lengthening of their duration, the fairs constituted a cycle covering the whole year. The length of their meetings distinguished them clearly from the numerous merely local fairs established in Champagne by Count Henry the Liberal and his successors.

The cycle in its final form was as follows:

591

Lagny	Fair of the Holy Innocents	2 January–19 February
Troyes	Fair of the Field at Troyes (formerly at Épernay)	22 January–5 February
Bar-sur-Aube	Lenten fair	24 February/30 March–13 April/17 May
Provins	May fair (St. Quiriace)	28 April/30 May
Troyes	St. John's	9/15 July–26 August/2 September
Lagny	St. Peter's	29 June
Provins	Fair of St. Ayoul	14 September–1 November
Troyes	Fair of St. Rémi	2 November–20 December
Provins	St. Martin's fair	11 November (disappeared by 1200)

Like all other fairs, those of Champagne often seem in contemporary descriptions to be primarily markets for agricultural products: cattle, horses, grain, wine, salt, and wool and hides. By the second third of the twelfth century cloth and haberdashery were sold. There were Flemings and men from Arras at Provins before 1137, and the Italians were beginning to bring silks and spices. Money changers were becoming more and more numerous. The imitation of coins of Provins by the Roman Senate in the second half of the twelfth century shows how important the fairs of Champagne had become. In spite of the significance of imports from Italy and the Orient, however, it was trade in cloth that assured the international success of the fairs of Champagne.

Probably by the end of the twelfth century, and certainly by 1230, the cloth towns of southern Flanders, Hainaut, and northern France had formed a league (the Seventeen Towns) to promote the sale of their goods. Other towns, such as Rheims and Châlons-sur-Marne, joined the group later. Besides cloth, furs from Russia and Scandinavia, cordovan leather from Spain, linen cloth from southern Germany, and avoirdupois were sold. This last category included anything sold by weight: metals, wool, dyes, drugs, perfumes, and spices.

The counts of Champagne protected their fairs and levied only moderate fees on them, a policy that assured their rapid growth during the twelfth and thirteenth centuries. The privileges of the fairs of Champagne were designed to counter the difficulties that hindered commerce at that time. The safety of the merchants was assured by protection along the trade routes and by laws of the fair that were more liberal than ordinary law.

At the end of the thirteenth century the Custom of the Fairs was a sort of commercial law code, drawn from mandates and regulations of the counts of Champagne and the "wardens of the fairs." There were two of these wardens; they are mentioned in documents from 1174 on, but their offices must have been established much earlier in order to provide security at the fairs and on the roads leading to them. They kept the market halls in repair and, assisted by lieutenants and clerks, conducted and judged trials concerning merchants. By the end of the thirteenth century contracts drawn up by the wardens were valid anywhere in Christendom.

The court they held was a fully developed court of justice with lawyers, agents, and notaries to draw up and guarantee contracts, bills of sale, and promissory notes. There was also a chancellor—mentioned for the first time in 1247—to attach the "seal of the fairs." By 1317 there were forty notaries. In the same year there were 140 "sergeants" (policemen), 120 on foot and the rest on horse. There were only twice that number at Paris during the same period.

The merchants had also formed their own organizations. They often traveled in caravans, but they could also hire professional carriers (vectuarii) to transport their goods. Groups of Italian merchants, beginning with those of Siena in 1246, had a consul who collected the taxes owed by his fellow citizens and represented them in the courts. After the mid thirteenth century the Italians and merchants from Provence formed companies to defend their interests; each company was headed by a "captain" elected by the group. Merchants from the same town or region stayed in the same inn and sold in the same market hall. There were brokers, couriers, and messengers to facilitate their dealings.

The multiplicity of monetary systems hindered trade, but at the fairs the Lombards, men of Cahors, and, occasionally, Jews acted as money changers. They also made loans, so that payments could be put off from one fair to another or from one country to another. These facilities reduced the numbers of national coinages needed for trading and lessened the risks of traveling with large amounts of gold and silver. It was the fairs of Champagne that first fully developed the instruments of credit and exchange which were necessary for an expanding economy. Once they were perfected, however, the techniques of financing exchanges between distant merchants made fairs less necessary, since one of their chief functions had disappeared.

In discussing the decline of the fairs of Champagne it is difficult to distinguish between cause and effect. The marriage in 1284 of the heiress of the county, Joan of Navarre, to Philip the Fair, soon to be king of France (1285–1314), united the county to the royal domain and exposed it to the financial demands of agents of the crown. This happened just as the Flemings and the Italians began to abandon the fairs. Cloth from the towns of Brabant (Brussels, Louvain, Malines) hardly ever appeared at the fairs; it was sent to Paris, and thus attracted many Italian merchants there.

At the same time the war between the King of France, who was the new lord of Champagne, and the count of Flanders barred the Flemings from the fairs. During the Hundred Years' War, Italian merchants tried to find a direct route to Flanders that avoided France, either by crossing the Alps and going down the Rhine, or by sailing to Bruges, London, or Southampton. Genoese and Venetian ships became numerous in these ports. Finally, the increasing industrialization of Italy diminished the demand for northern cloth; Florence and Milan supplied the market with as good materials. Further, the disorganization of financial companies and the increasing role of gold made it less necessary to go to centers of exchange and credit such as the fairs of Champagne had become.

About 1327 a proposal to reform the fairs was made to the king, but it had no results; the flow of commerce had turned in other directions. The solid organization of the fairs enabled them to continue up to the end of the fifteenth century, but the towns in which they were held saw their industries collapse. There had been 3,200 looms for weaving wool cloth at Provins in the thirteenth century; by 1393 there were only 30, and by 1433 only 4. The churches, as they lost income, had to reduce the number of benefices and thus of clergy. The fairs did not disappear completely, but after the fifteenth century they were essentially only large markets, of local interest at best.

BIBLIOGRAPHY

Robert-Henri Bautier, "Les foires de Champagne: Recherches sur une évolution historique," in Recueils de la Société Jean Bodin, V, La foire (1953); Félix Bourquelot, Études sur les foires de Champagne, 2 vols. (1865); Michel Bur, "Remarques sur les plus anciens documents concernant les foires de Champagne," in Cahiers de l'Association inter-universitaire de l'Est, 16: Les villes (1972) 45–62; Louis Carolus-Barré, "Les XVII villes: Une hanse vouée au grand commerce de la draperie," in Comptes rendus de l'Académie des inscriptions et belles-lettres (1965); Elisabeth Chapin, Les villes de foires de Champagne, dès origines au début du XIVe siècle (1937), ch. 5; R. D. Face, "Techniques of Business in the Trade Between the Fairs of Champagne and the South of Europe in the Twelfth and Thirteenth Centuries," in Economic History Review, 2nd ser., 10 (1957–1958), and "The 'vectuarii' in the overland commerce between Champagne and Southern Europe," ibid., 12 (1959–1960); Henri Laurent, Un grand commerce d'exportation au moyen âge (1935).

ANNE LOMBARD-JOURDAN

[See also **Champagne, County; Markets, Western European; Trade** (various articles).]

FAITS DES ROMAINS. See **Fet des Romains, Li.**

FALCHION (from the Latin for "sickle"), a short, broad, and slightly curved medieval sword with its cutting edge on the convex side.

LESLIE BRUBAKER

FALSE DECRETALS. See **Decretals, False.**

FAMILY. This topic is covered in a number of articles comprising the following: **Family, Byzantine; Family, Islamic; Family, Western European; Family and Family Law, Jewish;** and **Family and Marriage, Western European.**

FAMILY, BYZANTINE. The Byzantine family, as opposed to the Roman one, was for all intents and purposes a nuclear family, formed by the marriage bond. Its development was characterized by the gradual weakening in theory and disappearance in practice of patria potestas (paternal authority), and by the increasing role that women played in the family. The family unit, an economic as well as a biological and social cell, was protected by the church and the state.

The Isaurian law code *Ecloga* (issued in 741) has been considered the most important body of legislation concerning the Byzantine family. The legislators, issuing the code at a time of demographic decline, recognized and protected the nuclear family as the basic socioeconomic unit, which was formed by the marriage of a man and a woman, undertaken with the will of the participants and the consent of both parents (the requirement of the mother's consent being an innovation). The role of the woman in the family is further highlighted by the fact that her children owed her "honor and obedience."

According to this legislation, marriage created a unity of persons and goods, the essential family property consisting of the woman's dowry and the man's marriage gift to her. When the husband died, the wife acquired ownership and control of all the family property, from which she had to support her children and arrange for their marriages. If the wife remarried, she retained control of only her dowry and marriage gift. The family property was clearly designated for the support of the offspring, as is evident in the legislation regulating intestate succession, which made the children of a marriage the first heirs of the family property.

The interest of the state in the family unit is attested by the fact that the *Ecloga* regulates the legal age for marriage (fifteen for a boy, thirteen for a girl) and prohibits marriages within various degrees of consanguinity, affinity, or spiritual relationship. The *Ecloga* also includes the strictest Byzantine legislation on divorce, which was allowed only in the following cases: a woman might divorce her husband if he were impotent for three years after the celebration of the marriage, if he tried to kill her, or if he were a leper. Similarly, a woman could be divorced for adultery, leprosy, or designs against her husband's life. Neither the husband's adultery nor madness was seen as sufficient cause for dissolving the family.

Subsequent legislation elaborated on these principles, although some of the regulations of the *Ecloga* were changed. Specifically, the almost equal role of mother and father with regard to the children was weakened. The grounds of divorce, too, were somewhat extended. In general, however, the concern of Macedonian legislation continued to be the preservation and protection of the family, both as a biological unit and as an economic one.

The first concern is evident in legislation concerning the purpose of marriage and the prohibitions attending it. Leo VI the Wise (886–912) spoke of marriage as a great and honorable gift of the Creator, given to mankind for the purpose of ensuring the procreation of the species. Marriage was consequently forbidden to persons who could not produce offspring—eunuchs, for example. The importance of marriage for the reproduction of the human resources of the empire was also reflected in the law that abolished the *potestas* of a father over his daughter if she had reached her twenty-fifth year without his having made an effort to find her a husband. Divorce legislation remained relatively strict, and the further elaboration of the rules governing consanguinity and affinity as impediments to marriage attest to the concern of the legislator with the family unit.

The Byzantine church, too, established strict regulations concerning degrees of blood relationship within which marriage was forbidden, except occasionally for reasons of state. The basic ecclesiastical statement is the *Tomos* (997) of Patriarch Sisinnios II. The church's interest in the indissolubility of the matrimonial union is further indicated in the fact that betrothal was progressively made almost equivalent to marriage in law (see the legislation of John VIII Xiphilinos, 1066), although in practice betrothals were frequently broken or annulled.

The importance of childbearing in a society suffering from a chronic labor shortage is evident in the legislation governing second and third marriages. Second marriages were frowned upon (especially in the case of women) as endangering the rights of the children of the first union; third marriages were forbidden by Leo VI. But canonical legislation recognized the importance of second marriages in case of the absence of children, and even third marriages were permitted in the twelfth through fifteenth centuries when the person in question was young and childless.

It may have been the same concern that tended to push to an early age the decision of a boy or girl whether to marry or enter the monastery. The age of consent to betrothals was seven years, whereas the age of consent to enter monastic life was ten years. Furthermore, there was a tendency, at least in parts of the empire, for betrothals and marriages to take place at an age much below the canonical one: such was the case particularly in Epiros and western Greece, where the number of matrimonial unions sometimes exceeded three, as betrothals and marriages were made and revoked.

Paternal authority over children, which was affirmed by Byzantine legislation through the middle period, was nevertheless much weakened. Children were removed from parental control when they attained financial independence or, according to some eleventh-century interpretations of the law, at the point of marriage. In court decisions of the late period, neither paternal nor parental authority was much stressed.

In Byzantine society, the family was a very important economic unit. Legislation tried to preserve family property intact until the children grew up and married, or inherited it. Through the Middle Byzantine period, only the survival of children overrode the concern for the nonalienation of dowry goods, which could be sold if indigence threatened the lives of the children. In the eyes of the legislator, the property and the persons belonging to a family were considered an entity. The family was also the most important unit of production: household manufacture of some items (such as cloth) was common, and agricultural production, whether by independent peasants or by *paroikoi* (dependent peasants) was centered on the family plot (owned or rented), cultivated by family members.

The family unit functioned in a wider, though somewhat vague, set of kinship relations that never received a strict legal definition. Nevertheless, the economic importance of the larger kinship group is evident in the fact that alienation of family goods tended to take place within it, so that family property had a good chance of being reconstituted. The law of Romanos I on *protimesis* (preemption rights) in 922 gave the first right of purchase to close relatives of an individual who sold land. Legal practice also recognized the rights of family members as overriding those of others in the sale of property, thus affording a measure of stability and protection to the family in the wider sense.

In cases where we may establish the details of everyday life with some accuracy (for example, among the Macedonian peasantry in the Palaiologan period), it is clear that, whereas the nuclear family was the basic unit, kinship relations also played an important role. The kinship group may be defined, in economic terms, as those who shared inheritance rights over property; biologically, the group consisted of blood and affinal relatives, in various degrees of relationship. It protected those whose own nuclear families had not yet been established or had disintegrated: the old, the orphaned young, and the unmarried lived with their relatives, and a degree of economic cooperation between related households may have obtained. Thus, among the peasantry, the wider family tie supplemented that of the nuclear family.

In the aristocratic families, it is evident that similar phenomena were at work. The continuity of the family is marked by the appearance of stable inherited names during and after the tenth century. By the eleventh century, the major aristocratic families were linked to each other through marriage, so that an ambitious man could call on a network of relatives to help him achieve power. This was notably the case of Alexios I Komnenos, who came to power in 1081 first through the help of his immediate family and then through his relations by marriage.

Within the family the husband played a primary role as head of the household and financial manager. Women might assume these roles upon widowhood, at which point they acquired both ownership and control of their family property. Residence after marriage was commonly virilocal or patrivirilocal but occasionally uxorilocal. Family names were inherited usually through the male line; there are, however, many cases, both among the aristocracy and among the peasantry, in which names were inherited through the female line. Sometimes, but not always, this signals a superior economic or social position on the part of the woman.

Although the majority of families were nuclear, there are many examples of vertically or laterally extended families. These arrangements tended to be transitory, since the coresident members were either old or widowed parents, or siblings who would subsequently marry and form their own nuclear families and households.

The demographic characteristics of the Byzantine family may be discerned dimly in most periods, and with some clarity in the Palaiologan era. The mean household size of the peasant population of Macedonia in the fourteenth century was between four and five members. This population was barely reproducing itself, so that the average number of children born to a couple (and surviving beyond the first year) was between two and three and one-half. More children died before reaching their fifth year. Other parts of the empire in different periods had different demographic characteristics. In thirteenth-century Epiros, for example, family size appears to have been larger, and the number of children born to couples was often much greater than the one established for Macedonia; five or six children per couple were not uncommon. This area was also characterized by an earlier marriage age and a relatively high ratio of divorce and remarriage. In any case, high infant mortality was common throughout Byzantine history. There was also a high rate of early female mortality in the early period (fourth through seventh centuries), but not in the fourteenth century—a development that had parallels in western Europe.

These demographic patterns may lie at the basis of Byzantine family legislation. They also explain, to some extent, the fact that women in the empire were, at least from the eighth century, firmly relegated to family life, where their position was protected both by law and by a new ideology. That ideology resolved the earlier tension that existed in Christian thought between the need for procreation and the glorification of virginity in favor of the former. From that time on, as may be seen both in hagiographic prototypes and in other texts, woman's primary role was to be a wife and mother, and her primary justification was to be achieved through the excellence of her children. Thus it is clear that the efforts of the Byzantine state and church to protect the family unit were supplemented by an ideology that gave the family an exalted role in society.

BIBLIOGRAPHY

H. Antoniadis-Bibicou, "Quelques notes sur l'enfant de la moyenne époque byzantine (du VIe au XIIe siècle)," in *Annales de démographie historique* (1973); J. Beaucamp, "La situation juridique de la femme à Byzance," in *Cahiers de civilisation médiévale, Xe–XIIe siècles* (1977) 145–176; A. Guillou, "Il matrimonio nell'Italia bizantina nei secoli X e XI," in *Settimane di studio del Centro italiano di studi dell'alto medioevo* (1977); H. Hunger, "Christliches und Nichtchristliches im byzantinischen Eherecht," in *Österreichisches Archiv für Kirchenrecht*, 18 (1967), and "Byzantinisches Eherecht im 14. Jahrhundert: Theorie und Praxis," in *Zbornik Radova Vizantoloshkog Instituta*, 14–15 (1974); Angeliki E. Laiou, "The Role of Women in Byzantine Society," in *Jahrbuch der Österreichischen Byzantinistik*, 31 (1981); Angeliki E. Laiou-Thomadakis, *Peasant Society in the Late Byzantine Empire* (1977); Nikolaos P. Matses, *To oikogeneiakon dikaion kata ten nomologian tou Patriarcheiou Konstantinoupoleos ton eton 1315–1401* (1962); E. Patlagean, "L'enfant et son avenir dans la famille byzantine (IVe–XIIe siècles)," in *Annales de démographie historique* (1973); Dieter Simon, "Zur Ehegesetzgebung der Isaurier," in *Forschungen zur byzantinischen Rechtsgeschichte* (1976).

ANGELIKI E. LAIOU

[See also **Annulment of Marriage; Consanguinity; Domestic; Eclogue; Inheritance, Byzantine.**]

FAMILY, ISLAMIC. Pre-Islamic Arab society recognized both paternal and maternal lines of descent, but a child was named after its father. Society was divided into clans, each claiming descent from a common ancestor. Nuclear families within each clan lived in close proximity, especially among the desert bedouin, who migrated from place to place in search of pasture. Harsh environmental conditions dictated this type of tribal life, in which the individual's survival depended on the collaboration of the members of the clan. Therefore the individual's loyalty to his clan was undivided. Intertribal relations, however, could be hostile unless agreements of mutual respect between tribes were concluded.

Islam sought to do away with the evils of the tribal tie, replacing it with a bond uniting the entire community of the faithful into one political unit, the *umma*. All Muslims were equal under God, and each was to be treated with the dignity due to every human being. Although this religious bond transcended the consanguineous tie, special mutual rights and obligations still prevailed between relatives, especially when they lived in one neighborhood. This blood bond was called *raḥim* (pl.: *arḥām*), and people so related were called *ulu'l-arḥām* or *dhu'l-qurba*.

The Arab and Islamic social unit, even with the broad, all-embracing concept of *umma*, was conceived as the circle of the members of a blood group with recognizable mutual rights and obligations. Such a group was denoted by the terms *ḥayy*, *ᶜashīra*, or *qabīla*, but *ḥayy* had more territorial implications. The term *ahl* or *āl* denoted a lineage or lineages of which the members were closely knit, as opposed to lineages from the same clan. An example is the Alids versus the Abbasids; both groups were descendants of Hāshim, the great-grandfather of Muḥammad, but they were of separate *āl*. The terms *ᶜāᵓila* and *ᵓusra* later came to be used synonymously with *āl*, but with the consequences of urbanization in modern times they have come to indicate a nuclear or compound family.

Far from conflicting with the obligations and rights arising from family ties, Islam confirmed and reinforced these bonds. The family, nuclear or extended, remained the essential building block of society and retained its autonomy in its own sphere: the economic and cultural welfare of its own members under the guidance of Islam. As conceived by Muslims, the family was an institution through which human reproduction was effectively organized and administered. Perpetuation and increase of the human population was an Islamic imperative, but any birth outside the conjugal bond was unrecognized. Moreover, adoption of children was not legally permitted, though one might take a child into one's household as long as the child retained its original family name.

The family was always regarded as the only institution through which the biological impulse and psychological yearning for companionship could be productively fulfilled. It represented a union of a male and a female mutually attracted by their respective differences: male toughness tempered by female gentleness, his harshness soothed by her softness, and his aggressive nature complemented by her receptivity. The Koran describes humanity as divided into two categories, male and female, so that each individual can have a spouse from the opposite category of the same species; in the hearts of both, God has planted love and mercy. This system is described or implied in passages from the Koran: 4:1, 4:34, 7:189, and 30:20, in which we are reminded of God's wisdom in creating these two categories of humankind, so that a married couple could enjoy *sakīna* (psychological comfort and gratifying companionship). This ideal relationship cannot be achieved through companionship between two persons of the same sex.

Within the family unit and through cooperation of its members, the individual was an economic animal fulfilling his economic needs. Sometimes this end required the collaboration of the extended family. The labor of each family member had its economic value, whether it was cooking, sweeping, cleaning, spinning, food gathering, farming, trading, or working for wages. These domestic economic activities were motivated not merely by immediate needs but also by the future needs of the family and particularly its offspring.

Islam provided guidelines whereby a family unit and kinship network could be set up and maintained far more effectively than under the tribal system. A family was created by marriage, and the minimal nuclear domestic unit involved four types of relationships: conjugal, parental, filial, and sibling.

Marriage was encouraged as a virtuous practice; celibacy was discouraged. The Koran reads (24:32): "And marry those among you who are single, as well as the virtuous ones among your slaves, male or female. If they are in poverty, God will provide for them means out of his grace." In the process of mar-

riage, Islam recognized three steps: betrothal, contractual agreement, and consummation or wedding. The three steps could be taken together, but wisdom more often dictated short or long intervals between them.

The first step involved choosing a spouse from outside the prohibited circle, which, Islam taught, included a man's female ancestors, his female offspring, his sisters, his nieces, his father's sisters, and his mother's sisters, as well as these categories of foster relations (i.e., the same relatives of the woman who had fed the man from her breast and of that woman's husband). It also included a man's stepmother, stepdaughter, and mother-in-law. His wife's sister, her father's sister, and her mother's sister were likewise prohibited in a polygamous marriage. Outside these prohibitions, a man could make his choice, the less related the better—although marriages between first cousins were not forbidden. Racially mixed marriages were common throughout the history of Islam, and celebrated children of such marriages held positions of power. One example would be the Abbasid caliph al-Maʾmūn, son of Hārūn al-Rashīd and a Persian concubine, who defeated his half-brother (whose mother was Hārūn's noble wife Zubayda) in battle to assume the throne.

The Prophet declares that, in selecting a wife, a man should not be swayed by physical beauty, wealth, or nobility of origin, but should look first and foremost for good moral conduct. A father is also advised to choose for his daughter a God-fearing man, because he will not mistreat her even if he does not love her (al-Ghazzālī, *Revival of Religious Sciences* [1933], II, 38).

Once a choice had been made, the groom's family (usually with the father, elder brother, or a senior member of the family as spokesman) normally asked the girl's relatives for her hand in a simple religious ceremony at her father's home. The consent of the woman was to be secured: in view of a virgin's shyness, her silence would be taken to signify approval, but a previously married woman had to indicate her willingness in words. Usually a gift was given her on the occasion; and during the interval between betrothal and the contract, additional gifts—usually food—were sent on religious occasions such as the ʿIds, the *miʾrāj, niṣf shaʿbān, ʿĀshūrāʾ*, and the birthday of the Prophet.

When the parties were ready, the ceremony of the marriage contract was executed in a well-attended ceremony, in which (usually) the bride's father offered her by name to the bridegroom, who had to respond immediately and positively. The categorical use of the term "marriage" in both offer and acceptance was necessary. Also, a dower due the bride was specified, either in money or in kind. Whatever the value, payment was due on the execution of the contract, but could be fully or partially deferred until the death of either party, unless divorce should occur.

A groom and bride united by a marriage contract became full husband and wife (although consummation was often delayed to a convenient date). The approach of the wedding date was marked by festivities and music. On the day itself there was a procession in which either the bride or the groom traveled to the other's home, in full costume. There was also a wedding banquet. The bridal residence was whitewashed and duly decorated for the occasion. Islam did not prescribe a matrimonial locality; marriage could be patrilocal or matrilocal. The Prophet himself, when he married Khadījah, moved to her residence; but his daughters moved to the households of their in-laws. Therefore, when Islam spread outside Arabia, it tolerated either system.

In order to ensure domestic harmony and stability, the shariᶜa of Islam provided some guidelines to regulate marital relations. The husband was recognized as the head of the family. He bore the religious obligation of supporting the entire family, even if his wife was wealthy. A husband's kindness toward his wife, his endeavor to satisfy her biological and psychological needs, as well as his labor for her support were all of religious merit and promised tremendous rewards in paradise.

A good wife reciprocally respected her husband and devotedly obeyed his wishes. Although, strictly speaking, she was entitled to be fully served at her husband's expense (family finances permitting), she often volunteered to take care of the household chores. She usually stayed at home to look after the children and her domestic responsibilities, but she did not hesitate to venture out whenever those responsibilities required. Women of privileged families tended to stay at home, deliberately keeping themselves away from the public eye. When they went out they covered their faces with veils (ḥijāb). Ordinary women went about their work with their faces uncovered, but otherwise modestly dressed. A woman preserved modesty in public by allowing no part of her skin except the face and hands to be exposed.

Divorce, regarded as the most hated among all permissible acts, was rare and did not require cumbersome legal procedures. While in pre-Islamic days, women on the whole were badly treated and an estranged wife could be abandoned and completely ignored by her husband, Islam claimed full human and legal rights for women. Men were warned not to rush to divorce their wives. The Koran recommends that domestic disputes be amicably settled through the mediation of representatives of both parties (4:35). If reconciliation is untenable, a fair procedure of divorce was prescribed. Similarly, a woman could stipulate in her marriage contract the right to divorce her husband at will. If she did not do so, she could still apply to court for divorce on the grounds of cruelty or failure by her husband to provide for her maintenance or to perform conjugal duties.

Women's relative seclusion was not regarded as segregation or a mark of inferior status, nor were the traditional gender roles considered unjust or unequal: they were tacitly accepted as equitable, natural, and normal. Polygamy did occur, as it was conditionally permissible under the shariᶜa, but it was never a universal practice. It was common only among the wealthy and the rulers, and it led to dangerous dynastic rivalries between children of such marriages.

Conjugal faithfulness was highly praised. While adultery by a free woman was unthinkable among pre-Islamic Arabs, it was somewhat tolerated if committed by men. Islam condemned adultery by men and women alike, and all illicit sexual practices were considered as shameful abominations to be completely avoided. Stoning to death was the punishment for adultery, if it was confessed or witnessed by four lawful witnesses. Fornication between unmarried persons was punished by one hundred lashes.

The birth of a child was greeted with domestic celebration. The cost of a child's maintenance was the responsibility of the father until a daughter married or a son came of age. Reciprocally, a child was obliged to obey its parents and treat them with great respect. A child was not supposed to walk in front of its father, sit while he was standing, or call him by his name. Special honor was to be paid to the mother, and aging parents of no financial means were the responsibility of their children. The siblings' mutual obligations followed next in importance. A needy brother or sister with no parental, filial, or conjugal protection was the responsibility of his or her better-off siblings.

Ties existed also to members of the extended family, especially grandparents and grandchildren. Family bonds were further reflected in reciprocal rights to inheritance. The surviving spouse of a deceased person as well as his or her parents and children were all assured a share in the estate. Grandparents, siblings, nephews, and even sons of paternal cousins could inherit in the absence of a surviving male offspring or a father, though the shares due to each of these heirs varied. In the absence of all these categories of heirs, Muslim jurists were of two opinions: either to deliver the estate to the state treasury or to distribute it among relatives outside the circle of legal heirs, such as aunts, maternal uncles, nieces, and female cousins. Individuals were urged to make wills bequeathing not more than one third of their estates to such relatives if needy, or to charity.

The stability of the Muslim family throughout the Middle Ages, enhanced by the factors discussed above, sheltered the individual, sustained him at times of distress, and, with his belief in God, inspired him with a sense of confidence in the success of his endeavors and inculcated a belief in a meaningful and worthy life on earth leading to salvation of the righteous in the hereafter.

BIBLIOGRAPHY

Abul A^clā Maudūdī, *Purdah and the Status of Woman in Islam*, al-Ash^cari, ed. and trans. (1972); Qāsim Amīn, *Taḥrīr al-Mar³ah* (Woman's liberation) (1970); ^cAbbās Maḥmūd al-^cAqqād, *al-Mar³ah fi al-Qur³ān* (Women in the Koran) (1971); Zakarīyā Aḥmad al-Barrī, *al-Aḥkām al-Asāsiyah lil-Usrah al-Islāmīyah* (The basic rules for the Muslim family) (1974); Muḥammad al-Ghazzālī (Abu Hamid), *Iḥyaba³ ^cUlūm al-Dīn* (Revival of the sciences of religion) (1933); Hamilton A. R. Gibb and Harold Bowen, *Islamic Society and the West*, 1 vol. in 2 (1950–1957); ^cUmar ibn Muhammad al-Nafzāwī, *The Perfumed Garden*, Sir Richard F. Burton, trans. (1963); Mohammad Mazharuddin Siddiqi, *Women in Islam* (1959); Gertrude H. Stein, *Marriage in Early Islam* (1939); Ruth Frances Woodsmall, *Moslem Women Enter a New World* (1936, repr. 1960).

MUHAMMAD ABDUL-RAUF

[See also **Concubinage, Islamic; Contraception, Islamic; Domestic; Harem; Inheritance, Islamic; Law, Islamic.**]

FAMILY, WESTERN EUROPEAN. In order to understand family life during the Middle Ages, it is necessary to abandon many modern preconceptions. The word "family" comes from the Latin *familia,* meaning "household," and that was its primary meaning in medieval times. A family consisted of all the persons living in one house under one head, including parents, children, distant relatives, and servants. The term "family" was also used to refer to one's house, kindred, or lineage. The modern concept of the nuclear family, and the kind of relations it fosters, did not exist.

During the early Middle Ages, the customs of the Germanic tribes played a major role in shaping family life. The kinship group, called the *sippe* by the Saxons and Frisians and the *mægth* by the Anglo-Saxons, was an important influence on the Germanic family and the main institution of private law. The *sippe* consisted of a group of kindred descended from the grandchildren of two common ancestors. Since kinship was traced through both the father and the mother, each person belonged to two groups.

The *sippe* had considerable power and could protect a wife from her husband or a child from its father. A child did not become a member of the *sippe* until formally acknowledged by its father. Infanticide and child exposure were practiced in Europe during the early Middle Ages, in spite of the objections of the church. Nevertheless, a father's power of life and death over his offspring ended once the child had tasted food. Milk or honey was given to a newborn baby: once this food touched his or her lips, the child became a member of the kinship groups of the father and the mother and was protected by their laws.

The Germanic family was patriarchal, and the father had a great deal of power over his children in their early years. Among the Jutes, the father could beat his children freely as long as he broke no bones. He could sell his child into slavery up to the age of seven, although he was not supposed to do so unless faced by famine. He could place his child in a monastery to be dedicated to the life of a monk or nun. He could pledge his daughter in marriage without regard to her will. Nevertheless, the church encouraged free choice in marriage. The seventh-century *Penitentiale* of the English archbishop Theodore states that a girl is in the power of her parents up to the age of sixteen or seventeen; after that, she cannot be married against her will. Parents could betroth their children when they were as young as seven, but if the parent or child wished to terminate the contract when the child was ten, it could be done without penalty.

One consolation for children was that their minority did not last very long. There was nothing like the prolonged adolescence of modern times. Among most Germanic tribes, children reached their majority at twelve. At that age, boys were allowed to bear arms and become freemen, responsible to the law in their own person. Under feudalism, the age of majority for boys was raised to fifteen. Girls also reached their majority at twelve and were considered marriageable at that age, but they were not given as much personal or legal freedom as boys. In fact, women never attained full majority unless they became widows. They were first under the power of their fathers and then under the power of their husbands.

Marriage was an important event because it established people as free, responsible individuals, independent of their parents. The landless bachelor and the spinster were looked upon with suspicion and were seen as burdens on their families. For women of the upper class, the only alternatives were marriage or the convent. From a modern point of view, medieval marriage customs seem harsh and unnatural, but we must remember that expectations were entirely different. Marriage was seen as an institution for the raising of children and the provision of financial security and was not supposed to be based on romantic love.

A Germanic wife was subservient to her husband, but she did have some rights and some property of her own. Her property consisted of the bride-price, the morning gift, given to her by her husband on the morning after their marriage, and the *gerade,* a gift from her family to help set up her household, including house linen, furniture, ornaments, money, and sometimes the poultry and sheep she had tended before marriage. This personal property descended to her female heirs. The wife remained a member of her own kinship group and could appeal to them if her husband mistreated her. If her husband injured her or divorced her unjustly, her *sippe* would intervene. She supervised the household and all the activities that went on within it. Since the large medieval household was practically a self-sufficient economic unit, household management involved a great deal of responsibility. As manager of the household, a wife had a position of influence within the family.

The early medieval household was primitive and not very private, even for the wealthy. In Anglo-Saxon England, every freeholder surrounded his property with a low earthen wall and dug a ditch around it. Inside the wall was an open space, called the yard, and the buildings that made up the home of the wealthy Anglo-Saxon. The main building was the hall, which contained long trestle tables and benches where hospitality was dispensed to family,

friends, guests, and retainers. The wife and her servants served wine and mead to her husband and his followers as they sat on the benches, sometimes listening to tales of ancient heroes chanted by a poet. Retainers and male guests slept on pallets on the straw-strewn floor of the hall. Separate small buildings were constructed outside the hall to accommodate the women of the family. In the courtyard, clothing and loaves of bread were distributed to the poor. The homes of the poorer classes were rougher: there were no separate bedchambers, and many poor families lived in a single large room.

The household was a center not only of hospitality but also of economic activity. In the early Middle Ages, the manufacture of clothing and food was a home industry entirely in the hands of women. Theodore's *Penitentiale* forbids Anglo-Saxon women to shear sheep, card wool, beat flax, weave, spin, or sew on Sunday, implying that these were all common feminine occupations. "Spinster" was a common term for a woman because every woman knew how to spin. Women were the cooks, brewers, and bakers of the early Middle Ages. The terms "brewster" (brewer) and "baxter" (baker) were originally the feminine forms for these words. Women also made candles, soap, and dye, and they prepared their own medicines and cosmetics from herbal recipes.

Children were raised in a rough fashion with little sentimentality. They were brought into the world by superstitious midwives who placed an egg in the baby's bath to symbolize fruitfulness and a coin to ensure prosperity. Midwives bathed newborn babies, swaddled them, sprinkled them with water, and gave them to their fathers to be named. Children were not given much attention until the age of seven, since their chances of survival were small and it was believed that they were not capable of being trained until that age. Boys were taught mainly athletic skills, such as running, jumping, throwing the spear and javelin, hunting, and fighting. Girls learned mainly household skills. Few children received any formal education unless they were destined for the church.

During the later Middle Ages, feudalism codified many aspects of family life and curtailed the legal rights of women. Their right to inherit property was restricted in favor of male heirs, who were able to render military service to their feudal lords. The estate usually was left to the oldest son. There was a great deal of concern about carrying on the family line. A wife's first duty was to provide her husband with an heir, and she could be divorced if she were barren. In an age of high infant mortality, people had many children so as to ensure a surviving heir. Male heirs were preferred, but a daughter could inherit an estate if there were no sons. A daughter was a less desirable heir since she would not carry on the family name and her husband would acquire her property when she married. A husband had complete control over his wife's dower (the property given to her from his estate) and her dowry (the property bestowed upon her by her family at marriage). A widow was not allowed to be the legal guardian of her own children: she had to relinquish this right to her overlord, who took charge of the children's property and had to approve their marriage partners. A widow had to obtain the consent of her overlord if she wanted to marry again.

Although the legal position of women worsened under feudalism because of the favoring of men, who could serve as knights, the social position of women actually improved. The code of chivalry encouraged men to refine their manners and respect women. Life in the feudal castle was more civilized than life in the early Germanic hall. At first the castle was a rough fortress meant mainly for war, but later, together with the smaller manor house, it became adapted for comfortable living. Although the castle and the manor house still had a great hall as a center of hospitality, separate chambers, called "closets," were built for the retirement of the lord and lady. Improvement of the chimney made it possible to heat these small rooms. The life of the lord and lady thus became more private, even though they were still surrounded by a large group of servants. Walls were hung with elaborate tapestries, which helped to keep the rooms warm. Tables were set with fine linen and vessels of silver and gold.

While the men were off fighting in wars and crusades or conducting business at court, the women took over the management of the estates—a great responsibility not unlike running a business establishment. A list of officials for the barony of Eresby in the late thirteenth century reveals the enormous size of even a minor aristocratic household. There was a steward in charge of the estates and a wardrober who was the head clerk: together they checked the daily expenditures. The wardrober's deputy, the clerk of the offices, was responsible for writing letters and documents. Although their duties were mainly religious, the chaplain and almoner sometimes served as clerks or as controllers of expenses and the chaplain's offices could be performed by the

two friars or their boy clerk. There were, in addition, a chief buyer, a marshal, two pantrymen, two butlers, two cooks, two larderers (officials in charge of meat storage), a saucer (a cook who prepared sauces), a poulterer, two ushers, two chandlers, a porter, a baker, a brewer, and two blacksmiths, each with their boy helpers. Women servants tended to the laundry and the kitchen and provided personal services for the lady of the manor. Most of these officials and servants lived in the same household and were thus members of the "family."

The household account was a minutely detailed record of income and expenses. In large households it was not unusual to have two accounts, one for the lord and one for the lady. Since the lord was often away on business, it was primarily the lady's responsibility to oversee these accounts. She was expected to have a knowledge of the accounting procedures that applied to estate management, and she had to know her major expenditures and sources of income.

Rents and feudal fees were two important forms of income, but on an efficiently run estate a considerable amount of money could be made from items produced on the demesne lands (those retained by the lord and not rented out). These products were also used on the estate, which was a partially self-sufficient economic unit. Grain was used to make bread, ale, and fodder for livestock. Eggs, butter, milk, and cheese came from animals kept on the estate. Any surplus could be sold on the market. Animals were slaughtered at appropriate times of the year, and the meat that was not used was salted for consumption during the winter. Most estates had their own ponds for fresh fish, but salt fish such as herring had to be purchased. Most of the fruits and vegetables that were used were home-grown. Herbs for cooking and for medicinal purposes came from the garden. Medieval ladies were experts at the still and were adept at making all kinds of drinks, medicines, and cosmetics from plants grown on their lands. Dried fruits, salt, spices, and wines were purchased to enhance the bland home-grown diet. Wool from sheep kept on the estate was sold to merchants or woven into fabrics. The lady of the manor and her servants made many of the everyday clothes worn by members of the household; more elaborate garments were custom-made by professional tailors. Items such as shoes, belts, hats, purses, and laces were purchased from artisans. The lady of the manor had to manage production and maintain adequate supplies for the entire household.

Many noblemen owned more than one estate and

moved about from manor to manor bringing their families and many of their servants with them. This was the cheapest way to live when the produce of the land was the chief source of wealth. When the stores and supplies of one manor were exhausted, the owner and his family moved on to another one. The lady of the manor and her officials took charge of moving the household. Medieval aristocrats led a peripatetic existence: they were used to packing their precious belongings in chests and spending different times of the year at different places.

In the late Middle Ages, child rearing practices continued to be rough, impersonal, and unsentimental by modern standards. Among the upper and middle classes, children were nursed and raised by nurses, whose duties are described in Bartholomaeus Anglicus' thirteenth-century encyclopedia *On the Properties of Things*. The nurse fed the child, bathed him, placed him in swaddling bands, dressed him, gave him medicine when he was sick, and held him to comfort him when he cried. She chewed his food to make it easier for him to swallow, picked him up when he fell, helped him to walk, played with him, taught him his first words, and put him to sleep with lullabies. The nurse clearly performed many tasks that we would now consider "mothering": it was she rather than the mother who developed "maternal" feelings for the child.

Children were expected to participate in the adult world as soon as they were old enough to be free of their nurses and mothers, usually at the age of seven or eight, when boys were apprenticed to arms or to a trade. For girls, childhood was even briefer: they began to learn household tasks at an early age, and their parents might begin to plan their marriages when they were six or seven, particularly if they belonged to the aristocracy. By the time a girl was ten, she was expected to be able to run a household. Medieval art shows children freely mingling with adults, playing the same games and doing the same tasks.

Aristocratic parents often did not bring up their own children. Courtesy books written for children speak of their duties to their masters rather than to their parents. Throughout the Middle Ages, it was customary to send sons and daughters to the homes of other noblemen or churchmen to be educated. Young boys were trained as pages and went on to become squires at about fourteen and knights at about twenty-one. These boys performed various services for the nobleman who took them into his house. At meals they would serve as cupbearers,

carvers, or "sewers" (servers who brought in and arranged dishes). As they got older they learned to care for and to use horses and armor. In return for their services, the boys had a chance to observe courtly life closely. They were instructed by a tutor or master in subjects such as languages, grammar, rhetoric, reading, religion, riding, jousting, hunting, hawking, playing the harp and lute, singing, dancing, conversation, and courtesy.

Young girls were trained as ladies-in-waiting. Under the supervision of the lady of the house, they learned to spin, weave, embroider, sew, make clothing, dress wounds, and prepare medicines and cosmetics. They learned all the skills involved in running an estate, as well as dancing, singing, and playing musical instruments. They received rudimentary instruction in reading and writing in their native language, and sometimes in a foreign language. Since the rituals of the dining hall were particularly important, they learned proper table manners. During leisure hours, they might sit with pages and squires in the garden and listen to music, read romances, or engage in flirtatious dialogues. Parents sent their sons and daughters to other households in the hope that they would find suitable marriage partners or at least make good connections.

The life of the middle-class family was centered on the town rather than the country. Although a wealthy merchant might have a country estate, most of his time would be spent in the city, where he had his business. His townhouse was the urban equivalent of the manor house. At the back was a garden where vegetables, fruits, and herbs were grown. The ground floor consisted of a shop with warehouse space behind it. On the second floor was the main room, the hall, with an adjoining kitchen and pantry. The third floor contained sleeping chambers.

Shopkeepers and artisans had less comfortable dwellings. Their working areas were on the ground floor, and their living space consisted of a single large room built behind or above the shop. The poorest workers lived and worked in a single room, often in a crowded alley tenement.

Since merchants and artisans had their residence and place of business in the same building, home life and work life were not widely separated. A man's family was closely involved in his work. Merchants and artisans often taught their trades to their wives and children, who usually stood to inherit the business.

If a father did not teach his children his own trade, he usually apprenticed them to another one.

Some children attended school before their apprenticeship began. Middle-class families were the first to take advantage of formal schooling, and the guilds founded a considerable number of schools. Both boys and girls attended elementary schools, where they learned to read and write in their native language. Only boys attended grammar schools, where Latin was taught. For many children, instruction was delayed until the period of their apprenticeship, which was rather late by modern standards. Middle-class children were apprenticed at about twelve or in their early teens. Their apprenticeship lasted between seven and ten years. Many men remained apprentices until they were twenty-five or twenty-six. They attained their civic majority and became full citizens at twenty-four. Long apprenticeships tended to delay marriage for middle-class men, usually until their mid or late twenties.

An apprentice was brought up by his master as a member of his family. In addition to teaching the apprentice his trade and the rudiments of reading and writing, a master was expected to provide moral instruction. Chastisement of apprentices was considered a duty, and the master was allowed to beat them. Boys who wished to protest against ill treatment had to prove that they had been beaten more frequently or more severely than was considered reasonable. It was generally believed that children should be docile and obedient and should learn to respect authority. The proverb (from Prov. 14:24) rendered as "spare the rod and spoil the child" was popular in the Middle Ages.

A woman was expected to contribute to the financial well-being of the family by helping her husband in his trade or by practicing a trade of her own. She could work as a *femme sole* even if she were married, provided that her husband did not interfere in her business. In such a case, she could rent a shop of her own. She alone was responsible for the practice of her craft. If she were sued in court, she could plead as a *femme sole* and her husband would have nothing to do with the case. If she were condemned to make payment, she would be committed to prison until she made a settlement with her creditors, her husband remaining entirely untouched in person and property. If a married woman did not trade as a *femme sole,* she could plead coverture, and then her husband was responsible for her debts and misdeeds. A married woman in business had a legal advantage over a man, since she could either take full responsibility for her actions or place that responsibility upon her husband. After 1363, married women in

London had another advantage over men, for an act of Parliament passed in that year ordered men to keep to one trade, whereas women were left free to follow as many as they chose.

In the merchant class, married women often carried on trades even if there was no economic necessity for them to do so. It was a way to keep busy and to earn extra money for luxuries. In London, a fishmonger's heiress who married four times went in for tailoring and brewing. Another fishmonger's widow bequeathed a male apprentice all the equipment from a metalworking shop she had directed. Dame Elizabeth Stokton had cloth manufactured for export to Italy. Margery Kempe was the daughter of a mayor and alderman of Lynn and the wife of one of the town's wealthiest merchants, yet she took up brewing ale and grinding grain in a horsemill.

Many women thus developed considerable ability in business and led fairly independent lives. Consequently, they were treated with respect by their husbands. Middle-class men could accept the idea of their wives' pursuing a trade of their own and becoming successful businesswomen. City women had a great deal of freedom in their leisure activities: they attended sporting events and went to taverns on their own, although courtesy books told them not to. Men often made their wives their executors and the legal guardians of their children.

The peasant family most closely resembled the modern nuclear family in that it consisted solely of parents and children living together, but this was a matter of economic necessity rather than choice. Peasants were too poor to support any servants, and their cottages were too small to have other relatives or even grandparents living with them. When a son took over the holding of a widowed mother or elderly parents, he usually agreed to provide them with food and a cottage of their own on the land.

The peasant's house was rough and simply constructed. The framework was of wood beams. Walls were made of mud or twigs and plaster. Roofs were usually thatched, although wood shingles were not unknown. Usually there was no chimney, and smoke had to escape through the smoke hole, door, and windows. The family lived and worked together in very unprivate arrangements in a single room. The floor usually was of earth, strewn with straw for warmth and cleanliness. The fire was made on an iron or stone plate, and surrounding it were the cooking utensils: pots and pans of earthenware or iron; ladles and forks of metal; bowls and basins of wood. The wood utensils were carved by the father and sons from pieces of oak or beech during the long winter evenings. Furnishings were sparse: a few stools, a trestle table, and chests to hold clothes. Peasants usually slept on straw pallets covered by sheets or rough blankets. The whole family slept together in the same room.

Peasant children did not receive any education. Occasionally, a village priest might teach a promising boy the elements of Latin and even have him sent to a local grammar school so that he could become a servant of the church. Most peasant children, however, grew up to be entirely illiterate and began working at an early age. Boys learned how to plow and perform other agricultural tasks at their father's side. Girls learned to tend the family garden, care for domestic animals, clean, cook, bake, spin, sew, and care for the younger children of the family while helping their mothers.

Women and children shared in most of the agricultural labors. Sometimes they helped even with the plowing, although this was usually considered a man's job. Women gathered hemp and flax, dried it, and spun it into yarn to make thread, rope, and linen. They cultivated gardens where they grew vegetables, fruits, and herbs, and they looked after the poultry, pigs, cows, and other barnyard animals.

In addition, women were burdened with the traditional feminine household chores. They had to spin and weave linen and wool for their own family and sometimes made extra material for sale. Spinning was such a common occupation of peasant women that it was hardly regarded as a specialized craft. Women sometimes worked on yarn brought to them by entrepreneurs from the towns. Once the material was prepared, they turned it into clothing for their family. Clothes had to be washed and mended, and the house had to be cleaned. Soap and candles were not available for sale or could be purchased only in town or at markets, so the peasant housewife often made them herself. She baked her own bread, brewed her own ale, made cheese and butter, and cooked every meal. She served as the family doctor, using ancient charms and herbal recipes to cure common ailments. Whether a peasant woman was married to a free tenant or a serf, her way of life did not differ very much. Regardless of her legal position, she was tied to the soil, and her existence centered on her farm and family.

It can be seen that the family, which consisted of the entire household, was more of an economic unit in the Middle Ages than in modern times. Since having a large number of servants was a status symbol,

people employed as many as they could afford. The wealthier the family, the larger was their household and the less intimate their lives. The aristocratic family included all the officials, servants, retainers, and relatives living under one roof. Parents often sent their own children to be trained in other households and in turn trained the children of vassals or relatives. Thus, parents and children did not live in the same "family," if we use the term in the medieval sense, for a good part of their lives. Ties among the immediate family members were weak because they did not have much time to develop. The middle-class family consisted of a master and mistress, children who lived at home, apprentices, and servants. For an apprentice or worker, sharing his master's professional life meant sharing his private life.

Among peasants, parents and children lived together in a small dwelling, but this situation fostered discomfort rather than affection. Family members spent little time in their cramped cottage but sought sociability on the village green or at the tavern with neighbors. The village rather than the family was the peasant's real community.

Medieval people did not experience the intimacy of the conjugal family, and parents and children were not particularly sentimental toward each other. The concept of the conjugal family did not develop until the sixteenth and seventeenth centuries. Nevertheless, the medieval extended family had some advantages over the modern nuclear family. Parents and children were less limited by ties and responsibilities to each other: Adults did not have to devote as much of their lives to the raising of children, and children did not experience the frustration of a prolonged adolescence under the tutelage of parents and school officials. Adults and children of all ages mingled together in community settings where there were ties of intimacy among many people. Work life and home life were closely connected. The medieval family provided less careful nurturing for the individual than the modern family, but it provided more of a community and allowed for more extended sociability.

BIBLIOGRAPHY

Annie Abram, *English Life and Manners in the Later Middle Ages* (1913); Philippe Ariès, *Centuries of Childhood,* Robert Baldick, trans. (1965); Bartholomew Anglicus, *Medieval Lore from Bartholomew Anglicus,* Robert Steele, ed. (1924); Henry S. Bennett, *Life on the English Manor* (1937), and *The Pastons and Their England,* 2nd ed. (1968); Marc Bloch, *Feudal Society,* L. A. Manyon, trans.

(1963); Alfred Brittain and Mitchell Carroll, *Women of Early Christianity* (1907); Pierce Butler, *Women of Medieval France* (1907); George C. Coulton, *Social Life in Britain from the Conquest to the Reformation* (1918, repr. 1968), *Life in the Middle Ages*, 2 vols. (1928–1930, 2nd. ed. 1967), *The Medieval Village* (1931), and *Medieval Panorama* (1938); Norman Davis, ed., *Paston Letters and Papers of the Fifteenth Century* (1971–1976); Jean Louis Flandrin, *Families in Former Times* (1979); Ilene H. Forsyth, "Children in Early Medieval Art," in *Journal of Psychohistory*, 4 (1976); Willystine Goodsell, *A History of Marriage and the Family* (1934).

Sibylle Harksen, *Women in the Middle Ages*, Marianne Herzfeld, trans. (1975); Rodney Hilton, *Bond Men Made Free* (1973); Urban Holmes, *Daily Living in the Twelfth Century, Based on the Observations of Alexander Neckam in London and Paris* (1952); George C. Homans, *English Villagers in the Thirteenth Century* (1959); George E. Howard, *A History of Matrimonial Institutions* (1904); David Hunt, *Parents and Children in History* (1970); Margery Kempe, *The Book of Margery Kempe*, Sanford B. Meech and Hope Emily Allen, eds. (1940); Charles L. Kingsford, ed., *The Stonor Letters and Papers* (1919); Margaret Wade Labarge, *A Baronial Household of the Thirteenth Century* (1965); Peter Laslett and Richard Wall, eds., *Household and Family in Past Time* (1972); Andrée Lehmann, *Le rôle de la femme dans l'histoire de France au moyen âge* (1952); Gerald R. Leslie, *The Family in Social Context* (1967); John Leyerle, ed., "Marriage in the Middle Ages," in *Viator*, 4 (1973); Rosemarie T. Morewedge, ed., *The Role of Woman in the Middle Ages* (1975); Chilton L. Powell, *English Domestic Relations, 1487–1653* (1917); Eileen E. Power, *Medieval People* (1924, 10th ed. 1963); "The Position of Women," in Charles G. Crump and E. F. Jacobs, eds., *The Legacy of the Middle Ages* (1926, repr. 1943); and *Medieval Women*, Michael M. Postan, ed. (1975).

Theodore K. Rabb and Robert I. Rotberg, eds., *The Family in History* (1971, repr. 1976); Hermann Schoenfeld, *Women of the Teutonic Nations* (1907); Frank M. Stenton, "The Historical Bearing of Place-Name Studies: The Place of Women in Anglo-Saxon Society," in *Transactions of the Royal Historical Society*, 4th ser., 25 (1943); Doris Stenton, *The English Woman in History* (1957); Lawrence Stone, *The Family, Sex, and Marriage in England, 1500–1800* (1977); Susan M. Stuard, ed., *Women in Medieval Society* (1976); Sylvia L. Thrupp, *The Merchant Class of Medieval London, 1300–1500* (1948); Thomas Wright, *A History of Domestic Manners and Sentiments in England During the Middle Ages* (1862), and *Womankind in Western Europe from the Earliest Times to the Seventeenth Century* (1869).

DIANE BORNSTEIN

[See also **Annulment of Marriage; Antifeminism; Betrothal; Concubinage, Western; Consanguinity; Contra**ception, European; Courtly Love; Domestic; Family and Marriage, Western European; Inheritance, Western European.]

FAMILY AND FAMILY LAW, JEWISH. The most striking characteristic of medieval Jewish families is their uniformity despite the geographical and historical differentiation of Jewish life. To be sure, during the first part of the Middle Ages problems spread from the ancient centers of Judaism toward the West, and during the second part from western Europe toward the East. However, tradition and faith accompanied the family to the new surroundings, and the law was adapted to meet new situations.

The unique role of religion in Jewish life, in contrast to the relatively slight effects of socioeconomic factors, resulted in far-reaching similarities. Sexual asceticism, for instance, was almost unknown, and the building of a family was a basic commandment in medieval—as well as in ancient and modern—Judaism. The family was needed for the full celebration of the sabbath and festivals, for charity, for the observance of rites of passage into various life stages, and for the development of solidarity. Obviously, political factors still had an impact on the Jewish family; the wife's right to divorce, for instance, was recognized by Babylonian rabbis lest she bring her action before the local Muslim *qāḍī*. Similarly, the prohibitions of polygyny and unilateral divorce by the husband were adopted by the German communities in response to Christian mores, and communal control of marriage and divorce in Egypt arose from the impact of government policy on Jewish family law.

Changes in socioeconomic conditions, too, left their mark on Jewish family life. The scarcity of real property made it necessary to allow the collection of maintenance and capital payments from movable goods. Legislative measures against absentee husbands and changes in the stages of the marriage ceremony also illustrate this process of adaptation. The growing importance of the congregation vis-à-vis the authority of the exilarch in Babylonia reflects itself in the family legislation of the German, Egyptian, and Spanish traditions. The incidence, despite talmudic prohibitions, of child marriages, on the one hand, and greater legal capacity of women, on the other hand, are likewise the results of social changes.

Kinship was an important factor in public as well

as private life. A spiritual leader enhanced his authority by his pedigree, tracing his descent to King David if possible. The Jewish theory of evidence declared next of kin to be inadmissible witnesses, a factor that fostered the extension of kinship at least to second cousins. Burial rights also reflected the solidarity of kinship, as did the endogamic tendencies treated below.

Marriage was considered a means to a pure and saintly life, and the choice of a mate was often determined by pragmatic criteria. Sexual activity was considered meritorious if it took place between spouses and within prescribed limits. The consciousness of kinship led toward preference of a niece or cousin as a partner for life. Marriage into a scholarly and noble family was considered good preparation for an exemplary life, and financial considerations also played a major role, as reflected in dowries, marriage gifts, and successions, although the pious rejected these material considerations in choosing a mate. The decisive role of the respective parents in the selection process and in the marriage ceremonies served to balance the weight of personal attraction. But again, the pious still insisted on the personal acquaintance of the prospective spouses apart from the role played by parents and matchmakers.

Marriage was celebrated in three stages. The first formal ceremony was the engagement, when the two parents determined the financial arrangements and the date of the wedding. The second was the betrothal (kiddushin or erusin), including the acquisition and consecration of the bride. (Although she remained with her family and was prohibited from sexual relations with her future husband, she was already tied to him, and this bond could be severed only by a formal divorce.) The third ceremony, the nuptials (nissu'in), represented the symbolic entry of the bride into her husband's house, as witnessed by the marriage contract.

The initial engagement was a promise guaranteed by a pledge and witnessed by deed. Among German Jews a ban was declared or implied if either party violated the promise. The bride was acquired by (or consecrated to) her husband with the recitation of a formula and the delivery of a gift. Seventh-century Jews in the Holy Land began using a ring as the gift, a practice which may reflect Byzantine influence. Ten adult men were required to attend the betrothal ceremony to witness the recitation of the blessings; in spite of this rule, the consecration ceremony was relatively informal, and doubts about the status of the bride often remained.

Originally the first two stages took place on one occasion, but from the twelfth century on, the second stage was usually postponed. Finally, the plight of the bride separated from her bridegroom before the nuptials could take place led to the unification of the last two stages. The first two stages often took place while the bride was still underage; in addition to the political uncertainty that led many parents to marry off their children as early as possible, this custom also reflected a negative attitude toward premarital sex. Under the influence of Muslim law, a Babylonian bride was represented by her father even after she came of age, but a formal mandate issued from daughter to father prevented any unjustified claim that the bride had been betrothed without her knowledge. In the eighth century a Babylonian rabbi attempted to declare secret marriages void, but this rule was not generally followed. Licensing of marriages among eleventh-century Egyptian Jews was the result of government policy, while a fourteenth-century German rule requiring marriages to be performed by authorized rabbis served to prevent doubts about status.

The mutual rights and duties of the spouses were stipulated in a marriage contract written during the nuptials or sometimes even earlier. Financial arrangements covered the husband's marriage gift, including the sums payable in the case of divorce or if the husband predeceased, and also the bride's dowry. The husband assumed the duty of support, in return for which the wife promised assistance from her work and her income. A common promise on the husband's part was his acceptance of the bride's trustworthiness, which is equivalent to the Western "power of the key." Conjugal relations were regulated by custom, and the bridegroom often had to forego the right of polygyny or that of employing female servants without the wife's consent. In tenth-century Germany and France this arrangement developed into absolute monogamy, with exceptions granted only by the congregation; among the Karaites this had always been the rule. The husband's right of correction (wife beating) was entirely rejected in the West but recognized in the East. In discussing the disturbance of marital peace, commentators such as Rashi and Rabbi Meir ben Baruch of Rothenburg often mention interfering relatives. Difficulties also arose through migration and travels abroad, and provisions were often made for this eventuality in the marriage contract. In several twelfth-century French communities, a ban was declared against deserting husbands.

The death of a spouse did not sever the marital bond. The widower was obliged to care for his wife's tomb, since she remained his wife "until the resurrection of the dead." He was also entitled to her estate; marriage contracts sometimes stipulated against this right, especially if the wife's death occurred very soon after marriage and she left no child. The custom of Narbonne, limiting the surviving husband's right, extended throughout France and Germany during the twelfth and thirteenth centuries. In the takkanah of Toledo, the Spanish communities reduced his right to half her estate. Widows were much worse off. If the husband died without child, a widow became subject to the rule of levirate. While the Karaites had limited this rule to distant relatives, or to cases where the deceased man had only betrothed but not married the woman, the majority of medieval Jewry left the option of marrying or releasing the widow to any of the deceased husband's brothers. The frequent abuse of this right led Rabbi Ibn Abitur to suggest the abolition of the levirate duty if the brother-in-law was recalcitrant, and German Jewry tried to overcome this problem legally. While the widow normally had no right to her husband's estate, except for support, a husband often provided for such a right in the marriage contract or by will.

The husband's discretionary right to divorce was limited by the amount payable according to the marriage contract. Among the pious, moreover, it became a rule to refrain from witnessing an unjustified divorce. Following Rabbi Gershom, German communities during the eleventh century limited divorce by requiring consent of the wife or of the leaders. While the wife had originally enjoyed a very limited right of divorce, seventh-century Babylonian rabbis admitted it on grounds of incompatibility; this right had originally been provided in the marriage contract but by the seventh century was recognized ex lege. An attempt was made to adopt this rule in the West as well, but there it met with opposition. Rabbinic courts spent much time on reconciliation and, paralleling Muslim legal practice, often referred the dispute to neighbors and other arbitrators. The growing formality of the bill of divorce was sometimes abused by husbands who cast a slur on its validity after it had been issued. A ban was therefore declared against such a person, giving the divorce the force of a res judicata.

The Jewish family finds its greatest blessing in numerous children, especially sons. While parental rights were vested in the father, the custody of daughters went to the mother. According to the Babylonian academics this rule applied even after the mother's remarriage. Unlike sons, who were sent to school and received a general education, daughters were generally restricted to home instruction in practical matters. A number of women, however, were credited with knowledge, learning, and even leadership. Likewise, the Jewish law of inheritance did not recognize daughters as legal heirs, but it became customary to provide a dowry for unmarried daughters according to the accepted standard, either in the marriage contract or in a will. Among German Jews, the daughter was customarily allotted half of the son's share, a practice that may have been taken over from Muslim law.

The status of women in the medieval Jewish communities reflected a number of factors. In spite of important innovations in the law, Jewish marriage remained basically polygynous and male-centered; thus the opinion of the Babylonian rabbis granting the wife a right of divorce was rejected by the traditionalist French rabbi Jacob Tam in the twelfth century. The ban on polygyny and on unilateral divorce by the husband never became categorical enough to override another religious commandment, such as the levirate marriage. Moreover, most rabbis would not agree to annul certain marriages in order to overcome legal difficulties that otherwise caused hardship to the wife. Although the rabbis sympathized with the plight of the wife in such cases and although there were talmudic precedents, they did not have the courage of their Karaite colleagues, who declared the marriage to be dissolved.

On the other hand, Jewish women, like their Christian or Muslim sisters, often enjoyed a much higher status in practice than was expressed in the law. In both the Eastern and the Western diaspora, women owned property and often played a role in the economy. The German rabbi Elazar ben Natan described the activity of Jewish women in the twelfth century as a justification for granting them the capacity to contract and to act as guardians and trustees. Likewise, in the religious sphere women played a more active role than that provided for them by law and tradition. Among German Jews there were women learned in Scripture and liturgy and others who observed some of the traditionally "male" commandments and studied the law.

BIBLIOGRAPHY
Israel Abrahams, *Jewish Life in the Middle Ages* (1932); Louis M. Epstein, *The Jewish Marriage Contract* (1927,

repr. 1973), and *Marriage Laws in the Bible and the Talmud* (1942); Ze'ev W. Falk, *Jewish Matrimonial Law in the Middle Ages* (1966); Louis Finkelstein, *Jewish Self-Government in the Middle Ages*, 2nd. rev. ed. (1964); Aron H. Freimann, *Seder qidūshīn ve-nisu'īn* (1945); Mordechai A. Friedman, *Jewish Marriage in Palestine*, 2 vols. (1980); Solomon D. Goitein, *A Mediterranean Society: The Jewish Communities of the Arab World as Portrayed in the Documents of the Cairo Geniza*, III, *The Family* (1978); Jacob Katz, *Tradition and Crisis: Jewish Society at the End of the Middle Ages* (1961); Haim Tykocinski, *Die gaonäischen Verordnungen* (1929).

ZE' EV W. FALK

[See also: **Cairo Genizah; Jews** (various articles); **Responsum Literature, Jewish.**]

FAMILY AND MARRIAGE, WESTERN EUROPEAN. There was a rich diversity of family structures in western Europe during the Middle Ages. This diversity was the result of a complex history involving the movement of peoples during the migration periods, different degrees of cultural interpenetration, and later adjustments to new conditions in which families functioned. Celtic family forms survived on the northwest fringe of Europe. In the Mediterranean basin forms incorporating Roman traditions continued through the Middle Ages and beyond. The family structures of the Germanic peoples were somewhat different and developed in a variety of ways, there being a noticeable divergence of custom between those who entered the Roman Empire and those who remained in their homelands. Slavic and Hungarian tribes brought their family structures with them to their final areas of settlement. Furthermore, within each of these peoples the purpose and organization of the family varied considerably according to class. Finally, throughout the Middle Ages the different structures adjusted to many influences: economic, demographic, political, and ideological.

By and large, families were organized with a strong patriarchal bias. They tended to be extended in form (especially among the landed classes), though the degree and effectiveness of that extension shifted in accord with the changing ideals of family life in this period. Traditional views of medieval society, which saw a unidirectional development from a large household incorporating several married couples toward a smaller unit consisting essentially of the nuclear family, have had to be refined as more

detailed studies have shown that the balance between the degree of extension and the independence of the married couple shifted back and forth according to circumstances.

With such a variety of medieval family structures, marriage—meaning either the process whereby the recognized spousal relationship was established or the ongoing life of the couple—was realized in many ways. As a general rule, among the upper classes a spouse was expected to bring wealth, an alliance with an extended group, and new lives into the family. On the lower levels of society, marriage was seen more as a partnership of spouses who, in addition to their procreative and socialization functions, were expected to share the fruits of their labor, the major element in the support of a family, as well as the rather limited wealth they brought to the union. Even within these common patterns, the way in which union was brought about and its future quality varied greatly; but this variety of marriage customs was channeled toward a common pattern by political and religious pressures.

The first of these pressures, the right of lordship, was generally established across Europe during the Middle Ages. Whether at the feudal level or at that of the manor, the lord sought to protect his interests through partial control of marriages. The choices of spouses for his vassals and for their children—especially orphaned children—or a widow's decision to remarry or remain celibate, all affected the lord's ability to obtain suitable services from present and future generations. In varying ways, therefore, he exercised a degree of control over these choices. At the manorial level the lord's interest was largely financial and even more direct. During the early Middle Ages at least, he might separate a couple as the interests of an estate required, and in many parts of Europe his permission was expected before the marriage of an unfree tenant. Payment was usually exacted before the wedding of a peasant woman or when marriage involved the withdrawal of a villein from his lord's holdings. Thus, within the variety of customary arrangements that controlled the choice of a spouse, lordship tended to exercise a consistent influence that benefited a wider, extrafamilial institution.

The teaching of the Christian church was a greater and more lasting influence on marriage. Christianity did not have its own theory or ideal of family. Beginning with the usages of Jewish society, to which the first generation of believers belonged, it adapted itself (not without criticism) to the structures of the different peoples to which it spread. Nevertheless, a Christian ideal of marriage is discernible from the beginning. It emphasized the relation between the spouses rather than the view, characteristic of so many forms of extended family, that saw marriage in terms of the needs of the larger social structure. This ideal, essentially personal rather than proprietary, dominated Christian thinking throughout the Middle Ages. As it was elaborated, it provided a criticism of the different marriage customs of the Mediterranean basin and then of the regions north of the Alps. In time it was gradually accepted by society, and marriage customs were adjusted accordingly. Eventually changes in family structures resulted.

The basic principles and a few consequences of the Christian ideal of matrimony were stated by the early church. Of fundamental importance was the fact that the married state was confronted by the ideal of dedicated celibacy, which was seen not only as an honorable alternative to marriage but also as superior to it in many ways. Human sexuality was considered to have become disordered as a result of the fall of Adam and Eve, and marriage was seen as a means of channeling sexual energy in an acceptable way. Sexuality was properly exercised only within the married state and, since husband and wife were seen as equal before God, the conclusion was quickly if reluctantly drawn that they were equally obliged to marital continence. In spite of the preference for the celibate life stated by most writers of the early Christian period, marriage was considered the lot of most and a sacred relationship: bishops and priests soon began to take part in wedding ceremonies. The church emphasized the indissolubility of this union. Though it allowed, it did not encourage the remarriage of those whose spouses had died.

Thus Christianity had already become a critic of local marriage customs before the Middle Ages began. It insisted on monogamy and opposed the concubinage of the Roman Empire and the polygyny of the Celtic world. Similarly, its growing recognition of the consequences of Christ's teaching "What therefore God has joined together, let no man put asunder" (Matt. 19:6) soon led to conflict with forms of marriage that allowed the repudiation of wives or even of husbands.

During the first half of the Middle Ages, as Christianity reached the different peoples of western Europe and its leaders assumed positions of influence among them, its ideal of marriage became better known and, to a certain extent, accepted. Further-

more, in its desire to ascertain when unions had properly taken place, the church began to adopt rules touching such issues as the freedom to marry and the permitted degrees of relationship. Conflicts with other traditions and with the desires and plans of powerful individuals and families provided occasions for the examination and discussion of the Christian ideal of matrimony and its consequences. By the end of the eleventh century it was becoming accepted that a general supervision of marriage pertained to the bishop, and that decisions touching law or fact relating thereto lay with him and with the courts that exercised his jurisdiction.

A crucial stage in the history of marriage in the West was the reform period from the late eleventh to the mid thirteenth century. In the vibrant intellectual milieu of those years, the creation of the nuptial bond, its religious significance, the purpose of the union, and the quality of the relationship that resulted were examined in detail. One of the objectives of contemporary research is to ascertain how the resulting understanding of matrimony permeated a sometimes unreceptive society and the degree to which it was accepted and practiced, but even in the present state of research, it is possible to set out the main lines of marriage custom in western Europe.

As a preliminary to the selection of a spouse, capacity to marry had to be ascertained. The spouses were expected to be of sufficient age. The age of first marriage varied during the Middle Ages as a function of social usage and economic conditions. In many towns both merchants and artisans delayed marriage until they had established places for themselves in the local economy. A similar situation obtained in rural areas: eldest sons (assured of an inheritance in many family structures of the period) and women tended to marry younger. The church, espousing the position of Roman law, required a common minimum age: fourteen years for men and twelve for women. Those seeking to marry also had to be free of previous commitment, be it to a living spouse, to religious life, or, after regulations on the celibacy of the higher clergy were established in the councils of the twelfth century, to major orders.

Furthermore, the couple were to be free of relationship by blood or affinity within certain degrees. Regulations on this matter were confused during the early Middle Ages. In both the Roman and Germanic traditions marriage was forbidden between those related in the direct line and between brothers and sisters, but there was a wide freedom of choice between cousins. Church leaders tended to be more restrictive and, after considerable wavering during the missionary period (sixth–ninth centuries), forbade marriage between those related in the seventh degree (sixth cousins). This proved to be unworkable. In canon 50 of the Fourth Lateran Council (1215) the prohibition was reduced to the fourth degree (third cousins), a regulation that remained in force to the end of the Middle Ages. Even this limitation posed a serious restraint, especially among the rather small circle of royal and noble families that sought to intermarry and, more generally, among families that wished to strengthen their internal ties by endogamous unions. Dispensation lay with the papacy, which thus enjoyed a quasi-seignorial control over many marriages. At lower levels of society, bishops usually obtained papal permission to grant given numbers of dispensations at their discretion.

The procedures that led to the union of spouses included the assignment of property, the betrothal, and public expression of consent to the union by the couple and their families in the wedding ceremony. The first stage involved agreement on the endowment to be received and the betrothal. The form of contribution of the two parties was one of the key indicators of the future position of the wife within the nuclear family and, more generally, the position of the couple and their children within the extended group. In the early Middle Ages the general emphasis of the contribution of the husband found in the Germanic world—at first a bride price paid to the family of the prospective bride, then a dower promised to the woman for her support in the event that her husband predeceased her—tended to replace the dowry or contribution by the bride's family that had been common in the Mediterranean basin. During the later Middle Ages this tendency was reversed throughout much of Europe, especially the south, and the dowry was emphasized once more. This part of the proceedings was essentially familial, though by the thirteenth century some local churches ruled that the witnesses must include a priest.

Very young children, even infants, were sometimes betrothed. In these cases, where the agreement was clearly the decision of parents or guardians, the betrothal, to be binding, had to be validated when the children came to the age of discretion. According to a theory that obtained over much of Europe until late in the twelfth century, betrothal was the beginning of marriage; after that time it was considered to be only a promise to marry. The seriousness with which that promise was regarded varied: in France failure to honor it frequently led to litigation,

whereas such disputes seem to have been rare in England. In the earlier understanding of betrothal as *matrimonium initiatum,* the union was considered complete *(matrimonium ratum)* after it had been consummated. Even when betrothal came to be regarded as a promise, marriage was judged to take place if betrothal was followed by sexual union. Where procedures were properly observed, the neighborhood's general knowledge of the background of the betrothed was canvassed before the wedding, so that any objection to the union might be stated. A public announcement was made by reading the banns in the parish church at Sunday Masses. This usage was found in northwest Europe by 1200 and was imposed generally by canon 51 of the Fourth Lateran Council.

The marriage itself, the free exchange of consent *(per verba de presenti)* that, in canonical theory, established the nuptial bond, was expected to take place in public at the parish church. The ritual, often performed at the church door, usually included a symbolic transfer of endowment and an expression of family consent to the union as well as the essential act, the exchange of vows by the couple. The new husband and wife were then led to the sanctuary of the church, where the marriage Mass was offered and the nuptial blessing conferred.

Such was the ideal. Though much research remains to be done on the matter, it is already clear that a high proportion of medieval weddings, especially those in the poorer classes, were informal. Some incorporated parts of the ritual described, others were private exchanges of consent by the couple. Such unions were considered to be illicit but, if there were no impediments to the marriage of the pair, they were judged to be valid. Throughout most of Europe the children born to them were legitimate. Many bishops required that, when their situation became known, secretly married couples renew their vows in a public ceremony *(coram facie ecclesie).* In the acceptance by the church of the validity of these clandestine weddings, its teaching that the consent of the couple brought the marriage into existence is abundantly clear. However much it sought to reinforce the union by the expression of consent by the families involved and the association of the wider parish community, the church maintained that no other consent—be it that of family or of lord—no other ritual, and no endowment were necessary for the establishment of the marriage bond.

The conjugal life of the medieval couple can, for the most part, be described only in general terms.

Whatever their hesitations about praising its sexual aspect, theologians saw matrimony as a holy relationship, one that by the thirteenth century was commonly held to be a sacrament. It was a symbol of the union of Christ and the church, a means of salvation for most men and women. The church taught that marriage involved a mutual and exclusive sexual right and that it had a potential for friendship of a high order. Although the husband enjoyed superiority—as did Christ in that union of which marriage was the symbol—the spousal relationship was, at least in ideal, the nearest medieval society came to an equality of man and woman. The degree to which the wife exercised control over the property she brought to the union or gained by her labor varied according to family structure, as did the degree of independence of the married pair within a larger extended group in which it so often existed. Letters, testaments, and diaries occasionally reveal the intimate life of a couple. They suggest that, whatever custom stated as to the rights and duties of the married pair to the larger society, to their children, and to each other, much would be determined by the force of character of the spouses themselves.

Marriage was intended to endure for the lifetime of the couple. If it were desired to end the union, two roads were open, both of which respected the principle that a valid marriage was indissoluble. Where the marriage was judged to be valid, but married life proved to be intolerable, separation, in which property and maintenance rights of the parties and their children were stated and protected, could be sought from the courts. Husband and wife were freed from each other's society and, in accord with the decision of the court, controlled their own resources, but they remained married and there was hope of reconciliation. Registers of the ecclesiastical jurisdictions indicate that parties sometimes simply withdrew from an unacceptable union, a fact that is known because one of the spouses objected to the separation and asked the court to restore conjugal life. In cases where the union was found to have been invalid, the court judged that a true marriage had never existed and that the former spouses were free to live a celibate life or to marry. The most common basis of this declaration of nullity was the discovery that one of the parties was bound by an earlier, valid, and usually clandestine marriage.

The possibilities of abuse implicit in the position that the consent of a couple, so long as they were free to marry, was the sole requirement of a valid marriage, were considerable, and seem to have been the main weakness of the system. It was corrected for the Catholic world at the Council of Trent; the decree *Tametsi* (1563) prescribed that valid marriage between baptized persons required the presence of the parish priest or a delegate, appointed by him or the local ordinary, and at least two witnesses. A similar solution was adopted during the next two hundred years in those parts of Europe that accepted the Reformation. Recent analysis of the activity of the ecclesiastical courts, which had jurisdiction over these matters, suggests that they considered their role to be protector of the marriage bond, although, as cases required, they often found in favor of those who wished to withdraw from it.

In the difficult conditions of medieval life, many marriages did not long endure. Information gathered to date indicates that second unions were common. Acquittal of responsibilities, economic and social necessity, and personal desire led to the decision to remarry. The widow who held property was seen as a marriage prize, and she was subject to much pressure not only to remarry but also to choose a spouse who was acceptable to her lord. In other situations the preference of a deceased husband, as revealed in his testament, and the desires of his family, especially when the rights of children were involved, discouraged remarriage by the widow. Custom and civil and ecclesiastical law from the eleventh century on moved toward allowing the surviving spouse to remain single when that state was preferred. Although in individual cases religious leaders not only allowed but also counseled second marriages, the church assumed a position that involved some disapproval, as indicated by the denial of a second nuptial blessing and the limitation of the activities of a "bigamous cleric" who remarried or chose a widow as his spouse. Sometimes popes and bishops, as defenders of those who had no family (*miserabiles persone*), found it necessary to protect women who wished to remain in widowhood. Religious life, the beguinage, monastic corodies, and the custom of receiving private vows of chastity from widows who wished to remain in a family milieu were among the religious and social supports provided by medieval society for those who chose not to remarry.

BIBLIOGRAPHY

Marriage and family. Willystine Goodsell, *A History of Marriage and the Family,* rev. ed. (1934); David Herlihy, "Family Solidarity in Medieval Italian History" and "The Medieval Marriage Market," in his *The Social History of Italy and Western Europe, 700–1500* (1978); Diane Owen

Hughes, "From Brideprice to Dowry in Mediterranean Europe," in *Journal of Family History*, 3 (1978).

Theology of marriage. George H. Joyce *Christian Marriage*, 2nd ed. (1948).

Marriage and law. James A. Brundage, "Concubinage and Marriage in Medieval Canon Law," in *Journal of Medieval History*, 1 (1975); Jean Dauvillier, *Le mariage dans le droit classique de l'église, depuis le Décret de Gratian (1140) jusqu'à la mort de Clement V (1314)* (1933); Georges Duby, *Medieval Marriage*, Elborg Forster, trans. (1978); Ze'ev W. Falk, *Jewish Matrimonial Law in the Middle Ages* (1966); Jean Gaudemet, "Recherche sur les origines historiques de la faculté de rompre le mariage non consommé," in Stephen Kuttner and Kenneth Pennington, eds., *Proceedings of the Fifth International Congress of Medieval Canon Law* (1980); Rene Metz and Jean Schlick, eds., *Le lien matrimonial* (1970); Michael M. Sheehan, "Marriage Theory and Practice in the Conciliar Legislation and Diocesan Statutes of Medieval England," in *Medieval Studies, 40* (1978).

Marriage ritual. Jean-Baptiste Molin and Protais Mutembe, *Le rituel de mariage en France du XIIᵉ au XVIᵉ siecle* (1974); Korbinian Ritzer, *Formen, Riten und religiöses Brachtum der Eheschliessung in der christlichen Kirchen des ersten Jahrtausends* (1962), also in French: *Le mariage dans les églises chrétiennes du Iᵉʳ au XIᵉ siecle* (1970).

The married state. John F. Benton, "Clio and Venus: An Historical View of Medieval Love," in Francis X. Newman, ed., *The Meaning of Courtly Love* (1968); Christopher Brooke, *Marriage in Christian History* (1978); John T. Noonan, Jr., "Marital Affection in the Canonists," in *Studia Gratiana, 12* (1967).

Marriage and the courts. Richard H. Helmholz, *Marriage Litigation in Medieval England* (1974); Jean-Philippe Levy, "L'officialité de Paris et les questions familiales à la fin du XIVᵉ siecle," in *Etudes d'histoire de droit canonique, dédiées à Gabriel Le Bras*, II (1965); Rudolph Weigand, "Die Rechtsprechung des Regensburger Gerichts in Ehesachen unter besonderer Berücksichtigung der bedingten Eheschliessung nach Gerichtsbüchern aus dem Ende des 15. Jahrhunderts," in *Archiv für katholisches Kirchenrecht*, 17 (1968).

MICHAEL M. SHEEHAN

[See also **Annulment of Marriage; Betrothal; Law, Early German.**]

FAMILY SAGAS, ICELANDIC. The Norse word *saga* (related to *segja*, say or tell) refers to the large number of prose narratives produced chiefly in Iceland during the thirteenth century. The following main categories are distinguished, mainly on the basis of subject matter but also of style and structure:

Íslendinga sǫgur (literally sagas of Icelanders, also referred to as Icelandic or family sagas); *fornaldar sǫgur* (literally sagas of ancient times, also referred to as legendary or mythic-heroic sagas); *konunga sǫgur* (kings' sagas); *byskupa sǫgur* (bishops' sagas); *heilagra manna sǫgur* (saints' sagas); *samtíða sǫgur* (contemporary sagas—the *Sturlunga saga*); and *riddara sǫgur* (literally knights' sagas, assimilated prose versions of European works, chiefly romances and *chansons de geste*). The term "classical sagas" is often used to refer to the Icelandic family sagas and those kings' sagas produced during the classical period of saga writing (*ca.* 1220–1300). Closely related to the classical sagas are *þættir* (sing. *þáttr*, literally strand in a rope, used in literature to mean part of a whole), shorter narratives equivalent to sagas, or appended to or embedded in them.

Of these various categories, the Icelandic family sagas have enjoyed the greatest scholarly attention and literary popularity. There are about thirty examples, most ranging in length from about twenty pages in modern edition to over four hundred (*Njáls saga*). All are anonymous with the exception of *Droplaugarsona saga*, which in the concluding genealogy mentions a Þorvaldr Ingjaldsson "who told this saga." (The attribution of *Egils saga* to Snorri Sturluson is conjectural.) Written down, in most cases, in the thirteenth century, the family sagas purport to describe events of the settlement period in Iceland (*ca.* 870–1050).

Individually the family sagas tell dramatic and coherent stories of people's lives and of events in particular communities. But because they overlap considerably in content and character, the sagas may also be said to form a collective chronicle of the history of Iceland during the early Commonwealth period, providing a unique insight into the social and economic vicissitudes of frontier life, the conversion to Christianity (voted by the Althing in 1000), and the material realities of the Viking and post-Viking ages.

It is useful to divide the Icelandic sagas into two groups. One is biographical and includes *Egils saga, Fóstbrœðra saga, Kormáks saga, Gunnlaugs saga ormstungu, Hallfreðar saga, Bjarnar saga hítdœlakappa, Grettis saga, Víga-Glúms saga, Valla-Ljóts saga,* and *Hávarðar saga ísfirðings.* These sagas tell the life stories of men who were peerless fighters, Vikings, farmers, poets, and, in several cases, lovers. In *Kormáks saga, Gunnlaugs saga, Bjarnar saga, Hallfreðar saga,* and the part of *Fóstbrœðra saga* devoted to Þormóðr, the erotic interest is central, with two men, hero and antagonist, competing for and suffering over a heroine whose character (unlike Brynhild's) seldom transcends her narrative function as object. Bjǫrn and Þórðr *(Bjarnar saga)* feud at length with words and deeds over Oddný, as Gunnlaugr and Hrafn do over Helga the Fair. Kormákr falls desperately in love with Steingerðr at first sight and spends years overcoming the obstacles between them—a curse, her husband, various ill-wishers, and pirates—only to lose interest when she is finally within his grasp. Þormóðr's cognomen, Coal-Brow Poet *(Kólbrúnarskáld)*, derives from the nickname of the lady whose praises he sang in *Fóstbræðra saga*, and at the heart of *Hallfreðar saga* lies an adultery: Hallfreðr takes Kolfinna, wife of Gríss, as his lover. Erotic preoccupations take a different form, but play no less central a role, in *Gísla saga*, the first part of which builds on a barely concealed adultery, and the latter part of which is a protracted demonstration of spousal loyalty. Even the surly Egill Skallagrímsson is momentarily subject to love's agonies (ch. 56), though his saga, like those of Víga-Glúmr and Grettir, is otherwise uninterested in affairs of the heart.

It has been suggested that these "love sagas" are modeled on continental romances. Thomas' *Tristan* was translated into Norse in 1226, with *Yvain, Erec, Perceval,* and the *lais* of Marie de France following shortly thereafter. Individual motifs from romance are incorporated here and there in saga literature, notably in *Grettis saga* (from the end of the thirteenth century or later).

As characters, however, the Norse lovers differ dramatically from their counterparts to the south, as well as from native heroes of the Sigurd type, for they are fair in neither mind nor body but dramatically flawed in both. Egill, with his odd eyebrows and prematurely gray hair, is preternaturally ugly. Grettir is downright monstrous. The otherwise presentable Gunnlaugr is endowed with an unfortunate nose. A woman describes Kormákr as being dark and ugly, and having strange eyes and hair. Hallfreðr's disposition earned him the cognomen Troublesome, just as Gunnlaugr's penchant for verbal hostility is attested in his nickname Serpent-Tongue. The foster brothers Þorgeirr and Þormóðr, like Gunnlaugr, are decidedly "overbearing" and spend no small part of their time fleeing scrapes of their own making. Egill is a case study in truculence. Grettir is the ultimate misfit, spending the larger part of his life in outlawry and dying at the hands of bounty hunters. Gísli is in many ways a decent man, but his overdeveloped

sense of vengeance and general pugnacity earn him the same fate as Grettir.

Nor is it clear, despite the erotic trappings of the surviving versions, that these sagas were originally conceived as love stories. It is more likely that their heroes first attracted literary attention not as lovers but as poets—a role for which belligerence was not an uncommon qualification in early societies. (The word *skáld* originally connoted a person dealing in scorn and insults.) The rise of traditions about poets is on one hand a measure of the esteem in which skaldic practitioners were held in early Iceland, but it is equally a measure of the fascination their itinerant lives held for their insular friends and relatives. As the highly complex art form of skaldic poetry came to be concentrated in Iceland, Icelanders found themselves increasingly in demand at foreign courts. Their travels in Scandinavia, the British Isles, and the Continent brought Icelandic poets into contact with materially advanced cultures, introduced them to illustrious people, and involved them in epoch-making events. Many of their verses commemorate just such persons and places, and they form the basis of the prose sagas in which they are embedded. Sagas about professional poets, or about heroes whose poetic talent and production are central to their lives, are commonly referred to as "skald sagas" (the first six works on the above list).

A second group of sagas concerns not individuals but communities. Their titles reflect their collective focus: *Laxdœla saga, Reykdœla saga, Vatnsdœla saga, Eyrbyggja saga, Vápnfirðinga saga, Fljótsdœla saga, Kjalnesinga saga, Ljósvetninga saga, Svarfdœla saga* (sagas of the people of Laxárdalr, Reykdalr, and so on), *Heiðarvíga saga* (Saga of the heath slayings), *Bandamanna saga* (Saga of the confederate chieftains). Also collective in their focus, despite their being named for individuals, are *Njáls saga* (with its 600 characters), *Hœnsa-Þóris saga, Hrafnkels saga, Droplaugarsona saga,* and *Eiríks saga rauða.* But if these sagas are not biographies, neither are they district chronicles, as they are often called. Rather, they are chronicles of community feuds.

The paradigmatic feud saga has six phases, according to Theodore M. Andersson. The first, the introduction, presents characters and provides some genealogical information, which can itself assume the proportions of a miniature saga. From an irritation (quarrel over a woman, theft, slight on one's honor) arises a conflict, leading sooner or later to the climax, which nearly always takes the form of the death of one of the protagonists. Upon this follows a revenge, bloody in most cases, and in some sagas a counterrevenge as well. The situation is brought back to rights with a reconciliation, either personal or legal, and the saga ends with an aftermath, which gives further information on the survivors and their descendants.

Only two of the collective sagas depart emphatically from this general scheme: *Eyrbyggja saga* and *Vatnsdœla saga,* both of which consist of a loose assemblage of local traditions rather than chronicles of protracted feuds. Other sagas vary the pattern: *Ljósvetninga saga,* in which the middle stages are doubled and distributed over two generations (a pattern also found in *Egils saga*); *Heiðarvíga saga,* with its abnormally long and elaborate conflict phase; and *Njáls saga,* which is in effect two sagas. The remainder, despite their peculiar emphases and differences in temper and style, all build on the same plan. Classic feud narratives are *Laxdœla saga, Hœnsa-Þóris saga, Vápnfirðinga saga, Hrafnkels saga,* and *Njáls saga* (its bipartite construction notwithstanding). *Bandamanna saga,* which as the single comedy stands apart from the others, observes the pattern even as it mocks it.

The biographical sagas have their share of conflict, but because the hero's life necessarily imposes parameters, the feuding does not achieve the full proportions or the organic quality it has in those sagas where it is the subject. In the feud sagas the organizing principle is not the individual life but a social abstraction. This abstraction, having its own life cycle, determines where the saga begins and ends, and what characters it includes. It also entails a full exposure of both sides of the story, on the apparent premise that neither is simply right or wrong, but that both are culpable and aggrieved in roughly equal proportions.

The most heinous deed in saga literature is committed by one of its most admirable figures, Flosi Þórðarson, who orders the burning of Njáll's house because he understands, quite correctly, that the situation has come to the point where his choice is to kill or be killed: "We must either abandon the attack, which would cost us our own lives, or we must set fire to the house and burn them to death, which is a grave responsibility before God, since we ourselves are Christians." Like saga tragedy in general, this one is solely of human manufacture. It is not attributed to villains, traitors, cowards, or godless creatures, nor is it referred to a higher authority, Christian or otherwise. Real people's regrettable

lapses, and the part of human nature that cannot let grievances pass unrecompensed, are the operative categories in the sagas' reading of history. To the extent that the sagas are generally pessimistic about the ability of individuals to mend their ways and (hence) the ability of society to avoid repeating its tragedies, they may be said to be fatalistic. Of the sort of fatalism that holds lives and events to be preordained, however, there is no evidence. The occasional references to fixed destiny, like other supernatural elements (ghosts, omens, dreams), may indicate a once-viable belief system, but in the extant sagas they do little more than add to the sentimental decor.

Many features of saga violence are familiar remnants of older heroic legends: the drive for retaliation in kind, heroic posturing, preoccupation with personal and family honor, premonitory dreams, goading women, ritual insults. But the peculiar form and meaning of violence in the sagas, and their attitude toward traditional heroism, must be seen in the context of the historical period during which they took final shape. The twelfth century had, despite the progressive accumulation of wealth and influence by a few families, been a largely peaceful era. But the thirteenth century saw open conflict, not only among the chieftains but also between the church and the chieftain class and, further, between the Norwegian-controlled monarchists and the Commonwealth loyalists. It was during the Sturlung era, a period of virtual civil war ending only with the collapse of the Commonwealth in 1262, that the Icelandic sagas took their final form. The contemporary *Sturlunga saga* (describing events of the twelfth and thirteenth centuries) provides some evidence that recent experience conditioned the understanding of the historical feuds of the frontier period.

Also conditioned by contemporary experience is the sagas' ethical outlook. This is not expressed directly—the sagas maintain a stance of formal objectivity—but it is implicit in certain rhetorical conventions. A common device is the displacement of bias onto the community at large: "Everyone in the district condemned the killing" and "People agreed that the case had been settled fairly" have, in saga terms, the force of authorial intrusions. Equally tendentious are character descriptions. Characters are not thoroughly evil (with the exception of Mǫrðr in *Njáls saga*) or thoroughly good, but more or less subject to irresponsible behavior. The former are described with the unsympathetic adjectives "overbearing," "short-tempered," "unpopular," and "unlucky," whereas people less given to destructive behavior (or whose outbursts are seen as justified) are described as "moderate," "hardworking," "self-restrained," and "well-liked." Sententious statements—all the more conspicuous because of their scarcity—make much the same point: "With laws shall our land be built up, with lawlessness laid waste" (Njáll in *Njáls saga,* a quotation from the early laws); "The time has come for these family feuds to end" (Snorri goði in *Laxdæla saga*); "I don't know whether I am any less manly for being more reluctant than other men to kill" (Gunnarr in *Njáls saga*).

At stake are the traditional values of heroic individualism, not merely because they are unchristian but also because they are incompatible with the well-being, specifically the economic well-being, of the community. Nowhere is that incompatibility more compactly expressed, nor a medieval sensibility more evident, than in the miniature saga known as *Þorsteins þáttr stangarhǫggs* (The tale of Thorstein Staff-struck). This moral fable turns on the initial hesitation, and finally the downright refusal, of the two main characters, Þorsteinn and Bjarni, to play their appointed roles in a mounting vendetta. Here, as elsewhere, observance of the honor code is urged most vigorously by those who stand neither to carry it out nor to bear the brunt of its consequences, and for whom feud is a kind of spectator sport: women, old men, slaves (even children, in other sagas). When Bjarni and Þorsteinn lay down their weapons, they assert their authority as principals not only to settle their own affairs, but to do so in accordance with their own rational assessment of social and economic realities rather than the archaic dictates of personal pride. The case is put plainly by an unnamed character, who explains to Bjarni's scornful servants that their master's reluctance to claim Þorsteinn's life stems not from cowardice but from his understanding that to kill a man is to deprive a family of a provider and the community of a productive member. In effect, society needs live workers, not dead heroes. Even more pointed is the resolution, in which Þorsteinn gives up his status as an independent freeholder and, "with great courage and integrity," places himself in Bjarni's service, where he spends the rest of his life. Bjarni in turn becomes "better liked and more self-controlled" as he grows older, and he dies a devout Christian on pilgrimage to Rome.

Þorsteins þáttr thus encapsulates, in miniature and local form, the evolution of the Icelandic Commonwealth from a pagan and tribal system to a Christian and protofeudal society. Not all sagas are so programmatic in their analysis and recommendations; but the perception of an old and a new order, the one associated with violence and lawlessness, and the other with the forces of restraint and social responsibility, is a common denominator of the genre.

Yet the durability of the sagas as literary works lies less in their success in promulgating a consistent social message than in their ambivalence. The sagas' original anecdotes can be presumed to have circulated in the spirit of commemoration, not critical analysis. Admiration inheres in the stories of Gunnarr's last stand at Hlíðarendi, Gísli's stabbing of his best friend's killer, Grettir's epic land cleansings, the depictions of such decidedly old-style heroes as Egill Skallagrímsson and Skarpheðinn *(Njáls saga),* and in the accounts of proud ancestors who elected to emigrate rather than knuckle under to a king. These are the sagas' inherited data, originating in the wish to retain in public memory the history-making events of the district and the adventures and colorful personalities of particular neighbors, relatives, and forebears.

It is only in the context of whole sagas in their final form that the individual parts and characters come into ironic perspective. Grettir's individual deeds are commendable enough, but his life as a whole is sadly archaic, finally less like that of his analogue Beowulf than that of Don Quixote. Just when this new view of things established itself is not clear, though a plausible case could be made for the bloody and disillusioned context of the thirteenth century. Clearly, the new view was not so militant toward the old traditions that it condemned or dismissed them. On the contrary, the sagas' postmortem of the heroic ideal is performed with considerable residual sympathy for the people who lived it out, no matter what their shortcomings as actual citizens. It is no small part of the force of the sagas that they are able to glorify the warrior virtues and sympathize with the urge for vengeance even as they condemn violent solutions and the system of values that makes them inevitable.

Saga characters are all the more remarkable in light of the fact that they are constructed entirely from the outside—elucidated not by a narrator, but by their own words and actions. Certain of these external indications of inner states are clichés, to be sure—such as signaling anger by flushing red, falling silent, or exiting abruptly. Others are tailor-made and bear a more complicated message. A brief but emotionally loaded gesture occurs in the famous house-search episode in *Gísla saga* (ch. 17). Þorgrímr has just been found murdered. His best friend, Þorkell, who rushes to the room, apparently has reason to believe that the murderer is his own brother Gísli, from whom he has been estranged for some time. He deputizes sixty men, and they ride across the snowy fields to Gísli's house. Þorkell goes first, the saga says, and as he enters the bedroom, "He sees where Gísli's shoes are lying, all frozen and caked with snow; he pushes them under the footboard so that other men will not see them." No further explanation is given; but Þorkell's hasty hiding of the very evidence he was seeking speaks volumes about his attachment to the brother who has murdered his best friend.

Egill Skallagrímsson is at no point in his saga said to be greedy, yet in the moments when his face brightens at the sight of silver, and in his senile trek into the hills to hide his moneybags forever, he reveals himself as a miser on a par with Molière's Harpagon or Balzac's Grandet. Nor is he said to be self-important. That side of his personality too emerges from his words and actions—most strikingly, perhaps, in his three major poems, all manifestly more interested in their author than in their ostensible topics. In *Sonatorrek* (Loss of my sons) he begins by lamenting the accidental drowning of his son Bǫðvarr, but he reverts quickly to himself and his own remarkable talent; and he concludes, in effect, that for such a fine poetic gift as his, the loss of sons is not, after all, such an intolerable price. But Egill is more than a stingy egomaniac, just as he is more than a savage Viking; he is deeply loyal to his brother (on whose dead body he ceremoniously fastens two fine gold bracelets), and he is capable of falling so miserably in love that he sits for days with his head buried under his cloak.

The sagas have their share of types: shrewish wives, impertinent or loyal slaves, opportunists, berserks. Even major characters seem, in some cases, based on archetypes (Brynhild, Sigurd, the patriarch-sage). But within these broad categories, characters are individually conceived as full and often contradictory personalities. Even the femme fatale Hallgerðr is a loving and loyal wife and a resourceful housekeeper in her second marriage. Njáll, whose life is otherwise devoted to quelling the vengeance system and promoting the cause of peace, has his vindictive lapses. "May your hands prosper," he says to his sons when he learns that they have killed two men in defense of the family honor; and he refuses

the chance to save his life by saying, "I am an old man now and ill equipped to avenge my sons, and I do not want to live in shame." So lifelike are the personalities of such characters as these, and so remote in conception and execution from the general run of medieval characters, that one is tempted to ascribe them primarily to life and only secondarily to art—to assume, in other words, that the earliest versions of saga events were strongly person-oriented, and that at least the basic elements of the psychologies depicted there managed to survive the vicissitudes first of oral and then of literary transmission. If this is not so—if, that is, the characters are instead fictional creations—the saga authors may be regarded as the foremost portrait artists in medieval literature.

The origin of the sagas is obscure. They emerge abruptly, without known antecedents and without parallels in European literature, as a full-fledged phenomenon in the early thirteenth century. Given these circumstances, it is no surprise that saga scholarship has from the outset been preoccupied with questions of background and sources, in particular the relation of the extant texts to oral tradition. Two competing theories, termed "book prose" and "free prose" by Andreas Heusler, have dominated twentieth-century criticism. Generally speaking, the "free prose" view (represented mainly by Heusler, Knut Liestøl, and more recently, in modified form, by Theodore M. Andersson) holds that the sagas were orally composed and transmitted, and that they existed in something like their present form before they were written down (the word *saga* points to an oral origin). Although the transmission process admitted distortions, the sagas were by and large intended and understood as historical documents. The "book prose" view (represented mainly by Björn M. Ólsen, Sigurður Nordal, and Walter Baetke) holds that the sagas are the literary creations of medieval authors who may have had recourse to some oral traditions (though not in the form of whole sagas) but relied more heavily on written sources, both native and foreign, and their own imaginations. The sagas, according to this view, are the predecessors of the historical novel and were intended chiefly as literary entertainment. The "book prose"–"free prose" controversy has quieted in recent years, not because one side proved more successful but because the accumulated evidence did not support the terms of the original formulation. Scholars no longer ask whether the saga is literary *or* oral, but what in the received saga can be ascribed to the literary author (whose use of written sources is firmly established) and what to a native tradition (the existence of which is the only explanation for the survival of traditional material through the preliterate period).

Unmistakably oral in its origin is the sagas' prose style. Despite its idealized quality, presumably acquired during transmission, saga narrative has, in both its language and its peculiar use of discourse, strong affinities with folktale narrative—specifically, according to Liestøl, with traditions from western Norway (whence the original emigration to Iceland). Saga language is notoriously plain, relying on nouns and verbs, and using adjectives sparingly and in predicate position ("He owned the horse; it was a gray one" rather than "He owned the gray horse"). Metaphors and similes are virtually nonexistent. As affective conceits the sagas prefer litotes ("Hallgerðr showed great restraint that winter and was not disliked") and the ominous detail: "The sun was up and it was a clear day," "He was wearing a blue cloak," and "Two ravens flew with them all the way" all portend imminent tragedy. Description is otherwise strictly functional, limited to those features of landscape, personality, dress, and architecture that will figure in the forthcoming action.

Embedded in this laconic narrative setting, and often contrasting sharply with it, are the sagas' dialogues. Here are revealed characters' motives and reactions, sometimes in strongly emotional terms. There is a certain sexual disparity in the expression of personal feelings, particularly grief and hostility, which women put into plain words but men deflect into mannered understatements, proverbs, or skaldic verse. The dialogues form miniature dramas, framed by a narrative introduction that sets the scene and a narrative conclusion that mentions the outcome. A short example is the first dramatic scene of *Njáls saga:*

> There was a certain time when Hǫskuldr was holding a feast for his friends; Hrútr was there, sitting next to him. Hǫskuldr had a daughter called Hallgerðr, who was playing on the floor with some other girls. She was a beautiful child, tall for her age, with silken hair so long that it came down to her waist. Hǫskuldr called to her, "Come over here to me," and she went to him at once. Her father took her under the chin and kissed her, and she walked away again. Then Hǫskuldr said to Hrútr: "How do you like the girl? Don't you think she's beautiful?" Hrútr made no reply, and Hǫskuldr repeated the question. Then Hrútr said, "The girl is beautiful enough, and many will suffer for that; but I cannot imagine how thief's eyes have come into our kin." Hǫskuldr was furious, and for a long while the two of them had nothing to do with each other.

Sagas are made of such tripartite scenes as this one, sometimes abutting one another directly and sometimes separated by narrative. Their anecdotal, stylized quality and their appearance at the outset of saga writing and over the generic range point to an origin in oral prehistory.

If the framing and preservation of the sagas' particulars can be ascribed to oral tradition, the organization of those particulars in large, convoluted wholes appears to be a specifically literary development. A saga is not conceived as a unified plot but as several interlocking subplots; and these subplots are not related consecutively but woven together in such a way as to indicate that they are happening simultaneously ("Now the story returns to Þormóðr to tell what he was doing while Þorgeirr was on his journey" or "Now we shall let this side of the story rest while we turn our attention to Hrolleifr"). In this respect the sagas are in tune with continental literary fashion, especially in its thirteenth- and fourteenth-century prose manifestations. The correspondence between Icelandic and French prose practice cannot be explained by direct influence in the first instance, for saga writing was already established by the time interlace literature came into European vogue. It is more likely that the sagas and the prose romances represent independent responses to a common medieval aesthetic, the digressive chronicles (first Latin and the vernacular) being an important factor in both cases. To the extent that vernacular practice on the Continent played a role in saga evolution, it was by refining and reinforcing preexisting native tendencies. In any case, the sagas as whole compositions bear a strong resemblance to the French prose romances and may, like them, be regarded as medieval literary products.

A related puzzle is the long prose form. The "book prose" view of the sagas as epic-length folktales orally produced and reproduced finds little analogic support in documented oral traditions, where verse is the rule—hence the inapplicability of oral-formulaic theory to the sagas. (Scholars have not been able to establish a link between the Icelandic family sagas and the equally inexplicable prose sagas of Ireland.) In the literary sphere, too, verse was the normal vehicle for vernacular works in the imaginative mode until the advent of the prose romances. One popular theory holds that the family sagas are derived, via the skald sagas, from the slightly older kings' sagas, which are in turn derived from vernacular histories blending popular with learned elements in varying proportions (*Fagrskinna, Ágrip,*

Hryggjarstykki, Morkinskinna, and the clerical sagas of Óláfr Tryggvason and Óláfr Haraldsson), which are in their turn derived from the Latin synoptic histories (Theodoricus' *Historia de antiquitate regum Norwagiensium* and the *Historia Norwegiae*). The long prose form thus has its origins in historiography in the European tradition, although the narrative itself was rapidly popularized as the synoptic style gave way to a colloquial and anecdotal one.

The weak link in this model of development is the last one. There are, to be sure, pronounced affinities between the kings' sagas and the family sagas. They share a distinctive style, use of skaldic verse, and social attitude, and they overlap subject matter. (It should be recalled that the kings' sagas too were for the most part authored by Icelanders, and further that the Icelandic monasteries, especially Þingeyrar, as well as the two bishops' seats at Hólar and Skálaholt, were centers for historical study and writing.) Positing the skald sagas as a transitional stage between kings' and family sagas has the advantage of explaining the shift in orientation from Norway to Iceland, from individual to community history, and from kings to citizens. The problem with this scheme is that although the skald sagas are archaic, certain of the collective sagas appear to be equally so; and one of them, *Reykdœla saga,* is now believed to antedate not only the skald sagas and other family sagas but probably the bulk of classical kings' sagas as well. It thus appears that the Icelandic family sagas were not an outgrowth of the kings' sagas but a parallel phenomenon conditioned by historical writings in the learned mode. Those writings included *Landnámabók* and *Íslendingabók* as well as the Norwegian histories.

After about eighty years the classical sagas disappeared as abruptly as they had emerged, yielding to the *fornaldarsǫgur.* These simpler and, on the whole, shorter tales in a more popular idiom operate not in the historical world but in a timeless world of altered reality, with strongly typed or fantastic characters and in foreign or unspecified lands. The drift of Norse prose from the factual representation of history to fictional entertainment is thus complete.

Just where the family sagas lie on the continuum between these two poles remained a matter of controversy. But from the point of view of medieval literary history, the sagas' exact ratio of history to fiction is of less interest than the fact that these two traditionally separate spheres are synthesized in a highly developed prose form at an unexpectedly early date. The anomalous quality of the sagas in this and other respects points up the special nature of the society that produced them. Unlike Norway and Denmark, Iceland had no court and hence no exclusive forum for the production and consumption of literature. There was, to be sure, a culturally advantaged class (composed mainly of chieftains, clerics, and wealthy landowners) that was instrumental in the nation's literary production. Yet political and economic circumstances in Iceland were such that this elite necessarily remained in close association with the populace in cultural as well as practical matters.

It is generally assumed that after the advent of writing, the Icelandic sagas, like other types of sagas, were read aloud from manuscripts to entertain socially mixed groups. The eclectic composition of saga audiences—sophisticated readers on one hand and listeners of all ages, classes, and social levels on the other—puts into a social context the sagas' peculiar blend of oral and literary, fictional and historical, rational and supernatural, popular and learned. In Norway and Denmark, where the social elite separated from popular culture, native traditions were not cultivated to the same extent.

Two other circumstances must certainly have contributed to the literary industry in Iceland. One was the degree of literacy, which some scholars gauge to have been unusually high by medieval standards. The other was the extraordinary opportunity for cultural exchange in all forms provided by the parliamentary system, which involved both local meetings and a national assembly for all free men every summer. The decline of saga writing at the end of the thirteenth century may indicate that the underlying traditions were exhausted, but it may also have been related to the social and economic changes, the loss of national impetus, and the orientation toward Norwegian and continental cultural tastes that followed on the demise of the Commonwealth.

BIBLIOGRAPHY

Theodore M. Andersson, *The Problem of Icelandic Saga Origins* (1964), *The Icelandic Family Saga* (1967), and "The Icelandic Sagas," in Felix J. Oinas, ed., *Heroic Epic and Saga* (1978); Walter Baetke, "Über die Entstehung der Isländersagas," in *Berichte über der Verhandlungen der Sächsischen Akademie der Wissenschaften zu Leipzig, Philol.-hist. Kl.,* **102,** pt. 5 (1956); Carol J. Clover, *The Medieval Saga* (1982); Peter Hallberg, *The Icelandic Saga,* Paul Schach, trans. (1962); Andreas Heusler, "Die Anfänge der isländischen Saga," in *Abhandlungen der Königlich Preussischen Akademie der Wissenschaften, Phil.-hist. Kl.*

(1913), repr. in Stefan Sonderegger, ed., *Andreas Heusler: Kleine Schriften,* II (1969); William P. Ker, *Epic and Romance,* 2nd ed. (1908, repr. 1957); Knut Liestøl, *The Origin of the Icelandic Family Saga,* Arthur G. Jayne, trans. (1930, repr. 1974); Lars Lönnroth, *Njáls Saga: A Critical Introduction* (1976), considers the sagas in general; Sigurður Nordal, *Hrafnkels saga Freysgoða,* R. George Thomas, trans. (1958), and "Sagalitteraturen," in *Nordisk kultur,* 8, pt. b (1953); Kurt Schier, *Sagaliteratur* (1970); Einar Ól. Sveinsson, *Dating the Icelandic Sagas,* Gabriel Turville-Petre, trans. (1958).

CAROL J. CLOVER

[See also **Bandamanna Saga;** Bishops' Sagas; **Bjarnar Saga Hítdœlakappa;** Droplaugarsona Saga; Egils Saga Skalla-grímssonar; Eyrbyggja Saga; Fljótsdæla Saga; Fornaldar-sögur; Fóstbrœðra Saga; Gísla Saga Súrssonar; Grettis Saga Asmundarsonar; Gunnlaugs Saga Ormstungu; Hallfreðar Saga; Hávarðar Saga Ísfirðings; Heiðarvíga Saga; Hœnsa-Þóris Saga; Hrafnkels Saga Freysgoða; Iceland; Kjalnesinga Saga; Kormáks Saga; Laxdœla Saga; Ljósvetninga Saga; Njáls Saga; Reykdœla Saga; Svarfdæla Saga; Valla-Ljóts Saga; Vápnfirðinga Saga; Vatnsdæla Saga; Víga-Glúms Saga.]